Privacy Injunctions and the Media

Privacy Injunctions and the Media

A Practice Manual

Iain Goldrein QC MA (Cantab)

Recorder; Visiting Professor (The Sir Jack Jacob Chair) in Litigation: Nottingham Law School; Companion of the Academy of Experts; Fellow of the Royal Society of Arts; Fellow of the Institute of Advanced Legal Studies; Council Member: International Institute of Experts (Hong Kong); Editorial Board: Civil Court Practice; Advisory Editor: Hong Kong Civil Procedure

assisted by

Richard Brant LLB (Hons 1st Class)

• HART •
PUBLISHING

OXFORD AND PORTLAND, OREGON
2012

Published in the United Kingdom by Hart Publishing Ltd
16C Worcester Place, Oxford, OX1 2JW
Telephone: +44 (0)1865 517530
Fax: +44 (0)1865 510710
E-mail: mail@hartpub.co.uk
Website: http://www.hartpub.co.uk

Published in North America (US and Canada) by
Hart Publishing
c/o International Specialized Book Services
920 NE 58th Avenue, Suite 300
Portland, OR 97213-3786
USA
Tel: +1 503 287 3093 or toll-free: (1) 800 944 6190
Fax: +1 503 280 8832
E-mail: orders@isbs.com
Website: http://www.isbs.com

British Library Cataloguing in Publication Data

Data Available

ISBN: 978-1-84946-284-6

Typeset by Forewords, Oxon

Printed and bound in Great Britain by
TJ International Ltd, Padstow, Cornwall

MIX
Paper from responsible sources
FSC® C013056

To Rebecca Anne Goldrein

May the Lord make you as Sarah, Rebecca, Rachel and Leah.

May the Lord bless you, and keep you: May the Lord make his face to shine upon you, and be gracious unto you: May the Lord turn his face unto you, and give you peace.

Foreword

Privacy as a philosophical concept and as a value which society protects is both controversial in scope and content, and it therefore raises many difficult questions. Is it a right, as Warren and Brandeis put it, simply to be 'let alone'[1]? Or is it more than that? Is it a right which should be protected through a law of general application or should it only be protected in narrowly defined and limited circumstances? How should it relate to other rights? Should it, for instance, always trump freedom of expression when they come into conflict, should it always yield or should a balance be struck between them? If a balance should be struck, how should it be struck and in what circumstances?

The law of England and Wales has traditionally taken a narrow approach to privacy, its scope and content. The common law did not develop a general right of privacy, as the Court of Appeal in *Kaye v Robertson* affirmed in 1991,[2] nor did Parliament introduce one, despite many attempts to do so. In the absence of a general law, the common law developed a limited and fact-specific approach, protecting privacy through, for instance, as Lord Cottenham LC noted in *Prince Albert v Strange* in 1849,[3] the law of confidentiality. In 1998 there was, of course, a seismic shift when Parliament enacted the Human Rights Act, and through it incorporated Article 8 of the European Convention on Human Rights into English and Welsh law. This has not, as the House of Lords made clear in *Wainwright v Home Office*,[4] introduced a statutory general right of privacy into English and Welsh law. It has however, as Parliament understood and the government intended during the 1998 Act's passage, provided a very significant spur to the law of privacy's development, as Lord Phillips MR (as he then was) observed in *Douglas v Hello! (No 6)*,

> The enactment of the Human Rights Act 1998 provoked a lively discussion of the impact that it would have on the development of a law protecting privacy. The Government has made it clear that it does not intend to

[1] Warren and Brandeis, 'The Right to Privacy' (1890) 4 *Harvard Law Review* 193.

[2] (1991) FSR 62 at (66).

[3] (1849) 1 Mac & G 25, 'In the present case, where the privacy is the right invaded, the postponing of the injunction would be equivalent to denying it altogether. The interposition of this Court in these cases does not depend on any legal right; and, to be effectual, it must be immediate.'

[4] [2004] 2 AC 4 at [35].

> introduce legislation in relation to this area of the law, but anticipates that the judges will develop the law appropriately, having regard to the requirements of the Convention for the Protection of Human Rights and Fundamental Freedoms : see the comment of Lord Irvine of Lairg LC in the course of the debate on the Human Rights Bill (Hansard, HL Debates, 24 November 1997, col 771) and the submissions of the United Kingdom in Spencer (Earl) v United Kingdom (1998) 25 EHRR CD 105.[5]

In this welcome new book on *Privacy Injunctions and the Media: A Practice Manual*, Iain Goldrein QC provides a clear, insightful and, perhaps most importantly, practical guide to the way in which the courts have developed the law of privacy in the past decade or so. The book provides a readily accessible and properly comprehensive route through the substantive law of privacy as it now stands, its relationship with freedom of expression, and the balance to be struck between them. On its own, and given the ways in which the law has developed, this would be a significant achievement and should, deservedly, see this work become an essential reference work for lawyers, litigants and those generally interested in the law. In addition, Iain Goldrein has provided a detailed guide to the proper conduct of privacy litigation. Anyone wishing to prepare and prosecute a claim effectively ought to pay close attention to this guidance.

In the years to come it is inevitable that the law and practice relating to privacy will continue to develop. Those developments will further define how English and Welsh law deals with issues as to the scope and application of the law of privacy, and the procedure by which respect for privacy is protected and balanced against other substantive rights. That development will undoubtedly be greatly assisted, and shaped, by the insights contained in *Goldrein on Privacy Injunctions*. I commend it to all those who are interested in the development of the law in this important area, and particularly to those who want practical guidance.

Lord Neuberger of Abbotsbury, MR

[5] [2006] QB 125 at [46].

Preface

Purpose

The purpose of this book is to set out best practice in the field of privacy injunctions and the media.

For whom the book is intended

Such best practice is targeted not just at litigators. The intention of this book is also to embrace within its reach those who are the watchdogs of the freedoms of our society, journalists and other organs of the media. In this context, it reflects the agenda set by Lord Neuberger's Report of 2011 (*Report of the Committee on Super-Injunctions*), at p 33:

> 3.7 The Guidance should be available to everyone, not just to specialist lawyers in this area. It should ensure that all litigants, potential litigants, and their advisers, are fully aware of their obligations under the law. (p 33)

This agenda, to provide clarity of law beyond the frontiers traditionally set for legal practice, is part of a broader agenda of the genre struck by this book to provide access to law which is clearly intelligible, and thus to demystify its principles and practice.

Accordingly the book seeks to achieve a balance between the level of detail which meets the demands of the court and litigators, whilst securing sufficient clarity for a broader audience.

Style of writing

It is because of this broader agenda that the book is written in a style which it is intended should break the mould of legal writing.

The text is broken down into easily manageable sections. The fonts used are intended to launch the words off the page onto the reader's retina, rather than leave the impression of impenetrable learning.

These fonts are not just a characteristic of the primary text, but also of the Case Digest in Part 22.

Further to achieve clarity and best practice, checklists and quality-control protocols are a norm. In addition, the law and practice is set out in a way which is intended to be capable of immediate assimilation by trained lawyer and layperson alike.

Case driven

The legal principles and practice management which feature in the primary text are informed directly by the cases in the Case Digest in Part 22.

To facilitate this approach, the leading cases in the field in the last decade are to be found, edited into the Case Digest, which features in the latter part of the book. Thus a paragraph reference in a case cited in the primary text can be immediately cross-referenced with the relevant passage in the judgment, set out in the Case Digest. This brings with it the added advantage that the primary text does not need to be overburdened with citations, because the relevant passages can so readily be cross-referenced with the Case Digest.

Further, the focus has been on including material which is not just the source of legal principle, but rather puts that legal principle into a broader context.

The ease with which the cases can be located is facilitated by their being in chronological order, together with running titles at the top of each page indicating which case is dealt with on the respective page.

Lord Neuberger's Report

The thrust of this work has been immeasurably enriched by Lord Neuberger's Report[1] which provides a sturdy framework for practice in this field. This book is heavily indebted to, and necessarily draws upon, that Report to develop best practice.

Lord Neuberger has also distilled from ***LNR*** a **Practice Guidance: Interim Non-disclosure Orders**, which is included in this book at Part 17.

For ease of reference, through the text, the page and paragraph referencing are to ***LNR***; and if the reference is not to the body of the report, but to

[1] Report of the Committee on Super-injunctions: Super-injunctions, Anonymised Injunctions and Open Justice.

the **Practice Guidance,** that is explicitly stated and the relevant paragraph number in the Guidance set out.

Acknowledgement to the focal judiciary in this arena

This part of the preface would not be complete without fulsome acknowledgment of the contribution made so assiduously by the judiciary to the jurisprudence in this field, and particularly by Eady, Tugendhat and Sharp JJs.

Reading all the judgments intensively and with great care, as one must for a work such as this, brings home the meticulous commitment of these judges to achieving the balance that is demanded in an arena as sensitive as that where there is tension between public interest and privacy.

The work and research that has been invested in their judgments is manifest testimony to the quality of the jurisprudence.

Summary of contents

To ease the reader into the field, the book is divided into 22 Parts:

Part 1: Primary source material and legal principles.

Part 2: Applicant practice management: Article 6 derogations from open justice.

Part 3: The interaction of Articles 8 and 10.

Part 4: Proportionality.

Part 5: Practice principles underpinning an Article 8 application.

Part 6: Case management for Article 8 applications.

Part 7: Applicant proceedings checklist up to (but not including) service.

Part 8: Service checklist for applicants.

Part 9: Defence practice points in response to an Article 8 application.

Part 10: Quality control checklist for the courtroom.

Part 11: Journalists' checklist.

Part 12: Harassment and the media.

Part 13: Derogation from open justice and claims by children for approval of large personal injury awards.

Part 14: Reporting restriction orders in the Family Division together with the monograph *The Family Courts: Media Access and Reporting*. On behalf also of Hart Publishing, we are very grateful to the President of the Family Division, Sir Nicholas Wall, for permission to reproduce this document. That gratitude of course extends also to Adam Wolanski and Kate Wilson for the extensive and thorough work they have so effectively undertaken in writing the monograph. This Part is also used as the vehicle to draw attention to the important decision of Sir Nicholas Wall in *Doncaster v Haigh and others*.

Part 15: Template model statement.

Part 16: Mediation. On behalf also of Hart Publishing, we express our appreciation to the ADR Group—a pre-eminent service-provider in this arena—for the use of its Model Documents.

Part 17: On behalf also of Hart Publishing, we are particularly grateful to Lord Neuberger for his permission to publish his **Practice Guidance** in this Part; that gratitude of course extends to all those on his Committee who played such an important role in its preparation and in particular, Lord Judge CJ.

Part 18: Examples of orders from the cases.

Part 19: CPR provisions.

Part 20: Privacy codes.

Part 21: Key words highlighted in the Case Digest.

Part 22: Case Digest.

As a reading of these Parts will reveal, they begin with a succinct focus on the legal principles of privacy and freedom of expression. As the reader moves forward through that material, increasingly the legal principles are expressed through a procedural prism until, towards the end, the checklists are intensely practical and exclusively procedural.

In this way, it is intended that a clear grip on principle can run hand in hand with an accurate procedural presentation of the case. This should in turn enable material in the book to be readily cross-referenced with a skeleton argument, for ease and speed of preparation and presentation of an application.

Readily understandable

In this arena of privacy injunctions, there is so much room for misunderstanding, with pejorative phrases such as 'judge-made law' and 'gagging orders'.

It is with no disrespect to the media if one sensitively advances the point that they have a virtual monopoly over the dissemination to the public of the decisions in these cases. Such exposure to public attention is inevitable in the realm of an independent media which is much broader than the exposure which the judgments themselves enjoy (freely available though they are on BAILLI).

Lord Judge made the point with characteristic clarity in *R v (Binyam Mohamed) v Secretary of State for Foreign and Commonwealth Affairs* [2010] EWCA Civ 65 at para 38:

> In reality very few citizens can scrutinise the judicial process: that scrutiny is performed by the media, whether newspapers or television, acting on behalf of the body of citizens. Without the commitment of an independent media the operation of the principle of open justice would be irremediably diminished.

Indeed, one can readily understand that the nuances of a judgment demand much by way of legal analysis, and a journalist can reasonably and readily be forgiven for saying: *'Do not expect us to understand all the fine tuning; we are not trained lawyers—we are trained in serving the public interest as journalists.'*

And yet there is a tension here, with the courts, for as Tugendhat J said in the *Goodwin* case at para 87:

> So anyone commenting upon this case without reference to the specific evidence before the court will be approaching the issues in a way in which Parliament has not permitted judges to approach them.

Perhaps the time is therefore ripe, particularly in this very special arena, for a book which explains in terms readily understandable by all (trained lawyer or otherwise) what the principles are and how the judges work in practice within those principles.

If further encouragement were needed, it is perhaps to be found in the words of Richard de Bury, penned in 1344:

> Let us consider how great a commodity of doctrine exists in books—how easily, how secretly, how safely they expose the nakedness of human ignorance, without putting it to shame.

> Books are the masters which instruct us without rods, without hard words and anger, without money; if you approach them they are not asleep; if investigating, you interrogate them, they conceal nothing; if you mistake them, they never grumble; if you are ignorant, they cannot laugh at you.

Cost-effective litigation tool

This book is intended to serve a further purpose, namely to provide a cost-effective tool for the litigation process.

Inevitably perhaps, given the profile of so many of the claimants, this legal arena can so readily be regarded as restricted to the 'rich and famous'. It is hoped that with this book, the market can be further opened up, nationwide.

The result should be that those who fall outside the conventional category of 'celebrity' can still cost-effectively achieve a remedy if their Article 8 rights are to be wrongly infringed; and equally, journalists who wish to assert public interest are in this book given the tools to advance such argument, to empower them—where appropriate—to perform their function yet more effectively as a public watchdog.

The richness of diversity and 'One England'

Written as it is for a wider audience, this book is also intended to fulfil a further purpose.

We live in a society which is enriched by diversity. Yet the question can be asked: Are we all living, figuratively speaking, independently in hotel bedrooms? To what extent do the diverse cultures in our society genuinely mix? Do we share, as it were, at least a refectory? What binds us together as citizens?

There is one theme which binds us each to the other, which can afford to us a shared sense of being, of history and of culture, which binds us indeed from womb to tomb, from the clinical negligence action for a baby born with brain damage, to issues touching upon the essence of family life to an argument over a will.

That theme is, of course, the law of England and Wales, with its delightful cadences as reflected in passages in judgments, which have the eloquence to justify a readership much broader than that afforded just by the legal profession.

In its own modest way, this book is intended to tease out of the judgments, those very special cadences, and share them with a wider audience; so that whoever one is, from wherever one may have come, one can share a joint heritage with real pride—the heritage of a judiciary who, spanning the nation's history, have expressed their struggle to achieve the correct balance between individuals in society in language in which we are all stakeholders, and in which we can derive genuine pleasure.

Iain Goldrein QC
Liverpool, Nottingham and London
Trafalgar Day 2011

User's Guide

- Throughout, applicants for injunctive relief are referred to as 'A' and respondents, as R. The reason for the inverted commas vis-à-vis an applicant is to distinguish the reference from what otherwise could, in certain contexts, be misinterpreted as an indefinite article.
- All case references in the body of the text are to EWHC, UKHL, etc. The reason is:
    - These case references are immediately accessible by all users, for BAILLI is free of charge (www.bailli.org); and
    - Further references would clutter the text.

  The cases have been edited down, the earlier cases more than the more recent, to achieve a book of manageable proportions. The intention has consistently been to edit the cases in such a way as not to distort their context or thrust. If there is any issue as to the meaning of what the judge is reported as saying, please go to the full report to access the judgment as a whole.
- Fonts in bold and/or italics are editorial style; when they feature in passages cited from the cases, they are the emphasis of the book, not of the judgment cited.
- The key words set out in Part 21 (and indexed in the Case Digest Keywords Concordance) are highlighted throughout the primary text, and the Case Digest.
- The book is intended to be read as a book, rather than to be dipped into as one would a reference manual. It is advised that before using the book as a reference manual, time is spent going through Parts 1–10 sequentially, to understand how the book works and to assimilate an in-depth understanding of the topics.
- Part 1 is the foundation course for the book, and exclusively sets out principles as distinct from practice. It is therefore printed in a different font, so that it stands out from the rest of the book, which is practice driven.
- In Part 14, there is a template for a model statement, which seeks to provide triggers for the issues that are to be expected to arise in practice.
- Lord Neuberger has provided a Model Order in his Practice Guidance, which is set out in full in Part 17—together with an accompanying Explanatory Note.
- The Codes of Practice are set out (or references to the relevant websites) so that the reader can assimilate them together and have a grip on the policy issues advanced by the Codes.

- In the primary text, all emphases are those of the author, as are virtually all the emphases in the Case Digest.
- There are occasions when there is an appearance of repetition in the text. This however is to be seen in context: as the text unfolds, so different contexts arise.
- Throughout the book there are references to conduct which may be interpreted as reprehensible, eg blackmail, 'tipping off', etc. It should be kept firmly in mind that in the context of interlocutory relief, the court is addressing these issues on a preliminary basis and no final findings have been made.

Contents

Table of Cases

Table of Legislation

Note that the European Convention for the Protection of Human Rights is discussed and referred to throughout the work. For this reason, only references to specific Articles and the initial discussion of its provisions are cited below.

European/International

National

United Kingdom

Statutes

Statutory Instruments

Other Countries

Canada

Denmark

Germany

United States

Part 1

PRIMARY SOURCE MATERIAL AND LEGAL PRINCIPLES

The ECHR Articles

Article 6

> Right to a fair trial
>
> **In the determination of his civil rights and obligations or of any criminal charge against him, everyone is entitled to a fair trial and public hearing within a reasonable time by an independent and impartial tribunal established by law.** Judgment shall be pronounced ***publicly*** **but** the press and public ***may be excluded*** from ***all or part of the trial*** in the interest of morals, public order or national security in a democratic society, where the interests of juveniles or the ***protection*** of the ***private life*** of the parties so require, or to the extent ***strictly necessary*** in the opinion of the court in ***special circumstances*** where publicity would prejudice the interests of justice.

» **Introduction:** The issue under Article 6 is 'derogation from open justice.'

» **Anonymity as an exception:** The general rule is that the names of the parties to an action are included in orders and judgments of the court. This is the corollary of the general rule that hearings are carried out in, and judgments and orders, are public: Article 6 and CPR 39.2 There is no general exception for cases where private matters are in issue: *JIH v News Group Newspapers Ltd* [2011] EWCA Civ 42 at **para 21(1)** and **(2)**.

» **Necessity etc:** As to the meaning of the word '*necessary*' in this context, Maurice Kay LJ said the following in *Ntuli v Donald* [2010] EWCA Civ 1276 at **paras 51–53**:

> 51. It is submitted on behalf of Mr Donald that this is such a case. Mr Sherborne seeks to fortify that submission by inviting us to dilute **the test of necessity** referred to in the earlier authorities on the basis that they preceded the Human Rights Act which, in providing for competing qualified rights (private life and freedom of expression), requires a more nuanced approach. In this regard, he refers to the control order case of *Home Secretary v AP (No 2)* [2010] 1 WLR 1652, [2010] UKSC 26, in which the anonymity of a successful appellant against a control order was continued.
>
> 52. In my judgment, there is no need for a new approach. Indeed, it is significant that Article 6 of the ECHR itself prescribes a test of **strict necessity** in the context of publicity being permitted to be restricted in the interests of justice. However, as part of its consideration of all the circumstances of a case, a court will have regard to the respective and sometimes competing Convention rights of the parties. In *AP (No 2)*, this led Lord Rodger to formulate the question in these terms (at paragraph 7):
>
> > **". . . whether there is sufficient general, public interest in publishing a report of the proceedings which identifies [AP] to justify any resulting curtailment of his right and his family's right to respect for their *private* and *family* life."**
>
> 53. There, **anonymity** was continued because the public interest in publication '*has to give way to the need to protect AP from the* ***risk of violence***' and the same public interest '*would not justify curtailing AP's right to respect for his private and family life*' (paragraph 18). Whilst this is not the language of 'necessity', it is not significantly different. Indeed, '**has to give way**' is qualitatively similar to a **necessity** test. Necessity remains the test for the **residual power** to order a **private hearing** under the Civil Procedure Rules (CPR 39.2(3)(g)).

Also see in this context, *In re Guardian News and Media Ltd* [2010] 2 WLR 325 at **paras 50–52** and *Secretary of State for the Home Department v AP (No 2)* [2010] UKSC 26 at **para 7**.

» **Strictly etc.** As to the interaction of the word '*strictly*' with the word '*necessary*', see *JIH v News Group Newspapers Ltd* [2010] EWHC 2818 (QB) **para 34**, and at **para 64** (unaffected by subsequent appeal).

> I remind myself that where the proposed justification for **anonymity** is that identification would prevent the attainment of justice, the **test** that the Claimant has to satisfy is that of **strict necessity** (paras 33 and 34 above). The Claimant has not shown to that **high standard** that the object of achieving justice in this case would be rendered doubtful if the anonymity order were not made.

In this case, the order (stayed pending appeal) identified the Claimant but gave information about the subject matter of the action only in a *Confidential Schedule*; in this context, see also *Ambrosiadou v Coward* [2011] EWCA Civ 409 at **para 54**, and further see *Gray v UVW* [2010]

EWHC 2367 (QB) **paras 1** and **40** as to the need for '*necessity*' and '*proportionality*'. ***LNR* Practice Guidance**:

> 10. Derogations from the general principle [of open justice] can only be justified in exceptional circumstances, when they are strictly necessary as measures to secure the proper administration of justice. They are wholly exceptional: *R v Chief Registrar of Friendly Societies, ex parte New Cross Building Society* [1984] QB 227 art 235, and *Ntuli v Donald* [2010] EWCA Civ 1276 at **paras [52]–[53]**. Derogations should where justified, be no more than strictly necessary to achieve their purpose.
>
> . . .
>
> 14. When considering the imposition of any derogation from open justice, the court will have regard to the respective and sometimes competing Convention rights of the parties as well as the general public interest in open justice and in the public reporting of court proceedings. It will also adopt procedures which seek to ensure that any ultimate vindication of Article 8 of the Convention, where that is engaged, is not undermined by the way in which the court has processed an interim application. On the other hand, the principle of open justice requires that any restrictions **are the least that can be imposed** consistent with the protection to which the party relying on their Article 8 Convention right is entitled. The proper approach is set out in *JIH*.

LNR expressed it in these terms on p 8, at **para 1.19**:

> The principle of open justice must therefore yield to privacy or secrecy but normally only when, in the circumstances of a particular case, to adhere to it entirely would frustrate the court's ability to administer justice properly.

» **Whose right**? Note that *open justice* and *the right to be heard* is the right of a person affected by a court order, in particular a respondent, to be heard before the order is made. Apart from section 12 of the Human Rights Act 1998, that requirement is set out *twice* in the CPR: once in CPR 25.3(1),(3) and again in CPR PD 25, **para 4.3(3)**. CPR 25.3 and CPR PD 25A(1)–(5) apply to all interim injunction applications, including those for interim non-disclosure orders. Relevant case law is:

- *Kelly (A Minor) v BBC* [2000] EWHC 3 (Fam), [2001] Fam 59 at 94–95:

  > [I]f one party wishes to place evidence or other persuasive material before the court **the other parties must have an opportunity to see that material and to address the court about it**. One party may not make secret communications to the court. It follows **that it is wrong for a judge to be given material at an ex parte, or without notice, hearing which is not at a later stage revealed to the persons affected** by the result of the application.

- *G & G v Wikimedia Foundation Inc* [2009] EWHC 3148 (QB) at **para 30**—a *Norwich Pharmacal* application against Wikipedia:

> [W]here an order relates to freedom of expression, or may have the effect of interfering with freedom of expression, those applying for interim relief at a hearing at which the respondent or defendant is not present **should generally provide the respondent with a full note, whether or not the respondent asks for it**.

» **The classical circumstances for anonymity:** Per ***LNR*** at p 23, **para 2.23**:

> Historically however the use of anonymity, privacy and non-disclosure orders has tended to be limited to specific circumstances, eg, where **blackmail** is involved, where there is a **risk of violence** towards parties or witnesses, where publicity would frustrate the purpose of the order through **tipping-off** the subject of the order before it is served, or where **children are involved**.

» **Procedural steps:** The procedural steps to apply for a derogation from open justice are set out below in **Part 2**, and are to be read in the context of the balance to be struck between Article 8 and Article 10, set out in **Part 3**.

» **Ability to participate in proceedings:** As to how Article 6 rights could possibly interact with a mental condition and press intrusion, see *A Local Authority v A Mother & F & A* [2011] EWHC 1764 (Fam) per Baker J at **paras 44** and **68**.

Article 8

Right to respect for private and family life, home and correspondence

1. Every one has the right to respect for his private and family life, his home and his correspondence.
2. There shall be no interference by a public authority with the exercise of this right except such as is in **accordance** with the law and is **necessary** in a democratic society in the interests of national security, public safety or the economic well-being of the country, for the prevention of disorder or crime, for the protection of health or morals, or for the **protection** of the **rights** and **freedoms** of **others**.

» **What rights pre-exist Article 8 'privacy'?** Such rights are the derivatives of the following causes of action: nuisance, libel, breach of confidence, harassment, data protection and contempt of court.

» **What is embraced by '*privacy*'?** See *Bensaid v United Kingdom* [2001] 33 EHRR 10 at **paras 46** and **47**:

> 47. Private life is a broad term **not susceptible to exhaustive definition**. The

> Court has already held that elements such as **gender identification**, **name** and **sexual orientation** and **sexual life** are important elements of the personal sphere protected by Art 8. **Mental health** must also be regarded as a crucial part of private life associated with the aspect of **moral integrity**. Article 8 protects a right to **identity** and **personal development**, and the right **to establish and develop relationships** with other human beings and the outside world. The preservation of **mental stability** is in that context an **indispensable precondition** to effective enjoyment of the right to respect for private life.

Express recognition of Article 8 covering *physical* and *psychological* integrity was recognised in *R (Countryside Alliance) v A-G* [2007] UKHL 52 at **para 116** (essential reading). Per Lord Bingham at **para 10**:

> [Article 8 protects a] **private sphere** within which individual expect to be left alone to conduct their personal affairs and live their personal lives **as they choose**.

And per Baroness Hale at **para 116**:

> [Article 8] protects '**private space**' and 'the personal and **psychological space** within which each individual develops his or her **own sense of self** and relationships with other people.

Bensaid was expressly followed by Eady J in *Maxine Carr v News Group Newspapers Ltd* [2005] EWHC 971 (QB) at **para 3**.

» **The core principle:** There is no question of Article 8 furnishing an *absolute* right to privacy. Articl 8 (2) qualifies, in terms, the right conferred by Article 8(1); *Christopher Hutcheson (formerly known as 'KGM') v News Group Newspapers Ltd & Ors* [2011] EWCA Civ 808 at **para 27**. Laws LJ emphasised in *R (Wood) v Commissioner of Police for the Metropolis* [2009] EWCA Civ 414 at **para 22** that the purpose of the '*safeguards*' or '*qualifications*' to which he referred was to ensure that the '*core right protected by article 8 . . . should not be read so widely that its claims become unreal and unreasonable*'.

» **Horizontal approach:** Through the court being a public body, the Article 8 (and Article 10) rights are secured horizontally between the parties: *Campbell v MGN* Ltd [2004] UKHL 22 at **para 17**; In *Re S (A Child)* [2004] UKHL 47, [2005] 1 AC 593 at **paras 22–23**; *Niema Ash and another v Loreena McKennitt and Others* [2006] EWCA Civ 1714 at **paras 9–11**, and per Gross LJ in *Hutcheson v News Group Newspapers Ltd* at **para 22**.

» **The causes of action:** There is now recognised a distinct cause of action, '*misuse of private information*' (see Lord Nicholls in *Campbell v MGN Ltd* at **paras 14, 17 and 18**) as distinct from the traditional '*breach* *of confidence*'. As to the distinction between '*secrecy*' and '*privacy*', see *Michael Douglas v Hello! Ltd (No 6)* [2005] EWCA Civ 595 per Lord Phillips at **paras 50–82,** and per Lord Nicholls in *Michael Douglas v Hello! Ltd* [2007] UKHL 21 at **para 255.** This resonates with the distinction '*confidentiality*' and '*intrusion*' drawn by Tugendhat J in *Sir Frederick Goodwin v NGN Ltd and VBN (No 3)* [2011] EWHC 1437 (QB).

» **Meaning of 'private' as a principle:** Per Lord Nicholls in *Campbell v MGN Ltd* at **para 21**:

> Essentially the touchstone of private life is whether in respect of the disclosed facts the person in question had a **reasonable expectation of privacy** in respect of the information.

Also see in this context:

(a) *Campbell v MGN Ltd* at **para 50**.
(b) *Wood v Commissioner of Police for the Metropolis* at **paras 21** and **22**; and at **para 24**: '*legitimate expectation of protection*'.
(c) In *R v Broadcasting Standards Commission, Ex p BBC* [2000] EWCA Civ 116, **para 48**, Lord Mustill, sitting in the Court of Appeal, said:

> To my mind the privacy of a human being denotes at the same time the personal '**space**' in which the individual is free to be itself, and also the **carapace**, or shell, **or umbrella**, or whatever other metaphor is preferred, which **protects that space from intrusion**. An infringement of privacy is **an affront to the personality**, which is damaged both by the **violation** and by the **demonstration** that the personal space is not inviolate.

» **Reasonable expectation of privacy—objective or subjective?** The test is '*objective*'—established in *Campbell v MGN Ltd* [2004] UKHL 22, [2004] 2 AC 457, **para 99** per Lord Nicholls:

> The question is what a reasonable person of **ordinary sensibilities** would feel if she was placed in the **same position** as the claimant and faced with the same publicity.

This question refers to the sensibilities of a reasonable person placed in the situation of the *subject of disclosure* rather than to its recipient; see *Campbell v MGN Ltd* at **paras 99** and **136**. See also *TSE and ELP v News Group Newspapers Ltd* [2011] EWHC 1308 (QB) at **para 18**; *DFT v TFD* [2010] EWHC 2335 (QB) per Sharp J at **paras 16** and **17**; and the dicta of Ward LJ in *ETK v News Group Newspapers Ltd* [2011] EWCA Civ 439 at **para 10**.

» **Analysing the relevant material:** Per Tugendhat J in *Goodwin v NGN Ltd and VBN (No 3)* at **para 62(e)**:

> It is also clear from the authorities that the correct application of this approach requires the Court to give separate consideration to **different items** or **classes of information**. See, for example, *Lord Browne of Madingley v Associated Newspapers Ltd* [2008] QB 103 per Sir Anthony Clarke MR at [**37**].

In other words, the information should be refracted into its respective strands. Further as to '*strands*'; see *John Terry (previously 'LNS') v Persons Unknown* [2010] EWHC 119 (QB) per Tugendhat J at **para 6**; *Campbell v MGN Ltd* at **para 23**; and see *Ash v McKennitt* at **paras 12** and 20. As to '*strands*' and an analysis of Article 10 in the context of the press wishing to publish details as to a mother alleged to have killed her children, see *A Local Authority v A Mother & F &* A [2011] EWHC 1764 (Fam) at **para 57** per Baker J. As to '*degrees of privacy*' see *Goodwin v NGN Ltd and VBN (No 3)* at **para 106** and *Campbell v MGN Ltd* at **para 118.**

» **Reasonable expectation of privacy and photographs:** It depends on the circumstances; see *Von Hannover v Germany* [2005] 40 EHRR 1 where it was held that a photograph of Princess Caroline in the street did generate a reasonable expectation of privacy, as contrasted with a similar situation in (Sir Elton) *John v Associated Newspapers Ltd* [2006] EWHC 1611 (QB) where at **para 15** Eady J held that:

> . . . the circumstances are more akin to 'popping out for a pint of milk' . . .

» **Examples of private life through the English case law:** There is no comprehensive definition of 'private life'.

(a) In *Marper v UK* (Applications no 30562/04 and 30566/04, judgment delivered on 4 December 2008, [2008] ECHR 1581) it was held at **para 66** that the concept of 'private life' is a '*broad* term *not* susceptible to *exhaustive* definition'.

(b) The content of the phrase '*private and family life*' is *very broad* indeed; see *Wood v Commissioner of Police of the Metropolis* at **paras 18–21** (essential reading). Also in this context see *Mosley v UK* [2011] ECtHR 774 at **para 109** as to the state's margin of appreciation vis-à-vis Article 8.

(c) In *Murray v Express Newspapers* [2009] Ch 481 at **paras 24**, **27**, **35** and **40** it was held that the question at Stage 1 (is Article 8 engaged) is a '*broad one*' which '*takes account of all the circumstances of the case*'—and see the dicta of Sharp J on this issue at **para 16** in *DFT v TFD*, and *MJN v News Group Newspapers Ltd* [2011] EWHC 1192 (QB) per Sharp J at **para 9.** Further as to 'broad', see *TSE and ELP v News Group Newspapers Ltd* [2011] EWCH 1308 (QB) at **para 18.**

(d) *Campbell v MGN Ltd* at **para 51**; although it was not, on the facts, private information that Naomi Campbell suffered from drug addiction, it was private information that she was seeking treatment for that addiction, ie information in respect of which she had a reasonable expectation of privacy.

(e) As to the interaction of a '*confidential relationship*' and '*misuse of private information*', see Buxton LJ in *Ash v McKennitt* at **para 8** and at **para 15**; also see *CTB v NGN Ltd and Imogen Thomas (No 2)* [2011] EWHC 1326 (QB) per Eady J at **para 27**: '*The point of Article 8 is that it is not supposed to be any of NGN's business*.'

(f) Note also the particularly strong positive obligation of the state to *respect* and *promote* the interests of private and family life: *X & Y v Netherlands* [1985] 8 EHRR 235.

(g) It has yet to be decided whether a reasonable expectation of privacy embraces a conviction which is 'spent' under the Rehabilitation of Offenders Act 1974: *KJO v XIM* [2011] EWHC 1768 (QB) at **para 32.**

» **The 'public/private' concept is not necessarily a yardstick:** Per Eady J in *Jenifer Howlett v Terry Holding* [2006] EWHC 41 (QB) at para 26:

> A **zone** of interaction was recognised of one person with others, even in a public context, which would fall within the scope of *'private life'*. In the light of this case, and indeed others such as *P G & J H v United Kingdom* (Application 44787/98) and *Peck v United Kingdom* (2003) 26 EHRR 41, it may safely now be said that it is not possible for those who wish to intrude upon the lives of **individuals through surveillance, and associated photography**, to rely upon **a rigid distinction** being drawn in their favour between what takes place in **private** and activities capable of being witnessed in a **public** place by other people.

As to the so-called 'zonal' argument, see *KGM v NGN Ltd & AN Ltd* [2010] EWHC 3145 QB at para 38 per Eady J.

» **It is not just parties to the proceedings who are protected by Article 8:** see *JIH v News Group Newspapers Ltd* [2011] EMLR 9, [2010] EWHC 2818 (QB) (the subsequent judgment of the Court of Appeal did not affect this part of the judgment) per Tugendhat J:

> 59. **The widow and children were parties in the Plon case in the national courts.** But the obligation of the Court under s 6 of the HRA (not to act incompatibly with Convention rights) obliges the Court to have regard to the Art 8 rights of persons **who are not parties to the action**, as well as to the rights of the claimant.

Thus in *ETK v News Group Newspapers Ltd*, in the context of a married man with two teenage children who conducted an affair with a work colleague in the entertainment industry, Ward LJ said at **para 17**:

> The purpose of the injunction is both **to preserve the stability of the family** while the appellant and his wife **pursue reconciliation** and to save the children the ordeal of playground ridicule when that would inevitably follow publicity.

» **'Necessary':** *R (Wood) v Commissioner of Police for the Metropolis* [2009] EWCA Civ 414 at **para 83** per Dyson LJ:

> 83. In deciding whether the interference is **necessary**, the court must have regard to the **nature of the Convention right** in issue, **its importance** for the individual, the **nature of the interference** and **the object** pursued by the interference: see Marper at [102].

» **Boundaries:**

(a) An individual needs to know where his private life *ends* and his public life *starts*: see *Von Hannover v Germany* at **para 73**; contrast dicta of Eady J in *X & Y v Persons Unknown* [2006] EWHC 2783 (QB) **para 82** as to the uncertainty of the boundaries of Article 8.

(b) *Increased vigilance* in protecting private life is *necessary* to contend with *new* communication *technologies* which make it possible to store and reproduce personal data: *Von Hannover v Germany* at **para 70**; and this principle may be thrown into sharp relief in the context of internet publicity, social networking sites and the case of *CTB v News Group Newspapers Ltd (No 1)* [2011] EWHC 1232 (QB).

» **Right of others:** Article 8 rights fall within the scope of '*the rights of others*' in Article 10(2); see *Re Guardian News and Media* [2010] UKSC 1, **para 37**, and *Mosley v UK* [2011] ECtHR 774 at **para 113**:

> The press must not overstep the bounds set for, among other things, 'the protection of . . . the rights of others' including the requirements of acting in **good faith** and on an **accurate factual basis** and of providing **'reliable and precise' information** in accordance with the **ethics of journalism**.

As to 'responsible journalism', see **paras 174 et seq** below.

» **Interaction of 'intrusion' and 'harassment':** As to the interaction of '*intrusion*' and '*harassment*' (in the overall context of '*privacy*'), see *CTB v News Group Newspapers Ltd and Imogen Thomas* [2011] EWHC 1334 (QB) per Tugendhat J at **para 3** and his dicta in *Goodwin v NGN Ltd and VBN (No 3)* [2011] EWHC 1437 (QB) at **para 86**; and also at **para 114** (citing from *Thomas v News Group Newspapers Ltd* [2002] EMLR 78).

> 50. The court stated that the test for whether the articles amount to harassment requires the publisher to consider whether a proposed series of articles, **which is likely to cause distress to an individual**, will constitute an abuse of the freedom of press **which the pressing social needs of a democratic society** require should be curbed.

» **Versatility of the common law:** As to the innate ability of the common law to develop this field, see *Douglas v Hello! Ltd (No 1)* [2001] QB 967 at **para 88**, [2000] EWCA Civ 353.

» **Confidential relationship as an aspect of privacy:**

(a) **As to the existence of a confidential relationship:** See *Ash v McKennitt* at **para 15;** and *Associated Newspapers Ltd v HRH Prince of Wales* [2006] EWCA Civ 1776 at **para 28**. See also *Prince Albert v Strange* [1849] EWHC ChJ 20 per Cottenham LC where he observed that the real issue in the case was '*privacy*' in a situation arising out of a confidential relationship:

> In the present case, where the privacy is the right invaded, the postponing of the injunction would be equivalent to denying it altogether.

(Another way of expressing the 'ice-cube' point.)

(b) **The distinction between 'nature of the information' and a 'confidential relationship':** This was brought out by Buxton LJ in *Ash v McKennitt* at **para 15**:

(i) If the issue is unauthorised or purloined information, then one may look to the '*nature of the information*', because it is the recipient's perception of its confidential nature that imposes an obligation on him.

(ii) But in the vast majority of cases, the duty of confidence will arise from a '*transaction*' or '*relationship*' between the parties. That situation reverts to a more elemental enquiry into breach of confidence in the traditional understanding of that expression.

(c) **As to the 'nature of confidential information':** See *John Terry v Persons Unknown* per Tugendhat J at **paras 52** and **123** (the words said to be threatened were not yet known; see **para 76**), and *Leeds City Council v Channel Four Television Corporation* [2007] 1 FLR 678 at **para 18** (per Mumby J), [2005] EWHC 3522 (Fam):

> No doubt in its more recent extension into what for shorthand I will call the commercial context, the law of confidence focuses upon the confidential nature of the particular information in question, but there are many relationships or settings which have traditionally been

accepted as giving rise to a duty of confidence irrespective of the particular nature of the information in issue.

(d) **Is the test for breach of confidence 'objective' or 'subjective'?** The test is 'objective'; see *Napier v Pressdram Ltd* [2009] EWCA Civ 443 per Toulson LJ at **para 42**:

> For a duty of confidentiality to be owed (other than under a contract or statute), the information in question must be of a nature and obtained in circumstances such that **any reasonable person in the position of the recipient** ought to recognize that it should be treated as confidential.

(e) **What is covered by a cloak of confidence?** Not everything that happens between two persons in a confidential relationship is covered by a cloak of confidence; see *Ash v McKennitt* at **paras 17** and **18**, and **para 26**; and see *Maccaba v Lichtenstein* [2004] EWHC 1579.

(f) **The interaction between confidentiality and intrusion:** See Tugendhat J in *Goodwin v NGN Ltd and VBN (No 3)* at **para 85**:

> . . . unwanted access to private information and unwanted access to [or intrusion into] one's . . . personal space.

» **Examples of a confidential relationship:**

(a) **Doctor and patient:** *W v Egdell* [1989] EWCA Civ 13.

(b) **Legal professional privilege:** *R v Derby Magistrates' Court, ex p B* [1996] AC 487 at 507 per Lord Taylor CJ.

(c) **The relationship between informants and the police:** *R v Lewes Justices, ex p Home Secretary* [1973] AC 388 at 413.

(d) **Confidential information about a person's private life:** *Argyll (Duchess) v Argyll (Duke)* [1967] 1 Ch 302.

(e) **A journalist and his/her sources:** *R v Lewes Crown Court ex p Hill* [1991] 3 Cr App R 60 at 66–67 per Bingham LJ. As to '*the safety valve of effective investigative journalism*', see Judge LJ in *R (Bright) v Central Criminal Court* [2000] EWHC 560 (QB) at **para 98** and Lord Steyn in *R v Secretary of State for the Home Department, ex p Simms* [2000] 2 AC 115 at 131.

(f) **Medical condition:** *X v Y* [1990] 1 QB 220; *Author of a Blog v Times Newspapers Ltd* [2009] EWHC 1358 (QB) per Eady J at **para 9** (referring also to other categories of confidence, with the aphorism also of '*blogging is a public activity*' at **para 11**).

(g) **As to repetition, trade secrets and leakage:** See *JIH v NGN Ltd* [2010] EWHC 2818 (QB) **para 58**, and contrasting the position of trade secrets with privacy, **para 59**; in this context, also see *A Local*

Authority v A Mother & F & A [2011] EWHC 1764 (Fam) per Baker J at **para 36** set out below in Part 14 in relation to reporting restriction orders in the Family Division. See also *TSE and ELP v News Group Newspapers Ltd* at **para 29**, and *R v Dept of Health, ex p Source Infomatics Ltd* [2001] QB 424 (CA) at **paras 33–34**. In this context, also see *A Local Authority v A, F & A* per Baker J at **para 34** set out below in Part 14 in relation to reporting restriction orders in the family division.

(h) **Further references:** *David Murray v Express Newspapers plc and Big Pictures (UK) Ltd* [2007] EWHC 1908 (Ch) at **paras 19** and **20** (concerning photographs of JK Rowling's child); *Leeds City Council v Channel Four Television* per Munby J at **paras 18** *and* **39**; and see *Associated Newspapers v HRH Prince of Wales* at **para 48** (Prince of Wales's private diaries).

(i) **Sexual relationship:** See immediately below.

» **Between parties to a sexual relationship:**

(a) **Married woman's lesbian relationship:** *Stephens v Avery* [1988] Ch 449;

(b) **Kiss and tell:** *Barrymore v News Group Newspapers Ltd* [1997] FSR 600, per Jacob J:

> The fact is that when people kiss and later one of them tells, that second person is almost certainly breaking a confidential arrangement.

(c) **Adultery:** The fact that the relationship was adulterous does not affect the reasonable expectation of privacy; see *ASG v GSA* [2009] EWCA Civ 1574 per Waller LJ at **para 6**.

(d) **Sex lives**: Per Eady J in *Mosley v News Group Newspapers Ltd* [2008] EWHC 1777 (QB) at **paras 98** and **100**:

> Nevertheless, one is usually on safe ground in concluding that anyone indulging in sexual activity is entitled to a degree of privacy—especially if it is on private property and between consenting adults (paid or unpaid). . . .
> . . .
> . . . Nevertheless, the underlying sentiments are readily understood in everyday language; namely, that people's sex lives are to be regarded as essentially their own business—provided at least that the participants are genuinely consenting adults and there is no question of exploiting the young or vulnerable.

This resonates with earlier dicta vis-à-vis confidentiality—per Sir Nicholas Browne-Wilkinson V-C in *Stephens v Avery* [1988] 1 Ch 449 at 454:

> To most people the details of their sexual lives are high on their list of those matters which they regard as confidential.

(e) **Feelings expressed in correspondence:** Similarly, the feelings that people have for each other, as expressed in correspondence, may be confidential, subject of course to the specific facts: *Maccaba v Lichtenstein* [2005] EMLR 9, see Gray J at **para 4** where he addressed the principle in the context of the factual matrix:

> I agree with Mr. Sherborne that as a general rule **correspondence** between A and B on private matters such as their **feelings for one another** would be a prime candidate for protection. But the position appears to me to be different where A **is a married man expressing in unsolicited letters his love for a young woman married to another man**; referring to his sexual ambitions for her and making what I would for present purposes treat as **a semi-serious proposal to pay her husband a large sum for her release**. In those respects I accept that the Claimant's correspondence and poetry are properly described as shocking and immoral. Can it be said that an expectation on the part of the person responsible for those documents that the facts disclosed in them should be kept private would be a reasonable one? I think not.

(f) **A 'fleeting one night encounter':** Query if the '*expectation of privacy*' is not so '*reasonable*' if the matter in issue is fleeting (eg a '*one night stand*') as contrasted with a long-term relationship; see Eady J in *CC v AB* [2006] EWHC 3083 (QB) at **para 22.** In the context of a relationship with a prostitute, see *Theakston v MGN Ltd* [2002] EWHC 137 (QB) at **para 75** per Ouseley J. Equally, the expectation of privacy may not be reasonable if, for example, 'A' is a sportsman and his sexual relationship gives rise to a conflict of interest with his team or other professional interests etc: *Goodwin v NGN Ltd and VBN (No 3)* at **para 103.**

(g) **The limits on the role of the media:** It is not for the state or the media to expose sexual conduct which does not involve any significant breach of the criminal law; *Mosley v News Group Newspapers Ltd* at **paras 125–28**, and see *DFT v TFD* per Sharp J at **para 21** for a definitive expression of the law on sexual activity in this context, see also *Mosley v UK* [2011] ECtHR 774, at **para 114** (which should be read in full):

> **The Court also reiterates that there is a distinction to be drawn between reporting facts—even if controversial—capable of contributing to a debate of general public interest in a democratic society, and making tawdry allegations** about an individual's private life (see Armoniene, cited above, § 39).

» **The test for breach of a confidential relationship:** See *Douglas v Hello! Ltd (No 6)* [2005] EWCA Civ 595 at **paras 55–56** (Court of Appeal) echoing the test in *Coco v AN Clark (Engineers) Ltd* [1969] RPC 41 at 47.

(a) **First:** The information has to be of a *confidential nature*.
(b) **Second:** The information must have been communicated by the confider to the confidant in *circumstances of confidence*.
(c) **Third:** There had to be *unauthorised* use of the information to the detriment of the confider.

The actual wording in *Coco*, which was unanimously approved by the House of Lords in *Douglas v Hello! Ltd* [2007] UKHL 21 (and which does not include the words '*to the detriment of the provider*'), reads at **para 111**:

> **First**, the information itself . . . must 'have the necessary quality of confidence about it. **Secondly**, that information must have been imparted in circumstances importing an obligation of confidence. **Thirdly**, there must be an unauthorised use of that information to the detriment of the party communicating it.

Also see *A-G v Observer Ltd* [1990] 1 AC 109 at 281 per Lord Goff (second paragraph of his speech). Further as to factors to consider as to whether information is confidential, see *Thomas Marshall (Exports) v Guinle* [1979] Ch 227 at 248 per Megarry J.

» **Distinguishing between 'confidence' and 'misuse of private information':**

(a) **The distinction:** As to the maturing of the distinction between *secrecy* and *privacy*, see *Douglas v Hello! Ltd (No 6)* [2005] EWCA Civ 595 per Lord Phillips at **paras 50–82**.
(b) **Keeping 'privacy' and 'confidence' distinct:** As to the importance of keeping distinct, issues of *confidence* and *misuse of private information*, see *Douglas v Hello! Ltd* [2007] UKHL 21 per Lord Nicholls at **para 255**.

> As the law has developed breach of confidence, or misuse of confidential information, now covers **two distinct causes of action**, protecting **two different interests**: ***privacy***, and ***secret*** ('confidential') information. It **is important to keep these two distinct**. In some instances information may qualify for **protection both on grounds of privacy and confidentiality**. In other instances information may be in the **public domain**, and **not qualify for protection as confidential, and yet qualify for protection on the grounds of privacy**. Privacy can **be invaded** by **further publication** of information or photographs **already disclosed** to the public. **Conversely, and obviously, a trade secret may be protected as confidential information even though no**

> **question of personal privacy is involved**. This distinction was recognised by the Law Commission in its report on Breach of Confidence [1981] Cmnd 388, [1981] EWLC 110, pages 5–6.

In this context, also see: *Douglas v Hello! Ltd (No 3)* [2007] UKHL 21 at **para 255** per Lord Nicholls and see *CC v AB* per Eady J at **paras 40** and **49**.

(c) **Nature of the 'intrusion':** As to the relevance and significance of the actual '*intrusion*' vis-à-vis the law of privacy as contrasted with confidential secrecy, see *CTB v NGN Ltd and Imogen Thomas (No 2)* at **para 23** per Eady J:

> It is important always to remember that the modern law of privacy is not concerned solely with information or '**secrets**': it is also concerned importantly with **intrusion**. That is one reason why it can be important to distinguish between the way the law approaches **public domain** arguments in relation to **commercial or state secrets**, for example, and **that which is appropriate to personal information**. It also largely explains why it is the case that the **truth or falsity** of the allegations in question can often **be irrelevant**: see eg *McKennitt v Ash* [2008] QB 73 at [80] and [87]. In a 'family' context, see *A Local Authority v A Mother & F &* A [2011] EWHC 1764 (Fam) per Baker J at **para 65**.

» **A recent refinement:** Per Tugendhat J in *Goodwin v NGN Ltd and VBN (No 3)* at **para 85:**

> The right to respect for private life embraces more than one concept. **Dr Moreham** summarises what she calls the two core components of the rights to privacy: '**unwanted access to private information and unwanted access to [or intrusion into] one's . . . personal space**' (see Law of Privacy and the Media (2nd edn, 2011, Warby, Moreham and Christie eds) paras 2.07, 2.08, 2.16 and 12.71). I shall refer to the two components of the right as '**confidentiality**' and '**intrusio**n'.

» **Conflict of laws:** In *KJO v XIM* proceedings in England related to publication in Hong Kong. Eady J gives a succinct and clear summary of the issues vis-à-vis conflict of laws. He inter alia cited *Douglas v Hello! Ltd (No 2)* [2003] EMLR 28 at **paras 3** and **41**. At **para 30** Eady J said:

> It does not seem to me yet to be finally determined whether privacy claims are to be classified in English law as **tortious** in character: see eg the discussion on this subject in *Mosley v News Group Newspapers Ltd* [2008] EMLR 679. **The question of labelling may not be critical.** Ultimately, it may well turn in any event upon **where** the particular acts took place, or will take place, which are said to constitute the infringement of the rights in question. Mr Sinai submits that the question is determined by ss 11 and 12 of the Private International Law

> (Miscellaneous Provisions) Act 1995. He may be right, but I do not believe that it is necessary for me for present purposes to rule that such a claim is based on 'tort or delict'.

» **Phone-hacking:** Do the police have a duty to inform victims of phone hacking? Permission for judicial review on this issue was granted by Foskett J in *R (on the application of Bryant & Ors) v The Commissioner of Police of the Metropolis* [2011] EWHC 1314 (Admin).

Article 10

Freedom of expression

(a) Everyone has the right of freedom of expression. This right shall include freedom to hold opinions and to **receive** and **impart** information and **ideas** without interference by public authority and regardless of frontiers. This article shall not prevent states from requiring the licensing of broadcasting, television or cinema enterprises.

(b) The exercise of these freedoms, since it carries with it **duties** and **responsibilities**, may be subject to such **formalities, conditions, restrictions** or **penalties** as are prescribed by law and are necessary in a democratic society, in the interests of national security, territorial integrity or public safety, for the prevention of disorder or crime, for the protection of health or morals, for the **protection** of the **reputation** or **rights** of others, for preventing the disclosure of information received in **confidence**, or for maintaining the authority and impartiality of the judiciary.

» **The importance the Strasbourg jurisprudence attaches to freedom of expression:** This can be satisfactorily illustrated by this typical passage from the judgment of the court in *Nilsen and Johnsen v Norway* [1999] 30 EHRR 878 at **para 43**:

> According to the Court's well-established case law, **freedom of expression constitutes one of the essential foundations of a democratic society and one of the basic conditions for its progress and for each individual's self-fulfilment**. Subject to Article 10(2), it is applicable not only to '**information**' of '**ideas**' that are favourably received or regarded as inoffensive or as a matter of indifference, but also **those that offend, shock or disturb**. Such are the demands of that **pluralism, tolerance and broadmindedness without which there is no 'democratic society'**. As set forth in Article 10, **this freedom is subject to exceptions which must, however, be construed strictly**, and the need for any restrictions **must be established convincingly**. The test of '**necessity in a democratic society**' requires the Court to determine whether the '**interference**' corresponded to a '**pressing social need**', whether it was **proportionate** to

> the **legitimate aim** pursued and whether the reasons given by the national authorities to justify it are relevant and sufficient.

As to the issue of self-fulfilment and one party to a relationship wishing to invoke Article 10, see *Ntuli v Donald* [2010] EWCA 1276 Civ at **para 22.**

» **An essential foundation of a democratic society:** Freedom of expression constitutes one of the *essential foundations of a democratic society* and one of *the basic conditions* for its *progress* and the *self-fulfilment* of each individual: *Campbell v MGN Ltd* at **para 117.**

» **Interaction of public opinion and freedom of speech:** Per Tugendhat J in *John Terry v Persons Unknown* at **para 104**:

> It is as a result of public discussion and debate, that public opinion develops.

» **Interaction of freedom of expression and the press:** Strasbourg rightly considers that these principles are of particular importance where the freedom of the press is in play, as is apparent from the following passage, again typical, from the judgment of the Strasbourg court in *Observer and Guardian v United Kingdom* [1999] 14 EHRR 152 at **para 59**:

> These principles are of particular importance as far as the press is concerned. Whilst it must not overstep the bounds set, inter alia, in the 'interests of national security' or for 'maintaining the authority of the judiciary,' it is nevertheless **incumbent on it to impart information and ideas on matters of public interest**. Not only does the press **have the task of imparting** such information and ideas: **the public also has a right to receive them**. Were it otherwise, the press would be unable to play its vital role of 'public watchdog'.

» **'*Reputation*' and '*privacy*':** As to the interaction of '*reputation*' and '*privacy*', see **paras 121 et seq** below. As to the common law interpretation of the concept of '*reputation*' see *Reynolds v Times Newspapers Ltd* [1999] UKHL 45 at **para 201** per Lord Nichol.

» **Freedom of expression:**

(a) **Strasbourg:** As to the importance the Strasbourg jurisprudence attaches to freedom of expression vis-à-vis the *tension* between Articles 8 and 10, see *Esther Thomas v News Group Newspapers Ltd and Simon Hughes* [2001] EWCA 1233 at **paras 21–26** and **37.**

(b) **But freedom is not licence:** *Jersild v Denmark* [1994] 19 EHRR, **para 35** and *Lehideux and Isorni v France* [1998] 30 EHRR, **para 53.** The Convention right of freedom of expression does not extend to protect remarks *directly against the Convention's underlying values.*

(c) **Working example:** For a working example of the importance of freedom of expression: see the dicta of Munby J in *Leeds City Council v Channel Four Television Corporation* [2007] 1 FLR 678, [2005] EWHC 3522 at **para 33** (*'very powerful public interests which are here engaged'*).

(d) **Interaction of freedom of expression and the commercial interest of a free press:** See *Hutcheson v News Group Newspapers Ltd* per Gross LJ at **para 16,** and at **para 34:**

> To some, applicants in privacy claims may seem unattractive. However, to others, intrusive media coverage of matters of sexual conduct, particularly if it includes **salacious detail**, may be equally unattractive. That said, for sections of the media, developments in privacy law impinging on their ability to publish such matters, may not only give rise to issues of principle as to freedom of expression in the individual case but also **to real commercial concerns**—which, at least to the extent of the general public interest in having a thriving and vigorous newspaper industry, representing all legitimate opinions, may also be argued to give rise to a relevant factor for the court to take into account.

Query: Are these dicta a reflection of the impact on the conventional press of the internet and social networking sites?

» **As to the vital importance of freedom of expression:** See *ETK v News Group Newspapers Ltd* at **para 13** per Ward LJ:

> As for Article 10, everyone has the right to freedom of expression **but the ones with the greatest need for this constitutionally vital freedom are the organs of the media. In the interests of our democratic society we—and that includes the judges—must ensure that the press are freely able to enquire, investigate and report on matters of public interest. The press is the public watchdog. That freedom is, however, not unrestricted as Article 10(2) itself makes so clear** that it is worth repeating: . . .
>
> This restriction can only be justified if it is a **proportionate** and is **no more than is necessary** to promote the **legitimate object** of the **restriction**. To restrict **publication simply to save the blushes of the famous, fame invariably being ephemeral**, could have the **wholly undesirable chilling** effect on the necessary ability of publishers to sell their newspapers. **We have to enable sales if we want to keep our newspapers.** Unduly to fetter their freedom to report as editors judge to be responsible is **to undermine the pre-eminence of the deserved place of the press as a *powerful pillar of democracy.*** These considerations require the court **to tread warily** before granting this kind of injunction.

» **As to the meaning of 'chilling effect':** See ***LNR*** at p 40, **para 3.26**:

> There is an obvious danger that in the securing the Article 6 and 10 rights of

the respondents and of non-parties, an applicant's **Article 6 and 8 rights may be undermined**. This is particularly acute where private information is concerned, as a procedural imbalance may produce **a chilling effect** on the willingness of applicants to come to court to vindicate their rights.

» **As to the meaning of the 'public interest'**, see:

(a) ***CC v AB*** at **para 36** (by way of one of several such citations from the cases): what is interesting to the public may not necessarily be in the public interest; and see *Mosley v UK* [2011] ECtHR, **para 114**. In *Goodwin v NGN Ltd and VBN (No 3)* Tugendhat J said at **para 2**:

> [W]hat is of interest to the public is not the same as what it is in the public interest to publish. Newspaper editors have the final decision on what is of interest to the public interest: judges have the final decision on what it is in the public interest to publish.

(b) ***BKM Ltd v BBC*** [2009] EWHC 3151 (Ch) per Mann J at **para 25** as to the BBC's privacy code and its definition of what is in the public interest.

(c) ***John Terry v Persons Unknown*** per Tugendhat J at **para** 8:

> By the public interest I include the matters listed in ECHR Art 8(2) and in the PCC Code.

(d) ***Attorney General's Reference No 3 of 1999***: *Application by the British Broadcasting Corporation to set aside or vary a Reporting Restriction Order* [2009] UKHL 34 at **paras 25** and **26**:

> [T]here is a duty to impart information and ideas of public interest which the public has a right to receive.

and at **para 57**, Lord Brown of Eaton-under-Heywood indicated that the powers of the High Court to make such an Order '*arise under section 6 of the* [*Human Rights Act 1998*] *read in conjunction with section 37 of the* [*Senior Courts Act*] *1981*'.

(e) ***Guardian News and Media Ltd*** [2010] UKSC 1 at paras **63–64**:

> A requirement to report it in some austere, abstract form, devoid of much of its human interest, **could well mean that the report would not be read and the information would not be passed on**. Ultimately, such an approach could threaten the viability of newspapers and magazines, which can only inform the public if they attract enough readers and make enough money to survive.

Note the resonance between these dicta, and those of Gross LJ in *Hutcheson v News Group Newspapers Ltd* at **para 34**

(f) ***Von Hannover v Germany***: The court observed at **para 63** the vital role of the press as '*watchdog*'; see paras **63 and 64**. In *Ash v McKennitt*, Ward LJ said in relation to *Hannover* (at **para 37**) that it extended the reach of Article 8 beyond what had previously been understood.

(g) ***Mosley v NGN Ltd*** [2008] EWHC 1777 (QB) **para 135**: It is for the court, *objectively*, to decide whether a particular publication is in the public interest, whether or not a relevant party raises it: *TSE and ELP v News Group Newspapers Ltd* per Tugendhat J at **paras 18 and 27**.

(h) ***Mosley v UK*** [2011] ECtHR 774 at **para 112** vis-à-vis the interaction of publishing '*in the public interest*' and the '*rule of law*', and at **para 129** vis-à-vis restraints and penalties on the one hand, and freedom of expression on the other. Further as to the interaction of restraint and freedom of expression, see **para 131.**

(i) ***Hutcheson v News Group Newspapers Ltd*** at **para 35**: Freedom of expression in the public interest includes freedom to criticise.

(j) ***MJN v News Group Newspapers Ltd*** per Sharp J at **para 14:**

> No public interest justification has been advanced for its publication as I have said; but in any event I consider the Claimant is likely to establish there **is no public interest in the fact that the Claimant had a short-lived affair or in its sexual/salacious details and that publication of the relevant information would not make any contribution to any debate of public interest**: see also in this context, *ETK v News Group Newspapers* [2011] EWCA Civ 439. The relevant information here is **not in the public domain**.

» **The legal critical path analysis:** As to a paradigm expression of the law relating to what the author defines as the '*legal critical path analysis*' of the inter-action of Articles 8(1), 8(2) and Article 10, see *Wood v Commissioner of Police for the Metropolis* at **paras 22–26** (these paragraphs are essential reading).

» **As to the word 'necessary' in relation to the rights under Article 8 and Article 10:** What is the extent to which it is *necessary* to qualify the one right in order to protect the underlying value which is protected by the other? See *Campbell v MGN Ltd* at **paras 55** and **56**. Note that the court will be less concerned to allow freedom of expression in the context of sensationalism, than in the context of serious journalism and political debate; see *Mosley v UK* [2011] ECtHR 774 at **para 117**, and see also **para 121**:

> In particular, its implications for freedom of expression are not limited to the sensationalist reporting at issue in this case but **extend to political reporting and serious investigative journalism**. The Court recalls that the introduction of restrictions on the latter type of journalism requires careful scrutiny.'

Further as to sensationalism, see *BKM v BBC* at **para 38**.

» **As to '*degrees*' of freedom to express:** See Waller LJ in *ASG v GSA* as to the potential distinction between telling the press of an affair, and telling the cuckolded wife; and at **para 25**:

> . . . and it seems to me the answer to that question could be **different depending on whether the girl** was seeking to sell the story to the newspapers and the media or simply informing the claimant's wife.

And also see **para 26** as to remedies for alleged blackmail, including a report to the police.

Human Rights Act 1998, section 12

Freedom of expression

(1) This section applies if a court is considering whether to grant any relief which, if granted, might affect the exercise of the Convention right to freedom of expression.

(2) If the person against whom the application for relief is made ('the respondent') is neither present nor represented, no such relief is to be granted unless the court is satisfied—

(a) that the applicant has taken all practicable steps to notify the respondent; or

(b) that there are compelling reasons why the respondent should not be notified.

(3) No such relief is to be granted so as to restrain publication before trial unless the court is satisfied that the applicant is **likely** to establish that publication should not be allowed.

(4) The court must have particular regard to the **importance** of the Convention right to freedom of expression and, where the proceedings relate to material which the respondent claims, or which appears to the court, to be **journalistic**, **literary** or **artistic** material (or to **conduct** connected with such material), to—

(a) the extent to which—

(i) the material has, or is about to, become **available** *to the* ***public****; or*

(ii) it is, or would be, in the **public interest** for the material to be published;

(b) any relevant **privacy** code.

(5) In this section—

- 'court' includes a tribunal; and
- 'relief' includes any remedy or order (other than in criminal proceedings).

» **Issue:** The '*privacy*' injunction cases revolve primarily around one issue:

an interim non-disclosure order; see ***LNR***, p 77, where the following circumstances generating the potential for such a remedy are outlined:

- Rights guaranteed by the European Convention or on grounds of privacy or confidentiality;
- In respect of a threatened contempt of court;
- A threatened libel;
- A threatened malicious falsehood;
- Harassment;
- A Norwich Pharmacal application in support of such actions

All such orders will seek to restrict the exercise of the Article 10 Convention right of freedom of expression through prohibiting the disclosure of information.

» **When does section 12 apply?** Whenever the court is considering whether to grant relief which might affect the exercise of Article 10.

» **Policy:** See *CC v AB* per Eady J at **para 34**, for the policy of section 12(3), a policy endorsed by Mann J in *BKM v BBC* at **para 28**.

» **'Notification' to whom?** The statute refers in terms to a '*respondent*'. However, at first instance in *X & Y v Persons Unknown* at **paras 10–12** Eady J held that its ambit extended to non-parties who in practice are likely to have their Article 10 right constrained by an injunction. Per ***LNR***: the purpose of this rule is to enable non-parties to be in a position to mount, if they choose to do so, an effective challenge to the order, see p 40, **para 3.23**.

» **Leading judgment on the issue of *'likely'*:** Section 12(3) requires the applicant to satisfy the court that he/she is likely to establish, at trial, that publication should not be allowed; see Lord Nicholls in *Cream Holdings Ltd v Banerjee* [2004] UKHL 44 at **para 22**:

> Section 12(3) makes the **likelihood** of success at trial an essential element in the court's consideration of whether to make an interim order. But in order to achieve the necessary flexibility the **degree** of **likelihood of success** at the trial needed to satisfy section 12(3) **must depend** on the **circumstances**. There can be no single, rigid standard governing all applications for interim restraint orders. Rather, on its proper construction the effect of section 12(3) is that the court is not to make an interim restraint order unless satisfied that the applicant's **prospects** of success at trial are **sufficiently** favourable to justify such an order being made in the particular circumstances of the case. As to what degree of likelihood makes the prospect of success 'sufficiently favourable', the general approach should be that courts will be exceedingly slow to make interim restraint orders where the applicant has not satisfied the court that he

> will **probably** ('more likely than not') succeed at trial. In general, that should be the **threshold** an applicant must cross before the court embarks on exercising its **discretion**, duly taking into account the relevant jurisprudence on Article 10 and any countervailing Convention rights. But there will be cases where it is necessary for a court to **depart** from this general approach and a **lesser degree** of likelihood will suffice as a prerequisite. Circumstances where this may be so include . . . where the potential **adverse** consequences of disclosure are particularly **grave**, or where a **short-lived** injunction is needed to enable the court to hear and give proper consideration to an application for interim relief pending the trial or any relevant appeal.

This is in contrast to the ***American Cyanamid*** test of '*serious issue to be tried*'. Further as to a 'short-lived' injunction, and the principles so applying, see Waller LJ in *ASG v GSA* at **paras 3–5** and **26**. Insofar as the '*lesser degree of likelihood*' test is concerned, the Court of Appeal has emphasised that it would only apply in an exceptional case: *Ntuli v Donald* [2010] EWCA Civ 1276 at **paras 36–38**.

» **Vis-à-vis an argument that at trial a final order is '*likely*' to be made in similar terms; see section 12 of the Human Rights Act 1998:**

(a) **As to 'similar terms':** see *CC v A* at **paras 34** and **58**.
(b) **Likely, gravity and proportionality:** As to the interaction of these words, see *John Terry v Persons Unknown* at **para 149(viii)**.
(c) **What are the merits?** The court has to *assess merits*, looking forward to the final hearing; *Thomas v News Group Newspapers and Hughes* (case pleaded in *harassment*), and see *CC v AB* at **paras 34** and **56**; in an alleged '*blackmail*' category of case, see Sharp J in *KJH v HGF* [2010] EWHC 3064 (QB) where the court held at **para** 3 that the evidence established '*a high degree of probability*' that KJH was the victim of blackmail involving the threat of revelation of *stolen* private and *confidential* information. Note that the issue of blackmail inter alia goes to *the weight to be attached* to the Article 10 right—see *KJH v HGF* at **para 10**; it is also relevant to the issue of '*compelling reasons*' not to give advance notice of an application; see *ASG v GSA* at **paras 3–5**.
(d) **What is the gravity of the consequences to the applicant and/or any relevant others, if the risk materialises?** *Thomas v News Group Newspapers and Hughes* (in particular vis-à-vis whether an order should be granted even if Applicant cannot prove '*more likely than not*'); see *John v Associated Newspapers Ltd* per Eady J at **para 5** (*grave* consequences; need for *short-lived* injunction—drawing from Lord Nicholls at **para 22** in *Cream Holdings v Banerjee and Ors*).

(e) **Overall view:** An overall view should be formed as to *likelihood*: *Author of a Blog v Times Newspapers Ltd* [2009] EWHC 1358 (QB) Eady J at **para 12**. See also *BKM Ltd v BBC* per Mann J at **para 38**; proposed BBC programme '*strongly arguable*'—'*properly deployed*'. But note: the decision not to grant an injunction was not to be interpreted as *deciding that that broadcast would be justified or justifiable*.

(f) **Effect of court proceedings:** Once privacy has been infringed, the damage is done and the embarrassment is only augmented by pursuing a court action: *Mosley v News Group Newspapers Ltd* [2008] EWHC 1777 per Eady J at **para 230**; and see in a parallel context *Mosley v UK* [2011] ECtHR 774 at **para 80**:

> [S]ubjects often decided not to bring legal proceedings for fear of attracting further publicity in respect of the invariably embarrassing or damaging details about their private lives.

(g) **'No order' does not necessarily validate publication:** Per Munby J in *Leeds City Council v Channel Four Television Corporation* [2007] 1 FLR 678, [2005] EWHC 3522 (Fam) vis-à-vis *'likely'* at **para 24**: a working example of the fact that just because an injunction is not ordered does not mean that a broadcast is justified or justifiable:

(h) **Damages?** Vis-à-vis '*likelihood*' that damages would be an adequate remedy; see Lord Phillips of Worth Matravers *Attorney General v Times Newspapers Ltd* [1992] 1 AC 191, at p 1054F–G. As to the issue of *proportionality* between the sanction imposed and the degree of interference with the Article 8 right, see *Mosley v UK* [2011] ECtHR 774 at **para 116**.

(i) **Finding of fact?** Unless the facts are clear beyond doubt or are admitted, the court hearing an interim application for an injunction must not make findings of fact; *Gray v UVW* at **para 50**.

» **Ex parte/without notice—the test:** Per Waller LJ in *ASG v GSA*—cited by Tugendhat J in *JIH v News Group Newspapers Ltd* [2010] EWHC 2818 (QB) at **para 37**:

> Is there a sufficient degree of likelihood that the claimant will win at trial to justify an ex parte injunction for **a short period** before a full *inter partes* hearing?

Also see CPR 23.7 and PD23A at **para 3**.

» **As to section 12(4)(a)(i)**—'. . . *the material has, or is about to, become available to the public*': This highlights the 'public domain' issue—to what extent is the material already in the public domain? This is addressed at length in **Parts 2** and **4** below. Note in particular the '*about to be*' wording.

» **As to 'privacy codes':** ***LNR*** expressed the position thus on p 77, **para 7**:

> HRA s 12(4) . . . requires the court to have regard to any relevant privacy code. The code of the Press Complaints Commission is one such code.

And in this context, see *Mosley v UK* [2011] ECtHR 774 at **para 119:**

> A system of self-regulation of the press has been established in the United Kingdom, with guidance provided in the Editors' Code and Codebook and oversight of journalists' and editors' conduct by the PCC (see paragraphs 29–38 above). This system reflects the 1970 declaration, the 1998 resolution and the 2008 resolution of the Parliamentary Assembly of the Council of Europe (see paragraphs 55 and 58–59 above).

Part 2

APPLICANT PRACTICE MANAGEMENT: ARTICLE 6 DEROGATIONS FROM OPEN JUSTICE

Derogation from open justice in the context of an interim non-disclosure order application: overriding principles

1. Introduction: This Part starts with 'derogations from open justice' because:

(a) Article 6 (whence the jurisdiction derives) clearly precedes Articles 8 and 10.
(b) Open justice is important to the extent that as a matter of public interest it should be given a clear priority.
(c) If a consideration of 'derogation' reveals that anonymity cannot be justified, then that may in itself be the end of the enquiry vis-à-vis an application for an interim non-disclosure order.

2. Issues: The issues in an application for a derogation from open justice are:

(a) The respective Convention rights of the parties.
(b) The general public interest in open justice and in the public reporting of court proceedings.

3. Introduction: See ***LNR*** p iv, **para 2**:

- The principle of open justice is a fundamental constitutional principle, although it is not an absolute principle. It applies to interim injunction applications as it does to trials.
- Derogations from open justice can only properly be made where, and to

the extent that, they are strictly necessary in order to secure the proper administration of justice.
- Applications for such derogations must be supported by clear and cogent evidence, and should be subjected to careful scrutiny by the court. Where a derogation is appropriate the court should consider what information can properly be put into the public domain. Without such consideration it is not possible for the court to ensure that any derogation from open justice is the minimum necessary to secure the proper administration of justice.

4. *LNR* Practice Guidance:

> 10. Derogations from the general principle [of open justice] can only be justified in **exceptional circumstances**, when they are strictly necessary as measures to secure the proper administration of justice. They are wholly exceptional: *R v Chief Registrar of Friendly Societies, ex parte New Cross Building Society* [1984] QB 227 at 235 at [52]–[53]. Derogations should, where justified, be no more than strictly necessary to achieve their purpose.
>
> 11. The grant of derogations is **not a question of discretion**. It is **a matter of obligation** and the court is under a duty to either grant the derogation or refuse it when it has applied the relevant test: *AMM v HXW* [2010] EWHC 2457 (QB) at [34].
>
> 12. There is no general exception to open justice where privacy or confidentiality is in issue. Applications will only be heard in private if and to the extent that the court is satisfied that by nothing short of the exclusion of the public can justice be done. Exclusions must be no more than the **minimum strictly necessary** to ensure justice is done and **parties are expected to consider before** applying for such an exclusion whether something short of exclusion can meet their concerns, as will normally be the case: *Ambrosiadou v Coward* [2011] EWCA Civ 409 [50]–[54]. Anonymity will only be granted where it is strictly necessary, and **then only to that extent**.

Also see *R v Legal Aid Board ex p Kaim Todner* [1999] QB 966; see *Lord Browne of Madingley v Associated Newspapers Ltd* [2007] EWCA Civ 295, **para 3**, *JIH v News Group Newspapers Ltd* [2010] EWHC 2818 (QB) per Tugendhat J (which is essential reading on this issue) and *JXF v York Hospitals NHS Foundation Trust* [2010] EWHC 2800 per Tugendhat J at **paras 24–26**. As to the *minimum strictly necessary* see also *Ntuli v Donald* [2010]

EWCA Civ 1276 per Maurice Kay LJ at **para 54** and adopted by Sharp J in *KJF v HGF* [2010] EWHC 3064 (QB) at **para 8**.

5. Sources of jurisdiction: Article 6 of the Convention; and also Article 8—see Tugendhat J in *JXF v York Hospitals NHS Foundation Trust*; also see **CPR 39(2)** (hearings must be conducted in public).

6. Burden of proof: *LNR* Practice Guidance: Note the interaction between '*burden*' and evidence which is '*clear*' and '*cogent*'.

> 13. The burden of establishing any derogation from the general principle [of open justice] lies on the person seeking it. It must be established by clear and cogent evidence: *Scott v Scott* [1913] AC 417 at 438–439, 463 and 477; *Lord Browne of Madingley v Associated Newspapers Ltd [*2008] 1 QB 103 at [2]–[3]; *Secretary of State for Home Department v AP (No 2)* [2010] 1 WLR 1652 at [7]; *Gray v UVW* [2010] EWHC 2367 at [6]–[8]; and *JIH v News Group Newspapers* [2011] EWCA Civ 42 *(JIH)* at [21].

7. Litigation technique: As to how to make the application, see dicta of Sharp J in *DFT v TFD* [2010] EWHC 2335 at **para 4**:

> Evidence relating to **the substance** of the application and to **the reasons** why the court was being asked to make orders which **derogated** from the principles of open justice and from **the civil procedure rules** [*sic*] was placed before the court in **confidential schedules** to the **witness statements** of the applicant, his solicitor, Mr Benaim of Schillings, and from a member of a firm of **security consultants** engaged by the applicant.

Further as to the use of a *confidential schedule*, see *Ambrosiadou v Coward* [2011] EWCA Civ 409 at **para 54**. *Note also:* The retention of a *security consultant.*

8. Derogations from open justice in *DFT*: In *DFT v TFD*, the following derogations (see **para 8**) were ordered in the context of an interim injunction limited to seven days:

(a) **Anonymity** of the parties.
(b) **Restriction of access** to documents on the court file, so that none of the confidential annexures to the witness statements or the names of the parties would be provided to non-parties without further order of the court.
(c) **Derogation from CPR 25 PD 9.2** in that the applicant was not required to provide the material provided to the court, or a note of the hearing to those third parties served with the order *unless they specifically asked for*

that material and gave undertakings to protect the use of that material and the information it contained.

Derogation from open justice and practice management

9. If derogation strictly necessary, the least possible: If there is to be any derogation, it *should be the least* that can be imposed consistent with the protection to which an 'A' is entitled; *Ntuli v Donald* per Maurice Kay LJ at **para** 54 and adopted by Sharp J in *KJH v HGF* at **para 8**.

10. Rule compliance essential: There is an imperative to make the applications properly in accordance with the rules and for the judge to be apprised by the advocate of all relevant law; *G and G v Wikimedia Foundation Inc* [2009] EWHC 3148, **para 20**, and see ***LNR* Practice Guidance, para 32.**

11. Documentation and applications to derogate:

(a) **Statement and skeleton argument:** There must be a skeleton argument setting out the applicable law in addition to a statement setting out the relevant facts in support of anonymity/derogation: *JIH v News Group Newspapers Ltd* at **para 70** and ***LNR* Practice Guidance** at **paras 30–31**.

(b) **What 'A's' skeleton must cover in principle:** Why is it 'strictly necessary' to deprive the public of knowing either the substance of the material and/or the identity of 'A'? 'A's' statement should set out precisely the derogations sought: *John Terry (previously 'LNS') v Persons Unknown* [2010] EWHC 119 (QB) at **para 25**; including why any application has been made without notice, if indeed it has; and see *X & Y v Persons Unknown* [2006] EWHC 2783 (QB) per Eady J at **para 18**.

(c) **Example:** As an example of a statement in support of anonymity, see *Gray v UVW* [2010] EWHC 2367 (QB) **paras 20** and **21**:

> The Intended Claimant is concerned that if this action was reported, together with the names of the parties, this would **fuel speculation** in the media and **on the internet** as to what the injunction was designed to protect. This would inevitably cause further **distress** to the Intended Claimant and **his family** and defeat the intention of the injunction.

12. Urgency: Applications to restrain publication of private or confidential information, and related applications, are usually made in circumstances of urgency; *G and G v Wikimedia Foundation Inc* at **para 18**.

13. Restricting publicity to the contents of a judgment: The judgment of Tugendhat J in *Gray v UVW* is *essential reading* in its entirety:

(a) In this case an order was made restricting publicity to the contents of a judgment, in relation to which one party was anonymised but the other was not;
(b) The continued anonymity of R was justified by a significant risk that lifting his or her anonymity might have serious consequences for his or her private life, which consequences might not be remediable.
(c) *Gray* is also authority for the proposition that in cases of alleged blackmail, the court may be inclined to make an anonymity order: see para 61; and similarly if a threatened publication may be a contempt of court, or an interference with the course of justice: this may occur where the threatened media reporting will discourage 'A' or a witness from giving evidence, ie 'chilling effect'. Interference with the administration of justice is a crime.
(d) Further as to the interaction of alleged *blackmail* and *Article 10*, see *KJH v HGF* per Sharp J at **paras 10** and **11**.
(e) As to the interaction of alleged blackmail, Human Rights Act section 12(2) and advance notice of an application, see *ASG v GSA* [2009] EWCA Civ 1574 at **paras 3–5** and ***LNR* Practice Guidance** at **para 22**:

> Different considerations may however arise where a respondent or non-party is an internet-based organisation, tweeter or blogger, or where, for instance, there are allegations of blackmail.

14. *LNR* and the issue of the parties' consent to anonymity: At page 13, para 1.31:

> The court **cannot simply** give effect to an agreement between the parties to derogate from the principle of open justice. Unless the **strict necessity** test is satisfied, such agreements are both inconsistent with the public interest element of the proper administration of justice and infringe the Article 10 Convention rights of the public, which **parties cannot agree to waive** . . . it is incumbent on the court to assess **necessity** and to do so with as much **scrutiny** as it would on a contested application.

In this context, see also *JIH v News Group Newspapers Ltd* per Tugendhat J at **para 61**.

'Public' or 'private hearing' as a derogation from open justice

15. Strictly necessary? Can the derogation sought be justified by reference to what would otherwise be **unnecessary** or **disproportionate** interference? See *JIH v News Group Newspapers Ltd* at **para 60**, these dicta being unaffected by the appeal at [2011] EWCA 42. The following examples are taken from the case of *John Terry v Persons Unknown* per Tugendhat J, see **paras 15 et seq**.

16. A private hearing—striking the balance: For a paradigm example of how the Court can strike a balance, see the judgment of Sharp J in *MJN v News Group Newspapers Ltd* [2011] EWHC 1192 (QB) at **para 17**, a hearing in public with Orders restricting information flowing into the public domain by reference to **CPR 31.22** (subsequent use of disclosed documents).

17. Social networking sites and open justice: Given the nature of publication on social networking sites, should **the risk of such leakage** weigh in the balance vis-à-vis a public or private hearing? This appears to have been the determining factor in the **Northern Ireland case** of *Robinson v Sunday Newspapers* [2011] NICA 13, on the basis that reporting restrictions would not necessarily have been sufficient, per Morgan LCJ:

> [24] We are satisfied that we should take judicial notice of the fact that social networking sites, **Twitter and the internet generally now provides an alternative means of publication to traditional daily or Sunday newspapers.** Although the numbers of persons to whom the publication is made may be considerably less than the circulation of a popular Sunday newspaper publication on the **internet** is difficult to **control and in particular the source of the publication may be outside the jurisdiction of the court**. Publication can also occur on a more limited basis by word of mouth. **The hearing of the application will inevitably involve the discussion of aspects of the appellant's treatment and condition.** In view of the interest to which we have referred in the appellant's medical treatment in the preceding paragraph we consider that there is a real danger that if these proceedings were open to the public the information disclosed in the hearing would be disseminated on the internet even if a reporting restriction was imposed.

18. Comparing Northern Ireland practice with English practice: These dicta can be contrasted with the appeals in the following cases having been heard entirely in public: *JIH v News Group Newspapers Ltd* [2011] EWCA

Civ 42 and *Ambrosiadou v Coward*. In contrast, the following first-instance hearings were conducted in private: *MJN v News Group Newspapers Ltd* and *Sir Frederick Goodwin v NGN Ltd and VBN (No 3)* [2011] EWHC 1437 (QB). For dicta supporting a private hearing at first instance, see Sharp J in *MNB v News Group Newspapers Ltd* [2011] EWHC 528 (QB) at **para 12**.

19. Twitter etc: As to Twitter, other social networking sites and advance notification, see **para 22** in ***LNR* Practice Guidance**. One may anticipate case-law developing in this field, to set more specific parameters.

20. Should a judgment be delivered in private? See *John v Associated Newspapers* [2006] EWHC 1611 (QB) per Eady J at **para 2**:

> It is always undesirable for a judgment to be given in private unless it is absolutely necessary.

21. The interaction of disclosure and derogation: The following is to be kept immediately in mind: *the greater the disclosure*, the *less is the derogation* from open justice.

22. Can one have a public hearing and yet retain sufficient confidentiality? This was the position in the Court of Appeal in *JIH v News Group Newspapers Ltd* [2011] EWCA Civ 42 at **para 17.** Lord Neuberger MR expressed it thus:

> The hearing of the applications was **held in open court**. It was obviously right, as a matter of principle, to have the hearing in public **if it was possible to do so**. As both counsel very sensibly accepted, this was indeed possible, **on the basis that, at the hearing, the identity of JIH was not revealed**, and some of **the facts**, and some of the **contents of the documents** were referred to in rather **coded** or **referential terms.**

23. How as a matter of practice can one handle 'open court' in a confidentiality case? This fell for consideration in *Ambrosiadou v Coward*; see following dicta:

> **Lord Neuberger**
>
> *The hearing was in public*
>
> 50. When the appeal was called on, Mr Spearman applied for the hearing to take place in private, on the ground that it would be necessary to refer to material in the May application notice, which was arguably entitled to protection from public dissemination. **We took the view that the**

application should be refused, provided steps could be taken to ensure that arguably private information, whether mentioned in court or contained in a document referred to in court, could not be disseminated outside the court. As has been stated on many occasions, court hearings should take place in public and should be freely reported unless justice cannot be done on that basis in the particular case, and **in that event, the court should ensure that the restrictions on access and reporting are the minimum necessary to enable justice to be done in that case.**

51. In this case, we took the view that we should order that there should be no reporting of the contents of the May application notice, whether or not mentioned in court, without the permission of the court or the written agreement of both parties (or their solicitors). **On that basis, we could see no objection to the hearing proceeding in open court, on the basis that counsel could be expected to be able to avoid revealing any private information in their oral submissions**. If, for some reason it had been necessary to do so, counsel could have asked the court to sit in private temporarily; **if counsel had accidentally revealed any private information orally, the court could have made an appropriate order preventing its reporting. This did not appear to give rise to any difficulties.**

52. In many cases involving alleged confidential information, one or both of the parties wish the hearing to take place in private, because of understandable concern that confidential information may be revealed in the course of the hearing. **Before applying for the hearing to be in private, the parties and their advisers should consider whether such concerns can be accommodated by a less drastic course, such as that adopted in this case.** Experience suggests to me that it **normally can**, and I agree with what Leveson LJ has said in his short judgment.

Lord Justice Leveson

53. For the reasons that he gives and to the limited extent that he suggests, I agree with the judgment of the Master of the Rolls that this appeal should be allowed. I also agree with his general observations about the need to conduct proceedings in public **save only in the most unusual circumstances.**

54. As in this case, **it is almost invariably possible** to conduct a hearing of this nature in public and in such a way as demonstrates adherence to the **principle of open justice**, while at the same time ensuring that **truly confidential material is referenced on paper and does not enter the public domain**. When cases of this nature arise, therefore, it is **critically important** that parties conducting **them prepare documents (including**

> **submissions) in a way that facilitates that approach.** Without being prescriptive but by way of example, **this could involve placing confidential material in an annex which the court can readily identify and order not to be disclosed.**

Further as to '*confidential schedules*' see **paras 53 et seq** below and as to an example of splitting a hearing into public and private parts, see *Ferdinand v MGN Ltd* [2011] EWHC 2454 (QB) at **para 5**.

24. Position of third parties and derogation from open justice:

(a) Notwithstanding **CPR PD 25(A) para 9.2** the Order can contain a proviso that 'A' shall **not** be required to provide any third party served with a copy of the order, a copy of any materials read by the judge and/or a note of the hearing (including a telephone hearing); see *Gray v UVW* at **para 16**.
(b) Any such relief must be **specifically** applied for and explained in Article 6 and Article 8 terms.

'Anonymity' as a derogation from open justice

25 Issue: Is there a legally enforceable right to maintain *anonymity*? See *Author of a Blog v Times Newspapers Ltd* [2009] EWHC 1358 (QB) per Eady J, **para 4**. In this context, note the dicta of Sharp J in *XJA v NGN Ltd* [2010] EWHC 3174 at **para 14**:

> [N]aming a claimant at the interim stage may produce an undesirable restriction on what could be said in a subsequent judgment.

26. Definition of an anonymised injunction: ***LNR*** expressed the position as follows at p iv, **para 3**:

> An anonymised injunction is an interim injunction which restrains a person from publishing information which concerns the application and is said to be confidential or private where the names of either or both of the parties to the proceedings are not stated. The proper approach to anonymisation has been clarified in *JIH v News Group Newspapers Ltd* [2011] EWCA Civ 42.

27. The issues to be addressed in anonymity applications—the definitive judgment: Lord Neuberger MR prescribed the following definitive checklist in *JIH v News Group Newspapers Ltd* [2011] EWCA Civ 42 at **para 21**:

In a case such as this, where the protection sought by the claimant is an **anonymity order** or **other restraint on publication** of details of a case which are normally in the public domain, certain principles were identified by the Judge, and which, together with principles contained in valuable written observations to which I have referred, I would summarise as follows:

(1) The general rule is that the names of the parties to an action are included in orders and judgments of the court.

(2) There is no general exception for cases where private matters are in issue.

(3) An order for anonymity or any other order restraining the publication of the normally reportable details of a case is a **derogation** from the principle of open justice and an **interference with the Article 10 rights** of the public at large.

(4) Accordingly, where the court is asked to make any such order, it should only do so after **closely scrutinising** the application, and considering whether a **degree** of restraint on publication is **necessary**, and, if it is, whether there **is any less restrictive or more acceptable alternative** than that which is sought.

(5) Where the court is asked to restrain the publication of the **names of the parties** and/or the **subject matter** of the claim, on the ground that such restraint is necessary under Article 8, the **question is whether there is sufficient general, public interest in publishing a report of the proceedings which identifies a party and/or the normally reportable details to justify any resulting curtailment of his right and his family's right to respect for their private and family life.**

(6) On any such application, no special treatment should be accorded to public figures or celebrities: in principle, they are entitled to the same protection as others, no more and no less.

(7) An order for anonymity or for reporting restrictions should not be made simply because the parties consent: parties cannot waive the rights of the public.

(8) An **anonymity** order or any other order restraining publication made by a Judge at an interlocutory stage of an injunction application **does not last for the duration of the proceedings but must be reviewed at the return date**.

(9) Whether or not an anonymity order or an order restraining publication of normally reportable details is made, then, at least **where a judgment is or would normally be given, a publicly available judgment should normally be given, and a copy of the consequential court order should**

also be publicly available, although some editing of the judgment or order may be necessary.

(10) **Notice of any** hearing should be given to the defendant unless there is a **good reason not to do so**, in which case the **court** should **be told** of the **absence of notice** and the reason for it, and should be satisfied that the reason is a good one.

(11) Where, as here, the basis for any claimed restriction on publication ultimately rests on a judicial assessment, it is therefore essential that (a) the judge is first satisfied that the facts and circumstances of the case are **sufficiently strong** to justify encroaching on the open justice rule by restricting the extent to which the proceedings can be reported, and (b) if so, the judge ensures that the restrictions on publication are fashioned so as to satisfy the need for the encroachment in a **way which minimises the extent of any restrictions.**

These dicta were cited and adopted by Sharp J in *MNB v News Group Newspapers Ltd* at **para 29**; and see ***LNR*** at p 55, **para 4.8** as to judgments and orders containing derogations from the principle of open justice being publicly available (interpreting paragraph 21(9) in *JIH v News Group Newspapers Ltd* above) and the **Practice Guidance para 16** as to parties not being able to waive or give up the rights of the public.

28. The words in *JIH* '*Absence of notice*': Vis-à-vis these words, note the following passage in ***LNR*** at p 49:

3.22 . . . In future therefore, the default position will be, consistently with HRA s 12 and the CPR, one **of advance notice** to respondents and non-parties, including media organisations, whom the applicant intends to bring within the terms of the order. A failure to provide advance notice is only justifiable in exceptional circumstances.

3.23 . . . The obligation to provide a note of the hearing arises in the absence of any request for information under CPR PD 25A 9. **The purpose of this rule is to enable non-parties to be in a position to mount, if they choose to do so, an effective challenge to the order**. The provision of such information is moreover an '*elementary principle of natural justice.*'

3.24 Following implementation of the recommended Practice Guidance, the likelihood of this situation arising should decrease as non-attendance due to absence of notice will be confined to exceptional cases. It will also only arise in those cases where an applicant becomes aware following the grant of an order that a non-party has an interest in the information subject to the injunction, and at that point notifies the non-party of the order.

29. Anonymity for parties including '*listing*': Anonymity for 'A' and other relevant persons involved, including anonymity in listing and anonymisation of Order; see *John Terry v Persons Unknown* per Tugendhat J at **para 138**; *G and G v Wikimedia Foundation Inc* at **paras 1012** per Tugendhat J and *John v Associated Newspapers* at **paras 1–3** per Eady J.

30. Anonymisation of a judgment: See for example *A v B, C and D* [2005] EWHC 1651 (QB) per Eady J at **para 34**; but see *Lord Browne of Madingley v Associated Newspapers Ltd* at **para 3** per Sir Anthony Clarke MR.

31. The interaction of anonymity for an 'R' as relevant to the anonymity of 'A': See *G and G v Wikimedia Foundation Inc* at **para 12** and '*jigsaw*' identification, *NEJ v Helen Wood and Persons Unknown* [2011] EWHC 1972 (QB) at **para 11**, *JIH v NGN Ltd* [2011] EWCA Civ 42 at **para 40**, and also see *OPQ v BJM* [2011] EWHC 1059 per Eady J at **para 4**:

> It was obviously a case for the parties to be anonymised with a view to protecting the claimant's rights and to reduce the risk of jigsaw identification.

32. The risk of misidentification: As to the risk of misidentification flowing from an anonymity order, see *Ntuli v Donald* per Maurice Kay LJ at **para 55**:

> I do not consider that the same can be said of Mr Donald in the present case. In my view, it would have been possible and appropriate for Eady J to have written his judgment in a publishable form. **Moreover, to have done so would have avoided the risk that anonymisation can give rise to, namely that of 'jigsaw' identification, whereby anonymisation may be undermined** by correctly identifying someone as a result of relating separate snippets of information or, equally unfortunately, it may lead to the wrong person being identified by the media misaligning the snippets. We were shown one recent example of this.

These dicta were cited and adopted by Sharp J in *MNB v NGN Ltd* at **para 27** and she gave a classical explanation as to '*jigsaw identification*' at **para 33**. Further, these principles resonate with the following argument in *JIH v News Group Newspapers Ltd* per Tugendhat J at first instance in **para 52**:

> The naming of claimants may also be important, not because their identity is important, but because if they are named **it can be seen** that others are **not** the subject of suspicion as being the persons about whom rumours

> or true information is circulating. The number of individuals whom the public might suspect of being the claimant is in many cases quite small, and it is **unfair** on those who are not the claimant (and their families) for there to be **speculation** that they might be the claimant.

And also see *TSE and ELP v NGN Ltd* [2011] EWHC 1308 (QB) at **para 34** and *OPQ v BJM* at **para 4**, and in a matrimonial context, see *Hirschfeld v McGrath* [2011] EWHC 249 (QB) per Tugendhat J at **para 13b.**

33. The interaction of anonymity for family members and that of 'A': Ward LJ considered this in *ETK v News Group Newspapers Ltd* [2011] EWCA Civ 439 and said at para 14:

> As for Article 8, weight must be given not only to the right to respect for the private and family life of the appellant himself, **but also to the rights of X and, in addition, the rights of the appellant's wife and his children**. It is not at all clear to what extent if at all, Collins J. had regard to the Article 8 rights of anyone bar the appellant. He did say of X: . . .

And in the same context see **para 16** and separately from that, **para 17**; and vis-à-vis the interests of children as recognised in international convention, see **paras 18** and **19**. Also see the dicta of Eady J in *CC v AB* [2006] EWHC 3083 at **para 47**.

34. Non-disclosure of ['sealing'] parts of the court file: Non-disclosure in relation to parts of the court file or any part thereof falls within **CPR 5.4(C)** (Confidential Schedule, annex etc); *X & Y v Persons Unknown* at **para 81**; see *G and G v Wikimedia Foundation Inc* at **paras 13–20**; *John Terry v Persons Unknown* at **para 23**; and *Kelly v BBC* [2000] EWHC 3 (Fam) per Munby J (as to what to tell the media in an *ex parte contra mundum* case, if there is sensitive material).

35. As to the interaction of leakage into the public domain and a subsequent application for anonymity: see *In Private Poi v The Person Known as 'Lina'* [2011] EWHC 234 per Supperstone J at **para 11** citing from an earlier judgment in the same case from Tugendhat J:

> The evidence of **attempted blackmail** includes evidence that there is some information about the case that has been put in the **public domain**. If the name of the Applicant were to be identified, then it is likely that persons who knew, or learned, both that the Applicant had issued these proceedings and what is already in the public domain would be **able to deduce** information about the contents of the images, or the

> circumstances in which they were taken, which is private information, and which the Applicant is likely to establish should not be published. **It is likely that the policy of the law to protect those alleging they are victims of a blackmailer would be defeated**.

Also keep in mind in this context, the dicta of Lord Nicholls in *Campbell v MGN Ltd* [2004] UKHL 22 at **para 25**.

'Anonymity'—derogation from open justice—the need for 'intense factual analysis' and 'justification'

36. Focus/scrutiny: Each derogation from Art 6 and open justice must be **justified** on the **particular** facts of the case, in accordance with the **intense focus/scrutiny** required; see *John Terry v Persons Unknown* per Tugendhat J at **paras 108** and **109** (*essential reading*, cited in ***LNR*** inter alia on p 12 at **para 1.28**) and *CC v AB* at **para 13**, with particular relevance to the fact-sensitive nature of the inquiry tailored to the particular case.

37. The starting point: See the principles set out in *JIH v News Group Newspapers Ltd* at **paras 36** and **37** as to the need to engage Article 8, when seeking to secure anonymity, etc, as reasserted in the appeal at *JIH v News Group Newspapers Ltd* [2011] EWCA 42 [Civ] at **para 21**. As to the issue of whether disclosure of the general nature of the information in question would always engage a claimant's private life, see *Gray v UVW* at **para 55** per Tugendhat J:

> However, I do not accept that disclosure of the general nature of the information in question does always engage a claimant's private life. Almost everyone has information about their health, financial affairs, sex life and other matters, the details of which are private and confidential. The fact that a claimant has obtained an injunction to prevent disclosure of one or other of such categories of information is not in itself necessarily a matter which should not be published.

38. Test vis-à-vis anonymity: Is there is **sufficient** general, **public interest** in publishing a report of proceedings which **identifies** either or both parties to **justify** any resulting **curtailment** of the right of the party (and members of that party's family) to respect for their private lives? *Gray v UVW* at **para 44**; *JIH v News Group Newspapers Ltd* [2011] EWCA 42 at **para 21(5)**.

39. The fact-sensitive nature of an anonymity application:

(a) As has recently been re-emphasised by the Court of Appeal in *Donald v Ntuli*, at **para 54**, and by the Supreme Court in *Secretary of State for the Home Department v AP (No 2)* [2010] 1 WLR 1652 at para 7, the question of anonymity (as in all applications vis-à-vis derogations from open justice) is '*an essentially case-sensitive subject*'.
(b) This being the case, evidence of fact is relevant vis-à-vis an application as to the issue of anonymity.
(c) In *JIH v News Group Newspapers Ltd* [2011] EWCA Civ 42 the case against anonymity was supported by written submission from Ms Gillian Phillips, Director of Legal Services on Guardian News & Media, and from Mr Marcus Partington on behalf of The Media Lawyers Association, see **para 18**.

40. Detailed examination—how necessary? A more detailed examination of the material is available at a private hearing; **how necessary is such detailed examination to the facts** of the instant case? See *Niema Ash and another v Loreena McKennitt and others* [2006] EWCA Civ 1714 at **para 14.**

41. Necessity and proportionality: See *Gray v UVW* per Tugendhat J at **para 56**:

> There is a **range of measures** open to the court to protect the art 8 rights of the parties. These include a **variety of measures** to **prohibit or prevent** disclosure of the information sought to be protected, and an order prohibiting disclosure of the **identity** of one or both parties. But each measure is **cumulative**. The fact that one such measure may be necessary is **not** a reason for concluding that they are all necessary. On the contrary, the measures **as a whole** must be no more than is **necessary** and **proportionate**, and if one measure is adopted, then that may mean that an additional measure is not necessary.

42. Relevance of derogation vis-à-vis a respondent: See *Gray v UVW* at **paras 46** and **47** per Tugendhat J, where R was a person of positive good character, who was sincerely distressed by the whole matter, and for whom Article 8 privacy was relevant vis-à-vis identity.

43. Example of circumstances justifying derogation: See *DFT v TFD* at **para 5**: cogent evidence as to allegations of—

(a) **Blackmail or attempted blackmail** (which also goes to the weight to be attached to any Article 10 right), see *ASG v GSA* at **paras 3–5**; in *KJH* *v HGF* at **para 10** and *In Private POI v The Person Known as 'Lina'* [2011] EWHC 234 per Supperstone J at **para 9**. As to public policy and allegations of blackmail, see *CTB v NGN Ltd and Imogen Thomas (No 1)* [2011] EWHC 1232 per Eady J, **para 22**, where Eady J explained the over-arching legal principles in the context of blackmail being a crime, assuming it be established.

(b) **In touch with journalists:** Suspicion that R in touch with journalists with a view to fulfilling blackmail threat; *DFT v TFD* at **para 5**.

(c) **Alleged risk of 'tipping off':** See *DFT v TFD* at **paras 6** and **10**.

44. The interaction of the issue of *'anonymity'* and the *'subject matter of the action'*. A trade-off between **identity**, and the revealing of the **subject matter** of the action, may be the route to balance the Article 8 and 10 rights, consistent with section 12(3) of the Human Rights Act 1998, as Lord Neuberger MR explained in *JIH v News Group Newspapers Ltd* [2011] EWCA Civ 42 at **para 24**, citing from the judgment of Tugendhat J in *JIH v News Group Newspapers Ltd* at **paras 8** and **9**:

> [Where] the court has . . . accepted that the publication of private information **should be restrained** . . . if the court is to avoid disclosing the information in question **it must proceed in one of two alternative ways**:
>
> (1) If its public judgment or order directly or indirectly discloses the **nature** of the information in question then it **should be anonymised**;
>
> (2) If the claimant **is named** in the public judgment or order then the **information should not** be directly or indirectly identified.

But note the caveat in **para 25** (CA) which is essential reading. As to the use of the term 'trade-off' in this context, see **paras 35** and **36** (essential reading) in Lord Neuberger's judgment. As to a practical working example in a family context, see *Hirschfeld v McGrath* [2001] EWHC 249 (QB) at **para 11**:

> And an anonymity order would have the advantage that the Court could disclose to the public more details of the information which is the subject of the Defendant's undertakings than would otherwise be the case.

45. Anonymity—for how long required: For an example of where the need for anonymity had long since expired and was no longer necessary, see *Goldsmith v BCD* [2011] EWHC 674 (QB) **para 7**.

Derogations from open justice—cases of assistance in clarifying the principles

46. ***Ash v McKennitt*** at **paras 1–2** (claim for injunctions preventing further publication by a friend 'A', of a book describing 'A's' private life).

47. ***Browne v Associated Newspapers Ltd*** [2007] EWCA Civ 295 at **paras 2–7** per Sir Anthony Clarke MR. **Issue:** publishing of any details of the relationship between the Claimant and Mr Jeff Chevalier ('JC') and any confidential or private information that JC had obtained in the course of that relationship, **including 15 specific items of information**. In this context, note dicta of Eady J recited by Maurice Kay LJ in *Ntuli v Donald* at **para 18**:

> I would certainly grant an injunction in respect of '**salacious details**' (to adopt Lord Hoffmann's phrase), but I would go further and restrict the communication, with a view to publication to the media, of information as to **intimate** conversations or activities. Wording of that kind would not prevent references to appearances or activities in public or social circumstances. A similar distinction was recognized in *Lord Browne of Madingley*. It has been acknowledged in that case and, for example, in *Ash v McKennitt* that **private communications** between **intimates** will generally give rise to a **reasonable expectation of privacy** under Article 8 . . .
>
> The mischief towards which the injunction is directed is that of revealing *publicly*, for no good reason, **intimate details** relating to a **personal relationship** in which **each party** has a reasonable expectation of privacy.

48. ***John Terry (previously 'LNS') v Persons Unknown*** [2010] EWHC 119 (QB):

(a) Per Tugendhat J at **paras 21** and **22**:

> Substantial derogations have been ordered in cases involving **national security** and **risk to the lives** of others, as mentioned below.

(b) The draft order sought in that case provided at **para 206**:

> [A] prohibition on publishing 'all or any part of the information or purported information' and documents in four categories. I paraphrase this as follows: (1) the fact of a specified personal relationship ('the Relationship') between LNS and another person who is named ('the other person'); (2) details of that relationship including certain specific consequences of it; (3) information leading to the identification of LNS

or the other person and (4) any photographs evidencing or relating to the fact or details of these matters.

(c) Also note the following dicta in *In Re Guardian News and Media Ltd* [2010] UKSC 1 vis-à-vis those charged with criminal offences, deemed to be innocent until proved guilty, at **para 66**:

> The identities of persons charged with offences are published, even though their trial may be many months off.

Return date and service

49. CPR: CPR PD 25 para 5.1 provides that where orders are made without notice to any other party, there must be a return date.

50. *LNR* Practice Guidance:

> **Para 38:** Active case-management requires the court to ensure that a return date is specified in such orders and that, as a general rule, the return date is kept. The applicant is required to inform the court at the return date which, if any, non-parties have been served with any interim non-disclosure order granted at an earlier, without-notice, hearing.
>
> . . .
>
> **Para 40:** A return date is particularly important where an order contains derogations form the principle of open justice.

51. Time for service: Generally see CPR 7.5; CPR 7.6(1) provides that the time for service can be extended.

NB: As a general rule, when an application for an injunction is made before the issue of a claim form, 'A' will be required to *undertake* to the court to issue a claim form *immediately*; CPR 25 PD 25(A), para 4.4(1). For a working example of a breach of such an undertaking, see *Goldsmith & Anor v BCD* [2011] EWHC 674 (QB) per Tugendhat J at **para 5**.

52. Useful authorities on this topic: *John Terry v Persons Unknown* per Tugendhat J; particularly from **paras 17**, **22** and **135**; *Goldsmith v BCD* [2011] EWHC 674 (QB) at **para 15** and *G and G v Wikimedia Foundation Inc* at **paras 21–27** (the requirement of a return date).

Confidential schedules

53. Practice management at time of launch of application: As to the use (and wording) of a **Confidential Schedule** on the launch of an application for an interim injunction, see Lord Neuberger MR in *JIH v News Group Newspapers Ltd* [2011] EWCA Civ 42 at **paras 9** and **11**.

54. Private hearing—open judgment? As to how to handle a hearing in private yet with an open judgment, see *Ash & Anor v McKennitt & Ors* [2006] EWCA 1714 at **para 1** with reference to a **Confidential Schedule**: The judge enjoined further publication of a significant part of the work complained of. He dealt with the problem of publicity in the course of litigation by (if I may respectfully say so, very skilfully), delivering an open judgment that described the objectionable material in general terms, but appended a **confidential appendix** in which the actual enjoined material was fully described *X & Y v Persons Unknown* [2006] EWHC 2783 (QB) at **para 81** ('*This is becoming standard practice . . .*').

55. The interaction of a confidential schedule and jigsaw identification: In *DFT v TFD* at **paras 8** and **35–39**, Sharp J explained that the purpose of a **confidential schedule** in that case was to reduce the risk of **jigsaw** identification of 'A'.

56. The interaction of a '*public hearing*' and a *confidential schedule*: See *TSE and ELP v NGN Ltd* [2011] EWHC 1308 at **para 2** and *Ambrosiadou v Coward* at **para 54**

57. The interaction between a '*public hearing*', a '*confidential schedule*' with a CPR 31.22 order (subsequent use of disclosed documents), and anonymity: Further as to the use of confidential schedules to strike a balance between privacy and a public hearing/judgment, *Ambrosiadou v Coward* at **para 54**. Also see *MJN v News Group Newspapers Ltd* per Sharp J at **para 17**, where she conducted the hearing in public, having made an order pursuant to CPR Part 31.22 restricting subsequent use of disclosed documents:

> It is necessary further to consider the terms of the draft Order and any derogation it makes from the principles of open justice. I am satisfied that it remains necessary for the Claimant to be anonymised for the reasons I have already given. At the start of the hearing, Mr Tomlinson invited me to hear this matter in private. **In the event however, I was satisfied this was not necessary, provided an order was made pursuant to CPR 31.22 that no use may be made by any person who is not a party to the**

> **action of any of the confidential schedules to the witness statements or the skeleton arguments read by the court and referred to in the course of the hearing**; and that no person who is not a party to the action may obtain the documents from the court records. Accordingly, the hearing was in public, and I made an order pursuant to CPR 31.22 in those terms.

58. Practical working example of a confidential schedule: Per Sharp J in *MJN v News Group Newspapers Ltd* at **para 11**:

> Evidence has been put before the court in witness statements from the Claimant, and his solicitors, Mr Hobbs and Mr Oakley, and in **confidential schedules to those witness statements**. No evidence has been put before the court by NGN. In summary it is said that the Claimant, a married Premier league footballer as I have said, and Ms West had a brief sexual relationship and that their relationship was not conducted in public. **To the best of the Claimant's knowledge, only one person knew about it (a friend of the Claimant's) apart obviously from the Claimant and Ms West**. The Claimant understood that Ms West viewed the matter as confidential and did not speak to any one about it either. **It is also said the Claimant has never courted publicity in relation to any aspect of his private life**. He says that the information concerned here is private and sensitive, and its publication would cause him and his wife enormous distress and embarrassment.

59. The interaction between '*broad terms*' and a '*confidential schedule*': The **counterpart** to a **Confidential Schedule** is a judgment which is in **broad terms** and not in detail; see *Lord Browne of Madingley v Associated Newspapers Ltd* at **para 5** and *JIH v News Group Newspapers Ltd* at **para 41**, drawing from *Browne v Associated Newspapers Ltd.* Note the 'awkward language' per Tugendhat J in *John Terry v Persons Unknown* at **para 4**.

60. The importance of defining the strands of information—when considering '*broad terms*': When considering **broad terms**, see the following dicta in *JIH v News Group Newspapers Ltd* per Tugendhat J at **para 44:**

> In *Browne* there were three levels of information concerning the *relationship* between the claimant and the individual referred to as JC. The Court was considering whether or not to enjoin (or permit to be disclosed) in its order information as follows:
>
> (i) no information about the subject matter of the action
> (ii) 'the kind of information' the subject matter of the action
> (iii) 'the bare fact of the *relationship*'

(iv) 'details of the *relationship*'.

61. '*Bare fact*' and '*details*': As to the phrase '*bare fact of the relationship*' see the analysis of confidentiality in this context in *Goodwin v NGN and VBN* at **paras 95**, **96**, **97**, **100**, **102** and **104**; and the practical application of that concept in *Christopher Hutcheson (formerly known as 'KGM') v News Group Newspapers Ltd & Ors* [2011] EWCA Civ 808 at **para 8**, and at **para 26** for the contrast between '*bare fact*' and '*details*'. Equally see *Lord Browne of Madingley v Associated Newspapers Ltd* at **para 58**. '*Bare fact*' was also considered by Eady J in *CC v AB* at **paras 38–39**, in *Ntuli v Donald* at **para 9** and in *Ferdinand v MGN Ltd* [2011] EWHC 2454 per Eady J at **para 53**.

Part 3

THE INTERACTION OF ARTICLES 8 AND 10

Principles

Introduction

62. Limiting principles/scope of Article 8: The '*Spycatcher*' case, *A-G v Guardian Newspapers (No 2)* [1990] 1 AC 109, focused on the traditional concept of *confidence* prior to the emergence of the concept of a reasonable expectation of privacy. It continues, however, to provide a primary anchor point in relation to an analysis of Article 8.

63. The dicta of Lord Goff: He said at 282B–F:

> The **first** limiting principle (which is rather an expression of the scope of the duty) is highly relevant to this appeal. It is that the principle of confidentiality only applies to information to the extent that it is **confidential**. In particular, once it has entered what is usually called the **public domain** (which means no more than that the information in question is so generally accessible that, in all the circumstances, it cannot be regarded as confidential) then, as a general rule, the principle of confidentiality can have no application to it. . . .
>
> The **second** limiting principle is that the duty of confidence applies **neither** to **useless** information, nor to **trivia**. There is no need for me to develop this point.
>
> The **third** limiting principle is of far greater importance. It is that, although the **basis** of the law's protection of confidence is that there is **a public**

> **interest that confidences should be preserved** and protected by the law, nevertheless that public interest may be **outweighed** by some other **countervailing** public interest which favours disclosure. This limitation may apply as the learned judge pointed out to all types of confidential information. It is this limiting principle which may require a court to carry out a balancing operation, weighing the **public interest** in **maintaining** confidence against a **countervailing** public interest favouring **disclosure**.
>
> Embraced within this limiting principle is, of course, the so called **defence of iniquity**. In origin, this principle was narrowly stated, on the basis that a man cannot be made '**the confidant of a crime or a fraud**': see *Gartside v Outram* (1857) 26 LJ Charity 113, at p 114, *per* Sir William Page Wood V-C. But it is now clear that the principle extends to matters of which disclosure is required in the public interest: see *Beloff v Pressdram Ltd* [1973] 1 All ER 241, 260, *per* Ungoed-Thomas J, and *Lion Laboratories Ltd v Evans* [1985] QB 526, 550, *per* Griffiths LJ (as he then was). It does **not however follow** that the public interest will in such cases require disclosure to the media, or to the public by the media. There are cases in which **a more limited disclosure** is all that is required: see *Francome v Mirror Group Newspapers Ltd* [1984] 1 WLR 892.

The remainder of this Part should be read with these limiting principles in mind. As to where the Court of Appeal rejected a submission of more limited disclosure, see *Lord Browne of Madingley v Associated Newspapers Ltd* [2007] EWCA Civ 295 at **para 55**.

64. Exploring the 'limiting principles':

(a) '*Trivia*' is dealt with below, under '*seriousness*'.
(b) The principle of '*public interest*' is addressed below in the context of the Article 8/Article 10 balancing exercise.
(c) The '*defence of iniquity*' is considered below under *Defence Practice Points* in Part 9. Note, however, that a mere allegation of iniquity may not of itself be sufficient to justify disclosure in the public interest: see *Spycatcher*.

65. Public domain:

(a) By reference to the dicta of Lord Goff (above), whether or not the relevant material is in the 'public domain' may be of central relevance to the issue of confidentiality/reasonable expectation of privacy, ie if material is sufficiently in the public domain, then any question of a breach of Article 8 may not arise.

(b) In other words, 'public domain' is relevant to the 'scope' of Article 8 (as a condition precedent to invoking Article 8) as well as casting the burden of proof onto a Respondent if it is raised as a defence. This is of central relevance to Applicant file management, particularly in the context of a duty of full and frank disclosure. This is because the burden is throughout on the Applicant to prove 'likely' within the meaning of the Human Rights Act section 12(3). Accordingly, issues of 'public domain' and 'waiver' are considered next, before exploring whether Article 8 is 'engaged' or 'breached'.

Article 8 applications—public domain—principles

66. An aspect of Lord Goff's first '*limiting principle*': see *Spycatcher*, and in this context, see also *CTB v News Group Newspapers Ltd and Imogen Thomas (No 2)* [2011] EWHC 1326 (QB) per Eady J at **para 20**; and also **para 23**, where he said:

> It is important always to remember that the **modern law of privacy is not concerned solely with information or 'secrets'**: it is also concerned importantly with **intrusion**. That is one reason why it can be important to distinguish between the way the law approaches **public domain arguments in relation to commercial or state secrets, for example, and that which is appropriate to personal information**.

And in the same context, see *CTB vs News Group Newspapers Ltd and Imogen Thomas (No 1)* [2011] EWHC 1232 (QB) at **para 28**.

67. A '*public interest defence*': As with the *misleading* of the public, so with '*waiver*', '*public domain/waiver*' is a '*public interest defence*'; see *DFT v TFD* [2010] EWHC 2335 per Sharp J at **para 21**.

68. What is in the public domain? In *KJO v XIM* [2011] EWHC 1768 (QB) Eady J said at **para 21**:

> The test which has been applied to public domain arguments (albeit in different contexts) is whether, in the light of such accessibility as there is, **it is realistic to regard the information as any longer capable of protection**: see eg *Att-Gen v Guardian Newspapers (No 2)* [1990] 1 AC 109, 282B–F and *Venables v News Group Newspapers Ltd* [2001] Fam 430, 470–471. It is thus well established that the issue of **public domain** will often require **close analysis** of the particular facts. It is not simply a matter of

> black and white: see eg the discussion in *KGM v News Group Newspapers Ltd* [2010] EWHC 3145 (QB) at [30]–[31].

The emphasised words were adopted by Eady J in *KJO v XIM* at **para 21**. He went on, in **para 22**, to cite from Sir Roger Coulson's work on *Confidentiality* (2nd edn) at para 3-151:

> It is suggested that whether information is, or was once upon a time, a matter of 'public record' (whatever the meaning intended by that expression, as compared with **the broader expression 'public domain'**) is simply a factor in determining whether it **is so generally accessible** that it would not be just to require the party against whom a duty of confidentiality is alleged to treat it as confidential.

And see *CTB v News Group Newspapers Ltd and Imogen Thomas (No 1)* at **para 27** per Eady J.

69. The '*circle of friends*' criterion and the public domain? In this regard note the dicta in *Browne v Associated Newspapers Ltd* [2008] QB 103 at **para 61** cited by Tugendhat J in *Goodwin v NGN Ltd and VBN (No 3)* [2011] EWHC 1437 (QB) at **para 84**:

> [P]otentially an important distinction between information which is made available to **a person's circle of friends** or work colleagues and information which is widely published **in a newspaper**.

And in this context see also *CC v AB* [2006] EWHC 3083 (QB) per Eady J at **paras 19**, **34**, **35** and **49**:

70. Fact and degree: Whether what may start as information which is private has become information known to the public at large is a matter of *fact and degree*, for determination in each case, depending on its specific circumstances; and see *ETK v News Group Newspapers Ltd* [2011] EWCA Civ 439 at **para 10(3)**, and at **para 11**:

> Here the sexual relationship was essentially a private matter. One way or another it became known to work colleagues but their knowledge **does not put the information into the public domain**.

Further as to a '*limited circle*' see *Christopher Hutcheson (formerly known as 'KGM') v News Group Newspapers Ltd & Ors* [2011] EWCA Civ 808 at **para 25**.

71. Public domain and breach of confidence: Per Megarry J in *Coco v AN Clark (Engineers) Ltd* [1969] RPC 41 at 47:

Something which is public property and public knowledge cannot per se provide any foundation for breach of confidence.

72. If publication—what precisely is the information that has been published? Has the particular piece of information already been published (and if yes, by *whom*, from *what* source, on *whose* authority, in *what* circumstances)? Close *scrutiny* is required of *each* revelation and precisely how it came about; *X & Y v Persons Unknown* [2006] EWHC 2783 (QB) at **para 46** per Eady J.

73. How much has to be in the public domain before protection is lost—does leakage abrogate privacy? In the context of personal information (*as opposed to commercial secrets*) it *does not necessarily follow*, from the fact that something has been published, that further coverage cannot itself infringe a claimant's privacy; *X & Y v Persons Unknown* at **para 64**; and per Tugendhat J in *JIH v News Group Newspapers Ltd* [2010] EWHC 2818 (QB) at **paras 58–59**. In this context, also see *A Local Authority v A, F & A* [2011] EWHC 1764 (Fam) per Baker J at **para 34** set out below in Part 14 in relation to reporting restriction orders in the Family Division.

74. What about repetition of known facts? Repetition of known facts about an individual may amount to *unjustified* interference with the private lives not only of that person, but also of those who are *involved* with him/her in the matters which are the subject matter of the action; cited by Tugendhat J in *TSE and EPL v NGN* Ltd [2011] EWHC 1308 at **paras 29 and 30**; and also see *JIH v News Group Newspapers Ltd* per Tugendhat J at **paras 58–59** (not affected by subsequent appeal).

75. Saturation point? As to whether leakage/coverage has reached '*saturation point*' see *CTB v News Group Newspapers Ltd and Imogen Thomas (No 2)* per Eady J at **para 25** and in a Family Division context, see also *Re Stedman* [2009] EWHC 935 (Fam) in which an injunction had been refused after an avalanche of publicity about a 12-year-old boy who was (wrongly) alleged to have impregnated a 15-year-old girl.

76. Leakage/public domain/anonymity: As to the interaction of *leakage* into the *public domain* and a subsequent application for *anonymity*, see *In Private Poi v The Person Known as 'Lina'* [2011] EWHC 234 (QB) per Supperstone J at **para 11**. For a recent *definitive* expression of the law on this issue, see Eady J in *CTB v News Group Newspapers Ltd and Imogen Thomas (No 1)* at **para 28**. See also *A v B, C and D* [2005] EWHC 1651 (QB) per Eady J at

para 23. In this context, also see *A Local Authority v A Mother & F & A* at **para 34** set out below in Part 14 in relation to reporting restriction orders in the Family Division. Where a person was named in the press but anonymised in Strasbourg, see *A v United Kingdom* [2003] 36 EHRR 51.

77. Leakage and the internet: In *TSE and ELP v NGN Ltd* Tugendhat J said at **para 31**:

> In the course of his submissions Mr Caldecott referred to **the difficulty that claimants may have in enforcing injunctions against those who publish private information on the internet**. The difficulties are well known. However, as the ECHR confirmed in the *Mosley* case, **whether or not an injunction is granted, claimants continue to have the right to claim damages, whether or not those who publish the information have had notice of any injunction**.

In this context, also see *A Local Authority v A, F & A* per Baker J at **para 34** set out below in Part 14 in relation to reporting restriction orders in the Family Division.

78. Leakage and policy: In *CTB v News Group Newspapers Ltd and Imogen Thomas* Eady J said at **para 16**:

> The principle, however, is clear. One has only to pose the question for the answer to become obvious. **Should the court buckle every time one of its orders meets widespread disobedience or defiance?** In a democratic society, if a law is deemed to be unenforceable or unpopular, it is for the legislature to make such changes as it decides are appropriate.

And similarly, see Tugendhat J at **para 3** in *CTB v News Group Newspapers Ltd and Imogen Thomas (No 3)* [2011] EWHC 1334 (QB).

79. Leakage and contempt: Dominic Grieve as Attorney General said the following in the House of Commons on 24 May 2011 (Vol 528, part 163):

> Those who I think may take an idea that modern methods of communication mean they can act with impunity may well find themselves in for a rude shock.
>
> The courts do have the power to punish those who breach injunctions. Those who decide flagrantly to do so should bear that in mind.

80. What if the '*character*' of the applicant is in the public domain? It was argued in *Ntuli v Donald* [2010] EWCA 1276 (Civ) at **para 22** that Mr

Donald was a public figure, some of whose relationships had received media coverage, and he had been open about some immature sexual activity two decades before.

81. Disclosed in court? Information may be in the public domain if it has been disclosed in open court, even in another jurisdiction (unless subject to litigation privilege); see *Long Beach Ltd v Global Witness Ltd* [2007] EWHC 1980 (QB) and also *Commissioners for Her Majesty's Revenue and Customs v Banerjee* [2009] EWHC 1229 (Ch) and [2009] EMLR 24 per Henderson J, at **para 38**.

82. Proviso: It is now recognised that *generally* speaking an order restricting the communication of ideas and information should include a *public domain proviso*: see *X & Y v Persons Unknown* at **para 62**, ie an order will not restrain publication of that material already in the public domain.

83. Defining what is—and is not—covered by the '*public domain proviso*':

(a) The need for precision: If it is the court's intention to prevent further publication of specific material (even though it has apparently leaked into the public domain) on the basis that its confidentiality/ privacy has not thereby been utterly lost, it will need to be made expressly clear that such material is not to be treated as being within the proviso; *X & Y v Persons Unknown* at **para 66**.

(b) The distinction between '*secrecy*' and '*privacy*' in this context per Lord Nicholls: See Human Rights Act section 12(4)(a)(i) and as to the extent to which material in the public domain (or '*about to be*' adopting the statutory wording) undermines an application for an interim non-disclosure order, also see *Douglas v Hello! Ltd (No 3)* [2007] UKHL 21 at **para 255** per Lord Nicholls, and see *CC v AB* per Eady J at **paras 40** and **49**.

84. 'Confess and avoid?' If material is in the public domain and yet an injunction is still sought, is it possible to '**confess and avoid**' (*X & Y v Persons Unknown* at **paras 53** and **54**)?

Article 8 applications—waiver—principles

85. Issue in principle: Has any reasonable expectation of privacy been displaced by 'A's' own conduct—eg by his *courting* the relevant publicity? See *A v B, C, & D* [2005] EMLR 26; [2005] EWHC 1651 (QB) per Eady J **paras 22**

and **23**. Such courting, however, does not necessarily abrogate a reasonable expectation of privacy: *Campbell v Mirror Group Newspapers Ltd* [2004] UKHL 22 at **para 57**.

86. Genuine waiver: Could there have been a genuine '*waiver*' of privacy on the part of 'A'; if yes, on what grounds could that be so argued? See *X & Y v Persons Unknown* at **para 48**. For example, has the public, as it were, been *invited into* the area now claimed to engage Article 8? If yes, on what grounds is that contended? *X & Y v Persons Unknown* at **para 56**. Also see *X & Y v Persons Unknown* at **para 48**; and *Mosley v News Group Newspapers Ltd* [2008] EWHC 1777 (QB) at **para 13**.

87. Previous instances: Have similar instances of behaviour already been released into the public domain?

(a) If yes, the court will require the full details and circumstances of how such material came into the public domain and, if relevant, the limits of such information coming into the public domain (consider a Scott Schedule of dates cross-referencing with an internet trawl).

(b) If on the internet, see *CC v AB*, **para 57** explaining how far one needs to 'dredge'; and see *Niema Ash and another v Loreena McKennitt and others* [2006] EWCA Civ 1714, **paras 53** and **80** as to some material being in the public domain and other material 'in the same zone'—ie the same core area of private life—being held back; see also *X & Y v Persons Unknown* at **para 28** and *Howlett v Holding* [2006] EWHC 41 (QB) at **para 26**. As to the concept of a 'residual area of privacy', see Lord Hoffman in *Campbell v Mirror Group Newspapers Ltd* at **para 68**; and 'private space' vis-à-vis the Prince of Wales: *Associated Newspapers Ltd v HRH Prince of Wales* [2006] EWCA Civ 1776 at **para 70**. As to a working example of an internet search in this context, see *John Terry (previously 'LNS') v Persons Unknown* [2010] EWHC 119 (QB) at **para 27**.

(c) Have there been 'admissions as to his past behaviour'? See *Ntuli v Donald* at **para 24**, which on the facts resulted in placing 'relatively low value on it' in the context of 'it cannot be a determinative factor or anything like it'. In **para 35**, Maurice Kay LJ set out how the parties addressed this issue:

> The witness statements filed by and on behalf of Mr Donald and Ms Ntuli provide different accounts of the duration and intensity of their relationship. They also differ as to the extent to which it was

> conducted in public, although it seems to be common ground that it **was not wholly secret** and nor did Mr Donald ever seek to impose **a condition of secrecy**. It is unnecessary for me to rehearse the detail'

(d) Has 'A' made allegations involving other persons and, in particular, their personal lives so that it would be reasonable for such other persons to give another side of the story (again, if yes, give full details), *A v B, C and D* [2005] EWHC 1651 at **para 23** per Eady J.
(e) If anodyne, imprecise or already known to the public, the court will probably not enjoin; see *Ash v McKennitt* at **para 12** per Buxton LJ.

88. Might 'A's' own conduct have contributed to the nature and scale of the distress? If yes, give full details; see *Mosley v News Group Newspapers Ltd* at paras **224–26**, per Eady J. The resonance with this case and dicta in *Prince Albert v Strange* 64 ER 293 at 312 warrants citation:

> A man may employ himself in private in a manner very harmless, but which, disclosed to society, may destroy the comfort of his life, or even his success in it.

Prince Albert brought his claim on the basis of protecting property rights and breach of confidence, but the underlying principle was to secure privacy.

Article 8: what does 'engaged' mean?

89. '*Engaged*' does not mean '*breached*': Article 8 may be, in principle, applicable (or '*engaged*') but that does not by itself mean that there has been a breach of its provisions: *Harrow LBC v Qazi* [2003] UKHL 43 per Lord Hope at **para 47**.

90. The distinction: The *distinction* is between information that '*relates*' to family life and information in respect of which there is a '*reasonable expectation of privacy*'.

91. Example: 'A' did not have a reasonable expectation of privacy in keeping the identity of his second family secret, given that inter alia, the mother and children were known by the name of 'Hutcheson', and 'A' had played an active role in the their upbringing. This was clearly information relating to family life, but there was no reasonable expectation of privacy: *Hutcheson v News Group Newspapers Ltd*, **para 38**.

92. Fact-sensitivity: A complaint of misuse of private information is necessarily fact sensitive, and the nature of the information requires careful consideration: *Hutcheson v News Group Newspapers Ltd* per Gross LJ at **paras 26** and **37**.

93. Is the privacy in relation to the world—or to sections/groups/classes of people? See *Leeds City Council v Channel 4 Television* [2007] 1 FLR 678; [2005] EWHC 3522 (Fam) **para 32**:

> I also accept that although the consequence of obscuring their faces is that the children **will not be identifiable to the world at large**, in the nature of things, since the schools are identified in the film, and since the relevant classes are in some cases identified, e.g. Year 10, the overwhelming probability is that many of the children who are shown on the film **will be more or less readily identifiable** and in fact identified by their school friends, their relations and people in their immediate locality. This is an important factor which has to be fed into the Article 8 scale, because insofar as Article 8 protects privacy, the privacy is not merely privacy as against the world at large, it is also privacy as against particular sections of the world.

The control mechanisms for Article 8

As to a reasonable level of seriousness, see also *Ferdinand v MGN Ltd* [2011] EWHC 2454 per Eady J at **para 54**.

94. 'Safeguards': Per Laws LJ in *R (Wood) v Commissioner of Police for the Metropolis* [2009] EWCA Civ 414 at **para 22**:

> At the same time it is important that this core right protected by Article 8, however protean, should not be read so widely that its claims become unreal and unreasonable. For this purpose I think there are **three safeguards**, or qualifications. **First**, the alleged threat or assault to the individual's personal autonomy must (if Article 8 is to be engaged) attain '**a certain level of seriousness**'. **Secondly**, the touchstone for Article 8(1)'s engagement is whether the claimant enjoys on the facts a '**reasonable expectation of privacy**' (in any of the senses of privacy accepted in the cases). Absent such an expectation, there is no relevant interference with personal autonomy. **Thirdly**, the breadth of Article 8(1) may in many instances be **greatly curtailed by the scope of the justifications** available to the State pursuant to **Article 8(2)**. I shall say a little in turn about these three antidotes to the overblown use of Article 8.

95. Rationale for 'safeguards': Drawing from *R (Wood) v Commissioner of*

Police for the Metropolis at **para 22** (but also see **para 63**), Gross LJ said in *Hutcheson v News Group Newspapers Ltd* at **para 27** that the '**safeguards**' and '**qualifications**' in Article 8 are to ensure that the

> core right protected by article 8 . . . should not be read so widely that its claims become unreal and unreasonable.

96. Explaining these safeguards: There is detailed below the law relating to:

(a) what is 'serious';
(b) the meaning of a 'reasonable expectation of privacy'; and
(c) how Article 8 is curtailed by the operation of Article 8(2)/Article 10—'the balancing exercise'.

'Serious' as a 'safeguard'

97. What does '*serious*' mean in this context? Interference with private life *must* be of *some seriousness* before Article 8 is *engaged*, see *R (Wood) v Commissioner of Police for the Metropolis* at **para 22**.

98. The interaction of the word '*respect*' in Article 8 with the concept of '*seriousness*': Article 8 provides for '*respect*' for privacy rather than for 'privacy' as an absolute concept; see *M v Secretary of State for Work and Pensions* [2006] UKHL 11 per Lord Walker at **para 83**; and *Ash v McKennitt* at **para 12** ('*anodyne', imprecise or already known to the public*').

99. The relevance of '*identity*' and the '*nature of the information*' to the issue of '*seriousness*': The principle of 'seriousness' applies both to the identity of the claimant (the issue of 'anonymity') and to the nature of any information about the subject matter of the action; *JIH v News Group Newspapers Ltd* at para 40:

> To publish that a person has obtained an injunction restraining the publication of private information will not normally, of itself, cross that threshold, but will depend on all the circumstances. Whether the information is **sufficiently serious** may depend upon **the identity** of a claimant. **Resolution No 1165 (1998) of the Parliamentary Assembly of the Council of Europe** on the right to privacy includes:
>
> 6 . . . public figures must recognise that the special position they occupy in society—in many cases by choice—automatically entails increased pressure on their privacy.

> 7. Public figures are persons holding public office and/or using public resources and, more broadly speaking, all those who play a role in public life, whether in politics, the economy, the arts, the social sphere, sport or in any other domain.

100. Anodyne/salacious: In the context of '*public office*' Eady J said at first instance in *Ntuli v Donald* (cited in the CA at [2010] EWCA 1276 Civ at **para 14** in turn drawing from the dicta of Lord Hoffman in *Campbell v Mirror Group Newspapers Ltd* at para 60):

> The relatively **anodyne** nature of the additional details is in my opinion important and distinguishes this case from cases in which (for example) there is a public interest in the disclosure of a sexual relationship (say, between a politician and someone whom she has appointed to public office) but the addition of **salacious details** or intimate photographs is **disproportionate** and **unacceptable**. The latter, even if accompanying a legitimate disclosure of the sexual relationship, would be too obtrusive and demeaning.

101. Principle vis-à-vis public figures and their identity as celebrities: In this context, also see *Mosley v News Group Newspapers Ltd* per Eady J at **para 20**. All these dicta are consistent with the principle expressed by the Court of Appeal in *JIH v News Group Newspapers Ltd* [2011] EWCA Civ 42 at **para 21(6)**:

> On any such application, no special treatment should be accorded to public figures or celebrities: in principle, they are entitled to the same protection as others, no more and no less.

The House of Lords was unanimous in *Campbell v Mirror Group Newspapers Ltd* that Naomi Campbell did not lose her privacy rights just because she had attracted publicity and courted the media; see eg **paras 57 and 73–75** per Lord Hoffman, and at **para 120** per Lord Hope.

102. What about children? As with adults, so with children, the right to privacy is not an absolute; per Sir Anthony Clarke MR in *David Murray v Big Pictures (UK) Ltd* [2008] EWCA Civ 446 at **para 54,** and the following at **para 58**:

> It is important to note that so to hold does not mean that the child will have, as the judge puts it in [66], a guarantee **of privacy**. **To hold that the child has a** reasonable expectation of privacy **is only the first step**. **Then comes the balance** which must be struck between the child's rights to respect for his or her private life under article 8 and the publisher's rights

> to freedom of expression under article 10. This approach does not seem to us to be inconsistent with that in *Campbell*, which was not considering the case of a child.

103. 'Trivia'—examples through the cases: It may be possible to argue that '*trivia*' are not engaged by Article 8, subject to the *fact-sensitivity* of the individual case. As to examples of cases where the word '*trivia*' has been addressed, see:

(a) *Coco v AN Clark (Engineers) Ltd* [1969] RPC 41 at 48 per Megarry J (vis-à-vis confidential information, this will not be regarded as having the necessary quality of confidence if it is nothing more than '*trivial tittle-tattle*').

(b) *Campbell v Mirror Group Newspapers Ltd* [2004] UKHL 22, **para 56**:

> While there is no contrary public interest recognised and protected by the law, the press is free to publish anything it likes. Subject to the law of defamation, **it does not matter how trivial, spiteful or offensive the publication may be**. But when press freedom comes into conflict with another interest protected by the law, the question is whether there is a **sufficient public interest** in that particular publication to justify curtailment of the conflicting right.

(c) *Mosley v News Group Newspapers* [2008] EWHC 1777 at **para 13** (trivia) contrasted with **para 132** (titillation).

(d) *Author of a Blog v Times Newspapers Ltd* [2009] EWHC 1358 (QB) per Eady J at **para 20** where circumstances involving trivia in the context of a public servant could justify restraining publication.

(e) *CC v AB* per Eady J at **paras 6**, **19**, **36** and **44** ('*vapid tittle-tattle*'); as to the contrast with '*vapid tittle-tattle*' and publication to further 'rights to personal autonomy and self-development', see *Ntuli v Donald* at **para 22**; also see *CDE & FGH v MGN Ltd & LMN* [2010] EWHC 3308 at **para 73**. As to the autonomy of a prostitute to tell her story, see *Theakston v MGN Ltd* [2002] EWHC 137 (QB) at **para 75** per Ouseley J and also see Buxton LJ in *Ash v McKennitt* at paras 28–32. As to the interaction of 'tittle-tattle' and the public domain vis-à-vis colleagues at work, see *ETK v News Group Newspapers Ltd* at para 11. As to the interaction of 'tittle-tattle' and the right to a 'private life', see Eady J in *CTB v News Group Newspapers Ltd and Imogen Thomas (No 1)* at para 33.

(f) *Loreena McKennitt, Hampstead Productions Ltd and Quinlan Road Ltd v*

Niema Ash and Purple Inc Press Ltd [2005] EWHC 3003; [2006] EMLR 178 (QB) Eady J (first instance) at **para 135**.

(g) *Ash v McKennitt* [2006] EWCA 1714 (Civ) at **para 12** per Buxton LJ:

> [I]nterference with private life had to be **of some seriousness** before article 8 was engaged.

And see Buxton LJ at **para 26** and also the following at **para 21** citing dicta from first instance**:**

> Even relatively trivial details would fall within the protection simply because of the traditional security accorded to **hearth and home**.

This was cited with approval by Sir Anthony Clarke MR in *Lord Browne of Madingley v Associated Newspapers Ltd* at **paras 21**, **28**, **33** and **49** and also see **para 53.**

(h) *Jameel and ors v Wall Street Journal Europe Sprl* [2006] UKHL 44 at **para 147** per Baroness Hale:

> [T]he most **vapid tittle-tattle** about the activities of footballers' wives and girlfriends interests large sections of the public but no-one could claim any real **public interest** in our being told all about it.

(i) *R (Wood) v Commissioner of Police of the Metropolis* [2009] EWCA Civ 414 at **para 22** per Laws LJ (whilst going onto recognise the threshold of 'seriousness' to engage Article 8):

> This cluster of values, summarised as the personal autonomy of every individual and taking concrete form as a presumption against interference with the individual's liberty, is a defining characteristic of a free society. We therefore need to preserve it **even in little cases**.

(j) *Lord Browne of Madingley v Associated Newspapers Ltd* [2007] EWCA Civ 295 at **para 33**:

> The nature of the relationship is of considerable importance. For example, the mere fact that the piece of information can be regarded as trivial does not seem to us to be decisive against answering Lord Nicholls' question in the affirmative.

(k) *Ambrosiadou v Coward* [2011] EWCA Civ 409 at **paras 28–30**:

> 30. . . . **Just because information relates to a person's family and private life, it will not automatically be protected by the courts**: for instance, the information may be of **slight significance**, **generally expressed**, or **anodyne in nature**. While respect for family and private life is of fundamental importance, it seems to me that the courts

should, in the absence of special facts, **generally expect people to adopt a reasonably robust and realistic approach to living in the 21st century**.

(l) As to government secrets, secrets in the context of '*trivia*', see: *A-G v Observer Ltd* [1990] 1 AC 109 at 284.

'Reasonable expectation of privacy'—as a 'safeguard'

104. The test for a reasonable expectation of privacy—'objective' or 'subjective'? The test is '*objective*': *Murray v Express Newspapers and Big Pictures (UK) Ltd* [2008] EWCA 446, **para 35**; *Author of a Blog v Times Newspapers Ltd* per Eady J at **para 8**, and *Napier v Pressdram Ltd* [2009] EWCA Civ 443 at **para 42.**

105. Avoiding the 'partisan': Thus one must strive to avoid a partisan subjective perspective. This comes out particularly well in the following dicta of Eady J in *KJO v XIM* at **para 16**:

> . . . according to the standards of ordinary reasonable onlookers.

106. How to avoid partisan morality:

(a) **Judicial neutrality:** Judges need to be wary about giving the impression that they are ventilating, while affording or refusing legal redress, some personal moral or social views, and especially at a time when society is far less homogeneous than in the past; one must guard against allowing legal judgments to be coloured by personal attitudes; see *CC v AB* at **paras 22–27**, and see also *John Terry v Persons Unknown* at **paras 101** and **104**.
(b) **Litigator neutrality:** Correspondingly, personal, moral or social views will not be relevant to any party's argument.

107. Reasonable expectation of '*privacy*' and '*celebrity*' status:

(a) On any such application, no special treatment should be accorded just because 'A' is a public figure or a celebrity: in principle, they are entitled to the same protection as others, no more and no less; see *JIH v NGN Ltd* [2011] at **para 21(6)**.

(b) The fleeting nature of 'celebrity' was considered in *ETK v News Group Newspapers Ltd*: it is 'ephemeral', see **para 13** per Ward LJ.

108. Reasonable expectation—'public figures' and 'private lives': As Tugendhat and Christie say in *The Law of Privacy and the Media*, 2nd edn, at 7.18:

> [P]ublic figures should not be judged on information which is true but clearly irrelevant to their public lives.

Also see *Goodwin v NGN Ltd and VBN (No 3)* [2011] EWHC 1437 (QB) at **paras 59** and **92** and *Hutcheson v News Group Newspapers Ltd* per Gross LJ at **para 33**. Note how Sir Fred Goodwin, because of his profile, crossed a threshold, resulting in an expectation of privacy not being reasonable: *Sir Frederick Goodwin v NGN Ltd and VBN (No 3)* [2011] EWHC 1437 (QB) at **para 64**; and the following dicta at **para 103**:

> And he was Chief Executive of one the largest publicly quoted companies in the United Kingdom, doing business on a global scale. Whatever limits there may be to the legal concept of a public figure, or of a person carrying out official functions, in my judgment Sir Fred Goodwin came within the definition.

109. Examples drawn from *Bensaid v United Kingdom* [2001] 33 EHRR 10 at paras 46–47:

(a) **Gender identification.**
(b) **Name, sexual orientation.**
(c) **Sexual life:**
  (i) *Peck v The United Kingdom*, no 44647/98, § 57, ECHR 2003 I, 36 EHRR 41.
  (ii) Note in this context the interaction/possible overlap of '*intimate*', '*personal*' and '*sexually explicit*'; see *Ntuli v Donald* at **para 29** per Maurice Kay LJ:

> I accept that there is a degree of overlap between '**intimate**', '**personal**' and '**sexually explicit**'. They are not mutually exclusive epithets. However, that does not necessarily establish ambiguity or a lack of clarity. Words of restraint often overlap, as for example 'publishing, communicating or disclosing'. As developed before us, the issue seems to be whether '**intimate**' has an essentially **sexual connotation**. I am **convinced that it does not**. The same word was used in the order in *McKennitt v Ash*, where the relationship

between the parties was **not sexual**. What the judge had in mind in the present case is apparent from paragraph 17 of his judgment:

> . . . the court's protection should be extended to any facts communicated by the Defendant of a sexual nature **or other intimate personal details about their past relationship**.

(d) **Mental stability:** For a paradigm working example of this factor (in the context of an exemplary judgment on the overall issues of Articles 8 and 10), see *A Local Authority v A Mother & F & A* per Baker J at para 43 (to be found in Part 15 in the context of Reporting Restriction Orders in the Family Division).

Other examples of a reasonable expectation of privacy

110. A person's name: See *In Re Guardian News and Media Ltd* [2010] UKSC 1, **para 63,** by way of example.

111. Other means of personal identification and of linking to a family: See mutatis mutandis *Burghartz v Switzerland*, 22 February 1994; [1994] ECHR 2, § 24, Series A no 280B; and *Unal Tekeli v Turkey*, no 29865/96, §42, ECHR 2004 X (extracts), 42 EHRR 53.

112. Health: Information about the person's health is an important element of private life (see *Z v Finland,* 25 February 1997, § 71, Reports of Judgments and Decisions 1997 I, 25 EHRR 371); including a wish to die: *Pretty v UK* [2002] 35 EHRR 1. Also see Lord Hoffman at **para 53** in *Campbell v Mirror Group Newspapers Ltd.*

113. Ethnic identity: An individual's ethnic identity must be regarded as another such element; see in particular Article 6 of the *Data Protection Convention 1981* which lists personal data revealing *racial origin* as a special category of data along with other sensitive information about an individual (eg '*sexual life*'—see section 2(f)); this Article was a focus of the decision in *R (Wood) v Commissioner of Police of the Metropolis*, particularly at **para 18**.

114. Autonomy: A right to personal **development**, and the right to establish and develop **relationships** with other human beings and the outside world (see eg *Burghartz v Switzerland*, cited above, opinion of the Commission, p 37, § 47, and *Friedl v Austria*, judgment of 31 January 1995, Series A, no

305B, opinion of the Commission, p 20, § 45, 21 EHRR 83). This principle was expressed by Ryder J in *BBC v Rochdale MBC and X and Y* [2005] EWHC 2862 (Fam) in the following terms at **para 47**:

> [A]rticle 8 protects the right to establish, maintain and develop relationships with other human beings.

115. Elements relating to a person's right to their image: *Sciacca v Italy*, no 50774/99, § 29, ECHR 2005-I, 43 [2005] EHRR 20 at **para 29**:

> [T]he concept of private life includes elements relating to a person's right to their picture and that the publication of a photograph falls within the scope of private life.

116. The position of the police? What, however, is the right of privacy of a policeman to his own image, when acting in the execution of his duty. Is one permitted to film or photograph in a public place? Further, addressing the issue generically in the context of 'the police', what is the right (if any) so to film or photograph? The Metropolitan Police website, www.met.police.uk, contains the following passage:

> **Photography advice**
>
> The Metropolitan Police Service's approach towards photography in public places is a subject of regular debate.
>
> We encourage officers and the public to be vigilant against terrorism but recognise the importance not only of protecting the public from terrorism but also promoting the freedom of the public and the media to take and publish photographs.
>
> Guidance around the issue has been made clear to officers and PCSOs through briefings and internal communications. The following advice is available to all officers and provides a summary of the Metropolitan Police Service's guidance around photography in public places.
>
> **Freedom to photograph/film**
>
> Members of the public and the media do not need a permit to film or photograph in public places and police have no power to stop them filming or photographing incidents or police personnel.

This, however, should be seen in the broader context of the coverage of issues of terrorism, immediately below on the same website. To afford the full context, the relevant page of the website is included in Part 20 under Codes of Practice.

117. Storage: The mere storing of data relating to the private life of an individual amounts to an interference within the meaning of Article 8 (see *Leander v Sweden*, 26 March 1987, § 48, Series A, no 116, 9 EHRR 433). Questions arising in relation to data storage (taken from **para 18** in *R (Wood) v Commissioner of Police of the Metropolis*):

(a) the specific context in which the information in issue has been recorded and retained;
(b) the nature of the records;
(c) the way in which such records are used and processed and the results that may be obtained (see, mutatis mutandis, Friedl, cited above, §§ 49–51, and *Peck v the United Kingdom*, cited above, § 59).

118. Personal experiences including relationship: Relationships can retain their **private** character, even if shared with others; *Ash v McKennitt* [2006] EWCA Civ 1714; [2007] EMLR 113.

119. Business affairs: *Lord Browne of Madingley v Associated Newspapers Ltd*, **paras 33**, particularly **34** and also **54**. The issue is not whether the information was '**business**' or '**private**' but whether there was a **reasonable expectation of privacy**; see ibid, **para 50**, and vis-à-vis relations in **the workplace**, see *Goodwin v NGN Ltd* at **para 74** where the interested third party was not identified, but her job description (in the bank) was.

120. Information for personal gain—wedding photos: *OBG v Allan/ Douglas v Hello! Ltd.* And see *R (Wood) v Commissioner of Police of the Metropolis* at **para 18**.

The interaction of 'privacy' and 'reputation'

121. What is the real issue? Is the real issue the protection of a business reputation, or is it any other aspect of the applicant's private life? In this context, see *John Terry v Persons Unknown* at **para 95**, where Tugendhat J held that the nub of the claim was the protection of a commercial reputation as contrasted with his private life. The court did not believe there was some other serious interest to be protected other than commercial reputation. Note how the press in a family case argued that the nub of her claim did not engage Article 8: *A Local Authority v A & F &* A at **para 57** per Baker J at **para 59.**

122. The interaction of reputation as an aspect of personal integrity, as contrasted with commercial reputation:

(a) Article 8 embraces also reputation: 'Reputation' can fall within Article 8 because Article 8 protects the right to reputation, as part of the right to respect for family life; see *Greene v Associated Newspapers* [2004] EWCA Civ 1462, **para 68**; and *W v Westminster CC* [2004] EWHC 2866 (QB); [2005] 1 FLR 816 at **para 38**; *Von Hannover v Germany* [2005] 40 EHRR 1, **para 58**; *Prince Radu of Hohenzollern v Houston* [2007] EWHC 2735 (QB) at **para 44**. These dicta resonate also with those of Lord Hoffmann in *Wainwright v Home Office* [2003] UKHL 53 at **paras 16–18** which are essential reading as to the evolving concept of 'privacy', particularly as Lord Hoffman also parallels the US approach (and note also his reference to inadvertent intrusion at **para 51**: '*[I]t is one thing to wander carelessly into the wrong hotel bedroom . . .*').

(b) Interaction of 'reputation' and 'integrity': See *Gray v UVW* [2010] EWHC 2367 (QB) per Tugendhat J at **para 46**; and *Re Guardian News and Media* [2010] UKSC1 at **paras 39** and **40** for the ECtHR context:

> **40. . . . But the court took the view that, on the facts, the applicant had not shown** that the publication in question had constituted **such a serious interference** with his private life as to undermine his **personal integrity**.

Does such context connote something more in the nature of personal *integrity* than *reputation* is required to establish the engaging of Article 8?

123. Reputation and the identity of a journalist: Where a journalist was unsuccessfully seeking Article 8 protection to conceal his identity thus to protect his earning capacity and position as an investigative journalist, see *Mahmood v Galloway and Another* [2006] EWHC 1286.

124. The interaction of '*Article 8 Reputation*' with '*Defamation Justification*', in the context of Article 8/Article 10 balance: As to the issue of *privacy* as contrasted with *defamation*, see Tugendhat J in *Gray v UVW* [2010] EWHC 2367 (QB) **para 39**:

> **The reason I have not had to consider the question of defamation is that that** [*sic*] the Defendant **does not assert** a **right** to publish the information. In this respect the case is similar to *DFT v TFD* [2010] EWHC 2335 (QB) (see para [11]) and *AMM v HXW* [2010] EWHC 2457 (QB) para [4]. In a defamation action the Court will not refuse to grant an injunction simply because the action is one for defamation. It will refuse the **application if**

> **and when the defendant raises an issue or a defence**: see the discussion in Duncan & Neill on Defamation 3rd edn para 24.02.

And also see *John Terry v Persons Unknown* at **para 80**, where there is discussed the interaction of the defence of justification in defamation, and the balancing exercise between Article 8 and Article 10; and also **para 149**. Further in *Terry* at **para 80**, Tugendhat J went on to consider also the defamation defences of justification, fair comment and qualified privilege. See also *Ash v McKennitt* at **paras 79**, **80** and **86**.

The interaction of 'truth' and 'falsity' as an aspect of the issue: a 'reasonable expectation of privacy'

125. Is truth as contrasted with falsity, relevant? No, see *Prince Radu of Hohenzollern v Marco Huston and Sena Julia Publications Ltd* [2007] EWHC 2735 at **para 14**, and *McKennitt v Ash* at **para 86**.

> **The question** in a case of misuse of private information is whether the information is **private** not whether it is **true or false**.

And also see *CTB v NGN Ltd and Imogen Thomas* (*No 2)* per Eady J at **para 23**:

> **It is important always to remember that the modern law of privacy is not concerned solely with information or 'secrets'**: it is also concerned importantly **with intrusion**. That is one reason why it can be important to distinguish between the way the law approaches public domain arguments in relation to **commercial or state secrets**, for example, and that which is **appropriate to personal information**. It also largely explains why it is the case that the **truth or falsity** of the allegations in question can often be **irrelevant**: see eg *McKennitt v Ash* [2008] QB 73 at **[80] and [87]**.

In a 'family' context, see *A Local Authority v A Mother & F & A* per Baker J at **para 65** and see *Ferdinand v MGN Ltd* [2011] EWHC 2454 (QB) at **para 67**.

126. Confidentiality and false information: This principle vis-à-vis '**misuse of private information**' should be contrasted with traditional concepts of privacy where there can be no claim for confidentiality in respect of false information: *Khashoggi v Smith* [1980] 124 SJ 14 CA.

127. Practical working example: See *WER v REW* [2009] EWHC 1029 where at **para 6,** the following passage in a witness statement is quoted:

6The potential problem, however, as it appeared to me, is a different one. The sting of the publication as regards the claimant is that he has or has had an extra marital relationship. In his confidential statement annexed to his witness statement, the claimant confines himself to saying:

> 'Irrespective of whether this claim is true or false, it is immensely damaging to myself and my family for such a revelation to be published in the media.'

128. What is the relevance of inaccuracies vis-à-vis '*truth*' and '*falsity*'? See Lord Hope (*obiter*) in *Campbell v Mirror Group Newspapers Ltd* at para 102:

> In view of the conclusion that I have reached on this issue it is not necessary for me to say anything about the weight that the Court of Appeal attached to the **inaccuracies**, except to observe that there is a **vital difference between inaccuracies that deprive the information of its intrusive quality and inaccuracies that do not**. The inaccuracies that were relied on here fall into the latter category. The length of time that Miss Campbell had been attending meetings was understated, while the frequency of her attendance at meetings was exaggerated. And the caption to the photograph in the first article stated that she was arriving at the meeting, when the fact was that she was leaving it. **These were errors of a minor nature only, which did not affect the overall significance of the details that were published.** I would hold that they did not detract from the private nature of what was being published.

A further example of intrusive falsity is provided by *P, Q and R v Quigley* [2008] EWHC 1051 (QB) **para 7**: '*scandalous matter which serves no legitimate purpose*'.

129. Falsity can undermine the public interest defence: See Buxton LJ in *Ash v McKennitt* at **para 53**, citing from the first instance judgment at **para 79**:

> They came to court to contest the truth of the book's allegations, and the Judge made his findings about those allegations, **because the falsity undermined the public interest defence**, and not because an allegation of falsity was inherent in the basic claim itself.

And see Longmore LJ at **paras 85–87**, saying, inter alia:

> The question in a case of misuse of private information is whether the information is private **not whether it is true or false**. The truth or falsity of the information is **an irrelevant inquiry** in deciding whether the information is entitled to be protected and judges should be chary

of becoming **side-tracked into that irrelevant inquiry**. Cases such as Interbrew SA v Financial Times [2002] EWCA Civ 274, [2002] EMLR 446 (where a party claims protection on behalf of a source transmitting false information) are, of course, entirely different.

The interaction of Article 8(2) and Article 10

130. Article 8(2)—in accordance with the law, etc:

(a) **Certainty, precision and accessibility:**

(i) The proposed restriction on the Article 10 right must be '*in accordance with the law*' and must have a basis in national law which conforms to the ECHR standards of legality; see *Campbell v Mirror Group Newspapers Ltd* at **para 139(a)**.

(ii) Such drive for a '*legitimate aim*' also carries with it the need to establish legal *certainty*; see *R (Wood) v Commissioner of Police of the Metropolis* at **para 26**; because any putative legal justification for infringing Article 8(1) must be sufficiently *precise* and *accessible*; *R (Wood) v Commissioner of Police* at **paras 49**, **51**, **52** and **53**.

(b) **Legitimate aim:**

(i) Any restriction on publication of the material must pursue a legitimate aim as set out in Articles 8(2) and 10(b). For example, 'prevention of disorder or crime' or 'in the interests of . . . public safety or . . . for the protection of the rights and freedoms of others' (*R (Wood) v Commissioner of Police* at **para 48**).

(ii) Thus a story pursues a legitimate aim if it is in the public interest (as contrasted with 'interesting to the public'): *Leeds City Council v Channel Four Television* at **para 25**; [2005] EWHC 3522 (Fam). In *Goodwin v NGN Ltd* Tugendhat J said at **para 2**:

> [W]hat is of interest to the public is not the same as what it is in the public interest to publish. Newspaper editors have the **final decision** on what is of interest to the **public interest**: judges have the **final** decision on what it **is in the public interest to publish**.

(iii) Against that backdrop, a legitimate aim is contributing to a *debate of general interest*; *Author of a Blog v Times Newspapers Ltd* at **paras 22** and **23**.

(iv) Note the interaction between *good faith*, *legitimate aim*, *precision* and *certainty* of law together with accessibility thereto: *R (Wood) v Commissioner of Police of the Metropolis* at **paras 26**, **28**, **51**, **52**, **53** and **98**.

(c) **Examples of non-legitimate aims:**
  (i) Has either party *threatened* the other? If yes, in what terms? See *CC v AB* at **paras 54** and **55**.
  (ii) Has a party threatened to abuse the court's process for a *collateral* purpose? *CC v AB* at **para 55**.

131. Article 8(2)—necessity/need: Consider why publication is *necessary* in a democratic society.

(a) 'Pressing social need': The publication must meet a pressing social need. *Thomas v News Group Newspapers and Hughes* [2001] EWCA 1233, **para 21**; and in the context of '*necessary*' and '*legitimate aim*', '*relevant and sufficient*' and '*proportionate*', see *R (Woods) v. Commissioner of Police of the Metropolis* at **para 82** per Dyson LJ.

(b) **How wide?** The terms of the proposed injunction must be *no wider* than is necessary for any legitimate protection of the 'A's' Article 8 rights?

(c) **Conspiracy?** Issues which the jurisprudence on this issue raise are:
  (i) Is the *threatened publication* by more than one person?
  (ii) Working in *combination*?
  (iii) What is the purpose underlying the 'free speech' sought? Is the sole or *dominant* purpose of the (threatened) publication *deliberately to injure* 'A'? If yes, on what grounds is this stated? Inferred? For example, see *CC v AB* at **paras 5–7**.
  (iv) Without any just cause? If yes, on what grounds is this contended?

(d) **Would the intrusion expose illegality or prevent the public from being significantly misled?** As to the situation where 'A' had made vigorous public criticism of others apparently in breach of a *confidential relationship* with his employer, see *Author of a Blog v Times Newspapers Ltd* at **para 18**, where the words '*necessary*', '*proportionate*' and '*prescribed by law*' are considered in context. As to the use of the word '*burnishing*' as to one's own image, see *Theakston v MGN Ltd* per Ouseley J at **paras 48** and **75**.

(e) **Is the 'intrusion' necessary to make a contribution to 'a debate of general interest'?**
  (i) See *Von Hannover* at **paras 60** and **76**. As to the role of photographs vis-à-vis such debate, see Lord Hope at **para 24** [2009] UKHL 34.
  (ii) As to the relevance and significance of the very fact of an *intrusion*,

see *CTB v NGN Ltd and Imogen Thomas (No 2)* per Eady J at **paras 18**, **23** and **24**.

(iii) As to '*debate*' as an aspect of proportionality, see *Mosley v News Group Newspapers Ltd* per Eady J at **paras 14** and **131** and also *DFT v TFD* per Sharp J at **para 19** vis-à-vis the public interest.

(iv) As to '*debate'* and sexual activity, see *ETK v News Group Newspapers Ltd* at **paras 21** and **23**; *Mosley v UK* [2011] ECtHR 774 at **para 131**; and particularly in the context of a public figure and sexual relations with an employee in the same organisation, see *Goodwin v NGN Ltd* at **para 133**.

(f) **Is there a failure of a public servant to comply with a public law duty?** See Eady J in *Author of a Blog v Times Newspapers Ltd* at **para 20** and see also *R v Chief Constable of the North Wales Police, ex parte Thorpe* [1999] QB 396, 409–10, 415, 429, cited in *Author of a Blog*.

(g) **Is the nub of the claim in reality to suppress the fruits of legitimate detective work?** See *Author of a Blog v Times Newspapers Ltd* at **para 4**, where detective work by a Mr Foster had revealed the name of the 'blogger'.

(h) **Damages?** A relevant consideration to the exercise of the equitable jurisdiction to grant an injunction is whether damages be an adequate remedy?

(i) See *A-G v Steen* [2001] EWCA 403, per Lord Phillips at **para 84** and *Douglas v Hello!* [2005] EWCA 595, **paras 37** and **67**.

(ii) If the injunction is not granted, could there be irremediable harm? If that is contended for, then the court must be given full details as to how the facts and argument are articulated. The *potential* to cause *harm is* likely to be '*an important factor*' for the court to weigh here, as it was in *Campbell v Mirror Group Newspapers Ltd*; see *A v B, C and D* [2005] EWHC 1651 per Eady J at **para 33**.

(iii) Damages *must not exceed* that which is proportionate to the interference of the Article 8 right, for otherwise freedom of expression may be disproportionately impaired: *Mosley v UK* at **para 116**.

And see *John Terry v Persons Unknown* per Tugendhat J at **para 85.**

132. Balancing exercise: The above factors must be weighed in the Article 8/ Article 10 balance and calibrated by recourse to the issue of '*proportionality*'. This is a crucial aspect of the '*balancing exercise*' and is of such importance as to merit a sub-title dedicated to its explanation—see immediately below, as a separate part.

Part 4

PROPORTIONALITY

The 'balancing exercise' between Articles 8 and 10 in the context of the shifting burdens of proof

133. The interaction of Articles 8 and 10: Per Lord Nicholls at **para 20** in *Campbell v MGN Ltd* [2004] UKHL 22:

> Article 8(1) recognises the need to respect private and family life. **Article 8(2) recognises there are occasions when *intrusion* into private and family life may be justified.** One of these is where the **intrusion** is necessary for the **protection** of the rights and freedoms of others. Article 10(1) recognises the importance of **freedom of expression**. **But article 10(2), like article 8(2), recognises there are occasions when protection of the rights of others may make it necessary for freedom of expression to give way. *When both these articles are engaged a difficult question of proportionality may arise.***

134. The principle underpinning the balancing exercise: Per Gross LJ in *Christopher Hutcheson (formerly known as 'KGM') v News Group Newspapers Ltd & Ors* [2011] EWCA Civ 808 at **para 28**:

> *(4) Art 10 and the balancing exercise:* Art 10 enshrines another vitally important right in a free society, that of freedom of expression. It is unsurprising that **the balancing exercise** between the competing values of Arts. 8 and 10 may be difficult and necessarily requires an **'intense' focus on the facts of the individual case.** As US Appellate Judge and jurist, Richard A Posner observed (in *How Judges Think*, 2008, at p 246):
>
> > '. . . when cases are difficult to decide it is usually because the decision must strike a **balance between two legitimate interests**, one of which must give way.'

135. Burden of proof: Gross LJ covered this in *Hutcheson v News Group Newspapers Ltd* at **para 31**:

> *(6) Burden of proof:* So far as the burden of proof is concerned, it is, in my judgment, unnecessary to take time over a somewhat theoretical discussion as to legal, evidentiary and shifting burdens. Suffice to say that **it is for the applicant for interim relief to make out the case of an infringement of his Art 8 rights and for the respondent to raise a case of freedom of expression under Art 10**. But, ultimately, in a matter such as this, it is plain that **the burden rests on the applicant to satisfy the requirements of s 12(3), HRA, or fail.**

136. Further analysis: These principles are further analysed under the following discreet sub-titles:

(a) The *framework* within which to strike the Article 8/Article 10 balance.
(b) Lord Steyn's fourth proposition—*proportionality*.
(c) The margin of discretion as an aspect of 'balance' and 'proportionality'.
(d) The *nature of the privacy* sought (intrusion cases) as a factor in the balancing exercise.
(e) The *nature of the confidence* (secrecy cases) as a factor in the balancing exercise.
(f) *Particular factors* which weigh in the balancing exercise.
(g) '*Debate of general interest*' as an aspect of proportionality.
(h) The balancing exercise in the context of certain types of expression claimed as '*freedom*'.
(i) *Responsible journalism* and what is in the public interest as a factor in the balancing exercise.
(j) *Photographs* as a factor in the balancing exercise.
(k) Prior restraints.
(l) *Summarising the above:* quality control checklist for striking the balance.

The framework within which to strike the Article 8/Article 10 balance

137. Central issue: In all the circumstances, must the interest of the owner of the information under Article 8 *yield* to the right to freedom of expression conferred on the publisher by Article 10 buttressed as it is by section 12 of the Human Rights Act? See *Murray v Big Pictures (UK) Ltd* [2009] EWCA

Civ 446 at **para 27** (photographs of JK Rowling's child; authority for the principle that information *need not* be intimate or embarrassing to qualify for protection). Putting this another way, *is there sufficient public interest in publication to justify overriding the right to privacy?*

138. The generic analysis: Per Lord Steyn in *Re S (A Child) (Identification: Restrictions on Publication)* [2004] UKHL 47, [2005] 1 AC 593, **para 17** (followed by Ward LJ in *ETK v News Group Newspapers Ltd* [2011] EWCA Civ 439 at **para 10**):

> The interplay between articles 8 and 10 has been illuminated by the opinions in the House of Lords in *Campbell v Mirror Group Newspapers Ltd* [2004] 2 WLR 1232. For present purposes the decision of the House on the facts of *Campbell* and the differences between the majority and the minority are not material. What does, however, emerge clearly from the opinions are four propositions. **First**, neither article has **as such** precedence over the other. **Secondly**, where the values under the two articles are in conflict, **an intense focus** on the comparative importance of the specific rights being claimed in the individual case is necessary. **Thirdly**, the justifications for interfering with or restricting each right must be taken into account. **Finally**, the proportionality test must be applied to each. For convenience I will call this **the ultimate balancing test**. This is how I will approach the present case.

139. Neither having precedence: As to neither article having precedence over the other, see *Mosley v UK* [2011] ECtHR 774 at **para 58**.

140. Contrast between '*intense focus*' and '*generalisation*': As to the contrast between *'an intense focus'* in respect of individual circumstances on the one hand, and '*broad generalisations'* on the other, see:

(a) Eady J in *Mosley v News Group Newspapers Ltd* [2008] EWHC 1777 (QB) at **para 12**; and also see *X & Y v Persons Unknown* [2006] EWHC 2783 (QB), *Lord Browne of Madingley v Associated Newspapers Ltd* [2007] EWCA Civ 295 at **para 39** per Sir Anthony Clarke MR, and *CC v AB* [2006] EWHC 3083 (QB) at **paras 13** and vis-à-vis '*intense focus*' very specifically per Eady J, **paras 13**, **15** and **18**.
(b) In the context of '*legitimate aim*' perhaps yet more refinement is to be perceived in the dicta of Lord Hope in *A-G Reference No 3 of 1999* [2009] UKHL 34, **paras 23–26** (para 26 dealing with '*legitimate aim*'); and further see *KJO v XIM* [2010] EWHC 1768 per Eady J at **para 19**.

141. A gloss on the generic analysis when children are involved—the effect of *Neulinger*: In *ETK v News Group Newspapers Ltd* Ward LJ explained that the dicta of Lord Steyn in *Re S* long preceded the decision of the ECtHR in the case of *Neulinger* and that a further gloss is now required when adopting Lord Steyn's analysis, *in the context of children*. Ward LJ said at **para 20**:

> How then does this approach square with the way Lord Steyn advised in *In Re S* that the **ultimate balance** should be struck, see [10(4)] above. He was confining himself to articles 8 and 10 and not ranging more widely to take note of the other Convention rights of children. **He expressed his opinion long before Neulinger called for a re-appraisal of the position**. In any event, the emphasis he added makes it clear that he was concerned strictly with the balance between article 10 and article 8 *'as such'*, i.e. where the only rights in balance were those conferred by articles 8 and 10. If, as he requires, an intense focus on the comparative importance of the specific rights being claimed in the individual case is necessary, **then the additional rights of children are to be placed in the scale**. The question then is whether the force of the article 10 considerations outweigh them given what I have said in paragraph 19.

Reference should also be made to **para 19** of his judgment, as Ward LJ invites, and also to dicta of Lord Kerr in *ZH (Tanzania) v Secretary of State for Home Department* [2011] UKSC 4 at **para 46** that children's rights *'must rank higher'*.

142. Summary of *ETK v News Group Newspapers Ltd*: In the balancing exercise, '*particular weight*' is to be attached to the rights of any child likely to be affected by publication of private information (reminding oneself that in this case, both parties to the adulterous relationship wanted to keep the information private). The approach of the Court of Appeal to children's rights is in harmony with an equivalent approach in immigration law, and also the '*welfare*' provisions in childcare law.

143. The interests of children, in the context of the Code of the Press Complaints Commission: This fell particularly under the spotlight in *TSE and ELP v News Group Newspapers Ltd* [2011] EWHC 1308 per Tugendhat J at **para 23** (adulterous relationship, which if in the *public domain* would, inter alia, cause real harm to children) and *CDE & FGH v MGN Limited* [2010] EWHC 3308 (QB) at **para** 7. As to any suggestion that this area of law is '*judge made*' without more, see Eady J in *CTB v NGN Ltd and Imogen Thomas (No 1)* [2011] EWHC 1232 at **paras 18–21,** and in particular the reference to parliamentary debate as to this legal arena prior to the passing of the Human Rights Act 1998 (**para 19**).

Lord Steyn's fourth proposition—exploring the generic issue of '*proportionality*'—the framework for decision making

144. Balance: Any interference with the public interest in disclosure *has to be balanced against* the interference with the right of the individual to respect for their private life. The issue of '*public interest*' is one *for the court*, whether or not a relevant party raises it; see *TSE and ELP v News Group Newspapers Ltd* at **para 27**.

145. Legitimate aim in the context of proportionality: A prerequisite to publishing is that such publication must pursue a *legitimate aim.* Per Laws LJ in *R (Wood) v Commissioner of Police for the Metropolis* [2009] EWCA Civ 414 at **para 26**:

> Important for present purposes is the familiar question, whether the action is proportionate to the legitimate aim in whose service it was taken.

146. Risk/benefit ratio: Would the benefits that are to be achieved by publication be *proportionate* to the harm that may be done by interference with the right to privacy? See *In Attorney General's Reference No 3 of 1999: Application by the British Broadcasting Corporation to set aside or vary a Reporting Restriction Order* [2009] UKHL 34, **para 23.** Putting this another way, see Lord Hoffman in *Campbell v Mirror Group Newspapers Ltd* [2004] UKHL 22 at **para 55**:

> The question is rather the **extent** to which it is **necessary** to qualify the one right in order to **protect** the **underlying** value which is **protected** by the other. And the **extent** of the **qualification** must be **proportionate** to the **need**: see Sedley LJ in *Douglas v Hello! Ltd* [2001] QB 967, 1005, **para 137**.

Also see, in the same context, Sedley LJ in *Douglas v Hello! Ltd* [2000] EWCA Civ 353 at **para 137** and Lord Hope in *Campbell v Mirror Group Newspapers Ltd* at **paras 113–18**.

147. Striking the balance—practice management checklist: On the facts of any particular case (by recourse to a close examination of the factual justification for the restriction on the freedom of expression right):

(a) Is the *objective* of restricting the Article 10 right *sufficiently* important to justify limiting the *fundamental* right to freedom of expression which is to be asserted.
(b) If the answer to the first question is 'yes', are the means chosen to limit the Article 10 right *rational*, *fair* and not arbitrary and impair the right as *minimally* as is *reasonably* possible?

See *Campbell v Mirror Group Newspapers Ltd.* The factors explained below under separate sub-titles are integral to the generic issue of proportionality.

The margin of discretion as an aspect of 'balance'—'proportionality'

148. There is a margin: In the balancing exercise, subject always to context and the case's particular subject-matter, the ECtHR is likely to acknowledge and attribute a *margin* of discretion to the responsible state; see *R (Wood) v Commissioner of Police for the Metropolis* at **para 26** per Laws LJ.

149. Latitude—its extent: As to the *latitude* to be allowed to a state's margin of appreciation, see *R (Wood) v Commissioner of Police of the Metropolis* at **para 27**:

> [T]he scope of the State's margin of discretion must **vary** according to the **importance** of the impugned right. . . . Article 8(1) is generously applied, but the justifications properly available under 8(2), not least given the margin of discretion which the decision-maker is likely to enjoy, may sometimes **cut** its application **close to the quick**.

150. The interaction of '*margin*' and '*reasonable expectation of privacy*': This exercise therefore provides an *important contrast* with the court's task in assessing whether there is a '*reasonable expectation of privacy*' under Article 8(1). Such *margin* of discretion may amount to a *significant* restraint upon the bite of Article 8; see *R (Wood) v Commissioner of Police for the Metropolis* at **paras 26** and **27**.

151. Latitude and sexual intimacy: As to a margin of appreciation in the context of sexual intimacy, see *Mosley v UK* at **para 123**:

. . . intimate details of his sexual activities, which would normally result in a ***narrowing*** of the margin of appreciation.

Intrusion: nature of the 'privacy' protection sought as a factor in the balancing exercise

152. The degree of privacy to which 'A' is entitled: As to personal relationships, note the contrast between matters which are '*relatively anodyne*' on the one hand, and '*intimate/salacious details*' on the other: *Campbell v Mirror Group Newspapers Ltd* per Lord Hoffman (dissenting) at **paras 56** and **60**, *Ntuli v Donald* [2010] EWCA Civ 1276 at **paras 14** and **15**; *Mosley v News Group Newspapers Ltd* per Eady J at **para 20** and *Hutcheson v News Group Newspapers Ltd* per Gross LJ at **para 34**. In this context see also *Gray v UVW* [2010] EWHC 2367 (QB) **para 55**.

153. Promise of non-disclosure: As to the relevance of not seeking a promise of non-disclosure from the other party during a relationship, see the argument in *Ntuli v Donald* at **para 22.**

154. Example of an alleged 'blackmail' case: As to an example where the court expressed itself in limited and anodyne terms, see *KJH v HGF* [2010] EWHC 3064 (QB) **paras 4**, **5** and **6** (to reduce the risk of KJF's identity being published).

Secrecy: nature of the 'confidence' as a factor in the balancing exercise

155. The degree of confidentiality to which 'A' is entitled:

(a) Confidential relationship: If there is *a pre-existing relationship* of confidence, the approach of the courts is different from the situation where it is the recipient's *perception* of the *confidential nature* of information that imposes an obligation upon him in the context of unauthorised or purloined information; see *Niema Ash and another v Loreena McKennitt and others* [2006] EWCA Civ 1714 at **paras 15–24** per Buxton LJ; *Lord Browne of Madingley v Associated Newspapers Ltd* at **paras 25–26**, and *Associated Newspapers Ltd v HRH Prince of Wales* [2006] EWCA Civ 1776 at **paras 36–37** and **67–68**.

(b) Perception of confidential nature: This situation will arise when someone receives information which he or she knows, or ought to know, is fairly and reasonably to be regarded as:
   (i) confidential, eg unauthorised; or
   (ii) purloined material.

See *Napier v Pressdrum Ltd* [2009] EWCA Civ 443 at **para 42**; *Author of a Blog v Times Newspapers Ltd* [2009] EWHC 1358 **paras 9** and **19**. In *Venables v News Group Newspapers Ltd* [2001] Fam 430, Butler Sloss P held that no pre-existing relationship was required to give rise to an obligation of confidence. As to the use of the word '*purloined*', see *Ash v McKennitt* at **para 15** per Buxton LJ.

156. Questions thus arising: Has a duty of confidentiality arisen? And if yes:

(a) How? Purloined material, etc? If not:
(b) Was it expressly assumed under a contract or express agreement? If yes, give details.

157. Foundation for the above questions:

(a) **The nature of the relationship:** In the event of an issue involving matters touching upon confidence, in applying the test of proportionality, *the nature of the relationship* that gives rise to the duty of confidentiality may be important in respect of unauthorised or purloined information.
(b) **Interaction with a reasonable expectation of privacy:** The nature of such relationship is also relevant vis-à-vis the issue: *reasonable expectation of privacy*; see *Lord Browne of Madingley v Associated Newspapers Ltd* at **para 26**, but that does not necessarily secure privacy: see **paras 29** and **32**.
(c) **Primary focus:** In the case of purloined information, the primary focus has to be on *the nature of the information* because it is *the recipient's perception* of its *confidential* nature that imposes the *obligation* on him; see *Murray v Express Newspapers Plc and Ors* [2007] EWHC 1908 [Ch] per Patten J at **para 20**; and see per Lord Goff of Chieveley in *A-G v Guardian Newspapers (No 2) ['Spycatcher']* [1990] 1 AC 109 at 281, and also see *Ash v McKennitt* per Buxton LJ at **para 15** (a particularly helpful analysis).
(d) **The vast majority:** But, as Lord Goff immediately goes on to say in *'Spycatcher'*, in the *vast majority* of cases the duty of confidence will arise from a *transaction* or *relationship* between the parties; and see *Associated Newspapers Ltd v HRH Prince of Wales* at **paras 64–69** and **74**; and *Lord Browne of Madingley v Associated Newspapers Ltd* at **para 29**.

158. Factual matrices arising in 'confidence' cases:

(a) **State or commercial secrets:** *'Spycatcher'* explored the distinction between confidential information in the context of *state or commercial secrets* on the one hand, and *personal information* on the other: ibid at 260E–H and 287C–D; see also in this context *CTB v NGN Ltd and Imogen Thomas (No 2)* [2011] EWHC 1326 (QB) per Eady J at **paras 21–23** and **28**.

(b) **Commercially valuable information:** As to the interaction of commercially valuable confidential information and information of a private nature over which 'A' had sufficient control to impose duties of confidence, see *Douglas v Hello! Ltd* [2007] UKHL 21 per Lord Hoffman (agreeing with Baroness Hale and Lord Brown) at **para 124**. This case is also authority for the proposition that information can be protected even though it was intended to be used for personal gain, ie wedding photographs contracted to another; see **para 118** and also *Campbell v MGN Ltd* [2004] UKHL 22. The ruling in *Douglas* reflects the decision in *Barrymore v NGN Ltd* [1997] FSR 600 at 603 where Jacob J held that '*if something is expressly said to be confidential, then it is much more likely to be so held by the courts*'. This was in the context of a story described as being '*exclusive*'. In this context see also *Ferdinand v MGN Ltd* [2011] EWHC 2454 per Eady J at **para 52**.

(c) **Interaction of control and money:** See the dicta of Lord Hoffman in *Douglas v Hello! Ltd* [2007] UKHL 21 at **para 117**:

> In my opinion Lindsay J was right. The point of which one should never lose sight is that OK! had paid **£1m for the benefit of the obligation of confidence imposed upon all those present at the wedding** in respect of *any* photographs of the wedding. That was quite clear. Unless there is some conceptual or policy reason why they should not have the benefit of that obligation, I cannot see why they were not entitled to enforce it. And in my opinion there are no such reasons. Provided that **one keeps one's eye firmly on the money and why it was paid**, the case is, as Lindsay J held, quite straightforward.

159. How to strike a balance between a '*confidential relationship*' and the '*public interest*': In the context of breach of a confidential relationship, the test is

> not simply whether the information is a matter of public interest but whether, in all the circumstances, **it is in the public interest that the duty of confidence should be breached**.

See: *Associated Newspapers Ltd v HRH Prince of Wales* [2006] EWCA

Civ 1776; [2008] Ch 57, **para 68**; *John Terry (previously 'LNS') v Persons Unknown* [2010] EWHC 119 (QB) per Tugendhat J at **para 51**; and also see *Von Hannover v Germany* [2005] 40 EHRR 1, **para 54**:

> the public interest in being informed against the legitimate interests of the applicant.

Proportionality—particular factors which weigh in the balancing exercise

160. 'Fact' and 'degree': The weight to be attached to the various considerations (examples of which are given below) is a matter of fact and degree; *Mosley v News Group Newspapers* per Eady J at **para 14**:

> This '**ultimate balancing test**' has been recognised as turning to a large extent upon **proportionality**: see eg Sedley LJ in *Douglas v Hello! Ltd* [2001] QB 967 at [137]. The judge will often have to ask whether the intrusion, or perhaps the **degree of the intrusion**, into the claimant's privacy was **proportionate** to the **public interest** supposedly being served by it.

161. The interaction between 'breadth' and 'depth': The greater the *depth* and *breadth* of the intrusion, the more likely it is that Article 8 will be *engaged.* As to the concept of '*the degree of intrusion*', see also *Campbell v Mirror Group Newspapers Ltd* at **para 22.** Factors relevant to intrusion are therefore:

- nature;
- depth;
- extent;
- breadth;
- also consider the extent of any dissemination or proposed dissemination.

Also see *Dudgeon v United Kingdom* [1981] 4 EHRR 149, **para 52** where the European Court said that the more intimate the aspects of private life which are being interfered with, the more serious must be the reasons for doing so before the interference can be legitimate.

162. Different kinds of expression: The ECtHR has distinguished *three kinds* of expression, the distinction being relevant to '*proportionately*' and the balancing exercise:

(a) *political* expression;
(b) *artistic* expression; and
(c) *commercial* expression.

The ECtHR consistently attaches *great importance* to *political* expression and applies *rather less rigorous principles* to expression which is *artistic* or *commercial*. As to House of Lords authority vis-à-vis the important or political expression, see Baroness Hale in *Campbell v Mirror Group Newspapers* at **para 148**: '*Top of the list is political speech . . .*'. By way of example, selling a story to the tabloids (whether for revenge, money or any other reason) should be accorded a *lower* priority; *CC v AB* at **paras 6** and **36**.

163. Adverse consequences: See *DFT v TFD* [2010] EWHC 2335 per Sharp J at **paras 28** and **29**. These are also factors to be weighed in the balancing exercise:

(a) **Harm:** What is the potential for the disclosure of the information to cause *harm*? And *to whom*?
   (i) Consider the issue of *distress* flowing from press/internet speculation vis-à-vis *jigsaw identification.*
   (ii) As to internet, etc, speculation, see Lord Neuberger MR in *JIH v News Group Newspapers Ltd* [2011] EWCA Civ 42 at **para 38**, and as to *jigsaw identification* in this context, see **para 40**.
   (iii) As to damages being an *inadequate remedy*, see the arguments advanced by Max Mosley in *Mosley v UK* at **paras 67–72** and **76**.
   (iv) Note that '*harm*' and its extent can also fulfil the role of providing a yardstick as to whether information is confidential: see *Campbell v Mirror Group Newspapers Ltd* at **paras 119**, **124**, **157** and **158**.

(b) **Further harm:** If there has already been *intrusion*, the issue becomes: has there been harm, and if yes, *what further harm* (and to whom) would be caused by further *intrusion*?
   (i) In the context of internet publication as contrasted with the much greater dissemination through news media, see *Sir Frederick Goodwin v NGN Ltd and VBN (No 3)* [2011] EWHC 1437 (QB) per Tugendhat J at **para 125**, following the approach of Eady J in *CTB v NGN Ltd & Anor (No 2)* [2011] EWHC 1326 (QB) **para 24**.
   (ii) As to the significance of only a limited number of people knowing, not equating as such to '*carte blanche for the tabloids*, or *for any other section of the media*', see *Hutcheson v News Group Newspapers Ltd* per Gross LJ at **para 40**. As to disclosure to a limited number, see also Lord Hoffman in *Campbell v Mirror Group Newspapers Ltd* at **paras 73–75**, and *Stone v South East Coast Strategic Health Authority and Ors* [2007] UKHRR 137 at **paras 25** and **26**.

(iii) As to an argument vis-à-vis the further impact on mental state by press intrusion, and potentially narrowing the options for a child's future care, see *A Local Authority v A mother & F and A* [2011] EWHC 1764 (Fam) per Baker J at **para 51**, a case in which Baker J, vis-à-vis a mother alleged to have murdered her children, came down in favour of Article 10 prevailing over Article 8.

(c) **Intimate:** The *more intimate* the aspect of private life sought to be protected, the *more* there must be *particularly serious reasons* for interference: *Dudgeon v UK* at **para 52**:

> Accordingly, there must exist **particularly serious reasons** before interferences on the part of the public authorities can be legitimate for the purposes of paragraph 2 of Article 8.

As to the interaction of the *sexual* and *intimate* with Article 8, see *CTB v NGN Ltd and Imogen Thomas (No 1)* [2011] EWCA 1232 at **para 23**. As to *sexual activity* being *integral to Article 8* and private life, see *TSE and ELP v News Group Newspapers Ltd* per Tugendhat J, inter alia citing *Dudgeon v UK* at **para 24** (explaining that this is in no way new law but has a long and respected heritage). There are, however, limits as to the degree of confidence; see *Maccaba v Lichtenstein* [2005] EMR 109 at **para 4**.

164. 'Highly offensive': The issue of '*highly offensive*' is particularly relevant to '*proportionality*' when undertaking the balancing exercise; see *Murray v Big Pictures Ltd* at **para 26**:

> It is clear from that paragraph that Lord Nicholls regarded the '**highly offensive** test' as a stricter test than his own formulation of '**reasonable expectation of privacy**'. It seems to us therefore that, in so far as it is or may be relevant to consider whether publication of information or matter was '**highly offensive**', it is relevant to consider it in the context, not of whether article 8 is engaged, **but of the issues relevant to proportionality**, that is to the balance to be struck between article 8 and article 10.

Is the publication/proposed publication '*highly offensive*'? If yes, to what extent, in what way and why? See *Campbell v Mirror Group Newspapers Ltd* at **paras 21–22** per Lord Nicholls, per Lord Hope at **paras 94–96** and per Baroness Hale at **paras 135–37** and Lord Carswell at **para 166.**

The 'balancing exercise' in the context of certain types of expression claimed to be 'free'

165. 'Duty to impart'—'right to receive': There is the *duty to impart* information and ideas of public interest which the public have a *right to receive*: *Jersild v Denmark* [1994] 19 EHRR I, **para 26**. For a practical working example of striking the balance in this context, see *CTB v NGN Ltd and Imogen Thomas (No 1)* [2011] EWHC 1232 at **para 24**.

166. Has 'A' caused the public to be misled? If the public has been misled, this may justify a journalist in putting the *record straight*; see *Campbell v Mirror Group Newspapers Ltd* at paras **36**, **38**, **58**, **80** and **117**. This theme was part of the reasoning in *Hutcheson v News Group Newspapers Ltd* where at **para 45** Gross LJ inter alia said:

> There is a very real risk of a **distorted** and **partial** picture being presented to the public of this dispute, were an injunction to be granted as sought by Mr Hutcheson.

This is in the context of business and family matters becoming intertwined. In contrast, Tugendhat J found that the public had not been misled in *TSE and ELP v News Group Newspapers Ltd* at **para 23**. For an exceptional example of publishing details of a family to put the record straight in the Family Division, see the dicta of Sir Nicholas Wall P in *Doncaster MBC v Haigh and Tune and Others* [2011] EWEHC B16 (Fam).

167. Has 'A' *moralised* about his/her private life when behaving immorally? See *CC v AB* at **para 52**. However note: *misleading*, by itself, is *not* enough—it must still be established that publication is in the *public interest*.

168. If misbehaviour, to what degree/extent—the relevance of hypocrisy to proportionality? A *very high* degree of misbehaviour *may* be called for: *Loreena McKennitt, Hampstead Productions Ltd and Quinlan Road Ltd v Niema Ash and Purple Inc Press Ltd* [2005] EWHC 3003 (QB) per Eady J at **para 97** at first instance (the case was unsuccessfully appealed):

> I would nevertheless accept that Mr Browne is broadly correct when he submits that for a claimant's conduct to '**trigger the public interest defence**' a very **high** degree of misbehaviour must be demonstrated. Relatively trivial matters, even though falling short of the highest standards people might set for themselves, will not suffice. All of us try

> to behave well, no doubt, for most of the time but hardly anyone succeeds in achieving that ideal. The mere fact that a 'celebrity' falls short from time to time, like everyone else, could not possibly justify exposure, in the supposed public interest, of every **peccadillo** or **foible** cropping up in day-to-day life.

But this may go too far, given the dicta of Buxton LJ in this context in the Court of Appeal in *Ash v McKennitt*:

> 69. Some criticism is made of the Judge having said in his §97 that '*a very high degree of misbehaviour must be demonstrated*' to trigger a **public interest** defence. As an entirely general statement, divorced from its context, **that may well go too far**. But the Judge was speaking of the particular situation argued before him, where not the conduct in itself, but the fact that it had previously been lied about or treated with hypocrisy, was said to be the basis for disclosure. In *Campbell v Mirror Group Newspapers Ltd* it was the fact that Ms Campbell had not merely said that she did not take drugs but had **gone out of her way** to emphasise that she was in that respect **unlike** other fashion models that deprived otherwise private material of protection: see per Lord Nicholls of Birkenhead, [2004] 2 AC 457 [24]. By contrast, as the Judge clearly thought in his §97, the conduct complained of in the case of Ms McKennitt **fell well below** the level that would justify complaint on the ground of **hypocrisy**.

169. Public agencies: As to alleged *incompetence* or *wrongdoing* by public agencies to be exposed: *Leeds City Council v Channel Four Television Inc* [2007] 1 FLR 678; [2005] EWHC 3522 (Fam) at **paras 35** and **36** where OFSTED seems to have been misled by the school.

170. Has 'A' been guilty of criminality vis-à-vis proportionality? As to the mere allegation of iniquity not of itself being sufficient to justify disclosure in the public interest, see *'Spycatcher'*. If 'A' has been guilty of criminality, it is still not fatal to an Article 8 claim; it depends on all the circumstances; *Mosley v News Group Newspapers Ltd* per Eady J at **paras 111**, **112** and **118**; see also *Malone v Metropolitan Police Commissioner* [1979] Ch 344; *Hellewell v Chief Constable of Derbyshire* [1995] 1 WLR 804 (publication of photograph of a suspect, vis-à-vis the prevention and detection of crime). As to the traditional approach of the common law to the publication of wrong-doing, see *Initial Services v Putterill* [1968] 1 QB 396 per Lord Denning at 405:

> The exception should extend to crime, fraud and misdeeds, both those actually committed as well as those in contemplation, provided always—and this is essential—that the disclosure is justified in the public interest. The reason is because **no private obligations** can dispose with that **universal** one which lies on **every member** of the society to discover every design which may be formed, contrary to the laws of the society, to destroy the public welfare . . .
>
> The disclosure must, I should think, **be to one who has a proper interest to receive the information**. Thus it would be proper to disclose a crime to the police; or a breach of the Restrictive Trade Practices Act to the registrar. There may be cases where the misdeed is of such a character that the public interest may demand, or at least excuse, publication on a broader field, **even to the press**.

171. Examples where publication of alleged wrongdoing was *not* restrained:

(a) **Disclosure of suspected criminal conduct:** *Malone v Metropolitan Police Commissioner.*
(b) **Disclosure of fraudulent business practices:** *Gartside v Outram* [1857] 26 LJ Ch 113.
(c) **Alleged miscarriage of justice and corrupt police practices:** *Cork v McVicar* [1984] Times 31 October.
(d) **Alleged corruption by a public authority:** *Preston Borough Council v McGrath* [2000] Times 19 May; see also *Long Beach Ltd v Global Witness Ltd* [2007] EWHC 1980, para 52 (case also relevant to legal privilege and losing privacy).

> Once there is **good reason** to doubt the **propriety** of the financial affairs of a public official, there is a public interest in those affairs being **open** to public scrutiny.

(e) **Dangerous medical practices:** *Schering Chemicals Ltd v Falkman Ltd* [1982] 1 QB 1.

Also see the Code of the Press Complaints Commission and its definition of the public interest.

172. The '*social utility*' of what R threatens to publish: *John Terry v Persons Unknown* at **paras 102–04 (para 104** covering what is '*socially harmful*'). In this context, Eady J said at **para 25** in *CTB v NGN Ltd and Imogen Thomas (No 1)* [2011] EWHC 1232:

> I have to consider whether there would be a **legitimate public interest** in the revelation of this particular information, **in so far as it is not already in the public domain**, and whether publication would **contribute to 'a debate of general interest'**, in the sense conveyed by the European Court of Human Rights in such cases as *Von Hannover v Germany* (2005) 40 EHRR 1. Would it help to achieve some legitimate **social purpose**, such as the **prevention** or **detection of crime**? Or again, echoing the terminology of the Press Complaints Commission Code, would publication in some way **prevent the public from being seriously misled**?

And see the speech of Baroness Hale in *Campbell v Mirror Group Newspapers Ltd* at **para 149**:

> The political and social life of the community, and the intellectual, artistic or personal development of individuals, are **not obviously assisted by pouring over the intimate** details of a fashion model's private life.

173. Motive: As to a very clear explanation of the law as to the weight to be attached to material sought to be published by reference to motive, see *CC v AB* at **para 6**. That case is also authority for the proposition that *selling* a story to the tabloids (whether for revenge, money or any other reason) should be accorded *lower priority* (**para 36**).

'Responsible journalism' and what is in the public interest as a factor to be addressed in 'privacy' cases

174. The issue:

(a) **Vis-à-vis the law of defamation:** To what extent should there be civil sanctions against the media vis-à-vis a story *on a matter of public interest* where the facts are not, or cannot be proved to be, true? The means developed by the courts to address this tension between Articles 8 and 10 and strike the right balance are the qualified privilege defence of '*responsible journalism*'.

(b) **The cornerstone of this defence:** The essential point is that the publisher must have acted reasonably and responsibly; see in this context the dicta of Lord Nicholls in *Reynolds v Times Newspapers* [2001] 2 AC 127 at 200. The basis of the defence is that subject to the conditions afforded by the defence (as to which, see below), the public has a right to know; see *Reynolds v Times Newspapers* per Lord Nicholls at 197.

175. The 'calibration' of 'responsible journalism': Per Eady J in *Prince Radu of Hohenzollern v Marco Huston and Sena Julia Publications Ltd* [2007] EWHC 2735 (QB) at **para 42**, citing Sedley LJ in *Roberts v Gable* [2007] EWCA (Civ) 457 at **para 75**:

> [T]he English common law, now reinforced by the European Convention on Human Rights, seeks to hold . . . a sometimes difficult balance, **calibrated** by the concept of **responsible journalism**.

176. '*Responsible journalism*'—cross-fertilisation with the law of privacy:

(a) **The argument for cross-fertilisation:** It has been argued that '*responsible journalism'* (ie a reasonable belief on the part of an editor that a matter is of public interest) is a factor which the court can take into account when itself deciding what is in the public interest in a '*privacy*' case. Tugendhat J sets out the reasoning in *John Terry v Persons Unknown* at **paras 70–73** and **101–04** (an injunction application where R did not attend nor was he represented, and where Tugendhat J also drew upon data protection law).

(b) **The argument against:** To concede that a journalist (in a 'privacy' case) has a role to play in the interpretation of '*public interest*' could be interpreted as conceding that the court is not an absolute arbiter as to what is in the public interest. In the earlier case of *Mosley v News Group Newspapers Ltd* (which was a final trial on the merits) at **paras 135–41**, Eady J can be interpreted as inclining away from the position canvassed by Tugendhat J in *John Terry v Persons Unknown*. This is discussed further, immediately below.

177. Public interest—objective test—by the court:

(a) **The arbiter:** The *arbiter* of what in is in the *public interest* is the *court, not* the journalist, and the criteria for assessing such interest are *objective*: *Mosley v News Group Newspapers Ltd* at **paras 135–41** per Eady J:

> A decision on public interest must be capable of being tested by objectively recognised criteria.

(b) **Of its own motion:** The fact that the issue of public interest is one for the court falls into sharp relief in the following context: It is for the court *of its own motion,* to raise the issue even if the relevant parties do not; see *TSE and ELP v News Group Newspapers Ltd* per Tugendhat J at para

27. The position has been further clarified by Tugendhat J in *Goodwin v NGN and VBN* at **para 2**:

> [W]hat is of interest to the public is not the same as what it is in the public interest to publish. Newspaper editors have the **final decision** on what is of interest to the public interest: judges have the **final decision** on what it is in the public interest to publish.

178. The legal uncertainty vis-à-vis the issue of belief: In *John Terry v Persons Unknown* Tugendhat J addressed the issue that if the belief of an editor were relevant, how strong did that belief have to be? He said at **para 70**:

> The **uncertainty** is the extent to which, if at all, the **belief** of a person **threatening** to make a publication in the media is relevant on the issue of public interest.

Thus if the defence of '*responsible journalism*' does cross-fertilise into the law of privacy, then it is essential that the '*belief*' has to be *firmed up/buttressed* by those steps demanded of a journalist in the parallel context of the qualified privilege of '*responsible journalism*' to a claim in defamation.

179. Responsible steps:

(a) **The role of the court:** When the court is addressing the issue whether in defamation, a defence of '*responsible journalism*' is made out, it explores the *extent* to which a journalist has taken *such steps* as a *responsible* journalist would take to *try* and *ensure* that what is published is *accurate* and *fit* for publication: *John Terry v Persons Unknown* per Tugendhat J at para 71.

(b) **Rationale:** The rationale of this test is that there is *no duty* to *publish* and the public have *no interest* to read material which the publisher has *not taken* reasonable steps to *verify*, per Lord Hobhouse at 238, cited in *Jameel and ors v Wall Street Journal Europe Sprl* [2006] UKHL 44 at **para 32**:

> No public interest is served by publishing or communicating misinformation.

This resonates with the dicta of Baker J in *A Local Authority v A mother & F & A* at **para 46**:

> [P]ublication of inaccurate information was a breach of the PCC Code of Practice.

180. How to prove 'responsible journalism':

(a) Vis-à-vis defamation, the publisher is afforded the protection of qualified privilege if inter alia he has taken *such steps* as a *responsible* journalist would take to *try* and *ensure* that what is published is accurate and fit for publication and is information which the public has the right to know, ie he must inter alia verify the information to be published, see *Jameel v Wall Street Journal* at **paras 31–33** and **146–49**.

(b) This was a considered by Eady J in *Mosley v News Group Newspapers Ltd* at **paras 135–39** and at **para 141**, and see also Lord Nicholls's proposition in *Reynolds v Times Newspapers Ltd* [2001] AC 127 at 202; such test being repeated in *Bonnick v Morris* [2002] UK PC 31, **para 23**.

181. Checklist for '*responsible journalism*': As examples of such steps, see *Jameel v Wall Street Journal* at **paras 58**, **138** and **146–49**; these dicta help to inform the following checklist:

(a) **What steps?** The actual steps taken will vary with the *nature* and *sources* of the information. But one would normally expect that the source or sources were ones:
   (i) which the publisher had good reason to think it *reliable*;
   (ii) that the publisher himself *believed* the information to be *true*, and
   (iii) that he had done *what he could* to check it; and in this context, see *Gray v UVW* at **paras 14** and **15**; and *Mosley v UK* at **paras 52–54**, **80** and **91**, vis-à-vis contacting the subject of the proposed article for his/her comment before publication.
   (iv) As to the interaction of Article 10 '*prior restraints*', responsible journalism and contacting the subject of a feature before publication, see *Mosley v UK* at **para 117**. In this context see also the Editor's Code and the Code of Practice of the Press Complaints Commission and the interaction of that with '*responsible journalism*' set out in **para 35**.

(b) **Verify sources—making contact:** A publisher who is to avoid the risk of liability if the information cannot later be proved to be true would be *well advised* to check the truth of the story. Part of this is, of course, *taking reasonable steps to contact the people named for their comments*.

(c) **'Reportage' and verification:** The requirements in 'reportage' cases, where the publisher is simply reporting what others have said, may be rather different, but if the publisher *does not himself believe* the information to be true, he would be well advised to make this clear. In any case, the *tone* in which the information is conveyed will be relevant to whether or not the publisher has *behaved responsibly* in passing it on. As to this aspect in the context of defamation, see *Jameel v Wall Street Journal* at **para 62**.

A comprehensive questionnaire addressing the issue of '*responsible journalism*' is set out below in this book in Part 11.

182. The risk of irresponsible journalism: The *possibility* of some sectors of the press *abusing* their freedom to report cannot of itself, be a sufficient reason for curtailing that *freedom* for all members of the press; see *Gray v UVW* per Tugendhat J at **paras 57** and **58.** In a parallel context, Tugendhat J said in *Goodwin v NGN and VBN* at **para 87**:

> The court does **not** address questions of privacy in terms of **generalities**. According to the authorities set out above, the question must be whether **this particular person** (usually a claimant, but here also VBN) has a reasonable expectation of privacy **in respect of the particular information** at issue. **So anyone commenting upon this case *without reference to the specific evidence* before the court will be approaching the issues in a way in which Parliament has not permitted judges to approach them.**

183. Journalistic latitude: The following principles apply, once it is established that publication is in the public interest:

(a) **Credibility:** There is a need for the court to leave it to journalists to decide what material needs to be reproduced to ensure *credibility*: *Fressoz v France* [2001] EHRR I at **para 54** and *Campbell v Mirror Group Newspapers Ltd* at **para 143** (as to the speed with which editorial decisions have to be made), at **para 65** per Lord Hoffman and at **para 112** per Lord Hope.

(b) **Taste/modes of expression:** The press enjoys a wide discretion so far as *taste* and *modes* of expression are concerned, as part of editorial judgement; see *Mosley v News Group Newspapers Ltd* at **para 135**. Judges are *not* newspaper editors; *Campbell v Mirror Group Newspapers Ltd* at **para 59**.

(c) **Journalistic margin:** See *Campbell v Mirror Group Newspapers Ltd* at **paras 29**, **63–65**, **112**, **143** and **169**.

184. Summary: On the present state of the authorities, it is tentatively suggested that:

(a) If the court decides that publication is in the public interest, then the press is allowed latitude as to the editorial presentation of the material to be so published.

(b) When the court is deciding whether or not material is in the public interest, the issue of journalistic latitude may be tangentially relevant as suggesting that the view of a journalist may have a role to play on the issue of public interest; but that issue is one ultimately for the court.

(c) A journalist should in any event take the steps set out above, if inviting the court to take into account '*responsible journalism*' as a factor vis-à-vis an analysis of what is in the public interest.

Photographs as a factor in the balancing exercise

185. Special considerations: See *Douglas v Hello!* [2005] EWCA Civ 595 at **paras 84–87** per Lord Phillips:

> *Photographic information*
>
> 84. This action is about photographs. **Special considerations attach to photographs** in the field of privacy. They are **not merely** a method of conveying information that is an alternative to verbal description. They enable the person viewing the photograph to act as **a spectator**, in some circumstances **voyeur** would be the more appropriate noun, of whatever it is that the photograph depicts. As a means of **invading** privacy, a photograph is particularly **intrusive**. This is quite **apart** from the fact that the camera, and the telephoto lens, can give access to the viewer of the photograph to scenes where those photographed could **reasonably expect** that their appearances or actions would not be brought to the notice of the public.

Also see *R (Wood) v Commissioner for the Metropolis* per Laws LJ at **paras 30–36** (critical/essential reading). Note that in *Douglas* the nature of the information (photographs of the wedding) was not itself sensitive; thus publicity would not defeat the purpose of the proceedings.

186. The generic issue vis-à-vis the public interest and photographs: This was considered in *Mosley v UK* at **para 114**; and at **para 115** the court said:

> It is commonly acknowledged that the audiovisual media have often a **much more immediate and powerful** effect than the print media (see Jersild, cited above, para 31; and Peck v the United Kingdom, no 44647/98. . . . Accordingly, although freedom of expression also extends to publication of photographs, the Court recalls that this is an area in which the protection

of the rights of others **takes on particular importance**, especially where the images contain very personal and **intimate** 'information' about an individual or where they are taken on **private** premises and **clandestinely** through the use of **secret** recording devices.

Further as to the significance of visual images: *Mosley v News Group Newspapers Ltd* at first instance per Eady J at **paras 16-23**.

187. Examples of 'photograph' cases:

(a) **No right to one's own image:** English law gives no person a right to his own image: *Sports and General Press Agency v Our Dogs Publishing* [1916] 2 KB 880; nor is there a right to an image of one's home: *Baron Bernstein of Leigh v Skyviews and General Ltd* [1978] 1 QB 479, for '*the eye cannot by the laws of England be guilty of a trespass*': *Entick v Carrington* [1765] EWHC KB J98.

(b) **Photography and publishing:** There is therefore a distinction between a photograph being taken of one, and that photograph being published; see *Campbell v Mirror Group Newspapers Ltd* at **paras 73–74** per Lord Hoffman and *Murray v Big Pictures Ltd* at **para 54** per Sir Anthony Clarke MR. Also see Lord Nicholls in *Campbell v Mirror Group Newspapers Ltd* at **para 31** and Lord Hoffman at **paras 72–74**.

(c) **Brothel:** See *Theakston v MGN Ltd* [2002] EWHC 137 (QB) **para 78** (publication of the fact that 'A' had been in a brothel, but photographs of 'A' inside brothel restrained, as being particularly intrusive), this passage being approved by the Court of Appeal in *Douglas v Hello! Ltd (No 3)* [2005] EWCA Civ 595 at **paras 84** and **85** (wedding photos).

(d) **Princess Caroline:**

    (i) *Von Hannover* at **para 59**; going about mundane business in the street; all but one of the photographs (the publication of which was sought to be restrained) were taken in a public place. Thus *Von Hannover* is authority for the principle that the law is capable of extending its protection to public places and also to a '*social dimension*'; that is to say, to the relationships which people conduct with others; see *CC v AB* [2006] EWHC 3083 (QB) at **para 40**.

    (ii) Thus Eady J was able to say in *Howlett v Holding* [2006] EWHC 41 (QB) at **para 25**:

    > Princess Caroline of Monaco was described in the domestic courts in Germany as a figure of contemporary society **par excellence** but, even so, it was held in Strasbourg that such a

classification was **not sufficient** to justify constant intrusion into her private life by paparazzi. Thus her privacy was entitled to at least a **degree of protection** even in **public places**.

(e) **'Eavesdropping'—covert tape-recording:** Per Waller LJ in *D v L* [2003] EWCA Civ 1169 at **paras 23** and **24** (and see also **para 34** per Lord Phillips). This appeal was concerned with whether a party who did not know that a private conversation was being tape-recorded should be entitled to injunctive relief preventing publication of parts of that tape-recording. Waller LJ's dicta inter alia at **para 24** read:

> Just as a photograph can make a greater impact than an account of the matter depicted by that photograph, so **the recorded details of the very words** of a private conversation can make **more impact**, and cause more **embarrassment** and **distress**, than a mere account of the conversation in question.

Earlier authority supports the proposition that eavesdropping by private persons in the context of telephone-tapping generates an obligation of confidence; see *Francome v MGN Ltd* [1984] 1 WLR 892 at 900.

(f) **JK Rowling's child:**
   (i) *Murray v Big Pictures (UK) Ltd* [2008] EWCA 446; [2008] EMLR 12 at **para 50**, dealing with issues of profit and targeting a child—an important case because it also addresses an important point about the relationship between the decision of the House of Lords in *Campbell v Mirror Group Newspapers Ltd* [2004] UKHL 22; [2004] 2 AC 457 and that of the ECtHR in *Von Hannover v Germany.*
   (ii) In this context also see *R (Wood) v Commissioner for the Metropolis* at **para 58** with particular reference to *Kay v Lambeth LBC* [2006] 2 AC 465.
   (iii) Section 2 of the Human Rights Act requires the court to take into account Strasbourg jurisprudence, but subject to the rules of precedent in English law, when interpreting Convention rights

188. Photographs—checklist: With a view to defining the scope of the protection afforded by Article 8 against arbitrary interference by public authorities:

(a) **Is the actual act of photography a violation?** Whether the taking of the pictures, *along with their actual and/or apprehended use*, might amount to a violation; see *R (Wood) v Commissioner for the Metropolis* at **para 38**, per Laws LJ.

(b) **Public/private?** Whether the photographs related to *private* or *public matters*, are they exclusively of private life? See *Howlett v Holding* [2006] EWHC 41 (QB) at **para 26**.

(c) **Purpose?** What was the *purpose* in the photographs being taken? See *Re Guardian News and Media* [2010] UKSC 1? Was the material so obtained envisaged for a limited use, or was it likely to be made available to the *general public*? (see, *mutatis mutandis*, *Friedl v Austria*, judgment of 31 January 1995, Series A no 305-B, opinion of the Commission, 21, §§ 49–52); *PG and JH v the United Kingdom*, cited above, **para 58**; and *Peck v the United Kingdom*, no 44647/98 § 61); *Von Hannover v Germany*.

(d) **Public status of 'A':** Does 'A' have any public *official* function? See *JIH v News Group Newspapers Ltd* [2010] EWHC 2818 (QB) **para 40** and on appeal, at [2011] 42 (Civ) at **para 21(6)**.

(e) **Public interest:** What is the *contribution* (if any) that the published photos and articles make to *a debate of general interest*; see *Re Guardian News and Media* [2010] UKSC 1, **para 49**; also see the dicta of Ward LJ in *ETK v News Group Newspapers Ltd* at **para 10(5)**, together with those of Tugendhat J in *Goodwin v NGN and VBN* at **para 133** at **paras 67** and **68**. This issue also fell for consideration in *Von Hannover v Germany*, **paras 52** and **76**; the latter inter alia reads:

> [T]he decisive factor in balancing the protection of private life against freedom of expression should lie in the **contribution** that the **published photos** and articles make to a **debate of general interest**. It is clear in the instant case that they **made no such contribution** since the applicant exercises **no official** function and the photos and articles related **exclusively** to details of her private life.

This test of contribution to a *debate of general interest* was adopted by the Court of Appeal in *Ntuli v* Donald [2011] 1 WLR 294 at **para 20**; and see also *Campbell v Mirror Group Newspapers Ltd* per Baroness Hale at **paras 146–49**. Another way of expressing the same issue was given in *Mosley v UK* at **para 116**: '*discussion of matters of legitimate public concern*'.

Prior restraints

189. Exceptional:

(a) **Contact a subject:** An example of such a restraint could (speaking in the abstract) be a mandatory requirement to contact a subject of an article prior to publication.

(b) **The exception:** Prior restraints are viewed as *pernicious* and that, to be upheld as justifiable, their use will have to be viewed as *appropriate*, *proportionate* and *absolutely necessary*: C Munro, 'Prior Restraint of the Media and Human Rights Law' [2002] *Juridical Review* 1 at 23 (this passage is, of course, consistent with the terms of Article 10(2) itself) cited by Eady J in *CC v AB* at **para 17**; and also dicta on precisely this issue in *Mosley v UK* at **para 117**.

(c) **'A strong thing':** There is a brief discussion as to '*prior restraint*' in *Hutcheson v News Group Newspapers Ltd* at **para 30**, and at **para 48**:

> There is an important distinction between the desire to keep information private and invoking the full panoply of the Court's jurisdiction in order to do so. It is and should remain a strong thing to impose a prior restraint on publication.

190. Prior restraint in the context of defamation: In defamation, the rule in *Bonnard v Perryman* is a rule *against* prior restraint. The rule is that the court has a discretion whether or not to restrain publication of what is alleged to be a libel, but where there is a defence or claim of justification, the discretion is guided by the principle that it is *not normally just or convenient* to grant relief unless 'A' has proved the libel to be *plainly untrue* (ie to be a sham or to have no chance of success); for an example see *Howlett v Holding* [2006] EWHC 41 (QB) **para 15**.

191. Prior restraint, 'Mosley' and *LNR*: The ruling in *Mosley* is that there is *no* binding legal requirement on a newspaper to give prior notification to the subject of the news item prior to publication. In contrast, ***LNR*** provides at **paras 18–23** for the notification of non-parties prior to the making of an application for an injunction (ie 'advance notice').

Summarising the above: quality control checklist for striking the balance and proportionality

192. Presumptive parity: The starting point is *presumptive parity* between Articles 8 and 10.

193. No precedence: Neither Article has precedence over, or 'trumps', the other.

194. Parallel analysis: The exercise to be performed is one of *parallel analysis*; see *A Local Authority v W* [2005] EWHC 1564 (Fam) and at [2006] 1 FLR 1 at **para 53**. The exercise of *parallel analysis* requires the court intensely to examine the factual justification for interfering with *each* right.

195. Not a mechanical exercise: Parallel analysis is *not* a mechanical exercise to be decided upon the basis of *rival generalities*; see *CC v AB* per Eady J at **para 14**. *Careful, detailed* and *thorough* factual instructions are required because the issues raised by Articles 8 and 10 are essentially *questions of fact*; *Murray v Big Pictures* at **para 39** and **paras 55** and **56**; *Mosley v News Group Newspapers Ltd* at **paras 11** and **12.**

196. Intense focus: There must be an '*intense*' focus upon the comparative importance of the *specific rights* being claimed *in the individual case.* This is necessary *before* the *ultimate* balancing test in terms of *proportionality* is carried out. '*Proportionality*' calibrates the '*ultimate balancing test*', see *TSE and ELP v News Group Newspapers Ltd* at **paras 19** and **20** where the nature of the balancing exercise is expressed with singular authority and clarity. That the outcome is likely to be determined by considerations of *proportionality* was expressed by Sedley LJ in *Douglas v Hello! Ltd* [2000] EWCA Civ 353 at **para 137**, cited in *CC v AB* at **para 15**.

197. Legitimate aim: What is the legitimate aim contended for? On what grounds is it argued that the action is proportionate to the legitimate aim? See Laws LJ at **para 26** in *R (Wood) v Commissioner of Police for the Metropolis*.

198. Balancing out 'necessity': Do the civil and political *values* which underlie press freedom make it *necessary* to deny the citizen the right to protect such personal information? See *Campbell v Mirror Group Newspapers Ltd*, **paras 55** and **56**. For example, it may be that the result sought by R can be achieved *with a more limited disclosure*:

(a) See *Francome v Mirror Group Newspapers Ltd* [1984] 1 WLR 892 per Sir John Donaldson J, particularly at 901 where there is the interaction of the extent of disclosure and a *speedy trial*.

(b) If photographs, does '*every gory detail*' also need to be published to achieve the public interest objective; see Eady J at in *Mosley v News Group Newspapers Ltd* at **paras 16** and **17**.

Part 5

PRACTICE PRINCIPLES UNDERPINNING AN ARTICLE 8 APPLICATION

Introduction to the problems confronting the court at the interim hearing

199. The interaction of section 12(3) and '*merits*': The issue of public interest cannot be ignored at the interlocutory hearing. This is because section 12 of the Human Rights Act 1998 requires that an *overall view* should be formed as to the *likelihood* of 'A' succeeding at trial; *Author of a Blog v Times Newspapers Ltd* [2009] EWHC 1358 (QB) **para 12** per Eady J.

200. Incomplete material: It is not always easy for the court to come to a conclusion in respect of matters of public interest on an application for an interim injunction. Such a judgment has to be made almost always on an *incomplete* picture of the available evidence; *Author of a Blog v Times Newspapers Ltd* at **para 12**. Hence the *importance* of solicitors securing as much *detail* as reasonably practicable to put before the court.

201. Intense scrutiny: Because material is likely to be incomplete, the risk of the court reaching a wrong decision is enhanced. Hence the need for *intense judicial scrutiny*. ***LNR*** said at 81:

> 32. Each application shall be subject to intense scrutiny. The need for intense scrutiny is particularly acute on without-notice applications, or where non-parties are or have been served with orders containing restrictions on access to documents, because, for instance, the order contains derogations from CPR PD 25A 9.

202. Cases on the issue of difficulty and merits:

(a) *Mahmood v Galloway* [2006] EMLR 26, **para 24** ('. . . But that is not an issue that I could possibly determine at this stage in the proceedings').
(b) *X & Y v Persons Unknown* [2006] EWHC 2783 (QB) **paras 43–45**.
(c) *Ntuli v Donald* [2010] EWCA Civ 1276 at **paras 36–39** dealing with merits at the inter-parties stage (contrast at the *ex parte* stage: see *ASG v GSA* [2009] EWCA 1574).
(d) *Author of a Blog v Times Newspapers Ltd* [2009] EWHC 1358 per Eady J at **para 12**.

203. Risks of haste: As to guarding against a rushed judgment, see *X & Y v Persons Unknown* at **paras 43–45**.

The duty on the applicant—full and frank disclosure

204. Critically important: This is essential, particularly when moving *without notice*. Such a duty of *full and frank* disclosure should be seen in the broader context as being a layer of protection to the media, see *TUV v Persons Unknown* [2010] EWHC 853 (QB) at **para 25**. The three primary layers of such protection are—so that they can each be seen in context:

(a) The *duty to notify* the media (usually only with reference to those who have shown an interest in publishing).
(b) The duty of *full and frank* disclosure (and in this context see also *X & Y v Persons Unknown*).
(c) Application by the media can be made on very short notice to *vary or discharge*.

205. Overall rationale and principle: The ***LNR Practice Guidance*** sets out the following demands:

> 30. Particular care should be taken in every application for an interim non-disclosure order, and especially where an application is made without-notice, by applicants to comply with the high duty to make full, fair and accurate disclosure of all material information to the court and to draw the court's attention to significant factual, legal and procedural aspects of the case.

Similarly the words of Mummery LJ in *Memory Corporation v Sidhu and another (No 2)* [2000] EWCA Civ 9 at **para 65**:

> It cannot be emphasised too strongly that at an urgent without notice hearing for . . . any . . . form of interim injunction, there is a **high duty** to make **full, fair and accurate disclosure** of material information to the court and to draw the court's attention to **significant factual, legal and procedural aspects of the case**. It is the particular duty of the advocate to see **that the correct legal procedures and forms are used**; that a written **skeleton argument and a properly drafted order are prepared by him personally and lodged with the court before the oral hearing**; and **that at the hearing the court's attention is drawn by him to *unusual features*** of the evidence adduced, to the applicable law and to the **formalities and procedure to be observed**.

And in this overall context, see ***LNR*** at p 51, **para 3.60(i)**, citing *Beese & Others v Woodhouse & Others* [1970] 1 WLR 586 and at ***LNR*** **Practice Guidance** at **para 30**.

206. Stepping into R's shoes: 'A's' legal advisers should *step into the shoes* of the proposed Rs and make a conscientious determination, in the light of the information which has been obtained on the relevant topic, as to which points he or she would wish to make if instructed to represent media respondents on the other side. See *X & Y v Persons Unknown* at **paras 56** and **57**. Per Eady J at **para 57**:

> One would simply try to step into the shoes of a hypothetical opponent, just as one does when considering which authorities should be drawn to the court's attention as potentially undermining the submissions one is advancing.

207. Can one anticipate everything?

(a) **All reasonably practicable steps:** Whilst 'A' may be forgiven for not anticipating every '*non-disclosure*' point subsequently taken (*X & Y v Persons Unknown* at **paras 49–50**) that does not abrogate the need to take all reasonably practicable steps. However, the case must be looked at through the judge's eyes; *John Terry (previously 'LNS') v Persons Unknown* [2010] EWHC 119 (QB) **para 101**:

> If the judge is not permitted to hear from the other side, there is a **danger** that by **default** he will give more weight than he would wish to the views of the applicant or himself.

(b) **Duty on the advocate:** An advocate seeking interim relief without notice must consciously strive to understand what other perspectives there might reasonably be, bringing to bear his or her own knowledge and experience: *X & Y v Persons Unknown* at **para 55**.

(c) **The stand taken by R:** Thus any material relating to the stand taken by an R should be before the court, as was the published account of Imogen Thomas in the case of *CTB v NGN Ltd and Imogen Thomas (No 1)* [2011] EWHC 1232 per Eady J at **para 2**.

208. Celebrity cases—cuttings trawl: For an example of the argument and file management in this context, see *X & Y v Persons Unknown* at **paras 43–57**, essential reading as to how 'A' should go about disclosure in a celebrity case (internet trawl, etc)—previously called a "cuttings search"—**para 42**.

209. If reasonably possible, try and make contact with the proposed R: See *Gray v UVW* [2010] EWHC 2367 (QB) **paras 14** and **15** at least to seek to establish what the R's position is vis-à-vis the proposed proceedings/any threat to publish, thus to inform the judge.

210. If issue relates to sexual intimacy: Can 'A' give evidence as to how many people knew of the relationship in issue? See *MJN v NGN Ltd* [2011] EWHC 1192 (QB) at **para 11**. Query: is 'A' under an obligation to give full and frank disclosure as to other compromising relationships he or she has had, when seeking to enjoin publication of details involving a separate relationship? This must depend on the fact-sensitive nature of any particular case.

211. The interaction of full and frank disclosure with the real purpose of the injunction application: Is 'A' in fact seeking to secure a commercial reputation rather than protect his or her rights to privacy? Or is the motive to circumvent the rule in *Bonnard v Perryman*? The occasion to pin one's *genuine* colours to the mast is under the rubric of '*full and frank*' disclosure. As an example where the issue was held to be commercial reputation, see *John Terry v Persons Unknown*.

The duty on the applicant's advocate—strict compliance with procedure—*LNR* Practice Guidance

212. Checklist for the applicant's advocate: So far as is *consistent with the urgency* of the application, the advocate has a particular duty as to the following:

(a) That the *correct legal procedures* have been used;
(b) *Witness statements* are in order, if time;
(c) That the *correct forms* have been used;
(d) *Skeleton* argument in writing;
(e) *Properly drafted order* prepared personally by him or her and lodged with the court before the oral hearing;
(f) *At the hearing*, given the demand for the court to exercise an '*intense scrutiny*' that the court's attention is drawn to:
   (i) *unusual features* of the evidence adduced;
   (ii) the applicable *law*;
   (iii) the *formalities and procedure* to be observed, including how, if at all, the order submitted departs from the ***LNR* Model Order**;
   (iv) applications, especially those which seek derogations from open justice, must be *supported with clear and cogent evidence* which demonstrates that, without the specific exception, the underlying value could not be protected: see *Campbell v MGN Ltd* [2004] UKHL 22 at **para 55** per Lord Hoffman. In other words, that the derogation is strictly necessary, proportionate, and without which exception justice could not be done (and see also *Gray v UVW* [2010] EWHC 2367 (QB) at **para 1**).

213. If going *ex parte*/without notice: Checklist if application *ex parte*/*contra mundum*, taken from the judgment of Munby J in *Kelly v BBC* [2001] 1 FLR 197 [2000] EWHC 3 (Fam) (a children case):

(a) **Grounds—CPR 25.3:** Good reasons must be given supported by evidence for going without notice; see also *G and G v Wikimedia Foundation Inc* [2009] EWHC 3148 (QB), **para 25**. Note:
   (i) These reasons should be in 'A's' statement.
   (ii) Further, even if urgency prevents the giving of formal notice, 'A' is required to give informal notice unless '*the circumstances of the application require secrecy*'; CPR PD 23A 4.2.

   Reminder: the statutory hurdles to overcome for a without-notice application: Human Rights Act section 12(2)(a) and (b).
(b) **Efforts made:** What efforts have been made to serve the proposed Rs (giving full details including *all relevant documents and dates*)? To what effect? See *X & Y v Persons Unknown* at **paras 19** and **78** (essential reading).
(c) **Recital/schedule:** Any *ex parte* order containing injunctions should set out on its face, either by way of recital or in a schedule, a list of all

affidavits, witness statements and other evidential materials read by the judge.

(d) **Liaise:** The applicant's legal representatives should, whenever possible, *liaise* with the Court Associate with a view to ensuring that the *Order as drawn* contains this information.

(e) **Checking order:** On receipt of the order from the court, 'A's' legal representatives should *satisfy themselves* that the order is drawn correctly, that it sets out the *relevant information* and, if it does not, should take *urgent* steps to have the order amended under the slip rule.

(f) **Copies etc:** 'A's' legal representatives should respond forthwith to any reasonable request from the party injuncted or his legal representatives, *either for copies* of the materials read by the judge *or for information* about what took place at the hearing.

(g) **A full note** (see also CPR 25 PD(A)9.2 and ***LNR* Practice Guidance** at **paras 42–45**):

   (i) A full note must be taken and kept by those acting for an 'A', lest they find themselves embarrassed by a proper request for information which they were unable to file; see *G and G v Wikimedia Foundation Inc* at **paras 28** and **29** (inter alia citing White Book commentary as to indemnity costs). As to the importance of a full note for another judge at a subsequent hearing, see *MNB v NGN Ltd* [2011] EWHC 528 per Sharp J at **para 2**.

   (ii) The note should cover everything that was said and took place at the hearing; and all materials read by the judge including: *exactly* what *documents*, *bundles* or *other evidential materials* were lodged with the court either before or during the course of the hearing and what *legal authorities* were cited to the judge.

   (iii) The preparation and provision of a note of the hearing is important, not only to inform anyone notified of the order of what evidence was put before the court (in addition to that which is in the witness statements), but also to inform them of any points or queries that may have been raised by the judge; judges rarely have the time to write judgments in such cases after the event, and even if they give extempore reasons, there will be no transcript available unless that is requested and paid for. *G and G v Wikimedia Foundation Inc* at **para 31**.

(h) **Full disclosure:** On the principles of natural justice, it would be wrong for a judge to be given material at a *without-notice hearing* which would not at a later stage be revealed to the persons affected by the result of the application. In children cases this rule was qualified, but there was no justification for not making full disclosure to the media of the material upon which an injunction *contra mundum* had been granted.

(i) **Undertaking to swear and file:** In urgent cases, in which there was no time to prepare comprehensive evidence in proper form, the court must act upon the information provided by counsel, but in every such case there should be an *undertaking to swear* and file an affidavit, as soon as possible.

(j) **Confidential schedule for the media:** If, as would often be the case, it was not appropriate for the media to see the material in the form in which it was originally filed with the court, *the solution was to set out the relevant material in a separate and Confidential Schedule* which could be shown to the media, and this should be done even if there appeared to be no immediate likelihood of there being an application to discharge the injunction.

(k) **Public domain proviso:** An injunction in *rem* or *contra mundum* should *normally* be *qualified* with a *public domain proviso*: *Kelly v BBC* [2000] EWHC 3 (Fam) per Munby J.

And see ***LNR***, pp 12–13 at **para 1.29**.

Precision

214. Principle: Maurice Kay LJ said in *Ntuli v Donald* at **para 26**, it is axiomatic that any injunction

> should be to the highest degree clear and precise so that no publisher would be in any doubt whether he was infringing it or not. (*Times Newspapers Ltd v MGN Ltd* [1993] EMLR 443 at 447, per Sir Thomas Bingham MR)

215. The relevance of a '*Confidential Schedule*' to the issue of '*precision*': A loosely worded injunction is no use to an applicant, since the court will be reluctant to enforce by process of contempt if it clearly cannot be established that its terms have been infringed: *X & Y v Persons Unknown* at **para 81**; see also *Redwing Ltd v Redwing Forest Products Ltd* [1947] 64 RPC 67, 71 and *A-G v Greater Manchester Newspapers Ltd* [2001] All ER (D) 32 (Dec). It is to secure such precision that a *Confidential Schedule* is increasingly used; see *X & Y v Persons Unknown* at **para 81**; and at **para 84:**

> In the course of correspondence and submissions, with a certain amount of give and take, a ***Confidential Schedule*** has emerged which complies with these objectives. **It pinpoints effectively the relatively few items of information which are alleged (whether accurately or not) to be the immediate causes of, or to have contributed to, the marital difficulties. There is no real problem for any journalist or media lawyer served with such an order in identifying these 'hot spots' and avoiding any such coverage if someone tries to sell a story encroaching upon them.**

216. Precision and identifying with sufficient clarity '*persons unknown*': see *Bloomsbury Publishing Group Ltd v News Group Newspapers Ltd* [2003] EWHC 1205; [2003] 1 WLR 163, **para 21**:

> The crucial point, as it seems to me, is that the description used must be sufficiently certain as to identify both those **who are included** and those **who are not**. If that test is satisfied then it does not seem to me to matter that the description may apply to no one or to more than one person nor that there is no further element of subsequent identification whether by service or otherwise'.

Service

217. Principle: *LNR* at 79: The onus is to serve also non-parties with the application:

> 22. Where a respondent, or non-party, is a media organisation only rarely will there be compelling reasons why advance notification is or was not possible on grounds of either urgency or secrecy. It will only be in truly exceptional circumstances that failure to give a media organisation advance notice will be justifiable on the ground that it would defeat the purpose of an interim non-disclosure order. **Different considerations may however arise where a respondent or non-party is an internet-based organisation, tweeter or blogger, or where, for instance, there are allegations of blackmail.**

The question arises: to what extent is there an obligation also to give advance notice to internet-based organisations etc? This has still to be worked through, and it may be that case law will evolve to provide more specific guidance.

218. Context: In many cases where the identity of R is unknown, *the real value of the Order is the ability to serve it on media third parties* as it prohibits them from disclosing the information subject to the injunction pending the conclusion of proceedings: see *John Terry v Persons Unknown* at **para 20**. It is often the case that, where proceedings are brought against a person or persons unknown, media organisations are not joined as parties to the proceedings.

219. Whom to serve in the media: This is fact sensitive. As a general rule, the law will only impose an obligation to notify those who are *already believed to have shown some interest* in publishing; see *TUV v Persons Unknown* at **paras 23–26** per Eady J. In this context, see ***LNR*** **Practice Guidance**:

> 23. Where notice of the application is to be given to a media organisation it should be effected on the organisation's legal adviser, where it has one. The court will bear in mind that such legal advisers are:
>
> (i) used to participating in hearings at short notice where necessary; and
> (ii) able to differentiate between information provided for legal purposes and information for editorial use.

Note ***LNR*** at p 37, **para 3.18**:

> Adequate notice to defendants or respondents is a prerequisite of the right to be heard.

In this context, see also section 12(2) of the Human Rights Act.

220. Serving '*persons unknown*': As to the extent to which steps should be taken to serve the '*persons unknown*', see Eady J in *X & Y v Persons Unknown* at **para 2**.

> The Defendants had **not** been notified simply because their identity was **unknown**. It has subsequently been suggested by reason of s 12(2)(a) of the Human Rights Act 1998 that it was incumbent upon those representing the Claimants, who have been referred to throughout as X and Y, **to try and reach them** through **various newspapers**, with whom they have apparently been in contact; alternatively, there was a proposal that the Claimants should attempt to notify them by serving all **those friends** and **acquaintances** whom they suspected as **potential culprits** (according to the evidence the number involved is approximately 20). I shall need to return to this issue shortly.

And Eady J came back to this later in the judgment at **paras 75–80** inter alia saying:

> 75. It may be that **on some occasions it would be appropriate to request a newspaper editor or lawyer to notify the source**. If in the particular

case there is a willingness to co-operate, well and good. It would not be right, on the other hand, for the court routinely in such cases to order a newspaper to act as a process server. Nonetheless, because of the requirements under s 12 **all practicable steps** should be taken to notify defendants in advance (unless there are compelling reasons for not doing so), it might have been **worth at least making the request** in this case (however forlorn the hope of compliance). But this did not occur to the Claimants' advisers as being 'practicable'. **The prospect of any of the newspapers agreeing was surely, in the real world, remote**.

76. In any event, there may be **good reasons** from the newspaper's point of view **for not wishing** to perform this service. It might **antagonise** a particular source or, at least in theory, discourage others from coming forward with information on later occasions.

Notice and undertakings to the court—non-parties

221. ***LNR*:** This issue is covered in the ***LNR*** **Practice Guidance**, **paras 24–28**. The following points of practice management are distilled from the following passage, which sets out the policy:

> 24. . . . to provide effective protection of private and/or confidential information and information contained in private and/or confidential documents provide by applicants to non-parties.

222. Steps to take (see *LNR* Practice Guidance):

(a) **Irrevocable written undertaking to the court:**

> 24. . . . material supplied to the non-party by the applicant shall be supplied upon the applicant receiving an irrevocable written undertaking to the court that the material and the information contained within it, or derived from such material or information, will only be used for the purpose of the proceedings. A standard form of wording for the undertaking is set out in the notes to clause 13 of the Model Order, contained in the Model Order guidelines.

(b) **Advance notice–the significance of the Explanatory Note:**

> 25. **Where an applicant is to provide advance notice of an application** to a non-party they should first provide the non-party with a copy of the Explanatory Note, which may where strictly necessary refer to the applicant and/or respondent by three anonymised initials. If the non-party is willing

to provide the irrevocable written undertaking, the applicant should then supply the materials, including the applicant's and respondent's names, to the non-party upon receipt of the undertaking. Where the non-party is unwilling to provide the undertaking, no further information need be supplied by the applicant. (Information concerning when and where the application is to be heard should be set out in the Explanatory Note).

223. Notifying a non-party of an order—the interaction of service of materials and the irrevocable written undertaking:

26. Where an applicant notifies a non-party of an order, which should contain the provision set out in clause 13 of the Model Order, provision of material to a non-party shall be effected promptly by the applicant upon request, and upon receipt of the irrevocable written undertaking. Prior to notifying the non-party of the order where urgency does not preclude it, the applicant should ascertain whether the non-party will require a copy of any materials referred to in clause 13 of the Model Order. Where the non-party indicates that it will do so, it should at that stage provide the applicant with the written irrevocable undertaking. The applicant will then be in a position to, and should, serve a copy of the order and the relevant materials together. Where the non-party is unwilling to give the undertaking in advance of service of the order, the applicant will not be required to supply any relevant materials to the non-party until such time as the undertaking is given or further order of the court.

(a) **Who provides the undertaking?**

27. The undertaking should be provided on behalf of the non-party by its legal adviser where it has one. It should be provided by the non-party itself where it has no legal adviser. Breach of the undertaking may be held to be a contempt of court, which would render the non-party liable to imprisonment, a fine or having their assets seized.

(b) **What is the meaning of the word 'materials'?**

28. For the purpose of paragraph 24, material includes: the application and any supporting documentation; and a copy of any materials specified under CPR PD 25A 9.

That CPR PD defines such materials as (unless the court orders otherwise):

(i) A copy of any materials read by the judge, including material prepared after the hearing at the direction of the judge or in compliance with the order; or

  (ii) A note of the hearing.

(c) **The role of the explanatory note:** Such note enables those notified to do the following:
  (i) Readily understand the nature of the case;
  (ii) Ascertain whether they wish to attend the application hearing, and/or be legally represented at it; or
  (iii) Where the application was heard without notice, whether they wish to challenge the order.

  See ***LNR* Practice Guidance** at **para 32**.

Part 6

CASE MANAGEMENT FOR ARTICLE 8 APPLICATIONS

224. Explanation of Part 6: This Part is divided into three stages:

(a) **Stage 1:** Case management for Applicants.
(b) **Stage 2:** Case management for Respondents
(c) **Stage 3:** The balance between Article 8, its 'safeguards' and Article 10; case management checklist for all parties.

Stage 1: Case management for applicants

Checklist: identity of 'A'—relevant material and its source?

225. The identity/character of 'A'—or the person directly affected by the threatened disclosure/publication:

(a) Give full name, age, occupation, profile. (If a celebrity/famous /'a name'—in what context/circumstances?)
(b) If a child, why is he/she an apparent target?

226. The nature of the information:

(a) What is the *nature* of the information itself? See Eady J in *CC v AB* [2006] EWHC 3083 (QB) at **para 39**.
(b) What is the *intrusion*?
(c) If the alleged *intrusion* involves a particular *location*:
   (i) *Identify* precisely the location;
   (ii) What was the *activity* said to be taking place at that location?

(iii) How was the information *gathered/obtained* from that location?

(d) What were the *means* by which the information was obtained?

227. Sources: The following information should be addressed for 'A's' statement:

(a) **Principle:**
  (i) There must be available to the court the fullest particulars as to the *circumstances* in which, and the purposes for which, the information came *into the hands* of the person threatening to publish/disseminate?
  (ii) This goes to the *value* to be attached to the proposed exercise of R's Article 10 rights as compared with the *intrusive* effect it would have upon the Article 8 rights of 'A'; see *CDE & FGU v MGN Ltd & LMN* [2010] EWHC 3308 (QB) at **para 40** per Eady J, this being relevant to *proportionality*.

228. The importance of knowing the source: As to the right of the public to know whence the information comes, see *Author of a Blog v Times Newspapers Ltd* [2009] EWHC 1358 (QB), **para 21**:

> It is very often useful, in assessing the value of an opinion or argument, to now its source. As was pointed out, for example, by Lord Nicholls in *Reynolds v Times Newspapers Ltd* [2001] 2 AC 127 at 205A–B, one may wish to apply greater caution or scepticism in the case of a person with 'an axe to grind'.

229. The special position of a journalist: A journalist and his/her source are recognised as a confidential relationship: *A-G Mulholland* [1963] 2 QB 477; *In Re An Inquiry under the Company Securities (Insider Dealing) Act 1985*; [1988] AC 660; see also *John Terry (previously referred to as "LNS" v Persons Unknown* [2010] EWHC 119 (QB) at **para 20**:

> [J]ournalists do not normally reveal their sources and can rarely be obliged to do so.

230. Does it come from a reliable source? This information is relevant to the duty of full and frank disclosure:

(a) Is the source reliable, and on what grounds is that so contended? (And if not, why not?) The *less* strong the evidence, the less '*likely*' under section 12(3) of the Human Rights Act.

(b) Does anyone providing information appreciate the risk of sanctions (viz *statement of truth*) if the information is untrue: see *John Terry (previously 'LNS') v Persons Unknown* [2010] EWHC 119 (QB) per Tugendhat J at **paras 31–32**.

231. To what extent is 'A''s case verified/authenticated? See *John Terry v Persons Unknown* per Tugendhat J at **paras 31–32**; NB section 12(3) of the Human Rights Act *burden on 'A'*.

232. *Norwich Pharmacal*: Given relevant circumstances, consider a *Norwich Pharmacal* application to have the source revealed/to disclose identity of an online wrongdoer (eg internet protocol (IP) addresses left by internet users); see also (and this case is correctly spelt) *Bacon v Automattic Inc, Wikipedia Foundation and Denver Post LLC* [2011] EWHC 1072 (QB) per Tugendhat J. In **paras 1** and **2**, he said:

> 1. The difficult question raised by this application is: can a defendant domiciled in the United States of America be served by means of email with a claim form issued in England?
>
> 2. On 13 April 2011 the Claimant issued a Claim Form naming the three defendants. The first two are in California and the third in Colorado. The relief he seeks is a *Norwich Pharmacal* Order (*Norwich Pharmacal v Customs and Excise Commissioners* [1974] AC 133) requiring the Defendants to disclose to his solicitors the names, addresses, IP addresses and other information that will identify, or assist the Claimant's solicitors in identifying, the person or persons responsible for publishing statements about the Claimant which he alleges to be defamatory. These are publications on websites operated by the Defendants namely www.en.wikipedia.org, www.wordpress.com and www.denverpost.com respectively. He states that he has no other reasonable means of identifying the individual or individuals responsible for publishing those statements.

As to a *Norwich Pharmacal* application in relation to Wikipedia, see *G & G v Wikimedia Foundation Inc* [2009] EWHC 3148 (QB), and as against Microsoft, see *Goldsmith v BCD* [2011] EWHC 674 (QB) **para 4**.

233. The precise contents/ambit of the material: Set out precisely in the statement (or as appropriate, the Confidential Schedule) the corpus of material which the judge is to be invited to address; *CC v AB* at **paras 8**, **19** and **35** (case of alleged cuckolded husband). As part of this answer:

(a) **What is R likely to say/publish?** Close attention is required to this. On what grounds does 'A' argue that it is likely to be published (providing in the witness statement clear, precise and detailed facts vis-à-vis the source of information)?

(b) **To whom is R likely to say/publish it—setting out grounds for submission?** For example:
   (i) To a close friend;
   (ii) With members of the family;
   (iii) With a family doctor (see *Editions Plon v France* [2004] 42 EHRR 705), counsellor or social worker;
   (iv) With his lawyers or with expert witnesses; and/or
   (v) Through the press or on the internet/social networking site (and if to the press, directly or indirectly? This may have to be addressed in an order); see *CC v AB* at **paras 44** and **49**].

   See in this context, the dicta of Eady J in *CC v AB* at **paras 35–36.**

234. What is the type of speech involved in each scenario? Assuming more than one, in what detail?

235. Sexual: If the material is relevant to a sexual relationship, what is the *nature* of that *relationship*? *CC v AB* at **paras 22** and **39** (alleged cuckolded husband); also see *Lord Browne of Madingley v Associated Newspapers Ltd* [2007] EWCA Civ 295, **para 26**.

236. Analyse precisely the strands to that material:

(a) **Identifying strands:** The material which the court is to be invited to consider should be refracted into its constituent strands,
(b) **Which strand to injunct:** In relation to each strand of material the subject matter of scrutiny, explain whether it is sought to injunct that strand.
(c) **As to a practical working analysis of such strands:** see *JIH v News Group Newspapers Ltd* [2010] EWHC 2818 (QB) at **paras 41–45** and *Christopher Hutcheson (formerly known as 'KGM') v News Group Newspapers Ltd & Ors* [2011] EWCA Civ 808 at **para 4**. As to '*strands*' and an analysis of Article 10 in the context of the press wishing to publish details as to a mother alleged to have killed her children, see *A Local Authority v A & F & A* [2011] EWHC 1764 (Fam) at **para 57** per Baker J.
(d) **Relevant also to broadcasting:** Analyse the strands of subject matter as to whether they justify broadcasting, as did the BBC in *BKM v BBC* [2009] EWHC 3151 (Ch) per Mann J at **para 10**, a case of *clandestine* filming.

(e) As to **the interaction between 'strands' of information**, and how a draft Order may categorise information to be restrained, see *John Terry v Persons Unknown* per Tugendhat J at **paras 5** and **6**.

237. What is the nub of the complaint? What is the real issue? What is the gravity of the alleged interference with the private life? See *John Terry v Persons Unknown*, **para 149(viii)** with particular reference to the interaction of '*likely*', '*gravity*' and '*proportionality*'. Note how the press in a family case argued that the nub of her claim did not engage Article 8: *A Local Authority v A & F & A* per Baker J at **para 59**.

238. Photographs? If the proposed publication is in relation to photographs:

(a) *When* were they taken, *where*, by *whom*, in what *circumstances*, does the client have *access* to copies?
(b) In relation to any of the photographs, is there a *reasonable expectation* of privacy?
(c) If yes, on what *grounds*?

239. Analyse whose privacy—interests of third parties? Is there included in the proposed application, a claim to restrain *intrusion* into the private life *of another* person as being relevant to the privacy of 'A' (see *John Terry v Persons Unknown* per Tugendhat J at **para 95**; reference to 'altruism')? Such third parties are within the embrace of Article 8; see *CC v AB* at **para 47** per Eady J. If yes, how is the relevant evidence to be gathered and presented?

240. Primary data:

(a) What other person (giving full details of who, age, any relevant relationship, and why he/she comes *within the zone* of 'A's' privacy)?
(b) What aspect of that other person's private life?
(c) On what basis is it argued that their Article 8 rights to privacy would be affected?

241. Can such other persons argue the issue for themselves?

(a) **Independent evidence:** Is such other person/persons providing independent evidence?
    (i) If no, why not?
    (ii) For example, is that person unwell or otherwise abnormally susceptible, or not in a position to address this matter?

(b) **Representing themselves:** What is the problem with their representing themselves? Why have not such persons spoken for themselves?

(c) ***Locus standi*:**

  (i) Does the person seeking to represent them have *locus standi*, to protect the privacy rights of others, and is there any conflict of interest? *BKM v BBC* per Mann J at **paras 7**, **13** and **15**.

  (ii) These matters should be covered in a *witness statement*. See *John Terry v Persons Unknown* per Tugendhat J at **para 66**: '*they should speak for themselves*' on this; see also *CC v AB* at **para 46** and *Christopher Hutcheson v News Group Newspapers Ltd* at **para 47(ii)**.

242. Authority/independence of 'A':

(a) Does 'A' have the *necessary independence* to embrace the privacy of others within his application?

(b) In the event that 'A' enjoys *substantial earnings*, financial constraints cannot be invoked to justify omitting to take any steps that justice requires should be taken; see *John Terry v Persons Unknown* at **para 67**.

(c) Further as to the *impact* on others including *family*, see *Mosley v UK* [2011] ECtHR 774 at **para 97**.

243. Weight to be attached? To what extent should the court have regard to the rights of others and why is it so argued? See *John Terry v Persons Unknown* per Tugendhat J at **para 12**.

244. Determination: Should the court make a determination also vis-à-vis the rights of these other persons? *John Terry v Persons Unknown* at **para 150?**

245. Is the issue which is alleged to be 'private' a sexual relationship other than with the 'A's' spouse or long-term partner? See *John Terry v Persons Unknown* per Tugendhat J at **paras 28–30**, and *Mosley v News Group Newspapers Ltd* [2008] EWHC 1777 (QB) per Eady J at **para 20**.

(a) If yes, has that other person been *spoken to*?

(b) If yes, by whom, to *what agenda*?

(c) Does that other person *want publicity*, or is he/she willing to sign a *confidentiality agreement*? See *John Terry v Persons Unknown* at **paras 28–30** for a working example.

(d) Must that other person have realised that any relationship with 'A' must he been *expected* to be treated as discreet/confidential? If yes, set out in detail the grounds/facts/reasons for such averment.

(e) Is there correspondence which is properly described as *shocking and immoral*? See *Maccaba v Lichtenstein* [2005] EMR 109 at **para 4**.

246. What is the extent of the intrusion?

(a) As to the word '*intrusion*' approximating to a term of art, see *CTB v NGN Ltd and Imogen Thomas (No 2)* [2011] EWHC 1326 (QB) per Eady J and Tugendhat J in *Goodwin v NGN Ltd and VBN (No 3)* at **paras 85** and **125**.

(b) Thus the extent of the *intrusion* may aggravate; eg because of the *psychological profile of 'A'*, as it was in *Niema Ash and another v Loreena McKennitt and others* [2006] EWCA Civ 1714 at **para 23** where 'A' had been rendered more fragile through a bereavement.

(c) Further as to '*fragile state*' of a spouse whose husband had an extramarital relationship, see *CC v AB* at **para 43** per Eady J.

247. Threat to publish?

(a) Is the case to be argued on the basis of a *threat* to publish?

(b) If yes:

   (i) *From whom* is the threat coming?

   (ii) *What is the evidence* for such threat, and how serious is it claimed to be and on what grounds?

   (iii) If the threat is based on inference, what are the facts which form the foundation to the claimed inference, and on what *grounds* is it argued that the inference of a sufficient threat to publish can be drawn? See *John Terry v Persons Unknown* at **paras 11**, **65** and **68** (**para 65** deals with inferences to be drawn as to likelihood of the threat materialising).

(c) As to inferences to be drawn from the simple fact of a threat to publish, see *John Terry v Persons Unknown* per Tugendhat J at **paras 15** and **65** with particular reference as to *inferring the publication of detail and photographs* from a threat to publish, and also see **para 68**.

248. Sufficient? Is the threat sufficient for an injunction? Assuming it is, set out grounds for so arguing.

249. Can threat be otherwise restrained? Is the threat such that it can only be restrained by injunctive relief? See *KJH v HGF* [2010] EWHC 3064 (QB),

para 5. Set out the grounds for so arguing. What alternative approach does R contend for?

Is Article 8 'engaged' in the particular context of a 'confidential relationship'—practice management?

250. Does 'A' argue for a confidential relationship? If yes:

(a) **Was there a pre-existing relationship between the parties?** If yes, give full particulars. Issues which should be addressed in answering these questions are:

   (i) Does the confidential relationship arise out of a *contractual* or *equivalent* relationship? If yes, what was the nature of the relationship (give details and set out the precise provisions, including the duties of confidence to which the relationship is said to give rise)?

   (ii) Is the material complained of, conduct inconsistent with a pre-existing relationship? See *Mosley v News Group Newspapers Ltd* at **para 6**. If yes, give full details: *Ash v McKennitt* at **paras 8(v)** and **23**.

   (iii) If a duty of confidence is to be *implied*, on what grounds? For example, in *Barrymore v News Group Newspapers Limited* [1997] FSR 600, Jacob J said:

   > The fact is that when people kiss and later one of them tells, that second person is almost certainly breaking a confidential arrangement.

   (iv) Did the confider believe the information to be confidential? If yes, on what grounds? As to the law of confidence in this context, see *Thomas Marshall v Guinle* [1979] Ch 227 at 248.

   (v) Did the confider stipulate that the information was to be confidential? If yes, set out full particulars of what he/she so stipulated such as (just by way of example) if access to the information as controlled.

(b) **What is the nature of the information said to be confidential?**

   (i) Who has communicated/sought to communicate *what* to *whom*, *when*, *how* and in *what terms*?

   (ii) Identify any relevant *document* (exchange of letters, contract, emails, etc); if none, then the court's focus will be on the nature of the information asserted to be confidential.

(iii) In what *capacity*? (For example, personal capacity, or as a director, or as an employer, in the course of employment?)
(iv) Does *anyone else* have a claim to/interest in the information? If yes, who, and on what grounds could a claim/interest be asserted?
(v) Is there any evidence (by way of example) that any *photographs* there may be were produced or disclosed in confidence?

251. Has anyone received information which he knows, or ought to know, is fairly and reasonably to be regarded as confidential, eg unauthorised or purloined material? (See *Napier v Pressdram Ltd* [2009] EWCA Civ 443 at **para 42**; *Author of a Blog v Times Newspapers Ltd* at **paras 9** and **19**.) If yes:

(a) **What information?**
(b) **In what terms?**
 (i) Oral or in writing?
 (ii) Identify any relevant document.
(c) **What were the circumstances of the disclosure?** *Associated Newspapers Ltd v HRH Prince of Wales* [2006] EWCA Civ 1776, **para 68**:
 (i) When?
 (ii) Where?
 (iii) From whom?
 (iv) By/to whom?
 (v) What circumstances of confidence are contended for?
(d) **Grounds:** On what grounds is it alleged that R knew or ought to have known that it was fairly and reasonably to be regarded as confidential? See *David Murray v Express Newspapers plc and Big Pictures (UK) Ltd* [2007] EWHC 1908 (Ch) per Patten J at **para 36**; and see per Lord Goff of Chieveley in *A-G v Guardian Newspapers (No 2) ['Spycatcher']* [1990] 1 AC 109 at 281A and also see *Ash v McKennitt* per Buxton LJ at **para 15** (a particularly helpful analysis); *Associated Newspapers Ltd v HRH Prince of Wales* at **paras 64–69** and **74**; and *Lord Browne of Madingley v Associated Newspapers Ltd* at **para 29**.

252. Checklist of confidential situations—examples:

(a) **Doctor/patient**.
(b) **Husband/wife (long-term partners/personal and sexual relationships)**.
(c) **Employer/employee**.
(d) **Journalist and source**.
(e) **Diary.**

(f) **Business affairs**.
(g) **Photographs (including video tapes and recordings).**

Note: By way of contrast, the adjudication of the Solicitors' Complaints Tribunal is not confidential: *Department of Economic, Policy and Development of the City of Moscow v Bankers Trust Co* [2004] EWCA Civ 314; [2005] QB 207, **para 2** per Mance LJ.

Reasonable expectation of privacy—practice management

253. Introduction: In *David Murray v Big Pictures (UK) Ltd* [2008] EWCA Civ 446, Sir Anthony Clarke MR said at **para 36**:

> As we see it, the question whether there is a **reasonable expectation of privacy** is a **broad** one, which takes account of **all** the circumstances of the case. They include the **attributes** of the claimant, the **nature of the activity** in which the claimant was engaged, **the place** at which it was happening, **the nature and purpose of the intrusion**, the **absence of consent** and whether it was known or could be inferred, the **effect on the claimant** and the **circumstances** in which and the **purposes** for which the information came **into the hands of the publisher**.

The factors specifically identified by Sir Anthony Clarke MR are set out below.

254. What are the attributes of 'A'?

(a) **Does he/she have a robust personality?** If relevant:
   (i) Is his/her concern for any other's private life *altruistic* or otherwise?
   (ii) If otherwise, what? *John Terry v Persons Unknown* at **para 95**; and also see *MJN v News Group Newspapers Ltd* [2011] EWHC 1192 (QB) per Sharp J at **para 11** (sexual liaison involving a Premier League footballer, '*attributes*' included also those of 'A's' wife).
(b) **How offensive?**
   (i) What is the effect on 'A'? Consider *John Terry v Persons Unknown* at **para 55**.
   (ii) Is it contended that disclosure or observation of information or conduct would be '*highly offensive*' to a reasonable person of ordinary sensibilities, if he or she was placed in the same position as the

claimant and faced with the same publicity? See *Campbell v MGN Ltd* [2004] UKHL 22 at **paras 135–36**.

(iii) If yes, give detailed reasoning as to why. This is relevant not to the issue of whether there is a reasonable expectation of privacy, but to the issue of *proportionality*; see *Murray v Big Pictures* at **para 26** and *DFT v TFD* [2010] EWHC 2335 (QB) at **para 15**.

255. Activity: What is *the nature of any activity* in which 'A' was engaged? And see *John Terry v Persons Unknown* at **para 55**.

256. Place:

(a) Give details as to the *place* at which any occurrence was happening (including public or private, explaining if relevant the *characteristics* of the property, the *locality* and *disposition* of the owner of any relevant property); *Murray v Big Pictures* at **para 36**; *Campbell v NGN* at **para 135**.

(b) As to there not being a 'bright line' between public and private, see *Campbell v MGN Ltd* at **paras 91** and **135–36.**

257. Circumstances and purpose:

(a) What are the circumstances in which the *information* is said to be *imparted*, or *obtained*: *CC v AB* at **para 8**; *Lord Browne of Madingley v Associated Newspapers Ltd* at **para 33**.

(b) What was the *purpose* and *nature* of the *intrusion*? Has information been obtained unlawfully or surreptitiously? See *McKennitt v Ash* at **para 8(iii)** ('*information that he was not free to use*'); *John Terry v Persons Unknown* at **para 55**, and see also *A v B & C* [2002] EWCA Civ 337 [2003] QB 195 at **para 11(x)**.

(c) What are the *circumstances in which* and the *purposes for which* the information *came into the hands of the publisher*: see *Murray v Big Pictures* at **para 36** (where the purpose of the photographs, taken deliberately and in secret, was for publication for profit, see **para 50**), and *ETK v News Group Newspapers Ltd* [2011] EWCA Civ 439 at **para 10**.

(d) Did the person proposing to disclose the *information initially believe it to be confidential*? See *MJN v News Group Newspapers Ltd* [2011] EWHC 1192 (QB) per Sharp J at **para 11**.

258. Consent? Was there consent to disclosure, to the extent of publication?

(a) **If yes:**

(i) If oral or partly oral, between whom, when, where and in what terms?
(ii) If in writing or partly in writing, identify the document or documents.
(iii) Could consent be inferred from/by conduct?
(iv) If yes, on what grounds is that/could that be argued? See *Murray v Big Pictures* at **para 36** and *Theakston v MGN Ltd* [2002] EWHC 137 (QB) at **para 75**.

(b) **If no:** If consent is denied, confirm that there are no grounds for R to argue that he believed there was consent.
(c) **Codes:** Consider provisions as to consent in any relevant privacy code, and the extent of compliance/non-compliance in the context of section 12(4) of the Human Rights Act.

259. In what form is the information? See *Associated Newspapers Ltd v HRH Prince of Wales* at **para 36**:

> . . . the form in which it was conveyed . . .

260. Use: What is the use to which the proposed R has put, or intends to put, his or her right to freedom of expression? See *Mosley v News Group Newspapers Ltd* per Eady J at **para 15**.

261. 'All the circumstances of the case': Those circumstances can include:

(a) **Child:** If 'A' is a child, set out in detail the position of the child's parents and the way in which the child's life as part of that family has been conducted;
(b) **Harassment:** Any harassment? For example, abusive communications/emails? For an example of how harassment was handled by Eady J in *CC v AB* at **para 56**, and by Tugendhat J, see *ZAM v CFW & TFW* [2011] EWHC 476 (QB) at **para 25** (anonymised interim libel injunction). As to the interaction of '*intrusion*' and '*harassment*', see *CTB v NGN Ltd and Imogen Thomas (No 2)* [2011] EWHC 1326 (QB) per Tugendhat J at **para 3**.
(c) **Intrusion as evidence of a future threat:** Note the argument vis-à-vis *intrusion* into private lives, eg with a camera: '*leading to the possibility of further intrusion in the future*'; *Murray v Big Pictures* at **para 50**; and in the same context, see *JIH v News Group Newspapers Ltd* at **para 49** setting out the argument on this issue by Mr Tomlinson QC.

Article 8 practice management—how to handle the issue of 'photographs'/'filming'

262. Purpose of photographs: Do the photographs meet a particular public interest or do they merely satisfying curiosity? See *Leempoel v Belgium* App No 64772/01, 9 November 2006, cited at **para 133** in *Mosley v News Group Newspapers Ltd*; and see *Murray v Express Newspapers plc and Big Pictures (UK) Ltd* [2008] EWCA 446 at **para 50**.

> They were taken for the **purpose** of publication for profit, no doubt in the knowledge that the parents would have objected to them.

263. Consent? (See *Murray* (ibid) at **para 36**.)

(a) **If yes**, in what circumstances? (If oral or partly oral, between whom, when, where and in what terms? If in writing or partly in writing, identify the document or documents.)
(b) **If no**, can the inference be drawn that the person taking the photographs would have known that were consent to have been sought, it would have been refused? What are the grounds for such assertion? See *Murray v Big Pictures* at **para 50**.

264. Were the photographs taken intrusively/surreptitiously/clandestinely/otherwise in secret? If yes, give details of the following:

(a) **Nature and extent:** Full particulars of the *nature* and *extent* of the invasion; *Mosley v News Group Newspapers Ltd* per Eady J at **paras 17** and **18**.
(b) **Has distress been caused as a result?** If yes, give full particulars including who has suffered from such distress, and if relevant, how and why?

265. Was a zoom/telephoto lens used or the electronic equivalent? If yes, was it targeted/directed? If yes, at what/whom? Where was the camera *situated*? As to telephoto lenses in this context (photograph of suspect), see *Hellewell v Chief Constable of Derbyshire* [1995] 1 WLR 805 per Laws J. By way of analogy to a '*zoom lens*', see *Ash v McKennitt* at **paras 21** and **22** vis-à-vis intimate details of one's home ('*traditional sanctity accorded hearth and home*'). In this context at first instance in *Ash v McKennitt*, Eady J said (and the Court of Appeal agreed):

> To describe a person's home, the décor, the layout, the state of cleanliness, or how the occupiers behave inside it, is generally regarded as unacceptable. To convey such details, without permission, to the general public, is almost as objectionable as spying into the home with a long distance lens and publishing the resulting photographs.

266. Sexual relationship: Are the photographs linked to an alleged sexual relationship? See *Mosley v News Group Newspapers Ltd* per Eady J at **para 20**:

> It was acknowledged by Lord Hoffmann in *Campbell*, at [60], that there could be a genuine public interest in the disclosure of the existence of a sexual relationship (in, for example, a situation giving rise to favouritism or advancement through corruption), but he went on to warn that the addition of **salacious details or intimate photographs** would be disproportionate and unacceptable. 'The latter, even if accompanying a legitimate disclosure of the sexual relationship, would be too intrusive and demeaning.'

267. **Is a restraint on publication 'necessary'?** As to the meaning of the word '*necessary*' in this context, see for example *In Attorney General's Reference No 3 of 1999: Application by the British Broadcasting Corporation to set aside or vary a Reporting Restriction Order* [2009] UKHL 34 at **para 23.**

> [H]ow far is it 'necessary' for [Article 10] to be qualified in order to protect the values that [Article 8] seeks to protect?

268. Children? As to photographs, children and celebrity parents, see *Murray v Big Pictures* at **paras 45–52**.

269. Targeting? Were the photographs taken deliberately of the target person? *Murray v Big Pictures* at **para 47**:

> There is no authoritative case in England of a child being targeted as David was here.

This, of course, was JK Rowling's son.

270. Purpose: Is the inference to be drawn that the photographs were taken with a view to their subsequent publication (ie commercial interest), and if yes, on what grounds is that inference sought to be drawn?

271. Filming: If the alleged infringement is inter alia by way of film:

(a) **What type of film?** Identify precisely the film medium.

(b) **Pixellation.**

   (i) Can the film be pixellated? See *BKM v BBC* per Mann J at **paras 10** and **30**.

   (ii) If yes, can the relevant person(s) still be identified/identifiable—and if yes, by whom?

(c) **Consider Codes:** If surreptitious filming—was there another way of achieving the same result without the filming being surreptitious?

(d) **Broadcasting:** Is the application to restrain the broadcasting of a programme?

   (i) If yes, has the broadcaster volunteered to show the film to the other side/to the judge? See *BKM v BBC* at **paras 6**, **14** and **29**, or a trailer. If film is yet to be finalized, probably no inference adverse to the broadcaster in not giving a preview: see *BKM v BBC*, **para 29**, which paragraph deals also more generally with the issue of such inferences.

   (ii) The fact that the film has not been seen is not necessarily relevant; see *BKM v BBC* at **para 29** per Mann J:

   > I do not see what proper adverse inference about that (or any other inference, come to that) can be drawn from a failure to disclose the material in advance.

   (iii) Contrast this with *Leeds City Council and Ors v Channel Four Television Corp* [2007] FLR 678, [2005] EWHC 3522 Fam, where the judge was given an opportunity of viewing the programme whose making was challenged on privacy grounds.

   (iv) If a broadcast is vis-à-vis children, is it suggested that a broadcast can be achieved without photographs? See Munby J in *Leeds City Council v Channel Four Television* at **para 46**.

272. Photographs and a confidential relationship:

(a) **Was there an absence of consent?** Is that known or can it be inferred? See *Murray v Big Pictures* at **para 36**; *John Terry v Persons Unknown* at **para 55**.

(b) **What would R have known?** Does 'A' contend that R *would have known* that publication of the proposed material would be looked at as *unacceptable* in the eyes of 'A'? If yes, on what grounds is that contended? *CC v AB* at **para 22**.

(c) **Knowledge that confidential:** Does the person publishing/threatening to publish the photographs know, *or ought to know*, that there is a reasonable expectation that the information in question will be kept *confidential*? See Baroness Hale in *Campbell v MGN Ltd* at **para 134** and see also in this context *CC v AB* at **para 56.** See *Murray v Express Newspapers and Big Pictures (UK) Ltd* [2009] EWCA 446 at **para 39**.

Article 8—file management—losing protection through waiver/public domain

273. Introduction: The following factors constitute a file-management checklist. Full instructions will be required where appropriate, and where relevant an internet trawl.

274. Accurate? Is the information already published about 'A' accurate? (See *X & Y v Persons Unknown* [2006] EWHC 2783 (QB) at **paras 26** and **56**.) If no, in what respects is it not accurate?

275. Public eye: Is 'A' in the public eye? If yes, in what way and how did he/she come so to be?

276. Publicity seeker: Was he/she a publicity seeker? See *X & Y v Persons Unknown* per Eady J, at **para 29**.

(a) **Public domain:**
   (i) Is any information in the public domain?
   (ii) If yes, what information?
   (iii) How did it get there? And:
   (iv) What are its limits? (*X & Y v Persons Unknown* at **para 28**.)

(b) **When?** Just because information has long ago been in the public domain does not necessarily result in a bar to injunctive relief: see *R v Broadcasting Complaints Commission ex p Granada* [1995] EMLR 163 at 168 per Balcombe LJ:

> In my judgment it is clear that the fact that a matter has once been in the public domain cannot prevent its resurrection, possibly many years later, from being an infringement of privacy. Whether in such a case there is an **unwarranted infringement of privacy** is a matter of fact and degree and as such for the decision of the BCC with which the Court cannot interfere.

See also *TSE and ELP v NGN Ltd* [2011] EWHC 1308 at **para 31**; and *CTB v News Group Newspapers and Imogen Thomas (No 2)* [2011] EWHC 1326 (QB) at **para 16**.

277. Consent: Is the information already published about 'A' revealed with his/her consent (see *X & Y v Persons Unknown* at **para 16**). If yes, give full particulars/details of how such consent was given.

278. Contractual obligation: Is 'A' under contractual obligations to those whose products or services he/she promotes to give *interviews* from time to time? (See *X & Y v Persons Unknown* at **para 29**, ie as a counterpoint to 'self-promotion'.) If yes, identify the contract(s) and give full details of each interview so given; if possible, have copies available for the judge.

279. Public domain exposure—as evidence of risk/threat: If information is in the public domain without the agency of 'A' to achieve that, can the argument be turned to *'A's' advantage*? What is in the public domain may be evidence of what is likely to occur if the anonymity and other derogations from open justice are not continued? See *JIH v News Group Newspapers Ltd* at **para 30** (these dicta not being affected by the subsequent appeal).

280. 'Chilling effect': Would 'A' be in a worse position with no anonymity pursuant to an application to the court, than if he had not applied for the injunction in the first place? In this context see also *JIH v News Group Newspapers Ltd* at **paras 54**, **56** and **57**; and if 'A' is deterred from coming to court because of the threat of publication, see *Gray v UVW* [2010] EWHC 2367 (QB) **para 62**.

281. Prospective wording? Should the '*public domain proviso*' be worded prospectively to cover the situation where, if 'A' were to choose in the future to bring into the public domain the material which presently engages Article 8, that the proviso would be worded to ensure that the media were correspondingly released? *X & Y v Persons Unknown* at **para 67**.

282. The interaction of information in the '*public domain*' and '*relevance*'? Is a significant proportion of what is in the public domain not relevant to an application for injunctive relief? If it is so contended, on what grounds?

(a) **Outside Article 8:** That may be because the information already published is not such as to fall within the law's protection at all; or
(b) **Speculation:** Because it is speculation by journalists or purported revelations wrongly attributed to the particular 'A' (NB: ***speculation*** of itself can be intrusive, as infringing Article 8; *Standard Verlags GmbH v Austria (No 2),* judgment of 4 June 2009 ECtHR, **para 53**).

See also *X & Y v Persons Unknown* at **para 46**.

File management: losing Article 8 protection through material non-disclosure

283. Checklist as to pre-empting the issue of material non-disclosure: The following factors are taken from *X & Y v Persons Unknown* at **paras 47** and **55** and see also **para 58** vis-à-vis a celebrity client:

284. Instructions from the client: He/she should give the fullest details of all material which has been *broadcast/published by him/he*—on his/her behalf. If this information cannot be given, why not? And how can that be remedied?

285. Public relations consultant:

(a) Has 'A' retained a *public relations consultant*?
(b) Assuming yes, he/she should be asked as to what material he/she knows to be (or to have been put into) in the *public domain*, eg by way of interviews, etc, and for what purpose.
(c) There will have to be a *detailed examination* of such consultant by 'A's' solicitor—'one-word' answers to questions are *not sufficient.*

286. Public assertions:

(a) Have there been any public assertions or comments on the issue that is the subject matter of the proposed injunction?
(b) If yes, by whom, when, where and in what terms, giving full particulars including the circumstances of such disclosure and their context/intent? *X & Y v Persons Unknown* at **para 56**. For example, has 'A' *invited the public* into his marriage, in the context of a threatened publication as to marital infidelity?

287. 'Cuttings searches' (internet trawl):

(a) Is there a *'cuttings search'*? That is, has 'A' done such a search to pre-empt an argument as to material non-disclosure? Have A's solicitors pre-emptively got this ready on a data-base with the client's instructions?
(b) As to material which has been revealed in the *'cuttings search'*, how has such public revelation come about?
(c) Does the *'cuttings search'*, when carefully scrutinised on an individual basis, preclude the judge finding it *'likely'* that 'A' will succeed in restraining publication at trial?
(d) Is there material which shows that the public has been *misled* by 'A' in some respect, so as to justify a journalist putting the record straight by

revealing information which would otherwise fulfil the criteria for legal protection?

Losing Article 8 disclosure by failing properly to anticipate the defence case

288. Possible defences: What possible defences does 'A' anticipate R will advance? Consider the following—

289. Arguing the other side's case: Has 'A' taken all practical steps to reveal material/argument/assertion which is reasonably likely to assist *R's probable realistic defence* at trial (as contrasted with dredging up everything about 'A' in the public domain)? See *X & Y v Persons Unknown* at **para 50**.

290. As to possible defences: Consider by way of example:

(a) Have the public, as it were, been *invited* into the arena now claimed to engage Article 8?
(b) Is the information already sufficiently within the *public domain*?
(c) Or has the public been *misled* – false image?
(d) Hypocrisy?
(e) Right to tell the story – *Article 8 autonomy*?
(f) Protecting *public health* and safety?

Some guidance may be obtained by consulting the *Press Complaints Commission*'s Code of Conduct; see **para 51** in *John Terry v Persons Unknown* at **para 59** of which the relevant part of the Code is set out.

291. If a case of alleged marital disharmony: The fullest instructions are required as to the following:

(a) Has 'A' made *false assertions* as to marital harmony at a time after the stresses had emerged?
(b) Are the *tensions* in the relationship otherwise a matter of general *public interest*? *X & Y v Persons Unknown* at **para 51.**
(c) Is there any (alleged) criminality or other wrongdoing? See *Long Beach Limited v. Global Witness Limited* [2007] EWHC 1980 (QB) **para 52** (which is required reading).
(d) If there is material in the public domain, can 'A' *confess and avoid it*?

Adverse consequences flowing from infringement of Article 8—confidential relationship (ie 'secrecy' as contrasted with 'intrusion')

292. Is there a risk of any damage? If yes, particularise both the damage, and the likelihood of that risk materialising.

293. 'Kiss and tell': If a 'kiss and tell' breach of confidence, and the children of the other party may be expected to suffer harm, this is relevant damage; see *TSE and ELP v News Group Newspapers Ltd* [2011] EWHC 1308 (QB) per Tugendhat J at **para 25** (a sexual liaison case where the other woman also wanted to preserve her privacy—and not "kiss and tell" on the facts).

294. Sexual relations in the workplace: *ETK v News Group Newspapers Ltd* at **paras 19** and **20**, a case where the Court of Appeal upheld confidentiality in the context of a sexual relationship in the workplace; contrast the decision in *Goodwin v NGN Ltd and VBN (No 3)*.

295. Causation: How is it argued that these adverse consequences flow from the breach of confidence? Note the argument by counsel for the defendant in *Ntuli v Donald* [2010] EWCA 1276 (Civ) at **para 22** that there would not have been damage to Mr Donald's career or family life.

296. Evidence: What is the evidence for the information given pursuant to these questions?

Adverse consequences flowing from infringement of Article 8—reasonable expectation of privacy (ie 'intrusion' as contrasted with 'secrecy')

297. Adverse consequences in the context of a reasonable expectation of privacy (as contrasted with 'secrecy'): If there is an intrusion/proposed intrusion of privacy, with what (potential) adverse consequences?

(a) **Causation:** How is it argued that adverse consequences flow from infringement of the reasonable expectation of privacy? See *Associated Newspapers Ltd v HRH Prince of Wales* at **para 65**.
(b) **Public figure?** Is 'A' a public figure? Do different considerations apply? See *JIH v News Group Newspapers Ltd* at **para 40**, *Goodwin v NGN Ltd*

and VBN (No 3) at **paras 64–67**, and also *JIH v NGN Ltd* [2011] EWCA 42, [2011] EWCA Civ 42 at **para 21(6)**.

Article 8—adverse consequences—proving 'injury'

298. Is there is a risk of physical injury? If yes, what risk and what is the likelihood of it materialising? See *Author of a Blog v Times Newspapers Ltd* per Eady J at **para 31**; *Maxine Carr v News Group Newspapers* [2005] EWHC 971 (QB), **para 4**, and also see *Venables v News Group Newspapers Ltd* [2001] Fam 340.

299. Is there a risk of emotional injury? See *CC v AB* at **para 4**: Privacy extends to the establishment and development of emotional relationships with others: *X v Iceland* [1976] 5 DR 86, E Comm HR; *Von Vondel v Netherlands* [2007] ECHR 871, *JIH v News Group Newspapers Ltd* at **para 12**.

> The application was supported by a **witness statement** from the Claimant. In it he set out the facts, and gave reasons for his fear that, unless an injunction was granted, he and other individuals would suffer **distress** and **humiliation**, and he explained the **serious** effect upon him and them that he **feared** might result.

The risk is relevant, even if it is to a person who is *not a party* and who has not given evidence, see *Von Vondel v Netherlands*.

300. Is there a risk of emotional harm/damage to family/children?

(a) **Strains of the press:** See *CC v AB*, dealing inter alia with the pressures and strains of press *intrusion*; **paras 9** and **10**. This was an explicit factor taken into account by Baker J in *A Local Authority v A & F & A*, a case in which Baker J, vis-à-vis a mother alleged to have murdered her children, came down in favour of Article 10 prevailing over Article 8.

(b) **Damage to a marriage:** In the context of alleged marital disharmony, does the alleged material damage a marriage? If yes, give particulars; see *CC v AB* at **paras 43** and **45** (where 'A' argued that prevention of publication may save his marriage and R argued that publication would vindicate the institution of marriage); *XJA v News Group Newspapers Ltd* [2010] EWHC 3174 at **para 8** per Sharp J and *CTB v NGN Ltd and Imogen Thomas (No 1)* [2011] EWHC 1232 at **para 3**.

(c) **Wife and children:** As to adverse consequences vis-à-vis a wife and children of a marriage damaged by adultery, where there is a family wish to avoid publicity and rebuild relationships, see *ETK v News Group Newspapers Ltd* at **para 17** ('*the playground is a cruel place . . . etc*').

(d) **The need for evidence:** Thus in *Christopher Hutcheson v News Group Newspapers Ltd*, where 'A' expressed concern as to the distressing intrusion into the lives of his wife and children, Gross LJ highlighted that there was no evidence on the issue from either of the families, other than from Mr Hutcheson (see **para 13**). Note dicta of Tugendhat J in *John Terry v Persons Unknown* at **para 66**:

> Respect for the dignity and autonomy of the individuals concerned requires that, if practicable, they should speak for themselves.

Note the absence of evidence to resist a *contra mundum* injunction in the case of *OPQ v BJM* [2011] EWHC 1059 (QB) at **paras 24** and **26**.

301. Cases relevant to adverse consequences:

(a) ***John Terry v Persons Unknown*** per Tugendhat J at **para 127** (allegation of a relationship between Terry and another person etc).

(b) ***Mosley v News Group Newspapers Ltd*** per Eady J at **para 17** (as to adverse consequences) and at **para 212** et seq (as to damages/compensation in the context of a surreptitious video of sadomasochism in the context of an international sporting figure). As to Max Mosley not claiming an account of profits as contrasted with damages, see *Mosley v UK* at **para 74**.

(c) ***Venables v News Group Newspapers***.

(d) ***Maxine Carr v News Group Newspapers*** at **paras 4** and **9**: as to risk of physical injury. The background is explained in the first paragraph:

> The applicant, Maxine Carr, seeks an injunction, as it called [*sic*], *contra mundum;* that is to say, of general effect and binding upon anyone who knows of the order. The objective is to **protect her new** identity and to restrict information about her present and future whereabouts reaching the public domain. The terms of the order now sought are similar to those which have been in force since 13 May 2004 and the claim is founded upon the **confidential** nature of that information. In that application, she is supported by the probation service, by the Home Office and by the relevant police authority. (per Eady J)

(e) ***CTB v NGN Ltd and Imogen Thomas*** *(No 2)* per Eady J in the context of newspaper coverage in contrast to internet coverage:

> 24. It is fairly obvious that **wall-to-wall excoriation in national**

> **newspapers**, whether tabloid or 'broadsheet', is likely to be significantly more **intrusive** and **distressing** for those **concerned than the availability of information on the Internet or in foreign journals to those, however many, who take the trouble to look it up**. Moreover, with each exposure of personal information or allegations, whether by way of **visual images** or verbally, there is a **new intrusion** and occasion for **distress or embarrassment**. Mr Tomlinson argues accordingly that '**the dam has not burst**'. For so long as the court is in a position to prevent **some of that intrusion and distress**, depending upon the individual circumstances, it may be appropriate to maintain that degree of protection. **The analogy with King Canute to some extent, therefore, breaks down**.

And at **para 26** in the context of *adverse consequences* were there to be a lifting of anonymity: '*They* [ie the family] *would be engulfed in a cruel and destructive media frenzy.*' This theme was repeated by Tugendhat J in *Goodwin v NGN Ltd and VBN (No 3)* at **para 125**. In this context, also see *A Local Authority v A & F & A* per Baker J at **paras 36** and **65**, set out below in Part 15 in relation to '*Reporting Restriction Orders in the Family Division*'. *NEJ v Helen Wood and Persons Unknown* [2011] EWHC 1972 (QB) also addresses the issue of possible breach of an order and the 'dam' bursting; see **paras 13** and **21**.

(f) ***A Local Authority v A & F & A***—a case in which Baker J, vis-à-vis a mother alleged to have murdered her children, came down in favour of Article 10 prevailing over Article 8.

Stage 2: Case management for respondents

302. Introduction to Article 10:

(a) **Evidence/proof:**

(i) Article 10 invites evidence from those claiming the right to publish. So by way of example, there was no such evidence either from the newspaper or Imogen Thomas in the case of *CTB v NGN Ltd and Thomas (No 1)* [2011] EWHC 1232 (QB) **para 2**, the defence throwing its weight behind the '*public domain*' argument.

(ii) From another perspective, because Fred Goodwin or the other lady in the *Goodwin* case was not notified of the new '*public interest*' argument, they had no opportunity to give evidence or make submission to the court on that issue; see *Goodwin v NGN Ltd* [2011] 1309 (Civ) at **paras 21** and **27**.

(b) **'Legitimate aim':**
   (i) What aim is likely to be contended for? There must be identified a '*legitimate aim*' ('*prescribed by law*') which is '*necessary*'; see *Author of a Blog v Times Newspapers Ltd* at **para 18**.
   (ii) The legitimacy of the aim is always critical; *R (Wood) v Commissioner of the Police of the Metropolis* [2009] EWCA Civ 414, **para 26**:

   > [Is] the action ... **proportionate** to the **legitimate** aim in whose service it was taken . . . ?

   (iii) A '*legitimate aim*' includes a right to receive—see further, below.

(c) **'Necessary etc':** See Dyson LJ in *R (Wood) v Commissioner of Police of the Metropolis* at **paras 80–86**. The issue is:
   (i) *'The prevention of disorder or crime'* or
   (ii) *'For the protection of the rights and freedoms of others'?*
   (iii) *'In accordance with the law'?*
   (iv) *'Pressing social need'?*
   (v) Are the reasons adduced to justify the interference '*relevant and sufficient*'?
   (vi) As to the nature of the Convention right in issue, what is its *importance for the individual*, the *nature* of the *interference* and the *object* pursued by the interference? Note: '*parallel analysis*'.

303. Who, is it argued, has the *right to receive* the information?

(a) ***'Right to receive'*:** A '*legitimate aim*' (see above) includes that '*the public have a **right to receive***' (this is stated in terms in Article 10) the information. On what basis could it be argued that the public have the right to receive the information in question?

(b) ***Leeds City Council v Channel Four Television*:** public, parents of pupils, concerned citizens, council-tax payers, members of local authorities, councils and committees; and see *Von Hannover v Germany* [2005] 40 EHRR 1, **para 64**.

304. Who, is it argued, has the *right to impart* the information? Consider the role of the press as '*watchdog*', by way of example. Thus in *Von Hannover v Germany* the court observed at **para 63**:

> [T]he press exercises its vital role of 'watchdog' in a democracy by

> contributing to 'impart[ing] information and ideas on matters of public interest.

Further as to '*public watchdog*', see *Mosley v UK* at **para 114**.

305. Would publication make a contribution to '*a debate of general interest*'? If yes, explain in detail how such argument is articulated. *Note:*

(a) **'*Debate of general interest*' as an aspect of '*proportionality*':** See *Mosley v News Group Newspapers Ltd* per Eady J at **para 13;** and see also *DFT v TFD* per Sharp J at **para 19** vis-à-vis the public interest.
(b) **Public interest and sexual activity:** The concept of *public interest* was further explored by Ward LJ in *ETK v News Group Newspapers Ltd* at **para 21**; see also *Mosley v UK* at **para 131** (and also at **para 114**: '. . . *making* ***tawdry allegations*** *about an individual's private life* . . .').

306. What is the position vis-à-vis disclosure to friends and relatives—*limited disclosure*'? See *CC v AB* at per Eady J at **paras 19**, **34**, **35** and **49**:

> 19. It would be necessary as part of this process **to pay close attention to what the Defendant is likely to say, and to whom, and to evaluate the type of speech involved on each scenario**. For example, while it may conceivably [be] right to restrain the sale of celebrity **tittle-tattle** in which there is no real public interest, on the other hand there would **be no necessity or proportionate countervailing advantage in preventing him from conversing with relatives, friends or (say) doctors or counsellors about the subject of his own marital breakdown and what may have contributed to it**.
>
> . . .
>
> 35. It **would not be proportionate** to any reasonable expectation on the Claimant's part to prevent the Defendant, for example, discussing his wife's adultery with **a close friend**, or with **members of the family**, or (if he needed to do so) **with a family doctor**, **counsellor** or **social worker**, or with **his lawyers**.

Note the rejection by the Court of Appeal of the suggestion of limited disclosure to BP itself, in the case of *Lord Browne of Madingley v Associated Newspapers Ltd* at **para 55**.

307. Sweeping-up checklist: Can R pray in aid one or more of the following lines of defence, flowing from *OPQ v BJM* [2011] EWHC 1059 (QB) **para 25**?

(a) Is any of the material, sought to be protected, in the public domain?
(b) Is there a legitimate public interest in disclosure?
(c) Is there any question of exposing or detecting crime?
(d) Would disclosure make any contribution to a debate of general interest?

Stage 3: The balance between Article 8, its 'safeguards' and Article 10

Case-management checklist for all parties

Proportionality—the fulcrum of the balancing exercise between Articles 8 and 10

308. Intensely fact-sensitive: Upon an intense scrutiny of the fact-sensitive nature of *the instant* case, there must be very detailed instructions: see *R (Wood) v Commissioner of Police for the Metropolis* at **para 85**.

309. The centrality of 'proportionality': In the balancing exercise, one must pay the closest regard to '*proportionality*': *Howlett v Harding* [2006] EWHC 41 (QB) per Eady J at **para 12**.

310. Which category of publication? Into which of the brackets of information does the material in question fall (note the judicial emphasis on 'political expression': '[The Court] *consistently attaches great importance to political expression*')? See *Campbell v MGN Ltd* at **para 117**:

(a) *Political* expression;
(b) *Artistic* expression; or
(c) *Commercial* expression?

And in this context, see also section 12(4) of the Human Rights Act.

311. Right to receive:

(a) Why is it contended that the public *do not have the right* to receive this information?
(b) On what grounds is it to be argued that the means chosen to limit the

Article 10 right are *rational*, *fair* and *not arbitrary* and impair the right as *minimally* as is reasonably possible?

312. The freedom itself: Is the fact of freedom of expression (for the self-fulfilment of each individual) not so relevant here? If not, why not? See *A v B & C* at **para 11(xi)** (and see also in this context **para 45**), vis-à-vis the contrast between freedom of expression by a party to a sexual relationship, and disclosure of such relationship by a third party; see also *CC v AB* per Eady J:

> 32. So too, the Article 8 rights of the other party to that relationship (N) need to be taken into account. It is clear from *A v B plc* **that the court will be less inclined to protect the rights of one party to a sexual relationship if the other party wishes to reveal what happened**. Thus far, that does not appear to be so on the available evidence.

313. Freedom to impart – personal autonomy: As to the freedom of expression of a person to tell her story to a newspaper as to her life in care, see *Torbay Borough Council v News Group Newspapers Ltd* [2003] EWHC 2927 at **paras 14–17** and vis-à-vis an adult lacking capacity, see *E v Channel Four Television Corporation* [2005] EWHC 1144 (Fam). As to how such freedom to tell one's story can be an expression of personal autonomy, see *Ntuli v Donald* at **para 22** per Maurice Kay LJ. As to the autonomy of a prostitute to tell her story, see *Theakston v MGN Ltd* at **para 75** per Ouseley J and also see Buxton LJ in *Ash v McKennitt* at **paras 28–32**.

314. The tension between '*public interest*' and '*confidential information*': There is the potential inherent public interest in itself, in keeping matters received in breach of confidence, confidential; *Associated Newspapers Ltd v HRH Prince of Wales* at **para 68.** The test was set out by Tugendhat J in *John Terry v Persons Unknown* at **para 51**:

> 51. Where there is a confidential relationship the test is 'not simply whether the information is a matter of public interest but whether, in all the circumstances, **it is in the public interest that the duty of confidence should be breached**' (Associated Newspapers Ltd v HRH Prince of Wales [2006] EWCA Civ 1776; [2008] Ch 57 [68]). That case concerned an **unauthorised disclosure** by an employee of a travel journal, in breach of contract.

315. Exaggerated, etc:

(a) Is the degree of privacy sought *not over-exaggerated* and *not overstated*? Assuming yes, on what grounds is that contended, *supported* where possible with evidence?
(b) Are the *adverse consequences not over-exaggerated* and *not overstated*? Assuming that is the position—give grounds and explain, *supporting* where possible with evidence.

316. The harm/benefit ratio: Is the benefit to be achieved by Article 8 restriction *proportionate* to any adverse consequences flowing from interference with the Article 10 right? Any argument as to the harm/benefit ratio should be carefully articulated, and supported with facts which can be proved with evidence.

Codes of practice

317. Codes: The interpretation of section 12(4) of the Human Rights Act 1998 is that the court must have particular regard to any relevant *privacy codes*: *Douglas v Hello! Ltd (No 1)* [2001] QB 967 at **para 92**; see also *A v B & C* at **para 11(iv)** which concerned a married professional footballer (A) who sought to prevent publication by a newspaper (B) of his casual *sexual* relations with two women (C and D).

(a) **Check codes—Part 20 below:** Is there a relevant publishing code, against which to cross-reference, such as the BBC and Ofcom broadcasting codes? (See reference to this code in *Mosley v UK* at **para 82**.)
(b) **Code compliance:** Was a programme made (by way of example) in accordance with the provisions of such code; see *Leeds City Council v Channel Four Television* [2007] 1 FLR 675 at **para 25.**
(c) **Breaches?** Have there been breaches of such code(s)? Unlawful means used? If yes, what are the provisions of the code alleged to be breached and how are they said to be breached? Note how the codes were invoked in *A Local Authority v A & F & A*, a case in which Baker J, vis-à-vis a mother alleged to have murdered her children, came down in favour of Article 10 prevailing over Article 8.

318. Arbitrary conduct and the relevance of codes: Article 8 is primarily designed to prevent *arbitrary* interference by the state, but it also operates to impose on the court a duty to prevent *arbitrary* conduct between individuals, which will include the media. See *X and Y v The Netherlands* [1985] 8 EHRR 235, **paras 23** and **27**, the court said at **para 23**:

> The Court recalls that although the object of Article 8 is essentially that of protecting the individual **against arbitrary interference by the public authorities**, it does not merely compel the State to abstain from such interference: in addition to this primarily negative obligation, **there may be positive obligations inherent in an effective respect for family life**. These obligations may involve the adoption of measures designed to secure respect for private life even in the sphere of the **relations of individuals between themselves**.

The inference may therefore be drawn that the codes are intended to prevent *arbitrary* conduct. In this context, the fact that a programme was made *in accordance with the provisions of the Ofcom Code* was relevant to the issue of injunctive relief and Article 8: *Leeds City Council v Channel Four Television* [2007] 1 FLR, **para 25**, and see *Mosley v UK* at **para 82**.

Responsible journalism

319. Latitude—editorial style/presentation: Does the material in issue go *outside the latitude afforded* to a journalist's discretion? *Fressoz v France* [2001] 31 EHRR 2. Judges are not broadcasters or newspapers editors; see *In Attorney General's Reference No 3 of 1999: Application by the British Broadcasting Corporation to set aside or vary a Reporting Restriction Order* [2009] UKHL 34, **para 25**; *BKM v BBC* per Mann J at **paras 29** and **36**; and *In Re Guardian News and Media* [2010] UKSC 1, **para 35**.

320. The reasonable journalist—discharge of a journalist's duty:

(a) **Steps to be taken to fulfil responsible journalism:** As examples to such steps, see Baroness Hale in *Jameel and ors v Wall Street Journal Europe Sprl* [2006] UKHL 44 at **paras 146–49**. The following is a checklist of examples of such steps:
  - (i) What steps have actually been taken?
  - (ii) What has been verified?
  - (iii) Was the source (or sources) of information reliable?
  - (iv) Did the publisher believe the information to be true, and on what grounds?
  - (v) What had publisher done to check information?

(vi) What steps have been taken to contact the people named for their comments.

(vii) The requirements in 'reportage' cases, where the publisher is simply reporting what others have said, may be rather different, but if the publisher *does not himself believe* the information to be true, he would be well-advised to make this clear. In any case, the *tone* in which the information is conveyed will be relevant to whether or not the publisher has behaved responsibly in passing it on.

(b) **If steps not taken—detail them:** If the issue is publication by a journalist, has the journalist failed to take such steps as a responsible journalist would take to try and ensure that what is published is *accurate and fit for publication*? If yes, what steps have not been taken which should have been—*setting them out in detail*? See *John Terry v Persons Unknown* per Tugendhat J at **para 71**.

(c) **Examples:**

(i) As an example of responsible journalism, see *Christopher Hutcheson v News Group Newspapers Ltd* at **para 16**.

(ii) As to the potential for journalism not to be responsible: see *Goodwin v NGN Ltd* [2011] EWHC 1309 (QB) at **para 9**:

> 4. A third public interest argument was raised before me yesterday for the first time by Mr Caldecott QC for Associated Newspapers. It was to the effect that there might have been a breach of the corporate governance code of RBS, as suggested by Lords Oakeshott and Stoneham. I asked counsel whether any one had asked RBS, Sir Frederick Goodwin or the lady concerned about compliance with the code. He said they had not. He accepted that in those circumstances, if the imputation were published it would be damaging to others, and that a claim for defamation could not be defended as responsible journalism in accordance with *Reynolds v Times Newspapers Ltd* [2001] 2 AC 127.

Final 'balancing' checklist

321. '*Relevance*' and '*sufficiency*': Are R's reasons for restriction of the Article 8 right '*sufficient*' and '*relevant*'? See *Thomas v News Group Newspapers and Hughes* [2001] EWCA Civ 1233, **para 21**. Set out the argument in full, with the relevant facts supported by the evidence. Further, does such restriction pursue a *legitimate aim* and is it *necessary*?

322. *'Likely'*—*'Similar Terms'*—*'Merits'*? Is a final injunction *likely* to be made in similar terms (see section 12(3))? If yes, give grounds for that assertion - this issue goes to *merits*. It is a critical safeguard for freedom of expression.

323. *'Likely'* and the risk of a gap in the evidence: In this context, note the following dicta of Tugendhat J in *Goodwin v NGN Ltd and VBN (No 3)* at **para 92**:

> As I have noted above, both Sir Fred Goodwin and VBN have been **reticent as to the circumstances** of this case: paras 54 and 58 above. It is correct (as noted by Sir Fred Goodwin) that *information need not be true in order for it to attract a reasonable expectation of privacy.* But that *does not mean that the circumstances of the parties are irrelevant.* As I have already remarked**, if the parties choose not to give to the court details of the circumstances of their case, the court cannot take them into account**.

And continuing at **para 100**:

> Returning to the facts of the present case, the evidence about the relationship of the parties and their personal circumstances which they have put before the court **is so sparse** that **I cannot be satisfied that Sir Fred Goodwin and VBN are likely** to establish that they have a reasonable expectation of privacy in respect of the bare fact of their relationship.

Further as to '*bare fact*', see Eady J in *CC v AB* at **paras 38**, **39** and **41**.

324. A more limited disclosure? For example, in *Mosley v News Group Newspapers Ltd* Eady J considered disclosure of the Nazi theme to the Formula One Group but not beyond; see **para 122**. Consider whether a more limited disclosure would be proportionate. If yes, give reasons.

325. Undertakings: Have the proposed defendants/respondents/relevant third parties volunteered undertakings pending the interlocutory hearing? For an example, see *Author of a Blog v Times Newspapers Ltd* per Eady J at **para 1**. If yes:

(a) There must be full particulars with *supporting* documents/letters/emails.
(b) Do the terms of any proposed order *go beyond the ambit* of the undertaking volunteered? If yes, why?

326. Crosscheck as against Article 10(2).

Part 7

APPLICANT PROCEEDINGS CHECKLIST UP TO (BUT NOT INCLUDING) SERVICE

Pre-service checklist

327. Does 'A' have to pin his colours to the mast as to whether the proposed publication is true or untrue?

(a) **No:** See Sir Charles Gray in *WER v REW* [2009] EWHC 1029, **para 9**.
(b) **But make this clear if appropriate:** and see *Mosley v News Group Newspapers Ltd* [2008] EWHC 1777 (QB), per Eady J at **para 10**.
(c) **As to the rationale for this principle:** see *Prince Radu of Hohenzollern v Marco Huston and Sena Julia Publicatus Ltd* [2007] EWHC 2735 (QB), **para 14**; and further support for this principle is to be found in *Niema Ash and another v Loreena McKennitt and others* [2006] EWCA Civ 1714, **paras 86–87**.

328. Has 'A' stood in the other's side's shoes: Particularly if applying without formal notice, it is necessary for 'A' to anticipate any possible (ie realistically possible) defences; *X & Y v Persons Unknown* [2006] EWHC 2783 (QB) **para 51**. Such defences may include:

(a) Open justice.
(b) Abuse of process.
(c) Article 8 not engaged, because:
   (i) no reasonable expectation of privacy;
   (ii) threshold of 'seriousness' not crossed.
(d) Waiver.

(e) Information already in the public domain.
(f) Failure to make full and frank disclosure.
(g) Public interest in information being published, eg
  (i) the public have been misled;
  (ii) contribute to a general debate in the public interest.
(h) Proportionality.
(i) Damages an adequate remedy.
(j) Responsible journalism.
(k) Reliance on publishing/broadcasting codes.

329. Has a claim form been issued? With what causes of action? For example, in *John Terry (previously 'LNS') v Persons Unknown* [2010] EWHC 119 (QB) **para 48** the following causes of action were relied upon (flowing from the identification of these separate strands in *Campbell v MGN Ltd* [2004] UKHL 22 at **paras 13–15**, and per Lord Nicholls in *Douglas v Hello! Ltd* [2007] UKHL 21 at **para 255**):

(a) Breach of confidence; and
(b) Misuse of private information.
(c) And also consider:
  (i) *Protection from Harassment Act 1997* (see Part 12 below).
  (ii) *Data Protection Act 1998*. (This Act of 1998 is intended to protect privacy rather than confidentiality; it was considered by Eady J in *KJO v XIM* [2011] EWHC 1768 (QB) **paras 32–52**.)

330. Interaction of '*intrusion*' and '*harassment*' under the Act of 1997': See Tugendhat J in *CTB v News Group Newspapers Ltd and Imogen Thomas (No 2)* [2011] EWHC 1326 (QB) at **para 23**, and also per Tugendhat J at **paras 86** and **116** in *Sir Frederick Goodwin v NGN Ltd and VBN (No 3)* [2011] EWHC 1437 (QB), the dicta in **para 16** reading:

> In that case Ms Thomas's claim was under the 1997 Act, and under that Act the definition of harassment includes a requirement that there be **a course of conduct** which is unreasonable. **Intrusion** which the court could prohibit under the Human Rights Act does not necessarily have to amount to harassment within the meaning of the 1997 Act. But the test will otherwise be substantially the same.

331. If a claim form has not been issued:

(a) Why not? Have *CPR* provisions been complied with?
(b) Ensure that the *skeleton* is particularly full.

(c) Identify clearly the *causes of action* and the *grounds* on which they are based.
(d) 'A' must *undertake* to the court to issue a claim form *immediately* or the court will give directions for the commencement of the claim; and where possible the claim form should be served *with the order* for the injunction; see CPR PD(A)25 at **para 4.4(1)** and **(2)**.
(e) And once issued, the claim form *must be served*; see by way of practical example, *Goldsmith v BCD* [2011] EWHC 674 (QB) **paras 1** and **15**.

332. Serving on third parties before issue of claim: Under no circumstances can it be proper to serve on third parties an order made in proceedings which have not been commenced, *unless*:

(a) 'A' has *undertaken to the court* to issue (and as appropriate, serve) a claim form immediately (or as the judge may direct); and
(b) 'A' *intends to comply* with that undertaking; see *Goldsmith v BCD*, **para 17**. As to the importance of serving a claim form, see *Goldsmith v BCD*, **para 1**. As to the seriousness of failing to comply with an undertaking, see by way of example, *Goldsmith v BCD*, **paras 39**, **40** and **44**.

333. Service out of the jurisdiction? For a working example, see *ASG v GSA* [2009] EWCA Civ 1574 (CPR 6 PD(B) **para 3.1**).

Terms of order?

334. Precision as to who is the 'target': Maurice Kay LJ said in *Ntuli v Donald* [2010] EWCA Civ 1276 at **para 26**, it is axiomatic that any injunction:

> should be to the highest degree clear and precise so that no publisher would be in any doubt whether he was infringing it or not. [*Times Newspapers Ltd v MGN Ltd* [1993] EMLR 443 at page 447, per Sir Thomas Bingham MR].

(a) **Identification by class/category/individual:** The description used must be sufficiently certain as *to identify both those who are included and those who are not*.
(b) **Limits of description:** If that test is satisfied, then it does not seem to matter that the description may apply to no one or to more than one

person, or that there is no further element of subsequent identification whether by service or otherwise.

See *John Terry v Persons Unknown* per Tugendhat J at **para 144**, citing Sir Andrew Morritt V-C In *Bloomsbury Publishing Group and JK Rowling v News Group Newspapers* [2003] EWHC 1205 (Ch); [2003] 1 WLR 1633, at **para 21**.

335. Loopholes: Note the need to plug possible loopholes; see *X & Y v Persons Unknown* at **para 14.** Are there loopholes in the proposed order? If yes, what are they and can they be plugged?

336. Media third parties: As to *media third parties* being the *real target* as opposed to the respondent, see *John Terry v Persons Unknown* per Tugendhat J at **para 20** and **paras 143–46**, this also dealing with extending the time for service on *'Persons Unknown*'. Further as to service on the media, see *ASG v GSA* at **paras 29–30**.

337. Terms of order—length/breadth of injunction:

(a) **Policy:**
  - (i) It is in the *public interest* that it should be known *what* orders the court makes, and *why*; *G and G v Wikimedia Foundation Inc* [2009] EWHC 3148 (QB), **para 26**.
  - (ii) Further, the order should provide *maximum protection* for the person against whom the order is to be made, and the *least interference* with the right of freedom of expression necessary to protect 'A's' rights; *G and G v Wikimedia Foundation Inc* at **para 30**.
  - (iii) By requiring that orders should be drafted so as to take effect for *no longer* than is *necessary* and *proportionate*, the Practice Direction (PD 5.2) gives effect to the requirements of freedom of expression and open justice; *G and G v Wikimedia Foundation Inc* at **paras 23** and **24**. Hence the importance of a return date, where necessary: see ibid, **para 25**.

(b) **'Breadth' and public confidence:**
  - (i) If the terms of orders are *too wide*, the public's confidence in the administration of justice may be undermined (ibid, **para 26**).
  - (ii) Do the terms of the order go significantly more widely than is necessary for any legitimate protection of the C's Article 8 rights, assuming such rights are engaged?
  - (iii) Cases: *X & Y v Persons Unknown* at **paras 8**, **14** and **15**, and see

also **paras 17** and **18**; *Attorney General v Punch Ltd* [2002] UKHL 50 at **para 111**; see *BKM Ltd v BBC* [2009] EWHC 3151 (Ch) per Mann J at **para 39** for terms of an injunction sought, which were held to be too wide.

(c) **Limited to public at large:** If the material has already been circulated widely, then it may be sufficient for the order to be limited to '*publication to the public at large*'; see *John Terry v Persons Unknown* per Tugendhat J at **para 146**.

(d) **Confidential schedule:**

(i) Where 'A' anticipates, on the basis of evidence adduced, that a particular person is likely to reveal *only limited facts* or *make specific assertions*, it would be inappropriate to 'hack away' more broadly at his or anyone else's freedom to communicate than is necessary to prevent those identifiable revelations. *It would not be right to wield an axe where a scalpel would do*; see *X & Y v Persons Unknown* at **para 83**.

(ii) Means: Use a *confidential schedule* to specify precisely the information to be restrained; see **paras 81–84** in *X & Y v Persons Unknown* identifying the specific information or categories of information intended to be the subject of restriction. As to the use of *confidential schedules* as part of the *witness statements*, see *MJN v News Group Newspapers Ltd* [2011] EWHC 1192 (QB) per Sharp J at **para 11**.

(iii) For recent Court of Appeal authority as to *confidential schedules* and their interaction with a hearing in open court, see Leveson LJ in *Ambrosiadou v Coward* [2011] EWCA Civ 409 at **para 54**.

(e) **Delivery up?** If application is to restrain a television film, consider an order for delivery up of the broadcast or film?

(f) **If application is to restrain a broadcast:** See *BKM Ltd v BBC* per Mann J at **paras 8**, **9** and **39** for an example as to where the order sought was too wide to protect privacy.

338. Terms of order—purpose:

(a) **Precisely defining the purpose:** The purpose must be carefully and precisely defined, to cater for contempt proceedings vis-à-vis third parties and issues of *mens rea* (criminal intent) and *actus reus* (criminal act): see Lord Hope in *Attorney General v Punch Ltd* at **paras 86–120** and, in particular as to wording, **paras 105** and **111** ('precision' and 'clarity'). An example of an order in relation to intimacy, etc, which has been held to be sufficiently precise is *Ntuli v Donald*. The terms of the order inter alia challenged were (see **para 29**—the Defendant being '*Ntuli*'):

> [T]he court's protection should be extended to any facts communicated by the Defendant of a sexual nature **or other intimate personal details about their past relationship**.

See also **paras 30** and **31** which are essential reading vis-à-vis the meaning of the word '*intimate*'.

(b) **Proportionality:** Any *formalities, conditions, restrictions or penalties*, to be permitted by Article 10(b), must satisfy the principle of *proportionality*. They must be rational, fair and not arbitrary, and they must impair the fundamental right *no more than is necessary*: *Attorney General v Punch Ltd* at **para 116.**

(c) ***Contra mundum*?** Per Munby J in *Kelly v BBC* [2001] 1 FLR 198: *Per curiam*:

> Every injunction ***contra mundum*** therefore had to be treated as if it were an ex parte injunction granted without notice. The following principles applied to all without notice injunctions, including cases relating to children in which injunctive relief was sought against third parties or the world at large.

(See checklist at end of this Part, as to handling cases of urgency.)

(d) **If *contra mundum*, what can be disclosed to the media?** See *Kelly v BBC* [2000] EWHC 3 (Fam) per Munby J (these dicta clearly being said before ***LNR*** and before the procedural refinement of a confidential schedule was developed):
   (i) If it is not appropriate for the media to see the material in the form in which it was originally filed with the court, the solution is to set out the relevant material in a separate affidavit which could be shown to the media.
   (ii) This should be done even if there appeared to be no immediate likelihood of there being an application to discharge the injunction.

And now also see ***LNR*** **Practice Guidance** with particular reference to written irrevocable undertakings (**paras 24–28**) and an explanation as to their rationale, at ***LNR*** **paras 3.28–3.32**.

339. Does the draft order provide for the court being asked to adjudicate on a preliminary issue? Consider *David Murray v Express Newspapers plc and Big Pictures (UK) Ltd* [2007] EWHC 1908 (Ch) **para 12**:

> In the case of an application for summary judgment under CPR Part 24 the existence of unresolved factual issues may in itself be an answer.

If yes:

(a) What precisely is the preliminary issue? And
(b) On what basis is the court being asked to adjudicate?

340. How is the draft order phrased to cover information which has already been supplied, which is not to be further enjoined? See Lord Nicholls in *Cream Holdings v Banerjee* [2004] UKHL 44 at para 26:

> I recognise that without reference to the content of the confidential information this conclusion is necessarily enigmatic to those who have not read the private judgments of the courts below. But if I were to elaborate I would at once destroy the confidentiality the Cream group is seeking to preserve. Even if the House discharges the restraint order made by the judge, it would not be right for your Lordships to make public the information in question. The contents of your Lordships' speeches should not pre-empt Echo's publication, if that is what the newspaper decides now to do. **Nor should these speeches, by themselves placing this information in the public domain, undermine any remedy in damages the Cream group may ultimately be found to have against the Echo or Ms Banerjee** in respect of matters the Echo may decide to publish.

341. How should the draft order be phrased in the event of alleged wrongful appropriation of hardware/software? Draft the order thereby to put on R the obligation that once served, they are to provide information and deliver up property or copies of anything that may have been extracted or derived from the stored material. See dicta of Eady J in *TUV v Persons Unknown* [2010] EWHC 853 at **para 8**.

342. Derogations from open justice. Checklist:

(a) **Private hearing?** Is it strictly necessary that the hearing of the initial application and/or the appeal be *in private*? NB: If it is intended that a *telephone hearing* should be in private (as a derogation from open justice) this should be expressly applied for; see *MNB v News Group Newspapers Ltd* [2011] EWHC 528 (QB) per Sharp J at **para 1**.
(b) **Anonymity?**
(c) **Confidential schedule?** As to a 'private' judgment, see *Lord Browne of Madingley v Associated Newspapers Ltd* [2007] EWCA Civ 295, **para 2** and *Ambrosiadou v Coward* at **para 54**.

(d) **Restricting access to/sealing of court file:** see Eady J in *X & Y v Persons Unknown* at **para 11**.
(e) **Restriction on material to be served on a third party.**
(f) **Super-injunction?** See below.

If any such relief is sought, full grounds *must* be provided *with evidence*, anchored where appropriate to the relevant CPR provision and other equivalent anchor (eg case law). There must be a *detailed statement* in support from the 'A' (or relevant authorised person) and a *skeleton argument* setting out the applicable law: *JIH v News Group Newspapers Ltd* [2010] EWCH 2818 (QB) **para 70** and ***LNR* Practice Guidance, para 31**. Does 'strict necessity' demand that without the specific exception, justice could not be done?

The '*Spycatcher*' principle

343. Service on third parties on the '*Spycatcher*' principle: If third parties are to be served (whether with or without notice), consider carefully the terms of the draft injunction vis-à-vis them; per Eady J in *X & Y v Persons Unknown* at **para 61(vii)** to ensure that the terms of the injunction are applicable to the third parties as well as the respondents. The problem vis-à-vis drafting is addressed in **para 15** of the judgment. As to dicta on the '*Spycatcher*' principle, see:

(a) *Attorney General v Punch Ltd*, **paras 87–88**.
(b) *X & Y v Persons Unknown*, **paras 9–18**, **71–73** and **77–78**.
(c) *John Terry v Persons Unknown* per Tugendhat J at (**paras 18** and **para 112**) and *WER v REW* [2009] EWHC 1029, **para 16**.
(d) *Gray v UVW* [2010] EWHC 2367 (QB) **para 28**: it is not necessary to serve newspaper publishers where none is known to 'A' to have shown any interest in the matter.
(e) *Ambrosiadou v Coward* per Lord Neuberger MR at **para 38**:

> In the absence of an injunction, it would seem that there would be nothing to prevent a person, to whom an ineptly redacted copy of the May application notice was sent, actually reading the redacted material, and then publishing any information contained therein. An interlocutory injunction restraining the defendant from publishing such information would prevent such a person from doing so, provided that person had notice of the injunction, pursuant to the so-called *Spycatcher* principle—see *Attorney-General v Newspaper Publishing plc* [1988] Ch 333, 375, 380.

(f) *OPQ v BJM and CJM* [2011] EWHC 1059 (QB) at **para 7** per Eady J:

> Very shortly after I continued the injunction, copies of it were served on various media interests by the Claimant's solicitors, so as to notify them of the prohibition and of the court's intention to maintain the status quo until trial or further order. This was with a view to taking advantage of the so-called *Spycatcher* doctrine: see *Att-Gen v Newspaper Publishing Plc* [1988] Ch 333 and *Att-Gen v Times Newspapers Ltd* [1992] 1 AC 191. Anyone who revealed the confidential information, having knowledge of the court's order, and thereby thwarting its purpose, would be liable to be punished for criminal contempt of court. As Lloyd LJ explained in *Att-Gen v Newspaper Publishing* at p 380:
>
>> 'At common law, if the court makes an order regulating its own procedure and the purpose of the order is plainly to protect the administration of justice, then anyone who subverts that order will be guilty of contempt.'

'Super-injunctions'

344. Authoritative definition: Per ***LNR*** at p iv, **para 3**:

> A super-injunction is an interim injunction which restrains a person from: (i) publishing information which concerns the applicant and is said to be confidential or private; **and** (ii) publicising or informing others of the existence of the order and the proceedings.

345. When? The rarest of cases: ***LNR* Practice Guidance**:

> 15. It will only be in the rarest cases that an interim non-disclosure order containing a prohibition on reporting the fact of proceedings (a super-injunction) will be justified on grounds of strict necessity, ie, **anti-tipping off situations**, where short-term secrecy is required to ensure the applicant can notify the respondent that the order is made: *DFT v TFD* [2010] EWHC 2335 (*DFT)*. It is then only in truly exceptional circumstances that such an order should be granted for a longer period: *Terry v Persons Unknown* [2010] FCR (*Terry*) at [141].

Also see in this context, *Goldsmith v BCD* at **para 29** where Tugendhat J explains the approach of the court in the context of a risk of 'tipping-off'.

346. Potential for misuse: Maurice Kay LJ said in *Ntuli v Donald* at **para 47:**

Super-Injunctions attract understandable controversy. **Sometimes it is the product of more heat than light**. Although the concept carries the nomenclature of novelty, there is much that is simply a reflection of general principles. The starting point is the principle of open justice, most notably expounded in *Scott v Scott* [1913] AC 417, where Lord Haldane LC said (at page 438):

> '[The point] is one of principle . . . turning not on convenience but on **necessity**.'

Lord Atkinson added:

> '. . . in public trial is to [be] found, on the whole, the best security for the pure, impartial and efficient administration of justice, the best means for winning for it public confidence and respect.'

See also Lord Shaw of Dunfermline (at pages 476–478).

347. ***No*** **'super-injunction' without a return date:** As for an application for an order which prohibits the disclosure of the fact that an order has been made, and which is expressed to run for a period which is to continue after service on the respondent, and without a return date, see *John Terry v Persons Unknown* per Tugendhat J at **paras 141–42** and in particular **para 141**:

> If there ever has been an order which prohibits the disclosure of the fact an the order [*sic*] has been made, and which is expressed to run (as is sought here) for a period which is to continue after service on the respondent, and without a return date, then no example has been cited to me by Mr Spearman. I am not aware of what justification there might be for such an order, although I cannot exclude that there might be a justification in some case. But the grounds for applying for such an order would have be set out in the evidence. No grounds are given in the evidence in this case.

These dicta should be read also in the context of **paras 138–39**, cited by Sharp J in *DFT v TFD* [2010] EWHC 2335 (QB) at **para 10**. And see also *Goldsmith v BCD* [2011] EWHC 674 (QB) **para 15**, together with ***LNR*** at p v:

> Where super-injunctions and anonymised injunctions are granted they should be kept under review by the court.

Checklist for the 'super-injunction'

348. Strictly necessary: Is it argued that such an injunction is necessary to prevent the alleged wrongdoer from being *tipped-off* about the proceedings before an injunction could be applied for, or made against him or before he can be served and/or that there is a risk of evidence being destroyed? If yes, give full details as to the grounds of such assertions; see *John Terry v Persons Unknown* at **paras 109**, **138** and **139**. As to an example of an argument that failed: *Ntuli v Donald* at **para 46**, inter alia in the context of what in all the circumstances was truly '*necessary*'.

> It seems that the only argument advanced on behalf of Mr Donald at the *ex parte* stage was that a superinjunction provision was necessary because, without one, the media might publicise the fact that '**a well-known popular musician**' had obtained an injunction which prohibited the publication of (to put it neutrally) **salacious details**. This is unpersuasive because protection against personal identification could have been achieved by a **simple anonymity** order. **Alternatively**, the order could limit publicity to the fact that Mr Donald had obtained an injunction restraining Ms Ntuli from disclosing **details of the relationship** which existed between them.

349. Newspapers and tipping-off: It is less easy to show the need for such secrecy where the person *targeted* by the application is a national newspaper; *John Terry v Persons Unknown* per Tugendhat J at **para 109**; and **paras 138** and **139**. In this context see also ***LNR* Practice Guidance** at **para 22**.

350. Model form: For model form, see **para 20** of the Form of Search Order to CPR 25 (25 PD 10)and **para 140** in *John Terry v Persons Unknown*; further, such an order cannot run beyond service on R and a return date.

351. Working example: See dicta of Sharp J at **para 29** in *DFT v TFD*. In that case, Sharp J declined to extend a '*super-injunction*' and instead made an order limiting publication to what was contained in the order and in her public judgment—a *DFT* order; see also in this context *JIH v News Group Newspapers Ltd* per Tugendhat J at **para 67**.

352. The absolute necessity for a return date (note: the following factors also have a direct bearing on all interim non-disclosure applications):

(a) ***LNR* Practice Guidance, paras 37–41**:

- (i) A return date is particularly important where an order contains *derogations from* the principle of open justice.
- (ii) The need for active case management;
- (iii) A return date must *specified* and *kept* to;
- (iv) 'A' must inform the court at the return date *which non-parties* have been served;
- (v) It is not always necessary for parties to attend on the return date, *provided sufficient* material is before the court. Any order should be given *in public* and be publicly available.
- (vi) Is a *speedy trial* relevant? See *CTB v NGN Ltd and Imogen Thomas (No 1)* [2011] EWHC 1232 (QB) per Eady J at **para 38.**
- (vii) *If a trial is unlikely to take place:* The court should dismiss the substantive action, proceed to summary judgment, enter judgment by consent, substitute or add an alternative defendant, or direct that the claim and trial proceed in the absence of a third party. To continue an injunction after judgment, consider a *contra mundum* provision; see ***LNR* Practice Guidance** at **para 41**.

For a working example of what can go wrong without a return date, see *Goldsmith v BCD* at **para 15**.

(b) **'Must' and return dates:** See *Grey v UVW* per Tugendhat J (which is critically essential reading); per Eady J in *X & Y v Persons Unknown* at **paras 71** et seq, and per Tugendhat J in *John Terry v Persons Unknown* at **para 22** ('. . . *and orders made without the 3 days notice prescribed by CPR 23.7(1)(b) do not always provide for a return date* . . .') but see **para 135**: '. . . *there **must** be one if the order is made without notice to any other party* . . .' Also see *G and G v Wikimedia Foundation Inc* per Tugendhat J at **paras 21–27**. In *Thane Investments Ltd v Tomlinson* [2003] EWCA Civ 1272 the Court of Appeal at **para 21** emphasised the word '*must*' in the Practice Direction and in this context see ***LNR*** at **para 38** and *Goldsmith v BCD* at **para 15**.

(c) **As to the interaction of a return date, and the Court monitoring the proceedings:** See *John Terry v Persons Unknown* at **para 136** in the context of the *overriding objective* and *case management*, and ***LNR* Practice Guidance** at **paras 37–41**.

(d) **What *steps* are proposed by 'A' to progress the order/proceedings:** What would the court be *monitoring* if there were a return date? (Monitoring also as to propriety of the *continuing need* for any *extensions of* time and the continuing *derogations* from open justice etc.) Note: Indefinite extensions of time for service cannot be granted: *John Terry v Persons Unknown* at **para 143**.

(e) **Paramount importance of service:** If the claim form cannot be served *expeditiously*, then the action will be at risk of *dismissal*; see CPR Part 1; *John Terry v Persons Unknown* per Tugendhat J at **para 136**; *Goldsmith v BCD*; see immediately below.

(f) **Cost-effective technique when a return date:** As to how to avoid hearing costs in the context of a mandatory return date, see *Goldsmith v BCD* at **paras 60–61** and ***LNR* Practice Guidance** at **para 39**.

Undertakings by the applicant

353. As to taking a note of the hearing at which R is not present [see also CPR 25A 9]: See *G and G v Wikimedia Foundation Inc* per Tugendhat J at **paras 28–32** and particularly **para 30**, which must apply also to *telephone hearings*; *Gray v UVW* at **para 16**. For a case where the detailed note was the only recording of the hearing, see *TSE and ELP v News Group Newspapers Ltd* [2011] EWHC 1308 (QB) at **para 2**. Also see ***LNR* Practice Guidance**, **paras 42–45**, particularly as to when a note of a hearing may need to be *redacted.*

(a) **Damages:** There must be evidence as to the means of 'A'.

(b) **Signed statements:** (If relevant) that at the return date the evidence of 'A' (and any other relevant person) be in the form of *signed* statements (with confidential schedules if relevant) or that there be a satisfactory explanation of why it is not.

(c) **Form of undertaking:** See *Attorney General v Times Newspapers Ltd* [2001] 1 WLR 885 as to a form of undertaking (at **para 12**), and (**para 14**) the law as to their variation.

Checklist as to handling urgency—mitigation if a contempt

354. Has 'A' acted properly, given the time restraints? Checklist for mitigation (which should generate comprehensive witness statement(s)):

(a) Assuming any breach, was there an intention on the part of counsel or his instructing solicitors to mislead the court? Assuming not, what evidence is there to support such assertion?
(b) Have all reasonable steps been taken in the time available?
(c) Have extensive enquiries been made vis-à-vis full and frank disclosure, including looking at the case from a defence perspective?
(d) Have sufficient efforts been made vis-à-vis the following—giving full particulars:
    (i) To obtain undertakings in lieu of injunctive relief?
    (ii) Service on respondents?
    (iii) Service on third parties? See *Goodwin v NGN Ltd v VBN (No 3)* at **para 14** as to the regard a judge must have on the potential effect of an order on third parties.

These points were made in *X & Y v Persons Unknown* at **para 61**, and see also **paras 10–12** which are referred to in ***LNR*** at p 79, **para 19**.

355. Sanctions for breach etc: See *Gray v UVW* at **para 66**:

> Where there has been a breach of an undertaking to the court, or a breach of the legal representatives' duties to see that correct legal procedures and forms are used, there must be an **investigation** by the court. An **explanation** must be provided. If the explanation is inadequate, then **sanctions** must follow. The sanctions open to the Court may be limited, in that the sanction must not itself be a disproportionate interference with the rights of a claimant, in particular the right of access to the Court under Art 6, and the rights under Art 8. In the present case I do not have to consider that matter further.

As to a working example of a failure to comply with an undertaking to serve, see *Goldsmith v BCD* at **paras 5** and **7**.

Part 8

Service checklist for applicants

Notice/Human Rights Act section 12(2) and post-hearing Steps

Advance notice

356. Note *LNR* Practice Guidance as to 'advance notice':

(a) **Para 20**:

> Applicants will need to satisfy the court that all reasonable and practical steps have been taken to provide advance notice of the application. **At the hearing they should inform the court of any non-party which they intend to notify of the order as the court is required to ensure that the requirements of HRA s 12(2) are fulfilled in respect of each of them.** A schedule to any interim non-disclosure order granted should provide details of all such non-parties.

(b) And at **para 22**:

> Where a respondent, or non-party, is a media organisation only rarely will there be compelling reasons why advance notification is or was not possible on grounds of either urgency or secrecy. It will only be in **truly exceptional circumstances** that failure to give a media organisation advance notice will be justifiable on the ground that it would defeat the purpose of an interim non-disclosure order.

Service by reference to the '*Spycatcher*' principle

357. Who should be served to secure a '*Spycatcher*' effect? See Sir Charles Gray in *WER v REW* [2009] EWHC 1029 (QB) at **paras 16–18**. Per Eady J in *X & Y v Persons Unknown* [2006] EWHC 2783 (QB) at **para 78:** '*Some effort should be made to trace and serve the primary wrongdoer.*' Consider **CPR 6.8.**

358. Form of order for '*Spycatcher*': See *John Terry (previously 'LNS') v Persons Unknown* [2010] EWHC 119 (QB) per Tugendhat J, **para 18,** and *X & Y v Persons Unknown*, **paras 78** and **79** as to '*alternative*' service and '*best endeavours*'. Beware the risks of a scatter-gun approach: **para 79**. Note the '*half-way house*' approach at **para 80.**

> There may be a half way house available, in the sense that they may be able to approach some **friends**, tell them that someone has been trying to sell information to the newspapers about their domestic circumstances, and enquire if they have **any idea** who the **culprit** could be. This might help narrow the field to some extent. Much will depend on the individuals concerned and such an approach may not yield dividends. What would be the most appropriate '**best endeavours**' will inevitably have to be **tailored** to the circumstances by those best qualified to judge (ie in this instance X and Y).

359. Can there be an application without notice to secure the '*Spycatcher*' effect? Consistent with the terms of ***LNR*** (**para 21**) yes—see *John Terry v Persons Unknown* per Tugendhat J, **paras 1–4** and **109**; see also *RST v UVW* [2009] EWHC 2448 (QB) at **paras 7** and **13**. Situations:

(a) Evidence as to alleged risk of *tipping off* (eg *Goldsmith v BCD* [2011] EWHC 674 (QB) **para 29**).
(b) Convincing evidence that 'R' is seeking to *blackmail* the 'A': see *ASG v GSA* [2009] EWCA Civ 1574 at **para 3**, and *DFT v TFD* [2010] EWHC 2335 (QB) at **para 7**.

360. Can '*Spycatcher*' apply to a final order?

(a) **No status quo to preserve:** No—this doctrine has no application to a permanent injunction since there is no longer any need to preserve the status quo pending a trial.
(b) **The court's purpose fulfilled by a final order***:* This is because the court's purpose, in holding the ring until trial, has been overtaken by

events—there will be no need for a trial given the settlement; see *X & Y v Persons Unknown* at **para 72** cited by Tugendhat J in *JIH v News Group Newspapers Ltd* [2010] EWHC 2818 (QB) at **para 27**, and Eady J in *OPQ v BJM* [2011] EWHC 1059 (QB) at **para 9.**

(c) **A further relevance of the return date:** Thus a return date serves a number of purposes and in this particular context, also see *Gray v UVW* [2010] EWHC 2367 (QB) **para 37**.

361. Procedures to avoid the '*Spycatcher*' principle in the context of a final order:

(a) **Stay:** A technique for avoiding this problem is to invite the court *to stay proceedings* except for the purpose of carrying into effect the terms of the order, see *Gray v UVW*, **para 42**—a case in which such *a stay* was in fact ordered, but without argument as to jurisdiction (see **para 43**).

(b) ***Contra mundum*:**

(i) Alternatively the court can be invited to make an order *contra mundum* binding anyone notified of its terms, or to make an order against persons unknown, binding those who fit the description in the order once they are notified.

(ii) In *OPQ v BJM* Eady J avoided the '*Spycatcher*' principle not surviving a final order, by making an order *contra mundum* in the context of a submission that there was good reason to believe that the allegations may well be published in the media once it is thought that the *Spycatcher* restraints fall away. He said at **para 18**:

> It is now acknowledged, therefore, that the court's power to grant an injunction contra mundum is not confined to the wardship jurisdiction; nor to children; nor to 'individuals who cannot take care of themselves'. The remedy is available, **wherever necessary** and **proportionate**, for the protection of Convention rights **whether of children or adults**.

(iii) See **para 26**, for the making of the *contra mundum* order in *OPQ v BJM.*

(iv) Note that this jurisdiction was exercised, even though there was *no risk to life or limb* thus perhaps taking the law that much further beyond the position as expressed in *The Law of Privacy and the Media* (OUP, 2011) at **para 13.35**. Although there was evidence of serious adverse consequences to health (including mental health) were there not a *contra mundum* injunction, that does not seem to have been a prerequisite to the making of the order. As to mental health in this context, see *A Local Authority v A mother & F & A* [2011] EWHC 1764 (Fam), a case in which Baker J, vis-à-vis a mother alleged to have murdered her children, came down in favour of Article 10 prevailing over Article 8.

(v) ***LNR*** and *contra mundum*: At p 29, **para 2.33**:

> [T]he recent first instance decision of Eady J in *OPQ v BJM* [2011] EWHC 1059 (QB), making a final injunction *contra mundum* (against the world), although on the face of it extending privacy rights, may be a means of ensuring that there is no incentive to claimants to prolong the life of any interim injunction.

361. Interaction of an irrevocable undertaking and a final order: See ***LNR*** at p 42:

> 3.33 . . . Before formal notice or information needs to be given by the applicant to non-parties in advance of a hearing, the non-parties must give an irrevocable written undertaking to the court that they will use the documents and information provide solely and exclusively for the purpose of the proceedings subject to provisos set out in the undertaking. This undertaking will endure beyond the conclusion of the proceedings.
>
> 3.34 The court would have the power, on the same basis as set out in CPR 31.22, to release such a non-party from the undertaking.

If trying to notify/serve

362. *LNR*: The points made below are to be read subject to the '*advance notice*' provisions in ***LNR*** **Practice Guidance** at **paras 18 et seq**.

363. Notification of Rs: Unless there are compelling reasons, *all practicable steps* should be taken to notify respondents in advance: *X & Y v Persons Unknown* at **para 75.**

364. Notification of third parties:

(a) **Notifying newspapers:** If newspapers notified, how fully should they be notified? Eady J in *X & Y v Persons Unknown* at **paras 4** and **5**.

(b) **Service on persons unknown:** As to service on Rs presently unknown, see *X & Y v Persons Unknown* at **paras 68–70**, and **73–82**: some provision should be made for drawing the injunction to the attention of the unknown Rs; and see further, below.

(c) **Having regard to third parties:** Per Tugendhat J in *Sir Frederick Goodwin v NGN Ltd and VBN (No 3)* [2011] EWHC 1437 (QB) **para 14**:

> **VBN was not present or represented at the hearing**. There was no requirement that she should be. **But judges are required to have regard to the effect that any order might have on third parties who are not before the court**. So Henriques J enquired as to the position of VBN, and, after making his decision, **required the parties to inform her of the order he had made**.

(d) **The issue of a class broader than those to be served:** Sometimes it will be clear that the class of persons whose rights will be affected will be different from, and extend more widely than, those persons whom 'A' intends to serve: see *X & Y v Persons Unknown* at **para 12**.

365. Service out of the jurisdiction? See *ASG v GSA* [2009] EWCA Civ 1574.

If the order is to be against 'persons unknown'

366. Who is the real target? See *John Terry v Persons Unknown* per Tugendhat J at **para 143** where the newspaper was viewed as the real target.

367. Upon whom is it intended to serve the order? See *WER v REW* [2009] EWHC 1029 (QB), **para 15**.

(a) By what means?
(b) Why them—as opposed to anyone else?
(c) Is 'A' likely to serve a claim form on anybody? If yes, upon whom? If not, why not?
(d) Assuming they are not respondents, are the media third parties the real target of this application?
(e) Has sufficient attention been focused on the difficulties *from the third parties' point of view* in complying with the terms of the injunction, if it is tailored to the knowledge of the respondents? See *X & Y v Persons Unknown* at **para 61**.
(f) Consider whether the court should request a newspaper editor or lawyer to notify the source (*cautioning against using the media as process servers*); *X & Y v Persons Unknown*, **para 74**.

(g) If it is contended that there should be a '*leak enquiry*', see *John Terry v Persons Unknown* per Tugendhat J at **para 20** and *Goodwin v NGN Ltd and VBN (No 3*) at **para 80** ('*journalists do not normally reveal their sources and can rarely be obliged to do so*'); and in the context of journalists revealing their sources, see *Financial Times v UK* [2009] ECHR 2065.

Post-hearing steps

368. Notification:

(a) **Contact with the media:**
- (i) Has 'A's' solicitor been in contact with the media?
- (ii) If yes, with *whom*, *when* and for *what purpose* (identifying all relevant emails, correspondence, etc)?
- (iii) Statements required—see *DFT v TFD* per Sharp J at **paras 10** and **11** as to how to handle the file management in this context.

(b) **Newspapers:**
- (i) If notification to newspapers, which individual department should be given prior notification? NB importance of service, if possible to enable a counter-argument to be articulated: *John Terry v Persons Unknown* per Tugendhat J at **para 149(vii)**.
- (ii) As to a letter of explanation vis-à-vis the terms and effect of the order, see *JIH v News Group Newspapers Ltd (No 2)* [2010] EWHC 2979, **para 6**. As to the letter in response, see **paras 9** and **24**.

(c) **Informal contact:**
- (i) Has a proposed respondent or third party being contacted informally?
- (ii) If yes, in what terms, and with what response (identifying any relevant written/email communication)?

(d) **Third party application to vary/discharge?**
- (i) Is it anticipated that any third party would wish to apply to vary the order sought?
- (ii) If yes, give full details.
- (iii) If no, on what grounds is that contended? Note that if there is a *contra mundum* injunction to achieve a '*Spycatcher*' continuing effect, then presumably the order should contain provisions enabling a third party to apply to vary or discharge the order in the light of new information that affects the Article 8/Article 10 balance.

(e) **Applicant's continuing duty: *LNR* Practice Guidance, para 36**:

> Where an interim non-disclosure order is granted applicants are required to keep any respondent or non-party subject to the order, informed of any developments in the progress of proceedings which affect the status of the order. They are required to do so in order to satisfy the court that there has been compliance with the obligation imposed by CPR 1.3 and any requirements specified in any order or directions given by the court. Applicants are particularly required to inform any non-parties whom they have served with the order when it ceases to have effect.

369. What if a newspaper publishes in circumstances which may constitute a breach of the order? See *JIH v News Group Newspapers Ltd* [2010] EWHC 2979 (QB), **para 8**. Checklist for newspaper mitigation witness evidence:

(a) If published on the internet, how many 'hits' on the website?
(b) Apologise.
(c) Explain how publication came about.
(d) Explain what steps have been taken to ensure that it will not happen again.

And also see **para 24** vis-à-vis the speed with which the newspaper responded to a solicitor's letter and removed the allegedly offending material from the public domain.

370. Stay pending appeal: Does the losing party wish to have a *reasoned judgment* on the day of the hearing, for the purposes of an appeal? see *John v Associated Newspapers Ltd* [2006] EWHC 1611 per Eady J at **paras 22–25** and *Mahmood v Galloway and Another* [2006] EWHC 1286 (QB) per Mitting J at **para 27**; and for a working example, see the dicta of Lord Neuberger MR in *JIH v News Group Newspapers Ltd* [2011] EWCA Civ 42 at **para 15** and (as to the procedure adopted on the appeal) **para 16**; and *ETK v News Group Newspapers Ltd* [2011] EWCA Civ 439 at **para 2**. The court should wherever possible give a reasoned, necessarily *redacted*, judgment: ***LNR* Practice Guidance, para 45.**

371. Appeal:

(a) **Is there likely to be an appeal?** Grounds for so contending?
(b) **An undertaking expeditiously to apply for leave to appeal?** See, by way of example, *ETK v News Group Newspapers Ltd* at **para 2**.

(c) **Will there be an application for stay pending appeal?** Grounds for so contending?

(d) **If yes, has the Court of Appeal been notified?** Any appeal from an interim non-disclosure order may be expedited: *Unilever plc v Chefaro Proprietaries Ltd (Practice Note)* [1995] 1 WLR 243 at 246–47. It will depend on the circumstances of each case whether, and to what extent, expedition is necessary. The present system only requires those parties who desire expedition to take steps to persuade the court it is necessary.

(e) **Grounds:** As to whether in this context there can be grounds of appeal, see *Lord Browne of Madingley v Associated Newspapers Ltd* [2007] EWCA Civ 295 at **para 45** (correct approach on appeal).

(f) **'Balance' and the Court of Appeal:** As to how the Court of Appeal approaches issues of balance between Articles 8 and 10, see Lord Neuberger MR at **para 26** in *JIH v News Group Newspapers Ltd* [2011] EWCA Civ 42.

(g) **Anonymity and the Court of Appeal:** It is not to be presumed that anonymity granted early in proceedings remains justified on any appeal: *Pink Floyd Music Ltd v EMI Records* [2010] EWCA Civ 1429 at **paras 66–69**.

> 68. In a case where permission to appeal is required from this court, then, where the applicant wants a private hearing or anonymisation, the correct procedure is to apply for an appropriate order at the time permission to appeal is sought. If another party to such an appeal wants a private hearing or anonymisation, or in a case where permission to appeal has been granted below, if any party has such a wish, the party concerned should make an appropriate written application to this court. Where any application for a hearing in private or anonymisation is made, it will be referred to a single Lord Justice, who will, at any rate initially, consider it on paper. If such an application is granted *ex parte* and another party (or a representative of the media) objects, the order will, of course, be reconsidered.

372. File management checklist of post-hearing steps vis-à-vis third parties, etc: Taken from *JIH v News Group Newspapers Ltd* [2010] EWHC 2818 (QB) **para 72** (not affected by subsequent appeal).

(a) **Notice to media:** Have media organisations, who should have been given notice of the application, been given such notice? If not, why not?

(b) **What has been served?** Have those served been given copies of 'A's' statement (or the relevant deponent) and any skeleton argument? If not, why not?

(c) **Position of third parties:** Any third party affected by an injunction is entitled to attend a hearing; and see *Goodwin v NGN Ltd and VBN (No 3)* at **paras 14** and **28**.

(d) **Materials and note:**
   (i) Have the provisions of **CPR PD 25A, para 9.2** been dispensed with by the court?
   (ii) Persons served with the order to be provided on request with '*materials*' read by the judge and a note of the hearing; CPR 25A 9.
   (iii) If not, have these provisions been complied with? If not, why not?

   NB in this context: ***LNR*** p 12, **para 1.28** and **Practice Guidance, para 32**:

   > The need for intense scrutiny is particularly acute in respect of without-notice applications, or where the applicant seeks to serve, or has served, third parties with orders containing derogations from CPR PD 25A.9.

(e) **Service of 'derogation' materials:** Has information relied on in support of any application for a derogation from open justice been served on third parties? If not, why not?

(f) **Return date?** Have all relevant persons been notified of the return date?

(g) **Keeping third parties informed:**
   (i) Has 'A' kept non-parties, who have been served with an order, and who are bound by it under the *Spycatcher* principle, informed as to what is going to happen in the action, including prior notice of any hearings?
   (ii) As to the liability of third parties for breach of a '*Spycatcher*' order, see Butler-Sloss P in *A-G v Greater Manchester Newspapers* [2001] EWHC QB 451, at **para 19**, where she held that it was sufficient if someone was '*well aware of the spirit of the order*' (dicta focusing on a *contra mundum* order but seemingly of equal relevance to all *Spycatcher* third parties, and note the judicial advice for editors to have at hand a copy of the order).

   And see *TUV v Persons Unknown* [2010] EWHC 853 (QB) at **paras 10–16**.

Part 9

DEFENCE PRACTICE POINTS IN RESPONSE TO AN ARTICLE 8 APPLICATION

Checklist of possible lines of defence to be considered/anticipated

373. Abuse of process: For example, by framing the claim in '*breach of confidence/privacy*' to circumvent the rule in *Bonnard v Perryman* in defamation. This situation may arise if the nub of the case is in fact a claim in defamation vis-à-vis false information damaging '*reputation*'. See *Niema Ash and another v Loreena McKennitt and others* [2006] EWCA Civ 1714 at **paras 78**, **79**, **80**, **86**, **87**, **88**, **89** and **92**.

(a) **A claim of justification:** The *rule* in *Bonnard* is that the court has a discretion whether or not to restrain publication of what is alleged to be a libel, but where there is a defence or claim of justification, the discretion is guided by the principle that it is *not normally just or convenient* to grant relief unless 'A' has proved the libel to be *plainly untrue* (ie not be a sham or to have no chance of success); see *Bestobell Paints Ltd v Bigg* [1975] FSR 421.

(b) **Rationale for the rule:** The principle is not to interfere with freedom of speech.

(c) **The test:** The test is whether a jury could reasonably believe that the statement was true: *Compaq Computer Corp v Dell Computer Corp Ltd* [1992] FSR 93. For a development of the principles, see Auld LJ in *Holley v Smith* [1997] EWCA Civ 2914, [1998] QB 726 at 743–45.

(d) **Intense scrutiny:** Note the need for the court to scrutinize with greatest care any attempt to circumvent the rule in *Bonnard v Perryman*; *Gulf Oil (GB) Ltd v Page* [1987] Ch 327. For a practical working example where the rule in *Bonnard v Perryman* was not to be circumvented, see *John Terry (previously 'LNS') v Persons Unknown* [2010] EWHC 119 (QB) per Tugendhat J at **para 88**:

> It appears to me, in particular from the judgment of Ralph Gibson LJ, that it is a matter for the court to decide whether the principle of free speech prevails or not, and that it does not depend solely upon the choice of the claimant as to his cause of action.

374. Abuse of process—divorce 'ruse': Per Eady J in *CC v AB* [2006] EWHC 3083 (QB) at **para 55**:

> Reference has also been made to what has been called the 'the divorce ruse'. The Defendant has **threatened to use divorce proceedings** as a means of bringing the Claimant's name to the attention of the press. The proposal is that he would, unnecessarily, join him as a co-respondent. That strongly suggests that he intends to abuse the court's process for a collateral purpose. No one has the right to do that. Nor do professional advisers. But that threat appears to have subsided for the time being.

375. Is Article 8 engaged? Note:

(a) **Engaging Article 8—a precondition to Article 10:** If Article 8 is not engaged, then there is nothing to compete with the right under Article 10.
(b) **'Subject matter' and 'identity':** See Tugendhat J in *JIH v News Group Newspapers Ltd (No 2)* [2010] EWHC 2979 (QB) at **para 12**:

> Having considered the evidence, I too have no doubt that the private life considerations of **Art 8 are engaged** here, **both** as to the **subject matter of the action**, and, to a much lesser extent, as to **the identification of the Claimant**. The proceedings are likely to attract publicity, and if the Claimant is identified that will result in some interference with the private life of himself and his family. **There is no suggestion of any public interest or other possible justification in disclosure of the information which is the subject matter of the action**.

The focus on '*subject matter*' and '*identity*' was also made by Sharp J in *MNB v News Group Newspapers Ltd* [2011] EWHC 528 (QB) at **para 6**.
(c) **No reasonable expectation of privacy**:
  (i) By way of example, see the decision as to chance photographs in the street of Elton John; *John v Associated Newspapers Ltd* [2006] EWHC 1611 (QB) per Eady J at **para 17.**

(ii) Contrast the position in the JK Rowling case with that of *David Murray v Big Pictures (UK) Ltd* [2008] EWCA Civ 446 and see *Von Hannover v Germany* [2006] 43 EHRR 7.

(iii) If issue is publication of photographs, take a statement from the photographer as to all the circumstances surrounding their being taken.

(d) **Seriousness**:

(i) It is clear from ECHR jurisprudence that *intrusions* must reach a certain level of *seriousness* to engage the operation of the Convention; see *M v Secretary of State for Work and Pensions* [2006] UKHL 11 per Lord Walker at **para 83**; see *Ash v McKennitt* [2006] EWCA Civ 1714 at **para 12** (referring to **para 63** in *Minister for Work and Pensions v M* [2006] UKHL 11); *R (Gillan) v Commissioner of Police for the Metropolis* [2006] UKHL 12, **para 28** per Lord Bingham of Cornhill; and *R (Wood) v Commissioner of Police of the Metropolis* [2009] EWCA Civ 414; [2010] 1 WLR 123 per Laws LJ at **paras 22–23**. See also Eady J in *Ferdinand v MGN Ltd* [2011] EWHC 2454 at **para 54**.

(ii) As to the interaction of '*seriousness*' in the context of a public figure, see *JIH v News Group Newspapers Ltd* [2010] EWHC 2818 (QB) at **para 40** and on appeal at **para 21(6)** in [2011] EWCA 42 (Civ).

(iii) As to the phrase '*public figure*' as a term of art, see Tugendhat J in *Sir Frederick Goodwin v NGN Ltd and VBN (No 3)* [2011] EWHC 1437 (QB) at **para 64**, and also at **para 103**:

> Whatever limits there may be to the legal concept of a public figure, or of a person carrying out official functions, in my judgment Sir Fred Goodwin came within the definition. This distinguishes him from sportsmen and celebrities in the world of entertainment, who do not come within that definition. **But even in the case of sportsmen, there may be a public interest if the sexual relationship gives rise to conflicts with professional interest or duties, for example to his team.**

(e) **Criminality etc:** Is the subject matter of the proposed publication alleged to be criminality or other equivalent iniquitous wrongdoing (which may not be covered by Article 8)?

376. Public interest defences?

(a) **Waiver:**

(i) Can 'A' satisfy the court that he/she is not a person who willingly sets out for *self-promotion* to live her private life in the *public eye*, ie who does not invite the public into his/her private life? See *X & Y v Persons Unknown* [2006] EWHC 2783 (QB) at **paras 29**, **42**, **48** and **53** (M Tugendhat and I Christie, *The Law of Privacy and the Media* (OUP, 2002)).

(ii) For an example of a case where A claimed not to have courted publicity, see *MJN v News Group Newspapers Ltd* [2011] EWHC 1192 (QB) per Sharp J at **para 11**.

(iii) If it is contended that 'A' has behaved in such a way as to forfeit or waive any right to privacy, the fullest information must be given to the court including any relevant documents/publications; see *X & Y v Persons Unknown* at **para 28**. Note: In *CTB v News Group Newspapers Ltd and Imogen Thomas (No 2)* [2011] EWHC 1232 (QB), there was no suggestion of the relationship ever being conducted publicly.

(b) **Accessibility/public domain:**

(i) Is the information in question so *generally accessible* that, in all the circumstances, it *cannot* be regarded as *confidential* or having a *reasonable expectation* of privacy? (See the words of Lord Goff's '*first limiting principle*' in *A-G v Guardian Newspapers Ltd (No 2)* [1988] UKHL 26, [1990] 1 AC 109, at 282, a case where individuals had entered into public *debates* about matters of high public interest arising out of the proceedings, namely the appropriateness of government counter-terrorism measures; there was an obvious public interest in identifying such individuals.)

(ii) The test is '*objective*'; the subjective state of 'A's' mind is irrelevant.

(iii) In *CC v AB* at **para 57** Eady J did not consider that leakage into the internet brought into play a '*limiting principle*' preventing him from making an injunction, and in this context, also see *A Local Authority v A, F & A* [2011] EWHC 1764 (Fam) per Baker J at **para 34** set out below in Part 14 in relation to reporting restriction orders in the Family Division.

(iv) Dissemination of the Prince of Wales's journals to no more than 75 persons was not sufficient to bring these journals within the public domain: see *Associated Newspapers Ltd v HRH Prince of Wales* [2006] EWCA Civ 1776 at **para 42**:

> The judge proceeded on the basis that Mr Bolland was correct to say that those to whom Prince Charles sent his journals **totalled 50 to 75**, including politicians, media people, journalists and actors. The judge commented that the number and occupations

of the recipients of the journals were of no significance **in the absence of any suggestion that they would have felt free to publish the contents of the journals without Prince Charles' permission. Again we agree and again the significant fact is that over a period of some thirty years there is no evidence that any recipient of the journals breached the confidence under which they had received them**. If it be the fact that the circulation of the journals was as wide as Mr Bolland has suggested, this cannot, having regard to all the circumstances, lead to a conclusion that Prince Charles could not reasonably expect the contents of his journals, and in particular the Journal, to have been kept confidential.

377. Misleading: Has the public been misled? This is a '*public interest defence*' as is '*waiver*': see *DFT v TFD* [2010] EWHC 2335 (QB) at **para 24**; and see also *Campbell v MGN Ltd* [2004] UKHL 22 inter alia at **paras 24, 82, 126, 129, 151, 159** and **163**.

378. Material non-disclosure? Has 'A' presented a '*without notice*' application containing also what 'A' could properly have anticipated to be the defence case.

379. Accordance with the law, etc:

(a) Is the proposed restriction on the Article 8 right '*in accordance with the law*' and has a basis in national law which conforms to the ECHR standards of legality? *Campbell v MGN Ltd* at **para 139(a)**.
(b) Would publication of the material pursue a *legitimate aim* as set out in Article 8(2) and Article 10(a)?

380. Necessity/need:

(a) **Democratic purpose:** Why is publication *necessary* in a democratic society? Is it to expose wrongdoing; deceit; the public being *misled*; etc?
(b) **Pressing social need:** Does publication meet a pressing social need? Would publication contribute to a *debate* in the general interest? See *Mosley v News Group Newspapers Ltd* [2008] EWHC 1777 (QB), **paras 131** and **173**. Tugendhat J found this to be the position in *Goodwin v NGN Ltd and VBN (No 3)* at **para 133**. Further as to these dicta in additional context, see **para 130**.
(c) **Why not damages?** Are damages an *adequate remedy*? If not, why not? See by way of example for a case where damages would have been an

adequate remedy, *John Terry v Persons Unknown* per Tugendhat J at **para 149(ii)**.

(d) **Volunteering of an undertaking?**
   (i) Has a proposed respondent/defendant volunteered an undertaking?
   (ii) If yes, what are its terms (produce relevant documents)?
   (iii) Do the terms of the proposed order go beyond the ambit of the undertaking volunteered?

(e) **Consent to injunction:** Rs commonly consent to injunctions in order to avoid litigation while asserting that such injunctions are unnecessary: *Gray v UVW* [2010] EWHC 2367 (QB) **para 49** and *TSE and ELP v News Group Newspapers Ltd* [2011] EWHC 1308 (QB) per Tugendhat J at **para 35**; and also see *MJN v News Group Newspapers Ltd* per Sharp J where NGN did not oppose, but did not consent; and in particular see **para 6**. As to circumstances in which a newspaper did not resist an 'A's' application for an injunction or advance any form of defence, see *TSE and ELP v News Group Newspapers Ltd* at **para 35**.

(f) **Which category of publication?** Into which of the brackets of information does the material in question fall (note the emphasis on political expression)? See *Campbell v MGN Ltd* at **para 117**:
   (i) *Political* expression;
   (ii) *Artistic* expression; and
   (iii) *Commercial* expression.

   In *MJN v News Group Newspapers Ltd* NGN did not argue that the material fell into any '*public interest*' category.

381. Proportionality: Upon an intense scrutiny of the fact-sensitive nature of the case in question, set out in detail:

(a) **Principle:** Would the proposed interference with the Article 8 right be *no greater than is proportionate* to the legitimate aim pursued by R? Putting this another way, see Lord Hoffman in *Campbell v MGN Ltd* at **para 55**:

> The question is rather the extent to which it is *necessary* to qualify the one right in order to protect the underlying value which is protected by the other. And the extent of the qualification must be proportionate to the need: see Sedley LJ in *Douglas v Hello! Ltd* [2001] QB 967, 1005, para 137.

(b) **The harm/benefit ratio:** Is the *benefit* to be achieved by Article 10 publication *proportionate* to *adverse* consequences flowing from interference with the Article 8 right? *Attorney General's Reference No 3 of 1999:*

Application by the British Broadcasting Corporation to set aside or vary a Reporting Restriction Order [2009] UKHL 34, **paras 23** and **27**.

(c) **Has an undertaking been volunteered not to publish pending outcome?** If yes, set out *precisely* the terms of the undertaking **and** *evidence in support*; such may be sufficient in lieu of an injunction; see *X & Y v Persons Unknown* per Eady J at **para 83**.

(d) **Duty to impart:** Why is the duty to impart information in this particular case so important?

(e) **Right to receive:** Why is it contended that the public have the right to receive this information, and why is such right so important on the facts of this case?

(f) **Which category of publication?** Does the form of expression in issue fall into one of the higher brackets demanding publication, such as political expression? See *Campbell v MGN Ltd* at **para 117.**

(g) **The freedom itself:** Is the fact of freedom of expression (for the self-fulfilment of each individual) relevant here?

(h) **The ambit of journalistic discretion:** What is within the discretion of an editor—if relevant? Article 10 protects not only the substance of the ideas and the information expressed but also the form in which they are conveyed. As to the legitimate discretion of a journalist vis-à-vis presentation and credibility; see:

   (i) *In Re BBC* [2009] UKHL 34; [2009] 3 WLR 142, **paras 25–26**;

   (ii) Lord Hoffmann in *Campbell v MGN Ltd* [2004] UKHL 22, **para 59**, and see Lord Hope at **para 113** ('margin of appreciation'). Judges are not newspaper editors: **para 59** (ibid).

   (iii) *Mosley v News Group Newspapers Ltd* per Eady J at **paras 21** and **135**.

   (iv) *Attorney-General's Reference No 3 of 1999: Application by the British Broadcasting Corporation to set aside or vary a Reporting Restriction Order* [2009] UKHL 34, **para 25.**

(i) **Exaggerated etc:**

   (i) Is the degree of privacy sought over-exaggerated/overstated? If yes, set out the grounds for so arguing.

   (ii) Are the adverse consequences over-exaggerated/overstated—not supported by evidence—such as not to warrant restriction on freedom of expression? If yes, set out the grounds for so arguing.

   (iii) As to *exaggeration in reverse*, by the press, see *Von Hannover v Germany* [2005] 40 EHRR 1, **para 58**.

(j) **Codes:** Do the publishing codes *lend weight* to publication?

(k) **Discharge of a journalist's duty:** If the issue is publication by a journalist, has the journalist taken *such steps* as a *responsible* journalist would take to try and ensure that what is published is accurate and fit for publication? If yes, what *steps*—setting out in *detail*? As examples of such steps, see Baroness Hale in *Jameel and others v Wall Street Journal Europe Sprl* [2006] UKHL 44 at **paras 146–49**. File-management checklist of examples of such steps (answering the following questions in detail, with all relevant evidence):
   (i) What steps have actually been *taken*?
   (ii) What has been *verified*?
   (iii) Were the source or sources of information *reliable*?
   (iv) Did the publisher believe the information to be *true*, and on what grounds?
   (v) What had publisher done to *check* information?
   (vi) What steps have been taken to *contact* the people named for their comments.

(l) **'Reportage' cases:** As to whether a publisher has behaved responsibly in such a case:
   (i) Is the publisher *just reporting* what others have said?
   (ii) Does the publisher himself *believe* the information to be true? This should be made clear.
   (iii) *How*, *when*, *where* and in *what* circumstances and terms was the information passed on?
   (iv) What was the *tone* of the transaction?

(m) **More limited disclosure?** Would a more *limited* disclosure be consistent with achieving the result of what is sought to be published—a *proportionality* issue?

(n) **'Likely'—'Similar terms'?** Is a final injunction *likely* to be made in *similar terms* (see section 12(3) of the Human Rights Act)? If not, why not? What are the merits? See *BKM Ltd v BBC* [2009] EWHC 3151 (Ch) per Mann J, **para 37.**

(o) **'Relevance' and 'sufficiency':** Are R's reasons for restriction on the Article 8 Right sufficient and relevant? See *Thomas v News Group Newspapers and Hughes* [2001] EWCA Civ 1233, **para 21.**

382. Service: Analyse in full detail in relation to the following:

(a) **Clarity as to whom to serve:** Is it sufficiently clear to a respondent/third party whom it is intended to serve with the Order, and how? If not, why not?

(b) **Are those affected coextensive with those to be served?** Is the class of persons whose rights will be affected by the order different from, and/or extend more widely than, those persons whom 'A' intends to serve?
   (i) If yes, is that significant/ important?
   (ii) If yes, why?
   (iii) If not, why not?

383. Breadth of proposed order: Is the proposed order wider than is necessary for any legitimate protection of 'A's' Article 8 rights (assuming they are engaged at all)? Can the same be achieved with less?

384. Precision: Are the terms sufficiently precise? See *X & Y v Persons Unknown* at **para 6.** If yes, set out the grounds for so arguing.

385. The 'special weight' of section 12(3) and (4): see *BKM Ltd v BBC* [2009] EWHC 1351 (Ch) **para 33**; see *A v B & C* [2002] EWCA Civ 337, **para 48** for a working example.

386. Is there a Data Protection Act claim? See *Murray v Express Newspapers* at first instance and in the Court of Appeal; and see *Mosley v UK* [2011] ECtHR 774 at **paras 42–45**, **74**, **93** and **119**.

387. Should there be a 'public domain' proviso?

(a) *Attorney-General v Times Newspapers Ltd* [2001] EWCA Civ 97, [2001] 1 WLR 885, **paras 9**, **11**, **12** and **20**.
(b) *Harris v Harris; A-G v Harris* [2001] EWCA Civ 1645, [2001] 2 FLR at **paras 208** and **353** per Munby J.
(c) *A v B,C & D* [2005] EMLR 36; [2005] EWHC (QB) 1651 at **paras 16–17**.
(d) *X & Y v Persons Unknown* [2006] EWHC 2783 (QB) per Eady J at **paras 62–70**.
(e) *Attorney-General v Punch Ltd* [2002] UKHL 50, **paras 54–57**.

388. Has material been published infringing the order?

(a) **Infringement?** Has a newspaper, etc, in fact published material which oversteps the mark, and infringes an order already made? If yes, as to how to handle this situation, see *JIH v News Group Newspapers Ltd (No 2)* [2010] EWHC 2979 (QB) **paras 8**, **9**, **14** and **33**.
(b) **Prompt action:** Prompt action by a newspaper can work to support a defence argument that there is little or no risk of republication; see *JIH v News Group Newspapers Ltd* at **para 24**.

(c) **Details of what published:** The court will need to know precisely what was published, and if online, the number of 'hits'.

389. Derogation from open justice: As to the challenge confronting the court, see *JIH v News Group Newspapers Ltd* [2011] EWCA Civ 42 at **paras 1–4**. As to how such rationale expresses itself in practice, see the dicta of Sharp J in *KJF v HGF* [2010] EWHC 3064 (QB) at **paras 12** and **13** for a useful checklist, namely:

(a) Super-injunction order—no reporting of order?
(b) Anonymity—initials?
(c) If initials, one party or more?
(d) Restricting access to documents on the court file (so that none of the witness statements or annexures to the witness statements or the names of the parties would be provided to non-parties without further order of the court or an undertaking volunteered by them. NB where a non-disclosure order contains restrictions on access to documents, it must be accompanied by an explanatory note when served on any non-party who was not present at the hearing of the application: ***LNR*** **Practice Guidance, para 34**).
(e) Publication of any information as to the *subject matter* of the proceedings or the *identity* of the parties to be *limited* to that contained in the judgment.
(f) Material provided to the court—to be disclosed to third parties?
(g) If third parties have specifically asked for that information, have they given *undertakings* to protect the use of that material and the information it contains?

390. Clean hands doctrine and committal for contempt:

(a) Vis-à-vis any *leakage* of information, does R come to court with clean hands? See *CTB v NGN Ltd and Imogen Thomas* (*No 2)* [2011] EWHC 1326 (QB) at **paras 4–10.**
(b) In that case, 'A's' lawyers (unsuccessfully) made an application for *specific disclosure* in relation to the emails of Mr Kelvin Mackenzie; see also **para 9** for the details of the application seeking to establish how the leakage occurred: a practice management checklist.
(c) As to the law relating to self-incrimination in this context, see **para 11**.
(d) As to applications to *commit* for contempt, see **para 13**.

391. The interaction of '*contempt*' and third parties: This was explained in *X & Y v Persons Unknown* per Eady J at **para 9**:

This may be conveniently summarised in the words adopted by Lloyd LJ in *Att-Gen v Newspaper Publishing plc* [1988] Ch 333 at 380:

> 'Since the test of contempt is not a breach of the order but interference with the administration of justice, it follows that *at common law* a contempt may be committed if no specific order has been made by the court affecting anyone other than those involved in the proceedings. At common law, if the court makes an order regulating its own procedure and the purpose of the order is plainly to protect the administration of justice, then anyone who subverts that order will be guilty of contempt.'

It is therefore essential to ensure, if practicable, that anyone who has an existing interest in the information which is to be protected by an injunction is served (or at least notified) of the application; *WER v REW* [2009] EWHC 1029 (QB) at **para 18** and *TUV v Persons Unknown* [2010] EWHC 853 (Civ) at **para 24**. As to the position of third parties and the issue of contempt, see the application made by the third party, for a referral to the Attorney-General, in *Goodwin v NGN Ltd and VBN (No 3)* per Tugendhat J at **para 30**.

Part 10

Quality control checklist for the courtroom

Drawn inter alia from pages 79 et seq of *Lord Neuberger's Report* and from *ETK v NGN Ltd* Suggested use: in the court room at the hearing

1. Consent?

(a) Is there any consent to any part of an order sought? If yes, give details.
(b) Even if there is consent, the issue is one for the court and not for the parties.
(c) But the court is entitled to attach real weight to a consent given by a party who has been advised by very experienced legal advisers: *MJN v News Group Newspapers Ltd* [2011] EWHC 1192 (QB) per Sharp J at **para 8**.
(d) As to circumstances where an explanation for such consent is called for, see *JIH v News Group Newspapers Ltd* [2010] EWHC 2818 (QB) per Tugendhat J at **para 61**.

2. Is application to be made for any derogation from open justice? If yes:

(a) **What derogation?**
  (i) Without notice.
  (ii) Private hearing.
  (iii) Super-injunction—no reporting of Order?
  (iv) Anonymity—initials?
  (v) If initials, one party or more?
  (vi) Restricting access to documents on the court file.
  (vii) Extent of material to be disclosed to non-parties (including issue: a redacted note of hearing?).

(viii) Irrevocable written undertakings?

Give clear grounds for such derogation: eg grounds for any alleged risk of jigsaw identification (if appropriate, supported by an internet trawl).

(b) **Statement:** Any derogation to be established by clear and cogent evidence: 'A's' statement.

(c) **Human Rights Act section 12(2):**
   (i) Hurdles if moving '*without notice*'.
   (ii) Separately from that: the issue of '*likely*'.

(d) **Exceptional?** Strictly necessary (NB '*high standard*')? Is there any less restrictive or more acceptable alternative?

(e) **Listing:** How is the case to be referred to in the court lists?

(f) **Return date?** Critical to allow the court powers of adequate case management.

(g) **Terms of judgment:**
   (i) What should, and should not, go into the public judgment?
   (ii) Terms of any confidential schedule.

3. Is Article 8 engaged?

(a) **Applicant?**
   (i) Full particulars as to identity and character.
   (ii) Is the Applicant a child? For example, for approval of a damages award?

(b) **Others also?**
   (i) If others embraced within 'A's' '*zone of privacy*', in addition to 'A', precisely who and on what grounds?
   (ii) Why cannot these other people argue the case for themselves?
   (iii) What weight is to be attached to the Article 8 interests of these others and why?
   (iv) Are there rights of children to be placed in the scale?

(c) **Corpus of material:** What precisely is the corpus of material the judge is to be invited to address—setting out if helpful the separate '*strands*' of that material to invite particular judicial scrutiny?

(d) **Nature of information?**
   (i) Threatened publication?
   (ii) If yes, what is the extent of proposed dissemination? The court needs: details of nature of threat, and publication to whom; location/activity/how obtained—source/how did it come into hands of R? Was the receipt of the information unauthorised or purloined?

(iii) Reasonable expectation of privacy and/or confidentiality. If yes, on what grounds?
(iv) If confidentiality, what is the nature of the relationship? Court needs all circumstances: what is recipient's perception of the confidential nature? Does anyone else have a claim or interest in the information?

(e) **Degree/gravity of intrusion (depth/breadth/extent/expression as self-fulfilment/sale to the tabloids)?**
(i) Nature of interference (trivial)?
(ii) Importance for 'A'; object pursued by the interference (blackmail? Note the interaction between '*anonymity*' and allegations of '*blackmail*')? See also *CC v AB* [2006] EWHC 3083 (QB) at **paras 6** and **36**; and *DFT v TFD* [2010] EWHC 2335 (QB) per Sharp J at **para 35**:

> I also consider Mr Tomlinson is right when he says the blackmail element of this case brings extremely strong public interest considerations into play.

(f) **If photographs, extent of their intrusion:**
(i) Spectator or voyeur? Surreptitious? Clandestine? Zoom lens? Targeted? Of children?
(ii) Is the actual act of photography a violation? Were photographs taken with a view to publication?
(iii) Private or public matters?
(iv) Purpose?
(v) Public status of 'A'?
(vi) Consider Privacy Codes—could photographs have been taken in a manner that would secure any Code compliance? See *Michael Douglas v Hello! Ltd* [2005] EWCA Civ 595 at **paras 84–87** per Lord Phillips.

(g) **What is the objective to seeking to restrict the Article 10 right?**
(i) Adverse consequences? (To whom—family also?)
(ii) Harm?
(iii) How grave?
(iv) For how long?
(v) Medical evidence?

(h) **Is any material in the public domain?** If yes:
(i) How is that defined?
(ii) How much and how did it get there?
(iii) What has been published, by whom, when and in what circum-

stances? Internet/cuttings trawl, eg by a public relations consultant (if this reveals extensive articles).
  - (iv) Was 'A' under a contractual obligation to provide?
  - (v) What Article 8 right remains to be preserved?
  - (vi) What further harm could arise if no restraint?

(i) **How is the claim form to be phrased?** For example:
  - (i) Harassment?
  - (ii) Breach of confidence?
  - (iii) Misuse of private information?
  - (iv) Data Protection Act 1998?

  Ensure grounds for claims are contained in statement in support.

(j) **Prejudice a fair trial?** Could threatened media reporting discourage 'A' or a witness from giving evidence at a full hearing ('chilling effect')? If yes, give full particulars.

4. Is Article 10 engaged?

(a) **Does the public have a right to receive? Grounds?**

(b) **Public interest:**
  - (i) How is the '*public interest*' expressed? Political, artistic and commercial?
  - (ii) Is there sufficient public interest in publication to justify overriding the right to privacy?

(c) **If photographs:**
  - (i) What is the contribution contended for vis-à-vis a debate of general interest?
  - (ii) Can parts of the photographs be pixellated?
  - (iii) Can a broadcast be achieved without photographs?

(d) **If the material to be published flows from a sexual relationship with 'A':**
  - (i) Has that other person been spoken to?
  - (ii) To what agenda?
  - (iii) Does he/she want publicity, and why? If no, how was that expressed?
  - (iv) Does that person not consider the relationship to have been confidential; and if not, why not?
  - (v) Is there a conflict with professional interests or duties, eg to a sports team? See *Sir Frederick Goodwin v NGN Ltd and VBN (No 3)* [2011] EWHC 1437 (QB) **para 103**.

5. Balance?

(a) **Is legitimate public interest served by disclosure to the public?**
   (i) Does it contribute to a debate of general interest?
   (ii) Does it achieve some social purpose?

(b) **Harm/benefit ratio: proportionate?** Would the benefits that are to be achieved by publication be *proportionate* to the harm that may be done by interference with the right to privacy? Explain.

(c) **How wide are proposed terms?**
   (i) No more than is neccssary? (Is a full *inter partes* hearing sought? For how long is the injunction sought?)
   (ii) Are the means to restrict the Article 10 right rational, fair, not arbitrary, and impair the Article 10 right as minimally as is reasonably possible? If so contended, explain.
   (iii) Public domain proviso and if material already in the public domain to some extent, the order must make it expressly clear what material is not to be treated as coming within the proviso?

(d) **Legitimate object/aim?** Conspiracy to publish by more than one person?

(e) **Relevance of any Privacy Code—breaches?** As to the interaction of any relevant privacy code and a reasonable expectation of privacy, see *Goodwin v NGN Ltd and VBN (No 3)* per Tugendhat J at **para 83**.

(f) **Waiver?**
   (i) For example, by courting publicity, admissions as to past behaviour, made allegations as to others?
   (ii) Has 'A' invited public into the area now claimed to engage Article 8? If yes, grounds for so contending? In *Christopher Hutcheson (formerly known as 'KGM') v News Group Newspapers Ltd & Ors* [2011] EWCA Civ 808 the parties had chosen to conduct their quarrels publicly in such a fashion that they took the risk of not being able to insist on clear boundary lines between what was public and private (see **paras 5**, **10** and **45**).

(g) **Full and frank disclosure?**
   (i) Has 'A' made sufficient full and frank disclosure if moving without notice?
   (ii) Has he/she sufficiently stepped into the other side's shoes.

(h) **Undertaking:**
   (i) Has R volunteered an undertaking? If yes:
   (ii) In what terms?
   (iii) Why is that undertaking not sufficient?

(i) **Damages?**
   (i) Damage an adequate remedy?

(ii) If not, why not?

6. Can Human Rights Act section 12(2) likelihood be argued now?

(a) If yes, on what grounds.
(b) If no, why not?
(c) Is this a case for a 'short-lived' injunction pending an argument on the interim merits?
(d) If yes, give grounds.

7. Documents to be prepared by the Applicant (and see *LNR* Practice Guidance, para 17):

(a) **The application/claim form:** see HRA s 12(2), and CPR 25.3(2) and (3), and CPR 25A 4.3(3).
(b) **A witness statement or statements:** ('clear and cogent') justifying the need for each provision in the proposed order covering also in detail any reference to Articles 8 and 10, and any derogation sought from open justice.
(c) **Legal submissions.**
(d) **A draft order.**
(e) **An explanatory note**; see ***LNR***, p 79, **para 17**.

> In the rare or urgent case where it is not possible to prepare such documentation prior to the hearing, the applicant should file a statement at the earliest practicable opportunity, setting out the information placed orally before the court.

8. Notice:

(a) **Notice to respondent(s):**
  (i) Have all reasonable practicable steps been taken to provide advance notice of the application to R formally or informally? If yes, what are they? They should if necessary be in the statement.
  (ii) Are there compelling reasons why R should not be notified? If yes, on what grounds? For example, is there a real prospect that were R to be notified he/she would take steps to defeat the order's purpose—for instance, where there is convincing evidence that R is seeking to blackmail the applicant? If yes, this should be in the statement.
  (iii) Evidence as to alleged risk of 'tipping-off'? See by way of example *Goldsmith v BCD* [2011] EWHC 674 (QB) **paras 1**, **2** and **32**.

(b) Notice to non-parties:
  (i) Whom to serve? Those with an interest—similarly ('. . . because they

have an existing interest in the information which is to be protected by an injunction' *X & Y v Persons Unknown . . .*) [2007] EMLR 290 at **paras 10–12**.

(ii) *Who has/have been served?* Have all respondents and any non-parties been served with a copy of the application notice and any supporting documentation before the hearing? If not, why not? If relevant, precisely what efforts have been made?

(c) **Note: para 19** of the ***LNR*** **Practice Guidance** requires that non-parties should be given advance notice of the hearing. This is a substantial innovation, but *different considerations* may arise where a respondent or non-party is an internet-based organisation, tweeter or blogger, or where, for instance, there are allegations of blackmail: see ***LNR*** **Practice Guidance, para 22**. The question arises: to what extent is there an obligation also to give advance notice to internet-based organisations, etc? This has still to be worked through, and it may be that case law will evolve to provide more specific guidance.

(d) **Is a potential party outside the jurisdiction?** If yes, leave to serve? See *ASG v GSA* [2009] EWCA Civ 1574 at **paras 27–28** which paragraphs should be read carefully vis-à-vis such service and the documentary requirements.

(e) **Whom to serve in the media**: If service on the media, it should be effected on the organisation's legal adviser.

9. Post-hearing: notice and undertaking to the court—non-parties:

(a) **Material:** Is the material to be supplied to non-parties in order:
  (i) The application;
  (ii) Any supporting documentation;
  (iii) A copy of any materials as specified in CPR PD 25(A)9.

(b) **Order:** Is the order correctly drafted, with particular reference to what is clause 13 of the Model Order? See Part 17 below.

(c) **Irrevocable undertaking:** Is the irrevocable written undertaking properly drafted and complete? (See notes to clause 13 of the Model Order.)

(d) **Explanatory note:** Is the explanatory note to the Model Order properly drafted and complete?

(e) **Legal adviser:** Has the non-party a legal adviser? If yes, has she/he been identified?

(f) **Redacted note:** As to the interaction between an irrevocable written undertaking and a *redacted* note of hearing, see ***LNR*** at p 82, **para 44** and CPR 25(A)9.

10. Checklist vis-à-vis applicant compliance:

(a) **Applicant's statement and any other evidence?**
(b) **Correct legal procedures?**
(c) **Correct forms?**
(d) **Written skeleton?**
(e) **Properly drafted order?**
(f) **At the hearing**, that the court's attention is drawn to:
  (i) *unusual features* of the evidence adduced;
  (ii) *applicable law*,
  (iii) *formalities and procedure* (Does order depart from Model Order? If yes, how?)
  (iv) *Supported with clear and cogent evidence.*
(g) **A letter which sets out the effect of the order:** This is for service on any respondent and non-party? See *JIH v News Group Newspapers Ltd* [2010] EWHC (QB) 2979 at **para 6** per Tugendhat J.
(h) **Route map:** What steps are proposed by 'A' to progress the proceedings?
(i) **Court associate:** Advocate to liaise with the court associate with a view to ensuring that the order as drawn is accurate.
(j) **Full note:** Redacted if necessary.
(k) **Checking draft judgment:** To ensure that nothing included which is confidential; see *Goldsmith v BCD* at **para 12**, and *JIH v News Group Newspapers Ltd* [2010] EWHC 2818 (QB) per Tugendhat J at **paras 69** and **71** as to the judge personally serving a draft on media representatives.

11. Appeal?

(a) Is there likely to be an appeal? Grounds?
(b) Will there be an application for a stay pending appeal? Grounds?
(c) As to an undertaking expeditiously to apply for leave to appeal, see by way of example, *ETK v News Group Newspapers Ltd* [2011] EWCA Civ 439 at **para 2**.
(d) If yes, has the Court of Appeal been notified?

12. Service on a party?

(a) How?
(b) By when?
(c) Upon whom, precisely (eg named legal adviser)?
(d) With what?
(e) Service out of the jurisdiction? Leave?

13. Service of order/notification of—a non-party:

(a) Has 'A's' solicitor been in contact with the media? If yes, with whom, when and for what purpose, identifying all relevant emails, correspondence, etc? Is 'A' likely to serve a claim form on anybody? If yes, upon whom? If no, why not? See in this context, *Goldsmith v BCD*.
(b) Who is the real target? Why them as opposed to anyone else?
(c) Assuming they are not respondents, are the media third parties the real target?
(d) Consider whether the court should request a newspaper editor or lawyer to notify the source.
(e) Upon whom is it intended to serve the order?
(f) By what means? How?
(g) By when?
(h) Upon whom precisely?
(i) If 'persons unknown':
  (i) Are they defined with sufficient precision?
  (ii) Is it intended to notify them?
  (iii) If yes, how? What steps are proposed to be taken to find them?
(j) Any application to serve on non-parties material less than that which the judge has seen must be applied for and explained in Article 6 and Article 8 terms.

Note ***LNR*** at p 39 of the Main Report, footnote 131:

> An applicant may intend to serve a media organization because there is reason to believe it has an interest in the information: *WER v REW* [2009] EWHC 1029 (QB) at **para 18** and *TUV v Persons Unknown* [2010] EMLR 19 at [24].

And ***LNR*** at p 40, **para 3.24**:

> 3.25 Following implementation of the recommended Practice Guidance, the likelihood of this situation arising should decrease as non-attendance due to absence of notice will be confined to exceptional cases. It will also only arise in those cases where an applicant becomes aware following the grant of an order that a non-party has an interest in the information subject to the injunction, and at that point notifies the non-party of the order.

Part 11

JOURNALIST'S CHECKLIST

The following questions inter alia draw upon the dicta of Lord Nicholls in *Reynolds v Times Newspapers Ltd* [2001] 2 AC 127 at 205; and also upon the dicta in *Jameel and ors v Wall Street Journal Europe Sprl* [2006] UKHL 44 at **paras 58**, **138** and **149**.

1. Material: What precisely is the material which the journalist wishes to publish? Set it out clearly.

2. Public interest:

(a) **How serious is the issue** which the journalist wishes to publish?
(b) **How serious would be the damage** if the material published were not true? How much harm would be caused and to whom?
(c) **Has 'A' behaved** in such a way as to forfeit or waive any entitlement to privacy? High degree of misbehaviour (crime, fraud, misdeeds)? Has the public been seriously misled? Grounds?
(d) **Public interest in publication**?
    (i) To what extent is the material a matter of public concern?
    (ii) Does the material make a real contribution to the public interest/debate? Grounds?

3. Source:

(a) What is the **source/status** of the information?
(b) Does the **informant** have direct knowledge? If not, how did the informant come by the information?
(c) How **independent** is that source?
(d) Does the source have an **axe to grind**?

(e) Is the source being paid for the story? Is there a **profit motive**?

4. Has journalist acted in good faith? Give grounds for any answer to the following three issues:

(a) Has journalist worked on an accurate factual basis?
(b) What has been verified, by whom and how?
(c) How reliable and precise is the information?

5. What is the belief of the journalist vis-à-vis the information sought to be published?

(a) **What steps have been taken to try and ensure that what is published is accurate and fit for publication?** The steps will vary given the nature and source.
(b) **Does the journalist believe the source of information to be reliable?**
  (i) If yes, on what grounds? Has the information already been the subject of an investigation which commands respect?
  (ii) If no, why seek to publish?
(c) **Does the journalist believe the information to be true?**
  (i) If yes, on what grounds?
  (ii) If no, has he/she made this clear in the proposed publication—and if not believed to be true, why publish it?
(d) **What has journalist, etc, done to check information?**
(e) **Has journalist contacted the subject of any proposed article for his/her comment before publication?**
  (i) If yes, with what result?
  (ii) If not, why not?
(f) **Claimant's point of view:** Does the material proposed to be published give the gist of the story from the claimant's point of view?

6. Tone: What is the tone of the proposed publication?

(a) How the material is **to be treated** by the publisher has a bearing on responsible journalism.
(b) A newspaper can raise queries or call for an investigation. It **need not adopt** allegations as statements of fact.

7. Timing:

(a) **Circumstances:** The circumstances of the publication including the timing.

(b) **Urgency:** Is there any urgency in publishing? If yes, what? (Ice cube effect?)

8. Summary: Is the publication '*responsible*'? If the journalist has more to add than the issues raised above, state them here.

Part 12

HARASSMENT AND THE MEDIA

A. Protection from Harassment Act 1997

1997 CHAPTER 40

An Act to make provision for protecting persons from harassment and similar conduct

[21st March 1997]

Be it enacted by the Queen's most Excellent Majesty, by and with the advice and consent of the Lords Spiritual and Temporal, and Commons, in this present Parliament assembled, and by the authority of the same, as follows:—

England and Wales

1. Prohibition of harassment.

(1) A person must not pursue a course of conduct—

(a) which amounts to harassment of another, and

(b) which he knows or ought to know amounts to harassment of the other.

(2) For the purposes of this section, the person whose course of conduct is in question ought to know that it amounts to harassment of another if a reasonable person in possession of the same information would think the course of conduct amounted to harassment of the other.

(3) Subsection (1) does not apply to a course of conduct if the person who pursued it show's—

(a) that it was pursued for the purpose of preventing or detecting crime,

(b) that it was pursued under any enactment or rule of law or to comply with any condition or requirement imposed by any person under any enactment, or

(c) that in the particular circumstances the pursuit of the course of conduct was reasonable.

2. Offence of harassment.

(1) A person who pursues a course of conduct in breach of section 1 is guilty of an offence.

(2) A person guilty of an offence under this section is liable on summary conviction to imprisonment for a term not exceeding six months, or a fine not exceeding level 5 on the standard scale, or both.

3. Civil remedy.

(1) An actual or apprehended breach of section 1 may be the subject of a claim in civil proceedings by the person who is or may be the victim of the course of conduct in question.

(2) On such a claim, damages may be awarded for (among other things) any anxiety caused by the harassment and any financial loss resulting from the harassment.

(3) Where—

(a) in such proceedings the High Court or a county court grants an injunction for the purpose of restraining the defendant from pursuing any conduct which amounts to harassment, and

(b) the plaintiff considers that the defendant has done anything which he is prohibited from doing by the injunction, the plaintiff may apply for the issue of a warrant for the arrest of the defendant.

(4) An application under subsection (3) may be made—

(a) where the injunction was granted by the High Court, to a judge of that court, and

(b) where the injunction was granted by a county court, to a judge or district judge of that or any other county court.

(5) The judge or district judge to whom an application under subsection (3) is made may only issue a warrant if—

(a) the application is substantiated on oath, and

(b) the judge or district judge has reasonable grounds for believing that the defendant has done anything which he is prohibited from doing by the injunction.

(6) Where—

(a) the High Court or a county court grants an injunction for the purpose mentioned in subsection (3)(a), and(b)without reasonable excuse the defendant does anything which he is prohibited from doing by the injunction, he is guilty of an offence.

(7) Where a person is convicted of an offence under subsection (6) in respect of any conduct, that conduct is not punishable as a contempt of court.

(8) A person cannot be convicted of an offence under subsection (6) in respect of any conduct which has been punished as a contempt of court.

(9) A person guilty of an offence under subsection (6) is liable—

(a) on conviction on indictment, to imprisonment for a term not exceeding five years, or a fine, or both, or

(b) on summary conviction, to imprisonment for a term not exceeding six months, or a fine not exceeding the statutory maximum, or both.

4. Putting people in fear of violence.

(1) A person whose course of conduct causes another to fear, on at least two occasions, that violence will be used against him is guilty of an offence if he knows or ought to know that his course of conduct will cause the other so to fear on each of those occasions.

(2) For the purposes of this section, the person whose course of conduct is in question ought to know that it will cause another to fear that violence will be used against him on any occasion if a reasonable person in possession of the same information would think the course of conduct would cause the other so to fear on that occasion.

(3) It is a defence for a person charged with an offence under this section to show that—

(a) his course of conduct was pursued for the purpose of preventing or detecting crime,

(b) his course of conduct was pursued under any enactment or rule of law or to comply with any condition or requirement imposed by any person under any enactment, or

(c) the pursuit of his course of conduct was reasonable for the protection of himself or another or for the protection of his or another's property.

(4) A person guilty of an offence under this section is liable—

(a) on conviction on indictment, to imprisonment for a term not exceeding five years, or a fine, or both, or

(b) on summary conviction, to imprisonment for a term not exceeding six months, or a fine not exceeding the statutory maximum, or both.

(5) If on the trial on indictment of a person charged with an offence under this section the jury find him not guilty of the offence charged, they may find him guilty of an offence under section 2.

(6) The Crown Court has the same powers and duties in relation to a person who is by virtue of subsection (5) convicted before it of an offence under section 2 as a magistrates' court would have on convicting him of the offence.

5. Restraining orders.

(1) A court sentencing or otherwise dealing with a person ("the defendant") convicted of an offence under section 2 or 4 may (as well as sentencing him or dealing with him in any other way) make an order under this section.

(2) The order may, for the purpose of protecting the victim of the offence, or any other person mentioned in the order, from further conduct which—

(a) amounts to harassment, or

(b) will cause a fear of violence, prohibit the defendant from doing anything described in the order.

(3) The order may have effect for a specified period or until further order.

(4) The prosecutor, the defendant or any other person mentioned in the order may apply to the court which made the order for it to be varied or discharged by a further order.

(5) If without reasonable excuse the defendant does anything which he is prohibited from doing by an order under this section, he is guilty of an offence.

(6) A person guilty of an offence under this section is liable—

(a) on conviction on indictment, to imprisonment for a term not exceeding five years, or a fine, or both, or

(b) on summary conviction, to imprisonment for a term not exceeding six months, or a fine not exceeding the statutory maximum, or both.

6. Limitation.

In section 11 of the Limitation Act 1980 (special time limit for actions in respect of personal injuries), after subsection (1) there is inserted—

"(1A) This section does not apply to any action brought for damages under section 3 of the Protection from Harassment Act 1997."

7. Interpretation of this group of sections.

(1) This section applies for the interpretation of sections 1 to 5.

(2) References to harassing a person include alarming the person or causing the person distress.

(3) A "course of conduct" must involve conduct on at least two occasions.

(3A) A person's conduct on any occasion shall be taken, if aided, abetted, counselled or procured by another—

(a) to be conduct on that occasion of the other (as well as conduct of the person whose conduct it is); and

(b) to be conduct in relation to which the other's knowledge and purpose, and what he ought to have known, are the same as they were in relation to what was contemplated or reasonably foreseeable at the time of the aiding, abetting, counselling or procuring.

(4) "Conduct" includes speech.

. . .

B. Core summary of statutory provisions

(a) The statute creates two criminal offences (sections 2 and 4) and the right to bring a civil claim (section 3).
(b) There must be a '*course of conduct*' which involves conduct on at least two occasions; conduct can include speech.
(c) The course of conduct can be against an individual, or a group of individuals.
(d) Damages can include compensation for anxiety, and financial loss for harassment includes '*alarming the person to causing the person distress*'.
(e) A claim for an injunction can lie.
(f) Note the 'ought to know' provisions in section 1(2). See *R v C (Sean Peter)* [2001] EWCA Crim 1251 at **para 20** per Hughes J:

> We agree accordingly with the learned judge that except in so far as it requires the jury to consider the information actually in the possession of this defendant section 1(2) requires the jury to answer the question whether he ought to have known that what he was doing amounts to harassment by the objective test of what a reasonable person would think. Its words, we are satisfied, are abundantly clear.

(g) While the statute places the burden of proof on the defendant, that does not absolve the claimant from pleading facts which are capable of amounting to harassment.
(h) The conduct must be calculated, in an objective sense, to cause distress, conduct which the perpetrator knows or ought to know amounts to a harassment and conduct which a reasonable person would think amounted to harassment.

(i) **Summary:** See *Green v DB Group Services (UK) Ltd* [2006] EWHC 1898 (QB) at **para 14**:

> 14. Thus to constitute harassment within the meaning of the Act there must have been conduct:
>
> (a) occurring on at least two occasions
> (b) targeted at the claimant
> (c) calculated in an objective sense to cause distress and
> (d) which is objectively judged to be oppressive and unreasonable.

C. Case law

The central authorities vis-à-vis the media are:

(a) *Esther Thomas v News Group Newspapers Ltd and Simon Hughes* [2001] EWCA Civ 1233.
(d) *Jenifer Howlett v Terry Holding* [2006] EWHC 41 (QB).

D. Principles

(a) *Per Thomas*

(i) The issue in the case was whether it is arguable that the publications in question constituted '*harassment*' having regard to the effect that the respondent alleges they had upon her.
(ii) Statutory harassment is conduct targeted at an individual which is calculated to produce the consequences described in section 7 and which is oppressive and unreasonable. The practice of stalking is a prime example of such conduct.
(iii) Journalistic articles are not outside the ambit of the 1997 Act.
(iv) The 1997 Act applies to activities which go beyond stalking.
(v) Section 12 of the Human Rights Act 1998 emphasises the care which the court must take not to interfere with journalistic freedom unless satisfied that this is necessary. This is important in the context of publications by the media.
(vi) Section 7 of the 1997 Act does not purport to provide a comprehensive definition of harassment. Section 7 is dealing with that element of the offence which is constituted by the effect of the conduct rather than with the types of conduct that produce that effect.

(vii) When considering whether the conduct of the press in publishing articles is reasonable for the purposes of 1997 Act, the answer does not turn upon whether opinions expressed in the article are reasonably held. The question must be answered by reference to the right of the press to freedom of expression which has been so emphatically recognised by the jurisprudence both of Strasbourg and of this country.

(viii) In general, press criticism, even if robust, does not constitute unreasonable conduct and does not fall within the natural meaning of harassment.

(ix) Before press publications are capable of constituting harassment, they must be attended by some exceptional circumstance which justifies sanctions and the restriction on the freedom of expression that they involve. Such circumstances will be rare.

(x) The publication of press articles calculated to incite racial hatred of an individual provides an example of conduct which is capable of amounting to harassment under the 1997 Act.

(xi) The test requires the publisher to consider whether a proposed series of articles, which is likely to cause distress to an individual, will constitute an abuse of the freedom of press which the pressing social needs of a democratic society require should be curbed.

(b) *Howlett*

(i) The exercise of one's right of free speech can fall within the concept of harassment, provided the other necessary ingredients are present. For example, it would have to be classified as unreasonable and oppressive conduct.

(ii) Press publications, before being held capable of constituting harassment, would have to be attended by some exceptional circumstances which would justify sanctions and the restriction on the freedom of expression they involve.

(iii) Surveillance is capable of being harassment; see **para 19**:

> It is not his function to enforce the law as a vigilante. Still less is it his function to harass other citizens by having them watched or, reverting to the rather old fashioned word that was used in these situations in the past, to 'beset' people in their homes.

(iv) The statute does not set out to define harassment exhaustively but merely contains the proposition that it 'includes' certain matters. The relevant wording in section 7(2) of the Protection from Harassment Act 1997 is as follows:

> References to harassing a person include alarming the person or causing the person distress.

(v) Several acts of surveillance could be '*a course of conduct*' even if the victim was not aware of them:

> 23. . . . Just because she does not know, in any given instance, that surveillance is taking place, it does not make it any the less distressing for her.

(vi) The purpose of the proposed section 1(3)(a) is to prevent law enforcement agencies from being sued for harassment in circumstances where they were merely carrying out their duties of detection or crime prevention.

(vii) A private citizen before being able to avail himself of section 1(3)(a) would at least have to show that there was, objectively judged, some rational basis for the surveillance.

Esther Thomas v News Group Newspapers Ltd and Simon Hughes [2001] EWCA Civ 1233

1. LORD PHILLIPS, MR: This is an appeal from the judgment of His Honour Judge Cox sitting in Lambeth County Court on 7 March 2001. By that judgment he refused an application by the appellant to strike out the particulars of claim under Part 3 of the Civil Procedure Rules ("CPR"), or to give judgment in their favour under Part 24. The application turned on the meaning of "harassment" under the Protection from Harassment Act 1997 ("the 1997 Act"). Judge Cox recognised that this issue was one of general importance and gave permission to appeal. He directed that the appeal should be transferred to this court pursuant to CPR Part 52.14(1).
2. Under CPR 3.4(2) the court may strike out a particulars of claim where satisfied that it discloses no reasonable grounds for bringing the claim. Under CPR Part 24, the court may give summary judgment in favour of the defendant where satisfied that the claim has no real prospect of success and that there is no other compelling reason why the case should be disposed of at a trial.
3. The appellants contend that the judge should have found both tests satisfied in that the case pleaded by the respondent disclosed no cause of action and was bound to fail. In this case the appellants had taken out their

strike-out application before filing a defence. In such circumstances there is little to choose in practice between the two tests. The court proceeds on the assumption that the facts alleged by the claimants will be proved at the trial and considers whether, on that premise, the claim has any realistic prospect of success. If it does, it is permitted to proceed to trial; if it does not it is struck out unless there is some other compelling reason why the case should go to trial.

4. Before summarising the facts, it is helpful to set out the material provisions of the 1997 Act. These are as follows: . . .

. . .

The Facts

5. On 6 July 2000 the first respondents published in their newspaper "The Sun" an article written by the second respondent. It was headed "Beyond a Joke—Fury As Police Sarges Are Busted After Refugee Jest". The article read:

> "Two police sergeants have been demoted to constables over a 'private' remark about an asylum-seeker. Mark Pursey and John Saunders also face losing a total of more than £100,000 after their pay and pensions were cut.
>
> They were carpeted by bosses after a black clerk at their station complained about the way they treated a Somali woman trying to reach an asylum centre in Croydon, South London.
>
> The clerk claimed she overheard racist jokes about the Somali woman who was not in the room at the time.
>
> The clerk alleged Saunders, 42, said:
>
> 'She found her way 8,000 miles here from Somalia—surely she can find her way f***ing back'.
>
> But Saunders insisted he only said:
>
> 'She found her way here 8,000 miles from Somalia—surely she can find her way four miles to Croydon'.
>
> A fellow cop said last night: 'It was essentially light-hearted banter in private and the Somali never heard it. This is political correctness gone mad.'
>
> The incident happened last July at Bishopsgate in the City of London.
>
> The Somali—called Muna Ahmed—said she had been brought to England from France by a man who then robbed her and stole her passport.

She was given meals as cops arranged for her to get to Croydon and gave her money for fares - more than many UK forces would have done.

Pursey and two other officers were in an office away from the front desk discussing transport arrangements for the woman when Saunders arrived.

According to clerk Esther Thomas he then made his racist remark.

She told Pursey: 'If she was a blonde 6ft Australian you would have treated her differently'. Pursey replied: 'I'd have taken her out to dinner'. She hit back: 'You'd like to shoot us all'. Pursey said: 'I'd have you shot if you don't get on with your work'.

Esther Thomas reported the exchange to her bosses.

And last month the cops were found guilty of 'behaving in a derisive and racially discriminatory manner'.

Lose

Dad-of-two Pursey was also convicted of two procedural lapses.

The pair, who plan to appeal, were reduced to PCs and their annual salaries were slashed by £6,000 a piece. Their pensions will also be reduced.

Dad-of-two Saunders hoped to hold his rank for nine more years and will now lose £54,000.

Pursey planned to serve another six and will lose £36,000.

A woman cop was also found guilty and fined a maximum £7000 after saying of plans to help the Somali: 'Are we running a taxi service?' A fourth officer was cleared."

6. This article caused a number of readers to write to The Sun. Extracts from their letters were published in the edition of 12 July under the heading:

   "Don't punish cops over a joke made in private

   Beyond a Joke

   Fury as police sarges are busted after refugee jest

   The way we told it . . . our story about demoted officers

   The Big Issue."

7. The letters were introduced by the following comment:

> "You were furious over our story about two police sergeants demoted for racism after joking about a Somali woman who wanted help getting to an asylum centre.
>
> The crack—'She found her way here 8,000 miles from Somalia, surely she can find her way four miles to Croydon'—was overheard and reported by a clerk at their station in London. Here are some of your views."

8. I quote the more relevant extracts from the letters:

> "The treatment of these officers is diabolical. Had it been two black officers and a white asylum seeker it would have been dismissed as the trivial incident it was.
>
> Racism is an evil that must be stamped out but it won't be destroyed if it is promoted; and that is what these liberal-minded witch finders are doing by crying racism where it doesn't exist."
>
> "If the joke had been directed at a white person, no action would have been taken. If the politically correct brigade are saying that black people are less able to laugh at themselves than whites, then that in itself is racist."
>
> "Has the clerk who reported these two sergeants never witnessed the abuse police officers suffer in the course of their duties?Or is that all right for them to take? I'm disgusted at the treatment of these officers."
>
> "Is it any wonder that police morale is so low when two respectable police sergeants are about to lose £100,000 in wages and pensions because a clerk did not like a comment she overheard?
>
> By her actions, this woman has done harm to the working relationship between black and white people. While not condoning racism, sense must prevail."
>
> "Don't the police authorities realise they are only putting our backs up even more when they demote two sergeants for making a comment about a black refugee woman? If they had said it about a white person, nothing would have been done."

9. On 14 July a follow-up article was published in The Sun, again written by Simon Hughes, which included the following passage about the three officers who had been disciplined:

> "All three were hauled in front of a disciplinary tribunal after a black

civilian clerk complained about a series of exchanges at Bishopsgate last July."

10. The article went on to repeat part of what had appeared in the initial article.

11. The respondent's Statement of Case, based on these publications, reads as follows:

> "1. On Thursday 6 July the Sun Newspapers, owned and controlled by News Group International Ltd, published an article ('the article') written by Simon Hughes, which names the Claimant, Esther Thomas, and described her as a 'black clerk'. The article was entitled 'Beyond a Joke' and said that there was 'fury as police sarges are busted after refugee jest'. The police officers, both dads of two, were 'carpeted by bosses after a black clerk at their station complained about the treatment of a Somalia woman . . .'.
>
> 2. The article stated that the incident occurred at Bishopsgate police station.
>
> 3. The article amounted to harassment of the Claimant and caused her distress and anxiety.
>
> 4. The article was followed by a further article on 12 July in which it was stated that the newspaper's readers were 'furious' over the story. The newspaper received a lot of furious letters from its furious readers. Bishopsgate police station received race hate mail (three letters) addressed to Esther Thomas the same day.
>
> 5. Simon Hughes of The Sun wrote a third article on 14 July which was featured on the front page of the newspaper which stated that the police officers 'were hauled in front of a disciplinary tribunal after a black clerk complained of a series of exchanges . . .' The Sun stated that its readers could help one of the racist police officers by helping to pay off her disciplinary fine; to write a cheque to 'The Sun WPC Fine Fund NGN Ltd'.
>
> 6. The articles written by Mr Hughes, approved of by the Editor and published by the newspaper amount to a course of conduct which amounts to harassment of the Claimant. The article was written in an indignant tone which was designed to elicit a reaction.
>
> 7. The course of conduct caused the Claimant to be harassed by the Sun's readers. The course of conduct of itself amounted to harassment. The Claimant claims damages for breach of section 3 of the Protection from Harassment Act 1997.

8. The course of conduct was not reasonable. The Claimant did not have to be described as being black nor should her name and place of work be published. The facts stated in the articles were not accurate. In fact, the police officers were found guilty of race discrimination after both the Claimant and PC Bidmead, and others, gave evidence against the officers. The article incited racial hatred.

9. The articles caused the Claimant to be terrified and scared to go to work. She felt vulnerable to being physically attacked at work or en route to and from work. The Claimant has since transferred by her own choice to a new place of work."

12. The author of the Statement of Case is not stated. It was not, however, Mr Anthony Hudson, Junior counsel appearing before us.

The Appellants' case

13. Before Judge Cox the appellants argued that, as a matter of statutory interpretation, the meaning of "harassment" in the 1997 Act could not extend to a series of publications in a newspaper. In support of that submission they sought to rely on statements in Parliament when the Bill was being debated under the principle in *Pepper v Hart* [1993] AC 593. Judge Cox did not consider that that principle was engaged, for he did not find the provisions of the 1997 Act to be ambiguous. He rejected the appellants' argument of interpretation and dismissed their application.

14. Before this court, the appellants have abandoned their extreme argument on statutory interpretation. In his skeleton argument on their behalf, Mr Desmond Browne QC put their case as follows:

> "Whilst it is just possible to imagine circumstances in which newspaper articles could constitute a course of conduct amounting to harassment—in the same way that people can harass others by unwanted, unsolicited or vitriolic correspondence—such conduct would have to be extreme and be devoid of any true desire either to exercise freedom of speech or to fulfil the newspaper's responsibility to inform the public."

15. It follows that the appellants concede that publication of press articles is, in law, capable of amounting to harassment albeit in only very rare circumstances. This is an important concession, but I consider that it is a concession rightly made. **The suggestion that journalistic articles were implicitly outside the ambit of the 1997 Act was, in my view, unarguable**. In these circumstances, there can be no question of looking at Parliamentary material in order to resolve ambiguity of statutory interpretation. **The issue is whether it is arguable that the publications**

in question constituted "harassment" having regard to the effect that the respondent alleges they had upon her.

16. In this context, the appellants seek to place reliance on the "legislative intent" by reference to debates in Parliament and other material. I do not propose to embark upon an elaborate analysis of the extent to which these are admissible as an aid to interpretation. **I am prepared to proceed on the basis that the appellants are correct in their contention that the mischief which led to the legislation was the practice of stalking.** This much is common ground. Once it is conceded, however, that **the 1997 Act applies to activities which go beyond stalking**, the fact that the stalking was the principal mischief at which the Act was aimed, affords only limited assistance.

17. At the heart of the appellants' case **is the effect on the interpretation and application of the 1997 Act of the Human Rights Act 1998** ("the HRA") **and Article 10 of the European Convention on Human Rights** ("the Convention") which that Act incorporates into English domestic law.

18. Article 10 of the Convention provides:

. . .

19. Section 12(4) of the HRA provides . . .

. . .

20. The appellants have placed before the court a mass of jurisprudence, both from Strasbourg and this country, on the importance that has to be attached by the courts to freedom of expression and, more particularly, to freedom of the press. Over the last year this court has become extremely familiar with Strasbourg jurisprudence.

21. The **importance that the Strasbourg court attaches to freedom of expression** can be satisfactorily illustrated by this typical passage from the judgment of the court in *Nilsen and Johnsen v Norman* (1999) 30 EHRR 878 at paragraph 43:

> "According to the Court's well-established case law, freedom of expression constitutes one of the essential foundations of a democratic society and one of the basic conditions for its progress and for each individual's self-fulfilment. Subject to Article 10(2), it is applicable not only to 'information' of 'ideas' that are favourably received or regarded as inoffensive or as a matter of indifference, but also those that offend, shock or disturb. Such are the demands of that pluralism, tolerance and broadmindedness without which there is no 'democratic society'. As set forth in Article 10, this freedom is subject to exceptions which must, however, be construed strictly, and the need for any restrictions must be established convincingly.

The test of **'necessity in a democratic society'** requires the Court to determine whether the '**interference**' corresponded to a **'pressing social need'**, whether it was **proportionate** to the **legitimate aim** pursued and whether the reasons given by the national authorities to justify it are relevant and sufficient."

22. Strasbourg rightly considers that these principles are of particular importance where the freedom of the press is in play, as is apparent from the following passage, again typical, from the judgment of the Strasbourg court in *Observer and Guardian v United Kingdom* (1999) 14 EHRR 152 at paragraph 59:

"These principles are of particular importance as far as the press is concerned. Whilst it must not overstep the bounds set, inter alia, in the 'interests of national security' or for 'maintaining the authority of the judiciary,' it is nevertheless incumbent on it to impart information and ideas on matters of public interest. **Not only does the press have the task of imparting such information and ideas: the public also has a right to receive them**. Were it otherwise, the press would be unable to play its vital role of **'public watchdog'."**

23. Even before the HRA was enacted, English jurisprudence recognised that the principles set out above applied equally in our domestic law: *Attorney-General v Guardian Newspapers Ltd (No 2)* [1990] 1 AC 109, 283–4 per Lord Goff of Chieveley; *Derbyshire CC v Times Newspapers Ltd* [1993] AC 534 at 550–1 per Lord Keith of Kinkel. More recently Lord Steyn made these observations in *Reg v Home Secretary, Ex p Simms* [2000] AC 126:

"Freedom of expression is, of course, intrinsically important: it is valued for its own sake. But it is well recognised that it is also instrumentally important. It serves a number of broad objectives. **First**, it promotes the self-fulfilment of individuals in society. **Secondly**, in the famous words of Holmes J (echoing John Stuart Mill), 'the best test of truth is the power of the thought **to get itself accepted in the competition of the market**:' *Abrams v United States* (1919) 250 US, 616, 630 per Holmes J (dissenting).

Thirdly, freedom of speech is **the lifeblood of democracy**. The free flow of information and ideas informs political debate. It is a **safety valve**; people are more ready to accept decisions that go against **them if they can in principle seek to influence them**. It acts as a **brake on the abuse of power by public officials**. It facilitates the **exposure of errors in the governance and administration of justice** of the country."

24. Section 3 of the HRA requires the court, so far as it is possible to do so, to interpret and give effect to legislation in a manner which is compatible with Convention rights. Section 12 of the HRA **emphasises the care which the court must take not to interfere with journalistic freedom unless satisfied that this is necessary** according to the principles to which I have referred. Both these sections are important when considering the ambit of **the criminal offence and the civil tort of harassment created by the 1997 Act** in **the context of publications by the media.** Harassment **must not be given an interpretation which restricts the right of freedom of expression, save in so far as this is necessary in order to achieve a legitimate aim**. When considering that question, the court is required by section 2 of the HRA to have regard to the Strasbourg jurisprudence.

. . .

26. Both parties to this appeal recognise the importance of the right of freedom of expression and, in particular, press freedom. Both parties recognise that the duty to give effect to this right is an important consideration to any court when considering whether an offence or civil tort has been committed contrary to the 1997 Act.

. . .

The nature of harassment

29. **Section 7 of the 1997 Act does not purport to provide a comprehensive definition of harassment.** There are many actions that foreseeably alarm or cause a person distress that could not possibly be described as harassment. It seems to me that **section 7 is dealing with that element of the offence which is constituted by the effect of the conduct rather than with the types of conduct that produce that effect.**

30. **The Act does not attempt to define the type of conduct that is capable of constituting harassment. "Harassment"** is, however, a word which has a meaning which is generally understood. It **describes conduct targeted at an individual which is calculated to produce the consequences described in section 7 and which is oppressive and unreasonable. The practice of stalking is a prime example of such conduct.**

31. The fact that conduct that is reasonable will not constitute harassment is clear from section 1(3)(c) of the Act. **While that subsection places the burden of proof on the defendant, that does not absolve the claimant from pleading facts which are capable of amounting to harassment.** Unless the claimant's pleading alleges conduct by the defendant which is, at least, arguably unreasonable, it is unlikely to set out a viable plea of harassment.

The nature of reasonable conduct

32. Whether conduct is reasonable will depend upon the circumstances of the particular case. **When considering whether the conduct of the press in publishing articles is reasonable for the purposes of 1997 Act, the answer does not turn upon whether opinions expressed in the article are reasonably held.** The question must be answered **by reference to the right of the press to freedom of expression** which has been **so emphatically recognised** by the jurisprudence both of Strasbourg and this country.

33. Prior to the 1997 Act, the freedom with which the press could publish facts or opinions about individuals was circumscribed by the law of defamation. **Protection of reputation is a legitimate reason to restrict freedom of expression.** Subject to the law of defamation, the press was entitled to publish an article, or series of articles, about an individual, notwithstanding that it could be foreseen that such conduct was likely to cause distress to the subject of the article.

34. The 1997 Act has not rendered such conduct unlawful. **In general, press criticism, even if robust, does not constitute unreasonable conduct and does not fall within the natural meaning of harassment.** A pleading, which does no more than allege that the defendant newspaper has published a series of articles that have foreseeably caused distress to an individual, **will be susceptible to a strike-out on the ground that it discloses no arguable case of harassment.**

35. It is common ground between the parties to this appeal, and properly so, that **before press publications are capable of constituting harassment, they must be attended by some exceptional circumstance which justifies sanctions and the restriction on the freedom of expression that they involve**. It is also common ground that **such circumstances will be rare**.

. . .

37. It is not necessary for this court to rule on Mr Pannick's example, nor to attempt any categorisation of the types of abuse of freedom of the press which may amount to harassment. **That is because the parties are agreed that the publication of press articles calculated to incite racial hatred of an individual provides an example of conduct which is capable of amounting to harassment under the 1997 Act.** In so agreeing, Mr Browne recognises that the Convention right of freedom of expression does not extend to protect remarks directly against the Convention's underlying values (see *Jersild v Denmark* (1994) 19 EHRR paragraph 35 and *Lehideux and Isorni v France* (1998) 30 EHRR paragraph 53.

38. This agreement between the parties reduces the central issue in this case

to a relatively narrow one. **It is Mr Pannick QC's case for the respondent that she pleaded an arguable case that the series of publications in The Sun were intended to provoke hostility on the part of its readers against her on the grounds of her race.**

39. As to that, Mr Browne has taken two pleading points. The **first** is that paragraph 3 of the Statement of Case alleges that the article of 6 July amounted to harassment, whereas the 1997 Act prescribes a course of conduct that involves at least two incidents. The **second** is that there is no pleaded averment that the defendants knew, or ought to have known, that their conduct amounted to harassment. **Both these defects are capable of rectification by amendment without causing the appellant any prejudice** and they were not taken below or mentioned in the grounds of appeal. **They cannot affect the outcome of this appeal.**

40. The substantive argument advanced by Mr Browne is that the respondent's pleading does not raise even an arguable case of racism. **Before the judge the appellants conceded that the tone of their publication was strident, aggressive and inflammatory, but they denied that it was racist.** As to this, the judge held:

> "It seems to me that the colour of the Claimant's skin had no bearing whatever on the matters reported unless it was to be implied therefrom that it was because of her race that the Claimant had taken the action she did, action of which the Sun Newspaper profoundly disapproved."

41. **He held that the adjective "racist" was justified.** This court has to consider whether the judge's conclusion was wrong or, more precisely, whether his conclusion was one which was not fairly arguable.

42. Mr Pannick submitted that assuming, as we must, that the facts alleged in the Statement of Case are true, the pleading sets out an arguable case that the defendants' publications were racist. It is his case that the article suggested that the respondent complained of the police sergeants' comments because of her race, that, but for the fact that she was black, the police sergeants would not have been disciplined, and that both the complaint and the punishments imposed on the sergeants were unjustified.

43. The first point made by Mr Pannick in support of this submission is that the respondent was referred to as "black" both in the 6 July and 14 July articles. Mr Browne argued that the reference to the respondent's colour in the former article was legitimate because it was necessary, if her reported comment, "You would like to have us all shot", was to make sense to the readers. The 14 July article simply repeated much of the earlier article. Mr Pannick challenged this explanation, observing that in

the 6 July article the reference to the respondent's colour came at the beginning and her comment, "You would like to shoot us all", near the end of the article. Furthermore, the 14 July article did not repeat her comment, so that this explanation could not apply to it. **In my judgment, the judge's conclusion that the reference to the respondent's colour was gratuitous is at least arguable for the reasons advanced by Mr Pannick.**

44. The next point made by Mr Pannick is that, on the facts alleged in the Statement of Case, the articles gave a misleading impression that it was only because of the action of a black clerk that the sergeants were disciplined. The articles did not record that **a white police officer also gave evidence against the sergeants.**

45. Mr Browne submitted that no adverse inference could be drawn from this omission which did not have the effect of making the articles inaccurate. **I consider that it is at least arguable that the omission in question reflected an intention that the complaint criticised by The Sun should be seen to have been motivated by the fact that the respondent was black.**

46. Mr Pannick then drew attention to the fact that the respondent was named in the first article **and that the address of her place of work was published**. Mr Pannick suggested that this was an invasion of the respondent's right of privacy. Mr Browne challenged his assertion and it is not one upon which we need to rule. It is significant, however, that the Statement of Case alleges that a sequel to the publication of the respondent's name and address was that **she received hate mail and was too terrified to go to her work place**. I consider that it is **at least arguable that it was foreseeable that the publication would lead Sun readers to address hostile letters to the respondent causing her additional distress.**

47. Finally Mr Pannick turned to the letters published on 12 July. It was his case that it was arguable that the letters had been deliberately selected in order to emphasise the racist element in the story. Mr Browne argued that the Strasbourg jurisprudence showed that it was legitimate for the media to quote racist comments made by others. He suggested that this proposition received support from ***Jersild v Denmark*. In that case a Danish television documentary had included interviews with youths who had expressed highly offensive racist views. The makers of the programme had been fined for making racist statements under the Danish Penal Code. The Strasbourg court ruled that this had violated their right of freedom of expression**. An important part of the reasoning of the court was, however, that **the makers of the programme had disassociated themselves from the views expressed and that the purpose of compiling the programme was not racist.**

48. **The Sun did not disassociate itself from its readers' letters**. The opinions that these expressed **were in line with the tone of the article** that had provoked them. The letters were critical both of the complaint and of the punishment of the sergeants for allegedly racist remarks and, thus, inevitably, made comments about racism. However, none of the letters ostensibly suggested that the conduct of the respondent which was criticised was attributable to her race. **It seems to me that these letters add to the respondent's case that the appellants were pursuing a course of conduct which they could foresee was likely to cause her distress**, but do not, when taken in isolation, add to the respondent's case that this course of conduct was racist.

49. **When the three publications are considered together, however, and for the reason I have given, I am satisfied that the respondent has pleaded an arguable case that the appellants harassed her by publishing racist criticism of her which was foreseeably likely to stimulate a racist reaction on the part of their readers and cause her distress.**

50. Mr Browne argued that, if the test of whether a series of publications constitutes harassment is to turn on the question of whether the conduct of the publisher is reasonable, this test will lack the certainty that the Strasbourg court requires if it is to find that a restriction on freedom of expression is prescribed by law. **On my analysis, the test requires the publisher to consider whether a proposed series of articles, which is likely to cause distress to an individual, will constitute an abuse of the freedom of press which the pressing social needs of a democratic society require should be curbed**. This is a familiar test and not one which offends against Strasbourg's requirement of certainty.

51. For the reasons that I have given, I would dismiss the appeal.

52. LORD JUSTICE JONATHAN PARKER: I agree.

53. LORD MUSTILL: I also agree.

Jenifer Howlett v Terry Holding
[2006] EWHC 41 (QB)

The Hon Mr Justice Eady

1. On 14th December 2005 I granted an injunction against the Defendant **to restrain harassment** of the Claimant generally and in two particular respects. I now set out my reasons. This is the first occasion on which counsel were able to reassemble.

2. The evidence before me discloses **a clear and persistent campaign of**

harassment of the Claimant, Mrs Jenifer Howlett, which has been going on now intermittently for about four to five years. The Defendant has **been flying banners from his aircraft over the Castle Point area of Essex which are addressed to Mrs Howlett, or refer to her, in abusive and derogatory terms**. He has also **dropped leaflets** from time to time over the surrounding areas. This has undoubtedly caused her **anxiety and distress** and, what is more, because she never knows when she is likely to see another aircraft going past, she **is forced to live in a state of uncertainty and apprehension**.

3. Not surprisingly, it is contended by Mr McCormick on the Defendant's behalf that an injunction to restrain his client from flying banners with messages would constitute an infringement of his **right of free communication, as protected by Article 10 of the European Convention on Human Rights. There is no doubt that his rights are engaged. So too are the Claimant's rights to privacy and to the protection of her physical and psychological integrity under Article 8.**

4. The legal mechanism to which Mrs Howlett has on this occasion resorted is the Protection from Harassment Act 1997. It has already been held in *Thomas v News Group Newspapers Ltd* [2001] EWCA Civ 1233 that, in some circumstances, **the exercise of one's right of free speech can fall within the concept of harassment, provided the other necessary ingredients are present. For example, it would have to be classified as unreasonable and oppressive conduct.**

5. **It was explained by the Master of the Rolls in that case that press publications, before being held capable of constituting harassment, would have to be attended by some exceptional circumstances which would justify sanctions and the restriction on the freedom of expression they involve.** It was common ground in that case that **such circumstances would be rare**. It was also recognised that **the Convention right of freedom of expression does not extend to protecting remarks directly inconsistent with the Convention's underlying values**, and reference was made to *Jersild v Denmark* (1994) 19 EHRR at [35] and *Lehideux & Isorni v France* (1998) 30 EHRR at [53]. In *Thomas* itself, which was concerned only with whether a case of harassment was arguable, the respondent's case was permitted to go forward on the basis that the appellants were alleged to have harassed **her by publishing racist criticism of her which was foreseeably likely to stimulate a racist reaction on the part of The Sun's readers**. By contrast, in the present case, **what is objectionable in the exercise of Mr Holding's right of free expression is the impact it has had, and is likely to continue to have, on Mrs Howlett's privacy and psychological well-being**.

6. Predictably, it has been argued by Mr Holding that the Claimant's true complaint is that she has been libelled. No doubt she has. **The general message of his most recent publications is that she is in some unspecified way obtaining benefits to which she is not entitled.** But it is important to identify the true nature both of her complaint and of the conduct complained of. One of a number of unusual features in this case is **that the Claimant has already twice sued Mr Holding to judgment in defamation proceedings**, and **twice obtained the verdict and vindication of a jury** in respect of other allegations of dishonesty. Those cases were heard, respectively, in October 2003 and May 2005. It cannot be said of Mrs Howlett, for one moment, that she is afraid to sue for libel, that she lacks resolve, or that she is unwilling to face public cross-examination over whatever serious allegations Mr Holding chooses to make against her. **The outcome of the litigation has, however, not deterred Mr Holding from continuing with what is said to be a campaign against her.**
7. The second unusual feature of this litigation is that Mr Holding has been only too willing to reveal, and has done so in the witness-box in the second libel action last year, what it is that he hopes to achieve by his campaign of public vilification. **He seeks to cause Mrs Howlett "living hell" by way of retribution for her daring to speak out publicly in May 2000, in her then capacity as a councillor in Castle Point, on the subject of a planning application pending at that time by Mr Holding's company.** He expressed the hope that he had caused her "**hell**" because it was, in his rather sinister phrase, "**payback time**".
8. **The truth is that Mr Holding is a rich man who is prepared to use his wealth to victimise a woman of modest means**, who can only defend herself by resorting to the law (taking advantage of the relatively recent provisions governing conditional fee agreements). She has been fortunate to find lawyers to represent her and to attempt, as far as possible, to protect her interests. Even so, **Mr Holding is prepared to use his wealth to manipulate the system and to set her remedies at nought**. He made it clear, shortly after the first libel action, by the publication of abusive banners about the judicial system, that he thought nothing of the jury's verdict in that case.
9. **Mr Holding wants to use his Article 10 rights to go on inflicting damage on Mrs Howlett in a cruel and cynical way, while laughing up his sleeve at the processes available to her through the administration of justice.** He prefers to use his wealth to render such remedies ineffective. He is not prepared to accept a jury's verdict, and will seek by whatever means are available to him to extricate himself from the restrictions imposed by court orders.

10. It was held in the past, for example in *Crest Homes* v *Ascott* [1980] FSR 396, that in a libel context it would not be right to restrain by interim order publication of defamatory words - however offensively expressed and by whatever means - provided the relevant defendant indicated that it was genuinely his intention to justify his allegations. **That was an application of the rule in *Bonnard v Perryman* [1891] 2 Ch 269 in rather striking circumstances.** The Defendant had been driving his rather grand motor car around an estate recently developed by the claimant company, with his front door strapped to the top of the vehicle and rude remarks painted on it about the quality of its workmanship. The issues here are not that simple. **This is not an application for an interim order in a libel action. The proceedings are brought under CPR Part 8, as prescribed for harassment cases.**
11. It is now clear, at least since the House of Lords' decision in *Re S (FC) (A Child)* [2005] 1 AC 593, that it is not appropriate to accord automatic precedence to one Convention right over another. Once such rights are engaged, in any particular case, as they are here, then it is necessary to carry out what has been called "**the ultimate balancing exercise**" by bringing to bear "**an intense focus**" *upon the* circumstances of the individual case.
12. **As always, one must pay the closest regard to proportionality**. Mrs Howlett is not seeking to restrain Mr Holding from exercising his right of free speech, even to make derogatory allegations about her, for all purposes. If he has genuine concerns, even now, that Mrs Howlett may yet be breaking the law, he can go to the appropriate authorities and report those concerns. Indeed, he has already done so: he has been in communication with the Department of Work and Pensions. (He has declined, however, to reveal whatever response he has had.) Thus, as Miss Page QC for Mrs Howlett succinctly put it, "he has had his say".
13. **On the other hand, the anguish that Mrs Howlett has had to suffer at Mr Holding's hands over the last four years is out of all proportion to the value to be attached to the exercise of his right of free speech by the methods he has chosen.** It is no doubt desirable in a free society that, all things being equal, any individual citizen should be free to express whatever views and make whatever allegations he or she likes—subject to the usual constraints imposed, for example, by the law of **nuisance, libel, breach of confidence or contempt of court**. All things are not, however, equal. Mrs Howlett's right to lead a peaceful life and to enjoy her privacy are also to be protected.
14. When one applies the necessary "**intense focus**" to these circumstances, and one addresses the important issue of **proportionality**, there is in

my judgment only one answer. Mrs Howlett is entitled to call upon the protection of the law and to have Mr Holding's acts of **aerial harassment restrained by injunction.**

15. I should add that I expressed the view at a previous hearing, in the light of the evidence before me, that even if Mrs Howlett had claimed an interlocutory injunction on the basis of libel there was **insufficient material to warrant a plea of justification**. As I concluded, no responsible counsel could allege that Mrs Howlett was a benefit fraudster. It is not an allegation that can be advanced simply on the say-so of an obsessive client. Accordingly, on the facts of this case, *Bonnard v Perryman* would not avail Mr Holding.
16. Apart from questions of free speech, there is also the question of surveillance to be considered. **Mr Holding has revealed that he has had Mrs Howlett watched at various times and wishes to retain his right to do so, whatever anxiety and distress that may cause her.** It is another means by which he can twist the knife.
17. Various arguments have been raised by Mr Holding's legal team. It is, of course, by no means uncommon in the course of personal injury or clinical negligence litigation for defendants and their insurers to arrange for photographs or video recordings to be made of claimants purporting to have suffered certain consequences in terms of (say) pain and suffering, or loss of earnings, in order to test their veracity.
18. Reference was made to *Jones* v *University of Warwick* [2003] 1 WLR 954. There the court balanced various competing considerations, one of which was that in litigation it is generally desirable that the truth should be revealed. To take such steps in that context in order to protect oneself, if reasonably proportionate, is no doubt legitimate. Here there was no on-going litigation in which Mr Holding was seeking to protect himself. He wanted to expose Mrs Howlett, if at all possible, as a benefits cheat. His excuse was that he was anticipating that she *might* sue him for libel, and that the evidence *might* come in useful in that event. To put it more bluntly, he was goading her into having to launch a third set of libel proceedings. Effectively, therefore, unlike in the *Jones* case, **he was using the surveillance as a weapon of attack rather than by way of defending his own interests.**
19. He knows, however, because he has seen the medical evidence adduced in the libel litigation that **Mrs Howlett suffers from a degenerative disorder of the spine**. He has no medical evidence himself to contradict that. He is nevertheless determined to deprive her, if he can, of the benefits which she has been receiving in respect of her disability**. He suggests that the video material he has obtained casts doubt on whether she is as**

adversely affected as she claims. What is done cannot be undone. He may show his video footage to the relevant authorities if he wishes to do so. **But the surveillance must now cease**. He is an ordinary citizen, albeit a wealthy one; **it is not his function to enforce the law as a vigilante. Still less is it his function to harass other citizens by having them watched or, reverting to the rather old fashioned word that was used in these situations in the past, to "beset" people in their homes.** That is unacceptable and the true reason is that he simply wishes to cause Mrs Howlett a "living hell". He should not be permitted to do so.

20. Mr McCormick has raised other points in relation to surveillance. There is no doubt that Mrs Howlett has been distressed by discovering that she had been watched, and she is still anxious that she may at any moment be placed under surveillance as she goes about her daily life. It is said that there has been no surveillance since last September, but Mr Holding wishes to reserve the right to have her watched whenever he wishes in the future. The fact that she is aware that it might take place does not, however, necessarily mean that, if and when it does occur, she will find it distressing. If it is carried out efficiently, and in accordance with Mr Holding's intentions, she should not become aware of it. Moreover, applying the test in the statute, it is said for the same reason that there is no reason why Mr Holding should know, or ought to know, that secret surveillance would amount to harassment: see s 1(1)(b).

21. This gives rise to a potentially very sinister scenario. One citizen is aware that another wishes to keep her and her home under surveillance, whenever he feels like it. It seems counter-intuitive that the court should be able to do nothing to allay her concerns.

22. **It is to be noted that the statute does not set out to define harassment exhaustively but merely contains the proposition that it "includes" certain matters. The relevant wording in s 7(2) is as follows:**

> "References to harassing a person include alarming the person or causing the person distress."

This provision has encouraged Mr Holding to argue that he is, in effect, entitled to have Mrs Howlett and her house watched as often as the whim takes him, and to have her followed in the street, and into shops and restaurants, provided any individual act of surveillance does not involve alarming Mrs Howlett or causing her distress. Meanwhile, he can derive satisfaction from her suffering the anxiety and uncertainty of not knowing when "big brother" will strike. There can be little doubt that such behaviour would constitute a "course of conduct" for the purposes of s 1(1) of the statute. **I put to Mr McCormick in the course of argument the hypothesis that a victim of surveillance had been watched on six occasions but only**

realised what was happening on the seventh when he was caused alarm. On his case, there would be no "course of conduct" because there had been no alarm or distress on the previous occasions. Moreover, if the surveillance continued six more times, without the victim spotting it, those occasions would also have to be left out of account. I regard this as an artificial approach.

23. I am not persuaded that the source of Mrs Howlett's anxiety is, in this respect, beyond the protection of the law. To keep someone on tenterhooks, knowing that she is likely to be watched as she goes about her daily life, seems to me remarkably cruel. **Just because she does not know, in any given instance, that surveillance is taking place, it does not make it any the less distressing for her.** What causes the distress is the awareness that secret surveillance is taking place, or is likely to take place at any moment. I see no reason why that form of besetting should fall outside either the spirit or the letter of the Act.

24. Also, I need to bear in mind that what Mr Holding has done, and what he proposes to do, by way of surveillance comes close to the concept of "**stalking**" which, as it happens, is the very mischief to which the 1997 statute was primarily directed: see eg *Thomas v News Group Newspapers Ltd* at [16] and [30]. Also, as Miss Page has pointed out, **it would be artificial to address the aerial harassment and the surveillance as though they belonged in separate compartments**. In reality, they are each part of the continuing campaign (or "course of conduct") of giving her "hell".

25. It is necessary now for the court to have regard to the principles applied by the European Court of Human Rights in the recent case of *Von Hannover v Germany* (2005) 40 EHRR 1. The case illustrates how wide is the notion of "private life" which the court at Strasbourg is now prepared to recognise. **Princess Caroline of Monaco was described in the domestic courts in Germany as a figure of contemporary society par excellence but, even so, it was held in Strasbourg that such a classification was not sufficient to justify constant intrusion into her private life by paparazzi. Thus her privacy was entitled to at least a degree of protection even in public places.**

26. The notion of privacy was considered by the court, and especially at [50], where it was said that it included a person's physical and psychological integrity. The guarantee afforded by Article 8 of the Convention was primarily intended to ensure the development, without outside interference, of the personality of each individual in his or her relations with other human beings. **A zone of interaction was recognised of one person with others, even in a public context, which would fall within the scope of "private life". In the light of this case, and indeed others such as *P G & J H v***

***United Kingdom* (Application 44787/98) and *Peck v United Kingdom* (2003) 26 EHRR 41, it may safely now be said that it is not possible for those who wish to intrude upon the lives of individuals through surveillance, and associated photography, to rely upon a rigid distinction being drawn in their favour between what takes place in private and activities capable of being witnessed in a public place by other people.**

27. Miss Page submits that against the background of Article 8 the court is obliged to ensure that there are adequate safeguards, when construing a statute such as the Protection from Harassment Act, to protect rights of privacy and, in particular, to ensure that any encroachments expressly permitted should themselves be compliant with the Convention; that is to say, they must be necessary and proportionate to the legitimate objective pursued. Those can be identified from Article 8(2). She suggests

> **that I should construe any "defences" under the 1997 Act so as to be compatible with the exceptions recognised by Article 8(2).**

28. I should start by considering the terms of Article 8 itself:

> 1. Everyone has the right to respect for his private and family life, his home and his correspondence.
>
> 2. There shall be no interference by a public authority with the exercise of this right except such as is in accordance with the law and is necessary in a democratic society in the interests of national security, public safety or the economic well-being of the country, for the prevention of disorder or crime, for the protection of health or morals, or for the protection of the rights and freedoms of others.

29. I need, therefore, next to consider to what extent the exceptions or "defences" laid down in the 1997 Act marry up with the public policy considerations identified in Article 8(2). The relevant provisions are to be found in s 1(3):

> "Subsection (1) does not apply to a course of conduct if the person who pursued it shows—
>
> (a) that it was pursued for the purpose of preventing or detecting crime,
>
> (b) that it was pursued under any enactment or rule of law or to comply with any condition or requirement imposed by any person under any enactment, or
>
> (c) that in the particular circumstances the pursuit of the course of conduct was reasonable".

Mr McCormick placed reliance both upon (a) and (c).

30. There was a significant divergence between counsel as to the true extent of s 1(3)(a). Miss Page suggests that the section is directed only at preventing the ordinary law enforcement agencies from being sued for harassment in the carrying out of their regular duties. Mr McCormick, on the other hand, says no such restriction is to be found in the statute and, since in this respect the statutory words are not ambiguous, there is no warrant for resorting to Parliamentary debates or ministerial statements as an aid to interpretation in accordance with the principles in *Pepper v Hart* [1993] AC 593. The parties thus differed as to whether the words were ambiguous.

31. Miss Page invited me to look at *Hansard* by way of supporting her general submission but, in the alternative, argued that as a matter of construction it simply cannot be right that the relevant provision is intended to enable any Tom, Dick or Harry to set himself up as a vigilante and harass his neighbours under the guise of "preventing or detecting crime". That may be a rather contentious way of putting it, but I think the point is a fair one.

32. Going back to the words of Article 8(2), one sees that the emphasis is upon any interference with the right under Article 8(1) "by a public authority" being permitted only if it is "necessary... for the prevention of disorder or crime". In so far as there is a lack of clarity as to the scope of s 1(3)(a), **I would have no difficulty in concluding that it is not necessary to permit anyone to harass his fellow citizens by surveillance. It may well be necessary to leave room for security or law enforcement agencies to have such a power in appropriate circumstances, but that is a different matter.**

33. Furthermore I consider that, in view of the very differing interpretations put forward by counsel, it is legitimate and helpful to look at *Hansard.* **The purpose of the proposed s 1(3)(a) was explained clearly by the then Home Secretary as being to prevent law enforcement agencies from being sued for harassment in circumstances where they were merely carrying out their duties of detection or crime prevention.** What he said on 17th December 1996 was this:

> **". . . It will be a defence to show that the conduct was pursued for the prevention and detection of crime, or under an enactment or rule of law. Because of the nature of the activities pursued by stalkers, unless special provision is made, some police activities could be caught by the Bill. That, of course, is not our intention.** I am also aware that the activities of journalists, salesmen, religious activists, debt collectors, private investigators and even political canvassers might fall within the scope of the Bill. **We have therefore provided a**

defence of acting reasonably in the particular circumstances of the case in order to safeguard these legitimate activities."

It would thus appear that (a) was indeed framed with law enforcement agencies in mind and that (c) was directed towards others carrying out the miscellaneous functions described. Even if that is too rigid a construction, **a private citizen before being able to avail himself of (a) would at least have to show that there was, objectively judged, some rational basis for the surveillance.** Here there was none. It was merely carried out in the *hope* that something unlawful might be exposed. I respectfully agree with Tugendhat J's conclusion in *KD v Chief Constable of Hampshire* [2005] EWHC 2550 (QB) at [144] that an objective test must be applied.

34. Miss Page raised a further argument based on the requirement that any encroachment on a citizen's privacy rights contemplated in Article 8(2) would have to be "**in accordance with the law**". Thus it is necessary to consider whether there were any legal constraints restricting surveillance outside the specific context of the 1997 Act. She drew my attention to Part II of the **Regulation of Investigatory Powers Act 2000**, and submitted that any surveillance, even by the law enforcement agencies, would have to be authorised in writing. Obviously Mr Holding could not point to any such authorisation, and he could hardly be in a stronger position by virtue of his amateur status. **That is an attractive argument but, although I have found it persuasive, it is not essential to my determination of how s 1(3)(a) bears upon this case.**

35. As for s 1(3)(c), **I have already expressed the view that there was no rational basis for the surveillance of Mrs Howlett.** That is a proposition closely linked to whether or not Mr Holding's pursuit of that course of conduct was "reasonable". I am prepared to accept that the Home Secretary's list of occupations, given to the House of Commons in December 1996, was not intended to be exhaustive. Nor does it form part of the statutory wording. It is necessary, however, to remember that Parliament's objective was to prevent stalking and other forms of harassment and, accordingly, that arguments of "reasonableness" for the purpose of s 1(3)(c) need to be scrutinised carefully with that in mind. The terminology needs to be interpreted alongside the concepts of necessity and proportionality, as contemplated by Article 8(2). When invited to construe a course of conduct, which would otherwise qualify as harassment, as being "reasonable", the court will no doubt always guard against gullibility. **Here I see no reason at all why Mr Holding's behaviour should be classified as reasonable.**

36. Those are my grounds for granting the injunction now in force.

Model harassment order

The Defendants must not:

(a) Pursue or follow, 'doorstep' or otherwise harass the Claimant, whether by car, van, motorcycle, or by means of any other vehicle or other means howsoever; or
(b) Have the Claimant watched or in any other way have her under surveillance of any kind; or
(c) Approach within 100 metres of the curtilage of the Claimant's home at . . . . .; or
(d) In any way photograph or otherwise take pictures of the Claimant (whether in the course of 'doorstepping' or otherwise):
    (i) In any home in which she is living, or the home of any members of her family or friends where she is visiting or staying, or when she is in the garden or grounds of any such homes.
    (ii) In office blocks or buildings not open to the general public; or
    (iii) When she is entering or leaving her home, the home of any members of her family or friends, or when she is in the garden or grounds of the said homes;
    (iv) When she is being followed or pursued by photographers; or
    (v) Otherwise harass or intimidate the Claimant.

Checklist

1. What conduct is complained of?
2. Has it been persistent?
3. Is there a reasonable explanation for the conduct? If yes, set it out.
4. Is the order to prevent all photographs—or only those of paparazzi?
5. What effect is the conduct having on the Applicant?
6. What is the risk of the conduct continuing without a court order?

Part 13

DEROGATION FROM OPEN JUSTICE AND CLAIMS BY CHILDREN FOR APPROVAL OF LARGE PERSONAL INJURY AWARDS

1. Context: A Claimant minor recovers a large personal injury award and seeks anonymity vis-à-vis press reporting.

2. Issue: Should the court make an *anonymity order* in respect of the Claimant when *approving a compromise* by or behalf of a *protected* party?

3. *JXF v York Hospitals NHS Foundation Trust* [2010] EWHC 2800 (QB) per Tugendhat J: To ensure that C's identity was not disclosed, the relief sought (under CPR 39.2) was (see **para 3** of the judgment):

(a) That C be referred to only by the letters JFX;
(b) That any court documents to be disclosed to third parties had to be subject to appropriate adjustments.

4. Did Article 6 apply? Perhaps not—per Tugendhat J at **para 13**, on the basis that the proceedings may not have involved '*the determination of* [*a party's*] *civil rights and obligations*', this being an approval hearing.

5. Basis for jurisdiction in the *JXF* case: The court found jurisdiction to be based on Article 8, see **para 18**.

6. Issues in the case and how they were addressed:

(a) **Article 8 rights of 'A' engaged because:**
   (i) Sensitivity of the medical and financial information.
   (ii) He will be of full capacity when he reaches 18 for although the com-

pensation was very large, the disabilities were not in the catastrophic bracket.

(iii) He would be vulnerable to predators.

(b) **Article 10 rights of the press engaged:** A public hearing secures the following:

(i) Deters inappropriate behaviour on the part of the court.

(ii) Maintains the public's confidence.

(iii) Enables the public to know that justice is being conducted impartially.

(iv) Can result in evidence becoming available.

(v) Publicity can deter exaggerated claims.

7. Ruling: In favour of the relief sought, for the reasons explained in **paras 11** and **30**. (Note: An anonymity order was also made in *BJM v Eyre and Others* [2010] EWHC 2856 (QB) per Swift J.) For a further example of the exercise of this jurisdiction, see *A Child v Cambridge University Hospitals NHS Foundation Trust* [2011] EWHC 454 (QB), where in contrast to the *JXF* case, the primary application was for an order under the Children and Young Persons Act 1933.

Part 14

REPORTING RESTRICTION ORDERS IN THE FAMILY DIVISION

The recent case of *A Local Authority v A & F & A* [2011] EWHC 1764 (Fam), per Baker J provides a paradigm application of Article 8 and 10 jurisprudence in the specialist field of family law. It also provides an excellent working example of a Reporting Restriction Order in the context of a fully reasoned judgment.

The judgment is therefore set out below, together with the order. The editorial highlights are those of the book, not of the report itself.

IN THE HIGH COURT OF JUSTICE
FAMILY DIVISION

Before:

THE HONOURABLE MR JUSTICE BAKER
IN THE MATTER OF A (A MINOR)
AND IN THE MATTER OF THE CHILDREN ACT
AND
IN THE MATTER OF AN APPLICATION FOR A REPORTING RESTRICTION ORDER

Between:

A Local Authority	Applicant
and	
A mother	First Respondent
and	
F	Second Respondent
and	
A grandmother	Third Respondent

and

A (by her children's guardian) — Fourth Respondent

and

News Group Newspapers Ltd, Mirror Group Newspapers Ltd, Newsquest Ltd — Respondents to the application for a reporting restriction order

MR JUSTICE BAKER:

1. This is an application in care proceedings concerning a child, "A", born [a date] 2010 for a **reporting restriction order restraining publication of information concerning the family following the tragic deaths of A's two brothers.** The parties supporting the application **seek an order that would preclude, amongst other things, the naming of various members of the family, including not only A, but also adult family members, including the mother of all three children who has been arrested on suspicion of murdering the two boys.** The order sought is one that would apply contra mundum, **that is to say it would be of general effect and bind any person having notice of it.**
2. **The application is opposed in part by representatives of the media**. They accept that the name of the surviving child A should not be published, **but object to the order extending to cover the adult family members.**

BACKGROUND

3. The mother is a twenty-five-year-old woman with a very troubled background who has had extensive dealings with social services and a number of other agencies for most all her life. She has given birth to three children – B, born [a date] 2006, J, born [a date] 2008, and A, born [a date] 2010. B was conceived as a result of a very brief relationship and his father has had no further involvement with the family. J and A have the same father, F, who met the mother in a psychiatric unit. **Both the mother and F suffer ongoing long term psychiatric and psychological problems**. The mother has cognitive difficulties and a history of depression and self harm
4. It is the local authority's case that, throughout the lives of the children, the mother struggled to look after them. When he was about one year old, B was placed with his maternal grandmother under a residence order. Thereafter, he had regular contact with his mother, and after their births, his half-siblings, J and A. Because of the mother's long-term problems, social services were involved with the family from the outset. J and A

were placed on the child protection register in the category of neglect, and subsequently made the subject of child protection plans.

5. In the first few days of 2011, J was taken to hospital on two occasions but subsequently was discharged home. **Then, in the early hours of [a date] January 2011, he was taken to hospital by ambulance in a lifeless condition and pronounced dead shortly after arrival at hospital**. The mother was interviewed by police and a post-mortem examination carried out. A strategy meeting of professionals convened on [a date] January concluded that there were no grounds for carrying out any investigation under section 47 of the Children Act 1989 into the circumstances of J's death. A continued living with her mother, subject to the child protection plan, and the local authority continued to visit the family.

6. On [a date] April 2011, B, then aged four and a half, collapsed at his grandmother's home while his grandmother was out and he and A were being cared for by their mother. **He was taken to hospital but died three days later on [a date] April.** A preliminary post-mortem report stated that the cause of death was "undetermined pending further investigation". Extensive pathological investigations were commissioned from a number of specialists whose reports are expected in August 2011.

7. **Following B's death, the mother was arrested on suspicion of his murder.** She was interviewed under caution and released on police bail until [a date] August. After her release, she was detained in a psychiatric unit under section 136 of the Mental Health Act because of concern that she would harm herself.

8. On [a date] April, the Family Proceedings Court made an emergency protection order in respect of A, and the local authority placed her in the care of foster parents who live in the same town as the mother and maternal grandmother. The local authority started care proceedings which were transferred immediately to the county court and thence to the High Court. On [a date] April, HH Judge Marston, sitting as a judge of the Family Division, placed A under an interim care order and gave various directions, including joining the father and maternal grandmother as parties to the proceedings.

9. **The mother remained in a very disturbed state. When discharged from the psychiatric unit, she moved into in sheltered accommodation.** A psychological report dated 24 May discloses that**, in addition to her cognitive problems, she is suffering from a significant depressive disorder which "adversely affects her ability to interact with people, communicate with them, and answer probing or leading questions"**. The psychologist expressed the opinion that, in her condition, **she would be unable to manage questions posed by the media**, and would be likely to

make false statements as a result of being in a **highly suggestible state**. The psychologist described the mother as being in "a state of extreme grief" and expressed concerns that **prolonged pressure from the media may put her at risk of self harm.** He concludes: "I cannot stress strongly enough how vulnerable [the mother] is at the present time".

10. In early May, it became apparent that **the press were indeed interested in this case.** A reporter from **The Sun knocked on the maternal grandmother's door** wanting to ask questions about the death of the children. **The newspaper also contacted the police and social services seeking information**. On [a date] May, the police issued a press release stating that the police

    "can confirm that they are investigating the sudden death of two brothers . . . earlier this year. The two-year-old boy died in January, and his four year old brother died in April. Post- mortem examinations were carried out on both children and proved inconclusive. Police are currently awaiting the results of further tests to establish if their death should be treated as suspicious. A report has been submitted to HM Coroner. Following the deaths, police arrested a twenty-five-year old woman . . . on suspicion of murder. She has been questioned by detectives from the . . . constabulary's major crimes department and released on police bail until August [a date] while police carry out additional enquiries and await the results of further tests."

11. **The press interest also prompted the local authority to apply for a reporting restriction order**. In support of this application, the allocated social worker filed a **statement** saying inter alia **"that the publishing of any information which could identify A or her present or future placements, the fact of the care proceedings, or the detail contained within the care proceedings will be detrimental to A's welfare"**. The application was served on the media under the **CopyDirect service in accordance with the President's Direction and CAFCASS Practice Note dated [a date] March 2005.** On [a date] May, Her Honour Judge Sullivan QC, sitting as a judge of the High Court, made an order, paragraph 3 of which prohibited the publishing or broadcasting of (a) the name and address of A, her carers, any individual having day to day care of or medical responsibility of A, and any residential home or hospital or other establishment at which she was residing or being treated; (b) any picture of A, a carer or any such establishment, and, (c) **any other particulars or information relating to A. The order was, however, subject to the qualification that such publication was prohibited "IF BUT ONLY IF [it] is likely to lead to the identification of the child as being the child of [the mother or father]"**. It should be noted, therefore, the list of persons whose identification was

precluded did not at that stage include either the mother or the father or the maternal grandmother. The order also precluded any person from seeking information relating to the child from a list of named persons including the child herself, her foster carers, or any other carer. Again, that list did not include the mother, father or maternal grandmother. The order was subject to the proviso that it did not prevent the publication of information relating to a public court hearing, or information that was already in the public domain. **The order was expressed as lasting for seven days and was duly served on the media in accordance with the President's Direction and CAFCASS Practice Note.**

12. On [a date] May, the application was listed for further consideration before HH Judge Marston, also sitting as a judge of the High Court. On that occasion, the order was extended in the following ways.

    (1) The list of persons whose names and addresses were not to be published under paragraph 3 of the order was extended to include the A's mother, father, maternal grandmother, and maternal uncle.

    (2) The qualification on the publication of the names was amended so as to read as follows: "IF, BUT ONLY IF, such publication is likely to lead to the identification of the child as being the child of [the mother or father] and/or as a subject of care proceedings".

    (3) The list of people from whom the seeking of information relating to the child was prohibited was extended to include "any of the child's relatives."

    On [a date] May, The Sun published an article in its printed edition and on its web site under the heading "**Mum quizzed as two sons die in a month". The headline was inaccurate as the deaths were twelve weeks apart.** The report began: "Two vulnerable young brothers die within weeks of **after social workers 'ignored' warnings about them from neighbours, it is claimed**." The report continued by stating inter alia:

    (1) the mother's name and age;

    (2) the names of J and B;

    (3) the fact that they had died and that their deaths were "unexplained";

    (4) the fact that the mother was detained in a psychiatric unit;

    (5) an assertion that the children had been living in a state of neglect in the mother's care;

    (6) the maternal grandmother's name;

(7) an assertion that, after J's death, the mother had moved in with the maternal grandmother;

(8) the apparently erroneous assertion that B had sustained a head injury prior to being admitted to hospital;

(9) allegations by unnamed "sources" that the local authority had been informed about the family but have failed to take action – "nobody seemed to care. These children were let down by the system".

The article did not, however, name A or refer to her in any way.

14. Following the publication of this article, the mother's solicitor wrote to The Sun and **complained that publishing the mother's name would lead to the identification of A and that the order of 20th May had therefore been breached**. The newspaper denied that they had committed any breach of the order, but the story was duly removed from the newspaper's website.

15. **On the following morning, however, a local newspaper published a more extensive article, illustrated by photographs of the mother, J and B.** One of the photographs of J and B was allegedly taken from the maternal grandmother's Facebook page without her consent. The local paper reported, in addition to the material already published in The Sun,

    (1) the fact that the mother, who was named in the article, had been arrested on suspicion of killing her sons;

    (2) the address of the family flat where J had died;

    (3) the fact that J had been admitted to hospital in the days before his death;

    (4) the maternal grandmother's address at which B had died;

    (5) some details of the events around B's admission to hospital;

    (6) extensive comments from neighbours including further allegations about the state of neglect of the mother's home.

    Again, the report made no reference to A, although one of the photographs included part of a dress being worn by her.

16. Following this report, it is said that the press made further attempts to contact family members and attended at, and took photographs of, the mother's flat. **A new page was created on Facebook in the names of the deceased children containing negative and threatening comments directed towards the mother**.

17. Later that afternoon on 24th May, the mother's legal representatives returned to court before Judge Marston to seek an extension of the

injunction. **Short notice of their intention to seek an extension of the injunction was given to the CopyDirect media lawyer by telephone and a copy of an application form was sent by fax, although the full terms of the procedure laid down in the President's Directions and the CAFCASS Practice Note were not followed**. At the hearing, Judge Marston made the following amendments to the order.

(1) He deleted the "If but only if" qualification to paragraph 3 of the order prohibiting the naming of the individuals listed in that paragraph. The effect of this amendment was to prohibit the publication of the names of A, her parents, or maternal grandmother without qualification, save as mentioned below.

(2) He added a prohibition against the publication of the surname of the deceased children.

(3) He added a prohibition against the seeking of any information from the mother or father.

(4) He did not, however, amend paragraph 7 of the order which therefore continued to provide that nothing in the order would prevent the publication of information relating to the public court hearing, or information already in the public domain. The learned judge directed that the matter be listed before me (as the judge allocated to try the care proceedings) on 27th May.

18. **At that hearing before me on 27th May, representatives of the media attended seeking the reversal of the amendment to the order made by Judge Marston on 24th May**. It was clear that the hearing would involve consideration of extensive issues which could not be considered in the time available on that date. I therefore adjourned the matter to be heard on circuit on 21st and 22nd June. In the interim, I directed that the order of 24th May should continue. **It seemed clear to me, however, (and was accepted by representatives of the media) that the intention behind the order of 24th May had been to prevent any naming of the mother and father, and further that this aim was undermined by the retention of the public domain proviso in paragraph 7.** I therefore **deleted that proviso** in the interim in order to give effect what was the plain intention behind Judge Marston's order of 24th May, whilst indicating, that by doing so, **I was not giving any indication of the likely outcome of the contested hearing before me.**

19. Between 27th May and the full hearing before me on 21st June, the following further developments have taken place. **First**, the Facebook page containing allegedly negative and threatening comments directed

at the mother **has been taken down**. **Secondly**, a short psychiatric report has been filed given details of **the father's serious psychiatric condition**. **Thirdly,** a report had been filed by the team manager of the local learning disability team giving details of **recent incidents of self-harm committed by the mother**, each apparently requiring hospital treatment, and said to have been precipitated by the mother's "**distress around media intrusion**". The report described how, in her current sheltered accommodation, the mother requires additional one-to-one support fourteen and a half hours per day, plus waking night support. **Fourthly**, the local authority social worker reports in a statement filed for the hearing before me that, as a result of the press articles, contact visits between A and her mother and grandmother have been cancelled on four occasions, to ensure A's safety and privacy.

THE LAW

20. Since the implementation of the Human Rights Act 1998 passed by Parliament to incorporate the European Convention for the Protection of Human Rights and Fundamental Freedoms ("ECHR") into English law, the foundation of the jurisdiction to restrain publicity is now derived from ECHR. By section 6 of the Act, the court, as a public authority, is required to act in a way which is compatible with a right under ECHR, and by section 2(1) is obliged to take into account any relevant judgment of the European Court of Human Rights.

21. Applications for reporting restriction orders are determined by analysing and balancing the competing rights under ECHR. The approach was explained by the House of Lords in two cases, **Campbell v MGM Ltd** [2004] UKHL 22, [2004] 2 AC 457 and **Re S (A Child) (Identification: Restrictions of Publication)** [2004] UKHL 47, [2005] AC 593. Prior to the implementation of the 1998 Act, applications for orders restraining publicity in family cases had been made under the inherent jurisdiction – see the long line of cases beginning with *Re X (A Minor) (Wardship: Jurisdiction)* [1975] Fam 47 and culminating in *Re Z (A Minor) (Identification: Restrictions on Publications)* [1997] Fam 1. As explained in *Re S* (supra) by Lord Steyn at paragraph 23, the principles previously established under the inherent jurisdiction no longer apply, although the courts may in appropriate circumstances refer to the older cases to illustrate the way in which the competing rights under ECHR should be balanced.

22. Prior to the implementation of the Human Rights Act, the court's power to grant contra mundum injunctions of the type sought by the mother in this case was restricted to cases where the court was exercising its inherent jurisdiction in respect of children. Since the Act, however, as Eady J observed in **OBQ v BJM and CJM** [2011] EWHC 1059 (QB) at paragraph

18, *"the remedy is available, whenever necessary and appropriate, for the protection of Convention rights whether of children or adults"*. Initially it was thought that such orders could only be made in favour of an adult to protect interference with the right to life under article 3 or the prohibition of torture under article 3: see **Venables and Thompson v News Group Newspapers Ltd** [2001] Fam 430, the case concerning the murderers of Jamie Bulger. Following the decision of the European Court in **Bensaid v UK** (2001) 33 EHRR 10, in which it was recognised that *"the preservation of mental stability is . . . an indispensable precondition to effective enjoyment of the right to respect for private life"*, contra mundum injunctions have been granted, on the basis of evidence risk to mental health, **to protect an adult's rights under article 8**: see *X (formerly Bell) v O'Brien* [2003] EWHC 1101 (QB) **and Carr v News Group Newspapers Ltd** [2005] EWHC 971 (QB).

23. **The first step is therefore to identify the ECHR rights engaged. Normally, the only rights engaged will be articles 8 and 10.**

24. **Under article 8:**

> "(1) Everyone has the right to respect for his private and family life, his home and correspondence.
>
> (i2) There shall be no interference by a public authority with the exercise of this right except such as is in accordance with the law and is necessary in a democratic society in the interests of national security, public safety or the economic well-being of the country, the prevention of disorder or crime, for the protection of health or morals, or for the protection of the rights and freedoms of others."

25. **Under article 10:**

> "(1) Everyone has the right to freedom of expression. This right shall include freedom to hold opinions and to receive and impart information and ideas without interference by public authority ....
>
> (2) The exercise of these freedoms, since it carries with it duties and responsibilities, may be subject to such formalities, conditions, restrictions or penalties as are prescribed by law and are necessary in a democratic society, in the interests of national security, for the prevention of disorder or crime, for the protection of health or morals, for the protection of the reputation or rights of others or for preventing the disclosure of information received in confidence."

26. **Occasionally, as in this case, a party will assert that article 6 is engaged. Under article 6(1),**

> "in the determination of his civil rights and obligations . . . everyone is entitled to a fair and public hearing. . . . Judgment shall be pronounced publicly but the press and public may be excluded from all or part of the trial . . . where the interests of juveniles or the protection of the private life of the parties so require, or to the extent strictly necessary in the opinion of the court in special circumstances where publicity would prejudice the interests of justice."

27. Amongst the "**rights and freedoms of others**" which it may be necessary to protect by interfering with the article 8 rights are **the rights of the media to receive and report information.** Equally, amongst the "rights of others" which it may be necessary to protect by restricting the exercise of the article 10 freedom are **the rights of individuals to respect for their private and family life**. Thus, in most cases the two rights are likely to be in direct competition, and the court has to conduct a balancing exercise in each case to determine which right should prevail.

28. When conducting the balancing exercise between articles 8 and 10 of ECHR, the court applies the four well-known propositions identified by Lord Steyn in paragraph 17 of his judgment in Re S (supra) as emerging from the opinions of the House of Lords in the earlier case of Campbell v MGN Ltd (supra):

> "**First,** neither article has as such precedent of the other. **Secondly,** where the values under the two articles are in conflict, an *intense focus* on the comparative importance of the specific rights being claimed in the individual case is necessary. **Thirdly,** the justifications for interfering with or restricting each right must be taken into account. **Finally,** the proportionality test must be applied to each. For convenience I will call this the ultimate balancing test."

29. The House of Lords decisions in the **Campbell** case and in **Re S** emphasise that the terms of ECHR and the 1998 Act should not be read as giving presumptive priority to article 10. In **A Local Authority v W, L, W, T and R** [2005] EWHC 1564 (Fam), [2006] 1 FLR 1, Sir Mark Potter at Paragraph 53 summarised the approach as follows:

> "The exercise to be performed is one of parallel analysis in which the starting point is presumptive parity in that neither article has precedence over or "trumps" the other. The exercise of parallel analysis requires the courts to examine the justification of interfering with each right and **the issue of proportionality is to be considered in respect of each**. It is not a mechanical exercise to be decided upon the basis of rival generalities. An intense focus on the comparative importance of the specific rights being claimed in the individual

case is necessary before the ultimate balancing test in terms of proportionality is carried out. **Having so stated, Lord Steyn strongly emphasised the interest in open justice as a factor to be accorded great weight in both the parallel analysis and the ultimate balancing test . . ."**

30. In considering article 8, the court bears in mind, as explained by Tugenhat J in **Goodwin v NGN Ltd and VBN** [2011] EWHC 1437 (QB) at paragraph 85, that the right to respect for private and family life involves more than one concept, and that the right to privacy comprises **two core components** characterised in one academic authority (Law of Privacy and the Media, 2nd edition, 2011, Warby, Moreham and Christie) as "**unwanted access to private information and unwanted access to [or intrusion into] one's** . . . **personal space**" and labelled more succinctly by Tugenhat J as "**confidentiality**" and "**intrusion**". Manifestly, the intrusive component of the right includes unwanted interference into the life of the family as well as the private life of the individual.

31. When considering article 10, the court must have regard in particular to the provisions of **section 12 of the 1998 Act**, headed "Freedom of Expression":

> "(1) This section applies if a court is considering whether to grant relief which, if granted, might affect the exercise of the Convention right to freedom of expression.
>
> (2) If the person against whom the application for relief is made ('the respondent') is neither present nor represented, no such relief is to be granted unless the court is satisfied (a) that the applicant has taken all practicable steps to notify the respondent; or (b) there are compelling reasons why the respondent should not be notified.
>
> (3) No such relief is to be granted so as to restrain publication before trial unless the court is satisfied that the applicant is likely to establish that publication should not be allowed.
>
> (4) The court must have particular regard to the importance of the Convention right to freedom of expression and, where the proceedings relate to material which the respondent claims, or which appear to the court, to be journalistic, literary or artistic material (or to conduct connected with such material) to (a) the extent to which (i) the material has, or is about to, become available to the public, or (ii) it is, or would be, in the public interest for the material to be published, [and] (b) any relevant privacy code."

32. The **Press Complaints Commission Editors' Code of Practice** is a "**relevant**

privacy code" within the meaning of section 12(4)(b). Clause 1 of the Code, headed "Accuracy", provides inter alia:

> "(i) The press must take care not to publish inaccurate, misleading or distorted information . . ."

Clause 3, headed "Privacy" states:

> "(i) Everyone is entitled to respect for his or her private and family life, home, health and correspondence, including digital communications.
>
> (ii) Editors will be expected to justify intrusions into any individual's private life without consent ...."

Clause 5 is headed "Intrusion into grief and shock" and provides inter alia:

> "(i) In cases involving personal grief or shock, enquiries and approaches must be made with sympathy and discretion, and publication handled sensitively. This should not restrict the right to report legal proceedings such as inquests."

The section headed "The Public Interest" provides inter alia:

> "There may be exceptions to the clauses marked * [which includes the clause headed "Privacy" quoted above] where they can be demonstrated to be in the public interest.
>
> 1. The public interest includes, but is not confined to,
>
> (i) Detecting or exposing crime or serious impropriety
>
> (ii) Protecting public health and safety.
>
> (iii) Preventing the public from being misled by an action or statement of an individual or organisation.
>
> 2. There is a public interest in the freedom of expression itself.
>
> 3. Whenever the public interest is invoked, the PCC will require editors to demonstrate fully that they reasonably believed that publication, or journalistic activity undertaken with a view to publication, would be in the public interest.
>
> 4. The PCC will consider the extent to which material is already in the public domain, or will become so.
>
> 5. In cases involving children under 16, editors must demonstrate an exceptional public interest to override the normally paramount interests of the child."

33. Section 12(4)(a)(ii) reiterates the principle that, amongst the matters to be taken into account when determining where the balance lies in each case, is **the extent to which the information is already in the public domain**. This principle pre-dates the Human Rights Act. As Lord Goff of Chievely observed in *A-G v Guardian Newspapers (No 2)* [1990] 1 AC 109,

> "once [information] has entered what is usually called the public domain (which means no more than the information in question is so generally accessible that, in all the circumstances, it cannot be regarded as confidential) then, as a general rule, the principle of confidentiality can have no application to it."

One judge has likened **confidential information** to an **ice cube** so that, once melted, there is no effective remedy. In another colourful metaphor, Eady J in *Mosley v NGN Ltd* [2008] EWHC 687 (QB), warned (at paragraph 34) that the court "**should guard against slipping into playing the role of King Canute**". In recent times, however, the principle has undergone considerable refinement, for two reasons.

34. First, the concept of the public domain has changed as a result of the revolution in information technology, as acknowledged by Munby J (as he then was) in *F v Newsquest Ltd and others* [2004] EWHC 762 (Fam) [2004] EMLR 29 at paragraph 66:

> "There is, I think, considerable force in the point made by Mr Baker that, with the advent of the internet, and in a world where there is an almost infinite quantity of accessible information, **it is impossible to see the public domain as something which has clear boundaries.** As he says, although some information will be manifestly well-known so that re-publication will have comparatively little effect, **other information may be obscure so that re-publication could have a very significant effect.** As he also says, whereas some information, once in the public domain, will stay there permanently, **other information may in reality disappear from the public domain after time**, in the sense that although it remains in a cuttings file or a database it never or hardly ever sees the light of day."

35. It is sobering to recall that the judgment in **F v Newsquest** was delivered in April 2004 at the very moment when Facebook, launched only a few weeks earlier at Harvard, was starting to sweep through the campuses of America**. In the subsequent seven years, with the growth of Youtube and Twitter, the internet has had an even greater effect than was anticipated**. The range of information available to the public is infinitely greater than twenty years ago, but manifestly it does not follow that all that information can be described as being in the general public

consciousness. One consequence is that a court has to scrutinise an assertion that information is in the public domain even more carefully.

36. **Secondly,** it has been recognised that the application of the principle depends on which of the core components of article 8 – **confidentiality or intrusion** – is engaged. In most cases, once **confidential information** has been published to an extent that it has become generally accessible, **it will lose its essential quality of confidentiality and there will be nothing that the court can do to undo what has been done**. On the other hand, as Tugenhat J. explained in **JIH v News Group Newspapers Ltd** [2010] EWHC 2818 (QB) at paragraph 59, where the complaint is one of press intrusion, "**even when that information is not secret or unknown . . . the repetition of known facts about an individual may amount to unjustified interference with the private lives not only of that person but also of those who are involved with him**".

37. As Tugenhat J further observed in *CTB v News Group Newspapers Ltd and Thomas* [2011] EWHC 1326 (QB) at paragraphs 23 and 24, the fact that the modern law of privacy is concerned not only with confidential information but also with intrusion is

> "one reason why it can be **important to distinguish** between the was [*sic*] the law approaches **public domain arguments** in relation to **commercial or state secrets**, for example**, and that which is appropriate to personal information**. It also largely explains why **it is the case that the truth of falsity of the allegations in question can often be irrelevant**: see eg *McKennitt v Ash* [2008] QB 73 .... It is fairly obvious that **wall-to-wall excoriation in national newspapers** ... is likely to be significantly more intrusive and distressing for those concerned **than the availability of information on the internet or in foreign journals to those, however many, who take the trouble to look it up**. Moreover, with each exposure of personal information or allegations, whether by way of visual images or verbally, **there is a new intrusion and occasion for distress or embarrassment** .... For so long as the court is in a position to prevent some of that intrusion and distress, depending on individual circumstances, it may be appropriate to maintain that degree of protection. **The analogy with King Canute to some extent, therefore, breaks down**."

38. Further, when considering, as required by section 12(4)(a)(ii), the extent to which it is in the public interest for the material to be published, I bear in mind, in the words of Tugenhat J in *Goodwin v NGN Ltd and VBN* [2011] EWHC 1437 (QB) at paragraph 2, that

> "what is of interest to the public is not the same as what it is in the

public interest to publish. Newspaper editors have the final decision on what is of interest to the public interest: judges have the final decision on what it is in the public interest to publish."

39. On the other hand, **it is for editors, not judges, to decide how a story should be reported.** As Lord Rodger of Earlsferry said in *Re Guardian News and Media Ltd* [2010] UKSC 1 [2010] 2 AC 697, at paragraph 63:

> **"What's in a name? 'A lot', the press would answer**. This is because stories about **particular individuals are simply much more attractive to readers than stories about unidentified people**. It is just human nature. And this is why, of course, even when reporting major disasters, journalists usually look for a story about how particular individuals are affected. **Writing stories which capture the attention of readers is a matter of reporting technique, and the European Court holds that article 10 protects not only the substance of ideas and information but also the form in which they are conveyed**: *News Verlags GmbH & Co KG v Austria* (2001) 31 EHRR 8 . . . This is not just a matter of deference to editorial independence. **The judges are recognising that editors know best how to present material in a way that will interest the readers of their particular publication and so help them to absorb the information**. A requirement to report it in some austere, abstract form, devoid of much of its human interest, could well mean that the report would not be read and the information would not be passed on. Ultimately, such an approach could threaten the viability of newspapers and magazines, which can only inform the public if they attract enough readers and make enough money to survive."

SUBMISSIONS BY THE PARTIES TO THE CARE PROCEEDINGS

40. On behalf of the mother, Miss Frances Judd QC and Miss Margaret Pine-Coffin argued that the order of 24th May should be retained so that reporting restriction order continues to prevent identification of the mother as well as A. They were supported by Mr Douglas Taylor on behalf of the father, Miss Penny Howe on behalf of the maternal grandmother and Mr Stephen Cotton on behalf of the child's guardian. On behalf of the local authority, Miss Lucinda Davis supported the application concerning the child but was neutral as to whether or not the order should be extended to prevent publication of the names of the mother and other family members.

41. Miss Judd and Miss Pine-Coffin submitted that it is clear that the article 8 rights of A, the mother, and other family members, **are engaged by the publication of information about the mother, the state of the family home, the care of the children, and the circumstances of the death**

of the two boys, including the publication of names, addresses and photographs. They added that some of the descriptions of the home published by both The Sun and the local paper appeared to have **come from neighbours who were imparting information that was obviously private and confidential, whether or not it was accurate**. In oral submissions, Miss Judd characterised the publication of these details as a particular invasion of the mother's privacy. She drew my attention to the comment of Eady J at first instance, with which the Court of Appeal agreed, in *McKennitt v Ash* (2006) EWCA Civ 1714, [2008] QB73:

> "To describe a person's home, the décor, the layout, the state of cleanliness, or how the occupiers behave inside it, is generally regarded as unacceptable. To convey such details, without permission, to the general public, is almost as objectionable as spying into the home with a long distance lens and publishing the resulting photographs."

42. **Miss Judd proceeded to submit that the effect of the publication of such information was a very considerable interference with the article 8 rights of both A and her mother.** The naming of the mother was **likely to lead** to the identification in the local area of A as her daughter, given the fact that they had the same surname and **that both newspapers had reported considerable details about the family, in particular the addresses of both the mother and the maternal grandmother**. Miss Judd further submitted that the **photographs published would make it easier for the mother to be recognised and that, were she to be seen with A, for example at the contact centre, A would be identified as her daughter**. The risk of such identification had **led to the cancellation of a number of contact visits following the publication of the story in the local paper**. Further publication of information and photographs would be **likely to lead to further disruption of contact.**

43. So far as the mother is concerned, Miss Judd submitted on her behalf that the psychologists' report demonstrates that **the mother is a highly vulnerable individual who will find it extremely difficult to cope with press intrusion**. This evidence was supported by **the report filed by the team manager** of the local learning disability team giving details of recent incidents of self harm committed by the mother, precipitated by her distress around media intrusion, leading to hospital admissions and thereafter close personal supervision. On the basis of this evidence, Miss Judd described this as **a very extreme case.**

44. Miss Judd further pointed out that, depending on the outcome of the police investigations, it is likely that the mother will wish to argue in these care proceedings that she should be permitted to resume care of A at some point in the future. **Her poor mental state, allegedly attributable**

in part to the press reports, was likely to have an adverse effect not only on her capacity to care for A but also on her ability to participate in proceedings in which decisions about A's future care would be made. As a result, it was submitted that, in addition to her article 8 rights, **the mother's article 6 rights are engaged and in danger of being infringed.**

45. Miss Judd and Miss Pine-Coffin accept that article 10 is engaged. They acknowledge that the right to freedom of expression is of great importance, but add that "**it cannot be said that the publication of the matters set out in the articles of 23rd and 24th May based on information given by unnamed neighbours, were in the public interest, or that any further articles (other than reports of court proceedings) naming the mother and deceased children would likewise be in the public interest".** Miss Judd and Miss Pine-Coffin further submit that "**the press did not have any role to play in investigating any possible crime themselves**". In her oral submissions, Miss Judd added that the fact that press interest in the story appeared to have waned indicated that there was now less importance to be attached to the freedom of publication unless and until the mother is formally charged and brought to court.

46. The mother's counsel further add that information published about the state of the family home, and what is alleged to have happened to the boys, **would be highly prejudicial to the mother in the event of her being charged**. They point out that, under section 2(2) of the Contempt of Court Act 1981, the press are strictly liable for publication which carries "**a substantial risk that the course of justice in the proceedings will be seriously impeded or prejudiced**". In Miss Judd's submission there can be no public interest in publication that risks being in contempt of court. In addition, pointing to inaccuracies in the reports published to date, she contended that **there was no public interest in the publication of information that was untrue**, and reminded me that **publication of inaccurate information was a breach of the PCC Code of Practice**. She also asserted that the press had infringed clause 5 of the Code by **intruding into the mother's grief and shock.**

47. Miss Judd contended that little weight should be given to the argument that, as a result of the publication that has already taken place, the fact of the mother's arrest and the circumstances about the boys' deaths could be described as being in the public domain. **She submitted that repeated publication would continue to infringe the mother's article 8 rights**, citing in support the observation of Tugenhat J. at paragraph 59 of the judgment in *JIH v News Group Newspapers* (supra) quoted at above at paragraph 36. **She submitted that the level of publication that had occurred to date was not so significant as to render the continuation of**

the injunction meaningless. She contrasted this case with *Re Stedman* [2009] EWHC 935 (Fam) in which an injunction had been refused after an avalanche of publicity about a 12-year-old boy who was (wrongly) alleged to have impregnated a 15-year-old girl.

48. The mother's counsel concluded that the conduct of the ultimate balancing exercise in this case came down in favour of continuing the wider order made by Judge Marston on 24th May. **She conceded, however, that there is a different public interest in the reporting of a criminal trial and that, in the event of the mother being charged and brought to court, the conduct of the balancing exercise may well lead to a different outcome.**

49. As set out above, the mother's application is supported by counsel for the father, maternal grandmother and the guardian. Each counsel made further submissions in writing and orally. I have all of those submissions in mind and select only salient features for the purposes of this judgment.

50. On behalf of the maternal grandmother, Miss Howe sought an order which would preclude identification of her client. She based her case on the implications of further publications for A's welfare. She reminded me that, depending on the outcome of the forthcoming independent social worker's assessment, there was a prospect that the grandmother would seek to apply for an interim residence order before the conclusion of the care proceedings. **If the details concerning the grandmother which have already been published were to be repeated, or for there to be fresh publication about the grandmother's circumstances, there is a risk that the placement of A with the grandmother may be jeopardised.**

51. On behalf of the father, Mr Taylor in his written submissions made a number of observations about the impact of the internet upon publicity injunctions which, although interesting, do not in my judgment greatly impinge on the decision I have to make at this stage. In his oral submissions, he adopted Miss Judd's analysis and observed that further publication about details of the family of the sort that appeared in the earliest stories **might have the effect of narrowing the option for A's future care.** In this way, A's rights under article 8 and article 6 were in danger. Mr Taylor sought the continuation of the order on 24th May precluding publicity in respect of his client as well as other family members.

52. On behalf of the children, Mr Cotton fully supported the applications on behalf of the various family members for the continuation of Judge Marston's injunction. His stressed that the right to family life included the right to sustain family relationships and cited in support of this proposition the observation of **Ryder J in BBC v Rochdale MBC and X and Y [2005] EWHC 2862 (Fam), [2007] 1 FLR 101 that "article 8 of the Convention**

protects the right to establish, maintain and develop relationships with other human beings".

53. On behalf of the local authority, Miss Davis, as set out above, supported the continuation of the injunction covering A, but was neutral about the extension of the order to cover other family members. **She did, however, seek on behalf of the local authority an extension of the injunction so as to restrain the taking of any photographs of the mother, or any other family members, within five hundred metres of any contact venue**. This extension, which was not opposed by the media, was designed **to prevent the risk of press intrusion disrupting contact** and thereby adversely affecting A's welfare.

SUBMISSIONS ON BEHALF OF THE MEDIA

54. Mr Adam Wolanski appeared on behalf of News Group Newspapers Ltd, publishers of The Sun, MGN Ltd, publishers of the Mirror newspapers, and Newsquest Ltd, the publishers of the local paper.

55. Mr Wolanski indicated that the media parties took no issue with the initial order of Judge Sullivan QC, repeated by Judge Marston on 20th May, **but strongly resisted the current application by the mother.** He submitted that the relief sought by the mother would have a **far-reaching and unprecedented effect** in that she sought an order which would prevent the media from reporting the fact that an identified individual was being investigated, or had been arrested, in connection with the suspected crime. Mr Wolanski pointed out that the order granted by Judge Marston on 24 May, and as sought by the family members**, would have the effect of preventing anything at all being reported about the mother or the other family members covered by the order, save in relation to court proceedings.** Mr Wolanski submitted that this would provide the family members **with a level of protection which had only been afforded in very rare circumstances, for example, to the murderers of James Bulger** in *Venables and Thompson v News Group Newspapers Ltd* [2001] Fam 430. Mr Wolanski submitted that that case, and the other cases in which such orders had been made, **involved a background of public vilification and threats to the applicant which had no parallel in this case.**

56. In his written submissions, Mr Wolanski submitted that the application on behalf of the mother would have **serious implications for the freedom of the press to report the investigation of criminal offences.** Accounts in the media of police investigation, including arrests, are part of the daily diet of news reporting, and supported by the police, who frequently co-operate with the press and provide information intended for publication, including details of arrests. Such reporting not only informs the public, but assists

the process of encouraging prospective witnesses to come forward to contribute to the investigation.

57. Mr Wolanski amplified this argument in his oral submissions in which he identified **six interconnected strands of article 10 freedom in this case**.

(1) **The public interest in the freedom of the press generally**, as identified and explained by Lord Woolf MR in *A v B* [2003] QB 195 in particular his observation that: "any interference by the press has to be justified because it inevitably has some effect on the ability of the press to perform its role in society. This is the position irrespective of whether a particular publication is desirable in the public interest."

(2) The public interest being **known that the police are carrying out their investigatory functions.**

(3) The public interest **in enabling witnesses to possible offences to come forward;**

(4) **The importance of exposing crime;**

(5) The public interest in **reporting the involvement of the local authority in cases where children have died or sustained serious injury**; and

(6) The public interest in reporting the outcome of serious case reviews.

58. Mr Wolanski boldly submits that the mother's rights under article 8 are not engaged in this case. He cited the observation of Lord Nicholls in the Campbell case at paragraph 20 that:

"essentially the touchstone of private life is whether in respect of the disclosed facts the person in question had a reasonable expectation of privacy."

Mr Wolanksi submitted that the mother could have no reasonable expectation that information about her arrest and alleged involvement in the death of B and J would be kept private. He submitted that it was the information itself, not the consequences of the publication of that information, that was relevant to determining whether or not the article 8 rights were engaged. **He pointed out that Parliament has not legislated to prevent the reporting of arrests, and further argued that the terms of sections 2 and 32 of the Data Protection Act 1998 indicated that the Parliament has expressly recognised the importance of the rights of the press to report information on the alleged commission of offences.**

Accordingly, submitted Mr Wolanski, the mother's article 8 rights are not engaged in this case.

59. Mr Wolanski contended **that the mother's application is in reality a "libel injunction" because the evidence filed on her behalf indicates that the real nub of her complaint is that publication would damage her reputation and thereby cause her harm**. Mr Wolanski submitted, relying on observations by Tugendhat J in *Terry v Person Unknown* [2010] EWHC 119 (QB), [2010] EMLR 400 at paragraph 46, that in such circumstances an applicant was unlikely to succeed either at an interim application or at trial, whether under the law of defamation or the law of privacy, because, as explained in the Court of Appeal in *Initial Services v Putterill* [1968] 1 QB 396 there is **no confidence in iniquity.**

60. In the alternative, Mr Wolanski submitted that, if the court concluded that the article 8 rights of the mother and family members were engaged, the conduct of the "ultimate balancing exercise" should lead the court to refuse the wider injunctions sought in this case. **The importance of preventing any interference in the reporting of alleged crimes outweighed the importance of any infringement in the private and family lives of the adults involved in such cases, save in exceptional circumstances.** He argued that the only cases in which such an injunction has been granted were those cases, such as *Venables*, in which the applicant had been able to point not only to an interest in retaining privacy, but also a threat to lives. In other words, the circumstances engaged not merely the qualified right to respect for family life under article 8 but also the absolute right to life under article 2 or the absolute freedom from torture under article 3**. Mr Wolanski submitted that the threats made in this case on the so-called Facebook hate page were not of a scale of substance to engage the article 2 or 3 rights.**

61. Furthermore, Mr Wolanski submitted that the evidence did not support the argument that the press reporting had caused a significant infringement of the article 8 rights of the family members in this case. **In addition, he submitted that the information was already widely known within the local community as a result of the earlier publications, and could thus be said to be in the public domain.**

62. Finally, Mr Wolanski refuted the submission made on behalf of the mother that the publication of information about the state of the family home and what was alleged to have happened to the boys was highly prejudicial to the mother in respect of a criminal trial and therefore a matter to a contempt of court. He reminded me of the words of Lord Bridge in *Pickering v Liverpool Post* [1991] 2 AC 425 at page 425 .

"It is not, of course, possible to determine in advance what kind of public comment on pending proceedings would create a substantial risk on the course of justice will be seriously impeded or prejudiced. That is one reason why it is not commonly possible, save in . . . exceptional circumstances . . . to restrain, by injunction a threatened contempt in breach of the strict liability rule. But editors and publishers will be well advised to exercise great care and not to overstep the mark in this regard."

DISCUSSION

63. **The first issue is to identify the ECHR rights engaged. There is no dispute that article 10 is engaged and in this respect I accept Mr Wolanski's analysis.** The issue is therefore whether articles 6 and 8 are engaged.

64. **I find that the article 8 rights of all family members – A, the mother, F, and the maternal grandmother – are engaged in this case**. To my mind it is manifestly obvious that, in circumstances where two children have died there is a right to respect for private and family life. Furthermore, the lifestyle within the household, and the circumstances in which the children were being brought up, **are clearly aspects of family life which in most cases are kept shielded from public gaze**. Whatever the circumstances in which the children lived and died, the publication of reports in the press about the family **is an intrusion, that is to say an interference with the family's rights under article 8** which can only be justified by the reference to the exceptions in article 8(2). I reject Mr Wolanski's submission that there was no expectation that the information in this case would remain private. The question is whether the right to respect for family and private life is outweighed in the balancing exercise.

65. **I derive no assistance from Mr Wolanski's submission that the mother's application is, in reality, for a libel injunction. In my judgment, the fact that the statements made concerning the mother, or inferences derived from those statements, may be defamatory does not negate the need to adopt the approach set out by Lord Steyn in Re S**, that is to say the process of identifying, scrutinising and balancing the human rights engaged in the particular case. **As Tugenhat J explained in CTB in the passage cited above, the truth or falsity of the allegations is irrelevant because the modern law of privacy is concerned as much with intrusion as with confidentiality**. It would be absurd if the right to respect for private and family life was not engaged by publications of untrue statements. As Buxton LJ observed in *McKennitt v Ash* (supra) "**the defendant cannot deprive the claimant of his article 8 rights simply by demonstrating that the matter is untrue**." Excoriation in newspapers may be intrusive whether the reports are true or false.

66. **The article 8 rights of the family members are therefore engaged in this case.**

67. **So far as article 6 is concerned, as stated above, Miss Judd's supplemental argument is that her client's article 6 rights are engaged and in danger of being infringed because her poor mental state, allegedly attributable in part to the press reports, was likely to have an adverse effect on her ability to participate in the court proceedings concerning A.** Miss Judd relies on the first sentence of article 6 that "in the dissemination of his civil rights and obligations . . . everyone is entitled to a fair hearing". Miss Judd argues that the ability to participate in proceedings is an element of entitlement to such a fair hearing.

68. **I am not persuaded that this gives the mother any additional complaint in this case**. As explained below, I am persuaded that the publicity concerning the circumstances of the deaths of the children and the police investigation **assists the process of arriving at the truth, and may therefore ultimately contribute to the fairness of the litigation process to which, as article 6 states, everyone (not merely the mother) is entitled.** To my mind**, the submissions about article 6 add nothing of substance** to the balancing exercise to be conducted between articles 8 and 10 in this case.

69. **The publication of the articles in The Sun and the local paper were a clear interference with the family's article 8 rights. On the other hand, it is in the public interest for police investigations of serious crime to be fully reported providing such reports keep within the law, including the law of contempt of court. There are several reasons for permitting such reporting. First**, in general terms, crime is a disfiguring feature in our society which needs to be exposed to public view so that society as a whole can address the many issues it raises. **Secondly**, the suspicious death of a child is a particular issue of public importance which warrants appropriate scrutiny in the media. **Thirdly,** during the course of a difficult and important criminal investigation, the police need all the help they can get. The publication of reports of the investigation may trigger memories amongst readers or viewers and lead witnesses to come forward. Television programmes such as "Crimewatch" have been broadcast for many years with that specific aim in mind. Accordingly, **I reject Miss Judd's submission that the press did not have any role to play in the investigation.** On the contrary, as the success of "Crimewatch" demonstrates, the media may play a key role in the identification, investigation and solving of crimes. **Fourthly**, it is in my judgment in the public interest for there to be publicity about cases when children who are known to social services sustain

significant harm. **The performance and efficiency of public services is a matter of fundamental public interest.**

70. **Thus, to my mind, it is in the public interest for the press to be allowed to report that a woman has been arrested on suspicion of killing her two children, who were at the time known to social services. The question, again, is whether the freedom to report such matters is outweighed in the balancing exercise.**

71. **A's article 8 rights are particularly acute**. She has been taken from her family in the most tragic circumstances. She has lost two brothers, her mother is under suspicion for causing the death of her brothers and is displaying signs of significant mental health problems. Her grandmother, who cared successfully for her older brother, B, prior to his death, has put herself forward as a potential carer but finds herself caught up in the blaze of publicity.

72. The mother's article 8 rights are also acutely engaged. Two of her children have died and her third child is in care. After years of mental health problems, her psychiatric condition has deteriorated. The fact that she suffers from mental frailty is an aspect of her private life which must be given appropriate respect.

73. What is the impact of the fact that a considerable amount of this information has already been published? A distinction can be drawn between, on the one hand, the information that children known to social services have died and that their mother has been arrested in connection with their deaths, **and, on the other hand, intrusive reporting into the circumstances within the family home**. The fact of the children's deaths, that the mother has been arrested, and the involvement of social services is information already widely reported nationally and locally, and to my mind this is a factor against the injunction now sought on behalf of the mother. **These facts are widely known and the likely effect of any repetition on the mother's article 8 rights is to my mind limited so that the case for restraining republication is less strong**. On the other hand, detailed accounts of life in the home have amounted to significant intrusion. **To my mind, there is a stronger argument that re-publication of those details would have a significant impact on family members and would therefore amount to an interference with article 8 rights.**

CONCLUSION – THE ULTIMATE BALANCING EXERCISE

74. Mr Wolanski on behalf of the media concedes that his clients do not object to the Court reverting to the order made by Judge Marston on 20 May. By that concession, I understand him to be accepting that, **in A's case, the balance comes down in favour of protecting her article 8 rights.**

75. In my judgment, however, in order to achieve adequate and clear protection for A's article 8 rights, it is necessary to make the following amendments.

76. **First**, the proviso to paragraph 3 of the order (the "if, but only if" clause) should be amended to read as follows: "if but only if such publication is likely to lead to the identification of the child as being (a) the child of the mother and father named in schedule 3 to this order; (b) the child of a woman who has been arrested on suspicion of murdering children; (c) the sister of the deceased children named in schedule 3; (d) the sister of children who have died or (e) the subject of care proceedings."

77. **Secondly**, as the evidence demonstrates that there is a reasonable prospect that A will be placed in the interim care of her maternal grandmother in the next few months, I consider, balancing article 8 and 10, that it is right to add the following words to the "if but only if proviso": "if but only if such publication is likely to lead to the identification of the maternal grandmother named in schedule 3 to this order as being (a) the mother of the child's mother named in schedule 3; (b) the mother of woman arrested on suspicion of murder; (c) the grandmother of the child named in schedule 1; (d) the grandmother of the deceased children named in schedule 3; (e) the grandmother and/or carer of a child who is the subject of care proceedings, or (f) the grandmother and/or carer of a child whose siblings have died".

78. **Thirdly, no party has been able to provide me with full evidence as to the information that has been published on the internet about this case**. I therefore have no way of knowing the extent to which A's has been named or identified in such publications. **The fact that she may have been so named or identified is no justification for permitting repetition of such publication**. I therefore propose to delete paragraph 6(g) of the order of the 20 May, that is to say, the so-called public domain proviso. In other words, no one who breaks the order restraining publication of information concerning A will be able to rely on the fact that information about her had already been published.

79. **Fourthly**, I add the amendment agreed by the local authority and media precluding any person from approaching or photographing the mother within five hundred metres of any place at which she is having contact with A.

80. So much for the injunction restraining publication of information **concerning A.** In her case, the balance comes down clearly in favour of restraint, as recognised by the media parties.

81. **When I turn to M, however, the argument is more finely balanced**. The arguments deployed by Miss Judd are very persuasive. The mother is clearly someone with considerable **long term mental health problems**

which have been exacerbated by the publicity to date and likely to be effected by further publicity in future. As indicated, I do accept **that some of the reporting has been intrusive**, and that **the court has the power in appropriate circumstances to prohibit re-publication of such reports**. I also accept that the publicity has on occasions **prevented contact taking place**, although I do not consider that this presents insurmountable problems to the local authority **whose position will be buttressed by the agreed amendment precluding any person from approaching or photographing the mother within five hundred metres of any place at which she is having contact.**

82. Despite the strength of Miss Judd's arguments**, I find on balance, that, in the mother's case, her article 8 rights are outweighed by the importance of the media's freedom of expression**. In other words, I find that the interference in her right to respect for private and family life resulting from press reports of her arrest on suspicion of causing the death of her two sons **to be necessary in a democratic society** in the interests of the prevention of crime and for the protection of the rights and freedoms of others.

83. There is a **very great public interest** in the investigation of the deaths of children and the detection of cases in which such deaths are caused non-accidentally. **The reporting of police investigations satisfies justifiable public concern about the capabilities of the authorities to identify and deal with these difficult cases.** Such reporting may also unearth other witnesses and evidence. Equally, it is important that the public should be informed when children who die in such tragic cases are already known to social services so that local authorities can be held accountable.

84. Criticism has been made of **the tone** of some of the reporting which, it is said, has added to the intrusion in the lives of members of the family. But, as Lord Rodger noted in *Re Guardian News and Media* (supra), editors, not judges, know best how to present the material in a way that will interest the readers to their particular publication and so help them to absorb the information.

85. I therefore refuse the application on behalf of the mother to continue the order made by Judge Marston on 24th May, or to make any other order that prevents the media reporting details of the investigation. For the same reason, I decline to make any order in respect of other family members, save for the restrictions imposed in respect of the publication of information concerning A.

86. **But I add these caveats.**

87. **First**, the media need to consider carefully the terms of the reporting restriction order I am making protecting A's article 8 rights. It seems to

me, although I have not heard detailed argument on the point, that some of the reporting hitherto has come close to infringing the order of 20 May. Now that the order protecting A's article 8 rights has been tightened as set out above, **the media will need to tread even more carefully.**

88. **Secondly**, the media will need to bear in mind the provisions of the Contempt of Court Act. I make no findings whether or not the reporting to date has amounted to a contempt – that is not a matter for me. **But plainly, there is a risk that reports of an investigation may seriously impede or prejudice the course of justice**. I therefore echo the words of Lord Bridge in the Pickering case quoted above: "**editors and publishers will be well advised to exercise great care and not overstep the mark in this regard".**

89. **Thirdly**, the media will equally need to bear in mind the terms of the **PCC Editors Code of Practice** as quoted above, in particular, the passages in clause 5 concerning intrusion into grief and shock. The code requires that in such cases "**enquiries and approaches must be made with sympathy and discretion, and publication handled sensitively**".

90. **Finally**, this case is in a state of flux and uncertainty. The investigation is ongoing. At this stage, I have concluded that the balance comes down against the injunction sought on behalf of the mother, **but circumstances may change in future** so that the balance between the competing rights shifts. If so, the court will of course be prepared to hear a renewed application.

91. **At this stage, however, I make an order in the following terms:**

ORDER
REPORTING RESTRICTION ORDER
IMPORTANT

If you disobey this order you may be found guilty of contempt of court and may be sent to prison or be fined or have your assets seized. You should read the order carefully and are advised to consult a solicitor as soon as possible. You have the right to ask the Court to vary or discharge the order.

EXPLANATION

1. On 21 June 2011 and 5 July 2011 the Court considered an application for a reporting restriction order.
2. The following persons and/or organisations were represented before the Court;

    The local authority named in schedule 4 to this order.

The child's mother named in schedule 3 to this order.

The child's father named in schedule 3 to this order.

The child's maternal grandmother named in schedule 3 to this order.

The child named in schedule 1 to this order represented by her child's guardian.

News Group Newspapers Ltd, Mirror Group Newspapers Ltd and the publishers of the local newspaper named in schedule 5 to this order.

3. The court read the following documents;

   Reporting restrictions orders made on 13 May 2011, 20 May 2011, 24 May 2011 and 27 May 2011.

   Statements in support of the application by witnesses listed in schedule 6 of this order.

   Articles published by The Sun and the local paper named in schedule 5 of this order.

   A page from the Facebook internet site.

   Psychiatric reports on the mother and father.

   Position statements and skeleton arguments filed on behalf of all parties.

4. The court directs that copies of the Explanatory Note and reporting restriction order be made available to the applicant and any other person affected by this order.
5. The Court acknowledging that at present the addresses of the child and her foster carers' names and addresses are not public knowledge and in the exercise of the court's inherent jurisdiction, the said names and addresses will not therefore be published in the order.

ORDER

1. Subject to any different order made in the meantime, this order shall have effect until the child's 18th birthday in [a date] 2028.
2. This order binds all persons and all companies (whether acting by their directors, employees or any other way) who know that the order has been made.
3. This order prohibits the publishing or broadcasting in any newspaper, magazine, public computer network, internet website, sound or television broadcast or cable or satellite programme service of

a) the name and address of

i) the child whose name is listed in schedule 1 to this order ("the child");

ii) the child's carers whose details are set out in schedule 2 to this order;

iii) any individual having day to day care of or medical responsibility for the child.;

iv) any residential home or hospital, or other establishment in which the child is residing or being treated ("an establishment");

v) the child's mother who is named in schedule 3 to this order;

vi) the child's father who is named in schedule 3 to this order;

vii) the child's maternal grandmother who is named in schedule 3 to this order;

viii) the child's maternal uncle who is named in schedule 3 to this order;

ix) the child's deceased siblings who are named in schedule 3 to this order;

b) any picture being or including a picture of either the child or carer or an establishment;

c) any other particulars or information relating to the child,

IF BUT ONLY IF such publication is likely to lead to the identification of

(1)the child as being

a) the child of the mother and father named in schedule 3 to this order;

b) the child of a woman who has been arrested on suspicion of murdering children;

c) the sister of the deceased children named in schedule 3 to this order;

d) the sister of children who have died;

e) the subject of care proceedings;

(2) the maternal grandmother named in schedule 3 to this order as being

a) the mother of the child's mother named in schedule 3 to this order;

b) the mother of a woman arrested for murder;

c) the grandmother of the child named in schedule 1 to this order;

d) the grandmother of the deceased children named in schedule 3 to this order;

e) the grandmother and/or carer of the child who is a subject of care proceedings;

f) the grandmother and/or carer of a child whose siblings have died.

4. No publication of the text or summary of this order or supporting documents (except for service of the order under paragraph 7 below) shall include any of the matters referred to in paragraph 3 above, or the names in the schedules to this order.
5. This order prohibits any person from seeking any information relating to the children or a carer from any of the following;

   a) the child;

   b) the foster carers;

   c) a carer;

   d) the staff or residents of an establishment;

   e) the staff of a school;

   f) any of the child's relatives.

6. This order further prohibits any person approaching or photographing the child's mother named in schedule 3 to this order within five hundred metres of any place at which she is having contact with the child.
7. Nothing in this order shall prevent any person from

   a) publishing information relating to any part of a hearing in a court in England and Wales (including a coroner's court) in which the court was sitting in public and did not itself make any order restricting publication;

   b) seeking or publishing information which is not restricted by paragraph 3 above;

   c) enquiring whether a person or place falls within paragraph 3 (a) above;

d) seeking information relating to the children while acting in a manner authorised by statute or by any court in England and Wales;

e) seeking information from the responsible solicitor acting for the local authority , whose details are set out in schedule 4 to this order, or any press officer employed by the authority;

f) seeking or receiving information from anyone who before making of this order had previously approached that person with the purpose of volunteering information (but this paragraph will not make lawful the provision or receipt of private information which would otherwise be unlawful).

8. Copies of this order endorsed with a notice warning of the consequences of disobedience shall be served by the applicant (and may be served by any other parties to the proceedings):

a) by service on such newspaper and sound or television broadcasting or cable satellite or programme services as they see fit, by fax or first class post addressed to the editor (in the case of a newspaper) or senior news editor (in the case of a broadcasting, cable or satellite programme service) or website administrator (in the case of an internet website) and/or to their respective legal departments; and/or

b) on such other persons as the parties may think fit, by personal service.

9. The parties and any person affected by any the restrictions in paragraphs 3 to 6 of this order may make application to vary or discharge it to a judge of the High Court on no less than forty eight hours' notice to the parties, reserved to the Honourable Mr Justice Baker if available.

(The order concludes with schedules setting out names and other details of the parties and witnesses, and an explanatory note in accordance with the President's Direction and Cafcass Practice Note of [a date].)

The following is an exceptional example, from the Family Division, of revealing family names in order to put the record straight.

Doncaster Metropolitan Borough Council v Haigh and Tune and Others [2011] EWHC B16 (Fam) per Sir Nicholas Wall P

1. I am giving this judgment in open court.
2. The principal application with which I have to deal in this case is, in my experience, unprecedented. Doncaster Metropolitan Borough authority ("the local authority") seeks to put into the public domain aspects of care proceedings under Part IV of the Children Act 1989, which, in accordance with normal practice, were heard in private.
3. There is a second application made by the local authority, which is supported by both the father of the child concerned and her guardian in the proceedings, for an order against the mother under s 91 (14) of the Children Act 1989, designed to prevent any application by the mother in relation to the child under the Act without the court's permission for a period of two years. I will deal with that application at the conclusion of this judgment.
4. The local authority's principal application is supported by the father of the child and by the child's guardian, albeit with the important exception that in any publication of material the prohibition against naming the child herself should be maintained. This was the prohibition imposed by Baker J, sitting in the High Court earlier this year. During the course of argument on 15th August 2011 when I heard the case it became apparent that differences between the local authority and the guardian on this point could be accommodated, with the result that the order I propose to make at the conclusion of this part of my judgment will preserve the child's anonymity. I will amplify my reasons for taking this course later in the judgment. I propose, accordingly, to call the child "X".
5. X's mother is Victoria Haigh. She told me on 15 August 2011 that she now lives in the Irish Republic. Although it has been held that supervised contact between Ms Haigh and X is in the latter's interests, Ms Haigh has declined to take up the local authority's offer of such contact and has thus not seen X since X was removed from her care. The local authority now has an order under s 34 (4) of the Children Act 1989 permitting it to refuse to allow contact between Ms Haigh and the child. The absence of any contact between X and Ms Haigh is thus entirely the mother's choice and is an illustration of her inability to act in the child's best interests.
6. I recognise, of course, that many people know who X is. She goes, for example, to a local school. For the purposes of this judgment it is sufficient for me to say that X will be 8 later this year. She is currently in the care

of the local authority and living with her father, Mr David Tune. This is in accordance with the local authority's care plan which has been approved by the court. X is thus likely to be cared for by her father during the rest of her minority.

7. X's case has been before the court on a number of occasions. Two are of particular significance. The first is a finding of fact hearing conducted by His Honour Judge Robertshaw over a period of 10 days in January 2010. X was then 6. The principal issue before the judge was whether or not X had been sexually abused by her father. In a long and careful judgment the judge found not only that X had not been sexually abused by her father but that the allegations of abuse which she undoubtedly made, notably in two ABE interviews, had originated in the mind of the mother and were false. As Judge Peter Jones was later to summarise the position, Judge Robertshaw found the following (this is from Judge Jones):

   "Put shortly, the learned judge found that the father had not sexually abused X at all, nor had he behaved in a sexually inappropriate way towards her, but allegations of sexual abuse were first made by the mother and not by X. These were false and the mother knew them to be false. In 2009, X was coached by the mother to make a false allegation of sexual abuse against the father, which originated in the mind of the mother. As a result of inappropriate pressures and prompting, X came to make and believe the allegations. The mother used allegations of sexual abuse manipulatively as part of her irrational and longstanding hostility to contact which she sought to obstruct."

8. As will be apparent, Judge Robertshaw rejected the mother's conclusion that what the child was saying represented her own attitude and perception. He found the mother unconvincing and, at times, evasive as a witness. He rejected the submission made to him by counsel for the mother that she was seeking to distance herself from the allegations of sexual abuse and was not in fact seeking a finding that Mr Tune had sexually abused the child. He did not, however, change X's residence. She continued to reside with her mother. Judge Robertshaw concluded his judgment with the following words:

   "Those who are charged with the task of advising the court as to orders necessary to promote X's welfare in the future bear a burden more onerous than I have had to discharge at this hearing. The weapon of last resort, changing X's residence, will obviously need to be considered and a balance struck between the risks involved in that course against the risk of mother continuing to frustrate and impede contact in a way that will inevitably be emotionally damaging to X. Frustration at her past deplorable conduct must not be allowed to obscure the fact that the issue is welfare and that there are undoubtedly risks in employing the weapon of last resort. Direct contact will now need to be reinstated in some form. It will have to be regulated, not because of any risk posed by the father but simply because of the time that has elapsed since it last took place and, for the time being at least, to safeguard him from further allegations of abuse. Time alone will tell whether the mother is now able to embrace the letter and spirit of the principle that contact with a non-residential parent promotes the well-being of a child of separated parents. Any indication that she has not must involve the case being returned to me on short notice so that whatever steps may be appropriate, however draconian, can be taken."

9. The mother did not seek permission to appeal against Judge Robertshaw's order.

10. The second key judgment is that given by Judge Peter Jones on 22 November 2010. By this time Judge Robertshaw had retired. Like Judge Robertshaw, Judge Jones gave a long and careful judgment. At its conclusion he decided that X should be the subject of a full care order and that she should move to her father's care. Once again, the mother did not seek permission to appeal against that order.

11. As I propose to release both judgments, suitably anonymised, into the public domain, I will give only short extracts from the second judgment:

> "The mother's stance has, of course, severely circumscribed the arguments which could be deployed on her behalf, and counsel, who has put the case fully and in a measured and realistic fashion on her behalf, conceded as much in argument, accepting that the mother had to grasp at any straw in presenting her case. This is a mother who has been found to have caused her daughter emotional harm by the making of repeated, false allegations of sexual abuse which she knew to be false at the time she made them and, subsequently, to have coached X into making a false allegation which she knew to be untrue. She has also used those allegations manipulatively in the course of the family proceedings. Over several years the mother has made a number of allegations against the father, with the result X has been subjected to four medical examinations, police interviews and has had numerous contacts with professionals. Despite the court's findings, the mother accepts no responsibility for this state of affairs, complaining instead of the local authority's 'negligence' and that her treatment has been incredibly harsh 'with no-one really explaining the reasons why'. I am quite satisfied that this intelligent woman

knows exactly why X was removed from her care in January 2010 and why the professionals continue to take the view that X would suffer further emotional harm if rehabilitated to her. In addition, sadly, while professing her concern for X's well-being, the mother consistently prioritises her own needs over those of her daughter.

I have carefully considered all the papers. They make for rather depressing reading. The mother appears to be convinced that she is the only person in the right and everyone else involved with her and her family are wrong. As recently as 6th September 2010, she wrote in an email that she had made her decision and no amount of therapy would change her opinion of something she did not believe in. She accuses the guardian of bias and the local authority of negligence and, as recently as 8th November, of 'tyranny, scare tactics and bullying methods.

I am satisfied it would not be in the best interests of X to delay making a final decision in this case for further work to be done with the mother or with X and her father. In the light of the findings of Judge Robertshaw and all the evidence before this court, there are no good reasons why there should be any further delay in X moving to live permanently with her father, who I am satisfied is fully capable of meeting all her needs, including that for ongoing contact with her mother. I am equally satisfied that it would be contrary to X's best interests to move either now or in the foreseeable future to the full-time care of her mother, given the harm that she has already caused her daughter and the harm she will be likely to cause if X were placed in her care. I believe the mother does need help and she would be well advised to seek it out.

I invite the mother to consider my judgment carefully with her legal advisors. I do not believe that my decision will come as any surprise to her, though I ask her to take time to reflect on the reasoning behind it.

Her intransigent response to the court's findings in January 2010 and her intemperate reaction to the local authority's involvement provided her with little room for manoeuvre in the context of these proceedings. I have no doubt that she cares for X deeply, but she is demonstrating little insight into X's real needs and is failing to prioritise those needs over her own. If she continues on her present course, she runs the risk of alienating her daughter and permanently damaging their relationship. This would be a great loss for X, as everyone, including the father, acknowledges, and I hope it is a consequence which the mother, on further reflection, will seek to avoid."

12. As Judge Jones stated, Miss Haigh has not been able to accept the findings of either judge. What renders the case unique, however, is that Ms Haigh, aided and abetted by one Elizabeth Watson, is not only unable to accept the judges' findings but has put into the public domain the false allegations that she has not had justice and that X, contrary to both judges' findings, has been sexually abused by her father. Those allegations have been posted on the worldwide web and are in the public domain. In addition, the mother has circulated the allegations to the parents of X's school and to Mr Tune's fellow employees at his place of work. All this, of course, has been done illicitly and in breach of orders of the court.
13. The hyperbole which has been employed by Ms Watson might, it could be thought, categorise the allegations made by her and the mother as "absurd". I will give a flavour of these in this judgment. I will give more detail in the judgment I propose to give later in relation to the local authority's application to commit Ms Watson to prison for contempt of court. All the statutory authorities, they say, are "corrupt" and are only in it for the money. The police are "negligent and incompetent". The local authority is "motivated by financial gain and peopled by those whose sole aim is to snatch children from right-minded parents". The list is endless and extremely dispiriting.
14. In its skeleton argument prepared for the hearing on 15 August 2011 the local authority puts its case in the following way:

> "Doncaster shares parental responsibility with the mother and father in respect of their daughter X. At eight years of age X has lived virtually all her life in the centre of litigation and conflict. For the past 18 months, her mother, Victoria Haigh, has conducted an internet and media-based campaign designed to highlight what she now contends is a miscarriage of justice, namely, the court approved decision to place X in her father's care. In consequence of the mother's campaign the local community in which X lives has been made aware that Victoria Haigh accuses David Tune of being a paedophile, a rapist and of sexually abusing his daughter.
>
> For X and her father the present situation is intolerable: (1) the police have been called to X's school to protect her; (2) parents at [the school] are concerned about the information they have been sent by the mother and its significance in terms of the protection of their own children; (3) David Tune has been accosted in the street and called a 'paedophile'; (4) David Tune's work colleagues have had material sent to them both in a public forum and on their own Facebook pages, the contents of which have been to render David Tune's livelihood vulnerable and therefore his capacity to provide for his daughter.

Though the allegations are all false, neither David Tune nor Doncaster has felt able to respond publicly to them. The local authority is pursuing the mother and her fanatical campaigners by way of injunction and committal proceedings. It has not been possible, despite Doncaster's best efforts, to persuade the domain holders, voluntarily, to take the offending sites down or to close the relevant email accounts.

The present situation is self-evidently damaging to X and her father. The local authority, however, is also extremely concerned about the future. It will not be long before X and her school friends uncover the material which is presently on the internet. X's school, her social worker, if we may say so, and her father has all worked tirelessly and sensitively to shelter X from the allegations her mother makes. They have been broadly successful to date. However, it is beyond any doubt that if, and, perhaps now inevitably, when, that information comes to X's attention it will be extremely distressing to her. The repercussions are easy to predict. It is likely to impact on X's relationship with her peers and adults. It may destabilise her security at home with her father. It will be emotionally very confusing to her.

Even if the local authority was ultimately to remove the information from the internet, the fact remains that the mother's accounts have already been widely circulated and in a manner targeted to cause most damage to X and her father. This is a situation the local authority finds very difficult to manage. On the one hand, it seems clear that the false and tendentious material in the public domain must at least be counterbalanced by accurate and truthful information being made available to those who receive the mother's account. On the other hand, it must be recognised that information placed in the public domain cannot easily be regulated thereafter. There is a risk of widespread media interest that may have the consequence of making life for X and her father even more uncomfortable, particularly in the short term. Any course the court takes must, in our submission, contemplate both these possibilities.

Accordingly, the local authority has tried to evaluate the utility of taking no action at all on the issues and responding as best it can to events as they unfold, supporting X and her father with access to counselling services and practical help. Ultimately, the local authority has concluded that it would be failing in its obligations to X not to correct the false allegations and rumours that surround her. The real harm from the mother's actions, we would respectfully reiterate, has been to target her campaign, and so specifically, to those directly involved in her child's life."

15. By way of strategy the local authority suggest the following:

> "The local authority would propose that its information document, a document it has prepared, is incorporated into a public judgment which addresses the reasons for the release. It may be that the court will wish to vary the contents of the document perhaps, even to expand its ambit. The contemplated judgment would be a document in the public domain, and, as such, the local authority recognises it will have no control over its dissemination. It is proposed, however, that the social worker, the head teacher and Mr Tune's employer should work together in managing the release of the judgment to those concerned locally in a way that would be most sensitive to X. This, of course, can only be a strategy."

16. The particular mischief of what the mother and Ms Watson have done is, of course, that the internet providers, as the local authority points out, are not necessarily within or amenable to the jurisdiction of the court.

17. At the hearing on 15 August 2011 Ms Haigh sought to distance herself from Ms Watson's actions. In addition, she indicated to Baker J. on 13th April that she would abide in future by all orders in force and would email Ms Watson to advise her to cease acting on Ms Haigh's behalf. However, it seems to me, that Judge Robertshaw's assessment of Ms Haigh is amply borne out by the documents Ms Haigh gave me on 15 August 2011, in which she admits making both "a false statement" of her disbelief of the allegations against Mr Tune and also of making an "insincere apology" to him. Although she assured me that she was not in contempt of court, it is plain to me that she remains with a fixed and unaltered view that Mr Tune is a paedophile.

18. The question which thus arises is easy to state but more difficult to answer: what is to be done?

19. It seems to me this is a case in which it is necessary to go back to first principles and to state clearly what the law of England is. Parliament has passed the Children Act 1989. Parliament has decreed that courts hearing cases under the Children Act may sit in private. The object endorsed by parliament is to protect the confidentiality and the identity of those involved, particularly the confidentiality of children. The power to sit in private has, furthermore, been tested in Europe, and the European Court of Human Rights has upheld it (see B v United Kingdom [2001] 2 FLR 261 and Pelling v Bruce-Williams (Secretary of State for Constitutional Affairs Intervening) [2004] 2 FLR 823).

20. If parents cannot agree about an issue by negotiation, mediation or any other form of ADR (alternative dispute resolution), they take that issue

to court. The judge then decides it. As a matter of English law, an event either occurred or it did not; there is no halfway house: see the decision of the Supreme Court in Re B (Care Proceedings: Standard of Proof) [2008] UKHL 35 on the internet and in Re B (Care Proceedings: Standard of Proof) [2008] 2 FLR 141 in the specialist law reports.

21. In the instant case two judges have decided that Mr Tune is not a paedophile and that he has neither sexually abused X nor behaved inappropriately towards her. That is the end of the matter. Mr Tune is not a paedophile and X has not been sexually abused. That is the position which needs to be placed on record and in the public domain.

22. The disappointed party in English law is not left without a remedy. Ms Haigh has a number of avenues open to her, by means of which she can complain. The Family Proceedings Rules (now the Family Procedure Rules) were specifically amended to allow people in her position to do so. Moreover, she has the right, or had the right, to apply for permission to appeal against either order. Nothing, however, alters the rule that no party is entitled to breach the confidentiality of the proceedings by illicitly putting into the public domain material which is confidential to those proceedings and which, moreover, the judge in this case has ordered not to be published.

23. Judges of the High Court also have the power to make restraining orders in family cases. Mr Justice Baker plainly had the power and the jurisdiction to make the order of 25th February 2011 which forbade the mother and Ms Watson "from communicating via the internet or otherwise to the world".

24. I will read the relevant part of the order at this point. The order made by the judge against the world at large particularly prevented both the mother and Ms Watson, whether by themselves, individually or together or by instructing any other person:

> "from communicating to any media outlet, including to the makers of any television programme or radio programme or the publishers of any newspaper or magazine, or representatives of the same, or any digital media or via the internet, any information relating to any proceedings under the Children Act concerning X, namely, proceedings [and the number is then given]."

25. Ms Haigh and Ms Watson were forbidden from communicating the name of the child, the name of the child's parents, the name of the grandparents, the local authority, the school, the employees of the local authority. They were forbidden from distributing any picture of the child, any particulars or information related to the child and/or her parents or wider family

members and the name and address of the guardian. This is a standard order and was clearly made within the powers of the judge.

26. It follows that Baker J., as a Judge of the High Court, had the power to make his order on 25 February 2011. That proposition is plain. The contrary was not argued on 15 August 2011 and could not, in my judgment, be properly argued.
27. Why did Baker J make the order? He did so to protect the anonymity of the child and those caring for the child. His order has not been appealed, and it stands.
28. We live in a society which prides itself on the rule of law. Orders of the court are there to be obeyed. If they are wrong, there is a mechanism for putting them right. But whilst they stand – and Baker J's order still stands, as do the orders of Judge Robertshaw and Judge Jones – they are to be obeyed. As I said during the course of argument on this case, quoting a famous dictum much favoured by Lord Denning, "Be you never so great, the law is still above you". This applies to me as much as it applies to everyone else.
29. In the skeleton argument counsel for the local authority referred to the fact that parliamentary privilege has been invoked in this case: "A member of parliament has, on the basis of inaccurate and misleading information supplied to him, deployed parliamentary privilege to highlight the case. We would respectfully encourage the court to deprecate the use of parliamentary privilege in that way in circumstances where there is inevitably incomplete material available and the privacy of a child is threatened. It is perhaps helpful to emphasise that s 97 (2) of the Children Act 1989, which protects the privacy of children in the currency of proceedings, was enacted by parliament itself, not by judges. Indeed, it may be apt to observe here that the 2010 Act (Children, Schools and Families Act 2010) appears to impose a tightening of privacy principles in children cases, reversing the progress towards transparency made in the case of Clayton v Clayton [2006] EWCA Civ 878, [2007] FLR 11."
30. I have, of course, considered that submission very carefully, but I do not think it would be appropriate for me to become involved in matters which (a) are not my province, and (b) are not necessary for the proper resolution of the case before me.
31. What I think I can properly say is that orders of the court are not made capriciously and any disobedience of them is to be deplored. If a judge wishes to preserve the anonymity of a child and so orders, that order must be obeyed.
32. The nearest my researches have enabled me to come to the present

position is to be found in an article in the Family Law magazine for August 2003, [2003] Fam Law 594, by Mr Timothy Scott QC. He recounts a case in which parents were accused of abusing their child and vindicated by the court. They wished to publicise that vindication since they had been the victims of the "no smoke without fire" school of thought and had suffered an amount of local abuse. The matter was dealt with by consent, and the article does not relate what order the judge made. But, in my judgment, the situation is analogous. I anticipate that what happened is that the parents were permitted to publish the fact that they had been vindicated.

33. The researches of the guardian, his solicitor and counsel have revealed a New Zealand case reported at RR v EE [1999], case number 000621, in which a newspaper wanted to publish the name of a child. That application was refused. Mr Perkins accepts, however, that, whilst interesting, the case is illustrative rather than authoritative. It certainly does not bind me.

34. This leads me, however, to a second equally important point. Any person who embraces one party's version of events and treats it as the whole truth is making a serious mistake. In most family cases the version given by one side is partial and tendentious; on any view it does not give the other side. The only sensible course is to see what the court says in a judgment on all the evidence. Hence, the rule in English law that a court's judgment is authoritative, based as it is on all the evidence, is not only sound in law but founded in good sense.

35. In English law, therefore, issues between parties are decided by the courts, and in our courts are decided by judges. That is the system which operates.

36. There is, sadly, a tendency for those who wish to criticise the family justice system to publish the leaked version put forward by one side and to ignore any corrected version, notably the judgment given by the judge: – see, for example, the recent case of Re L (A Child: Media Reporting) [2011] EWHC B8 (Fam) in which a journalist published one side's version and ignored what the judge said about it. I called attention to the dangers of this course a long time ago: - see my reported decision of Re H (Freeing Orders: Publicity) [2005] EWCA Civ 1325, [2006] 1 FLR 815. I do so again. Ms Watson, for the reasons I will give later in my judgment, on the application to commit her for contempt, has fallen into this trap. She has publicised a tendentious version, which two judges, on investigation, have found to be untrue. In so doing, moreover, she has breached the court's order.

37. It follows, in my judgment, that the record must be put straight. How is this to be achieved? It is, I think, trite law that I have the power to release information into the public domain. Judges regularly do so, for example,

when an abducted child needs to be traced. My personal experience of this has been entirely positive. I have found the media helpful and cooperative, and, with their assistance, the child has usually been found. Here, of course, the situation is different. There is, however, a need to put material into the public domain. It is important for the world to know that two judges have found that Mr Tune is not a paedophile and that it is in the interests of his daughter to live with him. It is also important for me, having examined the record, having read all the papers in the case, to state that I have reached the same conclusion.

38. Since there is already much information about X in the public domain, including the names of her parents, why am I forbidding future publication of her name? The answer is not, I think, far to seek, and I have already touched upon it. Above all, I adhere strongly to the principle that children should not be named in Children Act proceedings. Children are nearly always the victims of their parents' misbehaviour. In this case the mother happens to be the abusive parent, but the principle is firm; the child should be protected as much as possible.

39. X, through her guardian, submits that the family justice system should maintain that principle. I agree with him. In his submission on this point Mr Perkins quoted from the Guardian and his solicitor when submitting the following:

> "[The children's guardian] is instinctively opposed to the release of information regarding X into the public domain. He has, throughout this case, supported the local authority in fighting to preserve her anonymity by way of injunctive measures and committal proceedings. He feels strongly that a child's interests are best met by her identity being kept confidential and likewise information which would tend to identify her as being the subject of proceedings, as it is enshrined within the Children Act 1989.
>
> The guardian feels, however, that this case is exceptional. The campaign conducted by Ms Haigh and her supporters has put an erroneous view of the court proceedings regarding X into the public domain. The impact of that has been immense on X, impacting on her day-to-day life and making her fearful.
>
> It is not clear whether, at the present time, she has any understanding that people in her school have knowledge of her situation, albeit knowledge of incorrect facts, but this could only be harmful to her as she grows up. The impact of the campaign being run by Ms Haigh and her supporters is affecting Mr Tune, and X is conscious of that.
>
> The guardian is also conscious that, in addition to the internet

campaign waged by Ms Haigh and her supporters, there is evidence that the more mainstream press has shown interest in X's case. A Member of Parliament has chosen to assist Ms Haigh by speaking of this case in the House of Commons, having alerted X's solicitor to his intentions and to the fact that he could not be prevented from this action. Again, this makes X's case very different from any other case the guardian has encountered.

Due to the very specific circumstances of this case, the guardian has reluctantly come to the position there should be disclosure of the true facts of X's case into the public domain. He has read the document prepared by leading counsel for the local authority and, whilst he would make some amendments to it, as shown in the attached document, he agrees to there being disclosure. He very strongly argues, however, that X should not be named. It could be argued that X can be easily identified because the parents are named and that refusing to name the child is therefore illogical. The guardian would argue that there is no necessity to name the child because clarity is achieved by naming the parents. Whilst for those familiar with this case it would be simple to identify X, the principle of a child's confidentiality should be maintained by those in the family justice system. Research evidence strongly suggests that children do not wish for their identities to become known, or indeed for their family details to be disclosed. The guardian would submit that X should not be named so that the document, if it is released by the court in its current form or an amended version, should not, in itself, come back to haunt X in the future.

The guardian will not support release of the document, therefore, as drafted by the local authority, and if the court were to countenance its release he would wish it to be clear that he has opposed it. The guardian believes that were X's name to appear publically it is important that the local authority takes immediate action to pursue an immediate remedy through the court. The guardian reaches this position after much thought. He remains concerned this case could open the floodgates to other breaches of children's confidentiality. He is clear that requests for release of information, as being considered here, should remain the exception, rather than the rule."

40. I accept the guardian's submissions. It does not seem to me that the court should be seen to derogate from the principle I have enunciated, whilst at the same time it criticises others for doing so. In one sense this case is no different from others. There are always people "in the know". There are always people who know who the parties to confidential proceedings are.

Those people, however, will not be at liberty to publish X's name, nor will the media, in any way in connection with these proceedings. I propose to release both the judgment of Judge Robertshaw and Judge Jones into the public domain, and both will be placed on the BAILII web site. As far as Judge Robertshaw's judgment is concerned, the child's name, whenever it appears, will be replaced by the letter "X". The names of the individuals (apart from those of the mother and the father, which can remain) should be replaced with their positions, ie the head teacher who is named can be called "the head teacher" and so on. Similarly, the social worker who is named can be "the social worker". As far as Judge Jones's judgment is concerned, similar considerations will apply. The named psychologist who gave evidence before Judge Jones can be called "the psychologist" and so on. Amendments will, I am afraid, have to be made by the local authority.

41. The local authority, as I have already indicated, has also prepared a document which it calls "the information". This document has been amended by the guardian. It contains the information which, in the view of the local authority, should be in the public domain. As originally drafted, it named X. For the reasons I have already given, I do not think X should be named. I have taken, therefore, the opportunity to alter the document myself, to anonymise it and to expand it. It will be attached to this judgment in the form in which I have drafted it. It will then be in the public domain in the form in which I have approved it.

42. In my papers there is also a statement from the head teacher of X's school. He is plainly a person of the highest respectability and responsibility. I propose to read substantial portions of his statement into this judgment. This is what he says:

> "I am the teaching head at the local school. I have been head teacher at the school for a year. I have been the head teacher for the last year and, prior to that, I was employed as a class teacher for the previous six years at the same school. I make this statement based on my knowledge of X, who has attended the school since March 2008 to the current date. I also make the statement based on discussions with X's class teachers, teaching assistants and from referring to school records in relation to X.
>
> This is a small local school with [a number less than 200] pupils, [a number less than 10] class teachers and [a number less than 10] teaching assistants. It is located in the heart of a village. The village consists of two pubs, a hairdresser, a church and no other local amenities. Children attending the school come from throughout the local geographical area. It is a closely knit community, with many of the families of children attending at school knowing each other

extremely well, including knowing X and her parents, Ms Haigh and Mr Tune. Ms Haigh is known in the local area ...In terms of X's educational attainments her assessment scores show that she is currently meeting age-appropriate milestones for a child her age.

However, X presents as a child who is extremely bright and, in my opinion, should be achieving over and above her age-appropriate milestones. X has many friends within her school and is a popular child with her peer groups.

X has plenty of friends within school, but I am unsure as to what friends she has contact with outside of school hours...With regard to X's emotional presentation at school, in my opinion, X is quieter this year than she has been in previous years, though she does not present at school as an unhappy child. In terms of her demeanour, she appears to be a more reserved child than in previous years and gives the impression she is capable of masking any emotional difficulties or concerns that she may have to professionals . . .

At the time the allegations were made by X there were several remarks that she made to teaching staff recorded in the concerns book. The concerns book is a document that is held within the school in which members of staff note their concerns in respect of any particular child at any one time so that I may consider the same to assess what is required or actually needed, or whether or not any support is required.

I do have some concerns with regard to X's ability to keep things to herself, which may cause her some emotional difficulty. For example, I was informed at a recent Looked After Child's review that X had begun to build herself a hiding place in the family home in the event that her mother attempted to come and remove her from home, from her father's care. I was concerned to learn that a child of X's age had the forethought to be able to formulate such a plan, which clearly had been given consideration for some considerable period of time.

I am of the opinion that if X did have some significant difficulties or concerns at a particular time she would report the same to one of the teaching assistants, and, as a result, they would bring it to my attention, but that, of late, no such discussions have taken place between X and any members of staff. I am clear that X is under a significant amount of pressure at this time. She appears to be a child who has the weight of the world on her shoulders. In the light of this, her educational attainments at this stage are not of any particular surprise to me, and I think she is coping extremely well with her current circumstances involving her mother."

43. Under the subheading "Mr David Tune" the headmaster comments:

> "I am aware that Mr Tune or his mother would be responsible for dropping off and collecting the child on a daily basis. I regularly meet with Mr Tune with regards to concerns and anxieties that he express in relation to X and the ongoing situation with X and Ms Haigh. Mr Tune himself appears to be under an extreme amount of pressure at the present time and struggling to come to terms with the nature and extent of the material which is presently on the internet about him, which I have observed first hand by looking at the same on the internet. Mr Tune always presents at school as extremely concerned for X's emotional welfare and relies on the school for a significant amount of support in protecting her whilst he is at work and X is at school. Mr Tune does talk to me about discussions he has had with X and her views with regard to having contact with her mother, although it has to be said that X herself has not spoken with regard to any of these issues.
>
> I am aware that a member of the public has recently approached Mr Tune and asked him whether or not he is a paedophile, which the internet reports refer. I am aware that such contact with Mr Tune further places more stress and anxiety upon him."

44. Under the subheading "Ms Victoria Haigh" the headmaster comments as follows:

> "I have known her since the summer of 2010. Following the orders having been made by the court in November/December 2010, I was, of course, informed by the children's services in Doncaster that Ms Haigh was not to have direct or indirect contact with the child unless authorised by the local authority and such an order was in place to keep Ms Haigh away from the school, away from X and away from her family home. Since that time Ms Haigh has sent presents for X at Christmas, has sent a school magazine with letters written inside, has emailed me photographs of her new baby directly to my email address at school, and packages of clothes, DVDs, CDs have also sent by Ms Haigh to be passed on to X. None of the above had been passed on to X by the school. They have been passed to children's services to assess how and when, if at all, the same could be forwarded to X for her attention. I have historically received emails from Ms Haigh via her iPhone, making requests for contact between herself and X, contact between her family members and X and making requests to

attend school at the various school events, including the nativity play and, more recently, the sports day.

Ms Haigh has recently emailed requesting a thorough report with regard to X. I confirmed that her report would be provided, as it would be provided to any non-resident parent, and that her emails concerning contact, or attempting to contact X via the school, should be forwarded to children's services for them to consider."

45. Under a subheading "The position of the school" the headmaster writes:

"I am aware that some, if not most, of the parents whose children attend the school have an understanding of the allegations made by Ms Haigh that are placed on the World Wide Web. None of the parents of the children have spoken to me with regards to any material that they have seen on the internet or have overheard in the community. However, on 27th May 2011, Ms Haigh emailed several of the parents whose children attend the school, having obtained the contacts list, inviting them to visit her web page.

Following that, an email having been sent, I understand that some of the parents may have followed the invitation, and have accessed the material on the internet. Some of the parents have spoken to me with regard to concerns regarding the content of the material on the webpage and the internet regarding X. However, none of the parents has made enquiries with regard to allegations made against Mr Tune by Ms Haigh.

In terms of the current proceedings and Ms Haigh's contact with the school, I have had, now on several occasions, to contact the local police with a view to seeking support from them following attendance by Ms Haigh at school .

Ms Haigh sent the email to the parents at the school, linking them to a petition and material on the internet concerning X."

46. The head teacher then deals with a number of incidents in which the police have been called to the school. He goes on:

"As a part-time teaching head, I am a class teacher for two and a half days a week. Whenever a particular incident takes place - for example, when Ms Haigh sent the email via the school web site to the parents of children at school, the entire day was spent liaising with Nottinghamshire children's services, Nottinghamshire legal services, South Yorkshire Police, Doncaster MBC children's services, liaising with the social worker, with the father and briefing members of the teaching staff at school as to advise them of the situation. The actions of Ms Haigh seemed to be made without any consideration for X, for Mr Tune or for the school itself. The resources which have been deployed in an attempt to keep the children of the school away from the material on the internet is having an adverse effect upon them, is significant and of monumental importance. Teaching time is affected as a result of the actions taken by Ms Haigh on the basis that I am responsible for ensuring the safety of the children. It is my paramount concern whilst at school that if my attentions are directed towards issues concerning X's welfare other members of staff have to resume my responsibilities on a particular day.

I am of the opinion the current proceedings and the actions of Ms Haigh in terms of the material which is on the internet are extremely damaging for a child of X's age. It is fortunate that at this time X is not yet of an age when she is likely to locate the information about her and her family on the internet and that none of the children within her peer group at school also have access to the material. There will, however, come a time when that material will be available to X, which I am of the opinion is extremely damaging. The impact of the current situation on Mr Tune is clearly impacting on him greatly and in turn his presentation at the present time is also likely to affect X."

47. It would be difficult, I think, to have a more responsible person showing how irresponsibly the mother and Ms Watson have behaved. I find it an intolerable situation for a responsible person such as the head to be in. He will therefore be in a position to use the document which I have approved as he thinks fit. I hope he will use it to dispel any lingering suspicions there are about Mr Tune.

48. The order made by Baker J on 25th February 2011 will, accordingly, continue. It will, however, be amended in para.3 to delete subparagraphs (ii), (IV) and (VI). These deal with X, her parents and, I think, the school. I would be grateful if counsel would look at the order and make the necessary amendments.

49. Finally, I turn to the application under s 91(14) of the Children Act 1989. The leading authority on the point is a case of which I am very familiar, Re P (A child) (Residence Order: A Child's Welfare) [1999] 2 FLR 573. It was an appeal from a decision of mine, and I took the opportunity in the judgment at first instance to go into s 91 (14) in considerable detail. The subsection reads as follows: "On disposing of any application for an order under this Act, the court may (whether or not it makes any other order in response to the application) order that no application for an order under this Act of any specified kind may be made with respect to the child

concerned by any person named in the order without the leave of the court."

50. I plainly thus have jurisdiction to make an order under s 91(14). I do not propose to go through the criteria identified by Butler-Sloss LJ. In Re P, although I bear the criteria very much in mind.

51. In essence, my view is that this is a wholly exceptional case. What the child and her father need above all is a period of respite from litigation. The mother recently applied for an emergency protection order. It was dismissed by the local Justices, with an order for costs made against her. It had, however, to be dealt with and no doubt caused considerable disruption. I am, therefore, entirely satisfied that an order under s 91(14) is justified, appropriate and proportionate. The mother is not prevented by it from negotiating contact with the local authority. If she has a reasonable application to be placed before the court, she will be heard. Thus, although the order represents a breach of her ECHR rights, I am satisfied that in the interests of X a respite of litigation is required and the order is proportionate.

52. I will, therefore, make an order under s 91(14) forbidding any application by the mother without the court's permission for a period of two years. That permission, in the first instance, is to be sought from me in writing without notice to the father. I will reserve the case generally to myself if available.

53. Ms Haigh, who was present on 15 August, argued that, as the child's mother, she should be entitled to make any application she liked about X. That, of course, would be the normal position. I am satisfied, however, that this case is exceptional and therefore an order under s 91(14) is called for.

Addendum: the local authority's "information document

"THE INFORMATION"

Below I have set out the core information regarding this case which, in my judgment, should now be placed into the public domain. Doncaster Metropolitan Borough Council and the other parties are to be free to use the document in whatever manner they think appropriate, provided, in particular, the injunction which I have made is obeyed, and the child in particular is not identified.

Nicholas Wall
5 September 2011

1. Victoria Haigh and David Tune married in May 2003 and their daughter, X was also born in that year. X appeared to have every advantage in life. The parents had both enjoyed successful sporting careers, they had a comfortable home and X was greatly loved by both of them. Sadly, by 2004 the parents began to experience difficulties in their marriage. In January 2005 Mr Tune vacated the former matrimonial home. At the early stages of the separation X had the benefit of frequent contact with her father, including overnight stays. In March 2005 Mr Tune began employment in Brussels but returned each weekend in order to exercise his overnight contact with X. X and her father also spoke daily on the telephone.
2. By August 2005 Ms Haigh sought a reduction in contact and in the Spring of 2006 she stopped contact altogether claiming that X was being emotionally affected by her contact with her father. A series of court orders made throughout 2006 sought to restore the contact in line with the expectations of both parents. The attachment of a penal notice to a Court order of 8 December 2006 evidences that the mother was still resistant to the Court ordered contact regime. She in fact assaulted the father at that Court hearing for which she received a formal caution.
3. On the day of that hearing Ms Haigh also made the first allegation of sexual abuse by Mr Tune against his daughter to Doncaster Social Services, followed 12 days later by a fresh application to the Court for permission to deny contact whilst her allegations were investigated. Thus began a continuing series of similar allegations. Each was taken seriously by the guardian ad litem, the Local Authority and the Court. Each was investigated by either Doncaster or Nottinghamshire social workers under their Child Protection procedures alongside the Police. Each time a fresh allegation was made by Ms Haigh, X's contact with her father was either suspended or only took place supervised by a social worker. On each occasion the investigations provided no evidence of sexual abuse but following the reinstatement of the father's contact a fresh allegation was in due course forthcoming from the mother resulting in a further period of contact suspension and a new investigation. In addition, Ms Haigh was invited, on three occasions, to present evidence for her allegations to be investigated by the court but on each occasion she either did not attend or did attend but produced no evidence. Ms Haigh has, however, not always been consistent as to her own beliefs. She has in the past told the Court that she was "totally wrong about the sexual abuse allegations", claiming that she may have overreacted to innocent or innocuous behaviour. She now tells me that this was untrue.
4. In due course and after many investigations, including four medical examinations of X herself, the case was heard before His Honour Judge

Robertshaw concluding on the 29th January 2010. At that hearing, which lasted two weeks, the mother was represented by Counsel. It is important to note that the mother's own case was not that X had been sexually abused but that allegations of sexual abuse, by this stage coming from X herself, were a reaction to the stressful relationships around her. In terms it was submitted, on the mother's behalf, X was saying things "she thinks the adults want to hear". By the adults, this, of course, could only have meant the mother. The Judge at that hearing gave Ms Haigh every opportunity to present a case that X had been abused, if that was what she believed, but Ms Haigh chose not to.

5. His Honour Judge Robertshaw rejected her analysis as put by Counsel on her behalf. He found Ms Haigh had been disingenuous in the way she ran her case. It was, he said, pursued to achieve 'tactical advantage'. The Judge found that Ms Haigh had 'coached' X into making her allegations of sexual abuse. Specifically, the Judge concluded that the allegations originated in the mind of the mother and were false allegations. Such was the evidence available to the Judge that he was able 'inevitably', as he termed it, to conclude that X had not been sexually abused.
6. The Judge found Ms Haigh had been motivated by her desire to obstruct X's contact with her father about which she had developed "a longstanding and irrational hostility". X as the Judge found, had been 'excessively' and 'inappropriately' questioned about possible abuse which actually sent unmistakable signals to X that 'disclosure' would be something that would please her mother. The Judge found undoubted influence of the mother in some of X's statements. Analysing the chronology of the allegations over a three year period, the Judge found that they correlated closely with the course of the protracted legal proceedings and had been deployed by the mother "manipulatively to support her case". The consequence, the Judge concluded, was that X had repeatedly incurred unnecessary and 'potentially distressing' intrusions into her life by professionals. The allegations had resulted in a cessation of X's contact to her father and the process had, in this way, been emotionally harmful to her.
7. Notwithstanding his findings His Honour Judge Robertshaw did not make immediate provision to transfer of X's care to the father. Rather he adopted a holding position of X living with her grandmother. Whilst viewing the mother's conduct as 'deplorable', the Judge was careful to recognise that the paramount concern of the Court was X herself. The responsibility and privilege of caring for her was not to be determined on the basis of a reward for unimpeachable parental conduct nor withdrawn as a punishment for a parent who had caused harm to a child. It was to be determined, as it always is in the Family Court, by reference to the

welfare criteria in section 1(1) and 1(3) of the Children Act 1989 where the interests of the child remain the paramount consideration. As the Judge put it, in terms easily accessible to the parties themselves, "Frustration at her [the mother's] past deplorable conduct must not be allowed to obscure the fact that the issue is welfare". The Judge made it clear, however, that X had a right to a relationship with both parents and that ultimately the Court might view it as necessary to transfer X's care to the parent who would allow her a relationship with both. This observation could not have been clearer or more child focused.

8. At no point has the mother sought to appeal the Judge's findings. However, Ms Haigh has been unable to accept the findings, despite her ambivalence as to their reliability within the litigation itself. In due course His Honour Judge Jones was asked to determine the question as to where X should live following a full assessment of both parents including a psychological assessment of Ms Haigh. In his Judgment of the 22nd November 2010, Judge Jones found Ms Haigh to be 'untruthful' and 'entrenched' in her position. He also found that the mother had continued to influence X and to manipulate her feelings whilst in effect 'placing her own as the priority'.

9. The Judge concluded that it would be contrary to X's best interest for her to live with her mother and that were she to do so, she would be likely to suffer further emotional harm in her care. The mother, Judge Jones found, had been "intransigent" in her response to the Court's findings and "intemperate" in her reaction to the Local Authority's involvement. He recognised that Ms Haigh "cares for X deeply" but emphasised "she is demonstrating little insight into X's real needs and is failing to prioritise these over her own". Foreshadowing the difficulties that were to come, the Judge observed if she [Ms Haigh] continues on her present course, she runs the risk of alienating her daughter and permanently damaging their relationship". The Judge considered "that would be a great loss for X (as everyone, including the father, acknowledges)" and expressed the hope that it would be a "consequence which the mother, on further reflection will seek to avoid".

10. During the course of the Judgment, HHJ Jones recorded his personal instinct that Ms Haigh needed "professional help". The mother advised the Court that she had sought out and received extensive therapeutic counselling, though no evidence of it was placed before the Court on her behalf. In her own account in evidence she said that at times during the litigation she recognised that she had been "a very poorly lady".

11. In the period that followed the original fact finding hearing before His Honour Robertshaw, the mother's professed ambivalence about the

abuse hardened to become a certainty which she expresses dogmatically. This, of course, reinforces the Court's own conclusion that the mother's position during the litigation had itself had been disingenuous and tactical. Following the transfer of X to her father's care, Ms Haigh became fixated on what by now had plainly become, in her own mind, a profound injustice.

12. Despite all that had happened Social Services considered that it was important to try to promote the relationship between X and her mother and provided contact facilities with that objective in mind. Inevitably, in the light of the Court's findings, that could only take place with a Social Worker present. It requires little imagination to recognise that contact for parents in such circumstances may be very difficult and artificial. From the child's perspective, however, it may prove to be reassuring and comforting. Parents who are able to appreciate this can, even within these limitations, contrive to ensure that contact is an enjoyable experience. Ms Haigh was unable to do this and decided that she would not see X at all in these circumstances. The Social Services wrote to Ms Haigh informing her of X's wish to see her mother and her concern that contact was not occurring but Ms Haigh's view was fixed and contact ceased.
13. Ms Haigh's attention then turned towards a media and internet based campaign designed to remedy what she claims to be a miscarriage of justice. She is highly critical of the child's Guardian, the police, the Social Workers, the teachers, the Judges and the lawyers (including her own). She has recruited a number of individuals to assist her in that campaign and there is much information on the internet about X which is in breach of the injunctive remedies the Court has put in place in its concern to protect X's privacy.
14. On the 1st May the mother e-mailed X's school with a document styled as a letter to X. In that email she observes "I am famous again darling, but this time it is not because I am a model or racehorse trainer. It is because I have fought my way to the top people in the country, to give me my daughter back and I will not stop until they do. When I see you I will keep all of the newspapers that I have been in and if you want to look at them you can. I have been in over 7 newspapers and I am going to be doing television programmes very soon". That e-mail may illuminate something of the mother's true motivation.
15. Ms Haigh has also contacted the father's employers through the Company's website and through the personal Facebook accounts of members of staff. Those communications have involved countless documents stating that Mr Tune is a paedophile and a rapist. They also assert an alleged conspiracy through the Court process, the police, all professionals and the Judiciary. Though his employers have been supportive to Mr Tune, they

are anxious about the damage done to the reputation of their business and accordingly Mr Tune's livelihood and thereby his capacity to provide for X, is jeopardised.

16. Perhaps most disturbingly Ms Haigh has caused profound difficulties for X at her school. The school has informed the Court that some, if not most, of the parents whose children attend X's primary school have an understanding of the allegations made by Ms Haigh that are placed on the web. On the 27th May 2011, Ms Haigh emailed several of the parents whose children attend at that school via the school contact list, (which she had obtained) inviting them to visit her webpage. This is a website primarily devoted to this case. It directs the reader by hyperlink to X's police interviews with the heading: VICKY HAIGH: REQUESTING HER DAUGHTER TO RETURN FROM HER PAEDOPHILE FATHER AND DONCASTER "SOCIAL" SERVICES. The site also extends it's scope to a campaign against "secrecy" in the Family Justice System. Ms Haigh has started a petition on this issue which as of the 11th July had 594 signatures. It seems some of the parents may have followed the invitation and have gained access to material which includes extracts of X's interviews to the police. The school informs the Court that the resources which have been deployed in an attempt to keep the other children away from the material on the internet has been significant and indeed of "monumental proportions". Teaching time has been considerably affected as a result of the actions taken by Ms Haigh and great pressure is placed on staff. The Head Teacher has expressed the view that the current proceedings and actions by Ms Haigh in terms of the material that is on the internet, is extremely damaging for a child of X's age:

> "It is fortunate that at this time X is not yet of an age where she is likely to locate the information about her and her family on the internet and that none of the children within her peer group at school also have access to that material. There will, however, become a time when that material will be available to X, which I am of the opinion is extremely damaging".

17. The extracts from X's police interviews contain the false allegations. In addition to the direct harm that causes to X and her father, it is perhaps important to remember that the material will be read by many different people with differing motivations. There are those who will read it for their own sexual gratification, victimising X in the process. The mother seems to be entirely unable to understand or empathise with the consequences to X of these actions. Her ability to focus on her child's needs have, in the Local Authority's analysis, been thoroughly exploited by a number of fanatical campaigners with whom the mother has been in contact.

18. On two occasions the school has had to call the Police both at the School Sports Day, when the mother despite her threats did not attend and at a Christmas Concert when the mother attended and had to be removed.

19. Such is the extent of the false, unauthorised and tendentious material now placed in the public domain that the Local Authority, who would otherwise be striving to protect the privacy of X, have concluded that the balance has shifted and that in this particular case X's best interests is served by the true facts being made available. This position has been supported by the Children's Guardian although he does not agree to X being named. It is ironic, of course, that the mother has complained about the privacy of the Family Court process and has historically argued for greater openness. Realising that the professionals in the case would be bound by their respect for X's privacy, the mother has utilised this to promote her own distorted view of the case which she has been able to advance thus far, unopposed by the true facts.

President's Practice Direction Applications for Reporting Restriction Orders (18 March 2005)

1.1 This direction applies to any application in the Family Division founded on Convention rights for an order restricting publication of information about children or incapacitated adults.

Applications to be heard in the High Court

2.1 Orders can only be made in the High Court and are normally dealt with by a Judge of the Family Division. If the need for an order arises in existing proceedings in the county court, judges should either transfer the application to the High Court or consult their Family Division Liaison Judge. Where the matter is urgent, it can be heard by the Urgent Applications Judge of the Family Division (out of hours contact number 020 7947 6000).

Service of Application on the National News Media

3.1 Section 12(2) of the Human Rights Act 1998 means that an injunction restricting the exercise of the right to freedom of expression must not be granted where the person against whom the application is made is neither present nor represented unless the court is satisfied—

(a) that the applicant has taken all practicable steps to notify the respondent, or

(b) that there are compelling reasons why the respondent should not be notified.

3.2 Service of applications for reporting restriction orders on the national media can now be effected via the Press Association's CopyDirect service, to which national newspapers and broadcasters subscribe as a means of receiving notice of such applications.

3.3 The court will bear in mind that legal advisers to the media—

(i) are used to participating in hearings at very short notice where necessary; and

(ii) are able to differentiate between information provided for legal purposes and information for editorial use.

Service of applications via the CopyDirect service should henceforth be the norm.

3.4 The court retains the power to make without notice orders, but such cases will be exceptional, and an order will always give persons affected liberty to apply to vary or discharge it at short notice.

Further Guidance

4.1 The Practice Note 'Applications for Reporting Restriction Orders' dated 18 March 2005 and issued jointly by the Official Solicitor and the Deputy Director of Legal Services, provides valuable guidance and should be followed.

4.2 Issued with the concurrence and approval of the Lord Chancellor.

PRACTICE NOTE

Official Solicitor: Deputy Director of Legal Services CAFCASS

Applications for Reporting Restriction Orders

1 This Note sets out recommended practice in relation to any application in the Family Division founded on Convention rights for an order which restricts freedom of expression. It is issued in conjunction with the President's Practice Direction "Applications For Reporting Restriction Orders" dated 18 March 2005 and is subject to decisions of the courts. It applies directly to any proceedings in which CAFCASS or the Official Solicitor represent a child or incapacitated adult, and follows discussions between the Official Solicitor, the Deputy Director of Legal Services CAFCASS, and representatives of media interests.

2 **Statutory Provisions**

An application founded on Convention rights need only be made where statutory provisions cannot provide adequate protection. Relevant provisions are Administration of Justice Act 1960, s 12(1); Children and Young Persons Act 1933, s 39; Contempt of Court Act 1981, s 11; Children Act 1989, s 8 (prohibited steps order preventing disclosure of information by parental figure) and s 97(2). While the President's Practice Direction is not aimed at applications under these provisions, s 12(2) of the Human Rights Act 1998 applies to any application for relief which might affect the exercise of the Convention right to freedom of expression and the procedures set out in this Note, including the arrangements for advance notification, can be used to secure compliance with this section in relation to any such application under these provisions.

An order founded on Convention rights may be required, for example, because:

- the need for protection is not linked to particular court proceedings
- the statutory provisions do not prevent publication of all kinds of information
- an injunction is needed to prevent approaches to family, doctors or carers.

3 **Application and Evidence**

The application may be a freestanding claim brought under the Part 8 procedure in the Civil Procedure Rules 1998 or it may be made within existing proceedings to which either the CPR or Family Proceedings Rules 1991 apply. It may be appropriate to seek a direction under CPR 39.2(4), where it applies, that the identity of a party or witness should not be disclosed, and for documents to be drafted identifying individuals by initials.

The applicant should prepare (a) the application/claim form (b) a witness statement justifying the need for an order (c) any legal submissions (d) a draft order and (e) an explanatory note.

Model Forms of Order and an example of an explanatory note are attached to this Practice Note and can be downloaded from the websites of either the Official Solicitor (www.offsol.demon.co.uk) or CAFCASS (www.cafcass.gov.uk).

In the rare event that it is not possible to draft such documentation in the time available before the hearing, the court is likely to require the applicant to file a statement at the earliest opportunity, setting out the information placed orally before the Court.

Subject to any contrary direction of the court, this material should be made available on request to any person who is affected by the order. See

W–v-H (Family Division: Without Notice Orders) [2001] 2 WLR 253; [2001] 2 FLR 927.

4 **Service of Application**

As required by the Practice Direction, advance notice should normally be given to the national media via the Press Association's CopyDirect service. Applicants should first telephone CopyDirect (tel. no 0870 837 6429). Documentation should be sent either by fax (fax no 0870 830 6949) or to the e-mail address provided by CopyDirect. CopyDirect will be responsible for notifying the individual media organisations. In the case of an application against the world at large this is sufficient service for the purposes of advance notice. The website:- http://www.medialawyer.press.net/court applications gives details of the organisations represented and instructions for service of the application. Unless there is a particular reason not to do so, copies of all the documents referred to above should be served. If there is a reason for not serving some or all of the documents (or parts of them), the applicant should ensure sufficient detail is given to enable the media to make an informed decision as to whether it wishes to attend or be legally represented.

The CopyDirect service does not extend to local or regional media or magazines. If service of the application on any specific organisation or person not covered is required it should be effected directly. The Official Solicitor and CAFCASS Legal hold lists of contact details for many national and some regional news organisations, and these are posted on their websites.

5 **The Hearing**

Any application invoking Convention rights will involve a balancing of rights under Article 8 (right to respect for private and family life) and Article 10 (freedom of expression). There is no automatic precedence as between these Articles, and both are subject to qualification where (among other considerations) the rights of others are engaged. Section12(4) of the Act requires the court to have particular regard to the importance of freedom of expression. It must also have regard to the extent to which material has or is about to become available to the public, the extent of the public interest in such material being published and the terms of any relevant privacy code (such as those of the Press Complaints Commission).

The court's approach is laid down in *Re S (a child)(identification: restriction on publication)* [2004] EWCA Civ 963, [2004], Fam 43(CA) and [2004] UKHL 47, 3 FCR 407(HL) and *Campbell-v-Mirror Group Newspapers Ltd.* [2004] UKHL 22. Guidance on the application of s 12(3) is now also provided in *Cream Holdings Ltd v Bannerjee* [2004] UKHL 44.

6 **Scope of Order**

Persons protected

The aim should be to protect the child or incapacitated adult, rather than to confer anonymity on other individuals or organisations. However, the order may include restrictions on identifying or approaching specified family members, carers, doctors or organisations in cases where the absence of such restriction is likely to prejudice their ability to care for the child or patient, or where identification of such persons might lead to identification of the child or patient and defeat the purpose of the order. In cases where the court receives expert evidence the identity of the experts (as opposed to treating clinicians) is not normally subject to restriction.

Identifying persons protected

Once an order has been made, the details of those protected by the order should normally be contained in the Schedule. In exceptional cases (for example *Leeds NHS Trust-v-A & B* [2003] 1 FLR 1091) where it is not appropriate for details to be given, a description by reference to the facts of the case should be contained in the Schedule to enable those reading the order to identify whether a person is likely to be the subject of the order.

Information already in the public domain

Orders will not usually prohibit publication of material which is already in the public domain, other than in exceptional cases such as *Venables and Thompson-v-News Group Newspapers Ltd* [2001] Fam 430.

Duration of Order

Orders should last for no longer than is necessary to achieve the purpose for which they are made. The maximum extent of an order in a child case will usually be the child's 18th birthday. In the case of an incapacitated adult the order will normally end on death. In some cases a later date may be necessary, to protect safety or welfare, or the anonymity of other children who are named in the order and who are still under age, or to maintain the anonymity of doctors or carers after the death of a patient. See for example:

Re C (Adult Patient: Publicity [1996] 2 FLR 251

Venables and Thompson-v-News Group Newspapers Ltd [2001] Fam 430

X (formerly known as Mary Bell)-v-Y and others [2003] EWHC QB 1101.

7 Service of Orders

Service of orders should be effected in the usual way, ie by fax or by post. Contact details for the national press and broadcasters can be found at http://www.medialawyer.press.net/courtapplications.

8 **Undertakings in Damages**

The court will consider whether it is appropriate to require an applicant to give such an undertaking in an individual case, particularly when an order is made without notice, and will bear in mind the applicant's capacity to fulfil any such undertaking.

9 **Explanatory Notes**

It is helpful if applications and orders are accompanied by an explanatory note, from which persons served can readily understand the nature of the case. In any case where notice of an application has not been given, the explanatory note should explain why.

10 **Advice and assistance**

Applicants or respondents are welcome to consult

Deputy Director
CAFCASS Legal Services and Special Casework
8th floor, Wyndham House,
South Quay Plaza, London E14 9SH
DX: 42691 Isle of Dogs

Telephone: 020 7510 7080
Fax: 020 7510 7104
Email: legal@cafcass.gov.uk
Website: www.cafcass.gov.uk
Official Solicitor
81 Chancery Lane
London WC2A 1D

Telephone: 020 7911 7127
Fax: 020 7911 7105
Email: enquiries@offsol.gsi.gov.uk
Website: www.offsol.demon.co.uk
Mike Hinchliffe,
Deputy Director of Legal Services, CAFCASS

Laurence Oates,
Official Solicitor

18 March 2005

Attached:

(1) Model Order

(2) Example of Explanatory Note

IN THE HIGH COURT OF JUSTICE **Case Number: [ ]**
FAMILY DIVISION
[PRINCIPAL REGISTRY]

BEFORE [*JUDGE*] IN PRIVATE
IN THE MATTER OF THE COURT'S INHERENT JURISDICTION
BETWEEN

[ ]
and
[ ]

REPORTING RESTRICTION ORDER

IMPORTANT

If you disobey this order you may be found guilty of contempt of court and may be sent to prison or be fined or have your assets seized. You should read the order carefully and are advised to consult a solicitor as soon as possible. You have the right to ask the Court to vary or discharge the order.

EXPLANATION

A On [*date*] the Court considered an application for a reporting restriction order.

B The following persons and/or organisations were represented before the Court: [*describe parties and their advocates*]

C The Court read the following documents: [*list the documents*]

and/or

The Court directed the [Applicant/Claimant] to file a statement no later than [*date*] setting out the information presented to the court at the hearing.

and/or

The Court directed that copies of the attached Explanatory Note and [*list any other documents*] be made available by the [Applicant/Claimant] to any person affected by this Order.

[D *In a case where an undertaking in damages is required by the Court:*
The Applicant gave an undertaking that if the Court later finds that this Order was obtained as a result of any deliberate or careless misrepresentation by the Applicant, and that this has caused loss to any person served with the Order, and that that person should be compensated, the Applicant will comply with any order the Court may make.]

E *In the case of an order made without notice:*
This order was made without notice to those affected by it, the Court having considered section 12(2) Human Rights Act 1998 and being satisfied (i) that the [Applicant/Claimant] has taken all practicable steps to notify persons affected and/or (ii) that there are compelling reasons for notice not being given, namely: [*set out the Court's reasons for making the order without notice*]

[F *In the case of an application by a local authority:*
The Court granted permission to the Applicant to apply for the exercise of the Court's inherent jurisdiction]

ORDER

1. *Duration*
Subject to any different order made in the meantime, this order shall have effect
[*in the case of an adult*] during the lifetime of the [Defendant], whose details are set out in Schedule 1 to this order.
[*in the case of a child*] until [date], the 18th birthday of the child whose details are set out in Schedule 1 to this order ("the Child").

2. *Who is bound*
This order binds all persons and all companies (whether acting by their directors, employees or agents or in any other way) who know that the order has been made.

3. *Publishing restrictions*
This order prohibits the publishing or broadcasting in any newspaper, magazine, public computer network, internet website, sound or television broadcast or cable or satellite programme service of:
(a) the name and address of
(i) the [Defendant/Child];
(ii) [*in the case of a child*] the Child's parents ("the parents"), whose details are set out in Schedule 2 to this order;
(iii) any individual having day-to-day care of or medical responsibility for the [Defendant/Child] ("a carer"), whose details are set out in Schedule 3 to this Order;
(iv) any residential home or hospital, or other establishment in which the [Defendant/Child] is residing or being treated ("an establishment");
(b) any picture being or including a picture of either the [Defendant/Child], a carer or an establishment;
(c) any other particulars or information relating to the [Defendant/Child];

IF, BUT ONLY IF, such publication is likely to lead to the identification of the [Defendant/ Child] as being [*set out the feature of the situation which has led to the granting of the order*].

4. No publication of the text or a summary of this order (except for service of the order under paragraph 7 below) shall include any of the matters referred to in paragraph 3 above.

[5. *Restriction on seeking information*
This Order prohibits any person from seeking any information relating to the [Defendant/Child] [or the parents] or a carer from any of the following:
(a) the [Defendant/Child];
[(b) the parents];
(c) a carer;
(d) the staff or residents of an establishment.]

6. *What is not restricted by this Order*
Nothing in this Order shall prevent any person from:
(a) publishing information relating to any part of a hearing in a court in England and Wales (including a coroner's court) in which the court was sitting in public and did not itself make any order restricting publication.
(b) seeking or publishing information which is not restricted by Paragraph 3 above.
(c) inquiring whether a person or place falls within paragraph 3(a) above.
(d) seeking information relating to the [Defendant/Child] while acting in a manner authorised by statute or by any court in England and Wales.
(e) seeking information from the responsible solicitor acting for any of the parties or any appointed press officer, whose details are set out in Schedule 4 to this order.
(f) seeking or receiving information from anyone who before the making of this order had previously approached that person with the purpose of volunteering information (but this paragraph will not make lawful the provision or receipt of private information which would otherwise be unlawful).
(g) publishing information which before the service on that person of this order was already in the public domain in England and Wales as a result of publication by another person in any newspaper, magazine, sound or television broadcast or cable or satellite programme service, or on the internet website of a media organisation operating within England and Wales.

7. *Service*
Copies of this Order endorsed with a notice warning of the consequences of disobedience shall be served by the [Applicant/Claimant] (and may be served by any other party to the proceedings)
   (a) by service on such newspaper and sound or television broadcasting or cable or satellite or programme services as they think fit, by fax or first class post addressed to the editor (in the case of a newspaper) or senior news editor (in the case of a broadcasting or cable or satellite programme service) or website administrator (in the case of an internet website) and/or to their respective legal departments; and/or
   (b) on such other persons as the parties may think fit, by personal service.
8. *Further applications about this Order*
The parties and any person affected by any of the restrictions in paragraphs 3-5 above may make application to vary or discharge it to a Judge of the High Court on not less than [*48 hours*] notice to the parties.

SCHEDULE 1

[*The [Defendant/Child]'s Full Name:*

Born:

Address:]

or

[*Information enabling those affected by order to identify the Defendant/Child*]

SCHEDULE 2

[*Similar details of parents*]

SCHEDULE 3

[*Similar details of carers or other persons protected*]

SCHEDULE 4

[*Contact details of responsible solicitor and/or press officer*]

Date of Order: [ ]

NHS TRUST X v AB
Application for a Reporting Restriction Order
EXPLANATORY NOTE

1 AB is in a permanent vegetative state. An application has been made by the NHS Hospital Trust responsible for his care for the Court's approval of the withdrawal of artificial nutrition and hydration. This course is supported by AB's family.

2 On [date] the application will be heard by the President of the Family Division, who will give judgment in open court.

3 A Reporting Restriction Order has been [made/applied for] to protect AB's right to confidentiality in respect of his medical treatment. This does not restrict publication of information or discussion about the treatment of patients in a permanent vegetative state, provided that such publication is not likely to lead to the identification of AB, those caring for him, the NHS Trust concerned or the establishment at which he is being cared for.

The Family Courts: Media Access & Reporting
July 2011

PRESIDENT OF THE FAMILY DIVISION

JUDICIAL COLLEGE

Society of Editors
www.societyofeditors.org

Preface

There is no more difficult issue in family justice than the reporting of cases. There is a tension between concerns about "secret justice" and legitimate expectations of privacy and confidentiality for the family. Both standpoints are valid, and the question is whether they are irreconcilable.

Against this background, and under the wise tutelage of the Lord Chief Justice, a group of lawyers and journalists, including representatives from both the print and broadcast media, have got together to talk to each other. As part of these discussions, they commissioned a paper which would set out a statement of the current state of the law in this most complex area.

The result is the document which follows this Preface. It has been drafted by two members of the bar, Adam Wolanski and Kate Wilson. It is an analysis of where we are at the moment: what we can and what we cannot do. It is, in our view, a substantial and very important piece of work. Its publication is all the more timely as the debate on increased transparency and public confidence in the family courts moves forward. It will serve to inform future consideration of this difficult and sensitive area, including the questions of access to and reporting of proceedings by the media, whilst maintaining the privacy of the families involved.

We are all very grateful to Adam and Kate for the enormous amount of hard work which has gone into the document and to Eddie Craven for proof reading it. We are confident it will be of practical use to journalists, judges and practitioners alike.

We commend it to you.

Sir Nicholas Wall President of the Family Division and Head of Family Justice	Bob Satchwell Executive Director Society of Editors

1

THE FAMILY COURTS: MEDIA ACCESS & REPORTING

ADAM WOLANSKI AND KATE WILSON

Assumptions

1. This paper seeks to draw together a number of interlocking and overlapping statutes, rules and common law principles which affect the ability of the media to inform the public about family proceedings. It does not address proposals which have not been enacted, specifically those in the Children, Schools and Families Act 2010.

2. The law is stated as of July 2011.

INTRODUCTION – PRINCIPLES

Open justice

3. The starting point for consideration of publicity in the family courts, as in all courts, is open justice.

4. Open justice promotes the rule of law[1]. It also promotes public confidence in the legal system[2]. The principle of open justice has two aspects:

   4.1. Proceedings should be held in open court to which the public and the media are admitted; and

   4.2. Nothing should be done to discourage the publication to the wider public of fair and accurate reports of proceedings that have taken place in court[3].

5. Since the enactment of the Human Rights Act 1998, the common law principle of open justice has been reinforced, in different terms, by Art. 6 and Art. 10 of the European Convention on Human Rights and Fundamental Freedoms.

---

[1] *Scott v Scott* [1913] AC 417; *Ex p. Guardian Newspapers Ltd* [1999] 1 WLR 2130 at [25] & [39]; and see *R(Binyam Mohamed) v SoS for Foreign and Commonwealth Affairs* [2010] EWCA Civ 65; [2011] QB 218 at [38]-[42] per Lord Judge CJ for a wide-ranging statement of the role of open justice and the principles it promotes

[2] *Re. Webster (A Child)* [2006] EWHC 2733; [2007] EMLR 7; [2007] 1 FLR 1146 at [24]-[25]

[3] *Attorney General v Leveller Magazine Ltd* [1979] AC 440 *per* Lord Diplock at 450

6. It has been held that the principle of open justice is to be derogated from only to the extent that it is strictly necessary to do so[4]. Applications for orders which amount to derogations must be supported by proper and convincing evidence; assertions or evidence of a generalised nature will not suffice[5].

Derogations from open justice in family courts

7. In *Scott v Scott*[6], the House of Lords recognized three exceptions to the principle of open justice, which justified hearings being held "in camera" [7]. The exceptions were founded in the nature of those proceedings. Two of the exceptions, wardship cases and cases dealing with the affairs of those suffering from mental incapacity, were founded in the jurisdiction being exercised[8]. The matters being dealt with were "truly domestic affairs"[9]. The court is not so much deciding contested questions as exercising what may be described as a paternalistic, parental, quasi-domestic and essentially administrative jurisdiction[10].

8. Statutory provisions have expanded the scope of the derogations from open justice. In addition to the specific class of cases involving children and cases of mental incapacity, ancillary relief proceedings, in which the parties' financial affairs are scrutinised, are also considered to concern private matters[11].

---

[4] *Scott v Scott* (See fn.1) at 438; *Attorney General v Leveller Magazine* (See fn.3) at 450. Note however that article 10 ECHR (freedom of expression) cannot be given a presumptive priority over other Convention rights: *Campbell v MGN* [2004] 2 AC 457 *per* Lord Hope at paragraph [111]; *Re S (A Child) (Identification: Restrictions on publication)* [2004] UKHL 47; [2005] 1 AC 593; [2005] EMLR 2; [2005] 1 FLR 591*per* Lord Steyn at [17]. See also *Re Guardian News & Media* [2010] UKSC 1; [2010] 2 AC 697; [2010] EMLR 15 at [43]-[52]

[5] *Kelly v BBC* [2001] Fam. 59 at 70, 85; See also *Re X (A Child) (Injunctions Restraining Publication)* [2001] 1 FCR 541

[6] See fn.1

[7] *Ibid.* at 436-439, *per* Viscount Haldane LC. *Scott v Scott* was concerned with the final adjudication of a matter which had taken place in camera. Earl Loreburn observed that it was not concerned with "what may be done in chambers, which is a distinct and by no means short subject" (at 445)

[8] The third exception was cases where publicity would defeat the very purpose of the case and would therefore amount to a denial of justice: see para 28 below

[9] See fn.1 at 482-483 *per* Lord Shaw. However, it has been recognized that not all cases involving children or those suffering from mental incapacity are "truly domestic affairs". For example, in care proceedings the intrusion (or potential intrusion) into the family life of those concerned is a serious interference by the state with family life: *Re L (Care: Assessment: Fair Trial)* [2002] EWHC 1379 (Fam), [2002] 2 FLR 730 at [150]; a point reiterated by Munby J, as he then was, in *Re. Webster (A Child)* (See fn. 2) at [74]-[75]. This position contrasts with *Re P-B (A Minor)* [1996] EWCA Civ 510; [1996] 2 FLR 765 at 60 & 63 in which all Children Act 1989 proceedings were considered to be analogous to wardship proceedings. Similarly, where a miscarriage of justice is alleged, the matter is not a purely domestic affair, even if the proceedings concern the welfare of a child: *Re Webster (A Child)* at [110]

[10] See fn 1 at 437 *per* Viscount Haldane

[11] See, for example, *Lykiardopulo v Lykiardopulo* [2010] EWCA Civ 1315; [2011] 1 FLR 1427 at [79]

3

9. There are therefore restrictions upon *access to* family proceedings and upon the *publication of information from* family proceedings.

SOURCES OF LAW

10. The sources of the restrictions upon access to proceedings and reporting of proceedings are:

10.1. Statute law and rules of court made under statute:

10.1.1. Access to hearings is governed by a variety of statutory provisions and rules of court depending on the court. These include the Family Procedure Rules 2010 (for the High Court, County Court and Family Proceedings Courts[12]), the Magistrates' Courts Act 1980 for Family Proceedings Courts[13], the Court of Protection Rules 2007 for that court and the Domestic and Appellate Proceedings (Restriction of Publicity) Act 1968, s1 for appellate courts.

10.1.2. The principal statutory provisions affecting the reporting of family proceedings are the Administration of Justice Act 1960 s12, the Children Act 1989 s97(2) and the Judicial Proceedings (Regulation of Reports) Act 1926 s1.

10.2. Common law

10.3. The European Convention on Human Rights and Fundamental Freedoms: Articles 6, 8 and 10. Under s6 of the Human Rights Act[14] the courts have an obligation to give effect to Convention rights. This has particular significance in respect of those Convention rights which impose a positive obligation on the Convention States to give effect to them[15].

10.4. The High Court has jurisdiction, by virtue of s6 of the Human Rights Act and/or the inherent jurisdiction, to strengthen or relax the default position in terms of access to the court, to documents and to reporting of cases (the disclosure and

[12] FPR 2010 r.2.1
[13] Although the Family Proceedings Courts (Children Act 1989) Rules 1991 have not been revoked, their provisions have been replaced by FPR 2010. It appears that other than where the transitional provisions are relevant, these rules, while technically still in force, can be ignored.
[14] See, for example, *Re Guardian News & Media* (fn. 4) at [28]
[15] *Marckx v Belgium* (1979) 2 EHRR 330; See, for example, in respect of Article 8 *McKennitt v Ash* [2006] EWCA Civ 1714; [2008] QB 73; [2007] EMLR 4 at [9]

restraint jurisdictions)[16]. When considering whether to make such an order, it must consider the competing Convention rights and undertake the "ultimate balancing exercise" mandated by the House of Lords in *Re. S (A Child)*[17]. This encompasses the jurisdiction to grant injunctions *contra mundum* (against the world) including orders providing anonymity to anyone involved in proceedings[18].

ACCESS TO COURT HEARINGS – AN OVERVIEW

11. **Courts which hear family cases**

11.1. A specially constituted magistrates' court, the Family Proceedings Court, has jurisdiction in respect of a wide variety of matters relating to families and children[19].

11.2. County Court, at first instance and on appeals from the Family Proceedings Courts.

11.3. High Court (Family Division) for difficult cases and on appeal.

11.4. High Court (QBD Administrative Court) for cases giving rise to mainly public law questions.

11.5. Court of Appeal and Supreme Court on appeal.

Hearings: introduction

12. Public access to hearings of family matters in the Family Proceedings Court, County Court and High Court (Family Division) is restricted (see below) whereas the default position in the High Court (QBD Administrative Court), Court of Appeal and Supreme Court is for hearings to be held in open court. As a matter of practice most family proceedings are heard in private[20].

Hearings in open court

---

[16] *Re B (A Child) (Disclosure)* [2004] EWHC 411 (Fam); [2004] 2 FLR 142
[17] *Re. Webster (A Child),* (See fn2), at [53]-[55]; *Re S (A Child) (Identification: Restrictions on Publication)* (See fn. 4)
[18] See paras 83-87 below
[19] Magistrates' Court Act 1980, s65 definition of "family proceedings"
[20] For consideration by the ECtHR of the regime for excluding the public from certain classes of case see *B v United Kingdom* [2001] 2 FLR 261; [2002] 34 EHRR 19

13. The media and members of the public may attend family proceedings held in open court.

Hearings in private

14. Most applications in the Family Proceedings Court, the County Court and the Family Division are heard "in private", as provided for by the relevant parts of FPR 2010[21]. The new rules, in force from 6 April 2011, have adopted the terminology of "in private" where the previous rules referred to hearings taking place "in chambers"[22]. Members of the public are not permitted to attend hearings held "in private".

Media attendance at family proceedings held "in private"

15. Duly accredited members of the media are entitled to attend hearings of family proceedings held in private in the Family Division, the County Court and Family Proceedings Courts, subject to the power to exclude them on specified grounds[23].

County Court, High Court (Family Division) and Family Proceedings Courts

16. FPR 2010 r.27.11(2) provides "duly accredited representatives of news gathering and reporting organisations" with a right to attend private hearings in "family proceedings"[24].

17. "Family proceedings" encompass, prima facie, all business conducted in the Family Division"[25]. However, there is no right to attend (i) judicially assisted conciliation or negotiation, including financial dispute resolution hearings[26] and First Hearing Dispute Resolution hearings in Children Act cases to the extent that the judge plays an active

---

[21] FPR 2010 r.27.10 provides for hearings under those rules to be in private unless any enactment provides otherwise or the court directs otherwise.

[22] This, it would appear, has disposed of the confusion arising from the contrast between the practice in the Family Division, where the public were not permitted to attend hearings "in chambers", and that adopted in other divisions of the High Court, where the principle is that the public should be admitted to hearings in chambers if they ask to attend: *Hodgson and Others v Imperial Tobacco and Others* [1998] 1 WLR 1056 *per* Lord Woolf at 1071G. It was held in *Clibbery v Allan* [2002] EWCA Civ 45, [2002] Fam 261; [2002] 1 FLR 565 at [21], [50] that *Hodgson* did not apply to the Family Division. See also Senior Courts Act 1981 s67 and *Re. Webster (A Child)* (See fn.2). The use of the term "in private" corresponds to CPR r.39.2.

[23] FPR 2010 r.27.11(2)(f) (re-enacting the provisions introduced by the Family Proceedings (Amendment) (No.2) Rules 2009/85).

[24] See generally *Practice Direction (Family Proceedings: Media Representatives)* [2009] 1 WLR 1111 on the previous provision in FPR 1991 r.10.28 in the same terms as FPR 2010 r.27.11(2)

[25] Matrimonial and Family Proceedings Act 1984, s32 and Senior Courts Act 1981, s61

[26] r.27.11(1)(a)

part; (ii) parental order applications[27]; (iii) hearings in adoption cases[28]; (iv) hearings in the Court of Protection, which is subject to its own rules. Practice Directions may provide for other types of hearings from which the media may be excluded[29].

18. A media representative is accredited if s/he carries a press card issued by the UK Press Card Authority[30].

19. The media may be excluded from all or part of the proceedings if it is necessary on one of the three grounds specified in r.27.11(3)(a) or justice will otherwise be impeded or prejudiced (r.27.11(3)(b)). The three grounds are that it is necessary (a) in the interests of any child concerned in, or connected with, the proceedings; (b) for the safety or protection of a party, a witness in the proceedings, or a person connected with such a party or witness; or (c) for the orderly conduct of the proceedings.

20. In determining whether the test of necessity is satisfied, the court should consider whether lesser measures would suffice[31]. If the applicant can satisfy one of the grounds for exclusion, then the court must carry out a balancing exercise and reach a value judgment about where the balance between the competing Convention rights lies (including, where relevant, of parties or witnesses and not just the child concerned)[32]. Ground (b) also enables the court to exclude the media to protect the article 8 rights of the parties where outrageous or intimate allegations were being made[33].

21. The court may exclude the media to protect the welfare of a vulnerable adult or child who is unrepresented, even if that party does not itself seek exclusion[34].

22. A person wishing to exclude the media must satisfy the court of the necessity of exclusion; it is not for the media to justify their attendance[35].

---

[27] r.27.11(1)(b)(i)
[28] r.27.11(1)(b)(ii). Hearings under the Adoption and Children Act 2002 are also governed by the Family Procedure (Adoption) Rules 2005
[29] r.27.11(1)(b)(iii)
[30] *Practice Direction* (See fn. 24) at para 4.2. Journalists from outside the jurisdiction are able to obtain UK Press Cards, but they may be beyond the court's contempt jurisdiction. The reporting risk arising from the presence of foreign reporters in court was a concern in *Re Child X* (*Residence and Contact: Rights of Media Attendance*) [2009] EWHC 1728; [2009] EMLR 26; [2009] 2 FLR 1467 at [66]
[31] *Practice Direction* (See fn.24) para 5.2
[32] *Re. Child X* (See fn. 30)
[33] *Ibid* at [45]
[34] *Practice Direction* (See fn.24) at para 5.2
[35] *Spencer v Spencer* [2009] EWHC 1529 (Fam); [2009] EMLR 25 at [35]; [2009] 2 FLR 1416

7

23. If a party seeks to exclude the media he should give advance notice of his intention to make his application to the court, to the other parties, to any representative of the child[36] and to the media by the Press Association's CopyDirect service[37]. The obligation to notify the media only arises when the application is made at the outset of the proceedings[38].

24. When the rules on media access were introduced (previously as FPR 1991 r.10.28 on 6 April 2009), the Practice Direction gave guidance that where contentious matters about media access arose in the Family Proceedings Courts or County Court, the matter should be transferred to the Family Division for consideration (Practice Direction of 22 April 2009, para 20). Despite the limited judicial scrutiny of the rules on media attendance, it is suggested that it will only be "necessary and appropriate" to transfer the matter to the High Court, where there are novel, difficult or important issues at stake.

25. If members of the public (as opposed to accredited media) wish to attend a hearing, then they must apply to the court to disapply FPR 2010 r.27.10(1) (or equivalent provision for particular proceedings). The court should upon such an application undertake a balancing exercise of the competing Convention rights engaged[39].

Hearings in secret ('in camera')

26. Neither media representatives nor members of the public may attend hearings which take place *in camera* (in secret)[40].

27. Hearings of family cases take place in secret only rarely. However:

   27.1. The court has the power to direct that the whole or part of any proceedings for a declaration of legitimacy shall be heard *in camera*[41]; and

---

[36] *Practice Direction* (See fn.24) at para 6.3. Use of this service enables an applicant to comply with the notification requirement of s12(2) of the Human Rights Act. See http://www.medialawyer.press.net/courtapplications/ where applicants can find a copy of the Practice Direction, the accompanying Practice Note explaining how to use the service and the Application for Reporting Restriction Orders Checklist which applicants should complete for the court before the hearing

[37] *Re Child X* (See fn. 30) at [86]

[38] On a decision to exclude the media, it is unclear what they can, or should, do if they wish to challenge that decision (i.e. seek judicial review or to appeal): see *Borrie & Lowe: The Law of Contempt* 4th ed at §9.13

[39] On an application under the old rules to disapply FPR 1991 r.4.16(7), which provided for hearings to take place in chambers, this was the approach which Munby J adopted, *Re Webster (A Child)* (See fn.2) at [77]

[40] The provisions addressed in this section for media attendance at hearings only apply to hearings "in private"

[41] Family Law Act 1986, s60(4)

27.2. Evidence of sexual capacity in the course of nullity proceedings is heard *in camera*, although the judge has a discretion to hear it in open court where the interests of justice so require[42].

28. The court has an inherent power to regulate its own proceedings and may hear cases *in camera* in exceptional circumstances. At common law a hearing may be held *in camera* where the hearing of the case in public would frustrate or render impracticable the administration of justice[43]. The test is one of necessity. In cases of abduction (of a child or a vulnerable adult) the Court will sit in camera when determining issues which are directed towards locating the abducted person (despite the fact that the orders being made are likely to be draconian e.g. freezing orders, orders compelling disclosure from anyone who may have knowledge of the persons whereabouts). To do otherwise would defeat the object of the hearing by alerting the abductor to the measures being taken[44].

29. Circumstances which may justify hearing a case *in camera* include situations where the evidence, if made public, would cause harm to national security. If the court can adopt a lesser measure it should do so.

30. The court has no power to direct that a court sit *in camera* because hearing the case in public may be painful, humiliating or a deterrent to parties or witnesses or because the evidence is of an unsavoury character[45].

MEDIA ACCESS TO COURT DOCUMENTS – GENERAL CONSIDERATIONS

31. In most family proceedings, media representatives have no entitlement to receive or peruse court documents referred to in the course of evidence, submissions, or judgment.

32. The communication of information relating to proceedings held in private (whether or not contained in a document filed with the court) is governed by chapter 7 of Part 12 of FPR 2010 and Practice Direction (PD) 12G. Nothing in FPR, however, permits the communication to the public at large, or any section of the public, of any information

---

[42] Matrimonial Causes Act 1973, s48(2)
[43] *AG v Leveller Magazine* (See fn.3) *per* Lord Diplock p. 450
[44] See the discussion of this "this small, discrete and necessarily discreet part of the Family Division's jurisdiction" in *Re HM (Vulnerable Adult: Abduction)* [2010] EWHC 870 (Fam); [2010] 2 FLR 1057 at [37].
[45] *Scott v Scott* (See fn.1) at 463

9

relating to the proceedings[46], and nothing in FPR 12.75 (Communication of information for purposes connected with the proceedings) permits the disclosure of an unapproved draft judgment handed down by any court[47].

33. The provisions in the FPR and PD 12G, which concern the disclosure of information from family proceedings generally (i.e. not only to the media), are described in detail at paragraphs 135-145 below.

34. If media representatives wish to see documents referred to in family proceedings, they may apply to the judge or, in some types of cases, may request the documents from a party. An exception is that in matrimonial and partnership proceedings under Part 7 of the Family Procedure Rules 2010 witness statements which stand as evidence in chief are available for public inspection[48].

35. The position is to be contrasted with that in proceedings governed by the CPR (which do not apply to most family proceedings). In such cases, where hearings take place in open court, there is what may be described as a presumption in favour of providing to third parties documents which were relied upon by the court in reaching its decision[49], though not the entire court file[50].

36. In family proceedings, if a media representative applies to the judge to see documents referred to during proceedings, the judge may exercise the disclosure jurisdiction to grant the application[51]. This involves considering the competing Convention rights and undertaking the "ultimate balancing exercise" mandated by the House of Lords in *Re. S*

[46] FPR 12.73(2). In other words, AJA 1960 s.12 continues to apply unless the court grants permission for disclosure to be made.
[47] FPR r.12.73(3)
[48] FPR 2010 r.22.19
[49] *Dain AO v Davis Frankel and Mead* [2004] EWHC 2662 (Comm); [2005] 1 WLR 2951; *Cleveland Bridge UK Ltd v Multiplex Constructions (UK) Limited* [2005] EWHC 2101 (TCC)
[50] Third parties must apply for permission to access the court file (save for the statements of case and orders: CPR r.5.4C). Skeleton arguments should also be made available in the Court of Appeal as a matter of course and also in other hearings where they are a substitute for oral submissions: Practice Direction (Court of Appeal: Leave to Appeal and Skeleton Arguments) [1999] 1 WLR 2; *GIO Personal Investment Services Ltd v Liverpool and London Steamship Protection and Indemnity Association Ltd* [1999] 1 WLR 984
[51] Recent ECHR authority supports the proposition that Article 10 provides the media with a protected right of access to official records: see *Tarsasag a Szabadsagjogokert v Hungary* (No 37374/05) considered by the Court of Appeal in *Independent News and Media Ltd v A* [2010] EWCA Civ 343; [2010] EMLR 22; [2010] 2 FLR 1290 and in *Sugar v BBC* [2010] EWCA Civ 715; [2010] 1 WLR 2278; [2010] EMLR 24 at [76]

(A Child)[52]. A highly relevant factor will be the extent to which provision of the documents will assist the media representatives in following the proceedings[53].

37. In *Re X, Y, Z (Morgan v A Local Authority)*[54], Sir Nicholas Wall P said he would like to see a practice develop whereby expert reports are routinely disclosed to media representatives, and media representatives made able to comment both on the reports and on the use to which they were put in the proceedings as long as this did not undermine the child's anonymity.

38. An order permitting media representatives to see documents referred to during proceedings does not, in itself, entitle the contents of those documents to be published to the world at large. The contents may be published in so far as this is not prohibited by section 12 of the Administration of Justice Act 1960, or that provision is disapplied, (see paras 47-54 below), section 97(2) of the Children Act 1997 (see paras 55-59 below) or by the restrictions applicable to information disclosed during proceedings for ancillary relief (see paras 71-75 below).

39. A party may provide documents or information from proceedings to representatives of the media in so far as this is not prohibited by the restrictions set out in the above paragraph, the general law of breach of confidence and misuse of private information or applicable rules of court, including FPR 2010 r.12.73 (proceedings relating to children). This rule permits the communication of information about the private proceedings to specified persons, but prohibits communication of information about the Children Act 1989 proceedings to the public generally[55].

40. FPR 2010 r.12.73 does not permit disclosure of documents or information to members of the media and to do so remains a contempt. However, a party may, because of r.12.75, be able to make disclosures to a journalist if this is necessary to enable that party to make a complaint against a person or body concerned in the proceedings or regarding the law, policy or procedure relating to private family proceedings. A journalist who

[52] *Re. Webster (A Child)* (See fn.2) at [53]-[55]; *Re S (A Child) (Identification: Restrictions on Publication)* (See fn.4)
[53] *Norfolk County Council v Webster* [2006] EWHC 2898 (Fam); [2007] 2 FLR 415 *per* Munby J at [40] to [43]
[54] [2011] EWHC 1157 (Fam)
[55] FPR 2010 r.12.73 lists persons to whom the communication of information about proceedings in private would not be a contempt, these include legal advisors, experts and a professional engaged in child protection (see paras 135-145 below)

receives such disclosures is, however, forbidden from putting that information into the public domain without the permission of the court[56].

The implied undertaking: information disclosed under compulsion

41. Where a party has disclosed information during proceedings under compulsion, rights of confidentiality in that information are preserved until that information is deployed in open court[57].

42. The implied undertaking operates to prevent a party from supplying to any third party, including a journalist, documents or information provided to him by another party under compulsion. This includes, by way of example, information about a party's means provided in Form E Affidavits during proceedings for ancillary relief and information provided in answer to questions before or after orders of the court[58].

43. The implied undertaking does not extend to information which a party chose to include in an affidavit, but which he was not compelled to provide[59]. Neither does it prevent a party from providing his own documents, or information about his own confidential affairs, to third parties, including journalists.

REPORTING THE COURTS – OVERVIEW

44. Unless restricted by statute or by court order, it is possible to report what happens in open court and, more importantly for the purposes of family law proceedings, what occurs in private. Subject to any statutory restrictions or court orders, the fact that a case is heard in private does not, in itself, mean it cannot be reported[60], except if it is accompanied by comment which substantially prejudices the administration of justice[61]. However, information put before a court sitting in private which is derived from compulsory disclosure cannot be reported unless that information is put into the public domain[62].

[56] *Re N (Family Proceedings: Disclosure)* [2009] EWHC 1663 (Fam); [2009] 2 FLR 1152 *per* Munby J at [52] to [81].
[57] *Home Office v Harman* [1983] 1 AC 280. For proceedings governed by the CPR, see CPR r.31.22
[58] *A v A, B v B* [2000] 1 FLR 701 *per* Charles J at 717
[59] *Clibbery v Allan* (See fn. 22) at [98].
[60] *AF Noonan (Architectural Practice) Ltd v Bournemouth and Boscombe Athletic Community Football Club Ltd* [2007] EWCA Civ 848; 1 WLR 2614
[61] *Hodgson* (See fn. 22) at 1072A; *Dobson v Hastings* [1992] Ch 394
[62] See paragraphs 42-43 above and 71-75 below

45. The law on reporting family proceedings is said to have been "unaffected" by the new rules on media access[63]. However, there is doubt as to whether a hearing with media representatives in attendance can properly said to be held 'in private'. In *Re Webster (A Child)*[64], a case decided before the implementation of the new rules on media access, Munby J held that a hearing with media representatives in attendance (but with the public excluded) was not "in private" within the meaning of s.12 of the AJA 1960 s.12, so that section did not apply. The 'premise' of the new rules that proceedings remain in private even when media representatives are present[65] has not been subjected to judicial scrutiny.

46. The following provides an overview of statutory restrictions which affect the reporting of family courts.

Administration of Justice Act 1960, s12(1)

47. The effect of section 12(1) is to prohibit publication of information about proceedings in private which relate to the High Court's exercise of the inherent jurisdiction, are under the Children Act 1989, the Adoption and Children Act 2002 or relate wholly or mainly to the maintenance or upbringing of a minor. Section 12 also applies where the proceedings are brought under the Mental Health Act 1983 authorising an application or reference to be made to a First Tier Tribunal or to a county court and under the Mental Capacity Act 2005. The prohibition is without time limit[66].

48. In addition to pure 'children cases', AJA 1960 s12 may apply to other proceedings, for example applications for an occupation order under Part IV of the Family Law Act 1996 because, on the facts of the particular case, the welfare of a child is a major issue[67].

---

[63] *Practice Direction* (See fn. 24) at para 2.4. Note that in *MNB v News Group Newspapers Limited* [2011] EWHC 528 (QB) at [14], Sharp J contrasted the position in the QBD with that in the Family Division. In the latter "*the jurisdictional basis for the attendance of accredited media representatives at hearings which are private and which are not open to the general public in the family courts is statutory: the relevant FPR (10.28) was inserted into the FPR by statutory instrument.*" There was, she held, no such statutory basis for such a distinction in the QBD.
[64] See fn. 2
[65] See President's Guidance Note 22 April 2009
[66] *Re E (A Minor) (Child Abuse: Evidence)* [1991] 1 FLR 420 concerning AJA s12(1)(a)(i)
[67] *Clibbery v Allan* (See fn. 22) at [79]; Likewise, it is possible that ancillary relief proceedings could relate "wholly or mainly to the maintenance or upbringing of a minor", although this is "unlikely", and the usual issues, like the accommodation needs of a child to the relationship, would not bring ancillary relief proceedings within s12, *Spencer v Spencer* (See fn. 35) at [12]-[15].

49. Section 12 does not operate to prohibit the reporting of the identity (name, address and photograph) of those involved in proceedings, whether as the child concerned or as a party or witness; it does not prohibit the identification of expert witnesses; nor does it prohibit reporting of the fact of that person's involvement in proceedings, including, in the case of witnesses, the party on whose behalf they gave evidence; the dates, times and places of hearings, what is observed by those lawfully in the open areas of the court building; the nature of the dispute; and the order or a summary of it.

50. Instead, it operates to prohibit dissemination of what went on in front of the judge and the documents filed for the proceedings, including written evidence, reports and written submissions. It also prohibits notes or transcripts of evidence and submissions, extracts from documents filed and summaries of them. The prohibition operates even if the documents are anonymised[68].

51. The question of what amounts to the 'nature of the dispute' is best illustrated by example, although each case will invariably turn on its own facts. In *Re B,* Munby J observed that it would not have been a contempt under section 12 for the media to report that the issues in that case included "whether the mother suffered from Munchausen's Syndrome by Proxy and whether she had killed (or attempted to kill) her child(ren) by, for instance, smothering or poisoning"[69]. While not expressing a final view, he indicated that the information which had in fact been published by a newspaper, namely that in evidence it had been suggested that the mother had injected her child with dirty water, was likely to be a contempt. In the earlier case of *X v Dempster*[70] (which Munby J expressly agreed with in *Re B*), it was held that the publication of the information, that in the proceedings the mother had been portrayed as a bad mother who was unfit to look after her children, went beyond a description of the nature of the dispute and was a discussion of the substance of the matters before the court; it was therefore not permissible.

52. Importantly, it is not a contempt for a person to communicate information or to disseminate documents which he or she could have done if there had never been any legal proceedings, so long as that information (or those documents) is not linked to those

[68] *Re B (A Child) (Disclosure)* (See fn. 16)
[69] *Ibid* at [80]
[70] [1999] 1 FLR 894

proceedings[71]. Section 12 does not does not operate to prohibit publication of the contents of documents which are lodged at court, or used in the proceedings, which already existed (e.g. many exhibits to witness statements) or information of an analogous quality. Therefore information in witness statements will not automatically fall within s12 merely because it is included in a witness statement.

53. Section 12(2) provides that the publication of the text or a summary of the whole or part of an order made by a court sitting in private shall not be a contempt of court unless prohibited by the court.

54. The court may disapply s12 where the balance of the competing private and public interests favours disclosure, as opposed to continued confidentiality. In *Re Ward (A Child)*[72], Munby J ordered that the s12 restrictions be relaxed. In that case, the information which would otherwise have been restricted did not engage the private interests of anyone other than the Ward family, who were the party seeking permission to publish the information. It is worth noting, however, that the Judge dealt with the anonymity of witnesses as a discrete issue. In that case there was an application for anonymity by some witnesses, but even in circumstances where the only application before the court is one to disapply s12, it may be necessary to consider whether other orders are necessary to protect legitimate interests in the event that the application is granted. In *Re X, Y, Z (Morgan v A Local Authority)*[73], Sir Nicholas Wall P relaxed s12 to permit reporting and discussion of an expert's report prepared by a doctor for the purpose of care proceedings.

Children Act 1989, s97(2)

55. The Children Act 1989, s97(2) prohibits the publication of material which identifies, or is likely to identify, a child involved in proceedings in which any power under the Children Act 1989, or the Adoption and Children Act 2002, may be exercised.

[71] *Re Ward (A Child)* [2010] EWHC 16 (Fam); [2010] 1 FLR 1497 at [105]-[114]. "Information relating to proceedings" within the meaning of AJA 1960 s12 distinguishes between documents and information which "relate to the proceedings" and documents and information which were merely deployed in proceedings. "Information relating to proceedings" includes documents prepared for that purpose (e.g. witness statements and position statements) and information (whether or not reduced to writing) which came to light as part of the information gathering process during, and for the purpose of, the proceedings.
[72] *Ibid.*
[73] See fn. 54

56. The prohibition only lasts for the duration of proceedings[74].

57. The Court has the power to dispense with the restriction where the "welfare of the child requires it", s97(4). However, s97(4) does not provide the only basis on which the restriction in s97(2) can be relaxed and it must be read in broad (i.e. Convention compliant) terms. Therefore it is not exercisable only when the welfare of the child requires it, but also when it is necessary and proportionate to do so to give effect to rights under Art.10 (or other Convention rights)[75].

58. At the conclusion of proceedings in which the identity of the child concerned has been protected by the operation of s97(2), the court should consider whether it is necessary to continue such protection, although an injunction is unlikely to be justified in most cases[76].

59. The prohibition in s97(2) does not apply in the Court of Appeal[77].

Judicial Proceedings (Restriction on Reports) Act 1926

60. The Judicial Proceedings (Regulation of Reports) Act 1926 s(1)(b) imposes restrictions in the following types of proceedings:

60.1. Any judicial proceedings for the dissolution or nullity of marriage or for judicial separation, or for the dissolution, annulment or order for separation of a civil partnership;

60.2. Proceedings under s27 of the Matrimonial Causes Act 1973 (proceedings by a wife against her husband, or by a husband against his wife, for financial provision)[78] and proceedings under the Civil Partnership Act 2004 Part 9 Sch 5;

60.3. Proceedings under the Family Law Act 1986 Part III (declarations of marital status, parentage and legitimacy)[79] and under the Civil Partnership Act 2004, s58 (declarations of subsistence of a civil partnership)[80].

---

[74] *Clayton v Clayton* [2006] Fam 83; [2007] EMLR 3; [2007] 1 FLR 11
[75] *Re Webster (A Child)* (See fn2) at [57]-[62] (For the balancing exercise, see para 10.4 above)
[76] *Pelling v Bruce-Williams* [2004] EWCA Civ 845; [2004] Fam 155; [2004] 2 FLR 823 at [51]; *Clayton v Clayton* (See fn.74) at [77] per Potter P and at [145] per Wall LJ
[77] *Ibid*
[78] Domestic and Appellate Proceedings (Restriction of Publicity) Act 1968 s2
[79] Inserted by Family Law Act 1996 s68(1) Sch 1 para 9b
[80] Civil Partnership Act 2004 Sch 27 para 29(2)

61. In the above cases, it is unlawful to publish anything except the following:

61.1. the names, addresses and occupations of the parties and witnesses;

61.2. a concise statement of the charges, defences and countercharges in support of which evidence has been given (or equivalent);

61.3. submissions on any point of law arising in the course of the proceedings and the decision of the court thereon;

61.4. the summing-up of the judge and the findings of the jury (if any) and the judgment of the court and observations made by the judge in giving judgment.

Does the 1926 Act restrict reports of hearings in applications for ancillary relief?

62. Munby J in *Clibbery v Allan* at first instance expressed the opinion that the 1926 Act applied to hearings in applications for ancillary relief[81].

63. However, upon appeal in *Clibbery*, Thorpe LJ said it was "self evident that the 1926 Act no longer bites on the business of the courts in our modern family justice system"[82]. Thorpe LJ also described as "inherently unsound" the proposition that the 1926 Act applied to applications for ancillary relief, but emphasised that his opinion on the matter was "provisional"[83].

64. There remains doubt over the issue[84].

Magistrates' Courts Act 1980

65. In respect of Family Proceedings Courts, MCA 1980 s71 prescribes the matters which may be reported, namely: the names, addresses and occupations of the parties and witnesses; the grounds of the application, and a concise statement of the charges,

[81] *Clibbery v Allan* [2001] 2 FLR 819
[82] *Clibbery v Allan* (See fn. 22) at [91]
[83] *Ibid* at [108] and [109]
[84] In *Spencer v Spencer* (See fn.35) Munby J declined to make any ruling as to whether the 1926 Act applied to reports of the ancillary relief application before the court. He pointed out that what he had said on the point in *Clibbery* had been *obiter*, since that had not been a claim for ancillary relief.

defences and counter-charges in support of which evidence has been given; submissions on any point of law arising in the course of proceedings and the decision of the court on the submissions; the decision of the court, and any observations made by the court in giving it[85].

Children and Young Persons Act 1933, s39

66. Although in practice the power to make orders under section 39 is not used much in family proceedings, it is of general application to all courts. It provides the court with the jurisdiction to restrain the publication in newspaper reports of matters, including photographs, which would lead to the identification of a child "concerned in the proceedings" (whether as a party, subject or witness)[86]. In *Harris v Harris*[87] Munby J held that, when possible, s39 orders should be made in preference to orders which imposed wider or greater restrictions.

Contempt of Court Act 1981, s11

67. Section 11 provides that in any case where a court (having power to do so) allows a name or other matter to be withheld from the public in proceedings before the court, the court may give such directions prohibiting the publication of that name or matter in connection with the proceedings as appear to the court to be necessary for the purpose for which it was so withheld.

68. Section 11 can only be invoked where the court allows a name or matter to be withheld from being mentioned in open court in the proceedings. It follows that it does not provide the court with a power to prohibit publication of any name or other matter which has been given in open court in the proceedings[88].

The jurisdiction to grant injunctions to give effect to a party's Convention rights

69. In addition to its powers under statute, the High Court has power to grant injunctions to restrain reporting of matters in order to give effect to the rights of both children and

[85] It is arguable that the provision, which is limited to *"newspapers, periodicals and programmes within the Broadcasting Act 1990"* does not apply to online publications and webcasts, save to the extent that newspapers' websites may be caught by s71(1B)(a)
[86] Extended to cover reports on television and sound broadcasting by the Children and Young Persons Act 1963, ss 57(1) and 64(3) and Schedule 5.
[87] [2001] 2 FLR 895 at [341].
[88] *Re Trinity Mirror plc* [2008] EWCA Crim 50; [2008] QB 770; [2009] EMLR 3

adults under the ECHR. This encompasses the power to restrain reporting of family cases. In *Spencer v Spencer* Munby J held that the court has jurisdiction to restrain reporting of hearings of applications for ancillary relief[89].

70. There has been no judicial consideration given to the circumstances in which the power to injunct the reporting of proceedings should be exercised. The general approach must, it is suggested, be in accordance with that applying to the restraint jurisdiction in general: see paragraph 10.4 above.

The implied undertaking: a further limitation upon reporting

71. In *Clibbery v Allan,* Butler Sloss LJ said, "information disclosed under the compulsion of ancillary relief proceedings is, in my judgment, protected by the implied undertaking before, during and after the proceedings are completed"[90].

72. Given the extent to which information disclosed under compulsion is referred to in proceedings for ancillary relief, Butler Sloss LJ concluded that "all cases involving issues of ancillary relief are also protected from publication by anyone without the leave of the court"[91].

73. Similarly, in *Lykiardopulo v Lykiardopulo* Stanley Burnton LJ said: "Parties to a matrimonial dispute who bring before the court the facts and documents relating to their financial affairs may in general be assured that the confidentiality of that information will be respected. They are required by the court to produce the information and documents, and it is a general principle, applicable to both civil and family proceedings, that confidential information produced by those who are compelled to do so will remain so unless and until it passes into the public domain"[92].

74. The position therefore is that the media will have considerable difficulty in reporting proceedings for ancillary relief and other cases in which reference is made to information disclosed under compulsion *unless the information passes into the public domain*.

[89] See fn. 35 at [25] to [28]. See also *D v D* [2009] EWHC 946 (Fam); [2009] 2 FLR 324
[90] See fn. 22 at [72]
[91] *Ibid* at [75]. See also Thorpe LJ at [106]
[92] *Ibid* at [76]

75. A question arises as to whether information put before a court sitting in private with media representatives lawfully in attendance has entered the public domain. If so, the implied undertaking ceases to have effect in respect of that information. This is not a matter which has received judicial consideration.

REPORTING THE COURTS – JUDGMENTS

76. There is no general statutory requirement for all judgments to be recorded in writing. FPR 2010 r.27.2(3) requires Family Proceedings Courts to give written reasons.

77. Whether or not a judgment is handed down in private or public (and if so, in what form) is primarily a matter for the judge's discretion. Although it remains a matter for the judge, senior members of the judiciary have encouraged the making of public judgments[93]. Furthermore judges should consider providing short written summaries in cases which have attracted media attention to assist the reporting of them[94].

78. These judgments may identify the parties and witnesses or may be anonymised and/or redacted so as to exclude sensitive material[95].

79. If parties are in the public eye anonymisation may achieve nothing, and for this reason judgments in financial cases involving celebrities have been released in unanonymised form in recent years[96].

80. Where a party has attempted to perpetrate a fraud by giving perjured evidence there may be strong reasons for releasing an unanonymised judgment, although publication of a judgment should not be used as an aid to enforcement of a judgment award[97].

81. A public judgment may be reported. A judgment handed down in private is however subject to the restrictions applicable to reporting cases in general. In particular, the effect of s12 of the Administration of Justice Act 1960 is to prohibit the publication of much of the contents of the judgment in cases to which that section applies[98].

[93] *Re H (Freeing Orders: Publicity)* [2005] EWCA Civ 1325; [2006] 1 FLR 815 at [26] per Wall LJ
[94] Ibid at [30]-[32]
[95] *Lykiardopulo v Lykiardopulo* (See fn. 11) at [52]
[96] For example *Mills McCartney v McCartney* [2008] EWHC 401 (Fam); [2008] 1 FLR 1508
[97] *Lykiardopulo v Lykiardopulo* (See fn. 11) at [73] [79] – [80]
[98] *Re B (A Child) (Disclosure)* (See fn.16) at [66]

The meaning and effect of rubrics

82. Anonymised public judgments generally contain a rubric prohibiting the identification of some or all of those involved in the proceedings. Since these rubrics permit the reporting of judgments (which would otherwise be prohibited by s.12 AJA 1960) *subject to* compliance with the rubric, publications which fail to comply with the rubric may contravene s12 AJA 1960 and be a contempt[99]. However such rubrics are not enforceable as injunctions[100].

ORDERS *CONTRA MUNDUM*

83. An order *contra mundum* is an injunction which effectively binds everyone with knowledge of the order. Such orders are founded on Convention rights, and in particular the right to a private and family right under ECHR article 8: *In Re S (A Child)*[101] . Applications for such orders should be made in the Family Division of the High Court[102].

84. The media must be served with applications for *contra mundum* orders in accordance with the President's Practice Direction[103]. Service on the media should be effected by the Press Association's CopyDirect service (and other means where appropriate)[104], in order to ensure compliance with s12(2) of the Human Rights Act.

85. Applications for *contra mundum* orders should only be made where other statutory restrictions are inadequate[105].

86. Public agencies (local authorities and hospital trusts for example) and professional witnesses (experts, treating clinicians and social workers) cannot expect to obtain injunctions *contra mundum* to restrain publication of the fact they have been involved in proceedings[106].

---

[99] See, for example, *Re B* [2007] EWHC 1622 (Fam); [2008] 1 FLR 482 *per* Munby J at [12] and *Re B* [2008] EWHC 270 (Fam) [2008] 1 FLR 1460 *per* Munby J at [12].
[100] *Re HM, (A Vulnerable Adult: Abduction)* [2010] EWHC 1579 (Fam); [2011] 1 FLR 97 at [12]–[23]
[101] See fn. 4
[102] President's Practice Direction [2005] 2 FLR 120
[103] *Ward v CAFCASS* [2007] EWHC 616 (Fam); [2007] 2 FLR 765; [2007] Fam Law 704 at [44]
[104] *Ibid*; *Harris v Harris* (See fn. 87) at 341. See http://www.medialawyer.press.net/courtapplications/ where applicants can find a copy of the Practice Direction, the accompanying Practice Note explaining how to use the service and the Application for Reporting Restriction Orders Checklist which applicants should complete for the court before the hearing
[105] Practice Note [2005] Fam Law 398, para 2
[106] *Re Ward (A Child)* (See fn 71). See, in a different context, *In re Guardian News and Media* (See fn. 4) at [52] *per* Lord Rogers: the test for whether to grant anonymity to a party is "whether there is sufficient general, public

87. In most cases it will be appropriate to include in an order *contra mundum* a public domain proviso, (and this will be consistent with s12(4) of the Human Rights Act), permitting the publication of information already in the public domain, although it is possible that on the facts of certain cases the balance of the rights will come down in favour of not including one[107].

interest in publishing a report of the proceedings which identifies [the party] to justify any resulting curtailment of his right and his family's right to respect for their private and family life".

[107] *Re Stedman* [2009] EWHC 935 (Fam); [2009] 2 FLR 852 at [90]-[91], considering *Re X, Y Children* [2004] EWHC 762 (Fam); [2004] EMLR 29 and *A v M* [2000] 1 FLR 562, which were, respectively, cases where "the public domain material was old and had been published only in local newspapers" or "was information from court proceedings … held in private" and "the injunction was capable of enforcement".

TYPES OF CASE

CHILDREN: PUBLIC LAW CASES

Family Proceedings Court

Access to the court

88. In proceedings in which powers under the Children Act 1989 may be exercised, the only persons who may attend a hearing are those directly concerned in the case and "representatives of newspapers and news agencies"[108]; and/or "duly accredited representatives of news gathering and reporting organisations"[109].

89. The above default position can be varied and the media (and others) excluded if it is "necessary in the interest of the administration of justice or of public decency"[110]; and/or it is necessary "in the interests of any child concerned in or connected with proceedings", for the safety of a person or for the orderly conduct of proceedings or justice will otherwise be impeded or prejudiced[111].

Access to documents

90. The Family Proceedings Courts are governed by FPR 2010 r.12.73 (see para 39 above). However, if an order is made in open court, any person may obtain a copy on payment of the prescribed fee (FPR 2010 r.29.12).

Reporting

91. The following restrictions will automatically apply, unless varied by the magistrates

91.1. MCA 1980 s71 (see para 65 above).

91.2. AJA 1960 s12(1) applies (see paras 47-54 above)

91.3. Children Act 1989, s97(2) (see paras 55-59 above)

[108] Magistrates' Courts Act 1980, s69(2)
[109] FPR 2010 r.27.11(2)
[110] Magistrates' Courts Act 1980, s69(4)
[111] FPR 2010 r.27.11(3)

Judgments

92. In Children Act proceedings, magistrates are required to record written reasons for decisions following a hearing[112] [113].

County Court and High Court (Family Division)

Access to the court

93. Hearings in proceedings under the Children Act 1989 are in private unless the court directs otherwise, FPR 2010 r.27.10. But FPR 2010 r.27.11(2) gives a right to "duly accredited representatives of news gathering and reporting organisations" to attend private hearings in children proceedings (see paras 15-25 above).

Access to documents

94. "Information relating to proceedings held in private (whether or not contained in a document filed with the court)" may not be communicated to the public or any section of the public; FPR 2010 r.12.73 (See paras 31-40 above). It would therefore seem that, except with permission of the court, the public/media may not gain access to, or copy, any document on the court file (although query whether there could be a document on the court file which did not contain "information relating to proceedings" and which could, therefore, be obtained). However, it appears that an equivalent to FPR 1991 r.10.20(3) has not been enacted in FPR 2010. The change in the statutory language appears to have no practical effect, but the new rule has not been subject to judicial scrutiny. There is a limited exception to the restriction on access to documents in respect of any order made in open court; any person may obtain a copy of such an order on payment of the prescribed fee (FPR 2010 r.29.12).

Reporting

95. The following provisions will automatically apply, unless varied by the court:

---

[112] FPR 2010 r.27.2(3)

[113] In 2009-2010, a one year pilot scheme was conducted in the magistrates' courts in Leeds, Cardiff and Wolverhampton in which anonymised judgments in certain types of public law children cases, including applications for care and supervision orders, were made available to the public: http://www.justice.gov.uk/news/newsrelease021109b.htm. A total of 99 judgments were published on the bailli website.

95.1. AJA 1960 s12(1) applies (see paras 47-54 above)

95.2. Children Act 1989, s97(2) (see paras 55-59 above).

Judgments

96. It is a matter for each judge whether or not to make his or her judgment publicly available (whether or not in anonymised form)[114]. There is no specific rule (such as there was under FPR 1991 r.10.20(3)) that judgments are not available to the public without permission.

CHILDREN: PRIVATE LAW CASES

Family Proceedings Court

97. The same rules govern private law Children Act 1989 proceedings as public law proceedings within that Act (see above).

County Court and High Court (Family Division)

98. See paras 93-96 above. In terms of media access to the courts, on an application to exclude the media in private law proceedings, although governed by the same rules as public law cases, there may be more compelling reasons to exclude the media[115].

CHILDREN: ADOPTION CASES

(Proceedings under the Adoption and Children Act 2002)

Family Proceedings Court

Access to the court

99. In proceedings under the Adoption and Children Act 2002, "no person shall be present" at the hearing other than those directly concerned in the case[116]. The default position is that the public and the media are excluded.

[114] The pilot scheme referred to in footnote 113 above included the County Courts in Cardiff and Wolverhampton. Under the scheme, bailli has published 64 judgments.
[115] See observations about residence and contact proceedings in *Re Child X* (See fn. 30)
[116] Magistrates' Courts Act 1980, s69(3)

25

Access to documents

100. The public has no right to inspect or copy documents or orders on the court file[117]. Furthermore, those involved in proceedings are restricted from communicating "information relating to proceedings held in private" to the public and media[118].

Reporting

101. The following restrictions will automatically apply, unless varied by the court:

101.1. The media is restricted to publishing submissions on any point of law which arises and the decision of court: Magistrates' Courts Act 1980, s71(2)

101.2. AJA 1960 s12(1) applies (see paras 47-54 above)

101.3. Children Act 1989, s97(2) (see paras 55-58 above)

Judgments

102. The default position is that judgments are not available to the public[119].

County Court and High Court (Family Division)

Access to the court

103. Proceedings under the Adoption and Children Act 2002 "may" be heard and determined in private[120], although it is unlikely that court would exercise its discretion to permit the media to attend[121].

104. It may be appropriate to allow the media to attend hearings for placement orders[122]. The fact that an application for a placement order is being heard together with care

[117] Family Procedure (Adoption) Rules 2005, r.83; See also FPR 2010 r.14.24
[118] Family Procedure (Adoption) Rules 2005, r.78; See also FPR 2010 r.14.14
[119] Family Procedure (Adoption) Rules 2005, r.83
[120] Adoption and Children Act 2002, s101; But see also FPR 2010 r.27.10
[121] *President's Guidance Note: Care Proceedings involving placement order applications – Attendance of the Media*, April 30, 2009, paras 5-6.
[122] *Ibid.*

proceedings is not, of itself, a reason to exclude the media when they would otherwise be entitled to attend the care proceedings hearing[123].

Access to documents

105. See para 100 above

Reporting

106. The following restrictions will automatically apply, unless varied by the court:

106.1. AJA 1960 s12(1) applies (see paras 47-54 above)

106.2. Children Act 1989, s97(2) (see paras 55-58 above)

Judgments

107. See para 102 above. However, as part of the above mentioned pilot scheme, courts were encouraged to provide anonymised judgments in contested adoption applications and on applications to make and revoke placement orders.

PARENTAL ORDER APPLICATIONS
(under Human Fertilisation and Embryology Act 2008)

Family Proceedings Courts, County Court and High Court (Family Division)

Access to the court

108. Hearings are in private[124]. The media have no presumptive right of access[125].

Access to documents

109. The public has no right to inspect documents or orders on the court file[126], and anyone who obtains any information in the course of, or relating to, parental order proceedings shall treat that information as confidential[127].

[123] *Ibid.* at para 7
[124] FPR 2010 r.27.10.
[125] FPR 2010 r.27.11(1)(b)

Reporting & Judgments

110. Judgments and orders are private and in light of access restrictions and the reporting restrictions of AJA s12 and the Children Act s97, there are almost no prospects of reporting such proceedings.

MATRIMONIAL AND CIVIL PARTNERSHIP CAUSES (DIVORCE, ANNULMENT, JUDICIAL SEPARATIONS AND CIVIL PARTNERSHIP DISSOLUTION)

County Court and High Court (Family Division)

Access

111. Contested divorce proceedings are rare. However, the rules provide that the substantive hearing of petitions for divorce or civil partnership orders takes place "in public"[128], subject to a discretion to sit in private on a number of grounds including that the hearing will damage the confidentiality of information or is necessary to protect the interests of any child[129]. These rules are also still subject to the exception that evidence of sexual capacity in the course of nullity proceedings is heard *in camera* unless the judge orders otherwise[130]. In practical terms undefended cases are more common and are referred to the district judge for making the decree (FPR 2010 r.7.20). This means that little takes place in open court, except the announcement of the divorce decree or the Civil Partnership Order.

Access to court file

112. Where there is a final hearing, then, during the course of it, a witness statement which stands as evidence-in-chief is open to inspection, subject to a discretion to order otherwise[131]. The public has a right to inspect and copy any order or decree made in

[126] FPR 2010 r.13.19
[127] FPR 2010 r.13.18(3)
[128] FPR 2010 r.7.16(1)
[129] FPR 2010 r.7.16(3)
[130] See para 27.2 above
[131] FPR 2010 r.22.19

open court[132]. There is also a specific right to obtain a copy of any decree absolute or final order from the central registry[133,134].

Reporting

113. Although contested petitions are heard in open court, the Judicial Proceedings (Regulation of Reports) Act 1926 s1(1)(b) restricts what may be reported (see paras 60-61 above).

114. In addition, there is a power to grant anonymity to a party or witness if that is necessary "to protect the interests" of that party or witness (FPR 2010 r.7.16(5)). The nature of the legitimate interests which can be protected is not elaborated upon.

APPLICATIONS FOR ANCILLARY RELIEF AND RELATED MATTERS[135]

Family Proceedings Court, County Court and High Court (Family Division)

Access to the court

115. Ancillary relief hearings and other proceedings for financial relief generally take place "in private"[136], but the media has a presumptive right of access, FPR 2010 r.27.11(2) (see above).

Access to documents

116. It appears that the public has no right of access to the court file, although there is no specific provision to that effect in FPR 2010[137].

117. See paragraphs 71-75 above for discussion of the effect of the implied undertaking on media access to documents[138].

[132] FPR 2010 r.29.12
[133] FPR 2010 r.7.36
[134] It appears that the new FPR 2010 has removed the right, in matrimonial and civil partnership cases (except in nullity proceedings), of the public to inspect not only the certificate but also the evidence in support for a period of 14 days after the decree or civil partnership order was made (FPR 1991 r.2.36(4))
[135] Causes falling within FPR 2010 Part 9, applications for financial remedies (as defined in r.2.3)
[136] FPR 2010 r.27.10
[137] There does not appear to be an equivalent to FPR 1991 r.10.20(3) See discussion in para 94
[138] *Clibbery v Allan*, (See fn. 22) per Butler-Sloss P. at [72]: "Information disclosed under compulsion of the ancillary relief proceedings is, in my judgment, protected by the implied undertaking, before during and after the

Reporting[139]

118. See the discussion at paragraphs 62-64 above. It is possible that a case for ancillary relief would be concerned "mainly with the maintenance or upbringing of a minor" and thereby engage AJA 1960 s12(1)(a)(iii), though such cases will be rare[140].

APPLICATIONS UNDER PART IV OF THE FAMILY LAW ACT 1996 (e.g. NON-MOLESTATION ORDERS, OCCUPATION ORDERS)

Family Proceedings Courts, County Court & High Court (Family Division)

Access to the court

119. Applications under Part IV of the Family Law Act 1996 are heard in private, unless the court directs otherwise[141], This is subject to the media's right of access under FPR 2010 r.27.11(2).

Access to documents

120. It appears that the public has no right of access to the court file although there is no specific provision to that effect in FPR 2010. (See the discussion in para 94 above)

Reporting

121. Proceedings under Part IV of the Family Law Act 1996 may raise issues concerning children and could therefore fall within the prohibitions of AJA 1960 s12(1). Reporting may also be constrained by the prohibition upon reporting material disclosed under compulsion[142].

VULNERABLE AND INCAPACITATED ADULTS: INHERENT JURISDICTION

proceedings are completed". Furthermore the implied undertaking was held to apply to cases analogous to ancillary relief (e.g. failure to provide maintenance) (at [73]).

139 The interaction of the operation of rules which restrict the ability of parties to give information to third parties (see for example under the Child Support Act 1991, (FPR r.10.21A)) and the ability of the media to report what they hear in chambers hearings appears to create the potential for anomalies.

140 *Spencer v Spencer* (See fn. 35) at [12]-[15]

141 FPR 2010 r.10.5

142 see paragraphs 41-43 & 71-75 above

High Court (Family Division)

Access to the court

122. As the exercise of the inherent jurisdiction arises in a variety of circumstances, the fact that an application is being made under that jurisdiction does not, of itself, dictate whether a hearing should be in public or private. The starting point is open justice. However, the court retains a wide range of powers and may make any order unless limited by statute or case law. It is suggested that the question of whether or not to sit in public or private must be decided by the court in each case, by reference to the principles set out above, namely the importance of open justice, the principles to be applied to derogations from that principle and the interests of the vulnerable adult and others involved in the proceedings. Note that there is no statutory regime in place (equivalent to FPR r.27.11(3)) under which the media, but not the public, may attend hearings. It may be possible for the court to make an order which has this effect, as was done in *Webster* (see paragraph 45 above). The power to sit in secret in cases involving the abduction of a vulnerable adult is addressed in para 28 above[143].

Reporting

123. It appears that the restrictions in AJA 1960 s12(1) do not apply. Section 12(1)(b) refers to the Mental Capacity Act 2005 and therefore applies to proceedings in the Court of Protection. It also covers proceedings brought under the Mental Health Act 1983, but makes no reference to proceedings concerning adults under the inherent jurisdiction. In the absence of an injunction there would appear to be no restraint upon reporting[144].

INCAPACITATED ADULTS: THE COURT OF PROTECTION

[143] *Re HM (Vulnerable Adult: Abduction)* (See fn.44)

[144] In cases where the adult concerned lacks capacity in certain issues but not in others, the matter is likely to take place in the High Court (Family Division) and not the Court of Protection because the former can make orders under the inherent jurisdiction as well as the Mental Capacity Act 2005. However, this illustrates a potentially anomalous position of someone in such proceedings, vis-a-vis a person who lacks mental capacity, in terms of automatic reporting restrictions.

124. The statutory regime governing the Court of Protection[145] "mirror and re-articulate one long-standing common law exception to the principle that justice must be done in open court."[146] The applicable rules are the Court of Protection Rules 2007.

Access to the court

125. The "general rule" is that the Court of Protection sits "in private"[147]. The meaning of a "private hearing" and persons entitled to attend are set out in r.90(2).

126. The media (or any person) may be permitted to attend a private hearing or part of it, r.90(3)(a). Furthermore, the court may order a hearing or part of a hearing to take place in open court, r.92(1), but if it does so it retains wide statutory powers to order reporting restrictions to protect identities and/or restrict publication of information (r.92(2)).

127. On an application to admit the media or conduct proceedings in public pursuant to r.93, the court should undertake a two-stage approach: (i) is there a "good reason" for permitting the media's attendance; and, if so (ii) where does the balance lie between the competing Convention rights engaged (namely the article 8 rights of the individual who is the subject of the proceedings and, where relevant, the article 8 rights of his family and the article 10 rights of the media)[148].

Access to documents for non-parties

128. A non-party may inspect or copy a judgment or order given or made in public (r.17(1), subject to rr.20 and 92(2)). A non-party may apply to inspect other documents on the court file and the court must consider editing them before allowing such an application (r.17(2)-(4)).

129. A party is bound by a collateral obligation in respect of documents disclosed to it for the purpose of proceedings, r.18(1), save where it has been read/referred to at a public hearing or the court gives permission.

---

[145] The Rules were made under the Mental Capacity Act 2005, s51. Of particular relevance is s51(2)(h) which provides that rules may provide for " *for enabling or requiring the proceedings or any part of them to be conducted in private and for enabling the court to determine who is to be admitted when the court sits in private and to exclude specified persons when it sits in public"*.

[146] *Independent News and Media Ltd and others v A* (See fn.51) at [19]

[147] Court of Protection Rules 2007, r.90(1); *Independent News and Media Ltd v A* (See fn.51) at [10]-[11]

[148] *Independent News and Media Ltd v A* (See fn.51) at [10]-[11]. See also *London Borough of Hillingdon v Neary* [2011] EWHC 413

Reporting

130. The default position is that the restrictions of AJA 1960, s12(1) apply (see paras 47-54 above)[149].

131. However, the Court may authorise the publication of information relating to the proceedings, r.91(2)(a), or impose restrictions on publication, r.91(3). The approach to be taken by the court on an application to relax reporting restrictions is the same as for applications under r.90 and r.92 (see above). Parties may be named, however, parties should not be named at the outset where there is a real possibility that the balance in terms of reporting restrictions/permission may change, because once the name is public the court's ability to control that information is lost[150].

APPEALS

Access to the court

132. A court hearing an appeal or an application for permission to appeal may sit in private (meaning in chambers or in camera) if the court whose decision is being appealed had the power to sit in private during those proceedings. But the appellate court must give its decision in public "unless there are good and sufficient grounds" for giving it in private (in which case the court must state those grounds in public)[151]. It appears that FPR 2010 r.27.10 applies equally to appeals as to first instance hearings.

Court of Appeal

Access to the court

133. Hearings in the Court of Appeal are open to the public, save where the court orders otherwise.

Reporting

[149] AJA 1960 s12(1)(b) includes "proceedings are brought under the Mental Capacity Act 2005" (Amendment introduced by Mental Capacity Act 2005, s67(1), Sch 6, para 10).
[150] *London Borough of Hillingdon v Neary* (See fn. 148) at [16]
[151] Domestic and Appellate Proceedings (Restriction of Publicity) Act 1968, s1

134. Reporting is prima facie not restricted unless the Court of Appeal makes an order in the proceedings[152]. It may do so under the inherent jurisdiction or the Children and Young Persons Act 1933 s39, if applicable. In the Court of Appeal, there was a standing practice for the court to make an order prohibiting the identification of a child concerned in a case, where the case has been heard in chambers below pursuant to FPR 1991, r.4.16(7)[153]. The Court of Appeal has since observed that it is necessary to consider whether, on the consideration of the competing rights in each case, anonymisation of proceedings and judgment is necessary[154]. Therefore merely because the case was heard in private (FPR 2010 r.27.10) does not mean that the Court of Appeal should automatically do so.

DISCLOSURE FROM FAMILY PROCEEDINGS

135. This section deals with the communication of information relating to proceedings held in private (whether or not contained in a document filed with the court).

136. The position is governed by chapter 7 of Part 12 of FPR 2010 and Practice Direction (PD) 12G.

137. Nothing in FPR, however, permits the communication to the public at large, or any section of the public, of any information relating to the proceedings[155], and nothing in FPR r.12.75 (Communication of information for purposes connected with the proceedings) permits the disclosure of an unapproved draft judgment handed down by any court[156].

138. A party (or his or her legal representative acting on instructions) is permitted to communicate information relating to the proceedings to a limited category of people. These comprise any person: where such communication is necessary to enable the party in question to obtain confidential legal advice or assistance[157], to engage in

[152] In children cases, Children Act 1989 s97(2) does not apply in the Court of Appeal, *Pelling v Bruce Williams* (See fn. 76) at [53])
[153] *In re R (Court of Appeal: Order against Identification)* [1999] 2 FLR 145
[154] *Pelling v Bruce-Williams* (See fn.76) at [49]
[155] FPR 2010 r.12.73(2). In other words, AJA 1960 s12 continues to apply unless the court grants permission for disclosure to be made.
[156] FPR 2010 r.12.73(3)
[157] *Ibid.* r.12.75(1)(a)

mediation or ADR[158], to make and pursue a complaint against a person or body concerned in the proceedings,[159] and "to make and pursue a complaint regarding the law, policy or procedure relating to a category of proceedings" to which Part 12 of the Rules applies[160].

139. Where information is communicated by a party for the purposes of support, advice or assistance in the context of the proceedings, no further communication is permitted.[161] In any other case the recipient may pass the information on provided that the person who initially communicated the information consents[162] and the further communication is made only for the purpose or purposes for which the party made the initial communication[163]. Successive communication of the information is then permitted on the same terms.[164]

140. However, information can be communicated to a party, the legal representative of a party, a professional legal adviser, a CAFCASS[165] or CAFCASS Cymru[166] Officer, a welfare officer, the Legal Services Commission, a court authorised expert, a child protection professional or an IRO[167], either where the court gives permission[168] or otherwise in accordance with the Rules or the Practice Direction[169]. Each of course owes a duty of confidentiality in the proceedings to the court and the information goes no further.

141. Unique to proceedings relating to children is the rule that nobody can instruct an expert for any purpose relating to the proceedings without the court's permission[170], and where an unauthorised expert is instructed, no evidence from that expert may be introduced without the court's permission[171].

---

[158] Alternative dispute resolution: FPR 2010 r.12.75(1)(b)
[159] *Ibid* r.12.75(1)(c)
[160] *Ibid* r.12,75(1)(d)
[161] *Ibid* r.12.75(2)
[162] *Ibid* r.12,75(3(a)(i)
[163] *Ibid* r.12.75(3)(a)(ii)
[164] *Ibid* r.12,75(3)(b)
[165] Children and Family Court Advisory and Support Service
[166] Its Welsh counterpart
[167] An Independent Reviewing Officer, provided he or she has been appointed in respect of a child who is or has been the subject of proceedings
[168] FPR 2010 r.12.73(1)(a)
[169] *Ibid* r.12,73(1)(b)
[170] *Ibid* r.12.74(1)
[171] *Ibid* r.12.74(2).

142. The Practice Direction lists in tabular form what information may be communicated by a party, to whom and for what purpose. It also lists information which may be communicated by a CAFCASS Officer or an officer of CAFCASS Cymru and it also deals with communications to and by a Minister of the Crown and Welsh Ministers.

143. It is to be noted that none of the communications listed in the Practice Direction is designed to breach the essential confidentiality of the court. The communications are either related directly to the proceedings, or designed to enable the recipient of the information to fulfil his or her statutory function.

144. There is no right given to any party to communicate information relating to proceedings to the media without the court's permission[172]. To do so remains a contempt of court, although see paragraph 40 above[173].

145. Parties may, however, for example communicate without fear of contempt with their Member of Parliament about the way they perceive they have been treated in proceedings under the Act, but the MP is not at liberty to publish the information to the world at large[174].

---

[172] See paragraphs 47 to 54 above

[173] Note, however, that FPR 2010 r.12.75(1)(d) uses the phrase "to make and pursue a complaint….." In *Re N (Family Proceedings: Disclosure)* (See fn. 56) at [58] to [62], Munby J (as he then was) suggested that the word "complaint" might have a wider meaning and be sufficiently broad as not to be confined to complaints made to disciplinary or regulatory bodies. The case itself concerned a "complaint" to the GMC, which was plainly within the rule, and the judge was at pains to say that the meaning of the crucial word "complaint" would have to be elucidated on a case by case basis.

[174] See FPR 2010 r.12.75(3) and *Re X, Y, Z (Morgan v A Local Authority)* (See fn.54)

Part 15

TEMPLATE MODEL STATEMENT

IN SUPPORT OF AN INTERIM NON-DISCLOSURE ORDER

On behalf of the Applicant
[setting out the name of person
giving statement]
First
Date:

[TITLE AS IN THE (INTENDED) ACTION]

SECTION 1: DATA COLLECTION

Introduction

1. Not all-embracing: This document is a file management aid. It cannot be all-embracing because each case is fact sensitive.

2. Two sections: This document is divided into two sections:

(a) **Section 1:** This is designed to assist in the gathering of the data required for the statement.
(b) **Section 2:** This is intended to provide a template for the decanting of the relevant material into the statement in support of the application for the interim non-disclosure order.

Preliminary data

3. Identity: Set out full details of the person making the statement.

(a) **If 'A':**

 (i) Identity (assuming he/she is the person directly affected by the threatened disclosure/publication).

 (ii) Full name, age, occupation, profile (eg if a celebrity/famous name, in what context/circumstances).

 (iii) If 'A' is a child, set out in detail the position/status of the child's parents and the way in which the child's life as part of that family has been conducted.

(b) **If not 'A':**

 (i) In what capacity (and if a solicitor, explaining his/her position and if appropriate, that he/she is subject to the supervision of principals)?

 (ii) If the statement is not made by 'A', set out in detail the authorisation to make this statement.

4. The corpus of material:

(a) Set out precisely in the statement (or as appropriate, the confidential schedule) the corpus of material which the judge is to be invited to address.

(b) Is there more than one strand to the material? If yes:

 (i) Identify each strand.

 (ii) In relation to each strand, explain whether/what it is sought to injunct.

(c) Is the material true or false/inaccurate?

 (i) If false, in what way?

 (ii) If inaccurate, in what way?

If the proposed publication is in relation to photographs

5. Generally: When were they taken, where, by whom, in what circumstances. Does the client have access to copies?

(a) In relation to any of the photographs, is there a reasonable expectation of privacy?

(b) If yes, on what grounds?

6. Public interest: Do the photographs meet a particular public interest or do they merely satisfy curiosity?

7. Consent to being photographed:

(a) **If yes,** in what circumstances?

(b) **If no**, can an inference be drawn that the person taking the photographs would have known that were consent to have been sought, it would have been refused? If yes, what are the grounds for such assertion?

8. Clandestine: Were the photographs taken intrusively/surreptitiously/clandestinely/otherwise in secret? If yes:

(a) Give full particulars of the nature and extent of the invasion.
(b) Has distress been caused as a result?
(c) Was a zoom/telephoto lens (or electronic equivalent) used? If yes:
   (i) Was it targeted/directed? If yes, at what/whom?
   (ii) Where was the camera situated?

9. Sexual relationship:

(a) Are the photographs linked to an alleged sexual relationship?
(b) If yes, give full details.

Source of information sought to be enjoined

10. Origin: What is the source of the information?

11. Reliability: Is that source reliable? (And if so contended, on what grounds?)

12. Cross-check as to reliability: Does anyone providing the information appreciate the risk of sanctions if the information is untrue?

13. Corroboration:

(a) To what extent is 'A's' case verified/authenticated?
(b) Give particulars/evidence/details?

14. Circumstances of receipt: Give the fullest particulars as to the circumstances in which, and the purpose for which, the information came into the hands of the person threatening to publish/disseminate.

15. The nature of the information:

(a) What is the *nature* of the information itself?
   (i) Political?
   (ii) Artistic?
   (iii) Commercial?
(b) Is the case about *secrecy* or *intrusion*?

Secrecy (confidential information)

16. Grounds: On what basis is it argued that the material is confidential?

17. What is the nature of the information said to be confidential?

(a) Who communicated/sought to communicate what to whom, when, how and in what terms?
(b) Identify any relevant document, including emails.
(c) In what capacity? For example, personal capacity or as a director, or as an employer or in the course of employment.
(d) Does anyone else have a claim to/interest in the information? If yes, who, and on what grounds could a claim/interest be asserted?

Reasonable expectation of privacy?

18. If it is contended that there has been an intrusion:

(a) What are the *characteristics* of the intrusion?
  (i) Nature?
  (ii) Depth?
  (iii) Extent?
  (iv) Breadth?
  (v) The extent of any dissemination or proposed dissemination?
(b) What was the *purpose* of the intrusion?
(c) Has information been obtained *unlawfully* or *surreptitiously*?
(d) *Consent*:
  (i) Was there consent to any intrusion, however limited? If yes, give details?
  (ii) If consent is denied, confirm that there were no grounds for R to argue that he believed there was consent (give full details).
(e) What is the nature of the '*activity*' in relation to which 'A' was engaged?
(f) Give details as to the *place* at which any occurrence was happening (including public or private, explaining if relevant the characteristics of the property, the locality and disposition of the owner of any relevant property).
(g) How was the information *gathered/obtained* from that location?
  (i) Means of obtaining?
  (ii) Circumstances in which imparted/obtained?
(h) Does past intrusion generate a *threat of future intrusion*? If yes, set out the facts for so arguing.

19. Attributes:

(a) What are the 'attributes' of 'A': Does he/she have a *robust personality*?
(b) What is the *effect* on 'A'? Harm? Further harm (emotional/physical)?

20. How offensive?

(a) Is it contended that disclosure or observation of information or conduct would be '*highly offensive*' to a reasonable person of ordinary sensibilities, if he or she was placed in the same position as the claimant and faced with the same publicity?
(b) If yes, give *detailed reasoning* as to why.

21. Sexual relationship: Is the issue which is alleged to be private, a sexual relationship other than with 'A's' spouse or long-term partner? If yes:

(a) Has that other person been *spoken* to?
(b) If yes, by whom? To what *agenda*?
(c) Does that other person *want publicity*, or is he/she willing to sign a confidentiality agreement?
(d) Must that other person have realised that any relationship with 'A' *must have been expected* to be treated as discreet/confidential? If yes, set out in detail the grounds for so contending.
(e) Is there any related correspondence?

22. Third parties: Is there included in the proposed application, a claim to restrain *intrusion* into the private life of another person as being relevant to the privacy of 'A'? If yes:

(a) What other person(s)? Give full details of who, age, any relevant relationship, and why he/she comes within the zone of 'A's' privacy.
(b) What aspect of that other person's private life?
(c) On what basis is it argued that their Article 8 rights to privacy would be affected?
(d) Can such a third party provide independent evidence for themselves? If not:
    (i) Why not?
    (ii) Does 'A' have the necessary independence to embrace the privacy of others within his application?
(e) To what extent should the court have regard to these rights of others and why is it so argued?

23. Central issue: What is the nub of the complaint—what is the real issue? For example, is it privacy or commercial reputation?

24. Threat to publish: Is the case to be argued on the basis of a threat to publish? If yes:

(a) *From whom* is the threat coming?
(b) On what grounds does 'A' argue that it is *likely to be* published?
(c) What is the *evidence* for such threat and *how serious* is it claimed to be—and on what *grounds* is it so claimed?
(d) If the threat is based on *inference*, what are the facts which form the foundation to the claimed inference, and on what grounds is it argued that the inference of a sufficient threat to publish *can be drawn*?
(e) On what grounds is it argued that the threat to publish is such as to *justify an injunction*?
(f) Is the threat such that it can *only be restrained* by injunctive relief? If yes, why is that contended? Does the proposed injunction have to be so wide?

25. To whom is R likely to say/publish it? Set out the grounds for the submission. For example:

(a) To a *close friend*?
(b) With members of the *family*?
(c) With a *family doctor*?
(d) With his *lawyers* or with *expert witnesses*?
(e) On the *internet*? On *social networking sites*?
(f) Through the *press*?

SECTION 2: DATA PRESENTATION IN STATEMENT

26. Claim form: If a claim form has yet to be issued, annex and exhibit the draft and explain:

(a) Why it has not been issued (give a full explanation); and
(b) When it is to be issued.

27. Factual matrix: Set out in as much detail as practicable the facts giving rise to the claim and the injunction application, explaining where appropriate (annexing, where appropriate, correspondence, emails and records of telephone calls).

(a) The material/story/publication sought to be enjoined and its nature (eg if about human relationships, explain).
(b) What were the means by which the information was obtained?
(c) What is the evidence that there is a threat of publication?
(d) Was any material (eg photographs) obtained by consent? If not, how, when and where were they obtained?
(e) Who is likely to publish it and why? Give grounds for so asserting with all relevant evidence.
(f) What is the gravity of the alleged interference with the private life? How serious is it for 'A' and why? Is there a risk of emotional injury? Is there a risk of damage to relationships? (NB: 'A' does not have to admit or deny the allegations made—the truth is not relevant—what is relevant is the privacy.)
(g) Is there a risk of harm to children/family life in that context?
(h) Whose privacy is involved—'A' alone, or beyond that, and why is that argued? And if someone else, how vulnerable would they be to the proposed publication?
(i) What is the extent of the intrusion into the private life?
(j) In relation to the material sought to be enjoined, was there a reasonable expectation of privacy? If yes:
    (i) On what grounds is that said?
    (ii) Has 'A' sought to maintain his privacy—and is that known to the press? (For example, has he made it clear to the press that he wishes to protect his privacy? If yes, give full particulars.)
(k) Would R know that the publication of the proposed material would be looked at as unacceptable in the eyes of 'A'? If yes, on what grounds?
(l) What is the nature of the activity in which A was engaged, the subject matter of the proposed injunction—when and where?
(m) What is the purpose and nature of the intrusion?
(n) How offensive is the intrusion?
(o) Has there been harassment?

28. As to the public interest: Explain in detail the case, taking into account the following factors:

(a) Is the proposed publication only of '*interest to the public*', as contrasted with being '*in the public interest*'?
(b) Would publication make a contribution to a debate of general interest? If not, why not?
(c) Would publication meet a pressing social need? If no, why not?

(d) Is it relevant to state that publication would not expose illegality or prevent the public from being significantly misled?
(e) If it is contended that nothing less than the injunction sought would be necessary, on what grounds?
(f) Has 'A' been approached by the anticipated publisher for his view? If yes:
    (i) If oral or partly oral, between whom, when, where and in what terms?
    (ii) If in writing or partly in writing, identify the document or documents.
(g) If 'A' can argue that a '*responsible journalism*' defence would be flawed, give details.
(h) Are there allegations of any blackmail, conspiracy or other form of threat?
(i) Set out clearly why 'A' contends that his/her right to privacy should prevail over the right of the proposed publisher to secure freedom of expression.
(j) Explain why damages would not be an adequate remedy (assuming this be the case) and volunteer an undertaking as to damages, supported by documentation evidencing sufficient means.
(k) Assistance from any code?

29. If the application is being made without notice, explain why.

(a) Explain fully why the urgency (if urgency claimed).
(b) If no informal notice given, explain why (eg risk of 'tipping off').
(c) If informal notice has been given, explain to whom it was given, when, where, in what terms—and what has been the response.

30. Set out (if they are sought) the derogations from open justice to be applied for, which can include:

(a) Anonymisation of court papers and judgment.
(b) Hearing in private.
(c) Restricting access to part of the court file.
(d) Certain material to remain confidential in its own confidential schedule.
(e) A 'super-injunction'.

31. Set out here all facts which are to be relied upon in support of any derogation from open justice in Article 6: Given the Article 6 right for open justice unless otherwise strictly necessary:

(a) Why should there be any derogation?
(b) In relation to each head of derogation applied for, what adverse consequences can be anticipated if the order is not made?
(c) Why should the private interest of 'A' prevail over the public interest in freedom of information?

(d) Would it be sufficient if 'A's' name were published, but not the story—ie that the fact of his bringing the injunction application was published, but no more? If not, why not? Why does the private interest prevail over the public's right to know?

32. Stepping into R's shoes: Identify the facts and arguments upon which R would rely if served in support of the argument of legitimate aim/public interest under Article 10 (this is particularly important if the application is without notice). For example:

(a) Is the material sought to be enjoined, partly or wholly in the public domain? If yes:
(i) What precisely has got into the public domain (internet trawl, etc)?
(ii) How is the public domain defined? The world at large? Or just the work-place? Or just friends, etc? Explain.
(iii) How has it got there?
(iv) Has 'A' been the cause, or is he innocent of such leakage?
(v) Has he invited the public into his private life? If not—and there has been leakage—how has it occurred? (Take instructions from the client's public relations consultant if he/she has one.)
(b) Has 'A' made any public assertions or comments on the issue the subject matter of the proposed injunction? If yes, give details.
(c) Has 'A's' solicitor undertaken an internet 'cuttings search'? Does that reveal intentional leakage by 'A'—and if yes, how does 'A' explain that (can he 'confess and avoid')?
(d) Has 'A' at any time misled the public in relation to the subject matter of the proposed injunction? If yes, how. If not, state it.

Harassment

33. Any harassment? If yes:

(a) Give full details in relation to each occasion of such harassment.
(b) Any abusive communications? Emails?

I believe the facts stated in this witness statement are true.

Signed etc

Dated etc.

Part 16

MEDIATION

The tension between Articles 8 and 10, reflected in the 'balancing exercise,' may provide opportunity for dispute resolution through mediation.

The *Hong Kong Mediation Handbook* (Thompson Reuters) quintissentially explains the role of mediation:

> Mediation is a flexible process of dispute resolution in which one or more impartial third parties intervenes in a conflict of dispute with the consent of the participants and assists them in negotiating a consensual and informed agreement. In mediation, the decision-making authority rests with the participants themselves. Recognising participants' needs, cultural differences and variations in style, the mediator facilitates the communication between the participants and assists them to define and clarify issues, reduce obstacles to communication, develop an empathic and constructive interaction, explore possible solutions and, when designed, reach a mutually acceptable agreement. Mediation presents the opportunity to express differences and improve relationships and mutual understanding, whether or not an agreement is reached. It provides a confidential and non-adversarial context for the participants to resolve their conflict in a collaborative manner.

For example, it may (depending on the fact-sensitive nature of any particular case) be appropriate to apply to the court for an interim non-disclosure order to run for a particular period of time, to allow for mediation between the parties to achieve a practical workable solution.

To cater for that contingency, there are set out below certain mediation documentation.

Gratitude is expressed to the ADR Group of Bristol for their permission to replicate this material.

Model ADR mediation documentation

Dispute Resolution Clauses

Introduction

The importance of including a Dispute Resolution clause in any contract is obvious: it introduces control and certainty by ensuring that all parties fully understand what will happen in the event of breach of the agreement or any of its terms. Once a dispute is raised by one party, the natural reaction is for the other party to go into defence mode. Although the parties may be able to remedy the breach through direct negotiation, the dispute may quickly escalate beyond the initial allegation. Professionalism, reputation and finance often block any early attempts to reach a compromise.

A tiered dispute resolution clause provides a logical framework for efficiently resolving a dispute at the earliest opportunity, cost effectively and to the mutual benefit of all parties. If the parties are unsuccessful in direct negotiations (internally and utilising appropriate senior management), then the parties are required to mediate (using a neutral third party to facilitate settlement discussions) and ultimately if mediation is unsuccessful, engaging in arbitration. As a last resort the dispute may be litigated, but the cost, delay and uncertainty of the judicial process mitigate in favour of an earlier and genuine attempt at settlement as a contractual obligation.

Mediation is the most commonly used process for resolving disputes as it provides a quick and confidential forum for the resolution of a dispute through the facilitation of a neutral third party. Mediation settlements are binding on all parties and seldom breached. This is because no decision is imposed: any settlement reached is by mutual agreement of all parties involved.

The inclusion of any dispute resolution clause in a contract requires careful consideration as the implications may have far reaching effects. It is advisable to seek independent legal advice.

Standard Mediation Clause: version 1

> *In the event of any dispute arising between the parties in connection with this agreement which cannot be settled by negotiation, the parties will in good faith, seek to resolve that dispute through mediation in accordance with ADR Group's mediation procedure before resorting to arbitration. If the dispute is not resolved by mediation within [30] days, or if one of the parties will not participate in the mediation, the dispute shall be referred to arbitration in accordance with the rules of the Chartered Institute of Arbitrators (London), whose rules are deemed to be incorporated by reference into this clause. The jurisdiction and law applicable to this contract is that of [England and Wales].*

Standard Mediation Clause: version 2

a. *The Parties shall attempt in good faith to resolve any dispute or claim arising out of or in connection with this agreement promptly through negotiations between their respective [managing directors].*

c. *If the parties are unable to resolve the dispute or claim through negotiation, the parties will in good faith, seek to resolve the dispute through mediation (or such other recognised Alternative Dispute Resolution ("ADR") Procedure) under the auspices of the ADR Group (UK).*

c. *The referral of this dispute to Mediation does not affect the rights that may exist under Article 6 of the European Convention on Human Rights and shall not prevent either party from issuing proceedings.*

d. *If the dispute is not settled by mediation, the parties right to a fair trial remain unaffected.*

Complex Mediation Clause

In the event of any dispute arising between the parties in connection with this agreement which cannot be settled by negotiation, the parties in good faith, seek to resolve that dispute through mediation under the auspices of the ADR Group (UK). The mediator shall be agreed upon within [15] days of one party requesting mediation, failing which the mediator will be appointed by the then Chairman of ADR Group. Unless otherwise agreed the parties shall share equally the costs of the mediation. If the dispute is not resolved within [30] days, or one of the parties refuses to participate in mediation, the dispute shall be referred to [arbitration in accordance with the rules of the Chartered Institute of Arbitrators, London whose rules are deemed to be incorporated by reference into this clause] or [litigation]. Nothing in this clause shall prevent either party seeking a preliminary injunction or other judicial relief at any time if in its judgement such action is necessary to prevent irreparable damage. The referral of this dispute to Mediation does not affect the rights that may exist under Article 6 of the European Convention on Human Rights and shall not prevent either party from issuing proceedings. The jurisdiction and law applicable to this contract is that of [England and Wales].

For further information please contact:
ADR Group
Grove House, Grove Road
Redland, Bristol
BS6 6UN
+44 (0) 117 946 7180

Mediation Procedure and Rules

ADR Group mediations are governed by the following procedure ('The Mediation Procedure') as amended by ADR Group from time to time. It will be taken that the parties have agreed that the mediation shall be conducted in accordance with the Mediation Procedure.

1. Mediation Procedure

1.1 The parties to the dispute or negotiation in question will attempt to settle by mediation. Representatives of the parties including, if desired, their advisers (legal representatives) and the mediator will attend the mediation session.

1.2 The representatives (Legal or otherwise) of the parties must have the necessary authority to settle the dispute. If a party is a natural person, that person must attend the mediation session. If a party is not a natural person it must be represented at the mediation session by an officer or employee with full authority to make binding agreements settling the dispute. If that person comes with ('limited') authority, that is, authority up to a certain amount, he or she must disclose this information to the mediator prior to the mediation.

1.3 Any and all communications relating to, and at, the mediation are private & confidential and will be without prejudice.

1.4 Upon request ADR Group will provide to the parties, details of recommended mediators drawn from its panel of mediators (ADR Net Limited). Consideration will be given to the nature of the dispute, the complexity, the location and the experience required. If the parties are unable to agree to the appointment of a mediator, ADR Group will appoint a mediator if requested to do so.

2. Mediation Agreement

2.1 The parties sign an agreement ('Agreement to Mediate') at the start of the mediation. This agreement governs the relationship between the parties before, during and after the mediation.

2.2 Each party, in signing the Agreement to Mediate, will be deemed to be agreeing on behalf of both itself and all such other persons to be bound by the confidentiality provisions of the Mediation Procedure.

3. The Mediator

3.1 The Mediator will:

- Attend any meetings with any or all of the parties preceding the mediation, if requested to do so, or if the mediator decides it is appropriate

- Prior to the commencement of the mediation read and familiarise him/herself with each party's Position Statement and any documents provided in accordance with paragraph 6.1
- Determine the procedure
- Assist the parties in drawing up any written settlement agreement
- Abide by the terms and conditions of the Mediation Procedure, the Agreement to Mediate and ADR Group's Code of Conduct

3.2 The Mediator will not:

- Analyse an party's legal position or rights
- Impose a settlement on the parties
- Offer legal advice or act as legal adviser to any party

3.3 The parties and mediator acknowledge that the mediator is an independent contractor and is not appointed as an agent or employee of any of the parties or ADR Group. Neither the mediator nor a member of his or her firm or business will act, or have acted, as a professional adviser, or in any other capacity, for any of the parties individually in connection with the dispute either before, during the currency of the mediation or at any time thereafter.

4. Mediation Agreement

4.1 ADR Group will in consultation with the parties and the mediator, make the necessary arrangements for the mediation including, as appropriate:

- Recommend mediators with regard to, inter alia, nature of the dispute, degree of complexity, location of parties etc and drawing up the Agreement to Mediate
- Liaise between the parties to agree suitable date and venue
- Assist the parties in preparing their Position Statement (see paragraph 6) and supporting documentation
- Discuss or meet with any or all of the parties or their representatives (and the mediator if appropriate), either together or separately, on any matter pursuant to the proposed mediation
- General administration in relation to the mediation

5. Representation

5.1 Parties do not require legal representation to attend the mediation.

5.2 Where a party is un-represented, ADR Group encourages such party to obtain independent legal advice prior to the mediation.

5.3 Each party is required to notify ADR Group and other parties involved in the mediation of the names of those people intended to be present on its behalf at the mediation.

6. Position Statements and Documentation

6.1 Each party will be required to prepare and deliver to the mediator, seven (7) days prior to the mediation, a concise summary ('Position Statement') of the case in dispute. Together with this statement should be copies of documents referred to in the Position Statement and those which parties will be seeking to refer to during the mediation.

6.2 ADR Group do not impose any obligation on the parties to exchange Position Statements, but parties are free to agree to the simultaneous exchange of the Position Statements, if so agreed or if considered appropriate.

6.3 The Position Statement is private and confidential and will not be disclosed (by the mediator) to any other third party unless expressly authorised to do so. ADR Group will provide to the parties a guide to position statement preparation.

6.4 Parties are encouraged to prepare and agree a joint bundle of documents where appropriate.

7. The Mediation

7.1 No formal record or transcript of the mediation will be made.

7.2 The mediation session is for the purpose of attempting to achieve a negotiated settlement and all information provided during the mediation session is without prejudice and will be inadmissible in any litigation or arbitration of the dispute. Evidence, which is otherwise admissible, shall not be rendered inadmissible as a result of its use in the mediation session.

7.3 If the parties are unable to reach a settlement during the mediation, the mediator may, if requested to do so, facilitate further negotiation after the mediation session itself has ended.

8. Settlement Agreement

8.1 Any settlement reached in the mediation will not be legally binding until it has been recorded in writing and signed by, or on behalf of, the parties.

9. Termination

9.1 Any of the parties may withdraw from the mediation at any time and shall immediately inform the mediator and the other representatives either orally or in writing. The mediation will terminate when:

- A party voluntarily withdraws from the mediation or

- A written settlement agreement is concluded or
- The mediator elects, in his/her sole discretion, that continuing the mediation is unlikely to result in a settlement or
- The mediator decides that he/she should retire for any of the reasons set our in the Code of Practice

10. Settlement Agreement

10.1 Where the dispute has been referred to mediation by the Court or where the Court has ordered that the parties consider mediation, and the mediation does not achieve settlement, the current litigation or arbitration in relation to the dispute may be commenced or continued, notwithstanding the mediation, unless the parties agree otherwise.

11. Settlement Agreement

11.1 Every person involved in the mediation will keep confidential and not use for any collateral or ulterior purpose:

- The fact that the mediation is to take place or has taken place and
- All information, (whether given orally or in writing or otherwise), produced for, or arising pursuant to, the mediation including the settlement agreement (if any) arising out of it

except in so far as is necessary to implement and enforce any such settlement agreement.

Not withstanding the above it would be prudent of the parties to include an express confidentiality clause (if so desired) in any settlement agreement.

11.2 All documents or other information produced for, or arising in relation to, the mediation will be privileged and not admissible as evidence or discoverable in any litigation or arbitration connected with the dispute (see paragraph 11.1 above). This does not apply to any information, which would in any event have been admissible or for disclosure in such proceedings.

11.3 The parties will not subpoena or otherwise require the mediator, ADR Group (or any employee, consultant, director or representative of ADR Group) or any other person attending the mediation under the auspices of ADR Group to testify or produce records, notes or any other information or material whatsoever in any future or continuing proceedings.

12. Mediation Costs

12.1 It is usual that the costs of the mediation are borne equally between the parties.

12.2 Payment of these costs will be made to ADR Group in accordance with its fee schedule and terms and conditions of business (as amended from time to time).

12.3 Each party attending the mediation is to bear its own costs and expenses of its participation in the mediation (including legal representative costs) and unless agreed otherwise, such costs will be costs in the cause.

13. Waiver of Liability

13.1 Neither the mediator nor ADR Group shall be liable to the parties for any act or omission in connection with the services provided by them in, or in relation to, the mediation, unless the act or omission is fraudulent or involves wilful misconduct.

14. Human Rights

14.1 The referral of a dispute to mediation does not affect any rights that may exist under Article 6 or the European Convention of Human Rights. Should the dispute not settle through the process of mediation, the parties right to a fair trial shall remain unaffected.

1. To refer your dispute to ADR Group you can either complete our Case Referral Form or call and discuss the case with one of our advisors. To help us identify suitable mediators we will need to know some basic information from you, in particular:
   - Nature of dispute, value and complexity
   - Current litigation status
   - Preferred timing and location
   - Available budget
   - Specific traits or areas of specialism required
2. Should you wish, ADR Group will also approach and discuss the possibility of a mediation meeting with the other parties.
3. Once all parties are in agreement to mediate, the mediation advisor will select up to three mediators who match, as closely as possible, the criteria you have stipulated and forward copies of their CV (or mediator profile) to you. In doing so ADR Group take account of:
   - Field of expertise relevant to the dispute
   - Level of experience
   - Location
   - Price
   - Specific mediator traits requested
4. Once all parties have confirmed their preferred choice of mediator, dates of availability are obtained and distributed. The mediation advisor

will then liaise with all the parties, including the mediator, to establish a suitable date for the mediation meeting.

5. The mediation advisor will continue to liaise with all those attending to finalise other arrangements such as venue, start time and duration. The issue of costs will also be discussed with you.
6. Once the arrangements have been agreed, confirmation will be sent to all parties. The parties are asked to prepare a Position Statement and send to the mediator. This document is to outline the details of the dispute, the reason for deadlock and what each party hopes to achieve out of the mediation (guidelines will be sent listing the information you need to include).
7. Together with the confirmation of the mediation arrangements, an Agreement to Mediate will also be sent. This should be read prior to the mediation. On the day of the mediation meeting all parties will be asked to sign the mediator's copy which will then be returned to ADR Group. The mediation cannot take place until this has happened.
8 It is usual for the mediator to contact the parties prior to the mediation to introduce themselves and to discuss the process. They may also request additional documentation.
9. Following the mediation ADR Group will ask you to complete our evaluation form so that we can monitor our service and that of the mediator. We address any points of concern raised in this form.

AGREEMENT TO MEDIATE

PARTIES:

A. «ePartyA» ("Party A" represented by..............)

B. «ePartyB» ("Party B" represented by............)

(collectively "the Parties")

MEDIATOR:

("the Mediator")

DISPUTE:

Matters which are subject to proceedings in Claim no XXX Division, High Court of Justice ("the Dispute")

The Parties agree that IDR Europe Ltd (hereinafter referred to as ADR Group) shall administer and the Mediator mediate the Dispute on the following terms and conditions ("the Mediation"):

1. MEDIATION PROCEDURES

1.1 The Mediation shall be held and conducted according to this Agreement to Mediate ("Mediation Agreement").

1.3 Parties will attend the Mediation personally or in the case of businesses, corporations or other legal entities, through their authorised representatives. The Parties will be represented at the Mediation as set out in Schedule 1. Each Party is to ensure that at least one of its representatives has full and unlimited authority to negotiate, compromise and settle the dispute on its behalf. Any restriction on this authority is to be raised with the Mediator or ADR Group prior to the mediation.

1.4 Any settlement reached in the mediation will not be legally binding until it has been reduced to writing and signed by, or on behalf of, each of the Parties ("settlement agreement").

2. MEDIATOR

2.1 The Mediator will

- 2.1.1 assist the Partries to compromise and resolve the Dispute
- 2.1.2 determine the Procedure at the Mediation, in consultation with the Parties
- 2.1.3 assist (if requested) in drawing up any settlement agreement
- 2.1.4 decline hereafter to act for any Party in any capacity in connection with the Dispute

2.2 The Parties and the Mediator recognise that the Mediator is an independent contractor and is not an agent (in any capacity) or employee of ADR Group or any Party, and that the Mediator has no personal or financial interest in the subject matter of the Dispute.

3. PLACE AND TIME OF THE MEDIATION

3.1 The Mediation will take place at .... on «eStartDate» starting at «eStartTime» am/pm.

4. MEDIATION FEES, EXPENSES AND COSTS

4.1 ADR Group's fees (which include the mediator's fees) and any other expenses associated with the Mediation will be borne equally by the Parties, unless as a result of mediated settlement, it is agreed otherwise. Where a party is represented at the mediation by a legal representative, that legal representative is liable for their client's share of the costs of the mediation in same way as they are liable for disbursements incurred in any litigation.

4.2 Payment of these fees and expenses will be made to ADR Group in accordance with ADR Group's terms and conditions of business.

4.3 Each Party will pay its own costs and expenses in instructing any legal representative to prepare for, and/or participate in, the Mediation. Unless agreed otherwise, these costs and expenses will be costs in the case.

5. CONSULTING WITH LEGAL ADVISERS

5.1 A Party does not require legal representation to attend the Mediation.

5.2 Where a Party is not legally represented, such Party is advised to obtain independent legal advice before, during and after the Mediation and prior to finalising any agreement reached pursuant to the Mediation.

5.3 The Parties recognise that neither ADR Group nor the Mediator offer legal advice or act as a legal advisor for any of the Parties of the Mediation nor will they provide any party with a legal analysis to protect any party's legal position or rights.

6. PRIVATE SESSIONS

6.1 The Mediator may hold private sessions with one Party at a time. These private sessions are designed to improve the Mediator's understanding of the Party's position and to facilitate the Mediator in expressing each Party's view point to the other side.

6.2 Information gained by the Mediator through such sessions is confidential unless (a) it is in any event publicly available or (b) the Mediator is specifically authorised by that Party to disclose it. This clause is subject to Clause 7.

7. CONFIDENTIALITY

7.1 Everyone involved in any manner in the Mediation hereby undertakes to each other that, unless otherwise agreed to in writing by the Parties or their respective advisers they shall maintain and respect the confidentiality of any and all information of any nature made or produced for, or arising in connection with, the Mediation, save

7.1.1 as may be required by law, whether under the Proceeds of Crime Act and/or any other regulations relating thereto or otherwise and/or

7.1.2 as may be necessary to implement and/or enforce any settlement agreement.

7.2 Everyone involved in the Mediation also agrees to keep confidential and regard as privileged, and shall not use what happened or what was said at the Mediation and/or the terms of any settlement (unless the settlement agreement has its own confidentiality terms in which case those terms shall prevail).

7.3 Everyone involved in the Mediation also recognises that the Mediation is for the purpose of attempting to achieve a negotiated settlement and as such all documents, correspondence, information or other material (in any format) and/or matters of any nature made or produced for, or arising in connection with, the Mediation information provided during the mediation is without prejudice and will be inadmissible in any litigation or arbitration of the Dispute.

7.4 Evidence which is otherwise admissible shall not be rendered inadmissible as a result of its use in the mediation.

7.5 The Parties, their advisers or representatives will not take steps in any jurisdiction to require or compel the Mediator, the ADR Group, a director or employee of ADR Group, or any other person attending the Mediation under the auspices of ADR Group to act as a witness in any proceedings connected in any way with the Mediation or the subject matter of the Dispute, or to testify or produce records, notes or any other information or material whatsoever in any future or continuing proceedings, unless such documents or information would have been admissible or discloseable in any event.

7.6 Every person involved in the Mediation will keep confidential and not use for any collateral or ulterior purpose the fact that the Mediation is to take place or has taken place, other than to inform a court dealing with any litigation relating to the dispute of that fact.

7.7 Where the Mediation has taken place as a result of a Court order, the Parties agree that the Court can be notified of the fact that the case has resolved through mediation. The notification will come from the parties and take the form of a letter agreed between the parties at the conclusion of the Mediation. The notification will not disclose the terms of any settlement, unless otherwise agreed by the Parties.

7.8 All documents, statements, information and other material produced prior to or during the course of the mediation, save to the extent those documents disclosed already and in the domain of the litigation, whether in writing or orally, shall be held in confidence by the Parties and shall be used solely for the purposes of the mediation.

8. TERMINATION OF THE MEDIATION

8.1 The Mediation shall terminate:

8.1.1 when a written settlement is executed and signed by the Parties, or

8.1.2 a written notice of withdrawal is given by any Party

8.1.3 the time set for the Mediation has expired without agreement for continuation or resumption, or

8.1.4 The Mediator decides, at his/her absolute discretion, and notifies the Parties, that continuing the Mediation is unlikely to result in a settlement, or is undesirable or inappropriate for any other reason.

8.2 The Parties or the Mediator may, at any time, adjourn the Mediation in order to consider further information or specific issues raised during the mediation, obtain further information or for any other reason which the Parties or the Mediator consider helpful in furthering the Mediation. ADR Group will liaise with the Parties and the Mediator to reconvene or resume the mediation.

9. EXCLUSION OF LIABILITY

9.1 Neither the Mediator nor ADR Group shall be liable to the Parties or their advisers or representatives for any view expressed by him/her during or in connection with the Mediation or for any act or omission in connection with his/her conduct in, or in relation to, the Mediation unless the view expressed or the act or omission is shown to be fraudulent or in bad faith. This exclusion clause applies subject to any applicable law.

10. HUMAN RIGHTS

10.1 The referral of this dispute to Mediation does not affect the rights that may exist under Article 6 of the European Convention on Human Rights. If the dispute is not settled by mediation, the Parties' right to a fair trial remain unaffected.

11. LAW AND JURISDICTION

11.1 The Mediation and this Mediation Agreement shall be governed by, construed and take effect in accordance with English Law. The High Court of Justice, London shall have exclusive jurisdiction to settle any claim, dispute or matter of difference which may arise out of or in connection with the Mediation and/or this agreement.

12. SIGNATURE OF THIS MEDIATION AGREEMENT

12.1 This Mediation Agreement is to be signed by the instructed legal representative of each Party attending the mediation (if represented) on behalf of that Party.

A. «ePartyA» (represented by ....)

Signed: ____
(Claimant)
Name: ____
(Claimant)
Signed: ____
(Representative)
Name: ____
(Representative)

B. «ePartyB» (represented by..............)

Signed: ____
(Defendant)
Name: ____
(Defendant)
Signed: ____
(Representative)
Name: ____
(Representative)

C. «MediatorForeName» «MediatorSurname» (The Mediator)

Signed: ____
Name: ____
Date: __________________________

D. Observer (if applicable)

Signed: ____
Name: ____
Date: __________________________

Schedule 1
MEDIATION ATTENDANCE SCHEDULE AND CONFIDENTIALITY RECORD

[NOTE: To be signed by all those in attendance at the Mediation, including the Parties, their representatives, advisers, lawyers, experts, Mediator(s) or any other parties invited to attend]

As I am attending the Mediation taking place under the provisions of this agreement to which this Schedule 1 is part, I agree to be personally bound by the confidentiality and without prejudice provisions of this agreement, including but not limited to paragraphs 7 (Confidentiality) and 9 (Exclusion of Liability).

NAME	SIGNATURE

Model ADR mediation: mediation case referral form

Claimant		**Defendant**	
Name		**Name**	
Add		**Add**	
Tel:		**Tel:**	
Nature of claim and brief description			

Approximate amount of dispute		£	
Complexity (low/medium/high)			
Claimant's Solicitors/Advisor		**Defendant's Solicitors/Advisor**	
Name		**Name**	
Firm		**Firm**	
Add		**Add**	
DX		**DX**	
Tel		**Tel**	
Fax		**Fax**	
Email		**Email**	
Ref		**Ref**	

1.	Have legal proceedings been issued? If so, please provide copies of relevant pleadings (if appropriate) and indicate stage reached	**Y/N**
2.	Is this a court referred mediation?	**Y/N**
3.	Has mediation been discussed with the other party(ies)? If yes, have all party(ies) agreed to mediation	**Y/N** **Y/N**
4.	If the mediation has not been proposed with the other party(ies), is ADR Group to approach them?	**Y/N**
5.	Please indicate preferred timing for the mediation	
6.	Please indicate preferred location for the mediation	

7.	Are any of the parties legally aided? If so, please provide a copy of the legal aid certificate (as amended)	**Y/N**
8.	Is it usual for the mediation fee to be split equally between the parties. Is there an alternative arrangement in this case?	**Y/N**
9.	Would there be any objection to the appointment of a mediator local to the parties and their advisors	**Y/N**
10.	Will the parties professional advisor(s) if any be in attendance at the mediation along with the parties?	**Y/N**
11.	Do you consider it likely that any other person(s) will attend the mediation e.g. expert witnesses, friends, insurers representatives?	**Y/N**
12.	Do the parties have any objection to an observer being present during the mediation?	**Y/N**
13.	Are there any other issues you or your client consider important and which may be relevant to in the choice of mediator?	
14.	How did you hear about ADR Group?	

Part 17

PRACTICE GUIDANCE: INTERIM NON-DISCLOSURE ORDERS

(1) GUIDANCE

1. This Guidance sets out recommended practice regarding any application for interim injunctive relief in civil proceedings to restrain the publication of information: an interim non-disclosure order. It is issued as guidance (not as a Practice Direction) by the Master of the Rolls, as Head of Civil Justice. Such applications may be founded on rights guaranteed by the European Convention on Human Rights (the Convention), or on grounds of privacy or confidentiality. They may also be made in respect of a threatened contempt of court, a threatened libel or malicious falsehood, harassment, or a Norwich Pharmacal application in support of such actions. All such orders will seek to restrict the exercise of the Article 10 Convention right of freedom of expression through prohibiting the disclosure of information.

2. It also provides guidance concerning the proper approach to the general principle of open justice in respect of such applications and explains the proper approach to the model interim non-disclosure order a copy of which is attached to this Guidance.

3. The law set out in this Guidance is correct as at 1 August 2011.

Statutory Provisions

4. Applications which seek to restrain publication of information engage Article 10 of the Convention and s12 of the Human Rights Act 1998 (HRA). In some, but not all, cases they will also engage Article 8 of the Convention. Articles 8 and 10 of the Convention have equal status and, when both have to be considered, neither has automatic precedence over the other. The court's approach is set out in *Re S (a child)* [2004] UKHL 47, [2005] 1 AC 593 at [17].

5. HRA s12 applies whenever the court is considering whether to grant relief which might affect the exercise of the Article 10 Convention right. HRA s12(2) requires advance notice to be given to persons against whom the application is made, except in the exceptional circumstances set out in HRA s12(2)(a) and (b).

6. HRA s12(3) requires the applicant to satisfy the court that they are likely to establish, at trial, that publication should not be allowed. Guidance on the application of s12(3) is set out in *Cream Holdings Ltd v Banerjee* [2005] 1 AC 253 at [22] – [23].

7. HRA s12(4) requires that court to have particular regard to the fundamental importance of the Article 10 Convention right of freedom of expression, where proceedings relate to material which a respondent claims, or which appears to the court, to be journalistic, literary or artistic material, or conduct connected with such material, the extent to which the material has or is about to become available to the public, or it is or would be in the public interest for it to be published. It also requires the court to have regard to any relevant privacy code. The code of the Press Complaints Commission is one such code.

Civil Procedure Rules

8. CPR 25.3 and CPR PD25A (1) – (5) apply to all interim injunction applications, including those for interim non-disclosure orders.

Open Justice

9. Open justice is a fundamental principle. The general rule is that hearings are carried out in, and judgments and orders, are public: see Article 6(1) of the Convention, CPR 39.2 and *Scott v Scott* [1913] AC 417. This applies to applications for interim non-disclosure orders: *Micallef v Malta* (17056/06) [2009] ECHR 1571 at [75]ff; *Ntuli v Donald* [2010] EWCA Civ 1276 (*Ntuli*) at [50].

10. Derogations from the general principle can only be justified in exceptional circumstances, when they are strictly necessary as measures to secure the proper administration of justice. They are wholly exceptional: *R v Chief Registrar of Friendly Societies, ex parte New Cross Building Society* [1984] Q.B. 227 at 235; *Nutuli* at [52] – [53]. Derogations should, where justified, be no more than strictly necessary to achieve their purpose.

11. The grant of derogations is not a question of discretion. It is a matter of obligation and the court is under a duty to either grant the derogation or refuse it when it has applied the relevant test: *AMM v HXW* [2010] EWHC 2457 (QB) at [34].

12. There is no general exception to open justice where privacy or confidentiality is in issue. Applications will only be heard in private if and to the extent that the court is satisfied that by nothing short of the exclusion of the public can justice be done. Exclusions must be no more than the minimum strictly necessary to ensure justice is done and parties are expected to consider before applying for such an exclusion whether something short of exclusion can meet their concerns, as will normally be the case: *Ambrosiadou v Coward* [2011] EWCA Civ 409 at [50] – [54]. Anonymity will only be granted where it is strictly necessary, and then only to that extent.

13. The burden of establishing any derogation from the general principle lies on the person seeking it. It must be established by clear and cogent evidence: *Scott v Scott* [1913] AC 417 at 438 – 439, 463 and 477; *Lord Browne of Madingley v Associated Newspapers Ltd* [2008] 1 QB 103 at [2] – [3]; *Secretary of State for Home Department v AP (No2)* [2010] 1 WLR 1652 at [7]; *Gray v UVW* [2010] EWHC 2367 at [6] – [8]; and *JIH v News Group Newspapers* [2011] EWCA Civ 42 (*JIH*) at [21].

14. When considering the imposition of any derogation from open justice, the court will have regard to the respective and sometimes competing Convention rights of the parties as well as the general public interest in open justice and in the public reporting of court proceedings. It will also adopt procedures which seek to ensure that any ultimate vindication of Article 8 of the Convention, where that is engaged, is not undermined by the way in which the court has processed an interim application. On the other hand, the principle of open justice requires that any restrictions are the least that can be imposed consistent with the protection to which the party relying on their Article 8 Convention right is entitled. The proper approach is set out in *JIH*.

15. It will only be in the rarest cases that an interim non-disclosure order containing a prohibition on reporting the fact of proceedings (a super-injunction) will be justified on grounds of strict necessity, i.e., anti-tipping-off situations, where short-term secrecy is required to ensure the applicant can notify the respondent that the order is made: *DFT v TFD* [2010] EWHC 2335 (*DFT*). It is then only in truly exceptional circumstances that such an order should be granted for a longer period: *Terry v Persons Unknown* [2010] 1 FCR 659 (*Terry*) at [141].

Consent Orders

16. Interim non-disclosure orders which contain derogations from the principle of open justice cannot be granted by consent of the parties. Such orders affect the Article 10 Convention rights of the public at large. Parties cannot waive or give up the rights of the public. The court's approach is set out in *JIH* at [21].

Application

17. The applicant should prepare (a) the application/claim form; (b) a witness statement or statements justifying the need for an order; (c) legal submissions; (d) a draft order; and (e) an Explanatory Note (see paragraph 33 below). In the rare or urgent case where it is not possible to prepare such documentation prior to the hearing, the applicant should file a statement at the earliest practicable opportunity, setting out the information placed orally before the court.

Notice of Application

18. Applicants must comply with the requirements set out in HRA s12(2), CPR 25.3(2) and (3), and CPR PD 25A 4.3(3).

19. HRA s12(2) applies in respect of both (a) respondents to the proceedings and (b) any non-parties who are to be served with or otherwise notified of the order, because they have an existing interest in the information which is to be protected by an injunction (*X & Y v Persons Unknown* [2007] EMLR 290 at [10] – [12]). Both respondents and any non-parties to be served with the order are therefore entitled to advance notice of the application hearing and should be served with a copy of the Application Notice and any supporting documentation before that hearing.

20. Applicants will need to satisfy the court that all reasonable and practical steps have been taken to provide advance notice of the application. At the hearing they should inform the court of any non-party which they intend to notify of the order as the court is required to ensure that the requirements of HRA s12(2) are fulfilled

in respect of each of them. A schedule to any interim non-disclosure order granted should provide details of all such non-parties.

21. Failure to provide advance notice can only be justified, on clear and cogent evidence, by compelling reasons. Examples which may amount to compelling reasons, depending on the facts of the case, are: that there is a real prospect that were a respondent or non-party to be notified they would take steps to defeat the order's purpose (*RST v UVW* [2009] EWHC 24 at [7] and [13]), for instance, where there is convincing evidence that the respondent is seeking to blackmail the applicant (*ASG v GSA* [2009] EWCA Civ 1574 at [3]; *DFT* at [7]).

22. Where a respondent, or non-party, is a media organisation only rarely will there be compelling reasons why advance notification is or was not possible on grounds of either urgency or secrecy. It will only be in truly exceptional circumstances that failure to give a media organisation advance notice will be justifiable on the ground that it would defeat the purpose of an interim non-disclosure order. Different considerations may however arise where a respondent or non-party is an internet-based organisation, tweeter or blogger, or where, for instance, there are allegations of blackmail.

23. Where notice of the application is to be given to a media organisation it should be effected on the organisation's legal adviser, where it has one. The court will bear in mind that such legal advisers are: (i) used to participating in hearings at short notice where necessary; and ii) able to differentiate between information provided for legal purposes and information for editorial use.

Notice and Undertakings to the Court – Non-Parties

24. In order to provide effective protection of private and/or confidential information and information contained in private and/or confidential documents provided by applicants to non-parties:

   (i) where an applicant is to provide advance notice of an application to a non-party; or
   (ii) where an applicant notifies a non-party of an order,

   material supplied to the non-party by the applicant shall be supplied upon the applicant receiving an irrevocable written undertaking to the court that the material and the information contained within it, or derived from such material or information, will only be used for the purpose of the proceedings. A standard form of wording for the undertaking is set out in the notes to clause 13 of the Model Order, contained in the Model Order guidelines.

25. Where an applicant is to provide advance notice of an application to a non-party they should first provide the non-party with a copy of the Explanatory Note, which may where strictly necessary refer to the applicant and/or respondent by three anonymised initials. If, the non-party is willing to provide the irrevocable written undertaking, the applicant should then supply the materials, including the applicant's and respondent's names, to the non-party upon receipt of the undertaking. Where the non-party is unwilling to provide the undertaking, no further information need be supplied by the applicant. (Information concerning

when and where the application is to be heard should be set out in the Explanatory Note.)

26. Where an applicant notifies a non-party of an order, which should contain the provision set out in clause 13 of the Model Order, provision of material to a non-party shall be effected promptly by the applicant upon request, and upon receipt of the irrevocable written undertaking. Prior to notifying the non-party of the order and where urgency does not preclude it, the applicant should ascertain whether the non-party will require a copy of any materials referred to in clause 13 of the Model Order. Where the non-party indicates it will do so, it should at that stage provide the applicant with the written irrevocable undertaking. The applicant will then be in a position to, and should, serve a copy of the order and the relevant materials together. Where the non-party is unwilling to give the undertaking in advance of service of the order, the applicant will not be required to supply any relevant materials to the non-party until such time as the undertaking is given or further order of the court.

27. The undertaking should be provided on behalf of the non-party by its legal adviser where it has one. It should be provided by the non-party itself where it has no legal adviser. Breach of the undertaking may be held to be a contempt of court, which would render the non-party liable to imprisonment, a fine or having their assets seized.

28. For the purpose of paragraph 24, material includes: the application and any supporting documentation; and a copy of any materials specified under CPR PD 25A 9.

Hearing – Scrutiny of Application

29. The onus is on the applicant to satisfy the court that an interim non-disclosure order is justified. Where the applicant seeks derogations from open justice reference should be made to paragraphs 8 – 13 of this Guidance.

30. Particular care should be taken in every application for an interim non-disclosure order, and especially where an application is made without-notice, by applicants to comply with the high duty to make full, fair and accurate disclosure of all material information to the court and to draw the court's attention to significant factual, legal and procedural aspects of the case. The applicant's advocate, so far as it is consistent with the urgency of the application, has a particular duty to see that the correct legal procedures and forms are used; that a written skeleton argument and a properly drafted order are prepared personally by her or him and lodged with the court before the oral hearing; and that, at the hearing, the court's attention is drawn to unusual features of the evidence adduced, to the applicable law and to the formalities and procedure to be observed including how, if at all, the order submitted departs from the model order.

31. Applications, especially those which seek derogations from open justice, must be supported with clear and cogent evidence which demonstrates that without the specific exception, justice could not be done.

32. Each application shall be subject to intense scrutiny. The need for intense scrutiny is particularly acute on without-notice applications, or where non-parties are or have been served with orders containing restrictions on access to documents, because, for instance, the order contains derogations from CPR PD 25A 9.

Explanatory Notes

33. It is helpful if applications and orders are accompanied by an Explanatory Note, from which persons served can (a) readily understand the nature of the case, (b) ascertain whether they wish to attend the application hearing, and/or be legally represented at it, or, (c) where the application was heard without-notice, whether they wish to challenge the order.

34. Where an interim non-disclosure order contains restrictions on access to documents it must be accompanied by an Ex planatory Note when served on any non-party who was not present at the hearing of the application.

35. An example of an Explanatory Note is attached to this Guidance.

Applicant's Continuing Duty

36. Where an interim non-disclosure order is granted applicants are required to keep any respondent or non-party subject to the order, informed of any developments in the progress of proceedings which affect the status of the order. They are required to do so in order to satisfy the court that that there has been compliance with the obligation imposed by CPR 1.3 and any requirements specified in any order or directions given by the court. Applicants are particularly required to inform any non-parties whom they have served with the order when it ceases to have effect.

Active Case Management

37. Interim non-disclosure orders, as they restrict the exercise of the Article 10 Convention right and, whether or not they contain any derogation from the principle of open justice, require the court to take particular care to provide active case management.

38. Active case management requires the court to ensure that a return date is specified in such orders and that, as a general rule, the return date is kept. The applicant is required to inform the court at the return date which, if any, non-parties have been served with any interim non-disclosure order granted at an earlier, without-notice, hearing.

39. It will not always be necessary for any parties to attend court on the return date: the hearing could be dealt with by the court on the papers, provided that sufficient material is before the court to enable scrutiny and effective case management to take place: see *BCD v Goldsmith* [2011] EWHC 674 (QB) at [60] – [62]. Any order should however be given in public and be publicly available.

40. A return date is particularly important where an order contains derogations from the principle of open justice. It is the means by which the court ensures that those derogations are in place for no longer than strictly necessary. It is also the means by which the court ensures that the interim non-disclosure order does not become

a substitute for a full and fair adjudication (*X & Y v Persons Unknown* [2007] EMLR 290 at [78]).

41. Where an interim non-disclosure order, whether or not it contains derogations from open justice, is made, and return dates are adjourned for valid reasons on one or more occasions, or it is apparent, for whatever reason, that a trial is unlikely to take place between the parties to proceedings, the court should either dismiss the substantive action, proceed to summary judgment, enter judgment by consent, substitute or add an alternative defendant, or direct that the claim and trial proceed in the absence of a third party (*XJA v News Group Newspapers* [2010] EWHC 3174 (QB) at [13]; *Gray v UVW* [2010] EWHC 2367 (QB) at [37]; *Terry* at [134] – [136]).

Hearing Notes and Judgments

42. The court's approach to judgments and hearing notes is set out in: *Terry* at [4]; *JIH* at [21(9)] & [35].

43. It is of particular importance that a full and accurate note of the hearing is taken of a without-notice hearing: *G & G v Wikimedia* [2010] EMLR 14 at [28] – [32]. It is the duty of counsel and solicitors to ensure that such a note is taken during the hearing, or, if that is not possible, to prepare such a note after the hearing is over. The note should be drafted so that anyone supplied with a copy of it is properly informed of: what documents were put before the court at the hearing; which legal authorities were relied on by the applicant; and what the court was told in the course of the hearing.

44. Where, and to the extent strictly necessary hearing notes may be redacted, if they are to be supplied under CPR PD 25A 9.2, to a non-party who is served with an order but who is unwilling or unable to provide a written irrevocable undertaking.

45. The court should wherever possible give a reasoned, necessarily redacted, judgment. Where a judgment of the type given in *Terry* or *JIH* would be disproportionate in terms of time or cost a short note or judgment should be given setting out any points of general interest, the reason why those points were raised and brief reasons for the decision: see *POI v The Person known as 'Lina'* [2011] EWHC 25 (QB).

Appeals

46. Any appeal from an interim non-disclosure order may be expedited: *Unilever plc v Chefaro Proprietaries Ltd (Practice Note)* [1995] 1 WLR 243 at 246 - 247. It will depend on the circumstances of each case whether, and to what extent, expedition is necessary.

(2) MODEL ORDER – GUIDELINES

The following guidelines should be read in conjunction with the model interim non-disclosure order.

Penal Notice

The penal notice should make clear that where the intended defendant or respondent is an individual they may be imprisoned as well as being liable to a fine or asset seizure. Where the intended defendant or respondent is a corporate defendant or respondent it should make clear that they can be fined or have their assets seized.

The penal notice should also make clear the effect it may have on non-parties who know of the order under the *Spycatcher* principle. The order will only bind non-parties who are notified of it while it is in force: *Jockey Club v Buffham* [2003] QB 462.

Clause 2(b)

Reference should be made to paragraphs 18 – 28 of the Practice Guidance.

Clause 3 (Anonymity)

This clause is **optional**. Reference should be made to paragraphs 9 – 14 of the Practice Guidance. Anonymity is an exception to the principle of open justice. It can only be ordered where it is strictly necessary. Guidance is set out in *JIH* at [21].

Clause 4(a)(ii) (Access to documents)

The court may need to decide which documents, e.g., statements of case, should not be available for public inspection. This decision may be prospective since there may be little if any opportunity to apply to court before some documents are served. While it may be the case that the claim form could be made anodyne by reference to a confidential schedule (subject to anonymity), subsequent statements of case or other documents in a case are unlikely to be dealt with so easily given that the purpose of the action, amongst other things, will be to seek a permanent injunction relating to the material protected on an interim basis under the order, and will involve a specific explanation of the material, how it is said to engage the applicant's Article 8 Convention rights and the effect such threatened disclosure would have if it is not so restrained (*Terry* at [23]; *G & G v Wikimedia* [2010] EMLR 14 at [14], [17] and [20]; *ABC Ltd v Y* [2010] EWHC 3176 (Ch) at [8] – [10].

(*In respect of any non-party notified or served with the order CPR PD 25A 9.2 applies: see clause 13 of the Model Order.*)

Clause 5(a) (Service of the claim form where defendant is not known or whereabouts unknown)

Where the respondent or defendant's identity is not known, or their whereabouts are unknown, there may be considerable problems in locating them in order to serve the claim form. This may necessitate an extension of time for service beyond the four month period. The court, by way of active case management, is required to ensure that the action is pursued with expedition. Indefinite extensions of time for service cannot be granted: *Terry* at [143]. A long-stop date may be inserted instead.

Clause 6 (Injunction)
CPR PD 25A 5 states that unless the court orders otherwise, the order must provide for a *return date* if the application was made without-notice. The need for, and importance of, a return date as a means to ensure the court can monitor the claim's progress and ensure it progresses properly was considered *G & G v Wikimedia* [2010] EMLR 14 at [21] – [27]; and in *Terry* at [134] – [136]. Reference should be made to paragraphs 37 – 41 of the Practice Guidance.

While there may be considerable practical and costs reasons which might render a return date in a claim against persons unknown unnecessary, especially given the safeguard of the liberty to vary or discharge provisions (*X & Y v Persons Unknown* [2007] EMLR 290 at [73]), the court should ensure that the order contains provision for periodical review by the court to ensure that the claim progresses, for instance, to default judgment, summary judgment, or to a trial in the absence of the persons unknown.

Clause 6(b)
This clause is **optional**. See clause 3 above. This provides a possible solution to the problem which arises from a jigsaw identification of the Claimant if the fact of the injunction is not prevented from being published: *DFT* at [36] – [39]. There should be a clear delineation in the order of what information can be released as to the fact of an order having been made.

Clause 7 (Reporting Restriction)
This is the super-injunction element. It is an **optional** clause. It is only likely to be necessary for example to prevent the respondent or a third party being tipped-off before the order is served, possibly precipitating disclosure of the information or destruction of evidence: see *Terry* at [138]; *G & G v Wikimedia* [2010] EMLR 14 at [41].

If the proceedings are anonymised, and an injunction is granted restraining disclosure or publication of the private information, there is generally no reason in principle to prohibit in addition any report of the fact that an order has been made: *Ntuli*. Consideration should be given to the risk of jigsaw identification if no reporting restriction is imposed: *DFT*.

Clause 13 (Provision of documents and information to third parties)
CPR PD 25A 9 requires any person served with the order not present at the application hearing to be provided with the order and supporting material read by the judge, and a note of the hearing.

This is the norm. Such notice is an elementary principle of natural justice:

Kelly v BBC [2001] Fam. 59 at 94 – 95, '. . . *if one party wishes to place evidence or other persuasive material before the court the other parties must have an opportunity to see that material and to address the court about it. One party may not make secret communications to the court. It follows that it is wrong for a judge to be given material at an ex parte, or without notice, hearing which is not at a later stage revealed to the persons affected by the result of the application.*';

G & G v Wikimedia [2009] EWHC 3148 (QB) at [30], '. . . *where an order relates to freedom of expression, or may have the effect of interfering with freedom of expression, those applying for interim relief at a hearing at which the respondent or defendant is not present should generally provide the respondent with a full note, whether or not the respondent asks for it.*'

Exceptions to the norm are exceptions to the principle of open justice, and natural justice, and are therefore only permissible where strictly necessary. If there is concern that information is particularly sensitive or confidential, it can be included in a separate witness statement which the court may agree should be specifically exempted from having to be provided under the CPR 25A PD 9, thus enabling as much information as possible to be provided to those, such as non-parties who request a hearing note under PD 9.2(2), not present at the application hearing.

Clause 13 Irrevocable written undertaking
The following standard wording should be used by third parties in respect of the irrevocable undertaking to be given to the Court under paragraph 24 of the Practice Guidance and in respect of clause 13 of the Model Order. Breach of the undertaking may amount to contempt of court. The wording provides for a Claimant to agree to information and material subject to the undertaking provided by the third party to be supplied, by the third party, to other parties in order, for instance, to ensure that the prohibition on disclosure is not inadvertently breached by that other party.

Undertaking to the Claimant and to the Court
The title of action or intended action is ....

1. I, [insert name, occupation] [for and on behalf of ....] (hereinafter "the receiver") promise that in consideration of the Claimant disclosing the material to the receiver, the receiver: will preserve the material in a secure place; use any material or information contained therein, or derived from such material or information, only for the purposes of the Proceedings except where:
(a) the information has been read to or by the court, or referred to, at a hearing which has been held in public;
(b) the court gives permission; or
(c) there is agreement in writing by the Claimant and by any other person who claims to be entitled to rights of property, privacy or confidentiality in respect of the information or the documents in which it is recorded;

and will only copy, disclose or deliver the material, or information contained therein or derived from such material or information, to the receiver's legal advisers, or as required by law, by order of the court or by agreement of the Claimant and by any other person who claims to be entitled to rights of property, privacy or confidentiality in respect of the information or the documents in which it is recorded.

2. Save as provided in para 1, this undertaking is irrevocable, and shall continue in force both before and after the conclusion of the Proceedings.

3. The receiver will give to the court an undertaking in writing in the same terms as herein, as soon as a judge is available to receive that undertaking.

4. For the purpose of this undertaking,
"Material" refers to: i) any claim form or application notice or statement of case (whether in draft or final form); ii) any evidence, whether in the form of witness statements or otherwise, in support of the proceedings, and any exhibits thereto; iii) and the material specified in CPR PD 25A para 9.2;
"Claimant" includes an intended claimant;
"Proceedings" means the proceedings identified above.

5. For the avoidance of doubt this promise only applies to those parts of the Material which contain the information alleged by the Claimant to be private and does not preclude the receiver (or anyone else) from making lawful use of any information that was already known to them prior to it being disclosed to the receiver pursuant to this undertaking, or of any information which is, or shall have come into, the public domain.

Clause 14 (Hearing in private)
This clause is **optional.** Reference should be made to paragraphs 9 - 14 of the Practice Guidance.

Private hearings can be reported without fear of contempt unless the material comes within the protection of the Administration of Justice Act 1960 s12. A specific order is required to prevent reporting under the Contempt of Court Act 1981 s11: *Clibbery v Allan* [2002] 2 WLR 151; *McKennitt v Ash* [2008] QB 73. Section 11 orders should only be made when strictly necessary.

This also incorporates the proviso, referred to in *JIH* at [42], regarding disclosure of material etc referred to in open court or in open judgments.

Clause 15 (Public Domain)
Orders will not usually, but may sometimes in cases of private information, prohibit publication of material which is already in the public domain. See *Terry* at [50].

Confidential schedule 2, paragraph 2
See the notes to **Clause 13 (Provision of documents and information to third parties)**.

(3) MODEL EXPLANATORY NOTE

Smith v Jones

or

AAA v BBB[1]

Application for an Interim Non-Disclosure Order

EXPLANATORY NOTE

1. The applicant is a well known professional sportsperson who has been in a long-term relationship with another person [XX]. A person [BBB/YY as appropriate] [or persons unknown] have threatened to take a story to the media about a relationship the applicant is alleged to have had with another person [YY], since the relationship with XX commenced.

2. An Interim Non-Disclosure Order has been [applied for/made] to protect the applicant's [right to privacy and/confidentiality] in respect of the information referred to in paragraph 1. This does not [will not] restrict publication of information which was in the public domain in England and Wales prior to this application being made or which is permitted by any order of the court to the extent permitted by the court

3. The [applicant applies for the application to be heard/the application was heard] in private. Judgment [will be/was] given in [public/private]. [The proceedings were anonymised.] [A private hearing/anonymity was applied for/granted on the grounds of strict necessity because . . .].

4. On [insert date] the application [will be heard by/was heard by] [Mr/Mrs Justice] in the High Court of Justice, [Queen's Bench Division/Chancery Division].

[1] Where the application is made or is intended to be made in anonymised form, three initials should be used.

Model Order

IN THE HIGH COURT OF JUSTICE **Claim No: [ ]**
[QUEEN'S BENCH/CHANCERY] DIVISION

BEFORE THE HONOURABLE [MR][MRS] JUSTICE [ ] [(IN PRIVATE)]
Dated: [ ]

B E T W E E N :

"AAA"

Intended Claimant/Applicant

- and -

(1) "BBB"
(2) [ ] NEWSPAPERS LIMITED
(3) THE PERSON OR PERSONS UNKNOWN
who has or have appropriated, obtained and/or offered or intend to offer for sale and/or publication the material referred to in Confidential Schedule 2 to this Order

Intended Defendant(s)/Respondent(s)

<u>PENAL NOTICE</u>

IF YOU THE RESPONDENT DISOBEY THIS ORDER YOU MAY BE HELD TO BE IN CONTEMPT OF COURT AND MAY BE IMPRISONED (IN THE CASE OF THE FIRST AND THIRD DEFENDANTS) OR FINED OR HAVE YOUR ASSETS SEIZED.

ANY PERSON WHO KNOWS OF THIS ORDER AND DISOBEYS THIS ORDER OR DOES ANYTHING WHICH HELPS OR PERMITS ANY PERSON TO WHOM THIS ORDER APPLIES TO BREACH THE TERMS OF THIS ORDER MAY BE HELD TO BE IN CONTEMPT OF COURT AND MAY BE IMPRISONED, FINED OR HAVE THEIR ASSETS SEIZED.

<u>NOTICE TO ANYONE WHO KNOWS OF THIS ORDER</u>

You should read the terms of the Order and the Practice Guidance on Interim Non-Disclosure Orders very carefully. You are advised to consult a solicitor as soon as possible. This Order prohibits you from doing the acts set out in Paragraphs 6 [, 7] and 10 of the Order and obliges you to do the acts set out in Paragraphs 8, 9, and 11 of the Order. You have the right to ask the Court to vary or discharge the Order. If you disobey this Order you may be found guilty of contempt of court and you may be sent to prison or fined or your assets may be seized.

THIS ORDER

1. This is an Injunction, with other orders as set out below, made against the Defendants on [insert date] by the Judge identified above (the **Judge**) on the application (the **Application**) of the Claimant. The Judge:

    (a) read the witness statements referred to in Schedule A at the end of this Order, as well as the witness statements referred to in Confidential Schedule 1 [or "was given information orally by Counsel on behalf of the Claimant"];

    (b) accepted the undertakings set out in Schedule B at the end of this Order; and

    (c) considered the provisions of the Human Rights Act 1998 (**HRA**), section 12.

2. [*This Order was made at a hearing without-notice to those affected by it, the Court having considered section 12(2) HRA and being satisfied:*

    (a) that the Claimant has taken all practicable steps to notify persons affected; and/or

    (b) that there are compelling reasons for notice not being given, namely: [set out in full the Court's reasons for making the order without-notice]. The Defendants (and anyone served with or notified of this Order) have a right to apply to the Court to vary or discharge the Order (or so much of it as affects them): see clause 17 below.]

[ONLY TO BE GRANTED IN AN EXCEPTIONAL CASE WHERE ANONYMITY IS STRICTLY NECESSARY]

ANONYMITY

3. *Pursuant to section 6 HRA, and/or CPR 39.2 the Judge, being satisfied that it is strictly necessary, ordered that:*

    (a) the Claimant be permitted to issue these proceedings naming the Claimant as "AAA" and giving an address c/o the Claimant's solicitors;

    (b) the Claimant be permitted to issue these proceedings naming the [First] Defendant as "BBB" [and the Third Defendant as "Person or Persons Unknown" and, once it is known to the Claimant, notifying the Defendant's home address by filing the same in a sealed letter which must remain sealed and held with the Court office subject only to the further order of a Judge or the Senior Master of the Queen's Bench Division/Chief Chancery Master];

    (c) there be substituted for all purposes in these proceedings in place of references to the Claimant by name, and whether orally or in writing, references to the letters "AAA"; and

    (d) if necessary, there be substituted for all purposes in these proceedings in place of references to the Defendant[s] by name once identified and whether orally or in writing, references to the letters "BBB" [and any subsequent letters of the alphabet].

[ONLY TO BE GRANTED IN AN EXCEPTIONAL CASE WHERE A RESTRICTION ON ACCESS TO DOCUMENTS IS STRICTLY NECESSARY]

ACCESS TO DOCUMENTS

4. Upon the Judge being satisfied that it is strictly necessary:

(a) (i) no copies of the statements of case; and

(ii) no copies of the witness statements and the applications,

will be provided to a non-party without further order of the Court.

(b) Any non-party other than a person notified or served with this Order seeking access to, or copies of the abovementioned documents, must make an application to the Court, proper notice of which must be given to the other parties.

SERVICE OF CLAIM FORM WHERE DEFENDANT NOT KNOWN OR WHEREABOUTS NOT KNOWN

5.

(a) The Claim Form should be served as soon as reasonably practicable and in any event by [ ] at the latest, save that there shall be liberty for the Claimant to apply to the Court in the event that an extension is necessary; and

(b) Any such application referred to in 5(a) must be supported by a witness statement. Such application may be made by letter, the Court having dispensed with the need for an application notice.

INJUNCTION

6. Until [ ] (the return date) / the trial of this claim or further Order of the Court, the Defendants must not:

(a) use, publish or communicate or disclose to any other person (other than (i) by way of disclosure to legal advisers instructed in relation to these proceedings (the **Defendants' legal advisers**) for the purpose of obtaining legal advice in relation to these proceedings or (ii) for the purpose of carrying this Order into effect) all or any part of the the information referred to in Confidential Schedule 2 to this Order (the **Information**);

(b) publish any information which is liable to or might identify the Claimant as a party to the proceedings and/or as the subject of the Information or which otherwise contains material (including but not limited to the profession [or age or nationality of the Claimant]) which is liable to, or might lead to, the Claimant's identification in any such respect, provided that nothing in this Order shall prevent the publication, disclosure or communication of any information which is contained in [this Order other than in the Confidential Schedules] or in the public judgments of the Court in this action given on [insert date].

[ONLY TO BE GRANTED IN AN EXCEPTIONAL CASE WHERE A REPORTING RESTRICTION IS STRICTLY NECESSARY]

REPORTING RESTRICTION/SUPER-INJUNCTION

7. *Until service of the Order/ the return date/ [ ] the Defendants must not use, publish or communicate or disclose to any other person the fact or existence of this Order or these proceedings and the Claimant's interest in them, other than:*

   (a) *by way of disclosure to the Defendants' legal advisers for the purpose of obtaining legal advice in relation to these proceedings; or*

   (b) *for the purpose of carrying this Order into effect.*

INFORMATION TO BE DISCLOSED

8. The Defendants shall within [24] hours of service of this Order disclose to the Claimant's solicitors the following:

   (a) the identity of each and every journalist, press or media organisation, press agent or publicist or any other third party with a view to publication in the press or media, to whom the Defendants have disclosed all or any part of the Information [since [insert date]]; and

   (b) the date upon which such disclosure took place and the nature of the information disclosed.

9. The Defendants shall confirm the information supplied in paragraph 8 above in a witness statement containing a statement of truth within 7 days of complying with paragraph 8 and serve the same on the Claimant's solicitors and the other parties.

PROTECTION OF HEARING PAPERS

10. The Defendants [, and any third party given advance notice of the Application,] must not publish or communicate or disclose or copy or cause to be published or communicated or disclosed or copied any witness statements and any exhibits thereto and information contained therein that are made, or may subsequently be made, in support of the Application or the Claimant's solicitors' notes of the hearing of the Application (the **Hearing Papers**), provided that the Defendants[, and any third party,] shall be permitted to copy, disclose and deliver the Hearing Papers to the Defendants' [and third party's/parties'] legal advisers for the purpose of these proceedings .

11. The Hearing Papers must be preserved in a secure place by the Defendants' [and third party's/parties'] legal advisers on the Defendants' [and third party's/parties'] behalf.

12. The Defendants [, and any third party given advance notice of the Application,] shall be permitted to use the Hearing Papers for the purpose of these proceedings provided that the Defendants' [third party's/parties'] legal advisers shall first inform anyone, to whom the said documents are disclosed, of the terms of this Order and, so far as is practicable, obtain their written confirmation that they understand and accept that they are bound by the same.

PROVISION OF DOCUMENTS AND INFORMATION TO THIRD PARTIES

13. The Claimant shall be required to provide the legal advisers of any third party [where unrepresented, the third party] served with advance notice of the application, or a copy of this Order promptly upon request, and receipt of their written irrevocable

undertaking to the Court to use those documents and the information contained in those documents only for the purpose of these proceedings:

(a) a copy of any material read by the Judge, including material read after the hearing at the direction of the Judge or in compliance with this Order [save for the witness statements referred to in Confidential Schedule 1 at the end of this Order] [the witness statements]; and/or

(b) a copy of the Hearing Papers.

[ONLY TO BE GRANTED IN AN EXCEPTIONAL CASE WHERE HEARING THE APPLICATION IN PRIVATE IS STRICTLY NECESSARY]
HEARING IN PRIVATE

14. The Judge considered that it was strictly necessary, pursuant to CPR 39.2(3)(a),(c) and (g), to order that the hearing of the Application be in private and there shall be no reporting of the same.

PUBLIC DOMAIN

15. For the avoidance of doubt, nothing in this Order shall prevent the Defendants from publishing, communicating or disclosing such of the Information, or any part thereof, as was already in, or that thereafter comes into, the public domain in England and Wales [as a result of publication in the national media] (other than as a result of breach of this Order [or a breach of confidence or privacy]).

COSTS

16. The costs of and occasioned by the Application are reserved.

VARIATION OR DISCHARGE OF THIS ORDER

17. The parties or anyone affected by any of the restrictions in this Order may apply to the Court at any time to vary or discharge this Order (or so much of it as affects that person), but they must first give written notice to the Claimant's solicitors. If any evidence is to be relied upon in support of the application, the substance of it must be communicated in writing to the Claimant's solicitors in advance. The Defendants may agree with the Claimant's solicitors and any other person who is, or may be bound by this Order, that this Order should be varied or discharged, but any agreement must be in writing.

INTERPRETATION OF THIS ORDER

18. A Defendant who is an individual who is ordered not to do something must not do it himself or in any other way. He must not do it through others acting on his behalf or on his instructions or with his encouragement.

19. A Defendant which is not an individual which is ordered not to do something must not do it itself or by its directors, officers, partners, employees or agents or in any other way.

[In the case of an Order the effect of which may extend outside the jurisdiction]
PERSONS OUTSIDE ENGLAND AND WALES

20. (1) Except as provided in paragraph (2) below, the terms of this Order do not affect or concern anyone outside the jurisdiction of this Court.

(2) The terms of this Order will affect the following persons in a country or state outside the jurisdiction of this Court –

(a) the Defendant or his officer or agent appointed by power of attorney;

(b) any person who –

(i) is subject to the jurisdiction of this Court;
(ii) has been given written notice of this Order at his residence or place of business within the jurisdiction of this Court; and
(iii) is able to prevent acts or omissions outside the jurisdiction of this Court which constitute or assist in a breach of the terms of this Order; and

(c) any other person, only to the extent that this Order is declared enforceable by or is enforced by a court in that country or state.

PARTIES OTHER THAN THE CLAIMANT AND THE DEFENDANT

21. **Effect of this Order**

It is a contempt of court for any person notified of this Order knowingly to assist in or permit a breach of this Order. Any person doing so may be imprisoned, fined or have their assets seized.

NAME AND ADDRESS OF THE CLAIMANT'S LEGAL REPRESENTATIVES

22. The Claimant's solicitors are -

[*Name, address, reference, fax and telephone numbers both in and out of office hours and e-mail*]

COMMUNICATIONS WITH THE COURT

23. All communications to the Court about this Order should be sent to:

Room WG08, Royal Courts of Justice, Strand, London, WC2A 2LL, quoting the case number. The telephone number is 020 7947 6010.

The offices are open between 10 a.m. and 4.30 p.m. Monday to Friday.

SCHEDULE A

The Claimant relied on the following witness statements:

1. ....
2. ....

SCHEDULE B

UNDERTAKINGS GIVEN TO THE COURT BY THE CLAIMANT

(1) If the Court later finds that this Order has caused loss to the Defendants, and decides that the Defendants should be compensated for that loss, the Claimant will comply with any order the Court may make.

(2) If the Court later finds that this Order has caused loss to any person or company (other than the Defendants) to whom the Claimant has given notice of this Order, and decides that such person should be compensated for that loss, the Claimant will comply with any Order the Court may make.

[(3) By 4.30pm on [ ] the Claimant will (a) issue a Claim Form and an Application Notice claiming the appropriate relief [and (b) cause a witness statement or witness statements to be made and filed confirming the substance of what was said to the Court by the Claimant's Counsel and exhibiting a copy of the Hearing Papers].

[(4) The Claimant will use all reasonable endeavours to identify and serve the Defendants within four months of the date of this Order and in any event will do so by [ ] at the latest. Once identified the Claimant will serve upon the Defendant together with this Order copies of the documents provided to the Court on the making of the Application and as soon as practicable the documents referred to in (3) above.]

(5) On the return date the Claimant will inform the Court of the identity of all third parties that have been notified of this Order. The Claimant will use all reasonable endeavours to keep such third parties informed of the progress of the action [insofar as it may affect them], including, but not limited to, advance notice of any applications, the outcome of which may affect the status of the Order.

(6) If this Order ceases to have effect or is varied, the Claimant will immediately take all reasonable steps to inform in writing anyone to whom he has given notice of this Order, or whom he has reasonable grounds for supposing may act upon this Order, that it has ceased to have effect in this form.

SCHEDULE C

This should contain details of who the Claimant has given advance notice of the application to, including how and when and by what means this was done.

SCHEDULE D

The detail required by paragraph 20 of the Guidance Note should go in here.

SCHEDULE E

The detail required by paragraph 38 of the Guidance Note should go in here.

CONFIDENTIAL SCHEDULE 1

The Claimant also relied on the following confidential witness statements:

1. ....
2. ....

CONFIDENTIAL SCHEDULE 2

Information referred to in the Order

Any information or purported information concerning:

(1) [Set out the material sought to be protected]

(2) [Any information liable to or which might lead to the identification of the Claimant (whether directly or indirectly) as the subject of the proceedings or the material referred to above, [the fact that he has commenced these proceedings or made the application herein].]

High Court & Court of Appeal Privacy Injunctions Statistics Form

See http://www.justice.gov.uk/courts/procedure-rules/civil/contents/form_section_images/practice_directions/pd51f_pdf_eps/pd51f_siform.pdf

Part 18

EXAMPLES OF ORDERS FROM THE CASES

(AND A MODEL NOTICE OF APPLICATION)

Introduction

1. ***LNR*:** The **Practice Guidance** sets out a Model Order.

2. **Purpose of this Part:** The purpose of this Part is to set out provisions in orders from individual cases which may be of assistance in tailoring any particular order to the fact-sensitive needs of the individual case.

3. **Refining the model order:** The following suggestions may provide for some refinement:

(a) A *Goodwin* exception vis-à-vis communications with the FSA, etc.
(b) A *DFT* proviso—with reference to a public judgment.
(c) A proviso to enable information to be used to gather evidence.
(d) A provision permitting an individual to tell her story, so long as intimate information is not disclosed nor the identity of the claimant revealed: *MJN* (ibid).

Draft Clauses from the Cases

4. **Bernard *Gray v UVW*** [2010] EWHC 2367 (QB). Terms of part of order at **para 22**:

> '1. **[Privacy]** The application be heard in private pursuant to CPR r 39.2(3) (a), (c) and (g).

2. **[Anonymised]** 'Until further Order the Claimant and Defendant shall be anonymised in this Order, and in any statements of case or application documents, pursuant to CPR r 39.2(4).

3. **[Confidential schedule—Order]** 'Schedule 1 to this order be treated as confidential and not open to inspection pursuant to CPR r5.4C(4).

4. [**Confidential information—statement of case**] 'Anything which may reveal any information or purported information described in the Confidential Schedule at the end of this Order shall be excluded from statements of case served in this intended action, and included in a separate confidential schedule served with the statement of case.

5. **[Restricted access by the public to the court file]** 'Pursuant to CPR r 5.4C(4) a person who is not a party to this intended action may not obtain from the court records any copy of the confidential schedule served with any statement of case. Any non party seeking access to or copies of any confidential schedule from the court file must make an application to the Court, having previously given at least 3 days notice of the application to the solicitors for all parties.

6. [**Notice of non-party application**] 'If any non party at any time makes an application to the Court under CPR r 5.4C(2) for permission to obtain from the court records a copy of any other document, other than a statement of case, or of any communication, such non party must give at least 3 days notice of the application to the solicitors for all parties.'

5. ***Lord Browne of Madingley v Associated Newspapers Ltd*** [2007] EWCA Civ 295. Order vis-à-vis confidential information.

7. On 6 January 2007 Underhill J, on the application of the claimant, Lord Browne of Madingley, granted an injunction in wide terms restraining the defendant ('the newspaper') from publishing any details of the relationship between the claimant and Mr Jeff Chevalier ('JC') and any confidential or private information that JC had obtained in the course of that relationship, including 15 specific items of information . . .

6. ***X and Y v Persons Unknown*** [2006] EWHC 2783 (QB). Terms of order restricting information:

3. I shall not set out the order in full for present purposes. It is unnecessary to do so. It was, however, primarily directed towards preventing the "persons unknown" from publishing confidential information to the following effect:

Until further order, the Defendants must not, whether by themselves or by any other person, publish, communicate or disclose to any other person (other than to legal advisers instructed in relation to the proceedings for the purpose of obtaining legal advice in relation to these proceedings) any information or purported information concerning

(i) [the Claimants'] personal relationship and any marital difficulties;

(ii) the fact that the Claimants have obtained an injunction.

7. ***A-G v Punch Ltd*** [2002] UKHL 50. At first instance Hooper J ordered that it be restrained—see **para 88**, and see also **para 124** (and paragraphs before that):

88. Until further order, whether by itself, its servants or agents or otherwise howsoever from publishing to any person any information obtained by it from the first defendant and obtained by the first defendant in the course of or as a result of his employment in and position as a member of the Security Service, whether in relation to the work of, or in support of, the security and intelligence services or otherwise; provided that this order does not apply to: (1) any information in respect of which the plaintiff (whether at the request of [the defendants or any of them] or any third party, or of his own motion) makes a statement in writing (either personally or by the Treasury Solicitor) that such information is not information in respect of which the Crown seeks to restrain publication; (2) the repetition of information disclosed in 'The Mail on Sunday' on 24 August 1997.

8. ***John Terry (previously referred to as "LNS") v Persons Unknown*** [2010] EWHC 119 (QB) Tugendhat J said:

6. [**As to strands of information**] The draft order seeks a prohibition on publishing "all or any part of the information or purported information" and documents in four categories. I paraphrase this as follows: (1) the fact of a specified personal relationship ("the Relationship") between LNS and another person who is named ("the other person"); (2) details of that relationship including certain specific consequences of it; (3) information leading to the identification of LNS or the other person and (4) any photographs evidencing or relating to the fact or details of these matters.

. . .

18. [**'*Spycatcher*' principle**] The draft order sets out correctly that (in accordance with what is known as the *Spycatcher* principle: see *A-G v Newspaper Publishing plc* [1988] Ch 333, 380):

"**Effect of this order**: It is a contempt of court for any person notified of this order knowingly to assist in or permit a breach of this order. Any person doing so may be imprisoned, fined or have their assets seized".

. . .

140. [**Super-injunction**] There is a standard form of prohibition on disclosure of the making of an injunction in para 20 of the Form of Search Order given in the Practice Direction to CPR Part 25. It reads:

"Except for the purpose of obtaining legal advice, the Respondent must not directly or indirectly inform anyone of these proceedings or of the contents of this order, or warn anyone that proceedings have been or may be brought against him by the Applicant until 4.30 p.m. on the return date or further order of the court."

9. ***JIH v News Group Newspapers Ltd*** [2010] EWHC 2818 (QB) per Tugendhat J.

A. **Claim form:** As to how the claim form read in *JIH* (ibid) at **para 21**:

21. On 16 August 2010 the Claimant gave Notice of an application for an Order continuing the Order of 13 August. On the same day he issued a claim form. The relief claimed was

"an injunction restraining the publication or disclosure of private information concerning the Claimant identified in the Confidential Schedule to the Order of Mr Justice Nicol dated 13 August 2010".

B. The terms of the Order made:

THE REVISED FORM OF ORDER

74. The revised form of draft order submitted by the parties includes the following as its substantive provisions, to run until the trial of this action or further order in the meantime:

"**The prohibited acts**

1. The Defendant must not publish, republish, syndicate, use, communicate or disclose to any person:

(a) Any information concerning the subject matter of these proceedings save for that contained in the public judgment of the Court handed down on 5 November 2010 and/or

(b) Any of the information set out in the Confidential Schedule to this Order (together "the Information").

PROVIDED THAT nothing in this Order shall prevent the publication, disclosure or communication of any of the Information:

(i) by the Defendant (1) to legal advisers instructed in relation to these proceedings for the purpose of obtaining legal advice in relation to these proceedings or (2) for the purposes of carrying this Order into effect or (3) for the purpose of these proceedings (including for the purpose of gathering evidence in relation to these proceedings) provided that any person to whom such information is disclosed must first be either given a copy of this Order or notified of its substance and effect;

(ii) by the Defendant of any part of the Information that is in the public domain as the result of national media publication (otherwise than as a result of breach of this Order).

[(iii) by or to any person named in the Confidential Schedule for purely private and personal purposes and in confidence, (that is, on the express understanding that there will be no further disclosure of the Information), with their closest friends, their immediate family and professional advisers.]

Confidential Information in Statements of Case

2. Anything which may reveal any information or purported information described in the Confidential Schedule to this Order shall be excluded from the statements of case served in this action, and included in a separate schedule served with the statement of case.

3. Pursuant to CPR 5.4C(4) any person who is not a party to this action may not obtain from the court records any copy of any confidential schedule served with any statement of case. Any non party seeking access to or copies of any confidential schedule from the court file must make an application to the Court, having previously given at least 3 days' notice of the application to the solicitors for the parties.

4. If any non-party at any time makes an application to the Court under CPR 5.4C(2) for permission to obtain from the Court records a copy of any other document, other than a statement of case, or of any communication, such non-party must give at least 3 days' notice of the application to the solicitors for all parties.

Provision of Documents and Information to Third Parties

5. The Claimant shall not be required pursuant to CPR 25 PD 9.2 or otherwise to provide any third party served with a copy of this order with:

(a) a copy of any materials read to or by the Judge, including material prepared after the hearing at the direction of the Judge or in compliance with the order; and/or

(b) a note of the hearing

save where the third party (1) specifically requests the same and (2) provides written undertakings to the court (i) that these documents will not be copied or reproduced except for the purposes of any application to vary or discharge this Order (ii) that they will be kept securely and (iii) that these documents and the information contained therein shall only be used (save to the extent that such information is already in the public domain) for the said purposes.

6. Any person who has made any such request may apply to the Court to vary these provisions or for directions.

Hearing in Private

7. Pursuant to CPR 39.2(3)(a)(c) and (g), the hearing of the application to which this order relates be heard in private and pursuant to section 6 of the Human Rights Act 1998, there be no reporting of the same. For the avoidance of doubt, nothing in this provision shall prevent the reporting of the Court's public judgment dated 5 November 2010.

Variation or Discharge of this Order

8. The Defendant or anyone served with or notified of this Order may apply to the Court to vary or discharge this Order (or so much of it as affects that person), but they must first give not less than 48 hours written notice to the Claimant's solicitors. If any evidence is to be relied upon in support of the application, the substance of it must be communicated in writing to the Claimant's solicitors at the time of giving notice or as soon as possible thereafter".

75. In addition, the undertakings given to the Court by the Claimant are:

"**Schedule 1**

Undertakings given to the Court by the Claimant:

(1) If the Court later finds that this Order has caused loss to the Defendant and decides that the Defendant should be compensated for that loss, the Claimant will comply with any Order the Court may make.

(2) If the Court later finds that this Order has caused loss to any person or company (other than the Defendant) to whom the Claimant has given

notice of this Order, and decides that such person should be compensated for that loss, the Claimant will comply with any Order the Court may make.

(3) If for any reason this Order ceases to have effect the Claimant will forthwith take all reasonable steps to inform, in writing, any person or company to whom he has given notice of this Order, or who he has reasonable grounds for supposing may act upon this Order, that this Order has ceased to be of effect.

(4) The Claimant will as soon as reasonably practicable give notice of this Order to the Defendant and will take all practicable steps to serve the Defendant with this Order and all supporting documents.

Schedule 2

Undertaking given to the Court by the Claimant's solicitors:

The Claimant's solicitors will prepare and retain until the conclusion of this intended action a full note of the hearing at which this Order was made."

76. The only provision not agreed between the parties is para 2(iii), which appears above underlined. This is referred to as a "friends and family clause".

77. Mr Spearman accepts that "NGN" is not entitled to seek the addition of this proviso in the light of the agreement between the parties.

78. Mr Tomlinson accepts that in principle such a clause may be appropriate in cases where the defendant is an individual, or where the claimant proposes to serve the order on a third party who is an individual, at least where the information the subject matter of the action is of a personal nature that such an individual may reasonably expect to discuss with friends and family. But he says that in this case there is no intention of serving the order on any third party who is an individual.

79. In the absence of full argument, I prefer to say nothing on this point, and to omit the proviso from my order.

CONCLUSION

80. This judgment is a public judgment. My conclusion is that the Claimant should not be granted anonymity. I will make the Order in the revised form agreed between the parties. But pending any order that may be made on any application for permission to appeal, the Claimant's name must remain anonymised.

10. ***Ntuli v Donald*** [2010] EWCA Civ 1276 at **paras 7** and **8**:

7. The principal substantive restraint in the original order restraining the publication of confidential information contains a proviso which was modified so as to read:

"PROVIDED THAT nothing in this paragraph of this Order shall prevent the Defendant from publishing, communicating or disclosing the following

(a) any material that before service of this Order was already in, or that thereafter comes into, the public domain ...; or

(b) the fact that the Claimant had a relationship with the Defendant; AND PROVIDED FURTHER THAT nothing in this paragraph of this Order shall prevent the Defendant from discussing any of the material which she has already discussed or wishes to discuss with any family member or close friend, nor from disclosing to any such family member or close friend the existence of these proceedings or the Claimant's interest in them."

8. The Schedule of confidential information subject to the restraint upon publication, communication use or disclosure included this provision:

"Any intimate, personal or sexually explicit details about the relationship ... including any facts of a sexual nature."

Another category referred to "intimate or sexual activity". The order also contained undertakings by Ms Ntuli.

. . .

Super-injunction and anonymity

43. If the injunction is to remain, the next question is whether it should retain its super-injunction and anonymity elements. The original order of 25 March 2010 included provisions under the headings "Anonymity of the Parties" (paragraph 3) and "Injunction and Related Relief" (paragraph 5). Paragraph 5 stated:

"Upon it appearing to the Judge (1) that these proceedings are likely to attract publicity, (2) that publicity revealing the identity of the Claimant or the Defendant [is] likely unfairly to damage the interests of the Claimant and (3) that accordingly publication of details revealing the Claimant's or Defendant's identity ought to be prohibited."

44. Paragraph 5 restrained Ms Ntuli from publishing, disclosing etc

"... the existence of these proceedings or the Claimant's interest in these proceedings."

11. ***MJN v News Group Newspapers Ltd*** [2011] EWHC 1192 (QB) per Sharp J:

> 3. The terms of the Order which the Claimant then invited the court to make (and which it did make) had been the subject of discussion between Mr Tomlinson, and Mr Spearman in advance of the hearing. The Order, discussed and made, permitted the publication of the story of the 'relationship' by Ms West provided only that (i) nothing is published which identifies or tends to identify the Claimant as the other party to the relationship or as the person who has applied to the court for an injunction; and (ii) what is published excludes sexual, salacious and/or other specified details. It is not conceded by the Claimant that there is any lawful justification for the publication of the story itself. But it was, and is accepted by Mr Tomlinson, that so far as the issue of prior restraint is concerned, the balance between the Article 8 and Article 10 rights engaged could be struck in the way allowed for by that part of the Order permitting Ms West to sell her story to NGN, and for its publication, but for it not to be told in a way which identifies the Claimant or which gives sexual or salacious details.
>
> . . .
>
> 16. Paragraph 1 (c) of the Order shall be varied so there shall be no publication of any photograph or video film of the Claimant or the Claimant's house (but only if that photograph or video identifies or tends to identify the Claimant as being the person who applied for this Order).
>
> 17. It is necessary further to consider the terms of the draft Order and any derogation it makes from the principles of open justice. I am satisfied that it remains necessary for the Claimant to be anonymised for the reasons I have already given. At the start of the hearing, Mr Tomlinson invited me to hear this matter in private. In the event however, I was satisfied this was not necessary, provided an order was made pursuant to CPR 31.22 that no use may be made by any person who is not a party to the action of any of the confidential schedules to the witness statements or the skeleton arguments read by the court and referred to in the course of the hearing; and that no person who is not a party to the action may obtain the documents from the court records. Accordingly, the hearing was in public, and I made an order pursuant to CPR 31.22 in those terms.'

12. ***Sir Frederick Goodwin v News Group Newspapers Ltd*** [2011] EWHC 1309 (QB) at **para 9(3)**:

> The injunctions of 1st and 9th March were not intended to prevent disclosure of any information to the FSA or to any regulatory authority.

There was a discussion between counsel on this in court at my request and there was unanimous agreement on this point, and that if anyone proposing to make any such disclosure was in doubt, then the order could and would have been varied accordingly upon the matter being drawn to the attention of the court.

13. ***Goldsmith and Khan v BCD*** [2011] EWHC 674 (QB) **para 1**: The substantive provisions of each of the two 2008 Orders and each of the two orders I made on 17 March 2011 were prohibitions on the disclosure of:

. . . any personal private information contained in or derived from personal and private e-mails received at or sent from [the Claimants'] personal email addresses set out in the Confidential Schedule 3 [to each of the orders].

14. ***Hirschfeld v McGrath*** [2011] EWHC 249 (QB) **para 17**:

The terms of the Defendant's undertaking are that he will:

". . . not publish, republish, syndicate, use, communicate or disclose to any person:

(a) any information concerning the intimate former relationship of the parties, their family life and/or the Claimant's health save for that contained in the public judgment of the Court in relation to the Application; and/or

(b) any of the information set out in the Confidential Schedule to this Oand will not cause or authorise any other person, firm or company to do any of those acts

PROVIDED THAT nothing in this Order shall prevent the use, disclosure, communication or publication of any of the Information:

(i) by the Defendant (1) to legal advisers instructed in relation to these proceedings for the purpose of obtaining legal advice in relation to these proceedings or (2) for the purposes of carrying this Order into effect provided that any person to whom such information is disclosed must first be either given a copy of this Order or notified of its substance and effect;

(ii) by the Defendant of any part of the Information that is in the public domain as the result of national media publication (otherwise than as a result of breach of this Order).

AND PROVIDED FURTHER THAT nothing in this paragraph of this Order shall prevent the Defendant from disclosing to or discussing with any member of his family, or any doctor or counsellor, any of the information referred to in paragraph (i) or (ii) of the Confidential Schedule to this Order.

MODEL APPLICATION FORM

Application for Interim Non-Disclosure Order

Title as in action.

APPLICATION NOTICE

1. [I/We on behalf of the/The] Applicant intend(s) to apply for an order (a draft of which is attached) that:
   (a) There be an injunction restraining a publication, and
   (b) There be the following derogations from Open Justice by reference to Article 6, namely [setting them out]; and
2. The grounds upon which the Applicant seeks the above relief are set out in the witness statement of . . . dated . . .
3. The Applicant wishes to have the application dealt with [at a hearing/ at a telephone conference/ orally at court/with a time estimate of [. . . Hour(s) . . . minutes] by a High Court Judge. The time estimate is [not] agreed. There is no trial period or fixed date. The parties to be served are . . .
4. The Applicant wishes to rely upon the said [witness statement/statement of case] in support of this application.

[Signature of solicitor/Applicant's representative]

[Position or office held]

Dated

[*Address to which documents about the claim should be sent, including reference, telephone number, fax number, DX number and email if applicable*].

I believe/the Applicant believes that the facts stated in this application notice are true.

Signed [set out position or office held]

Dated etc.

Part 19

CIVIL PROCEDURE RULES

Part 1 Overriding Objective

Contents of this Part

1.1 The overriding objective

(1) These Rules are a new procedural code with the overriding objective of enabling the court to deal with cases justly.
(2) Dealing with a case justly includes, so far as is practicable—
  (a) ensuring that the parties are on an equal footing;
  (b) saving expense;
  (c) dealing with the case in ways which are proportionate—
    (i) to the amount of money involved;
    (ii) to the importance of the case;
    (iii) to the complexity of the issues; and
    (iv) to the financial position of each party;
  (d) ensuring that it is dealt with expeditiously and fairly; and
  (e) allotting to it an appropriate share of the court's resources, while taking into account the need to allot resources to other cases.

1.2 Application by the court of the overriding objective

The court must seek to give effect to the overriding objective when it—
(a) exercises any power given to it by the Rules; or
(b) interprets any rule subject to rules 76.2 and 79.2.

1.3 Duty of the parties

The parties are required to help the court to further the overriding objective.

1.4 Court's duty to manage cases

(1) The court must further the overriding objective by actively managing cases.

(2) Active case management includes—
   - (a) encouraging the parties to co-operate with each other in the conduct of the proceedings;
   - (b) identifying the issues at an early stage;
   - (c) deciding promptly which issues need full investigation and trial and accordingly disposing summarily of the others;
   - (d) deciding the order in which issues are to be resolved;
   - (e) encouraging the parties to use an alternative dispute resolution(GL) procedure if the court considers that appropriate and facilitating the use of such procedure;
   - (f) helping the parties to settle the whole or part of the case;
   - (g) fixing timetables or otherwise controlling the progress of the case;
   - (h) considering whether the likely benefits of taking a particular step justify the cost of taking it;
   - (i) dealing with as many aspects of the case as it can on the same occasion;
   - (j) dealing with the case without the parties needing to attend at court;
   - (k) making use of technology; and
   - (l) giving directions to ensure that the trial of a case proceeds quickly and efficiently.

Part 5 Court Documents

Scope of this Part

5.1

This part contains general provisions about—
   - (a) documents used in court proceedings; and
   - (b) the obligations of a court officer in relation to those documents.

Preparation of documents

5.2

(1) Where under these Rules, a document is to be prepared by the court, the document may be prepared by the party whose document it is, unless—
   - (a) a court officer otherwise directs; or
   - (b) it is a document to which—
      - (i) Revoked

(ii) CCR Order 25, rule 8(9) (reissue of warrant where condition upon which warrant was suspended has not been complied with); or
(iii) CCR Order 28, rule 11(1) (issue of warrant of committal), applies.

(2) Nothing in this rule shall require a court officer to accept a document which is illegible, has not been duly authorised, or is unsatisfactory for some other similar reason.

Signature of documents by mechanical means

5.3

Where any of these Rules or any practice direction requires a document to be signed, that requirement shall be satisfied if the signature is printed by computer or other mechanical means.

Register of claims

5.4

(1) A court or court office may keep a publicly accessible register of claims which have been issued out of that court or court office.
(2) Any person who pays the prescribed fee may, during office hours, search any available register of claims.

(Practice Direction 5A contains details of available registers).

Supply of documents to Attorney-General from court records

5.4A

(1) The Attorney-General may search for, inspect and take a copy of any documents within a court file for the purpose of preparing an application or considering whether to make an application under section 42 of the Supreme Court Act 1981[1] or section 33 of the Employment Tribunals Act 1996[2] (restriction of vexatious proceedings).
(2) The Attorney-General must, when exercising the right under paragraph (1)—
   (a) pay any prescribed fee; and
   (b) file a written request, which must—
      (i) confirm that the request is for the purpose of preparing an application or considering whether to make an application mentioned in paragraph (1); and
      (ii) name the person who would be the subject of the application.

Supply of documents to a party from court records

5.4B

(1) A party to proceedings may, unless the court orders otherwise, obtain

from the records of the court a copy of any document listed in paragraph 4.2A of Practice Direction 5A.

(2) A party to proceedings may, if the court gives permission, obtain from the records of the court a copy of any other document filed by a party or communication between the court and a party or another person.

Supply of documents to a non-party from court records

5.4C

(1) The general rule is that a person who is not a party to proceedings may obtain from the court records a copy of—
  (a) a statement of case, but not any documents filed with or attached to the statement of case, or intended by the party whose statement it is to be served with it;
  (b) a judgment or order given or made in public (whether made at a hearing or without a hearing), subject to paragraph (1B).

(1A) Where a non-party seeks to obtain a copy of a statement of case filed before 2nd October 2006—
  (a) this rule does not apply; and
  (b) the rules of court relating to access by a non-party to statements of case in force immediately before 2nd October 2006 apply as if they had not been revoked.

(The rules relating to access by a non-party to statements of case in force immediately before 2nd October 2006 were contained in the former rule 5.4(5) to 5.4(9). Practice Direction 5A sets out the relevant provisions as they applied to statements of case.)

(1B) No document—
  (a) relating to an application under rule 78.24(1) for a mediation settlement enforcement order;
  (b) annexed to a mediation settlement enforcement order made under rule 78.24(5);
  (c) relating to an application under rule 78.26(1) or otherwise for disclosure or inspection of mediation evidence; or
  (d) annexed to an order for disclosure or inspection made under rule 78.26 or otherwise,

may be inspected without the court's permission.

(2) A non-party may, if the court gives permission, obtain from the records of the court a copy of any other document filed by a party, or communication between the court and a party or another person.

(3) A non-party may obtain a copy of a statement of case or judgment or order under paragraph (1) only if—
  (a) where there is one defendant, the defendant has filed an acknowledgment of service or a defence;

(b) where there is more than one defendant, either—
   (i) all the defendants have filed an acknowledgment of service or a defence;
   (ii) at least one defendant has filed an acknowledgment of service or a defence, and the court gives permission;
(c) the claim has been listed for a hearing; or
(d) judgment has been entered in the claim.

(4) The court may, on the application of a party or of any person identified in a statement of case—
(a) order that a non-party may not obtain a copy of a statement of case under paragraph (1);
(b) restrict the persons or classes of persons who may obtain a copy of a statement of case;
(c) order that persons or classes of persons may only obtain a copy of a statement of case if it is edited in accordance with the directions of the court; or
(d) make such other order as it thinks fit.

(5) A person wishing to apply for an order under paragraph (4) must file an application notice in accordance with Part 23.

(6) Where the court makes an order under paragraph (4), a non-party who wishes to obtain a copy of the statement of case, or to obtain an unedited copy of the statement of case, may apply on notice to the party or person identified in the statement of case who requested the order, for permission.

Supply of documents from court records—general

5.4D

(1) A person wishing to obtain a copy of a document under rule 5.4B or rule 5.4C must pay any prescribed fee and—
(a) if the court's permission is required, file an application notice in accordance with Part 23; or
(b) if permission is not required, file a written request for the document.

(2) An application for an order under rule 5.4C(4) or for permission to obtain a copy of a document under rule 5.4B or rule 5.4C (except an application for permission under rule 5.4C(6)) may be made without notice, but the court may direct notice to be given to any person who would be affected by its decision.

(3) Rules 5.4, 5.4B and 5.4C do not apply in relation to any proceedings in respect of which a rule or practice direction makes different provision.

Filing and sending documents

5.5

(1) A practice direction may make provision for documents to be filed or sent to the court by—
  (a) facsimile; or
  (b) other electronic means.

(2) Any such practice direction may—
  (a) provide that only particular categories of documents may be filed or sent to the court by such means;
  (b) provide that particular provisions only apply in specific courts; and
  (c) specify the requirements that must be fulfilled for any document filed or sent to the court by such means.

Footnotes

1. 1981 c.54.
2. 1996 c.17.

Part 6 Service of Documents

Service of the claim form where before service the defendant gives an address at which the defendant may be served

6.8

Subject to rules 6.5(1) and 6.7 and the provisions of Section IV of this Part—

(a) the defendant may be served with the claim form at an address at which the defendant resides or carries on business within the UK or any other EEA state and which the defendant has given for the purpose of being served with the proceedings; or

(b) in any claim by a tenant against a landlord, the claim form may be served at an address given by the landlord under section 48 of the Landlord and Tenant Act 1987[5].

(For Production Centre Claims see paragraph 2.3(7) of Practice Direction 7C; for Money Claims Online see paragraph 4(6) of Practice Direction 7E; and for Possession Claims Online see paragraph 5.1(4) of Practice Direction 55B.)

(For service out of the jurisdiction see rules 6.40 to 6.47.)

Footnote

5. 1987 c. 31

Part 7 How to Start Proceedings—The Claim Form

Where to start proceedings

7.1

Restrictions on where proceedings may be started are set out in the relevant practice directions supplementing this Part.

How to start proceedings

7.2

(1) Proceedings are started when the court issues a claim form at the request of the claimant.

(2) A claim form is issued on the date entered on the form by the court.

(A person who seeks a remedy from the court before proceedings are started or in relation to proceedings which are taking place, or will take place, in another jurisdiction must make an application under Part 23)

(Part 16 sets out what the claim form must include)

(The Costs Practice Direction sets out the information about a funding arrangement to be provided with the claim form where the claimant intends to seek to recover an additional liability)

('Funding arrangements' and 'additional liability' are defined in rule 43.2)

7.2A

Practice Direction 7A makes provision for procedures to be followed when claims are brought by or against a partnership within the jurisdiction.

Right to use one claim form to start two or more claims

7.3

A claimant may use a single claim form to start all claims which can be conveniently disposed of in the same proceedings.

Particulars of claim

7.4

(1) Particulars of claim must—
   (a) be contained in or served with the claim form; or
   (b) subject to paragraph (2) be served on the defendant by the claimant within 14 days after service of the claim form.

(2) Particulars of claim must be served on the defendant no later than the latest time for serving a claim form.

(Rule 7.5 sets out the latest time for serving a claim form)

(3) Where the claimant serves particulars of claim separately from the claim form in accordance with paragraph (1)(b), the claimant must, within 7 days of service on the defendant, file a copy of the particulars except where—
(a) paragraph 5.2(4) of Practice Direction 7C applies; or
(b) paragraph 6.4 of Practice Direction 7E applies.

(Part 16 sets out what the particulars of claim must include)

(Part 22 requires particulars of claim to be verified by a statement of truth)

Service of a claim form

7.5

(1) Where the claim form is served within the jurisdiction, the claimant must complete the step required by the following table in relation to the particular method of service chosen, before 12.00 midnight on the calendar day four months after the date of issue of the claim form.

Method of service	Step required
First class post, document exchange or other service which provides for delivery on the next business day	Posting, leaving with, delivering to or collection by the relevant service provider
Delivery of the document to or leaving it at the relevant place	Delivering to or leaving the document at the relevant place
Personal service under rule 6.5	Completing the relevant step required by rule 6.5(3)
Fax	Completing the transmission of the fax
Other electronic method	Sending the e-mail or other electronic transmission

(2) Where the claim form is to be served out of the jurisdiction, the claim form must be served in accordance with Section IV of Part 6 within 6 months of the date of issue.

Extension of time for serving a claim form

7.6

(1) The claimant may apply for an order extending the period for compliance with rule 7.5.

(2) The general rule is that an application to extend the time for compliance with rule 7.5 must be made—
  (a) within the period specified by rule 7.5; or
  (b) where an order has been made under this rule, within the period for service specified by that order.
(3) If the claimant applies for an order to extend the time for compliance after the end of the period specified by rule 7.5 or by an order made under this rule, the court may make such an order only if—
  (a) the court has failed to serve the claim form; or
  (b) the claimant has taken all reasonable steps to comply with rule 7.5 but has been unable to do so; and
  (c) in either case, the claimant has acted promptly in making the application.
(4) An application for an order extending the time for compliance with rule 7.5—
  (a) must be supported by evidence; and
  (b) may be made without notice.

Application by defendant for service of claim form

7.7
(1) Where a claim form has been issued against a defendant, but has not yet been served on him, the defendant may serve a notice on the claimant requiring him to serve the claim form or discontinue the claim within a period specified in the notice.
(2) The period specified in a notice served under paragraph (1) must be at least 14 days after service of the notice.
(3) If the claimant fails to comply with the notice, the court may, on the application of the defendant—
  (a) dismiss the claim; or
  (b) make any other order it thinks just.

Form for defence etc must be served with particulars of claim

7.8
(1) When particulars of claim are served on a defendant, whether they are contained in the claim form, served with it or served subsequently, they must be accompanied by—
  (a) a form for defending the claim;
  (b) a form for admitting the claim; and
  (c) a form for acknowledging service.
(2) Where the claimant is using the procedure set out in Part 8 (alternative procedure for claims)—

(a) paragraph (1) does not apply; and
(b) a form for acknowledging service must accompany the claim form.

Fixed date and other claims

7.9

A practice direction—

(a) may set out the circumstances in which the court may give a fixed date for a hearing when it issues a claim;
(b) may list claims in respect of which there is a specific claim form for use and set out the claim form in question; and
(c) may disapply or modify these Rules as appropriate in relation to the claims referred to in paragraphs (a) and (b).

Production Centre for claims

7.10

(1) There shall be a Production Centre for the issue of claim forms and other related matters.
(2) Practice Direction 7C makes provision for—
  (a) which claimants may use the Production Centre;
  (b) the type of claims which the Production Centre may issue;
  (c) the functions which are to be discharged by the Production Centre;
  (d) the place where the Production Centre is to be located; and
  (e) other related matters.
(3) Practice Direction 7C may disapply or modify these Rules as appropriate in relation to claims issued by the Production Centre.

Human Rights

7.11

(1) A claim under section 7(1)(a) of the Human Rights Act 1998[1] in respect of a judicial act may be brought only in the High Court.
(2) Any other claim under section 7(1)(a) of that Act may be brought in any court.

Electronic issue of claims

7.12

(1) A practice direction may make provision for a claimant to start a claim by requesting the issue of a claim form electronically.
(2) The practice direction may, in particular—
  (a) specify—
    (i) the types of claim which may be issued electronically; and

(ii) the conditions which a claim must meet before it may be issued electronically;
(b) specify—
(i) the court where the claim will be issued; and
(ii) the circumstances in which the claim will be transferred to another court;
(c) provide for the filing of other documents electronically where a claim has been started electronically;
(d) specify the requirements that must be fulfilled for any document filed electronically; and
(e) provide how a fee payable on the filing of any document is to be paid where that document is filed electronically.
(3) The practice direction may disapply or modify these Rules as appropriate in relation to claims started electronically.

(Practice Direction 5C deals with electronic issue of claims started or continued under the Electronic Working scheme.)

Footnote
1. 1998 c.42.

Part 8 Alternative Procedure for Claims

Types of claim in which Part 8 procedure may be followed

8.1
(1) The Part 8 procedure is the procedure set out in this Part.
(2) A claimant may use the Part 8 procedure where—
(a) he seeks the court's decision on a question which is unlikely to involve a substantial dispute of fact; or
(b) paragraph (6) applies.
(3) The court may at any stage order the claim to continue as if the claimant had not used the Part 8 procedure and, if it does so, the court may give any directions it considers appropriate.
(4) Paragraph (2) does not apply if a practice direction provides that the Part 8 procedure may not be used in relation to the type of claim in question.
(5) Where the claimant uses the Part 8 procedure he may not obtain default judgment under Part 12.
(6) A rule or practice direction may, in relation to a specified type of proceedings—
(a) require or permit the use of the Part 8 procedure; and

(b) disapply or modify any of the rules set out in this Part as they apply to those proceedings.

(Rule 8.9 provides for other modifications to the general rules where the Part 8 procedure is being used)

(Part 78 provides procedures for European orders for payment and for the European small claims procedure. It also provides procedures for applications for mediation settlement enforcement orders in relation to certain cross-border disputes.)

Contents of the claim form

8.2

Where the claimant uses the Part 8 procedure the claim form must state—

(a) that this Part applies;

(b)

  (i) the question which the claimant wants the court to decide; or

  (ii) the remedy which the claimant is seeking and the legal basis for the claim to that remedy;

(c) if the claim is being made under an enactment, what that enactment is;

(d) if the claimant is claiming in a representative capacity, what that capacity is; and

(e) if the defendant is sued in a representative capacity, what that capacity is.

(Part 22 provides for the claim form to be verified by a statement of truth)

(Rule 7.5 provides for service of the claim form)

(The Costs Practice Direction sets out the information about a funding arrangement to be provided with the claim form where the claimant intends to seek to recover an additional liability)

('Funding arrangement' and 'additional liability' are defined in rule 43.2)

Issue of claim form without naming defendants

8.2A

(1) A practice direction may set out circumstances in which a claim form may be issued under this Part without naming a defendant.

(2) The practice direction may set out those cases in which an application for permission must be made by application notice before the claim form is issued.

(3) The application notice for permission—

  (a) need not be served on any other person; and

(b) must be accompanied by a copy of the claim form that the applicant proposes to issue.

(4) Where the court gives permission it will give directions about the future management of the claim.

Acknowledgment of service

8.3

(1) The defendant must—
  (a) file an acknowledgment of service in the relevant practice form not more than 14 days after service of the claim form; and
  (b) serve the acknowledgment of service on the claimant and any other party.

(2) The acknowledgment of service must state—
  (a) whether the defendant contests the claim; and
  (b) if the defendant seeks a different remedy from that set out in the claim form, what that remedy is.

(3) The following rules of Part 10 (acknowledgment of service) apply—
  (a) rule 10.3(2) (exceptions to the period for filing an acknowledgment of service); and
  (b) rule 10.5 (contents of acknowledgment of service).

(4) Omitted

(The Costs Practice Direction sets out the information about a funding arrangement to be provided with the acknowledgment of service where the defendant intends to seek to recover an additional liability)

('Funding arrangement' and 'additional liability' are defined in rule 43.2)

Consequence of not filing an acknowledgment of service

8.4

(1) This rule applies where—
  (a) the defendant has failed to file an acknowledgment of service; and
  (b) the time period for doing so has expired.

(2) The defendant may attend the hearing of the claim but may not take part in the hearing unless the court gives permission.

Filing and serving written evidence

8.5

(1) The claimant must file any written evidence on which he intends to rely when he files his claim form.

(2) The claimant's evidence must be served on the defendant with the claim form.

(3) A defendant who wishes to rely on written evidence must file it when he files his acknowledgment of service.
(4) If he does so, he must also, at the same time, serve a copy of his evidence on the other parties.
(5) The claimant may, within 14 days of service of the defendant's evidence on him, file further written evidence in reply.
(6) If he does so, he must also, within the same time limit, serve a copy of his evidence on the other parties.
(7) The claimant may rely on the matters set out in his claim form as evidence under this rule if the claim form is verified by a statement of truth.

Evidence— general

8.6
(1) No written evidence may be relied on at the hearing of the claim unless—
  (a) it has been served in accordance with rule 8.5; or
  (b) the court gives permission.
(2) The court may require or permit a party to give oral evidence at the hearing.
(3) The court may give directions requiring the attendance for cross-examination of a witness who has given written evidence.

(Rule 32.1 contains a general power for the court to control evidence)

Part 20 claims

8.7
Where the Part 8 procedure is used, Part 20 (counterclaims and other additional claims) applies except that a party may not make a Part 20 claim (as defined by rule 20.2) without the court's permission.

Procedure where defendant objects to use of the Part 8 procedure

8.8
(1) Where the defendant contends that the Part 8 procedure should not be used because—
  (a) there is a substantial dispute of fact; and
  (b) the use of the Part 8 procedure is not required or permitted by a rule or practice direction,

  he must state his reasons when he files his acknowledgment of service.

(Rule 8.5 requires a defendant who wishes to rely on written evidence to file it when he files his acknowledgment of service)

(2) When the court receives the acknowledgment of service and any written evidence it will give directions as to the future management of the case.

(Rule 8.1(3) allows the court to make an order that the claim continue as if the claimant had not used the Part 8 procedure)

Modifications to the general rules

8.9

Where the Part 8 procedure is followed—

(a) provision is made in this Part for the matters which must be stated in the claim form and the defendant is not required to file a defence and therefore—
  (i) Part 16 (statements of case) does not apply;
  (ii) Part 15 (defence and reply) does not apply;
  (iii) any time limit in these Rules which prevents the parties from taking a step before a defence is filed does not apply;
  (iv) the requirement under rule 7.8 to serve on the defendant a form for defending the claim does not apply;
(b) the claimant may not obtain judgment by request on an admission and therefore—
  (i) rules 14.4 to 14.7 do not apply; and
  (ii) the requirement under rule 7.8 to serve on the defendant a form for admitting the claim does not apply; and
  (c) the claim shall be treated as allocated to the multi-track and therefore Part 26 does not apply.

Part 23 General Rules about Applications for Court Orders

Meaning of 'application notice' and 'respondent'

23.1

In this Part—

'application notice' means a document in which the applicant states his intention to seek a court order; and

'respondent' means—

(a) the person against whom the order is sought; and
(b) such other person as the court may direct.

Where to make an application

23.2

(1) The general rule is that an application must be made to the court where the claim was started.

(2) If a claim has been transferred to another court since it was started, an application must be made to the court to which the claim has been transferred.

(3) If the parties have been notified of a fixed date for the trial, an application must be made to the court where the trial is to take place.

(4) If an application is made before a claim has been started, it must be made to the court where it is likely that the claim to which the application relates will be started unless there is good reason to make the application to a different court.

(5) If an application is made after proceedings to enforce judgment have begun, it must be made to any court which is dealing with the enforcement of the judgment unless any rule or practice direction provides otherwise.

Application notice to be filed

23.3

(1) The general rule is that an applicant must file an application notice.

(2) An applicant may make an application without filing an application notice if—

  (a) this is permitted by a rule or practice direction; or

  (b) the court dispenses with the requirement for an application notice.

Notice of an application

23.4

(1) The general rule is that a copy of the application notice must be served on each respondent.

(2) An application may be made without serving a copy of the application notice if this is permitted by—

  (a) a rule;

  (b) a practice direction; or

  (c) a court order.

(Rule 23.7 deals with service of a copy of the application notice)

Time when an application is made

23.5

Where an application must be made within a specified time, it is so made if the application notice is received by the court within that time.

What an application notice must include

23.6

An application notice must state—

(a) what order the applicant is seeking; and
(b) briefly, why the applicant is seeking the order.

(Part 22 requires an application notice to be verified by a statement of truth if the applicant wishes to rely on matters set out in his application notice as evidence)

Service of a copy of an application notice

23.7

(1) A copy of the application notice—
   (a) must be served as soon as practicable after it is filed; and
   (b) except where another time limit is specified in these Rules or a practice direction, must in any event be served at least 3 days before the court is to deal with the application.
(2) If a copy of the application notice is to be served by the court, the applicant must, when he files the application notice, file a copy of any written evidence in support.
(3)When a copy of an application notice is served it must be accompanied by—
(a) a copy of any written evidence in support; and
(b) a copy of any draft order which the applicant has attached to his application.
(4) If—
(a) an application notice is served; but
(b) the period of notice is shorter than the period required by these Rules or a practice direction,
the court may direct that, in the circumstances of the case, sufficient notice has been given and hear the application.
(5) This rule does not require written evidence—
   (a) to be filed if it has already been filed; or
   (b) to be served on a party on whom it has already been served.

(Part 6 contains the general rules about service of documents including who must serve a copy of the application notice)

Applications which may be dealt with without a hearing

23.8

The court may deal with an application without a hearing if—

(a) the parties agree as to the terms of the order sought;

(b) the parties agree that the court should dispose of the application without a hearing, or
(c) the court does not consider that a hearing would be appropriate.

Service of application where application made without notice

23.9

(1) This rule applies where the court has disposed of an application which it permitted to be made without service of a copy of the application notice.
(2) Where the court makes an order, whether granting or dismissing the application, a copy of the application notice and any evidence in support must, unless the court orders otherwise, be served with the order on any party or other person—
   (a) against whom the order was made; and
   (b) against whom the order was sought.
(3) The order must contain a statement of the right to make an application to set aside or vary the order under rule 23.10.

Application to set aside or vary order made without notice

23.10

(1) A person who was not served with a copy of the application notice before an order was made under rule 23.9, may apply to have the order set aside or varied.
(2) An application under this rule must be made within 7 days after the date on which the order was served on the person making the application.

Power of the court to proceed in the absence of a party

23.11

(1) Where the applicant or any respondent fails to attend the hearing of an application, the court may proceed in his absence.
(2) Where—
   (a) the applicant or any respondent fails to attend the hearing of an application; and
   (b) the court makes an order at the hearing,
   the court may, on application or of its own initiative, re-list the application.

(Part 40 deals with service of orders)

Dismissal of totally without merit applications

23.12

If the court dismisses an application (including an application for permission

to appeal or for permission to apply for judicial review) and it considers that the application is totally without merit—
(a) the court's order must record that fact; and
(b) the court must at the same time consider whether it is appropriate to make a civil restraint order.

Part 24 Summary Judgment

Scope of this Part

24.1
This Part sets out a procedure by which the court may decide a claim or a particular issue without a trial.
(Part 53 makes special provision about summary disposal of defamation claims in accordance with the Defamation Act 1996)[1]

Grounds for summary judgment

24.2
The court may give summary judgment against a claimant or defendant on the whole of a claim or on a particular issue if—
(a) it considers that—
  (i) that claimant has no real prospect of succeeding on the claim or issue; or
  (ii) that defendant has no real prospect of successfully defending the claim or issue; and
(b) there is no other compelling reason why the case or issue should be disposed of at a trial.

(Rule 3.4 makes provision for the court to strike out a statement of case or part of a statement of case if it appears that it discloses no reasonable grounds for bringing or defending a claim)

Types of proceedings in which summary judgment is available

24.3
(1) The court may give summary judgment against a claimant in any type of proceedings.
(2) The court may give summary judgment against a defendant in any type of proceedings except—
  (a) proceedings for possession of residential premises against—
    (i) a mortgagor; or
    (ii) a tenant or a person holding over after the end of his tenancy

whose occupancy is protected within the meaning of the Rent Act 1977[2] or the Housing Act 1988[3] and;
(b) proceedings for an admiralty claim in rem.
(c) Omitted

Procedure

24.4

(1) A claimant may not apply for summary judgment until the defendant against whom the application is made has filed—
(a) an acknowledgement of service; or
(b) a defence,
unless—
(i) the court gives permission; or
(ii) a practice direction provides otherwise.

(Rule 10.3 sets out the period for filing an acknowledgment of service and rule 15.4 the period for filing a defence)

(1A) In civil proceedings against the Crown, as defined in rule 66.1(2), a claimant may not apply for summary judgment until after expiry of the period for filing a defence specified in rule 15.4.
(2) If a claimant applies for summary judgment before a defendant against whom the application is made has filed a defence, that defendant need not file a defence before the hearing.
(3) Where a summary judgment hearing is fixed, the respondent (or the parties where the hearing is fixed of the court's own initiative) must be given at least 14 days' notice of—
(a) the date fixed for the hearing; and
(b) the issues which it is proposed that the court will decide at the hearing.
(4) A practice direction may provide for a different period of notice to be given.

(Part 23 contains the general rules about how to make an application)

(Rule 3.3 applies where the court exercises its powers of its own initiative)

Evidence for the purposes of a summary judgment hearing

24.5

(1) If the respondent to an application for summary judgment wishes to rely on written evidence at the hearing, he must—
(a) file the written evidence; and
(b) serve copies on every other party to the application,

at least 7 days before the summary judgment hearing.

(2) If the applicant wishes to rely on written evidence in reply, he must—
  (a) file the written evidence; and
  (b) serve a copy on the respondent,

  at least 3 days before the summary judgment hearing.

(3) Where a summary judgment hearing is fixed by the court of its own initiative—
  (a) any party who wishes to rely on written evidence at the hearing must—
    (i) file the written evidence; and
    (ii) unless the court orders otherwise, serve copies on every other party to the proceedings,

    at least 7 days before the date of the hearing;
  (b) any party who wishes to rely on written evidence at the hearing in reply to any other party's written evidence must—
    (i) file the written evidence in reply; and
    (ii) unless the court orders otherwise serve copies on every other party to the proceedings,

  at least 3 days before the date of the hearing.

(4) This rule does not require written evidence—
  (a) to be filed if it has already been filed; or
  (b) to be served on a party on whom it has already been served.

Court's powers when it determines a summary judgment application

24.6

When the court determines a summary judgment application it may—

(a) give directions as to the filing and service of a defence;

(b) give further directions about the management of the case.

(Rule 3.1(3) provides that the court may attach conditions when it makes an order)

Footnotes

1. 1196 c.31.
2. 1977 c.42.
3. 1988 c.50.

Part 25 Interim Remedies and Security for Costs

Part 25 Interim Remedies and Security for Costs

I INTERIM REMEDIES

Orders for interim remedies

25.1

(1) The court may grant the following interim remedies—
  (a) an interim injunction;
  (b) an interim declaration;
  (c) an order—
    (i) for the detention, custody or preservation of relevant property;
    (ii) for the inspection of relevant property;
    (iii) for the taking of a sample of relevant property;
    (iv) for the carrying out of an experiment on or with relevant property;
    (v) for the sale of relevant property which is of a perishable nature or which for any other good reason it is desirable to sell quickly; and
    (vi) for the payment of income from relevant property until a claim is decided;
  (d) an order authorising a person to enter any land or building in the possession of a party to the proceedings for the purposes of carrying out an order under sub-paragraph (c);
  (e) an order under section 4 of the Torts (Interference with Goods) Act 1977[1] to deliver up goods;
  (f) an order (referred to as a 'freezing injunction')—
    (i) restraining a party from removing from the jurisdiction assets located there; or
    (ii) restraining a party from dealing with any assets whether located within the jurisdiction or not;
  (g) an order directing a party to provide information about the location of relevant property or assets or to provide information about relevant property or assets which are or may be the subject of an application for a freezing injunction;
  (h) an order (referred to as a 'search order') under section 7 of the Civil Procedure Act 1997[2] (order requiring a party to admit another party to premises for the purpose of preserving evidence etc.);
  (i) an order under section 33 of the Supreme Court Act 1981[3] or section 52 of the County Courts Act 1984[4] (order for disclosure of documents or inspection of property before a claim has been made);
  (j) an order under section 34 of the Supreme Court Act 1981[5] or section 53

of the County Courts Act 1984[6] (order in certain proceedings for disclosure of documents or inspection of property against a non-party);

(k) an order (referred to as an order for interim payment) under rule 25.6 for payment by a defendant on account of any damages, debt or other sum (except costs) which the court may hold the defendant liable to pay;

(l) an order for a specified fund to be paid into court or otherwise secured, where there is a dispute over a party's right to the fund;

(m) an order permitting a party seeking to recover personal property to pay money into court pending the outcome of the proceedings and directing that, if he does so, the property shall be given up to him;

(n) an order directing a party to prepare and file accounts relating to the dispute;

(o) an order directing any account to be taken or inquiry to be made by the court; and

(p) an order under Article 9 of Council Directive (EC) 2004/48 on the enforcement of intellectual property rights (order in intellectual property proceedings making the continuation of an alleged infringement subject to the lodging of guarantees).

(Rule 34.2 provides for the court to issue a witness summons requiring a witness to produce documents to the court at the hearing or on such date as the court may direct)

(2) In paragraph (1)(c) and (g), 'relevant property' means property (including land) which is the subject of a claim or as to which any question may arise on a claim.

(3) The fact that a particular kind of interim remedy is not listed in paragraph (1) does not affect any power that the court may have to grant that remedy.

(4) The court may grant an interim remedy whether or not there has been a claim for a final remedy of that kind.

Time when an order for an interim remedy may be made

25.2

(1) An order for an interim remedy may be made at any time, including—

(a) before proceedings are started; and

(b) after judgment has been given.

(Rule 7.2 provides that proceedings are started when the court issues a claim form)

(2) However—

(a) paragraph (1) is subject to any rule, practice direction or other enactment which provides otherwise;
(b) the court may grant an interim remedy before a claim has been made only if—
  (i) the matter is urgent; or
  (ii) it is otherwise desirable to do so in the interests of justice; and
(c) unless the court otherwise orders, a defendant may not apply for any of the orders listed in rule 25.1(1) before he has filed either an acknowledgment of service or a defence.

(Part 10 provides for filing an acknowledgment of service and Part 15 for filing a defence)

(3) Where it grants an interim remedy before a claim has been commenced, the court should give directions requiring a claim to be commenced.
(4) In particular, the court need not direct that a claim be commenced where the application is made under section 33 of the Supreme Court Act 1981 or section 52 of the County Courts Act 1984 (order for disclosure, inspection etc. before commencement of a claim).

How to apply for an interim remedy

25.3
(1) The court may grant an interim remedy on an application made without notice if it appears to the court that there are good reasons for not giving notice.
(2) An application for an interim remedy must be supported by evidence, unless the court orders otherwise.
(3) If the applicant makes an application without giving notice, the evidence in support of the application must state the reasons why notice has not been given.

(Part 3 lists general powers of the court)

(Part 23 contains general rules about making an application)

Application for an interim remedy where there is no related claim

25.4
(1) This rule applies where a party wishes to apply for an interim remedy but—
  (a) the remedy is sought in relation to proceedings which are taking place, or will take place, outside the jurisdiction; or
  (b) the application is made under section 33 of the Supreme Court Act 1981 or section 52 of the County Courts Act 1984 (order for disclosure,

inspection etc. before commencement) before a claim has been commenced.

(2) An application under this rule must be made in accordance with the general rules about applications contained in Part 23.

(The following provisions are also relevant—

- Rule 25.5 (inspection of property before commencement or against a non-party)
- Rule 31.16 (orders for disclosure of documents before proceedings start)
- Rule 31.17 (orders for disclosure of documents against a person not a party))

Inspection of property before commencement or against a non-party

25.5

(1) This rule applies where a person makes an application under—

(a) section 33(1) of the Supreme Court Act 1981 or section 52(1) of the County Courts Act 1984 (inspection etc. of property before commencement);

(b) section 34(3) of the Supreme Court Act 1981 or section 53(3) of the County Courts Act 1984 (inspection etc. of property against a non-party).

(2) The evidence in support of such an application must show, if practicable by reference to any statement of case prepared in relation to the proceedings or anticipated proceedings, that the property—

(a) is or may become the subject matter of such proceedings; or

(b) is relevant to the issues that will arise in relation to such proceedings.

(3) A copy of the application notice and a copy of the evidence in support must be served on—

(a) the person against whom the order is sought; and

(b) in relation to an application under section 34(3) of the Supreme Court Act 1981 or section 53(3) of the County Courts Act 1984, every party to the proceedings other than the applicant.

Interim payments— general procedure

25.6

(1) The claimant may not apply for an order for an interim payment before the end of the period for filing an acknowledgment of service applicable to the defendant against whom the application is made.

(Rule 10.3 sets out the period for filing an acknowledgment of service)

(Rule 25.1(1)(k) defines an interim payment)

(2) The claimant may make more than one application for an order for an interim payment.
(3) A copy of an application notice for an order for an interim payment must—
 (a) be served at least 14 days before the hearing of the application; and
 (b) be supported by evidence.
(4) If the respondent to an application for an order for an interim payment wishes to rely on written evidence at the hearing, he must—
 (a) file the written evidence; and
 (b) serve copies on every other party to the application,
 at least 7 days before the hearing of the application.
(5) If the applicant wishes to rely on written evidence in reply, he must—
 (a) file the written evidence; and
 (b) serve a copy on the respondent,
 at least 3 days before the hearing of the application.
(6) This rule does not require written evidence—
 (a) to be filed if it has already been filed; or
 (b) to be served on a party on whom it has already been served.
(7)The court may order an interim payment in one sum or in instalments.
(Part 23 contains general rules about applications)

Interim payments— conditions to be satisfied and matters to be taken into account

25.7
(1) The court may only make an order for an interim payment where any of the following conditions are satisfied—
 (a) the defendant against whom the order is sought has admitted liability to pay damages or some other sum of money to the claimant;
 (b) the claimant has obtained judgment against that defendant for damages to be assessed or for a sum of money (other than costs) to be assessed;
 (c) it is satisfied that, if the claim went to trial, the claimant would obtain judgment for a substantial amount of money (other than costs) against the defendant from whom he is seeking an order for an interim payment whether or not that defendant is the only defendant or one of a number of defendants to the claim;
 (d) the following conditions are satisfied—
  (i) the claimant is seeking an order for possession of land (whether or not any other order is also sought); and
  (ii) the court is satisfied that, if the case went to trial, the defendant would be held liable (even if the claim for possession fails) to pay the claimant a sum of money for the defendant's occupation and use of the land while the claim for possession was pending; or

(e) in a claim in which there are two or more defendants and the order is sought against any one or more of those defendants, the following conditions are satisfied—
  (i) the court is satisfied that, if the claim went to trial, the claimant would obtain judgment for a substantial amount of money (other than costs) against at least one of the defendants (but the court cannot determine which); and
  (ii) all the defendants are either—
(a) a defendant that is insured in respect of the claim;
(b) a defendant whose liability will be met by an insurer under section 151 of the Road Traffic Act 1988 or an insurer acting under the Motor Insurers Bureau Agreement, or the Motor Insurers Bureau where it is acting itself; or
(c) a defendant that is a public body.

(4) The court must not order an interim payment of more than a reasonable proportion of the likely amount of the final judgment.
(5) The court must take into account—
  (a) contributory negligence; and
  (b) any relevant set-off or counterclaim.

Powers of court where it has made an order for interim payment

25.8

(1) Where a defendant has been ordered to make an interim payment, or has in fact made an interim payment (whether voluntarily or under an order), the court may make an order to adjust the interim payment.
(2) The court may in particular—
  (a) order all or part of the interim payment to be repaid;
  (b) vary or discharge the order for the interim payment;
  (c) order a defendant to reimburse, either wholly or partly, another defendant who has made an interim payment.
(3) The court may make an order under paragraph (2)(c) only if—
  (a) the defendant to be reimbursed made the interim payment in relation to a claim in respect of which he has made a claim against the other defendant for a contribution, indemnity or other remedy; and
  (b) where the claim or part to which the interim payment relates has not been discontinued or disposed of, the circumstances are such that the court could make an order for interim payment under rule 25.7.
(4) The court may make an order under this rule without an application by any party if it makes the order when it disposes of the claim or any part of it.
(5) Where—
  (a) a defendant has made an interim payment; and

(b) the amount of the payment is more than his total liability under the final judgment or order,

the court may award him interest on the overpaid amount from the date when he made the interim payment.

Restriction on disclosure of an interim payment

25.9

The fact that a defendant has made an interim payment, whether voluntarily or by court order, shall not be disclosed to the trial judge until all questions of liability and the amount of money to be awarded have been decided unless the defendant agrees.

Interim injunction to cease if claim is stayed

25.10

If—

(a) the court has granted an interim injunction other than a freezing injunction; and

(b) the claim is stayed other than by agreement between the parties,

the interim injunction shall be set aside unless the court orders that it should continue to have effect even though the claim is stayed.

Interim injunction to cease after 14 days if claim struck out

25.11

(1) If–

(a) the court has granted an interim injunction; and

(b) the claim is struck out under rule 3.7 (sanctions for non-payment of certain fees),

the interim injunction shall cease to have effect 14 days after the date that the claim is struck out unless paragraph (2) applies.

(2) If the claimant applies to reinstate the claim before the interim injunction ceases to have effect under paragraph (1), the injunction shall continue until the hearing of the application unless the court orders otherwise.

II SECURITY FOR COSTS

Security for costs

25.12

(1) A defendant to any claim may apply under this Section of this Part for security for his costs of the proceedings.

(Part 3 provides for the court to order payment of sums into court in other circumstances. Rule 20.3 provides for this Section of this Part to apply to Part 20 claims)

(2) An application for sec(3) Where the court makes an order for security for costs, it will—
 (a) determine the amount of security; and
 (b) direct—
  (i) the manner in which; and
  (ii) the time within which
 the security must be given.

Conditions to be satisfied

25.13

(1)The court may make an order for security for costs under rule 25.12 if—
(a) it is satisfied, having regard to all the circumstances of the case, that it is just to make such an order; and
 (b)
  (i) one or more of the conditions in paragraph (2) applies, or
  (ii) an enactment permits the court to require security for costs.
(2) The conditions are—
 (a) the claimant is—
  (i) resident out of the jurisdiction; but
  (ii) not resident in a Brussels Contracting State, a State bound by the Lugano Convention or a Regulation State, as defined in section 1(3) of the Civil Jurisdiction and Judgments Act 1982[7];
 (c) the claimant is a company or other body (whether incorporated inside or outside Great Britain) and there is reason to believe that it will be unable to pay the defendant's costs if ordered to do so;
 (d) the claimant has changed his address since the claim was commenced with a view to evading the consequences of the litigation;
 (e) the claimant failed to give his address in the claim form, or gave an incorrect address in that form;
 (f) the claimant is acting as a nominal claimant, other than as a representative claimant under Part 19, and there is reason to believe that he will be unable to pay the defendant's costs if ordered to do so;
 (g) the claimant has taken steps in relation to his assets that would make it difficult to enforce an order for costs against him.

(Rule 3.4 allows the court to strike out a statement of case and Part 24 for it to give summary judgment)

Security for costs other than from the claimant

25.14

(1) The defendant may seek an order against someone other than the claimant, and the court may make an order for security for costs against that person if—
  (a) it is satisfied, having regard to all the circumstances of the case, that it is just to make such an order; and
  (b) one or more of the conditions in paragraph (2) applies.

(2) The conditions are that the person—
  (a) has assigned the right to the claim to the claimant with a view to avoiding the possibility of a costs order being made against him; or
  (b) has contributed or agreed to contribute to the claimant's costs in return for a share of any money or property which the claimant may recover in the proceedings; and
  (c) is a person against whom a costs order may be made.

(Rule 48.2 makes provision for costs orders against non-parties)

Security for costs of an appeal

25.15

(1)The court may order security for costs of an appeal against—
  (a) an appellant;
  (b) a respondent who also appeals,
  on the same grounds as it may order security for costs against a claimant under this Part.

(2) The court may also make an order under paragraph (1) where the appellant, or the respondent who also appeals, is a limited company and there is reason to believe it will be unable to pay the costs of the other parties to the appeal should its appeal be unsuccessful.

Footnotes

1. 1977 c.32; section 4 was amended by the Supreme Court Act 1981 (c.54), section 152(1), Schedule 5; by the County Courts Act 1984 (c.28), section 148(1), Schedule 2, Part V, paragraph 64 and by SI 1980/397 (NI3).
2. 1997 c.12.
3. 1981 c.54. Section 33 was amended by SI 1998/2940.
4. 1984 c.28. Section 52 was amended by the Courts and Legal Services Act 1990 (c.41), Schedule 18, paragraph 43 and by SI 1998/2940.
5. 1981 c.54. Section 34 was amended by SI 1998/2940.
6. 1984 c.28. Section 53 was amended by the Courts and Legal Services Act 1990 (c.41), Schedule 18, paragraph 44 and by SI 1998/2940.
7. 1982 c. 27, as amended by the Civil Jurisdiction and Judgments Act 1991

(c. 12) and by SI 1989/1346, SI 1990/2591, SI 1993/603, SI 2000/1824 and SI 2001/3929.

Practice Direction 25A—Interim Injunction

Practice Direction 25A—Interim Injunctions
This Practice Direction supplements CPR Part 25

Jurisdiction

1.1

High Court Judges and any other Judge duly authorised may grant 'search orders'[1] and 'freezing injunctions'[2].

1.2

In a case in the High Court, Masters and district judges have the power to grant injunctions:

(1) by consent,

(2) in connection with charging orders and appointments of receivers,

(3) in aid of execution of judgments.

1.3

In any other case any judge who has jurisdiction to conduct the trial of the action has the power to grant an injunction in that action.

1.4

A Master or district judge has the power to vary or discharge an injunction granted by any Judge with the consent of all the parties.

Making an application

2.1

The application notice must state:

(1) the order sought, and

(2) the date, time and place of the hearing.

2.2

The application notice and evidence in support must be served as soon as practicable after issue and in any event not less than 3 days before the court is due to hear the application[3].

2.3

Where the court is to serve, sufficient copies of the application notice and evidence in support for the court and for each respondent should be filed for issue and service.

2.4
Whenever possible a draft of the order sought should be filed with the application notice and a disk containing the draft should also be available to the court in a format compatible with the word processing software used by the court. This will enable the court officer to arrange for any amendments to be incorporated and for the speedy preparation and sealing of the order.

Evidence

3.1
Applications for search orders and freezing injunctions must be supported by affidavit evidence.

3.2
Applications for other interim injunctions must be supported by evidence set out in either:
(1) a witness statement, or
(2) a statement of case provided that it is verified by a statement of truth,[4] or
(3) the application provided that it is verified by a statement of truth,
unless the court, an Act, a rule or a practice direction requires evidence by affidavit.

3.3
The evidence must set out the facts on which the applicant relies for the claim being made against the respondent, including all material facts of which the court should be made aware.

3.4
Where an application is made without notice to the respondent, the evidence must also set out why notice was not given.
(See Part 32 and Practice Direction 32 for information about evidence.)

Urgent applications and applications without notice

4.1
These fall into two categories:
(1) applications where a claim form has already been issued, and
(2) applications where a claim form has not yet been issued,
and, in both cases, where notice of the application has not been given to the respondent.

4.2

These applications are normally dealt with at a court hearing but cases of extreme urgency may be dealt with by telephone.

4.3

Applications dealt with at a court hearing after issue of a claim form:

(1) the application notice, evidence in support and a draft order (as in 2.4 above) should be filed with the court two hours before the hearing wherever possible,

(2) if an application is made before the application notice has been issued, a draft order (as in 2.4 above) should be provided at the hearing, and the application notice and evidence in support must be filed with the court on the same or next working day or as ordered by the court, and

(3) except in cases where secrecy is essential, the applicant should take steps to notify the respondent informally of the application.

4.4

Applications made before the issue of a claim form:

(1) in addition to the provisions set out at 4.3 above, unless the court orders otherwise, either the applicant must undertake to the court to issue a claim form immediately or the court will give directions for the commencement of the claim[5],

(2) where possible the claim form should be served with the order for the injunction,

(3) an order made before the issue of a claim form should state in the title after the names of the applicant and respondent 'the Claimant and Defendant in an Intended Action'.

4.5

Applications made by telephone:

(1) where it is not possible to arrange a hearing, application can be made between 10.00 a.m. and 5.00 p.m. weekdays by telephoning the Royal Courts of Justice on 020 7947 6000 and asking to be put in contact with a High Court Judge of the appropriate Division available to deal with an emergency application in a High Court matter. The appropriate district registry may also be contacted by telephone. In county court proceedings, the appropriate county court should be contacted,

(2) where an application is made outside those hours the applicant should either—

 (a) telephone the Royal Courts of Justice on 020 7947 6000 where he will be put in contact with the clerk to the appropriate duty judge in the High Court (or the appropriate area Circuit Judge where known), or

- (b) the Urgent Court Business Officer of the appropriate Circuit who will contact the local duty judge,

(3) where the facility is available it is likely that the judge will require a draft order to be faxed to him,

(4) the application notice and evidence in support must be filed with the court on the same or next working day or as ordered, together with two copies of the order for sealing,

(5) injunctions will be heard by telephone only where the applicant is acting by counsel or solicitors.

Orders for injunctions

5.1

Any order for an injunction, unless the court orders otherwise, must contain:

(1) an undertaking by the applicant to the court to pay any damages which the respondent sustains which the court considers the applicant should pay.

(2) if made without notice to any other party, an undertaking by the applicant to the court to serve on the respondent the application notice, evidence in support and any order made as soon as practicable,

(3) if made without notice to any other party, a return date for a further hearing at which the other party can be present,

(4) if made before filing the application notice, an undertaking to file and pay the appropriate fee on the same or next working day, and

(5) if made before issue of a claim form—

- (a) an undertaking to issue and pay the appropriate fee on the same or next working day, or
- (b) directions for the commencement of the claim.

5.1A

When the court makes an order for an injunction, it should consider whether to require an undertaking by the applicant to pay any damages sustained by a person other than the respondent, including another party to the proceedings or any other person who may suffer loss as a consequence of the order.

5.2

An order for an injunction made in the presence of all parties to be bound by it or made at a hearing of which they have had notice, may state that it is effective until trial or further order.

5.3

Any order for an injunction must set out clearly what the respondent must do or not do.

Freezing Injunctions

Orders to restrain disposal of assets worldwide and within England and Wales

6.1
An example of a Freezing Injunction is annexed to this practice direction.

6.2
This example may be modified as appropriate in any particular case. In particular, the court may, if it considers it appropriate, require the applicant's solicitors, as well as the applicant, to give undertakings.

Search Orders

7.1
The following provisions apply to search orders in addition to those listed above.

7.2

The Supervising Solicitor
The Supervising Solicitor must be experienced in the operation of search orders. A Supervising Solicitor may be contacted either through the Law Society or, for the London area, through the London Solicitors Litigation Association.

7.3

Evidence:
(1) the affidavit must state the name, firm and its address, and experience of the Supervising Solicitor, also the address of the premises and whether it is a private or business address, and
(2) the affidavit must disclose very fully the reason the order is sought, including the probability that relevant material would disappear if the order were not made.

7.4

Service:
(1) the order must be served personally by the Supervising Solicitor, unless the court otherwise orders, and must be accompanied by the evidence in support and any documents capable of being copied,
(2) confidential exhibits need not be served but they must be made available for inspection by the respondent in the presence of the applicant's

solicitors while the order is carried out and afterwards be retained by the respondent's solicitors on their undertaking not to permit the respondent—

(a) to see them or copies of them except in their presence, and
(b) to make or take away any note or record of them,

(3) the Supervising Solicitor may be accompanied only by the persons mentioned in the order,

(4) the Supervising Solicitor must explain the terms and effect of the order to the respondent in everyday language and advise him—
   (a) of his right to take legal advice and to apply to vary or discharge the order; and
   (b) that he may be entitled to avail himself of—
      (i) legal professional privilege; and
      (ii) the privilege against self-incrimination.
   (5) where the Supervising Solicitor is a man and the respondent is likely to be an unaccompanied woman, at least one other person named in the order must be a woman and must accompany the Supervising Solicitor, and
   (6) the order may only be served between 9.30 a.m. and 5.30 p.m. Monday to Friday unless the court otherwise orders.

7.5

Search and custody of materials:

(1) no material shall be removed unless clearly covered by the terms of the order,
(2) the premises must not be searched and no items shall be removed from them except in the presence of the respondent or a person who appears to be a responsible employee of the respondent,
(3) where copies of documents are sought, the documents should be retained for no more than 2 days before return to the owner,
(4) where material in dispute is removed pending trial, the applicant's solicitors should place it in the custody of the respondent's solicitors on their undertaking to retain it in safekeeping and to produce it to the court when required,
(5) in appropriate cases the applicant should insure the material retained in the respondent's solicitors' custody,
(6) the Supervising Solicitor must make a list of all material removed from the premises and supply a copy of the list to the respondent,
(7) no material shall be removed from the premises until the respondent has had reasonable time to check the list,
(8) if any of the listed items exists only in computer readable form, the respondent must immediately give the applicant's solicitors effective

access to the computers, with all necessary passwords, to enable them to be searched, and cause the listed items to be printed out,

(9) the applicant must take all reasonable steps to ensure that no damage is done to any computer or data,

(10) the applicant and his representatives may not themselves search the respondent's computers unless they have sufficient expertise to do so without damaging the respondent's system,

(11) the Supervising Solicitor shall provide a report on the carrying out of the order to the applicant's solicitors,

(12) as soon as the report is received the applicant's solicitors shall—
  (a) serve a copy of it on the respondent, and
  (b) file a copy of it with the court, and

(13) where the Supervising Solicitor is satisfied that full compliance with paragraph 7.5(7) and (8) above is impracticable, he may permit the search to proceed and items to be removed without compliance with the impracticable requirements.

7.6

General

The Supervising Solicitor must not be an employee or member of the applicant's firm of solicitors.

7.7

If the court orders that the order need not be served by the Supervising Solicitor, the reason for so ordering must be set out in the order.

7.8

The search order must not be carried out at the same time as a police search warrant.

7.9

There is no privilege against self incrimination in—

(1) Intellectual Property cases in respect of a 'related offence' or for the recovery of a 'related penalty' as defined in section 72 Senior Courts Act 1981;

(2) proceedings for the recovery or administration of any property, for the execution of a trust or for an account of any property or dealings with property, in relation to—
  (a) an offence under the Theft Act 1968 (see section 31 of the Theft Act 1968[6]); or
  (b) an offence under the Fraud Act 2006 (see section 13 of the Fraud Act 2006[7]) or a related offence within the meaning given by section

13(4) of that Act— that is, conspiracy to defraud or any other offence involving any form of fraudulent conduct or purpose; or

(3) proceedings in which a court is hearing an application for an order under Part IV or Part V of the Children Act 1989 (see section 98 Children Act 1989).

However, the privilege may still be claimed in relation to material or information required to be disclosed by an order, as regards potential criminal proceedings outside those statutory provisions.

7.10

Applications in intellectual property cases should be made in the Chancery Division.

7.11

An example of a Search Order is annexed to this Practice Direction. This example may be modified as appropriate in any particular case.

Delivery-Up Orders

8.1

The following provisions apply to orders, other than search orders, for delivery up or preservation of evidence or property where it is likely that such an order will be executed at the premises of the respondent or a third party.

8.2

In such cases the court shall consider whether to include in the order for the benefit or protection of the parties similar provisions to those specified above in relation to injunctions and search orders.

Injunctions against third parties

9.1

The following provisions apply to orders which will affect a person other than the applicant or respondent, who:

(1) did not attend the hearing at which the order was made; and

(2) is served with the order.

9.2

Where such a person served with the order requests—

(1) a copy of any materials read by the judge, including material prepared after the hearing at the direction of the judge or in compliance with the order; or

(2) a note of the hearing,

the applicant, or his legal representative, must comply promptly with the request, unless the court orders otherwise.

Annex

FREEZING INJUNCTION

IN THE HIGH COURT OF JUSTICE
[ ] DIVISION

Before The Honour able Mr Justice [ ]

Claim No .

Dated

Applicant

Seal

Respondent

Name , address and reference of Respondent

PENAL NOTICE

IF YOU [ ][1] DISOBEY THIS ORDER YOU MAY BE HELD TO BE IN CONTEMPT OF COURT AND MAY BE IMPRISONED, FINED OR HAVE YOUR ASSETS SEIZED.

ANY OTHER PERSON WHO KNOWS OF THIS ORDER AND DOES ANYTHING WHICH HELPS OR PERMITS THE RESPONDENT TO BREA CH THE TERMS OF THIS ORDER MAY ALSO BE HELD TO BE IN CONTEMPT OF COURT AND MAY BE IMPRISONED, FINED OR HAVE THEIR ASSETS SEIZED.

1 Insert name of Re spondent .

THIS ORDER

1.

This is a Freezing Injunction made against [ ] ('the Respondent') on [ ] by Mr Justice [ ] on the application of [ ] ('the Applicant'). The Judge read the Affidavits listed in Schedule A and accepted the undertakings set out in Schedule B at the end of this Order.

2.

This order was made at a hearing without notice to the Respondent. The Respondent has a right to apply to the court to vary or discharge the order—see para 4.

If there is more than one Respondent—

(a) unless otherwise stated, references in this order to 'the Respondent' mean both or all of them; and

(b) this order is effective against any Respondent on whom it is served or who is given notice of it.

FREEZING INJUNCTION

[For injunction limited to assets in England and Wales]

5.

Until the return date or further order of the court, the Respondent must not remove from England and Wales or in any way dispose of, deal with or diminish the value of any of his assets which are in England and Wales up to the value of £ .

[For worldwide injunction]

5.

Until the return date or further order of the court, the Respondent must not—

(1) remove from England and Wales any of his assets which are in England and Wales up to the value of £ ; or

(2) in any way dispose of, deal with or diminish the value of any of his assets whether they are in or outside England and Wales up to the same value.

[For either form of injunction]

6.

Paragraph 5 applies to all the Respondent's assets whether or not they are in his own name and whether they are solely or jointly owned. For the purpose of this order the Respondent's assets include any asset which he has the power, directly or indirectly, to dispose of or deal with as if it were his own. The Respondent is to be regarded as having such power if a third party holds or controls the asset in accordance with his direct or indirect instructions.

7.

This prohibition includes the following assets in particular—

(a) the property known as *[title/address]* or the net sale money after payment of any mortgages if it has been sold;

(b) the property and assets of the Respondent's business [known as *[name]*] [carried on at *[address]*] or the sale money if any of them have been sold; and

(c) any money standing to the credit of any bank account including the amount of any cheque drawn on such account which has not been cleared.

[For injunction limited to assets in England and Wales]

8.

If the total value free of charges or other securities ("unencumbered value") of the Respondent's assets in England and Wales exceeds £ , the Respondent may remove any of those assets from England and Wales or may dispose of or deal with them so long as the total unencumbered value of his assets still in England and Wales remains above £ .

[For worldwide injunction]

8.

(1) If the total value free of charges or other securities ("unencumbered value") of the Respondent's assets in England and Wales exceeds £ , the Respondent may remove any of those assets from England and Wales or may dispose of or deal with them so long as the total unencumbered value of the Respondent's assets still in England and Wales remains above £ .

(2) If the total unencumbered value of the Respondent's assets in England and Wales does not exceed £ , the Respondent must not remove any of those assets from England and Wales and must not dispose of or deal with any of them. If the Respondent has other assets outside England and Wales, he may dispose of or deal with those assets outside England and Wales so long as the total unencumbered value of all his assets whether in or outside England and Wales remains above £ .

PROVISION OF INFORMATION

9.

(1) Unless paragraph (2) applies, the Respondent must [immediately] [within hours of service of this order] and to the best of his ability inform the Applicant's solicitors of all his assets [in England and Wales] [worldwide] [exceeding £ in value] whether in his own name or not and whether solely or jointly owned, giving the value, location and details of all such assets.

(2) If the provision of any of this information is likely to incriminate the Respondent, he may be entitled to refuse to provide it, but is recommended to take legal advice before refusing to provide the information. Wrongful refusal to provide the information is contempt of court and may render the Respondent liable to be imprisoned, fined or have his assets seized.

10.

Within [ ] working days after being served with this order, the Respondent must swear and serve on the Applicant's solicitors an affidavit setting out the above information.

EXCEPTIONS TO THIS ORDER

11.

(1) This order does not prohibit the Respondent from spending £ a week towards his ordinary living expenses and also £ [*or* a reasonable sum] on legal advice and representation. [But before spending any money the Respondent must tell the Applicant's legal representatives where the money is to come from.]

(2) This order does not prohibit the Respondent from dealing with or disposing of any of his assets in the ordinary and proper course of business.]

(3) The Respondent may agree with the Applicant's legal representatives that the above spending limits should be increased or that this order should be varied in any other respect, but any agreement must be in writing.

(4) The order will cease to have effect if the Respondent—

(a) provides security by paying the sum of £ into court, to be held to the order of the court; or

(b) makes provision for security in that sum by another method agreed with the Applicant's legal representatives.

COSTS

12.

The costs of this application are reserved to the judge hearing the application on the return date.

VARIATION OR DISCHARGE OF THIS ORDER

13.

Anyone served with or notified of this order may apply to the court at any time to vary or discharge this order (or so much of it as affects that person), but they must first inform the Applicant's solicitors. If any evidence is to be relied upon in support of the application, the substance of it must be communicated in writing to the Applicant's solicitors in advance.

INTERPRETATION OF THIS ORDER

14.

A Respondent who is an individual who is ordered not to do something must not do it himself or in any other way. He must not do it through others acting on his behalf or on his instructions or with his encouragement.

15.

A Respondent which is not an individual which is ordered not to do something must not do it itself or by its directors, officers, partners, employees or agents or in any other way.

PARTIES OTHER THAN THE APPLICANT AND RESPONDENT

16.

Effect of this order

It is a contempt of court for any person notified of this order knowingly to assist in or permit a breach of this order. Any person doing so may be imprisoned, fined or have their assets seized.

17.

Set off by banks
This injunction does not prevent any bank from exercising any right of set off it may have in respect of any facility which it gave to the respondent before it was notified of this order.

18.

Withdrawals by the Respondent
No bank need enquire as to the application or proposed application of any money withdrawn by the Respondent if the withdrawal appears to be permitted by this order.

[For worldwide injunction]

19.

Persons outside England and Wales
(1) Except as provided in paragraph (2) below, the terms of this order do not affect or concern anyone outside the jurisdiction of this court.
(2) The terms of this order will affect the following persons in a country or state outside the jurisdiction of this court—
  (a) the Respondent or his officer or agent appointed by power of attorney;
  (b) any person who—
    (i) is subject to the jurisdiction of this court;
    (ii) has been given written notice of this order at his residence or place of business within the jurisdiction of this court; and
    (iii) is able to prevent acts or omissions outside the jurisdiction of this court which constitute or assist in a breach of the terms of this order; and
  (c) anyother person, only to the extent that this order is declared enforceable by or is enforced by a court in that country or state.

[For worldwide injunction]

20.

Assets located outside England and Wales
Nothing in this order shall, in respect of assets located outside England and Wales, prevent any third party from complying with—
(1) what it reasonably believes to be its obligations, contractual or otherwise, under the laws and obligations of the country or state in which those assets are situated or under the proper law of any contract between itself and the Respondent; and
(2) any orders of the courts of that country or state, provided that reason-

able notice of any application for such an order is given to the Applicant's solicitors.

COMMUNICATIONS WITH THE COURT

All communications to the court about this order should be sent to—

[Insert the address and telephone number of the appropriate Court Office]

If the order is made at the Royal Courts of Justice, communications should be addressed as follows—

Where the order is made in the Chancery Division

Room TM 5.07, Royal Courts of Justice, Strand, London WC2A 2LL quoting the case number. The telephone number is 020 7947 6322.

Where the order is made in the Queen's Bench Division

Room WG08, Royal Courts of Justice, Strand, London WC2A 2LL quoting the case number. The telephone number is 020 7947 6010.

Where the order is made in the Commercial Court

Room EB09, Royal Courts of Justice, Strand, London WC2A 2LL quoting the case number. The telephone number is 0207 947 6826.

The offices are open between 10 a.m. and 4.30 p.m. Monday to Friday.

SCHEDULE A

AFFIDAVITS

The Applicant relied on the following affidavits–

[name] [number of affidavit] [date sworn] [filed on behalf of]

SCHEDULE B
UNDERTAKINGS GIVEN TO THE COURT BY THE APPLICANT

(1)
If the court later finds that this order has caused loss to the Respondent, and decides that the Respondent should be compensated for that loss, the Applicant will comply with any order the court may make.

[(2)
The Applicant will—
(a) on or before *[date]* cause a written guarantee in the sum of £ to be issued from a bank with a place of business within England or Wales, in respect of any order the court may make pursuant to paragraph (1) above; and

(b) immediately upon issue of the guarantee, cause a copy of it to be served on the Respondent.]

(3)
As soon as practicable the Applicant will issue and serve a claim form [in the form of the draft produced to the court] [claiming the appropriate relief].

(4)
The Applicant will [swear and file an affidavit] [cause an affidavit to be sworn and filed] [substantially in the terms of the draft affidavit produced to the court] [confirming the substance of what was said to the court by the Applicant's counsel/solicitors].

(5)
The Applicant will serve upon the Respondent [together with this order] [as soon as practicable]—
(i) copies of the affidavits and exhibits containing the evidence relied upon by the Applicant, and any other documents provided to the court on the making of the application;
(ii) the claim form; and
(iii) an application notice for continuation of the order.

[(6)
Anyone notified of this order will be given a copy of it by the Applicant's legal representatives.]

(7)
The Applicant will pay the reasonable costs of anyone other than the Respondent which have been incurred as a result of this order including the costs of finding out whether that person holds any of the Respondent's assets and if the court later finds that this order has caused such person loss, and decides that such person should be compensated for that loss, the Applicant will comply with any order the court may make.

(8)
If this order ceases to have effect (for example, if the Respondent provides security or the Applicant does not provide a bank guarantee as provided for above) the Applicant will immediately take all reasonable steps to inform in writing anyone to whom he has given notice of this order, or who he has reasonable grounds for supposing may act upon this order, that it has ceased to have effect.

[(9)
The Applicant will not without the permission of the court use any informa-

tion obtained as a result of this order for the purpose of any civil or criminal proceedings, either in England and Wales or in any other jurisdiction, other than this claim.]

[(10)

The Applicant will not without the permission of the court seek to enforce this order in any country outside England and Wales [or seek an order of a similar nature including orders conferring a charge or other security against the Respondent or the Respondent's assets].]

NAME AND ADDRESS OF APPLICANT'S LEGAL REPRESENTATIVES

The Applicant's legal representatives are—

[Name, address, reference, fax and telephone numbers both in and out of office hours and e-mail]

SEARCH ORDER

IN THE HI H COURT OF JUSTICE
[ ] DIVISION

Before The Honour able Mr Justice [ ]

Claim No .

Dated

Applicant

Seal

Respondent

Name, address and reference of Respondent

PENAL NOTICE

IF YOU [ ][1] DISOBEY THIS ORDER YOU MAY BE HELD T O BE IN CONTEMPT OF COURT AND MAY BE IMPRISONED, FINED OR HAVE YOUR ASSETS SEIZED.

ANY OTHER PERSON WHO KNOWS OF THIS ORDER AND DOES ANYTHING WHICH HELPS OR PERMITS THE RESPONDENT TO BREACH THE TERMS OF THIS ORDER MAY ALSO BE HELD TO BE IN CONTEMPT OF COURT AND MAY BE IMPRISONED, FINED OR HAVE THEIR ASSETS SEIZED.

1 Insert name of Re spondent .

THIS ORDER

1.

This is a Search Order made against [ ] ('the Respondent') on [ ] by Mr Justice [ ] on the application of [ ] ('the Applicant'). The Judge read the Affidavits listed in Schedule F and accepted the undertakings set out in Schedules C, D and E at the end of this order.

2.

This order was made at a hearing without notice to the Respondent. The

Respondent has a right to apply to the court to vary or discharge the order—see paragraph 27 below.

3.
There will be a further hearing in respect of this order on [ ] ('the return date').

4.
If there is more than one Respondent—
(a) unless otherwise stated, references in this order to 'the Respondent' mean both or all of them; and
(b) this order is effective against any Respondent on whom it is served or who is given notice of it.

5.
This order must be complied with by—
(a) the Respondent;
(b) any director, officer, partner or responsible employee of the Respondent; and
(c) if the Respondent is an individual, any other person having responsible control of the premises to be searched.

THE SEARCH

6.
The Respondent must permit the following persons[8]—
(a) [ ] ('the Supervising Solicitor');
(b) [ ], a solicitor in the firm of [ ], the Applicant's solicitors; and
(c) up to [ ] other persons[9] being *[their identity or capacity]* accompanying them,
(together 'the search party'), to enter the premises mentioned in Schedule A to this order and any other premises of the Respondent disclosed under paragraph 18 below and any vehicles under the Respondent's control on or around the premises ('the premises') so that they can search for, inspect, photograph or photocopy, and deliver into the safekeeping of the Applicant's solicitors all the documents and articles which are listed in Schedule B to this order ('the listed items').

7.
Having permitted the search party to enter the premises, the Respondent must allow the search party to remain on the premises until the search is complete. In the event that it becomes necessary for any of those persons to leave the premises before the search is complete, the Respondent must allow

them to re-enter the premises immediately upon their seeking re-entry on the same or the following day in order to complete the search.

RESTRICTIONS ON SEARCH

8.

This order may not be carried out at the same time as a police search warrant.

9.

Before the Respondent allows anybody onto the premises to carry out this order, he is entitled to have the Supervising Solicitor explain to him what it means in everyday language.

10.

The Respondent is entitled to seek legal advice and to ask the court to vary or discharge this order. Whilst doing so, he may ask the Supervising Solicitor to delay starting the search for up to 2 hours or such other longer period as the Supervising Solicitor may permit. However, the Respondent must—

(a) comply with the terms of paragraph 27 below;
(b) not disturb or remove any listed items; and
(c) permit the Supervising Solicitor to enter, but not start to search.

11.

(1) Before permitting entry to the premises by any person other than the Supervising Solicitor, the Respondent may, for a short time (not to exceed two hours, unless the Supervising Solicitor agrees to a longer period)—
  (a) gather together any documents he believes may be incriminating or privileged; and
  (b) hand them to the Supervising Solicitor for him to assess whether they are incriminating or privileged as claimed.

(2) If the Supervising Solicitor decides that the Respondent is entitled to withhold production of any of the documents on the ground that they are privileged or incriminating, he will exclude them from the search, record them in a list for inclusion in his report and return them to the Respondent.

(3) If the Supervising Solicitor believes that the Respondent may be entitled to withhold production of the whole or any part of a document on the ground that it or part of it may be privileged or incriminating, or if the Respondent claims to be entitled to withhold production on those grounds, the Supervising Solicitor will exclude it from the search and retain it in his possession pending further order of the court.

12.
If the Respondent wishes to take legal advice and gather documents as permitted, he must first inform the Supervising Solicitor and keep him informed of the steps being taken.

13.
No item may be removed from the premises until a list of the items to be removed has been prepared, and a copy of the list has been supplied to the Respondent, and he has been given a reasonable opportunity to check the list.

14.
The premises must not be searched, and items must not be removed from them, except in the presence of the Respondent.

15.
If the Supervising Solicitor is satisfied that full compliance with paragraphs 13 or 14 is not practicable, he may permit the search to proceed and items to be removed without fully complying with them.

DELIVERY UP OF ARTICLES/DOCUMENTS

16.
The Respondent must immediately hand over to the Applicant's solicitors any of the listed items, which are in his possession or under his control, save for any computer or hard disk integral to any computer. Any items the subject of a dispute as to whether they are listed items must immediately be handed over to the Supervising Solicitor for safe keeping pending resolution of the dispute or further order of the court.

17.
The Respondent must immediately give the search party effective access to the computers on the premises, with all necessary passwords, to enable the computers to be searched. If they contain any listed items the Respondent must cause the listed items to be displayed so that they can be read and copied[10]. The Respondent must provide the Applicant's Solicitors with copies of all listed items contained in the computers. All reasonable steps shall be taken by the Applicant and the Applicant's solicitors to ensure that no damage is done to any computer or data. The Applicant and his representatives may not themselves search the Respondent's computers unless they have sufficient expertise to do so without damaging the Respondent's system.

PROVISION OF INFORMATION

18.
The Respondent must immediately inform the Applicant's Solicitors (in the presence of the Supervising Solicitor) so far as he is aware—
(a) where all the listed items are;
(b) the name and address of everyone who has supplied him, or offered to supply him, with listed items;
(c) the name and address of everyone to whom he has supplied, or offered to supply, listed items; and
(d) full details of the dates and quantities of every such supply and offer.

19.
Within [ ] working days after being served with this order the Respondent must swear and serve an affidavit setting out the above information[11].

PROHIBITED ACTS

20.
Except for the purpose of obtaining legal advice, the Respondent must not directly or indirectly inform anyone of these proceedings or of the contents of this order, or warn anyone that proceedings have been or may be brought against him by the Applicant until 4.30 p.m. on the return date or further order of the court.

21.
Until 4.30 p.m. on the return date the Respondent must not destroy, tamper with, cancel or part with possession, power, custody or control of the listed items otherwise than in accordance with the terms of this order.

22.
[Insert any negative injunctions.]

23.
[Insert any further order]

COSTS

24.
The costs of this application are reserved to the judge hearing the application on the return date.

RESTRICTIONS ON SERVICE

25.
This order may only be served between [ ] a.m./p.m. and [ ] a.m./p.m. [and on a weekday][12].

26.
This order must be served by the Supervising Solicitor, and paragraph 6 of the order must be carried out in his presence and under his supervision.

VARIATION AND DISCHARGE OF THIS ORDER

27.
Anyone served with or notified of this order may apply to the court at any time to vary or discharge this order (or so much of it as affects that person), but they must first inform the Applicant's solicitors. If any evidence is to be relied upon in support of the application, the substance of it must be communicated in writing to the Applicant's solicitors in advance.

INTERPRETATION OF THIS ORDER

28.
Any requirement that something shall be done to or in the presence of the Respondent means—
(a) if there is more than one Respondent, to or in the presence of any one of them; and
(b) if a Respondent is not an individual, to or in the presence of a director, officer, partner or responsible employee.

29.
A Respondent who is an individual who is ordered not to do something must not do it himself or in any other way. He must not do it through others acting on his behalf or on his instructions or with his encouragement.

30.
A Respondent which is not an individual which is ordered not to do something must not do it itself or by its directors, officers, partners, employees or agents or in any other way.

COMMUNICATIONS WITH THE COURT

All communications to the court about this order should be sent to—

[Insert the address and telephone number of the appropriate Court Office]

If the order is made at the Royal Courts of Justice, communications should be addressed as follows—

Where the order is made in the Chancery Division

Room TM 5.07, Royal Courts of Justice, Strand, London WC2A 2LL quoting the case number. The telephone number is 020 7947 6322.

Where the order is made in the Queen's Bench Division

Room WG08, Royal Courts of Justice, Strand, London WC2A 2LL quoting the case number. The telephone number is 020 7947 6010.

Where the order is made in the Commercial Court

Room EB09, Royal Courts of Justice, Strand, London WC2A 2LL quoting the case number. The telephone number is 0207 947 6826.

The offices are open between 10 a.m. and 4.30 p.m. Monday to Friday.

SCHEDULE A
THE PREMISES

SCHEDULE B
THE LISTED ITEMS

SCHEDULE C

UNDERTAKINGS GIVEN TO THE COURT BY THE APPLICANT

(1)
If the court later finds that this order or carrying it out has caused loss to the Respondent, and decides that the Respondent should be compensated for that loss, the Applicant will comply with any order the court may make. Further if the carrying out of this order has been in breach of the terms of this order or otherwise in a manner inconsistent with the Applicant's solicitors' duties as officers of the court, the Applicant will comply with any order for damages the court may make.

[(2)
As soon as practicable the Applicant will issue a claim form [in the form of the draft produced to the court] [claiming the appropriate relief].]

(3)
The Applicant will [swear and file an affidavit] [cause an affidavit to be sworn and filed] [substantially in the terms of the draft affidavit produced to the court] [confirming the substance of what was said to the court by the Applicant's counsel/solicitors].

(4)
The Applicant will not, without the permission of the court, use any information or documents obtained as a result of carrying out this order nor inform anyone else of these proceedings except for the purposes of these proceedings (including adding further Respondents) or commencing civil proceedings in relation to the same or related subject matter to these proceedings until after the return date.

[(5)
The Applicant will maintain pending further order the sum of £ [ ] in an account controlled by the Applicant's solicitors.]

[(6)
The Applicant will insure the items removed from the premises.]

SCHEDULE D
UNDERTAKINGS GIVEN BY THE APPLICANT'S SOLICITORS

(1)
The Applicant's solicitors will provide to the Supervising Solicitor for service on the Respondent—

(i) a service copy of this order;
(ii) the claim form (with defendant's response pack) or, if not issued, the draft produced to the court;
(iii) an application for hearing on the return date;
(iv) copies of the affidavits *[or draft affidavits]* and exhibits capable of being copied containing the evidence relied upon by the applicant;
(v) a note of any allegation of fact made orally to the court where such allegation is not contained in the affidavits or draft affidavits read by the judge; and
(vi) a copy of the skeleton argument produced to the court by the Applicant's [counsel/solicitors].

(2)
The Applicants' solicitors will answer at once to the best of their ability any question whether a particular item is a listed item.

(3)
Subject as provided below the Applicant's solicitors will retain in their own safe keeping all items obtained as a result of this order until the court directs otherwise.

(4)
The Applicant's solicitors will return the originals of all documents obtained

as a result of this order (except original documents which belong to the Applicant) as soon as possible and in any event within [two] working days of their removal.

SCHEDULE E

UNDERTAKINGS GIVEN BY THE SUPERVISING SOLICITOR

(1)

The Supervising Solicitor will use his best endeavours to serve this order upon the Respondent and at the same time to serve upon the Respondent the other documents required to be served and referred to in paragraph (1) of Schedule D.

(2)

The Supervising Solicitor will offer to explain to the person served with the order its meaning and effect fairly and in everyday language, and to inform him of his right to take legal advice (including an explanation that the Respondent may be entitled to avail himself of the privilege against self-incrimination and legal professional privilege) and to apply to vary or discharge this order as mentioned in paragraph 27 above.

(3)

The Supervising Solicitor will retain in the safe keeping of his firm all items retained by him as a result of this order until the court directs otherwise.

(4)

Unless and until the court otherwise orders, or unless otherwise necessary to comply with any duty to the court pursuant to this order, the Supervising Solicitor shall not disclose to any person any information relating to those items, and shall keep the existence of such items confidential.

(5)

Within [48] hours of completion of the search the Supervising Solicitor will make and provide to the Applicant's solicitors, the Respondent or his solicitors and to the judge who made this order (for the purposes of the court file) a written report on the carrying out of the order.

SCHEDULE F

AFFIDAVITS

The Applicant relied on the following affidavits–

[name] [number of affidavit] [date sworn] [filed on behalf of]

NAME AND ADDRESS OF APPLICANT'S SOLICITORS

The Applicant's solicitors are–

[Name, address, reference, fax and telephone numbers both in and out of office hours.]

Footnotes

1. Rule 25.1(1)(h).
2. Rule 25.1(1)(f).
3. Rule 23.7(1) and (2) and see rule 23.7(4) (short service).
4. See Part 22.
5. Rule 25.2(3).
6. 1968 c. 60.
7. 2006 c. 35.
8. Where the premises are likely to be occupied by an unaccompanied woman and the Supervising Solicitor is a man, at least one of the persons accompanying him should be a woman.
9. None of these persons should be people who could gain personally or commercially from anything they might read or see on the premises, unless their presence is essential.
10. If it is envisaged that the Respondent's computers are to be imaged (i.e. the hard drives are to be copied wholesale, thereby reproducing listed items and other items indiscriminately), special provision needs to be made and independent computer specialists need to be appointed, who should be required to give undertakings to the court.
11. The period should ordinarily be longer than the period in paragraph (2) of Schedule D, if any of the information is likely to be included in listed items taken away of which the Respondent does not have copies.
12. Normally, the order should be served in the morning (not before 9.30 a.m.) and on a weekday to enable the Respondent more readily to obtain legal advice.

Part 31 Disclosure and Inspection of Documents

Subsequent use of disclosed documents and completed Electronic Documents Questionnaires

31.22

(1) A party to whom a document has been disclosed may use the document only for the purpose of the proceedings in which it is disclosed, except where—

(a) the document has been read to or by the court, or referred to, at a hearing which has been held in public;

(b) the court gives permission; or
(c) the party who disclosed the document and the person to whom the document belongs agree.

(2) The court may make an order restricting or prohibiting the use of a document which has been disclosed, even where the document has been read to or by the court, or referred to, at a hearing which has been held in public.

(3) An application for such an order may be made—
(a) by a party; or
(b) by any person to whom the document belongs.

(4) For the purpose of this rule, an Electronic Documents Questionnaire which has been completed and served by another party pursuant to Practice Direction 31B is to be treated as if it is a document which has been disclosed.

Part 39 Miscellaneous Provisions Relating to Hearings

Interpretation

39.1

In this Part, reference to a hearing includes a reference to the trial.

General rule— hearing to be in public

39.2

(1) The general rule is that a hearing is to be in public.

(2) The requirement for a hearing to be in public does not require the court to make special arrangements for accommodating members of the public.

(3) A hearing, or any part of it, may be in private if—
(a) publicity would defeat the object of the hearing;
(b) it involves matters relating to national security;
(c) it involves confidential information (including information relating to personal financial matters) and publicity would damage that confidentiality;
(d) a private hearing is necessary to protect the interests of any child or protected party;
(e) it is a hearing of an application made without notice and it would be unjust to any respondent for there to be a public hearing;
(f) it involves uncontentious matters arising in the administration of trusts or in the administration of a deceased person's estate; or

(g) the court considers this to be necessary, in the interests of justice.

(4) The court may order that the identity of any party or witness must not be disclosed if it considers non-disclosure necessary in order to protect the interests of that party or witness.

Failure to attend the trial

39.3

(1) The court may proceed with a trial in the absence of a party but—

(a) if no party attends the trial, it may strike out the whole of the proceedings;

(b) if the claimant does not attend, it may strike out his claim and any defence to counterclaim; and

(c) if a defendant does not attend, it may strike out his defence or counterclaim (or both).

(2) Where the court strikes out proceedings, or any part of them, under this rule, it may subsequently restore the proceedings, or that part.

(3) Where a party does not attend and the court gives judgment or makes an order against him, the party who failed to attend may apply for the judgment or order to be set aside.

(4) An application under paragraph (2) or paragraph (3) must be supported by evidence.

(5) Where an application is made under paragraph (2) or (3) by a party who failed to attend the trial, the court may grant the application only if the applicant—

(a) acted promptly when he found out that the court had exercised its power to strike out or to enter judgment or make an order against him;

(b) had a good reason for not attending the trial; and

(c) has a reasonable prospect of success at the trial.

Timetable for trial

39.4

When the court sets a timetable for a trial in accordance with rule 28.6 (fixing or confirming the trial date and giving directions— fast track) or rule 29.8 (setting a trial timetable and fixing or confirming the trial date or week—multi-track) it will do so in consultation with the parties.

Trial bundles

39.5

(1) Unless the court orders otherwise, the claimant must file a trial bundle containing documents required by—

(a) a relevant practice direction; and
(b) any court order.

(2) The claimant must file the trial bundle not more than 7 days and not less than 3 days before the start of the trial.

Representation at trial of companies or other corporations

39.6

A company or other corporation may be represented at trial by an employee if—

(a) the employee has been authorised by the company or corporation to appear at trial on its behalf; and
(b) the court gives permission.

Impounded documents

39.7

(1) Documents impounded by order of the court must not be released from the custody of the court except in compliance—
   (a) with a court order; or
   (b) with a written request made by a Law Officer or the Director of Public Prosecutions.
(2) A document released from the custody of the court under paragraph(1)(b) must be released into the custody of the person who requested it.
(3) Documents impounded by order of the court, while in the custody of the court, may not be inspected except by a person authorised to do so by a court order.

Practice Direction 39a— Miscellaneous Provisions Relating to Hearings This Practice Direction supplements CPR Part 39

Hearings

1.1

In Part 39, reference to a hearing includes reference to the trial[1].

1.2

The general rule is that a hearing is to be in public[2].

1.3
Rule 39.2(3) sets out the type of proceedings which may be dealt with in private.

1.4
The decision as to whether to hold a hearing in public or in private must be made by the judge conducting the hearing having regard to any representations which may have been made to him.

1.4A
The judge should also have regard to Article 6(1) of the European Convention on Human Rights. This requires that, in general, court hearings are to be held in public, but the press and public may be excluded in the circumstances specified in that Article. Article 6(1) will usually be relevant, for example, where a party applies for a hearing which would normally be held in public to be held in private as well as where a hearing would normally be held in private. The judge may need to consider whether the case is within any of the exceptions permitted by Article 6(1).

1.5
The hearings set out below shall in the first instance be listed by the court as hearings in private under rule 39.2(3)(c), namely:
(1) a claim by a mortgagee against one or more individuals for an order for possession of land,
(2) a claim by a landlord against one or more tenants or former tenants for the repossession of a dwelling house based on the non-payment of rent,
(3) an application to suspend a warrant of execution or a warrant of possession or to stay execution where the court is being invited to consider the ability of a party to make payments to another party,
(4) a redetermination under rule 14.13 or an application to vary or suspend the payment of a judgment debt by instalments,
(5) an application for a charging order (including an application to enforce a charging order), third party debt order, attachment of earnings order, administration order, or the appointment of a receiver,
(6) an order to attend court for questioning,
(7) the determination of the liability of an LSC funded client under regulations 9 and 10 of the Community Legal Service (Costs) Regulations 2000, or of an assisted person's liability for costs under regulation 127 of the Civil Legal Aid (General) Regulations 1989,
(8) an application for security for costs to be provided by a claimant who is a company or a limited liability partnership in the circumstances set out in rule 25.13(2)(c),
(9) proceedings brought under the Consumer Credit Act 1974, the Inheritance

(Provision for Family and Dependants) Act 1975 or the Protection from Harassment Act 1997,

(10) an application by a trustee or personal representative for directions as to bringing or defending legal proceedings.

1.6

Rule 39.2(3)(d) states that a hearing may be in private where it involves the interests of a child or protected party. This includes the approval of a compromise or settlement on behalf of a child or protected party or an application for the payment of money out of court to such a person.

1.7

Attention is drawn to paragraph 5.1 of Practice Direction 27 (relating to the hearing of claims in the small claims track), which provides that the judge may decide to hold a small claim hearing in private if the parties agree or if a ground mentioned in rule 39.2(3) applies. A hearing of a small claim in premises other than the court will not be a hearing in public.

1.7A

Attention is drawn to paragraph 24.5(8) of Practice Direction 52, which provides that an appeal to a county court against certain decisions under the Representation of the People Act 1983 is to be heard in private unless the court orders otherwise. Attention is also drawn to paragraph 24.5(9) of that practice direction, which provides that an appeal to the Court of Appeal against such a decision of a county court may be heard in private if the Court of Appeal so orders.

1.8

Nothing in this practice direction prevents a judge ordering that a hearing taking place in public shall continue in private, or vice-versa.

1.9

If the court or judge's room in which the proceedings are taking place has a sign on the door indicating that the proceedings are private, members of the public who are not parties to the proceedings will not be admitted unless the court permits.

1.10

Where there is no such sign on the door of the court or judge's room, members of the public will be admitted where practicable. The judge may, if he thinks it appropriate, adjourn the proceedings to a larger room or court.

1.11

When a hearing takes place in public, members of the public may obtain a transcript of any judgment given or a copy of any order made, subject to payment of the appropriate fee.

1.12
When a judgment is given or an order is made in private, if any member of the public who is not a party to the proceedings seeks a transcript of the judgment or a copy of the order, he must seek the leave of the judge who gave the judgment or made the order.

1.13
A judgment or order given or made in private, when drawn up, must have clearly marked in the title:
'Before [*title and name of judge*] sitting in Private'

1.14
References to hearings being in public or private or in a judge's room contained in the Civil Procedure Rules (including the Rules of the Supreme Court and the County Court Rules scheduled to Part 50) and the practice directions which supplement them do not restrict any existing rights of audience or confer any new rights of audience in respect of applications or proceedings which under the rules previously in force would have been heard in court or in chambers respectively.

1.15
Where the court lists a hearing of a claim by a mortgagee for an order for possession of land under paragraph 1.5(1) above to be in private, any fact which needs to be proved by the evidence of witnesses may be proved by evidence in writing.
(CPR rule 32.2 sets out the general rule as to how evidence is to be given and facts are to be proved.)

Failure to attend the trial

2.1
Rule 39.3 sets out the consequences of a party's failure to attend the trial.

2.2
The court may proceed with a trial in the absence of a party[3]. In the absence of:
(1) the defendant, the claimant may—
  (a) prove his claim at trial and obtain judgment on his claim and for costs, and
  (b) seek the striking out of any counterclaim,
(2) the claimant, the defendant may—

(a) prove any counterclaim at trial and obtain judgment on his counterclaim and for costs, and
(b) seek the striking out of the claim, or

(3) both parties, the court may strike out the whole of the proceedings.

2.3
Where the court has struck out proceedings, or any part of them, on the failure of a party to attend, that party may apply in accordance with Part 23 for the proceedings, or that part of them, to be restored and for any judgment given against that party to be set aside[4].

2.4
The application referred to in paragraph 2.3 above must be supported by evidence giving reasons for the failure to attend court and stating when the applicant found out about the order against him.

Bundles of documents for hearings or trial

3.1
Unless the court orders otherwise, the claimant must file the trial bundle not more than 7 days and not less than 3 days before the start of the trial.

3.2
Unless the court orders otherwise, the trial bundle should include a copy of:

(1) the claim form and all statements of case,
(2) a case summary and/or chronology where appropriate,
(3) requests for further information and responses to the requests,
(4) all witness statements to be relied on as evidence,
(5) any witness summaries,
(6) any notices of intention to rely on hearsay evidence under rule 32.2,
(7) any notices of intention to rely on evidence (such as a plan, photograph etc.) under rule 33.6 which is not—
  (a) contained in a witness statement, affidavit or experts report,
  (b) being given orally at trial,
  (c) hearsay evidence under rule 33.2,
(8) any medical reports and responses to them,
(9) any experts' reports and responses to them,
(10) any order giving directions as to the conduct of the trial, and
(11) any other necessary documents.

3.3
The originals of the documents contained in the trial bundle, together with copies of any other court orders should be available at the trial.

3.4

The preparation and production of the trial bundle, even where it is delegated to another person, is the responsibility of the legal representative[5] who has conduct of the claim on behalf of the claimant.

3.5

The trial bundle should be paginated (continuously) throughout, and indexed with a description of each document and the page number. Where the total number of pages is more than 100, numbered dividers should be placed at intervals between groups of documents.

3.6

The bundle should normally be contained in a ring binder or lever arch file. Where more than one bundle is supplied, they should be clearly distinguishable, for example, by different colours or letters. If there are numerous bundles, a core bundle should be prepared containing the core documents essential to the proceedings, with references to the supplementary documents in the other bundles.

3.7

For convenience, experts' reports may be contained in a separate bundle and cross referenced in the main bundle.

3.8

If a document to be included in the trial bundle is illegible, a typed copy should be included in the bundle next to it, suitably cross-referenced.

3.9

The contents of the trial bundle should be agreed where possible. The parties should also agree where possible:

(1) that the documents contained in the bundle are authentic even if not disclosed under Part 31, and
(2) that documents in the bundle may be treated as evidence of the facts stated in them even if a notice under the Civil Evidence Act 1995 has not been served.

Where it is not possible to agree the contents of the bundle, a summary of the points on which the parties are unable to agree should be included.

3.10

The party filing the trial bundle should supply identical bundles to all the parties to the proceedings and for the use of the witnesses.

Settlement or discontinuance after the trial date is fixed

4.1

Where:

(1) an offer to settle a claim is accepted,

(2) or a settlement is reached, or

(3) a claim is discontinued, which disposes of the whole of a claim for which a date or 'window' has been fixed for the trial, the parties must ensure that the listing officer for the trial court is notified immediately.

4.2

If an order is drawn up giving effect to the settlement or discontinuance, a copy of the sealed order should be filed with the listing officer.

Representation at hearings

5.1

At any hearing, a written statement containing the following information should be provided for the court:

(1) the name and address of each advocate,

(2) his qualification or entitlement to act as an advocate, and

(3) the party for whom he so acts.

5.2

Where a party is a company or other corporation and is to be represented at a hearing by an employee the written statement should contain the following additional information:

(1) The full name of the company or corporation as stated in its certificate of registration.

(2) The registered number of the company or corporation.

(3) The position or office in the company or corporation held by the representative.

(4) The date on which and manner in which the representative was authorised to act for the company or corporation, e.g. _________ 19____: written authority from managing director; or _________ 19____: Board resolution dated _________ 19____ .

5.3

Rule 39.6 is intended to enable a company or other corporation to represent itself as a litigant in person. Permission under rule 39.6(b) should therefore be given by the court unless there is some particular and sufficient reason why it should be withheld. In considering whether to grant permission the matters to be taken into account include the complexity of the issues and the experience and position in the company or corporation of the proposed representative.

5.4
Permission under rule 39.6(b) should be obtained in advance of the hearing from, preferably, the judge who is to hear the case, but may, if it is for any reason impracticable or inconvenient to do so, be obtained from any judge by whom the case could be heard.

5.5
The permission may be obtained informally and without notice to the other parties. The judge who gives the permission should record in writing that he has done so and supply a copy to the company or corporation in question and to any other party who asks for one.

5.6
Permission should not normally be granted under Rule 39.6:
(a) in jury trials;
(b) in contempt proceedings.

Recording of proceedings

6.1
At any hearing, whether in the High Court or a county court, the proceedings will be tape recorded unless the judge directs otherwise.

6.2
No party or member of the public may use unofficial recording equipment in any court or judge's room without the permission of the court. To do so without permission constitutes a contempt of court[6].

6.3
Any party or person may require a transcript or transcripts of the recording of any hearing to be supplied to him, upon payment of the charges authorised by any scheme in force for the making of the recording or the transcript.

6.4
Where the person requiring the transcript or transcripts is not a party to the proceedings and the hearing or any part of it was held in private under CPR rule 39.2, paragraph 6.3 does not apply unless the court so orders.

6.5
Attention is drawn to paragraph 7.9 of the Court of Appeal (Civil Division) Practice Direction which deals with the provision of transcripts for use in the Court of Appeal at public expense.

Exhibits at trial

7

Exhibits which are handed in and proved during the course of the trial should be recorded on an exhibit list and kept in the custody of the court until the conclusion of the trial, unless the judge directs otherwise. At the conclusion of the trial it is the parties' responsibility to obtain the return of those exhibits which they handed in and to preserve them for the period in which any appeal may take place.

Citation of Authorities Human Rights

8.1

If it is necessary for a party to give evidence at a hearing of an authority referred to in section 2 of the Human Rights Act 1998—

(1) the authority to be cited should be an authoritative and complete report; and

(2) the party must give to the court and any other party a list of the authorities he intends to cite and copies of the reports not less than three days before the hearing.

(Section 2(1) of the Human Rights Act 1998 requires the court to take into account the authorities listed there)

(3) Copies of the complete original texts issued by the European Court and Commission either paper based or from the Court's judgment database (HUDOC), which is available on the Internet, may be used.

Footnotes

1. Rule 39.1.
2. Rule 39.2(1).
3. Rule 39.3(1).
4. Rule 39.3(2) and (3).
5. For the definition of legal representative see rule 2.3.
6. Section 9 of the Contempt of Court Act 1981.

Part 20

CODES OF PRACTICE

Press Complaints Commission Editor's Code of Practice (www.pcc.org.uk)

THE EDITORS' CODE

All members of the press have a duty to maintain the highest professional standards. The Code, which includes this preamble and the public interest exceptions below, sets the benchmark for those ethical standards, protecting both the rights of the individual and the public's right to know. It is the cornerstone of the system of self-regulation to which the industry has made a binding commitment.

It is essential that an agreed code be honoured not only to the letter but in the full spirit. It should not be interpreted so narrowly as to compromise its commitment to respect the rights of the individual, nor so broadly that it constitutes an unnecessary interference with freedom of expression or prevents publication in the public interest.

It is the responsibility of editors and publishers to apply the Code to editorial material in both printed and online versions of publications. They should take care to ensure it is observed rigorously by all editorial staff and external contributors, including non-journalists, in printed and online versions of publications.

Editors should co-operate swiftly with the PCC in the resolution of complaints. Any publication judged to have breached the Code must print the adjudication in full and with due prominence, including headline reference to the PCC.

1 Accuracy

(i) The Press must take care not to publish inaccurate, misleading or distorted information, including pictures.
(ii) A significant inaccuracy, misleading statement or distortion once recognised must be corrected, promptly and with due prominence, and - where appropriate - an apology published. In cases involving the Commission, prominence should be agreed with the PCC in advance.
(iii) The Press, whilst free to be partisan, must distinguish clearly between comment, conjecture and fact.
(iv) A publication must report fairly and accurately the outcome of an action for defamation to which it has been a party, unless an agreed settlement states otherwise, or an agreed statement is published.

2 Opportunity to reply

A fair opportunity for reply to inaccuracies must be given when reasonably called for.

3 *Privacy

(i) Everyone is entitled to respect for his or her private and family life, home, health and correspondence, including digital communications.
(ii) Editors will be expected to justify intrusions into any individual's private life without consent. Account will be taken of the complainant's own public disclosures of information.
(iii) It is unacceptable to photograph individuals in private places without their consent.

Note—Private places are public or private property where there is a reasonable expectation of privacy.

4 *Harassment

(i) Journalists must not engage in intimidation, harassment or persistent pursuit.
(ii) They must not persist in questioning, telephoning, pursuing or photographing individuals once asked to desist; nor remain on their property when asked to leave and must not follow them. If requested, they must identify themselves and whom they represent.
(iii) Editors must ensure these principles are observed by those working for them and take care not to use non-compliant material from other sources.

5 Intrusion into grief or shock

(i) In cases involving personal grief or shock, enquiries and approaches must be made with sympathy and discretion and publication handled sensitively. This should not restrict the right to report legal proceedings, such as inquests.

*(ii) When reporting suicide, care should be taken to avoid excessive detail about the method used.

6 *Children

(i) Young people should be free to complete their time at school without unnecessary intrusion.

(ii) A child under 16 must not be interviewed or photographed on issues involving their own or another child's welfare unless a custodial parent or similarly responsible adult consents.

(iii) Pupils must not be approached or photographed at school without the permission of the school authorities.

(iv) Minors must not be paid for material involving children's welfare, nor parents or guardians for material about their children or wards, unless it is clearly in the child's interest.

(v) Editors must not use the fame, notoriety or position of a parent or guardian as sole justification for publishing details of a child's private life.

7 *Children in sex cases

1. The press must not, even if legally free to do so, identify children under 16 who are victims or witnesses in cases involving sex offences.
2. In any press report of a case involving a sexual offence against a child -
   (i) The child must not be identified.
   (ii) The adult may be identified.
   (iii) The word "incest" must not be used where a child victim might be identified.
   (iv) Care must be taken that nothing in the report implies the relationship between the accused and the child.

8 *Hospitals

(i) Journalists must identify themselves and obtain permission from a responsible executive before entering non-public areas of hospitals or similar institutions to pursue enquiries.

(ii) The restrictions on intruding into privacy are particularly relevant to enquiries about individuals in hospitals or similar institutions.

9 *Reporting of Crime

(i) Relatives or friends of persons convicted or accused of crime should not generally be identified without their consent, unless they are genuinely relevant to the story.

(ii) Particular regard should be paid to the potentially vulnerable position of children who witness, or are victims of, crime. This should not restrict the right to report legal proceedings.

10 *Clandestine devices and subterfuge

(i) The press must not seek to obtain or publish material acquired by using hidden cameras or clandestine listening devices; or by intercepting private or mobile telephone calls, messages or emails; or by the unauthorised removal of documents or photographs; or by accessing digitally-held private information without consent.

(ii) Engaging in misrepresentation or subterfuge, including by agents or intermediaries, can generally be justified only in the public interest and then only when the material cannot be obtained by other means.

11 Victims of sexual assault

The press must not identify victims of sexual assault or publish material likely to contribute to such identification unless there is adequate justification and they are legally free to do so.

12 Discrimination

(i) The press must avoid prejudicial or pejorative reference to an individual's race, colour, religion, gender, sexual orientation or to any physical or mental illness or disability.

(ii) Details of an individual's race, colour, religion, sexual orientation, physical or mental illness or disability must be avoided unless genuinely relevant to the story.

13 Financial journalism

(i) Even where the law does not prohibit it, journalists must not use for their own profit financial information they receive in advance of its general publication, nor should they pass such information to others.

(ii) They must not write about shares or securities in whose performance they know that they or their close families have a significant financial interest without disclosing the interest to the editor or financial editor.

(iii) They must not buy or sell, either directly or through nominees or agents, shares or securities about which they have written recently or about which they intend to write in the near future.

14 Confidential sources

Journalists have a moral obligation to protect confidential sources of information.

15 Witness payments in criminal trials

(i) No payment or offer of payment to a witness - or any person who may reasonably be expected to be called as a witness - should be made in any case once proceedings are active as defined by the Contempt of Court Act 1981.

This prohibition lasts until the suspect has been freed unconditionally by police without charge or bail or the proceedings are otherwise discontinued; or has entered a guilty plea to the court; or, in the event of a not guilty plea, the court has announced its verdict.

*(ii) Where proceedings are not yet active but are likely and foreseeable, editors must not make or offer payment to any person who may reasonably be expected to be called as a witness, unless the information concerned ought demonstrably to be published in the public interest and there is an over-riding need to make or promise payment for this to be done; and all reasonable steps have been taken to ensure no financial dealings influence the evidence those witnesses give. In no circumstances should such payment be conditional on the outcome of a trial.

*(iii) Any payment or offer of payment made to a person later cited to give evidence in proceedings must be disclosed to the prosecution and defence. The witness must be advised of this requirement.

16 *Payment to criminals

(i) Payment or offers of payment for stories, pictures or information, which seek to exploit a particular crime or to glorify or glamorise crime in general, must not be made directly or via agents to convicted or confessed criminals or to their associates – who may include family, friends and colleagues.

(ii) Editors invoking the public interest to justify payment or offers would need to demonstrate that there was good reason to believe the public interest would be served. If, despite payment, no public interest emerged, then the material should not be published.

THE PUBLIC INTEREST

There may be exceptions to the clauses marked * where they can be demonstrated to be in the public interest.

1. The public interest includes, but is not confined to:
   (i) Detecting or exposing crime or serious impropriety.
   (ii) Protecting public health and safety.
   (iii) Preventing the public from being misled by an action or statement of an individual or organisation.
2. There is a public interest in freedom of expression itself.
3. Whenever the public interest is invoked, the PCC will require editors to demonstrate fully that they reasonably believed that publication, or journalistic activity undertaken with a view to publication, would be in the public interest.
4. The PCC will consider the extent to which material is already in the public domain, or will become so.
5. In cases involving children under 16, editors must demonstrate an exceptional public interest to over-ride the normally paramount interest of the child.

Editor's Code Book

See: www.editorscode.org.uk

BBC Code of Practice

See: www.bbc.co.uk/commissioning/tv/how-we-work/business-requirements/code-of-practice.shtml

Ofcom Broadcasting Code of Practice 2009

See: http://stakeholders.ofcom.org.uk/broadcasting/guidance/programme-guidance/bguidance/

Part 21

KEY WORDS HIGHLIGHTED IN THE CASE DIGEST

(AND SPECIFICALLY INDEXED)

Artificial
Badge of confidentiality
Bare fact of a relationship
Blackmail
Bonnard v Perryman
Brothel
Celebrity
Certain level of seriousness.
Clandestine
Code (as in a broadcasting code)
Confidential information
Confidential Schedule
Contempt
Contra mundum
Covert
Curiosity
Data Protection Act 1998
Debate Proviso
Degree of privacy.
Disembodied
Embarrassment
Fragile
Harassment
Highly Offensive
Humiliation
Interest to the public
Interesting to the public
Internet
Intimate
Intrusive
Intrusion
John Doe
Latitude
Margin of appreciation.
Narrow
Narrowly
Photograph
Pixelated
Political speech
Politician[s]

Powder dry

Prevention from Harassment Act 1997

Prior restraint

Priority

Private thoughts

Prurience

Public at large

Public domain

Public eye

Public figure

Public watchdog

Purloin/purloined/purloining.

Purpose

Quality of confidence

Relationship

Repetition

Responsible journalism

Right to impart

Reputation

Salacious

Secretly

Sensationalism

Sexual relations

Shared

Surreptitious

Target (ed)

Tipped off

Tittle tattle

Trade secrets

Trivia: ***A v B, C, & D*** [2005] EMLR 26; [2005] EWHC 1651 (QB) per Eady J para 33

Waiver ***A v B, C, & D*** [2005] EMLR 26; [2005] EWHC 1651 (QB) per Eady J

Was in the public interest

Watchdog

Zone

Zone of interaction (in *Von Hannover v. Germany*)

Part 22

CASE DIGEST

R v Legal Aid Board ex p Kaim Todner [1999] 1 QB 96 per Lord Woolf MR

41. The need to be vigilant arises from the natural tendency for the general principle to be eroded and for exceptions to grow by accretion as the exceptions are applied by analogy to existing cases. This is the reason it is so important not to forget why proceedings are required to be subjected to the **full glare of a public hearing.** It is necessary because the public nature of proceedings **deters inappropriate behaviour on** the part of the court. It also **maintains the public's confidence in the administration of justice**. It enables the public to know that justice is being administered **impartially.** It can result in **evidence becoming available** which would not become available if the proceedings were conducted behind closed doors **or with one or more of the parties' or witnesses' identity concealed**. It makes **uninformed and inaccurate comment about the proceedings less likely.** If secrecy is restricted to those situations where justice would be frustrated if the cloak of anonymity is not provided, this reduces the risk of the sanction of **contempt** having to be invoked, with the expense and the interference with the administration of justice which this can involve.

R v Broadcasting Standards Commission, ex p BBC [2001] QB 885; [2000] 3 WLR 1327 per Lord Mustill

48. I do, however, wish to emphasise the degree to which this conclusion is dependent on the language and **purpose** of this particular statute, for in general I find the concept of a company's privacy hard to grasp. **To my mind the privacy of a human being denotes at the same time the personal *"space"***

in which the individual is free to be itself, and also the *carapace*, or *shell*, or *umbrella*, or whatever other metaphor is preferred, which protects that space from intrusion. An infringement of privacy is an affront to the personality, which is damaged both **by the violation** and **by the demonstration** that the personal space is **not inviolate**. The concept is hard indeed to define, but if this gives something of its flavour I do not see how it can apply to an impersonal corporate body, which has no sensitivities to wound, and no selfhood to protect.

Attorney General v Times Newspapers Ltd [2001] EWCA Civ 97

9. When the application came before Eady J, the first variation of their undertaking for which TNL applied, was the deletion of 1(a). As I have just explained, this was a formality as the Attorney General had already agreed to it. The substantial application was that the proviso A should be varied to read as follows:

> "Provided that:
>
> A. Nothing in this undertaking prevents the Defendants or any of them from republishing anything which at the date of publication or intended publication by the Defendant or Defendants:
>
> (i) has previously been published in The Sunday Times or in any other national newspaper; or
>
> (ii) has previous been published in any newspaper, magazine or other publication generally accessible to the **public at large** whether within or outside the jurisdiction of the Court (other than in a case where the only such publication was made by or was caused by the defendants or any of them);
>
> (iii) has previously been published or made generally accessible to the **public at large** on, by or through the **internet** or other electronic medium (other than a case where the only such publication was made or was caused by the defendants or any of them)."

10. The ground for seeking this variation was succinctly explained by Mr Martin Kramer, the Defendants' solicitor, in a witness statement dated 11 January 2001:

> "As will be seen from the correspondence exhibited to this Witness Statement, the Claimant's principal concern has been that the Defendants will obtain a copy of a book written by Richard Tomlinson which deals,

inter alia, with his employment in the Secret Intelligence Service. Once Mr Tomlinson's book becomes generally available, the Defendants believe that it will have entered the **public domain** as described by Lord Goff in Spycatcher (Attorney-General v Guardian Newspapers Ltd (No 2) [1990] AC 109 at 282C-D). If the book does come into the **public domain**, the First Defendant will wish to publish extracts from it relating to Mr Tomlinson's previous employment. At present, such information is caught by the Order of Toulson J, the proviso to which is too **narrowly** drawn."

11. At that stage the attitude of the Attorney General was apparent from correspondence between the Defendants' solicitors and the Treasury Solicitor in the previous months. On 30 November 2000, the Treasury Solicitor wrote as follows:

> "My clients would be content to vary the Order to permit publication of material put into the **public domain** by others without the involvement of your clients. Your proposed variation is not, however, acceptable.
>
> It is quite possible that, even if unauthorised disclosure of damaging material occurs abroad, the material may be disclosed to a 'section of the public' so small or obscure that no, or limited, damage may have been done until the story is picked up by a national newspaper, such as those of your clients.
>
> Your paragraph (ii) is therefore not acceptable, particularly since there have been instances of information being 'trailed' in obscure publications abroad, and then picked up by national newspapers, in circumstances where there must be a strong suspicion that the trailer has been contrived for the **purpose**.
>
> In order to guard against this possibility, **my clients would be content with a variation which makes it clear that publication is permitted only where the relevant information has previously come to the widespread attention of the public at large.** I attach some suggested wording which I trust you will find acceptable.
>
> In circumstances where there was any doubt about whether the publication had been on such a scale that confidentiality had been lost, **I would suggest your clients consult with my clients, as** they did about Mr Tomlinson's **photograph**. Should your clients decide to publish material in absence of such consultation, and this resulted in a breach of the injunction, it would be for them to explain to the court what steps they had taken to ensure no such breach occurred."

12. The suggested wording varied the undertaking as follows:

> "Provided that:

A. Nothing in this undertaking prevents the defendants or any of them from republishing anything which at the date of publication or intended publication by the defendant or defendants:

(i) **has previously been published in The Sunday Times or in any other national newspaper**; or

(ii) has previously been published in any newspaper, magazine or other publication, whether within or outside the jurisdiction of the court, **in circumstances where the Defendants can demonstrate that the publication has come to the widespread attention of the public at large** (other than in a case where such publication was made by or was caused by or on behalf of the Defendants or any of them): or

(iii) has previously been published **on or through the Internet,** or other electronic medium, in circumstances where the Defendants can demonstrate **that the publication has come to the widespread attention of the public at large** (other than in a case where such publication was made or was caused by or on behalf of the Defendants or any of them)."

13. By the time this matter came before Eady J, the attitude of the Attorney General had hardened. He was no longer prepared to agree to a variation of the wording of paragraph A of the proviso to the undertaking. **This was because TNL had failed to clarify certain matters which were of concern to the Attorney General.** A witness statement from the Head of Security and Counter Intelligence of the SIS, identified only as "H", spoke of contacts that had been monitored between TNL and Mr Tomlinson. **The speculative possibility was advanced that TNL had colluded with Mr Tomlinson to arrange publication of the book in Russia and that they were seeking to found on this to get out of their undertaking to the Court.**

14. Mr Crow, for the Attorney General, argued before Eady J that the law clearly demonstrated **that a party had to show good grounds for the variation of an undertaking given to the Court.** In the absence of any satisfactory explanation of their dealings with Mr Tomlinson, he submitted that TNL were not in a position to make out a good case. The reaction of Eady J to this argument appears at page 6 of the judgment:

"I am unable to come to any conclusion as to whether Mr Crow's submissions are in fact well founded. I must, therefore, take the Sunday Times application at face value."

15. A little later he said:

"I cannot assume, as Mr Crow invites me to do, that what the Sunday Times are actually trying to do is to steal a march on their rivals so as to be first in the field."

16. I cannot see that there is anything objectionable in a newspaper trying to obtain a **scoop** ahead of its rivals, provided it acts with propriety in doing so. **It would, however, plainly have been objectionable for TNL to procure publication by others abroad of that which they had undertaken not to publish themselves in order to found an application to be released from their undertaking.**

17. Before us, Mr Tugendhat QC, for TNL, reacted to the suggestion that his clients had been guilty of such conduct with **indignation**. He submitted that it appeared to amount to an unwarranted attempt to get TNL to **disclose their sources**. However, the eve of the hearing before us TNL had served a witness statement from Nicholas Fielding, a senior reporter on The Sunday Times, which explained in detail the limited nature of TNL's continued **relationship** with Mr Tomlinson. In the light of this, Mr Crow withdrew any suggestion that TNL had acted with impropriety. He also withdrew all objection, in principle, to the grant of permission to TNL to make an appropriate variation to their undertaking. **The only remaining issue was as to the appropriate terms of the variation.** This in fact resolved into two separate issues.

18. **The first issue was the formulation of the test of the degree of publicity which would have to occur before TNL could be permitted to republish matter that had already been published elsewhere**. There was no dispute between the parties that, so far as the book was concerned, the proposed publication described by Mr Korovin would, if it took place, suffice. **But what words should be used by way of general formula to describe the sufficiency of publication, not merely in the present circumstances, but in any other circumstances which might arise in the future?**

19. The legal principles that the test should reflect were not in issue. They were established by the well-known case of *Attorney-General v Guardian Newspapers (No 2)* [1990] 1 AC 109 (*"Spycatcher"*). They can be summarised as follows.

20. A right to restrain the publication of information, however damaging that information may be, must be founded on a claim that disclosure of the information will constitute an actionable breach of confidence. **No such action will lie once the information has been published elsewhere to such a degree that it is no longer confidential.** In *Spycatcher* the information, publication of which the Attorney General sought to restrain, **had received widespread publication abroad.** It was described by the House of Lords as "world wide dissemination". The **House of Lords found that, in these circumstances, publication in the United Kingdom would not bring about any significant damage to the public interest beyond that which had already occurred.** Thus, there was no justification for restraining such publication (see, for example, the speech of Lord Keith of Kinkel at page 259). Having

regard to the widespread publicity that had occurred, there was no need in *Spycatcher* to attempt to identify a formula that would suffice to describe the point at which publication destroys the confidentiality of information. **A phrase that is often used to describe this point is that the publication has brought the information into the public domain.**

21. The relevant term of the variation that was approved by Eady J was **that the information:**

> **". . . has previously been published in any newspaper, publication, magazine or other publication generally accessible to the public at large, whether within or without the jurisdiction of the court."**

22. The Attorney General objected to this formulation on the ground that publication might take place in some organ of the media that could be said to be generally accessible to the public, but in circumstances where it was so remote as to pass essentially unnoticed. In such circumstances, confidentiality would not have been destroyed. TNL, for their part, **objected to the width** of the alternative test proposed by the Attorney General, **ie "publication has come to the widespread attention of the public at large".** Such words were not apt to describe the proposed **publication in Russia**, although it was accepted that **such publication would suffice to destroy the Attorney General's assertion of confidentiality in respect of the contents of the book.**

23. Happily, in the course of argument before us, it became apparent that there was a formula that was satisfactory to both parties, subject to one important matter. The agreed variation altered the disputed terms of the undertaking so as to read as follows:

> **"A. Nothing in this undertaking prevents the Defendants or any of them from republishing anything which at the date of publication or intended publication by the Defendant or Defendants: . . .**
>
> **(ii) has previously been published in any other newspaper, magazine or other publication, whether within or outside the jurisdiction of the Court, to such an extent that the information is in the public domain (other than in a case where the only such publication was made by or was caused by the Defendants or any of them).**
>
> **(iii) has previously been published by or through the internet or other electronic media to such an extent that the information is in the public domain (other than in a case where the only such publication was made by or was caused by the Defendants or any of them)."**

24. There remains, however, **a bone of contention**, which is quite a big bone. That is the submission by the Attorney General that the relevant formula in the proviso should be preceded by the phrase:

" . . . where the Defendants can demonstrate that . . ."

25. This phrase was first introduced into the proposed formula by the Treasury Solicitor's letter of 13 November 2000. In the last paragraph of that letter, which I have previously quoted, he made it quite clear that he was not suggesting that the proposed formula would put TNL in breach of their undertaking if they had not, before publication, demonstrated to the Attorney General or to the Court that the matter to be published had entered the **public domain**. The phrase "**the Defendants can demonstrate"** seemed to do no more than attempt to **place on TNL, should publication by them be challenged after it had taken place, the obligation to demonstrate that what they had published was in the public domain.**

26. Before Eady J, and before us, Mr Crow took a different stance. **He submitted that the proposed variation should, in effect, require TNL to get clearance from the Attorney General or the Court that anything they wished to publish was indeed in the public domain before they would be entitled to publish it.** This had the effect of rendering the proposed variation nugatory. TNL would be little, if any, better off if they remained under an obligation to get clearance from the Attorney General or the Court before publishing.

27. **Mr Tugendhat** took strong objection to this proposal on a number of grounds.

    1. He said he was taken by surprise by the Attorney General's change of stance which had come very late.

    2. **He submitted that the proposed fetter on TNL's right to publish was without precedence.**

    3. He submitted that the usual position, where there is an injunction or undertaking subject to a proviso affecting the press, **is that it is for the editor to ensure that any condition in the proviso is satisfied.** An editor who gets it wrong will be in **contempt** of Court and this will have serious implications. **Editors should be trusted to be scrupulous in observing conditions to which they are subject under an order of the Court.**

    4. The requirement that the Attorney General sought to impose was **impractical.** How was the **duty Judge** to decide, when telephoned on Saturday on the eve of publication of The Sunday Times, whether a proposed publication had or had not come into the **public domain** as a result of prior publication?

    5. Finally, Mr Tugendhat invoked Article 10 of the European Convention on Human Rights. He submitted that the clause proposed by the Attorney General would **constitute an unjustified fetter** on the right to freedom of expression to the detriment both of the newspaper, which had the **right to impart** information, and the public which had the right to receive it. He

also relied upon section 12 of the Human Rights Act 1998, the material parts of which provide as follows:

> "(1) This section applies if a court is considering whether to grant any relief which, if granted, might affect the exercise of the Convention right to freedom of expression.
>
> . . .
>
> (4) The court must have particular regard to the importance of the Convention right to freedom of expression and, where the proceedings relate to material which the respondent claims, or which appears to the court, to be journalistic, literary or artistic material (or to conduct connected with such material), to-
>
> (a) the extent to which-
>
> (i) the material has, or is about to, become available to the public; or
>
> (ii) it is, or would be, in the public interest for the material to be published."

28. Mr Tugendhat recognised that part 2 of Article 10 permits, in the circumstances there specified, restriction of the right to freedom of expression. But he submitted that the **restriction proposed by the Attorney General was disproportionate** and could not be justified in the public interest in a democratic society. In that context he referred to the decision of the European Court of Human Rights in the case of *Bladet Tromso and Stensaas v Norway* (20 May 1999) and in particular to this passage from paragraph 62 of the judgment of the court:

> "It should further be recalled that Article 10 is applicable not only to information or ideas that are favourably received or regarded as inoffensive or as a matter of indifference, but also to those that offend, shock or disturb the State or any sector of the population (see Handyside v The United Kingdom judgment of 7 December 1976). Moreover, whilst the mass media must not overstep the bounds imposed in the interests of the protection of private individuals, it is incumbent on them to impart information and ideas concerning matters of public interest. Not only does the press have the task of imparting such information and ideas: the public also has a right to receive them. Consequently, in order to determine whether the interference was based on sufficient reasons which rendered it 'necessary', regard must be had to the public-interest aspect of the case."

29. Eady J was impressed by the arguments of Mr Tugendhat. The passages of his judgment relevant to the issue before this Court are as follows (page 11):

> "I wish to make one thing very clear about the decision I am about to

make. It is not at all based on any argument to the effect that what the Sunday Times wishes to do is in the public interest. I see no evidence of that whatever. The situation is simply the other way about. It is in practical terms for the Attorney General to demonstrate, particularly perhaps in the light of the European Convention, that any restriction on freedom of expression sought to be imposed, or continued, can itself by justified by some countervailing and substantial public interest. In the light of what is today going to be readily available in the **public domain** in Russia, the United States and elsewhere in the world, I am afraid I am not persuaded that the public interest requires the Sunday Times to be restricted, for reasons based on a duty of confidence, to any greater extent than any other organ of the media. In any event, the original provisos of the 1996 order were aimed at excluding from the undertaking any information in the **public domain**. It is just that the wording was not, as both parties seem at some stages to have recognised, entirely satisfactory. It seems to be arbitrarily **narrow** by being confined to what other newspapers publish."

30. At page 14 the Judge said:

> ". . . it might appear to the casual observer that the Sunday Times is keen to jump the gun for commercial reasons, on the footing that the material is about to enter the **public domain**, and to publish on Sunday, however widespread or not the publication of the book may by then have become. I am assured by Mr Tugendhat in clear terms that this is not their intention. He has made it clear that the editor wishes to make his judgment in the light of the circumstances prevailing tomorrow, and under no greater inhibition than any other editor in a similar position."

31. At page 18, in summarising the situation, the Judge said:

> **". . . all that is in issue here before me today, important though it is, is the question of whether or not the Sunday Times should be placed on the same footing as other media organisations or continue in the somewhat artificial position in which they now find themselves for purely historical reasons."**

32. Finally, at page 19 he concluded:

> ". . . it is necessary for me to bear in mind, as was mentioned in argument, that an important part of freedom of expression is not only the freedom to publish what one wishes but the ability to publish it when one wishes to do so.
>
> Once the information does enter the **public domain**, it seems to me to be **artificial** for the law to treat the Sunday Times on any different basis

from any other paper and I will, therefore, make the variation in the proviso sought in the Sunday Times' application."

33. Mr Crow attacked the reasoning of the Judge. He submitted that TNL should be treated differently from other newspapers; they were necessarily in a different position. Proceedings had been brought against them and they had given an undertaking. Having in the past, at least on the Attorney General's case, acted in such a way to attract a special restriction on publication, there was no reason why a distinction between their position and that of other newspapers should not be continued.

34. I think it is **desirable** that there should usually be **consultation between a newspaper** and **representatives** of the **SIS** before the newspaper publishes information that may include matters **capable of damaging** the Service or endangering **those who serve in it**. I understand from Mr Tugendhat that such consultation takes place. I would hope and expect that it does**. I do not, however, think it right to impose on TNL the requirement that they should seek confirmation from the Attorney General or the Court that facts that they intend to republish have been sufficiently brought into the public domain by prior publication so as to remove from them the cloak of confidentiality.** That is a matter on which an editor will be in a position to form **his own judgment** and he should be left **responsible for exercising that judgment**. That is consonant with Article 10 of the European Convention on Human Rights and section 12 of the Act. It also avoids the procedural problems raised by Mr Tugendhat, which seem to me to be very real potential problems.

35. **The terms of the agreed variation,** excluding the additional condition that the Attorney General sought to insert, **will impose on TNL a duty to the Court to comply with the law of confidentiality, and render TNL subject to the sanctions that exist for contempt of Court should they do not do so.** I agree with Eady J that it is not appropriate that TNL should be subject to a fetter on the freedom of expression that goes beyond this.

36. Subject to amending TNL's undertaking to substitute the wording that has been agreed, I dismiss this appeal.

37. LORD JUSTICE TUCKEY: I agree.

38. LORD JUSTICE LONGMORE: I agree also.

Harris v Harris; Att-Gen v Harris [2001] 2 FLR 285 at [353]

353. The word 'lawfully' which qualifies proviso (ii) in the order made by Wilson J in the present case was not, as I have said, included in the order in *Re C (A Minor)* (unreported) 15 March 1990. It was, so far as I am aware, first adopted in about 1996. **Its purpose is said to be to prevent the republication of information published in breach of, for example, an in personam injunction.** I have some doubts as to whether this reasoning was ever sound but the point, it seems to me, is now academic. **Assuming that a public domain proviso is appropriate at all,** and as I said in *Kelly* at 93A in my judgment, **any *contra mundum* injunction should normally be qualified by such a proviso**, it seems to me to follow that **the form of the proviso should from now on be in line with that approved by the Court of Appeal in** *Attorney-General v Times Newspapers Ltd and Others* [2001] EWCA Civ 97, [2001] 1 WLR 885. I reject Miss Wood's arguments that a more limited form of proviso is appropriate.

Kelly v BBC [2001] 1 FLR 197 per Mumby J

Headnote: After the 16-year-old boy left home to join a religious group, his grandmother applied to make him a ward of court. The boy's whereabouts were not known, and the grandmother feared that he might leave the UK with members of the group. The court made the wardship order, and a seek and find order, and enlisted the help of the media in tracing the boy. **A court order gave the Official Solicitor leave to give publicity about the boy, including the disclosure of any photograph, to the press and broadcasting companies.** In response to the media campaign the boy communicated from time to time with members of the media and his grandmother, by way of email and telephone call, stating that he was happy. **The BBC approached the religious group, and obtained a telephone interview with the boy.** The BBC informed the boy's family, who obtained an **injunction restraining publication** of the interview with the boy. The **BBC applied to discharge** the injunction.

Held—discharging the injunction, granting an injunction against solicitation, and making a statement in open court seeking the further assistance of the media—

1. So long as the media **took care** to avoid any breach of the restraints imposed by the **Administration of Justice Act 1960, s 12, Children Act 1989, s 97(2)**

and Contempt of Court Act 1981, s 2, no **contempt** was committed by the media interviewing a child who was known to be a ward of court or publishing or broadcasting such an interview. **An interview by the media was not an 'important' or 'major' step in a child's life, however interesting or exciting,** therefore the media did not require the leave of the court either to interview a ward of court, or to publish or broadcast such an interview, although they could be injuncted from doing so by the court.

2. **On the basis that the boy's participation in the interview did not raise any question with respect to his upbringing, the boy's welfare was not the paramount consideration in this case**. There was no burden on the media to establish why it should be allowed to publish, and **the issues were *whether* an injunction was *necessary* to *protect* the boy from clear and *identifiable harm*, and whether the injunction sought was *proportionate* to that aim and no wider than necessary**. No convincing case had been put forward that broadcasting the interview or other further publicity was going significantly to harm the boy, and an injunction framed as widely as that which the court was being invited to make would be wholly disproportionate to any aim that could legitimately be pursued on the boy's behalf. There was a **clear public interest in the boy's story, and in the interview,** and a particular **public interest in the media being encouraged to assist the court in cases such as this** in which the court had itself sought to enlist the media's assistance. In the circumstances, it would not be appropriate to restrain the media from publishing comments by other people about the boy.

Per curiam:

1. Even if some organs of the media were represented when an injunction ***contra mundum*** was granted, **the injunction would necessarily** still have been **granted ex parte**, or without notice, **to all the other organs of the media** *upon whom it might eventually be served.* **Every injunction *contra mundum* therefore had to be treated as if it were an ex parte injunction granted without notice.**
2. The following principles applied **to all without notice injunctions,** including cases relating to children in which injunctive relief was sought against third parties or the world at large.
3. **Any ex parte order containing injunctions should set out on its face, either by way of recital or in a schedule, a list of all affidavits, witness statements and other evidential materials read by the judge.**
4. The applicant's legal representatives should, whenever possible, **liaise** with the associate with a view to ensuring that the order as drawn contained this information.
5. **On receipt of the order** from the court, the applicant's legal representa-

tives should satisfy themselves **that the order as drawn correctly set out** the relevant information and, if it did not, should take **urgent steps** to have the order amended under the **slip rule**. The applicant's legal representatives should respond forthwith to any **reasonable request from the party injuncted** or his legal representatives, either for copies of the materials read by the judge or for information about what took place at the hearing. Persons injuncted ex parte were **entitled to proper information about the hearing**, and at the very least to be told, if they asked, ***exactly*** what *documents, bundles* or *other evidential materials* were lodged with the court either before or during the course of the hearing and what *legal authorities* were cited to the judge. It would be prudent for those acting for applicants in such cases to keep a *proper note* of proceedings, lest they find themselves embarrassed by a proper request for information which they were unable to find**. In urgent cases**, such as the instant case, in which there was no time to prepare comprehensive evidence in proper form, the court must act upon the information provided by counsel, but in every such case there should be an **undertaking to swear and file an affidavit** as soon as possible. **On the principles of natural justice, it would be wrong for a judge to be given material at a without notice hearing which would not at a later stage be revealed to the persons affected by the result of the application.** In children cases this rule was qualified, but there was no justification for not making **full disclosure to the media** of the material upon which an injunction ***contra mundum*** **had** been granted. **If, as would often be the case it was not appropriate for the media to see the material in the form in which it was originally filed with the court, the solution was to set out the relevant material in a separate affidavit which could be shown to the media, and this should be done even if there appeared to be no immediate likelihood of there being an application to discharge the injunction.** An injunction in rem or ***contra mundum*** should normally be qualified by a **public domain** proviso.

Dicta of Mumby J:

(iii) The public domain proviso

A question was raised as to whether, if I granted an injunction in the terms of either limb of para (1) of the draft, it should be **qualified by a proviso** making it clear that the injunction does not of itself prevent the further publication of material already in the **public domain.**

In the light of my conclusions this question does not arise for decision, but it is, I think, appropriate that I should indicate my views on it.

In **Re C (unreported)** 15 March 1990 Sir Stephen Brown, the President, was concerned with an application for an **injunction** ***contra mundum*** the **purpose** of which was in part to prevent the re-publication in the media of material **which**

had been the subject of extensive media coverage some 18 months previously. In his judgment the President said:

> '[Counsel] points out that a restriction on the publication of information already in the **public domain** directly raises the conflict between the interests of the person whom it is sought to protect and the interests of what is termed "freedom of speech". He has submitted that in carrying out a balancing exercise between these two competing interests, the court has to be very careful not to restrict too severely the publication of information which is already available.
>
> There is a risk that the minor C may suffer harm if the press or other organs of the media revive the publication of information, and more particularly pictures, which have already been published. On the other hand it would be taking a very strong line indeed if a court were to seek to restrict the media from publishing information which they have lawfully published in the past and which remains on their files and is readily available to members of the public, for example in libraries.'

And a little later he said:

> '**I do not find it possible to say that there should be a restriction on the publication of information or pictures already in the public domain.** It has been urged upon me that certain passages in the speeches of their Lordships in the "Spycatcher" case *The Attorney General v Guardian Newspapers Ltd (No 2)* [1990] 1 AC 109 relating to the publication of information generally are not strictly relevant to this case, because the circumstances are very different.
>
> 'The important matter in this case which has to be borne in mind is that information which has already been published is already lawfully available to persons in this country. I do not think that it would be appropriate for the court to attempt to prevent the re-publication of such information, although it may deprecate the way in which that may be done. Nevertheless there is an important principle to be borne in mind concerning the preservation of freedom of speech.'

Following that judgment it became, as I understand it, a general, though by no means the invariable, practice to **qualify injunctions *contra mundum* with a public domain proviso**.

A similar point arose recently before Charles J in *A v M (Family Proceedings: Publicity)* [2000] 1 FLR 562. That, as I have already observed, was not a case of an injunction ***contra mundum*** but a case where an injunction in personam was granted at the suit of one parent of the child against the other. Having said at 565D that:

> '. . . the **repetition** of material that has been placed in the **public domain** can be damaging to a child,'

Charles J declined to qualify the injunction which he granted with a **public domain** proviso, explaining, at 565D and again at 570F, that the injunction he was granting was not based upon duties of confidentiality. It appears that Charles J was not referred to the President's earlier decision, where, it will be recalled, the President had in fact been addressed on the difference between the injunctions he was being invited to grant in that case and injunctions based on duties of confidentiality.

Mr Murdoch says I should follow Charles J. Mr Tugendhat, supported on this point by Mr Kirk, says that I should follow the President. **Mr Kirk accepts that, if I am to grant an injunction, it should be qualified by a public domain proviso.**

I am far from saying that there is necessarily any conflict between *Re C* (unreported) 15 March 1990 and *A v M (Family Proceedings: Publicity)* [2000] 1 FLR 562. **The one deals with injunctions *contra mundum*, the other with an injunction in personam, and it may be that in this respect there is this distinction between them**. Be that as it may, it seems to me, as it seemed to the President in *Re C* (unreported) 15 March 1990, and for very much the same reasons, **that an injunction in rem or *contra mundum* should normally be qualified with a public domain proviso.** There is, after all, something rather odd about trying to restrain the world at large from publishing material which, being in the **public domain**, is already available to the world at large.

Accordingly, on this point I agree with Mr Tugendhat and Mr Kirk.

Thomas v News Group Newspapers and Hughes [2001] EWCA 1233

The respondent's Statement of Case, based on these publications, reads as follows:

"1. On Thursday 6 July the Sun Newspapers, owned and controlled by News Group International Ltd, published an article ('the article') written by Simon Hughes, which names the Claimant, Esther Thomas, and described her as a 'black clerk'. The article was entitled 'Beyond a Joke' and said that there was 'fury as police sarges are busted after refugee jest'. The police officers, both dads of two, were 'carpeted by bosses after a black clerk at their station complained about the treatment of a Somalia woman. . . . '.

2. The article stated that the incident occurred at Bishopsgate police station.

3. The article amounted to **harassment** of the Claimant and caused her distress and anxiety.

4. The article was followed by a further article on 12 July in which it was stated

that the newspaper's readers were 'furious' over the story. The newspaper received a lot of furious letters from its furious readers. Bishopsgate police station received race hate mail (three letters) addressed to Esther Thomas the same day.

5. Simon Hughes of The Sun wrote a third article on 14 July which was featured on the front page of the newspaper which stated that the police officers **'were hauled in front of a disciplinary tribunal after a black clerk complained of a series of exchanges. . . .** ' The Sun stated that its readers could help one of the racist police officers by helping to pay off her disciplinary fine; to write a cheque to 'The Sun WPC Fine Fund NGN Ltd'.

6. The articles written by Mr Hughes, approved of by the Editor and published by the newspaper amount to a course of conduct which amounts to **harassment of the Claimant**. The article was written in an indignant tone which was designed to elicit a reaction.

7. The course of conduct **caused the Claimant to be harassed by the Sun's readers.** The course of conduct of itself amounted to **harassment.** The Claimant claims damages for breach of section 3 of the **Protection from Harassment Act 1997.**

8. The course of conduct was not reasonable. **The Claimant did not have to be described as being black nor should her name and place of work be published.** The facts stated in the articles were **not accurate**. In fact, the police officers were found guilty of race discrimination after both the Claimant and PC Bidmead, and others, gave evidence against the officers. **The article incited racial hatred.**

9. The articles caused the Claimant to be **terrified and scared** to go to work. She felt **vulnerable** to being physically attacked at work or en route to and from work. The Claimant has since transferred by her own choice to a new place of work."

. . .

21. **The importance that the Strasbourg court attaches to freedom of expression** can be satisfactorily illustrated by this typical passage from the judgment of the court in *Nilsen and Johnsen v Norman* (1999) 30 EHRR 878 at paragraph 43:

> "According to the Court's well-established case law, freedom of expression **constitutes one of the essential foundations of a democratic society** and one of the **basic conditions for its progress** and for each individual's **self-fulfilment**. Subject to Article 10(2), it is applicable not only to 'information' of 'ideas' that are favourably received or regarded as inoffensive or as a matter of indifference, but also those that **offend**, **shock** or **disturb**. Such are **the demands of that pluralism, tolerance**

and broadmindedness without which there is no 'democratic society'. As set forth in Article 10, this freedom is subject to exceptions which must, however, be construed **strictly**, and the need for any restrictions must be established **convincingly.**

The test of **'necessity in a democratic society'** requires the Court to determine whether the **'interference'** corresponded to a **'pressing social need'**, whether it was **proportionate** to the **legitimate aim** pursued and whether the reasons given by the national authorities to justify it are relevant and sufficient."

22 Strasbourg rightly considers that these principles are **of particular importance** where the **freedom of the press** is in play, as is apparent from the following passage, again typical, from the judgment of the Strasbourg court in *Observer and Guardian v United Kingdom* (1999) 14 EHRR 152 at paragraph 59:

"These principles are of particular importance as far as the press is concerned. Whilst it must not overstep the bounds set, inter alia, in the **'interests of national security'** or for **'maintaining the authority of the judiciary**,' it is nevertheless incumbent on it to impart information and ideas on matters of public interest. Not only does the press have the task of imparting such information and ideas: **the public also has a right to receive them.** Were it otherwise, the press would be unable to play its vital role of **'public watchdog'."**

23. Even before the HRA was enacted, English jurisprudence recognised that the principles set out above applied equally in our domestic law: *Attorney-General v Guardian Newspapers Ltd (No 2)* [1990] 1 AC 109, 283–4 per Lord Goff of Chieveley; *Derbyshire CC v Times Newspapers Ltd* [1993] AC 534 at 550–1 per Lord Keith of Kinkel. More recently Lord Steyn made these observations in *Reg v Home Secretary, Ex p Simms* [2000] AC 126:

"**Freedom of expression** is, of course, intrinsically important: it is valued for its own sake. But it is well recognised that it is also instrumentally important. **It serves** a number of broad objectives. **First**, it promotes the self-fulfilment of individuals in society. **Secondly**, in the famous words of Holmes J (echoing John Stuart Mill), **'the best test of truth is the power of the thought to get itself accepted in the competition of the market:'** Abrams v United States (1919) 250 US, 616, 630 per Holmes J (dissenting).

Thirdly, freedom of speech is the **lifeblood of democracy.** The free flow of information and ideas informs political **debate**. It is a safety valve; people are more ready to accept decisions that go against them if they can in principle seek to influence them**. It acts as a brake on the abuse**

of power by public officials. It facilitates the **exposure of errors** in the **governance** and **administration** of justice of the country."

24. Section 3 of the HRA requires the court, so far as it is possible to do so, to interpret and give effect to legislation in a manner which is compatible with Convention rights. Section 12 of the HRA emphasises the care which the court must take not to interfere with journalistic freedom unless satisfied that this is necessary according to the principles to which I have referred. **Both these sections are important when considering the ambit of the criminal offence and the *civil tort of* harassment *created by the 1997 Act* in the context of publications by the media. Harassment** *must not be given an interpretation* which restricts the right of freedom of expression, save in so far as this is necessary in order to achieve a legitimate aim. When considering that question, the court is required by section 2 of the HRA to have regard to the Strasbourg jurisprudence.

25. The appellants have also referred us to extracts from United States decisions in relation to the First Amendment to their constitution. They illustrate the very robust approach that the Supreme Court has shown in upholding freedom of speech. The facts and issues in the cases in question were, however, very different from those which we have to address. **Nor is it right to equate the principles that the Supreme Court has developed when considering the First Amendment to the jurisprudence of the Strasbourg court when considering the Convention right of freedom of expression.** On this appeal I have not found that the American jurisprudence affords any assistance that is not available on this side of the Atlantic.

26. Both parties to this appeal recognise the importance of the right of **freedom of expression** and, in particular, **press freedom**. Both parties recognise that the duty to give effect to this right is an important consideration to any court **when considering whether an offence or civil tort has been committed contrary to the 1997 Act.**

. . .

37. It is not necessary for this court to rule on Mr Pannick's example, nor to attempt any categorisation of the types of abuse of freedom of the press which may amount to **harassment**. **That is because the parties are agreed that the publication of press articles calculated to incite racial hatred of an individual provides an example of conduct which is capable of amounting to harassment under the 1997 Act.** In so agreeing, Mr Browne recognises that the Convention right of freedom of expression **does not extend to protect remarks directly against the Convention's underlying values** (see *Jersild v Denmark* (1994) 19 EHRR paragraph 35 and *Lehideux and Isorni v France* (1998) 30 EHRR paragraph 53.

Douglas v Hello! Ltd (No 1) [2001] QB 967

82. An English judge interpreting the Act and the Convention is therefore confronted with something of a dilemma. On the one hand, Article 8(1) of the Convention appears to create a right, exercisable against all the world, to respect for private and family life. On the other hand, Article 8(2) of the Convention, Section 8 of the Act, and the general philosophy of both the Convention and the Act (namely that these rights are enforceable only against public authorities), **all appear to water down the value of the right created by Article 8(1).**

83. In a series of decisions the European Court of Human Rights has addressed this dilemma by relying on the positive duty imposed on the member states by Article 1 of the Convention (see paragraph 80 above). **A vivid example of this technique at work** can be seen in the judgment of the court in *A v United* Kingdom 27 EHRR 611 when it was concerned with a complaint under Article 3 by a boy who had been hit by his stepfather with a garden cane. The court said at paras 21–22:

> "The Court considers that treatment of this kind reaches the level of severity prohibited by Article 3. It remains to be determined whether the State should be held responsible, under Article 3, for the beating of the applicant by his stepfather. The Court considers that the obligation on the High Contracting parties under Article 1 of the Convention to secure to everyone within their jurisdiction the rights and freedoms defined in the Convention, taken together with Article 3, required States to take measures designed to ensure that individuals within their jurisdiction are not subjected to torture or inhuman or degrading treatment or punishment, including such ill-treatment administered by private individuals."

84. In other words, the court was saying that the boy had the right under Article 3 not to be subjected to inhuman or degrading treatment or punishment, and although it was his stepfather who had administered the treatment which breached that right, he was entitled to make a complaint against the state for its failure, in breach of Article 1, to secure his Article 3 right.

85. From time to time the court at **Strasbourg has adopted a similar approach** when applicants have complained to it that their Article 8(1) right to respect for their private and family life has been violated. Examples can be seen in *Airey v Ireland* 2 EHRR 305 paras 22 and 23, *X and Y v The Netherlands* 8 EHRR 235 paras 23 and 27, *Stjerna v Finland* 24 EHRR 194 para 38, *Lopez Ostra v Spain* 20 EHRR 277, paras 51 and 55, and *Botta v Italy* 26 EHRR 241 paras 33 and 34. In *X and Y v The Netherlands* the court said at para 23:

> "The Court recalls that although the object of Article 8 is essentially that of protecting the individual **against arbitrary interference by the public authorities,** it does not merely compel the State to abstain from such interference: in addition to this primarily negative obligation, **there may be positive obligations inherent in an effective respect for family life.** These obligations may involve the adoption of measures designed to secure respect for private life even in the sphere of the relations of individuals between themselves."

86. In *A v United Kingdom* it was the deficiencies of the common law, in relation to the physical chastisement of children, which led the court to conclude that the United Kingdom had violated the Convention. This country **narrowly** escaped a similar finding by the European Commission on Human Rights in the *Spencer* case. **A photograph of Lady Spencer had been taken with a telephoto lens while she was walking in the grounds of a private clinic at which she was receiving treatment. This photograph was published under the caption:**

> "SO THIN: Victoria walks in the clinic grounds this week".

Relying on the decision of this court in *Kaye v Robertson* , she did not pursue a claim in the English courts, but the Commission held that she should have pursued her remedies in these courts first. **It appears that the eloquence of the advocate for the United Kingdom government persuaded the Commission that English law provided her with a potentially satisfactory remedy in an action for breach of confidence.**

87. In this respect the Commission relied heavily on the strong and detailed case of the applicants in the domestic proceedings which pointed to their former friends as the direct source of the essential **confidential information** that had been published. Its determination ended in these terms:

> "Accordingly, the Commission considers that the parties' submissions indicate that the remedy of breach of confidence (against the newspapers and their sources) was available to the applicants and that the applicants have not demonstrated that it was insufficient or ineffective in the circumstances of their cases. It considers that, insofar as relevant doubts remain concerning the financial awards to be made following a finding of a breach of confidence, **they are not such as to warrant a conclusion that the breach of confidence action is ineffective or insufficient but rather a conclusion that the matter should be put to the domestic courts for consideration in order to allow those courts, through the common law system in the United Kingdom, the opportunity to develop existing rights by way of interpretation."**

88. **The Commission appears to be saying that since the authorities in this**

country have been content to leave it to the judges to develop the law in this sensitive field, it is the judges who must develop the law so that it gives appropriate recognition to Article 8(1) rights. Whether they do so in future by an extension of the existing frontiers of the law of confidence, or by recognising the existence of new **relationships** which give rise to enforceable legal rights (as has happened in relation to the law of negligence ever since the 3–2 decision of the House of Lords in *Donoghue v Stevenson* [1932] AC 562) is not for this court, on this occasion, to predict. **The versatility of the common law to adapt to new situations was well described by Scott LJ in Haseldine v Daw [1941] 2 KB 343, 362–3:**

> "The common law has throughout its long history developed as an organic growth, at first slowly under the hampering restrictions of legal forms of process, more quickly in Lord Mansfield's time, and in the last one hundred years at an ever-increasing rate of progress as new cases, arising under new conditions of society, of applied science, and of public opinion, have presented themselves for solution by the courts."

89. **Recent annual reports of the Law Commission show how successive Governments have been content to leave the development of the law in these fields to the judges.** As long ago as 1981 the Law Commission recommended to Parliament that the law of confidence should be reformed and codified (see its report on Breach of Confidence (1981) Law Com No 110), but although this recommendation was accepted by a former Government it was never implemented. The Commission's 1998 annual report (Law Com No 258, p 5) describes how in 1998, following the *Spencer* decision, a new Government rejected that report "because developing case law since its publication had clarified the scope and extent of the breach of confidence action, as confirmed by the European Commission on Human Rights".

90. In its 1993 Annual Report (Law Com No 223, p 25) the Commission described how one of the Commissioners had recently assisted in the preparation of a Government consultation paper on the infringement of privacy (which did not lead to the enactment of legislation). The Commission's anxieties, if the law of privacy was put on a statutory basis but not the law of confidence, were clearly articulated in paragraph 2.25 of that report. In the event, the executive and the legislature took the line of least resistance and left the development of both these fields of law to the judiciary, and that is how matters now stand. That members of the Appellate Committee of the House of Lords are uneasy about the present condition of our law is evident from the observations of Lord Browne-Wilkinson and Lord Nicholls in *R v Khan* [1997] AC 558, 571A–D and 582G–583A. On other occasions during the last 20 years some of our most senior judges have underlined the importance of the right to privacy: see Lord Scarman in *Morris v Beardmore* [1981] AC 446, 464C

("fundamental"), Lord Denning MR in *Schering Chemicals v Falkman* [1982] QB 1, 21C ("fundamental") and Lord Keith of Kinkel in *Attorney-General v Guardian Newspapers Ltd (No 2)* [1990] QB 109, 255 ("clearly one which the law should in this field seek to protect").

91. One difficulty which will confront the courts when they have to tackle this problematic issue head-on is that Article 1 of the Convention, on which a state's positive duty is founded when it is brought before the international court which has the duty of enforcing member states' duties under the Convention, does not find its way into the Schedule to the Human Rights Act 1998 which sets out the "Convention rights" referred to in Sections 2, 3, 4, 6 and 7 of the Act. **On the other hand, when a court determines a question which has arisen in connection with a Convention right, it must take into account any relevant judgment of the European Court of Human Rights (Section 2(1)(a)), and those judgments have made it clear that the law-making body of the member states has the positive duty identified in the judgments to which I have referred.** Where Parliament in this country has been so obviously content to leave the development of the law to the judges, it might seem strange if the absence of Article 1 from our national statute relieved the judges from taking into account the positive duties identified by the court at Strasbourg when they develop the common law. In this judgment, however, I have the luxury of identifying difficult issues: I am not obliged to solve them.

92. One matter, however, is clear, and this makes the task of the court that much easier on the present occasion. One of the Law Commission's anxieties in 1993 was that the law might develop in such a way that breaches of privacy, but not breaches of confidence, would be subject to statutory defences which the common law had not yet clearly recognised. In this respect, at least, Parliament has now intervened to provide that where proceedings relate to material which the respondent claims, or which appears to the court, to be journalistic, literary or artistic material, the court must have regard, among other things, to any relevant privacy code (Section 12(4)). **In this context we were shown by Mr Tugendhat the Code of Practice ratified by the Press Complaints Commission in November 1997, which states that all members of the press have a duty to maintain the highest professional and ethical standards, and that the code sets the benchmarks for those standards: "It both protects the rights of the individual and upholds the public's right to know".**

93. The code covers 16 discrete topics, the third of which is "Privacy". This is one of the topics where the code makes clear that there may be exceptions to the rules set out in the code where they can be demonstrated to be in the public interest. This phrase is said to include

(i) detecting or exposing crime or a serious misdemeanour;

(ii) protecting public health and safety; and

(iii) preventing the public from being misled by some statement or action of an individual or organisation. The rules on privacy are disarmingly simple:

"3. Privacy

(i) Everyone is entitled to respect for his or her private and family life, home, health and correspondence. A publication will be expected to justify **intrusions** into any individual's private life without consent;

(ii) The use of long lens photography to take pictures of people in private places without their consent is unacceptable.

Note—Private places are public or private property where there is a reasonable expectation of privacy."

94. It appears to me that the existence of these statutory provisions, coupled with the current wording of the relevant privacy code, mean that in any case where the court is concerned with issues of freedom of expression in a journalistic, literary or artistic context, it is bound to pay particular regard to any breach of the rules set out in Clause 3 of the code, especially where none of the public interest claims set out in the preamble to the code is asserted. **A newspaper which flouts Section 3 of the code is likely in those circumstances to have its claim to an entitlement to freedom of expression trumped by Article 10(2) considerations of privacy**. Unlike the court in *Kaye v Robertson*, Parliament recognised that it had to acknowledge the importance of the Article 8(1) respect for private life, and it was able to do so untrammelled by any concerns that the law of confidence might not stretch to protect every aspect of private life.

95. **It follows that on the present occasion it is not necessary to go beyond Section 12 of the 1998 Act and Clause 3 of the Press Complaints Commission's code to find the ground rules by which we should weigh the competing considerations of freedom of expression on the one hand and privacy on the other.** So far as privacy is concerned, the case of the first and second claimants is not a particularly strong one. They did not choose to have a private wedding, attended by a few members of their family and a few friends, in the normal sense of the words "private wedding". There is nothing in the court's papers to belie the suggestion at page 88 of the disputed Issue 639 of Hello! that they invited 250 guests, and the trappings of privacy in this context are identical with the trappings of confidentiality to which I have alluded earlier in this judgment. Although by clause 6 of their agreement with OK! they undertook to use their best efforts to ensure that their guests "shall not publish and/or broadcast . . . or write any article about, or give any extended comment, report or interview to any media concerning the Wedding", there is

no evidence before the court which shows that they took any steps to enforce that undertaking, so far as their guests were concerned.

96. Mr Carr did not seek to have recourse to any public interest defence, and I did not obtain any assistance from his citation of the very general principles stated by members of this court in *Woodward v Hutchins* [1977] 1 WLR 760, a case which preceded modern developments in practice (at any rate in the Queen's Bench Division) in relation to breach of confidence claims and which was concerned with the appropriateness of an injunction framed in astonishingly wide terms. Either the claimants will establish at trial that this particular occasion successfully retained the necessary indicia of confidentiality, **so far as the taking of photographic images is concerned**, or they will not. I do not consider that their privacy-based case, as distinct from their confidentiality-based case, adds very much. **I am satisfied, however, that on the present untested evidence the claimants are "likely to establish that publication should not be allowed" on confidentiality grounds**. This is not, however, the end of the matter, as I must turn to other factors affecting the balance.

. . .

LORD JUSTICE KEENE:

The Approach at this stage:

145. This appeal concerns an interlocutory injunction which has been granted in the High Court in advance of any trial of the issues in the case. That is a statement of the obvious, but it is nonetheless important, because it affects the approach to be adopted by a court. In most situations where such an injunction is sought, the court would be concerned merely with whether there was a serious issue to be tried and, if so, with the balance of convenience: *American Cyanamid v Ethicon Ltd* [1975] AC 396. However, in the present case that cannot be the appropriate approach, and neither party seeks to maintain that it is.

146. First, this is a case which falls within the principles established by this court in *Cambridge Nutrition Ltd v BBC* [1990] 3 All ER 523. In the words of Kerr LJ in that case: "**The subject matter concerns the right to publish an article, or to transmit a broadcast, whose importance may be transitory but whose impact depends on timing, news value and topicality**". p 535

147. **In such cases, the parties are principally interested in the grant or refusal of the interlocutory injunction, even though the damages claim may well remain as a secondary objective.** In such circumstances, the court must look beyond conventional *American Cyanamid* principle and seek to discern where the balance of justice lies. The present proceedings, where both OK!

magazine and Hello! magazine are published weekly, are undoubtedly concerned with material whose **topicality is of the essence.**

148. Secondly, **this court is required by section 12(1)** of the Human Rights Act 1998 to apply section 12(3) thereof.. Section 12(1) states:

> "This section applies if a court is considering whether to grant any relief which, if granted, might affect the exercise of the Convention right to freedom of expression."

It is then provided by section 12(3):

> "No such relief is to be granted so as to restrain publication before trial **unless the court** is satisfied that the applicant is **likely to establish** that publication should not be allowed."

149. It is not in dispute that section 12(3) is applicable in this case. Mr Tugendhat's submission is that the phrase "likely to establish" does not mean "more probable than not", because that interpretation in certain circumstances could bring it into conflict with the European Convention on Human Rights itself by giving **priority** to Article 10, the right to freedom of expression, over Article 8, the right to respect for private and family life. Such an automatic **priority**, it is said, would not be in conformity with the Convention. Since section 3(1) of the Human Rights Act requires the court to construe legislation in a way which is compatible with the Convention rights "so far as it is possible to do so", section 12(3) itself must be read in a way which avoids giving precedence to Article 10 rights. It is argued on behalf of the claimants that the words "likely to establish" in that subsection should be taken to mean "not fanciful" or "on the cards".

150. For my part, I do not accept that there is any need for conflict between the normal meaning to be attached to the words in section 12(3) and the Convention. **The subsection does not seek to give a priority to one Convention right over another. It is simply dealing with the interlocutory stage of proceedings and with how the court is to approach matters at that stage in advance of any ultimate balance being struck between rights which may be in potential conflict.** ***It requires the court to look at the merits of the case and not merely to apply the American Cyanamid test.*** **Thus the court has to look ahead to the ultimate stage and to be satisfied that the scales are likely to come down in the applicant's favour.** That does not conflict with the Convention, since it is merely requiring the court to apply its mind to how one right is to be balanced, **on the merits** against another right, without building in additional weight on one side. In a situation such as the one postulated by Mr Tugendhat, where the non-Article 10 right is of fundamental importance to the individual, such as the Article 2 right to life, the merits will include not merely the evidence about how great is the risk of that right being breached,

but also a consideration of the gravity of the consequences for an applicant if the risk materialises. The nature of the risk is part of the merits, just as it would be at trial when the balance had to be struck. That is as relevant at the interlocutory stage as it would be at trial. But that does not require any strained interpretation of section 12(3).

151. Certainly section 12(3) is making **prior restraint** (ie before trial) more difficult in cases where the right to freedom of expression is engaged than where it is not. That is not a novel concept in English law. **As was said by Laws J. in R v Advertising Standards Authority Ltd, ex parte Vernons Organisation Ltd [1992] 1 WLR 1289, at 1293 A–B: "there is a general principle in our law that the expression of opinion and the conveyance of information will not be restrained by the courts *save on pressing grounds.*** Freedom of expression is as much a sinew of the common law as it is of the European Convention for the Protection of Human Rights and Fundamental Freedoms."

152. Perhaps more to the point, the jurisprudence of the European Court of Human Rights is generally hostile to **prior restraint** by the courts. **Prior restraints** on publication are not prohibited by the Convention, as the European Court made clear in *The Observer and the Guardian v United Kingdom* [1992] 14 EHRR 153, the "Spycatcher" case, but in that same case it went on to say: **"**On the other hand, the **dangers inherent in prior restraints** are such that they call for the **most careful scrutiny** on the part of the court**.** This is especially so as far **as the press is concerned, for news is a perishable commodity** and to delay its publication, even for a short period, **may well deprive it of all its value and interest."** (p.191)

153. It is impossible to accept that a statutory provision requiring a court to consider the merits of the case and to be satisfied that the balance is likely to be struck in favour of the applicant before **prior restraint** is to be granted is incompatible with the Convention. It follows that no strained reading of the language of section 12(3) is needed to render it compatible with Convention rights. The wording can be given its normal meaning. **Consequently the test to be applied at this stage is whether this court is satisfied that the applicant is likely to establish at trial that publication should not be allowed. *Even then, there remains a discretion in the court.***

Bensaid v UK [2001] 33 EHRR 205

42. **The applicant complained that the expulsion would violate his right to respect for private life guaranteed under Article 8 of the Convention.**

46. Not every act or measure which adversely affects moral or physical integrity

will interfere with the right to respect to private life guaranteed by Article 8. However, the Court's case-law does not exclude that treatment which does not reach the severity of Article 3 treatment may nonetheless breach Article 8 in its private-life aspect **where there are sufficiently adverse effects on physical and moral integrity** (see *Costello-Roberts v the United Kingdom*, judgment of 25 March 1993, Series A no 247-C, pp 60–61, § 36).

47. **"Private life" is a broad term not susceptible to exhaustive definition. The** Court has already held that elements such as **gender identification, name** and **sexual orientation and sexual life** are important elements of the personal sphere protected by Article 8 (see, for example, *Dudgeon v the United Kingdom*, judgment of 22 October 1981, Series A no 45, pp 18–19, § 41; *B. v France*, judgment of 25 March 1992, Series A no 232-C, pp 53–54, § 63; *Burghartz v Switzerland*, judgment of 22 February 1994, Series A no 280-B, p 28, § 24; and *Laskey, Jaggard and Brown v the United Kingdom*, judgment of 19 February 1997, *Reports* 1997-I, p 131, § 36). **Mental health** must also be regarded as a crucial part of private life associated with the aspect of moral integrity. Article 8 protects a **right to identity and personal development**, and the **right to establish and develop relationships with other human beings and the outside world** (see, for example, *Burghartz*, cited above, opinion of the Commission, p 37, § 47, and *Friedl v Austria*, judgment of 31 January 1995, Series A no 305-B, p 20, § 45). **The preservation of mental stability is in that context an indispensable precondition to effective enjoyment of the right to respect for private life.**

Attorney General v Punch Ltd [2002] UKHL 50

LORD HOPE OF CRAIGHEAD

My Lords,

86. In this case the Attorney General invokes the inherent jurisdiction of the court to ensure the effective administration of justice. The relief which he seeks is punishment of the publisher ("the company") and the editor of "Punch" magazine ("the respondent") for **contempt** of court. The **contempt** which they are alleged to have committed was causing an article to be published containing material which the court had by means of interlocutory injunctions made clear that it intended was not to be published. **The injunctions were pronounced in proceedings to which neither the company nor the respondent were a party.** But that is not an obstacle to a finding that they were in **contempt**. The Attorney General's contention is that **their actions impeded or interfered with the administration of justice by the court** in the

proceedings in which the orders were made. He says that their actions did so by **thwarting or undermining the** intended effect of the injunctions.

87. The essential distinction between the liability of a party to the litigation for **contempt** of court and that of a third party was explained by Lord Oliver of Aylmerton in *Attorney General v Times Newspapers Ltd* [1992] 1 AC 191, 217F-218B. Where the alleged contemnor **is a party** to the litigation and bound by the order or is someone acting for him or at his direction, **all that has to be proved is that the order was served on that person and that he has done that which the order has prohibited.** But where it is alleged that **a stranger** to the litigation is in **contempt** the position is different. As Salmon LJ said in *Jennison v Baker* [1972] 2 QB 52, 61, **the public at large** no less than the individual litigant have **a very real interest in justice being effectively administered**. The power to commit for **contempt** ensures that acts and words tending to obstruct the administration of justice are prohibited. **So a stranger is liable for contempt if his act constitutes a wilful interference with the administration of justice by the court in the proceedings in which the order was made. *It has also to be shown there was an intention*** on his part to interfere with or impede the administration of justice. This is an essential ingredient, and it has to be established to the **criminal standard of proof**. But the **intent** need not be stated expressly or admitted by the defendant. As is the case where the question of intention, or mens rea, arises in criminal cases, it **can be inferred from all the circumstances including the forseeability of the consequences of the defendant's conduct**: *Attorney General v Newspaper Publishing plc* [1988] Ch 333, 374–375, per Sir John Donaldson MR

88. The interlocutory injunctions were pronounced on by Hooper J on 4 September 1997 in proceedings by the Attorney General against, first, David Michael Shayler and, second, Associated Newspapers Limited. Their effect was to continue interlocutory injunctions which had been obtained from Keene J on 30 August 1997. Neither Mr Shayler nor Associated Newspapers appeared when the action came before Hooper J, **but solicitors for Associated Newspapers had written a letter consenting to the order which Hooper J subsequently made against them.** The two orders were in similar terms, but the order which is most directly in point in this case is that which was pronounced against Associated Newspapers. Hooper J ordered that it be restrained:

> "until further order, whether by itself, its servants or agents or otherwise howsoever from publishing to any person any information obtained by it from the first defendant and obtained by the first defendant in the course of or as a result of his employment in and position as a member of the Security Service, whether in relation to the work of, or in support

of, the security and intelligence services or otherwise; provided that this order does not apply to: (1) any information in respect of which the plaintiff (whether at the request of [the defendants or any of them] or any third party, or of his own motion) makes a statement in writing (either personally or by the Treasury Solicitor) that such information is not information in respect of which the Crown seeks to restrain publication; (2) the **repetition** of information disclosed in 'The Mail on Sunday' on 24 August 1997."

89. The respondent was the **editor** of "Punch" when an article containing the relevant material was published in issue 111 of the magazine on 26 July 2000. Neither he nor the company **disputed the fact** that they were **aware of the terms** of the interlocutory injunctions. The principal issues at the trial were whether it had been proved to the **criminal standard of proof** that the **actus reus** of **contempt** had been committed by them and, as to **mens rea**, that **the conduct complained of was specifically intended to impede or prejudice the administration of justice.**

90. The trial judge, Silber J, held that both points that had to be established had been proved. He set out his reasons for doing so in a commendably clear and careful judgment. As to the **actus reus,** he held that it had been proved that **the defendants frustrated or thwarted the purpose of the court's order.** He said that the **purpose** of the order was to prevent disclosure of the material covered by the injunctions without the consent of the Attorney-General until after the trial, and that the defendants' conduct had a significant and adverse effect on the administration of justice: para 57. As to **mens rea,** he observed that the **purpose** of the court in granting the injunctions was to prevent publication or disclosure of information falling within paragraph 1 of the order but not covered by the **provisos**: para 76. **He said that he was satisfied that the defendants intended to impede or prejudice the administration of justice by thwarting or undermining the intended effect of the injunctions by publishing material which the court had intended by means of the injunctions not to be published pending trial of the action against Mr Shayler and Associated Newspapers:** para 78. The company did not appeal against this judgment. But the respondent did so, and his appeal was allowed by the Court of Appeal: [2001] EWCA Civ 403, [2001] QB 1028.

91. The facts are not now in dispute. But the case has raised **two important issues of principle.** The **first** is whether the judge was right to describe the **purpose** of the injunctions as being to prevent disclosure of the information until after the trial. The **second** is whether the terms of the injunctions went beyond what was necessary and appropriate, having regard to the **purpose** for which the orders were made.

*The **purpose** of the injunctions*

92. The respondent's challenge to the judge's decision in the Court of Appeal concentrated on the issue of ***mens rea.*** The essence of his defence was that he did not wish to do anything that might damage national security and that he did not believe that the article which he published contained any such information. This defence was rejected by the judge as irrelevant, in view of his finding as to the **purpose** of the injunctions. The judge held that it was sufficient that his conduct was intended to impede and prejudice the administration of justice by disclosing material which the court intended should not be published until after the trial. **The respondent's primary argument in the appeal was that that the judge should have accepted his evidence that he believed that the purpose of the injunctions was to prevent the publication of matter that might be damaging to national security, and that his mistake as to their true purpose meant that he did not have the necessary mens rea when he acted in a way that defeated that purpose**.

93. The Court of Appeal expressed unease about his proceeding on this **narrow** basis. As Lord Phillips of Worth Matravers MR explained, [2001] QB 1028, 1040H–1041C, para 38:

> "A court may have more than one **purpose** in granting an interlocutory injunction. The immediate **purpose** of restraining named defendants from publishing specific material will necessarily be to ensure that those defendants do not publish the material. An ulterior **purpose** may be to ensure that the material remains confidential until its status is determined at trial and the ultimate **purpose** may be to ensure that any parts of the material that are likely to damage the national interest remain permanently confidential. It seemed to us that the appellant's case raised the question of which **purpose** was the *relevant* **purpose** under the principles of the law of **contempt** developed in the *Spycatcher* cases: *Attorney General v Guardian Newspapers Ltd (No 2)* [1990] 1 AC 109; *Attorney General v Newspaper Publishing plc* [1988] Ch 333 and *Attorney General v Times Newspapers Ltd* [1992] 1 AC 191."

At the suggestion of the court a further ground of appeal was added, to the effect that the judge should have held that the **purpose** of the court in granting the injunctions was to prevent the publication of matter likely to harm national security and that, accordingly, the ***actus reus*** of the alleged **contempt** was publishing matter that was likely to harm national security.

94. The scope of the appeal having been thus enlarged, Lord Phillips of Worth Matravers MR conducted a detailed examination of the jurisprudence which is to be found in the *Spycatcher* cases. He then sought to define the issues in the case. He said that the Crown has no right to restrain a newspaper

from publishing information **about government unless** (i) disclosure of the information will be **contrary to the public interest** ***and*** (ii) **the information has not already been disclosed:** [2001] QB 1028, 1044C-D, para 46. He said that **the question that lay at the heart of the appeal was whether a third party who, with knowledge of an order that specific material is not to be published, publishes the material automatically commits a contempt of court, or whether he commits a contempt of court only if he thereby knowingly defeats the purpose for which the order was made**: p 1051C-D, para 73. I do not think that anything that he said in the course of this part of his judgment is controversial.

95. **I have more difficulty with the conclusion Lord Phillips of Worth Matravers MR reached as to the purpose of the injunctions in the present case.** Having examined the speeches in *Attorney General v Times Newspapers Ltd* [1992] 1 AC 191, he indicated at p 1054E–G, para 84 that he saw no difference in the application of the principle of **contempt** between material which was subject to an interlocutory injunction and the situation where the court had granted a final injunction against publication. At p 1054F–G he said:

> "It seems to me that in ordering an interim injunction in a case such as this the primary object of the court is to prevent what will *arguably* constitute a legal wrong for which damages will not be an adequate remedy. The party against whom the injunction is granted will be in criminal **contempt** if he breaches the injunction. **The effect, and, so it seems to me, the primary purpose, of the third party contempt jurisdiction is to render it a criminal offence for any third party who is aware of the injunction to commit the potential wrong which the injunction is designed to prevent.** That surely is the most serious aspect of the **contempt**, and the fact that it will **at the same time render the litigation pointless is a subsidiary consideration."**

He then examined the *Spycatcher* **contempt** case, *Attorney General v Newspaper Publishing plc*, The Times, 28 February 1990, i**n which Nicholls LJ had held that the purpose of the injunctions was that the material to which they related should remain unpublished until trial**. Having done so, he concluded that the ***actus reus*** of **contempt** was not the publication of the material covered by the order but the destruction of the confidentiality of the material which it had been the **purpose** of the injunction to preserve: p 1057E, para 97.

96. At p 1058B–C, para 100 Lord Phillips of Worth Matravers MR said:

> **"It has never been disputed that the purpose of the Attorney General in commencing the substantive proceedings and obtaining the interlocutory injunctions was to prevent the publication of material**

> **that might be prejudicial to national security. I consider that it is proper to infer that Hooper J had the same ultimate purpose in granting the interlocutory injunctions."**

At p 1060F–G, para 114 he again said that **the purpose of the injunction** was to preserve until trial the confidentiality of material whose disclosure *arguably posed a risk* of damaging national security [his emphasis]. At p 1064B-C, para 129 Simon Brown LJ said that he agreed with the conclusion of the Master of the Rolls in paras 100 and 114 of his judgment that the **purpose** of the injunctions was to preserve until trial the confidentiality of material whose disclosure "arguably posed a risk of damaging national security." At p 1065H, para 137 Longmore LJ said that that the **purpose** of the order was to prevent publication, before trial, of any information that **was not already in the public domain.**

97. Although Simon Brown LJ said that he agreed with Lord Phillips of Worth Matravers MR about the **purpose** of the injunctions, it is clear that in his dissenting judgment he reached a quite different conclusion on the question of mens rea. The Master of the Rolls said at p 1060H, para 115 that to establish **contempt** the Attorney General needed to demonstrate knowledge that the publication would interfere with the course of justice "by defeating the **purpose** underlying the injunctions." *The Attorney General had set out simply to prove that the respondent knew that the publication was one which the defendants to the action were enjoined from making under the terms of the injunctions.* This, he said, did not go far enough. There was no basis in the evidence for a finding that the respondent must have appreciated that publication might be a threat to national security, nor was it established that he knew that the article continued information not previously published. Longmore LJ agreed with the Master of the Rolls: p 1066A–B, para 138. Simon Brown LJ, on the other hand, expressed his conclusion as to mens rea in these words at p 1064H–1065B, para 131:

> "True it may be, as Mr Steen protests, that he had no *intention* of endangering national security and did not think he was doing so. That, however, is not the point. As he himself candidly admitted, he was not qualified to make that kind of judgment. If, as I would hold, he cannot have failed to appreciate that it was for this very reason that, pending a trial at which the court could have ruled on the substantive question, there was a bar on publication unless only the Attorney General consented to it, then he was guilty of the **contempt** alleged against him: he intended to take upon himself the responsibility for determining whether national security was risked and thereby he thwarted the court's intention."

98. I respectfully agree with everything that Simon Brown LJ said in that paragraph, and on this ground I would allow the appeal. But the fact that he

was able to reach that conclusion while agreeing with Lord Phillips of Worth Matravers MR's statements as to the **purpose** of the injunctions suggests there was in reality no common understanding on this vital point. I think that the point requires further examination. For this **purpose** it is necessary to go back to first principles.

99. The **purpose** for which the court grants an interlocutory injunction can be stated quite simply. In *American Cyanamid Co v Ethicon* Ltd [1975] AC 396, 405D Lord Diplock described it as a remedy which is both temporary and discretionary. Its **purpose** is to regulate, and where possible to preserve, the rights of the parties pending the final determination of the matter which is in issue by the court. That **purpose** should not be confused with the court's reasons for deciding that it would be appropriate to grant an interlocutory injunction. The court must of course have a good reason for granting an order of this kind. It must be satisfied in the first place that a sufficient ground has been stated to show that there is a real dispute between the parties. As Lord Diplock put it in *American Cynamid Co v Ethicon Ltd* at p 407, the court must be satisfied that there is a serious question to be tried. It must then consider whether the balance of convenience lies in favour of granting or refusing an interlocutory injunction. But it is in no position to reach a final decision at the interlocutory stage on the matters which are in dispute between the parties. It is no part of the court's function at that stage to resolve conflicts of evidence or questions of law that require detailed argument. All it can do is preserve the status quo in the meantime until these matters can be determined at the trial.

100. It is true, as Lord Phillips of Worth Matravers MR said at p 1054E-F, para 84, that in many cases the claimant's objective is achieved when an interlocutory injunction is granted and that the stage of a substantive hearing is never reached. This may be because the parties are content to settle their dispute at that stage or because the need for a final order has been overtaken by events. The grant or refusal of an interlocutory injunction is almost always decisive in industrial dispute cases because the dispute is usually settled one way or the other before there is time for the action to proceed to trial, as Lord Fraser of Tullybelton observed in *N W L Ltd v Woods* [1979] 1 WLR 1294, 1308F. But this does not alter the fact that the court's **purpose**, when it grants the order, is to preserve the rights of the parties pending a final determination of the issues between them by the court. Furthermore, as Lord Oliver said in *Attorney General v Times Newspapers Ltd* [1992] 1 AC 191, 223A-B, "**purpose**" in this context refers not to the litigant's **purpose** in obtaining the order or in fighting the action, but to the court's **purpose**. That is the **purpose** which the court was intending to fulfil in seeking to

administer justice between the parties in the particular litigation of which it has become seized.

101. **Confidential information** is, as Mr Sumption QC for the Attorney General said in the course of his speech, **particularly fragile**. It is not hard to see that litigation as to whether information is entitled to be protected on the ground that it is confidential would be rendered pointless if the information were to be published before trial. The **purpose** of an interim injunction in a case of this kind, **where the Attorney General sues in the public interest,** is not therefore difficult to identify. **It is to protect the public interest against an injury for which it could not be adequately compensated if the issue of confidentiality were to be resolved in favour of the Attorney at the trial.**

102. Lord Phillips of Worth Matravers MR sought to identify the immediate, ulterior and ultimate **purposes** of an interlocutory injunction: p 1040H–1041B, para 38. I doubt very much however, whether this is helpful. In my opinion the only **purpose** that is relevant to the question whether a **contempt** has been committed is the **purpose** which the court was seeking to serve in the interests of justice. The Master of the Rolls described this as the ulterior **purpose** of the injunction. He said that the ulterior **purpose** of the injunctions which were granted in this case was to ensure that the material remained confidential until its status was determined at trial. He then said that their immediate **purpose** was to restrain the defendants from publishing the material. I think that it would be more accurate to regard this as the means which were chosen by the court to ensure that the material remained confidential. He said that the ultimate **purpose** of the injunctions was to ensure that any parts of the material that were likely to damage the national interest remained permanently confidential.

103. The theme of Lord Phillips of Worth Matravers MR's judgment is that the primary **purpose** of the **contempt** jurisdiction is to render it **a criminal offence for any third party** who is aware of the injunction to commit the **potential wrong** which the injunction was designed to prevent: see p 1054G, para 84 [his emphasis]. But I think, that this tends to confuse the issue as to the **purpose** of the injunctions. It also overlooks a crucial distinction between injunctions which are final and those which are interlocutory. The question whether there was a need for a permanent order cannot be answered until the issues between the parties have been determined at the trial. Interlocutory injunctions are designed to ensure the effective administration of justice, so that the rights which it is the duty of the courts to protect can be fairly determined and effectively protected and enforced by the courts: *Attorney General v Times Newspapers Ltd* [1992] 1 AC 191, 216A-B, per Lord Oliver.

104. In my opinion the position can be stated more simply. The **purpose** of the

interlocutory injunctions which were pronounced in this case **was to ensure that the material as a whole remained confidential until its status had been determined by the court.** The *reason* why they were granted was because there was a serious question for the court to resolve as to the status of that information, and because the balance of convenience favoured this course. The *method* which was chosen was to prohibit publication of that information until further order of the court except to the extent which was permitted by the **provisos**.

105. It seems to me that this analysis, which separates **purpose** from *reason* and **purpose** from *method*, is more in keeping with the way the matter has been approached in the authorities. As Lord Oliver explained in *Attorney General v Times Newspapers Ltd* [1992] 1 AC 191, 223F, there can never be any doubt in anyone's mind what the court's **purpose** was in making an order prohibiting the publication of **confidential information** such as that obtained by a person in the course of his employment as a member of the security services. **It was to preserve the claimant's right to keep the information confidential until the action had been tried.** It was to ensure that the issues were determined by the court, without the claimant's rights being prejudiced in the meantime by the doing of the very act which the action sought to prevent. Moreover, if there is room for genuine doubt about what the court's **purpose** is, the party charged with **contempt** is likely to escape liability for want of the necessary mens rea. **That is why it is so important to define the purpose of the interlocutory injunction correctly.** In my opinion that must be done by examining the **purpose** which the *court* was intending to fulfil. That is the criterion. The court's **purpose** must not be confused with the issue between the parties. This is a matter which can ultimately only be resolved at the trial.

106. Lord Phillips of Worth Matravers MR said at p 1058C-D, para 100 that the court's **purpose** in granting the injunctions was "to prevent the disclosure of any matter that *arguably risked* harming the national interest." This was in keeping with his description of the primary **purpose** of the third party **contempt** jurisdiction at p 1054F-G, para 84. But it is plain that the effect of describing the court's **purpose** in this way was to deprive the claimant of the protection of the injunctions. The introduction of the word "arguably" may have been intended to recognise that the resolution of the issue lay in the future. But its effect was to remove the judgment as to whether or not to publish from the court and transfer it to the third party. **It enabled the respondent to avoid a finding of contempt by showing that he had an honest belief that the material which he published was not of that character.** This then enabled the Court of Appeal to conclude that he had an honest belief that the **purpose** for which the injunctions were granted did not apply to that material. It enabled the Master of the Rolls to say, at p 1060G-H, para 115,

that the respondent's evidence that he was anxious not to publish any material which would harm national security and that he did not believe that the material which he published carried the risk of causing such harm focused on the correct issue of fact so far as mens rea was concerned. All of this led directly to the Court of Appeal's finding that he was not in **contempt**.

107. **In my opinion the correct issue of fact was that identified by Simon Brown LJ at p 1065A–B, para 131. This was whether the respondent, who admitted that he was not qualified to judge whether publication of the material endangered national security, appreciated that there was a bar on publication unless the Attorney General consented to it.** The respondent cannot have failed to have understood this point, for the reasons given by judge which were not challenged in the appeal. **He admitted that the article offended against the wording of the injunctions.** As Silber J said in paragraph 74 of his judgment, the fact that he sought the approval of the Treasury Solicitor before publication shows that he knew that the material which the article contained fell within their terms when he published the article. I would respectfully disagree with majority in the Court of Appeal. I would hold that the necessary mens rea for a finding that the respondent was in **contempt** of court was established.

The wording of the injunctions

108. Lord Phillips of Worth Matravers MR said at p 1058H, para 103, that there were a number of objections to the Attorney General's contention that no newspaper could knowingly publish any matter that fell within the wide terms of the injunction against Associated Newspapers without first obtaining clearance from himself. At p 1059A-G, paras 104–109 he said that this was to subject the press to the censorship of the Attorney General, that it resulted in the imposition of a restriction on freedom of the press that was disproportionate to any public interest in breach of article 10 of the Convention and that the proposition could not be reconciled with the duty imposed on the court by section 12(3) of the Human Rights Act 1998, which applies if a court is considering whether to grant any relief which, if it were to be granted, might affect the exercise of the Convention right to freedom of expression. Section 12(3) provides:

> "No such relief is to be granted so as to restrain publication before trial unless the court is satisfied that the applicant is likely to establish that publication should not be allowed."

109. Lord Phillips of Worth Matravers MR had already expressed his concern on these points at p 1044E–H, paras 47 and 48 when he was considering the implications of Silber J's judgment. The trial judge recognised that the injunctions probably covered matters other than those affecting national

security. The Master of the Rolls said it followed from this that the injunctions extended beyond the categories of information that the Crown was entitled to require should remain confidential and that, by endorsing the terms of the injunction to which Associated Newspapers submitted by consent, the court in effect made it a criminal offence for newspapers to publish matter which they would otherwise have been lawfully entitled to publish. He saw this as imposing a significant fetter on the press.

110. These objections, if well founded, would indeed be formidable. They would justify the conclusion which Lord Phillips of Worth Matravers MR then reached at p 1059H, para 110, that the law of **contempt** was being extended in this case beyond the principle that it is an offence intentionally to interfere with the course of justice. Mr Price for the respondent did not address these objections, but they were addressed by Mr Sumption and I think that they are so important that they require to be dealt with. I am, not persuaded that they are based on a correct analysis of the **purpose** and effect of the **proviso** in the context of injunctions which are not final but interlocutory.

111. I take as my starting point for an examination of this issue the principle that an injunction must always be expressed with **precision and with clarity**. As Lord Deas put it in a Scottish case, if an injunction is to be granted at all, it must be in terms so plain that he **who runs may read:** *Kelso School Board v Hunter* (1874) 2 R 228, 230. This is because of the **penal consequences** that will follow if it is breached. Then there is another important principle. The prohibition **must extend no further** than is necessary to serve the **purpose** for which the order is to be made.

112. The background to the injunctions which were granted by Hooper J is to be found in section 1(1) of the Official Secrets Act 1989. It provides that it is an offence for a person who is or has been a member of the security and intelligence services without lawful authority to disclose to any person any information, document or other article relating to security or intelligence which is or has been in his possession by virtue of his position as a member of any of those services. As against that, Mr Shayler has asserted the right of the public to be provided with information which will enable it to assess whether the powers given to the security and intelligence services are being abused and whether these services are being run properly. He maintains that any disclosures by him were made in the public interest and in the exercise of his right of freedom of expression as guaranteed by the common law, the Human Rights Act 1998 and article 10 of the Convention.

113. Of course, any prohibition on the publication of information is a restraint on free speech. The right to freedom of expression which is guaranteed by article 10 of the European Convention for the Protection of Human Rights and Fundamental Freedoms is engaged. This is not an absolute right, as the

broad language of article 10(1) which protects the **right to impart** information and ideas without interference by public authorities is qualified by article 10(2). It provides:

> "The exercise of these freedoms, since it carries with it duties and responsibilities, may be subject to such formalities, conditions, restrictions or penalties as are prescribed by law and are necessary in a democratic society, in the interests of national security, territorial integrity or public safety, . . . for the protection of the . . . rights of others, for preventing the disclosure of information received in confidence . . . "

114. The word **"necessary"** in article 10(2) raises the question of **proportionality**. But in my opinion there can be no objection to an interim injunction against the publication of information on the ground of proportionality if **three requirements are satisfied**. The general principles which are to be applied where questions are raised about proportionality are now well established: see *R (Daly) v Secretary of State for the Home Department* [2001] 2 AC 532, 547A-B, per Lord Steyn; *R (Pretty) v Director of Public Prosecutions* [2001] 3 WLR 1598, 1637A-B; *R v Shayler* [2002] 2 WLR 754, 783F-H, 786A-B. In this context the requirements that must be met are: **(one)** that there is a genuine dispute as to whether the information is confidential because its publication might be a threat to national security, **(two)** that there are reasonable grounds for thinking that publication of the information before trial would impede or interfere with the administration of justice and **(three)** that the interference with the right of free speech is no greater than is **necessary**. Close attention to the facts is needed when consideration is given to the question whether the protection is necessary. The **purpose** of the order provides the context, and it is crucial to the whole exercise that this is correctly identified. Its **purpose** is to ensure that the other party to the dispute **does not assume the responsibility** of deciding for himself whether the material is of such a nature that the Attorney General is entitled in law to protection against its publication.

115. The question whether the statutory interference with the right to freedom of expression **was greater than was required** in order to **achieve the legitimate object** of acting in the **interests of national security** was examined by your Lordships in *R v Shayler* [2002] 2 WLR 754. It was held that sufficient safeguards were built into the Act, that the prohibition in section 1(1) came within the qualification in article 10(2) of the Convention and that it was a justified interference with the right to freedom of expression guaranteed by that article.

116. Any **formalities, conditions, restrictions** or **penalties,** to be permitted by article 10(2), must satisfy the principle of **proportionality.** In summary, they must be sensitive to the facts of the case, they must be rational, fair and

not arbitrary, and they must impair the fundamental right no more than is necessary. **In my opinion these tests must be satisfied at every stage in the judicial process that is liable to affect the exercise of the fundamental right.** This includes the stage when the court is deciding whether or not to make an **interlocutory injunction**, and if so in what terms. It also includes the stage when the court is considering whether the order **should be varied** following an application for that **purpose** by any third party before the trial. The need to have regard to these tests **at each stage** is reinforced by section 12(4) of the 1998 Act, which provides that the court must have regard to the importance of the Convention right if the court is considering whether to grant any relief which, if granted, may affect the exercise of the Convention right.

117. Lord Phillips of Worth Matravers MR said that he did not agree with the judge that the **purpose** of the injunctions extended to the restraint of publication of material which could not possibly be detrimental to the national interest and to material which had previously been published. This was because of the mechanism which was provided to avoid that result in the first **proviso**: p 1058E-H, paras 101–102. He recognised the attraction of this arrangement between the parties to the action. But he said that a critical issue was raised as to its effect on third parties who were not subject to the order. In his view it subjected the press to the censorship of the Attorney General.

118. Similar observations are to be found in *Attorney General v Times Newspapers Ltd* [2001] EWCA Civ 97; [2001] 1 WLR 885, although the context of that case was different as the order in question was not an interlocutory one made before trial. The judge ordered that no order be made in the action upon the defendants giving an undertaking. An application was later made for the undertaking to be varied to permit certain information to be published. **The Master of the Rolls observed that it was desirable that there should usually be consultation between a newspaper and representatives of the British Secret Intelligence Service before the newspaper published information that might include matters capable of damaging the service or endangering those who serve in it.** He then said at p 896C-D, para 34:

> "I do not, however, think it right to impose on TNL the requirement that they should seek confirmation from the Attorney General or the court that facts that they intend to republish have been sufficiently brought into the **public domain** by prior publication so as to remove from them the cloak of confidentiality. That is a matter on which an editor will be in a position to form his own judgment and he should be left responsible for exercising that judgment. That is consonant with article 10 of the Convention and section 12 of the 1998 Act."

119. **I agree with Lord Phillips of Worth Matravers MR that the way in which the orders in this case were framed can be regarded as satisfactory as**

between the parties to the action. Indeed, as I mentioned in para 3, solicitors for Associated Newspapers wrote a letter indicating their consent to the order which was to be pronounced against them. Any attempt to lessen the breadth of the opening words by identifying in advance items of information which were not to be covered by them would almost certainly have been too cumbersome. Some other way of providing relief had to be devised. **The method which was devised, and which was plainly regarded by Associated Newspapers as acceptable as they did not object to it, was to allow for decisions to be made as to the need for this protection to be taken ad hoc by the Attorney General subject to the overall supervision of the court. This is the method described in the first proviso.**

120. Leaving aside for the moment the question of interference with the Convention right to freedom of expression, I do not think that there can be any objection in principle to this method of relief. **It is normal practice in claims for infringement of copyright for injunctions to be pronounced against the defendant which permit infringing acts done with the licence of the holder of the copyright**. The same cannot be said of actions for breach of confidence between private individuals, where particulars are normally given of the information for which the claimant seeks protection. **But section 1(1) of the Official Secrets Act 1989 sets the scene for the wording that was needed in this case**. It casts its net widely across the entire range of information which is or has been in the person's possession as a member of the security and intelligence services. **It then creates an exception in favour of the disclosure of information where this is done with lawful authority.** The opening words of the injunctions which Hooper J pronounced in this case are in keeping with those of section 1(1) of the 1989 Act. **The system for providing relief, which is in equally broad terms, reflects the fact that the guardian of the public interest in these matters is the Attorney General.**

121. The question is whether Lord Phillips of Worth Matrvavers MR's criticism of the injunctions, and of the terms of the first **proviso** in particular, as an interference with the Convention right to freedom of expression is justified. I recognise the force of his criticisms, but I do not think that they are justified. **The system which allows for a statement in writing to be obtained from the Attorney General or the Treasury Solicitor is not an exercise in censorship. It is a mechanism for relaxing the scope of the injunction.** It provides a cheap, simple and convenient way of obtaining clearance before the trial for the publication of material to whose publication no objection can properly be taken on the grounds of confidentiality or national security. The whole process is then subject to the further order of the court. **A refusal of clearance by the Attorney General or the Treasury Solicitor is not the last word on the matter.**

122. Above all, full weight must be given to the **purpose** of these injunctions. They were interlocutory injunctions. It was not the intention when they were granted that they should be permanent. Their **purpose** was to serve the interests of the administration of justice by preserving the confidentiality of the information until trial. **As Simon Brown LJ observed at p 1065A-B, para 131, the court's intention would be thwarted if a third party to the action were to take upon himself the responsibility for determining whether or not the information risked national security**. That is the context in which the necessity for a restriction on the Convention right must be judged. The court remains available to give its own judgment before the trial as to whether publication of the material in the meantime would be objectionable, having regard to the **purpose** of the order and the requirements of the principle of proportionality.

123. So I do not think that the terms of the injunctions can be regarded as disproportionate in view of this safeguard. Nor do I think that there is any incompatibility with the respondent's right under article 10(1) of the Convention, to which particular regard must be had under section 12(4) of the Human Rights Act 1998. The restriction on the publication of the information before trial can be justified as being in the public interest in a democratic society. The requirement of **proportionality** is satisfied **(one)** because the opening words of the order are qualified by the first **proviso**, **(two)** because the extent of the injunction remains subject to the further order of the court and **(three)** because the court itself must observe the principle of proportionality when it deals with any application before the trial for relaxation of the scope of the injunction. It was not suggested that the orders made by Hooper J, which were made before the coming into force of the 1998 Act, were in conflict with section 12(3) of that Act. But the fact that this subsection is now in force, and that it will apply in the event of an application being made to the court for a further order before trial, supports the view which I favour that the interlocutory injunctions which were pronounced in this case are not incompatible with the article 10 Convention right.

124. That all having been said, I agree with my noble and learned friend Lord Nicholls of Birkenhead **that it would be better to avoid the appearance of delegating control of what may be published to the Attorney General by making it plain on the face of the order that anyone whose conduct is affected by the order has the right to apply to the court for a variation of its terms.** That could be done by inserting a further **proviso**. As for the width of the language, I have already mentioned the fact that the context for the words which were chosen in this case is provided by the width of the words used in section 1(1) of the Official Secrets Act 1989. But I agree that it would be wise not to regard the formula that was used in this case as the last word

on the subject, and that it would be preferable to use a more precise formula if this can be devised.

Conclusion

125. For these reasons, and for those given by Lord Nicholls and Lord Hoffmann whose speeches I have had the opportunity of reading in draft and with which I agree, I too would allow the appeal and restore the order of the trial judge.

A v B & C [2002] EWCA Civ 337

Concerning confidence and its interaction with privacy

2. A is a footballer with a **premier division** football club. B is a national newspaper. C is one of two women with whom A, who is a married man, **had affairs**. The injunction was granted to restrain B from publishing the stories which C and the other woman, D, had sold to B recounting their affairs with A. In using initials to describe the parties we are following the course adopted in the court below to protect the identity of A. D has taken no part in the proceedings.

3. Since the coming into force of the Human Rights Act 1998 ("the 1998 Act") there has been an increase in the number of actions in which injunctions are being sought to protect the claimants from the publication of articles in newspapers on the grounds that the articles contain **confidential information** concerning the claimants, the publication of which, it is alleged, would infringe their privacy. Such actions can be against any part of the media.

4. The applications for interim injunctions have now to be considered in the context of articles 8 and 10 of the European Convention of Human Rights ("ECHR"). **These articles have provided new parameters within which the court will decide, in an action for breach of confidence, whether a person is entitled to have his privacy protected by the court or whether the restriction of freedom of expression which such protection involves cannot be justified**. The court's approach to the issues which the applications raise has been modified because under section 6 of the 1998 Act**, the court, as a public authority, is required not to act "in a way which is incompatible with a Convention right". The court is able to achieve this by absorbing the rights which articles 8 and 10 protect into the long-established action for breach of confidence.** This involves giving a new strength and breadth to the action so that it accommodates the requirements of those articles.

. . .

GUIDELINES

11. We suggest that if judges direct themselves in accordance with the following paragraphs in many cases they will not need to be burdened by copious reference to other authorities:

i) The consideration of this type of application should generally begin with recognition that what is being considered is an interim application for an injunction. This means that whether any injunction is granted at all is **a matter of discretion for the judge**, to be exercised in accordance with what are now well-established principles which include the need to establish, as we will explain later, that after a trial it is **likely that an injunction would be granted** after a substantive hearing, while recognising that **the grant or refusal of an interim injunction could well determine the outcome of the entire proceedings.**

ii) The fact that the injunction is being sought to protect the privacy of the claimant, and **if the injunction is not granted, the claimant may be deprived of the only remedy which is of any value is a relevant consideration**. However, **this consideration has to be weighed against the defendant's rights of freedom of expression**. Even before the 1998 Act this would have been an important consideration. **Its importance has been enhanced by section 12 of the 1998 Act**. The relevant provisions of section 12 are:

> "12. (1) This section applies if the court is considering whether to grant any relief which, if granted, might affect the exercise of the Convention right to freedom of expression.
>
> (3) No such relief is to be granted so as to restrain publication before trial unless the court is satisfied that the applicant is likely to establish that publication should not be allowed.
>
> (4) The court must have particular regard to the importance of the Convention right to freedom of expression and, where the proceedings relate to material which the respondent claims, or which appears to the court, to be journalistic, literary or artistic material (or to conduct connected with such material), to –
>
> (a) the extent to which –
>
> (i) the material has, or is about to, become available to the public; or
>
> (ii) it is, or would be, in the public interest for the material to be published;
>
> (b) any relevant privacy code."

iii) As to the word "likely" in section 12(3) useful guidance is provided by

Sir Andrew Morritt VC in *Imutran Ltd v Uncaged Campaigns Ltd* [2002] FSR 20. He said of section 12:

> "17. Counsel for the defendants submitted that the requirement of likelihood imposed a higher standard than that formulated in American Cyanamid. I did not understand this to be disputed by counsel for Imutran. He submitted that whatever the standard was his case satisfied it. **Theoretically and as a matter of language likelihood is slightly higher in the scale of probability than a real prospect of success. But the difference between the two is so small that I cannot believe that there will be many (if any) cases which would have succeeded under the American Cyanamid test but will now fail because of the terms of s 12(3).** Accordingly I propose to apply the test of likelihood without any further consideration of how much more probable that now has to be."

There is no conflict between section 12 (3) and the Convention. (See *Douglas v Hello! Ltd* [2001] QB 967; Keene LJ paragraph 150)

iv) The fact that if the injunction is granted it will interfere with the freedom of expression of others and in particular the freedom of the press is a matter of particular importance. This well-established common law principle is underlined by section 12 (4). **Any interference with the press has to be justified because it inevitably has some effect on the ability of the press to perform its role in society. *This is the position irrespective of whether a particular publication is desirable in the public interest.*** *The existence of a free press is in itself desirable and so any interference with it has to be justified.* Here we would endorse the approach of Hoffmann LJ in *R v Central Independent Television PLC* [1994] Fam 192 at p 201–204, where he said:

> **"Publication may cause needless pain, distress and damage to individuals or harm to other aspects of the public interest.** But a freedom which is restricted to what Judges think to be responsible or in the public interest is no freedom. **Freedom means the right to publish things which Government and Judges, however well motivated, think should not be published.** It **means the right to say things which "right thinking people" regard as dangerous or irresponsible.** This freedom is subject only to clearly defined exceptions laid down by common law or statute **. . . the principle that the press is free from both Government and judicial control is more important than the particular case."**

v) The fact that under section 12 (4) the court is required to have particular regard to whether it would be in the public interest for the material to be published **does not mean that the court is justified in interfering with the freedom of the press where there is no identifiable special public interest**

in any particular material being published. Such an approach would turn section 12 (4) upside down. Regardless of the quality of the material which it is intended to publish *prima facie* the court should not interfere with its publication. **Any interference with publication must be justified.**

vi) It is most unlikely that any **purpose** will be served by a judge seeking to decide whether there exists a new cause of action in tort which protects privacy. In the great majority of situations, if not all situations, **where the protection of privacy is justified, relating to events after the Human Rights Act came into force, an action for breach of confidence now will, where this is appropriate, provide the necessary protection.** This means that at first instance it can be readily accepted that it is not necessary to tackle the vexed question of whether there is a separate cause of action based upon a new tort involving the infringement of privacy.

vii) Furthermore in the majority of cases the question of whether there is an interest capable of being the subject of a claim for privacy should not be allowed to be the subject of detailed argument. There must be some interest of a private nature which the claimant wishes to protect, **but usually the answer to the question whether there exists a private interest worthy of protection will be obvious.** In those cases in which the answer is not obvious, an answer will often be unnecessary. **This is because the weaker the claim for privacy the more likely that the claim for privacy will be outweighed by the claim based on freedom of expression**. The advantage of not having to distinguish between acts which are public and those which are private in a difficult case is made clear by what Gleeson CJ had to say on the subject in *Australian Broadcasting Corporation v Lenah Game Meats Pty Ltd* [2001] HCA 63. He explained the difficulty of distinguishing between public and private information when he said at para 42:

> "[42] There is no bright line which can be drawn between what is private and what is not. Use of the term "public" is often a convenient method of contrast, **but there is a large area in between what is necessarily public and what is necessarily private.** An activity is not private simply because it is not done in public. It does not suffice to make an act private that, because it occurs on private property**, it has such measure of protection from the public gaze as the characteristics of the property, the nature of the activity, the locality, and the disposition of the property owner combine to afford**. Certain kinds of information about a person, such as information relating to health, personal **relationships**, or finances, may be easy to identify as private; as may certain kinds of activity, which a reasonable person, applying contemporary standards of morals and behaviour, would understand to be meant to be unobserved. **The requirement that disclosure or observation of information or**

conduct would be *highly offensive* to a reasonable person of ordinary sensibilities is in many circumstances a useful practical test of what is private."viii) The same is true in cases in which the public interest in publication is relied on to oppose the grant of an injunction. We have already made clear that **even where there is no public interest in a particular publication** interference with freedom of expression has to be justified. **However, the existence of a public interest in publication strengthens the case for not granting an injunction**. Again in the majority of situations whether the public interest is involved or not will be obvious. In the grey area cases the public interest, if it exists, is unlikely to be decisive. Judges should therefore be reluctant in the difficult borderline cases to become involved in detailed argument as to whether the public interest is involved. **In a borderline case the application will usually be capable of being resolved without deciding whether there is a public interest in publication.** In any event, the citation of authority is unlikely to be helpful. **The circumstances in any particular case under consideration can vary so much that a judgment in one case is unlikely to be decisive in another case, though it may be illustrative of an approach.**

ix) The need for the existence of a confidential **relationship** should not give rise to problems as to the law. The difficulty will be as to the relevant facts. **A duty of confidence will arise whenever the party subject to the duty is in a situation where he either knows or ought to know that the other person can reasonably expect his privacy to be protected**. (See Lord Goff of Chieveley, in *Attorney General v Guardian Newspapers Ltd* [No 2] [1990] 1 A C 109 at 281.) The range of situations in which protection can be provided is therefore extensive. Obviously, the necessary **relationship** can be expressly created. More often its existence will have to be inferred from the facts. Whether a duty of confidence does exist which courts can protect, if it is right to do so, will depend on all the circumstances of the **relationship** between the parties at the time of the threatened or actual breach of the alleged duty of confidence.

x) If there is an **intrusion** in a situation where a person can reasonably expect his privacy to be respected then that **intrusion** will be capable of giving rise to liability in an action for breach of confidence unless the **intrusion** can be justified. (See the approach of Dame Elizabeth Butler-Sloss p in *Venables v Newsgroup Newspapers Ltd* [2001] 1038 at para 81) The bugging of someone's home or the use of other surveillance techniques are obvious examples of such an **intrusion**. **But the fact that the information is obtained as a result of unlawful activities does not mean that its publication should necessarily be restrained by injunction**

on the grounds of breach of confidence (see the Lenah Game decision). Dependent on the nature of the unlawful activity there may be other remedies. **On the other hand, the fact that unlawful means have been used to obtain the information could well be a compelling factor when it comes to exercising discretion.**

xi) More difficult is the situation where the alleged intrusion into privacy is as a result of the reporting of the information to a third party by a party to the relationship which creates the privacy. This is a material factor in situations where two people have **shared** a **sexual relationship** outside marriage. If one wishes to exercise his or her article 10 rights that must impact on the other's right to maintain confidentiality. For example the information may relate, as in this case, to a situation where there is a **sexual relationship** between two parties **and one of the parties informs the media about the relationship without the consent of the other party.** Here the conflict between one party's right to privacy and the other party's right of freedom of expression is especially acute. **In situations where the parties are not married (when they are, special considerations may arise) the fact that the confidence was a shared confidence which only one of the parties wishes to preserve *does not extinguish the other party's right to have the confidence respected, but it does undermine that right*.** While recognising the special status of a lawful marriage under our law, the courts, for present purposes, have to recognise and give appropriate weight to the extensive range of **relationships** which now exist. **Obviously, the more stable the relationship the greater will be the significance which is attached to it.**

xii) Where an individual is a **public figure** he is entitled to have his privacy respected in the appropriate circumstances. **A public figure is entitled to a private life.** The individual, however, should recognise that because of his public position he must expect and accept that his actions **will be more closely scrutinised** by the media. Even trivial facts relating to a **public figure** can be of great interest to readers and other observers of the media. Conduct which in the case of a private individual would not be the appropriate subject of comment can be the proper subject of comment in the case of a **public figure**. **The public figure may hold a position where higher standards of conduct can be rightly expected by the public.** The **public figure** may be a role model whose conduct could well be emulated by others. He may set the fashion. **The higher the profile of the individual concerned the more likely that this will be the position.** Whether you have courted publicity or not you may be a legitimate subject of public attention. **If you have courted public attention then you have less ground to object to the intrusion which follows**. In many of these situations it would be overstating the position to say that there is a public interest in the information being published. **It would be more accurate to say that the public have an understandable and so a legitimate interest in being told the information.** If this is the situation then it can be appropriately taken into account by a court when deciding on which side of the line a case falls. The courts must not ignore the fact that **if newspapers do not publish information which the public are interested in, there will be fewer newspapers published, which will not be in the public interest**. The same is true in relation to other parts of the media. On the difficult issue of finding the right balance, useful guidance of a general nature is provided by the Council of Europe Resolution 116 5 of 1998. We set out paragraphs 6, 7, 8, 9, 10, 11 and 12 which are in these terms:

> "6. The Assembly is aware that personal privacy is often invaded, even in countries with specific legislation to protect it, as people's private lives have become a highly lucrative commodity for certain sectors of the media. The victims are essentially **public figures**, since details of their private lives serve as a stimulus to sales. **At the same time, public figures must recognise that the special position they occupy in society—in many cases by choice—automatically entails increased pressure on their privacy.**
>
> 7. **Public figures are persons holding public office and/or using public resources and, more broadly speaking, all those who play a role in public life, whether in politics, the economy, the arts, the social sphere, sport or in any other domain.**
>
> 8. It is often in the name of a one-sided interpretation of the right to freedom of expression, which is guaranteed in Article 10 of the European Convention on Human Rights, that the media invade people's privacy, claiming that their readers are entitled to know about **public figures**.
>
> 9. Certain facts relating to the private lives of **public figures**, particularly **politicians**, may indeed be of interest to citizens, and it may therefore be legitimate for readers, who are also voters, to be informed of those facts.
>
> 10. It is therefore necessary to find a way of balancing the exercise of two fundamental rights, both of which are guaranteed by the European Convention on Human Rights: the right to respect for one's private life and the right to freedom of expression.
>
> 11. The Assembly reaffirms the importance of every person's right to privacy, and of the right to freedom of expression, as fundamental to a democratic society. These rights are neither absolute nor in any hierarchical order, since they are of equal value.

12. However, the Assembly points out that the right to privacy afforded by Article 8 of the European Convention on Human Rights should not only protect an individual against interference by public authorities, **but also against interference by private persons or institutions, including the mass media."**

xiii) In drawing up a balance sheet between the respective interests of the parties **courts should not act as censors or arbiters of taste**. This is the task of others. **If there is not a sufficient case for restraining publication the fact that a more lurid approach will be adopted by the publication than the court would regard as acceptable is not relevant**. If the contents of the publication are untrue the law of defamation provides prohibition. **Whether the publication will be attractive or unattractive should not affect the result of an application** if the information is otherwise not the proper subject of restraint.

xiv) Section 12 (4) requires the court to take into account "any relevant privacy code" but it is only one of a number of factors to be taken into account. The *Press Complaints Commission Code of Practice provides* that:

"It is essential to the workings of an agreed code that it be honoured not only to the letter but in the full spirit. The code should not be interpreted so **narrowly** as to compromise its commitment to respect the rights of the individual, nor so broadly that it prevents publication in the public interest.

Privacy

(i) Everyone is entitled to respect for his or her private and family life, home, health and correspondence. A publication will be expected to justify **intrusions** into any individual's private life without consent.

(ii) The use of long lens photography to take pictures of people in private places without their consent is unacceptable.

Note—Private places are public or private property where there is a reasonable expectation of privacy.

Harassment

They must not **photograph** individuals in private places (as defined by the note to clause 3) without their consent; must not persist in telephoning, questioning, pursuing or photographing individuals after having been asked to desist; must not remain on their property after having been asked to leave and must not follow them.

The public interest

1. The public interest includes:

(i) Detecting or exposing crime or a serious misdemeanour.

(ii) Protecting public health and safety.

(iii) Preventing the public from being misled by some statement or action of an individual or organisation."

Courts may well find this statement of practice of assistance. While recognising that section 12 (4) was primarily concerned with preserving the freedom of the press regard should be had to the guidance given by Lord Justice Brooke in *Douglas v Hello! Ltd* at paragraph 94, where he says;

"94. It appears to me that the existence of these statutory provisions, coupled with the current wording of the relevant privacy code, mean that **in any case where the court is concerned with issues of freedom of expression in a journalistic, literary or artistic context, it is bound to pay particular regard to any breach of the rules set out in clause 3 of the code,** *especially where none of the public interest claims set out in the preamble to the code is asserted.* **A newspaper which flouts clause 3 of the code is likely in those circumstances to have its claim to an entitlement to freedom of expression trumped by article 10(2) considerations of privacy.** Unlike the court in *Kaye v Robertson* [1991] FSR 62, Parliament recognised that it had to acknowledge the importance of the article 8(1) respect for private life, and it was able to do so untrammelled by any concerns that the law of confidence might not stretch to protect every aspect of private life."

xv) However, the court should discourage advocates seeking to rely on individual decisions of the Press Commission which at best are no more than illustrative of how the Press Commission performs its different responsibilities.

. . .

44. Although the criticisms which we make of the approach of Jack J are not individually of great significance, collectively we do believe they resulted in his coming to a wrong decision. **The degree of confidentiality to which A was entitled, notwithstanding that C and D did not wish their relationships with A to be confidential,** ***was very modest.***

45. **Relationships** of the sort which A had with C and D **are not the categories of relationships which the court should be astute to protect** when **the other parties to the relationships do not want them** to remain confidential. Any injunction granted after a trial would have to be permanent. It is most **unlikely** such an injunction would ever be granted.

46. On an issue which depends to such a substantial extent on the discretion of the judge, his decision is entitled to a considerable degree of deference from

an appellate court. However here, it can be shown there are significant flaws in Jack J's approach and we are satisfied that his decision is wrong.

47. Ouseley J in *Theakston v MGM Limited* [2002] EWHC 137 (QB) made reference to this case saying that if the **relationship** between A and C and D was entitled to confidentiality—that degree of protection represents to my mind the outer limit of what is confidential. We do not go so far as to say the **relationships** of the class being considered here can never be entitled to any confidentiality. **We prefer to adopt Ouseley J's view that the situation is one at the outer limits of relationships which require the protection of the law.** The fact that it attracts the protection of the law does not mean, however, that an injunction should be granted to provide that protection. In our view to grant an injunction would be an unjustified interference with the freedom of the press.

48. **Once it is accepted that the freedom of the press should prevail, then the form of reporting in the press is not a matter for the courts but for the Press Commission and the customers of the newspaper concerned.**

49. In relation to certain communications between A and C and D, A could be in a position to contend that their publication would constitute a breach of copyright. Restraining B in respect of the limited area to which the law of copyright would apply would serve no **purpose** if that was the only relief granted to A, and so the claim based on copyright is accepted as being of no practical significance.

50. We set aside the injunction and allow this appeal.

Pretty v United Kingdom [2002] 35 EHRR 1

Para 65 as to assisted suicide:

61. As the Court has had previous occasion to remark, the concept of 'private life' is a broad term not susceptible to exhaustive definition. It covers the physical and psychological integrity of a person. It can sometimes embrace aspects of an individual's physical and social identity. Elements such as, for example, gender identification, name and sexual orientation and sexual life fall within the personal sphere protected by article 8. Article 8 also protects a right to personal development, and the right to establish and develop **relationships** with other human beings and the outside world. Though no previous case has established as such any right to self-determination as being contained in article 8 of the Convention, the Court considers that the notion of personal autonomy is an important principle underlying the interpretation of its guarantees."

. . .

65. The very essence of the Convention is respect for human dignity and human freedom. Without in any way negating the principle of sanctity of life protected under the Convention, the Court considers that it is under Article 8 that notions of the quality of life take on significance. **In an era of growing medical sophistication combined with longer life expectancies**, many people are concerned that they should not be forced to linger on in old age or in states of advanced physical or mental decrepitude which conflict with strongly held ideas of self and personal identity.

Wainwright v Home Office [2003] UKHL 53

18. **The need in the United States to break down the concept of "invasion of privacy" into a number of loosely-linked torts must cast doubt upon the value of any high-level generalization which can perform a useful function in enabling one to deduce the rule to be applied in a concrete case.** English law has so far been unwilling, perhaps unable, to formulate any such high-level principle. There are a number of common law and statutory remedies of which it may be said that one at least of the underlying values they protect is a right of privacy. Sir Brian Neill's well known article "Privacy: a challenge for the next century" in *Protecting Privacy* (ed B Markesinis, 1999) contains a survey. Common law torts include trespass, nuisance, defamation and malicious falsehood; there is the equitable action for breach of confidence and statutory remedies under the **Protection from Harassment Act 1997** and the **Data Protection Act 1998.** There are also extra-legal remedies under Codes of Practice applicable to broadcasters and newspapers. But there are gaps; cases in which the courts have considered that an invasion of privacy deserves a remedy which the existing law does not offer. Sometimes the perceived gap can be filled by judicious development of an existing principle. The law of breach of confidence has in recent years undergone such a process: see in particular the judgment of Lord Phillips of Worth Matravers MR in *Campbell v MGN Ltd* [2003] QB 633. On the other hand, an attempt to create a tort of telephone **harassment** by a radical change in the basis of the action for private nuisance in *Khorasandjian v Bush* [1993] QB 727 was held by the House of Lords in *Hunter v Canary Wharf Ltd* [1997] AC 655 to be a step too far. The gap was filled by the 1997 Act.

[ie Lord Hoffman rejected suggestions in some earlier cases that the courts might be willing to develop a tort of "right to privacy"—see *Douglas v Hello!* [2001] QB 967, *H (A Healthcare Worker) v Associated Newspapers* [2002] EMLR 23 para 40, *Campbell v MGN* [2004] 2 AC 457 at para 79].

In Re S [2003] 3 WLR 1425 at paras 54–60

[Court of Appeal—this went to the House of Lords—appeal dismissed—Court of Appeal dicta instructive.]

54. This is the approach which should have been followed in this case. **The concept of proportionality means that the proposed interference or restriction must be supported by 'relevant and sufficient grounds'; it must respond to a 'pressing social need'; and it must be no greater than necessary to meet the legitimate aim pursued.**

55. In considering the proportionality of the proposed interference with freedom of expression, a court must not only consider the importance of press freedom in principle: as Lord Woolf CJ also said in *A v B plc*, at para 11(iv), **'The existence of a free press is in itself desirable and so any interference with it has to be justified'**. It must also consider those features which enhance its importance in the particular case. In this case, these include **(a) the particular importance to be attached to the reporting of criminal trials; these have to be subject to the scrutiny, not only of those in the courtroom but also of the wider public, not only to protect individuals against arbitrariness but also to preserve public confidence in the administration of justice; (b) in this context, therefore, *the importance of the press's freedom of expression is enhanced by the corresponding freedom of the public to receive the information in question;* and (c) this particular trial will raise more than usually important issues, about an unusual and controversial form of child abuse and about the conduct of the world famous children's hospital in which it was allegedly allowed to take place. The factors mentioned in section 12(4) of the 1998 Act are also relevant at this point.56. But that does not mean that no restriction, however limited, can be justified under Article 10(2). The court must consider what restriction, if any, is needed to meet the legitimate aim of protecting the rights of CS.** If prohibiting publication of the family name and **photographs** is needed, the court must consider how great an impact that will in fact have upon the freedom protected by Article 10. **It is relevant here that restrictions on the identification of defendants before conviction are by no means unprecedented.** The situation may well change if and when the mother is convicted. **There is a much greater public interest in knowing the names of persons convicted of serious crime than of those who are merely suspected or charged.** These considerations are also relevant to the extent of the interference with CS's rights.

57. In considering the proportionality of the proposed interference with the right of CS to respect for his private and family life, the judge must again consider the magnitude of the interference proposed. He must consider among other

things **(a)** the extent to which this additional **intrusion** would add to the interference which has already taken place and is bound to take place in future; **(b)** the extent of any further harm that identifying publicity about the trial will do to this child's private and family life, in which his mental health is a 'crucial part'; **(c)** the impact, not only directly upon the child but also upon his father and others who are looking after him, and his school, and the extent to which their task will be made harder by this kind of publicity; **(d)** the impact on this child's **relationship** with his mother in the short and the longer term and the extent of the damage this will do to this aspect of his family life.

58. **The court must then consider what steps, if any, are necessary to prevent or minimise this interference.** Again, there may be an important difference between the impact of prolonged identifying publicity, with **photographs**, during the trial and the rather shorter period during which the family might be identified if there is a conviction.

59. **These considerations may be helpful in thinking carefully about the extent of the interference or limitation proposed and the necessity for each.** A comparatively small additional harm to a child who has already suffered so much may not be a sufficient reason to limit reporting of such an important trial. **But the extent of the limitation proposed is not so great in relation to the reasons why reporting criminal trials is so important as to suggest that it could never be justified to impose it.** No-one is seeking to limit what can be said about the trial, however much the terms of some court reporting by some newspapers may be disliked in some quarters. **Mere distaste or disapproval, as Hoffman LJ indicated in R v Central Independent Television plc, can never be a ground for interference.**

60. It would be so much easier if there were a trump card or governing principle, whether it be press freedom or the rights of the child. **But there is in my judgment no escape from the difficult balancing exercise which the Convention requires.** ***Because the judge did not consider each Article independently, and thus did not conduct that exercise, I consider that this appeal should be allowed.***

Torbay Borough Council v News Group Newspapers [2004] EMLR 8

Mr Justice Munby:

. . .

The legal framework

13. So much for the facts. I turn to the law.

14. As is notorious this is a branch of the law where there has been much judicial activity over the last 25 years. This is certainly not the place for yet another general survey: that task was comprehensively performed by Ward LJ in *In re Z (A Minor) (Identification: Restrictions on Publication)* [1997] Fam 1.

15. Shortly before the Human Rights Act 1998 came into force in October 2000 I summarised the matter in *Kelly v British Broadcasting Corpn* [2001] Fam 59 at p 74:

> "in relation to the media the exercise of the court's inherent parens patriae or wardship jurisdiction is divided into three parts: the **first part**, in which the jurisdiction is not exercisable at all and the child is left to whatever remedies against the media the law would give an adult in comparable circumstances; a **second part** in which the jurisdiction is exercisable, but in circumstances where, because the court is exercising only its "protective" jurisdiction, the child's interests are *not* paramount and where a so-called balancing exercise has to be performed; and the **third part**, in which, because the court is exercising its "custodial" jurisdiction, the child's interests *are* paramount. Well known examples of cases falling into the first category, where no injunction can be granted, are *In re X (A Minor) (Wardship: Jurisdiction)* [1975] Fam 47; *R v Central Television plc* [1994] Fam 192 and *M v British Broadcasting Corpn* [1997] 1 FLR 51."

I went on to suggest that a case would fall into the second rather than the first category:

> **"only where the proposed publication is directly about a child whose care and upbringing are already being supervised by the court and is such as might threaten the effective working of the court's jurisdiction or the ability of the child's carers to carry out their obligations to the court for the care of the child."**

16. This analysis has had to be revisited in the light of the Human Rights Act 1998. **And all the earlier learning has now to be reviewed in the light of the recent decision of the Court of Appeal in Re S (A Child)** [2003] EWCA Civ 963**.** Even if the effect of *Re S* is not simply to collapse the first and second categories into one, it establishes that there is no longer any bright-line boundary between them and that it is no longer a forensically useful exercise to analyse the facts of a particular case with a view to establishing at the outset whether it properly falls into the first or into the second category.

17. The proper approach now is that encapsulated in a passage in Latham LJ's judgment at para [75]:

> "Whatever the theoretical limit of the jurisdiction may be, the authorities suggest that the court should not even consider exercising that jurisdiction in cases where publicity is not directed at the child or the child's carers unless it could have an adverse affect on the court's ability to deal properly with the care proceedings in question. I prefer the view that the jurisdiction is, as Ward LJ said in *re Z* and Millett LJ said in *R v Central Television plc,* theoretically unlimited, but that as Waite LJ said in the latter case at page 207: "The courts have nevertheless found it necessary to set self-imposed limits upon its exercise." It seems, to me, however, that the limitations so far imposed on its exercise have to be reconsidered in the light of the Human Rights Act 1998. As there is a proper foundation for the court to exercise jurisdiction, the child's rights under Article 8 must be taken into account by the court if it is to comply with its obligations under section 6 of the Act. **It follows that the court is at least entitled to consider the grant of an injunction in cases such as this even if publicity is not directed at the child or his carers and could not be shown to have an adverse effect on the care proceedings, although that will undoubtedly be a significant factor in deciding whether or not an injunction should ultimately be granted."**

As Hale LJ said at para [40]:

> "If the existence of the jurisdiction is accepted, it may now be unnecessary to resolve the tension between the various statements made in the earlier decisions of this court. These cases all preceded the implementation of the Human Rights Act 1998. Now that the Human Rights Act is in force, the relevance of the jurisdiction may simply be to provide the vehicle which enables the court to conduct the necessary balancing exercise between the competing rights of the child under Article 8 and the media under Article 10."

Lord Phillips of Worth Matravers MR said much the same thing at para [108]:

> "The cases to which I have referred predate the Human Rights Act At the same time they reflect, to a large degree, an attempt to balance the rights conferred by Article 8 of the Human Rights Convention with the Article 10 right to freedom of expression I consider, however, that the principles to be derived from the pre Human Rights Act authorities cannot be rigidly applied. It is necessary in the individual case to balance Article 8 rights which are engaged against Article 10 rights."

18. Thus the exercise of the jurisdiction now requires the court first to decide whether the child's rights under Article 8 are engaged and, if so, then to conduct the necessary balancing exercise between the competing rights under

Articles 8 and 10, considering the proportionality of the potential interference with each right considered independently.

19. The whole of Hale LJ's judgment in *Re S* repays careful study but the central core of her analysis is to be found in paras [52]—[60], and particularly in the following passages:

> "[52] . . . the court, in deciding whether to exercise its jurisdiction to restrain publication, whether under the inherent jurisdiction or under section 39 or any other statutory provision, has to consider both Article 8 and Article 10 as independent elements . . . As Sedley LJ said in *Douglas v Hello! Ltd* [2001] QB 967, at p 1005,
>
>> "Neither element is a trump card. They will be articulated by the principles of legality and proportionality which, as always, constitute the mechanism by which the court reaches its conclusion on countervailing or qualified rights. It will be remembered that in the jurisprudence of the Convention proportionality is tested by, among other things, the standard of what is necessary in a democratic society."
>
> [53] In *A v B plc* [2003] QB 195, Lord Woolf CJ observed at para 6:
>
>> "There is a tension between the two articles which requires the court to hold the balance between the conflicting interests they are designed to protect. This is not an easy task but it can be achieved by the courts if, when holding the balance, they attach proper weight to the important rights which both articles are designed to protect. Each article is qualified expressly in a way which allows the interests under the other article to be taken into account."
>
> [54] This is the approach which should have been followed in this case. The concept of proportionality means that the proposed interference or restriction must be supported by 'relevant and sufficient grounds'; it must respond to a 'pressing social need'; and it must be no greater than necessary to meet the legitimate aim pursued.
>
> [55] In considering the proportionality of the proposed interference with freedom of expression, a court must not only consider the importance of press freedom in principle: as Lord Woolf CJ also said in *A v B plc*, at para 11(iv), 'The existence of a free press is in itself desirable and so any interference with it has to be justified'. It must also consider those features which enhance its importance in the particular case.
>
> [60] It would be so much easier if there were a trump card or governing principle, whether it be press freedom or the rights of the child, But there is in my judgment no escape from the difficult balancing exercise

> which the Convention requires . . . the judge did not consider each Article independently, and thus did not conduct that exercise . . . "

Lord Phillips MR and Latham LJ agreed. At para [64] Latham LJ described the exercise now required under the Human Rights Act as being:

> "identifying the extent to which refusing to grant the relevant terms of the injunction asked for would be a proportionate interference with the private life of the child on the one hand and their grant would be a proportionate interference with the rights of the press under Article 10 on the other hand."

20. It is, no doubt, ultimately a somewhat fruitless exercise to reconsider in the light of the decision in *Re S* all the many cases that were decided before the Human Rights Act 1998. But it is, perhaps, worth noting that there is, so far as I can see, nothing whatever in any of the judgments in *Re S* to suggest that the outcome in either *In re X (A Minor) (Wardship: Jurisdiction)* [1975] Fam 47 or *R v Central Television plc* [1994] Fam 192 would have been any different had the new approach been adopted. If anything quite the contrary, for at para [37] Hale LJ made this observation:

> "The information in this case lies somewhere in between that in *Re X* and *R v Central Television* and that in *Re M and N* or *Re W*. The proposed publication will not relate directly to how CS is currently being brought up . . . On the other hand, this is not the sort of remote and unconnected information about a deceased or long-absent parent with which the cases of *Re X* and *R v Central Independent Television plc* were concerned. The publication will relate to events within his recent family life in which he has been directly involved. These have already had and will continue to have a serious impact upon the way in which he is brought up."

In re X, it will be recalled, was the case in which, as I said in *Kelly v British Broadcasting Corpn* [2001] Fam 59 at p 73,

> "an ultimately unsuccessful attempt was made to invoke the wardship jurisdiction to suppress a book describing the aberrant private activities of a 14-year-old girl's dead father, publication of which would be 'psychologically grossly damaging' to the child and where the injury to her emotional psychological health would be 'very grave indeed'."

21. In *Re S* the balancing exercise was not particularly complicated. Although Article 6 was also implicated the essential contest was between the rights of the child under Article 8 and the rights of the media under Article 10. In the present case, as we shall see, the exercise is more complicated. On one side there are ranged ANL's rights under Article 10 and, as she would have it, Angela's rights under both Article 10 and Article 8. On the other side there are ranged Article 8 rights asserted on behalf of both X and Y and also, on

one view, Angela's rights under Article 8. But although the exercise may be more complicated (though no more complicated than the somewhat similar exercise I had to undertake in *Clibbery v Allan* [2001] 2 FLR 819, affirmed on appeal, *Clibbery v Allan* [2002] EWCA Civ 45, [2002] Fam 261) the essential task remains that identified by Hale LJ in *Re S*.

22. Mr Warby was thus, in my judgment, right to accept in the light of *Re S* that the present case has to be viewed as one where I can *consider* the exercise of the protective jurisdiction, even though neither Angela nor Y is any longer the subject of a care order (and X, so far as I am aware, was never the subject of a care order) and even though the proposed article is not directed at the way in which any of them is being brought up now. Likewise, in my judgment, Mr Warby was right to accept that I can in principle *exercise* the jurisdiction if I conclude that Article 8 is engaged.

. . .

The Convention

25. I turn therefore to consider the relevant provisions of the European Convention for the Protection of Human Rights and Fundamental Freedoms. Mr Warby and Mr Arnot are rightly agreed that the Articles which here either are or may be in play are Articles 8 and 10.

26. Article 10 affirms "the right to freedom of expression", including "freedom to hold opinions and to receive and impart information and ideas without interference by public authority". That, of course, is subject to the well-known exceptions in Article 10(2). Article 8 guarantees, subject to the exceptions in Article 8(2), the "right to respect for . . . private and family life".

27. The Article 10 jurisprudence is familiar and needs little exposition here. So too is the jurisprudence relating to the right to respect for "family life" guaranteed by Article 8. But central to the arguments in the present case is the perhaps somewhat less familiar jurisprudence relating to the right to respect for "private life" also guaranteed by Article 8. To that I therefore turn.

28. First, however, there is one aspect of Article 10 that requires emphasis. Article 10 protects both the right to "receive" and the right to "impart" information and ideas. As I said in *Kelly v British Broadcasting Corpn* [2001] Fam 59 at p 79:

> "Press conferences held by those who wish to attract attention to their views, and interviews conducted by the media, are both essential mechanisms for facilitating the exercise of the rights guaranteed by article 10. Both the press conference and the interview are means by which those wishing to disseminate their views exercise their Convention right to 'impart' information and ideas and by which the

> media exercise their Convention rights both to 'receive' and in turn to 'impart' information and ideas."

So, in a case such as this, one is concerned with the Article 10 rights not merely of the press and of those who read newspapers but also of those who wish to tell—or sell—their stories to the press. And just as I stressed in *Kelly* at p 79 that I was concerned with the Article 10 rights not merely of the BBC but also of Bobby Kelly, so here I stress that I am concerned not merely with the Article 10 rights of ANL and the *Mail on Sunday* but also—and every bit as important—with Angela's Article 10 rights.

29. I turn to Article 8. The starting point is *Niemietz v Germany* (1993) 16 EHRR 97 at para [29], where the Court indicated that "private life" includes at least two elements. The first is the notion of "an "inner circle" in which the individual may live his own personal life as he chooses"; the second is "the right to establish and develop **relationships** with other human beings". Applying *Niemietz v Germany*, the Court in *Botta v Italy* (1998) 26 EHRR 241 at para [32] said:

> "Private life, in the court's view, includes a person's physical and psychological integrity; the guarantee afforded by Art 8 of the Convention is primarily intended to ensure the development, without outside interference, of the personality of each individual in his relations with other human beings."

30. This was elaborated by the Court in *Bensaid v United Kingdom* (2001) 33 EHRR 205 at paras [46]–[47]:

> "[46] Not every act or measure which adversely affects moral or physical integrity will interfere with the right to respect to private life guaranteed by Article 8. However, the Court's case-law does not exclude that treatment which does not reach the severity of Article 3 treatment may nonetheless breach Article 8 in its private life aspect where there are sufficiently adverse effects on physical and moral integrity.
>
> [47] Private life is a broad term not susceptible to exhaustive definition. The Court has already held that elements such as gender identification, name and sexual orientation and sexual life are important elements of the personal sphere protected by Article 8. Mental health must also be regarded as a crucial part of private life associated with the aspect of moral integrity. Article 8 protects a right to identity and personal development, and the right to establish and develop **relationships** with other human beings and the outside world. The preservation of mental stability is in that context an indispensable precondition to effective enjoyment of the right to respect for private life."

31. In *Pretty v United Kingdom* (2002) 35 EHRR 1, [2002] 2 FLR 45, at para [61] the Court drew the inevitable conclusion:

> "As the Court has had previous occasion to remark, the concept of 'private life' is a broad term not susceptible to exhaustive definition. It covers the physical and psychological integrity of a person. It can sometimes embrace aspects of an individual's physical and social identity. Elements such as, for example, gender identification, name and sexual orientation and sexual life fall within the personal sphere protected by Article 8. Article 8 also protects a right to personal development, and the right to establish and develop **relationships** with other human beings and the outside world. Though no previous case has established as such any right to self-determination as being contained in Article 8 of the Convention, the Court considers that the notion of personal autonomy is an important principle underlying the interpretation of its guarantees."

32. In addition to its emphasis on the importance of personal autonomy as one of the principles underlying Article 8 (as to which see also what the Court said at para [66]) the Court stressed at para [65] tha"The very essence of the Convention is respect for human dignity and human freedom."

33. This Strasbourg jurisprudence has of course been recognised and applied in our domestic case law. A striking example is the decision of the President in *X and Y v News Group Newspapers and MGN Limited* [2003] EWHC 1101 (QB)—the Mary Bell case—but there are many others. In *R (A, B, X and Y) v East Sussex County Council* [2003] EWHC 167 (Admin) at para [86] I said:

> "True it is that the phrase [human dignity] is not used in the Convention but it is surely immanent in article 8, indeed in almost every one of the Convention's provisions. The recognition and protection of human dignity is one of the core values—in truth *the* core value—of our society and, indeed, of all the societies which are part of the European family of nations and which have embraced the principles of the Convention. It is a core value of the common law, long predating the Convention."

34. There is one final aspect of private life that needs to be remembered in this context. *As Gaskin v United Kingdom* (1990) 12 EHRR 36 shows, amongst the aspects of private life respect for which is guaranteed by Article 8 is knowledge about, and the right to obtain from public records information about, one's childhood, development and history.

35. Article 8 thus protects two very different kinds of private life both the private life lived privately and kept hidden from the outside world and also the private life lived in company with other human beings and **shared** with the outside world. For, as the Strasbourg jurisprudence recognises, the ability to lead one's own personal life as one chooses, the ability to develop

one's personality, indeed one's very psychological and moral integrity, are dependent upon being able to interact and develop **relationships** with other human beings and with the world at large. And central to one's psychological and moral integrity, to one's feelings of self-worth, is the knowledge of one's childhood, development and history. So amongst the rights protected by Article 8, as it seems to me, is the right, as a human being, to share with others—and, if one so chooses, with the world at large—one's own story, the story of one's childhood, development and history. Man is a sociable being. Long ago Aristotle said that "He who is unable to live in society, or who has no need because he is sufficient for himself, must be either a beast or a god". More recently, Blackstone observed that, "Man was formed for society". And, somewhat earlier, John Donne had memorably written that, "No man is an Island . . . any man's death diminishes me, because I am involved in Mankind". That is what distinguishes mankind from the brute creation. We are able to think and to communicate with each other. We have self-awareness. It is natural for us to want to talk to others about ourselves and about our lives. It is fundamental to our human condition, to our dignity as human beings, that we should be able to do so. This, after all, is why totalitarian regimes seek to silence those who will not conform not merely by taking away their right to speak in public but also by depriving them of human companionship.

36. The personal autonomy protected by Article 8 embraces the right to decide who is to be within the "inner circle", the right to decide whether that which is private should remain private or whether it should be **shared** with others. **Article 8 thus embraces both the right to maintain one's privacy and, if this is what one prefers, not merely the right to waive that privacy but also the right to share what would otherwise be private with others** or, indeed, with the world at large. So the right to communicate one's story to one's fellow beings is protected not merely by Article 10 but also by Article 8.

37. A child is, of course, as much entitled to the protection of the Convention—and specifically of Articles 8 and 10—as anyone else. But, as Mr Arnot correctly pointed out, the personal autonomy guaranteed by Article 8 (and, I would add, by Article 10) is necessarily somewhat qualified in the case of a child. For, depending on the circumstances, decision—making power may rest not with the child but with the child's parents or even with the court. I must return to this topic in due course. For the moment I observe only that there may well be cases where a child wishes to go to the media—wishes, in other words, to avail himself of what he asserts are his Article 10 and Article 8 rights to make public that which would otherwise be private—whilst his parents, or the court, may think that his interests are better served by asserting his right under Article 8 to keep such matters private.

The Convention in the present case

38. I approach the present case on the footing that neither X nor Y (nor their parents on their behalf) wish to waive their privacy. And both have a family life which, I imagine, they and their parents are anxious to preserve and protect. Angela, on the other hand, not merely wishes to waive her privacy: she is anxious to communicate her story to the whole world. She is, however, still a child. It can therefore be seen that the following Convention rights are or may be engaged:

    i) X's rights under Article 8 (a) to keep his private life private and (b) to preserve and protect the family life he enjoys with his parents and other members of his family;

    ii) Y's rights under Article 8 (a) to keep her private life private and (b) to preserve and protect the family life she is now enjoying with her adoptive parents;

    iii) Angela's rights under Articles 8 and 10, as she wishes to assert them, to tell her story to the world through the medium of the *Mail on Sunday;*

    iv) Angela's rights under Article 8, as Angela's parents or the court might wish to assert them on her behalf, (a) to keep her private life private and (b) to preserve and protect the family life she enjoys with her parents and other members of her family;

    v) ANL's rights under Article 10 (a) to obtain the story that Angela wishes to tell and (b) to publish Angela's story in the *Mail on Sunday.*

. . .

Concluding observations

88. There is one final matter I must deal with. Mr Arnot invited me to make an order requiring ANL to file with the court and serve on the local authority a copy of each article that it proposes to publish. I would in any event have declined to do so. I am not aware of any case in which such an order has been made and I can think of no case other than *In re W (A Minor) (Wardship: Restrictions on Publication)* [1992] 1 WLR 100 in which a newspaper has volunteered an article in draft. In my experience both the print and the broadcast media usually decline to share their story with the court in advance of publication or broadcast.

89. Now quite apart from any editorial reasons the media may have for adopting this stance there is, as it seems to me, very good reason why the court should not go down the road suggested by Mr Arnot. A judge can assess what is lawful or unlawful, A Judge in the Family Division may be called on to assess whether some publication is sufficiently harmful to a child as to warrant preventing it. But judges are not arbiters of taste or decency. As

Neill LJ said in *In re W (A Minor) (Wardship: Restrictions on Publication)* [1992] 1 WLR 100 at p 104:

> "The court has seen a copy of the article to be published by the newspaper. It is not for me to comment on the style of the article. . . . But I have no doubt whatever that the newspaper should be free to publish this story and to publish it in a manner which will engage the interest of their readers."

It is not the function of the judges to legitimise "responsible" reporting whilst censoring what some are pleased to call "irresponsible" reporting. The days are past when the business of the judges was the enforcement of morals. A judge, although it may be that on occasions he can legitimately exercise the functions of an aedile, is no censor. And as the Strasbourg jurisprudence establishes (see *Harris v Harris, Attorney-General v Harris* [2001] 2 FLR 895 at para [373]), the freedom of expression secured by Article 10 is applicable not only to information or ideas that are favourably received, or regarded as inoffensive, but also to those that offend, shock or disturb the State or any section of the community. Article 10 protects not only the substance of the ideas and information expressed, but also the form in which they are conveyed. It is not for the court to substitute its own views for those of the press as to what technique of reporting should be adopted by journalists. Article 10 entitles journalists to adopt a particular form of presentation intended to ensure a particularly telling effect on the average reader. As Neill LJ recognised, a tabloid newspaper is entitled to tell the story in a manner which will engage the interest of its readers and the general public. If there is no basis for injuncting a story expressed in the temperate or scholarly language of a legal periodical or the broadsheet press there can be no basis for injuncting the same story simply because it is expressed in the more robust, colourful or intemperate language of the tabloid press.

90. At the end of the hearing on Friday 28 November 2003 I made an order in the following terms, saying that I would give my reasons in due course: this I have now done:

> "IT IS ORDERED that:
>
> 1 The Order of Mr Justice Munby made herein on 7 July 2000 be discharged.
>
> 2 Until 4 December 2004 or further order in the meantime no person including the defendant (whether by himself', his servants or agents or otherwise howsoever or in the case of a company, whether by its directors, servants or agents or otherwise howsoever) shall do any of the following things except to the extent permitted by paragraphs 3 and 7 of this Order:

(i) publish in any book, magazine or newspaper or broadcast in any sound or television broadcast or by means of any cable or satellite programme services:

(a) the name and/or address of:

(1) Angela Roddy;

(2) any school or any other educational institution attended by Angela Roddy;

(b) any picture being or including a picture of Angela Roddy;

(c) any other matter calculated to lead to the identification of Angela Roddy as being the girl who became pregnant at the age of 12;

(ii) solicit any information relating to Angela Roddy (other than information already in the **public domain**):

(a) from Angela Roddy;

(b) from any natural person believed to have or have had day-today care of Angela Roddy;

(c) from her parents;

(d) from any other person who is believed to be a relative of Angela Roddy;

(e) from the staff and/or pupils of any school or educational institution that Angela Roddy is believed to attend or to have attended;

(iii) (notwithstanding the provisions of section 12(2) of the Administration of Justice Act 1960 as amended . . .) include, in any publication of the text or a summary of the whole or any part of this Order, any of the matters referred to in paragraph 2(i) above;

(iv) give or seek information or conduct any negotiation for publication from the home in which Angela Roddy resides or in the presence of Angela Roddy;

(v) publish any information (other than information already in the **public domain**) relating to Angela Roddy that has been obtained directly or indirectly from Angela Roddy's father, Anthony Roddy.

3 The injunctions in paragraph 2 above shall not of themselves prohibit any person from publishing information falling within paragraphs 2(i), (iii) or (v) above if the publication is made:

(i) with the prior consent of Angela Roddy; or

(ii) at a time when the information is already in the **public domain**.

4 Until 4 December 2004 or further order in the meantime no person including the defendant (whether by himself, his servants or agents or otherwise howsoever or in the case of a company, whether by its directors, servants or agents or otherwise howsoever) shall do any of the following things except to the extent permitted by paragraph 7 of this Order:

(i) publish in any book, magazine or newspaper or broadcast in any sound or television broadcast or by means of any cable or satellite programme services, any matter calculated to lead to the identification of [X] as the putative father of Angela Roddy's child;

(ii) solicit any information relating to [X] (other than information already in the **public domain**):

(a) from [X];

(b) from any natural person believed to have had day to day care of [X];

(c) from his parents;

(d) from any other person who is believed to be a relative of [X];

(e) from the staff and/or pupils of any school or educational institution that [X] is believed to attend or to have attended;

(iii) (notwithstanding the provisions of section 12(2) of the Administration of Justice Act 1960 as amended . . .) include in any publication of the text or a summary of the whole or in any part of this Order, any of the matters referred to in paragraph 4(i) above;

(iv) publish any **intimate** medical or educational information or other **confidential information** (other than information already in the **public domain**) relating to [X] that has been obtained directly or indirectly from Angela Roddy's father, Anthony Roddy.

5 Until 27 January 2018 or further order in the meantime (but without prejudice to paragraph 3(i) above in so far as it relates to the information in paragraph 2) no person including the defendant (whether by himself, his servants or agents or otherwise howsoever or in the case of a company whether by its directors, servants or agents otherwise howsoever) shall:

(i) publish in any book, magazine or newspaper or broadcast in any sound or television broadcast or by means of any cable or satellite programme service:

(a) the name and/or address of [Y];

(b) any picture being or including a picture of [Y];

(c) any other matter calculated to lead to the identification of [Y] as being the child of Angela Roddy, or [X] (as the putative father of [Y]);

(ii) solicit any information relating to [Y] (other than information already in the **public domain**) from any natural person other than Angela Roddy believed to have or have had day to day care of [Y];

(iii) solicit any information within paragraph *5(i)* above at any time from any person.

6

(i) Until 4.00 pm on Thursday 4 December 2003 or further order in the meantime no person including the defendant (whether by himself, his servants or agents or otherwise howsoever or in the case of a company whether by its directors, servants or agents otherwise howsoever) shall publish in any book, magazine or newspaper or broadcast in any sound or television broadcast or by means of any cable or satellite programme service any information which identifies [the local authority] as the Authority which has had responsibility for and has made decisions in respect of the care of Angela Roddy or [Y].

(ii) If the claimant wishes to apply for an extension of this injunction notice must be given to Associated Newspapers Limited by 12.00 noon on Wednesday 3 December 2003 together with, if possible, and if need be in draft, the evidence in support.

7. Nothing in this Order shall of itself prevent any person:

(a) inquiring of another person:

(i) as to whether that person is a person referred to in paragraph 2(ii) or 4(ii) or 5(ii) above;

(ii) whether any particular information is information within paragraph 5;

(b) publishing any particulars of or information relating to any part of the proceedings before any Court other than a court sitting in private,

(c) soliciting information relating to Angela Roddy or [X] or [Y] in the course of or for the **purpose** of the exercise by the person soliciting such information of any duty or function authorised by statute or by any Court of competent jurisdiction."

91. There remains the question of costs. Each side sought at least a partial order for costs against the other. Neither side has been completely successful. And the fact is that ANL would have been put to the cost of appearing before the court even if the matter had been wholly unopposed. Subject to any further

submissions that either party may wish to make I propose to direct that there should be no order as to costs.

Postscript (4 December 2003)

92. On 3 December 2003 the local authority informed ANL and the court that it was not seeking any further order. Accordingly the injunction contained in paragraph 6(i) of the order I had made on 28 November 2003 expired by effluxion of time at 4pm on 4 December 2003. It follows that there is no longer any reason why the local authority should not be named. It is in fact Torbay Borough Council.

93. I have been told that the parties wish to make further submissions in relation to costs. I shall deal with that matter in due course.

In Re S (a child) [2004] UKHL 47

17. The interplay between articles 8 and 10 has been illuminated by the opinions in the House of Lords in *Campbell v MGN Ltd* [2004] 2 WLR 1232. For present purposes the decision of the House on the facts of *Campbell* and the differences between the majority and the minority are not material. What does, however, emerge clearly from the opinions are four propositions. **First**, neither article has *as such* precedence over the other. **Secondly**, where the values under the two articles are in conflict, **an intense focus** on the comparative importance of the specific rights being claimed in the individual case is necessary. **Thirdly**, the justifications for interfering with or restricting each right must be taken into account. **Finally**, the proportionality test must be applied to each. For convenience I will call this the ultimate balancing test. This is how I will approach the present case.

. . .

34. **Thirdly**, it is important to bear in mind that from a newspaper's point of view a report of a sensational trial without revealing the identity of the defendant would be a very much **disembodied** trial. If the newspapers choose not to contest such an injunction, they are less likely to give prominence to reports of the trial. Certainly, readers will be less interested and editors will act accordingly. Informed **debate** about criminal justice will suffer.

35. **Fourthly**, it is true that newspapers can always contest an application for an injunction. **Even for national newspapers that is, however, a costly matter which may involve proceedings at different judicial levels. Moreover, time constraints of an impending trial may not always permit such proceedings.**

Often it will be too late and the injunction will have had its negative effect on contemporary reporting.

R (Razgar) v Secretary of State for the Home Department [2004] UKHL 27

Meaning of 'private life'

9. This judgment establishes, in my opinion quite clearly, that reliance may in principle be placed on article 8 to resist an expulsion decision, even where the main emphasis is not on the severance of family and social ties which the applicant has enjoyed in the expelling country but on **the consequences for his mental health** of removal to the receiving country. *The threshold of successful reliance is high, but if the facts are strong enough article 8 may in principle be invoked.* **It is plain that "private life" is a broad term, and the Court has wisely eschewed any attempt to define it comprehensively**. *It is relevant for present purposes that the Court saw mental stability as an indispensable precondition to effective enjoyment of the right to respect for private life.* In *Pretty v United Kingdom* (2002) 35 EHRR 1, paragraph 61, the Court held the expression to cover "the physical and psychological integrity of a person" and went on to observe that

> *"Article 8 also protects a right to personal development, and the right to establish and develop* **relationships** *with other human beings and the outside world."*

Elusive though the concept is, I think one must understand **"private life" in article 8 as extending to those features which are integral to a person's identity or ability to function socially as a person.** Professor Feldman, writing in 1997 before the most recent decisions, helpfully observed ("The Developing Scope of Article 8 of the European Convention on Human Rights", [1997] EHRLR 265, 270):

> **"Moral integrity in this sense demands that we treat the person holistically as morally worthy of respect, organising the state and society in ways which respect people's moral worth by taking account of their need for security."**

Campbell v MGN Ltd [2004] UKHL 22

Note Lord Nicholls and Lord Hoffman dissenting

Breach of confidence: misuse of private information

11. In this country, unlike the United States of America, there is no over-arching, all-embracing cause of action for 'invasion of privacy': see *Wainwright v Home Office* [2003] 3 WLR 1137. But protection of various aspects of privacy is a fast developing area of the law, here and in some other common law jurisdictions. The recent decision of the Court of Appeal of New Zealand in *Hosking v Runting* (25 March 2004) is an example of this. In this country development of the law has been spurred by enactment of the Human Rights Act 1998.

12. The present case concerns one aspect of invasion of privacy: wrongful disclosure of private information. The case involves the familiar competition between freedom of expression and respect for an individual's privacy. Both are vitally important rights. Neither has precedence over the other. **The importance of freedom of expression has been stressed often and eloquently, the importance of privacy less so. But it, too, lies at the heart of liberty in a modern state. A proper degree of privacy is essential for the well-being and development of an individual. And restraints imposed on government to pry into the lives of the citizen go to the essence of a democratic state**: see La Forest J in *R v Dymont* [1988] 2 SCR 417, 426.

13. The common law or, more precisely, courts of equity have long afforded protection to the wrongful use of private information by means of the cause of action which became known as breach of confidence. **A breach of confidence was restrained as a form of unconscionable conduct, akin to a breach of trust. Today this nomenclature is misleading.** The breach of confidence label harks back to the time when the cause of action was based on improper use of information disclosed by one person to another in confidence. To attract protection the information had to be of a confidential nature. But the gist of the cause of action was that information of this character had been disclosed by one person to another in circumstances 'importing an obligation of confidence' even though no contract of non-disclosure existed: see the classic exposition by Megarry J in *Coco v A N Clark (Engineers) Ltd* [1969] RPC 41, 47–48. The confidence referred to in the phrase 'breach of confidence' was the confidence arising out of a confidential **relationship**.

14. **This cause of action has now firmly shaken off the limiting constraint of the need for an initial confidential relationship. In doing so it has changed its nature.** In this country this development was recognised clearly in the judgment of Lord Goff of Chieveley in Attorney-General v Guardian Newspapers Ltd (No 2) [1990] 1 AC 109, 281**. Now the law imposes a 'duty of confidence' whenever a person receives information he knows or ought to know is fairly and reasonably to be regarded as confidential.** Even this formulation is awkward. The continuing use of the phrase 'duty of confidence' and the

description of the information as 'confidential' is not altogether comfortable. Information about an individual's private life would not, in ordinary usage, be called 'confidential'. The more natural description today is that such information is private. **The essence of the tort is better encapsulated now as misuse of private information.**

15. In the case of individuals this tort, however labelled, affords respect for one aspect of an individual's privacy. That is the value underlying this cause of action. **An individual's privacy can be invaded in ways not involving publication of information. Strip-searches are an example.** The extent to which the common law as developed thus far in this country protects other forms of invasion of privacy is not a matter arising in the present case. It does not arise because, although pleaded more widely, Miss Campbell's common law claim was throughout presented in court exclusively on the basis of breach of confidence, that is, the wrongful publication by the 'Mirror' of private information.

16. The European Convention on Human Rights, and the Strasbourg jurisprudence, have undoubtedly had a significant influence in this area of the common law for some years. The provisions of article 8, concerning respect for private and family life, and article 10, concerning freedom of expression, and the interaction of these two articles, have prompted the courts of this country to identify more clearly the different factors involved in cases where one or other of these two interests is present. Where both are present the courts are increasingly explicit in evaluating the competing considerations involved. When identifying and evaluating these factors the courts, including your Lordships' House, have tested the common law against the values encapsulated in these two articles. **The development of the common law has been in harmony with these articles of the Convention**: see, for instance, Reynolds v Times Newspapers Ltd [2001] 2 AC 127, 203–204.

17. **The time has come to recognise that the values enshrined in articles 8 and 10 are now part of the cause of action for breach of confidence. As Lord Woolf CJ has said, the courts have been able to achieve this result by absorbing the rights protected by articles 8 and 10 into this cause of action**: A v B plc [2003] QB 195, 202, para 4. Further, it should now be recognised that for this **purpose** these values are of general application. **The values embodied in articles 8 and 10 are as much applicable in disputes between individuals or between an individual and a non-governmental body such as a newspaper as they are in disputes between individuals and a public authority.**

18. In reaching this conclusion it is not necessary to pursue the controversial question whether the European Convention itself has this wider effect. Nor is it necessary to decide whether the duty imposed on courts by section 6 of

the Human Rights Act 1998 extends to questions of substantive law as distinct from questions of practice and procedure. **It is sufficient to recognise that the values underlying articles 8 and 10 are not confined to disputes between individuals and public authorities.** This approach has been adopted by the courts in several recent decisions, reported and unreported, where individuals have complained of press **intrusion**. A convenient summary of these cases is to be found in Gavin Phillipson's valuable article 'Transforming Breach of Confidence? Towards a Common Law Right of Privacy under the Human Rights Act' (2003) 66 MLR 726, 726–728.

19. In applying this approach, and giving effect to the values protected by article 8, courts will often be aided by adopting the structure of article 8 in the same way as they now habitually apply the Strasbourg court's approach to article 10 when resolving questions concerning freedom of expression. **Articles 8 and 10 call for a more explicit analysis of competing considerations than the three traditional requirements of the cause of action for breach of confidence identified in Coco v A N Clark (Engineers) Ltd [1969] RPC 41.**

20. I should take this a little further on one point. Article 8(1) recognises the need to respect private and family life. **Article 8(2) recognises there are occasions when intrusion into private and family life may be justified**. One of these is where the **intrusion** is necessary for the protection of the rights and freedoms of others. Article 10(1) recognises the importance of freedom of expression. **But article 10(2), like article 8(2), recognises there are occasions when protection of the rights of others may make it necessary for freedom of expression to give way.** When both these articles are engaged a difficult question of proportionality may arise. This question is distinct from the initial question of whether the published information engaged article 8 at all by being within the sphere of the complainant's private or family life

21. Accordingly, in deciding what was the ambit of an individual's 'private life' in particular circumstances courts need to be on guard against using as a touchstone a test which brings into account considerations which should more properly be considered at the later stage of proportionality. **Essentially the touchstone of private life is whether in respect of the disclosed facts the person in question *had a reasonable expectation of privacy.***

22. Different forms of words, usually to much the same effect, have been suggested from time to time. The second Restatement of Torts in the United States (1977), article 652D, p 394, uses the formulation of disclosure of matter which 'would be **highly offensive** to a reasonable person'. In Australian Broadcasting Corporation v Lenah Game Meats Pty Ltd (2001) 185 ALR 1, 13, para 42, Gleeson CJ used words, widely quoted, having a similar meaning. This particular formulation should be used with care, for two reasons. **First**, the '**highly offensive**' phrase is suggestive of a stricter test of

private information than a reasonable expectation of privacy. **Second**, the '**highly offensive**' formulation can all too easily bring into account, when deciding whether the disclosed information was private, considerations which **go more properly to issues of proportionality**; for instance, **the degree of intrusion into private life, and the extent to which publication was a matter of proper public concern.** This could be a recipe for confusion.

The present case

23. I turn to the present case and consider first whether the information whose disclosure is in dispute was private. Mr Caldecott QC placed the information published by the newspaper **into five categories**: **(1)** the fact of Miss Campbell's drug addiction; **(2)** the fact that she was receiving treatment; **(3)** the fact that she was receiving treatment at Narcotics Anonymous; **(4)** the details of the treatment—how long she had been attending meetings, how often she went, how she was treated within the sessions themselves, the extent of her commitment, and the nature of her entrance on the specific occasion; and **(5)** the visual portrayal of her leaving a specific meeting with other addicts.

24. It was common ground between the parties that in the ordinary course the information in **all five categories would attract the protection of article 8.** But Mr Caldecott recognised that, as he put it, Miss Campbell's 'public lies' precluded her from claiming protection for categories (1) and (2). **When talking to the media Miss Campbell went out of her way to say that, unlike many fashion models, she did not take drugs.** By repeatedly making these assertions in public Miss Campbell *could no longer have a reasonable expectation* that this aspect of her life should be private. Public disclosure that, contrary to her assertions, she did in fact take drugs and had a serious drug problem for which she was being treated was not disclosure of private information..**As the Court of Appeal noted, where a public figure chooses to present a false image and make untrue pronouncements about his or her life, the press will normally be entitled to put the record straight**: [2003] QB 633, 658. Thus the area of dispute at the trial concerned the other three categories of information.

. . .

29. . . . **The need to be free to disseminate information regarding Miss Campbell's drug addiction is of a lower order than the need for freedom to disseminate information on some other subjects such as political information.** *The degree of* **latitude** *reasonably to be accorded to journalists is correspondingly reduced, but it is not excluded altogether.*

. . .

LORD HOFFMANN

My Lords,

36. The House is divided as to the outcome of this appeal, but the difference of opinion relates to a very **narrow** point which arises on the unusual facts of this case. The facts are unusual because the plaintiff is a **public figure who had made very public false statements** about a matter in respect of which even a **public figure** would ordinarily be entitled to privacy, **namely her use of drugs.** It was these **falsehoods** which, as was conceded, made it justifiable, for a newspaper to report the fact that she was addicted. **The division of opinion is whether in doing so the newspaper went too far in publishing associated facts about her private life**. But the importance of this case lies in the statements of **general principle on the way in which the law should strike a balance between the right** to privacy and the right to freedom of expression, on which the House is **unanimous**. The principles are expressed in varying language but speaking for myself I can see no significant differences.

37. Naomi Campbell is a famous fashion model who lives by publicity. What she has to sell is herself: her personal appearance and her personality. **She employs public relations agents to present her personal life to the media in the best possible light just as she employs professionals to advise her on dress and make-up**. That is no criticism of her. It is a trade like any other. **But it does mean that her relationship with the media is different from that of people who expose less of their private life to the public.**

38. **The image which she has sought to project of herself to the international media is that of a black woman who started with few advantages in life and has by her own efforts attained international success in a glamorous profession.** There is much truth in this claim. Unfortunately she has also given wide publicity, in interviews with journalists and on television, **to a claim which was false,** namely that **(unlike many of her colleagues in the fashion business)** she had not succumbed to the temptation to take drugs.

. . .

50. What human rights law has done is to identify private information as something worth protecting **as an aspect of human autonomy and dignity.** And this recognition has raised inescapably the question of why it should be worth protecting against the state but not against a private person. There may of course be justifications for the publication of private information by private persons which would not be available to the state—I have particularly in mind the position of the media, to which I shall return in a moment—but **I can see no logical ground for saying that a person should have less protection against a private individual than he would have against the state**

for the publication of personal information for which there is no justification. Nor, it appears, have any of the other judges who have considered the matter.

[As to the interaction of breach of confidence and privacy]

51. The result of these developments has been a shift in the centre of gravity of the action for breach of confidence when it is used as a remedy for the unjustified publication of personal information. It recognises that the incremental changes to which I have referred do not merely extend the duties arising traditionally from a **relationship** of trust and confidence to a wider range of people. **As Sedley LJ observed in a perceptive passage in his judgment in Douglas v Hello! Ltd** [2001] QB 967**, 1001, the new approach takes a different view of the underlying value which the law protects.** Instead of the cause of action being based upon the duty of good faith applicable to confidential personal information and **trade secrets** alike**, it focuses upon the protection of human autonomy and dignity—the right to control the dissemination of information about one's private life and the right to the esteem and respect of other people.**

. . .

55. I shall first consider the **relationship** between the freedom of the press and the common law right of the individual to protect personal information. Both reflect important civilised values, but, as often happens, neither can be given effect in full measure without restricting the other. How are they to be reconciled in a particular case? **There is in my view no question of automatic priority**. **Nor is there a presumption in favour of one rather than the other**. The question is rather the extent to which it is **necessary** to qualify the one right in order to protect the underlying value which is protected by the other. **And the extent of the qualification must be *proportionate* to the *need*:** see Sedley LJ in *Douglas v Hello! Ltd* [2001] QB 967, 1005, para 137.

56. If one takes this approach, there is often no real conflict. Take the example I have just given of the ordinary citizen whose attendance at NA is publicised in his local newspaper. The violation of the citizen's autonomy, dignity and self-esteem is plain and obvious. Do the civil and political values which underlie press freedom make it necessary to deny the citizen the right to protect such personal information? Not at all. While there is no contrary public interest recognised and protected by the law, the press is free to publish anything it likes. Subject to the law of defamation, **it does not matter how trivial, spiteful or offensive the publication may be**. But when press freedom comes into conflict with another interest protected by the law, **the question is whether there is a sufficient public interest in that particular publication to justify curtailment of the conflicting right. In the example I**

have given, there is no public interest whatever in publishing to the world the fact that the citizen has a drug dependency. The freedom to make such a statement weighs little in the balance against the privacy of personal information.

57. One must therefore proceed to consider the grounds why the *Mirror* say there was a public interest in its publication of information about Ms Campbell which it would not have been justified in publishing about someone else. First, there is the fact that she is a **public figure** who has had a long and symbiotic **relationship** with the media. In my opinion, **that would not in itself justify publication**. *A person may attract or even seek publicity about some aspects of his or her life without creating any public interest in the publication of personal information about other matters.* I think that the history of Ms Campbell's **relationship** with the media does have some relevance to this case, to which I shall return in due course, but that would not without more justify publication of confidential personal information" [That is, great interest by the public does not correspond to a great public interest].

58. The reason why Mr Caldecott **concedes** that the *Mirror* was entitled to publish the fact of her drug dependency and the fact that she was seeking treatment is that she had specifically given publicity to the very question of whether she took drugs and **had falsely said** that she did not. I accept that this creates a sufficient public interest in the correction of the impression she had previously given.

59. The question is then whether the *Mirror* should have confined itself to these bare facts or whether it was entitled to reveal more of the circumstantial detail and print the **photographs**. If one applies the test of necessity or proportionality which I have suggested, this is a matter on which different people may have different views. That appears clearly enough from the judgments which have been delivered in this case. **But judges are not newspaper editors**. It may have been possible for the *Mirror* to satisfy the public interest in publication with a story which contained less detail and omitted the **photographs**. But the *Mirror* said that they wanted to show themselves sympathetic to Ms Campbell's efforts to overcome her dependency. For this **purpose**, some details about her frequency of attendance at NA meetings were needed. I agree with the observation of the Court of Appeal, at p 660, para 52, that it is harsh to criticise the editor for "painting a somewhat fuller picture in order to show her in a sympathetic light."

60. . . . "The anonymity of participants and the general nature of the therapy is common knowledge. The details of her frequency of attendance (which were in fact inaccurate) could not be said to be discreditable or embarrassing. The relatively anodyne nature of the additional details is in my opinion important and distinguishes this case from cases in which (for example) **there is**

a public interest in the disclosure of the existence of a sexual relationship (say, between a **politician** and someone whom she has appointed to public office) **but the addition of salacious details or intimate photographs is disproportionate and unacceptable.** The latter, even if accompanying a legitimate disclosure of the **sexual relationship**, would be too **intrusive** and demeaning."

. . .

62. In my opinion, it would be inconsistent with the approach which has been taken by the courts in a number of recent landmark cases for a newspaper to be held strictly liable for exceeding what a judge considers to have been necessary. **The practical exigencies of journalism demand that some latitude must be given.** Editorial decisions have to be made quickly and with less information than is available to a court which afterwards reviews the matter at leisure. And if any margin is to be allowed, it seems to me strange to hold the *Mirror* liable in damages for a decision which three experienced judges in the Court of Appeal have held to be perfectly justified.

. . .

66. It is only in connection with the **degree of latitude** which must be allowed to the press in the way it chooses to present its story that I think it is relevant to consider **Ms Campbell's relationship with the media.** She and they have for many years both fed upon each other. **She has given them stories to sell their papers and they have given her publicity to promote her career.** ***This does not deprive Ms Campbell of the right to privacy in respect of areas of her life which she has not chosen to make public.*** But I think it means that when a newspaper publishes what is in substance a legitimate story, **she cannot insist upon too great a nicety of judgment** in the circumstantial detail with which the story is presented.

. . .

68. To that question I would certainly answer yes, but it was not the question which arose in this case. Accepting that Ms Campbell has a "**residual area of privacy**", the question is whether it was infringed by the publication in this case. To answer that question one must assess the disclosures said to be objectionable in the light of the disclosures conceded to be legitimate. One must then ask whether the journalists exceeded the **latitude** which should be allowed to them in presenting their story.

. . .

70. "**. . . The question of the effect of the publication upon Ms Campbell's therapy was not pleaded . . .**"

. . .

72. That leaves the question of the **photographs**. In my opinion a **photograph** is in principle information no different from any other information. It may be a more vivid form of information than the written word **("a picture is worth a thousand words").** That has to be taken into account in deciding whether its publication infringes the right to privacy of personal information. The publication of a **photograph** cannot necessarily be justified by saying that one would be entitled to publish a **verbal description** of the scene: see *Douglas v Hello! Ltd* [2001] QB 967. But the principles by which one decides whether or not the publication of a **photograph** is an unjustified invasion of the privacy of personal information are in my opinion the same as those which I have already discussed.

73. In the present case, the pictures were taken **without** Ms Campbell's **consent.** That in my opinion is not enough to amount to a wrongful invasion of privacy. **The famous and even the not so famous who go out in public must accept that they may be photographed without their consent, just as they may be observed by others without their consent.** As Gleeson CJ said in *Australian Broadcasting Corporation v Lenah Game Meats Pty Ltd* (2001) 185 ALR 1, 13, para 41:

> "Part of the price we pay for living in an organised society is that we are exposed to observation in a variety of ways by other people."

74. But the fact that we cannot avoid being photographed **does not mean that anyone who takes or obtains such photographs can publish them** to the world at large. In the recent case of *Peck v United Kingdom* (2003) 36 EHRR 41 Mr Peck was filmed on a public street in an embarrassing moment by a CCTV camera. Subsequently, the film was broadcast several times on the television. The Strasbourg court said (at p 739) that this was an invasion of his privacy contrary to article 8:

> "the relevant moment was viewed to an extent which far exceeded any exposure to a passer-by or to security observation and to a degree surpassing that which the applicant could possibly have foreseen when he walked in Brentwood on August 20, 1995."

75. ". . . As Lord Mustill said in *R v Broadcasting Standards Commission, Ex p BBC* [2001] QB 885, 900, **"An infringement of privacy is an affront to the personality, which is damaged both by the violation and by the demonstration that the personal space is not inviolate."**

. . .

The background

80. The business of fashion modelling, in which the appellant Naomi Campbell has built up such a powerful **reputation** internationally, is conducted under

the constant gaze of the media. It is also highly competitive. It is a context where public **reputation** as a forceful and colourful personality adds value to the physical appearance of the individual. Much good can come of this, if the process is carefully and correctly handled. But there are aspects of Miss Campbell's exploitation of her status as a **celebrity** that have attracted criticism. **She has been manipulative and selective in what she has revealed about herself.** She has engaged **in a deliberately false presentation of herself** as someone who, in contrast to many models, has managed to keep clear of illegal drugs. The true position, it is now agreed, is that she has made a **practice of abusing drugs.** This has caused her medical problems, and it has affected her behaviour to such an extent that she has required and has received therapy for her addiction.

. . .

82. . . . Miss Campbell cannot complain about the fact that publicity was given in this article to the fact that she was a drug addict. **This was a matter of legitimate public comment, as she had not only lied about her addiction but had sought to benefit from this by comparing herself with others in the fashion business who were addicted.** As the Court of Appeal observed [2003] QB 633, 658, para 43, where a **public figure** chooses to make untrue pronouncements about his or her private life, the press will normally be entitled to put the record straight.

. . .

85. [Lord Hope] The questions that I have just described seem to me to be essentially questions of fact and degree and not to raise any new issues of principle. As Lord Woolf CJ said in *A v B plc* [2003] QB 195, 207, paras 11(ix) and (x), **the need for the existence of a confidential relationship should not give rise to problems as to the law because a duty of confidence will arise whenever the party subject to the duty is in a situation where he knows or ought to know that the other person can reasonably expect his privacy to be protected.** The difficulty will be as to the relevant facts, bearing in mind that, if there is an **intrusion** in a situation where a person can reasonably expect his privacy to be respected, that **intrusion** will be capable of giving rise to liability unless the **intrusion** can be justified: see also the exposition in *Attorney-General v Guardian Newspapers Ltd (No 2)* [1990] 1 AC 109, 282 by Lord Goff of Chieveley, where he set out *the three limiting principles* to the broad general principle that a duty of confidence arises when **confidential information** comes to the knowledge of a person where he has notice that the information is confidential. The **third limiting principle** is particularly relevant in this case. This is the principle which may require a court to carry out a balancing operation, weighing the public interest in maintaining confidence against a countervailing public interest favouring disclosure.

. . .

92. The underlying question in all cases where it is alleged that there has been a breach of the duty of confidence is whether the information that was disclosed was private and not public. There must be some interest of a private nature that the claimant wishes to protect: *A v B Ltd* [2003] QB 195, 206, para 11 (vii**). In some cases, as the Court of Appeal said in that case, the answer to the question whether the information is public or private will be obvious. Where it is not, the broad test is whether disclosure of the information about the individual ("A") would give substantial offence to A, assuming that A was placed in similar circumstances and was a person of ordinary sensibilities.**

. . .

99. "The approach which the Court of Appeal took to this issue seems to me, with great respect, to be quite unreal. I do not think that they had a sound basis for differing from the conclusion reached by the trial judge as to whether the information was private. They were also in error, in my opinion, when they were asking themselves whether the disclosure would have offended the reasonable man of ordinary susceptibilities. The mind that they examined was the mind of the reader: para 54. This is wrong. It greatly reduces the level of protection that is afforded to the right of privacy. **The mind that has to be examined is that, not of the reader in general, but of the person who is affected by the publicity.** The question is what a reasonable person of ordinary sensibilities would feel if she was placed in the same position as the claimant and faced with the same publicity."

. . .

105. The context for this exercise is provided by articles 8 and 10 of the Convention. The rights guaranteed by these articles are qualified rights. Article 8(1) protects the right to respect for private life**, but recognition is given in article 8(2) to the protection of the rights and freedoms of others.** Article 10(1) protects the right to freedom of expression, **but article 10(2) recognises the need to protect the rights and freedoms of others**. The effect of these provisions is that **the right to privacy which lies at the heart of an action for breach of confidence** has to be balanced against the right of the media to impart information to the public. And the right of the media to impart information to the public has to be **balanced** in its turn against the respect that must be given to private life.

106. There is nothing new about this, as the need for this kind of balancing exercise was already part of English law: *Attorney General v Guardian Newspapers (No 2)* [1990] 1 AC 109, per Lord Goff of Chieveley. But account must now be taken of the guidance which has been given by the European Court on the

application of these articles. As Sedley LJ pointed out in *Douglas v Hello! Ltd* [2001] 1 QB 967, 1004, para 135:

> "The European Court of Human Rights has always recognised the **high importance of free media of communication in a democracy,** but its jurisprudence does not—and could not consistently with the Convention itself—give article 10(1) the presumptive **priority** which is given, for example, to the First Amendment in the jurisprudence of the United States' courts. Everything will ultimately depend on the proper balance between privacy and publicity in the situation facing the court."

. . .

Striking the balance

112. There is no doubt that **the presentation** of the material that it was legitimate to convey to the public in this case without breaching the duty of confidence was a **matter for the journalists.** The **choice of language** used to convey information and ideas, and decisions as to whether or not to accompany the printed word by the use of **photographs**, are **pre-eminently editorial matters** with which the court will not interfere. The respondents are also entitled to claim that they should be accorded **a reasonable margin of appreciation** in taking decisions as to what details needed to be included in the article to give it credibility. This is an essential part of the journalistic exercise.

113. But decisions about the publication of material that is private to the individual raise issues that are not simply about presentation and editing. **Any interference with the public interest in disclosure has to be balanced against the interference with the right of the individual to respect for their private life.** The decisions that are then taken are open to review by the court. **The tests which the court must apply are the familiar ones. They are whether publication of the material pursues a *legitimate aim* and whether the benefits that will be achieved by its publication are *proportionate* to the *harm* that may be done by the interference with the right to privacy**. The jurisprudence of the European Court of Human Rights explains how these principles are to be understood and applied in the context of the facts of each case. **Any restriction of the right to freedom of expression must be subjected to very close scrutiny**. *But so too must any restriction of the right to respect for private life.* Neither article 8 nor article 10 has any pre-eminence over the other in the conduct of this exercise. As Resolution 1165 of the Parliamentary Assembly of the Council of Europe (1998), para 11, pointed out, they are neither absolute not in any hierarchical order, since **they are of equal value in a democratic society**.

The article 10 right

114. In the present case it is convenient to begin by looking at the matter from

the standpoint of the respondents' assertion of the article 10 right and the court's duty as a public authority under section 6(1) of the Human Rights Act 1998, which section 12(4) reinforces, not to act in a way which is incompatible with that Convention right.

115. **The *first question* is whether the objective of the restriction on the article 10 right—the protection of Miss Campbell's right under article 8 to respect for her private life—is sufficiently important to justify limiting the fundamental right to freedom of expression which the press assert on behalf of the public**. It follows from my conclusion that the details of Miss Campbell's treatment were private that I would answer this question in the affirmative. The ***second question*** is whether the means chosen to limit the article 10 right are rational, fair and not arbitrary and impair the right as minimally as is reasonably possible. It is not enough to assert that it would be reasonable to exclude these details from the article. A **close examination of the factual justification** for the restriction on the freedom of expression is needed if the fundamental right enshrined in article 10 is to remain practical and effective. **The restrictions which the court imposes on the article 10 right must be rational, fair and not arbitrary,** and they must impair the right no more than is necessary.

116. "In my opinion the factors that need to be weighed are, on the one hand, the duty that was recognised in *Jersild v Denmark* (1994) 19 EHRR 1, para 31 to impart information and ideas of public interest **which the public has a right to receive**, and the need that was recognised in *Fressoz v France* (2001) 31 EHRR 28, para 54 **for the court to leave it to journalists to decide what material needs to be reproduced to ensure credibility**; and, on the other hand, the **degree of privacy** to which Miss Campbell was entitled under the law of confidence as to the details of her therapy. Account should therefore be taken of the respondents' wish to put forward a story **that was credible** and to present Miss Campbell in a way that commended her for her efforts to overcome her addiction."

117. "But it should also be recognised that **the right** of the public to receive information about the details of her treatment was of a **much lower order** than the undoubted **right** to know that she was misleading the public when she said that she did not take drugs. In *Dudgeon v United Kingdom* (1981) 4 EHRR 149, para 52 the European Court said that **the more intimate the aspects of private life which are being interfered with, the more serious must be the reasons for doing so before the interference can be legitimate**. *Clayton and Tomlinson, The Law of Human Rights* (2000), para 15.162, point out that the court has distinguished **three** kinds of **expression: political expression, artistic expression and commercial expression**, and that it consistently **attaches great importance to political expression** and applies rather less

rigorous principles to expression which is **artistic** and **commercial**. According to the court's well-established case law, **freedom of expression constitutes one of the essential foundations of a democratic society and one of the basic conditions for its progress and the self-fulfilment of each individual:** *Tammer v Estonia* (2001) 37 EHRR 857, para 59. **But there were no political or democratic values at stake here, nor has any pressing social need been identified:** contrast *Goodwin v United Kingdom* (1996) 22 EHRR 123, para 40."

118. As for the other side of the balance, Keene LJ said in *Douglas v Hello! Ltd* [2001] QB 967, para 168, that any consideration of article 8 rights must reflect the fact that there are **different degrees of privacy**. In the present context the potential for disclosure of the information to cause harm is an **important factor to be taken into account** in the assessment of the extent of the restriction that was needed to protect Miss Campbell's right to privacy.

The article 8 right

119. Looking at the matter from Miss Campbell's point of view and the protection of her article 8 Convention right, publication of details of the treatment which she was undertaking to cure her addiction—that she was attending Narcotics Anonymous, for **how long**, **how frequently** and at **what times of day** she had been attending this therapy, the nature of it and **extent of her commitment** to the process and the publication of the **covert**ly taken **photographs** (the third, fourth and fifth of the five elements contained in the article)—had the **potential to cause harm** to her, for the reasons which I have already given. So I would attach a good deal of weight to this factor.

120. "As for the other side of the balance, **a person's right to privacy may be limited by the public's interest in knowing about certain traits of her personality and certain aspects of her private life,** as L'Heureux-Dubé and Bastarache JJ in the Supreme Court of Canada recognised in *Aubry v Les Éditions Vice-Versa Inc* [1998] 1 SCR 591, paras 57–58. **But it is not enough to deprive Miss Campbell of her right to privacy that she is a celebrity and that her private life is newsworthy.** A **margin of appreciation** must, of course, be given to the journalist. Weight must be given to this. But to treat these details merely as background was to undervalue the importance that was to be attached to the need, if Miss Campbell was to be protected, to keep these details private. **And it is hard to see that there was any compelling need for the public to know the name of the organisation that she was attending for the therapy, or for the other details of it to be set out.** The presentation of the article indicates that this was not fully appreciated when the decision was taken to publish these details. **The decision to publish the photographs suggests that greater weight was being given to the wish to publish a story that would attract interest rather than to the wish to maintain its credibility**."

121. "The reasonable person of ordinary sensibilities would also regard publication of the **covertly** taken **photographs**, and the fact that they were **linked with the text in this way**, as **adding greatly overall** to the **intrusion** which the article as a whole made into her private life."

122. ". . . The question then arises, balancing the rights at issue, where the public's right to information **can justify dissemination of a photograph taken without authorisation**: *Aubry*, para 61."

123. ". . .They were taken **deliberately, in secret** and with a view to their publication in conjunction with the article. The **zoom** lens was directed at the doorway of the place where the meeting had been taking place. The faces of others in the doorway were **pixilated** so as not to reveal their identity. Hers was not, **the photographs were published and her privacy was invaded.** The **argument** that the publication of the **photograph** added **credibility** to the story has **little weight**. The **photograph** was not self-explanatory. Neither the place nor the person were instantly recognisable. The reader only had the editor's word as to the truth of these details.130. ". . . **bore the badge of confidentiality** . . . It was, viewed objectively, likely to **affect adversely** her attendance and participation in therapy meetings."

. . .

134. This begs the question of how far the Convention balancing exercise is premissed on the scope of the existing cause of action. Clearly outside its scope is the sort of **intrusion** into what ought to be private which took place in *Wainwright*. Inside its scope is what has been termed the protection of the **individual's informational autonomy'** by prohibiting the publication of **confidential information**. How does the scope of the action for breach of confidence accommodate the Article 8 rights of individuals? As Randerson J summed it up in *Hosking v Runting* [2003] 3 NZLR 385, 403, para 83 at p 403:

> "[The English Courts] have chosen to develop the claim for breach of confidence on a case by case basis. In doing so, it has been recognised that no pre-existing **relationship** is required in order to establish a cause of action and that an obligation of confidence may arise from the nature of the material or may be inferred from the circumstances in which it has been obtained."

The position we have reached is that the exercise of balancing article 8 and article 10 may begin when the person publishing the information **knows or ought to know that there is a reasonable expectation that the information in question will be kept confidential**. That is the way in which Lord Woolf CJ put it in *A v B plc*, at paras 11(ix) and (x) (in which he also referred to the approach of Dame Elizabeth Butler-Sloss P in *Venables v News Group Newspapers Ltd* [2001] Fam 430). It is, as I understand it, also the way in which it is put by my noble and learned friends, Lord Nicholls of Birkenhead (at paragraph 21) and Lord Hope of Craighead (at paragraph 84) in this case.

138. The parties agree that neither right takes precedence over the other. This is consistent with Resolution 1165 (1998) of the Parliamentary Assembly of the Council of Europe, para 10:

> "The Assembly reaffirms the importance of everyone's right to privacy, and of the right to freedom of expression, as fundamental to a democratic society. These rights are neither absolute nor in any hierarchical order, since they are of equal value."

139. Each right has the same structure. Article 8(1) states that "everyone has the right to respect for his private and family life, his home and his correspondence". Article 10(1) states that "Everyone has the right to freedom of expression. This right shall include freedom to hold opinions and to receive and impart information and ideas without interference by public authorities and regardless of frontiers. . . ." **Unlike the article 8 right, however, it is accepted in article 10(2) that the exercise of this right *'carries with it duties and responsibilities.'*** Both rights are qualified. They may respectively be interfered with or restricted provided that three conditions are fulfilled:

(a) The interference or restriction must be **'in accordance with the law'**; it must have a basis in national law which conforms to the Convention standards of legality.

(b) It must pursue one of the **legitimate aims** set out in each article. ***Article 8(2)*** provides for **"the protection of the rights and freedoms of others"**. ***Article 10(2)*** provides for *"the protection of the* **reputation** *or rights of others"* and for **"preventing the disclosure of information received in confidence".** The rights referred to may either be rights protected under the national law or, as in this case, other Convention rights.

(c) Above all, the interference or restriction must be "**necessary in a democratic society**"; it must meet a "**pressing social need**" and be **no greater than is proportionate** to the **legitimate aim** pursued; the reasons given for it must be both "**relevant**" and "**sufficient**" for this **purpose**.

140. The application of the proportionality test is more straightforward when only one Convention right is in play: the question then is whether the private right claimed offers sufficient justification for the degree of interference with the fundamental right. It is much less straightforward when two Convention rights are in play, **and the proportionality of interfering with one has to be balanced against the proportionality of restricting the other. *As each is a fundamental right, there is evidently a "pressing social need" to protect it.*** The Convention jurisprudence offers us little help with this. The European Court of Human Rights has been concerned with whether the state's interference

with privacy (as, for example, in *Z v Finland* (1997) 25 EHRR 371) or a restriction on freedom of expression (as, for example, in *Jersild v Denmark* (1994) 19 EHRR 1, *Fressoz and Roire v France* (2001) 31 EHRR 2, and *Tammer v Estonia* (2001) 37 EHRR 857) could be justified in the particular case. **In the national court, the problem of balancing two rights of equal importance arises most acutely in the context of disputes between private persons.**

141. Both parties accepted the basic approach of the Court of Appeal in In re S [2003] 3 WLR 1425, 1451–1452, at paras 54 to 60. **This involves looking first at the comparative importance of the actual rights being claimed in the individual case; then at the justifications for interfering with or restricting each of those rights; and applying the proportionality test to each.** The parties in this case differed about whether the trial judge or the Court of Appeal had done this, the appellant arguing that the Court of Appeal had assumed primacy for the Article 10 right while the respondent argued that the trial judge had assumed primacy for the Article 8 right.

. . .

145. It has always been accepted that information about a person's health and **treatment for ill-health** is both private and confidential. This stems not only from the confidentiality of the **doctor–patient relationship but from the nature of the information itself**. As the European Court of Human Rights put it in *Z v Finland* (1997) 25 EHRR 371, 405, para 95:

> "Respecting the confidentiality of health data is a vital principle in the legal systems of all the Contracting Parties to the Convention. **It is crucial not only to respect the sense of privacy of a patient but also to preserve his or her confidence in the medical profession and in the health services** in general. Without such protection, those in need of medical assistance **may be deterred from revealing such information of a personal and intimate nature as may be necessary in order to receive appropriate treatment** and, **even, from seeking such assistance,** thereby **endangering their own health** and, in the case of **transmissible diseases**, that of the community."

. . .

148. "What was the nature of the freedom of expression which was being asserted on the other side? *There are undoubtedly different types of speech, just as there are different types of private information, some of which are more deserving of protection in a democratic society than others.* Top of the list is **political speech**. **The free exchange of information and ideas on matters relevant to the organisation of the economic, social and political life of the country is crucial to any democracy.** Without this, it can scarcely be called a democracy at all. *This includes revealing information about* **public figures**,

especially those in elective office, which would otherwise be private but is relevant to their participation in public life. Intellectual and educational speech and expression are also important in a democracy, not least because they enable the development of individuals' potential to play a full part in society and in our democratic life. **Artistic speech and expression is important for similar reasons, in fostering both individual originality and creativity and the free-thinking and dynamic society we so much value.** No doubt there are other kinds of speech and expression for which similar claims can be made."

149. "But it is difficult to make such claims on behalf of the publication with which we are concerned here. **The political and social life of the community, and the intellectual, artistic or personal development of individuals, are not obviously assisted by pouring over the intimate details of a fashion model's private life**."

. . .

151. "The answer which she herself accepts is that she had presented herself to the public as someone who was not involved in drugs. It would have been a very good thing if she were not. If other young women do see her as someone to be admired and emulated, then it is all to the good if she is not addicted to narcotic substances. It might be questioned why, if a role model has adopted a stance which all would agree is beneficial rather than detrimental to society, it is so important to reveal that she has feet of clay. **But the possession and use of illegal drugs is a criminal offence and a matter of serious public concern. The press must be free to expose the truth and put the record straight."**

. . .

154. Publishing the **photographs** contributed both to the revelation and to the harm that it might do. By themselves, they are not objectionable. Unlike France and Quebec, **in this country we do not recognise a right to one's own image:** cf *Aubry v Editions Vice-Versa Inc* [1998] 1 SCR 591. We have **not** so far held that the mere fact of **covert** photography is sufficient to make the information contained in the **photograph** confidential. The activity photographed must be private. **If this had been, and had been presented as, a picture of Naomi Campbell going about her business in a public street, there could have been no complaint.** She makes a substantial part of her living out of being photographed looking stunning in designer clothing. **Readers will obviously be interested to see how she looks if and when she pops out to the shops for a bottle of milk. There is nothing essentially private about that information nor can it be expected to damage her private life**. It may not be a high order of freedom of speech **but there is nothing to justify interfering with it**. (This was the view of Randerson J in *Hosking v Runting*

[2003] 3 NZLR 385, which concerned a similarly innocuous outing; see now the decision of the Court of Appeal, 25 March 2004.)

155. **But here the accompanying text made it plain that these photographs were different.** They showed her coming either to or from the NA meeting. They showed her in the company of others, some of whom were undoubtedly part of the group. They showed the place where the meeting was taking place, which will have been entirely recognisable to anyone who knew the locality. **A picture is 'worth a thousand words' because** it adds to the impact of what the words convey; but it also adds to the information given in those words. If nothing else, it tells the reader what everyone looked like; in this case it also told the reader what the place looked like. In context, it also added to the potential harm, by making her think that she was being followed or betrayed, and deterring her from going back to the same place again.

. . .

157. ". . . **The risk of harm is what matters at this stage, rather than the proof that actual harm has occurred.** People trying to recover from drug addiction need considerable dedication and commitment, along with constant reinforcement from those around them. That is why organisations like Narcotics Anonymous were set up and why they can do so much good. **Blundering in when matters are acknowledged to be at a 'fragile' stage may do great harm."**

. . .

165. I am unable to agree with the distinction drawn by the Court of Appeal and for the reasons given by Lord Hope and Lady Hale **I consider that the information was private.** It seems to me that the publication of the details of the appellant's course of treatment at NA and of the **photographs** taken **surreptitiously** in the street of her emerging from a meeting went significantly beyond the publication of the fact that she was receiving therapy or that she was engaged in a course of therapy with NA. It revealed where the treatment was taking place and the text went into the frequency of her treatment. **In this way it intruded into what had some of the characteristics of medical treatment and it tended to deter her from continuing the treatment which was in her interest and also to inhibit other persons attending the course from staying with it, when they might be concerned that their participation might become public knowledge**. This in my view went beyond disclosure which was, in the words of the Court of Appeal, "peripheral to" the publication of the information that the appellant was a drug addict who was receiving treatment and was capable of constituting breach of confidence. **One cannot disregard the fact that photographs are a powerful prop to a written article and a much valued part of newspaper reporting, especially in the tabloid**

or popular press (hence the enthusiasm of paparazzi to obtain pictures of celebrities for publication in the newspapers). I think that the Court of Appeal dismissed them too readily as adding little to the reports already published and that they were not justified in rejecting the judge's conclusions on this.

. . .

168. Resolution of this question depends on the weight which one attributes to *several factors*, the **extent of the distress** to the appellant and the **potential adverse effects** on her drug therapy, the extent to which one judges the material in categories 3, 4 and 5 to have gone beyond that contained in categories 1 and 2, and **the degree of latitude** which should be allowed to the press in the way in which it chooses to present a story. Weighing and balancing these factors is a process which may well lead different people to different conclusions, as one may readily see from consideration of the judgments of the courts below and the opinions given by the several members of the Appellate Committee of your Lordships' House.

Cream Holdings Ltd and Ors v Banerjee and Ors [2004] UKHL 44

Section 12(3) and "Likely"

22. In my view section 12(3) calls for a similar approach. **Section 12(3) makes the likelihood of success at the trial an essential element in the court's consideration of whether to make an interim order.** But in order to achieve the necessary flexibility the degree of likelihood of success at the trial needed to satisfy section 12(3) must depend on the circumstances. **There can be no single, rigid standard governing all applications for interim restraint orders. Rather, on its proper construction the effect of section 12(3) is that the court is not to make an interim restraint order unless satisfied the applicant's prospects of success at the trial are sufficiently favourable to justify such an order being made in the particular circumstances of the case**. As to what degree of likelihood makes the prospects of success 'sufficiently favourable', **the general approach should be that courts will be exceedingly slow to make interim restraint orders where the applicant has not satisfied the court he will probably ('more likely than not') succeed at the trial.** In general**, that should be the threshold an applicant must cross before the court embarks on exercising its discretion, duly taking into account the relevant jurisprudence on article 10 and any**

countervailing Convention rights. ***But there will be cases where it is necessary for a court to depart from this general approach and a lesser degree of likelihood will suffice as a prerequisite.*** **Circumstances where this may be so include those mentioned above: where the potential adverse consequences of disclosure are particularly grave, or where a short-lived injunction is needed to enable the court to hear and give proper consideration to an application for interim relief pending the trial or any relevant appeal.**

23. This interpretation achieves the **purpose** underlying section 12(3). Despite its apparent circularity, this interpretation emphasises the importance of the applicant's prospects of success as a factor to be taken into account when the court is deciding whether to make an interim restraint order. It provides, as is only sensible, that the weight to be given to this factor will depend on the circumstances. By this means the general approach outlined above does not accord inappropriate weight to the Convention right of freedom of expression as compared with the right to respect for private life or other Convention rights. **This approach gives effect to the parliamentary intention that courts should have particular regard to the importance of the right to freedom of expression and at the same time it is sufficiently flexible in its application to give effect to countervailing Convention rights.** In other words, this interpretation of section 12(3) is Convention-compliant.

. . .

26. I recognise that without reference to the content of the **confidential information** this conclusion is necessarily enigmatic to those who have not read the private judgments of the courts below. But if I were to elaborate I would at once destroy the confidentiality the Cream group are seeking to preserve. Even if the House discharges the restraint order made by the judge, it would not be right for your Lordships to make public the information in question. The contents of your Lordships' speeches should not pre-empt Echo's publication, if that is what the newspaper decides now to do. Nor should these speeches, by themselves placing this information in the **public domain**, undermine any remedy in damages the Cream group may ultimately be found to have against the Echo or Ms Banerjee in respect of matters the Echo may decide to publish.

Von Hannover v Germany [2005] 40 EHRR 1

THE LAW

I. ALLEGED VIOLATION OF ARTICLE 8 OF THE CONVENTION

43. The applicant submitted that the German court decisions had infringed her

right to respect for her private and family life, guaranteed by Article 8 of the Convention, which is worded as follows:

> "1. Everyone has the right to respect for his private and family life, his home and his correspondence.
>
> 2. There shall be no interference by a public authority with the exercise of this right except such as is in accordance with the law and is necessary in a democratic society in the interests of national security, public safety or the economic well-being of the country, for the prevention of disorder or crime, for the protection of health or morals, or for the protection of the rights and freedoms of others."

A. Submissions of the parties and interveners

. . .

B. The Court's assessment

1. As regards the subject of the application

48. The Court notes at the outset that the photos of the applicant with her children are no longer the subject of this application, as it stated in its admissibility decision of 8 July 2003.

The same applies to the photos published in *Freizeit Revue* magazine (issue no 30 of 22 July 1993) showing the applicant with Vincent Lindon at the far end of a restaurant courtyard in Saint-Rémy-de-Provence (see paragraph 11 above). In its judgment of 19 December 1995, the Federal Court of Justice prohibited any further publication of the photos on the ground that they infringed the applicant's right to respect for her private life (see paragraph 23 above).

49. **Accordingly, the Court considers it important to specify that the present application concerns the following photos, which were published as part of a series of articles about the applicant:**

(i) the photo published in *Bunte* magazine (issue no 32 of 5 August 1993) showing the applicant on horseback (see paragraph 12 above)

(ii) the photos published in *Bunte* magazine (issue no 34 of 19 August 1993) showing the applicant shopping on her own; with Mr Vincent Lindon in a restaurant; alone on a bicycle; and with her bodyguard at a market (see paragraph 13 above);

(iii) the photos published in *Bunte* magazine (issue no 10 of 27 February 1997) showing the applicant on a skiing holiday in Austria (see paragraph 14 above);

(iv) the photos published in *Bunte* magazine (issue no 12 of 13 March 1997) showing the applicant with Prince Ernst August **von Hannover** and alone leaving her Parisian residence (see paragraph 15 above);

(v) the photos published in *Bunte* magazine (issue no 16 of 10 April 1997) showing the applicant playing tennis with Prince Ernst August **von Hannover** and both of them putting their bicycles down (see paragraph 16 above);

(vi) the photos published in *Neue Post* magazine (issue no 35/97) showing the applicant tripping over an obstacle at the Monte Carlo Beach Club (see paragraph 17 above).

2. Applicability of Article 8

50. The Court reiterates that the concept of private life extends to aspects relating to **personal identity,** such as a **person's name** (see *Burghartz v Switzerland*, judgment of 22 February 1994, Series A no 280-B, p 28, § 24), or a person's picture (see *Schüssel v Austria* (dec.), no 42409/98, 21 February 2002).

Furthermore, private life, in the Court's view, includes a person's **physical** and **psychological integrity;** the guarantee afforded by Article 8 of the Convention is primarily intended to ensure the development, **without outside interference**, of the **personality** of each individual in his relations with other human beings (see, *mutatis mutandis*, *Niemietz* v **Germany**, judgment of 16 December 1992, Series A no 251-B, pp 33–34, § 29, and *Botta v Italy*, judgment of 24 February 1998, *Reports of Judgments and Decisions* 1998-I, p 422, § 32). There is therefore a **zone of interaction** of a person with others, **even in a public context,** which may fall within the scope of "private life" (see, *mutatis mutandis*, p *G. and J.H. v the United Kingdom*, no 44787/98, § 56, ECHR 2001-IX, and *Peck v the United Kingdom*, no 44647/98, § 57, ECHR 2003-I).

51. The Court has also indicated that, in certain circumstances, a person has a "legitimate expectation" of protection and respect for his or her private life. Accordingly, it has held in a case concerning the interception of **telephone calls on business** premises that the applicant "would have had a reasonable expectation of privacy for such calls" (see *Halford v the United Kingdom*, judgment of 25 June 1997, *Reports* 1997-III, p 1016, § 45).

52. As regards **photos**, with a view to defining the scope of the protection afforded by Article 8 against arbitrary interference by public authorities, the European Commission of Human Rights had regard to whether the **photographs** related to **private** or **public matters** and whether the material thus obtained was envisaged for a limited use or was likely to be made available to the **general public** (see, *mutatis mutandis*, *Friedl v Austria*, judgment of 31 January 1995, Series A no 305-B, opinion of the Commission, p 21, §§ 49–52; p *G. and J.H. v the United Kingdom*, cited above, § 58; and *Peck*, cited above, § 61).

53. In the present case there is no doubt that the publication by various German

magazines of photos of the applicant in her daily life either on her own or with other people falls within the scope of her private life.

3. Compliance with Article 8

(a) The domestic courts' position

54. The Court notes that, in its landmark judgment of 15 December 1999, the Federal Constitutional Court interpreted sections 22 and 23 of the Copyright (Arts Domain) Act (see paragraphs 40–41 above) by balancing the requirements of the freedom of the press against those of the protection of private life, **that is, the public interest in being informed against the legitimate interests of the applicant.** In doing so the Federal Constitutional Court took account of two criteria under German law, one functional and the other spatial. It considered that the applicant, as a figure of contemporary society "*par excellence*", enjoyed the protection of her private life even outside her home but only if she was in a secluded place out of the **public eye** to which persons retire "with the objectively recognisable aim of being alone and where, confident of being alone, they behave in a manner in which they would not behave in public". In the light of those criteria, the Federal Constitutional Court held that the Federal Court of Justice's judgment of 19 December 1995 regarding publication of the photos in question was compatible with the Basic Law. The court attached decisive weight to the freedom of the press, even the entertainment press, and to the public interest in knowing how the applicant behaved outside her representative functions (see paragraph 25 above).

55. Referring to its landmark judgment, the Federal Constitutional Court did not entertain the applicant's appeals in the subsequent proceedings brought by her (see paragraphs 32 and 38 above).

(b) General principles governing the protection of private life and the freedom of expression

56. In the present case the applicant did not complain of an action by the State, **but rather of the lack of adequate State protection of her private life and her image.**

57. The Court reiterates that, although the object of Article 8 is essentially that of protecting the individual against arbitrary interference by the public authorities, it does not merely compel the State to abstain from such interference: in addition to this primarily negative undertaking, there may be positive obligations inherent in an effective respect for private or family life. **These obligations may involve the adoption of measures designed to secure respect for private life even in the sphere of the relations of individuals between themselves** (see, *mutatis mutandis*, *X and Y v the Neth-*

erlands, judgment of 26 March 1985, Series A no 91, p 11, § 23; *Stjerna v Finland*, judgment of 25 November 1994, Series A no 299-B, pp 60–61, § 38; and *Verliere v Switzerland* (dec.), no 41953/98, ECHR 2001-VII). **That also applies to the protection of a person's picture against abuse by others** (see *Schüssel*, cited above).

The boundary between the State's positive and negative obligations under this provision does not lend itself to precise definition. The applicable principles are, nonetheless, similar. In both contexts regard must be had to the fair balance that has to be struck between the competing interests of the individual and of the community as a whole; **and in both contexts the State enjoys a certain margin of appreciation** (see, among many other authorities, *Keegan v Ireland*, judgment of 26 May 1994, Series A no 290, p 19, § 49, and *Botta*, cited above, p 427, § 33).

58. That protection of private life has to be balanced against the freedom of expression guaranteed by Article 10 of the Convention.

In that context, the Court reiterates that freedom of expression constitutes one of the essential foundations of a democratic society. Subject to paragraph 2 of Article 10, it is applicable not only to "information" or "ideas" that are favourably received or regarded as inoffensive or as a matter of indifference, **but also to those that offend, shock or disturb. Such are the demands of that pluralism, tolerance and broadmindedness without which there is no "democratic society"** (see *Handyside v the United Kingdom*, judgment of 7 December 1976, Series A no 24, p 23, § 49).

In that connection, the press plays an essential role in a democratic society. Although it must not overstep certain bounds, in particular in respect of the **reputation** and rights of others, its duty is nevertheless to impart—in a manner consistent with its obligations and responsibilities—information and ideas on all matters of public interest (see, among many authorities, Observer *and* Guardian v *the United Kingdom*, judgment of 26 November 1991, Series A no 216, pp 29–30, § 59, and Bladet Tromsø *and Stensaas v Norway* [GC], no 21980/93, § 59, ECHR 1999-III). **Journalistic freedom also covers possible recourse to a degree of exaggeration, or even provocation** (see *Prager and Oberschlick v Austria*, judgment of 26 April 1995, Series A no 313, p 19, § 38; *Tammer v Estonia*, no 41205/98, §§ 59–63, ECHR 2001-I; and *Prisma Presse v France* (dec.), nos. 66910/01 and 71612/01, 1 July 2003).

59. Although freedom of expression also extends to the publication of **photos**, this is an area in which the protection of the rights and **reputation** of others takes on **particular importance**. The present case does not concern the dissemination of "ideas", but of images containing very personal or even **intimate** "information" about an individual. **Furthermore, photos appearing**

in the tabloid press are often taken in a climate of continual harassment which induces in the person concerned a very strong sense of intrusion into their private life or even of persecution.

60. In the cases in which the Court has had to balance the protection of private life against freedom of expression, it has always stressed the contribution made by photos or articles in the press **to a debate of general interest** (see, as a recent authority, *Tammer*, cited above, §§ 59 et seq.; *News Verlags GmbH & Co. KG v Austria*, no 31457/96, §§ 52 et seq., ECHR 2000-I; and *Krone Verlag GmbH & Co. KG v Austria*, no 34315/96, §§ 33 et seq., 26 February 2002). The Court thus found, in one case, that the use of certain terms in relation to an individual's private life was not "justified by considerations of public concern" and that those terms did not "[bear] on a matter of general importance" (see *Tammer*, cited above, § 68) and went on to hold that there had not been a violation of Article 10. In another case, however, the Court attached particular importance to the fact that the subject in question was a news item of "major public concern" and that the published **photographs** "did not disclose any details of [the] private life" of the person in question (see *Krone Verlag GmbH & Co. KG*, cited above, § 37) and held that there had been a violation of Article 10. Similarly, in a recent case concerning the publication by President Mitterrand's former private doctor of a book containing revelations about the President's state of health, the Court held that "**the more time that elapsed, the more the public interest in discussion of the history of President Mitterrand's two terms of office prevailed over the requirements of protecting the President's rights with regard to medical confidentiality"** (see *Editions Plon* v *France*, no 58148/00, § 53, ECHR 2004-IV) and held that there had been a breach of Article 10.

(c) Application of these general principles by the Court

61. The Court notes at the outset that in the present case the photos of the applicant in the various German magazines show her in scenes from her **daily life**, thus involving activities of a **purely private nature** such as engaging in **sport,** out **walking**, **leaving a restaurant** or on **holiday**. The photos, in which the applicant appears sometimes alone and sometimes in company, illustrate a series of articles with such innocuous titles as "Pure happiness", "Caroline . . . a woman returning to life", "Out and about with Princess Caroline in Paris" and "The kiss. Or: they are not hiding anymore" (see paragraphs 11–17 above).

62. The Court also notes that the applicant, as a member of the Prince of Monaco's family, represents the ruling family at certain cultural or charitable events. However, she does not exercise any function within or on behalf of the State of Monaco or any of its institutions (see paragraph 8 above).

63. The Court considers that a fundamental distinction needs to be made between reporting facts—even controversial ones—capable of contributing to a ***debate*** in a democratic society relating to **politicians** in the exercise of their functions, for example, and reporting details of the private life of an individual who, moreover, as in this case, **does not exercise official functions**. While in the former case the press exercises its vital role of "**watchdog**" in a democracy by contributing to "impart[ing] information and ideas on matters of public interest (see Observer *and* Guardian, loc. cit.), it does not do so in the latter case.

64. Similarly, although the public has a right to be informed, which is an essential right in a democratic society that, in certain special circumstances, can even extend to aspects of the private life of **public figure**s, **particularly where politicians are concerned** (see *Editions Plon*, loc. cit.), this is not the case here. The situation here does not come within the sphere of any political or public **debate** because the published photos and accompanying commentaries **relate exclusively to details of the applicant's private life.**

65. As in other similar cases it has examined, the Court considers that the publication of the photos and articles in question, **the sole purpose of which was to satisfy the *curiosity* of a particular readership** regarding the details of the applicant's private life, cannot be deemed to contribute to any **debate** of general interest to society despite the applicant being known to the public (see, *mutatis mutandis*, *Campmany y Diez de Revenga and Lopez Galiacho Perona v Spain* (dec.), no 54224/00, ECHR 2000-XII; *Julio Bou Gibert and El Hogar Y La Moda J.A. v Spain* (dec.), no 14929/02, 13 May 2003; and *Prisma Presse*, cited above).

66. In these **conditions freedom of expression calls for a narrower interpretation** (see *Prisma Presse*, cited above, and, by converse implication, *Krone Verlag GmbH & Co. KG*, cited above, § 37).

67. In that connection, the Court also takes account of the resolution of the Parliamentary Assembly of the Council of Europe on the right to privacy, which stresses the "one-sided interpretation of the right to freedom of expression" by certain media which attempt to justify an infringement of the rights protected by Article 8 of the Convention by claiming that "their readers are entitled to know everything about **public figure**s" (see paragraph 42 above, and *Prisma Presse*, cited above).

68. The Court finds another point to be of importance: even though, strictly speaking, the present application concerns only the publication of the photos and articles by various German magazines, the context in which these photos were taken—**without the applicant's knowledge or consent**—and the **harassment** endured by many **public figure**s in their daily lives cannot be fully disregarded (see paragraph 59 above).

In the present case this point is illustrated in particularly striking fashion by the photos taken of the applicant at the Monte Carlo Beach Club **tripping over an obstacle and falling** down (see paragraph 17 above). It appears that these photos were taken **secretly** at a distance of several hundred metres, probably from a neighbouring house, whereas journalists' and photographers' access to the club was strictly regulated (see paragraph 33 above).

69. The Court reiterates the fundamental importance of protecting private life from the point of view of the development of every human being's personality. That protection—as stated above—extends beyond the private family circle and **also includes a social dimension.** The Court considers that anyone, even if they are known to the general public, must be able to enjoy a "legitimate expectation" of protection of and respect for their private life (see paragraph 51 above and, *mutatis mutandis*, *Halford*, cited above, p 1016, § 45).

70. Furthermore, **increased vigilance in protecting private life is necessary to contend with new communication technologies which make it possible to store and reproduce personal data** (see point 5 of the Parliamentary Assembly's resolution on the right to privacy, paragraph 42 above, and, *mutatis mutandis*, *Amann v Switzerland* [GC], no 27798/95, §§ 65–67, ECHR 2000-II; *Rotaru v Romania* [GC], no 28341/95, §§ 43–44, ECHR 2000-V; p *G. and J.H. v the United Kingdom*, cited above, §§ 57–60; and *Peck*, cited above, §§ 59–63 and 78). **This also applies to the systematic taking of specific photos and their dissemination to a broad section of the public.**

71. Lastly, the Court reiterates that the Convention is intended to guarantee not rights that are theoretical or illusory but **rights that are practical and effective** (see *Artico v Italy*, judgment of 13 May 1980, Series A no 37, pp 15–16, § 33).

72. The Court finds it hard to agree with the domestic courts' interpretation of section 23(1) of the Copyright (Arts Domain) Act, which consists in describing a person as such as a figure of contemporary society "*par excellence*". Since that definition affords the person very limited protection of their private life or the right to control the use of their image, it could conceivably be appropriate for **politicians** exercising official functions. However, it cannot be justified for a "private" individual, such as the applicant, in whom the interest of the general public and the press is based solely on her membership of a reigning family, **whereas she herself does not exercise any official functions**.

In any event the Court considers that, in these conditions, the Act has to be interpreted **narrowly** to ensure that the State complies with its positive obligation under the Convention to protect private life and the right to control the use of one's image.

73. **Lastly, the distinction drawn between figures of contemporary society "par excellence" and "relatively" public figures has to be clear and obvious so that, in a State governed by the rule of law, the individual has precise indications as to the behaviour he or she should adopt. Above all, they need to know exactly when and where they are in a protected sphere or, on the contrary, in a sphere in which they must expect interference from others, especially the tabloid press.**

74. The Court therefore considers that the criteria on which the domestic courts based their decisions were not sufficient to protect the applicant's private life effectively. As a figure of contemporary society "*par excellence*" she cannot—in the name of freedom of the press and the public interest—rely on protection of her private life unless she is in a secluded place out of the **public eye** and, moreover, succeeds in proving it (which can be difficult). Where that is not the case, she has to accept that she might be photographed at almost any time, systematically, and that the photos are then very widely disseminated even if, as was the case here, the photos and accompanying articles relate exclusively to details of her private life.

75. In the Court's view, the criterion of spatial isolation, although apposite in theory, is in reality too vague and difficult for the person concerned to determine in advance. **In the present case, merely classifying the applicant as a figure of contemporary society "par excellence" does not suffice to justify such an intrusion into her private life.**

(d) Conclusion

76. As the Court has stated above, it considers that the decisive factor in balancing the protection of private life against freedom of expression should lie in the contribution that the published photos and articles make to **a debate of general interest**. It is clear in the instant case that they made no such contribution, since the applicant exercises **no official function** and the photos and articles **related exclusively to details of her private life.**

77. Furthermore, the Court considers that the public **does not have a legitimate interest in** knowing where the applicant is and how she behaves generally in her private life even if she appears in places that cannot always be described as secluded and **despite the fact that she is well known to the public.**

Even if such a public interest exists, as does a commercial interest of the magazines in publishing these photos and these articles, in the instant case those interests must, in the Court's view, yield to the applicant's right to the effective protection of her private life.

78. Lastly, in the Court's opinion the criteria established by the domestic courts were not sufficient to ensure the effective protection of the applicant's private

life and she should, in the circumstances of the case, have had a "legitimate expectation" of protection of her private life.

79. Having regard to all the foregoing factors, **and despite the margin of appreciation afforded to the State in this area,** the Court considers that the German courts did not strike a fair balance between the competing interests.

80. There has therefore been a breach of Article 8 of the Convention.

81. Having regard to that finding, the Court does not consider it necessary to rule on the applicant's complaint relating to her right to respect for her family life.

A v B, C, & D [2005] EWHC 1651 (QB) per Eady J (allegations about private life)

The relevance of the Claimant's own revelations of personal information

16. An important consideration when assessing the background of this case is that the **Claimant has himself made public through the media** a great deal of information that might usually be considered as falling within the protection afforded to private or personal information, including matters concerning B and the child of the marriage. Mr Caldecott submits that this conduct is highly material to the question of whether the Claimant has a **reasonable expectation of privacy** in relation to any proposed publication touching upon the subject-matter in respect of which he has already revealed such information. It is also material to the **closely related question of what is, and what is not, in the public domain**. That is of immediate concern because it is clear, as Mr Spearman acknowledges, that any order the court grants should have incorporated within what is now called a "**public domain proviso**": see eg *Kelly v BBC* [2001] Fam 59 at 93 (Munby J); *Att.-Gen. v Times Newspapers Ltd* [2001] 1 WLR 885, CA, and *Harris v Harris; Att.-Gen. v Harris* [2001] 2 FLR at [208] (Munby J).

17. It was in this context that Mr Spearman drew my attention to two principles which seem to have emerged in the recent authorities:

i) In the context of personal information, which is treated differently in this respect from **confidential information** of a commercial nature, **the fact that something has been published does not necessarily mean that further revelation cannot itself infringe the claimant's right to protect his privacy.** That is especially the case perhaps where it is the defendant who has himself put the information into the **public domain** in the first place and would otherwise be enabling himself to profit from his own wrong: see eg *Att.-Gen. v Guardian Newspapers (No 2)* [1990] 1 AC 109.

ii) Where it is the claimant who has chosen to put personal information into the **public domain**, even though it may be such as to attract *prima facie* the protection of the law, **it does not necessarily follow that it is open season** for the media to publish any other information pertaining to the same subject-matter: see eg *Douglas v Hello!* [2005] EWCA Civ 595. **Individuals are permitted some degree of control over how much they choose to reveal.**

Those are important matters which I need to bear in mind.

18. It emerges from the correspondence which I have been shown that the relevant journalist contacted the Claimant on 8th June in order to ask questions in relation to certain specific areas. Undertakings were sought not to publish matters in those categories, on the basis that it was anticipated that, whether he answered the queries or not, there would be publications of some kind on that subject-matter. It was at that stage assumed that the information came from B. **Some of it, however, appeared to relate to earlier material revealed by the Claimant in published articles in the Evening Standard and The Tatler.**

19. Mr Caldecott highlighted at the outset of his submissions the importance of keeping clearly in mind throughout the two separate questions of **(i)** whether article 8 is engaged at all and, if so, **(ii)** whether an interim injunction should be granted to protect A's rights having regard to proportionality. **The two stages are quite distinct:** see eg the observations of Lord Nicholls in *Campbell* at [20]–[21].

20. A major difference of principle between the parties was whether the Claimant's incursions into the **public domain** in respect of his private affairs **were relevant to the first stage or only to the second.** Mr Spearman submitted that the subject-matter of the proposed article was clearly such as to fall within the category of information which the Claimant was reasonably entitled to expect would be afforded protection by the developing law of privacy and confidence. His client's article 8 rights were, he submitted, plainly engaged.

21. **Mr Caldecott, on the other hand, argued that the Claimant's own intimate revelations should be taken into account in determining whether it was reasonable for him to expect information of the relevant kind *still* to be protected.** It would not suffice to pass the stage one threshold that the information fell, in general terms, in certain categories. That would mean that everyone would pass that test automatically and the only scope for differentiation between individual applicants would arise at the stage of assessing proportionality. No one doubts that at any rate most of the categories which

give rise to the Claimant's concern in this case would be such as to attract *prima facie* the protection of the law. The critical question for stage one appears to me to be whether *the Claimant* has a reasonable expectation that such information should be protected. **That depends to a large extent upon his own circumstances and conduct.** I agree therefore with the thrust of Mr Caldecott's submission.

22. I do not take the argument to entail that article 8 is not engaged at all. I would rather construe Mr Caldecott's submission as being directed towards whether the Claimant's *prima facie* right to the protection of such information **has been displaced by his own conduct,** in the sense that it has rendered it no longer reasonable for that protection to be maintained by legal process. **It is by no means clear that this should necessarily be analysed in terms of a doctrine of *waiver*: see eg the discussion in Tugendhat and Christie, The Law of Privacy and the Media (OUP), 2002, at 9.29–9.37.** Such authority as there is rather suggests that the situation is to be judged **not by out and out waiver** but according to the particular circumstances of the case. It was observed, for example, in *A v B plc* [2003] QB 195 that "if you have courted public attention then you have less ground to object to the **intrusion** that follows". As a general statement, that is surely unobjectionable, but I would not accept that the law supports the proposition sometimes advanced by journalists, for obvious reasons, to the effect that those who live in the spot-light of publicity, or actively seek it out, are thereby automatically deprived of the protection of privacy accorded to other citizens. As was also noted in *A v B plc* at [11(xii)], **"a public figure is entitled to a private life"**.

23. It is consistent with European jurisprudence and with more recent decisions within this jurisdiction, such as *Douglas v Hello! Ltd* (cited above), to take into account the voluntary revelations on a case by case basis in determining whether any particular information is such that the claimant can any longer *reasonably* expect to keep it private. This question is likely to involve consid-erations such as whether, for example, **the particular piece of information has itself already been published, whether similar instances of behaviour have already been out in the public domain, whether the claimant has made allegations involving other persons and, in particular, their personal lives so that it would be reasonable for such other persons to give another side of the story.**

The precise terms of the order sought against C and D

24. On the morning of 16th June Mr Spearman presented Mr Caldecott with the wording of the primary order he was seeking against his clients:

> "2. Until Trial or further Order in the meantime the Second and Third Defendants and each of them must not publish any details relating to the

Claimant's health, medical history, past or present medical condition or treatments, sexual life, finances, drug use, drug rehabilitation, alleged involvement in telephone bugging or computer hacking, childhood, **relationship** with and marriage to the First Defendant, **relationship** with the child of his marriage to the First Defendant, and the divorce proceedings between the First Defendant and the claims made in those proceedings (save details which have already been published in the news media) and must not cause or authorise any other person, firm or company to do any of those acts".

Mr Caldecott's first submission was that this was **hopelessly wide.**

The applicable principles of law

25. He said that his clients were now presented with "the devil" rather than, as on the first day, "the deep blue sea". He emphasised that the protection of article 8 does not extend to everything that is not in the **public domain**. There must be something which has the **quality of confidence** about it in order to give rise to a reasonable expectation of privacy for personal information. Before even needing to address the second (or "proportionality") stage, the Claimant needed to pass the threshold test. This he was unable to do. In order to satisfy the "reasonable expectation" test, Mr Spearman needed to focus not merely on the subject-matter of the proposed revelation, in broad terms, but had rather to demonstrate that he had a reasonable expectation in the circumstances confronting the court.

26. Mr Caldecott relied particularly in this context upon the following passage in the speech of Lord Nicholls in *Campbell v MGN Ltd* at [25]–[26]:

> ". . . it is important to note this is a highly unusual case. On any view of the matter, this information related closely to the fact, which admittedly could be published, that Miss Campbell was receiving treatment for drug addiction. Thus when considering whether Miss Campbell had a reasonable expectation of privacy in respect of information relating to her attendance at Narcotics Anonymous meetings the relevant question can be framed along the following lines: Miss Campbell having put her addiction and treatment into the **public domain**, did the further information relating to her attendance at Narcotics Anonymous meetings retain its character of private information sufficiently to engage the protection afforded by article 8?
>
> I doubt whether it did. Treatment by attendance at Narcotics Anonymous meetings is a form of therapy for drug addiction which is well known, widely used and much respected. Disclosure that Miss Campbell had opted for this form of treatment was not a disclosure of any more significance than saying that a person who had fractured a limb has his

limb in plaster or that a person suffering from cancer is undergoing a course of chemotherapy. Given the extent of the information, otherwise of a highly private character, which admittedly could properly be disclosed, the additional information was of such an unremarkable and [in]consequential nature that to divide the one from the other would be to apply altogether too fine a toothcomb. Human rights are concerned with substance, not with such fine distinctions".

27. My attention was also drawn to the following passages in the speech of Lord Hoffmann at [57] and [66]:

> "A person may attract or seek publicity about some aspects of his or her life without creating any public interest in the publication of personal information about other matters. I think that the history about Ms Campbell's **relationship** with the media does have some relevance to this case, . . . but that would not without more justify publication of confidential personal information.
>
> . . . It is only in connection with the degree of **latitude** which must be allowed to the press in the way it chooses to present its story that I think it is relevant to consider Ms Campbell's **relationship** with the media. She and they have for many years both fed upon each other. She has given them stories to sell their papers and they have given her publicity to promote her career. That does not deprive Ms Campbell of the right to privacy in respect of areas of her life which she has not chosen to make public. But I think it means that when a newspaper publishes what is in substance a legitimate story, she cannot insist upon too great a nicety of judgment in the circumstantial detail with which the story is presented".

28. In the light of these statements, Mr Caldecott submits **first** that, once a claimant has chosen to exercise his own article 10 rights, so as to introduce potentially private or personal information into the **public domain**, the reasonableness of his expectation of continuing protection must be judged in that particular context. **Secondly**, in identifying the scope of material within the **public domain**, once such a claimant has chosen to lift the veil on his personal affairs, the test will be "**zonal**"; that is to say, the court's characterisation of what is truly in the **public domain** will not be tied specifically to the details revealed in the past but rather focus upon the general area or **zone** of the claimant's personal life (eg drug addiction) which he has chosen to expose. Both these considerations are germane to the present case.

29. It so happens that A too, like Miss Campbell, has revealed information through press interviews about his drug addiction and his experiences in connection with that problem. **One of the categories of information in respect of which**

he seeks to impose restraint upon the Defendants concerns drug-related incidents in the past similar to those about which he chose to make revelations. Mr Caldecott was prepared to concede, in principle, that a drug addict, or former addict, who has chosen to speak about his past experiences is not necessarily precluded thereafter, on a once for all basis, from seeking protection in respect of other experiences. Suppose he had chosen to speak about his addiction and the unpleasant experiences he had suffered in the past, and recounted how he had overcome his addiction. **If he were later to lapse, it would not necessarily follow that his new health problems would also automatically be open to media intrusion.** On those hypothetical facts, his revelations would have related to a particular period in his life and would thus not cover the later lapse; nor, for that matter, would there be any question, on the facts I have posited, of the public being in any way misled by the information he had supplied.

30. Nevertheless, Mr Caldecott argues that on the facts of the present case the categories of information which his clients wish to be free to publish fall squarely within the area of A's earlier revelations; they are merely "**more of the same".** Moreover, if the court were to prevent publication of the new information, notwithstanding the revelations on the earlier occasions, this would involve the application of "altogether too fine a toothcomb". All these factors are relevant, submits Mr Caldecott, at the threshold stage of determining to what extent there still remains a reasonable expectation on the Claimant's part of concealing information of this kind.

31. One has to recognise in this context that it is inherent in any communication of personal information to the public through the media that it may invite discussion. It would thus be unrealistic to confine future coverage to the precise details in the original revelations. People might wish to **debate**, for example, whether the revelations were accurate or whether they were so selective as to be misleading. It would be difficult to envisage circumstances in which this could be prevented on grounds of privacy.

32. Another important consideration (which is also relevant to the present case, but not determinative) is that for public policy reasons there would be powerful arguments against concealing, with the assistance of the court, information about **one's criminal activities.** This could not be an inflexible rule, **as there might be circumstances in which the court would think it right for spent convictions or past acquittals not to be revealed to the general public**. One example might be where the defendant was **blackmailing** the claimant. Nevertheless, it would be hard to justify the concealment of information about (say) domestic violence or tax evasion simply because it has taken place behind closed doors. It could hardly be categorised as information in respect of which there would be a reasonable expectation

of confidentiality. Nor would the law generally imply a duty of confidence. As it used to be said, "**there is no confidence in iniquity**": see eg *Gartside v Outram* (1857) 26 LJ Ch 113. The courts might well baulk at assisting in the concealment of Class A drug consumption, especially if it has taken place in public. On the other hand, as Mr Spearman pointed out, the law is prepared to acknowledge in some circumstances, as the *Campbell* case illustrates, that problems of addiction may be kept private—notwithstanding that it will often be implicit in such information that illegal supply must have occurred or other offences under the misuse of drugs legislation.

33. As Lord Nicholls observed in the passage cited above, **human rights are concerned with matters of substance.** A similar point was made by Lord Goff in *Att-Gen v Guardian Newspapers (No 2)* [1990] 1 AC 109 at 282 to the effect that the law of confidence is not concerned with the protection of useless information or **trivia**. This too is potentially relevant to some of the matters raised by this Claimant. Specifically in the context of health, it has been recognised that it is not every statement that will carry **the badge of confidentiality** or risk doing harm to the person's physical or moral integrity. To publish that someone in the **public eye** has a bout of flu or a broken wrist is generally likely to do no harm: by contrast, for the media to "blunder in" when treatment for drug addiction is at a **fragile** stage may do great harm: see eg *Campbell v MGN* at [157] *per* Baroness Hale**. The potential to cause harm is likely to be "an important factor" for the court to weigh here, as it was in Campbell: ibid at [118] per Lord Hope.**

The particular categories of information the Claimant wishes to protect

34. There is no doubt that the Claimant's problems with drug addiction would constitute the most significant aspect of the material he wishes to keep secret, but Mr Caldecott went on to address all the parts of the Claimant's personal life with regard to which he seeks to restrain publication—as variously identified at different stages. He turned first to paragraph 3 of the Claimant's witness statement and contrasted the comparative specificity of that evidence with the breadth of the injunction sought. **I shall turn to consider these categories, while taking such steps as I reasonably can to minimise the risk, at least for the time being, of any parties being identified from the contents of my judgment.**

35. The "type of confidential and private information" identified by the Claimant was as follows:

    a) **"Medical information":** He described a particular disorder from which he was suffering and the medication he was prescribed. The Defendants, however, indicated that they did not wish to publish any of this material.

    b) **"Childhood":** Reference was made to particular childhood experiences but, again, the Defendants confirmed that there was no intention to publish any information in this category. They wished, however, to reserve the right to include within the article general information relating to his childhood period which was already in the **public domain.**

c) "My use of drugs during our marriage and rehabilitation process": As I have already made clear, this was the central area of dispute between the parties for the purposes of the present application. The Claimant acknowledges certain lapses into drug use during the period of his marriage but contends, despite the coverage to which I have already referred, that "**a lot of information** including the effect of drugs upon me, my conduct when using drugs and details of my rehabilitation and use of N.A. meetings **is not publicly known**". This is the context in which Mr Caldecott urges me not to apply "too fine a toothcomb".

d) **"Sexual life":** A referred to **intimate** aspects of his **relationship** with his wife, but Mr Caldecott indicated that his clients have no wish to cover this area at all.

e) "**Financial":** The Claimant was concerned to protect information relating to his income, trust funds, general financial standing and the financial aspects of the pending divorce proceedings. Again, however, save in the most general terms, the Defendants made it clear they had no wish to go into such matters.

f) "**Matrimonial proceedings":** Save in certain very limited respects, previously identified in correspondence, and to which I shall return briefly in due course, there was no wish on the Defendants' part to include material within this category.

36. There was a "catch all" paragraph in the Claimant's statement as follows:

> "I also claim to be entitled to protect any other confidential and private information that my wife is aware of arising out of my first meeting with her . . . , our subsequent **relationship**, marriage and divorce".

This was unsatisfactory from the Defendants' point of view, since it would be impossible for them to govern their conduct by reference to an order couched in **such general and vague terms**. The Defendants would need to know, apart from anything else, what exactly B was "aware of". That would be impractical from their point of view.

37. In the letter of 14th June 2005, the same day on which his witness statement was signed, the Claimant's solicitors sent a letter marked "extremely urgent" to the publishers' solicitors, in which they identified a list of concerns as to information which the Defendants might be about to publish. This to some extent overlapped with the material in paragraph 3 of the Claimant's witness

statement but also listed some rather more specific points. Mr Caldecott addressed each of these in turn:

i) **The Claimant's "frequent disappearances":** The Claimant spoke extensively in earlier articles about his drug taking, where it took place, and consequent absences from his family. He also addressed the impact of these disappearances on them. Information was supplied about attendances for treatment, the identity of those treating him, and how he responded to it. **Mr Caldecott made the following submissions:**

a) Drug taking in a social context could not sensibly be regarded as being personal or **confidential information** or as falling within the notion of marital confidence.

b) The Claimant had already chosen to speak publicly about the impact of his drug related problems on his marriage.

c) Information the Defendants wished to cover in the course of the article belonged to the same period of time about which the Claimant had apparently chosen to speak freely.

d) The Claimant's position was to be **contrasted** to that adopted by Princess Caroline of Monaco (the subject of a recent case in the European Court of Human Rights: *Von Hannover v Germany* (2005) 40 EHRR 1) and by Mr and Mrs Michael Douglas, **who had striven to keep the subject-matter of the relevant articles private.** He could not thus expect reasonably to maintain the same degree of protection which the law would otherwise afford.

ii) **The details of a particular "drug binge" in a specific location:** For the Defendants it was argued that this was not, as such, about the Claimant's addiction but about a "specific and rather disgraceful episode of drug-taking". It was merely a particular instance of his behaviour about which the Claimant had spoken in general terms.

iii) "**Details of paranoid fantasies" in particular locations:** The Defendants did wish to publish the fact that the Claimant had paranoid fantasies, but without any description of the fantasies themselves. Since the Claimant has publicly admitted large scale drug abuse, it would hardly come as a surprise to readers that he would be likely to suffer from such fantasies. It was accepted in argument, without any formal concession, that descriptions of his particular fantasies might be too **intrusive**.

iv) **The "first relapse during the marriage" on a specific trip:** Reference was made to the *Evening Standard* article, in the light of which it was submitted that the Claimant could no longer have a reasonable expectation of privacy in relation to any similar "chapter of drug-taking in the same historic period".

v) **The allegation that the Claimant "freebased and disappeared for several days at a time in different cities using [a pseudonym]" and visited a crack den:** The Defendants resist any restriction on a similar basis; namely, the information was confined to the same historic period and, furthermore, "crack" is not so qualitatively different from cocaine as to be still covered by a reasonable expectation of privacy.

vi) **"Details concerning our client's divorce proceedings":** The Defendants had no wish to go into these matters.

vii) **A promise made to his wife that he would "stay clean" during his marriage:** The Defendants submit that this cannot be the subject of protection in the light of the fact that he had himself referred to private arrangements and promises made to his wife in connection with drug taking in the course of the earlier article. This could be categorised simply as "more of the same".

viii) **Certain problems the Claimant had with his trustees and to the use of his wife's funds:** The Defendants made clear there was no intention to refer to the trustees in the article; moreover, it was submitted that there could be no objection to B referring in the article to the Claimant having used some of her money. He himself had already chosen in one of the earlier articles to go into some detail as to his personal wealth.

ix) **An incident concerning the child of the marriage**: The Defendants have no intention of referring to this.

x) **The subject of ancillary relief in the current matrimonial proceedings:** The Defendants will not be referring to the merits of the dispute but wish to reserve the right to identify in general terms the nature of the relief sought.

xi) **An allegation relating to the seizure of the Claimant's computer system:** This is said to be in the **public domain**, and the Defendants accordingly reserve their right to refer to it.

xii) **The subject of the Claimant's current sobriety and the fact that he visits the child of the marriage regularly:** This is said to be anodyne and complimentary and thus a matter which, in all the circumstances, could not be said to be covered by any reasonable expectation of keeping the subject-matter private.

Conclusion

38. I came to the conclusion that in the light of the evidence the Claimant had failed to establish:

i) that the second and third Defendants were proposing to publish anything

in respect of which he had a reasonable and continuing expectation of privacy;

ii) that an injunction would be likely to be effective in protecting any of his rights (whether at common law or under the European Convention) or in preventing significant harm;

iii) that any of the criteria identified in Cream Holdings could be fulfilled.

39. It was for these reasons that I informed the parties at the close of the hearing on 16th June that the application against the relevant Defendants would be refused. Unfortunately, it was not possible for the parties to reassemble for the handing down of my reasons until today.

Mahmood v Galloway and Another [2006] EWHC 1286 per Mitting J

22. **Mr Spearman submits that the publication of photographs of Mr Mahmood would provide valuable information to those who may wish to cause serious harm to Mr Mahmood. I disagree**. For **photographs** of Mr Mahmood to be of any use to such people they would have to have a whole package of further information, not least information as to his whereabouts and habits. Armed with such information, the **photographs** might be of some assistance, but one would have expected anybody who had got that information also to have been able to obtain at a minimum a description—more likely a **photograph**—of Mr Mahmood to permit them to inflict whatever harm it was that they might have in mind.

23. **I am satisfied that the true purpose of this application is not protection of Mr Mahmood's life and physical integrity but the protection of his earning capacity and position as an investigative journalist and his utility to his employers in that respect.** Neither of those beneficial objectives are the subject of the European Convention. Accordingly, it would not, in my view, be at all likely that any court would extend rights of privacy to include and uphold those rights.

24. It is submitted by Mr Spearman that it is in the public interest that Mr Mahmood's identity should be protected by injunction. That is debatable. Mr Galloway's view is that it is in the public interest that his identity should be exposed so that people like him are not subject to the activities of a man whom he regards as an unscrupulous agent provocateur. Were I to have to decide the case on the balance of where the public interest lay, I would decide it in favour of Mr Mahmood because it seems to me that his track record establishes that on balance his activities have been in furtherance

of the public interest by bringing criminals to book rather more than they have been against the public interest by encouraging those who might not otherwise have committed crimes to do so. But that is not an issue that I could possibly determine at this stage in the proceedings.

25. The mere fact that it might be, in a sense, generally beneficial to the public that Mr Mahmood's identity should be protected could not itself give rise to or support a cause of action based on confidence or privacy. It is but a factor to be borne in mind. In my view, it is a factor that would have to be weighed, and weighed with care, against Mr Galloway's right under Article 10 to give public vent to the views that he holds.

. . .

27. Accordingly, applying, as I am obliged to, section 12 of the Human Rights Act, I conclude that it is more likely than not that this claim would at final trial fail. Accordingly, I am obliged to refuse the injunction sought.

MR PRICE: My Lord, it is five past five, so the injunction terminated at five o'clock.

MR JUSTICE MITTING: Yes.

MR PRICE: No doubt my learned friend and I can put together an order recording the undertaking that has been proffered that you require.

MR JUSTICE MITTING: Yes.

MR PRICE: My client is grateful to your Lordship. I would ask for costs of this application. I do so on the basis that there has been—well, first of all, my client is a defendant and he has successfully contested the grant of the injunction.

MR JUSTICE MITTING: Well, he has won.

MR PRICE: He has won.

MR JUSTICE MITTING: So therefore on ordinary principles he is entitled to costs.

MR PRICE: Yes. In any event, for what it is worth, he signified his intention to publish the material a week ago in an article in the Guardian. Mr Mahmood said he did not take it seriously and that is why he left —

MR JUSTICE MITTING: These are very minor matters by contrast to the major one, that he has won.

MR PRICE: Yes, my Lord.

MR JUSTICE MITTING: Yes, Mr Spearman?

MR SPEARMAN: Well, it does not sound a very promising start on costs.

MR JUSTICE MITTING: No

MR SPEARMAN: But the position is that it is only one part of the action. Your Lordship plainly has a practice in these matters or has a view on this case.

MR JUSTICE MITTING: It is not just me, everybody does. It is a discrete question.

MR SPEARMAN: Yes.

MR JUSTICE MITTING: The answer is either yes or no and, as far as you are concern, it has turned out to be no

MR SPEARMAN: Yes. But what I say, in terms of practice, what I mean is that many judges take the view that the appropriate order is either costs in case or the successful party's costs in case, which is obviously less favourable for the . . . party rather than an outright order and some judges take the view that costs reserved is best. But if I say costs in case is the right order, then the result follows the merits at the end of the day which obviously at this stage your Lordship is only able to form a provisional view about.

MR JUSTICE MITTING: Quite, but, as I think everybody recognises, the substance of these cases is in the interim application and not later on.

MR SPEARMAN: Yes.

MR JUSTICE MITTING: Save very occasionally when well known fashion models are engaged.

MR SPEARMAN: That is often the way, my Lord, but if that is so, then the case will go away sooner or later on a costs in case order. So I would say it ought to be costs in case or, at the very worst, defendants' costs in case.

MR JUSTICE MITTING: The claimant will pay the defendants' costs to be assessed on a detailed basis if not agreed.

MR PRICE: Just for the avoidance of doubt, if we cannot agree those costs now, we can pursue the assessment now. As your Lordship says it is possible —

MR JUSTICE MITTING: Indeed. My intention is that because you have won on a discrete issue you are entitled to have your costs the moment that they have been assessed.

MR PRICE: I am grateful, my Lord.

MR JUSTICE MITTING: Any other matters?

MR SPEARMAN: My Lord, two small things. The question of time for compliance with the undertaking as to the further evidence.

MR JUSTICE MITTING: Yes. I can see no reason why that cannot be done overnight.

MR SPEARMAN: Yes. So something like midday tomorrow or something of that sort.

MR JUSTICE MITTING: By 4.00 p m. tomorrow.

MR SPEARMAN: 4.00 p m. tomorrow. The other is, and I will not take long on this, may we have permission to appeal?

MR JUSTICE MITTING: On what basis?

MR SPEARMAN: On the basis that we have a real prospect of success.

MR JUSTICE MITTING: I think it is something you will have to ask the Court of Appeal for. I refuse the application.

MR SPEARMAN: And would your Lordship extend the injunction to give us the time to ask the Court of Appeal for a short period such as 24 hours?

MR JUSTICE MITTING: Mr Price?

MR PRICE: My Lord, this is precisely what section 12 is designed to avoid. I think in *A v B* this issue arose and that was a case of real principle. I do not need to take you to para 115 in *Campbell*, Baroness Hale's speech where she says in terms that there is no right to one's own image and one cannot complain about the publication of a **photograph** —

MR JUSTICE MITTING: All that is being sought now is an overnight stay pending an application to the Court of Appeal for permission to appeal.

MR PRICE: My Lord, yes, but then if this stay is granted, there will be a further stay until the appeal is heard.

MR JUSTICE MITTING: No That is up to the Court of Appeal.

MR PRICE: If your Lordship is prepared to grant the stay and to effectively hold the ring, that is what you are being asked to do —

MR JUSTICE MITTING: Ordinarily, if I had made my ruling by, let us say, half past two, then I would have granted a stay for half an hour to enable Mr Spearman to go up to the Court of Appeal and say: "Can I have a stay, please, as well as permission to appeal?" But because of the time of day, if I refuse a stay now, then a member of the Court of Appeal is going to have to be disturbed outside normal business hours to consider an application.

MR PRICE: Alternatively, no application would be made. This is, with respect—I know time is moving on but, with respect, this is an important issue if this stay is granted in effect—well, I mean, if a stay is granted—let us think this through logically. At the moment the order has been discharged.

MR JUSTICE MITTING: Yes.

MR PRICE: There is no order. There is nothing to stay.

MR JUSTICE MITTING: I can re-impose it for a short period. That is the effect of —-

MR PRICE: But that is what section 12 is telling you you cannot—your Lordship cannot do that having ruled on that that section 12 is not satisfied.

MR JUSTICE MITTING: Can you give me the page number again? (After a pause): 1108.

MR PRICE: 1108. But the position now is that there is no restriction on Mr Galloway's freedom of expression. The order has expired and your Lordship has refused to continue it. So it is not a question of granting a stay. Your Lordship is going to have to grant an injunction in the same terms —

MR JUSTICE MITTING: In circumstances where I have already said that I do not believe he will get one at final trial.

MR PRICE: And we have not had any particularisation of the basis of the appeal, and Lord Woolf in *A v B* makes it absolutely clear that these matters are supposed to come before the judge, be dealt with by the judge, so that if freedom of expression is to prevail, that freedom of expression can be exercised. There is simply no jurisdiction basis to make the order in any event. Furthermore, before the order was going to be made, your Lordship would need to have some cogent grounds on which your Lordship's order might be overturned, and it is incumbent upon the judge at first instance . . . whether permission to appeal should be granted and whether a stay should be granted. If the judge at first instance forms the view that there should be no permission and there should be no stay, the judge exercising his own discretion without worrying what the Court of Appeal may do, the net result is that if this claimant wants to go to the Court of Appeal, he is going to have to go to the Court of Appeal now. The timing issue is all his own fault because this notification was made last week and Mr Mahmood did not take it seriously. That is in his own witness statement. He did not think it was serious. So it was not until six o'clock yesterday afternoon that he decided maybe it is serious, notwithstanding that clear statement of intention in the media that —

MR JUSTICE MITTING: What about what Lord Nicholls says at p 262B-C that "circumstances where this may be so", that is where you do not apply the ordinary standard, "include those mentioned above" and they are:

> " . . . where a short-lived injunction is needed to enable the court to hear and give proper consideration to an application for interim relief pending the trial or any relevant appeal."

MR SPEARMAN: I hate to interrupt my friend but in fact more germane is the end of 18 on p 260, the very last sentence:

> "So if a judge refuses to grant an interlocutory injunction preserving confidentiality until trial, the court ought not to be powerless to grant interim relief pending the hearing of any interlocutory appeal against the judge's order."

MR JUSTICE MITTING: Yes.

MR SPEARMAN: That is expressly envisaging where you are not satisfied that it is likely but you apply the lesser standard in all the circumstances to give the protection over an application to the Court of Appeal.

MR JUSTICE MITTING: Yes. I am entitled, I think, to require you to undertake to apply to the Court of Appeal tomorrow.

MR SPEARMAN: Yes.

MR JUSTICE MITTING: For permission to appeal and for a stay or for continuation of the injunction pro tern. I am minded at the moment to extend the injunction until 4.00 p m.

MR SPEARMAN: Yes.

MR JUSTICE MITTING: So as to ensure that you do bring the matter before the Court of Appeal within a short time frame.

MR SPEARMAN: Yes, I understand that, but is your Lordship saying that we have only got until 4.00 p m. tomorrow to apply to the Court of Appeal?

MR JUSTICE MITTING: Yes.

MR SPEARMAN: That is right?

MR JUSTICE MITTING: Yes.

MR SPEARMAN: Not that I have got to undertake to you that I definitely will appeal.

MR JUSTICE MITTING: No, no, of course not. If you do not

MR SPEARMAN: Then that is the end of that.

MR JUSTICE MITTING:—then the whole thing lapses.

MR SPEARMAN: Yes. We have got until 4.00 p m. tomorrow to do it. There is a stay pending that.

MR JUSTICE MITTING: Yes. Mr Price, I think I have got to do that otherwise, if I am wrong, then the value of the claim to the claimant is lost as a result of what would be held necessarily to be my error.

MR PRICE: Yes. Well, I mean, that could be said of any application.

MR JUSTICE MITTING: I appreciate that.

MR PRICE: And the net result is that it just gets put off.

MR JUSTICE MITTING: It gets put off for 23 hours.

MR PRICE: Yes. But practically then the Court of Appeal have got to be summoned —

MR JUSTICE MITTING: No, there is no problem about doing that because the matter can be put before a single Lord Justice tomorrow morning without any difficulty. But I am terribly reluctant to cause a single Lord Justice, let alone a full court, to be assembled at this time. They are very busy people, they have plenty to do and it is unreasonable to impose upon them additional burdens if it can be avoided. I am going to continue an injunction until 4.00 p m. tomorrow. I think in view of the submissions that have been made to me, it ought not to be an "against the whole world" injunction but against the two —

MR SPEARMAN: My Lord, that, with the greatest of respect, is just a matter of form.

MR JUSTICE MITTING: Yes.

MR SPEARMAN: It is a question of taking out the words in paral. If you go to our skeleton argument, it is a question of taking out the words "and any person with notice of this order" from the wording.

MR JUSTICE MITTING: Yes.

MR SPEARMAN: And then that can just go. Then that is just a matter of putting the usual words that tell people that if anybody gets notice and they frustrate it, they will be in trouble, putting it colloquially.

MR JUSTICE MITTING: Yes.

MR SPEARMAN: But those words can come out.

MR JUSTICE MITTING: Yes. Subject to that, I will extend your injunction until 4.00 p m. tomorrow.

MR SPEARMAN: I am obliged, my Lord.

MR JUSTICE MITTING: Thank you, both. Will you lodge a draft, please?

MR SPEARMAN: Yes, my Lord.

MR JUSTICE MITTING: Mr Spearman, it is probably better coming from you as you have had the conduct of it so far.

MR SPEARMAN: Yes.

MR JUSTICE MITTING: Thank you.

MR SPEARMAN: In the morning?

MR JUSTICE MITTING: Yes.

MR SPEARMAN: Thank you very much. Thank you very much indeed for the time.

MR JUSTICE MITTING: Not at all.

[Elton] *John v Associated Newspapers* Ltd [2006] EWHC 1611 (Eady J)

MR JUSTICE EADY:

1. This afternoon I have heard an application made on behalf of Sir Elton John by Mr Browne QC for injunctive relief. The defendants are Associated Newspapers Limited who publish, among other journals, the Daily Mail. They have made it clear in correspondence that they wish to publish in tomorrow's edition **a photograph** of Sir Elton John of which a clear copy has been put in evidence.
2. The application was heard in **private** for the **usual reasons**, namely that the application, being based on an alleged **breach of confidence** or **infringement of privacy**, might be set at nought if the application were upheld and the information had meanwhile been revealed or discussed in public. There is, however, no reason why the content of this judgment should be restricted. **It is always undesirable for judgments to be given in private unless it is absolutely necessary, and I do not regard it as necessary in this case.**
3. It is important to note that the terms of the injunction sought are directed towards the publication of a **photograph** or **photographs**. **There is no attempt made to inhibit or restrict in any way the publication of text.** In some ways that is not surprising because the defendants have not revealed the text which they intend to publish if and insofar as it has already crystallised, which it may not have done, and they are entitled to keep their **powder dry** in that respect.
4. **The specific photograph which it is intended to publish consists of an image of Sir Elton John in the street abutting his London home, together with his driver.** Apparently they have just driven from another home near Windsor and arrived in this London street. He is dressed in a baseball cap and a tracksuit. He has his hand on the gate through which he is just about to pass. Insofar as it matters, in this **photograph** both **his feet are still on the public street,** by contrast with some of the other **photographs** in the series, which include at least one showing one of his feet having gone through the gateway into what is presumably his private front garden.
5. It is necessary for me to bear in mind certain well-known principles about

the grant of interim relief, particularly insofar as it impinges upon a defendant's rights of freedom of expression as protected or enshrined in Article 10 of the European Convention. I need to bear in mind specifically section 12 of the Human Rights Act 1998, as subsequently interpreted in the courts, and in particular by their Lordships in *Cream Holdings v Banerjee* [2005] 1 AC 253. My attention was invited by both counsel to paragraph [22] of the speech of Lord Nicholls, where he said this:

> "Section 12(3) makes the **likelihood** of success at the trial an **essential element** in the court's consideration of whether to make an interim order. But in order to achieve the necessary flexibility the degree of **likelihood** of success at the trial needed to satisfy section 12(3) must depend on the circumstances. There can be no single, rigid standard governing all applications for interim restraint orders. Rather, on its proper construction the effect of section 12(3) is that the court is not to make an interim restraint order unless satisfied the applicant's prospects of success at the trial are sufficiently favourable to justify such an order being made in the particular circumstances of the case. As to what degree of likelihood makes the prospects of success `sufficiently favourable', the general approach should be that courts will be **exceedingly slow to** make interim restraint orders where the applicant has not satisfied the court that he will probably (**'more likely than not'**) succeed at the trial. In general, that should be the threshold an applicant must cross before the court embarks on exercising its discretion, duly taking into account the relevant jurisprudence on Article 10 and any countervailing Convention rights. **But there will be cases where it is necessary for a court to depart from this general approach and a lesser degree of likelihood will suffice as a prerequisite.** Circumstances where this may be so include those mentioned above: where the **potential adverse consequences of disclosure are particularly grave,** or where a **short-lived injunction** is needed to enable the court to hear and give proper consideration to an application for interim relief pending the trial or any relevant appeal."

That seems to me to be the guideline which I should adopt in approaching this application.

6. Mr Browne has urged upon me the proposition that the circumstances of this case give rise to one of the exceptional situations contemplated by Lord Nicholls towards the end of paragraph [22]. I believe he relied in the alternative upon both the examples given, that is to say that a lesser degree of likelihood would suffice because either the adverse consequences to his client of disclosure would be particularly grave or because it is necessary

to have protection for the court to hear and give proper consideration to the evidence and legal principles.

7. I am satisfied here **that neither of those circumstances arises** and therefore the appropriate test for me to apply is the more general one of whether the claimant is **more likely than not** to succeed at the trial with regard to this remedy of an injunction restraining publication.

8. My attention was also drawn to the decision of the Court of Appeal in the case of *A v B Plc* [2003] QB 195 which, although it was handed down only a few years ago, might be thought in certain respects to have been **overtaken by later developments.** Nevertheless, it is right that it **should be accorded consideration and respect**. My attention was particularly focused by Mr Warby QC on certain principles upon which he placed particular reliance. The first was this:

> "Any interference with the press has to be justified because it inevitably has some effect on **the ability of the press to perform its role in society.** This is the position irrespective of whether a particular publication is desirable in the public interest."

That, if I may say so with respect, is a general statement of the law which **remains valid.** In other words, **it is not necessary to demonstrate, in the case of a tabloid publication in particular, that the contents of an article or the content of photographs is desirable in the public interest**. It may very well be that, in certain circumstances, it will be necessary to focus upon whether or not it is in the public interest to publish material in respect of which there is a prima facie legitimate expectation of privacy. **But that is a consideration which has to be addressed later down the line.**

9. The other proposition which was referred to was this. **Regardless of the quality of the material which it is intended to publish, prima facie the court should not interfere with its publication.** Again, that is a statement of the obvious and a principle which has long applied ever since **Blackstone's** observations on prior or "previous" restraint: **Commentaries** (1765), Book IV, pp 151–2.

10. Furthermore, guideline (vii) in Lord Woolf's judgment was identified:

> ". . . . Usually the answer to the question whether there exists a private interest worthy of protection will be obvious. In those cases where the answer is not obvious an answer will often be unnecessary. This is because the weaker the claim for privacy the more likely that the claim for privacy will be outweighed by the claim based on freedom of expression."

11. Finally, reference was made to "guideline (xii)":

> "Where an individual is a **public figure**, he is entitled to have his privacy respected in the appropriate circumstances. The individual, however, should recognise that because of his public position he must expect and accept that his actions will be more closely scrutinised by the media. Even **trivial** facts relating to a **public figure** can be of great interest to readers and other observers of the media. . . . Whether you have courted publicity or not, you may be a legitimate subject of public attention."

12. Needless to say, my attention was also drawn to guidance given by the House of Lords in *Campbell v MGN* [2004] 2 AC 457, and also by the New Zealand Court of Appeal in *Hosking v Runting* [2004] NZCA 34, [2003] NZLR 385, and to the second hearing before the Court of Appeal in *Douglas v Hello*! [2006] QB 125, when the matter came before Lord Phillips MR I do not propose to analyse any of those decisions in any detail for the purposes of the present application, but I emphasise that I am familiar with them. I am grateful for the submissions of counsel with regard to them and I have them very much in mind.

13. Here one of the questions I have to address is whether or not on the evidence before me, it could be said that there is a reasonable expectation of privacy on the part of Sir Elton John in relation to the **content of the photograph**, that is to say **the information conveyed** by the **photograph**.

14. In *Campbell v MGN*, as is well known, the material **photograph** concerned **Ms Naomi Campbell emerging from a drug rehabilitation clinic into the street.** The **photograph** and the story contained information which was relevant to her health in general terms, and more particularly to a course of drug rehabilitation treatment which she was undergoing at the time, **in respect of which it was recognised that the publication might have some impact**. That was a special factor and it was contrasted, in the words of one of the members of the House of Lords, with a situation where a well-known person is observed or photographed in more casual circumstances "**popping out for a pint of milk".**

15. In the present case there is **no question** of the **photograph** revealing information which touches upon or is relevant to Sir Elton John's **health**. Nor is there any information about **social** or **personal relationships** or, as sometimes happens in these cases, **sexual relationships**. Those are all matters in respect of which, to a greater or lesser extent, as with allegations about health, an individual has a reasonable expectation of privacy. Here it seems to me that the circumstances are much more akin to "popping out for a pint of milk". In other words, it is simply an individual leaving his car and going to his front gate.

16. An important factor in *Von Hannover v Germany* (2005) 40 EHRR 1 was the

element of **harassment**, as in the recent case of *Howlett v Holding* [2006] EHWC 41 (QB), where a woman was being followed by a person who had a grudge against her and whom she had sued on more than one occasion for libel. **There is nothing here in the evidence before me to disclose a case of harassment**. There is no question, either, of **anything which discloses a course of conduct** (to use the phrase which appears in the **Protection from Harassment Act 1997).**

17. **There was some evidence before the court from the photographer who had taken the photographs about the circumstances in which he came to take them**. Mr Browne for the claimant has expressed considerable scepticism about that evidence, particularly because the **photographer says that he happened to be in the street**, was not there intending to **photograph** Sir Elton or to keep an eye out for him or to harass him. He did not know, he said in his evidence, that he lived in this street. The reason given by the photographer was that he was there because it was a particularly good area for him to be able to make an **internet** connection from his lap-top and he was sitting in his car for about 15 or 20 minutes using his lap-top. He happened to notice Sir Elton and, when he saw him and identified him, he got out of his car and took some **photographs** from a spot which he indicated by a mark on a **photograph**. He also showed where, in relation to that spot, Sir Elton was standing or walking at the time of the **photographs**.

18. It may be that in due course Mr Browne will be able successfully to challenge some or all of that evidence, **but at the moment I have no reason to suppose that it is untruthful.** I therefore take it into account as part of the background to this application. I have already said that there is nothing here which touches upon subject matter which is traditionally regarded as having about it **"the quality of confidence" or a reasonable expectation of privacy (such as health or personal relationships).**

19. An unusual case, where **photographs** in a public street were held to give rise to a claim, was that of *Peck v United Kingdom* (2003) 36 EHRR 41, where Mr Peck had taken the opportunity late at night in Brentwood High Street to **attempt suicide** without realising that he was being photographed by CCTV cameras. He was not aware of the presence of anyone else. **Publishing the photographs of someone attempting to commit suicide is exceptionally intrusive and insensitive** There is nothing here which is remotely comparable to that tragic situation.

20. Against that background, and applying the test which I have already identified in *Cream Holdings v Banerjee*, **I am not satisfied that the claimant is more likely than not to obtain injunctive relief at trial,** in the sense of establishing the threshold requirement that there was a reasonable expectation of privacy in the circumstances in which he found himself, or, alternatively, that if there

was such a reasonable expectation, the claimant's Article 8 rights would at trial prevail over the defendant's Article 10 rights. **I have no doubt that the article is likely to cause offence and embarrassment to Sir Elton**. There is reason to suppose from correspondence, which I need not refer to in this judgment, that **the article is likely to be dismissive and personally offensive.** That, however, in this day and age is regarded as quite a distinct matter from coverage which gives rise to a cause of action, whether in breach of confidence or for that matter libel. I must put to one side, as is made clear by the judgment of Lord Woolf in *A v B Plc*, considerations about whether or not the material has any particular worth or quality, and I do so.

21. **The photograph was not taken with consent,** but I am not persuaded that there is, as yet, any doctrine operative in English law whereby it is necessary to demonstrate that to publish a **photograph** one has to show that the subject of the **photograph** gave consent. **It may be a relevant factor, but it is to my mind one of relatively little weight in these particular circumstances**.

22. For those reasons I refuse the injunction.

MR WARBY: My Lord, I invite you to do so and order costs in favour of the defendants.

MR JUSTICE EADY: Mr Browne?

MR BROWNE: My Lord, could I just take instructions for a moment in relation to the matter of an appeal?

MR JUSTICE EADY: Yes, certainly. Do you want me to rise?

MR BROWNE: Yes, for five minutes.

(*The court adjourned for a short time*)

MR BROWNE: My Lord, I ask first for permission to appeal and for an injunction to be granted pending either the prosecution of the appeal, if your Lordship grants permission, or in the event that you do not, to enable us to go to the Appeal Court and seek permission. Your Lordship will recall that, clearly if the boot had been on the other foot, an application would have been made by Mr Warby. That was made clear in the letter that we received today. Can I just indicate the basis upon which I suggest that, in addition to there obviously being, as the defendants have said, an issue of great importance here and an issue where the law needs clarifying because this is the sort of case that can occur very often and leads to public concern, that the reason that I suggest that there is an arguable point of appeal here is that one is not concerned in applying section 12(3) with a direction question of discretion. Your Lordship is concerned with an **issue of law:** whether or not the claimant is more likely than not to succeed at trial. **It is not the usual case where it can be said that this is all a matter for the discretion of the judge**. The judge has to weigh the law and weigh the law in a developing area. In that area obviously, as Mr Warby has indicated, consideration has to be given to the differing emphases in the judgments of the house in *Campbell*. Your Lordship approached this on the basis of the informational content of the **photograph**. With great respect, that fails to give adequate weight to the approach at any rate of Lord Hope and Lady Hale, which was to treat the tort as one of **intrusion**. In other words, we have gone beyond simply a tort whose basis is the law of **confidential information** to look at what is **intrusive** in relation to Article 8 rights of privacy in the home. In other words, in Lord Hope's words, this is not an ordinary street scene. What is intended here is clearly going to be, as your Lordship acknowledged, **derisive of his baldness and personally offensive**, all added to the breach of Article 8 rights.

The second point that I would made is that your Lordship, although mentioning *Douglas v Hello* in passing, did not consider—and this is extremely important in the context of the *Cream* assessment—the point that was made in *Douglas* that **damages would be an inadequate remedy**. That is a matter which swayed the Court of Appeal in *Douglas v Hello* the second time and was said to be a criticism of their predecessors three or four years before.

So, my Lord, I do ask, as Mr Warby would be asking were the boot on the other foot, for permission to appeal and for your Lordship to extend the grant of an injunction to enable us to go to the Court of Appeal. This is a **photograph** that was taken last Monday. There is no conceivable urgency if the Daily Mail wish deride Sir Elton John, it is no matter to them whether the do so tomorrow or two or three weeks hence.

MR JUSTICE EADY: May I just ask **whether any contact has been made with the Court of Appeal?**

MR BROWNE: Not by us. It may well be that Mr Warby may have set it up.

MR JUSTICE EADY: Sometimes one is told that the Court of Appeal is as it were standing by.

MR BROWNE: I do not know whether Mr Warby has put that in hand. We have not.

MR WARBY: No, we have not. Mr Browne has misunderstood some of the things we said. **We said that we would go there if necessary, but we did not say that we had it all lined up.**

MR BROWNE: No, I was not suggesting that, but it is quite clear that they regarded this as much a matter of importance requiring issues to be resolved of some complexity and difficulties to justify going to the Court of Appeal, and we feel the same, particularly given the nature of the article which is likely to be published, coupled with the **intrusive photograph** capitalising on a physical feature of Sir Elton, just as humiliating and **intrusive** in its way as if they had capitalised on his state of health. Indeed, one could perhaps treat baldness as a feature of health.

MR JUSTICE EADY: Yes, thank you. Mr Warby?

MR WARBY: My Lord, it is an evaluative exercise, your Lordship's decision, and what your Lordship has done is to apply the existing principles laid down in the authorities to the facts of this particular case. Mr Brown says it is an issue of great importance. What we said was that the ramifications would be considerable if the novel proposition advanced by his side was accepted. The converse does not apply. It certainly does not mean that there is any merit in the proposition that lay behind the application. So the point of principle does not really arise at all. Your Lordship did refer to the informational content of the **photograph**, but you also noted the clear reference the question of whether distress and **embarrassment** would be caused. Your Lordship took all the relevant factors into account and the Court of Appeal would have no basis for interfering with the evaluative exercise your Lordship carried out.

The second point that was made was that your Lordship mentioned *Douglas*, but not the point about **damages being an adequate** remedy. Well, your Lordship having given sufficient grounds for the decision, that point did not really arise. Your Lordship has dismissed the application on the basis that it did not cross the threshold. You were not satisfied it **crossed the threshold** and you were not satisfied that it would succeed when balancing Article 8 with Article 10. So damages being an adequate remedy, it quite simply was not necessary for your Lordship to address. So I invite you to refuse permission and leave it to Mr Browne, if so advised and instructed, to take his application to the Court of Appeal.

MR BROWNE: My Lord, it is obviously very late and it will be difficult now, as the Court of Appeal pointed out in *Douglas v Hello* if an injunction is refused, that represents a considerable **intrusion** on the claimant's Convention rights, obviously assuming that he is right, as I would ask your Lordship to do for the purposes of this argument.

My Lord, so far as the section 12(3) point is concerned, this is not simply a question of evaluation. Your Lordship has to evaluate the factual evidence, but the real question is the application of the law. I will not repeat myself, save to this extent. Where, with great respect, a point of great importance arises is whether it is right in a case like this to be concerned solely with the informational content of the **photograph** or whether one has regard to the **intrusive** nature of a **covert**, non-consensual **photograph**, which is the approach we say that was taken in *Von Hannover*. So, my Lord, we do say that issues of great importance arise here, not least because, as has been said by these defendants, these matters arise so frequently. In those circumstances, having regard to the stress that is obviously likely to be caused to Sir Elton **by the publication of the photograph focusing, as that photograph did, on his baldness,** and **speculating about whether he wears a wig or a hairweave**, my Lord, we say that we should be permitted to have the injunction for as long as it takes us to get this matter before the Court of Appeal. But I do ask your Lordship to say that this is a case where permission to appeal would be proper and justified, bearing in mind the lack of urgency to publish.

MR JUSTICE EADY:

23. Yes, thank you. This afternoon I have refused an interim injunction for reasons set out in the ex tempore judgment I delivered a few minutes ago. I am now asked to grant an interim injunction, nevertheless, so that the claimant can have the opportunity of applying to the Court of Appeal at some stage, perhaps (I was told) several weeks away.

24. Sometimes it is the case, where an urgent application for an injunction is made**, that the Court of Appeal has been notified so that Lords Justices can be standing by** in order to deal with an appeal in circumstances of urgency. I am told that that has not been done on this occasion.

25. In all the circumstances it does not seem to me to be right to grant an interim injunction *despite* the reasons I gave in my earlier judgment. It is said that there are matters of developing law and of great importance here which require the attention of the Court of Appeal. On the particular circumstances of this case I am not persuaded that that is so. Therefore, insofar as it is necessary, I refuse permission to appeal. I also refuse to grant an interim injunction for the same reasons I gave earlier.

26. Do you want to say something about the question of costs, Mr Browne?

    MR BROWNE: Your Lordship will have to form a view as to the need to have spent as much as twelve hours.

    MR JUSTICE EADY: I am concerned for the moment with the principle. **MR BROWNE:** I am so sorry, my Lord. So far as costs are concerned, the only argument that I could mount is that it should be costs in the action. That, of course, assumes that it will go on. That in the ordinary way would be the appropriate order because it does not necessarily follow from your Lordship's ruling on section 12(3) that the case is doomed, even if your Lordship is right. So that is the order that I would seek, costs in the action, and in due course a detailed assessment if the action goes not further. One does not know quite what will be published and what Sir Elton will wish to do, having regard to the advice from the Court of Appeal that damages are an inadequate remedy once the cat is out of the bag.

    MR JUSTICE EADY: All right. Thank you. I think you are entitled to your costs as a matter of principle, Mr Warby. Are you asking me to make a summary assessment?

MR WARBY: Yes, we have done the decent thing and produced a statement of costs.

MR JUSTICE EADY: Have you done the decent thing in serving it on the other side 24 hours beforehand?

MR WARBY: Yes, we have. That is what I meant, but I did not say it.

MR JUSTICE EADY: Yes, I see.

MR WARBY: Yes, we have provided this to the other side. That is what Mr Browne began by talking about.

MR JUSTICE EADY: Yes.

MR WARBY: Could I have a copy handed up to your Lordship and invite you to assess the costs in the sum specified?

MR JUSTICE EADY: Thank you.

MR WARBY: The focus of Mr Browne's submission, half made before he had second thoughts, was the second count, the apparently extravagant amount of twelve hours spent by Miss Hartley dealing with this matter. Of course, there being no costs statement from the other side, we are not to know how many hours –

MR JUSTICE EADY: I never find that terribly helpful anyway. People always like to refer to it, but I would rather concentrate on what has been –

MR WARBY: I always find it rather intriguing.

MR JUSTICE EADY: Well, that is a different point.

MR WARBY: Your Lordship's views are what matter. My Lord, I can say that that time was principally spent from between about six o'clock yesterday when the question of a threatened injunction was raised again and the time this hearing began. From personal experience, to-ing and fro-ing was going on throughout the course of last evening, as your Lordship will understand. Taking the statement of the journalist whose e-mail confirming and proofing the statement came in at some time after ten o'clock.

MR JUSTICE EADY: Yes.

MR WARBY: So, in my submission, twelve hours at that rate is remarkably modest compared to many that one sees. It is a thoroughly reasonable sum in a matter of this kind.

MR JUSTICE EADY: Can I check with you whether in this case VAT is properly claimed?

MR WARBY: VAT is not charged, no

MR JUSTICE EADY: It is claimed here.

MR WARBY: Yes, I apologise for that.

MR JUSTICE EADY: That ought to come out?

MR WARBY: Yes, because that can be reclaimed.

MR JUSTICE EADY: That is what I thought, yes.

MR WARBY: So I drop the claim for VAT. The fee is £7,081.

MR JUSTICE EADY: Do you want to say anything about the detail? You were about to say something about the twelve hours, Mr Browne?

MR BROWNE: Well, your Lordship has to approach this with a fairly broad brush and twelve hours does seem an awful lot. I will not speculate about what Mr Taite has worked out. As your Lordship said, it would not be helpful, but in our submission the sum of £7,000 odd, which remains after the VAT is deducted, ought to be knocked down by a reasonable percentage.

MR JUSTICE EADY: Mr Warby, unless you want to persuade me to the contrary, I think the right figure for summary assessment is £6,000.

MR WARBY: My Lord, I will leave it there.

MR JUSTICE EADY: Thank you very much.

Douglas v Hello! Ltd (No 3) [2006] QB 125

Lord Phillips, MR:

This is the judgment of the court, to which all members have contributed.

The Background

The basic facts

1. Hello! Ltd ("Hello!"), the publishers of Hello! magazine, appeal against awards of damages made by Lindsay J in favour of Mr Michael Douglas and his wife Ms Catherine Zeta-Jones ("the Douglases"), and Northern & Shell Plc ("OK!"), the publishers of OK! magazine. The appeal against the award of £14,600 in favour of the Douglases is in respect of liability only; the appeal against the award of £1,033,156 in favour of OK! is in respect of liability and quantum. The Douglases and OK! contingently cross-appeal; the issues raised on the cross-appeals concern the liability of Hello! Ltd to OK!, and the damages awarded to the Douglases.
2. The complex factual and procedural history of this matter is fully and clearly set out in paragraphs 1 to 179 of Lindsay J's judgment on liability, which is

reported as *Douglas v Hello! Ltd (No 3)* at [2003] 3 All ER 996. We shall limit ourselves to the essential facts necessary to determine the issues raised before us.

On 18th November 2000, Mr Douglas and Ms Zeta-Jones, who were and are very well-known film stars, were married at the Plaza Hotel, New York. As soon as the couple's engagement was announced in early 2000, there was intense interest in this event from certain sections of the media; in particular, from the publishers of OK! and Hello! magazines. As the judge said, in paragraph 12 of his judgment, both those magazines "provide a regular diet of **photographs** and text about royal, but, more usually, entertainment, sporting, and social celebrities, with **photographs** taking precedence over text." Most of those **photographs** are posed, and many of those that are not will have been taken with the consent of their subjects. As the judge said (at paragraph 15), the two magazines are "plainly keen rivals in the same market", and they each had an average weekly circulation in the UK of just over 450,000 copies.

4. Both publishers approached the Douglases with a view to obtaining the exclusive right to publish **photographs** of the wedding reception. The Douglases decided, with a view to reducing what Ms Zeta-Jones called "the media frenzy", that they would grant that right to one publisher. According to Mr Douglas, they regarded this course as "the best way to control the media and to protect our privacy". After some negotiations, they entered into a contract with OK! ("the OK! contract") on 10th November, eight days before the wedding.

5. In its preamble, the OK! contract referred to "the publication of an article, including story and **photographs** (collectively "the Article") relating to the Wedding". By clause 1, OK! agreed to pay £500,000 each to Mr Douglas (therein "MKD"), and to Ms Zeta-Jones (therein "CZJ"). By clause 2, it was agreed that:

> "MKD and CZJ hereby transfer to OK! the exclusive right to publish . . . the **Photographs** (as defined in paragraph 6 below) and the text referred to herein from the date of the Wedding and for nine months thereafter."

. . .

The issues in relation to confidence and privacy: the principles

Introductory

. . .

43. It is convenient to consider the issues in relation to the Douglases' claim separately from those in relation to OK!'s claim. The issues in relation to the Douglases' claim are as follows:

- (Disregarding the effect of the OK! contract) did the law of confidence protect information about the wedding as being private information? If so,

- Did the OK! contract destroy that protection?
- Did the law of confidence protect the Douglases' commercial interest in the information about their wedding?

44. The issues in relation to OK!'s claim are as follows:

- Did the OK! contract have the effect of extending to OK! the protection of the law of confidence in respect of the information about the wedding? If so
- Was that protection lost when OK! published the authorised **photographs**?

45. There is one issue common to both claims. Is this area of the law so uncertain that it cannot be invoked to justify interference with Hello!'s freedom of expression?

. . .

The United Kingdom's Convention obligation in respect of privacy

47. We are not the first to acknowledge the assistance to be derived from Gavin Phillipson's lucid article, *Transforming Breach of Confidence? Towards a Common Law Right of Privacy under the Human Rights Act* (2003) 66 MLR 726. At p 729 he observes that the Strasbourg jurisprudence provides no definite answer to the question of whether the Convention *requires* states to provide a privacy remedy against private actors. **That is no longer the case. In von Hannover v Germany (24 June 2004) the ECtHR gave judgment in respect of a series of complaints by Princess Caroline of Monaco.** They all related to press **photographs** of her that had been taken in public places. She contended that these infringed her privacy and had sought a remedy in a series of actions in the German courts, which had been unsuccessful. She alleged that these decisions of the German courts infringed her Article 8 right to respect for her private and family life. The ECtHR agreed:

> "The Court reiterates that although the object of Article 8 is essentially that of protecting the individual against arbitrary interference by the public authorities, it does not merely compel the State to abstain from such interference: in addition to this primarily negative undertaking, there may be positive obligations inherent in an effective respect for private or family life. **These obligations may involve the adoption of measures designed to secure respect for private life even in the sphere of the relations of individuals between themselves** (see, *mutatis mutandis, X and Y v the Netherlands*, judgment of 26 March 1985, Series A no 91, p 11, ss 23; *Stjerna v Finland*, judgment of 25 November

1994, Series A no 299-B, p61, ss38; and *Verliere v Switzerland* (dec.), no 41953/98, ECHR 2001-VII). That also applies to the protection of a person's picture against abuse by others " .

48. The ECtHR went on at paragraph 72 to state that the relevant German statute should have been interpreted **narrowly** by the German courts:

    "to ensure that the State complies with its positive obligation under the Convention to protect private life and the right to control the use of one's own image"

49. **It follows that the ECtHR has recognised an obligation on member states to protect one individual from an unjustified invasion of private life by another individual and an obligation on the courts of a member state to interpret legislation in a way which will achieve that result.**

What obligation is placed on the courts in respect of the protection of privacy?

. . .

53. We conclude that, in so far as private information is concerned, **we are required to adopt, as the vehicle for performing such duty as falls on the courts in relation to Convention rights, the cause of action formerly described as breach of confidence**. As to the nature of that duty, it seems to us that sections 2, 3, 6 and 12 of the Human Rights Act all point in the same direction. **The court should, insofar as it can, develop the action for breach of confidence in such a manner as will give effect to both Article 8 and Article 10 rights**. In considering the nature of those rights, account should be taken of the Strasbourg jurisprudence. In particular, when considering what information should be protected as private pursuant to Article 8**, it is right to have regard to the decisions of the ECtHR.** We cannot pretend that we find it satisfactory to be required to shoe-horn within the cause of action of breach of confidence claims for publication of unauthorised **photographs** of a private occasion.

The law of confidence

54. We now turn to consider the law of confidence as it has developed up to this point. We start with *Prince Albert v Strange* (1849) 1 Mac & G 25. Prince Albert obtained an injunction restraining the defendant from publishing a catalogue of etchings made by himself and Queen Victoria**. One ground for the grant of this equitable remedy was that the information in the catalogue must have been obtained by breach of trust, confidence or contract**. The information in question was personal, not commercial, although the defendant intended to make money out of it, and Lord Cottenham LC remarked that "privacy is the right invaded".

55. We can advance well over a century to *Coco v A N Clark (Engineers) Ltd* [1969]

RPC 41, a case in which Megarry J analysed three elements of breach of confidence as established by the authorities up to that point in time. **First** the information had to be **'of a confidential nature'**. In explaining this phrase Megarry J first cited the statement of Lord Greene MR in *Saltman Engineering Co Ltd v Campbell Engineering Co Ltd* (1948) 65 RPC 203 at p 215 that it must not be "**something which is public property and public knowledge**". This is not the clearest of definitions. **It seems to us that information will be confidential if it is available to one person (or a group of people) and not generally available to others, provided that the person (or group) who possesses the information does not intend that it should become available to others**. Megarry J went on to hold that "whether it is described as originality or novelty or ingenuity or otherwise, I think **that there must be some product of the human brain which suffices to confer a confidential nature upon the information"**. While this may have been an appropriate statement on the facts before him, it is plainly not of general application, as the *Spycatcher* litigation demonstrates.

56. The **second** requirement was that the information must have been communicated by the confider to the confidant in circumstances of confidence. As to this requirement, Megarry J advanced the following test at p 48:

> **". . . if the circumstances are such that any reasonable man standing in the shoes of the recipient of the information would have realised that upon reasonable grounds the information was being given to him in confidence, then this should suffice to impose on him the equitable obligation of confidence."**

The **third** requirement was that there had to be an **unauthorised** use of the information to the **detriment** of the confider. We would observe that the essential feature creating the duty of confidence was the circumstances in which the information was communicated from the confider to the confidant.

58. The information that was the subject matter of *Coco v A N Clark* was technical information of value for commercial purposes. It was held not to be of a confidential nature as it was already in the **public domain**.

59. In *Attorney-General v Guardian Newspapers Limited (No 2)* [1990] 1 AC 109 Lord Goff of Chieveley observed that an obligation of confidence could arise even where the information in question had not been confided by a confider to a confidant. He said at p 281:

> "I realise that, in the vast majority of cases, in particular those concerned with **trade secrets**, the duty of confidence will arise from a transaction or **relationship** between the parties—often a contract, in which event the duty may arise by reason of either an express or an implied term of that contract. It is in such cases as these that the expressions "confider"

and "confidant" are perhaps most aptly employed. **But it is well settled that a duty of confidence may arise in equity independently of such cases**; and I have expressed the circumstances in which the duty arises in broad terms, not merely to embrace those cases where a third party receives information from a person who is under a duty of confidence in respect of it, knowing that it has been disclosed by that person to him in breach of his duty of confidence, **but also to include certain situations, beloved of law teachers—where an obviously confidential document is wafted by an electric fan out of a window into a crowded street, or where an obviously confidential document, such as a private diary, is dropped in a public place, and is then picked up by a passer-by."**

59. Lord Goff went on to say that he had deliberately avoided the fundamental question whether, contract apart, the duty lay simply "in the notion of an obligation of conscience arising from the circumstances in or through which the information was communicated or obtained". We would observe that the reference to an *obviously confidential document* might be said to have begged the question of what made the document confidential. We would also observe that in Lord Goff's examples the nature of the information, together possibly with the form in which it was recorded, coupled with the circumstances in which it came to the notice of the person fixed with the duty of confidence, were such as to lead a reasonable person to conclude that the information in question was private.

60. **Lord Goff also deliberately avoided the question of whether confidential information might be regarded as property, a question of particular importance in the context of the appeal before us.**61. The potential that Lord Goff's analysis had for protecting private information that was not recorded in a document was not immediately appreciated. In *Kaye v Robertson* (1991) 19 IPR 147 journalists had gained unauthorised access to the hospital bedside of a **celebrity** recovering from a brain injury and taken **photographs** of his appearance to which he was in no condition to consent. The Court of Appeal held that the law provided no protection for the photographic information so obtained. It was not even argued that the law of confidence could provide a remedy.

62. The significance of Lord Goff's approach was, however, appreciated by Laws J who, in *Hellewell v Chief Constable* [1995] 1 WLR 804 at p 807, made the following *obiter* observation:

> **"If someone with a telephoto lens were to take from a distance and with no authority a picture of another engaged in some private act, his subsequent disclosure of the photograph would, in my judgment, as surely amount to a breach of confidence as if he had found or stolen a letter or diary in which the act was recounted and proceeded to**

> **publish it. In such a case, the law would protect what might reasonably be called a right of privacy**, although the name accorded to the cause of action would be breach of confidence. **It is, of course, elementary that, in all such cases, a defence based on the public interest would be available."**

. . .

67. The Court discharged the injunction on the basis that the OK! contract had substantially weakened The Douglases' claim to relief based on invasion of privacy and that damages or an account of profits was likely to provide an adequate remedy should breach of duty be established at the trial.

68. Perhaps the most dramatic use of the law of confidence to protect privacy occurred within weeks of the interlocutory decision in this case. In *Venables and Thompson v New Group Newspapers Ltd and others* [2001] Fam 430 Dame Elizabeth Butler-Sloss P granted injunctions against the whole world restraining the disclosure of any information that might lead to the identification of the murderers of James Bulger after their release from prison. The President held that, taking into account the Convention, the law of confidence could extend to cover the injunctions sought. **Disclosure of the information in question might lead to grave, and possibly fatal, consequences for the claimants**. This factor not merely rendered the information confidential**, but outweighed** the freedom of expression that would otherwise have underpinned the right of the press to publish the information.

69. A remarkable feature of this decision was that **the nature of the information alone gave rise to the duty of confidence** regardless of the circumstances in which the information might come to the knowledge of a person who might wish to publish it.

70. In *A v B* [2003] QB 195 the Court of Appeal had to consider an application to set aside an interim injunction preventing the first defendant newspaper from publishing details of the claimant's **sexual relationships** with the second defendant and a woman to whom he was not married. The injunction had been granted on the ground that the information was confidential and subject to the protection of Article 8 of the Convention and there was no public interest in publication that enabled the defendant's rights of freedom of expression to prevail.

71. In introducing the judgment of the court, Lord Woolf CJ said this at paragraph 4: . . .

72. Lord Woolf went on to deal with the circumstances where a person can and cannot reasonably expect details of his **sexual activities** to be treated as confidential. This was a matter that later fell for consideration by Ouseley J in *Theakston v MGN* [2002] EWHC 137 and, in the nature of things, is likely

to call for consideration not infrequently in the future. Having regard to the facts of the present case this is not an area that we need explore. We would simply observe that to date the English courts appear to have taken a less generous view of the protection that the individual can reasonably expect in respect of his or her sexual activities than has the Strasbourg court.

. . .

77. **We have already referred to Lord Nicholls's statement that the essence of the tort was better encapsulated as a misuse of private information. That statement was preceded by the following passage:**

> **"Now the law imposes a "duty of confidence" whenever a person receives information he knows or ought to know is fairly and reasonably to be regarded as confidential. Even this formulation is awkward. The continuing use of the phrase "duty of confidence" and the description of the information as "confidential" is not altogether comfortable. Information about an individual's private life would not, in ordinary usage, be called "confidential". The more natural description today is that such information is private"**

78. **Later at paragraph 21 Lord Nicholls commented:**

> **"Essentially the touchstone of private life is whether in respect of the disclosed facts the person in question had a reasonable expectation of privacy."**

He drew attention to the distinction between identifying whether information is private and identifying whether it is proportionate to prevent disclosure of such information, having regard to the competing Convention right of freedom of expression. He suggested that the test of whether disclosure would be "**highly offensive** to a reasonable person", advanced by Gleeson CJ when considering the test of what is private in *Australian Broadcasting Corpn v Lenah Game Meats Pty Ltd* (2001) 208 CLR 199, paragraph 42, was more relevant to the latter issue.

79. **Lord Hoffmann identified two developments of the law of confidence. The first was the recognition of the artificiality of distinguishing between confidential information obtained through a violation of a confidential relationship and similar information obtained in some other way. The second was the acceptance, under human rights instruments such as Article 8 of the Convention, of the privacy of personal information as something worthy of protection in its own right.** As to the latter there was no logical ground for affording a person less protection against a private individual than against the state. In the result (paragraph 51):

> **"Instead of the cause of action being based upon the duty of good faith applicable to confidential personal information and trade secrets** alike,

> **it focuses upon the protection of human autonomy and dignity—the right to control the dissemination of information about one's private life and the right to the esteem and respect of other people."**

80. **Lord Hope of Craighead (paragraph 85) approved Lord Woolf CJ's statement in** *A v B* that a duty of confidence will arise whenever the party subject to the duty is in a situation where he knows or ought to know that the other person can reasonably expect his privacy to be protected. He considered that Gleeson CJ's test was useful **where there was room for doubt, but:**

> **"If the information is obviously private, the situation will be one where the person to whom it relates can reasonably expect his privacy to be respected. So there is normally no need to go on and ask whether it would be *highly offensive* for it to be published." (paragraph 96)**

81. **Baroness Hale held that the cause of action of breach of confidence had within its scope what has been termed "the protection of the individual's informational autonomy". Where the person publishing the information knows or ought to know that there is a reasonable expectation that the information in question will be kept confidential the threshold is reached where the court will have to balance the claimant's interest in keeping the information private against the countervailing interest of the recipient in publishing it** (paragraph 137). Lord Carswell at paragraph 166 observed that it was not necessary to apply Gleeson CJ's test. It was sufficiently established by the nature of the material that it was private information which attracted the duty of observing the confidence in which it was imparted to the respondents.

82. Some of the comments that we have cited underline the validity of Lord Nicholls's observation that the use of the phrase "duty of confidence" and the description of private information as "confidential" are not altogether comfortable. **What the House was agreed upon** was that **the knowledge, actual or imputed, that information is private** will **normally impose on anyone publishing** that information **the duty to justify what, in the absence of justification, will be a wrongful invasion of privacy.** The House was also agreed that, when Article 8 and Article 10 are both engaged, one does not start with the balance tilted in favour of Article 10.

'Private information'

83. Megarry J in *Coco v A N Clark* identified two requirements for the creation of a duty of confidence. The first was that the information should be confidential in nature and the second was that it should have been imparted in circumstances importing a duty of confidence. As we have seen, it is now recognised that the second requirement is not necessary if it is plain that the information is confidential, **and for the adjective 'confidential' one can**

substitute the word 'private'. What is the nature of **'private information?'** It seems to us that it **must include information that is personal to the person who possesses it and that he does not intend shall be imparted to the general public.** The nature of the information, or the form in which it is kept, may suffice to make it plain that that the information satisfies these criteria.

Photographic information

84. This action is about **photographs**. **Special considerations attach to photographs in the field of privacy.** They are not merely a method of conveying information that is an alternative to verbal description. **They enable the person viewing the photograph to act as a spectator, in some circumstances voyeur would be the more appropriate noun, of whatever it is that the photograph depicts.** As a means of invading privacy, a **photograph is particularly intrusive**. This is quite apart from the fact that the camera, and the telephoto lens, can give access to the viewer of the **photograph** to scenes where those photographed could reasonably expect that their appearances or actions would not be brought to the notice of the public.

85. The intrusive nature of photography is reflected by the various media codes of practice. It is also recognised by the authorities. In *Theakston v MGN* Ousley J refused an injunction restraining publication of a verbal depiction of the claimant's activities in a **brothel**. **He granted, however, an injunction restraining the publication of photographs taken of these activities**. He held, at paragraph 78:

> **"The authorities cited to me showed that the Courts have consistently recognised that photographs can be particularly intrusive** and have showed **a high degree of willingness to prevent the publication of photographs, taken without the consent of the person photographed but which the photographer or someone else sought to exploit and publish.** This protection extended to **photographs**, taken without their consent, of people who **exploited the commercial value of their own image** in similar **photographs**, and to **photographs** taken with the consent of people **but who had not consented to that particular form of commercial exploitation,** as well as to **photographs** taken in pubic or from a public place of what could be seen if not with a naked eye, then at least with the aid of powerful binoculars. I concluded that this part of the injunction involved no particular extension of the law of confidentiality **and that the publication of such photographs would be particularly intrusive into the Claimant's own individual personality.** I considered that even though the fact that the Claimant went to the **brothel** and the details as to what he did there were not to be restrained from publication, the publication of **photographs** taken there without his consent could still constitute an **intrusion** into his private and personal

life and would do so **in a peculiarly humiliating and damaging way.** It did not seem to be remotely inherent in going to a **brothel** that what was done inside would be photographed, let alone that any **photographs** would be published."

86. In *D v L* [2004] EMLR 1 at p 10 Waller LJ remarked:

> **"A court may restrain the publication of an improperly obtained photograph even if the taker is free to describe the information which the photographer provides or even if the information revealed by the photograph is in the public domain. It is no answer to the claim to restrain the publication of an improperly obtained photograph that the information portrayed by the photograph is already available in the public domain."**

87. In *von Hannover v Germany* the ECtHR remarked at paragraph 59:

> **"Although freedom of expression also extends to the publication of photos, this is an area in which the protection of the rights and reputation of others takes on particular importance. The present case does not concern the dissemination of "ideas", but of images containing very personal or even intimate "information" about an individual.** Furthermore, photos appearing in the tabloid press are often taken in a **climate** of **continual harassment** which induces in the person concerned a **very strong sense of intrusion** into their private life of even of persecution."

88. In *Campbell v MGN*, although Naomi Campbell made no complaint that the publication of her **photographs** itself constituted a breach of confidence, both Lord Hope and Baroness Hale placed particular weight on the **intrusive** nature of **photographs**. Lord Hope said at paragraph 123:

> **"Miss Campbell could not have complained if the photographs had been taken to show the scene in the street by a passer-by and later published simply as street scenes.** But these were not just pictures of a street scene where she happened to be when the **photographs** were taken. **They were taken deliberately, in secret, and with a view to their publication in conjunction with the article.** The zoom lens was directed at the doorway of the place where the meeting had been taking place. The faces of others in the doorway were **pixelated** so as not to reveal their identity. Hers was not, the **photographs** were published and her privacy was invaded."

89. Lord Hope had earlier held applicable the reasoning of the Supreme Court of Canada in *Aubry v Editions Vice-Versa Inc* [1998] 1 SCR 591. The court had held that publication in a magazine of an unauthorised **photograph** of a 17 year old girl sitting on the steps of a public building had violated her right to

respect for private life conferred under Article 5 of the 'Quebec Charter' of Human Rights and Freedoms.

90. Baroness Hale was not prepared to go this far. She said that by themselves the **photographs** would not have been objectionable, contrasting the law of England with that applied in the *Vice-Versa* case. She held the **photographs** objectionable because (paragraph 155):

> **"A picture is "worth a thousand words"** because it adds to the **impact** of what the words convey; but it also adds to the information given in those words. If nothing else, it tells the reader what everyone looked like; in this case it also told the reader what the place looked like."

91. With this summary of English law, we turn to the issues raised by the facts of this case.

...

The effect of the OK! contract

103. Hello!'s argument, as advanced by Mr Price, is that, once the Douglases had committed themselves by the OK! contract to putting before the public **photographs** of their wedding, it was no longer possible for them to advance a claim that events at their wedding were private or confidential. Thereafter, publication of other **photographs** of that event could not possibly infringe Article 8 of the Convention or give rise to a claim for breach of confidence.

104. We have seen that the first element of breach of confidence identified by Megarry J in *Coco v A N Clark* was that the information had to be 'of a confidential nature', as opposed to being public property and public knowledge. The *Spycatcher* litigation concerned republication in English newspapers of extracts from a book, published without legal restraint in Australia and elsewhere, which had been written by a former member of the British secret service in breach of contract and confidence applicable under English law. In that litigation, which culminated in the decision of the House of Lords in *Attorney-General v Guardian Newspapers Limited (No 2)* [1990] 1 AC 109, **it was held, after much discussion, that the protection of the law of confidence had been lost as a result of the information coming into the public domain**. Care must be exercised in applying that decision generally, for **there is a special principle of law which precludes the State from asserting breach of confidence where it cannot be shown that this is in the public interest**.

105. **In general, however, once information is in the public domain, it will no longer be confidential or entitled to the protection of the law of confidence, though this may not always be true**: see *Gilbert v Star Newspaper Company Limited* (1894) 51 TLR 4 and *Creation Records Limited v News Group Newspapers Ltd* [1997] EMLR 444 at p 456. **The same may generally be true of**

private information of a personal nature. Once intimate personal information about a celebrity's private life has been widely published it may serve no useful purpose to prohibit further publication. ***The same will not necessarily be true of photographs.*** **Insofar as a photograph does more than convey information and intrudes on privacy by enabling the viewer to focus on intimate personal detail,** ***there will be a fresh intrusion of privacy when each additional viewer sees the photograph*** **and even** ***when one who has seen a previous publication of the photograph,*** **is confronted by a fresh publication of it.** To take an example, ***if a film star were photographed, with the aid of a telephoto lens, lying naked by her private swimming pool, we question whether widespread publication of the photograph by a popular newspaper would provide a defence to a legal challenge to repeated publication on the ground that the information was in the public domain.*** **There is thus a further important potential distinction between the law relating to private information and that relating to other types of confidential information.**

106. Nor is it right to treat a **photograph** simply as a means of conveying factual information. A **photograph** can certainly capture every detail of a momentary event in a way which words cannot, but a **photograph** can do more than that. **A personal photograph can portray, not necessarily accurately, the personality and the mood of the subject of the photograph.** It is quite wrong to suppose that a person who authorises publication of selected personal **photographs** taken on a private occasion, will not reasonably feel distress at the publication of **unauthorised photographs** taken on the same occasion.

107. There is a further point. **The objection to the publication of unauthorised photographs taken on a private occasion is not simply that the images that they disclose convey secret information, or impressions that are unflattering. It is that they disclose information that is private.** The offence is caused because what the claimant could reasonably expect would remain private has been made public. **The intrusion into the private domain is, of itself, objectionable.** ***To the extent that an individual authorises photographs taken on a private occasion to be made public, the potential for distress at the publication of other, unauthorised, photographs, taken on the same occasion, will be reduced. This will be very relevant when considering the amount of any damages.*** **The agreement that authorised photographs can be published will not, however, provide a defence to a claim, brought under the law of confidence, for the publication of unauthorised photographs.** It follows that we do not accept Mr Price's submission that the effect of the OK! contract precluded the Douglases' right to contend that their wedding was a private occasion and, as such, protected by the law of confidence.

W v Westminster City Council [2005] 1 FLR 816

Headnote: The claimant took proceedings for libel against the council and two social workers regarding **a document presented at a child protection case conference suggesting that the claimant was grooming for prostitution an 11-year-old girl who was the half-sister of his son**. The case came before the court where defences were raised of **absolute** or **qualified privilege**. The allegations in the report were **subsequently withdrawn**. The judge reconsidered the defences in the light of recent developments in the law, in particular the Human Rights Act 1998, and delivered a reserved judgment on the issue.

Held –

1. Absolute privilege attached at common law and by statute to a number of different types of occasion, but while there were many statutes making provision for local authorities there was no statute assisting the defendants in the present case. The courts could extend the common law to new circumstances, the test to be applied being one of necessity. **Earlier attempts to establish that absolute privilege applied in relation to certain child care proceedings had failed.** Furthermore in rejecting these attempts the courts had the European Convention for the Protection of Human Rights and Fundamental Freedoms 1950 in mind, notwithstanding that the Human Rights Act 1998 was not yet in force. **The courts have since recognised that the right to reputation was one of the rights generated by Art 8,** therefore both the claimant and the child had rights under Art 8. However, **nothing encouraged the recognition of new examples of common law absolute privilege.** Given that a case-by-case approach was required, **qualified privilege was the more appropriate route to approach the matter.**
2. It was common ground that **subject to factual issues, in particular as to relevance and malice, a communication made to a child protection case conference would be protected by qualified privilege.** It had been submitted on behalf of the claimant, **first**, that **irrelevant** statements were not privileged, and, **secondly**, that the statement had been **reckless**. In a case like the present, however, where the defendants had a duty to raise matters that might be of vital importance to the child, **the fact that the statement was irrelevant went to the question of malice, not to qualified privilege.** The court must decide whether either or both the defendants **had acted in good faith in the discharge of their duty under the Children Act 1989** or whether the claimant could establish some **dominant motive other than a sense of duty**. On the facts of the case, therefore, the statement complained of was **protected by qualified privilege, subject to proof of malice.**
3. Since the coming into force of the Human Rights Act 1998 there was another

cause of action, under s 7, by which claimants could ensure their rights under Art 8. **If the outcome of a libel action against a public authority appeared not to give a remedy for interference with a claimant's right under Art 8, then it might be that he had a remedy under s 7.** Given the letter of apology from the first defendant it might be that the case should be viewed in the light of s 7, whether or not it was also a libel action.

. . .

38. The European Court of Human Rights has said more than once recently that the ***right to* reputation is one of the rights guaranteed by Art 8 of the European Convention:** *Radio France v France* (Application No 53984/00) (unreported) 30 March 2004, para 31; *Cumpana and Mazare v Romania* (Application No 33348/96) (unreported) 10 June 2003, paras 48, 56 **(a case where the publication complained of was a cartoon suggesting the complainant was having an extra-marital affair).** The Court of Appeal has assumed that to be the law: *Greene v Associated Newspapers* [2004] EWCA Civ 1462, [2005] 1 All ER 30, at [57]. I must do so also. **The claimant s Art 8 rights were in any event engaged in the child protection conference**, because **he was a member of S's family,** and if any action had been taken as a result of the concerns expressed in the words complained of, relating as they did to possible **sexual** abuse by him, that could have led to the most serious consequences for him, **including on his relationship with both S and H.**

CC v AB [2006] EWHC 3083

The Hon Mr Justice Eady:

1. In this case the Claimant (CC) conducted an **adulterous relationship** for some months with the **Defendant's wife,** and now seeks the court's assistance in preventing him from telling anybody about it. **There is no direct precedent for this, so far as I am aware, and it does not at first glance appear to be a very compelling case.**

2. What is the cause of action? **(Clearly, if reliance were placed on defamation, there would be no prospect of an injunction if the words the Defendant wishes to publish would be susceptible to a defence of justification: *Bonnard v Perryman* [1891] 2 Ch 269.)** Since it is not yet recognised that English domestic law offers an enforceable right to privacy, as such, it has been put on the basis that any such communication would be a breach of confidence; alternatively, that the Defendant (AB) should be restrained from **harassing** the Claimant contrary to the provisions of the **Protection from Harassment Act 1997**. That is based primarily upon certain **abusive communications**

which the Claimant has received from the Defendant by way of e-mail and telephone.

3. The first of the causes of action relied upon entails the striking proposition that a spouse whose partner has committed adultery owes a duty of confidence to the third party adulterer to keep quiet about it—even without any voluntary assumption of such an obligation.

4. Before proceeding further, however, it is appropriate to add in some further elements revealed by the evidence in this particular case.

5. **First**, the Defendant has made it clear in a number of **threatening** communications, and indeed in his evidence to the court, that he wishes to reveal the information partly out of **revenge** and partly to **make money** for himself by selling the story to the media.

6. Whether the Defendant's motive has anything to do with it is a matter for closer consideration. **It may be thought that a citizen's right of free speech is not dependent on the *motive* or the motives governing its exercise: see eg the observations of Lord Nicholls, in the context of fair comment, in Tse Wai Chun Paul v Albert [2001] EMLR 31.** On the other hand, ***it is a factor* which Mr Warby QC for the Claimant argues is at least relevant to be taken into account when, if that stage is reached, it becomes necessary to weigh competing rights against one another.** It is now recognised in Strasbourg and domestic jurisprudence that there are different categories of "speech" to which greater or lesser importance may be attached (eg what has been called "**political speech**" versus "**vapid tittle-tattle"):** see *Campbell v MGN Ltd* [2004] 2 AC 457 at [147]–[149]. **The purpose for which the Defendant wishes to exercise his freedom of speech could be relevant in that context.**

7. **Secondly**, the evidence at the moment appears to indicate that **neither of the parties to the sexual relationship in question wishes either the fact of it, or any details about how it was conducted, to be made public**. Certainly not the Claimant and, although there is nothing directly from the Defendant's wife (N), such evidence as is currently available suggests that she takes the same view.

8. There is a **powerful argument** that the conduct of an **intimate** or **sexual relationship** is a matter in respect of which there is **"a reasonable or legitimate expectation of privacy**". Accordingly, anyone who obtains such information **would be expected to recognise** that, either from the **nature of the information itself** or from the **circumstances in which it was imparted.** If that is so for journalists, or for scandal mongers in general, it is a matter for consideration whether, and to what extent, a **"cuckolded" husband** is under a lesser obligation.

9. **Thirdly**, the Claimant says that he is now seeking to reconstruct his family

life and is concerned for the interests of his own wife and young children. Even if the Defendant is correct in attributing the blame for their problems to the Claimant himself, Mr Warby argues that there is **no reason why the wife and children should suffer more than is necessary and**, in particular, through the **stresses and strains** of press **intrusion**. He suggests that the court should have regard to their rights, especially in the context of Article 8 of the European Convention on Human Rights and Fundamental Freedoms, in determining the current dispute, even though they are not themselves parties.

10. **Fourthly**, there is an extra dimension to this aspect of the case which is perhaps even more troubling. The Claimant's wife is suffering stress and anxiety which requires medical attention (attested to by medical evidence) and **which is quite likely to be made worse by press exposure.** There is also (non-medical) evidence of **self-harm and of threats to commit suicide**. It is this factor, in particular, which has led editors so far to hold back from publication and has meant that the Defendant has hitherto been frustrated in his efforts to exploit the situation for gain. He himself has not been deterred by this at all. He says it is just "bullshit" and portrays himself as the victim, absolved from any responsibility for the consequences of his actions. His attitude is that he is entitled to his revenge on the Claimant, and if possible also to some financial gain; if his own wife, or the Claimant's wife or his children, suffer incidental fallout, then that is the Claimant's fault.

11. **Fifthly**, it is the Claimant's case (albeit contested) that at the time of the "affair" he did not know that N was married. She did not wear a wedding ring and made no mention of having a current partner.

12. Against this unhappy background, Mr Bartley Jones QC for the Defendant has argued strongly for a principle to the effect that "a party to an adulterous **relationship** can never, as a matter of law, obtain injunctive relief (interim or permanent) against the wronged party preventing him from disclosing the **relationship**".

13. If no such principle of law can be demonstrated from case law in the 19th or 20th centuries, it seems curious that it should now emerge fully formed in the 21st. So broadly stated, it cannot be correct. The approach now adopted by domestic courts, in the light of Strasbourg jurisprudence, is to determine particular conflicts between Convention rights, where they are shown to be engaged, by bringing to bear an "**intense focus**" on **the facts of the individual case**, rather than by purporting to create **general** principles of law judicially: see eg *Re S* [2005] 1 AC 593 at [17] and *Campbell v MGN Ltd* [2004] 2 AC 457.

14. It may be helpful to have in mind in this context the **observations of Sir Mark**

Potter P in *A Local Authority v W* [2005] EWHC 1564 (Fam) at [53] on how the court is to apply the new methodology once it is clear that conflicting Convention rights are engaged:

> "The exercise to be performed is one of **parallel analysis** in which the starting point is **presumptive parity**, in that neither Article has precedence over or 'trumps' the other. The exercise of parallel analysis **requires the court to examine the justification for interfering with each right** and the issue of **proportionality** is to be considered in respect of each. **It is not a mechanical exercise to be decided upon the basis of rival generalities.** An **intense focus** upon the comparative importance of the specific rights being claimed **in the individual case** is necessary before the **ultimate balancing test** in terms of **proportionality** is carried out".

15. Applying this language, is seems to me that the principle tentatively fashioned by Mr Bartley Jones could properly be characterised as a **"generality",** which would simply pre-empt the required **" parallel analysis"** and "intense focus" on the unique facts of the case. The approach of the House of Lords in the recent cases would appear to confirm the validity of a comment made by Sedley LJ, in *Douglas v Hello! Ltd* [2001] QB 967 at [137], to the effect that **the outcome is likely to be determined by considerations of proportionality.**

16. The starting point must be to determine whether relevant Convention rights are here engaged. There is no doubt that the Defendant's right of freedom of expression is indeed engaged. The whole object is to restrain him in this regard. The European Court of Human Rights has noted that "**the dangers inherent in prior restraint are such that they call for the most careful scrutiny":** *Observer Ltd and Guardian Newspapers Ltd v United Kingdom* (1991) 14 EHRR 153 at [60]. So too in *Wingrove v United Kingdom* (1996) 24 EHRR 1 at [58] it was said that where **prior restraint** is involved "**special scrutiny by the court"** is required.

17. "There cannot as yet be said to be a 'bright-line' rule against judicial **prior restraint** in ECHR law. **However, it is clear that prior restraints are viewed as pernicious and that, to be upheld as justifiable, their use will have to be viewed as appropriate, proportionate, and absolutely necessary":** C Munro, **Prior restraint** *of the Media and Human Rights Law,* (2002) Juridical Review 1 at 23. This passage is, of course, consistent with the terms of Article 10 (2) itself.

18. The question would seem to be whether I come to the conclusion, having applied "**careful scrutiny"** and "**an intense focus**" to the facts disclosed in the evidence before me, that there is a **countervailing requirement of public policy** which renders it **necessary** and **proportionate** to restrain the

Defendant from communicating certain information in order to protect the Convention rights of any other person(s).

19. It would be necessary as part of this process **to pay close attention** to what the Defendant is **likely to say,** and **to whom**, and to **evaluate the type of speech** involved on **each scenario**. For example, while it may conceivably right to restrain the sale of **celebrity tittle-tattle** in which there is **no real public interest**, on the other hand there would be **no necessity** or **proportionate** countervailing advantage in preventing him from conversing with relatives, friends or (say) doctors or counsellors about the subject of his own marital breakdown and what may have contributed to it.

20. I need to consider next whether there is any countervailing Convention right against which those of the Defendant need to be balanced. Mr Bartley Jones submits quite simply that the stage of "balancing" should not even be reached in this case.

21. In **personal** and **sexual relationships** the courts have for some time recognised that there is what is now generally referred to as a reasonable or legitimate "expectation of privacy": see eg the terminology of Lord Nicholls in *Campbell v MGN Ltd* [2004] 2 AC 457 at [20]–[21] and that of the European Court of Human Rights in *Von Hannover v Germany* (2005) 40 EHRR 1 at [51] and [69].

22. I was reminded, in particular, of the decision of Sir Nicolas Browne-Wilkinson V.-C. (as he then was) in *Stephens* v *Avery* [1988] 1 Ch. 449. It demonstrates two propositions relevant for present purposes. First that an **intimate lesbian relationship** could be within the scope of the law's protection as being confidential. This has been recognised more recently in the context of other **sexual relationships**, subsequently to the advent of the Human Rights Act, in such cases as *Theakston* v *MGN Ltd* [2002] EMLR 398 and in *A v B plc* [2003] QB 195, **although it may be necessary to have regard to the nature of the relationship.** ***It may yet be the case, for example, that a fleeting one night encounter will attract less protection, if any, than a long term*** **relationship.** This is an uncertain area, because it is by **no means fully determined how appropriate it is for individual judges to apply moral evaluation to such encounters**. But it is not an issue that I need to address too closely for present purposes.

23. I am certainly not prepared to accept Mr Bartley Jones' submission that there is, or should be, a general legal principle that "there is no legitimate expectation of privacy for a person who conducts a **relationship** with another person's wife".

24. The other proposition which Mr Warby sought to derive from *Stephens* v *Avery,* since one of the protagonists happened to have been a married woman, is

that it is hardly likely that a modern court would regard an adulterer as beyond the pale when it comes to the protection of **intimate** personal **relationships**. Indeed, **if the commission of a crime does riot deprive a citizen of the opportunity to enforce his or her Article 8 rights** (see eg *Polanski v Condi Nast Publications Ltd* [2005] 1 WLR 637), it is difficult to see how adultery could do so.

25. **Judges need to be wary about giving the impression that they are ventilating, while affording or refusing legal redress, some personal moral or social views, and especially at a time when society is far less homogeneous than in the past**. At one time, when there was, or was perceived to be, a commonly accepted standard in such matters as **sexual** morality, it may have been acceptable for the courts to give effect to that standard in exercising discretion or in interpreting legal rights and obligations. Now, however, there is a **strong argument** for **not holding forth** about adultery, or **attaching greater inherent worth** to a **relationship** which has been **formalised** by marriage than to any other **relationship**.

26. A judge, like any one else, is obviously entitled to hold personal moral views about the issues of the day, **but it is important not to let them intrude when interpreting and applying the law**. Such issues are best avoided—at least without some statutory sanction. No doubt many people, especially those with a strong religious faith, will disapprove of adultery. Many others, on the other hand, will not give it a. second thought, while moving easily through a series of medium or short term **relationships** as they feel it appropriate.

27. With such a wide range of differing views in society, perhaps more than for many generations, **one must guard against allowing legal judgments to be coloured by personal attitudes.** Even among judges, there is no doubt a wide range of opinion. It is all the more important, therefore, that the outcome of a particular case should not be determined by the judge's personal views or, as it used to be said, by "the length of Chancellor's foot". There is a risk that with greater emphasis on applying an "**intense focus**" to the **particular facts,** with the room this leaves for the making of individual judgments, differing outcomes on what may seem to be broadly comparable facts may be interpreted by onlookers as being explicable on the basis of **arbitrary personal differences** between the judges. That is plainly undesirable because it would undermine faith in the rule of law, but the danger has to be recognised as inherent in the "new methodology" of balancing Convention rights.

28. It is not for judges when applying the European Convention, **which is a secular code applying to those of all religions and none**, to give an appearance of sanctimony by damning adulterers or seeking, as I was invited to do by Mr Bartley Jones, to "vindicate" the state of matrimony. Indeed, if the Defendant is pretending that his desire to "spill the beans" to a tabloid newspaper has

anything to do with "vindicating" the institution of marriage, that would be remarkable hypocrisy in the light of his own evidence. **He wishes to expose and humiliate not only the Claimant but also incidentally his own wife and to do so, on his own ready admission, for revenge and for financial profit.**

29. Both counsel referred, in the context of adultery, to *Tammer* v *Estonia* (2001) 29 EHRR CD 257. I am not sure that it assists greatly. A criminal sanction had been imposed over insults directed at someone for alleged adultery and poor parenting. It seems to have been concerned with the mode of expression rather than the substance of what was said.

30. I have come to the conclusion that there can be no rule of "**generality**" that an adulterer can *never* obtain an injunction to restrain the publication of matters relating to his adulterous **relationship**; or, to put it another way, ***even an adulterous* relationship *may attract, at least in certain respects, a legitimate expectation of privacy.*** **That being so, there is no rule which exempts a "wronged" husband from restraint automatically, by virtue of his status**, although in any given situation there may be particular respects in which his right to free speech should be accorded greater **priority**.

31. It follows that the Claimant's Article 8 rights are engaged once there is a threat to publish, to the world at large (whether for payment or otherwise), the fact of his **sexual relationship** and the details of how it was conducted.

32. So too, **the Article 8 rights of the other party to that relationship (N) need to be taken into account**. It is clear from *A v B plc that the court will be less inclined to protect the rights of one party to a* **sexual relationship** *if the other party wishes to reveal what happened*. Thus far, that does not appear to be so on the available evidence.

33. In these circumstances, what is required is an intense focus on the particular facts so as to achieve an **appropriate balance** between the **competing rights,** bearing in mind that freedom of speech should only be constrained if it is **necessary** to do so to protect the rights of other persons concerned; what is more, any such restraint should be limited to what is **proportionate.**

34. At this stage, what is sought is an interlocutory injunction and I need to take into account the requirements of s 12(3) of the Human Rights Act and its interpretation by the House of Lords in *Cream Holdings Ltd v Banerjee* [2005] 1 AC 253. I should not grant an injunction unless I am satisfied that the Claimant is **likely to obtain** an order **in similar terms** following a trial. I can only decide that in the light of the evidence currently before me and should not speculate as to what further material may be available at that stage, or what might happen in cross-examination. Nevertheless, **I have to make a preliminary assessment of the merits on what I have.** It is not simply a question of deciding that there is a good arguable case. The task may not

always be an easy one to carry out, but that it is necessary follows from the interpretation of s 12 by their Lordships.

35. I recognise straight away that the Claimant is unlikely to obtain at trial a blanket restraint on *any* communication about the fact of the adulterous **relationship**. **It would not be proportionate to any reasonable expectation on the Claimant's part to prevent the Defendant, for example, discussing his wife's adultery with a close friend, or with members of the family**, or (if he needed to do so) **with a family doctor, counsellor or social worker, or with his lawyers.** What is in contention is the Defendant's desire, directly or indirectly, to put the **relationship** into the **public domain through the press,** and to support it with detail.

36. The distinction I have just drawn can be analysed in terms of differing categories of "speech". Communication **genuinely** aimed at the **persons, or for the purposes**, I have suggested above would be accorded a **relatively high priority**, whereas **selling the story** to the **tabloids** (whether for revenge, money or any other reason) should be accorded **lower priority.** The analogy is with what has been described in the House of Lords as "the most vapid **tittle-tattle** about the activities of footballers' wives and girlfriends": *Jameel* v *Wall Street Journal (Europe)* [2006] UKHL 44 at [147]. That phrase was used in the context of what is or is not **"in the public interest", in the true sense of the term, as contrasted with what is merely "interesting to the public".** That is a contrast which has long been recognised: see eg the observations of Lord Wilberforce in *British Steel Corporation* v *Granada Television* [1981] AC 1096, 1168G. The point is of equal validity, however, in the context of assessing the relative value of different kinds of "speech". The communication of material to the world at large in which there is a genuine public interest is naturally to be rated more highly than the right to sell what is mere "**tittle-tattle**".

37. I have little doubt that **sexual relationships** involving those who are in the **public eye**, whether they merit the appellation "**public figures**" or not, are generally likely to be **interesting to the public**, but they will not necessarily be of genuine public interest. Sometimes, as for example long ago in the case of the **"Profumo scandal",** the information will fulfil both criteria. The fact that the then Minister for War had a mistress in common with a Russian diplomat or defence attaché, at the height of the cold war, would plainly be of legitimate public interest. I am quite satisfied, however, that there is nothing remotely comparable about the present facts. I shall consider the arguments put forward in a little more detail.

38. Mr Bartley Jones draws a distinction between certain documents, which evidence the **relationship** between N and the Claimant, in respect of which it is conceded that the test under s 12(3) has been satisfied, and the bare fact

of the **relationship** itself. As to the latter, he submits that the Defendant is entitled to inform "whomsoever he wishes about the fact of the **relationship** and detail thereof as known to the Defendant derived otherwise than from the documents". The reason for this dichotomy is, presumably, that the personal documents (including a hotel receipt and a personal note) could by virtue of their nature be the subject of a duty of confidence, whereas if the information came from some other source it could not.

39. **Sometimes, however, the court will recognise a legitimate expectation of privacy, not on the basis of the means by which the information was imparted, but rather because of the nature of the information itself.** Quite often, for a variety of reasons, people prefer to conduct **sexual relationships**, at least temporarily, **on a secret basis.** They would appear to be entitled to do so and, **until they choose to "go public", to enjoy a legitimate expectation of privacy vis a vis the world at large**. That is to say, such information is capable of being regarded as confidential.

40. It is said here that the **relationship** was conducted in public, in the sense that the Claimant and N stayed in hotels together and were seen in various cities—not merely in England but in the United States and on the continent. **They were not recognised,** although it could be said that they "took the chance" of being spotted. I doubt whether that is the same as "going public", and especially since the decision of the European Court of Human Rights in *Von Hannover v Germany* (2005) 40 EHRR 1, where it was recognised that **the law is capable of extending its protection to public places and also to a "social dimension"**; that is to say, to the **relationships** which people conduct with others.

41. I would not accept, therefore, that nowadays such a clear distinction can be drawn, as a matter of "**generality**", between private documents and the **bare fact of a relationship**. It may depend on the circumstances, which have to be carefully scrutinised.

42. Here, the **relationship** is over and the respective parties no doubt wish to "move on". **On the face of it, the Claimant and N ought to be able to keep their past indiscretion to themselves rather than suffer public humiliation and embarrassment—not only for themselves but for completely "innocent" third parties such as the Claimant's wife and children.**

43. The Claimant's **relationship** with his wife is ongoing and he wishes to rebuild it. Exposure in the press could frustrate that project and, on the evidence, **damage his wife's fragile mental state.** I can hardly ignore that if the consequence of the order which Mr Bartley Jones seeks would have these effects. **I need to act compatibly with the Convention and have regard to the impact on the Claimant's family life.**

44. Thus, if I come to the conclusion that, in order to protect it, it is necessary to prevent the Defendant going directly **or indirectly** to the media for no better reason than spite, money-making or "**tittle tattle",** then I would be obliged to restrain him. The fact that he may be, or may see himself as, **an "injured party" does not accord him a special status**, not given to others, which inherently raises the value of the communications he wishes to make to the tabloids on to some higher plane or renders them more valuable in Article 10 terms.

45. Nor is it an answer to Article 8 concerns to say, in Mr Bartley Jones' words, that "it is his own voluntary conduct which has put that marriage and family life in jeopardy". Mr Bartley Jones characterised the Claimant's reliance on the threat to his wife's health by saying that he is "bolstering his claim of confidence through the damage he has caused [her] by the very fact of having the **relationship** [with N]".

46. Quite simply, that factor does not absolve the court from having to take into account the impact on the Claimant's family life. Indeed, Mr Bartley Jones expressly acknowledges that her position becomes relevant if the Claimant is held to have a reasonable expectation of privacy in respect of the adulterous **relationship** (contrary to his primary submission). Nonetheless, he argues that it would be wrong for me to give very much weight to the Claimant's wife's rights under Article 8, or for that matter those under Articles 2 and 3, since **she is not a party and has provided no evidence herself.**

47. It is worth noting, however, that even before the Human Rights Act came into effect the courts always **had an eye to the rights of any third party who might be adversely affected by the grant of an injunction.** Now a judge is certainly required to ensure that court orders and determinations are compatible with the Convention, and thus to have regard to such rights in arriving at decisions.

48. I do not accept the analogy which Mr Bartley Jones draws with the **brothel** in respect of which Ouseley J declined to grant protection in *Theakston v MGN Ltd* (cited above).

49. One of Mr Bartley Jones' arguments is that "once the wronged party is entitled to tell some people, the information cannot as such be protected in any meaningful way". I do not believe this to be correct as a matter of law. **Exceptions are regularly incorporated in the terms of court orders to enable limited communications to take place,** the most typical example being to facilitate discussions with **lawyers** or **expert witnesses**. If the Defendant were restricted from communicating with the press, but chose to do so through a friend or family member, he would be on risk of imprisonment for **contempt** of court. That would be "meaningful".

50. Another point was that it would be wrong to restrain the Defendant when the Claimant, his wife and N are not so restrained. I see no logic in this at all. An injunction is granted because there is evidence that, otherwise, the party to be enjoined will commit a wrong. There is obviously no point in granting restrictions against other people in respect of whom no such risk is perceived to arise.

51. Mr Bartley Jones has put forward the proposition that the Claimant has a "public persona" and also that "the fact, that the **relationship** goes to inform that public persona": *ergo,* he submits, "there is a public interest in the disclosure of information about the **relationship**". He says that the Claimant "cannot complain if his public persona is negated".

52. I need to bear in mind that, as Lord Woolf emphasised in *A* v *B plc*, **even a public figure is entitled to a private life**. Moreover, this is not a case (such as eg *Campbell* v *MGN Ltd)* where the Claimant has **misled the public by false denials**; nor has he **moralised publicly on family life,** or his own **continence** in **sexual** matters. I cannot accept that there is any genuine interest so far as the public is concerned in the disclosure of this information.

53. It is important to have regard to the Defendant's attitude demonstrated in an e-mail of 24 September 2006. Having described the Claimant's wife's suicide threat as "bullshit", he went on to threaten:

> " . . . as you know the **internet** is a huge uncensored world so wat ive decided to do is put u in the shit no matter wat! . . . cause I think you're a twat an I reckon the stress is getting to u . . . "

This was explained in terms of publishing to the world at large, **or as he put it "every fuckin person in the world"**.

54. There was also a telephone call made by the Defendant to the Claimant on the evening of 4 November 2006, which was tape-recorded and contained the following (apparently drunken) remarks by way of explaining that the Claimant could not possibly succeed in his litigation:

> "Listen mate. You're going to be fucked. You're fucked, I'm just telling you when this goes to court. You can't even afford the House of Lords. This is going to go to the House of Lords, and you can't even afford it. I'm on legal aid. I'm on legal aid. It's all paid for me. Because I'm a good guy. I'm a good guy. I've done nothing . . . "

55. Reference has also been made to what has been called the "the divorce ruse". **The Defendant has threatened to use divorce proceedings as a means of bringing the Claimant's name to the attention of the press.** The proposal is that he would, unnecessarily, join him as a co-respondent. **That strongly suggests that he intends to abuse the court's process for a collat-**

eral purpose. No one has the right to do that. Nor do professional advisers. But that threat appears to have subsided for the time being.

56. **All in all, the Defendant's behaviour so far demonstrates the need for an interim order under the Protection from Harassment Act 1997** (which indeed Mr Bartley Jones does not oppose). More than that, these documents lay a clear foundation for **reasonable apprehension** that, unless restrained by a court order, the Defendant will publish as many details as he knows about the Claimant's **relationship**, whatever the consequences likely to flow for the Claimant and his family.

57. There were communications by the Defendant on the **internet** about the **relationship**, but the stage **has not yet been reached, in my judgment, where it could be said, in the words of Lord Goff s first "limiting principle" in Att.-Gen. v Guardian Newspapers (No 2) [1990] 1 AC 189, 282 that the information is so generally accessible** that, in all the circumstances, it cannot be regarded as confidential.

58. For the reasons I have outlined above, I am satisfied that the Claimant is also likely to obtain a permanent injunction **in similar terms** to that which I now propose to grant. Accordingly, the test under S.12 (3) is fulfilled. Subject to any further submissions as to its terms, I would propose to grant an injunction restraining the Defendant from communicating, directly or indirectly, **with the media** or on the **internet** on the subject of the Claimant's former **relationship** with N. That is in addition to an order under the **Protection from Harassment Act** and to restricting the use of the private documents (neither of which is at present opposed).

Maxine Carr v News Group Newspapers [2005] EWHC 971 (QB)

4. **There is before the court a wealth of evidence of a continuing danger of serious physical and psychological harm to the applicant**. There is also evidence which demonstrates convincingly that the subsistence of the injunctions since last May has been very effective in reducing those risks and in permitting the police, the Home Office and the probation service to carry out their responsibilities of protection, treatment and rehabilitation.

Greene v Associated Newspapers [2004] EWCA 1462 (Civ)

PART III

8. The Law of Prior restraint in Defamation Actions: the Beginnings

. . .

42. Blackstone (see para 1 above) made a **clear distinction** between the press's freedom to publish without **prior restraint** and the **post-publication** penalties it might incur if it published "what is improper, mischievous or illegal". **After publication the publisher must take the consequences of his own temerity.**

43. In 1792 Fox's Libel Act established that the question, "libel or no libel", was one for the jury to determine, and although the rule was made in a criminal law context it was rapidly adopted in civil litigation as well. In those days the danger to press freedom came from the executive and the licensing systems it might introduce, which Blackstone castigated in these terms:

> "To subject the press to the restrictive power of a licenser, as was formerly done, both before and since the revolution, is to subject all freedom of sentiment to the prejudices of one man, and make him the arbitrary and infallible judge of all controverted points in learning, religion, and government."

44. In those days the judges did not have the power of **prior restraint**. Until the enactment of the Common Law Procedure Act 1854 the judges of the common law courts had no power to grant an injunction, and even after 1854 they never used it in a libel case. The judges of the Court of Chancery, who did possess such a power, had no jurisdiction to try a libel action.

45. It was only when the Judicature Acts fused equity with the law, sweeping away the old jurisdictional boundaries, that the courts had to grapple seriously with **two new questions**. The **first** was whether they possessed jurisdiction to grant an injunction in a libel case where the defendant averred that he had a defence. The **second** related to the principles on which they should exercise any jurisdiction they might be found to possess. The story has recently been told by Auld LJ in ***Holley v Smyth*** [1998] QB 726 at pp 737–743, and we derived much benefit from that judgment.

46. The **rule in *Bonnard v Perryman* [1891] 2 Ch 269 was laid down by five judges,** including the Lord Chief Justice and the Master of the Rolls, who constituted the majority of the full Court of Appeal in that case. **The libel in issue was a very damaging one.** North J at first instance said (at p 274) that

unless it could be justified at the trial it was one in which a jury would give the plaintiff "very serious damages". He went on to say (at pp 277–8):

> "I have this to bear in mind, that, if in such a case as this an interlocutory injunction is not granted, I cannot imagine any case in which an interlocutory injunction to restrain a libel could be granted, whereas it is clear on the authorities that there are cases in which it would be proper to grant it.
>
> "Then there is this further matter to be considered with reference to the point made, that the matter ought to be tried before a jury. I am satisfied of this, that if the matter was before a jury now, upon the evidence which is before me—that is to say, the evidence of the Plaintiffs uncontradicted, not cross-examined to, and merely resting on the Defendant's evidence in answer to it—I am perfectly satisfied there is not any jury in *England* who would say there should be a verdict for the Defendant in such a case, and, what is more, if they did, I am quite satisfied it is a case in which a new trial would be directed. This, of course, does not touch what may be the case when the action comes to be tried. There may be evidence before the Court then which would satisfy a jury who tries it that the Defendant has made out a justification. I am merely referring to the materials before me, which are all I can look to now in considering what I am to do in the matter. In these circumstances I have come to the conclusion that an injunction must be granted in the terms which I have mentioned."

47. In overruling that decision Lord Coleridge CJ quoted with approval what Lord Esher MR had said four years earlier in *William Coulson and Sons v James Coulson and Co* (1887) 3 TLR 846:

> ". . . the question of libel or no libel was for the jury. It was for the jury and not for the Court to construe the document and to say whether it was a libel or not. **To justify the Court in granting an interim injunction it must come to a decision upon the question of libel or no libel before the jury decided whether it was a libel or not.** Therefore, the jurisdiction was of a delicate nature. **It ought only to be exercised in the clearest cases,** where any jury would say that the matter complained of was libellous, and where, if the jury did not so find, the Court would set aside the verdict as unreasonable. **The Court must also be satisfied that in all probability the alleged libel was untrue, and if written on a privileged occasion that there was malice on the part of the defendant.** It followed from those three rules that the Court could only on the rarest occasions exercise the jurisdiction."

48. In *Coulson* Lindley LJ (concurring, as he was later to concur in ***Bonnard v Perryman***)

> "agreed with the rules laid down by the Master of the Rolls, and he was not prepared to say that the jury might not find that this was no libel, or that the alleged libel was true. The injunction, therefore, ought not to have been granted. Both the Judge at Chambers and the Divisional Court had suggested a form of circular; but it was no part of a Judge's duty to do so, except for the purposes of putting an end to litigation, and the Court ought not to settle a draft form of what might turn out to be a libel."

49. This dictum illustrates an unusual feature of this particular jurisdiction, which is **that the judge does not know in advance exactly what the publisher is going to say**. Since he cannot determine the question "libel or no libel" at the trial, still less at the pre-trial stage, he must not get himself involved in the process of drafting what the defendant may or may not be permitted to say.

50. In ***Bonnard v Perryman*** Lord Coleridge CJ resolved North J's dilemma by saying (at p 285) that although the courts undoubtedly possessed the requisite jurisdiction, **"in all but exceptional cases"** they should not issue an interlocutory injunction to restrain the publication of a libel which the defence sought to justify except where it was clear that that defence would fail. He based his approach on the particular need not to restrict the right of free speech in libel cases by interfering before the final determination of the matter by a jury otherwise than in a clear case of an untrue libel. At p 284 he said:

> "**[T]he subject-matter of an action for defamation is so special as to require exceptional caution in exercising the jurisdiction to interfere by injunction before the trial of an action to prevent an anticipated wrong.** The right of free speech is one which it is for the public interest that individuals should possess, and, indeed, that they should exercise without impediment, so long as no wrongful act is done; and, unless an alleged libel is untrue, there is no wrong committed; but, on the contrary, often a very wholesome act is performed in the publication and **repetition** of an alleged libel. Until it is clear that an alleged libel is untrue, it is not clear that any right at all has been infringed; and the importance of leaving free speech unfettered is a strong reason in cases of libel for dealing most cautiously and warily with the granting of interim injunctions . . . In the particular case before us, indeed, the libellous character of the publication is beyond dispute, but the effect of it upon the Defendant can be finally disposed of only by a jury, and we cannot feel sure that the defence of justification is one which, on

the facts which may be before them, the jury may find to be wholly unfounded; nor can we tell what may be the damages recoverable."

9. The Law of Prior restraint in Defamation Actions: the Modern Law

51. It is necessary to refer only to five modern cases in which the rule in ***Bonnard v Perryman*** was authoritatively restated. In *Fraser v Evans* [1969] 1 QB 349 Lord Denning MR said at pp 360–1:

> "The court will not restrain the publication of an article, even though it is defamatory, **when the defendant says he intends to justify it or to make fair comment on a matter of public interest.** That has been established for many years ever since ***Bonnard v Perryman***. The reason sometimes given is that the defences of justification and fair comment are for the jury, which is the constitutional tribunal, and not for a judge. But a better reason is the importance in the public interest that the truth should out. . . . There is no wrong done if it is true, or if [the alleged libel] is fair comment on a matter of public interest. The court will not prejudice the issue by granting an injunction in advance of publication."

52. In *Herbage v Pressdram Ltd* [1984] 1 WLR 1160 Griffiths LJ restated the effect of the rule and then said (at p 1162H):

> "These principles have evolved **because of the value the court has placed on freedom of speech and I think also on the freedom of the press,** when balancing it against the **reputation** of a single individual who, if wrong, can be compensated in damages."

53. He refused to water the principles down. After summarising an argument by counsel which suggested that the combined effect of the Rehabilitation of Offenders Act 1974 and the decision of the House of Lords in *American Cyanamid Co v Ethicon Ltd* [1975] AC 396 justified a radical departure from the rule, he went on to say (at p 1163B):

> "If the court were to accept this argument, the practical effect would I believe be that in very many cases the plaintiff would obtain an injunction, for on the *American Cyanamid* principles he would often show a serious issue to be tried, that damages would not be realistic compensation, and that the balance of convenience favoured restraining **repetition** of the alleged libel until trial of the action. It would thus be a very considerable incursion into the present rule which is based on freedom of speech."

54. In *Khashoggi v IPC Magazines Ltd* [1986] 1 WLR 1412 Sir John Donaldson MR applied the rule in a new context, where the defendants had asserted that they would justify what they said at trial by reference to a *Polly Peck* defence (see *Polly Peck Holdings Plc v Trelford* [1986] QB 1000). He said (at p 1417G-H):

"I cannot see why the ***Bonnard v Perryman*** principle should not be applied. **Quite apart from any question of public interest in the freedom of the press, there is a much wider principle which covers it, and that is this.** The injunctive powers of the court can only be invoked in support of a right or in defence of an interest. If the *Polly Peck* defence were to succeed the plaintiff would have no right. She therefore cannot expect to have it defended. That does not of course answer the question which arises as to how likely she is to succeed. That is a problem which always arises in libel and elsewhere. **The point is that *Bonnard v Perryman*, apart from its reference to freedom of speech, is based on the fact that courts should not step in to defend a cause of action in defamation if they think that this is a case in which the plea of justification might, not would, succeed.**"

55. By now it was firmly established by this court that the principles underlying the grant of interlocutory injunctions which Lord Diplock laid down in *American Cyanamid* did not apply to cases covered by the rule in ***Bonnard v Perryman***. This was reaffirmed by Lord Denning MR in *Herbage v Times Newspapers Ltd*, The Times, 30th April 1981. In that case Sir Denys Buckley, who had a great understanding of practice and procedure in relation to equitable remedies, observed that:

" **. . . the question what meaning the words complained of bore was primarily one for the jury.**

"Suppose the words bore the second meaning alleged and an injunction were granted restraining further publication, if application were made to commit the defendants for **contempt** of court for breach of that injunction, the judge hearing the application would have to form a view as to whether there had been a breach of the injunction and decide whether the words used implied that Mr Herbage had been made bankrupt and discharged without paying his debts in full. **It could not be right in a defamation action to grant an action of that kind.** *There were special circumstances in defamation actions*". (Emphasis added)

56. In *Holley v Smyth* [1998] QB 726, where the potency of the rule was reaffirmed, Sir Christopher Slade, another experienced Chancery judge, said at p 749:

"I accept that the court may be left with a residual discretion to decline to apply the rule in ***Bonnard v Perryman*** in **exceptional circumstances.** One exception, recognised in that decision itself, **is the case where the court is satisfied that the defamatory statement is clearly untrue**. In my judgment, however, that is a discretion which must be exercised in accordance with established principles."

10. The Law of **Prior restraint** in Defamation Actions: the Rationale of the Rule

57. This survey of the caselaw shows that in an action for defamation a court will not impose a **prior restraint** on publication unless it is clear that no defence will succeed at the trial. This is partly due to the importance the court attaches to **freedom of speech**. ***It is partly because a judge must not usurp the constitutional function of the jury unless he is satisfied that there is no case to go to a jury.*** The rule is also partly founded on the pragmatic grounds **that until there has been disclosure of documents and cross-examination at the trial a court cannot safely proceed on the basis that what the defendants wish to say is not true**. And if it is or might be true the court has no business to stop them saying it. This is another way of putting the point made by Sir John Donaldson MR in *Khashoggi*, to the effect that **a court cannot know whether the plaintiff has a right to his/her reputation until the trial process has shown where the truth lies**. And if the defence fails, the defendants will have to pay damages (which in an appropriate case may includes aggravated and/or exemplary damages as well).

Part IV

11. The Effect of the Human Rights Act 1998

58. **But Mr Spearman says that the Human Rights Act 1998 has changed all this. He relies in part on the express effect of section 12(3) of the Act. And if he is wrong about that, he relies on section 6 of the Act which inhibits a court from acting in a way which is incompatible with a Convention right**. He says that his client has a right to a **reputation** which is protected by Article 8 of the European Convention on Human Rights, and that the rigidity of the rule in ***Bonnard v Perryman*** runs roughshod over that right, giving a court no power to weigh competing rights in the balance and give a proportionate response.

12. Section 12(3) of the Human Rights Act 1998

59. We can deal with the first of these points quite quickly. Section 12 of the Act is entitled "Freedom of Expression" and sub-section (1) makes it clear that it applies "if a court is considering whether to grant any relief which, if granted, might affect the exercise of the Convention right to freedom of expression." This language does not suggest that Parliament intended within this very section to whittle down a defendant's right to freedom of expression in a case like this, but Mr Spearman told us that this was the effect of section 12(3) which provides that:

> "No such relief is to be granted so as to restrain publication before trial

unless the court is satisfied that the applicant is **likely to establish** that publication should not be allowed."

60. As Fulford J observed (see paras 28–29 above), in *Cream Holdings Ltd v Banerjee* [2003] EWCA Civ 103, [2003] Ch 650, the majority of this court took it for granted that the rule in ***Bonnard v Perryman*** was still good law notwithstanding the enactment of section 12 of the Human Rights Act, and although the House of Lords differed from their approach to the meaning of section 12, **it did not avert to this aspect of the matter at all**. That case was concerned with an entirely different subject-matter (the protection of **confidential information**). As Lord Nicholls observed (see [2004] UKHL 44 at [18]), **"Confidentiality, once breached, is lost for ever, so that the granting or withholding of a pre-trial injunction is of critical importance to a claimant."** But before explaining what the word "likely" meant in the context of section 12(3) he said (at para 15):

> "When the Human Rights Bill was under consideration by Parliament concern was expressed at the adverse impact the Bill might have on the freedom of the press. Article 8 of the European Convention, guaranteeing the right to respect for private life, was among the Convention rights to which the legislation would give effect. The concern was that, applying the conventional *American Cyanamid* approach, orders imposing **prior restraint** on newspapers might readily be granted by the courts to preserve the status quo until trial whenever applicants claimed that a threatened publication would infringe their rights under article 8. **Section 12(3) was enacted to allay these fears.** Its principal **purpose** was **to buttress the protection afforded to freedom of speech at the interlocutory stage**. It sought to do so by setting a higher threshold for the grant of interlocutory injunctions against the media than the *American Cyanamid* guideline of a 'serious question to be tried' or a 'real prospect' of success at the trial."

61. **This has got nothing at all to do with practice in defamation cases, where as we have observed (see para 55 above) the American Cyanamid guidelines are not applied.** There are "special circumstances in defamation actions", as Sir Denys Buckley put it in *Herbage v Times Newspapers Ltd*) (*ibid*). In a section of an Act of Parliament which is expressly concerned with the protection of freedom of expression and not with undermining it, Parliament cannot be interpreted as having abrogated the rule in ***Bonnard v Perryman*** by a sidewind. In any event the very language of section 12(3) does not require such an interpretation. Nor do we consider that section 12(4) has any bearing on questions relating to **prior restraint** in the context of the case with which we are concerned.

62. First principles in statutory interpretation would also rule out the disman-

tling of judge-made law by stealth (in the absence of necessary implication). In *Black-Clawson International Ltd v Papierwerke-Aschaffenburg AG* [1975] AC 591, Lord Reid said at p 614:

> "There is a presumption which can be stated in various ways. One is that in the absence of any clear indication to the contrary **Parliament can be presumed not to have altered the common law further than was necessary to remedy the 'mischief.'** Of course it may and quite often does go further. But the principle is that if the enactment is ambiguous, that meaning which relates the scope of the Act to the mischief should be taken rather than a different or wider meaning which the contemporary situation did not call for."

63. In *In re F* [1977] Fam 58, a case concerned with the interpretation of section 12(1) of the Administration of Justice Act 1960, Scarman LJ said (at p 99E):

> "The words, in their context, need mean no more than that there is a **contempt** in the absence of a defence recognised by law. If Parliament had intended to treat publication of information relating to proceedings before a court sitting in private as a **contempt** irrespective of circumstances, I would have expected express provision to that effect. Circumstances can and do arise in which Parliament must have intended the old law to continue, for example, where the court authorises publication or where by the passage of time 'the rule of publicity [is] resumed' (Lord Shaw of Dunfermline, *Scott v Scott* [1913] AC 417 at 483). Similarly, if, as I believe, the pre-existing law recognised a defence that the publisher neither knew nor ought to have known that the information published related to proceedings before a court in private, one would have expected express provision if such a defence was to be taken away."

64. More recently, in *R (Rottman) v Commissioner of Police for the Metropolis* [2002] UKHL 20, [2002] 2 AC 692, a case concerned with the question whether any part of the police's common law powers of search and seizure had survived the enactment of the Police and Criminal Evidence Act 1984 ("PACE") Lord Hutton said (at para 75):

> **"It is a well established principle that a rule of the common law is not extinguished by a statute unless the statute makes this clear by express provision or by clear** implication."

65. Mr Spearman submitted that this well established principle did not apply to constitutional enactments like the Human Rights Act, but the House of Lords had no compunction about applying it in order to preserve the state's power to search a citizen against his will, overruling a Divisional Court, of which Brooke LJ was a member, which had believed that the **purpose** of PACE was

to clarify and codify what the police might or might not lawfully do in this very sensitive area.

66. **We therefore have no hesitation in holding that there is nothing in section 12(3) of the Human Rights Act 1998 that can properly be interpreted as weakening in any way the force of the rule in *Bonnard v Perryman*.**

13. Section 6 of the Human Rights Act

67. Section 6(1) of the Human Rights Act provides that it is unlawful for a public authority to act in a way which is incompatible with a Convention right. It is well known that by section 6(3)(a) the expression "public authority" is defined so as to include a court within the scope of its meaning.

68. **For the purposes of this judgment we are content to assume that a person's right to protect his/her reputation is among the rights guaranteed by ECHR Article 8** (see *Affaire Radio France et autres v France* (No 53984/00) at para 31). In its judgment in that case the court at Strasbourg recognised this **right as an element of the right to respect for private life**. (Compare Lord Hoffmann's observations to similar effect in *Wainwright v Home Office* [2003] UKHL 23 at [16]—[18]).

69. Against this background Mr Spearman showed us a number of recent cases which demonstrate **the techniques to be adopted where two Convention rights are in apparent conflict**. That this is the case in the field of defamation was made very clear by Cooke P in *Bell-Booth Group Ltd v Attorney-General* [1989] 3 NZLR 148, in which he said:

> "The common law rules, and their statutory modifications, regarding defamation and injurious falsehood represent compromises gradually worked out by the Courts over the years, with some legislative adjustments, between competing values. Personal **reputation** and freedom to trade on the one hand have to be balanced against freedom to speak or criticise on the other."

70. More recently, in *Reynolds v Times Newspapers Ltd* [2001] 2 AC 127 Lord Nicholls said at p 190:

> "My Lords, this appeal concerns the interaction between two fundamental rights: freedom of expression and protection of **reputation**."

71. Mr Spearman argued that a rights-based approach requires a careful balancing at every stage of every case between the competing rights. He relied in this context on passages in the speeches in the House of Lords in *Campbell v MGN Ltd* [2004] UKHL 22, [2004] 2 WLR 1292 (see Lord Nicholls at paras 19–20; Lord Hoffmann at paras 55–56; Lord Hope of Craighead at paras 105–111; and Baroness Hale of Richmond at paras 139–142).

72. Mr Caldecott QC, who appeared for the defendants, submitted that it is at

the trial of a defamation action that English law shows itself appropriately solicitous of the claimant's right to a fair **reputation**. **At the trial the burden lies on defendants to prove** that their defamatory statement was true, or that it represented fair comment on a matter of public interest, or that it was made on an occasion that attracted privilege. If they fail to do so, they have to pay the penalty for infringing the claimant's right, and the claimant thereby sees his/her **reputation** vindicated in a very public way. Even if the case is settled before trial, rules of court uniquely allow a statement to be made in open court by way of vindication.

73. At the pre-trial stage, he argued, the position is different. As Stuart-Smith LJ said in *Lonrho v Fayed* [1993] 1 WLR 1489 at p 1502:

> ". . . [N]o one has a right to a **reputation** which is unmerited. Accordingly one can only suffer an injury to **reputation** if what is said is false. **In defamation the falsity of the libel or slander is presumed; but justification is a complete defence."**

74. If a claimant were able to stop a defendant from exercising its ECHR Article 10 right merely by arguing on paper-based evidence that it was more likely than not that the defendant could not show that what it wished to say about the claimant was true, it would seriously weaken the effect of Article 10. In *The Observer and The Guardian v UK* (1992) 14 EHRR 153 the court at Strasbourg said (at para 60);

> ". . . [T]he dangers inherent in **prior restraint** are such that they call for the most careful scrutiny on the part of the Court. This is especially so as far as the press is concerned, for news is a perishable commodity and to delay its publication, even for a short period, may well deprive it of all its value and interest."

75. **Scoops, as Mr Caldecott observed, are the lifeblood of the newspaper industry.** He might have added that stale news is no news at all. If Mr Spearman was correct, people with a fair **reputation** they do not deserve could stifle public criticism by obtaining injunctions simply because on necessarily incomplete information a court thought it more likely than not that they would defeat a defence of justification at the trial.

76. In our judgment Mr Caldecott's submissions are well-founded. As Sir John Donaldson MR observed in the *Khashoggi* case, **once a claimant's right to a fair reputation is put in issue it is the function of the trial, and the duty of the jury, to determine whether he/she does have a right to be vindicated.** ***One cannot speak sensibly of the violation of the right until it is established at the trial,*** and at the trial the rules of evidence will favour the claimant.

77. In the passage quoted at para 31 above the editors of the current edition of *Gatley* correctly refer to "**the usually impossible task of investigating sum-**

marily the merits of the defence of justification which is so often dependent on the credibility of witnesses and detailed consideration of documents". The judicial authors of the rule in ***Bonnard v Perryman*** recognised this phenomenon when they created the rule in the first place. This court recognised it a generation ago when it refused to apply *American Cyanamid* principles in a defamation action. And in our judgment **there is nothing in the European Convention of Human Rights that requires the rule to be done away with.**

78. In cases involving **confidential documents**, the confidentiality of the documents will be lost completely if an injunction against disclosure is not granted when appropriate. In cases involving **national security,** great damage may similarly be done if an injunction is not granted when appropriate. In a defamation action, on the other hand, while some damage may be done by permitting the publication of what may later turn out to be false, everyone knows that it is at the trial that truth or falsehood will be tested and the claimant vindicated if the defendant cannot prove that the sting of the libel is justified or that he has some other defence the law will recognise. The damage that may on occasion be done by refusing an injunction where a less strict rule would facilitate its **grant pales into insignificance compared with the damage which would be done to freedom of expression and the freedom of the press** if the rule in ***Bonnard v Perryman*** was relaxed.

79. Since argument in this case was completed, the members of the appellate committee of the House of Lords have delivered their opinions in the case of *In re S (FC)* [2004] UKHL 47. That appeal was concerned with the appropriateness of an injunction which restrained the publication of the name of a defendant and her deceased child in the context of the reporting of a pending criminal trial in which a mother is charged with murdering her child. The **purpose** of the injunction was to protect the welfare of the mother's younger child.

80. In paragraphs 17 and 18 of his speech, with which the other members of the House of Lords agreed, Lord Steyn said:

> "17. The interplay between articles 8 and 10 has been illuminated by the opinions in the House of Lords in *Campbell v MGN Ltd* [2004] 2 WLR 1232. For present purposes the decision of the House on the facts of *Campbell* and the differences between the majority and the minority are not material. What does, however, emerge clearly from the opinions are four propositions. **First**, neither article has *as such* precedence over the other. **Secondly**, where the values under the two articles are in conflict, an intense focus on the comparative importance of the specific rights being claimed in the individual case is necessary. **Thirdly**, the justifications for interfering with or restricting each right must be taken into account. **Finally**, the proportionality test must be applied to each.

For convenience I will call this the ultimate balancing test. This is how I will approach the present case.

VI. The general rule

"18. In oral argument it was accepted by both sides that the ordinary rule is that the press, as the **watchdog** of the public, may report everything that takes place in a criminal court. I would add that in European jurisprudence and in domestic practice this is a strong rule. It can only be displaced by unusual or exceptional circumstances. It is, however, **not a mechanical rule**. The duty of the court is to examine with care each application for a departure from the rule by reason of rights under article 8."

81. On the facts of that case Lord Steyn said, in effect, that the Article 8 rights of the younger child paled into insignificance when compared with the importance to be attached to the freedom of the press to report a criminal trial. **Similarly, the relevant Article 8 rights of the claimant in the present case cannot be accorded great weight (before the trial of this action takes place) when compared with the importance to be attached to the freedom of the press to report matters of public interest, for the reasons already set out in this judgment.** Once again we need to stress the distinction between a defamation case (where the claimant's right to a **reputation** has been put in issue and the issue cannot be effectively resolved before the trial) and a case which raises direct issues of privacy or confidentiality.

82. For these reasons we decided to dismiss this appeal.

Niema Ash & anor v Loreena McKennitt & ors [2006] EWCA 1714 (Civ)

1. I set out no more than is necessary to understand the issues in the appeal. Much of what follows is taken largely verbatim from the judgment of Eady J, which was described by the constitution of this court that granted permission to appeal as detailed and careful. **The case before Eady J was heard in private.** The claim seeks to prevent the further publication of certain material, so this was a case where a **public hearing would have defeated** the object of that hearing, one of the cases for privacy that is provided by CPR **39.2(3)(a)**. The judge enjoined further publication of a **significant** part of the work complained of. **He dealt with the problem of publicity in the course of litigation by (if I may respectfully say so, very skilfully), delivering an open judgment that described the objectionable material in general terms,**

but appended a confidential appendix in which the actual enjoined material was fully described.

2. **Before us, an application was made to hear in private those parts of the appeal that required reference to the material in the appendix. We granted that application, for the same reason as the judge had sat in private.** However, we were able without undermining the judge's order to hear the major part of the appeal, including all of the legal argument, **in public**. That was achieved by the **care exercised** by Mr Price and by Mr Browne QC in presenting their arguments, and we are grateful to them for their skill and co-operation in that respect.

. . .

A taxonomy of the law of privacy and confidence

8. It will be necessary to refer to the underlying law at various stages of the argument, and it would be tedious to repeat such reference more than is necessary. Since the content of that law is in some respects a matter of controversy, I set out what I understand the present state of that law to be. I start with some straightforward matters, before going on to issues of more controversy:

i) **There is no English domestic law tort of invasion of privacy**. Previous suggestions in a contrary sense were dismissed by Lord Hoffmann, whose speech was agreed with in full by Lord Hope of Craighead and Lord Hutton, in *Wainwright v Home Office* [2004] 2 AC 406 [28]–[35].

ii) Accordingly, in developing a right to protect private information, including the implementation in the English courts of articles 8 and 10 of the European Convention on Human Rights, the English courts have **to proceed through the tort of breach of confidence, into which the jurisprudence of articles 8 and 10 has to be "shoehorned":** *Douglas v Hello! (No3)*[2006] QB 125[53].

iii) That feeling of discomfort arises from the action for breach of *confidence* being employed where there was **no pre-existing relationship of confidence between the parties,** but the "confidence" arose from the defendant having acquired by **unlawful** or **surreptitious** means information that he should have known he was not free to use: as was the case in *Douglas*, and also in *Campbell v MGN* [2004] 2 AC 457. Two further points should however be noted:

iv) At least the verbal difficulty referred to in (iii) above has been avoided by **the rechristening of the tort as misuse of private information**: per Lord Nicholls of Birkenhead in *Campbell* [2004] 2 AC 457[14]

v) Of great importance in the present case, as will be explained further below, **the complaint here is of what might be called old-fashioned**

breach of confidence by way of conduct **inconsistent with a pre-existing relationship,** rather than simply of the **purloining** of private information.

Something more now needs to be said about the way in which the rules laid down by articles 8 and 10 enter English domestic law.

9. Most of the articles of the Convention impose negative obligations on the state and on public bodies. That accordingly affects the content of the articles and the obligations that they create, which are obligations owed only by public bodies. When those articles were introduced into English law by the medium of the Human Rights Act 1998, and recited in Schedule 1 to that Act, that content did not change and could not have changed. That is why, whatever the structure adopted by English law for giving effect to the Convention, most of the articles, since their content is restricted to creating obligations on public bodies, do not and cannot create obligations owed by private parties in private law. Article 8 has, however, always been seen as different; as, in this regard, has article 11, freedom of assembly, on which latter see *das Leben v Austria* (1988) 13 EHRR 204[32]. Not in its terms, but as extended by jurisprudence**, article 8 imposes not merely negative but also positive obligations on the state: to respect, and therefore to promote, the interests of private and family life. That means that a citizen can complain against the state about breaches of his private and family life committed by other individuals.** That has been Convention law at least since *Marckx v Belgium* (1979) 2 EHRR 330, and a particularly strong statement of the obligation is to be found in *X and Y* v *Netherlands* (1985) 8 EHRR 235.

10. More difficulty has been experienced in explaining how that state obligation is articulated and **enforced in actions between private individuals**. However, judges of the highest authority have concluded that that follows from section 6 (1) and (3) of the Human Rights Act, placing on the courts the obligations appropriate to a public authority: see Baroness Hale of Richmond in *Campbell* at §132; Lord Phillips of Worth Matravers in *Douglas v Hello!* at §53; and in particular Lord Woolf in *A v B plc* [2003] QB 195[4]:

> Under section 6 of the 1998 Act the court, as a public authority, is required not to act "in a way which is incompatible with a Convention right". The court is able to achieve this **by absorbing the rights which articles 8 and 10 protect into the long-established action for breach of confidence.** This involves giving a new strength and breadth to the action so that it accommodates the requirements of those articles.

Confidence/privacy

11. **The effect of this guidance is, therefore, that in order to find the rules of the English law of breach of confidence we now have to look in the jurisprudence of articles 8 and 10. Those articles are now not merely of**

persuasive or parallel effect but, as Lord Woolf says, are the very content of the domestic tort that the English court has to enforce. Accordingly, in a case such as the present, where the complaint is of the wrongful publication of private information, the court has to decide two things. ***First,*** *is the information private in the sense that it is in principle protected by article 8?* If no, that is the end of the case**. If yes**, the second question arises: *in all the circumstances, must the interest of the owner of the private information **yield** to the right of freedom of expression conferred on the publisher by article 10?* The latter enquiry is commonly referred to as the balancing exercise, and I will use that convenient expression. I take the two questions in turn. Some aspects of the jurisprudence overlap between the two questions, but it remains necessary to keep the underlying issues separate. I have well in mind, in addressing article 8, the warning given by Lord Nicholls of Birkenhead in §21 of his speech in Campbell:

> "21. Accordingly, in deciding what was the ambit of an individual's 'private life' in particular circumstances courts need to be on guard against using as a touchstone a test which brings into account considerations which should more properly be considered at the later stage of proportionality. **Essentially** the touchstone of private life is whether in respect of the disclosed acts the person in question had **a reasonable expectation of privacy."**

The pre-existing relationship of confidence

. . .

12. The judge listed a large number of parts of the book that were said by Ms McKennitt to consist of private information. He refused protection for many of them because he regarded their content as **"anodyne", imprecise or already known to the public.** In an authority shown to us after argument had closed, M v Secretary of State for Work and Pensions [2006] 2 AC 91[83] Lord Walker of Gestingthorpe pointed out that interference with private life had to be of some seriousness before article 8 was engaged. The spirit of that guidance was indeed respected by the Judge in the analysis just described. It will be necessary to describe the remaining matters, in respect of which the judge did grant injunctive relief, with some particularity, but the general nature of the information sought to be restrained was indicated by the Judge in his §11:

    - Ms McKennitt's personal and **sexual relationships**.
    - Her **personal feelings** and, in particular, in relation to her deceased fiancé and the circumstances of his death.
    - Matters relating to her **health** and **diet.**

- Matters relating to her **emotional vulnerability.**
- The detail of an **unhappy dispute** between Ms McKennitt, on the one hand, and Ms Ash and Mr Fowkes on the other, concerning monies advanced to them by Ms McKennitt to assist in the purchase of a property in 1997 and the subsequent litigation in the Chancery Division (which was settled on the basis of a Tomlin order without ever coming to a public hearing).

13. I should say straightaway that the last matter, which I shall refer to as the property dispute, raises issues different from the other matters complained of, and I will deal with it separately towards the end of the judgment. The other parts of the book in respect of which relief was granted can be identified as follows, for convenience repeating the numeration in the claim, which was also used by the judge:

    i) Item 4: what the Judge describes in his §17 as "a rather **intimate** conversation between Ms McKennitt and Ms Ash (which would otherwise certainly not have been in the **public domain**)"

    ii) Item 5: what the Judge describes in his §18 as "extensive references in the book to Ms McKennitt's **relationship** with her fiancé, who died in the boating accident in 1998"

    iii) Item 9: a detailed account of events at Ms McKennitt's cottage in Ireland, and of the physical arrangements there, including a period when Ms Ash and Mr Fowkes did building work at the cottage.

    iv) Item 13: what the Judge described in his §13 as "**intimate** revelations" about the state of Ms McKennitt's health after the bereavement described in (ii) above.

    v) Item 14: revelations about Ms McKennitt's **fragile** condition during a visit to Tuscany after the bereavement

    vi) Item 15: discussion of terms and conditions of a contract entered into by Ms McKennitt with a recording company

    vii) Item 34: an incident in a hotel bedroom **shared** by Ms McKennitt and Ms Ash; and a report of a telephone conversation in which Ms McKennitt revealed the state of her health.

14. The **nub** of Mr Price's argument in this part of the case, based both on the account given in the judgment and repeated above, **and also on the more detailed examination of the book that we undertook in the private part of the hearing,** was that the judge's finding that all of the above was private information went far beyond anything previously decided. That, it was suggested, could be seen by comparison with the facts of cases like *Campbell* and *Douglas*. I am not at all sure that that argument is correct, even on its

own terms. *Campbell* concluded that although it was not, on the facts, private information that Ms Campbell suffered from drug addiction **it was private information that she was seeking treatment for that addiction**. *Douglas* concluded that **unauthorised photographs of a wedding were private even though the couple were perfectly content, indeed contractually bound, to allow authorised tphotographs of the same event to be published.** I would be hard pressed to say that the matters listed by Eady J were less obviously **intrusive** into Ms McKennitt's life. But there is a much more formidable reason why this assault on Eady J's conclusions must fail. That is to be found **in the nature of the relationship between Ms McKennitt and Ms Ash**, to which I now turn.

A pre-existing relationship of confidence

15. Recent leading cases in this area, such as *Campbell*, *Douglas* and the most recent case in the ECtHR, *Von Hannover v Germany* (2005) 40 EHRR 1, have wrestled with the problem of identifying the **basis for claiming privacy or confidence in respect of unauthorised or purloined information:** see § 8(iii) above. There, the primary focus has to be on **the nature of the information, because it is the recipient's perception of its confidential nature that imposes the obligation on him**: see for instance per Lord Goff of Chievely in *A-G v Guardian Newspapers (No2) ["Spycatcher"]* [1990] 1 AC 109 at p 281A. **But, as Lord Goff immediately goes on to say, in the vast majority of cases the duty of confidence will arise from a transaction or relationship between the parties.** And that is our case, which accordingly reverts to a more elemental enquiry into breach of confidence in the traditional understanding of that expression. That does not of course exempt the court from considering whether **the material obtained during such a relationship is indeed confidential;** but to enquire into that latter question without paying any regard to **the nature of the pre-existing relationship between the parties**, as the argument for the appellant in this court largely did, is unlikely to produce anything but a **distorted outcome**.

. . .

18. The Judge accordingly approached, and correctly approached, his consideration of the passages complained of **against the background of a pre-existing relationship of confidence, known to be such by Ms Ash, while at the same time *not assuming* that that covered everything that happened between the two women with the *cloak of confidence***. I will briefly review his findings on the items listed in §13 above, all of which findings are unassailable.

19. Item 4 concerned what the Judge in his §132 described as "private and **intimate** observations": Ms Ash must have known that she was not at liberty to broadcast them to the world.

20. Item 5 deals with Ms McKennitt's **relationship** with her fiancé and the outcome of his death in 1998. The Judge in his §133 described the passages in the book as **"remarkably intrusive and insensitive".** Having had the benefit, if that is the right word, of reading the whole of the book's treatment of this subject, I would think that the Judge's characterisation was if anything restrained.

21. Item 9 was addressed by the Judge in his §§ 135–136. He said:

> 135. Item 9 concerns Ms McKennitt's Irish cottage. It is not her only house, but it is nevertheless a home. That is one of the matters expressly addressed in Article 8(1) of the Convention as entitled to "respect". Correspondingly, there would be an obligation of confidence. **Even relatively *trivial* details would fall within this protection simply because of the *traditional sanctity accorded to hearth and home*.** To describe a person's home, the décor, the layout, the state of cleanliness, or how the occupiers behave inside it, is generally regarded as unacceptable. **To convey such details, without permission, to the general public is almost as objectionable as spying into the home with a long distance lens and publishing the resulting photographs.**
>
> 136. True it is that over five or six years Mr Fowkes was engaged, from time to time, in renovation works at the cottage. Ms Ash, too, did a lot of hard work to make it habitable after Ms McKennitt acquired it in 1992. Some of the work was remunerated and some was not. That seems to me to make no significant difference. **Whether one is allowed into a person's home professionally, to quote for or to carry out work, or one is welcomed socially, it would clearly be understood that the details are not to be published to the world at large.**

22. Criticism was made of the introduction to this passage, in that article 8 cases have tended to be concerned with the security or stability of residence, rather than with privacy within the home. But the Judge clearly spoke only by analogy, pointing out that it should have been and was obvious that **events in a person's home cannot be lightly intruded upon;** and in the event, as he said in his §138, "it is **intrusive** and distressing for Ms McKennitt's household minutiae to be exposed to curious eyes". And **I would also respectfully agree with his comparison with *long distance photography*,** an exercise generally considered to raise privacy issues. If anything, on the Judge's findings as set out in §17 above Ms Ash knew a good deal better than might a casual photographer that publication of the fruits of her inspection of the cottage and **of what happened there was unacceptable.**

23. **Item 13 concerns revelations about the state of Ms McKennitt's health, their instrusive nature being made the worse by her fragility having been**

associated with the bereavement. *A person's health is in any event a private matter, as the Campbell case demonstrated. It is doubly private when information about it is imparted in the context of a* **relationship** *of confidence.* The Judge was entirely right to say in his §142 that there is a reasonable expectation of privacy in relation to such matters. The same is true of his holding in his §143 in relation to item 14.

24. Item 15 relates to Ms McKennitt's **contractual dealings,** dealings that we were told, and the Judge assumed, were not public knowledge. If the contractual documents had **fallen off the back of a lorry** and been picked up by a third party there might be some question as to whether they were of such a nature that he was bound to hold them in confidence. **The documents might not come within the category of self-evident privacy that was in the mind of Laws J in his famous example in Hellewell v Chief Constable of Derbyshire [1995] 1 WLR 804 at 807.** But there is no such issue in the case of a person who finds out details of contractual terms because she is in a **relationship** of confidence with the contracting party. As the Judge said in his §144:

    There is a general discussion on page 26 [of the book] of the contractual terms and of concessions made. Even though it is general, it seems to me that Ms McKennitt is entitled to a reasonable expectation of privacy as to her contractual terms. They are certainly not for Ms Ash to reveal.

25. Item 34 was seen by the Judge as more of a borderline case, but he thought that both occasions were ones on which privacy was to be expected by Ms McKennitt of Ms Ash. He was clearly entitled so to hold.

26. I would therefore respectfully agree with all of the Judge's conclusions as to the reach of article 8. It may also be added, as an indication that he did not approach the case with any preconception, nor any unreasonable hostility to Ms Ash, that **there were many stories about the relationship between the two women reproduced in the book that the Judge held not to have been breaches of confidence.** I would only comment that in some of those cases I myself might have taken a different view.

. . .

29. Some support was sought from passages in the judgment of this court in A v B plc [2003] QB 195. We shall have to return to that case in more detail when addressing article 10. **It is sufficient here to say that it concerned a married professional footballer [A] who sought to prevent publication by a newspaper [B] of his casual sexual relations with two women [C and D].** C and D had sold their story to B. In the course of a wide-ranging review of how a court should handle such a claim, this court said that the right of protection of one party to a **bilateral relationship** ***might be affected by the attitude of the other party,*** and continued, at its § 43(iii):

> "Although we would not go so far as to say there can be no confidentiality where one party to a **relationship** does not want confidentiality, the fact that C and D chose to disclose their **relationships** to B does affect A's right to protection of the information. **For the position to be otherwise would not acknowledge C and D's own right to freedom of expression."**

By the same token, it was suggested, Ms Ash's decision that her **shared relationship** with Ms McKennitt should not be treated as confidential undermined Ms McKennitt's contention that it was confidential.

30. On the facts of our case, as found by the Judge, that argument was **wholly misconceived**. **First**, the **relationship** between Ms McKennitt and Ms Ash, testified to in many places, and not least in the Judge's citations from the book set out in §17 above, was miles away from the **relationship** between A and C and D. In the preceding paragraph I deliberately and not merely conventionally described the latter as a **relationship** of **casual sex.** A could **not** have thought, and did not say, that when he picked the women up they realised that they were entering into a **relationship of confidence with him**. Small wonder that Lord Woolf said, A v B at §45:

> **"Relationships of the sort which A had with C and D are not the categories of relationships which the court should be astute to protect when the other parties to the relationships do not want them to** remain confidential."

Lord Woolf would have been unlikely to say the same about the **relationship** between Ms McKennitt and Ms Ash.

. . .

Woodward v Hutchins [1977] 1 WLR 760

33. This case dates back to an era when the Convention had not invaded the consciousness of English lawyers. I bear well in mind the warning of Lord Woolf in §9 of *A v B* that

> **authorities which relate to the action for breach of confidence prior to the coming into force of the 1998 Act . . . are largely of historic interest only.**

Nevertheless, *Woodward v Hutchins* has never been overruled; and its subject-matter has some commonalty with our case, since it concerned the dismissed publicity agent of a well-known group of singers who wished to write a series of articles dealing with their private lives and conduct.

34. The group failed to obtain an interlocutory injunction to prevent publication. The decision was based on two grounds. **First**, the only reason given by Lawton LJ, with whom Bridge LJ agreed in full, was that to grant interlocutory relief in a case where there were concurrent claims in breach of

confidence and defamation would or might undermine the rule in ***Bonnard v Perryman***, preventing interlocutory relief in a defamation case where it is proposed to justify. Lord Denning MR took the same view; but his main reason was that articulated by Bridge LJ at p 765D:

> It seems to me that those who seek and welcome publicity of every kind bearing upon their private lives so long as it shows them in a favourable light are in no position to complain of the invasion of their privacy by publicity that shows them in an unfavourable light.

35. Eady J, at his § 103, thought that the application in *Woodward v Hutchins* failed because the revelations were in the public interest. It would however seem that the view of Lord Denning MR and Bridge LJ was more fundamental than that, in that they thought that in the circumstances the enjoined material was not confidential at all.

36. *Woodward v Hutchins* has come in for a good deal of criticism, of which the point most relevant to our enquiry is **that the court was not reminded of the relevance of the contractual relationship between the agent and his former employers**. That largely deprives the decision of any direct authority in or relevance to our case. But there is another reason why in any event *Woodward v Hutchins* is of no assistance to us. We were constantly reminded, not least by the appellant, that all of these cases are **fact-sensitive.** I have set out the Judge's findings of fact about Ms McKennitt's attitude to publicity in §6 above. That is very far different from the sort of conduct and attitude that, in the view of Bridge LJ, would deprive a person's behaviour of the **quality of confidence**.

. . .

41. Perhaps realising the force of observations such as the foregoing, the media parties, in particular, were most anxious to persuade us that the ECtHR went no further in Von Hannover than to hold that the Princess's privacy had been invaded **by a campaign of media intrusion into her life**, of which the enjoined **photographs** were the fruit. The taking and publication of the **photographs** would otherwise not have been in itself an invasion of privacy. They cited in support some observations of Fenwick and Phillipson at p 768 of their book, though it is fair to say that the learned authors also say that that analysis is not without its difficulties. **The judge, at his §53, did not accept that analysis, nor would I.** While it is quite correct that there is reference in the judgment of the ECtHR to media **intrusion**, it is not possible to say that the general statements of principle set out in §38 above are so limited. **And Mr Browne was able to show us authority from the ECtHR decided since Von Hannover that applies those statements in situations that were not ones of media intrusion**. Of those, the most significant is **Sciacca v Italy**

(Application 50774/99), §§ 27 and 29 of the judgment of the ECtHR applying Von Hannover to a case that was not one of press **harassment**, and citing the jurisprudence of Von Hannover in entirely general terms.

. . .

The Judge's methodology

46. In a passage headed "A need to balance Convention rights" the Judge, basing himself on Campbell and on Re S(FC)(A child) [2005] 1 AC 593, set out the principles to be applied when article 8 rights were relied on to restrain publication. No criticism was made of the formulation or the relevance of those principles, nor could it have been made. The Judge's principles were:

i) Neither article has as such precedence over the other.

ii) Where conflict arises between the values under Articles 8 and 10, an "intense focus" is necessary upon the comparative importance of the specific rights being claimed in the individual case.

iii) The court must take into account the justifications for interfering with or restricting each right.

iv) So too, the proportionality test must be applied to each.

. . .

Ms Ash's right to tell her own story

50. A concern that Ms Ash might have been deprived of her article 10 right to tell her own story was one of the matters that weighed with the court that was persuaded to grant permission to appeal. The point featured heavily in the appellant's argument, strong reliance being placed on the observation at § 11(xi) of A v B that

> The fact that the confidence was a **shared** confidence which only one of the parties wishes to preserve does not extinguish the other party's right to have that confidence respected, but it does undermine that right.

Based on that, the argument then moved to the striking proposition that the Judge should have held that Ms McKennitt's article 8 rights, if any, were to be subordinated to the article 10 rights of Ms Ash.

51. That argument again completely ignores the Judge's findings of fact. He held that **the confidence was "shared" only in the sense that Ms McKennitt had admitted Ms Ash to her confidence, which confidence Ms Ash knew should be respected**: see §16 above. As a result, Ms Ash **had no story to tell that was her** own as opposed to being Ms McKennitt's: see §§ 30–31 above. And, even if that were not so, it needs no intense focus to conclude that on the facts the right of Ms Ash must **yield** to the right of Ms McKennitt.

. . .

53. It is perhaps inevitable that, although the enquiry is now under article 10, it still tends to be conducted in the traditional terms of the English law of confidence. As we shall in due course see, that is particularly the case in A v B. But the general principle is no doubt correct in both cases, that information that is already known cannot claim the protection of private life. **Mr Price however advanced a striking extension of that principle, that once a person had revealed or discussed some information falling within a particular "*zone*" of their lives they had a greatly reduced expectation of privacy in relation to any other information that fell within that *zone*.** This argument was used in particular in respect of Ms Ash's revelations about Ms McKennitt's health and her distress at the death of her fiancé. The material said to contain revelations by Ms McKennitt falling within the same **zone** were remarkably sparse, which is in itself an indication of how protective Ms McKennitt has been of her privacy. The Judge dealt with the argument in these terms, in his §§ 79–80:

. . .

79. Ms Ash produced a number of articles on the basis of which she argued that, at least in certain respects, Ms McKennitt had revealed aspects of her personal life and beliefs to the general public. She chose to confine her submissions to a limited number of articles, partly for reasons of time, although it is reasonable for me to proceed on the basis that she selected the examples which she thought best illustrated her point. If that is so, I did not find the submission very compelling in the light of the material contained in the book. **Conversations with, or behaviour in the presence of, close personal friends would appear to me to be significantly different from the sort of material revealed by Ms McKennitt in the past.** Also, as I have already pointed out, there is in this context a **significant difference between choosing to reveal aspects of private life with which one feels "comfortable" and yielding up to public scrutiny every detail of personal life, feelings, thoughts and foibles of character**.

80. In any event, it is important that a large proportion of the material Ms Ash relied upon was **specifically revealed by Ms McKennitt in the context of her attempts to promote water safety** and to support the **Cook-Rees Memorial Fund.** A classic example is provided by an interview in May 1999 with the journal Le Lundi. **It is somewhat surprising that Ms Ash should think that this carefully measured, and no doubt in itself distressing, exposure of her own feelings in a particular context should give her the right to reveal at considerable length what Mr Browne described as "her pitifully grief-stricken reaction to the death of [her fiancé], his brother and a friend".** It goes on for some eight pages. One's reactions and communications to

a friend in the immediate aftermath of personal bereavement are surely a **classic example** of material in respect of which there would a "**reasonable expectation**" that one's privacy would be respected.

The public interest: and Ms McKennitt as a public figure

56. One might instinctively think that there was little legitimate public interest in the matters addressed by the book, and certainly no public interest sufficient to outweigh Ms McKennitt's article 8 right to private life. That is what the Judge thought and, as already pointed out, in the absence of error of principle his view will prevail. That conclusion **was contested** under this head in two respects, which it is necessary to keep separate. **First**, there was a legitimate public interest in the affairs of Ms McKennitt because she was a **public figure**, *and for that reason alone*. **Second**, if a **public figure** had misbehaved, the allegation in the present case being of hypocrisy, the public had a right to have the record put straight. The parallel for that argument was the case of Ms Campbell, who could not retain privacy for the fact that she was a drug addict because she had lied publicly about her condition.

57. The first of these arguments involves consideration of two recent authorities, already introduced, *Von Hannover* and *A v B*, to which I must now return.

. . .

64. However that may be, and wherever that leaves courts that would have to apply the guidance given in *A v B*, **it seems clear that A v B cannot be read as any sort of binding authority on the content of articles 8 and 10.** To find that content, therefore, we do have to look to *Von Hannover*. The terms of that judgment are very far away from the automatic limits placed on the privacy rights of **public figure**s by *A v B*.

65. But, in any event, even if we were to follow *A v B*, the guidance that that case gives does not produce the outcome in our case that is sought by the appellant. **First,** as to the position of Ms McKennitt, she clearly does not fall within the first category mentioned by Lord Woolf, and "hold a position where higher standards of conduct can be rightly expected by the public": that is no doubt the preserve of **headmasters** and **clergymen**, who according to taste may be joined by **politicians, senior civil servants**, **surgeons** and **journalists. Second**, although on one view Ms McKennitt comes within Lord Woolf's second class, of involuntary role models, I respectfully share the doubts of Lord Phillips, set out in §63 above, as to the validity of that concept; and it would in any event seem difficult to include in the class a person such as Ms McKennitt, **who has made such efforts not to hold herself out as someone whose life is an open book**. **Third**, it is clear that Lord Woolf thought that role models were at risk, or most at risk, of having to put up with the reporting of **disreputable conduct**: such as was the conduct of claimant before him.

Ms McKennitt does not fall into that category; but to make that good I need to go on to the second part of this argument, that exposure is legitimate to demonstrate improper conduct or dishonesty.

66. In so doing I have not overlooked Lord Woolf's second general point, that weight must be given to the commercial interest of newspapers in reporting matter that interests the public. That view has also received criticism, and it seems clear that this court in *Campbell*, in the passage cited above, was not entirely happy with it. It is difficult to reconcile with the long-standing view that what interests the public is not necessarily in the public interest, a view most recently expressed by Baroness Hale of Richmond in *Jameel v Wall Street Journal* [2006] 2 AC 465[147]:

> The public only have a right to be told if two conditions are fulfilled. First, there must be a real public interest in communicating and receiving the information. This is, as we all know, very different from saying that it is information that interests the public-the most vapid **tittle-tattle** about the activities of footballers' wives and girlfriends interests large sections of the public but no-one could claim any real public interest in our being told all about it.

> It is fortunately not necessary to pursue that issue further, because it is merely a general factor, that cannot be said to have any significant impact on the present case.

Hypocrisy

67. This is the charge brought against Ms McKennitt, which is said to justify telling the world about her private behaviour and attitudes. Much of the book (for instance the matters about health or bereavement) does not fall into this category in any event. The complaint is that Ms McKennitt treated Ms Ash, and others, badly in two main respects, in the Irish cottage and in connexion with the property dispute, and that that was inconsistent with her public position about proper behaviour and respect for others.

68. Once again, this argument simply fails on the facts. The Judge made findings in his §§ 98–100 about the material on which Ms McKennitt's alleged announcement of her principles was based, the "compass points". He found them, as I do, a **fragile** basis for any public interest defence; and indeed said, at §100, that they were

> simply being used as an excuse by Ms Ash to enable her to escape her obligations of confidence and, in her own phrase, "unqualified loyalty"

And the Judge concluded that in any event Ms McKennitt had not behaved disreputably or insincerely in any way."

69. Some criticism is made of the Judge having said in his §97 that "a very high

degree of misbehaviour must be demonstrated" to trigger a public interest defence. **As an entirely general statement, divorced from its context, that may well go too far**. But the Judge was speaking of the particular situation argued before him, where not the conduct in itself, but the fact that it had previously been lied about or treated with hypocrisy, was said to be the basis for disclosure. In *Campbell* it was the fact that Ms Campbell had not merely said that she did not take drugs but had gone out of her way to emphasise that she was in that respect unlike other fashion models that deprived otherwise private material of protection: see per Lord Nicholls of Birkenhead, [2004] 2 AC 457[24]. By contrast, as the Judge clearly thought in his §97, the conduct complained of in the case of Ms McKennitt fell well below the level that would justify complaint on the ground of hypo70. The most sustained attack in the book on Ms McKennitt's probity and honesty is to be found in the last forty pages,that address the property dispute. **The Judge found that all or almost all of the allegations were untrue, and that the incident revealed nothing whatever to Ms McKennitt's discredit:** see §41 of the judgment. But since this part of the case involves other difficulties I deal with it separately.

. . .

The falsity of the allegations: and herein of defamation

78. Mr Price however had a further answer. The Judge had found that most or all of the book's allegations about the property dispute were **untrue**. There could therefore be no claim in breach of confidence. Whatever the position in defamation, the falsity of what Ms Ash had written was a complete defence, a defence in no way undermined by the appellant's case at trial having been that the whole of the book was true.

. . .

86. This argument, in my judgment, is untenable. *The question in a case of misuse of private information is whether the information is private not whether it is true or false.* The truth or falsity of the information **is an irrelevant inquiry** in deciding whether the information is entitled to be protected and judges should be chary of becoming side-tracked into that irrelevant inquiry. Cases such as Interbrew SA v Financial Times [2002] EWCA Civ 274, [2002] EMLR 446 (where a party claims protection on behalf of a source transmitting false information) are, of course, entirely different.

87. Eady J, however, had no option but to become involved in that inquiry in the present case. It was only shortly before trial that Ms Ash's counsel withdrew the allegation contained in the book that Ms McKennitt had brought the Chancery proceedings dishonestly knowing that she had no legal right to do so. The watered-down claim that Ms McKennitt was being vindictive in

pursuing an immoral claim, said now to be the public interest justification for publishing the private information, could not be intelligently adjudicated upon without the judge deciding whether that claim was true or false. That meant that he had also to decide the truth or falsity of other incidental allegations made by Ms Ash in seeking to re-argue through her book the matters already disposed of by the Tomlin order. **But the fact that it may be relevant to decide the truth or falsity of matters raised in support of an Article 10 claim to freedom of expression does not mean that, if matters are shown to be false, the claim to misuse of private information then disappears.**

X & Y v Persons Unknown [2006] EWHC 2783 (QB)

The applications by Mirror Group Newspapers and News Group Newspapers

4. Now there is before the court an application on behalf of MGN Ltd ("MGN") and News Group Newspapers Ltd ("NGN") to discharge the injunction. **They are not, of course, parties to the litigation but they are just as effectively restrained by the terms of the order served upon them.** There is also **an application by Associated Newspapers Group Ltd to vary the terms of the order (if it survives at all).** It is said that it would have been desirable for the newspapers to have been notified of the nature of the application on 5 October prior to its being made. They were told no more than that a "**John Doe**" application was to be made against persons unknown. **The reasoning of Mr Nicklin, who appeared before me on that occasion on the Claimants' behalf, was that representatives had given assurances on behalf of each of the relevant newspaper groups, or undertakings, that no such information would be published until a certain period of time had elapsed.** Those assurances were taken at face value and his application was therefore confined to those persons perceived to be the sources or potential sources.

5. **Upon reflection, no doubt, it would have been better to notify the newspaper publishers more fully—not least because the scope of the order obtained by Mr Nicklin was wider than the undertakings given.** They would all have had an interest in addressing the terms of the order because it affects them and, in particular, by restricting the exercise of their freedom of expression protected by Article 10 of the European Convention on Human Rights and Fundamental Freedoms.

6. Mr Spearman QC, appearing now for MGN and NGN, raises a battery of arguments in support of his application for discharge. **He relies primarily on the merits**, arguing that the Claimants are not entitled to this protection, either because their Article 8 rights under the Convention are not engaged at all,

in the sense that there is no reasonable expectation on their part to have information of this kind protected by the law, or because it is not likely, when the court comes to balance those rights with the Article 10 rights of the persons unknown and also, for that matter, of the newspaper groups, that the scales would come down in favour of the Claimants. That is arguably a question primarily of proportionality: See eg *Douglas v Hello! Ltd (No1)* [2001] QB 967 at [137], *per* Sedley LJ.

7. It is necessary to have regard to the various principles canvassed by the House of Lords in *Campbell v MGN Ltd* [2004] 2 AC 457 and *Re S (FC) (A Child)* [2005] 1 AC 593.

8. I should explain that Mr Spearman relies upon alternative arguments, such as that there was material non-disclosure on 5 **October and that the terms of the order go significantly more widely than is necessary for any legitimate protection** of the Claimants' Article 8 rights (assuming that they are engaged at all, which is contrary to his primary submission).

. . .

11. In principle, an extension of the requirements of notification to third parties would be unobjectionable and entirely consistent with Parliament's intention. **I have in mind also the (limited) provision made for third parties by CPR Part 25, 25 PD 9.2. They are entitled to a copy of any material read by the judge, once they have been served with an order, together with a note of the hearing.** This would clearly enable them *ex post facto* to mount a more effective challenge to the terms of the order in so far as it affects them. The argument of Associated Newspapers is, in effect, that prevention would be even better than cure.

12. There may be theoretical difficulties in defining or identifying how far the category of interested third parties extends, but that will sometimes be less of a hurdle in practice where the applicant for injunctive relief will know, when coming before the court, **whom it is intended to serve with the order and, in the case of media groups at least, it would be easy to determine which individual department should be given prior notification.** Sometimes, however, it will be clear that the class of persons whose rights will be affected will be different from, and extend more widely than, those persons whom the applicant intends to serve.

13. When counsel came before the court on 5 October no restrictions were sought against Associated Newspapers **because a form of undertaking had already been offered which**, albeit limited in point of time, was acceptable to the Claimants. **The need at that stage was to restrain the source of the allegations** who was, apparently, a **disloyal friend or acquaintance** hawking the story round various media groups in the hope of making some money.

14. Accordingly, both Mr Nicklin and I were focussing on a draft which might capture as many permutations of misconduct as possible on the part such confidants. **One is naturally conscious of the risk that a would-be infringer may be looking for loopholes.** That is why it is helpful to have someone put the other side of the case, and especially the risks of casting the net too widely.

15. What has displeased Associated Newspapers is that not only was the injunction served on it any way, **but its terms were actually wider than those of the undertaking which had been proffered and accepted.** I understand the frustration of the Associated Newspapers legal team, but I am quite satisfied that there was no intention to mislead the court or "pull a fast one" on the newspaper. It was simply a question of thinking on the hoof in a developing situation.

16. Another factor which played its part was that the Claimants' solicitor genuinely got the impression from a conversation with one of Associated Newspapers' in house lawyers that all interest had been lost in the story. Whether he read too much into his words is neither here nor there for present purposes, but from the evidence I am quite satisfied that this was another reason why Associated Newspapers were put out of mind.

17. Nonetheless, it was unfortunate that this should have happened and, if the suggestions now put forward by Associated Newspapers are accepted, as a matter of best practice for the future, it will be less likely that such misunderstandings will arise.

. . .

22. In the light of the House of Lords' decision in *Re S (A Child)*, cited above**, it is clear that the first step is for me to decide whether the Claimants' Article 8 rights are engaged at all.** It goes without saying that the grant of the injunction affects the Article 10 rights of anyone, party or not, who would be restrained from publishing the specified category of information. **Thus, if the Article 8 rights are engaged, the next stage would be to carry out a balancing exercise as between the competing Convention rights without according automatic priority to either.** It is no longer fashionable, as it was for a short time a few years ago, to describe Article 10 as a "trump card": *cf R v Central Independent Television plc* [1994] Fam 192, 203; *Venables v News Group Newspapers Ltd* [2001] 1 All ER 908 at [36]–[41]; *Douglas v Hello! Ltd* [2001] QB 967 at [137].

. . .

28. **In the present context, that distinction can be of some importance. It by no means follows that an individual who is photographed and described in print, and about whom information or speculation is published regarding**

his or her private life, must have so behaved as to forfeit or waive the entitlement to privacy with regard to (say) intimate personal relationships or the conduct of a private life generally. ***Close attention may need to be paid as to how such information came into the*** **public domain** ***and as to its limits.*** Some well known people are prepared to go along with "lifestyle" pieces which reveal, for example, their likes and dislikes, and how they spend their spare time, **without wishing to cross boundaries into personal relationships**. Others, on the other hand, will be less fastidious **and take the view that any publicity is good publicity, being prepared to reveal any titbit to attract attention to themselves or to make money**. There is no hard and fast rule, since the general proposition has to be recognised **that even well known people are entitled to some private life: see eg the observations in A v B plc** [2003] QB 195 **at 208.** The court will in every case have to examine the specific evidence and make an evaluation (on which, inevitably, there may be room for differing opinions).

29. There is a significant volume of material in the papers about X. That is clear from the evidence, and Mr Spearman has highlighted those articles which he regards as best making his case. I am quite satisfied, in the light of X's evidence in particular, and the other material before me which I find consistent with it, **that X is not a person who willingly sets out for self-promotion to live her private life in the public eye.** Yet she is under contractual obligations to those whose products or services she promotes to give interviews from time to time. That is an important part of the context in which the court has to reach its conclusion.

Non-disclosure: "The punitive expedition"

41. Mr Spearman's alternative stance is that, even though the court would otherwise be inclined to grant some form of interlocutory protection to these Claimants, it should in this instance be refused because of the way **they and their advisers went about the application of 5 October.**

42. It is becoming increasingly common for media defendants to carry out what used to be called a "**cuttings**" search in these cases. Such investigations can obviously be executed more quickly and efficiently by electronic means and, in the case of newsworthy people, **a huge amount of published material can be conjured up at the press of a button.** The object is obviously **to demonstrate, or at least give the impression, that the individual concerned has forfeited rights to privacy or confidentiality and become, to all intents and purposes, public property**. It is important not to be beguiled into drawing such a conclusion simply because of bulk.

43. The coverage in question, and especially that expressly relied upon by the relevant media defendant, **needs to be scrutinised carefully on an individual**

basis in order to see whether the proposition is made out. It involves, after all, drawing the conclusion at an early stage of the litigation, **and often without detailed evidence or full argument,** that the citizen who seeks protection from the court (albeit only on a temporary footing) is already precluded from reliance on an increasingly significant Convention right. **The court will naturally guard in that context against a rush to judgment.**

44. This is especially so, perhaps, in a situation where it is clear from s 12 of the Human Rights Act, and the House of Lords' interpretation of it in *Cream Holdings v Banerjee* [2005] 1 AC 253, that the threshold usually to be passed is not that of an "arguable case", or even a "strong *prima facie* case"**, but rather whether the particular claimant is likely to succeed in restraining publication at trial.** The court thus cannot generally avoid coming to a conclusion on the merits. Such a decision, inevitably at that stage to a greater or lesser extent inchoate, **will have the consequence if it is adverse to the claimant that the publication will take place and any confidentiality will be gone for ever.**

45. In this context, each party will wish to provide the court with as much relevant information as possible **on the merits** to enable a favourable conclusion to be reached. So far as a claimant is concerned, it has always been necessary on an application without notice to give **full and frank disclosure of material** which is likely to have a **genuine bearing,** one way or the other, on the chances of success. It is right to note, in the developing area of protecting privacy, that there is room for differing interpretations on what is truly relevant.

46. There is a natural tendency on the part of newspaper lawyers to dredge up everything yielded by an electronic search on the relevant "**celebrity**" in order to persuade the court that he or she has indeed become **public property.** As I have already suggested, however, close **scrutiny is required of each private revelation and how it came about.** The claimant's lawyers may genuinely come to the conclusion that a significant proportion of what is in the **public domain** is **not relevant** to an application for injunctive relief. That may be because the information already published is not such as to fall within the law's protection at all, or because it is speculation by journalists or purported revelations wrongly attributed to the particular claimant. It is only too easy in these uncertain waters for a media defendant to point the finger of criticism at an applicant's lawyers for supposed non-disclosure. **Yet a claimant is not necessarily to be criticised for not having disclosed everything which a defendant subsequently chooses to dredge up in support of its argument.**

47. That is, however, a practical difficulty which arises from the fluid nature of the law and the inevitable uncertainties as to how material came into the

public domain. Yet the principle remains clear. If and in so far as the exigencies of the occasion permit, **anyone applying for an injunction must comply with his or her obligation of full and frank disclosure.** In cases of this kind, that will generally involve a search of the **internet** or previous publications relating to the same category of information now sought to be protected. The court will need all the assistance available, for the **purpose** of deciding "**likelihood" of success, and in particular for making a preliminary judgment as to whether "the information in question is so generally accessible that, in all the circumstances, it cannot be regarded as confidential" (in the words of Lord Goff's "first limiting principle" in Att.-Gen. v Guardian Newspapers Ltd (No2)** [1990] 1 AC 109, **282).**

48. Depending upon the circumstances, it may also be necessary for the court to decide whether the evidence shows that there has been a **genuine "waiver" of privacy** on the part of the applicant (which, of course, is not necessarily the same as Lord Goff's **public domain** test). I use the term "waiver" somewhat loosely as a convenient label, while bearing in mind the analysis in Tugendhat & Christie, *The Law of Privacy and the Media* (OUP 2002), at 9.29–9.37, **which suggests that the doctrine of waiver may not be a relevant consideration. Each situation must be judged according to the circumstances of the case**. For example, it should be **assessed objectively**, and without having to determine the claimant's state of mind, whether it is any longer reasonable for there to be an expectation of privacy in respect of material in the **public domain** (and that will include material which the claimant has revealed).

49. Another question which may have to be determined, if it is relevant to the case, is **whether there is information which shows that the public has been misled by the applicant in some respect, so as to justify a journalist putting the record straight** by revealing information which would otherwise fulfil the criteria for legal protection (*cf* Miss Campbell's denials of drug-taking). Of course, at the stage of applying for an interlocutory injunction a claimant will not necessarily be aware of which or how many of these possible arguments a defendant is likely to deploy. In some cases, it may be obvious: **in others not.** For the **purpose** of discharging the obligation of disclosure, an applicant and his or her advisers will sometimes be operating in **uncertain territor50. A reasonable test against which to judge non-disclosure may be whether the applicant has taken all practical steps to reveal material which is reasonably likely to assist the respondent's probable defence(s) at trial.** That obligation is not to be identified, however, or confused with a need to dredge up everything about the claimant in the **public domain**.

51. It is therefore necessary for an applicant to anticipate any possible (ie realistically possible) defences. Some guidance may be obtained by consulting the **Press Complaints Commission's Code of Conduct** and its attempts to

grapple with the concept of "public interest". In the present case, there could be no suggestion of the public having been misled. There is no evidence, for example, of X having made false claims of marital harmony at a time after the stresses had emerged. (**One could argue that she would be entitled to keep them to herself anyway, but that is a separate point.**) Nor are the tensions in the Claimants' **relationship** otherwise a matter of general public interest. Still less could there be any suggestion here of what used to be called **"iniquity"**; in other words, **criminal or other wrongdoing** on the Claimants' part requiring to be exposed in the public interest.

52. The most likely areas for **debate** (confirmed by the submissions which have now been made on the present applications) would appear to be whether Article 8 is engaged at all in relation to these particular circumstances or, if it is, whether there has been an effective "waiver". Accordingly, the obligation on the Claimants' part (subject to questions of urgency) was to disclose to the court any material (specifically, published articles) which could *reasonably* be thought to assist on one or other of those arguments.

53. Naturally, it is open to an applicant to **"confess and avoid"** when any such material is presented to the court, as X has done here, but it should nevertheless be disclosed.

54. On 5 October, Mr Nicklin touched upon the subject of the Claimants' public disclosures, specifically the fact that wedding **photographs** had been permitted, but gave the impression that (so far as he knew) there was nothing they had put into the **public domain** concerning the more private or personal aspects of their **relationship**. (As we now know, there had also been some "exclusive" coverage of the honeymoon.) This represented a reasonable summary of the position as he personally understood it at the time, but the court will generally need, and be entitled to, greater assistance than this.

55. This is a recently developing area of law and practice, and the interpretation of s 12 by the House of Lords is being implemented in a rather experimental environment. Practitioners are still feeling their way, and I do not make any criticism of Mr Nicklin. The court, however, **has to be supplied with as complete a picture as possible of the knowledge of the applicants and their advisers, so that the** judge can come to a personal and informed conclusion on the **chances of success at trial**—rather than being simply given general reassurance (albeit in good faith) from an inevitably partisan source relying, quite possibly, on partisan or incomplete information. Despite the room for differing interpretations of (say) what is in the **public domain**, or as to those matters in respect of which there is a reasonable expectation of privacy**, it is sometimes easy to think that one's own perspective is the only valid way of looking at the available facts**. But an advocate seeking interim relief without notice must consciously **strive to understand what other perspectives** there

might reasonably be, bringing to bear his or her own knowledge and experience.

56. With the benefit of hindsight, one can see that there should have been some **scrutiny of any public assertions or comments by the Claimants, and X in particular, on the subject of her marriage or relationship with Y**, with a view to seeing whether the relevant media might be able to construct a respectable argument to the effect, for example, **that the public had been *invited in*, so to speak, to follow the progress of the relationship,** or had **genuinely been misled by the volunteering of information which**, at the time it was imparted, was known to be inaccurate. (As it happens, in the event that has not even been suggested by either Mr Spearman or Mr Caldecott.)

57. I emphasise again that this is not to say that an applicant has to carry out the "dredging" exercise which defendants tend to undertake. There must be some discrimination. **What would appear to be reasonable is that the applicant's advocate should make a conscientious determination, in the light of the information which has been obtained on the relevant topic, as to which points he or she would wish to make if instructed to represent media defendants on the other side**. One would simply try **to step into the shoes of a hypothetical opponent**, just as one does when considering which authorities should be drawn to the court's attention as potentially undermining the submissions one is advancing. It is not necessarily always easy to do this in situations where conflicting rights come into play under Articles 8 and 10, as so much is ultimately a matter of impression. Nevertheless, **this exercise needs routinely to be carried out.** Obviously, it cannot be addressed merely on an *a priori* basis. A conclusion can only be reached after enquiry and establishing the true factual position to the extent that circumstances permit.

. . .

61. In the particular circumstances of the case I would list the following mitigating circumstances which lead me to conclude that the Claimants should not, on this occasion, be penalised by the refusal of injunctive relief:

(i) There was no intention on the part of Mr Nicklin or his instructing solicitors to mislead the court.

(ii) It was perceived on 5 October that urgent action was required to restrain the "persons unknown" from approaching yet further newspapers or taking other steps to profit from the Claimants' misfortunes. The hearing was arranged in hurry at the last minute. The pressure of time meant that corners were cut.

(iii) Enquiries were made of X's public relations consultant, as I have said, to find out whether any interviews had been given on the subject of the

marriage, such as might be thought effectively to "waive" the reasonable expectation of privacy: a negative response was received.

(iv) The court was informed about the willingness to have wedding photographs published in the media (that being the extent of counsel's knowledge at the time).

(v) The emphasis at the hearing on 5 October was upon restraining the "persons unknown", which was given priority in the light of the undertakings/assurances given by the individual newspaper lawyers.

(vi) Accordingly, the drafting was directed to restraining the Defendants from revealing any confidential information about the relationship within their knowledge.

(vii) Although it was in the minds of the Claimants' legal team to serve third parties to discourage them from relying on information sourced from the Defendants, insufficient attention was focussed at that point on the difficulties *from the third parties' point of view* in complying with the terms of the injunction, tailored as it was to the knowledge of the Defendants. As a counsel of perfection, no doubt, the Claimants should have raised the concerns which have now been articulated on the part of Associated Newspapers, but this is the first case to arise (so far as I am aware) in which these matters have been addressed, and the omission was more understandable than is likely to be the case on future applications.

In all the circumstances, I decline to exercise my discretion against the grant of an injunction which I consider otherwise to be appropriate. The non-disclosure was, on these particular facts, not such as to merit this disciplinary or punitive step.

. . .

The need for a **public domain** proviso

62. It is now recognised that generally speaking an order restricting the communication of ideas and information should include a **public domain** proviso: see *Att.-Gen. v Times Newspapers Ltd* [2001] 1 WLR 885; *Harris v Harris; Att.-Gen. v Harris* [2001] 2 FLR at [208] and [353] (Munby J); *A v B, C & D* [2005] EMLR 36 at [16]–[17].

63. In the order of 5 October such a proviso was omitted—it seems again through haste. Mr Nicklin recognised that his draft should have included this exemption but suggested that a reasonable construction of the order would have taken such a term to be implied. Things are not so straightforward unfortunately. **Those who are on risk of contempt proceedings cannot afford to assume that the express wording of the court's order is subject to an implied qualification.** They are entitled and bound to take it at face value.

64. In any event, **in the context of personal information (as opposed to commercial secrets) it does not necessarily follow, from the fact that something has been published, that further coverage cannot itself infringe a claimant's privacy:** see eg the observations of Lord Keith in *Att-Gen v Guardian Newspapers Ltd (No 2)*, cited above, at p 260. It may be more difficult to establish that confidentiality has gone for all purposes by virtue of such information having come to the attention of certain readers or categories of readers.

65. Also, even where a claimant has chosen to put personal information into the **public domain**, it does not necessarily entail that the media is free to publish any other details relating to the same subject-matter. **Individuals appear to be permitted some degree of control over how much information is released**: *Douglas v Hello! Ltd* [2005] EWCA Civ 595; [2005] EMLR 609.

66. These are other factors which illustrate how unrealistic it would be to expect anyone served with an injunction simply to assume a **public domain** proviso and, correspondingly, that any topic which has already received press coverage can be pursued further with impunity. **On the other hand, if it is the court's intention to prevent further publication of material even though it has apparently reached the public domain, on the basis that its confidentiality has not thereby been utterly lost, it will need to be made expressly clear that it is not to be treated as being within the proviso.**

67. The wording of such a proviso may be directed to matters already in the **public domain** at the time of the order or may cover, additionally, information published subsequently. So, for example, if X or Y were to choose in the future to discuss the reasons underlying their temporary problems, then a suitably worded proviso could ensure that the media were correspondingly released to cover the same subject-matter. **Whether a prospectively worded proviso is appropriate will depend on the circumstances of the case**. Here, I believe that it would be apt, since matters are fluid and the situation could well go on developing.

"Persons unknown"

68. It is submitted by Mr Spearman that, by contrast with the circumstances in the *Bloomsbury Publishing* case (cited above), the description of the "persons unknown" is not sufficiently certain as to identify those who are, and those who are not, included within the restrictions. He is making two points. First, he says that the description of the "persons" is in itself too wide. Secondly, they are restrained by the terms of the original order in respect of too wide and uncertain a class of information about X and Y. I address the second point elsewhere and accept that a narrower formulation, by reference to a **confidential schedule**, is to be preferred. I propose at this stage to consider the first argument.

69. The *Bloomsbury Publishing* case concerned persons who had offered an advance copy of the novel *Harry Potter and the Order of the Phoenix* to *The Sun*, the *Daily Mail* and the *Daily Mirror* newspapers, and persons who had physical possession of a copy of the book, or any part of it, without the consent of the publishers. **The Vice-Chancellor said that it was crucial that the description used must be sufficiently certain to identify both those who are included and those who are not**. It had been submitted by the publishers' counsel that no confusion should arise because anyone to whom it was shown would know immediately whether it was descriptive of and therefore directed to him or her.

70. True it is that a copy of the relevant novel was a more specific concept than "information about the status of the Claimants' marriage". But it is unlikely to cause confusion because anyone served is likely to know whether or not they have been offering such information to the relevant newspapers. **I cannot accept that X and Y are powerless to take any step to protect the dissemination of information, in respect of which there is a reasonable expectation of privacy, just because they do not yet have the identity of the person(s) concerned or know the precise nature of the titbits offered.**

. . .

Other submissions on the scope of the order

71. The order was **criticised** for a number of reasons, including the **absence of any return date or** provision for serving the "persons unknown" (either with any evidence or the order itself). It was therefore argued that the Claimants had effectively obtained permanent relief and restricted the media indefinitely from venturing into the prohibited topics.

72. One consequence would be that the Spycatcher doctrine would go on inhibiting third parties from publishing the relevant information notionally pending a trial which would never actually take place. **The Spycatcher doctrine, as a matter of logic, has no application to a permanent injunction** since, obviously, there is no longer any need to preserve the status quo pending a trial. **This doctrine is directed at preventing a third party from frustrating the court's purpose of holding the ring**: see eg the discussion in *Att-Gen v Punch Ltd* [2003] 1 AC 1046 at [87]–[88] in the Court of Appeal and at [95] in the House of Lords; and *Jockey Club v Buffham* [2003] QB 462 (Gray J).

73. This sounds Draconian, but of course there was liberty to apply forthwith for discharge or variation accorded to any interested person without the need to issue a formal application. **In a case where the only parties to the action are "persons unknown", there may be little point in fixing a return date, since it is likely to be ineffective and cause the claimant to incur unnecessary**

costs. Some provision should, however, be made **for drawing the injunction to the attention of the unknown defendants,** which will have to be tailored to the particular case in hand. That is relatively straightforward where they are known to attend at a specific location, as in the case of "travellers": see *South Cambridgeshire District Council v Persons Unknown* [2004] EWCA Civ 1280. But that clearly has no application in the instant case. The Claimants can only guess who or where the relevant persons are.

74. As I mentioned earlier, **one suggestion was that an attempt should be made to serve them through some or all of the newspapers who have apparently been approached with a view to selling the private information.** It is being assumed that someone on the newspaper's staff will, in each case, know the identity of the source(s) and have some means of making contact.

75. It may be that on some occasions it would be appropriate to request a newspaper editor or lawyer to notify the source. If in the particular case there is a willingness to co-operate, well and good. **It would not be right, on the other hand, for the court routinely in such cases to order a newspaper to act as a process server.** Nonetheless, because of the requirements under s 12 **all practicable steps should be taken to notify defendants in advance (unless there are compelling reasons for not doing so),** it might have been worth at least making the request in this case (however forlorn the hope of compliance). But this did not occur to the Claimants' advisers as being "practicable". The prospect of any of the newspapers agreeing was surely, in the real world, remote.

76. In any event, there may be good reasons from the newspaper's point of view for not wishing to perform this service. It might **antagonise** a particular source or, at least in theory, **discourage others** from coming forward with information on later occasions.

77. On the other hand, if a claimant is content to sit back and make no attempt at all to serve the defendant against whom an injunction has been obtained, with the order or the evidence on which it was based, then the tail will be wagging the dog. The *Spycatcher* doctrine has been acknowledged by the Court of Appeal and the House of Lords over the past twenty years **because it is recognised that third parties should not knowingly frustrate orders of the court *whether made inter partes or contra mundum:*** see eg *Att-Gen v Punch Ltd* [2003] 1 AC 1046 at [32]. The primary relief will usually have been obtained against a party who, it is anticipated, will otherwise infringe the claimant's rights. **It is not desirable that this remedy should be sought as matter of formality, while depending primarily on the ancillary Spycatcher doctrine**—salutary though it is.

78. Some effort should be made to trace and serve the primary wrongdoer. If appropriate, advantage can be taken of the provisions of **CPR 6.8 for service by an alternative method (formerly "substituted service").** Otherwise, the litigation will go to sleep indefinitely, which is hardly consistent with the policy underlying the CPR, and what is supposed to be a temporary holding injunction becomes a substitute for a full and fair adjudication.

79. In some cases, and this would appear to be an example, **it would be appropriate to direct *that best endeavours* be used to trace and serve the individual concerned.** How could that be achieved in circumstances such as these? As I mentioned at [2] above, it appears that so far the Claimants have whittled down in their own minds the field of suspects to about 20 of their acquaintances who are likely to know at least some of the relevant information. It has been suggested that they should therefore serve all of those potential "suspects". That is all very well from the point of view of the media, but it is a rather scattergun approach and may be counter-productive for these Claimants. **It may alienate people unnecessarily and alert interest in their difficulties among some who had not been aware of them.**

80. There may be a **half way house available, in the sense that they may be able to approach some friends, tell them that someone has been trying to sell information to the newspapers about their domestic circumstances, and enquire if they have any idea who the culprit could be.** This might help **narrow** the field to some extent. Much will depend on the individuals concerned and such an approach may not yield dividends. What would be the most appropriate "best endeavours" will inevitably have to be tailored to the circumstances by those best qualified to judge (ie in this instance X and Y).

81. I referred earlier to the proposal for a ***confidential schedule* identifying the specific information or categories of information intended to be the subject of restriction.** This is becoming standard practice and it recognises the need for certainty. A loosely worded injunction is no use to a claimant, since the court will be reluctant to enforce by process of **contempt** if it clearly cannot be established that its terms have been infringed: see eg *Redwing Ltd v Redwing Forest Products Ltd* [1947] 64 RPC 67, 71 and *Att.-Gen. v Greater Manchester Newspapers Ltd* [2001] All ER (D) 32 (Dec).

82. There is **a particular need for specificity in this type of case** because **the scope of the legal protection for Article 8 rights is itself somewhat uncertain**, and in a state of apparent development at the moment. The nature of the information so protected will also vary from case to case, depending on such factors as I have been considering. Whereas it may not be too difficult, in a defamation context, to construe "the said or any similar words defamatory of the Claimant", **it is much more problematic to ascertain in relation to particular individuals what information is or is not, for example, "subject to a duty of confidence", or "is not in the public domain",** or in respect

of which there remains **"a reasonable expectation of privacy".** Hence the need to identify it clearly in the order (preferably having afforded a **reasonable opportunity** to hear submissions from any persons with a **legitimate interest** in the outcome).

83. Having regard not only to s 12 of the Human Rights Act, but also to the need for "**necessity**" and "**proportionality**" whenever the court is **contemplating a restriction on anyone's freedom of expression**, it is important for an advocate making submissions, and to the court itself, to have enough information on which to decide whether any proposed restriction fulfils those criteria. Thus, where a claimant anticipates, on the basis of evidence adduced**, that a particular person is likely to reveal only limited facts or make specific assertions, it would be *in*appropriate to hack away more broadly at his or anyone else's freedom to communicate** than is necessary to prevent those identifiable revelations. It would not be right to wield an axe where a scalpel would do.

Confidential schedule

84. In the course of correspondence and submissions, with a certain amount of give and take, a **confidential schedule** has emerged which complies with these objectives. It pinpoints effectively the relatively few items of information which are alleged (whether accurately or not) to be the immediate causes of, or to have contributed to, the marital difficulties. There is no real problem for any journalist or media lawyer served with such an order in identifying these **"hot spots"** and avoiding any such coverage if someone tries to sell a story encroaching upon them.

M v Secretary of State for Work and Pensions [2006] UKHL 11

83. My Lords, in my opinion that is not the effect of the Strasbourg case law which I have attempted to summarise. The ECHR has taken a more nuanced approach, reflecting the unique feature of article 8 to which I have already drawn attention: that it is concerned with the failure to accord respect. To criminalise any manifestation of an individual's **sexual** orientation plainly fails to respect his or her private life, even if in practice the criminal law is not enforced (Dudgeon; Norris); so does **intrusive** interrogation and humiliating discharge from the armed forces (Smith and Grady; Lustig-Prean and Beckett). Banning a former KGB officer from all public sector posts, and from a wide range of responsible private-sector posts, is so draconian as to threaten his leading a normal personal life (Sidabras and Dziautas). Less

serious interference would not merely have been a breach of article 8; it would not have fallen within the ambit of the article at all.

"In R v G [2008] 1 WLR 1379 at para 54, Baroness Hale said that Article 8 does not mean 'that every **sexual relationship**, however brief or unsymmetrical is worthy of respect, nor is every **sexual** act which a person wishes to perform' [although this approach does not seem to have been supported by other members of the House]."

Associated Newspapers Ltd v HRH Prince of Wales [2006] EWCA Civ 1776

Approach to the law

28. This action is not concerned, however, with **a claim for breach of privacy** that involves an extension of the old law of breach of confidence. There is an issue in this case as to whether the information disclosed was private so as to engage Article 8 and there is an obvious **overlap** between this question and the question of whether the information was capable of being the subject of a duty of confidence under the old law. Assuming that it was, there are in this action all the elements of a claim for breach of confidence under that law. The information was disclosed **in breach of a well recognised relationship of confidence, that** which exists between master and servant. Furthermore, **the disclosure was in breach of an express contractual duty of confidentiality.** The Newspaper was aware that the journals were disclosed in breach of confidence.

29. Article 10.2 provides that the freedom to receive and impart information and ideas 'may be subject to such formalities, restrictions or penalties as are prescribed by law and necessary in a democratic society for preventing the disclosure of information received in confidence'. **Information received in confidence may not be of such a nature as to engage Article 8. A trade secret will not necessarily do so.** Thus the Convention recognises that it may be necessary in a democratic society to give effect to a duty of confidence in the old sense at the expense of freedom of expression.

. . .

36. It is not easy in this case, as in many others, when concluding that information is private to identify the extent to which this is because of the nature of the information, the form in which it is conveyed and the fact that the person disclosing it was in a confidential **relationship** with the person to whom it relates. Usually, as here, these factors form an interdependent amalgam of circumstances. **If, however, one strips out the fact of breach of a confiden-**

tial relationship, and assumes that a copy of the Journal had been brought to the Newspaper by someone who had found it dropped in the street, we consider that its form and content would clearly have constituted it private information entitled to the protection of Article 8(1) as qualified by Article 8(2).

. . .

48. **We do not believe that Lord Hoffman intended to suggest that the fact that information has been disclosed in breach of the duties of good faith that arise in a relationship of trust and confidence is irrelevant when considering the balance between the requirements of Article 8 and Article 10.** In that case the press had been informed of Ms Campbell's treatment **as a result of a breach of confidence,** either on the part of a fellow participant at meetings of Narcotics Anonymous or on the part of one of her staff or entourage. But the House of Lords did not have to consider the extent to which this weighed in the balance to be struck between Article 8 and Article 10 rights. It was common ground that, had Ms Campbell not herself put her experience of drugs into the **public domain**, all the information published would have constituted an interference with her Article 8 rights which was not justified by Article 10 considerations."

The impact of Article 10 on an action for breach of confidence

51. Where the published information invades an individual's right of privacy, as protected by Article 8, the court gives careful consideration to whether the information is **truly of public interest rather than of interest to the public.** Thus in *Von Hannover v Germany* (2005) 40 EHRR 1 the Court observed at paragraph 63:

> "The Court considers that a fundamental distinction needs to be made between reporting facts—even controversial ones—capable of contributing to a **debate** in a democratic society relating to **politicians** in the exercise of their functions, for example, and reporting details of the private life of an individual who, moreover, as in this case, does not exercise official functions. While in the former case the press exercises its vital role of '**watchdog**' in a democracy by contributing to 'impart[ing] information and ideas on matters of public interest' it does not do so in the latter case."

[This is an example of the policy of the courts that it does not follow from the fact that the public is interested in the information that the disclosure of that information is in the public interest.]

52. In *In re S (a child)* [2004] UKHL 47; [2005] 1 AC 593 Lord Steyn, in a speech with which the other members of the House concurred, deduced the following principles from the decision of the House in *Campbell v MGN* :

> "**First**, neither article has as such precedence over the other. **Secondly**, where the values under the two articles are in conflict, an intense focus on the comparative importance of the specific rights being claimed in the individual case is necessary. **Thirdly**, the justifications for interfering with or restricting each right must be taken into account. **Finally**, the proportionality test must be applied to each."

. . .

[NB: paras 64–69 suggest balancing exercise even if Art 8 and/or Art 10 not caught—but cf speeches of HL in ***OBG v Allan*** [2008] 1 AC 1 per Clayton: the speeches in the HL might arguable be read as taking a more traditional approach where commercial confidence as opposed to privacy is at issue.]

Discussion

64. In *Hosking v Runting* [2004] NZCA 34 the Court of Appeal of New Zealand suggested that there were now in English law two quite distinct versions of the tort of breach of confidence.

> "**One** is the long-standing cause of action . . . under which remedies are available in respect of use or disclosure where the information has been communicated in confidence. Subject to possible '**trivia**' exceptions and to public interest (**iniquity**) defences, those remedies are available irrespective of the 'offensiveness' of the disclosure. The **second** gives a right of action in respect of publication of personal information of which the subject has a reasonable expectation of privacy irrespective of any burden of confidence"

65. Time has moved on since that judgment, which was delivered in March 2004 and its **summary of the position under English law can be seen to be inaccurate.** Whether a publication, or threatened publication, involves a breach of a **relationship** of confidence, an interference with privacy or both, **it is necessary to consider whether these matters justify the interference with Article 10 rights that will be involved if the publication is made the subject of a judicial sanction**. A balance has to be struck. Where no breach of a confidential **relationship** is involved, that balance will be between Article 8 and Article 10 rights and will usually involve **weighing the nature and consequences of the breach of privacy** against the **public interest,** if any, in the disclosure of private information.

66. What is the position where the disclosure relates to **'information received in confidence'**? The authors of *The Law of Privacy and the Media* in their Second Supplement at 6.111 express the view that it would be surprising if this consideration was ignored. We agree. It is a factor that Article 10(2) recognises is, of itself, capable of justifying restrictions on freedom of expression.

67. There is an **important *public interest* in the observance of *duties of confidence.*** Those who engage employees, or who enter into other **relationships** that carry with them a duty of confidence, ought to be able to be **confident that they can disclose, without risk of wider publication, information that it is legitimate for them to wish to keep confidential.** Before the Human Rights Act came into force the circumstances in which the public interest in publication overrode a duty of confidence were very limited. The issue was whether exceptional circumstances justified disregarding the confidentiality that would otherwise prevail. **Today the test is different.** It is whether a fetter of the right of freedom of expression is, in the particular circumstances, 'necessary in a democratic society'. **It is a test of proportionality. *But a significant element to be weighed in the balance is the importance in a democratic society of upholding duties of confidence that are created between individuals.*** It is not enough to justify publication that the information in question is a matter of public interest. To take an extreme example, the content of a budget speech is a matter of great public interest. But if a disloyal typist were to seek to sell a copy to a newspaper in advance of the delivery of the speech in Parliament, there can surely be no doubt that the newspaper would be in breach of duty if it purchased and published the speech.

68. For these reasons, **the test** to be applied when considering whether it is necessary to restrict freedom of expression in order to prevent disclosure of information **received in confidence** is not simply whether the information is a matter of public interest but whether, in all the circumstances, **it is in the public interest that the duty of confidence should be breached**. The court will need to consider whether, having regard to the nature of the information and all the relevant circumstances, it is legitimate for the owner of the information to seek to keep it confidential or whether it is in the **public interest** that the information should be made public.

69. In applying the test of proportionality, the nature of the relationship that gives rise to the duty of confidentiality may be important. Different views have been expressed as to whether the fact that there is an express contractual obligation of confidence affects the weight to be attached to the duty of confidentiality. In *Campbell v Frisbee* [2002] EWCA Civ 1374; [2003] ICR 141 at paragraph 22 this court drew attention to this conflict of view, and commented:

> "We consider that it is arguable that a **duty of confidentiality** that has been expressly assumed **under contract** carries **more weight,** when balanced against the right of freedom of expression, than a duty of confidence that is not buttressed by express agreement"

We adhere to this view. But the extent to which a contract adds to the weight of duty of confidence arising out of a confidential **relationship** will depend upon the facts of the individual case.

. . .

Conclusions

70. The information at issue in this case is private information, public disclosure of which constituted an interference with Prince Charles' Article 8 rights. As heir the throne, Prince Charles is an important **public figure**. In respect of such persons the public takes an interest in information about them that is **relatively trivial.** For this reason public disclosure of such information can be particularly **intrusive**. The judge rightly had regard to this factor when he said at paragraph 133:

> "Not the least of the considerations that must be weighed in the scales is the claimant's countervailing claim to what was described in argument as '**his private space**': the right to be able to commit his **private thoughts** to writing and keep them private, the more so as he is inescapably a **public figure** who is subject to constant and intense media interest. **The fact that the contents of the Hong Kong Journal are not at the most intimate end of the privacy spectrum does not, to my mind, lessen the force of this countervailing claim.** The claimant is as much entitled to enjoy confidentiality for his **private thoughts** as an aspect of his own '**human autonomy and dignity**' as is any other."

Douglas v Hello! [2007] UKHL 21

LORD HOFFMANN

My Lords,

The three appeals

1. These three appeals are principally concerned with claims in tort for economic loss caused by intentional acts

(a) . . .

(b) In *Douglas v Hello! Ltd* the magazine *OK! [2006] QB 125* contracted for the exclusive right to publish **photographs** of a **celebrity** wedding at which all other photography would be forbidden. The rival magazine *Hello!* published **photographs** which it knew to have been **surreptitious**ly **taken by an unauthorised photographer pretending to be a waiter or guest.** OK! says that this was interference by unlawful means with its contractual or business relations **or a breach of its equitable right to confidentiality in photographic images of the wedding.**

(c) . . .

. . .

Douglas v Hello! Ltd.

108. Northern & Shell plc publishes *OK!* magazine and I shall refer to it as *OK!*. In November 2000 *OK!* entered into a contract with Michael Douglas and Catherine Zeta-Jones, whom I shall call "the Douglases", for the exclusive right to publish **photographs** of their forthcoming wedding on 18 November 2000 at the Plaza Hotel, New York. The Douglases dealt with *OK!*, **who paid them £1m for the rights, in preference to the rival magazine Hello!, published by the respondent.** The Douglases agreed to engage a photographer and to supply *OK!* with pictures they had chosen. **By clause 6 of the agreement they agreed to use their best efforts to ensure that no one else would take any photographs.**

109. The Douglases went to some lengths to comply with this obligation and no criticism is made of their security precautions, but a freelance photographer named Rupert Thorpe infiltrated the wedding and took **photographs** which he sold to *Hello!*. *OK!* obtained an ex parte injunction restraining publication by *Hello!* but on 23 November 2000 the injunction was discharged by the Court of Appeal and the **photographs** were published on the following day. A few hours earlier on the same day *OK!* published its own **photographs**, having brought forward its date of publication on account of what it knew to be the imminent publication by *Hello!* Also on the same day, some of the unauthorized pictures were, without objection by *Hello!*, published in national daily newspapers.

110. **OK! sued Hello! for breach of confidence and for the tort of causing loss by unlawful means.** (The Douglases brought separate proceedings against *Hello!* and recovered modest damages, but these are not in issue in this appeal, to which the Douglases are not parties.)

111. Lindsay J held *Hello!* liable for breach of confidence. He applied the well-known criteria summarized by Megarry J in *Coco v AN Clark (Engineers) Ltd* [1969] RPC 41, 47:

> "**First,** the information itself . . . must 'have the necessary **quality of confidence** about it. **Secondly**, that information must have been imparted in circumstances importing an obligation of confidence. **Thirdly**, there must be an unauthorised use of that information to the detriment of the party communicating it."

112. For this **purpose** the judge identified the information as being photographic images of the wedding. **Not information about the wedding generally; anyone was free to communicate the information that the Douglases had been married, describe what the bride wore and so forth.** The claim was

only that there had been a breach of an obligation of confidence in respect of photographic images.

113. Lindsay J held that the **three conditions were satisfied**. As for the **first**, **photographs** of the wedding were **confidential information** in the sense that **none were publicly available**. As to the **second**, the Douglases had **made it clear** that anyone admitted to the wedding was not to make or communicate photographic images. They allowed people to witness their marriage, **but only on the basis that the information which the spectators thereby obtained was not communicated in the form of a photographic image.** The judge said (at para 197):

> "the very facts that *Hello!* and *OK!* competed for exclusivity as they did and that each was ready to pay so much for it **points to the commercial confidentiality of coverage of the event**. The event was private in character and the **elaborate steps** to exclude the uninvited, to include only the invited, **to preclude unauthorized photography, to control the authorized photography** and to have had the claimants' intentions in that regard **made clear** all conduce to that conclusion. Such images as were, so to speak, radiated by the event were imparted to those present, including Mr Thorpe and his camera, in **circumstances importing an obligation of confidence**. Everyone there knew that was so."

114. Furthermore, everyone knew that the obligation of confidence was imposed for the benefit of *OK!* as well as the Douglases. To no one could this have been clearer than to Mr Thorpe. The judge then went on to make findings about the circumstances in which *Hello!* had acquired his **photographs**:

> "198. As for the *Hello!* defendants, their consciences were, in my view, tainted; they were **not acting in good faith nor by way of fair dealing.** Whilst their position might have been worse had I held that the taking of unauthorised pictures for use by them had been truly commissioned in advance, even without that there is in my view enough to afflict their conscience. **They knew that OK! had an exclusive contract;** as persons long engaged in the relevant trade, they **knew what sort of provisions any such contract** would include and that it would include provisions intended to preclude **intrusion** and unauthorised photography. Particularly would that be so where, as they **knew, a very considerable sum** would have had to have been paid for the exclusive rights which had been obtained. . . . **The surrounding facts were such that a duty of confidence should be inferred from them**. The *Hello!* defendants had indicated to paparazzi in advance that they would pay well for **photographs** and **they knew the reputation of the paparazzi** for being able to intrude. The unauthorised pictures themselves plainly indicated they were taken **surreptitious**ly. Yet these defendants **firmly kept their**

eyes shut lest they might see what they undeniably knew would have become apparent to them."

115. The **obligation of confidence** was therefore **binding upon Hello!** and the third *Coco* requirement of use to the detriment of *OK!* was plainly satisfied. Lindsay J therefore decided that *Hello!* was liable to *OK!* for the loss caused by the publication, which he later assessed at £1,033,156.

116. The Court of Appeal (Lord Phillips of Worth Matravers MR, Clarke and Neuberger LJJ) reversed the judge's **decision on the ground that the obligation of confidence for the benefit of OK! attached only to the photographs which the Douglases authorized them to publish**. They did not have the benefit of an obligation of confidence in respect of any other **photographs**. **Their publication may have invaded a residual right of privacy retained by the Douglases but did not infringe any right of OK!**

117. *In my opinion Lindsay J was right*. The point of which one should never lose sight is that OK! had paid **£1m for the benefit of the obligation of confidence** imposed upon all those present at the wedding in respect of *any* **photographs** of the wedding. That was quite clear. Unless there is some conceptual or policy reason why they should not have the benefit of that obligation, I cannot see why they were not entitled to enforce it. And in my opinion there are no such reasons. **Provided that one keeps one's eye firmly on the money and why it was paid, the case is, as Lindsay J held, quite straightforward.**

118. It is first necessary to avoid being distracted by the concepts of privacy and personal information. **In recent years, English law has adapted the action for breach of confidence to provide a remedy for the unauthorized disclosure of personal information**: see *Campbell v MGN Ltd [2004] 2 AC 457*. This development has been mediated by the analogy of the right to privacy conferred by article 8 of the European Convention on Human Rights and has required a balancing of that right against the right to freedom of expression conferred by article 10. **But this appeal is not concerned with the protection of privacy.** Whatever may have been the position of the Douglases, who, as I mentioned, recovered damages for an invasion of their privacy, **OK!'s claim is to protect commercially confidential information and nothing more.** So your Lordships need not be concerned with Convention rights. *OK!* has no claim to privacy under article 8 nor can it make a claim which is parasitic upon the Douglases' right to privacy. The fact that the information happens to have been about the personal life of the Douglases is irrelevant. It could have been information about anything that a newspaper was willing to pay for. What matters is that the Douglases, by the way they arranged their wedding, **were in a position to impose an obligation of confidence. They were in control of the information.**

119. Is there any conceptual problem about the fact that the obligation of confidence was imposed only in respect of a particular form of information, namely, photographic images? I do not see why there should be. If *OK!* was willing to pay for the right to be the only source of that particular form of information and did not mind that others were free to communicate other forms of information about the wedding, then I think the Douglases should be able to impose a suitably limited obligation of confidence.

120. My noble and learned friends, Lord Nicholls of Birkenhead and Lord Walker of Gestingthorpe, are troubled by the fact that the information in the photographic images was not intended to be kept secret but to be published to the world by *OK!* and was so published at much the same time as the unauthorised **photographs** in *Hello!*. **But I see no reason why there should not be an obligation of confidence for the purpose of enabling someone to be the only source of publication if that is something worth paying for**. Why should a newspaper not be entitled to impose confidentiality on its journalists, sub-editors and so forth to whom it communicates information about some scoop which it intends to publish next day? That does not of course prevent publication by someone who receives the information otherwise than under an obligation of confidence. **And I say nothing about cases in which there is a public interest in communicating the information to others or the public at large.** But otherwise it is simply information of commercial value.

121. My noble and learned friend, Lord Nicholls, is also of opinion that once the approved **photographs** were published, the publication of the unauthorised **photographs** was not a breach of confidence. I cannot understand this. **Mr Thorpe was subject to an obligation of confidence in respect of the pictures which he took. Hello!, by reason of the circumstances in which they acquired the pictures, were subject to the same obligation. How could it be destroyed by OK!'s publication of other photographs a few hours earlier?** He says that the differences between the **photographs** were "insufficiently significant to call for legal protection"; "the unapproved pictures contained nothing not included in the approved pictures".

122. My Lords, it is certainly the case that once information gets into the **public domain**, it can no longer be the subject of confidence. Whatever the circumstances in which it was obtained, there is no point in the law providing protection. But whether this is the case or not depends on the nature of the information. **Whether there is still a point in enforcing the obligation of confidence depends on the facts.** If the **purpose** of publishing the pictures was simply to convey the information that the Douglases had married, the bride wore a wedding dress and so forth, then the publication of any **photographs** would have put that information in the **public domain**. So would a description of the event. In this case, however, **the point of the transaction**

was that each picture would be treated as a separate piece of information which OK! would have the exclusive right to publish. The pictures published by *OK!* were put into the **public domain** and it would have had to rely on the law of copyright, not the law of confidence, to prevent their reproduction. But no other pictures were in the **public domain** and they did not enter the **public domain** merely because they resembled other pictures which had. **Why was Hello! willing to pay Mr Thorpe so much money for information which was already in the public domain?** Why did the judge find that the publication of information which did not, in Lord Nicholls's words, "call for legal protection", had caused substantial financial loss to *OK!*? My Lords, this seems to me a point on which theory is in danger of losing touch with reality.

123. The Court of Appeal's analysis, which treats the obligation of confidence as having been imposed in favour of *OK!* only in respect of the **photographs** with which it was supplied by the Douglases, also **seems to me to make no commercial sense.** The essential **purpose** of the security arrangements and the prohibition of unauthorised photography **were to impose an obligation of confidence in respect of any pictures of the wedding.** Only in that way could the commercial interests of *OK!* be protected. And it was clear to everyone, Mr Thorpe and Senor Sanchez Junco in particular, that this obligation was imposed for the benefit of *OK!* as well as the Douglases. As the Court of Appeal put it when stating OK's argument, ([2006] QB at para 138) **"the photographs published by Hello! fell within a generic class of commercially confidential information . . . which OK! were entitled to protect".**

124. Is there any reason of public policy why the law of confidence should not protect information of this form and subject-matter? There is in my opinion no question of creating an "image right" or any other unorthodox form of intellectual property. **The information in this case was capable of being protected, not because it concerned the Douglases' image any more than because it concerned their private life, but simply because it was information of commercial value over which the Douglases had sufficient control to enable them to impose an obligation of confidence**. Some may view with distaste a world in which information about the events of a wedding, which Warren and Brandeis in their famous article on privacy in (1890) 4 Harvard LR 193 regarded as a paradigm private occasion, should be sold in the market in the same way as information about how to make a better mousetrap. **But being a celebrity or publishing a celebrity magazine are lawful trades and I see no reason why they should be outlawed from such protection as the law of confidence may offer.**

125. **I therefore think that the Court of Appeal was wrong to reverse the judge on this point**. Mr Price QC, who appeared for *Hello!*, also relied upon two other arguments. First, he said that to hold that participants in a "**celebrity**

event" can impose a duty of confidence upon those who attend would give rise to inconsistency with the "carefully constructed" scheme of statutory performing rights in Part II of the Copyright, Designs and Patents Act 1988. I cannot see how there can be a conflict between such statutory rights and any additional rights which may exist under the common law. One might as well say that the law of contract is inconsistent because it allows for the possibility of a performer bargaining for greater rights than he would have under the statute.

. . .

127. **I would therefore allow the appeal of OK! and restore the order of the judge**. Mr Price submitted that the award of damages should not be allowed in full because, on the evidence, a substantial part of the loss was caused by the publication of the unauthorized **photographs** in national daily newspapers rather than in *Hello!* But the judge considered this point in his supplemental judgment on damages and came to the conclusion that **the full losses were "sufficiently consequential upon the breach and sufficiently foreseeable as to make Hello! liable for them in the ordinary way"** (paragraph 48). Further, in paragraph 53 he said that —

> "I do not regard the newspaper publications of the pictures as so remote a consequence of Hello!'s publication as not to be laid at Hello!'s door and plainly the newspaper publications would not have occurred as they did but for Hello!'s publication of the unauthorized **photographs**."

128. In the light of these findings of fact I would not disturb the judge's award.

. . .

LORD NICHOLLS OF BIRKENHEAD

Confidential information

255. As the law has developed breach of confidence, or misuse of **confidential information**, now covers two distinct causes of action, protecting two different interests: privacy, and secret ('confidential') information. It is important to keep these two distinct. In some instances information may qualify for protection both on grounds of privacy and confidentiality. In other instances information may be in the **public domain**, and not qualify for protection as confidential, and yet qualify for protection on the grounds of privacy. Privacy can be invaded by further publication of information or **photographs** already disclosed to the public. Conversely, and obviously, a trade secret may be protected as **confidential information** even though no question of personal privacy is involved. This distinction was recognised by the Law Commission in its report on Breach of Confidence (1981) Cmnd 388, [1981] EWLC 110, pages 5–6.

. . .

BARONESS HALE OF RICHMOND

My Lords,

302. I have read your lordships' opinions with admiration. On many issues, in particular the general shape of the economic torts, there is complete agreement. On three issues, there is disagreement**. On two of these, I agree with the conclusions and reasoning of my noble and learned friend, Lord Hoffman**n: these are "what should count as unlawful means" in the tort of causing economic loss by unlawful means **and "what should count as a secret" in the law of breach of confidence.** On the third issue, the application of the tort of conversion to contractual rights of action, I agree with the conclusions and reasoning of my noble and learned friend, Lord Nicholls of Birkenhead.

303. **On the first two issues, Lord Hoffmann's view is shared by a majority.** The least said by the rest of us who take the same view, therefore, the better. There should be no doubt, and no room for argument, about what has been decided and why. Any perceived inconsistency between what I say and what he says is to be resolved in favour of the latter. Indeed, there would be much to be said for our adopting the practice of other supreme courts in having a single majority opinion to which all have contributed and all can subscribe without further qualification or explanation. There would be less grist to the advocates' and academics' mills, but future litigants might thank us for that.

. . .

307. **Commercial confidentiality is a different matter.** It is moving forward rather than drawing back. The law took a big leap forward with the *Spycatcher* case (*Attorney-General v Guardian Newspapers Ltd [1990] 1 AC 109*). It was, incidentally, a leap which would have been impossible had the Law Commission's Report on *Breach of Confidence* (1981, Law Com No 110, *[1981] EWLC 110*) been implemented by statute. Rather as *Lumley v Gye* had expanded liability for breach of contract beyond the contract breaker to the person who persuaded him to break his contract**, Spycatcher expanded liability for failing to keep a secret beyond the person to whom it had originally been confided to the person who knowingly took advantage of the secret**. There are some secrets which the law will not protect. They may be so **trivial** or useless that the law should not concern itself with them. **There may be a public interest in disclosure greater than the private interest in secrecy.** But **we have not been given any principled reason why photographic images of this wedding should not be protected**. They were undoubtedly a secret unless and until *OK!* chose to publish the images authorised by the Douglases. *Hello!* **did its best to break what it knew was a secret.** There may not have been an

entirely identical case before but it is consistent with existing principles to apply them to this case, as the judge did. I confess to having some difficulty in understanding what this has to do with the law of intellectual property. Parliament has devised ways in which an author, inventor or creator can continue to profit from his creativity long after the product has passed into the **public domain**. Although in both cases the subject matter can be called information, **one set of remedies is about rewarding its creator, the other about keeping it quiet**. Parliament has intervened in the former but not the latter.

. . .

318. For these reasons, I would allow the appeals in the cases of OBG and OK! but, in agreement with all your lordships, I would dismiss the appeal in the Mainstream case.

LORD BROWN OF EATON-UNDER-HEYWOOD

My Lords,

319. I have had the privilege of reading in draft the opinions of my noble and learned friends, Lord Nicholls of Birkenhead, Lord Hoffman and Lord Walker of Gestingthorpe. All three agree on many of the issues arising in these appeals and where that is so I too agree. Where, however, they disagree—notably with regard to (i) the precise nature and ambit of the economic tort of causing loss by unlawful means, (ii) whether the tort of conversion should be extended to cover the appropriation of choses in action, and (iii) OK's claim based on confidentiality—I have come in the end to accept in each instance the reasoning and conclusions of Lord Hoffmann. I add only the following brief observations.

. . .

Confidentiality

323. The facts giving rise to the claim by OK! against Hello! are sufficiently summarised by Lord Hoffmann at paras 108–109 and by Lord Nicholls at paras 242–246 (and are to be found in altogether greater detail in the judgments below). **Nobody disputes that the Douglases were perfectly entitled, quite irrespective of any right of privacy, to sell the exclusive right to publish photographs of their wedding, and nobody doubts that the right was worth the £1m which OK! paid for it.** Indeed Hello! had earlier made an unsuccessful bid for the same right in the same sum. **It is no less plain that in publishing as they did the rogue photographs deceitfully taken by an infiltrator at the wedding, Hello! not only lent themselves to this outwitting of the strenuous efforts made by the Douglases to safeguard OK!'s exclusive but intentionally destroyed the very right itself.**

324. **The loss of their exclusive right cost OK! £1m; that was the judge's assessment of damages here and there are no good grounds for impugning it.** Hello!, however, contend that vis-à-vis OK! they committed no actionable wrong: **all is fair in love and war and so too, they submit, between publishers of celebrity magazines.** Spike your competitor's exclusive if you can and use whatever means you must.

325. If the law were indeed to sanction such an approach I for my part would regret it. Having paid £1m for an exclusive right it seems to me that OK! ought to be in a position to protect that right and to look to the law for redress were a third party intentionally to destroy it. Like Lord Hoffmann, I would uphold OK!'s claim, as Lindsay J did at first instance, on the ground of breach of confidence.

326. What is the information to which the confidence here attached? Plainly the information as to how the wedding looked—the photographic images which bring the event to life and make the viewer a virtual spectator at it. How can one doubt that this was commercially **confidential information** or, if one prefers, a trade secret? It was, after all, secret information for which OK! had been prepared to pay £1 million, in the expectation, obviously, that it was to remain secret until they chose to make use of it. And that is certainly how it would also have been perceived by Hello! (who had themselves hoped to acquire and exploit the secret in the same way).

327. **Like Lord Hoffmann I find the Court of Appeal's criticism of the judge at para 136 of their judgment unpersuasive.** I cannot agree that OK!'s complaint, properly analysed, is not about Hello!'s breach of their exclusive right to publish authorised **photographs** but rather that Hello! published images which no one had a right to publish and about which only the Douglases had a right to complain. This to my mind entirely overlooks that the Douglases had granted OK! the exclusive right to publish any photographic images of the wedding and had undertaken to do their best to ensure that no **photographs** were taken by anyone else so that nobody else would be in a position to defeat their exclusive right.

328. Assume, for example, that the Douglases were themselves magazine publishers and had wished to market the visual images of their wedding as an exclusive in their own magazine. Could it then be suggested that they had no right to complain against Hello! for behaving as they did here? Surely not. Or assume that the contract had stipulated that if other **photographs** of the wedding came to be published, the £1m paid by OK! (or, say, £½m) would be repayable. Would not the Douglases have been entitled to claim that loss against Hello! on the ground of breach of confidence? Why then not OK! too?

329. **The one hesitation I must own to having had with regard to the claim for**

breach of confidence concerns the situation which arises upon publication by OK! of the authorised photographs in pursuance of their exclusive right. At that moment, it may be suggested, the secret is out, the world now knows what the wedding looks like, and no commercial confidence remains to be protected. The answer, however, I am persuaded is this. **The secret consists no less of each and every visual image of the wedding than of the wedding as a whole**. Assume, for example, that OK! had chosen to publish **photographs** of the bride and groom in one issue, the guests in the next, and the presents later still. The confidence would, I think, continue throughout and I see no reason why at some point bootlegged **photographs** should suddenly become acceptable on the grounds that the look of the wedding was now in the **public domain** so that no confidentiality in its photographic image remained to be protected

Conclusion

330. It follows from all this that I too would dismiss the appeals respectively by OBG and by Mainstream Properties but allow the appeal by OK! on the ground of breach of confidence, reinstating Lindsay J's damages award accordingly.

Leeds City Council v Channel Four Television Corporation [2005] EWHC 3522

18. I am also very far indeed from persuaded that the law of confidence does not extend to the kind of situation with which I am here concerned. No doubt in its more recent extension into what for shorthand I will call the **commercial context**, the law of confidence **focuses upon the confidential *nature* of the particular information in question,** but there are many **relationships** or settings which have traditionally been accepted as giving rise to a duty of confidence irrespective of the particular nature of the information in issue; such obvious examples as the **doctor/patient**, the **lawyer/client** and the **banker/customer relationship** come readily to mind. **The class** of cases in which a claim in confidence can arise on that jurisprudential basis **is not, I believe, closed.** It seems to me highly arguable that the **relationship** of **parent or pupil and school** is such as in principle not merely engages Article 8 (as it undoubtedly does), but also in principle gives rise to **enforceable duties of confidentiality**. Of course, if a schoolchild goes to a school sports day or takes part in the Christmas nativity play or some other similar production it is probably the anticipation of both the pupil and the parent that the event may be filmed. It is not, however, I should have thought the normal expectation or assumption of either a pupil or a parent that the ordinary

school day will be **surreptitiously** filmed by an organ of the media. If, in the final analysis, the most convenient form of words to identify the touchstone of an enforceable duty of confidence is Lord Nicholls of Birkenhead's formulation in *Campbell v MGN Ltd.* [2004] UKHL 22, [2004] 2 AC 457, at paragraph [21], Was there a **"reasonable expectation of privacy"?** then I am inclined to think that the answer to that question in a case such as this is, in principle, yes.

. . .

24. **This being an interim hearing I have of course ultimately to direct myself by reference to section 12(3) of the Human Rights Act 1998. In other words,** Mr Hudson does not have to demonstrate, as he would at trial, that he does have a cause of action. He does not have to demonstrate, as he would at trial, that the balance will come down in favour of his clients. It suffices if he can demonstrate that it is **"likely"** that it will; likely for this **purpose** having the meaning given to it by the House of Lords in *Cream Holdings Ltd v Banerjee* [2004] UKHL 44, [2005] 1 AC 253.

25. The other matter which I have to take into account, again by reason of s 12 of the 1998 Act, is the **OFCOM Broadcasting Code,** that being the relevant **code** which governs Channel 4. My attention has been directed in particular to rr 8.1, 8.13, 8.20 and 8.21 of the **Code**. Summarising the matter shortly, these indicate that **surreptitious** filming is acceptable only where it is **'warranted',** and moreover that it will only be 'warranted' in that sense if a number of conditions set out in r 8.13 are met, including a requirement that there are **reasonable grounds to suspect** further material can be obtained by **surreptitious** filming, and most important of all that 'it is necessary to the **credibility** and **authenticity** of the program' that there be **surreptitious** filming. In other words, **surreptitious** filming is permissible in principle if, but only if, a **legitimate story** which is in the **public interest**—a requirement also spelled out in r 8.13—can be achieved only by means of **surreptitious** rather than open filming. Rule 8.20 directs broadcasters 'to pay particular attention to the **privacy of people** under 16'. Rule 8.2 specifically directs that where a program features an **individual under the age of 16** in a way that infringes privacy, consent 'must' be obtained from a parent, guardian or other person in loco parentis, and if possible the individual .concerned, and this is the important qualification, **unless the subject matter . . . is warranted to proceed without consent.**

. . .

32. I also accept that although the consequence of **obscuring** their faces is that the children will not be identifiable to the world at large, in the nature of things, since the schools are identified in the film, and since the relevant

classes are in some cases identified, eg Year 10, the **overwhelming probability is that many of the children who are shown on the film will be more or less readily identifiable and in fact identified by their school friends, their relations and people in their immediate locality**. This is an important factor which has to be fed into the Article 8 scale, because in so far as Article 8 protects privacy, the privacy is not merely privacy as against the world at large **it is also privacy as against particular sections of the world.**

33. As against all that there are, as I have indicated, very powerful public interests which are here engaged and which are protected by Article 10. This is **not** in my assessment, having seen it, a **trivialising** film whose **purpose** is merely prurient entertainment; it is a **serious documentary film** seeking in a serious, if nonetheless in many ways **shocking,** fashion to bring to public attention matters which ought to be of concern to many people.

. . .

35. The fact is that the particular problem which Channel 4, as it seems to me in the public interest, wishes to bring to the attention of the public is capable of being brought to public attention only if **surreptitious** methods are used. A school which is prepared, so it would seem, to **deceive OFSTED** is hardly going to allow itself to be filmed, warts and all, by a commercial broadcaster. One does not, I think, have to be unduly cynical to believe that a request for permission to film, even if that request had been granted, would have led to a presentation very different from that which in the event Channel 4 was able to obtain by **surreptitious** means.

36. Mr Hudson suggests that this, as I would see it pressing and important, public interest is not such as to justify, let alone require, the public broadcasting of the film. He says that if the objective of Channel 4 is to expose matters of concern then that can equally effectively be done by taking matters up with the appropriate authorities and without a public broadcast. That, as it seems to me, is to adopt an **unduly optimistic** view of the consequences which would be achieved if, without general publicity, there is a merely private disclosure to those directly concerned with what the film shows. Also, and perhaps more fundamentally, it seems to me to attach wholly insignificant weight to the importance in a democracy, as has been repeatedly pointed out both by the European Court of Human Rights in Strasbourg and by the highest tribunal in our Country, of an **investigative press** which in the public interest **exposes wrongdoing or incompetence by those public agencies who serve the citizen.**

. . .

39. At the end of the day, in my judgment, the balance comes down fairly heavily against granting the injunction. I attach considerable weight, as I have said,

to the circumstances in which the filming took place, to the fact that there is on the face of it a compelling case to be made that there was here, **absent lawful justification**, a breach of **privacy** and a breach of the duty of **confidentiality**. I attach more weight than Mr Nicklin would have me attach to the fact that the children, although **obscured**, are nonetheless highly likely to be identified by those who know them. I also, as I have made clear, proceed on the assumption that each of the children would vigorously resist the broadcasting of the film and will, as I have already said, feel **embarrassment**, **humiliation** and it may well be worse, if the film is broadcast.

. . .

46. Amongst the difficulties with that submission is this: in truth, since Mr Hudson explicitly disavowed any claim based upon particular damage to a child because of that child's particular circumstances, his arguments if good in relation to A and B must equally be good in relation to all the children who are the subject of the film. His case was not based upon specific problems in relation to either A or B. It was based upon the Convention rights of all the children, of whom A and B are merely examples. It seems to me wrong in principle, if that is the reality, to restrain the broadcasting of a film showing A and B but not the others, not X, Y and Z as it were, merely because A and B have commenced proceedings and X, Y and Z have not, in circumstances where had X, Y and Z also commenced proceedings they would, on Mr Hudson's argument, have been entitled to the same relief. Moreover, there is a further practical point**. If the principle once be established, as Mr Hudson would have me accept, that any child can obtain an injunction preventing the broadcasting of that child, what will there be to prevent X, Y, Z, D, E, F and G from making application tomorrow morning saying, in effect, well if the court has accepted that A and B are entitled to prevent their images being broadcast, then the same must go for any other claimant who—I do not put this pejoratively—seeks to climb on the bandwagon.**

WER v REW [2009] EWHC 1029 (QB) per Sir Charles Gray

1. Gross J on Friday evening granted an injunction after hearing argument over the telephone. He granted injunctive relief until 2.00pm this afternoon, Monday, 26 January 2009.
2. Mr Richard Spearman, QC, who represented the **anonymised** claimant and who has appeared before me today, indicated to the learned judge that the claimant's solicitors intended to serve copies of the injunction on the legal

representatives of a considerable number of **third-party media organisations.** I have been given the list of those media organisations; it seems to me to cover every single Sunday and national newspaper.

3. Gross J granted the injunction over the weekend in order to enable the anonymised **defendant to oppose the continuance of the injunction** today. I received earlier today an email from solicitors acting for the defendant saying they were not going to oppose the continuation of the injunction until trial or further order. Mr Lamont has been courteous enough to appear this afternoon but did not make any submissions.

4. However, that e-mail would not necessarily or invariably be an end of the matter. For a reason that I will explain, I invited Mr Spearman to come to court in order to **satisfy me that this is indeed a proper case for the grant of an injunction**. The facts are within a remarkably short compass. The defendant published on to its e-mail subscribers an item which referred to an unnamed person and to the effect than [sic] aspect of his family life might have on a member of his family.

5. Neither the claimant nor the member of his family was named in that publication. Having read paragraph 7 of Mr Spearman's skeleton argument, **I am prepared to accept that the claimant would be identifiable to some at least of those who read the item complained of in the defendant's e-mails.**

6. The potential problem, however, as it appeared to me, is a different one. The sting of the publication as regards the claimant is that he has or has had an **extra marital relationship**. In his **confidential statement** annexed to his witness statement, the claimant confines himself to saying:

> "**Irrespective of whether this claim is true or false, it is immensely damaging to myself and my family** for such a revelation to be published In the media."

7. Mr Spearman in his skeleton argument says, consistently with his client's witness statement, that the applicant has not advanced any case as to whether this information is **true or false.** Mr Spearman submits that such a stance is legitimate given what was said by the Court of Appeal in *McKennitt v Ash* [2007] 3 WLR 194 at paragraph 86:

> "**The question in a case of misuse of private information is whether the information is private not whether it is true or false.** The truth or falsity of the information is an *irrelevant inquiry* in deciding whether the information is entitled to be protected and judges should be chary of becoming side-tracked into that irrelevant inquiry."

8. I have to confess that at first blush I found it troubling that a judge should be asked to grant an injunction restraining not just the defendant publication but a whole number of other media organisations from publishing certain

information, **in complete ignorance whether the information is true or false** and in complete ignorance **of the extent to which the information, true or false, had entered the public domain.**

9. I readily accept that in *McKennitt* it was said by the Court of Appeal in broad terms **that truth or falsity is not an issue on an application for a privacy injunction**. I will assume, in favour of the present claimant, that the Court of Appeal in *McKennitt* would not have been critical of the claimant in that case if she had remained tight-lipped as to whether the information she was seeking to protect was true information. My recollection of that case is that the claimant did go into the truth or falsity of the information recounted by the defendant, albeit perhaps in the context of a public interest defence or an issue of hypocrisy rather than as an entitlement to a privacy injunction.

10. The point which troubles me, however, is a rather different one. **Suppose, for the sake of argument, that the allegation concerning the claimant is true.** Suppose further that he is **still married.** On those hypotheses, it appears to me that before continuing the injunction until trial or further order **it is legitimate for the court to enquire as to the extent to which the information sought to be protected by injunction had entered into the public domain.** I accept that information may **remain confidential** despite having become known to a significant number of people; **it is question of degree**. The problem, as I saw it on reading the papers, is that the court is being invited to interfere with the Article 10 rights of **a large number of media defendants in ignorance of what *might* be material facts.** In this connection it is material also to have in mind the provisions of section 12(3) and (4) of the Human Rights Act 1998.

11. In the present case, the claimant not only declined to tell the court whether the information is **true or false;** in addition **he has vouchsafed no information about the availability of the information he now seeks to injunct in particular about the availability of that information to the public.** I felt when I read the papers that a judge being invited to grant wide-ranging injunctive relief was entitled to look for rather greater candour than the claimant has displayed hitherto.

12. Mr Spearman is a considerable authority in this field. He has represented both defendants and claimants in many privacy cases. He has drawn my attention this afternoon to the **dilemma confronting claimants in many privacy cases**. The dilemma arises in this way: if a claimant comes clean, if I may use that expression, as to the truth or falsity of allegedly private information or at least gives some detail of the extent to which the information may be true information, then after having obtained and served his order on the media defendants, he is confronted with the provision to be found in CPR

part 25 Practice Direction at paragraph 9.2, which deals with the rights of non-parties on whom the claimant has served the injunction. It reads:

> **"Where such a person served with the order requests—**
>
> > **(1) a copy of any materials read by the judge, including material prepared after the hearing at the direction of the judge or in compliance with the order; or**
> >
> > **(2) a note of the hearing,**
>
> **the applicant, or his legal representative, must comply promptly with the request, unless the court orders otherwise."**

13. As Mr Spearman said, if the large number of media defendants who have been served with the injunction in the present case are to be made aware of the claimant's explanation as to the extent to which the information sought to be injuncted is true information or partially true information, **then those media non-parties are, naturally enough, going to make what they can of the information supplied to them.** True it is that the Practice Direction provides that the judge can "order otherwise" when it comes to the question whether the non-parties should be served with all the material placed before the judge including the claimant's witness statement. Mr Spearman submits that, if the Judge does so order, those served with the injunction may well realise that a judge has ordered otherwise and, at all events in a case such as the present, are likely to **smell a rat**. They will deduce that the information or some of it is true.

14. I am quite satisfied that Mr Spearman's decision to limit the information which he put before the court was a **proper exercise of discretion on his part as counsel** and that his reasons for taking that course were legitimate and not such as to deprive his client of an entitlement to the injunction which was granted by Gross J. I remain unhappy about the **invidious position** in which the judge is placed in having to decide whether to grant an injunction when he is, in effect, **blindfolded** as regards the facts of the case before him. However, for the reasons I have endeavoured to articulate and having heard Mr Spearman's explanation of the problems confronting privacy claimants such as the present claimant, I am satisfied that this is an injunction which should be continued until trial or further order. I repeat that Mr Lamont indicated that his **client did not oppose** the grant of an injunction and has not sought to resile from that position.

15. I should mention a further point which had been ventilated in the course of argument. It arises from the fact that it was, for obvious reasons, **always the intention of this claimant to serve notice of the injunction obtained against the defendant on a large number of media organisations.** One of those media organisations was Mirror Group Limited, publishers of the Daily

Mirror and Sunday Mirror. In consequence of being served with a copy of the order, Mr Marcus Partington on behalf of the Mirror Group emailed the solicitor representing the claimant in the present case asserting that Mirror Group should have been given notice of the hearing of the application for an injunction before Gross J on Friday. **He disputed Mr Spearman's assertion in the skeleton argument put before Gross J that it was unnecessary to serve any media defendant who had not, in one way or another, indicated an interest in the story.**

16. Mr Partington, understandably, placed reliance on what was said by Eady J in *X v Persons unknown* [2006] EWHC 2783 (QB), and in particular paragraph 18 of that judgment:

> "It is not for me to lay down practice directions, but what I can say is that a proper consideration for the Article 10 rights of media publishers, and indeed their rights under Article 6 as well, would require **that where a litigant intends to serve a prohibitory injunction upon one or more of them, in reliance on the Spycatcher principle, those individual publishers should be given a realistic opportunity to be heard on the appropriateness or otherwise of granting the injunction, and upon the scope of its terms**. As is well known, it is relatively easy for the media in such circumstances to instruct their lawyers to come to court at short notice and, if they are content to do so and no conflict arises, to arrange for common representation (just as, here, Mr Spearman represents the interests both of MGN and NGN)."

17. I should, for completeness, read paragraph 19 of Eady J's judgment as well:

> "The point of principle for which Mr Caldecott contends [I interpolate that Mr Caldecott was acting for one of the media defendants] can be encapsulated in the terms of the draft placed before the court for this hearing, which obviously mirrors closely the provisions contained in section 12 of the Human Rights:
>
> > 'A claimant, who applies for an interim order restraining a defendant from publishing allegedly private or **confidential information**, should give advance notice of the application and of the injunctive relief sought to any non-party on whom the claimant intends to serve the order so as to bind that party by application of the *Spycatcher* principle . . . unless:(a) The claimant has no reason to believe that the non-party has or may have an existing specific interest in the outcome of the application; or
> >
> > > (b) The claimant is unable to notify the non-party having taken all practicable steps to do so; or

(c) There are compelling reasons why the non-party should not be notified.'

It was no part of Mr Caldecott's case to argue that the injunction should be discharged altogether. As to that, he was neutral. His clients were only concerned to ensure that, in so far as the restrictions survive, they should be proportionate and not inhibit their freedom of communication beyond what the court believes necessary for the claimants' legitimate purposes. It is Mr Spearman who seeks to set the order aside in its entirety. To that I now turn."

18. I can well understand why Mr Partington read those words of Eady J as in effect obliging a claimant such as the present claimant **to notify in advance all those media defendants** intended to be served with the injunction. However, I have been provided today with information by Mr Spearman about the facts of *X v Persons unknown*. As is apparent from its title, it was a case where the claimants themselves were **unaware of the identity of the individual defendants** whom they sued. As I understand it, the claimants limited their notification of the application to non-parties to third-**party to a selected number who had shown some interest in the story**. In those circumstances, it appears to me (and I hope I do not misapprehend what the judge said) that Eady J cannot have been contemplating an obligation being imposed on individual claimants, who may be of limited means, to arrange through their legal advisers to serve what might be a substantial body of evidence on a large number of media non-parties. It seems to me that the obligation to serve them must, as a matter of common sense and economy, be **confined to those media organisations whom the claimant has reason to believe have displayed an interest** in publishing the story which the claimant is seeking to injunct.

19. **I direct there should be redacted from my judgment the quotation which I took from paragraph 6 of Mr Spearman's skeleton argument and, to make doubly sure, I also direct, in accordance with the Practice Direction quoted in the judgment, that in the event that any third-party seeks a copy of the judgment it should be supplied in that redacted form and not in its totality.**

Prince Radu of Hohenzollern v Houston [2007] EWHC 2735 (QB) per Eady J

11. Since the case was argued partly on **reportage** and partly on the basis of a more general **"public interest" defence**, it is right to have regard to two very recent decisions of the Court of Appeal (both presided over by Ward LJ)

which address these forms of privilege and the **relationship** between them. I have in mind *Roberts v Gable* [2007] EMLR 457 and *Charman v Orion Publishing Group* [2007] EWCA Civ 972. I should adhere to that guidance, while naturally applying the principles expounded to the circumstances of this particular case. It has been emphasised recently on a number of occasions that the courts should be "flexible" in their approach to privilege defences.

12. It is said, first, that the Claimant has fulfilled various public roles, both in Romania and internationally, so that the subject-matter of the allegation is of genuine public interest. In judging whether this is so, it would be right no doubt to have in mind not merely the **narrow** perspective of the **public interest** in this jurisdiction, but also the **international dimension.** As I suggested in *Lukowiak v Unidad Editorial SA* [2001] EMLR 46 at [45]–[46]:

> " . . . .In theory, it might be possible for the publishers and proprietors of a newspaper selling copies throughout Europe to take legal advice as to the defences available in each jurisdiction and the differences between them. Yet it is difficult to see how, if they were *required* to do so as a matter of law, this constraint could have other than a severely chilling effect on their freedom of expression.
>
> 46. Specifically when the courts in England have to consider whether a particular defendant had, or may have had, a duty (legal, social or moral) to publish the particular words complained of, it must surely be necessary to take into account the circumstances confronting a hypothetical defendant at or prior to publication. These would include circumstances applying outside this jurisdiction. It cannot be right, as a matter of principle, that the issue of duty should be judged by an English court on the hypothetical basis that the publication was only taking place in England and Wales. **The court is considering whether or not there is a duty to communicate the relevant information to the world at large; that is to say, to place it in the public domain generally**. It would not be appropriate to attempt to draw fine distinctions in such cases between duties that might be owed, for example with reference to one jurisdiction and not others. This international dimension would have to be borne in mind, or so it seems to me, when addressing most, if not all, of Lord Nicholls' ten non-exhaustive tests set out in *Reynolds v Times Newspapers Ltd* . . ."

13. The nature of the public roles carried out by the Claimant upon which the Defendants place particular reliance is pleaded on the basis of the letter before action dated 25 November 2004; that is to say, that he has held "meetings with the Prince of Wales, with Members of Parliament and members of the House of Lords, with representatives of the British-Romanian Chamber

of Commerce". That passage related to activities within this jurisdiction. It had also been explained that on a wider stage:

> "Our client has been appointed Special Representative of the Romanian Government for Integration, Co-operation and Sustainable Development, a post with ministerial rank, by the Romanian Government. In this capacity he works with the ministries of Integration and Foreign Affairs and other government institutions in, amongst other matters, promoting Romania's membership of the NATO and the European Union, encouraging foreign investment in Romania and promoting Romania's economic, commercial and business interests, culture and history. He is extremely concerned at the impact which the publication of these allegations might have on his work and **reputation**"

14. I have little doubt that the subject-matter of the article taken as a whole is of public interest. **It used to be said that the test to apply was whether or not it was in the public interest to publish the defamatory allegations about the claimant:** see eg *Blackshaw v Lord* [1984] QB 1. That is because it was thought necessary to focus on the tortious element of the publication. **More recently, however, it seems that the appropriate criterion is rather whether the subject-matter of the publication, more broadly, can be categorised as being of public interest. T**hen it becomes necessary to decide whether it is in the public interest for the allegations, **irrespective of their truth or falsity**, to be published to the world at large: see eg *Loutchansky v Times Newspapers Ltd (Nos. 2–5)* [2002] QB 783 at [41(iii)]. If it is, then there is deemed to be a duty so to publish: see eg *Jameel (Mohammed) v Wall Street Journal Europe* [2007] 1 AC 359 at [48]–[50]. When the court comes to the conclusion, in relation to the article as a whole, **that the public has a right to be told,** the specific inclusion in the story of the allegations about the claimant has to be assessed according to whether it was reasonable to include them as part of the overall picture: *ibid.* at [51]. **That is a different approach from the traditional one, at least in theory, since the court used to ask whether there was a duty to publish the defamatory words themselves**. In the present case, it makes no difference since the Claimant is at the heart of the story. Here, the defamatory allegations about him cannot be characterised as merely incidental to a wider theme.

15. **Lord Nicholls observed in Reynolds, the court should be slow to conclude that a publication was not in the public interest and any ongoing doubts should be resolved in favour of publication.**

16. Critical questions would appear to be whether the allegations are an example of "**responsible journalism**", appropriate to the gravity of the allegations and the circumstances in which the Defendants published them, and (as far

as the *reportage* defence is concerned) whether or not the Defendants were fairly and neutrally covering both sides of a debate or controversy.

The law of "reportage"

17. It is necessary to consider first the recent developments so far as *reportage* is concerned. It is interesting to note that in *Roberts v Gable* at [74] Sedley LJ warned that this defence **"needs to be treated restrictively".** In his view, it has had the effect of modifying the **repetition** rule, and that is the express reason he gave. It would be right, however, in this context to remember also that **in a true reportage case the journalist does not need to verify the allegations being reported.** Indeed, as Simon Brown LJ commented in *Al-Fagih v HH Saudi Research & Marketing (UK) Ltd* [2002] EMLR 13, the process of verification could be regarded as inconsistent with objective reporting. **That is because it is the accuracy (and balance) of the reporting which is important, rather than the accuracy of the underlying allegations.**

18. As it was put by Ward LJ at [61] in *Roberts v Gable*:

    "If upon a proper construction of the thrust of the article the defamatory material is attributed to another and is not being put forward as true, then a responsible journalist would not need to take steps to verify its accuracy. He is absolved from that responsibility because he is simply reporting in a neutral fashion the fact that it has been said without adopting the truth".

    One can well understand, against that background, why it was thought that the defence should be applied "restrictively". It is important to scrutinise the particular circumstances of each case to make sure that it is indeed an example of true *reportage*.

19. On the other hand, reliance on this form of privilege does not entail that any special "tone" needs to be adopted. As Sedley LJ made clear, **nothing in the law denies the reportage defence to a defendant who is "taking a perceptible pleasure" in reporting the controversy.**

20. Similarly, in *Roberts v Gable* itself, I had made the point that a journalist or publisher will not be deprived of such a defence merely by reason of having a particular personal or corporate political stance**. What is important is not so much the political stance of the defendant, but rather the way in which the particular dispute or controversy is being reported**. Thus, in the present case, even if Mr Houston happens to sympathise or agree with the case put forward in his article by the Hohenzollerns, that in itself would not deprive him of the opportunity to rely on a *reportage* defence. **All depends on whether the particular controversy is, notwithstanding his personal views, being fairly presented to the readers**. Naturally, **a journalist is entitled to take a particular stance, and indeed vigorously to advocate the merits of**

one side, in a public dispute. What he cannot do, however, is then to pray in aid the form of privilege known as reportage. As was said in *Charman* at [48]:

> **"The protection is lost if the journalist adopts what has been said and makes it his own or if he fails to report the story in a fair, disinterested, neutral way".**

21. Because the Court of Appeal in *Roberts v Gable* wished to arrive at its conclusions in the light of a thorough analysis of the law's recent developments, reference was made to broadly comparable American jurisprudence and, in particular, to the case of *Edwards v National Audubon Society* 556 F. 2d 113. I bear in mind that both Ward LJ (with whom Moore-Bick LJ expressed his agreement) and Sedley LJ sounded a "cautionary note" in relation to the principles there set out. As Sedley LJ commented:

> "Where rights to **reputation** and privacy have wilted somewhat in the bright light of First Amendment jurisprudence, the English common law, now reinforced by the European Convention on Human Rights, seeks to hold the two in a sometimes difficult balance, **calibrated by the concept of responsible journalism**".

It is nonetheless important to note that, even in the American context, it is a requirement of the *reportage* defence that the reporting of "charges", regardless of the reporter's private views as to their validity, must be "accurate and disinterested". Reference was also made to "the press's right of neutral *reportage*": see the citation in the judgment of Ward LJ at [45].

22. It was noted also (at [46]) that those criteria had been met in relatively few cases in the United States, since *Audubon*, and that "neutral reportage had, therefore, rarely been applied by the courts to immunise publication". It is thus reasonable to proceed on the basis that the courts in the United States, consistently with the remarks of Sedley LJ, have also approached this defence in a "restrictive" way.

. . .

The concept of "responsible journalism"

41. In the circumstances I must now turn to the alternative argument based on "**responsible journalism**" (as most recently explained in *Charman*).

42. The role of "**responsible journalism**" has been addressed more than once in recent years. I have already quoted Sedley LJ in *Roberts v Gable* at [75]:

> " . . . the English common law, now reinforced by the European Convention on Human Rights, seeks to hold . . . a sometimes difficult balance, calibrated by the concept of **responsible journalism**".

43. Lord Nicholls also explained the concept of "**responsible journalism**" in terms of trying to achieve an acceptable balance or reconciliation: see *Reynolds* at pp 200–201. On the one side, obviously, is freedom of speech and the corresponding right of the public to be told; **on the other, the reputation of the individual concerned.**

44. Now, perhaps, this tension would be expressed more overtly as being between competing Convention rights under Article 10 and Article 8, since it has subsequently been acknowledged in Strasbourg that the **protection of reputation** is one of the functions of Article 8: see eg *Radio France v France* (2005) 40 EHRR 29; *Lindon v France* [2007] ECHR 836. Be that as it may, Lord Nicholls went into some detail about the considerations to be put in the scales alongside freedom of speech, albeit without express reference to Article 8:

> "To be justified, any curtailment of freedom of expression must be **convincingly established** by a **compelling** countervailing consideration, and the **means employed must be proportionate to the end sought to be achieved.**
>
> "Likewise, there is no need to elaborate on the importance of the role discharged by the media in the expression and communication of information and comment on political matters. **It is through the mass media that most people today obtain their information on political matters**. Without freedom of expression by the media, freedom of expression would be a hollow concept. **The interest of a democratic society in ensuring a free press weighs heavily** in the balance in deciding whether any curtailment of this freedom bears a **reasonable relationship** to the **purpose of the curtailment**. In this regard it should be kept in mind that one of the contemporary functions of the media is **investigative journalism.** This activity, as much as the traditional activities of reporting and commenting, is part of the **vital role** of the press and the media generally.
>
> **"Reputation is an integral and important part of the dignity of the individual.** It also forms the basis of many decisions in a democratic society which are fundamental to its well-being: **whom to employ or work for, whom to promote, whom to do business with or to vote for.** Once besmirched by an unfounded allegation in a national newspaper, **a reputation can be damaged for ever,** especially if there is no opportunity to vindicate one's **reputation**. **When this happens, society as well as the individual is the loser.** For it should not be supposed that protection of **reputation** is a matter of importance only to the affected individual and his family. ***Protection of* reputation *is conducive to the public good.*** It is in the public interest that the **reputation** of **public**

figures should **not be debased falsely.** In the political field, in order to make an informed choice, the electorate needs to be able to identify the good as well as the bad. Consistently with these considerations, human rights conventions recognise that freedom of expression is not an absolute right. Its exercise may subject to such restrictions as are prescribed by law and are necessary in a democratic society for the protection of the **reputation**s of others."

OBG v Allan [2007] UKHL 81

118. It is first necessary to avoid being distracted by the concepts of privacy and personal information. In recent years, **English law has adapted the action for breach of confidence to provide a remedy for the unauthorized disclosure of personal information**: see *Campbell v MGN Ltd* [2004] 2 AC 457. This development has been mediated by the analogy of the right to privacy conferred by article 8 of the European Convention on Human Rights and has required a balancing of that right against the right to freedom of expression conferred by article 10. **But this appeal is not concerned with the protection of privacy.** Whatever may have been the position of the Douglases, who, as I mentioned, recovered damages for an invasion of their privacy, **OK!'s claim is to protect commercially confidential information and nothing more**. So your Lordships need **not** be concerned with Convention rights. **OK! has no claim to privacy under article 8 nor can it make a claim which is parasitic upon the Douglases' right to privacy**. ***The fact that the information happens to have been about the personal life of the Douglases is irrelevant.*** It could have been information about anything that a newspaper was willing to pay for. **What matters is that the Douglases, by the way they arranged their wedding, were in a position to impose an obligation of confidence. They were in control of the information.**

. . .

122. My Lords, it is certainly the case that once information gets into the **public domain**, it can no longer be the subject of confidence. **Whatever the circumstances in which it was obtained**, there is no point in the law providing protection. But whether this is the case or not **depends on the nature of the information**. Whether there is still a point in enforcing the obligation of confidence **depends on the facts.** If the **purpose** of publishing the pictures was simply to convey the information that the Douglases had married, the bride wore a wedding dress and so forth, then the publication of any **photographs** would have put that information in the **public domain**. So would a description of the event. In this case, however, **the point of the transaction was that**

each picture would be treated as a separate piece of information which OK! would have the exclusive right to publish. The pictures published by *OK!* were put into the **public domain** and **it would have had to rely on the law of copyright, not the law of confidence, to prevent their reproduction.** But no other pictures were in the **public domain** and they did not enter the **public domain** merely because they resembled other pictures which had. Why was *Hello!* willing to pay Mr Thorpe so much money for information which was already in the **public domain**? Why did the judge find that the publication of information which did not, in Lord Nicholls's words, "call for legal protection", had caused substantial financial loss to *OK!*? My Lords, this seems to me a point on which theory is in danger of losing touch with reality.

. . .

Confidential information

255. As the law has developed breach of confidence, or misuse of **confidential information**, **now covers two distinct causes of action**, protecting **two different interests**: **privacy,** and **secret ('confidential') information.** It is important to keep these two **distinct**. In some instances information may qualify for protection both on grounds of privacy and confidentiality. In other instances information may be in the **public domain,** and not qualify for protection as confidential, and yet qualify for protection on the grounds of privacy. **Privacy can be invaded by further publication of information or photographs already disclosed to the public.** Conversely, and obviously**, a trade secret may be protected as confidential information even though no question of personal privacy is involved**. This distinction was recognised by the Law Commission in its report on Breach of Confidence [1981] Cmnd 388, [1981] EWLC 110, pages 5–6.

R (Countryside Alliance) v A-G [2007] UKHL 52

116. As yet, however, as my noble and learned friend Lord Bingham of Cornhill has shown, the Strasbourg jurisprudence has not gone so far in its interpretation of the rights protected by article 8; and for the reasons given above, I am not sure that I share the desire of my noble and learned friend Lord Brown of Eaton-under-Heywood that it should. Article 8, it seems to me, reflects **two separate** but related fundamental values. **One** is the **inviolability of the home and personal communications** from official snooping, entry and interference without a very good reason. It protects a private space, whether in a building, or through the post, the telephone lines, the airwaves or the ether, within which people can both be themselves and communicate privately with

one another. **The other** is the inviolability of a different kind of space, the **personal and psychological space** within which each individual develops his or her own sense of self and **relationships** with other people. This is fundamentally what families are for and **why democracies value family life so highly.** Families are subversive. **They nurture individuality and difference.** One of the first things a totalitarian regime tries to do is to distance the young from the individuality of their own families and indoctrinate them in the dominant view. Article 8 protects the private space, **both physical and psychological**, within which individuals can develop and relate to others around them. But that falls some way short of protecting everything they might want to do even in that private space; and it certainly does not protect things that they can **only** do by leaving it and engaging in a very public gathering and activity.

Jameel and others v Wall Street Journal Sprl [2007] 1 AC 359

31. The necessary precondition of reliance on **qualified privilege** in this context is that the matter published should be one of **public interest.** In the present case the subject matter of the article complained of was of undoubted public interest. But that is not always, perhaps not usually, so. **It has been repeatedly and rightly said that what engages the interest of the public may not be material which engages the public interest.**

32. **Qualified privilege as a live issue only arises where a statement is defamatory and untrue.** It was in this context, and assuming the matter to be one of public interest, that Lord Nicholls proposed [in *Reynolds v Times Newspapers Ltd*], at p 202, a **test of responsible journalism**, a test repeated in *Bonnick v Morris* [2003] 1 AC 300, 309. The rationale of this test is, as I understand, that **there is no duty to publish and the public have no interest to read material which the publisher has not taken reasonable steps to verify**. As Lord Hobhouse observed with characteristic pungency, at p 238, 'No public interest is served by publishing or communicating misinformation.' **But the publisher is protected if he has taken such steps as a responsible journalist would take to try and ensure that what is published is accurate and fit for publication.**

33 **Lord Nicholls, at p 205, listed certain matters which might be taken into account in deciding whether the test of responsible journalism was satisfied.** He intended these as pointers which might be more or less indicative, depending on the circumstances of a particular case, and not, I feel sure,

as a series of hurdles to be negotiated by a publisher before he could successfully rely on qualified privilege. Lord Nicholls recognised, at pp 202–203, inevitably as I think, that it had to be a body other than the publisher, namely the court, which decided whether a publication was protected by qualified privilege. **But this does not mean that the editorial decisions and judgments made at the time, without the knowledge of falsity which is a benefit of hindsight, are irrelevant.** Weight should ordinarily be given to the **professional judgment of an editor or journalist** in the absence of some indication that it was made in a casual, cavalier, slipshod or careless manner."

. . .

The Reynolds defence

146. It should by now be entirely clear that the **Reynolds defence** is a "different jurisprudential creature" from the law of privilege, although it is a natural development of that law. **It springs from the general obligation of the press, media and other publishers to communicate important information upon matters of general public interest and the general right of the public to receive such information**. It is not helpful to analyse the particular case in terms of a specific duty and a specific right to know. That can, as experience since *Reynolds* has shown, very easily lead to a **narrow** and rigid approach which defeats its object. **In truth, it is a defence of publication in the public interest.**

147. This does not mean a free-for-all to publish without being damned. **The public only have a right to be told if two conditions are fulfilled. First**, there must be a **real public interest** in communicating and receiving the information. This is, as we all know, very different from saying that it is information which interests the public—the most vapid **tittle-tattle** about the activities of footballers' wives and girlfriends interests large sections of the public but no-one could claim any real public interest in our being told all about it. It is also different from the test suggested by Mr Robertson QC, on behalf of the Wall Street Journal Europe, of whether the information is "newsworthy". That is too subjective a test, based on the **target** audience, inclinations and interests of the particular publication. **There must be some real public interest in having this information in the public domain**. But this is less than a test that the public "need to know", which would be far too limited.

148. If ever there was a story which met the test, it must be this one. In the immediate aftermath of 9/11, **it was in the interests of the whole world that the sources of funds for such atrocities be identified and if possible stopped.** There was and should have been a lively public **debate** about this. Given the nationalities of the hi-jackers, this focussed particularly upon the efforts of the Saudi Arabian authorities. Anti-Saudi feeling was running high in some

places. Information that the Saudis were actively co-operating, not only with the United Nations, but also with the United States was of great importance to that debate. This was, in effect, a pro-Saudi story, but one which, for internal reasons, the Saudi authorities were bound to deny. Without names, its impact would be much reduced.

149. **Secondly,** the publisher must have taken the care that a **responsible publisher would take to verify** the information published. The actual steps taken will vary with the nature and sources of the information. But one would normally expect that the source or sources were ones which the publisher had good reason to think **reliable, that the publisher himself believed the information to be true, and that he had done what he could to check it.** We are frequently told that "fact checking" has gone out of fashion with the media. But a publisher who is to avoid the risk of liability if the information cannot later be proved to be true **would be well-advised to do it. Part** of this is, of course, **taking reasonable steps to contact the people named for their comments**. The requirements in "reportage" cases, where the publisher is simply reporting what others have said, may be rather different, but if the publisher does not himself believe the information to be true, he would be well-advised to make this clear. In any case, the tone in which the information is conveyed will be relevant to whether or not the publisher has behaved responsibly in passing it on.

150. Once again, as my noble and learned friend Lord Hoffmann has demonstrated, the publication of this story passed this test. We have to judge the steps which are known to have been taken against the background of the style and tone of the publication in general and the article in particular. This is not a newspaper with an interest in publishing any sensational information however inaccurate (or even in some cases invented). It is, as the journalist quoted by my noble and learned friend said, "gravely serious" (indeed some might find it seriously dull). We need more such serious journalism in this country and our defamation law should encourage rather than discourage it.

151 In short, My Lords, if the public interest defence does not succeed on the known facts of this case, it is hard to see it ever succeeding.

Lord Browne of Madingley v Associated Newspapers Ltd [2007] EWCA Civ 295

As to information to be gathered to test whether reasonable expectation of privacy see paras 24–37.

This judgment [Sir Anthony Clarke MR]

1. As is explained much more fully below, in these proceedings Lord Browne of Madingley seeks to enjoin on grounds of breach of confidence the publication by the *Mail on Sunday* of various items of information or allegations. The proceedings are still at an interlocutory stage, and Eady J, from whom the appeal is brought, was therefore constrained, as we are, by the rule in section 12(3) of the Human Rights Act 1998. We have concluded that Eady J was right in holding that the publication of some, but not all, of the matters alleged by the newspaper should not be enjoined. That means that in preparing our judgments explaining our decision we are constrained by various considerations.

2. **First**, the general rule is that hearings must be in public unless there is good reason to take another course: *Scott v Scott* [1913] AC 417, and CPR 39.2(2). In this case, in order to protect the subject-matter of the appeal until determination **we exercised the power given by CPR 39.2(3)(a) to sit in private,** as had the trial judge. And under the same rubric we have prepared, solely for the information of the parties and not for any further use, **a private judgment** that sets out in full the facts of the case and our conclusions on them.

3. **Second**, however, we now have to recognise the imperative of public justice and the need to explain the outcome of the appeal, while continuing to accord proper protection to the appellant until trial. In that connexion **it is clear that matter that the court has ruled should not be published until trial should not be set out in this judgment.** However, on the other hand, granted that the judgment relates to some matters concerning the parties, there is no good reason why they should continue to be referred to anonymously, **a course to be avoided unless justice requires it:** *R v Legal Aid Board ex p Kaim Todner* [1999] QB 966.

4. The most difficult question arises in respect of the handling of the matters that we have concluded are publishable by the newspaper in advance of trial. That question has been addressed by the House of Lords in *Cream Holdings v Banerjee* [2005] 1 AC 263. At [5] of the leading speech Lord Nicholls of Birkenhead indicated the nature of case:

> "In January 2001 Cream dismissed Mrs Banerjee. When she left she took with her copies of documents she claims show illegal and improper activity by the Cream group. She passed these to the 'Echo' with additional information . . . ..On 13 and 14 June 2002 the 'Echo' published articles about alleged corruption involving one director of the Cream group and a council official. On 18 June 2002 the Cream group

sought injunctive relief to restrain publication by the newspaper of any further **confidential information** given it by Ms Banerjee.

The House discharged that injunction in respect of information already supplied by Ms Banerjee to the newspaper, but not otherwise. That was because the allegations about Cream raised matters of serious public interest, and Cream was not likely to succeed at trial in rebutting those public interest arguments in support of publication."

5. The House then considered what it should say in its judgment about that conclusion. Lord Nicholls said this at his [26]:

> I recognise that without reference to the content of the **confidential information** this conclusion is necessarily enigmatic to those who have not read the private judgments of the courts below. But if I were to elaborate I would at once destroy the confidentiality the Cream group are seeking to preserve. **Even if the House discharges the restraint order made by the judge, it would not be right for your Lordships to make public the information in question.** The contents of your Lordships' speeches should not pre-empt the 'Echo's' publication, if that is what the newspaper decides now to do. Nor should these speeches, by themselves placing this information in the **public domain**, undermine any remedy in damages the Cream group may ultimately be found to have against the 'Echo' or Ms Banerjee in respect of matters the Echo may decide to publish.

The present judgment respects that guidance. **In doing so, we note that it does not follow that the principle of open justice has to be trespassed on to the extent that a judgment is not merely enigmatic but incomprehensible**. As we have seen, in *Cream* the House set out the general nature or category of the information sought to be enjoined, and the **broad reason** why that injunction was not in law available. We have taken that course in explaining our decision in this judgment, by referring in **broad terms** to the kind of information that the newspaper is entitled to publish, but not in any way going on to the degree of detail that may appear in any published report.

6. **We have invited the comments of the parties on a draft of the present judgment and have taken note of what they have said. That step was without prejudice to the determination of what should appear in the judgment being a matter for the court.**

. . .

23. As we see it, the approach required by section 12 arises in this way. The court should first consider whether this is a case in which article 8 is engaged. **It should then consider whether article 10 is engaged and, critically, whether** the applicant for relief has shown that he is likely to establish at a trial that

publication should not be allowed within the meaning of section 12(3) of the HRA.

Article 8

. . .

26. The cases make it clear that, in answering the question whether in respect of the disclosed facts the claimant **has a reasonable expectation of privacy** in the particular circumstances of the case the **nature of any relationship** between the relevant persons or parties is of considerable potential importance. This can be seen from proposition v) in [8] (quoted above) and from [15] to [24] of *McKennitt*. It can also be seen from *The Prince of Wales* case at [67] to [68], albeit in the context of the balance to be struck between rights under article 8 and article 10.

27. The issue between the parties in this appeal centers on the relevance of the nature of the information which it is sought to publish. Ms Sharp QC submits that the mere fact that the parties had a pre-existing **relationship**, such as **marriage** or a **relationship of friendship,** as in *McKennitt*, **or an intimate** and **sexual relationship**, such as that between the claimant and JC, does not create a reasonable expectation of privacy in relation to all information learned or activities witnessed during the **relationship**. In this regard Ms Sharp relies, for example, upon this statement of Lord Hope in *Campbell* at [92]:

> "The underlying question in all cases where it is alleged that there has been a breach of the duty of confidence is whether the information that was disclosed was private and not public. There must be some interest of a private nature that the claimant wishes to protect: see *A v B* [2003] QB 195, 206, para 11(vii)."
>
> Lord Hope added:
>
> "In some cases, as the Court of Appeal said in that case, the answer to the question whether the information is public or private will be obvious. Where it is not, the broad test is whether disclosure of the information about the individual ("A") would give substantial offence to A, assuming that A was placed in similar circumstances and was a person of ordinary sensibilities."

28. Mr Price reminded us of the wide scope that has been accorded to the notion of privacy. For instance, Lord Mustill said in this court in *R v Broadcasting Standards Commission ex p BBC* [2001] QB 885 at [48] that the privacy of a human being denotes at the same time the **personal 'space'** which should be free from **intrusion**. He added that **"an infringement of privacy is an affront to the personality, which is damaged both by the violation and by**

the demonstration that the personal space is not inviolate. Also, in *McKennitt* [2005] EWHC 3003, [2006] EMLR 178 (QB) Eady J found at first instance that it was the **intrusive** nature of the revelation of the minutiae of one's home life which is offensive to article 8. When considering publication of details of Ms McKennitt's home, Eady J said at [135]:

> "[Home] is one of the matters expressly addressed in Article 8(1) of the Convention as entitled to "respect". Correspondingly, there would be an obligation of confidence. Even **relatively trivial details** would fall within this protection simply because of the traditional sanctity accorded to hearth and home. To describe a person's home, the décor, the layout, the state of cleanliness, or how the occupiers behave inside it, is generally regarded as unacceptable. To convey such details, without permission, to the general public is almost as objectionable as spying into the home with a long distance lens and publishing the resulting **photographs**."

This court approved Eady J's approach: see eg [22].

29. **Nevertheless we accept Ms Sharp's submission that the mere fact that the information was imparted in the course of a relationship of confidence does not satisfy Lord Nicholls' test of "expectation of privacy".** An example would be **a husband telling his wife that Oxford or Cambridge won the boat race in a particular year.** However, **the relationship may be of considerable importance in answering the question whether there was an expectation of privacy**. Buxton LJ put the point thus in McKennitt at [15]:

> "Recent leading cases in this area, such as Campbell, Douglas [ie Douglas v Hello! (No 3) [2006] QB 125] and the most recent case in the ECtHR, von Hannover v Germany (2005) 40 EHRR 1, have wrestled with the problem of identifying the basis for claiming privacy or confidence **in respect of unauthorised or purloined information:** see § 8(iii) above. **There, the primary focus has to be on the nature of the information, because it is the recipient's perception of its confidential nature that imposes the obligation on him:** see for instance per Lord Goff of Chievely in A-G v Guardian Newspapers (No2) ["Spycatcher"] [1990] 1 AC 109 at p 281A. But, as Lord Goff immediately goes on to say, **in the vast majority of cases the duty of confidence will arise from a transaction or relationship between the parties.** And that is our case, which accordingly reverts to a more elemental enquiry into breach of confidence in the traditional understanding of that expression. **That does not of course exempt the court from considering whether the material obtained during such a relationship is indeed confidential**; but to enquire into that latter question without paying any regard to the nature of the pre-existing **relationship** between the parties, as

the argument for the appellant in this court largely did, is unlikely to produce anything but a distorted outcome."

. . .

31. In our judgment, the cases support the conclusion that **the relationship between the relevant persons or parties is of considerable importance** in answering Lord Nicholls' question, namely whether there was a reasonable expectation of privacy. In answering that question there are **a number of potentially relevant questions,** depending upon the circumstances. **They include whether the person concerned (here JC) received information which he knew or ought reasonably to have known was fairly and reasonably to be regarded as confidential or private.**

32. There was some discussion in the course of the argument as to whether it was sufficient for the claimant to show that there was a **relationship** of confidence and whether, once such a **relationship** is shown, all information obtained in the course of the **relationship** is confidential without regard to the nature of the information. **In our judgment, the answer to those questions is no** That is clear, for example from Lord Nicholls' formulation of the test, **namely whether in respect of the disclosed facts the claimant has a reasonable expectation of privacy—our emphasis.** As we see it, the test must be applied to each item of information communicated to or learned by the person concerned in the course of the **relationship**.

33. **The nature of the relationship is of considerable importance**. For example, the mere fact that the piece of information can be regarded as **trivial** does not seem to us to be decisive against answering Lord Nicholls' question in the affirmative. As the passage quoted above from [135] of Eady J's judgment in McKennitt shows, **it may or may not be.** We agree with the general proposition advanced by Ms Sharp that the question whether any particular piece of information qualifies as private and the claimant has a reasonable expectation of privacy in respect of it, **requires a detailed examination of all the circumstances on a case by case basis.** The circumstances include **the nature of the information itself** and **the circumstances in which it has been imparted or obtained.** We will return to this consideration in the context of the facts

34. Ms Sharp submits that there is no authority for the proposition that information relating to business activities will be characterised as private merely because it is communicated or learned in a domestic environment, or in the course of a personal **relationship**. We accept that that is so but, again, **it appears to us that all depends upon the circumstances of the particular case**. The judge suggested at [33] that as a matter of first impression the characterisation of business information as private would appear incon-

sistent with the policy objectives behind article 8, namely that this is a human right concerned with protecting personal integrity, dignity and domestic life. **We are not sure that that is quite right because it seems to us that business information passed by a company director to his *sexual* partner could** readily be held to be information which the latter knew or ought reasonably to have known was **fairly and reasonably to be regarded as confidential or private and in respect of which the former had a reasonable expectation of privacy**. However, it seems to us that the judge recognised that that was or might be so at [33] and [34]. . .

Correct approach on appeal

45. **The approach which should be adopted on an appeal of this kind is not, we think, in dispute**. Although the exercise upon which the judge was engaged was not the exercise of a discretion it was similar in that it involved carrying out a balancing exercise upon which different judges could properly reach different conclusions**. In these circumstances it is now well settled that an appellate court should not interfere unless the judge has erred in principle or reached a conclusion which was plainly wrong or, put another way, was outside the ambit of conclusions which a judge could reasonably reach:** see eg *Assicurazioni Generali SpA v Arab Insurance Group* [2003] 1 WLR 577 at [9] and [16] to [20], *Campbell v MGN* at [87] to [101], [158] and [165], *Galloway v Daily Telegraph* [2006] EWCA Civ 17 at [68], [2006] EMLR 221, *McKennitt* at [45] and *Mersey Care NHS Trust v Ackroyd* [2007] EWCA Civ 101 at [35] .

. . .

48. **For the reasons given earlier, the relationship between the claimant and JC was central to the question whether article 8 was engaged in respect of particular items of information and how the balance between the claimant's rights under article 8 and the newspaper's rights under article 10 should be struck.** When setting out his task at [11] of his judgment, the judge correctly directed himself that **he had to ask himself whether a prima facie duty of confidence would arise in respect of *each of the items* sought to be enjoined by virtue of the fact of the relationship**. There is no doubt that, in determining items b) and d), the judge followed that direction by having the implications of the **relationship** well in mind. **In each case the judge held that the claimant had no legitimate expectation of privacy with regard to the information** and, in any event, that, if he did, he had not shown that publication was 'likely to establish that publication should not be allowed' at the trial.

49. The judge's conclusions can be seen at [43] to [46] of his judgment as follows:

"43. For example, there are two matters which directly concern the claimant's conduct in relation to [BP] information, personnel and resources. There is the alleged use of some of its equipment and personnel for the benefit of JC and, also, the revelation of **confidential information** and documents to him. One may ask whether there can be a reasonable expectation that the law will protect the privacy of a senior executive, in relation to the use of corporate information and resources, when the effect would be to keep such allegations from those who might ordinarily be expected to make the relevant judgments, or exercise supervision; that is to say, shareholders and colleagues on the board of directors. For example, they might wish to know that a company was set up (to enable JC to deal in ring-tones for mobile phones) with the assistance of [BP] personnel. It is at least accepted by the claimant that his personal assistant helped with "secretarial tasks". The company no longer trades.

44. Mr Spearman has argued that these matters, if they are to be criticised at all, should be regarded as relatively **trivial**. There is, for example, a dispute as to the *extent* to which [BP] personnel were involved in the project. He may well be right, but it seems to me that it is not desirable for the court to make a value judgment on such behaviour in a corporate context: more specifically, if the circumstances call for a judgment to be made on relative gravity, it is not for a judge to help him keep the information from those whose right and responsibility it is to make it.

45. **On the other side of the line,** or so it seems to me, would fall private conversations in a domestic environment (including at any rate some discussion about business matters). For example, one would expect most people from time to time to come home from work and to feel free to unburden themselves about the horrors of the day—whether to a wife, husband, lover, mistress or partner (homo**sexual** or otherwise). **People feel free in the privacy of their own homes to have a moan about colleagues or employers.** What puts such communications, potentially, under the protection of the law is that revelations of such information would infringe the reasonable expectation people have that **intimate** and uninhibited discussions in a domestic environment will be respected.

46. It is not the subject-matter which determines the issue in those cases, but the circumstances in which the opinions or information may be imparted. **The entitlement to protection springs from the nature of the confidential relationship itself: cf Argyll v Argyll (cited above) at 329–30.** It is necessary to have regard to any such pre-existing **relationship**, and the duties of confidence to which it correspondingly

gives rise. **This kind of case calls for what Buxton LJ in McKennitt at [15] termed " . . . a more elemental inquiry into breach of confidence in the traditional understanding of that expression" (rather than addressing the different question of whether a stranger could be restrained, who has "purloined" confidential or private information outside the context of such an existing relationship).** Of course, even within a domestic environment or **relationship**, there may be circumstances where the public interest genuinely requires the confidence to be overridden (eg in order to reveal significant wrongdoing or perhaps to protect the public from being seriously misled)."

50. The judge had already concluded, in his [42], that he should not seek to isolate particular items as falling into a 'business' or 'personal' category, but should ask **directly in relation to each separate item whether there was a reasonable expectation of privacy.** That demonstrates, contrary to the submission made to us at one point, that the judge did not simply hold that the claimant could not establish an article 8 right because the information concerned was characterised as business information or business activity. **He asked himself the correct question.** We do not think that the judge's conclusions of principle in those paragraphs can fairly be criticised. The question in this appeal is not whether we would have answered the question in the same way but whether the judge was wrong to reach the conclusion he did.

. . .

53. Further, it was in our view open to the judge to conclude that, while some may regard the assistance provided to JC, **whatever it was, as relatively *trivial*,** that was a matter for BP and not for the court to decide. In short it was open to the judge to hold that the claimant had no reasonable expectation of privacy with regard to the use of BP equipment and resources. In reaching this conclusion it was not necessary for the judge or this court to resolve the issues between the parties as to what precise use was made of what laptops by JC.

. . .

61. The judge gave two other reasons in [54] and [55]. The first was that the **relationship** was already in the **public domain**, such that it would be unrealistic to restrain publication and the second, which is closely related to the first, is that the information had become "so generally accessible that, in all the circumstances, it cannot be regarded as confidential". The judge referred to A-G v Guardian Newspapers (No 2) [1990] 1 AC 109, per Lord Goff at 282. We doubt whether we would have concluded that these were sufficient reasons to permit publication of the fact of the **relationship**, if it were not for the

judge's decision on items b) and d). **It appears to us that there is potentially an important distinction between information which is made available to a person's circle of friends or work colleagues and information which is widely published in a newspaper.** However, in the light of our decision with regard to b) and d), it is not necessary to discuss this point further.

David Murray v Express Newspapers plc and Big Pictures (UK) Ltd [2007] EWHC 1908 [Ch] Patten J

12. One argument which sometimes surfaces in relation to the trial of issues of law on an interlocutory basis is that the judgment should be deferred until after a full trial because of the difficulty of applying the principles of a developing part of law to a set of assumed facts. In the case of an application for summary judgment under CPR Part 24 the existence of unresolved factual issues may in itself be an answer to the application**. But in this case it is difficult to see how oral evidence would assist the Court to decide whether the taking of the photograph was or was not a breach of the Claimant's rights if it did no more than to confirm the facts pleaded in the Particulars of Claim**. On the more limited basis on which this application is made I would not be assisted by such evidence. The only **purpose** of a trial would be to enable BPL to substantiate its own pleaded case. In these circumstances, the Court has to apply the law as it sees it to the facts on which the Claimant relies. There is nothing to suggest that the principles to be applied will change materially between now and a trial and BPL is, I think, entitled to test the Claimant's case as a matter of law on the basis of how things now stand. In the recent case of *HRH The Prince of Wales v Associated Newspapers Ltd* [2007] 3 WLR 222 the Court of Appeal felt able to determine the Prince's claim to confidentiality in his journals under CPR Part 24 by applying the law to largely uncontested facts. Although the facts in this case have to be assumed to be true it is open to me at least under CPR 3.4 to adopt the same approach.

. . .

19. The speeches of Lord Nicholls and Lord Hoffmann in the case of *Campbell v MGN Ltd* [2004] 2 AC 457 **trace this development of the action for breach of confidence from its source in the protection of confidential information from disclosure by those in an intimate or confidential relationship to the imposition of a duty of confidence on any person who receives information which he knows or ought to know is fairly and reasonably to be regarded**

as confidential: see *AG v Guardian Newspapers Ltd (No 2)* [1990] 1 AC 109 at p 281.

20. The incorporation of convention values into this branch of the law widens the focus of the cause of action t**o include private information which would never have been regarded as confidential by a court of equity** in the days of *Prince Albert v Strange (1849) 2 De G & Sm* , (BAILII [1849] EWHC Ch J20) or even those of *Coco v AN Clark (Engineers) Ltd [1969] RPC41.* **Conduct, however intimate or embarrassing, in a public place is not as a matter of ordinary language confidential, not least because it takes place in circumstances which could never have been expected or perhaps intended to be secret**. The Courts have therefore had to recognise that they are not protecting information with a personal or industrial value but are imposing limitations on the publication of events which were visible to any member of the public who happened to be around at the time. **In the case of confidential information properly so called, the starting point is the confidential nature of the information itself which requires a justification for its disclosure**. In the case of allegedly private information consisting of public conduct, the ultimate issue for the court is whether any restraints should be imposed on the wider dissemination of what begins as public information.

. . .

37. In paragraph 62 of the judgment the ECtHR refers to the use of the CCTV footage by the media as far exceeding any exposure to a passer-by or to security observation. This was to take account of the nature of **Mr Peck's complaint, which was not that his activities were captured on CCTV but that they had been subsequently broadcast to a much wider audience whom he could never have anticipated would have been shown the images in question**. That distinction does not however take the matter any further in this (or I suspect in any) case where the private or personal conduct of an individual is exposed by the media to the world at large**. Mr Spearman made it clear that his client was not objecting (and probably could not object) to photographs taken casually by members of the public for their own purposes which would have a very limited circulation**. The essence of the complaint in virtually all of these cases **centres on the degree of publicity which the occasion photographed ultimately receives**. A **photograph** taken by a member of the public which remains the property of that person and is at most shown to family and friends **does not infringe any right of privacy because it does not lead to any real public exposure of the events portrayed.** They remain essentially private and unseen. It is only when the **photograph** is sold to an agency or a newspaper for publication that any appreciable invasion of privacy can be said to occur. **This, I think, has relevance when one comes to consider cases like Hosking v Runting which do not involve the depiction of**

conduct or events that could in any sense be described as embarrassing or intimate. In such cases the actionable complaint is not and cannot be that the claimant was photographed or that press photographers were present to witness the events in question. **Some degree of public exposure (at least to the eyes of those around at the time) is the inevitable consequence of operating in a public place.** If absolute privacy is required then it can only be secured behind closed doors or a high garden wall. The question whether there has been an actionable invasion of privacy in cases such as this therefore turns on whether activities which probably could be protected from widespread public scrutiny if conducted in private qualify for the same degree of protection when they are open to public view. The stance of the English courts in the decisions up to and including *Campbell* (like those in New Zealand) has been to limit the protection in such cases to conduct or information of a personal or embarrassing kind. **But Von Hannover is said to have changed all that.**

. . .

The Post Von-Hannover English authorities

50. These begin with the decision of Eady J in McKennitt v Ash [2006] EMLR 178. This was not a case about **photographs**. It concerned a book written by the Defendant about her friendship and travels with Loreena McKennitt, the Canadian folk musician. The book contained a variety of anecdotes including revelations about Ms McKennitt's **personal** and **sexual relationships**, her emotional reaction to her fiancé's death, a detailed description of her home and the history of a property dispute between the parties which led to litigation.

. . .

56. Mr Spearman submitted that Buxton LJ was wrong to elevate the reference in Lord Walker's speech to the seriousness of the interference required in order to engage Art. 8 into a statement of principle that ordinary, familiar activities cannot qualify for protection. The remarks have, he said, to be considered in the context in which they were made: ie in response to a submission in that case that since the concept of respect for private and family life was so wide, any act of sexual discrimination (in that case in relation to a child support scheme) within Art. 14 also fell within the ambit of Art. 8.

57. **I do not believe that it is helpful to over-analyse Lord Walker's dictum which was not made in relation to a case like the present one or by reference to the decision in Von Hannover.** It was not in any event central to Buxton LJ's reasoning in McKennitt v Ash. **The important passage in his judgment is where he deals in terms with the effect of Von Hannover on the scope of Art. 8.** In paragraph 37 of the judgment **he begins by stating**

that there is little doubt that Von Hannover has extended the reach of Art. 8 beyond what had previously been understood. At paragraphs 39–42 he says this:

> "[39] Eady J suggested, at his para 58, that that approach was consistent with the assumption in Campbell that art 8 protected a person's reasonable expectation of privacy. That is so in broad terms, but at the same time it is far from clear that the House of Lords that decided Campbell would have handled Von Hannover in the same way as did the ECtHR. Very extensive argument and discussion was seen as required before Ms Campbell was able to enjoin the publication of **photographs** of her in the public street, and then only because of their connection with her medical condition. Had the House had the benefit of Von Hannover a shorter course might have been taken.
>
> [40] That does not however mean (to anticipate an argument that will arise again under art 10) that the English courts should not now give **respectful attention** to Von Hannover. The House of Lords in Campbell made no specific findings as to the content of art 8 save in the very general terms extracted by Eady J. As it is put in a work shown to us by the media parties, Professor Fenwick and Mr Phillipson's Media Freedom Under the Human Rights Act (2006), at p 764, "the test propounded-of a reasonable expectation of privacy, of whether the information is obviously private-is to be structured by reference to the art 8 case law". It thus remains for the national court to apply that case law, as it currently stands, to the facts before it. It was therefore certainly open to Eady J to have regard to Von Hannover in relation to the very different facts of the present case.
>
> [41] Perhaps realising the force of observations such as the foregoing, the media parties, in particular, were most anxious to persuade us that the ECtHR went no further in Von Hannover than to hold that the Princess's privacy had been invaded by a campaign of media **intrusion** into her life, of which the enjoined **photographs** were the fruit. The taking and publication of the **photographs** would otherwise not have been in itself an invasion of privacy. They cited in support some observations of Fenwick and Phillipson at p 768 of their book, though it is fair to say that the learned authors also say that that analysis is not without its difficulties. The judge, at his para 53, did not accept that analysis, nor would I. While it is quite correct that there is reference in the judgment of the ECtHR to media **intrusion,** it is not possible to say that the general statements of principle set out in para 38 above are so limited. **And Mr Browne was able to show us authority from the ECtHR decided since Von Hannover that applies those statements in situations that**

were not ones of media intrusion. Of those, the most significant is ***Sciacca v Italy*** (Application 50774/99), paras 27 and 29 of the judgment of the ECtHR applying Von Hannover to a case that was not one of press **harassment**, and citing the jurisprudence of Von Hannover in entirely general terms.

[42] I would therefore conclude that to the extent that it is the Appellant's case that the judge should not have had regard to Von Hannover when considering the first question of whether art 8 was engaged; and to the extent if at all that the issue matters for the determination of this part of the case; **that complaint is unfounded**."

. . .

65. It seems to me that a distinction can be drawn between a child (or an adult) engaged in family and sporting activities and something as simple as a walk down a street or a visit to the grocers to buy the milk. The first type of activity is clearly part of a person's private recreation time intended to be enjoyed in the company of family and friends. Publicity on the test deployed in Von-Hannover is **intrusive** and can adversely affect the exercise of such social activities. But if the law is such as to give every adult or child a legitimate expectation of not being photographed without consent on any occasion on which they are not, so to speak, on public business then it will have created a right for most people to the protection of their image. If a simple walk down the street qualifies for protection then it is difficult to see what would not. For most people who are not **public figures** in the sense of being **politicians** or the like, there will be virtually no aspect of their life which cannot be characterized as private. Similarly, even celebrities would be able to confine unauthorized photography to the occasions on which they were at a concert, film premiere or some similar occasion.

Long Beach Limited v Global Witness Limited [2007] EWHC 1980 (QB) Stanley Burnton J

20. There are conflicting interests in this case. The first is the Claimants' interest in preventing the further publication of sensitive and at least originally confidential documents and information about them, ie the alleged misuse of private information. The Second Claimant's rights under Article 8 are undoubtedly engaged. But this case also concerns the Convention and common law rights of freedom of expression. The Convention right is defined by Article 10 as follows:

1. Everyone has the right to freedom of expression. This right shall

> include freedom to hold opinions and to receive and impart information and ideas without interference by public authority and regardless of frontiers. . . .
>
> 2. The exercise of these freedoms, since it carries with it duties and responsibilities, may be subject to such formalities, conditions, restrictions or penalties as are prescribed by law and are necessary in a democratic society, . . . for the protection of the **reputation** or rights of others, for preventing the disclosure of information received in confidence, . . .

. . .

52. However, there may never be a trial in Hong Kong of the issue whether the Claimants are "unsavoury or corrupt". The specified documents, unless explained, frankly suggest that they are. There is no obvious reason why the Second Claimant should not publicly explain that the transactions shown by these documents are consistent with his honest performance of his duties as President and Director General of Cotrade and his disclosed personal income. **Once there is good reason to doubt the propriety of the financial affairs of a public official, there is a public interest in those affairs being open to public scrutiny.** The approach of Deputy High Court Judge Carlson is inconsistent with our law as to the publication of documents referred to in court open to the public**, and to the general principle that the courts will not enforce an obligation of confidentiality in relation to material that is alleged to show misconduct:** *Initial Services Ltd v Putterill* [1968] 1 QB 396, in which the Court of Appeal refused to strike out the defence that the confidential documents showed that the plaintiff had failed to register an agreement as required by the Restrictive Trade Practices Act 1956 and had issued a misleading circular. Manifestly, in that case the defendant had not proved the misconduct alleged. The judgment of Lord Denning MR in *Initial Services Ltd v Putterill* was subsequently approved by the House of Lords in *British Steel v Granada Television* [1981] AC 1096.

Max Mosley v News Group Newspapers Ltd [2008] EWHC 687 (QB) Eady J

33. The other "limiting factor" to be considered is whether the information contained in the edited footage has lost its privacy **to the extent that there is nothing left for the law to protect**. I have found this more difficult. I am prepared to accept that the material has been seen by thousands of people around the world and that it continues to be available. Mr Millar asks

rhetorically, therefore, what can be achieved by an injunction in these circumstances? **The Court must always be conscious of the practical realities and limitations as to what can be achieved.** I have in mind, of course, what was said in *Douglas v Hello!* at [105] (cited above). Nevertheless, a point *may* be reached where the information sought to be restricted, by an order of the Court, is so widely and generally accessible "in the **public domain**" that such an injunction would make no practical difference.

34. As Mr Millar has pointed out, if someone wishes to search on the **Internet** for the content of the edited footage, there are various ways to access it notwithstanding any order the Court may choose to make imposing limits on the content of the *News of the World* website. The Court should guard against slipping into playing the role of King Canute. Even though an order may be desirable for the protection of privacy, and may be made in accordance with the principles currently being applied by the courts, there may come a point where it would simply serve no useful **purpose** and would merely be characterised, in the traditional terminology, as a *brutum fulmen*. It is inappropriate for the Court to make vain gestures.

Max Mosley v News Group Newspapers Ltd [2008] EWHC 1777 Eady J

The nature of the claim

1. The claimant in this litigation is Mr Max Mosley, who has been President of the Fédération Internationale de l'Automobile ("FIA") since 1993 and **is a trustee of its charitable arm**, the FIA Foundation. He sues News Group Newspapers Ltd as publishers of the *News of the World*, complaining of an article by Neville Thurlbeck in the issue for 30 March 2008 under the heading "F1 BOSS HAS SICK NAZI ORGY WITH 5 HOOKERS". It was claimed as an "EXCLUSIVE" and was accompanied by the subheading **"Son of Hitler-loving fascist in sex shame".** It concerned an event which took place on 28 March, described variously as a "party" (by the Claimant and his witnesses) and "an orgy" (by the Defendant). He also complains of accompanying images published alongside the article.

2. **He sues additionally over the same information and images on the newspaper's website, which also contained video footage relating to the same event.** Reference is also made to a "follow up article" contained in the issue of 6 April headed "EXCLUSIVE: MOSLEY HOOKER TELLS ALL: MY NAZI ORGY WITH F1 BOSS". **This consisted primarily of a purported interview with one of the women who had been present at the event in question and had filmed what took place clandestinely with a camera concealed in her**

clothing, which had been supplied by the *News of the World*. It is relied upon primarily in the context of aggravation of damages and in support of a claim for exemplary damages.

3. The cause of action is breach of confidence and/or the unauthorised disclosure of personal information, said to infringe the Claimant's rights of privacy as protected by Article 8 of the European Convention on Human Rights and Fundamental Freedoms ("the Convention"). **There is no claim in defamation and I am thus not directly concerned with any injury to reputation.**

4. It is argued not only that the content of the published material was **inherently private in nature,** consisting as it did of the portrayal of sado-masochistic ("S and M") and some **sexual** activities, but that there had also been a **pre-existing relationship of confidentiality** between the participants. They had all known each other for some time and took part in such activities on the understanding that they would be private and that none of them would reveal what had taken place. I was told that there is a fairly tight-knit community of S and M activists on what is known as "the scene" and that it is an **unwritten rule that people are trusted not to reveal what has gone on.** That is hardly surprising. (It is apparently more common nowadays to refer to "BDSM", a term which embraces bondage, discipline, domination and submission or sado-masochistic practices, but I shall continue to use the more familiar "S and M" for convenience.)

5. It is alleged against the woman in question (known as "Woman E") that she breached that trust **and that the journalist concerned must have appreciated that she was doing so.** That could not in reality be disputed, since the whole object of supplying her with a **concealed** camera, and **instructing her how to use it**, was to ensure that she could record the events **without being suspected** by her fellow participants.

6. Against that background, it is clear that the present claim is partly founded, as in *McKennitt v Ash* [2008] QB 73, upon **" . . . old-fashioned breach of confidence by way of conduct inconsistent with a pre-existing relationship, rather than simply of the purloining of private information**": see eg *ibid* at [8], *per* Buxton LJ.

The "new methodology"

7. Although the law of "old-fashioned breach of confidence" has been well established for many years, and derives historically from equitable principles, these have been extended in recent years under the stimulus of the Human Rights Act 1998 and the content of the Convention itself. The law now affords protection to information in respect of which there is a reasonable expectation of privacy, **even in circumstances where there is no pre-existing relationship** giving rise of itself to an enforceable duty of confidence. That is

because the law is concerned to prevent **the violation of a citizen's autonomy, dignity and self-esteem.** It is not simply a matter of "unaccountable" judges running amok. Parliament enacted the 1998 statute which *requires* these values to be acknowledged and enforced by the courts. In any event, the courts had been increasingly taking them into account because of the need to interpret domestic law consistently with the United Kingdom's international obligations. It will be recalled that the United Kingdom government signed up to the Convention more than 50 years ago.

8. The relevant values are expressed in Articles 8 and 10 of the Convention, which are in these terms:

. . .

9. It was recognised in *Campbell v MGN Ltd* [2004] 2 AC 457 that these values are as much applicable in disputes between individuals, or between an individual and a non-governmental body such as a newspaper, as they are in disputes between individuals and a public authority: see eg Lord Nicholls at [17]–[18] and Lord Hoffmann at [50]. Indeed, " . . . **in order to find the rules of the English law of breach of confidence we now have to look in the jurisprudence of articles 8 and 10":** *per* Buxton LJ in *McKennitt v Ash* [2008] QB 73 at [11].

10. If the first hurdle can be overcome, by demonstrating a reasonable expectation of privacy, it is now clear that the court is required to carry out the next step of weighing the relevant competing Convention rights in the light of an "**intense focus**" upon the individual facts of the case: see eg *Campbell* and *Re S (A Child)* [2005] 1 AC 593. It was expressly recognised that no one Convention right takes automatic precedence over another. In the present context, for example, **it has to be accepted that any rights of free expression, as protected by Article 10, whether on the part of Woman E or the journalists working for the News of the World, must no longer be regarded as simply "trumping" any privacy rights that may be established on the part of the Claimant.** Language of that kind is no longer used. **Nor can it be said, without qualification, that there is a "public interest that the truth should out"**: cf *Fraser v Evans* [1969] 1 QB 349, 360F-G, *per* Lord Denning MR

11. In order to determine which should take precedence, *in the particular circumstances*, it is necessary **to examine the facts closely as revealed in the evidence** at trial and to decide whether (assuming a reasonable expectation of privacy to have been established) some countervailing consideration of public interest may be said to justify any **intrusion** which has taken place. This is integral to what has been called "the new methodology": *Re S (A Child)* at [23].

12. This modern approach of applying an "**intense focus**" is thus obviously

incompatible with making broad generalisations of the kind to which the media often resorted in the past such as, for example, "**Public figures** must expect to have less privacy" or "People in positions of responsibility must be seen as 'role models' and set us all an example of how to live upstanding lives". **Sometimes factors of this kind may have a legitimate role to play when the "ultimate balancing exercise" comes to be carried out**, but generalisations can never be determinative. In every case "it all depends" (ie upon what is revealed by the intense focus on the individual circumstances).

13. The exercise is sometimes still described, in terminology used by Lord Goff in the *Spycatcher* litigation, as determining whether any **"limiting principles"** come into play: see *Att-Gen v Guardian Newspapers (No 2)* [1990] 1 AC 109, 282B-F:

> " . . . **The first limiting principle** (which is rather an expression of the scope of the duty) is highly relevant to this appeal. It is that the principle of confidentiality only applies to information to the extent that it is **confidential**. In particular, once it has entered what is usually called the **public domain** (which means no more than that the information in question is **so generally accessible that, in all the circumstances, it cannot be regarded as confidential**) then, as a general rule, the principle of confidentiality can have no application to it. . . .
>
> **The second limiting principle** is that the duty of confidence applies neither to useless information, nor to **trivia**. There is no need for me to develop this point.
>
> The **third limiting principle** is of far greater importance. It is that, although the basis of the law's protection of confidence is that there is a public interest that confidences should be preserved and protected by the law, nevertheless that public interest may be outweighed by some other **countervailing public interest** which favours disclosure. This limitation may apply . . . to all types of **confidential information**. It is this **limiting principle** which may require a court to carry out a balancing operation, weighing the public interest in maintaining confidence against a countervailing public interest favouring disclosure.
>
> Embraced within this **limiting principle** is, of course, the so called **defence of iniquity**. In origin, this principle was **narrowly** stated, on the basis that a man cannot be made 'the confidant of a crime or a fraud': see *Gartside v Outram* (1857) 26 LJ Charity 113, 114, *per* Sir William Page Wood V-C. But it is now clear that the principle extends to matters **of which disclosure is required in the public interest**: see *Beloff v Pressdram Ltd* [1973] 1 All ER 241, 260, *per* Ungoed-Thomas J, and *Lion Laboratories Ltd v Evans* [1985] QB 526, 550, *per* Griffiths LJ.

It does not however follow that the public interest will in such cases require disclosure to the media, or to the public by the media. **There are cases in which a more limited disclosure is all that is required:** see *Francome v Mirror Group Newspapers Ltd* [1984] 1 WLR 892."

14. This "ultimate balancing test" has been recognised as turning to a large extent upon proportionality: see eg Sedley LJ in *Douglas v Hello! Ltd* [2001] QB 967 at [137]. The judge will often have to ask whether the **intrusion**, or perhaps the **degree of the intrusion,** into the claimant's privacy was **proportionate to the public interest supposedly being served by it.**

15. One of the more striking developments over the last few years of judicial analysis, both here and in Strasbourg, is the acknowledgment that the balancing process which has to be carried out by individual judges on the facts before them **necessarily involves an evaluation of the use to which the relevant defendant has put, or intends to put, his or her right to freedom of expression.** That is inevitable when one is weighing up the **relative worth** of one person's rights against those of another. It has been accepted, for example, in the House of Lords that generally speaking **"political speech" would be accorded greater value than gossip or "tittle tattle":** see eg *Campbell* at [148] and also *Jameel (Mohammed) v Wall Street Journal Europe Sprl* [2007] 1 AC 359 at [147].

The significance of visual images

16. This naturally has particular significance in the context of **photographs** or other visual images. Sometimes there may be a good case for revealing the fact of wrongdoing to the general public; **it will not necessarily follow that photographs of "every gory detail" also need to be published to achieve the public interest objective.** Nor will it automatically justify **clandestine** recording, whether visual or audio. So much is acknowledged in the relevant section of the Press Complaints Commission ("PCC") Editors' **Code** at Clause 10:

"i) The press must not seek to obtain or publish material acquired by using hidden cameras or **clandestine** listening devices; or by intercepting private or mobile telephone calls, messages or emails; or by the unauthorised removal of documents or **photographs** or by accessing digitally-held private information without consent.

ii) Engaging in misrepresentation or subterfuge, including by agents or intermediaries, can generally be justified only in the public interest and then only when the material cannot be obtained by other means."

17. Naturally, the very fact of **clandestine recording** may be regarded as an **intrusion** and an unacceptable infringement of Article 8 rights. That is one issue. Once such recording has taken place, however, a separate issue may

need to be considered as to the appropriateness of onward publication, either **on a limited basis** or more generally to the world at large. In this case, **the pleaded claim is confined to publication of the information; it does not include the intrusive method by which it was acquired.** Yet obviously the nature and scale of the distress caused is in large measure due to the **clandestine** filming and the pictures acquired as a result.

18. The **intrusive nature of photography** has been fully discussed in the European Court of Human Rights in *Von Hannover v Germany* (2005) 40 EHRR 1 and also in domestic jurisprudence. The point was articulated by Waller LJ in *D v L* [2004] EMLR 1 at [23]:

> "A court may restrain the publication of an improperly obtained **photograph** even if the taker is free to describe the information which the photographer provides or even if the information revealed by the **photograph** is in the **public domain**. It is no answer to the claim to restrain the publication of an improperly obtained **photograph** that the information portrayed by the **photograph** is already available in the **public domain**."

19. Later, in *Douglas v Hello! Ltd (No 3)* [2006] QB 125 at [84] the Court of Appeal explored the underlying reasons in terms which resonate in the factual circumstances now before the court:

> **"This action is about photographs.** Special considerations attach to **photographs** in the field of privacy. They are **not merely** a method of conveying information that is an alternative to verbal description. They enable the person viewing the **photograph** to act as **a spectator**, in some circumstances **voyeur** would be the more appropriate noun, of whatever it is that the **photograph** depicts. **As a means of invading privacy, a photograph is particularly intrusive.** This is quite apart from the fact that the camera, and the **telephoto lens**, can give access to the viewer of the **photograph** to scenes where those photographed could reasonably expect that their appearances or actions would not be brought to the notice of the public."

20. It was acknowledged by Lord Hoffmann in *Campbell*, at [60], that there could be a genuine public interest in the disclosure of the existence of a **sexual relationship** (in, for example, a situation giving rise to **favouritism** or advancement through corruption), but he went on to warn that **the addition of salacious details or intimate photographs would be disproportionate and unacceptable**. "The latter, even if accompanying a legitimate disclosure of the **sexual relationship**, would be **too intrusive and demeaning".**

21. At the Court of Appeal stage of *Campbell* [2003] QB 633 at [64], Lord Phillips stated that provided the publication of particular **confidential information**

is justifiable in the public interest, **the journalist must be given reasonable latitude as to the manner in which the information is conveyed to the public:** see too *Fressoz v France* (2001) 31 EHRR 2. Yet, for the reasons given by Lord Hoffmann, it should not be assumed that, even if the subject-matter of the meeting on 28 March *was* of public interest, the showing of the film or the pictures was a reasonable method of conveying that information. In effect, it is a question of **proportionality.**

22. It is always important to remember that a number of the comments made about **intrusion** by photography or video recording in Strasbourg have been made in the context of images recorded in **more or less public spaces.** This was so in *Von Hannover v Germany* itself and in *Peck v United Kingdom* (2003) 36 EHRR 41. It was true also of the decision of the Supreme Court of Canada in *Aubry v Éditions Vice-Versa Inc.* [1998] 2 SCR 591, in which it was held that there had been a violation of a young woman's right of privacy under Article 5 of the Quebec Charter of Human Rights and Freedoms, **notwithstanding the fact that she had been sitting on the steps of a public building.**

23. The present complaint relates to the recording on **private property** of **sexual activity**. The situation may be at the **extreme of intimate intrusion**, but the matter is by no means outside the scope of existing authority. An injunction was granted, for example, by Ouseley J in *Theakston v MGN Ltd* [2002] EMLR 22 in respect of **photographs taken inside a brothel,** even though he recognised that it was not appropriate to restrain verbal descriptions of what the claimant did there. The passage in his judgment giving reasons for restraining publication of the **photographs** was cited and endorsed by the Court of Appeal in *Douglas v Hello! Ltd (No 3)* at [85].

A brief summary of the Defendant's case on Article 8

24. In the present case, the Defendant advances two alternative propositions in the light of the legal principles developed over recent years. **First**, it is said that the Claimant had no reasonable expectation of privacy in relation to the information concerning the events of 28 March, or in relation to the visual images contained in the newspaper, or in relation to the video material. **Alternatively**, the argument is raised that the Claimant's right to privacy under Article 8 of the Convention is outweighed by a greater public interest in disclosure, such that the Defendant's right to freedom of expression under Article 10 should, in these particular circumstances, be allowed to prevail.

25. The public interest argument has somewhat shifted as matters have developed. The primary case would appear to be that the public has an interest in knowing of the newspaper's and/or Woman E's **allegation** that the events of 28 March involved Nazi or concentration camp role-play. A somewhat later variation on the theme, perhaps primarily attributable to the Defendant's

legal team, **is that what took place was at least partly illegal.** It was said that the Defendant was committing offences such as assault occasioning actual bodily harm and **brothel**-keeping. When the editor of the newspaper went into the witness-box on 8 July, he went so far as to claim, *irrespective of any Nazi element*, that the nature of the **sexual** activities was such that the public had a right to know that the Claimant indulged in them. **This was because of his role as President of the FIA.**

The publication of 6 April 2008

33. The following Sunday the front page was again largely taken up with the headline "MY NAZI ORGY WITH F1 BOSS" accompanied by the claim "**EXCLUSIVE: MOSLEY HOOKER TELLS ALL".** There is another strap across the bottom of the page claiming, "Secret S&M tapes expose his lies". There is a full-length **photograph** of Woman E dressed in a peaked cap, white shirt, leather skirt and thigh-length boots. She is carrying a cane. This time it is her face which is blocked out. There is the caption "POSING: Mosley hooker in Nazi outfit".

. . .

99. There is now a considerable body of jurisprudence in Strasbourg and elsewhere which recognises that sexual activity engages the rights protected by Article 8. As was noted long ago in *Dudgeon v UK* (1981) 4 EHRR 149, **there must exist particularly serious reasons before interferences on the part of public authorities can be legitimate for the purposes of Article 8(2) because sexual behaviour "concerns a most intimate aspect of private life".** That case concerned the criminal law in the context of buggery and gross indecency (in Northern Ireland). It was said at [60] that Article 8 rights protect in this respect "an essentially private materialisation of the human personality".

. . .

(i) The allegation of criminality

110. There are various strands to the argument that need to be considered. **First,** it is said that it is legitimate sometimes to infringe an individual's privacy for the greater good of exposing or detecting crime. So much is expressly recognised in the PCC Code in a form of words originally deriving from the draft attached as a schedule to the report of the Committee on Privacy and Related Matters (the Calcutt Report): (1990) Cm 1102.

111. **The *question* has to be asked whether it will always be an automatic defence to intrusive journalism that a crime was being committed on private property, however technical or trivial**. Would it justify installing a camera in someone's home, for example, in order to catch him or her smoking a spliff?

Surely not. There **must be some limits and, even in more serious cases, any such intrusion should be no more than is proportionate**.

112. One of Mr Price's submissions, strongly challenged by Mr Warby, is that a defendant may only rely in support of a public interest defence on matters of which he was aware at the time of publication *and* which were actually communicated to the public. He argues that significant parts of the Defendant's case here did not occur to the journalists at the time and were thought up by the lawyers after the event. Mr Thurlbeck was cross-examined to that effect; in particular, because it was being suggested that he did not choose to publish all these **salacious** allegations for the reason that he thought that certain specific offences had been committed. Nor did he inform the public that this was the reason he felt compelled to draw them to their attention. That may well be so. **But I do not believe that it would, as a matter of law, be fatal to the public interest defence. If the facts are published, I see no reason why the relevant defendant should be precluded from later teasing out their implications more fully, when brought before the court, or from refining the way the case is presented in jurisprudential terms.** Nor is there, as yet, any authority for the proposition that a defendant's state of mind, in a privacy case, is relevant to the issue of public interest at all—still less capable of depriving him of such a defence which would otherwise be upheld.

. . .

115. Mr Warby placed considerable reliance on the case of *Brown* [1994] 1 AC 212, in which the majority held that neither consent nor the sexual context could afford a defence in a case concerning extreme sado-masochistic activity. Thus, it was argued that the consent of these women to the spanking, despite their evident enjoyment, does not excuse the fact that a technical assault contrary to the 1861 Act was committed by the Claimant with every thwack. **Yet again, however, I must try to maintain some sense of reality. In any event, consent is a valid defence so far as common assault is concerned.**

116. The facts of *Brown* involved cruelty of an altogether different order and activities that were extremely dangerous. One of the considerations which justified the criminalisation of such activities, according to the Strasbourg court, **was the potential impact on health:** see *Laskey, Jaggard and Brown v UK* (1997) 24 EHRR 39 at [63]. There was also the issue, which does not arise here by any stretch of the imagination, **that some very young people were victimised or corrupted.**

117. It is well known that the Attorney-General and the Crown Prosecution Service exercise discretion in deciding whether to institute criminal proceedings and frequently acknowledge that it would not be in the public interest to pros-

ecute every crime—**however trivial**. I have little doubt that such a discretion would be exercised in cases of this kind. **This was rather confirmed by the CPS prosecution guidelines and "Charging Standard" introduced by Mr Price**. It would **hardly be appropriate to clutter up the courts with cases of spanking between consenting adults taking** place in private property and without disturbing the neighbours. That would plainly not be in the public interest. It would not be logical, therefore, to pray in aid the public interest when seeking to justify hidden cameras and worldwide coverage.

118. **It is worth remembering that even those who have committed serious crimes do not thereby become "outlaws" so far as their own rights, including rights of personal privacy, are concerned:** see eg *Silver v UK* (1983) 5 EHRR 347 and *Polanski v Condé Nast Publications Ltd* [2005] 1 WLR 637 .

119. So too, it was recognised in *Campbell* at [56] that drug dependency was a matter which ordinarily a person might expect to keep private (as in the case of other problems affecting health). That is notwithstanding that it is implicit in that information that the person concerned has regularly been in possession of prohibited drugs. Again, it can be seen that illegal behaviour does not automatically undermine a person's rights under Article 8.

. . .

(ii) The Nazi and concentration camp theme

122. The principal argument on public interest related to the Nazi theme. I have come to the conclusion (although others might disagree) **that if it really were the case**, as the newspaper alleged, that the Claimant had for entertainment and **sexual** gratification been "mocking the humiliating way the Jews were treated", or "parodying Holocaust horrors", **there could be a public interest in that being revealed at least to those in the FIA to whom he is accountable**. He has to deal with many people of all races and religions, and **has spoken out against racism in the sport**. If he really were behaving in the way I have just described, that would, for many people, **call seriously into question his suitability for his FIA role.** It would be information which people arguably should have the opportunity to know and evaluate. It is probably right to acknowledge that private fantasies should not in themselves be subjected to legal scrutiny by the courts, but when they are acted out that is not necessarily so.

[The court seems to have countenanced a limited disclosure.]

. . .

(iii) "Depravity and adultery"

124. I need to consider, therefore, whether the residual S and M behaviour and

other admitted aspects of what took place on 28 March **could be said in themselves to be matters of legitimate journalistic investigation or public interest.** Mr Warby described it as immoral, depraved and to an extent adulterous. Everyone now, thanks to the *News of the World*, probably holds an opinion on that, but even if there was adultery and even if one happens to agree that it was "depraved", **it by no means follows that they are matters of genuine public interest**, as that is understood in the case law.

125. The modern approach to personal privacy and to **sexual** preferences and practices is very different from that of past generations. **First**, there is a greater willingness, and especially in the Strasbourg jurisprudence, to accord respect to an individual's right to conduct his or her personal life without state interference or condemnation. It has now to be recognised that **sexual** conduct is a significant aspect of human life in respect of which people should be free to choose. That freedom is one of the matters which Article 8 protects: governments and courts are required to afford remedies when that right is breached.

126. **Secondly**, as Lord Nicholls at [17]–[18] and Lord Hoffmann at [50] observed in *Campbell* in 2004, remedies should be available against private individuals and corporations (including the media) because, **absent any serious element of public interest, they are obliged to respect personal privacy as much as public bodies**. It is not merely state **intrusion** that should be actionable. Moreover, the Council of Europe Resolution 1165 of 1998 had already made this clear:

> "11. The Assembly reaffirms the importance of every person's right to privacy, and of the right to freedom of expression, as fundamental to a democratic society. These rights are neither absolute nor in any hierarchical order, since they are of equal value.
>
> 12. However, the Assembly points out that the right to privacy afforded by article 8 of the European Convention on Human Rights should not only protect an individual against interference by public authorities, but also against interference by private persons or institutions, including the mass media."

127. **Thirdly**, it is not for the state or for the media to expose **sexual** conduct **which does not involve any significant breach of the criminal law.** That is so whether the motive for such **intrusion** is merely **prurience** or a moral crusade. It is not for journalists to undermine human rights, or for judges to refuse to enforce them, **merely on grounds of taste or moral disapproval**. Everyone is naturally entitled to espouse moral or religious beliefs to the effect that certain types of **sexual** behaviour are wrong or demeaning to those participating. That does not mean that they are entitled to hound those who practise them or to detract from their right to live life as they choose.

129. It is important, in this new rights-based jurisprudence, to ensure that where breaches occur remedies are not refused because an individual journalist or judge finds the **conduct distasteful or contrary to moral or religious** teaching. **Where the law is not breached, as I said earlier, the private conduct of adults is essentially no-one else's business.** The fact that a particular **relationship** happens to be adulterous, or that someone's tastes are unconventional or "perverted", does not give the media *carte blanche*.

129. I was referred by Mr Price to the judgment in *CC v AB* [2007] EMLR 11 at [25]–[27] where it was said:

> "25. **Judges need to be wary about giving the impression that they are ventilating, while affording or refusing legal redress, some personal moral or social views, and especially at a time when society is far less homogeneous than in the past.** At one time, when there was, or was perceived to be, a commonly accepted standard in such matters as **sexual morality**, it may have been acceptable for the courts to give effect to that standard in exercising discretion or in interpreting legal rights and obligations. **Now, however, there is a strong argument for not holding forth about adultery, or attaching greater inherent worth to a relationship which has been formalised by marriage than to any other relationship.**
>
> 26. A judge, like anyone else, is obviously entitled to hold personal moral views about the issues of the day, **but it is important not to let them intrude** when interpreting and applying the law. Such issues are best avoided—at least without some statutory sanction. No doubt many people, especially those with a strong religious faith, will disapprove of adultery. Many others, on the other hand, will not give it a second thought, while moving easily through a series of medium or short-term **relationships** as they feel it appropriate.
>
> 27. With such a wide range of differing views in society, perhaps more than for many generations, **one must guard against allowing legal judgments to be coloured by personal attitudes.** Even among judges, there is no doubt a wide range of opinion. . . ."

It was only, of course, a decision at first instance which did not go to appeal, but that is because permission was refused (in January 2007).

130. I am conscious that the decision in *CC v AB* was subjected to a number of criticisms, the more restrained of these being directed to its "moral relativism". This is, I believe, largely because of a failure to appreciate the task which judges are now required to carry out in the context of the rights-based environment introduced by the Human Rights Act, hitherto largely unfamiliar in our common law tradition. In deciding whether a right has been infringed,

and in assessing the relative worth of competing rights, **it is not for judges to make individual moral judgments or to be swayed by personal distaste.** It is not simply a matter of personal privacy versus the public interest. The modern perception is that there is a public interest in respecting personal privacy. It is thus a question of taking account of conflicting public interest considerations and evaluating them according to increasingly well recognised criteria.

131. When the courts identify an infringement of a person's Article 8 rights, and in particular in the context of **his freedom to conduct his *sex life* and personal relationships as he wishes**, it is right to afford a remedy and to vindicate that right. The only permitted exception is where there is a countervailing public interest which in the particular circumstances is strong enough to outweigh it; that is to say, because one at least of the established "**limiting principle**s" comes into play. **Was it necessary and proportionate for the intrusion to take place, for example, in order to expose illegal activity or to prevent the public from being significantly misled by public claims hitherto made by the individual concerned** (as with Naomi Campbell's public denials of drug-taking)? Or was it necessary because the information, in the words of the Strasbourg court in *Von Hannover* at [60] and [76], **would make a contribution to "a *debate* of general interest"?** That is, of course, a very high test. It is yet to be determined how far that doctrine will be taken in the courts of this jurisdiction in relation to **photography in public places.** If taken literally, it would mean a very significant change in what is permitted. It would have a profound effect on the tabloid and **celebrity** culture to which we have become accustomed in recent years.

132. The facts of this case are far removed from those in *Van Hannover*. There can be little doubt that **intimate photographs** or recording of private **sexual activity**, however unconventional, **would be extremely difficult to justify at all by Strasbourg standards:** see eg *Dudgeon v UK* (cited above) at [49]–[53]. It is those to which we are now required by the Human Rights Act to have regard. Obviously, ***titillation* for its own sake could never be justified.** Yet it is reasonable to suppose that it was this which led so many thousands of people to accept the *News of the World*'s invitation on 30 March to "See the shocking video at notw.co.uk". **It would be quite unrealistic to think that these visits were prompted by a desire to participate in a "*debate* of general interest" of the kind contemplated in Von Hannover.**

133. More recently the principles have been affirmed in Strasbourg in the case of *Leempoel v Belgium*, App No 64772/01, 9 November 2006:

> "In matters relating to striking a balance between protecting private life and the freedom of expression that the Court had had to rule upon, it has always emphasised . . . the requirement that the publication of

> **information, documents** or **photographs** in the press **should serve the public interest** and make **a contribution to the *debate*** of general interest . . . Whilst the right for the public to be informed, a fundamental right in a democratic society that under particular circumstances may even relate to aspects of the private life of public persons, **particularly where political personalities are involved** . . . **publications whose sole aim is to satisfy the *curiosity*** of a certain public as to the details of the private life of a person, whatever their fame, **should not be regarded as contributing to any *debate* of general interest to society."**

134. In the light of the strict criteria I am required to apply, in the modern climate, **I could not hold that any of the visual images, whether published in the newspaper or on the website, can be justified in the public interest**. Nor can it be said in this case that even the information conveyed in the verbal descriptions would qualify.

Public interest: the journalists' perception

135. As the law stands, it seems clear that **it is for the court to decide whether a particular publication was in the public interest**. This may require further explanation. It is important to have in mind that some authorities (here and in Strasbourg) have in recent years placed emphasis on the need to make **due allowance for editorial judgment** and also **for a wide discretion so far as taste and modes of expression** are concerned: see eg *Jameel (Mohammed) v Wall Street Journal Sprl* [2007] 1 AC 359 at [31]–[33] in the context of privilege in the **law of defamation,** where Lord Bingham made these observations:

> "31 The necessary precondition of reliance on **qualified privilege** in this context is that the matter published should be one of **public interest.** In the present case the subject matter of the article complained of was of undoubted public interest. But that is not always, perhaps not usually, so. **It has been repeatedly and rightly said that what engages the interest of the public may not be material which engages the public inter32 Qualified privilege as a live issue only arises where a statement is defamatory and untrue**. It was in this context, and assuming the matter to be one of public interest, that Lord Nicholls proposed [in *Reynolds v Times Newspapers Ltd*], at p 202, **a test of responsible journalism**, a test repeated in *Bonnick* **v** *Morris* [2003] 1 AC 300, 309. **The rationale of this test is, as I understand, that there is no duty to publish and the public have no interest to read material which the publisher has not taken reasonable steps to verify.** As Lord Hobhouse observed with characteristic pungency, at p 238, 'No public interest is served by publishing or communicating misinformation.' **But the publisher is protected if he has taken such steps as a responsible journalist would**

take to try and ensure that what is published is accurate and fit for publication.

33 Lord Nicholls, at p 205, **listed certain matters** which might be taken into account in deciding whether the test of **responsible journalism** was satisfied. He intended these as pointers which might be more or less indicative, depending on the circumstances of a particular case, and not, I feel sure, as a series of hurdles to be negotiated by a publisher before he could successfully rely on qualified privilege. Lord Nicholls recognised, at pp 202–203, inevitably as I think, that it had to be a body other than the publisher, namely the court, which decided whether a publication was protected by qualified privilege. But this does not mean that the editorial decisions and judgments made at the time, without the knowledge of falsity which is a benefit of hindsight, are irrelevant. **Weight should ordinarily be given to the professional judgment of an editor or journalist in the absence of some indication that it was made in a casual, cavalier, slipshod or careless manner.**"

. . .

137. **In the defamation context, it seems clear that it is for the court alone to decide "whether the story as a whole was a matter of public interest", but there is scope for editorial judgment as to what details should be included within the story and as to how it is expressed (see eg also Lord Hoffmann at [51]).** That distinction seems to be clear, although in individual cases the line may be difficult to draw. Here the situation is that the journalists' perception was, or may have been, that the story was about Nazi role-play. Even though I concluded that this was not the case, should some allowance be made for a different view on the matter? The answer is probably in the negative, **because it is only the court's decision which counts on the central issue of public interest**.

138. It might seem reasonable to allow in this context for some difference of opinion. **I cannot believe that a journalist's sincere view on public interest, however irrationally arrived at, should be a complete answer.** A decision on public interest **must be capable of being tested by objectively recognised criteria**. But it could be argued as a matter of policy that allowance should be made for a decision reached which falls within a range of reasonably possible conclusions. Little was said in submissions on this aspect of the case.

139. It would seem odd if the only determining factor was the decision reached by a judge after leisurely debate and careful legal submission—luxuries not available to a hard-pressed journalist as a story is breaking with deadlines to meet. **Obviously, on the other hand, the courts could not possibly abdicate the responsibility for deciding issues of public interest and simply leave**

them to whatever decision the journalist happens to take. As Sir John Donaldson MR observed in *Francome v Mirror Group Newspapers Ltd* [1984] 1 WLR 892, 898, "The media . . . are peculiarly vulnerable to the error of confusing the public interest with their own interest".

140. Against this background, it would seem that there may yet be scope for paying regard to the concept of "**responsible journalism**", **which has been referred to over recent years in the context of public interest privilege in libel.** There is an obvious analogy. This rather vague term has been illuminated and defined in such a way that it could now be regarded as approaching a legal term of art. It has to be assessed in the round, **but there are certain guidelines which have been listed to assist in making a judgment: see eg Lord Nicholls' 10 non-exhaustive "factors" in *Reynolds v Times Newspapers Ltd*** [2001] 2 AC 127, **205.**

141. There may be a case for saying, when "public interest" has to be considered in the field of privacy, that a judge should enquire whether the relevant journalist's decision prior to publication was reached as a result of carrying out enquiries and checks consistent with "**responsible journalism**". In making a judgment about that, with the benefit of hindsight, a judge could no doubt have regard to considerations of that kind, **as well as to the broad principles set out in the PCC Code** as reflecting acceptable practice. Yet I must not disregard the remarks of Lord Phillips MR in *Campbell* [2003] QB 633 at [61] to the effect that the same test of public interest should *not* be applied in the "two very different torts".

. . .

The nature of compensatory damages in privacy cases

212. So far there have been very few awards of damages for infringement of privacy and they have all been pitched at **relatively modest levels** compared with some defamation awards: see eg *Campbell* (cited above), *Lady Archer v Williams* [2003] EMLR 38, *Douglas v Hello! Ltd* [2003] 3 All ER 996 and *McKennitt v Ash* [2006] EMLR 178. There have been some settlements which have been mentioned in the newspapers, but those are of no value as precedents or as setting any kind of tariff.

213. The claim is limited to damage inflicted in this jurisdiction and there are, or may be, other claims to be pursued in foreign jurisdictions. This may be **artificial** in some respects, but it has to be acknowledged.

214. Because both libel and breach of privacy are concerned with compensating for infringements of Article 8, there is clearly some scope for analogy. **On the other hand, it is important to remember that this case is *not* directly concerned with compensating for, or vindicating, injury to reputation.** The claim was not brought in libel. The distinctive functions of a defamation claim

do not arise. **The purpose of damages, therefore, must be to address the specific public policy factors in play** when there has been "an old fashioned breach of confidence" and/or an unauthorised revelation of personal information. **It would seem that the law is concerned to protect such matters as *personal dignity, autonomy and integrity.***

215. It has to be recognised, of course, that at first sight these notions appear somewhat incongruous when introduced in the present context. But, as I have already said in the context of liability, one must beware of being distracted by considerations which relate purely to taste or moral disapproval. **One should be careful not to dismiss matters going to *personal dignity* because a particular sexual activity or inclination itself may seem undignified.** After all, **sexual activity** is **rarely dignified.** That is far from saying, however, that **intrusions** into a person's **sexual** tastes and privacy cannot infringe the right to dignity protected by Article 8. The Strasbourg jurisprudence demonstrates the contrary.

216. Thus it is reasonable to suppose that damages for such an infringement may include ***distress, hurt feelings and loss of dignity***. The scale of the distress and indignity in this case is difficult to comprehend. It is probably unprecedented. Apart from distress, there is another factor which probably has to be taken into account of a less tangible nature. **It is accepted in recent jurisprudence that a legitimate consideration is that of vindication to mark the infringement of a right**: see eg *Ashley v Chief Constable of Sussex* [2008] 2 WLR 975 at [21]–[22] and *Chester v Afshar* [2005] 1 AC 134 at [87]. Again, it should be stressed that this is different from vindication of **reputation** (long recognised as a proper factor in the award of libel damages). **It is simply to mark the fact that either the state or a relevant individual has taken away or undermined the right of another—*in this case taken away a person's dignity and struck at the core of his personality.*** It is a relevant factor, but the **underlying policy is to ensure that an infringed right is met with "an adequate remedy".** If other factors mean that significant damages are to be awarded, in any event, the element of vindication does **not need** to be reflected in an even higher award. As Lord Scott observed in *Ashley, ibid,* " . . . **there is no reason why an award of compensatory damages should not also fulfil a vindicatory purpose".**

217. **If the objective is to provide an adequate remedy for the infringement of a right, it would not be served effectively if the court were merely to award nominal damages out of distaste for what the newspaper had revealed. As I have said, that should not be the court's concern.** It would demonstrate that the judge had been **distracted from the main task.** The danger would be that the more unconventional the taste, and the greater the **embarrassment**

caused by the revelation, the less effective would be the vindication. **The easier it would be for the media to hound minorities.**

218. These are the elements which need to be recognised in an award of damages in this field but, of course, they must be **proportionate** and **not open to the criticism of arbitrariness:** see eg *Tolstoy Miloslavsky v UK* (1995) 20 EHRR 442. It has been recognised since the Court of Appeal decision in *John v MGN Ltd* [1997] QB 586 that there must be a readily identifiable scale in the field of defamation so as to avoid, as far as possible, the vices pointed out in Strasbourg. The guidance there provided can to that extent be transferred to the present environment. **Thus, it will be legitimate, in particular, to pay some attention to the current levels of personal injury awards in order to help maintain a sense of proportion.**

219. It is common knowledge that general damages for pain and suffering are relatively low compared to awards made in the past in respect of some of the more serious defamation claims. In recent years, however, the practice has developed of acknowledging informally a ceiling in the libel context, broadly geared to that in personal injury awards. There are difficulties about this, as the editors of *Gatley on Libel and Slander* (10th edn) point out at para 9.6, because in truth there is no real comparison.

220. The ceiling in personal injury cases is now of the order of £220,000, which is intended to be appropriate for the worst types of injury, such as quadriplegia or severe brain damage. At every level of compensation, there are obvious incongruities if one tries to compare a possible libel award with the level of harm which a similar figure would reflect in the personal injury field. An award of £50,000, for example, would probably be appropriate for a moderately serious libel published in the national newspapers, but there is something of a mismatch if one tries to equate it in any real sense to injuries that would attract a similar level of award. Examples might include severe back injuries with unsightly scarring and impaired bowel and bladder function, or asbestos-related lung cancer with protracted symptoms (although less painful than in a case of mesothelioma). People recover significantly less, usually, for the total loss of one eye.

221. This merely illustrates the limits of useful comparison. It is as well to have in mind the remarks of Hirst LJ in *Jones v Pollard* [1997] EMLR 233, 257:

> **"I cannot accept that the main purpose of** *John* was to establish a ceiling, if by that is meant that in the most serious cases awards of general damages at the very top of the JSB range would normally be appropriate. Such cases comprise quadriplegia, very severe brain damage where 'in the most severe cases the plaintiff will be in a vegetative state . . . unable to obey commands, with no language functions and the need for 24

hour nursing care', and total blindness and deafness. For my part, save possibly in the most exceptional cases, I find it difficult to imagine any defamation action where even the most severe damage to **reputation**, accompanied by maximum aggravation, would be comparable with such appalling physical injuries. **The purpose of the personal injuries comparison sanction in John is in my judgment to assist juries and the Court of Appeal to maintain a sense of proportion,** by drawing a comparison between any prospective award of damages for defamation with the type of personal injury which would lead to a similar award, without of course seeking any precise correlation."

It is also to be borne in mind that some heads of damage reflected in libel awards, such as aggravation and vindication, have no direct point of comparison in personal injury cases.

222. It must be recognised that it may be appropriate to take into account any **aggravating conduct** in privacy cases on the part of the defendant which increases the hurt to the claimant's feelings or "rubs salt in the wound". As Lord Reid said, in the context of defamation, in *Cassell v Broome* at p 1085:

> **"It has long been recognised that in determining what sum within that bracket should be awarded, a jury, or other tribunal, is entitled to have regard to the conduct of the defendant. He may have behaved in a highhanded, malicious, insulting or oppressive manner in committing the tort or he or his counsel may at the trial have aggravated the injury by what they there said. That would justify going to the top of the bracket and** awarding as damages the largest sum that could fairly be regarded as compensation."

223. **It would thus seem to be appropriate to pay regard to such matters as the "follow up" of 6 April. I was asked by Mr Warby not to hold it against the Defendant that it had fought the case—a factor which would often be relevant to libel damages.** It is fair to say that in defamation cases it would be less likely to aggravate damages where the defendant had not chosen to renew the attack on the claimant's **reputation**; in other words, **there could be a significant difference in this respect as between a defence of (say) qualified privilege and one of justification**. In this litigation, the conduct of the Defendant's case has not involved further **intrusions** into privacy. **Considerable discretion has been shown in not referring, more than absolutely necessary, to embarrassing or intimate matters from the video recordings.** There have, it is true, been attacks on the Claimant's character (references to "depravity" and so forth), but **this is not a defamation case and reputation is not in issue**. It would not be right to increase damages because of attacks on character which the Defendant, if sued for libel, would wish to defend. Nevertheless, in advancing its case on public interest, the Nazi and con-

centration camp allegations were persisted in publicly and without success. **That is therefore a legitimate element to take into account and to reflect in any award.**

224. So too, it may be appropriate that a **claimant's conduct** should be taken into account (as it is in libel cases). Logically, it may be said, a claimant's conduct has nothing to do with whether or not his privacy has been invaded or the impact upon his feelings caused by such an **intrusion**. There is no doctrine of contributory negligence. On the other hand, **the extent to which his own conduct has contributed to the nature and scale of the distress might be a relevant factor on causation.** Has he, for example, put himself in a predicament by his own choice which contributed to his distress and loss of dignity?

225. **To what extent is he the author of his own misfortune?** Many would think that if a prominent man puts himself, year after year, into the hands (literally and metaphorically) of prostitutes (or even professional dominatrices) he is gambling in placing so much trust in them. There is a risk of exposure or **blackmail** inherent in such a course of conduct. **In this particular case, the evidence is that the Claimant had received a warning from Lord Stevens that he was being watched by some unidentified group of people hostile to him.** This was at the end of February. **He had also received a similar tip from Mr Bernie Ecclestone** in January. He had taken the matter sufficiently seriously to arrange instruction for himself in spotting or avoiding surveillance. Yet he continued to arrange parties, such as those on 8 and 28 March, knowing of the heightened risk.

226. To a casual observer, therefore, and especially with the benefit of hindsight, **it might seem that the Claimant's behaviour was reckless and almost self-destructive.** This does not excuse the **intrusion** into his privacy **but it might be a relevant factor to take into account when assessing causal responsibility for what happened**. It could be thought unreasonable to absolve him of all responsibility for placing himself and his family in the predicament in which they now find themselves. **It is part and parcel of human dignity that one must take at least some responsibility for one's own actions.** On the other hand, I have no evidence to suggest that the surveillance he was warned against had any connection with Woman E or the *News of the World*.

227. An issue to which attention was directed in counsel's submissions was that of **deterrence.** Passing reference has been made in the authorities from time to time to this concept, but it seems at least questionable whether deterrence should have a distinct (as opposed to a merely incidental) role to play in the award of compensatory damages. It is a notion more naturally associated with punishment. It often comes into the court's assessment of an appropriate punishment for prevalent criminal offences. There is also the anomaly to be considered, already mentioned in the context of exemplary

damages; namely, that if damages are paid to an individual for the **purpose** of deterring the defendant (or others) it would naturally be seen as an **undeserved windfall.**

228. Furthermore, if deterrence is to have any prospect of success it would be necessary to take into account (as with exemplary damages) the means of the relevant defendant (often a newspaper group). **Any award against the present Defendant would have to be so large that it would fail the test of proportionality when seen as fulfilling a compensatory function**. There is also a concomitant danger in including a large element of deterrence by way of "chilling effect".

229. It would in my judgment **not** be consistent with the approach of the Court of Appeal in *John v MGN Ltd* to impose, **solely for the sake of deterrence**, a large award of damages unrelated to any recognised scale or tariff. For this **purpose**, as I have said, I need to have well in mind the tariff applied over the last 10 years so far as defamation awards are concerned. It is true that the approach was questioned in *Gleaner Company Ltd v Abrahams* [2004] 1 AC 628, but I must nevertheless do my best to avoid any appearance of arbitrariness and keep the award in proportion.

230. I am conscious naturally that the analogy with defamation can only be pressed so far. I have already emphasised that **injury to reputation is not a directly relevant factor,** but it is also to be remembered that libel damages can achieve one objective that is impossible in privacy cases. Whereas **reputation** can be vindicated by an award of damages, in the sense that the claimant can be restored to the esteem in which he was previously held, **that is not possible where embarrassing personal information has been released for general publication**. As the media are well aware, once privacy has been infringed, the damage is done and the **embarrassment** is only augmented by pursuing a court action. Claimants with the degree of resolve (and financial resources) of Mr Max Mosley are likely to be few and far between. **Thus, if journalists successfully avoid the grant of an interlocutory injunction, they can usually relax in the knowledge that intrusive coverage of someone's sex life will carry no adverse consequences for them** and (as Mr Thurlbeck put it in his 2 April email) that the news agenda will move on.

231. Notwithstanding all this, it has to be accepted that an infringement of privacy cannot ever be effectively compensated by a monetary award. **Judges cannot achieve what is, in the nature of things, impossible.** That unpalatable fact cannot be mitigated by simply adding a few noughts to the number first thought of. Accordingly, it seems to me that the only realistic course is to select a figure which marks the fact that an unlawful **intrusion** has taken place while affording some degree of *solatium* to the injured party. That is all that can be done in circumstances where the traditional object of *restitutio*

is not available. **At the same time, the figure selected should not be such that it could be interpreted as minimising the scale of the wrong done or the damage it has caused.**

[The figure awarded was £60,000.]

David Murray v Big Pictures (UK) Ltd [2008] EWCA Civ 446

1. Dr Neil Murray and Mrs Joanne Murray are the parents of David Murray. Mrs Murray is the author of the Harry Potter books which, as everyone knows, she wrote under the name JK Rowling. **David was born on 23 March 2003**. On Monday 8 November 2004 Dr and Mrs Murray were out walking in an **Edinburgh street** some time after 9 o'clock in the morning. Dr Murray was pushing a **buggy** with David in it. **The respondent ('BPL') took a colour photograph of the family group which was subsequently published in the Sunday Express magazine on 3 April 2005 ('the Photograph').**
2. On 24 June 2005 proceedings were issued in David's name through his parents as his litigation friends against the publishers of the **Photograph**, Express Newspapers Plc as first defendant and against BPL as second defendant. The action against the first defendant was settled leaving BPL as the sole defendant**. In the action David asserts** an infringement of his right to respect for his privacy contrary to article 8 of the European Convention on Human Rights ('the Convention'). He also puts his claim under the **Data Protection Act 1998 ('the DPA').**
3. BPL applied for an order striking out the claim under CPR 3.4 or for summary judgment under CPR 24. The application was heard by Patten J ('the judge') on 20, 21 and 22 June 2007. By an order dated 7 August 2007 the judge struck out the claim and gave judgment for BPL. In reaching his conclusion he assumed that the facts alleged in the particulars of claim were true. **This appeal is brought with the permission of the judge, who gave permission on the ground that the case raises an important point about the relationship between the decision of the House of Lords in Campbell v MGN** [2004] UKHL 22**,** [2004] 2 AC 457 **and that of the ECtHR in Von Hannover v Germany** (2005) 40 EHRR 1.

. . .

The correct approach

19. As already indicated, the judge struck the action out under CPR 3.4 on the assumption that the facts alleged are true. The facts now alleged are some-

what more extensive than they were before the judge. **This was not the trial of a preliminary issue but an application to strike the action out without a trial.** The claimants are entitled to have the action tried unless the defendant's case is plainly correct on the assumed facts. We do not think that this principle is in dispute.

Privacy—the principles

20. The two most important recent cases that have considered the relevant principles are of course the decision of the House of Lords in *Campbell v MGN* and the decision of the ECtHR in *Von Hannover v Germany*, which were concerned with well-known celebrities, namely **Naomi Campbell** and **Princess Caroline** respectively. **In this court we are bound by the former and not the latter** and we fully recognise that the House of Lords made it clear in *Kay v Lambeth LBC* [2006] UKHL 10, [2006] 2 AC 465, that, in the event of a conflict between a decision of the House and a later decision of the ECtHR, lower courts, including this court, **must follow the former**: see per Lord Bingham at [43–44] in a passage quoted by the judge at [61]. We will therefore focus in particular upon the decision in *Campbell*.

Campbell v MGN

21. The facts are well-known but were shortly these. Naomi Campbell is an internationally famous fashion model. On 1 February 2001 the *Daily Mirror* **published articles and photographs** which Ms Campbell said infringed her right to respect for her private life contrary to article 8 of the Convention. The **photographs** included a **photograph** of her in the **street leaving Narcotics Anonymous ('NA'),** which had been taken by a freelance photographer specially employed for the **purpose**. The source of the information that Ms Campbell went to NA was either an associate of hers or a fellow addict. **Ms Campbell admitted that she was a drug addict and that she had lied about it publicly**. It was accepted on her behalf that, as Lord Hoffmann put it at [36], it was those falsehoods that entitled the newspaper to publish the fact that she was addicted to drugs. This left **three matters** which were said to infringe her rights under article 8: **first**, the fact that she attended meetings of NA; **secondly**, the published details of her attendance and what happened at the meetings; and **thirdly,** the **photographs** taken in the street without her knowledge or consent: see eg per Lord Hoffmann at [42].

22. Ms Campbell succeeded before Morland J and, although she failed in this court, she succeeded by a majority in the House of Lords. Lord Hope, Baroness Hale and Lord Carswell were in the majority, with Lord Nicholls and Lord Hoffmann dissenting. However, the difference of opinion was a difference on the facts. So, for example, Lord Hoffmann said at [31] that, although the principles were stated in varying language, **he could discern no**

significant differences between the views of the members of the appellate committee. In these circumstances, we naturally accept that their reasoning does not significantly differ, although there is we think scope for argument that it is not quite the same in every case.

23. Articles 8 and 10 of the Convention provide so far as relevant:

> "*Article 8—Right to respect for private and family life*
>
> 1. Everyone has the right to respect for his family and private life . . .
>
> 2. There shall be no interference by a public authority with the exercise of this right except such as is in accordance with the law and is necessary in a democratic society . . . for the protection of the rights and freedoms of others.
>
> *Article 10—Freedom of expression*
>
> 1. Everyone has the right of freedom of expression. . . .
>
> 2. The exercise of these freedoms, since it carries with it duties and responsibilities may be subject to such formalities, conditions, restrictions or penalties as are prescribed by law and are necessary in a democratic society, . . . for the protection of the **reputation** or rights of others . . . "

24. The principles stated by Lord Nicholls can we think be summarised in this way:

> i) The right to freedom of expression enshrined in **article 10** of the Convention and the right to respect for a person's privacy enshrined in **article 8** are **vitally important rights**. Both lie at **the heart of liberty** in a modern state and neither has precedence over the other: see [12].
>
> ii) Although the origin of the cause of action relied upon is breach of confidence, since information about an individual's private life would not, in ordinary usage, be called 'confidential', the more natural description of the position today is that such information is private and the essence of the tort is better encapsulated now as **misuse of private information**: see [14].
>
> iii) The values enshrined in articles 8 and 10 are now part of the cause of action and should be treated as of general application and as being as much applicable to disputes **between individuals** as to disputes between **individuals and a public authority:** see [17].
>
> iv) Essentially the **touchstone** of private life is whether in respect of the disclosed facts the person in question had a reasonable expectation of privacy: see [21].
>
> v) In deciding whether there is in principle an invasion of privacy, it is important to distinguish between that question, which seems to us to be

the question which is often described as whether article 8 is engaged, **and the subsequent question whether, if it is, the individual's rights are nevertheless *not infringed* because of the combined effect of article 8(2) and article 10:** see [22].

25. This last point seems to us to be of potential significance because of the view that Lord Nicholls took of the suggestion that one of the requirements which a claimant must satisfy is that publication of matter must be ***'highly offensive*** *in order to be actionable'*. He said this at [22]:

> "Different forms of words, usually to much the same effect, have been suggested from time to time. The second Restatement of Torts in the United States (1977), article 652D, p 394, uses the formulation of disclosure of matter which *'would be **highly offensive** to a **reasonable** person'*. In *Australian Broadcasting Corporation v Lenah Game Meats Pty Ltd* (2001) 185 ALR 1, 13, para 42, Gleeson CJ used words, widely quoted, having a similar meaning. This particular formulation should be used with care, for two reasons. **First,** the '**highly offensive**' phrase is suggestive of a stricter test of private information than a reasonable expectation of privacy. **Second,** the '**highly offensive**' formulation can all too easily bring into account, when deciding whether the disclosed information was private, considerations which go more properly to issues of *proportionality*; for instance, the degree of **intrusion** into private life, and the extent to which publication was a matter of proper public concern. This could be a recipe for confusion."

26. It is clear from that paragraph that Lord Nicholls regarded **the *'highly offensive*** *test'* as a stricter test than his own formulation of 'reasonable expectation of privacy'. It seems to us therefore that, in so far as it is or may be relevant to consider whether publication of information or matter was '**highly offensive**', **it is relevant to consider it in the context,** not of whether article 8 is engaged, but of the issues relevant to **proportionality,** that is to the balance to be struck between article 8 and article 10.

27. In the subsequent decision of this court in *McKennitt v Ash* [2006] EWCA Civ 1714, [2008] QB 73, Buxton LJ, with whom Latham and Longmore LJJ agreed, underlined at [11] the point that articles 8 and 10 of the Convention are now the very content of the domestic tort that the English court must enforce, and **identified two key questions** which must be answered in a case where the complaint is of the wrongful publication of private information. They are **first**, whether the information is private in the sense that it is in principle protected by article 8 (ie such that article 8 is in principle engaged) and, **secondly**, if so, *whether in all the circumstances the interest of the owner of the information must yield to the right to freedom of expression conferred on the publisher by article 10.* In expressing that conclusion Buxton LJ quoted

the last part of the extract from [22] of Lord Nicholls' speech which we have set out above.

28. Baroness Hale's approach was the same as that of Lord Nicholls. **She said at [134] that the balancing exercise may begin when the person publishing the information knows or ought to know that that there is a reasonable expectation that the information in question will be kept confidential.** At [135] she added that that test is much simpler than the test in the *Australian Broadcasting Corporation* case that publication would be **highly offensive** to a reasonable person. Then, importantly, she again stressed (at [137]) that **the 'reasonable expectation of privacy' is the threshold test which brings the balancing exercise into play**. In the latter part of her speech, she considered *how the balance should be struck.*

29. It is perhaps arguable that Lord Hope took a somewhat different view on the relevance or potential relevance of the '**highly offensive**' test: see eg [100]. However, he said at [92] that in some cases the question whether the information is public or private will be obvious and added:

> "Where it is not, the broad test is whether disclosure of the information about the individual ("A") would give substantial offence to A, assuming that A was placed in similar circumstances and was a person of ordinary sensibilities."

At [93], after referring to the judgment of Gleeson CJ in the *Australian Broadcasting Corporation* case, **Lord Hope said that that test was useful in cases where there was room for doubt** but that there was no room for doubt on the facts of the *Campbell* case.

30. Thus, Lord Hope's view was that the first question is whether the information is obviously private. He explained what he meant by 'obviously private' in the first sentence of his [96]:

> "**If the information is obviously private,** the situation will be one where the person to whom it relates can reasonably expect his privacy to be respected. So there is normally no need to go on and ask whether it would be **highly offensive** for it to be published."

On that approach, there is no difference between Lord Nicholls, Baroness Hale and Lord Hope, namely that the first question is whether there is a reasonable expectation of privacy and, if there is, that article 8 is in principle engaged. Nor is there any difference between their opinions and that of Lord Carswell, who expressly agreed with Lord Hope and Baroness Hale.

31. As we said earlier, Lord Hoffmann took the view that he too was applying the same principles. At [51] he emphasised that **the law now focuses upon the protection of human autonomy and dignity**—

> "the right to control the dissemination of information about one's private life and the right to the **esteem** and **respect** of other people."

At [72] Lord Hoffmann said that the same principles applied to **photographs** but added at [73] that the famous and the not so famous who go out in public must accept that they may be photographed without their consent, just as they may be observed without their consent. He concluded:

> "As Gleeson CJ said in *Australian Broadcasting Corporation v Lenah Game Meats Pty Ltd* (2001) 185 ALR 1, 13, para 41:
>
> > "Part of the price we pay for living in an organised society is that we are exposed to observation in a variety of ways by other people."

Lord Hoffmann then drew an **important distinction between the mere taking of a photograph and its publication**:

> "74. But the fact that we cannot avoid being photographed does not mean that anyone who takes or obtains such **photographs** can publish them **to the world at large**. In the recent case of *Peck v United Kingdom* (2003) 36 EHRR 41 Mr Peck was filmed on a public street in an embarrassing moment by a CCTV camera. Subsequently, the film was broadcast several times on the television. The Strasbourg court said (at p 739) that this was an invasion of his privacy contrary to article 8:
>
> > "the relevant moment was viewed to an extent which far exceeded any exposure to a passer-by or to security observation and to a degree surpassing that which the applicant could possibly have foreseen when he walked in Brentwood on August 20, 1995."

33. Lord Hoffmann then distinguished in [75 and 76] between the widespread publication of a **photograph** of someone in a situation of **humiliation** or severe **embarrassment** and the **photograph** taken of Ms Campbell. He concluded, in **disagreement with the majority**, that there was no invasion of Ms Campbell's privacy. He did not analyse the facts by specific reference to the two stages identified above. Lord Nicholls doubted whether the disputed **photographs** were taken in circumstances in which there was a reasonable expectation of privacy at [25–27] but concluded at [28–35] that the balance between article 8 and article 10 came down in favour of permitting publication.

34. The members of the majority concluded that the **photographs** were **taken in circumstances** in which there was **a reasonable expectation of privacy** and held that **the balance** between Ms Campbell's rights under article 8 and the newspaper's rights of freedom of expression under article 10 came down in favour of the conclusion that the publication of the disputed **photographs** involved **a breach of Ms Campbell's rights under article 8**. The balance was

considered in considerable detail: see per Lord Hope at [112–125], especially at [122–124], Baroness Hale at [142–158] and Lord Carswell at [169–170].

35. In these circumstances, so far as the **relevant principles** to be derived from **Campbell** are concerned, they can we think be **summarised in this way**. The **first question** is whether there is a reasonable expectation of privacy. This is of course **an objective question**. The nature of the question was discussed in *Campbell*. Lord Hope emphasised that the reasonable expectation was that of the person who is affected by the publicity. He said at [99]:

> "The question is what **a reasonable person of ordinary sensibilities** would feel if she was placed in the same position as the claimant and faced with the same publicity."

We do not detect any difference between Lord Hope's opinion in this regard and the opinions expressed by the other members of the appellate committee.

36. As we see it, the question whether there is a reasonable expectation of privacy is a broad one, which takes account of all the circumstances of the case. They include the **attributes** of the claimant, the **nature** of the activity in which the claimant was engaged, the **place** at which it was happening, the **nature and purpose of the intrusion,** the **absence of consent** and whether it was known or could be inferred, the **effect on the claimant** and **the circumstances in which and the purposes for which the information came into the hands of the publisher.**

37. In the case of a **child** the position is somewhat **different** from that of an adult. The judge recognised this in [23] of his judgment, where he said this, albeit in the context of a somewhat differently formulated test discussed by Lord Hope at [100] in *Campbell*:

> "This test cannot, of course, be applied to a child of the Claimant's age who has no obvious sensitivity to any invasion of his privacy which does not involve some direct physical **intrusion** into his personal space. **A literal application of Lord Hope's words would lead to a rejection of any claim by an infant unless it related to harassment of an extreme kind.** A proper consideration of the degree of protection to which a child is entitled under Art. 8 has, I think, for the reasons which I gave earlier to be considered in a wider context by taking into account not only the circumstances in which the **photograph** was taken and its actual impact on the child**, but also the position of the child's parents and the way in which the child's life as part of that family has been conducted**. **This merely reinforces my view about the artificiality of bringing the claim in the name of the child.** The question whether a child in any particular circumstances has a reasonable expectation for

privacy must be determined by the Court taking an objective view of the matter **including the reasonable expectations of his parents in those same circumstances as to whether their children's lives in a public place should remain private.** Ultimately it will be a matter of judgment for the Court with every case depending upon its own facts. The point that needs to be emphasized is that the assessment of the impact of the taking and the subsequent publication of the **photograph** on the child cannot be limited by whether the child was physically aware of the **photograph** being taken or published or personally affected by it. **The Court can attribute to the child reasonable expectations about his private life based on matters such as how it has in fact been conducted by those responsible for his welfare and upbringing."**

38. Subject to the point we made earlier that ***we do not share the judge's view that the proceedings are* artificial,** *we agree with the approach suggested by the judge in that paragraph.* **Thus, for example, if the parents of a child *courted publicity* by procuring the publication of photographs of the child in order to promote their own interests, the position would or might be quite different from a case like this,** where the parents have taken care to keep their children out of the public gaze39. As applied in this case, which, unlike *McKennitt v Ash*, is **not a case** in which there was a **pre-existing relationship** between the parties, the first question at any trial of the action would be whether article 8 was in principle engaged; that is whether David had a reasonable expectation of privacy in the sense **that a reasonable person in his position would feel that the Photograph should not be published**. On Lord Nicholls' analysis, that is a lower test than would be involved if the question were whether a reasonable person in his position would regard publication as either offensive or **highly offensive**. That question would or might be relevant at the second, balancing stage, assuming article 8 to be engaged on the footing that David had **a reasonable expectation that commercial picture agencies like BPL would not set out to photograph him with a view to selling those photographs for money without his consent, which would of course have to be given through his parents.**

40. At a trial, if the answer to the **first question** were yes, the next question would be how the balance should be struck as between the individual's right to privacy on the one hand and the publisher's right to publish on the other. If the balance were struck in favour of the individual, publication would be an infringement of his or her article 8 rights, whereas if the balance were struck in favour of the publisher, there would be no such infringement by reason of a combination of articles 8(2) and 10 of the Convention.

41. At each stage, the questions to be determined are essentially **questions of fact**. The question whether there was a reasonable expectation privacy is **a**

question of fact. If there was, the next question involves determining the relevant factors and balancing them. As Baroness Hale put it at [157], the weight to be attached to the various considerations is a matter of fact and degree. That is essentially a matter for the trial judge.

. . .

Discussion

45. We have reached a different conclusion from that of the judge. In our opinion it is at least arguable that David had a reasonable expectation of privacy. **The fact that he is a child is in our view of greater significance than the judge thought.** The courts have recognised the importance of the rights of children in many different contexts and so too has the international community: see eg *R v Central Independent Television Plc* [1994] Fam 194 per Hoffmann LJ at 204–5 and the United Nations Convention on the Rights of the Child, to which the United Kingdom is a party. More specifically, clause 6 of the Press Complaints Commission Editors' **Code** of Practice contains this sentence under the heading Children:

> **"v) Editors must not use the fame, notoriety or position of the parent or guardian as sole justification for publishing details of a child's private** life."

There is also a publication called The **Editors' Codebook**, which refers to the **Code** and to the above statement. Although it is true that the **Codebook** states (at page 51) in a section headed **'Intrusion'** that the Press Complaints Commission has ruled that the mere publication of a child's image cannot breach the **Code** when it is taken in a public place and is unaccompanied by any private details or materials which might embarrass or inconvenience the child, which is particularly unlikely in the case of babies or very young children, it seems to us **that everything must depend on the circumstances**.

46. So, for example, in **Tugendhat and Christie on The Law of Privacy and the Media th**e authors note at paragraph 13.128 (in connection with a complaint made by Mr and Mrs Blair) that the PCC has stated that:

> **"the acid test to be applied by newspapers in writing about the children of public figures who are not famous in their own right (unlike the Royal Princes) is whether a newspaper would write such a story** if it was about an ordinary person."

It seems to us to be at least arguable that a similar approach should be adopted to **photographs**. **If a child of parents who are not in the public eye could reasonably expect not to have photographs of him published in the media, so too should the child of a famous parent.** In our opinion it is at least arguable that a child of 'ordinary' parents could reasonably expect that the press would not **target** him and publish **photographs** of him. The same is true of David, especially since on the alleged facts here the **Photograph** would not have been taken or published if he had not been the son of JK Rowling.

47. Neither *Campbell* nor *Von Hannover* is a case about a child. **There is no authoritative case in England of a child being *targeted* as David was here.** There is an unreported decision of Connell J in *MGN Ltd v Attard*, 9 October 2001, in which he expressed doubts as to whether article 8 was engaged in respect of the publication of a **photograph** taken **in a Malta street of the survivor of the conjoined twins.** However, the facts were very different from this case because the parents would have permitted publication if they could have **agreed a price** with the newspaper.

48. The case that particularly struck the judge was, however, *Hosking v Runting*, which he regarded as on all fours with this. The facts are indeed similar to those here. However, for the reasons we gave earlier, we are of the opinion that the test applied in that case is not the same as the test of reasonable expectation of privacy, which falls to be applied at the first stage of the analysis. In giving the leading judgment of the New Zealand Court of Appeal, Gault P and Blanchard J (with whom Tipping J substantially agreed) described at [117] the two fundamental requirements for a successful claim for interference with privacy:

> "1. The existence of facts in respect of which there **is a reasonable expectation of privacy**; and
>
> 2. publicity given to those private facts that would be considered **highly offensive** to an objective reasonable person."

49. As can be seen, those are separate considerations. For the reasons given earlier, as explained by Lord Nicholls in *Campbell*, it is **only the first question** that has to be asked in order to decide whether article 8 is in principle engaged. If it is, **the second question** may be relevant in carrying out the **balancing exercise** as between the rights under article 8 and the rights under article 10. It is true that the court decided both questions in favour of the defendants but the underlying basis for the conclusions of Gault and Blanchard JJ can be seen from [161–165] quoted by the judge at [34]:

> "161. The real concern of the appellants as parents relates not to the publication of **photographs** of their two children in the street, but to publication of the **photographs** along with identification and the association of them with a "**celebrity**" parent. We accept the sincerity of their anxiety for the wellbeing of the children and their concern at the prospect of recurring unwanted media attention. They wish to protect the freedom of the children to live normal lives without constant fear of

media **intrusion.** They feel that if publication of the present **photographs** is prevented there will be no incentive for those who, in the future, might pursue the children in order to capture marketable images.

162. We must focus on the issues now presented. If there is no case for relief now, we cannot address the future. We are inclined to the view, however, that the concerns are overstated.

163. We are **not** persuaded that a case is made out for an injunction to protect the children from a **real risk of physical harm.** We do not see any substantial likelihood of anyone with ill intent seeking to identify the children from magazine **photographs**. We **cannot** see the intended publication **increasing any risk** that might exist because of the public prominence of their father.

164. The inclusion of the **photographs** of Ruby and Bella in an article in New Idea would not publicise any fact in respect of which there could be a reasonable expectation of privacy. The **photographs** taken by the first respondent do not disclose anything more than could have been observed by any member of the public in Newmarket on that particular day. They do not show where the children live, or disclose any information that might be useful to someone with ill intent. The existence of the twins, their age and the fact that their parents are separated are already matters of public record. **There is a considerable line of cases in the United States establishing that generally there is no right to privacy when a person is photographed on a public street.** Cases such as *Peck* and perhaps *Campbell* qualify this to some extent, so that in exceptional cases a person might be entitled to restrain additional publicity being given to the fact that they were present on the street in particular circumstances. That is not, however, this case.

165. We are not convinced a person of ordinary sensibilities would find the publication of these **photographs highly offensive** or objectionable even bearing in mind that young children are involved. One of the **photographs** depicts a relatively detailed image of the twins' faces. However, it is not sufficient that the circumstances of the photography were considered **intrusive** by the subject (even if that were the case, which it is not here because Mrs Hosking was not even aware the **photographs** had been taken). The real issue is whether publicising the content of the **photographs** (or the "fact" that is being given publicity) would be offensive to the ordinary person. We cannot see any real harm in it."

50. **It seems to us that, although the judges regarded the parents' concerns as overstated, the parents' wish, on behalf of their children, to protect the**

freedom of the children to live normal lives without the constant fear of media intrusion is (at least arguably) entirely reasonable and, other things being equal, should be protected by the law. It is true, as the judges say at [164], that the **photographs** showed no more than could be seen by anyone in the street **but, once published, they would be disseminated to a potentially large number of people on the basis that they were children of well-known parents,** ***leading to the possibility of further*** **intrusion** ***in the future.*** If the **photographs** had been taken, as Lord Hope put it at [123] of *Campbell*, to show the scene in a street by a passer-by and later published as street scenes, that would be one thing**, but they were not taken as street scenes but were taken** ***deliberately,*** **in** ***secret*** **and with a** ***view to their subsequent publication.*** They were taken for the **purpose** of publication for profit, **no doubt in the knowledge that the parents would have objected to them.**

51. We recognise that the facts of *Hosking v Runting*, as in this case, are not the same as in *Campbell*, but in our opinion the judges' view of whether the children would have a reasonable expectation of privacy, in the sense that they could reasonably expect to be left alone without **photographs** of them being published in the media without their consent, **is at least arguably a view which should not be adopted here.** It does not seem to us to follow from the reasoning of the House of Lords in *Campbell* that the judges were correct (let alone plainly correct) on the reasonable expectation of privacy point.

52. As to [165], as the judge observed at [35], the approach is different from that approved in *Campbell*. The approved test is not whether a person of **ordinary sensibilities** would find the publication **highly offensive** or objectionable, even bearing in mind that young children are involved, but (as Lord Hope put it in the passage quoted at [35] above) **what a reasonable person of ordinary sensibilities would feel if he or she was placed in the same position as the claimant and faced with the same publicity.** The judges did not consider either of the two questions posed through the eyes of the reasonable child, **or (more realistically) through the eyes of the reasonable parent on behalf of the child**. Although the judge recognised the error, he said that neither Lord Hope nor Baroness Hale expressed any doubts about the decision in *Hosking v Runting*. That is true but the question whether *Hosking v Runting* would be followed here was not the question which the House of Lords had to decide. In these circumstances, the decision in *Hosking v Runting* was in our opinion not a sufficient reason to hold that the claimant cannot show a reasonable expectation of privacy at a trial. Yet, as we read [68], the judge's reliance on *Hosking v Runting* was a significant part of his reasoning.

53. We note in passing that in *Rogers v Television New Zealand Limited* [2007] NZSC 91, although four of the five judges in the Supreme Court said that they

were willing to proceed on the footing that *Hosking v Runting* represented the law, Elias CJ and Anderson J (who were admittedly dissenting) expressed doubts: see [23, 25, 26 and 144].

54. As to the judge's [65] and [66], as we read his reasoning he focuses on the taking of the **Photograph**. As we indicated earlier, it is our opinion that the **focus** should not be on the taking of a **photograph** in the street, but **on its publication.** In the *absence of distress* or the like caused when the **photograph** is taken, **the mere taking of a photograph in the street may well be entirely unobjectionable**. We do not therefore accept, as the judge appears to suggest in [65], that, if the claimant succeeds in this action, the courts will have created an image right.

55. **We recognise that there may well be circumstances in which there will be no reasonable expectation of privacy, even after *Von Hannover*. However, as we see it all will (as ever) depend upon the facts of the particular case.** The judge suggests that a distinction can be drawn between a child (or an adult) engaged in family and sporting activities **and something as simple as a walk down a street or a visit to the grocers to buy the milk.** This is on the basis that the first type of activity is clearly part of a person's private recreation time intended to be enjoyed in the company of family and friends and that, on the test deployed in *Von Hannover*, publicity of such activities is **intrusive** and can adversely affect the exercise of such social activities. We agree with the judge that that is indeed the basis of the ECtHR's approach **but we do not agree** that it is possible to draw a clear distinction in principle between the two kinds of activity. **Thus, an expedition to a café of the kind which occurred here seems to us to be at least arguably part of each member of the family's *recreation time* intended to be enjoyed by them and such that publicity of it is intrusive and such as adversely to affect such activities in the future.**

56. We do not share the predisposition identified by the judge in [66] that routine acts such as a visit to a **shop or a ride on a bus** should not attract any reasonable expectation of privacy. **All depends upon the circumstances. The position of an adult may be very different from that of a child.** In this appeal we are concerned only with the question whether David, as a small child, had a reasonable expectation of privacy, not with the question whether his parents would have had such an expectation. Moreover, we are concerned with the **context** of this case, which was not for example a single **photograph** taken of David which was for some reason subsequently published.

57. It seems to us that, subject to the facts of the particular case, **the law should indeed protect children from intrusive media attention,** at any rate to the extent of holding that a child has a reasonable expectation that he or she will not be ***targeted*** in order to obtain **photographs** in a **public place** for publica-

tion which the person who took or procured the taking of the **photographs knew would be objected to** on behalf of the child. That is the **context** in which the **photographs** of David were taken.

58. It is important to note that so to hold does not mean that the child will have, as the judge puts it in [66], a guarantee of privacy. To hold that the child has a reasonable expectation of privacy is only the first step. Then comes the balance which must be struck between the child's rights to respect for his or her private life under article 8 and the publisher's rights to freedom of expression under article 10. **This approach does not seem to us to be inconsistent with that in Campbell, which was not considering the case of a child.**

59. In these circumstances we do not think that it is necessary for us to analyse the decision in *Von Hannover* in any detail, especially since this is not an appeal brought after the trial of the action but an appeal against an order striking the action out. Suffice it to say that, in our opinion, the view we have expressed **is consistent with that in Von Hannover, to which, as McKennitt v Ash makes clear, it is permissible to have regard.** We do not disagree with the judge's summary of the decision in *Von Hannover* which we have quoted at [43 ix)] above. Mr Warby drew our attention to the oral submissions made to the ECtHR by Mr Prinz on behalf Princess Caroline, where he emphasised the **campaign of harassment** conducted against her by the German media. That was indeed part of the **context** in which the decision was made. For his part Mr Spearman stressed the fact that some of the **photographs**, the publication of which was held to infringe Princess Caroline's rights under article 8, showed her doing no more than walking in public.

60. The **context** of *Von Hannover* was therefore different from this but we have little doubt that, **if the assumed facts of this case were to be considered by the ECtHR, the court would hold that David had a reasonable expectation of privacy and it seems to us to be more likely than not that, on the assumed facts, it would hold that the article 8/10 balance would come down in favour of David**. We would add that there is nothing in the Strasbourg cases since *Von Hannover* which in our opinion leads to any other conclusion: see eg *Reklos and Davourlis v Greece*, petition no 1234/05, 6 September 2007.

61. In these circumstances, **the judge was in our judgment wrong to strike out David's claim on the ground that he had no arguable case that he had a reasonable expectation of privacy.** Understandably, the judge did not consider whether, if article 8 was engaged, David had an arguable case that the balance should be struck in his favour. In our opinion David has an arguable case on both points and his parents should be permitted to take his claim to trial on his behalf.

In Attorney General's Reference No 3 of 1999: Application by the British Broadcasting Corporation to set aside or vary a Reporting Restriction Order [2009] UKHL 34

7. But broadcasting these details will not just be of **interest to the public**. **Revealing D's name** will affect him too. As Lord Hoffmann observed in *Jameel (Mohammed) v Wall Street Journal Europe Sprl* [2007] 1 AC 359, para 91, **the reputation of an individual is part of his personality.** It is, as he said, an "**immortal part of himself**". So it is right that he should be able to vindicate it. *But control under the common law over information which is objectionable and false is one thing. The law of defamation will usually provide a remedy.* **Not so where information which the individual wishes to screen from others is accurately reported and is true.**

. . .

The article 8 right

18. The first question, as to whether D's article 8 right is engaged, requires careful scrutiny. **As I said earlier, the common law of defamation offers no assistance where information which the individual wishes to screen from others will be broadcast accurately and is true**. But the area of the law to which Lord Pannick's submissions direct attention is the wrongful disclosure of private information. Like everyone else, there are **facets** of D's **personality** that are unique to him. They include aspects of his identity such as his **name**, his **character** and his **appearance**. In *R v Broadcasting Standards Commission, Ex p BBC* [2001] QB 885, para 48, Lord Mustill, sitting in the Court of Appeal, said:

> "To my mind the privacy of a human being denotes at the same time the personal **'space'** in which the individual is free to be itself, and also the **carapace**, or shell, **or umbrella**, or whatever other metaphor is preferred, which **protects that space from intrusion**. An infringement of privacy is **an affront to the personality,** which is damaged both by the **violation** and by the **demonstration** that the personal space is not inviolate."

It has come to be accepted, under the influence of human rights instruments such as article 8 of the European Convention, that **the privacy of personal information is something that is worthy of protection in its own right**: *Campbell v MGN Ltd*, para 46, per Lord Hoffmann. As he put it in para 50, human rights law has identified private information as something worth protecting **as an aspect of human autonomy and dignity.**

19. In *Von Hannover v Germany* (2005) 40 EHRR 1, para 50 the European court said that the concept of private life extends to aspects relating to personal identity, such as a **person's name** or a **person's picture**, and that it includes **a person's physical and psychological integrity**. As Clayton and Tomlinson, *The Law of Human Rights*, 2nd ed (2009), para 12.288, put it, **identity involves the manner in which a person presents himself to the state and to others.** *So there is a **zone of interaction** of a person with others, even in a public context, which may fall within the scope of private life.* The issue in this case is about the publication of a name, linked to an allegation that the person is guilty of the crime of rape. In *Burghartz v Switzerland* (1994) 18 EHRR 101 it was about the use of name as a means of personal identity and of linking it to a family: see para 24. It is not about whether the article 8 right is engaged by the publication of a **photograph**. **So the familiar trilogy of cases that have addressed that issue**—*Campbell v MGN Ltd* [2004] 2 AC 457 (Naomi Campbell), *Von Hannover v Germany* (Princess Caroline of Monaco) and *Murray v Express Newspapers plc* [2008] EWCA Civ 446, [2008] 3 WLR 1360—offer no direct assistance. It has been suggested that the European court in *Von Hannover v Germany* took a wider view of what falls within an individual's private life than *Campbell v MGN Ltd*: see *Murray v Express Newspapers plc*, para 43 (viii). But it is not necessary to resolve that issue in this case. The principles on which all those cases proceed indicate that **the publication of D's name will engage article 8 if this is done in circumstances where D has a reasonable expectation of privacy.** This, as Lord Nicholls said in *Campbell v MGN Ltd*, para 21, is **the touchstone** of what falls within the ambit of "private life".

20. The fact that D was acquitted of the rape is not of itself private information the publication of which would be incompatible with his right to privacy. This has nothing to do with his private life. The trial was held in public, and the media were at liberty to publish D's name along with other details of the case other than the identity of the complainant. But the point to which the BBC wish to draw attention is not confined to his acquittal. At the heart of the broadcast will be the fact that a DNA profile obtained from a saliva sample that was taken from him when he was arrested for an offence of burglary was matched with the DNA profile obtained from swabs taken from the rape victim. The judge's ruling that the DNA evidence was inadmissible having been held to have been wrong in *Attorney General's Reference (No 3 of 1999)* [2001] 2 AC 91, it is arguable that it is available as new and compelling evidence for the **purpose** of a retrial within the meaning of section 78 of the Criminal Justice Act 2003. What the BBC wish to do is to undermine his acquittal and to campaign for his retrial. Lord Pannick's response is that if the keeping and storing of his DNA sample was an interference with the right guaranteed to D by article 8(1), so too must be the programme that the BBC wish to make which will refer to him by name and to the circumstances of

his acquittal on the assumption that his DNA profile is available as new and compelling evidence.

21. D was acquitted of the burglary, and it was conceded in that case that his DNA profile ought to have been removed from the database before the match was made under section 64(1) of the Police and Criminal Evidence Act 1984, as it was prior to the substitution of section 64(1A) by section 82 of the Criminal Justice and Police Act 2001. In *R (S) v Chief Constable of the South Yorkshire Police* [2004] UKHL 39, [2004] 1 WLR 2196, differing views were expressed as to whether retention of fingerprints or samples amounted to an interference with the right to respect for private life. In para 31 Lord Steyn said that he inclined to the view that article 8(1) was not engaged and that, if he was wrong in this view, any interference was very modest indeed. Baroness Hale of Richmond disagreed. In para 78 **she said that it would be surprising if Strasbourg were not to consider it incumbent upon the state to justify its retention and storage of DNA samples and profiles**. Her prediction was borne out by the court's decision in *S and Marper v United Kingdom*, Application Nos 30562/04 and 30566/04, 4 December 2008. In that case the Grand Chamber drew attention in para 122 to the risk of stigmatising those who have not been convicted of any offence and are entitled to the presumption of innocence. **It held that the blanket and indiscriminate nature of the power of retention under the substituted section 64(1A) of PACE failed to strike a fair balance between the competing public and private interests, and that there had been a violation of article 8: para 125.**

22. **As the indiscriminate retention of samples of a person's DNA must now be held to be incompatible with his rights under article 8(1), so too must be the publication of the fact that his retained DNA has been used to link him to the commission of a crime of which he has been acquitted.** I think that it must follow that the test as to whether this was information in respect of which D had a reasonable expectation of privacy is satisfied. He was acquitted of the burglary in connection with which his DNA samples were taken. He has been acquitted of the rape too. The double jeopardy rule has been abolished but the Attorney General has not taken steps to seek his retrial for that offence. **He remains entitled to the presumption of innocence. This is not just an article 6 point. It has a direct bearing on the approach that must be taken to his article 8 right.** The link that his DNA sample provides to the commission of the rape is personal information. **The giving of publicity to the link will inevitably suggest that he is guilty of the offence.** Lord Pannick described this **as the *jigsaw* effect**. His **reputation,** his **personality**, the **umbrella** that protects his **personal space** from **intrusion,** will just as inevitably be damaged by it. The conclusion that broadcasting this

information will engage his right to respect for his private life seems to me to be inescapable.

The article 10 right

23. **The question then is whether publication of the facts that the BBC wish to publish in the exercise of their right of freedom of expression under article 10 can be justified under article 8(2).** The tests that must be applied are well settled. **They are whether publication of the material pursues a legitimate aim, and whether the benefits that will be achieved by its publication are proportionate to the harm** *that may be done by the interference with the right to privacy.* Any restriction of the right of freedom of expression must be subjected to **very close scrutiny**. *But **so too** must any restriction on the right to privacy.* The protection of private life has to be balanced against the freedom of expression guaranteed by article 10: *Von Hannover v Germany* (2005) 40 EHRR 1, para 58. One must start from the position that **neither** article 8 **nor** article 10 has any **pre-eminence** over the other. The values that each right seeks to protect are **equally important**. The question is how far, as article 8(2) puts it, it is **"necessary"** for the one to be qualified in order to protect the values that the other seeks to protect.

24. Further guidance as to the approach that is to be adopted was given in *Von Hannover v Germany*. In **para 60** the European court said that in the cases in which it has had to balance the protection of private life against freedom of expression, **it has always stressed the contribution that photographs or articles in the press make to a debate of general interest**. In para 63 it pointed out that a **fundamental distinction** had to be **drawn between** reporting facts which were capable of contributing to **imparting information** and **ideas** on matters of public interest and reporting **details of the private life** of an individual. In **para 76** it said that the decisive factor in balancing the protection of private life against freedom of expression **should lie in the contribution that the published material makes to a debate of general interest**. So the extent to which the programme that the BBC wish to make will satisfy that test must be examined with just as much care as the question whether the broadcast will engage D's right under article 8.

25. Lord Pannick suggested it would be open to the BBC to raise the issue of general interest without mentioning D's name or in any other way disclosing his identity. But I think that Mr Millar was right when he said that the BBC should not be required to restrict the scope of their programme in this way. **The freedom of the press to exercise its own judgment in the presentation of journalistic material has been emphasised by the Strasbourg court. In Jersild v Denmark (1994) 19 EHRR 1, para 31, the court said that it was not for it, nor for the national courts for that matter, to substitute their own views for those of the press as to what technique of reporting should be**

adopted by journalists. It recalled that article 10 protects not only the substance of the ideas and the information expressed **but also the form in which they are conveyed**. In essence **article 10 leaves it for journalists to decide what details it is necessary to reproduce to ensure credibility:** see *Fressoz v France* (1999) 31 EHRR 28, para 54. So the BBC are entitled to say that the question whether D's identity needs to be disclosed to give weight to the message that the programme is intended to convey is for them to judge. As Lord Hoffmann said in *Campbell v MGN Ltd* [2004] 2 AC 457, para 59, **judges are not newspaper editors.** They are **not broadcasting editors either.** The issue as to **where the balance is to be struck** between the competing rights must be approached **on this basis.**

26. Will the revealing of D's identity in connection with the proposed programme pursue a **legitimate aim**? **I would answer that question in the affirmative.** In *Jersild v Denmark*, para 31 it was recognised that there is a duty to impart information and ideas of public interest **which the public has a right to receive.** The programme that the BBC wish to broadcast has been inspired by the removal of the double jeopardy rule. What this means in practice for our system of criminal justice is a matter of legitimate public interest. Among the issues which can be so described are the kinds of offences to which Part 10 of the 2003 Act applies, and the circumstances in which an application for a person who has been acquitted to be retried would be appropriate. These issues could, of course, be discussed in the **abstract** by reference to hypothetical facts and circumstances. **But the arguments that the programme wishes to present will lose much of their force unless they can be directed to the facts and circumstances of actual cases.** The point about **D's name** is that the producers of the programme believe that its disclosure **will give added credibility to the account** which they wish to present. This is a view which they are entitled to adopt and, given the content of the programme as a whole, it is an aim which can properly be regarded as **legitimate**.

27. There remains the question of **proportionality.** As against the public's right to receive information there is D's right to be protected against publication of details of his private life**. But the weight that is to be given to his right has to be judged against the potential for harm if publication does take place**. The fact that he was acquitted of the rape is already legitimately in the **public domain. He cannot complain of a violation of his rights under article 8 if, as a result of the programme, an application is made for him to be put on trial again for that offence.** This is because the statute provides for this, and because the interests of a democratic society in the prevention of crime and disorder lie in the bringing of those who have committed crimes before the courts so that, if convicted, they can be punished for them.

28. **There is a risk, as Lord Pannick has pointed out, of D's being tried by the**

media. That, of course, is to be deprecated. If this happens it will add to the effects on his personality that will flow inevitably from the mention of his name in the broadcast. But I do not see this additional feature as a reason for holding that his article 8 right to the protection of his **reputation** outweighs the right of freedom of expression on a matter of legitimate public interest. **It may increase the pressure on the authorities, which will be there anyway as a result of the broadcast, to take steps for him to be retried**. If that happens, the system of justice will take its course. **Procedures are available for protecting D's identity so that he can receive a fair trial:** section 82 of the 2003 Act: see also *Montgomery v HM Advocate* [2003] 1 AC 641. The conclusion which I would draw is that the interference with D's article 8 right will be significant, but that it is **proportionate** when account is taken of the weight that must be given to the competing right to freedom of expression that the BBC wish to assert.

. . .

63. In my opinion there is nothing in this article 6 argument: by discharging the order your Lordships would be saying no more than that is it perfectly proper for the BBC if they wish (and no doubt at the risk of a defamation action) **to call D's innocence into question. Indeed it is difficult to see why the position here is any different from that of a court, say, refusing to strike out as hopeless a claim for damages by the victim of a rape against her alleged attacker notwithstanding his acquittal**—or, say, the Court of Appeal acceding to a prosecutor's application under Part 10 of the 2003 Act to re-try an acquitted defendant. Nor is there any sensible risk of the BBC's proposed broadcast here compromising the fairness of any possible retrial of D even supposing one were eventually to be sought and permitted. One could hardly be further from proceedings which are "active" within the meaning of section 2(3) of the 1981 Act.

Napier v Pressdram Ltd [2009] EWCA Civ 443

42. The answer to that question depends on the application of simple principles. For a **duty of confidentiality** to be owed (other than under a contract or statute), the information in question must be of a nature and obtained in circumstances such that any reasonable person in the position of the recipient ought to recognise that it should be treated as confidential. As Cross J observed in *Printers and Finishers Limited v Holloway* [1965] RPC 239, 256, the law would defeat its own object if it seeks to enforce in this field standards which would be rejected by the ordinary person. Freedom to report the truth is a precious thing both for the liberty of the individual (the libertarian

principle) and for the sake of wider society (the democratic principle), and it would be unduly eroded if the law of confidentiality were to prevent a person from reporting facts **which a reasonable person in his position would not perceive to be confidential.**

Author of a Blog v Times Newspapers Ltd [2009] EWHC 1358 (QB) per Eady J

Mr Justice Eady:

1. On 4 June 2009 I heard an application in private whereby the Claimant, who is the author of a blog known as "Night Jack", sought an interim injunction to restrain Times Newspapers Ltd from publishing any information that would or might lead to his identification as the person responsible for that blog. **An undertaking had been given on 28 May 2009 that such information would not be published pending the outcome.** I indicated at the conclusion that I would refuse the injunction but, in the meantime, I granted temporary cover to restrain publication until the handing down of the judgment, when the matter could be considered afresh if need be.
2. The Claimant's case, advanced on his behalf by Mr Tomlinson QC, is based both on the traditional law of confidence and upon the more recently developed doctrine acknowledging an independent cause of action arising from the **improper disclosure of private information**: see eg *Campbell v MGN Ltd* [2004] 2 AC 457 and *McKennitt v Ash* [2008] QB 73. It is **suggested that The Times is subject to an enforceable duty of confidence not to reveal the Claimant's identity** as the author of the blog; **alternatively**, that he has a **reasonable expectation of privacy in** respect of that information, in respect of which there is no countervailing public interest justification for its publication.
3. It was asserted in the Claimant's skeleton for the hearing of 28 May that his identity had been disclosed to *The Times* in breach of confidence. By the time the matter came before me, on the other hand, Mr Tomlinson was prepared to proceed on the basis that the evidence relied upon from Mr Patrick Foster, the relevant journalist, was correct; that is to say, **that he had been able to arrive at the identification by a process of deduction and detective work, mainly using information available on the Internet.**
4. Mr Tomlinson submitted that the thousands of **regular bloggers** who communicate nowadays via the **Internet, under a cloak of anonymity,** would be horrified to think that the law would do nothing to protect their anonymity if someone carried out the necessary detective work and sought to unmask

them. That may be true. I suspect that some would be very concerned and others less so. Be that as it may, Mr Tomlinson needs to demonstrate that there would be a **legally enforceable right to maintain anonymity,** in the absence of a genuine breach of confidence, **by suppressing the fruits of detective work such as that carried out by Mr Foster.**

5. Mr Tomlinson's primary argument was simply that the Claimant wished to remain anonymous and has taken steps to preserve his anonymity accordingly. He says that the Defendant is fully aware of the Claimant's wish and that, in the circumstances, there is no justification for "unmasking" him, as he is entitled to keep his identity as the author of the blog private and confidential. Indeed, **it is submitted as a general proposition that "there is a public interest in preserving the anonymity of bloggers".**

6. It is necessary to examine the matter more closely, however, since the mere fact that the Claimant wishes to remain anonymous does not mean either that he has **a reasonable expectation** of doing so or that *The Times* is under an **enforceable obligation** to him in that respect.

7. It is well known that the court nowadays adopts a **two stage** approach, when addressing claims based upon the publication of allegedly private information in contravention of Article 8 of the European Convention on Human Rights and Fundamental Freedoms. One must ask, **first**, whether the claimant had a reasonable expectation of privacy in relation to the particular information in question and, if so, then move to the **second stage** of enquiring whether there is some countervailing public interest such as to justify overriding that *prima facie* right. Whereas Mr Tomlinson focused most of his attention upon the second stage, and rather took it for granted that the stage one test had been passed, **Mr White QC made it clear on behalf of The Times that it was most certainly not accepted that this Claimant had a reasonable expectation of maintaining his anonymity.**

8. The **test is an objective one** (both for privacy and breach of confidence) and the importance of that has recently been underlined by the Court of Appeal in *Napier v Pressdram Ltd* [2009] EWCA Civ 443 at [42], where Toulson LJ commented:

   " . . . For a duty of confidentiality to be owed (other than under a contract or statute), **the information in question must be of a nature and obtained in circumstances such that any reasonable person in the position of the recipient ought to recognise that it should be treated as confidential**. As Cross J observed in *Printers and Finishers Limited v Holloway* [1965] RPC 239, 256, the law would defeat its own object if it seeks to enforce in this field standards which would be rejected by the ordinary person. **Freedom to report the truth** is a precious thing both for the liberty of the individual (the libertarian principle) and for the sake of wider society (the democratic principle), **and it would be unduly eroded if the law of confidentiality were to prevent a person from reporting facts which a reasonable person in his position would not perceive to be confidential**."

9. Hitherto, in those cases which have come before the courts where the claimant relied successfully upon the recently developed cause of action, in the absence of any pre-existing **relationship** of confidence, the information in question has been of a strictly personal nature concerning, for example, **sexual relationships**, **mental** or **physical health**, **financial affairs**, or the **claimant's family** or **domestic arrangements**. I am not aware of a case in which, as here, there is a significant public element in the information sought to be restricted. I have in mind, of course, that what the Claimant seeks to withhold from scrutiny is the identity of the person communicating to the public through his blog. Those who wish to hold forth to the public by this means often take steps to disguise their authorship, but it is in my judgment a significantly further step to argue, if others are able to deduce their identity, that they should be restrained by law from revealing it.
10. Mr White drew my attention to the case of ***Mahmood v Galloway*** [2006] EMLR 26. Mr Tomlinson challenged him to identify any useful *ratio decidendi* from this case, to which Mr White responded by advancing the proposition that a journalist who writes under a pseudonym for the **purpose** of functioning more effectively in his undercover work has no reasonable expectation of privacy in respect of his identity and, in particular, in relation to **photographs** which would, when published widely, reveal his identity. **It seems to me that Mr White's interpretation is correct** and, although the decision is not strictly binding upon me, the reasoning of Mitting J is nonetheless, if I may respectfully say so, **entirely persuasive**. Although the Claimant here is not a journalist, the function he performs via his blog is closely analogous. **I see no greater justification for a reasonable expectation of anonymity in this case than in that concerning Mr Mahmood.**
11. I consider that the Claimant fails at stage one, **because blogging is essentially a public rather than a private activity.**
12. When I move, therefore, to the second stage, the exercise becomes somewhat **artificial**. That is because I have to proceed on the hypothesis that one or more public interest considerations have to be identified which would be capable of outweighing the Claimant's right to privacy—when I have already held that no such right exists. Nevertheless, I should address the arguments raised. **It is not always easy to come to a conclusion on matters of public interest on an application for an interim injunction**, as Mitting J observed in *Mahmood* at [24], but it cannot be ignored since s 12 of the Human Rights

Act 1998 requires that an **overall view should be formed as to the likelihood** of the Claimant succeeding at trial. **Such a judgment has to be made almost always on an incomplete picture of the available evidence**. But that is what Parliament intended.

13. At this stage it is necessary to address the background circumstances in more detail. **The Claimant is a serving detective constable and his blog mostly deals with his police work** and his opinions on a number of social and political issues relating to the police and the administration of justice. He expresses strong opinions about these matters including on subjects of political controversy. In particular, **he has criticised a number of ministers**. In so far as he has written about cases of which he has obtained direct knowledge through his police duties, it is said that he has taken particular care to disguise the information. Moreover, he has tried to make it a practice not to comment on cases which were pending or "active" within the meaning of the **Contempt** of Court Act 1981. Nor has he flouted any court reporting restrictions. Whether he has always succeeded in achieving these aims may be a matter of **debate**. Such an exercise will often involve fine questions of judgment.

14. Nevertheless, on the basis of the evidence before me, it has always been apparent that **if his employing police authority became aware** (as it now has) that one of its officers was communicating information and opinions to the **public at large** about the conduct of police operations, there would be **a significant risk of disciplinary action.** This is recognised by the Claimant and is reflected in the evidence of his solicitor. Indeed, this would appear to be one of the main reasons why he was keen from the outset to maintain his anonymity.

15. My attention was drawn to the relevant Police (Conduct) Regulations. Those governing his conduct prior to 1 December 2008 were to be found in SI 2004 No 645 and those applicable subsequently in SI 2008 No 2864. The wording of the provisions differs somewhat, but perhaps not to any material extent. The relevant passages prior to 1 December 2008 were contained in Schedule 1 to the 2004 Regulations under the heading "**Code** of Conduct":

> "**Confidentiality**
>
> 7. Information which comes into the possession of the police should be treated as confidential. It should not be used for personal benefit and nor should it be divulged to other parties except in the proper course of police duty. Similarly, officers should respect, as confidential, information about force policy and operations unless authorised to disclose it in the course of their duties.
>
> . . .

> **General Conduct**
>
> 12. Whether on or off duty, police officers should not behave in a way which is likely to bring discredit upon the police service."

16. Under the more recent 2008 Regulations, the corresponding wording is to be found under the heading "Standards of Professional Behaviour":

> "**Confidentiality**
>
> Police officers treat information with respect and access or disclose it only in the proper course of police duties.
>
> . . .
>
> **Discreditable Conduct**
>
> Police officers behave in a manner which does not discredit the police service or undermine public confidence in it, whether on or off duty."

17. It may be said that the wording is in some respects woolly and imprecise. After all, it clearly cannot be intended that police officers have to treat *all* information "with respect" or be restrained so as not to disclose it except "in the proper course of police duties". There must be some limit. Presumably what is intended is that they should show such restraint in relation to information acquired in the course of, and connected with, their police duties. What would appear to be tolerably clear, however, **is that the regulation would certainly apply to information obtained by a police officer about cases on which he is working or has in the past been engaged.** It is obvious that the regulations should not be read subject to a proviso such that information of this kind may be "disclosed" or "divulged" *if the officer does it anonymously or in his spare time*.

18. **Mr Tomlinson argues that if The Times were to reveal the Claimant's identity this would not only infringe his rights under Article 8 but also those under Article 10, since it would inhibit his right to impart information and ideas to the general public.** It has not been argued, however, that the statutory restrictions on police officers disclosing information are not "**necessary",** not "**proportionate**", or not "**prescribed by law**" (ie that they are not compatible with the exceptions recognised in Article 10(2) of the Convention).

19. Against this background, Mr White submits that the obligations contained in the two relevant sets of regulations are imposed in the public interest to maintain appropriate standards of conduct in the police service. **It is said that there is a corresponding public interest in the disclosure of any significant non-compliance by a police officer with his obligations under the statutory *code*.**

20. Moreover, it is argued that there is a general public law duty on police officers not to reveal information obtained in the course of a police investigation

otherwise than for the **purpose** of performing public duties: see eg *R v Chief Constable of the North Wales Police, ex parte Thorpe* [1999] QB 396, 409–410, 415, 429. Failure to comply with that duty would also, it is said, justify public exposure. **There is much force in the argument that any wrongdoing by a public servant (save perhaps in trivial circumstances)** is a matter which can legitimately be drawn to the attention of the public by journalists. There is a growing trend towards openness and transparency in such matters.

21. Although Mr Tomlinson rather dismissed it, a further argument was advanced by Mr White to the effect that the Claimant's writings, being "overtly political and highly critical of central and local policing strategies", are such that **the public is entitled to receive information about the author,** so as to enable it to make an assessment of the weight and authority to be attached to them. Mr Tomlinson submitted that all the Claimant's readers need to know is that the author is a serving police officer. I disagree. **It is very often useful, in assessing the value of an opinion or argument, to know its source.** As was pointed out, for example, by Lord Nicholls in *Reynolds v Times Newspapers Ltd* [2001] 2 AC 127 at 205A-B, **one may wish to apply greater caution or scepticism in the case of a person with "an axe to grind".** For so long as there is anonymity, it would obviously be difficult to make any such assessment. More generally, when making a judgment as to the value of comments made about police affairs by "insiders", it may sometimes help to know how experienced or senior the commentator is.

22. Mr Tomlinson also submits that there is no public interest in the disclosure of the Claimant's identity and (echoing the language used by the European Court of Human Rights in *Von Hannover v Germany* (2005) 40 EHRR 1) that the publication of such information would make no "**contribution to a *debate* of general interest".**

23. If it were the case that the Defendant's Article 10 right of freedom of expression here is indeed conditional upon establishing a public interest (which I do not believe it is), **it would seem to me quite legitimate for the public to be told who it was who was choosing to make, in some instances, quite serious criticisms of police activities and, if it be the case, that frequent infringements of police discipline regulations were taking place.** Correspondingly, if the allegations and observations made by the Claimant through his blog were themselves contributing to **a *debate* of general interest,** as he undoubtedly thinks they are, I cannot see why the proposed publication in *The Times* would not be worthy of the same classification.

24. Much of what the Claimant publishes could be characterised as "**political speech**", since he criticises and ridicules a number of senior **politicians**. It is well recognised both here and in Strasbourg that considerable value must be attached to a citizen's right to express his opinions on matters of

this kind. Nevertheless, constraints are placed upon the rights of civil servants and police officers to become involved in party political **debate**. Some such restraint may be regarded as legitimate and proportionate for reasons which are fairly obvious; namely, **that for some people the discharge of public duties requires them to stand aside from the cut and thrust of such *debate*.** Such constraints are recognised as appropriate, for example, for judges, teachers and civil servants. I sought assistance from counsel as to the precise nature of the restraints placed on police officers in this respect, but they were unable to provide much information save to the extent that it was accepted that police officers are not permitted to stand for elected office.

25. Even though the Claimant believes that he was doing nothing wrong, he suspected that as and when his employing authority discovered his activities, he might be subjected to **disciplinary action** or, at least, some kind of **"pressure**" to limit the use of his freedom of expression.

26. I have drawn attention to the wording of the regulations **relating to an officer's obligation of confidentiality** in relation to "information", but there is also the more general prohibition against "discreditable conduct". This is a notoriously flexible concept, of course, but it might well be thought that some of the Claimant's publications would "discredit the police service or undermine public confidence in it". It would not be appropriate for me to come to any conclusion about that, but I recognise that his superiors might, at least, take that view.

27. It is clear from his own evidence that one of the reasons why the Claimant originally sought the court's assistance to maintain his anonymity was to protect him against disciplinary measures being brought to bear. His solicitor said in his witness statement that:

> "26. Publication of the identification of the identity [*sic*] of the Claimant as the author of the Blog would be likely to cause him significant damage.
> 27. Firstly, while it appears to be true that the Force has been notified of his identity by the Defendants (in breach of confidence), the Claimant believes that if the matter is subject to publicity in the media this could lead to more serious disciplinary charges being brought—on the basis that the publicity itself might be regarded as damaging to the force and having brought it into disrepute.
>
> 28. Secondly, the Claimant has no reason to believe that his identity as the author of the Blog is known beyond his immediate supervisor and the Professional Standards Department of the Force. If this became now [*sic*] beyond this was group [*sic*], the Claimant considers that there would be inevitable disruption to his work as a detective. In particular,

the Claimant is concerned that his identification as the author of the Blog might have an adverse effect on his working **relationships** and could make it very difficult for him to carry on his job. Some of his colleagues may be hostile to the Blog and may have objections to working with him as a result. Moreover, if his picture is published, it will also make it far harder for him to undertake the surveillance and informant handling work for which he is trained."

28. As he points out, his identity has been revealed to the police service by the Defendant. Even if this had not happened, **however, I would agree with Mr White's observation that any such justification for seeking an injunction would be "unattractive", to say the least**. I do not accept that it is part of the court's function to protect police officers **who are, or think they may be, acting in breach of police discipline regulations** from coming to the attention of their superiors (whose task it is to make judgments about such matters, at least in the first instance).

29. An alternative argument advanced by Mr Tomlinson is founded on the fact that now, for better or worse, the police authority does know about the Claimant's identity. In those circumstances, he suggests, there is no need for the information to be released more widely (ie to the readership of *The Times*). I do not accept that this necessarily follows**. It seems to me that the public is entitled to know how police officers behave and the newspaper's readers would be entitled to come to their own conclusions about whether it is desirable for officers to communicate such matters publicly (whether there is an infringement of the disciplinary regulations or not).** Of course, generally speaking, there would be no reason to publicise genuinely private matters about police officers, such as their domestic arrangements or personal **relationships**, **but blogging is not a wholly private activity** (as I have already noted in the context of addressing the arguments at stage one).

30. Mr Tomlinson sought to draw a distinction between the Claimant's police duties and what he does in his own spare time "off duty". That is nevertheless, in the context of a police officer, a somewhat hazy distinction. It is clear, for example, that police officers should not behave in a manner which brings discredit on the police force "whether on or off duty". Furthermore, the restraints upon disclosing **confidential information** are not qualified by any wording to the effect that the information can be disclosed otherwise than "in the proper course of police duties" provided that the disclosure takes place when the officer is "off duty". That would make a nonsense of the regulatory requirements.

31. I return briefly to the subject of **photographs**, to which the Claimant's solicitor referred in his witness statement. I was asked to bear in mind that rather blurred pictures of the Claimant have apparently from time to time

appeared in the local press. I am not sure that this assists Mr White's argument, since the **photographs** are not relevant to the Claimant's identity as the author of the blog in question. On the other hand, his solicitor seems concerned about possible prejudice to **undercover work**. **I would require more convincing evidence before considering the restraint of photographs, especially having regard to the Mahmood decision.** *There is no suggestion here of physical risk to the Claimant, as there was in that case.*

32. As I have already noted, it is necessary for me to have in mind the provisions of s 12 of the Human Rights Act 1998, since the injunction sought would restrain *The Times* from exercising its right of freedom of expression. I have properly been reminded by both counsel of these provisions and, in all the circumstances, I have come to the conclusion that it is not likely that the Claimant would succeed at trial in restraining *The Times* from publishing his identity as the author of the blog, whether on grounds of traditional breach of confidence or by way of reliance upon the more recently developed remedies in respect of "private information".

33. I conclude that he fails at stage one, in the sense that the information does not have about it the necessary "**quality of confidence**", as contemplated by Megarry V.-C. in *Coco v A N Clark (Engineers) Ltd* [1969] RPC 41; nor does it qualify as information in respect of which the Claimant has a reasonable expectation of privacy—essentially because **blogging is a public activity.** Furthermore, even if I were wrong about this, I consider that any such right of privacy on the Claimant's part would be likely to be outweighed at trial by a countervailing public interest in revealing that a particular police officer has been making these communications.

G and G v Wikimedia Foundation Inc [2009] EWHC 3148

10. As the title to this judgment shows, I made orders giving **anonymity** to the Applicants. One provision which was sought, but which I did not grant, was an order giving **anonymity** to the Respondent.

11. There has been an exchange of letters and e-mails between lawyers for the Applicants and for the Respondent. The Respondent indicated that it would not disclose the IP information without a court order being made, but neither would it oppose the making of an order requiring such disclosure. It gave no indication that it required **anonymity** for itself, and I could see no grounds for giving **anonymity** to it. I set out below the gist of the correspondence between the Applicants' solicitors and lawyers for the Respondent.

12. There are some cases in which **anonymity** must be given to a respondent, because if it is not, then the naming of the respondent may indirectly enable readers who already know other information about the case to identify of the claimant **(sometimes referred to as *jigsaw* identification)**. But the Applicants do not suggest that applies in this case.

OPEN JUSTICE—ACCESS TO THE COURT FILE

13. A second provision which was sought but which I granted only in a limited form was as follows:

> "Pursuant to CPR 5.4C(4), a non-party may not obtain a copy of any statement of case in the proposed claim between the Applicant and the Respondent until further order".

14. No reason was advanced, in evidence or argument, as to why the statement of case against the Respondent should not be obtained by a non-party in the normal way. A statement of case includes a Claim Form (CPR 2.3). The corresponding order which I made (subject to a right to apply to vary it) reads:

> "Pursuant to CPR 5.4C(4), a non-party may not until further Order obtain a copy of any statement of case in the proposed claim between the Applicant and the Respondent other than one edited to remove any reference to the names of the Claimants or the user name shown in the confidential annex."

15. CPR 5.4C provides:

> "*Supply of documents to a non-party from court records*
>
> 5.4C (1) The general rule is that a person who is not a party to proceedings may obtain from the court records a copy of –
>
> (a) a statement of case, but not any documents filed with or attached to the statement of case, or intended by the party whose statement it is to be served with it;
>
> (b) a judgment or order given or made in public (whether made at a hearing or without a hearing) . . .
>
> (3) A non-party may obtain a copy of a statement of case or judgment or order under paragraph (1) only if –
>
> . . .
>
> (c) the claim has been listed for a hearing; or
>
> (d) judgment has been entered in the claim.
>
> (4) The court may, on the application of a party or of any person identified in a statement of case –

(a) order that a non-party may not obtain a copy of a statement of case under paragraph (1);

(b) restrict the persons or classes of persons who may obtain a copy of a statement of case;

(c) order that persons or classes of persons may only obtain a copy of a statement of case if it is edited in accordance with the directions of the court; or

(d) make such other order as it thinks fit.

(5) A person wishing to apply for an order under paragraph (4) must file an application notice in accordance with Part 23.

(6) Where the court makes an order under paragraph (4), a non-party who wishes to obtain a copy of the statement of case, or to obtain an unedited copy of the statement of case, may apply on notice to the party or person identified in the statement of case who requested the order, for permission."

16. **Open justice** has been an essential principle of English law for centuries. It is provided for today in CPR 39.2(1) which states: **"The general rule is that a hearing is to be in public".** There are exceptions to the principle. The relevant provisions applicable in this case are set out in CPR 39.2(3):

"A hearing, or any part of it, may be in private if –

(a) publicity would defeat the object of the hearing; . . .

(c) it involves **confidential information** . . . and publicity would damage that confidentiality;

(d) a private hearing is necessary to protect the interests of any child . . ."

17. Hearings in private under CPR 39.2(3) and orders under CPR 5.4C(4) are derogations from the principle of open justice. They must be ordered only when it is necessary and proportionate to do so, with a view to protecting the rights which claimants (and others) are entitled to have protected by such means. When such orders are made, they must be limited in scope to what is required in the particular circumstances of the case.

18. **Applications to restrain publication of private or confidential information, and related applications, are usually made in circumstances of urgency.** Provision is made for such applications by CPR Part 25: in particular the Practice Direction to Part 25 para 4. CPR 25(3)(2) requires that

"An application for an interim remedy must be supported by evidence, unless the court orders otherwise".

19. In the preparation of such applications, it is not uncommon for the legal representatives of claimants to focus their attention largely on the substantive

application, and to omit to give the same degree of attention to subsidiary orders, including those providing for a derogation from the principle of open justice. That is what happened in this case. There was no evidence, and nothing in the Skeleton argument, to support the width of some of the restrictions on open justice that were sought in the draft order.

20. In this case, as in most cases, this was certainly not the result of any bad faith. **But it is the duty of the court to scrutinize such draft orders**. However, the court is commonly asked to hear such applications in circumstances where there are other cases in the list requiring attention, or out of hours, where there may be limited access to books, and pressure of time. **It is important that counsel and others who apply for such orders do not overlook the need to adapt any restriction on reporting or open justice to what is no more than is necessary and proportionate in the circumstances of the particular case.**

THE REQUIREMENT OF A RETURN DATE

21. CPR Part 25 Practice Direction para 5.1 sets out the provisions which any order for an injunction must contain, unless the court orders otherwise. So:

> "5.1 Any order for an injunction, unless the court orders otherwise, **must** contain: . . . (3) if made without notice to any other party, a return date for a further hearing at which the other party can be present".

22. In *Thane Investments Ltd v Tomlinson* [2003] EWCA Civ 1272 the Court of Appeal at para 21 emphasized the word "**must**" in this Practice Direction.

23. The Practice Direction at para 5.2 provides that:

> "An order for an injunction made in the presence of all parties to be bound by it or made at a hearing of which they have had notice, may state that it is effective until trial or further order".

24. **By requiring that orders should be drafted so as to take effect for no longer than is necessary and proportionate, the Practice Direction gives effect to the requirements of freedom of expression and open justice.**

25. Notwithstanding the clear terms of the Practice Direction, Claimants applying for injunctions without notice commonly ask for orders **without a term, or return date,** by including the words "until further order". That **may be appropriate** in the case of some injunctions to restrain publication of private information, for example where it appears that there is **unlikely to be a dispute** as to the sensitive private nature of the information. Including a **return date** has the disadvantage of putting the applicants to the cost of attending before the court a second time. **But advocates applying for a departure from the requirements of the Practice Direction should draw to the attention of the judge that that is what the draft order provides, and they should**

explain in the evidence or Skeleton argument (as may be appropriate) why the departure from the Practice Direction is sought. In the words of Mummery LJ in *Memory Corporation v Sidhu and another (No 2)* [2000] 1 WLR 1443, at p 1459H-1460A:

> "It cannot be emphasised too strongly that at an urgent without notice hearing for . . . any . . . form of interim injunction, there is a **high duty** to make **full, fair and accurate disclosure of** material information to the court and to draw the court's attention to **significant factual, legal and procedural aspects of the case**. It is the particular duty of the advocate to see **that the correct legal procedures and forms are used;** that a written **skeleton argument and a properly drafted order are prepared by him personally and lodged with the court before the oral hearing;** and *that at the hearing the court's attention is drawn by him to* **unusual features** *of the* evidence adduced, to the applicable law and to the **formalities and procedure to be observed."** (emphasis added)

26. As a general rule the Practice Direction should be complied with. If it is not, orders may last longer than is required. If orders are drafted too widely, or made to apply for too long a period, the public's confidence in the administration of justice may be undermined. It is in the public interest that it should be known what orders the court makes, and why.

27. The draft order in the present case included a provision that the order under CPR 5.4C should apply "until further order", instead of including a return date. That would have been objectionable, if I had been minded to make the order in the form set out in para 13 above. But having limited the scope of the restriction on public access, I have included those words in the order I have made. I have done this in spite of the fact that the hearing was *without notice*. In this case the hearing was only technically *without notice*, in that the Respondent has not been served with the Application Notice, but the Respondent has been notified of the intention to make the application today, and has indicated that it does not wish to oppose it. **This situation is sometimes said to be without notice on notice.**

UNDERTAKINGS BY THE APPLICANT

28. There is an undertaking that should normally be included in any order for an injunction, but which is not mentioned in the Practice Direction para 5.1, and was not included in the draft order put before me. **It is an undertaking to provide *full notes* of the hearing with all expedition to any party that would be affected by the relief sought.**

29. The following appears in the White Book (2009 edn) in note 25.3.5.

> "Applicants without notice for relief are under a duty to provide full notes of the hearing with all expedition to any party that would be affected by

the relief sought; a failure to do so may result in an award of **indemnity costs** in favour of the party affected (*Interoute Telecommunications (UK) Ltd v Fashion Gossip Ltd*, The Times, November 10, 1999 (Lightman J.)) . . . **Counsel and solicitors have responsibility for taking full notes of what was said at the hearing and they should not expect that a transcript of the hearing would be available or would suffice if it were** (*Cinpres Gas Injection Ltd v Melea Ltd*, [2005] EWHC 3180 (Pat) . . . . Where a freezing order is granted, the duty to provide the respondent with a full note arises whether or not the respondent asks for it (*Thane Investments Ltd v Tomlinson* [2003] EWCA Civ 1272 ([approving remarks by] Neuberger J.))."

30. **So too, where an order relates to freedom of expression, or may have the effect of interfering with freedom of expression**, those applying for interim relief at a hearing at which the respondent or defendant is not present should generally provide the respondent with a full note, **whether or not the respondent asks for it.** To adapt the words of Neuberger J (as he then was) cited by the Court of Appeal at para 21 of *Thane*: Orders which may interfere with freedom of expression should only be granted in circumstances which **provide maximum protection for the person against whom the order is to be made,** and the least interference with the right of freedom of expression necessary to protect the claimant's rights.

31. The preparation and provision of a note of the hearing is important, **not only to inform anyone notified of the order of what evidence was put before the court (in addition to that which is in the witness statements), but also to inform them of any points or queries that may have been raised by the judge.** See also *Memory Corporation v Sidhu* at p 1459B. Judges rarely have the time to write judgments in such cases after the event, and even if they give ex tempore reasons, there will be no transcript available unless that is requested and paid for.

32. In the present case, I required an undertaking that a note be kept. But the undertaking permits that the note need only be provided on request, since the Respondent had made clear that it did not oppose the application.

R (Wood) v Commissioner of Police of the Metropolis [2009] EWCA Civ 414

ARTICLE 8

15. The principal issue in the case as the argument has developed is whether the appellant's right to respect for his private life, guaranteed by ECHR Article 8,

was violated by the police taking and retaining photographs of him on 27 April 2005.

(1) The Scope of Article 8

16. Article 8 is one of the provisions of the ECHR most frequently resorted to in our courts since the HRA came into force. It falls to be considered most often in immigration cases, where the nature of the actual or putative interference with private and family life is plain enough: **the claimant complains that if he is removed or deported he will be separated from family members**, often a spouse and children, settled in the United Kingdom. **In this present case, however, the nature of the claimed interference is more elusive**. So is the nature of the private or family life interest which is said to be assaulted. It is useful therefore to have in mind the many facets of the Article 8 right acknowledged by the European Court of Human Rights, and—if it can be ascertained—what it is that links them.

17. The leading case of *Von Hannover v Germany* (2005) 40 EHRR 1 concerned the publication of **photographs** of Princess Caroline of Monaco engaged in various everyday activities such as horse riding, shopping, **dining in a restaurant** with a **companion**, on a **skiing holiday,** leaving **her Paris home** with **her husband** and **tripping over an obstacle** at a **private beach club in Monaco**. The Strasbourg court held that there had been a violation of Article 8, even though all the **photographs** were taken when the Princess was in a public place except those, **taken at long range**, when she was at the private beach club. I should cite the following passages from the judgment:

> "50. The Court reiterates that the concept of private life extends to aspects relating to **personal identity,** such as a **person's name**, or a **person's picture.**
>
> Furthermore, private life, in the Court's view, includes a person's **physical** and **psychological integrity;** the guarantee afforded by Art. 8 of the Convention is primarily intended **to ensure** the development, **without outside interference**, of the **personality of each individual** in his relations with other human beings. **There is therefore a zone of interaction of a person with others, even in a public context, which may fall within the scope of 'private life'.**
>
> 51. The Court has also indicated that, in certain circumstances, a person has a 'legitimate expectation' of protection and respect for his or her private life. Accordingly, it has held in a case concerning the **interception of telephone calls on business premises that the applicant 'would have had a reasonable expectation of privacy for such calls'.**
>
> 52. As regards **photos**, with a view to defining the scope of the protection afforded by Art.8 against arbitrary interference by public authorities,

the Commission had regard to whether the photographs related to private or public matters and whether the material thus obtained was envisaged for a limited use or was likely to be made available to the general public.

53. In the present case there is no doubt that the publication by various German magazines of photos of the applicant in her daily life either on her own or with other people falls within the scope of her private life . . . "

18. In *Marper v UK* (Applications no 30562/04 and 30566/04, judgment delivered on 4 December 2008, BAILII: [2008] ECHR 1581) the applicants were arrested on suspicion of serious offences and their **fingerprints and DNA samples were taken.** They were in due course acquitted (or the charge not pressed). They asked for their fingerprints and DNA samples to be destroyed, but in both cases the police refused. They brought judicial review proceedings to challenge the police decision, culminating in an appeal to their Lordships' House, but were unsuccessful. The Strasbourg court said this, under the heading "General Principles":

"**66. The Court recalls that the concept of 'private life' is a broad term not susceptible to exhaustive definition**. It covers the physical and psychological integrity of a person (see Pretty v the United Kingdom, no 2346/02, § 61, ECHR 2002 III, 35 EHRR 1, and Y.F. v Turkey, no 24209/94, §33, ECHR 2003 IX, 39 EHRR 34). It can therefore embrace multiple aspects of the person's physical and social identity (see Mikulic v Croatia, no 53176/99, § 53, ECHR 2002-I, BAILII: [2002] ECHR 27). Elements such as, for example, **gender identification, name** and **sexual orientation** and **sexual life** fall within the personal sphere protected by Article 8 (see, among other authorities, Bensaid v the United Kingdom, no 44599/98, § 47, ECHR 2001, 33 EHRR 10, I with further references, and Peck v the United Kingdom, no 44647/98, § 57, ECHR 2003 I, 36 EHRR 41). Beyond a person's name, his or her private and family life may include other means of personal identification and of **linking to a family** (see mutatis mutandis Burghartz v Switzerland, 22 February 1994, BAILII: [1994] ECHR 2, § 24, Series A no 280 B; and Unal Tekeli v Turkey, no 29865/96, §42, ECHR 2004 X (extracts), 42 EHRR 53). Information about the **person's health** is an important element of private life (see Z v Finland, 25 February 1997, §71, Reports of Judgments and Decisions 1997 I, 25 EHRR 371). The Court furthermore considers that an **individual's ethnic identity must be** regarded as another such element (see in particular Article 6 of the Data Protection Convention quoted in paragraph 41 above, which lists personal data revealing **racial origin** as a special category of data along with other sensitive information about an individual). Article

> 8 protects in addition **a right to personal development**, and the right **to establish and develop relationships** with other human beings and the outside world (see, for example, Burghartz, cited above, opinion of the Commission, p 37, § 47, and Friedl v Austria, judgment of 31 January 1995, Series A no 305-B, opinion of the Commission, p 20, § 45, 21 EHRR 83). The concept of private life moreover includes **elements relating to a person's right to their image** (Sciacca v Italy, no 50774/99, § 29, ECHR 2005-I, 43 EHRR 20).
>
> 67. **The mere storing of data relating to the private life of an individual amounts to an interference within the meaning of Article 8 (see Leander v Sweden, 26 March 1987, §48, Series A no 116**, 9 EHRR 433). The subsequent use of the stored information has no bearing on that finding (Amann v Switzerland [GC], no 27798/95, §69, ECHR 2000-II, 30 EHRR 843). However, in determining whether the personal information retained by the authorities involves any of the private-life aspects mentioned above, the Court will have due regard to the specific context in which the information at issue has been recorded and retained, the nature of the records, the way in which these records are used and processed and the results that may be obtained (see, mutatis mutandis, Friedl, cited above, §§ 49–51, and Peck v the United Kingdom, cited above, § 59)."

19. **These and other cases show that the content of the phrase "private and family life" is very broad indeed.** Looking only at the words of the Article, one might have supposed that the essence of the right was the protection of close personal **relationships**. While that remains a core instance, and perhaps the paradigm case of the right, the jurisprudence has accepted many other facets; so many that **any attempt to encapsulate the right's scope in a single idea can only be undertaken at a level of considerable abstraction.** But it is an endeavour worth pursuing, since we need if possible to be armed at least with a sense of direction when it comes to disputed cases at the margin.

20. The phrase **"physical and psychological integrity"** of a person (*Von Hannover* paragraph 50, *Marper* paragraph 66) is with respect helpful. So is the person's **"physical and social identity"** (*Marper* paragraph 66 and other references there given). These expressions reflect what seems to me to be the **central value** protected by the right. I would describe it as the **personal autonomy of every individual. I** claim no originality for this description. In *Murray v Big Pictures (UK) Ltd* [2008] EWCA Civ 446 Sir Anthony Clarke MR, giving the judgment of the court, referred at paragraph 31 to Lord Hoffmann's emphasis, at paragraph 51 of *Campbell v MGN Ltd* [2004] 2 AC 457, upon the fact that "**the law now focuses upon the protection of human autonomy and**

dignity—'the right to control the dissemination of information about one's private life and **the right to the esteem and respect of other people.'"**

21. **The notion of the personal autonomy of every individual marches with the presumption of liberty enjoyed in a free polity**: a presumption which consists in the principle that every interference with the freedom of the individual stands in need of objective justification. Applied to the myriad instances recognised in the Article 8 jurisprudence, this presumption means that, subject to the qualifications I shall shortly describe, **an individual's personal autonomy makes him—should make him—master of all those facts about his own identity, such as his name, health, sexuality, ethnicity, his own image, of which the cases speak; and also of the "zone of interaction" (*Von Hannover* paragraph 50) between himself and others.** *He is the presumed owner of these aspects of his own self; his control of them can only be loosened, abrogated, if the State shows an objective justification for doing so.*

22. This cluster of values, summarised as the **personal autonomy** of every individual and taking concrete form as a presumption against interference with the individual's liberty, is a defining characteristic of a free society. **We therefore need to preserve it even in little cases.** At the same time it is important that this core right protected by Article 8, **however protean**, should not be read so widely that its claims become unreal and unreasonable. For this **purpose** I think there are **three safeguards**, or qualifications. **First**, the alleged threat or assault to the individual's personal autonomy must (if Article 8 is to be engaged) attain "**a certain level of seriousness**". **Secondly**, the touchstone for Article 8(1)'s engagement is whether the claimant enjoys on the facts a "**reasonable expectation of privacy**" (in any of the senses of privacy accepted in the cases). **Absent such an expectation, there is no relevant interference** with personal autonomy. **Thirdly**, the breadth of Article 8(1) may in many instances **be greatly curtailed** by the scope of the justifications available to the State pursuant to Article 8(2). I shall say a little in turn about these three antidotes to the overblown use of Article 8.

23. **As for the first—"a certain level of seriousness"**—see for example *R (Gillan) v Commissioner of Police for the Metropolis* [2006] 2 AC 307, paragraph 28 *per* Lord Bingham of Cornhill:

> "It is true that 'private life' has been **generously** construed to embrace wide rights to personal autonomy. **But it is clear Convention jurisprudence that intrusions must reach a certain level of seriousness to engage the operation of the Convention,** which is, after all, concerned with human rights and fundamental freedoms, and I incline to the view that an ordinary superficial search of the person and an opening of bags, of the kind to which passengers uncomplainingly submit at airports, for example, can scarcely be said to reach that level."

24. **As for the second—a "reasonable expectation of privacy"**—I have already cited paragraph 51 of *Von Hannover*, with its reference to that very phrase, **and also to a "legitimate expectation" of protection.** One may compare a passage in Lord Nicholls' opinion in *Campbell* at paragraph 21:

> "Accordingly, in deciding what was the ambit of an individual's 'private life' in particular circumstances courts need to be on guard against using as a touchstone a test which brings into account considerations which should **more properly be considered at the later stage of proportionality.** Essentially the touchstone of private life is whether in respect of the disclosed facts the person in question had **a reasonable expectation of privacy**."

In the same case Lord Hope said at paragraph 99:

> **"The question is what a reasonable person of ordinary sensibilities would feel if she was placed in the same position as the claimant and faced with the same publicity."**

In *Murray v Big Pictures (UK) Ltd* Sir Anthony Clarke MR referred to both of these passages, and stated:

> "35 . . . [S]o far as the relevant principles to be derived from *Campbell* are concerned, they can we think be summarised in this way. The **first question** is whether there is a reasonable expectation of privacy. This is of course **an objective question**. . . .
>
> 36. As we see it, the question whether there is a reasonable expectation of privacy is a **broad** one, which takes account of all the circumstances of the case. They include the **attributes** of the claimant, **the nature** of the activity in which the claimant was engaged, **the place** at which it was happening, the **nature** and **purpose** of the **intrusion**, the **absence of consent** and whether it was known or could be inferred, the **effect on the claimant** and the **circumstances** in which and the **purposes** for which the information came **into the hands of the publisher**."

25. We can see, then, that while an individual's personal autonomy makes him the master of all those facts about his own identity of which the cases speak, **his *ownership* of them depends by law on there being a reasonable expectation in the particular case that his privacy will be respected.** This may operate as a factor limiting the scope of the Article 8 right. As I will shortly explain, it is a major dimension of Mr Grodzinski's case on behalf of the respondent Commissioner that what happened here took place in a public street, where people may take **photographs** at any time; there was, he says, no reasonable expectation that the appellant would not be photographed.

26. The **third safeguard** against too pervasive an application of Article 8 consists in the relation between Article 8(1) and 8(2). **The *first two* antidotes, *a* certain**

level of seriousness and ***a reasonable expectation of privacy,*** **though clearly important, still allow an open gate to Article 8(1) in very many circumstances; but it will often be closed by Article 8(2).** Once the 8(2) stage is reached, and the court is looking for a justification from the State for what would otherwise amount to a violation, the first question will be whether the action complained of was taken or to be taken in pursuance of a **legitimate aim**; that is **always crucial**. If that condition is met, there will be other issues (such as compliance with **the requirement of legal certainty**). Important for present purposes is the familiar question, whether **the action is proportionate to the legitimate aim in whose service it was taken.** At ***that*** stage, subject always to context and the case's particular subject-matter, **the court is likely to acknowledge and attribute a margin of discretion to the responsible State.** This exercise provides an important contrast with the court's task under 8(1). Its application may amount to a significant restraint upon the bite of Article 8.

27. I recognise, of course, that the court's assessment of proportionality will always and necessarily be sensitive to the facts of the particular case, and **the scope of the State's margin of discretion must vary according to the importance of the impugned right** in the particular instance, the force of the legitimate aim involved, and other balancing factors. The overall point to be made is that while the application of 8(1) and that of 8(2) are logically separate, and the second arises only if the first is fulfilled, there is a symbiosis: Article 8(1) is **generously** applied, **but the justifications properly available under 8(2), not least given the margin of discretion which the decision-maker is likely to enjoy, may sometimes cut its application close to the quick.**

28. The value of this approach is I think to be understood in light of the important fact that the paradigm case of Article 8's application is where the putative violation is by the State itself. It seems to me entirely in harmony with the fair balance which falls to be struck throughout the Convention provisions between the rights of the individual and the interest of the community (see for example *Sporrong v Sweden* (1983) 5 EHRR 35, paragraph 69) that where State action touches the individual's personal autonomy, it should take little to require the State to justify itself, but equally—if (and I repeat, this is critical) the action complained is **taken in good faith** to further a **legitimate aim**—a proper justification may be readily at hand. This is no more than the rule of law in action. Thus the State organ in question, here the police, is subjected by Article 8 to proper standards of conduct; but through the margin of discretion recognised in the jurisprudence, the law will allow it proper practical scope to fulfil its public duty.

(2) Article 8(1)—Was There a Prima Facie Violation?

29. Against that background I turn to the issues in this appeal. It is useful first to refer to the respondent Commissioner's case. Mr Grodzinski on his behalf contends that the actions of the police in taking and retaining the pictures did not touch the appellant's right under Article 8: there was no *prima facie* violation of Article 8(1), and therefore nothing for the respondent to justify by reference to any of the considerations set out in Article 8(2). In the course of his submissions he drew a distinction between the *taking* of the **photographs** and the *retention* of the images. His case is that neither involved any *prima facie* violation of Article 8(1). The learned judge below agreed. Although for reasons I shall explain I consider that this distinction is in the end unhelpful (at least in the present case) for the **purpose** of ascertaining the reach of the Convention right, **it is nevertheless convenient first to consider whether Article 8(1) was engaged by the mere taking of the photographs.**

(2a) Is Article 8(1) Engaged by the Mere Taking of the Photographs?

30. Mr Grodzinski supports his position as regards the taking of the **photographs** principally by reference to two propositions given by the authorities, one **broad**, the other **narrow**. I have already introduced the broad proposition. It recalls that the ECHR is concerned with the protection of fundamental rights and freedoms; and is to the effect that the facts said to constitute an interference with the right guaranteed by Article 8 must attain **"a certain level of seriousness".** This is supported by a wealth of authority; Mr Grodzinski cites *R (Gillan) v Commissioner of Police for the Metropolis* [2006] 2 AC 307, *per* Lord Bingham of Cornhill at **paragraph 28,** a passage which I have set out above at **paragraph 22.**

31. I have also foreshadowed **the second,** and **narrower**, proposition advanced by Mr Grodzinski. It is that ordinarily the taking of **photographs** in a public street involves no element of interference with anyone's private life and therefore will not engage Article 8(1), **although the later publication of such photographs may be a different matter.** Here I should again cite *Campbell v MGN Ltd*. The facts in barest outline were that a well-known fashion model was photographed in a public street leaving a narcotic addiction therapy session, and the **photographs** (or some of them) were later published. The House of Lords was divided as to the outcome of Miss Campbell's privacy/confidence claim, albeit on a very **narrow** aspect of the case. The force of the following *dicta* is unaffected by their authors' concurrence in the result or otherwise. Lord Hoffmann said this at paragraphs 73–74:

> "In the present case the pictures were taken without Miss Campbell's consent. That in my opinion is not enough to amount to a wrongful invasion of privacy. The famous and even the not so famous who go

> out in public must accept that they may be photographed without their consent . . . But the fact that we cannot avoid being photographed does not mean that anyone who takes or obtains such **photographs** can publish them to the world at large . . . "

Lord Hope of Craighead said this at paragraph 122:

> "The **photographs** were taken of Miss Campbell while she was in a public place, as she was in the street outside the premises where she had been receiving therapy. **The taking of photographs in a public street must, as Randerson J said in Hosking v Runting [2003] 3 NZLR 385, 415, para 138, be taken to be one of the ordinary incidents of living in a free community.** ***The real issue is whether publicising the content of the* photographs *would be offensive*** . . ." (see also: [2003] 3 NZLR 385)

Finally, Baroness Hale of Richmond at paragraph 154:

> "Publishing the **photographs** contributed both to the revelation and to the harm that it might do. **By themselves, they are not objectionable.** Unlike France and Quebec, in this country we do not recognise a right to one's own image: cf *Aubry v Editions Vice-Versa Inc* [1998] 1 SCR 591. We have not so far held that the mere fact of **covert** photography is sufficient to make the information contained in the **photograph** confidential. The activity photographed must be private. **If this had been, and had been presented as, a picture of Naomi Campbell going about her business in a public street, there could have been no complaint . . . "**

32. In the present case there was, of course, no question of the **photographs** being published. Mr Grodzinski says there are no aspects of the facts that could elevate the case to "**a certain level of seriousness**": the fact that more than one picture was taken, or that the police followed the appellant down Duke St, cannot suffice. He submits that in the end this is no more than an instance of **photographs** being taken in a public street and there can be no Article 8 complaint.

33. It is clear that the **real vice** in *Campbell* (and also *Von Hannover* and *Big Pictures*, which concerned the **covert** photographing of a well known author, J K Rowling, her husband and young child in a public street in Edinburgh) **was the fact or threat of publication in the media,** and not just the snapping of the shutter. Can Mr Westgate for the appellant sustain a claim that the mere taking of the pictures, irrespective of the use made of them (a claim he vigorously pursued), engages Article 8(1)?

34. I would certainly acknowledge that the **circumstances** in which a **photograph** is taken **in a public place** may of themselves turn the event into one in which Article 8 is not merely engaged but grossly violated**. The act of taking the picture, or more likely pictures, may be intrusive or even violent,**

conducted by means of hot pursuit, face-to-face confrontation, pushing, shoving, bright lights, barging into the affected person's home. The subject of the photographers' interest—in the case I am contemplating, there will usually be a bevy of picture-takers—may be seriously harassed and perhaps assaulted. He or she may certainly feel frightened and distressed. Conduct of this kind is simply brutal. It may well attract other remedies, civil or criminal, under our domestic law. It would plainly violate Article 8(1), and I can see no public interest justification for it under Article 8(2). But scenarios of that kind are very far from this case. **I accept Mr Grodzinski's submission that the fact that more than one picture was taken, or that the police followed the appellant down Duke St, cannot turn this episode into anything remotely so objectionable.**

35. The core of Mr Westgate's case is however that it was the police—and thus the State—who took the pictures. As I have stated (paragraph 28), the paradigm case of Article 8's application is where the putative violation is by the State. Can that make all the difference, simply as regards the taking of the **photographs** and nothing more? In my judgment it cannot. **It is no surprise that the mere taking of someone's photograph in a public street has been consistently held to be no interference with privacy.** The snapping of the shutter of itself breaches no rights, unless something more is added.

36. **Accordingly I conclude that the bare act of taking the pictures, by whoever done, is not of itself capable of engaging Article 8(1) *unless there are aggravating circumstances.*** I have already referred (paragraph 34) to the case where the subject of the photographer's attention is harassed and hounded, and perhaps assaulted. As I have said that is plainly not this case. And as for this particular case, I have already rejected (again paragraph 34) the suggestion that the fact that more than one picture was taken, or that the police followed the appellant down Duke St, could give rise to a *prima facie* violation of the Article. **I would add that notwithstanding the appellant's apprehensions, there is in my view every reason to accept Mr Williams' evidence that he was generally at pains "to keep a safe distance from the subject and try not to invade their 'personal space'",** for reasons he gives at paragraph 5 of his statement. It is also obvious that the new material I have described, based on Superintendent Hartshorn's interview, cannot advance the case as regards the bare act of taking the pictures.

37. I should note that Mr Westgate also submits, somewhat more generally, that the use of overt photography by the police has actually become an intimidating feature of London life. He relies on a second witness statement from Mr Gask, an employee of Liberty, for whose introduction in evidence we gave permission at the hearing. Mr Gask gives particulars of three press publications on the subject. One of these (the Guardian, 30 May 2008) describes an

operation by Essex police involving intensive surveillance of youths (including repeated photography) in a bid to curb anti-social behaviour; an operation which was welcomed by some very muscular observations by the Secretary of State. In my view all this puts the matter far too high. **None of Mr Gask's instances suggests, far less demonstrates, that the snapping of the shutter by the police in a public place is capable without more of engaging Article 8(1), or that the facts of this case (so far as they concern only the taking of the pictures) do so.**

38. **The real issue is whether the taking of the pictures, *along with their actual and/or apprehended use,* might amount to a violation.**

(2b) Article 8(1): the Taking of the Photographs and their Use

39. **It might be thought that if (as I would hold) the mere taking of the pictures does not engage Article 8(1)**, there follows a wholly separate question: whether **their retention and intended use** might do so. But I do not think this is the right way to analyse the case**. I stated earlier (paragraph 29) that the supposed distinction between the taking of the photographs and the retention of the images is in the end unhelpful for the purpose of ascertaining the reach of the Article 8 right.** We have seen that **the respondent's policy** is that "cameras are deployed overtly . . . officers should clearly identify themselves as police officers or police staff and not hide the fact that they are filming". This is certainly as it should be; **if it were done covertly, there would be other very substantial arguments to consider which in this case do not arise.** As it is, the subject—here, the appellant—observes who is taking his picture and knows it is a police photographer. He is bound to assume that the picture will be kept, and that it will, or at least might, be used for a police **purpose**. Mr Grodzinski submitted that if the taking of the pictures is not itself any interference with the appellant's Article 8(1) right, it cannot become so by reason of the pictures' potential use; but this I think is too simplistic. The subject's complaint—absent any question of intimidation or **harassment**—is that his image is being recorded by State authorities, an act to which he does not consent, which he believes to be unjustified, and whose precise **purpose** is unknown to him. The police operation, from the taking of the pictures to their actual and intended retention and use, must in my opinion be judged as a whole. Accordingly I am inclined to agree with Mr Westgate's submission recorded by the learned judge below as follows:

> "24 . . . **It is impossible . . . to 'compartmentalise' the taking of the photographs without regard to the circumstances in which they were taken, the purposes of their retention, whether, for example, it is intended thereby to identify the individual and whether there is proper and certain legal control over the photography as a whole.** He submits that here the Claimant's identity was discovered and there was

a degree of systematic gathering of information about CAAT activity and its members. He pointed also to evidence from the Claimant's solicitor of other occasions when members of CAAT have been similarly photographed."

40. Mr Grodzinski cited two decisions of the Strasbourg Commission, *X v UK* (Application no 5877/72) and *Friedl v Austria* (1995) 21 EHRR 83, which I think tend to confirm that (at least in a case about the taking of pictures by the police) **we are to look at all the circumstances of the case in order to see whether Article 8(1) is engaged.** The facts of *X v UK* involved a protest against the apartheid laws in South Africa. The applicant was arrested during a rugby match in England involving the South African national team and was photographed upon arrest and thereafter at the police station. She said that she was told that the **photographs** would be kept in case she made trouble at future matches. The Commission's decision, **declaring the claim inadmissible,** stated as follows:

> "The Commission has noted here the following elements in the case as it has been presented: **first**, that there was no invasion of the applicant's privacy in the sense that the authorities entered her home and took **photographs** of her there; **secondly**, that the **photographs** related to a public incident in which she was voluntarily taking part; and **thirdly**, that they were taken solely for the **purpose** of her future identification on similar public occasions and there is no suggestion that they have been made available to the general public or used for any other **purpose**. Bearing these factors in mind, the Commission finds that the taking and retention of the **photographs** of the applicant could not be considered to amount to an interference with her private life within the meaning of Article 8 . . .
>
> An examination by the Commission of the applicant's complaint . . . shows that **the taking of her photographs was part of and solely related to her voluntary public activities** and does not therefore disclose any appearance of a violation of the rights and freedoms set out in the Convention and in particular in the two articles just considered."

41. ***Friedl*** (in which *X v UK* was cited) was a case where there had been a demonstration involving a round-the-clock "sit in" of about fifty persons in an underground pedestrian passage in Vienna, held with a view to drawing public attention to the plight of the homeless. The police took **photographs** and also recorded images on a video cassette for use in the event of a prosecution. The applicant also claimed that he was photographed individually, his identity was checked and his particulars noted down. **The Commission held the applicant's Article 8 claim to be admissible but in the event found there was no violation, stating:**

"49. In the present case, the Commission has noted the following elements: **first**, there was **no intrusion** into the 'inner circle' of the applicant's private life in the sense that the authorities entered his home and took the **photographs** there; **secondly**, the **photographs** related to a **public incident,** namely a manifestation of several persons in a public place, in which the applicant was voluntarily taking part; and **thirdly**, they were solely taken for the purposes, on 17 February 1988, of recording **the character of the manifestation and the actual situation at the place in question,** *eg* the sanitary conditions, and, on 19 February 1988, of recording the conduct of the participants in the manifestation in view of ensuing investigation proceedings for offences against the Road Traffic Regulations.

50. In this context, the Commission attaches weight to the assurances given by the respondent Government according to which the individual persons on the **photographs** taken **remained anonymous in that no names were noted down,** the personal data recorded and **photographs** taken **were not entered into a data processing system,** and **no action was taken to identify** the persons photographed on that occasion by means of data processing.

51. Bearing these factors in mind, the Commission finds that the taking of **photographs** of the applicant and their retention **do not amount to an interference** with his right to respect for his private life within the meaning of Article 8(1) of the Convention."

42. What, then, of the Article 8(1) issue on the facts of the present case? In his first witness statement the appellant says:

"9 . . . I was . . . confused as to why this was happening to me, as I knew I had not done anything wrong.

. . .

11. I felt threatened and uncomfortable throughout this. At no point would any of the officers explain why we were being photographed or questioned. It was my unease at this and my knowledge that I had not done anything wrong which meant that I chose not to give them my identity . . .

. . .

15. The knowledge that I have nothing to hide in terms of my own actions does not make this situation any easier for me. Instead it makes me more anxious that the **photographs** were taken when there did not seem to be any reasonable explanation as to why there was a need to do so.

16. I feel that I do not know how any information might be used by the police in the future, and that I had no control over the **photographs** being taken. I feel very uncomfortable that the information might be kept on my file by police indefinitely . . . "

43. The appellant has not been cross-examined, and his witness statement has of course been crafted, perfectly properly, by his solicitor. **But the essential point being made is clearly right: he found himself being photographed by the police, and he could not and did not know why they were doing it and what use they might make of the pictures.** The case is in my judgment quite different from *X v UK*, in which the **photographs** were taken on and after the applicant's arrest, when the police might well have been expected to do just that. It is possibly closer to *Friedl*, but in that case there had been a demonstration—a sit-in—where again the taking of police **photographs** could readily have been expected. In *R (Gillan) v Commissioner of Police for the Metropolis*, which I have cited at paragraph 23, Lord Bingham referred to "an ordinary superficial search of the person and an opening of bags, of the kind to which passengers uncomplainingly submit at airports": another instance in which the putative violation of Article 8 (if any violation were suggested) consists in something familiar and expected. In cases of that kind, where the police or other public authority are acting just as the public would expect them to act, it would ordinarily no doubt be **artificial** and unreal for the courts to find a *prima facie* breach of Article 8 and call on the State to justify the action taken by reference to Article 8(2).

44. I do not of course suggest that there is a rigid class of case in which, once it is shown that the State actions complained of (such as taking **photographs**) are expected and unsurprising, Article 8 cannot be engaged; nor likewise that where they are surprising and unexpected, Article 8 will necessarily be applicable. **The Strasbourg court has always been sensitive to each case's particular facts,** and the particular facts must always be examined. And the first two limiting factors affecting Article 8's application—**a certain level of seriousness** and a reasonable expectation of privacy—are not sharp-edged.

45. But in my judgment it is important to recognise that State action may confront and challenge the individual as it were out of the blue. It may have no patent or obvious contextual explanation, and in that case it is not more apparently rational than arbitrary, nor more apparently justified than unjustified**. In this case it consists in the taking and retaining of photographs, though it might consist in other acts. The Metropolitan Police, visibly and with no obvious cause, chose to take and keep photographs of an individual going about his lawful business in the streets of London. This action is a good deal more than the snapping of the shutter. The police are a State authority. And as**

I have said, the appellant could not and did not know why they were doing it and what use they might make of the pictures.

46. **In these circumstances I would hold that Article 8 is engaged. On the particular facts the police action, unexplained at the time it happened and carrying as it did the implication that the images would be kept and used, is a sufficient intrusion by the State into the individual's own space, his integrity, as to amount to a prima facie violation of Article 8(1).** It attains a sufficient level of **seriousness** and in the circumstances the appellant enjoyed a reasonable expectation that his privacy would not be thus invaded. Moreover I consider with respect that this conclusion is supported by the judgment of the Strasbourg court in *Marper*. It will be recalled that the first sentence of paragraph 67 reads:

> "The mere storing of data relating to the private life of an individual amounts to an interference within the meaning of Article 8 . . . "

And at paragraph 121 the court said:

> "The Government contend that the retention could not be considered as having any direct or significant effect on the applicants unless matches in the database were to implicate them in the commission of offences on a future occasion. **The Court is unable to accept this argument and reiterates that the mere retention and storing of personal data by public authorities, however obtained, are to be regarded as having direct impact on the private-life interest of an individual concerned, irrespective of whether subsequent use is made of the data (see paragraph 67 above).**"

However the impact of these observations on the present case is I think weakened by the fact that the appellant's image was not placed on the CO11 database, which I have described in dealing with the new material arising from the Guardian article, nor on any other database. And I should make clear my view that this new material does not assist the appellant in any respect. The fact that the CO11 database exists cannot conceivably support the appellant's contention that his Article 8 rights have been interfered with, since his image was never placed upon it; and he has no proper business advancing any arguments—if this is what he seeks to do—to assault the practice or procedure of the respondent (as regards the storage and use of information) in circumstances where any such arguments cannot actually bear on his claim.

47. In arriving at this conclusion on the application of Article 8(1) I intend no criticism of the police. Their action's merits will be for consideration under Article 8(2). Their subjection to the discipline of Article 8 means that the fair balance which falls to be struck throughout the Convention provisions

between the rights of the individual and the interest of the community has to be struck on the facts of this case. That I think is as it should be.

(3) Article 8(2)

48. ***First*, it seems to me that there can be no question but that the taking and retention of photographs of the appellant on 27 April 2005 were in pursuit of a legitimate aim.** As I have stated (paragraph 4), the pictures were taken **(1)** so that if disorder erupted and offences were committed (or it transpired that offences had already been committed inside the hotel), offenders could be identified, albeit at a later time if necessary; and **(2)** so that persons who might possibly commit public order offences at the DESi fair in September could be identified in advance: this would or might assist the police operation at the forthcoming event. In Article 8(2) terms, the action was taken "**for the prevention of disorder or crime"**; perhaps also "**in the interests of . . . public safety or . . . for the protection of the rights and freedoms of others".** So much is not I think disputed.

49. Mr Westgate's argument on this part of the case is twofold. He submits first that the police action was not "in accordance with the law", **because any putative legal justification for it (certainly for the retention and use of the pictures) is not *sufficiently clear and precise.*** Secondly he says that the police action was disproportionate to the legitimate aim in view.

(3a) "In Accordance with the Law"

50. Mr Grodzinski submits that the taking and retention of the **photographs** was done pursuant to the respondent's common law powers to detect and prevent crime. He cites *Rice v Connolly* [1966] 2 QB 414 *per* Lord Parker CJ at 419: with respect I need not set out the passage. **As regards the requirements of clarity and certainty**, Mr Grodzinski relied on the striking decision of the Strasbourg court in *Murray v UK* (1994) 19 EHRR 193. In that case the first applicant was arrested and detained under the Northern Ireland (Emergency Provisions) Act 1978. She was suspected of collecting money for the purchase of arms for the Irish Republican Army. At an Army screening centre she refused to answer questions, was photographed without her knowledge and consent and the **photographs** were kept on record along with personal details about her, her family and her home. She was later released without charge. The Strasbourg court (seventeen judges: the equivalent of today's Grand Chamber) roundly stated:

> "The taking and, by implication, also the retention of a **photograph** of the first applicant without her consent had no statutory basis but, as explained by the trial court judge and the Court of Appeal, were lawful under common law.
>
> The impugned measures thus had a basis in domestic law. The Court

discerns no reason, on the material before it, for not concluding that each of the various measures was 'in accordance with the law', within the meaning of Article 8(2)."

51. McCombe J had this to say:

"69. Mr Westgate submitted that the decision in *Murray* was 'wrong'. He was prepared to accept that *Rice v Connolly* might provide the outline of a legal basis for what was done here and prevents the conduct in issue from being actionable in tort, but it does not address the recognised requirements of accessibility, certainty and precision now recognised in European jurisprudence. In answer, Mr Grodzinski submitted that the decision in *Murray* was that of the Full Court and post-dated *Malone* (1985) 7 EHRR 14, *Silver v UK* (1983) 5 EHRR 347 and *Sunday Times v UK* 2 EHRR 245 in which the principles of **precision, certainty and accessibility** were fully considered; it was inconceivable, it was submitted, that the Court would not have had those principles well in mind.

70. I recognise that the European Court in *Malone* stated (at paragraph 68 of its judgment, (1985) 7 EHRR 14 at p 41) **that the degree of precision required of the law will depend on the subject matter and, on any footing, any interference with the Claimant's rights under Article 8 must, in my view, be no more than modest.** In the circumstances, it appears that the common law power relied upon by the defendant must, in the circumstances of this case, be sufficiently in accordance with the law to satisfy Article 8(2). Further, as the Defendant rightly submits, the exercise of that power is subject to public law control reaching over and above the inherent 'lawfulness' of the actions. In addition, I cannot accept that it is my place simply to dismiss the decision of the Full Court in *Murray* as 'wrong', as Mr Westgate would have me do. That would do quite inadequate respect for the decisions of that court, the ultimate arbiter of these matters, in a case in close proximity of subject matter to the present one."

52. It appears that on seeing a draft of the judgment Mr Westgate disavowed having made so stark a submission; but the judge indicates (footnote 8 to the judgment) that paragraph 69 accurately records his note of the argument. In his skeleton argument for this appeal Mr Westgate submits (paragraph 39) that "*Murray* dealt only with the source of the power to take **photographs** and not with the other established requirements that the law be **sufficiently precise, certain and accessible",** and refers to *Malone* and *Silver*. However it is to be noted, as Mr Grodzinski pointed out (skeleton argument paragraph 74), that the court in *Murray* upheld the earlier decision of the Commission, which had referred expressly (p. 216, paragraph 80) to the *Malone* case.

53. **It seems to me that the judge's reasoning is correct.** I would attach particular importance to the nature of the **intrusion** said to violate Article 8. There is some suggestion in the cases of a relativist approach, so that the more **intrusive** the act complained of, the more precise and specific must be the law said to justify it. Thus in *Gillan*, to which I have already referred, Lord Hope said this:

> "56. As the concluding words of para 67 of the decision in *Malone v United Kingdom* (1985) 7 EHRR 14 indicate**, the sufficiency of these measures must be balanced against the nature and degree of the interference with the citizen's Convention rights which is likely to result from the exercise of the power that has been given to the public authority.** The things that a constable can do when exercising the section 44 [sc. of the Terrorism Act 2000] power are limited by the provisions of section 45(3) and 45(4). He may not require the person to remove any clothing in public except that which is specified, and the person may be detained only for such time as is reasonably required to permit the search to be carried out at or near the place where the person or vehicle has been stopped. **The extent of the intrusion is not very great given the obvious importance of the purpose for which it is being resorted to. In my opinion the structure of law within which it is to be exercised is sufficient in all the circumstances to meet the requirement of legality."**

Malone concerned telephone intercepts. As McCombe J observed at paragraph 70, the Strasbourg court in that case stated at paragraph 68 that **the degree of precision required of the law will depend on the subject matter**. The previous paragraph, referred to by Lord Hope in *Gillan*, has this:

> "Undoubtedly, as the Government rightly suggested, the requirements of the Convention, notably in regard to foreseeability, cannot be exactly the same in the special context of interception of communications for the purposes of police investigations as they are where the object of the relevant law is to place restrictions on the conduct of individuals. In particular, the requirement of foreseeability cannot mean that an individual should be enabled to foresee when the authorities are likely to intercept his communications so that he can adapt his conduct accordingly. **Nevertheless, the law must be sufficiently clear in its terms to give citizens an adequate indication as to the circumstances in which and the conditions on which public authorities are empowered to resort to this secret and potentially dangerous interference with the right to respect for private life and correspondence."**

It is also interesting to note this observation by the Strasbourg court in *Marper*:

> "**96. The level of precision required of domestic legislation—which cannot in any case provide for every eventuality—depends to a considerable degree on the content of the instrument in question, the field it is designed to cover and the number and status of those to whom it is addressed** (*Hasan and Chaush v Bulgaria* [GC], no 30985/96, § 84, ECHR 2000-XI, with further references, 34 EHRR 55)."

54. In the present case, though for reasons I have given the Article 8(1) threshold is crossed, the nature of the respondent's interference with the appellant's private life was, as the judge observed, **no more than modest.** In those **circumstances the requirement of legality is in my judgment satisfied** by the general common law power referred to in *Murray*, and the judge was right so to hold.

55. There were some other points on this part of the case. Mr Westgate relied on the respondent's failure to disclose the "Standard Operating Procedures for 'Use of Overt Filming/Photography'", to which I referred at paragraph 13. I should in fairness note that this document has been withheld, as I understand it, on grounds permitted under the Freedom of Information Act 2000. The respondent says that throws no light on the circumstances in which police **photographs** may be taken. **In any event, however, the respondent in my judgment does not need to rely on the terms of his policy, or any established internal procedures relating to overt photography, in order to establish compliance with the requirement of legality.** ***The common law power suffices.*** For the same reason I do not find it necessary to enter into the further debate between the parties as to whether the legality requirement might be met by the provisions of the **Data Protection Act 1998.** Likewise, the new material arising out of the Guardian article does not affect the matter.

(3b) Proportionality

56. McCombe J dealt with this aspect very shortly. He considered (paragraph 74) that "it was entirely reasonable and proportionate for the police to **photograph** persons who, as it might turn out, had been engaged or might be likely to engage in criminal disorder". Ironically, as it has turned out, he relied on some observations of Lord Steyn in *Marper* in the House of Lords ([2004] 1 WLR 2196, paragraph 1):

> "My Lords, it is of paramount importance that law enforcement agencies should take full advantage of the available techniques of modern technology and forensic science. Such real evidence has the inestimable value of cogency and objectivity. It is in large measure not affected by the subjective defects of other testimony. It enables the guilty to be detected and the innocent to be rapidly eliminated from inquiries. Thus

in the 1990s closed circuit television ('CCTV') became a crime-prevention strategy extensively adopted in British cities and towns. The images recorded facilitate the detection of crime and prosecution of offenders. Making due allowance for the possibility of threats to civil liberties, this phenomenon has had beneficial effects."

57. As I have indicated their Lordships' House considered that the retention of the applicants' DNA and fingerprints did not offend their rights under Article 8. The Strasbourg court took a very different view. They held:

> "117. While neither the statistics nor the examples provided by the Government in themselves establish that the successful identification and prosecution of offenders could not have been achieved without the permanent and indiscriminate retention of the fingerprint and DNA records of all persons in the applicants' position, the Court accepts that the extension of the database has nonetheless contributed to the detection and prevention of crime.
>
> 118. **The question, however, remains whether such *retention* is proportionate and strikes a fair balance between the competing public and private interests.**
>
> 119. In this respect, the Court is struck by the blanket and indiscriminate nature of the power of retention in England and Wales. The material may be retained irrespective of the nature or gravity of the offence with which the individual was originally suspected or of the age of the suspected offender; fingerprints and samples may be taken—and retained—from a person of any age, arrested in connection with a recordable offence, which includes minor or non-imprisonable offences. The retention is not time-limited; the material is retained indefinitely whatever the nature or seriousness of the offence of which the person was suspected. Moreover, there exist only limited possibilities for an acquitted individual to have the data removed from the nationwide database or the materials destroyed . . . ; in particular, there is no provision for independent review of the justification for the retention according to defined criteria, including such factors as the seriousness of the offence, previous arrests, the strength of the suspicion against the person and any other special circumstances.
>
> . . .
>
> 125. In conclusion, the Court finds that the blanket and indiscriminate nature of the powers of retention of the fingerprints, cellular samples and DNA profiles of persons suspected but not convicted of offences, as applied in the case of the present applicants, fails to strike a fair balance between the competing public and private interests and

that the respondent State has overstepped any acceptable **margin of appreciation** in this regard. **Accordingly, the retention at issue constitutes a disproportionate interference with the applicants' right to respect for private life and cannot be regarded as necessary in a democratic society.** This conclusion obviates the need for the Court to consider the applicants' criticism regarding the adequacy of certain particular safeguards, such as too broad an access to the personal data concerned and insufficient protection against the misuse or abuse of such data."

58. **Plainly there might be a question whether this court should follow the House of Lords or the European Court of Human Rights in Marper. If this court were required to confront such a question, it would follow the House of Lords: *Kay v Lambeth LBC*** [2006] 2 AC 465**.** But in my judgment ***Marper*** is wholly distinguishable on its facts. **Pictures of the appellant were taken because the police believed that he had contact with EA who had a history of unlawful activity, and there was the possibility that he had been involved in unlawful activity in the meeting from which EA had been ejected. The taking of the pictures was in no sense aggressively done. The retention of the pictures was carefully and tightly controlled. The appellant's image was not placed on any searchable database, far less a nationwide database indefinitely retained**. But for the commencement of these proceedings the images of the appellant would have been destroyed after the DSEi exhibition.

59. In my judgment no useful comparison can be made between the facts of this case and the features of *Marper* which led the Strasbourg court to reject the State's Article 8(2) justification. There is a qualitative difference between photographic images on the one hand and fingerprints and DNA on the other, not least as regards the reach of the use to which they might be put. **The appellant's photograph was in my judgment taken, and retained, in the course of a properly controlled operation undertaken for perfectly good policing reasons consistently with a balanced and reasonable published policy.**

60. I acknowledge that any link between the appellant and EA is disputed; that the appellant is a person of good character; that any suspicion that the appellant might have committed an offence at or in connection with the AGM must have been quickly dissipated; and that the only justification for keeping the images thereafter was to monitor his conduct at the DSEi fair several months later. **But that was a legitimate aim, in service of which the images were kept.** For my part I find it impossible to categorise what was done as outwith **the margin of operational discretion** which, it must surely be acknowledged, the police possess in such circumstances. In my judgment

the retention of the images was proportionate to the legitimate aim of the exercise.

ARTICLES 10, 11 AND 14

61. I hope it will not be thought discourteous to Mr Westgate if I deal with these further complaints summarily. I consider it fanciful to suppose that in the events which happened there was any interference with the appellant's rights under Article 10 and 11. Apart from anything else he was not purporting to exercise either such right on the occasion in question.

62. As for Article 14, the police had good reason, arising from their perception of events which was itself reasonable, to **photograph** the appellant. There was no discrimination contrary to Article 14.

CONCLUSION

63. I would dismiss the appeal.

Lord Justice Dyson:

64. I gratefully adopt the account of the facts and issues set out so fully by Laws LJ. I agree with his valuable analysis of the article 8(1) issue and his reasons for concluding that article 8 is engaged on the facts of this case. **For the reasons that follow, however, I have reached a different conclusion on the article 8(2) issue**. Before I explain why in my judgment the interference with the appellant's article 8 rights was disproportionate, I need to emphasise some of the relevant facts. I regret that this will inevitably involve some **repetition** of the account already given by Laws LJ.

The relevant facts

65. Chief Inspector Weaver was Operations Chief Inspector at West End Central Police Station at the material time. The police had been informed that there might be some form of protest by members of CAAT at the AGM of Reed on 27 April 2005. A second demonstration was due to take place on the same day outside the premises of BP by an environmental campaigning group and Chief Inspector Weaver was concerned that the two protest groups might combine and exacerbate the problem. Her concerns that there might be trouble at the AGM were further increased when it became known that a named individual (EA), who had a history of unlawful demonstrations against companies involved in the arms trade and who had a number of previous convictions for offences in this context, had been nominated as a proxy to vote at the AGM. It was these concerns which led Chief Inspector Weaver to decide that the AGM had to be policed: see paras 4 to 6 of her witness statement.

66. 24 officers were allocated to the policing of the event. In addition, intelligence

gathering officers were deployed. The **purpose** of the intelligence gathering teams was to "gather intelligence, primarily by taking **photographs** and making notes which may be of subsequent evidential value should offences be committed or disorder break out" (para 10 of Chief Inspector Weaver's statement).

67. At para 13, she says:

> "The reason why I decided to request the use [of] FITs and EGs was because of the ongoing nature of the protests against companies involved in the arms trade and the attendance of known trouble makers so that I believed that public disorder may result. In such situations it is vital that the police know who has attended and what their involvement is".

68. And again at para 15:

> "Intelligence had to be gathered at the time so that, should disorder result or offences subsequently come to light, those guilty of an offence could be identified so that they could be arrested, if not at the time then in the future. Thus if those attending the AGM caused trouble they could be identified and either arrested at the time or if appropriate, shortly after. Further, I took the view that if those individuals who might attend and commit public order or other offences at the DSEi fair in September could be identified in advance, by ascertaining their identity at the Reed AGM, that would help to police the DSEi event and deal with any such offences".

69. Police Sergeant Dixon was an officer in one of the intelligence gathering teams on 27 April. In his statement, he says (para 5) that of particular interest to the team were two activists (EA and RH) both of whom had a history of violent protests and who, it was believed, had a tendency to encourage otherwise peaceful protesters to commit offences.

70. The AGM was conducted peacefully, although EA and RH were ejected by private security officials for disrupting the meeting. The appellant left the hotel after the conclusion of the AGM at about 12.30 pm with another man (IP). They stopped to speak to KB and were joined by EA. It was in these circumstances (ie because the appellant and IP were seen associating with EA) that PS Dixon says that he directed the photographer to take the **photographs** which have given rise to these proceedings. PS Dixon says at para 10 of his statement:

> "The decision to take the **photographs** of the claimant and IP was not solely because of their association with EA but also because the **photographs** could be of subsequent evidential value if any, as yet undiscovered, offences had been committed inside the hotel. Such

offences are not always immediately apparent and may have become known only after the meeting was over."

71. The evidence as to the extent of the association between EA and the appellant is as follows. The appellant has no recollection of being joined by or seeing EA after the AGM. IP says that he and the appellant had a "brief chat" with EA lasting about one minute before they dispersed. PS Dixon says that the group comprising the appellant, IP and KB was joined by EA, but he does not say how long they stayed together. Neal Williams, the photographer, says that at about 12.44, the two females who had been ejected from the meeting joined other protesters outside the hotel and that was when he was asked to take the **photographs**. He does not say how long the two females remained with the appellant.

72. **The only other evidence to which I should refer is that the appellant is a man of good character with no previous convictions.** Some time after 27 April (on a date which has not been disclosed), the police discovered his identity. This they did by discovering the names of the new shareholders in Reed and working out by a process of elimination that the person photographed in the company of IP and others was the appellant.

73. A number of points need to be emphasised. **First**, the only evidence of a link between the appellant and EA is the brief association between them when the appellant was speaking to IP and they were joined by EA for about one minute. There is no evidence that the appellant went to the meeting with EA or that after he had been photographed outside the hotel, he was accompanied by her as he went along Duke Street and into Bond Street underground station.

74. **Secondly,** the principal reason why Chief Inspector Weaver involved the intelligence gathering teams was her concern that there might be disorder and criminal conduct at the AGM and/or in the vicinity of the hotel. Moreover, the reason why PS Dixon requested **photographs** to be taken of the appellant (and IP) was because of their association with EA and because such **photographs** could be of evidential value if it transpired that offences had been committed inside the hotel. Chief Inspector Weaver did, however, also see advantage in gathering evidence which would enable those who might attend the DSEi fair in September to be identified as well. The possible use of the **photographs** to identify persons who attended the DSEi fair does not, however, seem to have been a factor which led to the decision of PS Dixon to require the **photographs** to be taken.

75. **Thirdly,** it was acknowledged by Chief Inspector Weaver (and as is obvious), that if any offences had been committed in the hotel, this would have become apparent shortly after the conclusion of the AGM.

76. **Fourthly,** although it is not clear when the police first became aware that the appellant was a man of good character, they did know on 27 April that, unlike EA and RH, he had not been ejected from the meeting and that he was not guilty of any misconduct outside the hotel; and they must have known within a few days of 27 April (at the latest) that there was no evidence that he had been guilty of any misconduct inside the hotel either.

77. It follows that, within at most a few days of the conclusion of the meeting, there could no longer be any justification for retaining the **photographs** as evidence of the identity of a person who might have committed an offence at the meeting. The justification for retaining the **photographs** thereafter must have been as evidence of the identity of a person who might attend the DSEi fair several months later and who might commit an offence at that meeting.

78. It is against this background that it is necessary to consider whether the interference with the appellant's article 8 right to a private life constituted by the taking and retaining of the **photographs** was justified pursuant to article 8(2).

Article 8(2)

Legitimate aim

79. **I agree with Laws LJ that the taking and retention of the photographs were in pursuit of a legitimate aim, namely "for the prevention of disorder or crime" or "for the protection of the rights and freedoms of others": article 8(2). The phrase "prevention of disorder or crime" includes the detection of disorder or crime: see, for example, Marper v UK (Application 30562/04 and 30566/04, judgment of ECtHR 4 December 2008, BAILII:** [2008] ECHR 1581**). The contrary was not argued by Mr Westgate.**

"In accordance with the law"

80. The next question is whether the interference with the appellant's article 8 rights was **"in accordance with the law".** In view of the conclusion that I have reached on the issue of proportionality, I do not find it necessary to express a view on this question. I do, however, wish to express one reservation about Laws LJ's analysis.

81. At [53], Laws LJ attaches particular importance to the nature of the **intrusion** said to violate article 8 and suggests that, broadly, the more **intrusive** the act complained of, the more precise and specific must be the law said to justify it. **I would merely say that I have some doubt as to whether [56] of the speech of Lord Hope in Gillan supports such a proposition or that, if it does, it is supported by the concluding words of [67] of the decision in Malone v UK** (1985) 7 EHRR 14**.** In any event, I see no support for this proposition in the speech of Lord Bingham in *Gillan.* It is to be noted that all

the other members of their Lordships' House (including Lord Hope himself) agreed with the reasoning of Lord Bingham.

"Necessary in a democratic society": proportionality

82. The phrase "necessary in a democratic society" has been considered and applied by the ECtHR on many occasions. In *Marper* at [101], the court said:

> "An interference will be considered "necessary in a democratic society" for a legitimate aim if it answers a "**pressing social need"** and, in particular, if it is **proportionate** to the legitimate aim pursued and if the reasons adduced by the national authorities to justify it are **"relevant and sufficient".**

83. **In deciding whether the interference is *necessary,* the court must have regard to the nature of the Convention right in issue, its importance for the individual, the nature of the interference and the object pursued by the interference:** see *Marper* at [102]. At [103], the court went on to say that the protection of personal data is of fundamental importance to a person's enjoyment of his or her article 8 rights and the domestic law must afford appropriate safeguards to prevent any such use of personal data as may be inconsistent with the guarantees of article 8. **The need for such safeguards is all the greater where the protection of personal data undergoing automatic processing is concerned, not least when such data are used for police purposes.**

84. In other words, the court is required to carry out a careful exercise of **weighing** the **legitimate aim** to be pursued, the **importance of the right** which is the subject of the interference and the extent of the interference. **Thus an interference whose object is to protect the community from the danger of terrorism is more readily justified as proportionate than an interference whose object is to protect the community from the risk of low level crime and disorder.** The importance of the former was emphasised by the House of Lords in *R (Gillan) v Commissioner of Police of the Metropolis* [2006] UKHL 12, [2006] 2 AC 307: see per Lord Bingham of Cornhill at [29] and Lord Scott of Foscote at [62].

85. I agree that *Marper* is wholly distinguishable on the facts. **Whether an interference with a Convention right is proportionate is a fact-sensitive question.** I accept that the retention of the **photographs** by the police was not an interference of the utmost gravity with the appellant's article 8 rights. Nor, however, should it be dismissed as of little consequence. **The retention by the police of photographs taken of persons who have not committed an offence, and who are not even suspected of having committed an offence, is always a serious matter.** I say this notwithstanding the fact that I accept that the retention of the **photographs** in this case was tightly controlled and

that there is **a qualitative difference between photographic images on the one hand and fingerprints and DNA on the other.** It should also be recorded that the evidence is that, had these proceedings not been commenced, the **photographs** would have been destroyed after the DSEi fair. That is because the appellant did not attend that event and there was no intelligence suggesting that he had prior to that event (and after the AGM) participate in any other unlawful activities: see para 13 of the statement of Superintendent Gomme.

86. **The retention by the police of photographs of a person must be justified and the justification must be the more compelling where the interference with a person's rights is, as in the present case, in pursuit of the protection of the community from the risk of public disorder or low level crime, as opposed, for example, to protection against the danger of terrorism or really serious criminal activity.**

87. I return to the facts of this case. Within a few days of the AGM, the **retention of the photographs** could not rationally be justified as furthering the aim of detecting the perpetrators of any crime that may have been committed during the meeting. There was no realistic possibility that evidence that a crime had been committed at the meeting would only be obtained weeks or months after the event. The meeting was well attended. There were Reed officers and private security officials present who were on the look-out for trouble-makers and who did indeed eject two of them (although there is no evidence that even they committed any offence). **I repeat that the principal object of the evidence-gathering operation was to obtain evidence about possible disorder and criminal** conduct at the AGM and/or in the vicinity of the hotel and the sole reason given by the officer who instructed the photographer to take the **photographs** was to obtain evidence which would be of value if offences had been committed at the AGM.

88. The fact that the appellant had been seen briefly in the company of EA after the AGM may have provided further justification for retaining the **photographs** for a few days after 27 April. But thereafter, in my judgment, neither the brief association with EA nor anything else relating to the AGM provided any justification for retaining the **photographs** any longer.

89. **It follows that the only justification advanced by the police for retaining the photographs for more than a few days after the meeting was the possibility that the appellant might attend and commit an offence at the DSEi fair several months later. But in my judgment, even if due allowance is made for the margin of operational discretion, that justification does not bear scrutiny**. **First**, the DSEi fair was not the principal focus of the evidence-gathering operation. The principal concern of the police was what might happen at the AGM and/or in the vicinity of the hotel. But for that concern,

the evidence would suggest that the operation would not have taken place in the first place. **Secondly**, the sole reason why the **photographs** were taken was to obtain evidence in case an offence had been committed at the AGM. **Thirdly**, once it had become clear that, notwithstanding his brief association with EA, the appellant had not committed any offence at the AGM, there was no reasonable basis for fearing that, even if he went to the DSEi fair, he might commit an offence there. His behaviour on 27 April was beyond reproach, even though he was subjected to what he considered to be an intimidating experience. There was no more likelihood that the appellant would commit an offence if he went to the fair than that any other citizen of good character who happened to go to the fair would commit an offence there.

90. It is for the police to justify as proportionate the interference with the appellant's article 8 rights. For the reasons that I have given, I am of the opinion that they have failed to do so. I would allow this appeal.

Lord Collins of Mapesbury:

91. **I agree with Dyson LJ that the appeal should be allowed**. Plainly the court must not be quick to second guess, or interfere with, operational decisions of the police force. All that in fact happened at the AGM of Reed Elsevier plc on April 27, 2005 was that two people, EA (who had a criminal record of unlawful activity against organisations in the defence industry) and RH, were ejected by private security staff after chanting slogans, without any suggestion of any involvement in criminal activity. There was a very substantial police presence. It consisted of a chief inspector, 3 sergeants, 21 constables, 5 officers in forward intelligence teams, and 3 officers in an evidence gathering team (together with a civilian photographer in uniform). With the benefit of hindsight, of course, the deployment of 33 police officers and a photographer in uniform was not necessary.

92. When I first read the papers on this appeal, I was struck by the chilling effect on the exercise of lawful rights such a deployment would have. I was also disturbed by the fact that notwithstanding that the police had no reason to believe that any unlawful activity had taken place, and still less that Mr Wood had taken part in any such activity, when he (with Mr Prichard) walked from the hotel in Grosvenor Square where the meeting had taken place towards Bond Street Underground station via Duke Street he was followed by a police car, and then questioned about his identity by 4 police officers, two of whom then followed him on foot and tried to obtain the assistance of station staff to ascertain Mr Wood's identity from his travel card.

93. The reason for the police presence was that demonstrators against the arms trade might try to disrupt the AGM. The **purpose** of the evidence gathering

team with the photographer was "to gather intelligence, primarily by taking **photographs** and making notes which may be of subsequent evidential value should offences be committed or disorder break out" (Chief Inspector Weaver, para 10). Chief Inspector Weaver decided to use the evidence gathering team because public disorder might break out, and it was therefore vital that the police knew who had attended and what their involvement was (para 13). Intelligence had to be gathered at the time, so that, should disorder result or offences subsequently come to light, those guilty of an offence could be identified: para 15. She also added that she "took the view that if those individuals who might attend and commit public order or other offences at the DSEi [Defence Systems and Equipment International] fair in September could be identified in advance, by ascertaining their identity at the Reed AGM, that would help to police the DSEi event and deal with any such offences."

94. Police Sergeant Dixon headed the evidence gathering team. Chief Inspector Weaver told him that one of her fears was that once inside the hotel demonstrators might commit acts which would only subsequently come to light. EA was of specific interest to the evidence gathering team, and the decision to take the **photographs** was "not solely because of their association with EA but also because the **photographs** could be of subsequent evidential value if any, as yet undiscovered, offences had been committed inside the hotel" (PS Dixon, para 10). PS Dixon says that such offences are not always immediately apparent and may become known only after a meeting is over. But unless there was absolutely no communication between Reed Elsevier's staff or security officers and the police, I do not find it easy to imagine what undiscovered offences might have been committed.

95. There is conflicting evidence on whether Mr Wood and EA were together in Grosvenor Square after the meeting. But what is not in doubt is that Mr Wood is a person of good character with no previous convictions; and that the police had no reason to believe that he had taken any part in unlawful activities at the AGM, or indeed been guilty of any misconduct at all. To the extent that the **photographs** were taken in case any unlawful activity inside the hotel were subsequently to come to light, it would have been apparent very soon after the meeting (as Dyson LJ says, within a few days at most) that no criminal offences had been committed.

96. **I agree with Laws and Dyson LJJ that Article 8(1) was engaged, but that the taking and retention of the photographs were in pursuance of a legitimate aim, namely "for the prevention of disorder or crime" or "for the protection of the rights and freedoms of others" for the purposes of Article 8(2).**

97. **But I agree with Dyson LJ that the interference was not proportionate. He has referred to the crucial facts, of which it seems to me that the following**

are the most important. First, the main object of the evidence gathering operation was to obtain evidence about possible disorder and criminal conduct at the AGM and/or in the vicinity of the hotel, and the sole reason given by PS Dixon who instructed the photographer to take the **photographs** was to obtain evidence which would be of value if offences had been committed at the AGM. **Second**, the retention of the **photographs** for more than a few days could not be justified as furthering the aim of detecting the perpetrators of any crime that may have been committed during the meeting. **Third**, a possible brief association between Mr Wood and EA on the day did not provide any justification for a lengthy retention of the **photographs**. **Fourth**, the suggestion that retention of the **photographs** was justified by the possibility that Mr Wood might attend and commit an offence at the DSEi fair several months later is plainly an afterthought and had nothing to do with the decision to take the **photographs**.

98. Like Dyson LJ, I prefer to express no concluded view on the question whether the interference was "in accordance with the law". In many cases the European Court of Human Rights has said that not only must the impugned act have some basis in domestic law, but also that it should be compatible with the rule of law and be accessible to the person concerned who must be able to foresee its consequences for him: for recent examples see, eg *Liberty v United Kingdom* [2008] ECHR 58243/00, July 1, 2008; *Marper v United Kingdom*, December 4, 2008 BAILII: [2008] ECHR 1581; *Iordachi v Moldova*, February 10, 2009, BAILII: ([2009] ECHR 256. The taking of the **photographs** in the present case was lawful at common law, and there is nothing to prevent their retention. There is a published policy by the Metropolitan Police on the use of overt filming and photography, but not on the retention of **photographs**.

99. As Laws LJ says, there is a striking decision of the full court of the European Court of Human Rights in *Murray v United Kingdom* (1995) 19 EHRR 193. **That case concerned the right of the Army in Northern Ireland to take and retain photographs of a person who was being questioned at an Army screening centre on suspicion of being involved in the collection of money for IRA arms purchases**. The Court noted (at [40]) that the common law rule entitling the Army "to take a **photograph** equally provides the basis for its retention" and said (at [88]): "The taking and, by implication, also the retention of a **photograph** of the first applicant without her consent had no statutory basis but, as explained by the trial court judge and the Court of Appeal, were lawful under the common law." The Court concluded (ibid): "The impugned measures thus had a basis in domestic law. The Court discerns no reason, on the material before it, for not concluding that each of the various measures was 'in accordance with the law', within the meaning of Article 8(2)."

100. Nevertheless, **it is plain that the last word has yet to be said on the implications for civil liberties of the taking and retention of images in the modern surveillance society.** This is not the case for the exploration of the wider, and very serious, human rights issues which arise when the State obtains and retains the images of persons who have committed no offence and are not suspected of having committed any offence.

ASG v GSA [2009] EWCA Civ 1574

Lord Justice Waller:

1. This is an appeal from a decision of Blair J who refused to grant an injunction on a without notice application restraining the disclosure of certain information. The appeal has been **held in privat**e for reasons which are or will become obvious, that is to say, **unless the proceedings are held in private the very remedy which the appellant is seeking will be denied him**. For the same reason**, the least said about the facts in this judgment the better**. Suffice it to say, **a well known person, married with children**, had an **adulterous relationship** with a girl that he met at a **night club**. He says that she is now attempting to **blackmail** him, demanding money under threat that she will otherwise publish in the press and/or tell his wife.
2. Blair J **refused a without notice injunction** on two bases: **first,** that the claim should not have come to the court without giving notice to the defendant girl; second, he expressed the view, applying section 12(3) of the Human Rights Act, that the claimant **was unlikely to succeed at trial** and therefore the injunction should not be granted.
3. As regards the point about the application being made without notice, it seems to me that **if the allegation of blackmail is established, it would also be established that there was a serious risk that if given notice of the application of an injunction, the girl would have simply gone to the media and either sought to obtain money for publication or simply published**. I would therefore respectfully disagree with the judge that it was not appropriate to bring this without notice application.
4. As regards the chances of success at the trial, I accept that section 12(3) of the Human Rights Act does require the court to look ahead and only grant an injunction at an interlocutory stage if the **claimant is likely to succeed at trial.** But I would also say that **there will be cases where it may be necessary to grant an injunction ex parte to hold the ring until a proper inter partes hearing can be held and in which it can be finally explored as to whether the claimant will succeed at trial.** In such cases, of course, the

claimant must show even at the ex parte stage **a sufficient likelihood** that he will succeed at the inter partes hearing, but a **more flexible approach is appropriate**. Lord Nicholls put the matter in this way in *Cream Holdings Ltd v Banerjee* [2005] 1 AC 253 at paragraph 22:

> "Section 12(3) makes the likelihood of success at the trial an essential element in the court's consideration of whether to make an interim order. But in order to achieve the necessary flexibility the degree of likelihood of success at the trial needed to satisfy section 12(3) must depend on the circumstances. There can be no single, rigid standard governing all applications for interim restraint orders. Rather, on its proper construction the effect of section 12(3) is that the court is not to make an interim restraint order unless satisfied the applicant's prospects of success at the trial are sufficiently favourable to justify such an order being made in the particular circumstances of the case. As to what degree of likelihood makes the prospects of success 'sufficiently favourable', the general approach should be that courts will be exceedingly slow to make interim restraint orders where the applicant has not satisfied the court he will probably ('more likely than not') succeed at the trial. In general, that should be the threshold an applicant must cross before the court embarks on exercising its discretion, duly taking into account the relevant jurisprudence on article 10 and any countervailing Convention rights. But there will be cases where it is necessary for a court to depart from this general approach and a lesser degree of likelihood will suffice as a prerequisite. Circumstances where this may be so include those mentioned above: where the potential adverse consequences of disclosure are particularly grave, or where a short-lived injunction is needed to enable the court to hear and give proper consideration to an application for interim relief pending the trial or any relevant appeal."

5. The question I would therefore pose is: is there a sufficient degree of likelihood that the claimant will succeed at trial to justify an ex parte injunction for a short period pending an inter partes hearing? As *Browne v Associated Newspapers* [2007] EWHC 202 and indeed other cases show, the court must first consider whether this is a case in which **Article 8 is engaged**. It must then consider whether **Article 10 is engaged**. If both are engaged, the court must then make **an assessment of whether there is a likelihood** at trial that, having regard to the claimant's Article 8 rights, the publication sought by the defendant will be restrained.

6. It seems to me that the claimant is likely to establish that his Article 8 rights are engaged. **The sexual relationship with the girl was private as between them.** The cases indicate that **the fact that it was adulterous will not affect the conclusion that Article 8 is engaged**. In *CC v AB* [2007] EMLR 11, a case

where the cuckolded husband was seeking to publish details of a **relationship** between his wife and the other man, it was argued that an adulterer simply had no rights under Article 8 and Eady J said this at paragraphs 24 and 25:

> "24. The other proposition which Mr Warby sought to derive from *Stephens* v *Avery,* since one of the protagonists happened to have been a married woman, is that it **is hardly likely that a modern court would regard an adulterer as beyond the pale** when it comes to the protection **of intimate personal relationships**. Indeed, if the commission of a crime does riot deprive a citizen of the opportunity to enforce his or her Article 8 rights (see eg *Polanski v Condi Nast Publications Ltd* [2005] 1 WLR 637), it is difficult to see how adultery could do so.
>
> 25. Judges need to be wary about giving the impression that they are ventilating, while affording or refusing legal redress, **some personal moral or social views, and especially at a time when society is far less homogeneous than in the past.** At one time, when there was, or was perceived to be, a commonly accepted standard in such matters as sexual morality, it may have been acceptable for the courts to give effect to that standard in exercising discretion or in interpreting legal rights and obligations. Now, however, there is a strong argument for not holding forth about adultery, or attaching greater inherent worth to a **relationship** which has been formalised by marriage than to any other **relationship**."

In looking at the question of arguability at this stage, I would adopt that approach of Eady J.

25. I then turn to the **Article 10 rights of the defendant girl**. Clearly those are also engaged. Leaving aside for the present any question of **blackmail**, the question is whether the claimant would be likely to succeed in obtaining an injunction restraining publication by the girl, **and it seems to me the answer to that question could be different depending on whether the girl was seeking to sell the story to the newspapers and the media or simply informing the claimant's wife**. This seemed to be a point which Eady J was referring to at paragraph 32 of his judgment in *CC v AB*. In *A v B Plc* [2003] QB 195, which is a case referred to in that paragraph, the original decision of Jack J, he in fact confined his injunction to publication by the girl to the media, and it may thus be that there is a distinction between publication to others and publication to the media. Thus, though without any **blackmail** element, there is as it seems to me a sufficient likelihood of the claimant succeeding at a trial to justify an ex parte injunction restraining publication by the girl from publication to the media, **I am more doubtful as to whether**

without the blackmail element there would be a case for restraining the claimant from divulging the information to the claimant's wife.

26. Does the **blackmail** element make any difference? **What is said is that the claimant is entitled to an injunction to take away the basis on which the blackmail can operate.** That as it seems to me raises possibly a good point. On the one side it could be said that until the girl stops **blackmail**ing threats, she cannot rely on her entitlement to exercise her rights of freedom of speech. On the other side it could be said that the claimant's remedies are available without having to go to the court. **He could refuse to bow to the blackmail and he can report the matter to the police.** It is then up to the girl whether she exercises her right to divulge the information to, for example, the claimant's wife without insisting on any payment. **But at this stage we are only concerned with whether an injunction should be granted for a short period of time pending full argument as to whether an interlocutory injunction should be granted until trial**. While there is (as there is) on the evidence before us, a **blackmail** element, it seems to me that the right course is to **grant the wider injunction for a limited period of time.** By the time the inter partes hearing comes on, the factual situation may become clearer and the point can be more fully considered. Thus I would allow the appeal and grant an injunction.

27. But there are aspects so far as determining the terms of that injunction are concerned which it is important just to record. **First,** it is actually not known where the defendant is at present. The evidence would indicate that she was in communication with the claimant while she was in Portugal and that she was on her way to Brazil, so that the likelihood is that she is outside the jurisdiction. It follows from that that in order for these proceedings to be served on her, there is a requirement that **leave be given to serve out of the jurisdiction**. When one examines the paragraphs of 6BPD.3, which established the gateways for service out of the jurisdiction, the obvious candidate is one in which an injunction is sought ordering the defendant to do or refrain from doing an act within the jurisdiction. **That Mr Tomlinson ultimately accepted, and thus the injunction should be in the terms of must not disclose or publish within the jurisdiction, and then continue as the draft we have got, and leave to serve out should be granted. It should appear under paragraph six, that leave has been given, and there should be an undertaking that a statement in accordance with the requirements for leave to serve out should be adduced and served with the claim form.28. So what will be necessary is that a statement is prepared and on that undertaking leave to issue a concurrent claim form for service out of the jurisdiction should be granted**. In the present draft order it should also be made clear that under paragraph 8 the appellant should not be required, (and there should appear

at the end of that paragraph) without further order from the court; and in the schedule of undertakings the undertaking four should be the appellant will as soon as reasonably practicable give notice of this order to the respondent and will take all practical steps to serve the defendant with this order and all supporting documents.

29. I think I should also record finally that we have in debate with Mr Tomlinson recorded some anxiety about precisely the way in which this order might operate. **Clearly it will be the intention of those acting for the claimant to notify newspapers or members of the media of the existence of the order**. In so doing Mr Tomlinson has told us that the name of the claimant will be disclosed, so that if any person were to contact the newspaper or media suggesting that they have some **confidential information** about the claimant, the newspaper will be on notice that some form of order has been obtained from the court and the media or newspaper will then be able to get in contact with those acting for the claimant.

30. The anxiety which I have so far as that process is concerned is that it seems to put the newspaper and media in a difficult situation insofar as they may be contacted by any person, and any person with some **confidential information** about this claimant will then impose on the newspaper or the media the requirement to ring those acting for the claimant. My understanding is that that may be putting the burden the wrong way round, and I would have thought it possible that the right course is that if notification is going to be given to the media of the name of the claimant so that they at least know about whom disclosure might be made, they also ought to be told of the name of the defendant so that they appreciate precisely in relation to whom the injunction has been obtained. But having listened to argument, I would not be prepared myself to make it a condition of the granting of this order at this stage that a notification should be given of both claimant and defendant. It is a matter that needs further consideration and should be considered on the inter partes hearing.

31. But with those observations I would allow the appeal and I would grant an injunction in the terms indicated for a period of seven days, a return date being sought within that period.

BKM Ltd v BBC [2009] EWHC 3151 (Ch) per Mann J

Mr Justice Mann:

Introduction

1. On 25th November I indicated that I would refuse to grant an interim injunc-

tion sought by the claimant to restrain the broadcast of a programme, or certain material in a programme, which it was the intention of the BBC to broadcast on the evening of the same day . . .

2. The application before me was an application for an interim injunction to restrain the broadcast of a television programme on BBC Wales in the series "Week In Week Out", and bearing the further title "Who cares in Wales?". The application was made on 23rd November, on which occasion Norris J restrained the broadcast of a trailer, refused an order for delivery up of the broadcast or film and adjourned the case for further argument the next day on the injunction in relation to the main programme . . . ..

3. BKM operates a care home in Ystrad Rhondda in Wales called the Glyndwr Nursing Home. It has a number of very elderly residents, some of whom need a significant amount of care and assistance in their day to day personal activities. It is subject to regulation and control by the by the Care and Social Services Inspectorate for Wales ("CSSIW"), and the local authority and local health board have certain responsibilities to the residents as well. In inspections over recent years the inspectors have found **shortcomings** in the standards of care offered by Glyndwr in areas such **as record-keeping, wound care** and **staffing levels**. The reports in question were in evidence before me but time constraints meant that their detail was not examined. The level of complaints was not gone into, so that I do not know the level of seriousness of the shortcomings, **save that the BBC would say they were not insignificant.** I myself say nothing about them other than to describe them generally.

4. The BBC in Wales wished to make a programme which had as at least part of its theme that **regulation of care homes was not working**. It wished to portray this in relation to Glyndwr, and apparently took the view that there were still significant shortcomings in the standards of that home. It therefore sent in an **undercover reporter** (Ms Kirsty Hemming), who worked alongside carers for a week and who, after a day and a half, **conducted some secret filming in the home**. The content of her filming is **not known**; nor is the detail of her "findings", but the latter are said to be **not favourable**. In correspondence the BBC claims to have identified:

   i) failings in the lifting of patients (hoists not used where they ought to have been, insufficient numbers of carers lifting and lifting in an inappropriate manner);

   ii) failings in staffing levels that are such that the dignity and care of residents was compromised (though only a couple of examples were given, one being bedroom doors being left open when residents were being assisted with private functions);

iii) one carer who did not follow hygiene guidelines on the use of gloves;

iv) the references provided for the journalist were not in fact checked;

v) an instance where the reporter herself was allowed to wash and dress residents without supervision, and to feed a disabled resident unsupervised.

5. **On 11th November 2009 the BBC wrote to BKM inviting the latter to contact them in relation to unparticularised allegations. This was followed the next day by another letter which put some flesh on the bones of the generalised allegation. BKM sought some more detail, and it was provided in an e-mail of 13th November, this time giving some detailed particulars of the incidents in question. In the end the directors of the home declined to be interviewed. One of their complaints is that they have not been able to see the film footage.**

6. **No-one other than the BBC has seen that footage**, or the footage that is sought to be broadcast (indeed at the time of the hearing before me the programme contents were said still to be under construction). It is, however, apparent that the BBC proposes to broadcast film taken **surreptitious**ly in the home and which, presumably, will back up (to some extent) the allegations made against BKM.

BKM's case in outline

7. **BKM brought this application to restrain broadcast of the programme not in pursuit of any rights of its own, but in order to protect the rights of the home's residents to privacy and family life under the Human Rights Act**. It says that filming in the home was an infringement of their privacy rights and was offensive to their dignity (*Green Corns Limited v Claverley [2005] EMLR 748* at 31. So far as necessary, BKM also says that the filming was illegal under more general legal principles. Broadcasting film taken inside the home would be a further infringement, particularly if it showed residents and enabled them to be identified. While the privacy rights had to be balanced against the BBC's rights to free expression, the balance came down in favour of granting an injunction because the use of **surreptitious filming**, and the **consequential invasion of privacy**, was **disproportionate** when measured against any **public interest** in standards of care at the home. BKM put in evidence various **complaints from relatives** of residents (and one resident herself) about the **clandestine filming**, and expressions of **support** for and satisfaction with the **standards of care** at the home. Apart from one former resident's son who had complained about treatment, there were no other complaints about care standards from those residents who now commented.

8. BKM originally sought an injunction restraining the broadcast of the pro-

gramme as such pending trial of the action. That was the form of the relief sought when I started hearing the application on 24th November. One of the prime reasons why it was said that that was justified was that the footage, and I think the material for the programme, was obtained illegally. That was always a tall order where the real basis of the claim, as propounded, was the protection of the privacy of the individual residents, and before I sat to resume the case on 25th November Miss Heal proposed a modified injunction in the following form:

> **"IT IS ORDERED THAT**
>
> **Until further Order, the Defendant is restrained from broadcasting by television or otherwise howsoever (including on BBC IPlayer):**
>
> **(i) any audio and/or film (including such audio and/or film which subsequently has been pixilated and/or distorted** in whole or in part) obtained at the Glyndwr Nursing Home between 2-6 November 2009 (inclusive) by the Defendant's journalist Kirsty Jayne Hemming of either:
>
> (a) any of the 32 residents of the Glyndwr Nursing Home resident during the period 2—6 November 2009; and/or
>
> (b) any part of the bedrooms, toilets, bathrooms and/or lounges including the entrances thereto within the Glyndwr Nursing Home
>
> (i) (the **Surreptitious** Film) ;
>
> (ii) any audio or film of comment by an expert or experts in any field on the whole or any part of the **Surreptitious** Film; and
>
> (iii) any audio or film of editorial or journalistic comment on the whole or any part of **Surreptitious** Film ; and
>
> (iv) any audio or film in which there is described the whole or any part of the **Surreptitious** Film."

9. **This was an attempt to limit the use of filmed material so that it excluded any visual or audible reference to the individual residents themselves**—BKM consider that filming in bedrooms or lounges may reveal material such as personal items like **photographs** which would enable residents to be identified. Any individual such as those referred to in the latter half of the draft order might identify residents if they commented on film footage of the residents (or, apparently, the accommodation, judging by the order). It was not clear to me why film of empty bathrooms or toilets was an infringement of privacy rights.

The BBC's case in outline

10. The BBC relied on its rights to free expression under Article 10, and said that to the extent that there was an infringement of privacy rights, **its Article 10**

rights were stronger and that an injunction would **not be granted** at trial; so section 12(3) of the Human Rights Act 1998 meant that an injunction could not be **granted** at this stage. It defended its decision on the facts to conduct **clandestine** filming operations and said that it intended to show that this particular home had not been improved, or sufficiently improved, by the **regulatory regime**. The privacy of the residents would be acknowledged and the broadcast material would **not enable the identification** of any of the residents. In pre-action correspondence the BBC said that the residents would not be "identif*ied*". The evidence which was placed before me went further (and it was supplemented by assurances given by Miss Rogers in relation to response to additional concerns voiced by Miss Heal). Steps would be taken to make sure that residents were not "indentif*iable*". This would include **pixilation of faces** and, **where necessary, hair, clothing and whole body outlines**, to prevent any residents from being identifiable from the footage, **and no shots of any private areas of the home** (such as rooms) would be used in a manner which would show **personal effects** from which residents could be identified. It would also **modify voice recording** to disguise the identity of the speaker. The decision to film **clandestinely**, and to broadcast such material, was justified by reference to **the guidelines of the BBC.** Ultimately it **was in the public interest** to allow the material to be broadcast because the general area of care home standards was of **legitimate public interest**, the **failure of regulation was of public interest**, and the manner in which this care home in particular still fell short of proper standards was also of **public interest.** It was never intended to broadcast all the material that was filmed. The broadcast film would be confined to the areas of concern (outlined above). The decision as to what to broadcast was an editorial matter with which the court should not be concerned.

11. So far as the expressed attitude of the residents was concerned, Miss Rogers said that not all of their complaints about what had happened related to invasion of their privacy (though some did). Some related to other matters, including the standard of their care (which was not criticised) and the fairness of criticism of that standard. The letters from residents or their families came after a director, Dr Choudhary, had called a meeting of residents and families, and **it might** be that at that meeting **he told them that all the film** would be broadcast (without any assurances as to the obscuring of identities) since that is what he seemed to believe would happen. **Accordingly, the letters might have been written on a false premise.**

The locus of the claimant

12. I have already pointed out that BKM does not rely on any of its own rights in relation to this application. It seems to rely on the rights of its residents. **It claims that it is entitled, and indeed obliged, by legislation and by contract**

to protect the privacy and dignity of its residents. The regulators have not done so (though they have been given little opportunity to consider doing so); nor has the local authority.

13. The BBC accepted, for the purposes of this application, **that BKM arguably had locus to make this application (and indeed bring this action) to protect the privacy rights of others,** and I have therefore proceeded on the footing that it does have that right. This is not wholly satisfactory. There are elements in the evidence, and elements in the way that the case is put, which **indicate that BKM is (understandably) sensitive to its own reputational position**, and concerned about the **effect on its business**. I sometimes got the impression that that was **a significant underlying factor** to the decision to bring this application. **BKM clearly has a potential conflict of interest. Its commercial interests lie in playing down the allegations, and not having them broadcast. The interests of the residents might (I say no more than "might") lie in having them broadcast in order to improve standards**. I think that this might explain why a lot of the emphasis of Miss Heal in submissions was to prevent the broadcast of the programme at all, as opposed to a broadcast which did not render residents identifiable though Miss Heal expressly disclaimed any intention to prevent comment on the running of the home. **However, there is a privacy point to be addressed, and BKM is the only person taking it**. In the circumstances they must be taken to be **entitled to do** so. So far as I am concerned, I shall focus on only the privacy rights of the residents, and not be distracted by the private interests of BKM.

The trailer

14. BBC Wales prepared a **short trailer** for the programme. I have seen it. It was broadcast a number of times. The trailer contains a voice-over, some comments which I take to be voiced by Ms Hemmings explaining that a resident was dumped "like a sack of potatoes", and a snippet of what seem to be some strong opinions on standards at the home voiced by an expert on care who refers to the absence of dignity and says that "that's just unacceptable". It is not clear precisely on what piece of detail she is commenting. **The overall tone can, I think, be described as somewhat sensationalised, and suggests very serious failings**. The outside of what I take to be part of the home is shown, and there is a brief, **extremely fuzzy,** shot of what is presumably an interior sitting room. The **vague outline** of a couple of residents can be vaguely (but only very vaguely) be seen. There is also a 5 second shot which is presumably part of the **clandestine** filming. It shows the chest, lap and hands of an elderly lady sitting a wheelchair. It is somewhat wobbly, but the impression is clear. **No features are shown which would enable a viewer to identify the person, save for her clothing.** Nonetheless, she has apparently been **identified by a relative** (presumably from that clothing and

a knowledge that the lady was in the home in question). BKM relies on that sort of identification. **Norris J barred the further broadcast of that trailer pending the final determination of this application.**

The competing Human Rights Act rights

15. The right to privacy which is relied on is contained in Article 8 of the European Convention on Human Rights, given some force in this jurisdiction by the Human Rights Act 1998. Article 8 reads:

> **"Article 8:**
>
> **1. Everyone has a right to respect for his private and family life, his home and his correspondence.**
>
> **2. There shall be no interference by a public authority with the exercise of this right except such as is in accordance with the law and is necessary in a democratic society in the interests of national security, public safety or the economic wellbeing of the country, for the prevention of disorder or crime, for the protection of health and morals, or for the protection of the rights and freedoms of others."**

16. The BBC does not dispute (at least for the purposes of this action) that the residents in their care home have rights of privacy which are entitled to protection, and that **the surreptitious** filming, and its **broadcast**, is **capable** of infringing those rights. The Article is **engaged**. The residents have a **reasonable expectation of privacy**—see *Campbell v MGN [2004] AC 457*. This last part seems to me to be right. The home is the home of the residents, and **their need for privacy** is reinforced by the fact that their various **disabilities** mean that they **need assistance in activities** which for most people are **most private,** and they have an even greater need for **their dignity to be respected. Non-consensual filming is capable of being a very serious infringement of their rights to privacy**, whether it merely films them in their home or whether it goes further and intrudes into their disabilities.

17. However, the BBC has its own rights. For these purposes they are contained in Article 10:

> **"Article 10:**
>
> 1. Everyone has the right to freedom of expression. This right shall include freedom to hold opinions and to receive and impart information and ideas without interference by public authority and regardless of frontiers. This Article shall not prevent States from requiring the licensing of broadcasting, television and cinema enterprises.
>
> 2. The exercise of these freedoms, since it carries with it duties and responsibilities, may be subject to such formalities, conditions, restrictions or penalties as are prescribed by law and are necessary

in a democratic society, in the interests of national security, territorial integrity or public safety, for the prevention of disorder or crime, for the protection of health or morals, for the protection of the **reputation** or rights of others, for preventing the disclosure of information received in confidence, or for maintaining the authority and impartiality of the judiciary."

18. It also has the benefit of section12(3) of the Act:

"12(3) No such relief is to be granted so as to restrain publication before trial unless the court is satisfied that the applicant is likely to establish that publication should not be allowed."

19. Section 12(4) contains provisions which have to be taken into account in freedom of expression cases:

"12(4) The Court must have particular regard to the importance of the Convention right to freedom of expression and, where the proceedings relate to material which the respondent claims, or which appears to the court, to be **journalistic**, **literary** or **artistic** material (or to conduct connected with such material), to –

(a) the extent to which –

(i) the material has, or is about to, become available to the public; or

(ii) it is, or would be, in the public interest for the **material to be published;**

(b) any relevant **privacy code**."

20. The parties each relied on a code promulgated by Ofcom and the BBC's own editorial guidelines.

The operation and interaction of those rights in the present case

21. The competition between the two rights is resolved by a balancing exercise. Lord Steyn explained this in *Re S (A Child)* [2005] 1 AC 593 at para 17:

"First, neither article has *as such* precedence over the other. **Secondly,** where the values under the two articles are in conflict, an **intense focus** on the comparative importance of the specific rights being claimed in the individual case is necessary. **Thirdly,** the justifications for interfering with or restricting each right must be taken into account. **Finally,** the proportionality test must be applied to each. For convenience I will call this the ultimate balancing test."

22. By the end of their submissions each party was conducting the case on the basis of such an exercise.

23. I therefore have to conduct such an exercise, but with a very firm eye on

section 12(3). I have to determine not only how the competition between the rights is to be resolved for present purposes, but also to do so with an eye to determining whether an injunction would be granted to restrain a broadcast at a trial. An injunction should not be granted unless I am satisfied that at a trial it would be likely to be determined (in the sense of more probable than not—see *Cream Holdings v Bannerjee [2005] 1 AC 253*) that the broadcast should not be allowed.

24. Each side relied on guidelines about **clandestine** filming, both **the BBC's and Ofcom's**. Section 12(4) requires that to be done. **Ofcom's guidelines state:**

> "**Deception—set-ups and wind-up calls**
>
> 7.14 Broadcasters or programme makers should not normally obtain or seek information, audio, pictures or an agreement to contribute through **misrepresentation or deception** (deception includes **surreptitious** filming or recording). However:
>
> - It may be warranted to use material obtained through misrepresentation or deception **without consent** if it is in the **public interest** and **cannot reasonably be obtained** by other means;
> - Where there is **no adequate public interest** justification, for example some unsolicited wind-up calls or entertainment set-ups, **consent should be obtained** from the individual and/or organisation concerned before the material is broadcast;
> - If the individual and/or organisation is/are **not identifiable** in the programme, then consent for broadcast will **not** be required . . . .
>
> 8.13 **Surreptitious filming or recording** should only be used where it is warranted. Normally, it will only be warranted if:
>
> - There is prima facie evidence of a story in the **public interest; and**
> - There are reasonable grounds to suspect that **further material evidence could be obtained;** and
> - It is necessary to the **credibility and authenticity** of the programme."

25. The BBC has its own guidelines in the form of an editorial policy statement. They state:

> "Introduction
>
> Secret Recording is a **two stage** process: the **gathering** of **secretly** recorded material, and as a **transmission** of the material. Each process could amount to an **intrusion** and they must be considered and approved separately **to ensure any invasion of privacy is justified** by a clear public interest.

. . . ..

[Chapter 6]

The BBC must not infringe privacy **without good reason** wherever in the world it is operating. It is essential in order to exercise our rights of freedom of expression and information that we work within a framework which respects an individual's privacy and treats them fairly, while investigating and establishing matters which it is in the public interest to reveal. **Private behaviour, correspondence** and **conversation** should not be brought into the **public domain** unless there is a clear public interest. There are also a number of ways in which the law protects privacy in the United Kingdom, including the Human Rights Act 1998.

. . .

Public Interest

There is no single definition of public interest, it includes but is not confined to:

- **Exposing or detecting crime;**
- Exposing significantly **anti-social behaviour**;
- Exposing **corruption or injustice;**
- Disclosing significant **incompetence or negligence;**
- Protecting people's **health and safety.**

. . .

Secret Recording

Secret recording must be justified by a clear **public interest.** It is a **valuable tool** for the BBC because it enables **the capture of evidence or behaviour that our audiences would otherwise not see or hear.** However, secret recordings should normally be a method **of last resort**—misuse or overuse could discredit or devalue its impact.

The BBC will normally only use secret recordings for the following purposes:

(a) As an investigative tool to expose issues of public interest where:

- **There is clear existing documentary or other evidence** of such behaviour or of an intention to commit an offence.
- It can be shown that an open approach would **be unlikely to succeed.**
- The recording is necessary for **evidential purposes."**

26. Miss Heal says that these guidelines are engaged, which they clearly are . . .

She drew a contrast with the facts of *Lakeside Homes Ltd v BBC,* (unreported, 14th November 2000, available on Westlaw with the reference 2000 WL 1841602). That was a case where filming was over a much more extended period, and some very serious shortcomings were revealed. 4 residents actually consented to the broadcast. Broadcasting was allowed in the public interest. The present case was nothing like that on the facts; no residents consented; and the balance produced a very different result.

27. Miss Heal also **invited me to draw inferences from fact that the BBC has not shown the programme to me (or to her client),** for which **purpose** she drew a contrast with the facts of *Leeds City Council v Channel 4 Television Corporation* [2007] FLR 678, where the judge was given the opportunity of viewing the programme whose making was challenged on privacy grounds. I think that the inference I was invited to draw was that the programme contained material which went too far and was an unjustifiable invasion of privacy.

28. The BBC for its part said it was acting within Ofcom's guidelines and its own editorial policy. The defaults were significant and serious. Revealing them fully and clearly required, or at least justified, **clandestine** filming in order to make the desired point. Its right to broadcast was within Article 10, and it **was in the public interest** that it should do so. It, too, relied on *Lakeside,* and said that there were parallels between the facts of that case and the present one, so far as the defaults went. . . .

The resolution of the dispute

29. This is an application to restrain the broadcasting of **some material that the claimant has not seen, and I have not seen**. I can dispose of one of Miss Heal's submissions about that at this stage. **I cannot draw any inferences adverse to the BBC about that for at least three reasons**. **First**, I was told, and I accept, that the material is **not finalised** yet, so to that extent there is nothing yet to see. This is therefore **not** a case in which it would be right to **draw inferences** against someone **who has withheld** some material adverse to its case. **Second,** it is the usual practice of the media not to disclose material in advance of publication unless it wants to, and **the courts have respected that conduct**—see eg *Re Roddy [2004] EMLR 127* at paragraph 88. This is doubtless partly as a matter of principle, **and partly because an evaluation of the material might require a judge to perform an editorial function**, which is not desirable. **Third,** it is not clear to me what adverse inference could be justifiable. The claimants have brought this application on the factual basis that there will be broadcasting of material which will or might infringe rights to privacy. That is accepted by the BBC for the purposes of the present argument. The justification lies elsewhere, in the balancing exercise, on the assumption that infringing material will be broadcast. **I do not see what proper adverse inference about that (or any**

other inference, come to that) can be drawn from a failure to disclose the material in advance. I certainly **cannot draw the inference that the BBC knows that the material will be improperly broadcast**. I therefore do not accede to that submission of Miss Heal.

30. I therefore have to embark on the balancing exercise which is referred to in the cases, including those identified above. I do so on the assumption that Article 8 is engaged; the BBC has something to justify. Its justification comes from two principal sources—first, the fact (so far as the broadcast is concerned) the **infringement of privacy rights will be removed, or at least ameliorated, by pixilation and other processes that will render the residents unidentifiable;** and second, the public interest in the subject matter and the justifiable desire to give effect to that by broadcasting footage of residents and their surroundings.

31. I deal first with the **obscuring mechanisms and techniques**. Miss Heal has said this case is not about identification. There can be an infringement of privacy rights even if a resident is not identifiable. If there is, for example, a depiction of a resident being assisted in an **intimate** process (using a commode, to use one example given in at the hearing), that resident's privacy may well be wrongfully interfered with even if the image **is completely pixilated or otherwise blurred out**. Anyone whose acts are thus depicted would still consider that their privacy has been seriously interfered with if their activities are broadcast, even if their image cannot be discerned at all. So obscuring identities is not a complete answer. **The answer, according to Miss Heal, is getting the consent of the residents, and the BBC does not have that.**

32. Miss Heal has a limited point. She may well be right about any broadcast of, for example, a resident's use of a commode is a contravention of his or her privacy and dignity rights**, however heavily pixilated.** On the other hand, there is little if any invasion of privacy if a resident merely sitting in the lounge is shown heavily **pixilated** (of course the act of filming will probably already have been an invasion, but that is not the immediately relevant point). And in any event**, these factors are not automatically determinative of the significance of the invasion of privacy**. The circumstances are important. Consent is obviously important, and if present would be determinative**. But its absence does not determine the case the other way.**

33. Thus it may be that contraventions of the Article 8 rights are not completely removed by taking cinematic steps to obscure the identities of those depicted. That is both for the reason given above, and because (as the trailer broadcast indicated) residents might still be identifiable by those who know them and who know they are in the home, though in many cases if that is the extent of the identification then the privacy infringement may be very slight. However,

that does not mean that those means are irrelevant. **The level of an invasion of privacy is relevant to the balancing act that I have to perform**. An invasion of privacy should not be allowed beyond that which is **necessary** in the **public interest.** It is hard to imagine that the public interest would ever justify the **un-pixilated** broadcasting of an image of a resident using a commode. **It might well justify broadcasting a heavily obscured image**. Other examples can be given. So one cannot say that any portrayal of the residents will give rise to a sufficiently serious infringement of privacy rights to outweigh any public interest justification coupled with Article 10 rights.

34. So I apply that in the balancing exercise to which I have referred. **The real issue between the parties is whether the resort to clandestine filming was justified in the first place, and whether broadcasting its fruits is justified now**. Since there is a privacy code (if not two) in place, then those matters have to be justified in the light of those codes as well as in the light of more general legal considerations. Those **codes provide**, in essence (and reducing them to their most relevant points), that **the use of clandestine techniques and their fruit is not to be lightly undertaken**. The matter has to be **sufficiently serious to justify** it, and it should not be done if there are **other means available** to achieve the same ends. BKM says those criteria are not fulfilled; the BBC says they are.

35. Doing the best I can on the material available, and bearing in mind that I have only a general description of the areas to which the filming is said to go rather than the film itself**, I have come to the conclusion that there are serious factors which can be said to justify or out-balance any infringement of privacy rights.** The general areas of standards in care homes, and the ability of a regulator to maintain them, are matters which are **firmly in the territory of the public interest (as BKM has itself acknowledged in correspondence)**. So, potentially, is the manner of running this care home if it is badly run. So the question then becomes whether the matters relied on by the BBC are matters which legitimately raise that public interest in the present case, and if so whether they raise it **to such an extent**, and in circumstances, which **would justify the clandestine filming** which involves the home of the residents and the residents themselves. It seems to me to be **firmly arguable that they do.** It is true that on one view of the facts, what the reporter saw (and may have filmed) might be mainly errors of judgment and isolated incidents which do not reflect a home that is badly run. She was only there for a week. But on another view they might be symptomatic of something wrong with its management. **The context is likely to be very important.** I bear in mind that there is some short evidence, albeit hearsay, **that two experts** in the field have said that the faults are significant and serious.

36. I reject Miss Heal's submissions that it is apparent that the BBC did not need to indulge in **clandestine** filming because there was material in the inspection reports, and Ms Hemmings could have narrated what she saw in the home. In this connection she relied on the codes so far as they provide that **clandestine** filming is not appropriate **if the point can be made as well in other ways**. It is not at all clear to me that the point could be made just as well by other means so as to render the **clandestine** filming unnecessary, **and in any event this is probably the sort of consideration that judges, who are not editors or journalists**, should not embark on at all, and certainly not on an interim application such as the one before me.

37. So the balancing process produces some weight on each side. At present it seems to me that if the BBC lives up to its word and **obscures the identity** of residents, the invasion of their privacy from broadcasting is likely to be **relatively slight**. The greater weight lies on the public interest side of the argument. That would be my assessment on the evidence that I have. That points against granting an injunction. **However, the BBC has the additional weight of sections 12(3) and 12(4) on its side of the scales**. I must give special weight to free speech, and then should only grant an injunction if I thought it were likely at a trial that publication would be restrained. **The burden of the latter point is on the claimant**. They have not fulfilled it. I do not think it likely that an injunction would be granted at trial, on the present state of the evidence.

38. However, on the facts of this case I should make it clear what I am not deciding. **I am not deciding that any particular form of broadcasting of images would not be an actionable infringement of the privacy rights of the residents in the light of the conduct that the BBC claims to have encountered**. I am not saying that the evidence clearly demonstrates that here is a nursing home whose conduct plainly needs to be exposed. There may well be some real merit in the argument that in its proper context the conduct found demonstrates no more than the sort of shortfall from standards which one suspects can be found in nearly every care home (because of human failings) but which do not demonstrate a general unfitness. **The management of the home have tendered explanations which, if true, would remove the sting and real force of some of the complaints.** It is fair to BKM to give a couple of examples. The matron of the home has stated that sometimes hoists are not used because they frighten a particular resident. She has also said that one of the residents will not allow her bedroom door to be closed when carers are in the room with her. On any view, this case is nothing like the facts of the *Lakeland* case, and I confess that I was very surprised that the BBC sought to draw that parallel. **I also confess that I detected a slightly unattractive whiff of sensationalism in the presentation of some of the BBC's material.**

However, my decision is based on the deployment of material for Article 10 purposes which it is strongly arguable has been obtained **within guidelines**, and which it is clearly if not strongly arguable can be properly deployed in the public interest with all proper steps being taken to ensure either that there is no (further) infringement of the residents' Article 8 rights, or no infringement beyond that which can be justified by that public interest. **It is, of course, the case that the BBC will have to consider very carefully whether the clandestinely obtained material can be properly deployed in the programme, particularly in the light of the points made during the hearing before me.** I am deciding that I will not restrain the broadcast of any material. **I am not deciding that that broadcast will be justified or justifiable.** That will depend on the ultimate content.

39. **Lastly**, I add something about the **form of the injunction sought.** I would not, in any event, have granted an injunction in those terms even if I had been minded to consider any injunction at all. **It is far too wide**. An injunction barring the whole programme was always out of the question. The most that would be ordered would be an injunction necessary to protect the privacy of the residents. The last three sub-paragraphs of the injunction would not be necessary for that **purpose**. **I fail to see how rights to privacy would be necessarily infringed by expert or journalistic comment of the kind referred to there.** Neither would the injunction contained in paragraph 1(i)(b) be justified. Again, it is far too wide. Again, not all **pixilated** images would infringe privacy rights, in my view, so even paragraph 1(i)(a) would have its difficulties. However, in the light of my actual decision I do not have to address those difficulties.

40. It is for those reasons that I declined to grant the injunction sought. I understand that the parties have reached an agreement on the general content, if not the precise form, of the order which follows from my decision, but if there remains an area of non-agreement the parties are at liberty to restore the application so that I can rule on it.

In Re Guardian News and Media Ltd [2010] UKSC 1

This is the unanimous judgment of the court delivered by:

LORD RODGER

1. **"Your first term docket reads like alphabet soup."** With these provocative words counsel for a number of newspapers and magazines highlighted the issue which confronts the Court in this application. In all the cases down for hearing in the first month of the Supreme Court's existence at least one of

the parties was referred to by an initial or initials. Thanks to the relevant Practice Note, the same goes for the very last case heard by the House of Lords (*BA (Nigeria) v Secretary of State for the Home Department* [2009] UKSC 7; [2009] 3 WLR 1253) and the very first judgment handed down by the Supreme Court (*In re appeals by Governing Body of JFS* [2009] UKSC 1; [2009] 1 WLR 2353). See *Practice Note (Court of Appeal: Asylum and Immigration Cases)* [2006] 1 WLR 2461. **Indeed, so deeply ingrained has the habit of anonymisation become that the judgment of the Court of Appeal in AM (Somalia) v Entry Clearance Officer** [2009] EWCA Civ 634 **was published under that name, and came on appeal to the Supreme Court under the same name, even though Maurice Kay LJ had begun his judgment by saying that anonymity was unnecessary.** At the hearing of the appeal that assessment proved to be correct. See *Mahad v Entry Clearance Officer* [2009] UKSC 16; [2010] 1 WLR 48.

2. **These are simply examples of what is now a widespread phenomenon.** For instance, on a rough calculation, in 8 out of the 58 appeals decided by the House of Lords in 2007 at least one of the parties appeared under an initial; the same applied in 15 out of 74 cases in 2008. Admittedly, cases reaching the House of Lords and the Supreme Court are not necessarily typical of those going through the court system as a whole**, but the general impression is that the practice of referring to parties by initials has increased at all levels in recent years**. Even assuming that the use of initials was justified in many cases, the present appeals show that an order ("anonymity order") may be made, often by consent of both parties, without the court considering in any detail what is the basis or justification for it. This happens despite Sir Christopher Staughton's warning, in *Ex p P*, The Times 31 March 1998, that **"when both sides agreed that information should be kept from the public, that was when the court had to be most vigilant." Lord Woolf MR quoted the warning with approval in R v Legal Aid Board, Ex p Kaim Todner** [1999] QB 966**, 977D-E. The application challenging the anonymity orders in these appeals provides an opportunity for reviewing the position.**

3. The appeals involve five individuals: four of them, A, K, M and G, are appellants; the fifth, HAY, is the respondent and cross-appellant in an appeal by the Treasury. For simplicity's sake, and unless the context otherwise requires, references to "the appellants" include HAY. When the appeals were lodged, the appellants' names were concealed by the use of letters. This was the result of orders first made at the outset of the proceedings in the administrative court. Take, for instance, the case of A. On 15 February 2008 Collins J ordered that **"The claimant be granted anonymity throughout these proceedings and be referred to as A. No report of these proceedings shall directly or indirectly identify him or any member of his family**." ***The***

practice is for such orders to be* intimated *to the Press Association. In these cases, therefore, the orders were in place during the substantive hearings. Following those hearings, with the consent of the Treasury, Collins J continued the anonymity orders in the cases of A, K and M. In the case of G, he continued the order, but left it to the Court of Appeal "to make the final decision as to whether the anonymity order in his case should or should not be lifted."

4. When allowing the Treasury's appeal, [2009] 3 WLR 25, the Court of Appeal included an order, apparently of consent, that "The respondents shall be granted anonymity and no report of these proceedings shall directly or indirectly identify them or any member of their families." That was the position when the appeals came before this Court and the press and media ("the press") made their application to have the anonymity orders set aside. The Court decided to set aside the order in the case of one of the appellants, G, but to postpone consideration of the application relating to the others until after the substantive hearing. A separate hearing to consider the application in respect of those appellants took place on 22 October when the Court also considered the application to set aside the anonymity order in the separate case of HAY.

5. Counsel for the applicants suggested that, since rule 27 of the Supreme Court Rules 2009 provides for every contested appeal to be heard in open court, the appellants should have made an application for a fresh anonymity order to cover the appeal to this Court. We would reject that contention. **There was never any question of departing from rule 27: the hearing of the appeals was always going to be in open court. The anonymity orders simply restricted the form of any report of the hearing. *So far as anonymity orders are concerned, the practical approach is that, where an open-ended order has been made, it should remain in force throughout the proceedings, at whatever level, unless and until it is set aside, either spontaneously on a change of circumstances, or as the result of an application by the press. That approach promotes certainty and avoids unnecessary applications.***

6. Although the courts below appear to have granted the anonymity orders without any very prolonged consideration and without explaining their thinking, **the appellants contend that the orders are necessary because identifying them as the claimants in these proceedings would infringe their rights under article 8 of the European Convention on Human Rights and Fundamental Freedoms to respect for their private and family life.** To understand that contention, it is necessary to outline the events giving rise to the proceedings.

The Background Events

7. The three appellants A, K and M are brothers in their thirties. **On 2 August 2007 each of them was informed that the Treasury had reasonable grounds for suspecting that he was, or might be, a person who facilitated the commission of acts of terrorism.** All three had, accordingly, been designated under article 4 of the Terrorism (United Nations Measures) Order 2006 ("TO 2006"). Subsequently, the Treasury indicated that in 2004 an Al-Qaida-linked operative had alleged that A and M were Al-Qaida facilitators based in East London, with M as the leader of the group. It was further suggested that K and M were involved, with others, in funding Al-Qaida contacts in the tribal areas of Pakistan. The three men deny all the allegations and maintain that they are of good character.

8. In the case of these appellants the Treasury decided, in accordance with article 5(1)(a)(ii) of the TO 2006, to inform only certain persons about the order. In that situation article 6 applied:

> "(1) Where the Treasury propose (in accordance with article 5(1)(a)(ii)) to inform only certain persons of a direction, they may specify in the direction that information contained in it is to be treated as confidential.
>
> (2) A person who obtains information which is to be treated as confidential in accordance with paragraph (1), or to whom such information is provided, must not disclose it except with lawful authority.
>
> (3) **Confidential information** is disclosed with lawful authority only if and to the extent that any of the following applies—
>
> (a) the disclosure is by the Treasury;
>
> (b) the disclosure is with the consent of the person who is the subject of the information;
>
> (c) the disclosure is to (and is necessary to) give effect to a requirement under this Order;
>
> (d) the disclosure is required, under rules of court or a court order, for the purposes of legal proceedings of any description.
>
> (4) This article does not prevent the disclosure of information which is already, or has previously been, available to the public from other sources.
>
> (5) A person who contravenes the prohibition in paragraph (2) is guilty of an offence.
>
> (6) In proceedings for an offence under this article, it is a defence for a person to show that he did not know and had no reasonable cause to suspect that he was disclosing **confidential information**.

(7) The High Court or, in Scotland, the Court of Session may grant an injunction to prevent a breach of paragraph (2) in relation to any information upon the application of—

(a) the person who is the subject of the information, or

(b) the Treasury."

The letters sent to the appellants informed them that the Treasury had "specified in the direction that your identity is to be treated as confidential in accordance with article 6 of the order."

9. It followed that, unless the appellants consented or a court ordered that their names were to be disclosed for the purposes of these proceedings (article 6(3)(b) and (d)), their identities were to be treated as confidential.

10. Counsel for the Treasury could not explain the precise basis upon which the Treasury had chosen to specify that the identities of A, K and M were to be treated as confidential. **But he indicated that there would have been some input from the Security Services.** Plainly, the attitude of the Treasury could not be determinative for the courts. But the point is now academic, since—subject to one qualification which it is unnecessary to explore—the Treasury has changed its position. By the time of the hearing of the application by the press, the Treasury no longer opposed setting aside the anonymity orders granted in the courts below.

11. In fact, in July 2009 Her Majesty had made The Terrorism (United Nations Measures) Order 2009 ("TO 2009"). On 30 October 2009—after the hearing of the present application—the Treasury revoked the designations of A, K and M under the TO 2006, but made fresh directions designating them under article 4 of the TO 2009. In accordance with the change of position explained at the hearing of the application, when it made the fresh directions the Treasury considered that it was no longer necessary to apply any restrictions on their publication under the TO 2009. The Treasury decided, however, that, "in the interests of justice", pending this Court's decision on the anonymity issue, it would actually restrict publication of the directions pursuant to article 6(2)(b)(iii) of the TO 2009.

12. In the result the Treasury does not oppose the Court making an order that disclosure is required for the **purpose** of these proceedings. That order would have the effect of making disclosure of these appellants' identities lawful by virtue of article 8(3)(d) of the TO 2009.

13. Under the anonymity orders granted below, the other appellant was to be referred to as G. On 13 December 2006 he received a letter informing him that the Treasury had made a similar direction under article 4 of the TO 2006. In his case, however, the letter told him that the Bank of England, acting as agent for the Treasury, had issued a notice and press release pub-

licising the direction generally. And the Bank of England's News Release dated 13 December does indeed name G as Mr Mohammed al-Ghabra, living in East London. A few days later he received a letter from the Foreign and Commonwealth Office indicating that the 1267 Committee (i e the Sanctions Committee) of the United Nations Security Council had added him to its consolidated list of Usama Bin Laden, Al Qaida and the Taliban and other individuals, groups, undertakings and entities associated with them. This meant that his funds, assets and economic resources were frozen. In March of the following year he was told that he was subject to the Al-Qaida and Taliban (United Nations Measures) Order 2006 ("AQO"). This is because any person designated by the 1267 Committee is automatically designated for purposes of United Kingdom law by virtue of article 3(1) of the AQO.

14. In G's case, at the outset of the hearing of the substantive appeal, the Court was shown material confirming that, as just narrated, his identity as someone who was subject to a freezing order was already in the **public domain**. It had been given in the Bank of England's press notice and had also been contained in the relevant list published by the 1267 Committee. These matters had been reported in the press. In the circumstances, the anonymity order made by the lower courts served no effective or legitimate **purpose** and so, as already mentioned, this Court decided to lift the order in his case. The press were therefore able to report that G is actually Mr Mohammed al-Ghabra. Articles containing that information were published the following day. No evidence was produced to the Court on behalf of Mr al-Ghabra or any of the other appellants to show that either the Bank of England's original press release or the lifting of the anonymity order by this Court had led to any particular social, far less physical, harm to him or to any members of his family.

15. Subsequently, by letter dated 22 October 2009 Mr al-Ghabra was informed that the Treasury had designated him afresh under article 4 of the TO 2009. But, in view of the fact that his identity was already known (partly as a result of the order of this Court), no restriction was placed on the publication of the Treasury's direction in his case. His designation under the AQO remained unchanged.

16. Finally, as already explained, the respondent in a separate appeal by the Treasury, which raises similar substantive issues, is known under the initials HAY. By a letter dated 6 October 2005 the Foreign and Commonwealth Office informed him that on 29 September the 1267 Committee had added him to their consolidated list. Persons included on the list were subject to the freezing of their funds, economic resources and other financial assets. On 10 October the Bank of England issued a press release naming HAY as one of seven people whose names had been added to the list, as a result

of which they fell within the financial sanctions régime under the AQO. He was named as Mr Hani al-Sayyid Al-Sebai, also known by a variety of other names, including Hani Youssef ("Mr Youssef"). He was described as an Egyptian living in London. In fact, shortly after HAY's designation, in about January 2006 the Government started trying to persuade the 1267 Committee and the designating state to provide disclosure to HAY. In June 2009 the Government went further and began trying to persuade them to agree that his name should be removed from the list. By the time of the hearing of this application those efforts had not been successful.

A and K

. . .

Press Reporting of Judgments in the United Kingdom

22. **In the United Kingdom, until the recent efflorescence of anonymity orders, the general rule both in theory and in practice was that judicial proceedings were held in public and the parties were named in judgments. Their names would also be given in newspaper reports and in the law reports. That is still usually the position—as can be seen from the frequent press reports of, say, employment tribunal hearings and decisions where details of personal and sexual relationships among the warring parties are a common feature.**

23. In the nineteenth century many couples would doubtless have been only too pleased to agree to have their divorce heard in private. **But the court sat in public and reports of the evidence, often recounting high-class intrigues, were published in the newspapers**. These reports gave rise to concern in some quarters, especially since they were particularly popular reading-matter among servants. So, during the nineteenth and early twentieth centuries, various attempts were made to introduce legislative controls. **The attempts foundered, partly because the unpleasant publicity was thought to act as a welcome deterrent against couples divorcing.** Against that background, in ***Scott v Scott [1913] AC 417*** the House of Lords affirmed in the strongest possible terms the long-established stance of the English courts that hearings should be held in public. The first instance judge was criticised for hearing the nullity proceedings in private.

24. **Eventually, however, in the Judicial Proceedings (Regulation of Reports) Act 1926 Parliament intervened to restrict the freedom of the press to report any indecent matter, the publication of which would be calculated to injure public morals. Special limitations were placed on what could be reported about divorce and other matrimonial proceedings.** But, even so, the right to report the names, addresses and occupations of the parties and witnesses and a concise statement of the charges, defences and counter-

charges was affirmed. The **purpose** of the legislation was therefore not the protection of the parties' privacy but the prevention of injury to public morals throughout Great Britain: *Friel v Scott* 2000 JC 86, 88D-89C. See G Savage, "Erotic Stories and Public Decency: Newspaper Reporting of Divorce Proceedings in England" (1998) 41 The Historical Journal 511–528.

25. Over the years Parliament has gone on to create a considerable number of exceptions to the ordinary rule that proceedings must be held in public. Similarly, Parliament has gone beyond the Judicial Proceedings (Regulation of Reports) Act 1926 and has introduced other statutory restrictions on what may be reported in various kinds of cases, especially those involving children. See, for instance, section 39 of the Children and Young Persons Act 1933, section 97 of the Children Act 1989 and section 45 of the Youth Justice and Criminal Evidence Act 1999. "Given the number of statutory exceptions," Lord Steyn observed in **In re S (A Child) (Identification: Restrictions on Publication)** [2005] 1 AC 593**, 604,**

> "it needs to be said clearly and unambiguously that the court has no power to create by a process of analogy, except in the most compelling circumstances, further exceptions to the general principle of open justice."

Anonymity Orders to Give Effect to Article 8 Convention Rights

26. In **an extreme case**, identification of a participant in legal proceedings, whether as a party or (more likely) as a witness, might put that person or his family in peril of their lives or safety because of what he had said about, say, some powerful criminal organisation. In that situation, he would doubtless ask for an anonymity order to help secure his rights under articles 2 and 3 of the European Convention. Those Convention rights are not in play in these appeals, however, since counsel accepted that the appellants could not show that publication of their names would put any of them or their families at risk of physical violence.

27. **States are, of course, obliged by articles 2 and 3 to have a structure of laws in place which will help to protect people from attacks on their lives or from assaults, not only by officers of the state but by other individuals. Therefore, the power of a court to make an anonymity order to protect a witness or party *from a threat of violence* arising out of its proceedings can be seen as part of that structure. And in an appropriate case, where threats to life *or safety* are involved, the right of the press to freedom of expression obviously has to yield: a newspaper does not have the right to publish information at the known potential cost of an individual being killed or maimed. In such a situation the court may make an anonymity order to protect the individual.**

28. **Under the Human Rights Act 1998 article 8(1) requires public authorities, such as the court, to respect private and family life. But M does not need to ask for the anonymity order to prevent the court itself from infringing his article 8 Convention rights. Suppose the court considers, whether in the light of submissions or not, that, by publishing its judgment in the usual form, it will itself act unlawfully under section 6 of the Human Rights Act because it will infringe a party's article 8 Convention rights. In that eventuality, the court does not deal with the matter by issuing anonymity orders to other people; rather, it ensures that it acts lawfully by taking appropriate steps of its own. That presumably explains why, for instance, the letter M, instead of the appellant's name, is used in the judgments below. In this way the courts avoid what they perceive to be the problem that they would act unlawfully if they named M in their judgments and so infringed his article 8 rights.**

29. In fact, however, in these cases the courts have gone further: they have not only used initials in their judgments but have made anonymity orders addressed to other people—in effect, to the press. Having the power to make orders of this kind available is one of the ways that the United Kingdom fulfils its positive obligation under article 8 of the Convention to secure that other individuals respect an individual's private and family life. In *Von Hannover v Germany* (2005) 40 EHRR 1, 25, para 57, the European Court of Human Rights reiterated that:

> "although the object of article 8 is essentially that of protecting the individual against arbitrary interference by the public authorities, **it does not merely compel the State to abstain from such interference:** in addition to this primarily negative undertaking, there may be positive obligations inherent in an effective respect for private or family life. These obligations may involve the adoption of measures designed to secure respect for private life even in the sphere of the relations of individuals between themselves . . .
>
> "The boundary between the State's positive and negative obligations under this provision does not lend itself to precise definition. The applicable principles are, nonetheless, similar. In both contexts regard must be had to the fair balance that has to be **struck between the competing interests of the individual and of the community as a whole . . .**" (internal citations omitted).

So, when M applied to the courts below for an anonymity order, he was asking them to exercise their power to secure that other individuals, viz the press and journalists, showed respect for his private and family life.

30. To comply with article 8, United Kingdom law must have a remedy of this

kind available for use in appropriate cases. This means that the Human Rights Act has removed any doubts that might otherwise have existed (cf *Raybos Australia Pty Ltd v Jones* (1985) 2 NSWLR 47) about the availability of the remedy in English law. In *In re S (A Child) (Identification: Restrictions on Publication)* [2005] 1 AC 593, a woman had been charged with the murder of her son. The guardian of her remaining son sought an order restraining the media from identifying the woman and the victim, in order to protect the privacy of her remaining son. The House of Lords held that no such order should be made. **But, speaking for all members of the appellate committee, Lord Steyn affirmed, at p 605, para 23, that the court did have jurisdiction to make an order of this kind and that "the foundation of the jurisdiction to restrain publicity in a case such as the present is now derived from Convention rights under the ECHR."** More recently, in *In re British Broacasting Corpn* [2009] UKHL 34; [2009] 3 WLR 142, 161, para 57, Lord Brown of Eaton-under-Heywood indicated that the powers of the High Court to make such an order "arise under section 6 of the [Human Rights Act 1998] read in conjunction with section 37 of the [Senior Courts Act 1981]."

31. Incidentally, **Collins J appears to have thought that section 11 of the Contempt of Court Act 1981 was the source of the power to make anonymity orders that is in play in these cases. That view was mistaken.** Section 11 is dealing with the particular situation where a court, having power to do so, allows a name or other matter to be withheld from the public in proceedings before the court. An obvious example is a court allowing the victim to withhold his name when giving evidence for the Crown in a prosecution for **blackmail**. Section 11 then gives the court the ancillary power to give directions prohibiting a newspaper which actually knows the name of the individual from publishing it. The section resolves any doubt about the power of the court in these circumstances to prevent persons, other than the parties, from naming the individual or mentioning the matter outside court. Cf *Ex p P*, The Times 31 March 1998, per Sir Christopher Staughton.

32. Counsel for the press argued, however, that M's **reputation** does not fall within the scope of article 8. The argument is best addressed after looking at article 10.

The Press and Article 10 Convention Rights

33. The press found their case for setting aside the anonymity order in favour of M on their article 10 Convention rights to freedom of expression. **Although article 10(1) does not mention the press, it is settled that the press and journalists enjoy the rights which it confers.**

34. In asserting their right to publish M's name, the press are not asking to be supplied with information which would otherwise not be available to them.

On the existing Strasbourg case law, a right to obtain that kind of information is not within the scope of article 10(1): *Leander v Sweden* (1987) 9 EHRR 433, 456, para 74. **Here, however, the cases are heard in public and, were it not for the use of his initial and the anonymity orders, M's name would be available to the press and they would be free to report it. Indeed, the effect of the orders is that, even if the press are aware of M's name from other sources (which may well be the case), they cannot use it when reporting the proceedings.** ***So, by making the orders, the courts have interfered with the article 10 Convention rights of the press to impart information*** **which either is, or normally would be, available to them.**

35. **Equally clearly, the court interferes with the article 10 rights of the press when it takes a step, such as making an anonymity order, which interferes with their freedom to report proceedings as they themselves would wish**— in the present case, by making their report refer to the situation of named, identifiable, individuals, including M. See, for instance, *News Verlags GmbH & Co KG v Austria* (2000) 31 EHRR 246, 256, para 39:

> "The Court recalls that it is not for the Court, or for the national courts for that matter, to substitute their own views for those of the press as to what technique of reporting should be adopted by journalists. **Article 10 protects not only the substance of ideas and information but also the form in which they are conveyed."**

36. Nevertheless, under article 10(2), the right of the press to freedom of expression can be subjected to restrictions which are prescribed by law and are necessary in a democratic society "for the protection of the **reputation** or rights of others". The "rights of others" include their rights under article 8.

Article 8 and **Reputation**

37. **On behalf of the press, Mr Robertson QC did not dispute that article 8 rights fall within the scope of "the rights of others" in article 10(2).** But, under reference to the judgment of the European Court of Human Rights in *Karakó v Hungary* (application no 39311/05, BAILII: [[2009] ECHR 712], 28 April 2009, he submitted that article 8 does not confer a right to have your **reputation** protected from being affected by what other people say. So the only article in play in relation to M's **reputation** was article 10.

38. In *Karakó* the applicant was a **politician**. During an election campaign an opponent had said in a flyer that the applicant was in the habit of putting the interests of his electors second. The applicant accused his opponent of criminal libel, but the prosecutor's office terminated the investigation on the ground that the flyer concerned the applicant as a candidate rather than as a public official and so its publication was not a matter for a public prosecution. Then, acting as a private prosecutor, the applicant submitted an indictment

for libel. The district court dismissed the indictment on the ground that the opponent's statement was a value judgment within the limits of acceptable criticism of a **politician**. The applicant complained of a violation of his article 8 rights. The European Court held that there had been no such violation.

39. As the European Court's judgment in *Karakó* itself shows, in *Petrina v Romania* (application no 78060/01, BAILII: [2009] ECHR 2252), 14 October 2008, the court had confirmed, at para 19, that the right to **protection of reputation is a right which, as an element of private life, falls within the scope of article 8** ("le droit à la protection de la réputation est un droit qui relève, en tant qu'élément de la vie privée, de l'article 8 de la Convention"). The court had gone on, at para 29, to survey its previous case law, ending up with the statement in *Pfeifer v Austria* (2007) 48 EHRR 175, 183, para 35, that "**a person's reputation, even if that person is criticised in the context of a public debate, forms part of his or her personal identity and psychological integrity** . . . ".

40. In *Karakó* the European Court did not depart from that earlier jurisprudence. Rather, it accepted, at para 23, that **some attacks on a person's reputation could be of such a seriously offensive nature as to have an inevitable direct effect on the victim's private life.** But the court took the view that, on the facts, the applicant had not shown that the publication in question had **constituted such a serious interference with his private life as to undermine his personal integrity**. That being so, the applicant's **reputation alone was at stake** in the context of the expression which was said to have damaged it.

41. Contrary to what Mr Robertson suggested, however, this conclusion did not mean that the court was proceeding on the basis that the applicant's claim in respect of his **reputation** did not fall within the scope of article 8. That would have been inconsistent with the court's previous case law and would also have made nonsense of the reasoning in paras 24–29 of the judgment. In particular, in paras 24 and 25 the court is concerned with the inter-**relationship** of articles 8 and 10 in the circumstances. The outcome of that discussion (para 26) is that, even though the applicant is founding on article 8, the court must consider whether the Hungarian authorities properly applied the principles inherent in article 10. The court concludes that they did (para 27). **Putting the two strands together, the court goes on to find, in para 28, that the applicant's claim that his reputation as a politician has been harmed is not sustainable under article 8 and that a limitation of his opponent's right to freedom of expression under article 10 would have been disproportionate.** That leads, finally, to the conclusion that there has been no violation of article 8.

42. In short, in *Karakó* the European Court was concerned with the application of articles 8 and 10 in a situation where, in the court's view, the applicant had

not shown that the attack on his **reputation** had so seriously interfered with his private life as to undermine his personal integrity. In fact, the court does not mention any specific effects on the applicant's private life. In the present case, however, as already set out at para 21 above, M does explain how he anticipates that his private life would be affected if his identity were revealed. Admittedly, he appears at one point to single out the alleged damage to his **reputation**. **Nevertheless, the Court is really being invited to consider the impact of publication of his name on his reputation as a member of the community in which he lives and the effect that this would have on his relationship with other members of that community. In that situation the alleged effect on his reputation should be regarded as one of the reasons why, he contends, a report that identified him would seriously affect his private life. On that basis the report would engage article 8(1).**

The Approach when Article 8 and Article 10 are both in play

43. The case is, accordingly, one where both articles 8 and 10 are in play and the Court has to weigh the competing claims of M and his family under article 8 and of the press under article 10. More particularly, the Court is being asked, on the one hand, to give effect to the right of the press to freedom of expression and, on the other, to ensure that the press respect M's private and family life.

44. M objects to being identified as a person who is challenging the freezing orders against him which proceed on the basis that the Treasury suspects on reasonable grounds that he facilitates, or may facilitate, terrorism. **In other words, what he really objects to is being identified as a person who the Treasury suspects, on what it regards as reasonable grounds, facilitates or may facilitate terrorism.** He maintains that, if he is identified as such a person, his article 8 Convention rights will be infringed in the various ways outlined in para 21.

45. Two particular effects of an anonymity order of this kind should be noted.

46. **First**, M accepts, of course, that the freezing orders have been made against him under the TO 2006 and the TO 2009. And he does not challenge the fact that the Treasury made them because it claims to have reasonable grounds for suspecting that he facilitates, or may facilitate, terrorism. So the effect of the anonymity order is to prevent the publication of these matters of fact which M does not—indeed cannot—challenge.

47. **Secondly**, the anonymity orders granted by the courts below are blanket orders: in the words of the Court of Appeal, "no report of these proceedings shall directly or indirectly identify [the appellants] or any member of their families." Sweeping orders of that kind proceed on the basis that the mere publication of *any* report of the proceedings which identified any of

the appellants, including M, as a person suspected of facilitating terrorism would infringe his article 8 rights. This is clear from the fact that the ban prevents a newspaper, which is wholly sympathetic to the plight of M, from publishing a report of the proceedings that identifies him and from then going on to support his case and criticise the Government in the strongest possible terms for subjecting him to the ordeal of the freezing order. The Court has to be satisfied that a ban with this far-reaching effect is necessary in a democratic society in order to ensure due respect for M's private and family life.

48. **The European Court gave guidance on the approach to be adopted when articles 8 and 10 are both in play in *Von Hannover v Germany*** (2005) 40 EHRR 1. The circumstances were, of course, very different from those in the present cases: Princess Caroline was complaining of **intrusions** into her private life by the paparazzi taking **photographs** of her while she was engaged in ordinary, everyday, pursuits. The court held that, when so engaged, she was entitled to the protection of article 8. So it had to consider whether German law, which permitted these **intrusions** by the press, had properly balanced the rights of the press under article 10 and the rights of Princess Caroline under article 8. The European Court held that it had not.

49. The European Court recalled, at p 25, para 58, that "**the press plays an essential role in a democratic society. Although it must not overstep certain bounds, in particular in respect of the reputation and rights of others, its duty is nevertheless to impart—in a manner consistent with its obligations and responsibilities—information and ideas on all matters of public interest** . . . ". Hence "in the cases in which the Court has had to balance the protection of private life against the freedom of expression it has always stressed the contribution made by photos or articles in the press to a debate of general interest . . . " (p 25, para 60). **The decisive factor in balancing the protection of private life against freedom of expression should lie in the contribution that the published photos and articles make to a debate of general interest** (p 28, para 76). But, where publication of the **photographs** and articles was simply intended to satisfy the **curiosity** of a particular readership regarding the details of the applicant's private life, it could not be deemed to contribute to any debate of general interest to society. In that situation freedom of expression called for a **narrower** interpretation (p 27, paras 65 and 66).

50. The European Court's exposition in *Von Hannover* really echoed what Lord Hoffmann had said, a few weeks earlier, in *Campbell v MGN Ltd* [2004] UKHL 22; [2004] 2 AC 457, 473–474, paras 55 and 56:

> "55. I shall first consider the **relationship** between the freedom of the press and **the common law right of the individual to protect personal**

information. Both reflect important civilised values, but, as often happens, neither can be given effect in full measure without restricting the other. How are they to be reconciled in a particular case? There is in my view no question of automatic **priority**. Nor is there a presumption in favour of one rather than the other. The question is rather the extent to which it is ***necessary*** to qualify the one right in order to protect the underlying value which is protected by the other. And the extent of the qualification must be proportionate to the need: see Sedley LJ in *Douglas v Hello! Ltd* [2001] QB 967, 1005, para 137.

56. If one takes this approach, there is often no real conflict. Take the example I have just given of the ordinary citizen whose attendance at NA is publicised in his local newspaper. The violation of the citizen's autonomy, dignity and self-esteem is plain and obvious. **Do the civil and political values which underlie press freedom make it necessary to deny the citizen the right to protect such personal information? Not at all.** While there is no contrary public interest recognised and protected by the law, the press is free to publish anything it likes. **Subject to the law of defamation, it does not matter how trivial, spiteful or offensive the publication may be.** But when press freedom comes into conflict with another interest protected by the law, the question is whether there is a sufficient public interest in that particular publication to justify curtailment of the conflicting right. In the example I have given, there is no public interest whatever in publishing to the world the fact that the citizen has a drug dependency. The freedom to make such a statement weighs little in the balance against the privacy of personal information."

51 Lord Hoffmann's formulation was adopted by Lord Hope of Craighead in *In re BBC* [2009] 3 WLR 142, 149, para 17. Since "neither article has *as such* precedence over the other" (*In re S (A Child) (Identification: Restrictions on Publication)* [2005] 1 AC 593, 603, para 17, per Lord Steyn), the weight to be attached to the rival interests under articles 8 and 10—and so the interest which is to prevail in any competition—will depend on the facts of the particular case. In this connexion it should be borne in mind that—picking up the terminology used in the *Von Hannover* case—the European Court has suggested that, where the publication concerns a question "of general interest", article 10(2) scarcely leaves any room for restrictions on freedom of expression: *Petrina v Romania* (application no 78060/01, BAILII: [2009] ECHR 2252), 14 October 2008, para 40 ("l'article 10(2) de la Convention ne laisse guère de place pour des restrictions à la liberté d'expression dans le domaine . . . des questions d'intérêt général").

52. In the present case M's private and family life are interests which must be respected. On the other side, publication of a report of the proceedings,

including a report identifying M, is a matter of general, public interest. **Applying Lord Hoffmann's formulation, the question for the court accordingly is whether there is sufficient general, public interest in publishing a report of the proceedings which identifies M to justify any resulting curtailment of his right and his family's right to respect for their private and family life.**

Anonymity in Europe

53. Unfortunately, no real additional help with the question of anonymity orders can be obtained from examining the practices of courts in Europe when issuing judgments. In all the principal systems, at least, steps can apparently now be taken, where appropriate, to anonymise reports of matrimonial disputes and disputes relating to children. Apart from that, however, what is striking is the variety of approaches.

. . .

Article 8 Arguments in favour of an Anonymity Order

58. In para 21 above, we have summarised the effects which, M says, publication of his name would have on the lives of himself and his family as members of the local Muslim community. It is more a comment than a criticism to point out that this evidence is somewhat speculative. Moreover, the impact of the publication of M's name is particularly hard for a court to judge when it does not know how he is currently regarded by other members of the community.

59. As one of the witness statements lodged on his behalf acknowledges, if publication were permitted, **M would not be identified as someone who facilitated terrorism, but as someone whom the Treasury claims to have reasonable grounds to suspect of facilitating terrorism**. But his fear is that, however accurate the reporting, members of the public would simply proceed on the basis that he *is* a terrorist. So the ban on publication, he says, should remain in place to prevent this.

60. **That argument raises an important point of principle. It really amounts to saying that the press must be prevented from printing what is true as a matter of fact, for fear that some of those reading the reports may misinterpret them and act inappropriately**. Doubtless, some may indeed draw the unjustified inference that M fears. **But the public are by now very familiar with the argument that various measures, including control orders, have been taken against people who are merely suspected of involvement in terrorism, precisely because the authorities cannot prove that they are actually involved**. **Politicians** and the press have frequently debated the merits of that approach, the debates presupposing that members of the public, including members of the Muslim community, are more than capable of drawing the distinction between mere suspicion and sufficient evidence to

prove guilt. Any other assumption would make public discussion of these and similar serious matters impossible. **We therefore see no reason to assume that most members of the local Muslim community would be unable to draw the necessary distinction and to respond appropriately to any revelation that the Treasury suspects that M facilitates, or may facilitate, terrorism.**

61. Mr Tomlinson QC submitted, however, that the fact that M cannot challenge the substance of the allegation against him is crucial. Admittedly, the House of Lords held in *In re S (A Child) (Identification: Restrictions on Publication)* [2005] 1 AC 593 that the press was entitled to name a woman who had been charged with murdering one of her children, even though this would affect the private life of her other son. The public interest in publishing the defendant's name outweighed the impact on the second son's private life. Nevertheless, Mr Tomlinson argued, the press should not reveal that the Treasury suspects M of facilitating terrorism**, since this allegation will never be brought to trial and cannot be effectively challenged by M**. In this situation the rights of M and his children to respect for their private life should outweigh the public interest in receiving a report of the proceedings which identifies him. **An order which keeps M's identity confidential, but otherwise allows a full report of the proceedings to be published should be regarded as a fair compromise that gives due weight to M's right to respect for his private and family life, on the one hand, and to the interest of the public in being informed about the proceedings, on the other.**

62. This is perhaps the main argument in favour of the anonymity order. Along with the others, it has to be considered against the points advanced by the press in favour of lifting the anonymity order and allowing M's identity to be revealed.

Article 10 Arguments against an Anonymity Order

63. **What's in a name? "A lot", the press would answer.** This is because stories **about particular individuals** are simply much more attractive to readers than stories about unidentified people. It is just human nature. And this is why, of course, even when reporting major disasters, journalists usually look for a story about how particular individuals are affected. **Writing stories which capture the attention of readers is a matter of reporting technique,** and the European Court holds that article 10 protects **not only** the substance of ideas and information **but also** the form in which they are conveyed: *News Verlags GmbH & Co KG v Austria* (2000) 31 EHRR 246, 256, para 39, quoted at para 35 above. More succinctly, Lord Hoffmann observed in *Campbell v MGN Ltd* [2004] 2 AC 457, 474, para 59, "**judges are not newspaper editors**." See also Lord Hope of Craighead in *In re British Broadcasting Corpn* [2009] 3 WLR 142, 152, para 25. This is not just a matter of deference to editorial independence.

The judges are recognising that editors know best how to present material in a way that will interest the readers of their particular publication and so help them to absorb the information. A requirement to report it in some austere, abstract form, devoid of much of its human interest, **could well mean that the report would not be read and the information would not be passed on.** Ultimately, such an approach could threaten the viability of newspapers and magazines, which can only inform the public **if they attract enough readers and make enough money to survive.**

64. Lord Steyn put the point succinctly in *In re S* [2005] 1 AC 593, 608, para 34, when he stressed the importance of bearing in mind that

> "from a newspaper's point of view a report of a sensational trial **without revealing the identity of the defendant would be a very much disembodied trial**. If the newspapers choose not to contest such an injunction, they are less likely to give prominence to reports of the trial. Certainly, readers will be less interested and editors will act accordingly. Informed debate about criminal justice will suffer."

> Mutatis mutandis, the same applies in the present cases. A report of the proceedings challenging the freezing orders which did not reveal the identities of the appellants would be **disembodied**. Certainly, readers would be less interested and, realising that, editors would tend to give the report a lower **priority**. In that way informed debate about freezing orders would suffer.

65. On the other hand, **if newspapers can identify the people concerned, they may be able to give a more vivid and compelling account which will stimulate discussion about the use of freezing orders and their impact on the communities in which the individuals live.** Concealing their identities simply casts a shadow over entire communities.

66. Importantly, **a more open attitude** would be consistent with the true view that freezing orders are merely indicative of suspicions about matters which the prosecuting authorities accept they cannot prove in a court of law. **The identities of persons charged with offences are published, even though their trial may be many months off.** In allowing this, the law proceeds on the basis that most members of the public understand that, even when charged with an offence, **you are innocent unless and until proved guilty in a court of law.** That understanding can be expected to apply, a fortiori, if you are someone whom the prosecuting authorities are not even in a position to charge with an offence and bring to court. **But, by concealing the identities of the individuals who are subject to freezing orders, the courts are actually helping to foster an impression that the mere making of the orders justifies sinister conclusions about these individuals.** That is particularly

unfortunate when, as was emphasised on the appellants' behalf, they are unlikely to have any opportunity to challenge the alleged factual basis for making the orders.

67. It might be argued that, nevertheless, in this particular case naming M in any report would be an unnecessary luxury. **After all, it could be said, what actually matters are the legal and constitutional issues raised in the proceedings and these can be understood and debated on the basis of an anonymised report.** But the very fact that **M and the other appellants are not accepting, but challenging, the whole system of freezing orders** based on mere suspicion means that they are presenting the orders as wrongs done to them, rather than as indications that they themselves have done something wrong. **Concealing their identities runs counter to the entire thrust of that case.** Should their appeals be allowed, concealment would be even less appropriate. Not E but Mr John Entick of Stepney has gone down in history as the plaintiff in the great case of *Entick v Carrington* (1765) 19 Howell's State Trials 1030; 95 ER 807.

68. Certainly, the identities of the claimants cannot affect the answers that this Court gives to the legal questions in the substantive appeals. So those identities may not matter particularly to the judges. **But the legitimate interest of the public is wider than the interest of judges qua judges or of lawyers qua lawyers.** Irrespective of the outcome, the public has a **legitimate interest in not being kept in the dark about who are challenging the TOs and the AQO.** The case of HAY is instructive in this respect. Most people will be astonished, for example, to learn that, up until now, the courts have prevented them from discovering that one of the claimants, Mr Youssef, has already successfully sued the Home Secretary for wrongful detention after a failed attempt to deport him to Egypt. Equally importantly, even while the Treasury is defending these proceedings brought by him, the Government are trying to have his name removed from the 1267 Committee list. Meanwhile, he is busy writing and broadcasting from London on Middle East matters.

69. By lifting the anonymity order in HAY's case the court allows members of the public to receive relevant information about him which they can then use to make connexions between items of information in the **public domain** which otherwise appear to be unrelated. **In this way the true position is revealed and the public can make an informed judgment**. There may well, of course, be no similar revelations in the case of M. But, assuming that is so, this would, in itself, be important, since it would contribute to showing how the freezing-order system affects different people in different situations—a point to be considered in any debate on the merits of the system. At present, the courts are denying the public information which is relevant to that debate,

even though the whole freezing-order system has been created and operated in their name.

70. Along with A, K and G, M has himself sought to enter the debate about the merits of freezing orders. After the judgment of Collins J in these proceedings in April 2008, **his solicitors issued a press release which included the following:**

> "The five British nationals bringing this challenge who have been designated under the Orders have had their assets frozen, are only allowed to access enough money to meet basic expenses, and are compelled to account to a civil servant for every penny they spend. They are subject to unprecedented levels of **intrusion** and control without end or review. They require permission for all economic activity, however modest. The complex regime governed by permissions and licences is not merely harsh but at points absurd. We have the madness of civil servants checking Tesco receipts, a child having to ask for a receipt every time it does a chore by running to the shops for a pint of milk and a neighbour possibly committing a criminal offence by lending a lawnmower . . .
>
> The court ruling today has shown that the Government is willing to sacrifice the fundamental rights and liberties of its citizens, including the fundamental constitutional right that only Parliament can take away basic freedoms, when they think it convenient to do so. They have dishonoured their pledge of accountability and oversight through Parliament."

71. **It is unusual, to say the least, for individuals to enter a debate, using highly charged language and accusing the Government of dishonouring a pledge, but at the same time to insist that they should have the right to hide behind a cloak of anonymity.** It is also unusual for someone to assert the need for the press to respect his private and family life by not reporting his identity **while simultaneously inviting them to report his version of the impact of the freezing orders on himself and members of his family.** The public can hardly be expected to make an informed assessment of the argument if they are prevented from knowing who is making these points and, therefore, what his general stance is.

72. Of course, allowing the press to identify M and the other appellants would not be risk-free. It is conceivable that some of the press coverage might be outrageously hostile to M and the other appellants—even though nothing particularly significant appears to have been published when Mr al-Ghabra's identity was revealed. **But the possibility of some sectors of the press abusing their freedom to report cannot, of itself, be a sufficient reason**

for curtailing that freedom for all members of the press. James Madison long ago pointed out that "Some degree of abuse is inseparable from the proper use of everything, and in no instance is this more true than in that of the press": "Report on the Virginia Resolutions" (1800), in *Letters and Other Writings of James Madison* (1865) Vol 4, p 544. **The Press Complaints Commission is the appropriate body** for dealing with any lapses in behaviour by the press. The possibility of abuse is therefore simply one factor to be taken into account when considering whether an anonymity order is a proportionate restriction on press freedom in this situation.

73. Although it has effects on the individual's private life, the **purpose** of a freezing order is public: it is to prevent the individual concerned from transferring funds to people who have nothing to do with his family life. So this is not a situation where the press are wanting to publish a story about some aspect of an individual's private life, whether trivial or significant. Rather, they are being prevented from publishing a complete account of an important public matter involving this particular individual, for fear of the incidental effect that it would have on M's private and family life.

74. So far as the potential effect on M's private and family life is concerned, the evidence is very general and, for that reason, not particularly compelling. The apparent lack of reaction to the naming of Mr al-Ghabra is relevant in this respect, since it suggests that the impact of identifying an individual on **relationships** with the local community is not likely to be as dramatic as the judges who made the orders appear to have anticipated. **The fact that, through his solicitors, M has himself gone out of his way to put into the public domain what he says are the effects of the freezing order on his family life, is also significant.**

75. On the other hand, **publication of M's identity would make a material contribution to a debate of general interest.**

Conclusion

76. In these circumstances, when carrying out the ultimate test of balancing all the factors relating to both M's article 8 rights and the article 10 rights of the press, we have come to the conclusion that there is indeed a powerful general, public interest in identifying M in any report of these important proceedings which justifies curtailment, to that extent, of his, and his family's, article 8 Convention rights to respect for their private and family life.

77. For all these reasons, we would set aside the anonymity order in respect of M. It follows that there is nothing to prevent the order in favour of A and K from being set aside for the reasons given in para 17. As explained in paras 18–20, the order in favour of HAY must also be set aside. Therefore, A, K, M and HAY will be named here and in the judgments on the substantive

appeals, as Mr Mohammed Jabar Ahmed, Mr Mohammed Azmir Khan, Mr Michael Marteen (formerly known as Mohammed Tunveer Ahmed) and Mr Hani El Sayed Sabaei Youssef (or Hani al-Seba'i), respectively. In addition, in relation to article 8(3)(d) of the TO 2009, the Court will order that the identities of A, K and M should be disclosed for the **purpose** of these proceedings. The anonymity order in respect of the appellant, G, has, of course, already been set aside and he has been identified as Mr Mohammed al-Ghabra.

Anonymity in Control Order Cases

78. During the course of the argument, incidental reference was made to anonymity orders in proceedings relating to control orders made under section 2 of the Prevention of Terrorism Act 2005. The present proceedings do not concern control orders and therefore it would not have been possible on any view for the Court to set aside the anonymity orders in the proceedings relating to them. Many of the same issues would obviously arise if an application were made to set aside the anonymity orders made in any outstanding control order proceedings. **The same principles would also have to be applied, but there may be arguments and considerations in those cases which were not explored at the hearing in this case.** Conceivably, also, the position might not be the same in all of the cases. We would accordingly reserve our opinion on the matter of anonymity orders in control order cases.

R (Binyam Mohamed) v Secretary of State for Foreign and Commonwealth Affairs [2010] EWCA Civ 65:

" . . . Judgment shall be pronounced publicly but the press and public may be excluded from all or part of the trial . . . where the protection of the private life of the parties so require[s], or to the extent strictly necessary in the opinion of the court in special circumstances where publicity would prejudice the interests of justice."

John Terry (Previously referred to as "LNS") v Persons Unknown [2010] EWHC 119 (QB)

Mr Justice Tugendhat:

1. This application for an interim injunction raises issues as to how the court is at the same time to act compatibly with rights under each of **Arts 6, 8 and**

10 of ECHR, and to give effect to corresponding common law principles, from which those rights are derived. These relate to **open justice**, to the right to a **fair hearing**, to the right to **private life** and to **reputation,** and to the right to **speak freely.**

2. The application was made by LNS at 1445 on Friday 22 January 2010. I heard submissions from Mr Spearman for about two hours. **No notice had been given to any Respondent or other person.** The applicant states that the order is **"likely to be served on media third parties". No third party is identified in the draft order,** but one, the publisher of The News of the World ("NGN"), is named in the evidence.

3. At that hearing I made orders for there to be a **private hearing** and **anonymity (CPR39.2(3) and (4))** and I granted an order substantially in the form sought. This prohibited the publication of certain information. But that order is expressed to last only until I delivered my decision on the application, which I now do.

4. **This judgment is drafted in a form which should be publishable in the usual way,** whatever the outcome of this hearing, or any subsequent hearing in any court in these proceedings. **It is necessary to use awkward language to achieve this aim,** which is necessary to protect the rights of individuals referred to in this judgment.

THE SUBSTANCE OF THE ORDER SOUGHT—ARTS 8 AND 10

5. There is a **Confidential Schedule** to the **draft Order** submitted to the court, and a **confidential annex** to this judgment.

6. The draft order seeks a prohibition on publishing "**all or any part of the information or purported information**" and documents in four categories. I paraphrase this as follows: **(1)** the fact of a specified personal **relationship** ("the **Relationship**") between LNS and another person who is named ("the other person"); **(2)** details of that **relationship** including certain specific consequences of it; **(3)** information leading to the identification of LNS or the other person and **(4)** any **photographs** evidencing or relating to the fact or details of these matters.

7. The applicant accepts **the truth** of certain information which is sought to be protected by the draft order. *I do not know whether or not LNS considers that those matters were acceptable for a person in LNS's position in life.* But the application is to stop further publication of such information, **at least to the public to large**. I shall consider below what reasons are given for that. LNS does not know what NGN or anyone else may be intending to publish, **so there is no admission that whatever may be published will be true.**

8. Evidence is before the court of LNS's position in life, both professional and

personal. In my view, there is a real prospect that this information could form the basis for a submission for a respondent (or a third party given notice of the order) that publication of at least the fact of the **Relationship** ought to not to be prohibited, on the ground that publication would be in the public interest, alternatively on the ground that the respondent (or person given notice of the order) believes that publication would be in the public interest. **By the public interest I include the matters listed in ECHR Art 8(2) and in the PCC Code.** I express no view, at this stage, as to whether that submission would succeed. I merely state that there is a **real prospect** that it could properly be advanced. The reasons for this conclusion are set out below.

9. In the language of defamation, **the information, if published, would be capable of lowering LNS in the estimation of right thinking members of society generally.** That is all that a judge could say at this **interim** stage. Whether it would so lower him, would be a matter for a jury to decide.

10. **Nothing** in or about the **Relationship** appears likely to be **unlawful.** Mr Spearman submits that the information is all **private**, and that a publication would be a **misuse** of the information.

11. There is reference in the evidence to some **unspecified details** of the **Relationship**, and some **unspecified photographs.** Publication of these would **undoubtedly be prohibited,** ***if*** it were established that they are as **intrusive** as the applicant suggests, and if there is **sufficient evidence of a threat** to publish them to justify the making of a court ord12. There is also reference in the evidence to individuals (other than LNS and the other person) whose rights of privacy the applicant says would also be affected by any publication. I shall call these "the first interested person", and so on. Neither the other person, nor any of the interested persons, is a party to this application. **In principle all or any of them could be joined as applicants,** if they wished to be, so far as I have understood. I shall have to consider to what extent I should have regard to rights which LNS, but not they themselves, are choosing to seek to establish in these proceedings.

13. The upshot thus far is that, subject to the other issues I shall consider, this is a case where the applicant could expect an injunction to be granted in some form, including at least some of the information in category **(2)**, **if there is sufficient evidence** of a threat in relation to that category.

14. I will consider below whether there is sufficient evidence of a threat to publish details of the **Relationship** or **photographs** relating to it. Save for one mention of the existence of **photographs**, the only evidence relates to the alleged threat of publication of the fact of the **relationship**. **The case that there is a threat to publish detailed information or photographs is largely based on inference from the threat to publish the fact of the Relationship.**

15. The issues raised in this application include:

    (1) whether the limitations upon, or **defences** to, a **claim in misuse of private information** on grounds of **public interest** are such that an injunction ought, or ought not, to be granted; and whether or not the law to be applied to this application is that set out in ***Bonnard v Perryman*** (recently re-affirmed in *Greene v Associated Newspapers* [2004] EWCA Civ 1462; [2005] QB 972);

    (2) whether the court should order the **derogations** sought from **open justice**, the **requirements of fairness,** and Art 6;

    (3) whether the court should order the **derogations** sought from **other provisions** of the CPR;

    (4) what should be the **scope of any prohibition** granted: the order sought is unqualified in form, but according to the evidence the **information is already circulating widely by word of mouth**, and what appears to be sought is in reality a prohibition of publication to the **public at large** by **broadcast** in the **press** or **other media**.

THE DEROGATIONS FROM OPEN JUSTICE, THE REQUIREMENTS OF FAIRNESS, Art 6 and CPR

16. The following derogations from open justice, the requirements of fairness, and Art 6, are sought in the draft order: **(1)** a private hearing, **(2)** anonymity for the persons involved in the **Relationship**, **(3)** that the entire court file should be sealed pursuant to CPR5.4C(7), **(4)** that the order should prohibit publication of the existence of these proceedings, and that it should do so not just until service of the proceedings, or until a return date, but that it do so "until after the conclusion of the trial of this claim or further Order in the meantime", **(5)** that (notwithstanding the provision of CRP PD 25 para 9.2), the applicant shall *not* be required to provide any third party served with a copy of the order a copy of any materials read by the judge and/or a note of the hearing.

17. There are further derogations from the CPR sought in the draft order as follows: **(a)** that the order shall be made until trial or further order (whereas in orders made without notice CPR PD para 5 provides that there must be a return date); **(b)** that time for service of the Claim Form pursuant to CPR 7.5 and CPR 7.6(1) be extended "generally until 21 days after the identification of the Respondent(s) by the Claimant".

18. The draft order sets out correctly that (in accordance with what is known as the *Spycatcher* principle: see *A-G v Newspaper Publishing plc* [1988] Ch 333, 380):

    "Effect of this order: It is a contempt of court for any person notified

of this order knowingly to assist in or permit a breach of this order. Any person doing so may be imprisoned, fined or have their assets seized".

19. Of course, **the draft order also provides that the order itself, including all of these derogations from the norms, are to be subject to the right of the respondent, and of anyone served with or notified of the order, to apply to the court to vary or discharge the order (or so much of it as affects them)**. But the effect of this is to place upon a respondent or third party **the burden** of making an application to the court. A person considering making an application to vary the order would do so **without knowing anything about the basis** upon which it had been granted. He would **not** even know whether, and if so to what extent, the court will permit **disclosure to him of the** material upon which the order was granted. **The draft order thus seeks to transfer to third parties notified of the order the financial risk of incurring costs which they might not incur if they had been informed (as required by CPR PD 25 para 9) of the grounds of the application.** CPR PD 25 para 9 provides:

"**9.1** The following provisions apply to orders which will affect a person other than the applicant or respondent, who:

(1) did not attend the hearing at which the order was made; and

(2) is served with the order.

9.2 Where such a person served with the order requests—

(1) a copy of any materials read by the judge, including material prepared after the hearing at the direction of the judge or in compliance with the order; or

(2) a note of the hearing,

the applicant, or his legal representative, must comply promptly with the request, unless the court orders otherwise".

20. The overall likely effect of the order sought appeared to me to be as follows. **The applicant was likely to notify a limited number of media third parties promptly**. After the hearing that was done, as set out below. If it were not intended to do that, there would be no point in the court making the order (since it is admitted the Respondent has not been identified). **In my view, on the information now before me, the applicant is unlikely ever to serve the Claim Form on any respondent**. **Journalists do not normally reveal their sources and can rarely be obliged to do so:** *Financial Times v UK* (Application no 821/03) 15 December 2009. *As that case showed, even leak enquiries conducted with the resources of a major corporation, backed up by specialist investigators, commonly fail to identify the source of a leak*. But that will not trouble the applicant. There is no provision for a return date. **Since service**

on the Respondent is unlikely, it follows that no trial is likely to be held. Unless a third party is prepared to take the **risk in costs** of applying to vary this order, this interim application is likely to be **the only occasion** on which the matter comes before the court. **The real target of this application is the media third parties who are not respondents.** The only third parties who will ever hear of the proceedings are those whom the applicant chooses to notify. **According to the terms of the draft order,** no one else will have any means of discovering that an order has been made at all. **The third parties who will be notified will be told nothing by the applicant about the grounds for the claim, or any possible defence to it.** If they want to know more, they will be at risk as to costs in making an application to the court. **In short,** the effect of the interim order sought is likely to be that of **a permanent injunction (without any trial) binding upon any person to whom LNS chooses to give notice that the order exists.**

21. The CPR provide for departures from the rules if the court so orders, and from time to time, when justice so requires, court orders are made which include significant derogations from normal procedural requirements. **I do not recall** any order that has been made with derogations as comprehensive as those sought in this case, although Mr Spearman informs me that there have been some. **Substantial derogations have been ordered in cases involving national security and risk to the lives of others, as mentioned below.**

22. Other derogations, including provisions for a private hearing, and for anonymity for the applicant, are **not uncommon**: see for example *McKennitt v Ash* [2006] EWCA Civ 1714, [2008] QB 73 at p75 (claim for an injunctions preventing further publication by a friend of the claimant of a book describing the claimant's private life). Without these provisions an application for an order prohibiting the disclosure of private or **confidential information** would in many cases be self-defeating. **And orders made without the 3 days notice prescribed by CPR 23.7(1)(b) do not always provide for a return date**. That is often **because** a respondent has been contacted **informally** and **indicated he will not oppose** the application. In other cases, too, the court from time to time dispenses with a return date for various reasons. Mr Spearman submits that in this case a return date "would probably achieve no more than to ensure that further costs and Court time are expended on that hearing". Mr Spearman did not envisage that any third party would wish to ask the court to vary the order sought.

23. Orders have from time to time been made providing for **sealing the whole court file.** But such a wide order under CPR 5.4C is very rarely necessary. Normally sufficient protection to the claimant is given if there is an order for the **anonymity** of the claimant, and for **statements of case,** and **witness**

statements, to include any **private** or **confidential information** in a **separate confidential schedule**. **Any order under CPR 5.4C can then be confined to the confidential schedule.**

24. Orders have from time to time been made prohibiting the disclosure of the fact that an order has been made and providing for sealing the whole court file. Some newspapers refer to these as '**super injunctions**'. I shall consider such orders below.

25. The grounds for any derogation from the normal provisions of the CPR **should be set out in evidence put before the court** asked to make the order. CPR 25.3 provides:

> "**25.3(1)** The court may grant an interim remedy on an application made without notice if it appears to the court that there are good reasons for not giving notice.
>
> **(2)** An application for an interim remedy must be supported by evidence, unless the court orders otherwise.
>
> **(3)** If the applicant makes an application without giving notice, the evidence in support of the application must state the reasons why notice has not been given."

26. That has not been done in this case. The grounds have been advanced by Mr Spearman in his Skeleton argument.

THE FORM OF THE EVIDENCE

27. The evidence submitted is in the form of a short witness statement made by the applicant's solicitor. *In order to maintain confidentiality, all the substantive evidence is contained in a nine page exhibit headed "Confidential" ("the exhibit").* **The exhibit has 111 pages of attachments. All but 4 of these are print outs from the internet,** mainly of results of searches against the name of LNS and the other person.

28. In the exhibit the solicitor describes LNS as a person well known in the field of professional sport. He goes on to state:

> "On Wednesday evening, 20 January 2010, and together with [another solicitor of the same firm] I spoke with [LNS]'s business partners [BP1 and BP2—"the business partners"]. [The business partners] told me of [LNS]'s very grave concern over the possibility of **intrusion** into [LNS's] personal life. This concern has arisen as a result of [LNS] being aware of rumours circulating among the [relevant sporting] community concerning [LNS's] private life. It is that concern that leads to the present application being made . . . In the afternoon of 22 January 2010 [the business partners] met with [the other person] at a London hotel. [The other person] confirmed to [the business partners] that [the

other person] considered the fact and detail of [the other person's] **relationship** with [LNS] to be private and that [the other person] did not want any such information . . . to become public. For the avoidance of doubt however it should be made clear that a substantial amount of information is **in the public domain concerning** [the other person] which in the case of a less well known person would not be in the **public domain**, at least some of it at [the other person's] instigation or with [the other person's] consent I refer by way of illustration . . . [and illustrations of this are attached to the exhibit]. **At the meeting, [the other person] executed a confidentiality agreement and side letter confirming these wishes.** A copy of these documents is attached . . . .".

29. The side letter is dated 21 January 2010 and addressed to the applicant's solicitors. It consists of seven lines signed by the other person personally. The other person writes:

> **"I understand that there have been claims made concerning a relationship between [LNS] and myself. Whilst I do not make any admission as to the truth or otherwise of such rumours, speculation concerning [LNS, the other person and the Relationship] is private and I agree to keep such information private and confidential. If I receive any enquiries from the media concerning the above, I agree that I shall notify [BP1] about this as soon as possible".**

30. The confidentiality agreement bears the same date and signature. It consists of 15 clauses covering two full pages. It starts:

> **"As a result of my dealings with you there has been speculation about a relationship with you. Whilst I do not make any admission as to the truth or otherwise of such speculation, I do not want such information to be disclosed. In order to assist you in keeping such matters confidential and in consideration of £1 receipt of which is hereby acknowledged I agree as follows:**
>
> . . .
>
> **2. I agree not to disclose any Confidential information to any third parties (save to my legal advisors or as required by law).**
>
> **3. I agree not to disclose any Confidential information to any media organisations, journalists or any 3rd party who may provide such Confidential information to any media organisation . . .**
>
> **14. The terms of this agreement are confidential . . ."**

31. So the source for the information contained in the document is not the applicant directly, nor the other person. **It is the business partners.** This is a matter of concern. It is not said that the business partners are solicitors,

or have received any advice from solicitors as to how they should go about collecting information to be put before the court. **I infer that they are not solicitors**. The significance of this is that solicitors owe duties to the court and are skilled in taking statements from witnesses. It is very important that information from witnesses should be what the witness truly believes, and that words should not be put into the mouth of a witness: see White Book (2010) **note 32.8.1**. An applicant for interim relief owes duties of **full and frank disclosure to the court**. **No one but a solicitor** will be in a position to assess what that duty requires in the context of an application such as this. When the evidence before the court is not verified by the person who is the source for the information, there is not the assurance that that person feels at **risk of sanctions if the information is untrue.**

32. There is no information given as to the business in which the two "business partners" are partners of the applicant. As noted below, the exhibit includes a statement that LNS has "**a number of high profile sponsorship or endorsement deals for companies** . . . " That is a business which successful sporting figures commonly engage in. It is a matter of common knowledge that for very successful professionals, income earned in this way can be very large indeed. **But high profile sponsors are sensitive to the reputation of the sports professionals to whom they pay the large sponsorship fees demanded for promoting the sponsor's products**. They may cease to use a famous face if it is associated with behaviour of which the sponsor or the public may disapprove.

33. I infer that the business partners are engaged in the promotions of LNS for sponsorship deals, and that their business interest is to protect LNS's **reputation. I am left in serious doubt as to whether the information sourced through the business partners is full and frank.**

. . .

44. But I am **not satisfied**, on the information and submissions before me, that the applicant is **likely to succeed** on this point. The burden under HRA s **12(3)** lies on the applicant, and LNS has not discharged the burden on the present application.

. . .

BREACH OF CONFIDENCE

48. No Claim Form had been issued before the application was made to me. **But Mr Spearman has prepared a very full skeleton argument**. Pages 5 to 24 set out in some details the two causes of action upon which he relies. They are **breach of confidence** and **misuse of private information**. I can set out the elements of those two causes of action briefly.

. . .

51. Where there is a confidential **relationship** the test is **"not simply whether the information is a matter of public interest but whether, in all the circumstances, it is in the public interest that the duty of confidence should be breached"** (*Associated Newspapers Ltd v HRH Prince of Wales* [2006] EWCA Civ 1776; [2008] Ch 57 [68]) . **That case concerned an unauthorised disclosure by an employee of a travel journal, in breach of contract.**

52. I am not satisfied that LNS is likely to establish that there has been a breach of a duty of confidence owed to LNS under this cause of action. **There is insufficient evidence as to what LNS and the other person have each told to whom and in what circumstances**. In so far as details of the **Relationship** are concerned, it may well be that *if* either of them has told details, then I would infer that those details were likely to have been communicated in confidence. **But the evidence before me does not identify any details which are said to be known by anyone other than LNS and the other person, from which I would draw the inference that there has been a breach of confidence of which LNS can complain**. The evidence goes no further than to make it likely that LNS will establish that the fact of the **Relationship** is known to persons other than the two parties to it. There is no evidence that any **photographs** there may be were produced or disclosed in confidence. In *X v Persons Unknown* [2006] EWHC 2783 (QB); [2009] EMLR 290 the information in question was about the applicants' marriage and was allegedly disseminated to the media by unknown friends. As Eady J put it in that case, **at [38], some facts about the existence or otherwise of a relationship between two persons are "naturally accessible to outsiders**". And outsiders can draw inferences from such facts. I do not know enough about the other person's view of it to conclude whether or not it is likely that the other person would have disclosed information only in confidence.

53. I shall **consider below possible defences,** and whether, if I were satisfied that LNS would succeed on liability, I would also be satisfied that he would be likely to obtain a permanent injunction restraining publication. What applies to misuse of private information in this connection also applies to breach of confidence.

MISUSE OF PRIVATE INFORMATION

54. The second cause of action relied on by Mr Spearman is misuse of private information. Here he is on somewhat stronger ground.

55. At a trial of a claim for misuse of private information a claimant must first establish that he has a reasonable expectation of privacy in relation to the information of which disclosure is threatened. That is **"whether a reasonable person of ordinary sensibilities would feel if he or she was placed**

in the same position as the claimant and faced the same publicity" in all the circumstances. These include "**the *attributes* of the claimant, the *nature of the activity* in which the claimant was engaged, *the place* at which it was happening, the *nature and* purpose *of the* intrusion, *the absence of consent* and whether it was known or could be inferred, the *effect on the claimant* and the circumstances in which and the *purposes for which* the information came into the hands of the publisher**": see *Murray v Express Newspapers* [2008] EWCA Civ 446; [2008] Fam Law 732 [24], [36], [52]. That case concerned **photographs** of a young child in a public place taken **covertly** and published without the parents' permission. **Photographs** attract special protection because they can be much more **intrusive** and informative than words: *Douglas v Hello! (No 3)* [2006] QB 125. That case concerned **photographs** taken **surreptitiously** at a wedding part56. If there is such a reasonable expectation, the next question is whether there is a justification for the disclosure, eg public interest and **public domain, as set out in Art 8(2) and 10**, and whether a permanent injunction would be a **necessary** and **proportionate** remedy, having regard to Art 10. As noted in *Murray* [21], in *Campbell v MGN Ltd* [2004] 2 AC 457 [36] it was accepted on Ms Campbell's behalf that falsehoods she had told entitled the newspaper to publish the fact that she was addicted to drugs. There is no corresponding concession in the present case.

. . .

59. Mr Spearman cites in his skeleton argument the provisions of the **PCC Code** as follows:

"**3 *Privacy**

(i) Everyone is entitled to respect for his or her private and family life, home, health and correspondence, including digital communications.

(ii) Editors will be expected to justify **intrusions** into any individual's private life without consent. **Account will be taken of the complainant's own public disclosures of information.**

(iii) It is unacceptable to **photograph** individuals **in private places** without their consent.

Note—Private places are public or private property where there is a **reasonable expectation of privacy.**

The public interest

There may be exceptions to the clauses marked * where they can be demonstrated to be in the public interest.

1. The public interest includes, but is not confined to:

(i) Detecting or exposing **crime** or **serious impropriety**.

(ii) Protecting **public health** and **safety**.

(iii) Preventing the public from being **misled** by an action or statement of an individual or organisation.

2. There is a public interest in **freedom of expression** itself.

3. Whenever the public interest is invoked, the PCC will require editors to demonstrate fully that they reasonably believed that publication, or journalistic activity undertaken with a view to publication, would be in the public interest.

4. The PCC will consider the extent to which material is **already in the public domain**, or **will become so**.

5. In cases involving **children under 16**, editors must demonstrate an **exceptional public interest** to over-ride the normally paramount interest of the child".

60 In a section of his Skeleton Argument addressed to fulfilling an applicant's duty to the court to draw attention to **possible defences**, Mr Spearman referred to the **need to prevent the public from being misled.** He wrote this:

> "In the present case the applicant has made claims [about LNS's conduct] and it could be argued that he cannot complain if the true position is exposed. However the court has to have regard not only to [LNS's] Art 8 rights **but also those of [the other person] and [the interested persons],** and it is submitted that it would be an unduly heavy price for them to pay to the end of correcting any false public image that the applicant may have cultivated. In addition, the question for the court is not so much whether there is a contrast or contradiction between the position . . . which was stated at the time and that which prevails now, but whether previous claims that were false and misleading **at the time when they were made**".

61. Mr Spearman reminds me, and I accept, that in relation to misuse of private information, there is a conflict between rights under Art 8 and 10, and I must follow the course set out in *Re S (A Child) (Identification: Restriction on Publication)* [2004] UKHL47; [2005] 1 AC 593. That case concerned the reporting of a trial of a parent charged with murder of a son. Lord Steyn said at [17]:

> "**First**, neither article has as such precedence over the other. **Secondly**, where the values under the two articles are in conflict, an intense focus on the comparative importance of the specific rights being claimed in the individual case is necessary. **Thirdly**, the justifications for interfering with or restricting each right must be taken into account. **Finally**, the proportionality test must be applied to each. For convenience I will call this *the ultimate balancing test*".

62. I also have in mind that **there is a public interest in naming individuals in some circumstances**. For example, in relation to a report of a trial, in the same case Lord Steyn said at para 34:

> ". . . it is important to bear in mind that from a newspaper's point of view a report of a sensational trial without revealing the identity of the defendant would be a very much **disembodied** trial. If the newspapers choose not to contest such an injunction, they are less likely to give prominence to reports of the trial. Certainly, readers will be less interested and editors will act accordingly. Informed **debate** about criminal justice will suffer."

63. Similar statements have been made in *In re BBC* [2009] UKHL 34; [2009] 3 WLR 142 para 25–26 (also a case about reporting of criminal proceedings) by Lord Hope of Craighead and 65–66 by Lord Brown of Eaton-under-Heywood. Lord Hope said:

> "25. Lord Pannick suggested it would be open to the BBC to raise the issue of general interest without mentioning D's name or in any other way disclosing his identity. But I think that Mr Millar was right when he said that the BBC should not be required to restrict the scope of their programme in this way. **The freedom of the press to exercise its own judgment in the presentation of journalistic material has been emphasised by the Strasbourg court. In Jersild v Denmark (1994) 19 EHRR 1,** the court said, at para 31, that it was not for it, nor for the national courts for that matter, to substitute their own views for those of the press as to what **technique of reporting** should be adopted by journalists. It recalled that **article 10 protects not only the substance of the ideas and the information expressed but also the form in which they are conveyed**. In essence article 10 leaves it for journalists to decide **what details it is necessary to reproduce to ensure credibility**: see *Fressoz and Roire v France* (1999) 31 EHRR 28, para 54. So the BBC are entitled to say that the question whether D's identity needs to be disclosed to give weight to the message that the programme is intended to convey is for them to judge. As Lord Hoffmann said in *Campbell v MGN Ltd* [2004] 2 AC 457, para 59, judges are **not newspaper** editors. They are **not broadcasting** editors either. The issue as to where the balance is to be struck between the competing rights must be approached on this basis.
>
> 26. Will the revealing of D's identity in connection with the proposed programme pursue a legitimate aim? I would answer that question in the affirmative."

64. Lord Brown said at [66] that the short answer to Mr Pannick's submission

was to be found in para 34 of Lord Steyn's speech in *In re S (A Child)* [2005] 1 AC:

> "such a programme would indeed be 'very much **disembodied**' and have a substantially lesser impact upon its audience".

65. As I indicated in my summary of the evidence, the evidence of the existence of such a threat is **limited to one reference** to unspecified **photographs** on 18 or 19 January, and to **an inference** from the interest of the media in the story. **That is not enough for me** to be satisfied that there is a real threat to publish **photographs** or details in respect of which LNS has a reasonable expectation of privacy.

66. The court is being asked by LNS to have regard to the Art 8 rights of the other person **and the interested persons**. Respect for the dignity and autonomy of the individuals concerned requires that, if practicable, **they should speak for themselves**. There is no suggestion that **the first interested person is unwell or otherwise abnormally susceptible, or not in a position to address this matter**. If it is not practicable or just that the other person or anyone else should not give evidence personally, **the court should know why.** The evidence does include a statement that LNS has not told one of the interested persons about the **Relationship**. That is not the same as saying that person does not know about. **I do not find it credible that rumours that have circulated as widely as the rumours in this case are said to have circulated have not yet reached the ears of at least the first interested person**. If they have not yet got that far, they surely will do very soon.

67. As to any other interested person, in my view LNS **is not well placed to represent their interests.** LNS lacks **the necessary independence** to do that. It is relevant to this, and to other aspects of this case, that I infer that LNS enjoys the **very large earnings** which **comparable sporting professionals** are well known to enjoy. **Financial constraints cannot be invoked to justify omitting to take any steps that justice requires should be taken.**

68. I accept that LNS has shown **a real threat** exists to publish information about the fact of the **Relationship**, and no doubt some unspecified details. **But I am not satisfied that LNS is likely to succeed in establishing that publication of *the fact of the* Relationship (and possibly some relatively *un*intrusive details), should not be allowed.**

69. As to any threat to publish **intrusive details** of the **Relationship**, **or photographs** relating to the **Relationship**, I am not satisfied that there is a real threat. But if there were, then that seems to me to be a **different level of speech from disclosing the fact of the Relationship and details which are at a low level of intrusiveness**. If there were a threat to publish any **intrusive details** of the **Relationship**, **or photographs relating to the Relationship,**

then I would be satisfied that LNS **would be likely to** establish at trial that publication should *not* be allowed to that extent.

70. There is a further reason why I am unable to be satisfied that LNS is likely to establish that publication should not be allowed. This reason relates to an **uncertainty in the law** of misuse of private information (and for that matter the law of confidence). **The uncertainty is the extent to which, if at all, the belief of a person threatening to make a publication in the media is relevant on the issue of public interest.**

71. Eady J referred to this point in *Mosley v News Group Newspapers Ltd* [2008] EWHC 1777 (QB); [2008] EMLR 679 (the trial of a claim about a report of **clandestine** sado-masochistic activities). He said:

> "135 As the law stands, **it seems clear that it is for the court to decide whether a particular publication was in the public interest.** This may require further explanation. It is important to have in mind that some authorities (here and in Strasbourg) have in recent years placed emphasis on the need **to make due allowance for editorial judgment** and also for a **wide discretion** so far as **taste** and **modes of expression** are concerned: see eg *Jameel (Mohammed) v Wall Street Journal Sprl* [2007] 1 AC 359 at [31]–[33] **in the context of privilege in the law of defamation,** where Lord Bingham made these observations:
>
> {SUB}"31 The necessary precondition of reliance on **qualified privilege** in this context is that the matter published should be one of **public interest.** In the present case **the subject matter of the article complained of was of undoubted public interest.** But that is not always, perhaps not usually, so. **It has been repeatedly and rightly said that what engages the interest of the public may not be material which engages the public interest.**
>
> 32 **Qualified privilege** as a live issue only arises where a statement is **defamatory and untrue.** It was in this context, and assuming the matter to be one of public interest, that Lord Nicholls proposed [in *Reynolds v Times Newspapers Ltd*], at p 202, **a test of responsible journalism**, a test repeated in *Bonnick v Morris* [2003] 1 AC 300, 309. **The rationale of this test is, as I understand, that there is no duty to publish and the public have no interest to read material which the publisher has not taken reasonable steps to verify**. As Lord Hobhouse observed with characteristic pungency, at p 238, **'No public interest is served by publishing or communicating misinformation.'** But the publisher is **protected if he has taken such steps as a responsible journalist would take to try and ensure that what is published is accurate and fit for publication.**

33 Lord Nicholls, at p 205, **listed certain matters** which might be taken into account in deciding whether the test of **responsible journalism** was satisfied. He intended these as pointers which might be more or less indicative, depending on the circumstances of a particular case, and not, I feel sure, as a series of hurdles to be negotiated by a publisher before he could successfully rely on qualified privilege. Lord Nicholls recognised, at pp 202–203, inevitably as I think, that it had to be a body other than the publisher, **namely the court, which decided whether a publication was protected by qualified privilege.** But this does not mean that the editorial decisions and judgments made at the time, without the knowledge of falsity which is a benefit of hindsight, are irrelevant. **Weight should ordinarily be given to the professional judgment of an editor or journalist in the absence of some indication that it was made in a casual, cavalier, slipshod or careless manner.""**

72. Also relevant to an argument that the belief of the journalist may be **relevant to a defence** are **the PCC Code (Public Interest, para 3)** and, where the **Data Protection Act** might apply, to s 32(1)(b) and 55(2)(d). The passage in s 32 reads:

> "Personal data which are processed only for the special purposes **[journalism, literature and art]** are exempt from any provision to which the subsection relates if . . . (b) the data controller reasonably believes that, having regard in particular to the special importance of the public interest in freedom of expression, publication would be in the public interest, and (c) the data controller reasonably believes that, in all the circumstances, compliance with that provision is incompatible with the special purposes".

73. The **Data Protection Act** might well apply to a newspaper publication, **and in particular to an online publication**. If that Act did apply, it would be anomalous if the public interest defence under s 32 required the court to have regard to the reasonable belief of the journalist, but that the same defence under the general law did not. **I cannot decide that any reasonable belief on the part of a journalist or editor would be irrelevant without hearing argument for that proposition, if it is to be advanced.**

DEFAMATION

74. I raised with Mr Spearman whether the facts LNS relies on in this case should not be regarded as constituting a cause of action in defamation. In *Letang v Cooper* [1965] 1 QB 232 Diplock L.J. stated a well known and much followed dictum:

> "A cause of action is simply a factual situation the existence of which

entitles one person to obtain from the court a remedy against another person".

75. A libel or slander is commonly defined as the publication in permanent or spoken form (as the case may be) of words referring to the claimant **that would tend to lower the claimant in the estimation of right thinking people generally.**

76. As I have already indicated, although the words which the NGN, and/or other media, are allegedly threatening to publish **are not yet known,** it is very likely that there will be an arguable case that they are defamatory in that sense.

77. Of course, **LNS would not choose to sue in defamation** because Mr Spearman recognises that any person or media intending to publish this story is likely to do so in words for which he will be able to say that he has a defence in law, under one or other of the **defences available in defamation**. If so, applying the rule in ***Bonnard v Perryman,*** no interim injunction could be granted.

78. **The relationship between defamation and the new cause of action of misuse of private information is not yet clear.** Breach of confidence was also a developing cause of action in and from the 1970s. Some remarks have been made, in cases in confidence and in conspiracy, about the **relationship** between those causes of action and defamation.

79. Mr Spearman submits that the substantive law of defamation has also come under challenge **on the grounds that none of the defences in defamation appear to allow for the ultimate balancing test**. **If the defence is established, no regard is paid to the impact of publication on the reputation of the claimant.** He cites Clayton and Tomlinson on the Law of Human Rights, 2nd Edn at §12.19, where the editors say that **the English courts have effectively avoided engaging directly with the extent to which**

> "the tort of defamation—which has developed to take account of Article 10 rights of defendants—may now have to be further adapted to take into account the Article 8 rights of claimants".

80. A challenge to the defence of absolute privilege on that basis failed in Strasbourg: *A v United Kingdom* (Application 35373/97) (2002) 36 EHRR 917 [88], [103]. I accept that it might be argued that a similar challenge in respect of the defences of **justification**, **fair comment**, and **qualified privilege** could also be mounted. **The point in relation to Justification is that the defendant is free to say anything that is true, however harmful or distressing even if there is no public interest or public benefit.** See Lord Denning MR's statement in *Fraser v Evans* [1969] 1 QB 349, 360–1, and the citation by Lord Nichols from Littledale J, set out below. But I note that **the harshness of this rule has been tempered by the recent development of the law against harassment**. **Reputation** is an Art 8 right. So the argument is that English law requires

reform along the lines of what was recommended by The Select Committee of the House of Lords on the Law of Defamation in 1843. **The Committee recommended that the defendant who pleads justification should also have to establish "it was for the benefit of the community that the words should be spoken".** Or there is the model of French law, which has imported from Arts 8 and 10 the concepts of legitimate aim and proportionality. In the case of a defence of justification, the **reputation** of a successful claimant can be vindicated by an award of damages if the words are not true**. In the case of a successful defence of common law and statutory *qualified privilege*, a claimant has no means of vindicating his reputation at all**. It is not just that damages are not an adequate remedy: **there is no remedy in damages and no declaration of falsity.**

81. I mention this point at this stage, because I am addressing the substantive law. The main challenge to the HRA compatibility of the law of defamation has been in relation to the rule in ***Bonnard v Perryman*** in interim applications, which I address below. But the criticisms that are made of that rule (and **which were made unsuccessfully in Greene v Associated)** are ones which logically relate also to the substantive law. However, as Mr Spearman rightly accepted, a judge at first instance is bound by existing authority. So I must apply the law of defamation as it is.

82. In *Reynolds v Times Newspapers Ltd* [2001] 2 AC 127 at p192 Lord Nicholls said:

> ". . . as Littledale J said in *M'Pherson v Daniels* (1829) 10 B & C 263, 272, "the law will not permit a man to recover damages in respect of an injury to a character which he does not, or ought not, to possess". **Truth, is a complete defence.** If the defendant proves the substantial truth of the words complained of, he thereby establishes the defence of justification. With the minor exception of proceedings to which the Rehabilitation of Offenders Act 1974 applies, this defence is of universal application in civil proceedings. **It avails a defendant even if he was acting spitefully."**

83. In *Fraser* Lord Denning MR said this in relation to interim injunctions at pp 360–1, but it applies as much to a trial:

> "The court will not restrain the publication of an article, even though it is defamatory, when the defendant says he intends to justify it or to make fair comment on a matter of public interest. . . . **The reason sometimes given is that the defences of justification and fair comment are for the jury,** which is the constitutional tribunal, and not for a judge. But a better reason is the importance in the public interest that the truth should out. As the court said in that case:

"The right of free speech is one which it is for the public interest that individuals should possess, and, indeed, that they should exercise without impediment, so long as no wrongful act is done."

There is no wrong done if it is true, or if it is fair comment on a matter of public interest. The court will not prejudice the issue by granting an injunction in advance of publication".

84. Lord Denning went on to say at p362:

"It was said: Seeing that no injunction should be granted in respect of the defamatory aspect of the article, likewise no injunction should be granted in respect of the breach of confidence. The plaintiff should not be able to avoid the salutary rule of law in libel by framing the case in breach of confidence. Reliance was placed on *Sim v H J Heinz Co. Ltd.* I do not think it necessary to rule on this point today. I can well see that there may be cases where it would be wrong to grant an injunction on breach of confidence when it would not be granted on libel: **but I can equally well see that there are some cases of breach of confidence which are defamatory, where the court might intervene, even though the defendant says he intends to justify."**

85. In *Gulf Oil (GB) Ltd v Page* [1987] Ch 327 the Court of Appeal granted an injunction in conspiracy **to restrain the publication of words that were true.** After citing the first of the passages from *Fraser* set out above, Parker LJ said at p333:

"It is true that there is no wrong done if what is published is true provided that it is not published in pursuance of a combination and even if it is, there is still no wrong **unless the sole or dominant purpose of the combination and publication is to injure the plaintiff**. If, however, there is both combination and **purpose** or dominant **purpose** to injure, there *is* a wrong done. When a plaintiff sues in conspiracy there is, therefore, a potential wrong even if it is admitted, as it is in the present case, that the publication is true and thus that there is no question of a cause of action in defamation. In such a case the court can, and in my view should, proceed on the same principles as it would in the case of any other tort.

. . . I have no doubt that the court would scrutinise with the greatest care any case where a cause of action in conspiracy was joined to a cause of action in defamation and would require to be satisfied that such joinder was not merely an attempt to circumvent the rule in defamation".

At p 334 Ralph Gibson LJ said:

"Although that principle, which is applied in defamation cases, is not directly applicable in its terms to a case where the basis of claim is conspiracy to inflict deliberate damage without any just cause, **nevertheless it seems to me that that principle, namely the individual and the public interest in the right of free speech, is a matter of great importance in the consideration of the question whether in the exercise of the court's discretion an interlocutory injunction should be made and, if yes, what should be the extent of any restriction upon publication of any statement pending trial."**

Browne-Wilkinson LJ agreed with both judgments.

88. It appears to me, in particular from the judgement of Ralph Gibson LJ, that **it is a matter for the court to decide whether the principle of free speech prevails or not, and that it does not depend solely upon the choice of the claimant as to his cause of action.**

89. There have been a number of other references to the point in the interval, and in a number of cases injunctions have been refused on this basis, where the claim was brought in some cause of action other than defamation. Examples are given in Duncan & Neill on Defamation (3rd ed) in the footnotes to para 24.10. The most recent observations of the Court of Appeal on this point are to be found in *McKennitt v Ash* [2006] EWCA Civ 1714, [2008] QB 73. At [79] Buxton LJ said:

> **"If it could be shown that a claim in breach of confidence was brought where the *nub* of the case was a complaint of the falsity of the allegations, and that that was done in order to avoid the rules of the tort of defamation, then objections could be raised in terms of abuse of process."**

90. The reference to falsity in that passage is because the claimant in that case contested the truth of the book's allegations. **The point would have had more force, not less, if the claimant admitted the truth of the allegations, and was attempting to protect an undeserved reputation by recourse to the cause of action in misuse of private information, at least where there was a public interest in her not doing so.**

91. Mr Spearman relied on the following passages from the judgment of Longmore LJ, who had expressed his entire agreement with Buxton LJ at [83]:

> "85. . . . It was then said that there was no right of privacy in relation to false statements, in respect of which the tort of defamation was, in any event, available.
>
> 86 This argument, in my judgment, is untenable. **The question in a case of misuse of private information is whether the information is private not whether it is true or false.** The truth or falsity of the information is an irrelevant inquiry in deciding whether the information is entitled to

be protected and **judges should be chary of becoming side-tracked into that irrelevant inquiry".**

Mr Spearman submits that:

"In light of the latter decision, claimants have been able to sidestep the problems which might otherwise be presented by the Rule [in ***Bonnard v Perryman]*** by bringing (and seeking interim injunctions in) claims **for misuse of private information** in respect of allegations which concern private or personal activities even if they also adversely affect rights of **reputation**, contending that, **in that context**, the truth or falsity of the allegations is irrelevant: see, for example, *WER v REW* [2009] EMLR 304. As in the case of claims brought in reliance on other causes of action (such as under the **Protection of Harassment Act 1997:** see *Gatley* [on Libel and Slander 11th ed], §27.17 and the cases there cited) **this is an entirely legitimate tactic, provided that the claim is brought genuinely and not merely to circumvent the Rule**".

93. I accept that submission in so far as it relates to **harassment**: it is entirely consistent with *Gulf Oil*. But I do not accept that the court in *McKennitt* was overruling earlier decisions of that court, or distinguishing the decisions of the House of Lords, made in cases which were not referred in the judgments in *McKennitt*.

94. I do not read Longmore LJ as saying anything different from what the court had said in *Gulf Oil*. **He did not address his own remarks to an attempt to circumvent or avoid the rule in defamation.**

95. On the evidence available to me now, I have reached the view that it is likely that the **nub** of LNS's complaint in this case is the protection of **reputation, and not of any other aspect of LNS's private life**. I note that in the evidence the most LNS is said to have expressed is "grave concern over the possibility of **intrusion** into [LNS's] private life". **There is no mention of any personal distress.** As to **personal attributes**, LNS appears to have a **very robust personality**, as one might expect of a **leading professional sportsman**. It does not seem likely to me that the concern expressed on [LNS's] behalf for the private lives of the other person and the interested persons is **altruistic**. This claim is **essentially a business matter** for LNS. That is why the assembling of the evidence has been put into the hands of the **business partners** and not of the solicitors. **My present view is that the real basis for the concern of LNS is likely to be the impact of any adverse publicity upon the business of earning sponsorship and similar income.**

96. Before leaving the topic of **defamation**, I note that **it is only in limited classes of cases that the law of privacy gives rise to an overlap with the law of defamation.** In broad terms the cases may be considered in at least **four**

different groups. **The first group** of cases, where there is **no overlap**, is where the information cannot be said to be defamatory (eg *Douglas v Hello!*, and *Murray*). **It is the law of confidence, privacy and harassment that are likely to govern such cases.** There is a **second group** of cases where there **is an overlap**, but where it is unlikely that it could be said that **protection of reputation** is the **nub** of the claim. These are cases where the information would in the past have been said to be defamatory even though it **related to matters which were involuntary eg disease.** There was always a difficulty in fitting such cases into defamation, but it was done because of the absence of any alternative cause of action. There is a **third group** of cases where there **is an overlap**, but no inconsistency. These are cases where the information relates to conduct which is voluntary, and **alleged to be seriously unlawful,** even if it is personal (eg **sexual** or financial). The claimant is unlikely to succeed whether at an interim application or (if the allegation is proved) at trial, whether under the law of defamation or the law of privacy. The **fourth group** of cases, where it may make a difference which law governs, is where the information relates to **conduct which is voluntary, discreditable, and personal** (eg **sexual** or financial) **but not unlawful (or not seriously so).** In defamation, if the defendant can prove one of the libel defences, he will not have to establish any public interest (except in the case of **Reynolds privilege**, where the law does require consideration of the seriousness of the allegation, including from the point of view of the claimant). **But if it is the claimant's choice alone that determines that the only cause of action which the court may take into account is misuse of private information, then the defendant cannot succeed unless he establishes that it comes within the public interest exception (or, perhaps, that he believes that it comes within that exception).**

THE SOCIAL UTILITY OF THE THREATENED SPEECH

97. Mr Spearman submits that the level of social utility of the threatened speech is very low. . . .

98. It is of course one of the essential features of the protection of private life, and Art 8 in particular, that it **enables people to live freely according to their own choices.** Art 8 even promotes freedom of speech, as well as of conduct, since much speech can only be conducted freely if the parties are in private.

. . .

101. **It is not for the judge to express personal views on such matters, still less to impose whatever personal views he might have**. That is not the issue. **The issue is what the judge should prohibit one person from saying publicly about another.** If the judge is not permitted to hear from the other side,

there is a danger that by default he will give more weight than he would wish to the views of the applicant or himself.

102. By not giving notice, the applicant has **deprived** me of the opportunity to hear the case for the other side, including as to the **social utility** of whatever it is that the media might be threatening to say about the applicant. In *Francome v Mirror Group Newspapers Ltd* [1984] 1 WLR 892, at p 989 Sir John Donaldson MR (as he then was) said:

> "The "media," to use a term which comprises not only the newspapers, but also television and radio, are an essential foundation of any democracy. In exposing crime, anti-social behaviour and hypocrisy and in campaigning for reform and propagating the view of minorities, they perform an invaluable function."

103. This expresses part of the reason why I am not able to form a view on the material before me as to the **social utility** of the speech that might be in question here, and why that must be left to argument, if the application for an injunction to restrain the threatened speech is opposed.

104. There is much public **debate** as to what conduct is or is not **socially harmful**. Not all conduct that is **socially harmful** is unlawful, and there is often said to be much inconsistency in the law. For example, some commentators contrast the law on consumption of alcohol with that on other intoxicating substances. The fact that conduct is private and lawful is not, of itself, conclusive of the question whether or not it is in the public interest that it be discouraged. **There is no suggestion that the conduct in question in the present case ought to be unlawful, or that any editor would ever suggest that it should be.** But in a plural society there will be some who would suggest that it ought to be discouraged. That is why sponsors may be sensitive to the public image of those sportspersons whom they pay to promote their products. **Freedom to live as one chooses is one of the most valuable freedoms. But so is the freedom to criticise (within the limits of the law) the conduct of other members of society as being socially harmful, or wrong.** Both the law, and what are, and are not, acceptable standards of lawful behaviour have changed very considerably over the years, particularly in the last half century or so. During that time these changes (or, as many people would say, this progress) have been achieved as a result of public discussion and criticism of those engaged in what were, at the time, lawful activities. The modern concept of public opinion emerged with the production of relatively cheap newspapers in the seventeenth century. Before that there was no medium through which public **debate** could be conducted. **It is as a result of public discussion and debate, that public opinion develops**. Recent examples in the financial field include insider dealing and dealing in works of art which have been acquired lawfully but in debateable circum-

stances (eg taken indiscriminately but lawfully from sites of archaeological interest). Examples in the field of personal behaviour include some of the new offences created by the Sexual Offences Act 2003, and the increased protection given to employees, both financially and in terms of privacy and **harassment**. Exploitation of weaker persons by those who are richer and more powerful commonly occurs in private places, including within families. Those who are exploited do not always protest, or welcome protest by outsiders. They may believe that they have more to fear than to hope from the outcome of a protest.

105. I emphasise that I have expressed no view of the **social utility** of the speech in question here, because I have heard no argument from any opponent of the injunction sought.

OPEN JUSTICE

106. **Open justice is one of the oldest principles of English law**, going back to before Magna Carta. It is now set out in **CPR39,** and in Art 6, in terms which it is unnecessary to repeat here. In *R v Legal Aid Board ex p Kaim Todner* [1999] 1 QB 966 Lord Woolf MR gave reasons for open justice at p 977:

> "The need to be vigilant arises from the natural tendency for the general principle to be eroded and for exceptions to grow by accretion as the exceptions are applied by analogy to existing cases. This is the reason it is so important not to forget why proceedings are required to be subjected to the full glare of a public hearing. It is necessary because the public nature of proceedings **deters inappropriate behaviour on the part of the court.** It also maintains the public's confidence in the administration of justice. It enables the public to know that justice is being administered impartially. It can result in evidence becoming available which would not become available if the proceedings were conducted behind closed doors or with one or more of the parties' or witnesses' identity concealed. It makes uninformed and inaccurate comment about the proceedings less likely. If secrecy is restricted to those situations where justice would be frustrated if the cloak of anonymity is not provided, this reduces the risk of the sanction of **contempt** having to be invoked, with the expense and the interference with the administration of justice which this can involve."

107. The opening words of that citation are particularly apt here, because it seems that claimants' advisers have come under the impression that extensive derogations from open justice should be routine in claims for misuse of private information.

108. There is of course an obvious difficulty in at the same time complying with the principle of open justice and giving an effective remedy for threatened

misuse of private information. But as was stated in *Re S*, **there is no presumptive priority between ECHR rights. That applies as much to tensions between Art 6 and Art 8 as it does to tensions between Art 8 and Art 10.** Art 8 does not have a presumptive **priority** over Art 6 and open justice. Each derogation from Art 6 and open justice must be justified on the particular facts of the case, in accordance with the intense scrutiny required. And it is not just open justice that is in issue: **it is the right of a person affected by a court order, in particular a respondent, to be heard before the order is made. Apart from HRA s 12, that requirement is set out twice in the CPR, once in CPR 25.3(1), (3), cited above, and again in CPR PD 25 para 4.3(3):**

> "(3) except in cases ***where secrecy is essential,*** the applicant should take steps to notify the respondent informally of the application".

109. **Secrecy may be essential in the case of a respondent who, if tipped off,** *is likely to defeat the purposes of an application by publishing the material before he can be shown to have had notice of the injunction, or before it can be granted.* **It is less easy to show the need for such secrecy where the person targeted by the application is a national newspaper.** There may be a need to work out ways to address the problems which arise in such cases, but giving privacy claimants comprehensive derogations from Art 6 and Art 10 cannot be the answer.

THE OMISSION TO GIVE NOTICE

110. The fact that no notice of this application has been given means that no one but the applicant knows what occurred last Friday, or why I did what I have done. **All the factors mentioned by Lord Woolf are relevant in this case.**

111. Mr Spearman submitted that "there are compelling reasons why the respondent should not be notified" in this case. He submits that because there is no present means of identifying and so serving the Respondent the requirement is satisfied.

112. However, he rightly drew to my attention that the position is not as simple as that. Eady J has considered this point in **X v Persons Unknown. He said at [18]:**

> "18 It is not for me to lay down practice directions, but what I can say is that a proper consideration for the Article 10 rights of media publishers, and indeed their rights under Article 6 as well, would require that where a litigant intends to serve a prohibitory injunction upon one or more of them, in reliance on the *Spycatcher* principle, **those individual publishers should be given a realistic opportunity to be heard on the appropriateness or otherwise of granting the injunction, and upon the scope of its terms.**

19 The point of principle for which Mr Caldecott contends [I interpolate that Mr Caldecott was acting for one of the media defendants] can be encapsulated in the terms of the draft placed before the court for this hearing, which obviously mirrors closely the provisions contained in section 12 of the Human Rights:

> **'A claimant, who applies for an interim order restraining a defendant from publishing allegedly private or confidential information, should give advance notice of the application and of the injunctive relief sought to any non-party on whom the claimant intends to serve the order so as to bind that party by application of the *Spycatcher* principle . . . unless:**
>
> **(a) The claimant has no reason to believe that the non-party has or may have an existing specific interest in the outcome of the application; or**
>
> (b) **The claimant is unable to notify the non-party having taken all practicable steps to do so; or**
>
> **(c) There are compelling reasons why the non-party should not be notified"**

113. The **first reason** advanced for not notifying anyone of the application is that LNS "does not know of any media organisation which has a specific interest in the story".

. . .

117. **I cannot accept that explanation.** The evidence shows that NGN were intending to publish a story about LNS on the Sunday.

118. The **second reason** Mr Spearman advanced for not giving notice was based on what Sir Charles Gray said in *WER v REW* 2009] EWHC 1029 (QB); [2009] EML:R 17, 304. At [18] Sir Charles Gray referred to Eady J's judgement in *X v Persons Unknown* at [19] and said:

> "I can well understand why Mr Partington read those words of Eady J as in effect obliging a claimant such as the present claimant to notify in advance all those media defendants intended to be served with the injunction. However, I have been provided today with information by Mr Spearman about the facts of *X v Persons unknown*. As is apparent from its title, it was a case where the claimants themselves were unaware of the identity of the individual defendants whom they sued. As I understand it, the claimants limited their notification of the application to non-parties to third-party **to a selected number who had shown some interest in the story.** In those circumstances, it appears to me (and I hope I do not misapprehend what the judge said) that Eady J cannot

have been contemplating an obligation being imposed on individual claimants, who may be of limited means, to arrange through their legal advisers to serve what might be a substantial body of evidence on a large number of media non-parties. **It seems to me that the obligation to serve them must, as a matter of common sense and economy, be confined to those media organisations whom the claimant has reason to believe have displayed an interest in publishing the story which the claimant is seeking to injunct."**

119. But LNS is not of limited means, and in any event I have held that on the evidence before me **NGN had shown a sufficient interest.**

. . .

DEFAMATION AND THE RULE IN *Bonnard v Perryman*

123. **Having decided that the nub of this application is a desire to protect what is in substance reputation, it follows that in accordance with *Bonnard v Perryman* no injunction should be granted.** I do not know what words any newspaper threatens to publish. But it is likely that whatever is published, the editors will choose words that they **will contend are capable of being defended in accordance with the law of defamation.**

IF THE PRIVACY RULE APPLIES

124. If I am wrong about that, I turn to consider what I should do on the footing that this is in substance a claim for misuse of private information.

125. I have already concluded that I cannot decide that s 12(3) is satisfied ("**likely to establish that publication should not be allowed**"), having regard to the potential defence of public interest. It follows from that that no injunction should be granted.

126. But if I am wrong about that, I must consider what I would do as a matter of discretion.

. . .

THE NEED FOR A RETURN DATE

134. I would require a return date. And Mr Spearman did not oppose that.

135. On the need for a return date I repeat what I said in *G and G v Wikimedia Foundation* [2009] EWHC 3148 (QB). CPR PD25 para 5.1 says **there must be one if the order is made without notice to any other party.** There is no reason in the present case why I should order otherwise. Mr Spearman did not contest this when I raised the point.

136. And as stated above, a return date would serve two important purposes in this case, if I granted an injunction. The **first** is that it would enable the

evidence of the applicant and of any other witness to be put before the court in a statement which was made personally. **Second**, it would enable the court to monitor the progress of any attempts to find a Respondent and to serve him. As Eady J noted in *X v Persons* Unknown [78], **it is not consistent with the CPR for litigation to be commenced and for the subsequent steps required of claimant to be deferred indefinitely to suit the interests of the claimant.** CPR 1 provides that cases are to be dealt with **expeditiously and fairly**, and that the court has a duty to manage the case, including by fixing timetables and otherwise controlling the progress of the case, and giving directions to ensure that the trial of a case proceeds quickly and efficiently. **If the Claim Form cannot be served expeditiously, then the action will be at risk of dismissal.** Or a substitute defendant who can be served may be added by amendment.

PROHIBITION OF REPORTING THE FACT OF THE ORDER

137. When I queried with Mr Spearman the provision in the draft order prohibiting reports of the fact of the injunction he accepted that it was not necessary. I would not make that part of the order.

138. **The reason why, on some occasions, applicants wish for there to be an order restricting reports of the fact that injunction has been granted is in order to prevent the alleged wrongdoer from being tipped off about the proceedings before an injunction could be applied for, or made against him, or before he can be served**. In the interval between learning of the intention of the applicant to bring proceedings, and the receipt by the alleged wrongdoer of an injunction binding upon him, **the alleged wrongdoer might consider that he or she could disclose the information, and hope to avoid the risk of being in contempt of court.** Alternatively, in some cases, the alleged wrongdoer may **destroy any evidence** which may be needed in order to identify him as the source of the leak. **Tipping off of the alleged wrongdoer can thus defeat the purpose of the order.**

139. If a prohibition of the disclosure of the making of the injunction is included in an order for the **purpose** of preventing **tipping off**, and if the order provides for a return date (as the Practice Direction envisages) then the prohibition on disclosure may normally be expected to expire once the alleged wrongdoer has been served with an injunction, or at the return date (whichever is earlier).

140. There is a standard form of prohibition on disclosure of the making of an injunction in para 20 of the Form of Search Order given in the Practice Direction to CPR Part 25. It reads:

> **"Except for the purpose of obtaining legal advice, the Respondent must not directly or indirectly inform anyone of these proceedings or**

of the contents of this order, or warn anyone that proceedings have been or may be brought against him by the Applicant until 4.30 p m. on the return date or further order of the court."

141. If there ever has been an order which prohibits the disclosure of the fact an the order has been made, and which is expressed to run (as is sought here) for a period which is to continue after service on the respondent, and without a return date, then **no example** has been cited to me by Mr Spearman. I am not aware of what justification there might be for such an order, although I cannot exclude that there might be a justification in some case. But the grounds for applying for such an order would have be set out in the evidence. No grounds are given in the evidence in this case.

142. There is one unreported case which I recall. It was commenced in 1999 against a known defendant who, it was alleged, was threatening disclose information which the claimant considered to be **in breach of confidence and in breach of national security and which exposed other people to the risk of torture and even death.** There was **difficulty in serving the defendant**, and that was not effected for some six months. In due course the action was settled on the basis of undertakings. The order in force for the period before service contained a number of provisions similar to those sought in the present case to ensure secrecy. There was no record on the court file available to the public. But significantly, **there was a return date, and the matter came back before the court on a number of occasions** at which the court was able to monitor the continuing need for extensions of time and other derogations from the rules of court. Such cases engaging Arts 2 and 3 are more extreme than those where the risk is to no more than Art 8 rights.

OTHER MATTERS

143. The paragraphs under this head are subject to any further submissions that may be made, since Mr Spearman was not able to address all these points at the hearing last Friday. I accept that the proceedings against Persons Unknown are properly constituted (subject to any further argument that any other party may make). **But I would not grant an indefinite extension of time for service**. I will hear argument on this from the applicant in due course. But as indicated above, the **claim must proceed expeditiously.** So in a case such as the present, there may be little point in bringing proceedings against persons unknown, instead of against the newspaper publisher which is the real **target**.

144. In *Bloomsbury Publishing Group and J.K.Rowling v News Group Newspapers* [2003] EWHC 1205 (Ch); [2003] 1 WLR 1633 an injunction had been granted by Laddie J against **persons unknown** to prevent a breach of pre-publication embargo on a Harry Potter book. It therefore ran **only for a brief period.** Sir

Andrew Morritt V-C held that there was **power to make** such an order. He then said at [21]:

> "The crucial point, as it seems to me, is that the description used must be sufficiently certain as **to identify both those who are included and those who are not**. If that test is satisfied then it does not seem to me matter that the description may apply to no one or to more than one person, nor that there is no further element of subsequent identification whether by service or otherwise".

145. In *X v Persons Unknown* [2006] EWHC 2873 (QB) [68]–[70] Eady J explained a similar order he had made at an earlier hearing. But he went on to say what is cited above in relation to giving notice to the newspapers.

146. If I were to make a substantive order prohibiting any publication, it seems to me that **it ought to be limited to restraining publication to the public at large.** The information has already circulated widely by word of mouth, and further disclosure in that way cannot be stopped.

147. I would not order the sealing of the whole court file, **but at most a *confidential schedule.***

148. **I would require undertakings that at the return date the evidence of the applicant and the other person be in the form of signed statements, or that there be a satisfactory explanation of why it is not.**

CONCLUSION

149. I decline to make any order as sought by LNS, who is the only applicant, for the following main reasons:

i) There is a threat to publish information about the fact of the **Relationship**, but I am not satisfied that the applicant is likely to establish that publication should not be allowed;

ii) I think it likely that the **nub** of the applicant's complaint is to protect [LNS's] **reputation, in particular with sponsors,** and so **(a)** that the rule in ***Bonnard v Perryman*** precludes the grant of an injunction; and **(b)** in any event damages would be an adequate remedy for LNS;

iii) I am not satisfied that the double hearsay account I have been given of the evidence of LNS and the other person is **full and frank** (this may not be a criticism of the lawyers or of the individuals concerned, but arises from the fact that their evidence has been collected and reported by non-lawyers: I do not know who is responsible for this);

iv) I am not satisfied that the applicant is **likely** to establish that there has been a **breach of a duty of confidence** owed to LNS;

v) I have had regard to the extent to which it would be in the public interest for the material to be published, but, without having heard the Respondent or the media, I am **not** satisfied that the applicant **is likely to succeed** in defeating a defence that it would be in the public interest for there to be a publication;

vi) There is insufficient evidence of a threat to publish **photographs** or *sensitive details* about the **Relationship**;

vii) **Notice has not been given to any newspaper when it should have been,** and, as a result, I have not had **the benefit of arguments in opposition** to the application, which might have assisted me to be satisfied of the matters of which I am not satisfied;

viii) I do **not** consider that an interim injunction is **necessary** or **proportionate** having regard **to the level of gravity of the interference with the private life** of the applicant that would occur in the event that there is a publication of the fact of the **Relationship**, or that LNS can rely in this case on the interference with the private life of anyone else.

150. I draw particularly to the attention of editors and others what I have said in paras 11, 69 and 129 above. This claim has been brought by LNS **alone**. I have not had **to determine what may be the rights of any other person who may be referred to in any story** that NGN, or another publisher, may be proposing to publish.

151. Subject to any submissions to be made as to the form in which this judgment should be published, I adopt the course set out in *Browne v Associated Newspapers Ltd* [2007] EWCA Civ 295; [2008] 1 QB 103 [5] and [80]–[85], and hand down the judgment **in this anonymised form and without the confidential schedule**. The contents of this judgment should not pre-empt the publication by any newspaper, if that is what any newspaper decides now to do. **Nor should this judgment, by placing information in the public domain, undermine any remedy in damages LNS, or any one else, may ultimately be found to have against any publisher** in respect of matters that may be published about the events to which this judgment relates.

TUV v Persons Unknown [2010] EWHC 853 (QB)

8. The relief sought on the return date was concerned with the following matters:

i) The continuation until trial or further order of what Mr Spearman QC, for the Applicant, refers to as the "principal protection"; that is to say, restrictions imposed upon the Respondents preventing their dealing with, or parting with possession of, the goods identified as having been stolen in the burglary on the night of 29–30 March 2010; restrictions upon infringement of copyright; restrictions upon the use or communication of any information derived from the stolen goods and also upon revealing the fact that the Applicant had an interest in these proceedings (ie restraining any reference to her identity as the Applicant); and a prohibition against causing or authorising any other person to do any of those acts.

ii) An extension was sought until 21 days after the identification of the Respondents of the time within which the claim form is to be served upon them.

iii) A restriction in the following terms:

"Pursuant to CPR 25 APD 9.2, . . . , the Applicant shall be required to provide the legal advisers of any third party served with a copy of this Order promptly on request with (a) a copy of any materials read by the Judge, including material prepared after the hearing at the direction of the Judge or in compliance with the Order and/or (b) a note of the hearing on their written undertaking to use those documents and the information contained in those documents only for the purposes of these proceedings AND PROVIDED ALWAYS that before complying with any such request the Applicant shall be permitted to redact the name of the individual who assigned copyright to the Applicant."

DFT v TFD [2010] EWHC 2335 (QB)

Mrs Justice Sharp:

1. This is the return date hearing of an application by the applicant to restrain the publication of what is said to be **private** and **confidential information.**

The first hearing

2. On 9 September 2010 (the first hearing) I heard an urgent without notice application for an interim injunction in this matter to restrain the publication of what was said to be private and **confidential information**. **No proceedings had yet been issued, and the application was made without notice** to the (then intended) respondent, or to the media. Hugh Tomlinson QC appeared for the applicant, as he does at this return date hearing.

3. At the outset of the first hearing, and indeed this one, I made orders pursuant to CPR 39.2(3) (a), (c) and (g) that each should be conducted in private. I was satisfied it was necessary to do so having regard to the nature of the application (which would otherwise be self- defeating).

4. Evidence relating to the substance of the application and to the reasons why the court was being asked to make orders which derogated from the principles of open justice and from the civil procedure rules was placed before the court **in confidential schedules to the witness statements of the applicant**, his solicitor, Mr Benaim of Schillings, and from a member of a firm of security consultants engaged by the applicant.

5. Broadly, it was (and is) said t**hat the respondent had been blackmailing or attempting to blackmail** the applicant, and has **threatened to make public private and confidential information concerning a sexual relationship between them unless she was paid very substantial sums**. There was evidence that she may not have been acting alone, and that some of her family may have been involved. **Shortly before the application it had been made clear to her that no money would be paid, and it was now suspected that the respondent had been in touch with journalists with a view to fulfilling the blackmail threat**. However, there was no evidence as to the identity of those journalists, or that any media organisation had shown an interest in the information. **There was (and is) in my view, cogent evidence before the court which supports the applicant's case in all these respects.**

6. There was also a real concern having regard to these matters**, that if the respondent found out (or was 'tipped off') about the application she might avoid service and/or attempt to frustrate any order made before she could be served.**

7. In these circumstances I considered it appropriate for an order to be made without notice **either to the respondent or to the media** (see *ASG v GSA* [2009] EWCA Civ 1574 at [3] for the position when there is an allegation of **blackmail**; and *TUV v Persons Unknown* [2010] EWHC 853 (QB) where Eady J considered the issue of prior notification of the media, in particular his observations at [23] to [26]).

8. I granted the injunction for the limited period asked for (that is for 7 days) until the return date. **The order provided for the anonymity of the parties, for the restriction of access to documents on the court file, so that none of the confidential annexures to the witness statements or the names of the parties would be provided to non parties without further order of the court; and for a derogation from CPR 25 PD. 9.2 in that the applicant was not required to provide the material provided to the court, or a note of the hearing on those third parties served with the order unless they specifically asked for that material and gave undertakings to protect the use of that material and the information it contained.**

9. The need for such provisions has to be considered on a case by case basis, but they are not uncommon in privacy cases providing (in essence) practical

solutions to **the inevitable danger that the application itself will result in what is said to be private information becoming public** (see for example, what is said in *Terry (previously LNS) v Persons Unknown* [2010] EWHC 119 (QB) at at [22]).

10. **The order also provided that there should be no report of the existence of the proceedings themselves.** I considered that provision in particular to be necessary for a short period because of the 'tipping off' risk to which I have referred. As Tugendhat J said in *Terry*:

> "138. The reason why, on some occasions, applicants wish for there to be an order restricting reports of the fact that injunction has been granted is in order to prevent the alleged wrongdoer from being **tipped off** about the proceedings before an injunction could be applied for, or made against him, or before he can be served. In the interval between learning of the intention of the applicant to bring proceedings, and the receipt by the alleged wrongdoer of an injunction binding upon him, the alleged wrongdoer might consider that he or she could disclose the information, and hope to avoid the risk of being in **contempt** of court. Alternatively, in some cases, the alleged wrongdoer may destroy any evidence which may be needed in order to identify him as the source of the leak. Tipping off of the alleged wrongdoer can thus defeat the **purpose** of the order.
>
> 139. If a prohibition of the disclosure of the making of the injunction is included in an order for the **purpose** of preventing tipping off, and if the order provides for a return date (as the Practice Direction envisages) then the prohibition on disclosure may normally be expected to expire once the alleged wrongdoer has been served with an injunction, or at the return date (whichever is earlier)."

After the hearing

11. **In a second witness statement Mr Benaim has set out what has happened since the first hearing.** The respondent was served with the order on the day it was made. She instructed solicitors only yesterday, and a brief witness statement from her was put before the court yesterday. **She says that she strongly disputes the allegations made against her, but she consents to the continuation of the injunction granted last week until trial or further order for what are said to be pragmatic reasons**. This was confirmed to me by Mr John Critchley who appears on her behalf. It is nonetheless necessary for the court to be satisfied that the order should be continued because of the provisions of section 12 (3) of the Human Rights Act 1998.

12. **A number of media organisations have also been served with copies of the order**, as I was told they would be at the first hearing. Two of them

including Guardian News Media Limited, asked for copies of the material supplied to the court on the last occasion; and I have received a letter from Ms Gill Phillips, the Director of Editorial Legal Services of Guardian News Media. Ms Phillips says that this does not appear to be the sort of case that Guardian News Media would wish to be further involved with, **but sets out some general considerations and various points about the terms of the order which I have considered.**

The law

13. The relevant principles may be summarised as follows.

14. *Interim relief before trial.* Since this is an application which, if granted, might affect the exercise of the right to freedom of expression, section 12 of the Human Rights Act 1998 applies and no relief is to be granted so as to restrain publication before trial unless the court is satisfied that the applicant is likely to establish that publication should not be allowed.

> "As to what degree of likelihood makes the prospects of success 'sufficiently favourable', the general approach should be that courts will be exceedingly slow to make interim restraint orders where the applicant has not satisfied the court he will probably ('more likely than not') succeed at the trial." See *Cream Holdings Ltd v Banerjee* [2005] 1 AC 253, at [22] per Lord Nicholls.

15. **Private information**. When considering whether the publication of information which is said to be private should be permitted, the court must first decide whether the information in question is private, that is whether the claimant has a **reasonable expectation of privacy** in respect of that information such that the claimant's rights under Article 8 of the European Convention on Human Rights are engaged (stage 1). If yes, the Court must then engage in a balancing exercise, weighing the Article 8 rights of the claimant against the Article 10 rights of the defendant (stage 2). See eg *Murray v Express Newspapers Plc* [2009] Ch 481 at [24], [27], [35] and [40].

16. In *Murray* the Court of Appeal said at [35] that the question at stage 1 is "**a broad one**" which "**takes account of all the circumstances of the case**". The Court of Appeal also quoted with approval Lord Hope's formulation of the test in *Campbell v MGN* [2004] 2 AC 457, [99]:

> "The question is what a reasonable person of ordinary sensibilities would feel if she was placed in the same position as the Claimant and faced the same publicity"

17. Relevant considerations include the attributes of the claimant, **the nature of the activity in which** the claimant was engaged, the place at which it was happening, the nature and **purpose** of the **intrusion**, the absence of consent,

whether it was known or could be inferred that consent was absent and the effect (of disclosure) on the claimant (see *Murray* at [36]).

18. The Court should approach the balancing exercise at stage 2 in this way:

> "**First**, neither article has as such precedence over the other. **Secondly**, where the values under the two articles are in conflict, an intense focus on the comparative importance of the specific rights being claimed in the individual case is necessary. **Thirdly**, the justifications for interfering with or restricting each right must be taken into account. Finally, the proportionality test must be applied to each"

per Lord Steyn in *Re S (a child)* [2005] 1 AC 593 at [17].

19. *Public Interest.* It is not enough for information to be **interesting to the public**. Publication of the information must be in the public interest. The modern approach in any event is to consider public interest as an aspect of proportionality: see *HRH Prince of Wales v Associated Newspapers Ltd* [2008] Ch 57 at [68].

This case

20. Bearing those principles in mind, is the applicant likely to establish at trial that the information he seeks to protect is private and/or confidential and that he is likely to succeed overall at trial? Having regard to the evidence presently before the court, I am satisfied that he is.

21. As to stage one, I respectfully agree with what was said by Eady J in *Mosley v News Group* [2008] EWHC 1777 (QB) at [98] that "**anyone indulging in sexual activity is entitled to a degree of privacy—especially if it is on private property and between consenting adults"** and that "**people's sex lives are essentially their own business**" at [98]; see also *RST v UVW* [2009] EWHC 2448 (QB) and *ASG* at [6]. The information in this case concerns the fact and details of private sexual encounters, including during the course of a **relationship, between the applicant and the respondent at his home.** They had **nothing to do with any "public functions" or with the applicant's profession. He holds no public office. The information is known only to a few individuals and is not in the public domain.**

22. In relation to the second stage, Mr Tomlinson submits that looking at the matter from the perspective of Article 8, there is a plain interference with the applicant's right to respect for privacy and family life which cannot be justified under Article 8(2).

23. As to the Article 10 rights of the respondent, the evidence before me currently suggests the applicant is likely to establish at trial that **disclosure of the information (whether to the media or generally) would be the fulfilment of a blackmailing threat.** I accept Mr Tomlinson's submission **that the**

expression rights of blackmailers are extremely weak (if they are engaged at all).

24. At the first hearing evidence was put before the court of information in the **public domain** about the applicant, in media reports dating back over a number of years. **I consider there is nothing in them which arguably gives rise to any "public interest defence" by suggesting for example that the applicant had waived his privacy rights or that he had sought to mislead the public**

25. Bearing these matters in mind, as I have already said in my view the applicant is entitled to a continuation of the injunction already granted subject to consideration of some of the terms which are asked for.

The terms of the order

26. Any provisions derogating from the principles of open justice and the provisions of the CPR must be necessary on the facts of the case. In the light of some the points made by Ms Phillips, Mr Tomlinson has addressed in particular the provision in the order for anonymity and the prohibition against reporting the existence of the proceedings.

27. Mr Tomlinson submits both provisions should remain in place until trial or further order. Anonymity orders have been considered twice by the Supreme Court in 2010; and he has referred me to the judgment given by Lord Rodger in *Secretary of State for the Home Department v AP (No2)* [2010] UKSC 26 where he summarises the test to be applied as follows:

> "the Court must ask itself "whether there is sufficient general, public interest in publishing a report of the proceedings which identifies [AP] to justify any resulting curtailment of his right and his family's right to respect for their private and family life."" [7]

28. He submits the answer to this question in the present case is plainly "no". In particular, he says the publication of the applicant's name would lead to large scale media **intrusion** which would, in itself, constitute a very substantial **intrusion** into his private and family life and would be very distressing for him and his family. There is in addition a very strong public interest in the prevention of **blackmail** and in encouraging victims of **blackmail** not to give in. It would be contrary to that public interest to publish the fact that the applicant was being **blackmail**ed. As a result, all that any report of the proceedings could do would be to identify the applicant as the person who has obtained an injunction.

29. As for the prohibition of publication of the fact of the order, he submits if no such provision is made then experience suggests that the press will publicise the fact of the order adding "snippets" of identifying information with a

substantial risk of a "jigsaw identification" of the applicant, thus defeating the **purpose** of the action. Such "jigsaw identification" has taken place in the recent past when other injunctions have been granted, as explained in the evidence. In addition, if the fact that the injunction has been granted is publicised this will, inevitably, lead to press and **internet** speculation as to the identity of the applicant. Such speculation will itself cause the applicant distress and will interfere with his Article 8 rights. Such speculation risks breaches of the injunction taking place in forums on the **internet**. There is a temptation for journalists who become aware of the identity of the applicant to release this anonymously. This has happened in previous cases. There is no substantial public interest served by the public availability of the fact of an order—without any background information.

30. He says that in her letter to the Court, Ms Phillips reiterates the well known and uncontroversial point that private hearings and reporting restrictions should be ordered only where strictly necessary. Such necessity is established in this case as there are strong grounds for believing that the respondent is a **blackmail**er, seeking to extort money by threatening to disclose private information about the applicant.

31. It is not correct he submits (as Ms Phillips has suggested) that the "jigsaw identification" point is purely speculative. The evidence demonstrates that this has taken place in the recent past. It is submitted that there is a serious and substantial risk of it taking place again in the present case.

32. If, contrary to the above submissions, the Court takes the view that information should be released to the public as to the fact of an order in the present proceedings then he submits this should be restricted to information clearly delineated by the terms of the Order. This would avoid the "drip drip" effects of partial revelations in different newspapers and the attendant risk of "jigsaw identification".

33. In my view, it is necessary for the proceedings to continue to be anonymised, but I do not consider it is any longer necessary for there to be an order prohibiting the fact that the order has been made.

34. It seems to me that when assessing need, the court must consider the need for each provision in the context of the protection which may be given by any other terms an order may contain.

35. **If the applicant is identified by name, in my view there is a serious risk that the private information which the order is supposed to protect would emerge and that the purpose of the order in protecting private information would therefore be frustrated. I also consider Mr Tomlinson is right when he says the blackmail element of this case brings extremely strong public interest considerations into play. The fact that the applicant has been**

blackmailed should not be published. A report of the applicant's identity on its own, and absent the underlying details, would not be of sufficient public interest to justify the very substantial interference with his private and family life which would in my view, inevitably result from his identification for the reasons Mr Tomlinson has given.

36. **Whether and in what circumstances the court should prohibit the fact that an order has been made at all is in itself a matter of public interest, and indeed particular controversy at the moment. It raises in an acute form the obvious difficulty which arises "in at the same time complying with the principles of open justice and giving an effective remedy for threatened misuse of private information." (See Terry at [108]).**

37. **Indeed it is this very controversy which leads to the practical risks to which Mr Tomlinson referred to of jigsaw identification or that information as to the applicant's identity will be made public anonymously—for example by being placed on the internet. I agree that the examples he has drawn the Court's attention to, provide concrete evidence that this has happened when such orders have been made in the past.**

38. **I also agree with Mr Tomlinson that the Court must take a realistic view. There is it seems to me a risk which cannot be discounted, that what has happened in the past, may happen in this case. The significance of this risk must be considered when addressing the question which, as Mr Tomlinson said is simple at least to formulate, namely whether the effective protection of the applicant's Article 8 rights requires the substantial derogation of the Article 10 rights and Article 6 rights that making such an order involves.**

39. **The answer in my view is that it does not but only if the other parts of the order granted at the first hearing remain in place, and there is added to the order the proviso suggested by Mr Tomlinson so the order itself clearly delineates the information which should be released as to the fact of an order. In those circumstances, the risk of jigsaw identification should be minimal. The difficulties posed by the possibility of an anonymous leak can never be eliminated, whatever order is made by the court, in circumstances where an order such as this requires, as is necessary if it is to be effective, the identity of the parties and material relied on in support of an application to be supplied to third parties. But the risk that this may occur of itself, in my view does not make it necessary to prohibit publication of the fact that this particular order has been made.**

Addendum

40. Since the hearing on 17 September 2010 I have received further submissions from the parties as to the terms of the proviso mentioned in paragraph 39

above; and as to the judgment, to ensure so far as possible, this judgment itself does not contain material which would lead to the identification of the parties. It was necessary to delay the handing down of this judgment in public until these matters could be addressed.

41. It should be noted that the effect of the proviso to the order (contained in paragraph 1 (a) of the order now made) is that publication of any information as to the subject matter of these proceedings or the identity of the parties to these proceedings, is limited to that contained in this judgment.

Bernard Gray v UVW [2010] EWHC 2367 (QB)

Mr Justice Tugendhat:

1. The general rule is that the names of the parties to an action should be included in the orders and judgments of the Court: **In re Guardian News and Media Ltd** [2010] 2 WLR 325; [2010] UKSC 1 para 22 ("*Guardian*"). There is no general exception for cases where private matters are in issue. Such matters are commonly litigated in public, for example in the employment tribunal, and in claims for personal injury and medical negligence, and in the criminal courts: *ibid* para [22] and *Re S (a child)* [2004] UKHL 47, [2005] 1 AC 593. Nor is there any general exception to this principle for claims for injunctions to restrain publication of private information: see eg *Argyll v Argyll* [1967] Ch 302, *Lord Browne of Madingley v Associated Newspapers Ltd* [2008] 1 QB 103, [2007] EWCA Civ 295, [2007] EMLR 538 at para [3] and *Commissioners for HMRC v Banerjee* [2009] EWHC 1229 (Ch).

2. When an application for an injunction is made **before the issue** of a claim form the applicant will be required to **undertake** to the court to issue a claim form immediately: **CPR 25 PD25A para 4.4(1). It is of the utmost importance that applicants and their legal representatives ensure that such undertakings are complied with.**

3. **It is the duty of legal representatives, both counsel and solicitors, to see that correct legal procedures and forms are used**. This principle is established in relation to applications made without notice **(Memory Corpn v Sidhu (No 2) [2000] 1 WLR 1442, 1460).** But it must apply equally in cases where the court is obliged to have regard not only to the interests of the parties, but also to the interests of the public. **In such cases the public are in a position analogous to a defendant against whom an order has been sought without notice.**

4. **An application for an order that the names of the parties or the subject matter of the action be not disclosed is a derogation from the principle of**

open justice and an interference with the rights of freedom of expression of the public at large. The jurisdiction of the court to restrain publication of names and the subject matter of the dispute is **derived from the Human Rights Act 1998 ("HRA") s 6** (duty of the Court not to act in a way which is incompatible with Convention rights) and Arts 2, 3 and 8. Where the court is asked to restrain the publication of the names of the parties and the subject matter of a claim on the ground that restraint is necessary under Art 8, the question for the court is **whether there is sufficient general, public interest in publishing a report of proceedings which identifies a party to justify any resulting curtailment of the right of the party (and members of that party's family) to respect for their private life.** For these propositions see ***Guardian*** paras **27, 28, 30, 34–5 and 60.**

5. This judgment requires consideration of each of these three principles.

6. The principle of open justice in English law long preceded the ECHR and the HRA. For its importance see *R v Legal Aid Board ex p Kaim Todner* [1999] 1 QB 966 per Lord Woolf MR at 977 and *R (Binyam Mohamed) v Secretary of State for Foreign and Commonwealth Affairs* [2010] EWCA Civ 65 at [38]–[42]. So far as material to this case the relevant parts of arts 6 are:

> **"Art 6: . . . Judgment shall be pronounced publicly but the press and public may be excluded from all or part of the trial . . . where the protection of the private life of the parties so require[s], or to the extent strictly necessary in the opinion of the court in special circumstances where publicity would prejudice the interests of justice".**

7. Art 6 is similar in substance to the common law as summarised in *Guardian.* In *Scott v Scott* [1913] AC 417 at 438 and 463 Lords Haldane and Atkinson said:

> "(438) . . . unless it be strictly necessary for the attainment of justice, there can be no power in the Court to hear in camera either a matrimonial cause or any other where there is a contest between the parties. He who maintains that by no other means than by such a hearing can justice be done may apply for an unusual procedure. But he must make out his case strictly, and bring it up to the standard which the underlying principle requires. He may be able to show that the evidence can be effectively brought before the Court in no other fashion. He may even be able to establish that subsequent publication must be prohibited for a time or altogether. But this further conclusion he will find more difficult in a matrimonial case than in the case of the secret process, where the objection to publication is not confined to the mere difficulty of giving testimony in open Court. In either case he must satisfy the Court that by nothing short of the exclusion of the public can justice be done. The

mere consideration that the evidence is of an unsavoury character is not enough, any more than it would be in a criminal Court, and still less is it enough that the parties agree in being reluctant to have their case tried with open doors . . . If the evidence to be given is of such a character that it would be impracticable to force an unwilling witness to give it in public, the case may come within the exception to the principle that in these proceedings, . . . a public hearing must be insisted on in accordance with the rules which govern the general procedure in English Courts of justice. A mere desire to consider feelings of delicacy or to exclude from publicity details which it would be desirable not to publish is not, I repeat, enough as the law now stands. I think that to justify an order for hearing in camera it must be shown that the paramount object of securing that justice is done would really be rendered doubtful of attainment if the order were not made.

[463] . . . in public trial is to found, on the whole, the best security for the pure, impartial, and efficient administration of justice, the best means for winning for it public confidence and respect".

8. Art 6 also qualifies the word "**necessary**" with the word "**strictly**". It requires that an order be "strictly necessary" where the reason for making the order is that "publicity would prejudice the interests of justice".

9. The relevant parts of Arts 8 and 10 are:

"Article 8 Right to respect for private and family life

1 Everyone has the right to respect for his private and family life, his home and his correspondence.

2 There shall be no interference by a public authority with the exercise of this right except such as is in accordance with the law and is necessary in a democratic society . . . for the prevention of disorder or crime, for the protection of health or morals, or for the protection of the rights and freedoms of others.

Article 10 Freedom of Expression

1 Everyone has the right to freedom of expression. This right shall include freedom to hold opinions and to receive and impart information and ideas without interference by public authority . . .

2 The exercise of these freedoms, since it carries with it duties and responsibilities, may be subject to such formalities, conditions, restrictions or penalties as are prescribed by law and are necessary in a democratic society, . . . for the prevention of disorder or crime, for the protection of health or morals, for the protection of the **reputation** or rights of others, for preventing the disclosure of information received

in confidence, or for maintaining the authority and impartiality of the judiciary."

THE FACTS GIVING RISE TO THE APPLICATION FOR AN INJUNCTION

10. A brief outline of the facts that can be disclosed in this judgment is as follows.

11. The Claimant is a businessman, writer and sometime adviser to the Ministry of Defence and other bodies. He is a well known figure within certain political, educational, business and publishing circles. Over one year ago, the Claimant communicated to the Defendant private information. On 12 October 2010 the Defendant made a communication to the Claimant, following which they exchanged a number of messages. The Claimant became concerned and instructed solicitors. Miss Harris, the solicitor, spoke to the Defendant. The Defendant expressed a willingness to sign an undertaking not to disclose information personal to the Claimant, but the Defendant also made conflicting statements.

12. On the evidence before me, there were two conversations between Miss Harris and the Defendant in the afternoon of 13 October. According to the evidence, in these conversations the statements of the Defendant were inconsistent, or at least unclear, as to whether there are one or more third persons who have come to know the information in question, and if so whether any such third person is a journalist who is threatening to publish the information more widely. Miss Harris did not receive answers to questions she asked about the third party, if there is one.

13. In a witness statement the Claimant said that without protection from the court he felt vulnerable to publication by the Defendant of private information. There is no suggestion of **blackmail** in the present case.

14. At 11pm on 13 October, before making the application to the duty Judge, but at his request, Miss Addy called the Defendant to ascertain the attitude that the Defendant was adopting to the application for an injunction. The Judge hearing applications made out of hours was Nicol J ("the Judge"). At that stage the Defendant had not seen the witness statements or other documents what were to be submitted to the Judge. The Judge and Miss Addy had in mind HRA s 12(2)(a) (notice to be given to the defendant before an application is made for an order that might interfere with the right of freedom of expression).

15. In speaking to Miss Addy the Defendant opposed the granting of an injunction, saying that the Claimant and the Defendant could sort it out by speaking directly. In that conversation the Defendant protested that s/he had not told anyone about it and was not going to tell it to anyone. The Defendant protested that s/he had made his/her position clear to Miss Harris, but that

Miss Harris had not believed him/her. The Defendant admitted having made inconsistent statements, and repeated that s/he had no documents to disclose. The Defendant again gave explanations for the inconsistencies in what s/he had previously stated to Miss Harris.

THE HEARING BY TELEPHONE

16. This application was made on the basis of the evidence summarised above. Miss Addy has provided me with the note of the telephone hearing and a copy of the draft order that she submitted to the Judge. The hearing took 46 minutes. It is clear from the note that Miss Addy gave detailed disclosure to the Judge. There was a draft witness statement from the Claimant (which has since been signed) and a witness statement from Miss Harris. Miss Addy made submissions to the Judge on the balancing exercise that he was required to perform. She informed the Judge, as was the case, that the Defendant was not asserting a right to publish the information. She submitted that there was no public interest in the disclosure of the information. The information has no bearing on the Claimant's profession or public work.
17. During the telephone hearing Miss Addy referred the Judge to well known authorities where the court had granted injunctions protecting private and **confidential information**.
18. The Judge noted a reference in the evidence to the Claimant's clients and invited Miss Addy to address him as to whether the Claimant was simply seeking to an injunction to protect his **reputation**.
19. During the application to the Judge Miss Addy made clear that she was not seeking an order prohibiting the disclosure of the fact of the injunction (a so-called super-injunction).
20. Miss Addy asked the Judge to make an anonymity order, which he did. An anonymity order is may be made under CPR Part 39.2(4), or by the court's powers under HRA s 6. CPR Part 39.2(4) reads:

    "The court may order that the identity of any party or witness must not be disclosed if it considers non-disclosure necessary in order to protect the interests of that party or witness".
21. The grounds advanced for the making of an anonymity order are set out in the witness statement of the Claimant. They are as follows:

    "The Intended Claimant is concerned that if this action was reported, together with the names of the parties, this would fuel speculation in the media and on the internet as to what the injunction was designed to protect. This would inevitably cause further distress to the Intended Claimant and his family and defeat the intention of the injunction".
22. Between about 11.15 to 12pm the Judge heard the application and granted

the injunction in the form sought by Miss Addy, subject to variations which are not material for the purposes of this judgment. The Order set a Return Date for Friday 15 October. The Order included:

> **"1. The application be heard in private pursuant to CPR r 39.2(3)(a), (c) and (g).**
>
> **2. Until further Order the Claimant and Defendant shall be anonymised in this Order, and in any statements of case or application documents, pursuant to CPR r 39.2(4).**
>
> **3. Schedule 1 to this order be treated as confidential and not open to inspection pursuant to CPR r5.4C(4).**
>
> **4. Anything which may reveal any information or purported information described in the Confidential Schedule at the end of this Order shall be excluded from statements of case served in this intended action, and included in a separate confidential schedule served with the statement of case.**
>
> **5. Pursuant to CPR r5.4C(4) a person who is not a party to this intended action may not obtain from the court records any copy of the confidential schedule served with any statement of case. Any non party seeking access to or copies of any confidential schedule from the court file must make an application to the Court, having previously given at least 3 days notice of the application to the solicitors for all parties.**
>
> **6. If any non party at any time makes an application to the Court under CPR r5.4C(2) for permission to obtain from the court records a copy of any other document, other than a statement of case, or of any communication, such non party must give at lease 3 days notice of the application to the solicitors for all parties."**

23. Para 12 is an order prohibiting the reporting of the hearing. This is an order under HRA s 6, and not under the Administration Act 1960 or the **Contempt** of Court Act 1980, as mistakenly stated: *Guardian* para [31]. Nothing turns on that detail in this case, because the Judge is very experienced in this field of the law, as is Miss Addy. But in other cases the reference to a wrong basis of jurisdiction could mislead the court into omitting to carry out the balancing of the Convention rights in question.

24. By Sch 3, para 2 the Claimant undertook to the Court to issue a claim form by 4pm on Thursday 14th October, and to serve that, the witness statements, and a note of the hearing upon the Defendant. The Practice Direction 25A para 4.4 provides:

> **"Applications made before the issue of a claim form:**

> **(1) in addition to the provisions set out at 4.3 above, unless the court orders otherwise, either the applicant must undertake to the court to issue a claim form immediately or the court will give directions for the commencement of the claim,**
>
> **(2) where possible the claim form should be served with the order for the injunction, . . . "**

25. It follows that the effect of the Judge setting a time limit of 4pm was to define what was to be meant by "**immediately**" in the context of this case. The Judge did not add any requirement not already specified in the Practice Direction.

EVENTS AFTER THE HEARING BEFORE THE JUDGE

26. At 11.58 on 13th October the Defendant sent to Miss Harris an e-mail in which the Defendant gave an explanation for what s/he had said previously, agreed to sign "any form of agreements in writing to confirm . . . my promise not to disclose any of this private information", and confirmed that the Defendant did not retain any information in documentary form. By the time this was read, the Judge had granted the application.

27. There then occurred a serious failure on the part of the Claimant and his legal representatives. The Order and witness statements were duly served on the Defendant, but no Claim Form was issued. This omission was a breach of the undertaking to the Court.

28. Nevertheless, Miss Addy has informed me that the Order has been served on a number of newspaper publishers. None of these were notified in advance of the application. It is not necessary to serve newspaper publishers where none is known to a claimant to have shown any interest in the matter. There is no evidence before me that any newspaper publisher had any information about the matter prior to being served with the Order by the Claimant's solicitors.

29. On 14th October the Defendant signed a letter acknowledging service of the Judge's Order. The letter states that the Defendant has no intention of disclosing to anyone the Claimant's private information, and that the Defendant also regards the information as his/her own private information. The Defendant expresses deep sorrow for what had occurred.

30. Later on 14th October there was provided to the Court on behalf of the Claimant a form of consent order signed by the Defendant personally and by solicitors for the Claimant, together with the letter signed by the Defendant. This was submitted to the Court that day.

31. On the morning of 15th October there was an oral hearing attended by Miss Addy and his solicitors for the Claimant and by the Defendant in person.

THE NEED FOR A RETURN DATE AND AN ORAL HEARING

32. **There were the following reasons why an oral hearing was necessary.**

33. **First**, an order providing for anonymity and reporting restrictions cannot be made by the consent of the parties. "**When both sides agree that information should kept from the public, that [is] when the court [has] to be most vigilant**": *Guardian* para [2]. The Court has to consider the rights of the public under Arts 6 and 10, and not just the rights of the parties. Parties to civil litigation can waive or give up their own rights: they cannot waive or give up the rights of the public.

34. **Second, an anonymity order made by a Judge out of hours cannot be interpreted as intended to last for the duration of the proceedings. A provision for anonymity and other provisions derogating from open justice must be reviewed at the Return Date, whether the original order provides for that or not. The Judge's Order granting anonymity was limited by the words "Until further Order". The court's obligation to ensure open justice is a continuing one, as is its obligations to comply with Arts 10 and 8.** On the Return Date the court may, and in this case did, hear submissions from the defendant. And in the meantime a defendant may, as the Defendant did, make written statements which **may be relevant to the continuation of the anonymity order.**

35. The **third** reason why an oral hearing was necessary was that it became apparent that the undertaking to issue a claim form **had not been complied with**. Where an undertaking to the court is not complied with there must be an enquiry by the Court as to why that has happened and what, if any, sanction or consequential order should be imposed.

36. **An undertaking to the court cannot be disregarded:** if a party wishes to be discharged from performing an undertaking, then he must apply to the court to be released from it. ***Under no circumstances* can it be proper to serve on third parties an order made in proceedings which have not been commenced, unless the party has undertaken to the court to issue a claim form immediately (or as the judge may direct), and that party intends to comply with that undertaking.**

37. Subject to any order of the court, if parties to a dispute such as the present one have settled their differences, then the claimant must either discontinue the action or proceed with it. Of course, if the claimant discontinues the action, or asks to be released from the undertaking to issue a claim form, then there will be no order of the court to serve on third parties, and any undertaking by the defendant will be contractual only, and not an undertaking to the court. **For a claimant there is no third option to discontinuance and continuing with proceedings, subject to any order of the court.** As I said

in *Terry v Persons Unknown* [2010] 1 FCR 659, [2010] Fam Law 453, [2010] EWHC 119 (QB), [2010] EMLR 16 para [38], a Return Date serves a number of purposes.

THE SUBSTANCE OF THE APPLICATION

38. As to the substance of the application, Miss Addy submitted, and I accept, that the information the subject of the application is clearly within Art 8. As noted above, Miss Addy referred the Judge to authorities where private information had been protected by non-disclosure orders in the past. The Defendant consented to the Order.

39. I have not had to consider further whether the claim is in substance for the protection of the Claimant's private information or for protection of his **reputation**. The reason I have not had to consider the question of defamation is that that the Defendant does not assert a right to publish the information. In this respect the case is similar to *DFT v TFD* [2010] EWHC 2335 (QB) (see para [11]) and *AMM v HXW* [2010] EWHC 2457 (QB) para [4]. In a defamation action the Court will not refuse to grant an injunction simply because the action is one for defamation. It will refuse the application if and when the defendant raises an issue or a defence: see the discussion in Duncan & Neill on Defamation 3rd edn para 24.02.

40. Nor have I had to consider whether this was a case in which I would have continued the injunction, if continuation had been opposed. **A claimant is not entitled to any injunction, still less one which interferes with freedom of expression, unless there is a threat to interfere with his own rights such that an injunction is necessary and proportionate.** I express no view as to whether or the Defendant would have been successful in opposing the continuation of the injunction, if the Defendant had persisted before me in the stance that there should be no injunction (as was the Defendant's stance when telephoned on the evening of 13 October). I have formed no view as to whether or not the Defendant's explanation for the inconsistent statements is to be believed.

41. Unlike the Judge, I have had the benefit of seeing and hearing from the Defendant. I was able to ask the Defendant questions and to hear his/her submissions**. The fact that an injunction may be necessary at the time the out of hours judge considers the matter does not of itself mean that an injunction will still be necessary by the time of the Return Date.**

42. In the present case Miss Addy has asked for an order that **all further proceedings *be stayed* except for the purpose of carrying into effect the terms of the order I have made**. I have included that provision in the order I have made. **An alternative would have been to enter final judgment.** That can be done where there is consent or where the requirements of CPR Part 24

are satisfied. **The disadvantage of that from a claimant's point of view is that whereas an interim injunction has been held to be binding on third parties, it has been held that a final injunction is not.** As Eady J said in *X & Y v Persons Unknown* [2006] EWHC 2783 (QB), [2007] EMLR 290 at para 72:

> " . . . the *Spycatcher* doctrine [*Attorney-General v Newspaper Publishing Plc* [1988] Ch 333 at 375, 380] would go on inhibiting third parties from publishing the relevant information notionally pending a trial which would never actually take place. **The Spycatcher doctrine, as a matter of logic, has no application to a permanent injunction since, obviously, there is no longer any need to preserve the status quo pending a trial.** This doctrine is directed at preventing a third party from frustrating the court's **purpose** of holding the ring: see eg the discussion in *Att.-Gen. v Punch Ltd* [2003] 1 AC 1046 at [87]–[88] in the Court of Appeal and at [95] in the House of Lords; and *Jockey Club v Buffham* [2003] QB 462 (Gray J)."

43. **The fact that I have ordered a stay in the present case should not be taken as authority that that is the right course to take.** I have heard not argument on the point.

THE ANONYMITY ORDER AND OTHER DEROGATIONS FROM OPEN JUSTICE

44. As noted above, **the question** that the Judge had to ask himself, and which I have to ask myself afresh is**: is there is sufficient general, public interest in publishing a report of proceedings which identifies either or both parties to justify any resulting curtailment of the right of the party (and members of that party's family) to respect for their private lives?**

45. Each of the Claimant and the Defendant submitted that I should grant an anonymity order in respect of both parties, and the further derogations from open justice that I have ordered to apply. But their arguments were different.

46. The Defendant submitted, and I have no hesitation in accepting, that his/her right to private life is engaged by these proceedings. **I find that disclosure of the Defendant's identity at this stage would be an unjustifiable interference with the Defendant's private life and that that outweighs the rights of the public under Art 10, and the need for open justice. *I recall that the right to private life protected by Art 8 includes the right to* reputation**. My reasons are as follows.

47. The **allegations** made against the Defendant are **very serious** for a person in the Defendant's position. There is no suggestion that the Defendant is anything other than a person of positive good character. On appearing in court before me the Defendant was distressed by the whole matter, and this was plainly sincere distress. **For an individual to be brought to court in**

the circumstances in which this Defendant was brought to court is a very serious matter.

48. If the claims of a claimant are properly made, then the effect upon a defendant of those claims being advanced may be a consequence that a defendant must accept in the interests of justice. But if the claims of a claimant ought not to have been made or pursued, the pursuit of the proceedings may have caused to a defendant distress, and possibly damage to **reputation**, which may not be remediable.

49. In the present case I can form no view as to whether or not I would have granted the continuation of the injunction the Claimant claims if the Defendant had opposed it (as was his/her stance when speaking to Miss Addy on 13 October). Nothing in this judgment should be taken as casting any doubt upon the Claimant's justification for bringing these proceedings as he has, or of the correctness of the decision of the Judge. But nor do I cast any doubt on the Defendant's stance that no injunction was necessary. Defendants commonly consent to injunctions in order to avoid litigation while asserting that such injunctions are unnecessary.

50. **Unless the facts are clear beyond doubt, or are admitted, the court hearing an interim application for an injunction must make no findings of fact.** Disclosure, or the threat of disclosure, of confidential or private information may be a serious wrong. But applications for injunctions can also be made oppressively.

51. Since that question will not now be resolved, I find on the evidence before me, including what I heard orally from the Defendant, that it is necessary for the court to protect the Art 8 rights of the Defendant by ordering that the Defendant be not identified.

52. For the reasons given above in relation to the order for anonymity of the Defendant, **I also find that it is necessary to order that there be no report of these proceedings or their subject matter of any information which is not included in this judgment.**

53. Miss Addy for the Claimant advanced quite different reasons why I should order that the names of both parties be anonymised. The cases Miss Addy cited are well known. But it is to be noted that they were mostly reported cases where the names of both parties were published in the usual way. Lord Rodger noted in *Guardian* para [2], that "the general impression is that the practice of referring to parties by their initials has increased at all levels in recent years". That observation also applies to applications for injunctions to restrain publication of private information.

54. **As Miss Addy submitted, in a claim for misuse of private or confidential information, the public will often infer from the identity of the defendant**

the nature of the information which the claimant is seeking to protect. She submitted that that will, at least to some extent, defeat the purpose of the order. For example, if the defendant is a financial adviser or healthcare worker or a young man or woman, members of the public may infer (perhaps quite wrongly) that the information is financial, medical or sexual.

55. **However, I do not accept that disclosure of the general nature of the information in question does always engage a claimant's private life. Almost everyone has information about their health, financial affairs, sex life and other matters, the details of which are private and confidential. The fact that a claimant has obtained an injunction to prevent disclosure of one or other of such categories of information is not in itself necessarily a matter which should not be published.**

56. **There is a range of measures open to the court to protect the art 8 rights of the parties. These include a variety of measures to prohibit or prevent disclosure of the information sought to be protected, and an order prohibiting disclosure of the identity of one or both parties. But each measure is cumulative. The fact that one such measure may be necessary is not a reason for concluding that they are all necessary. On the contrary, the measures as a whole must be no more than is necessary and proportionate, and if one measure is adopted, then that may mean that an additional measure is not necessary.**

57. In the present case the reason advanced by the Claimant for why his identity should not be disclosed is ***weak.*** **He refers to the possibility that the media may speculate as to what the information is.** But in this connection I remind myself of the approach of the Supreme Court in *Guardian* at para [72]:

> "72 . . . the possibility of some sectors of the press abusing their freedom to report cannot, of itself, be a sufficient reason for curtailing that freedom for all members of the press. James Madison long ago pointed out that "**Some degree of abuse is inseparable from the proper use of everything, and in no instance is this more true than in that of the press":** "Report on the Virginia Resolutions" (1800), in *Letters and Other Writings of James Madison* (1865) Vol 4, p 544. . . . **The possibility of abuse is therefore simply one factor to be taken into account when considering whether an anonymity order is a proportionate restriction on press freedom in this situation."**

58. At para [59] Lord Rodger considered an argument based on fears about how the matter might he reported if the identity of the individual concerned was disclosed. He said:

> "That argument raises an important point of principle. It really amounts to saying that the press must be prevented from printing what is true

as a matter of fact, for fear that some of those reading the reports may misinterpret them and act inappropriately. Doubtless, some may indeed draw the unjustified inference that [the applicant] fears. . . . . **Politicians** and the press have frequently debated the merits of that approach, the debates presupposing that members of the public, . . . are more than capable of drawing the distinction between mere suspicion and sufficient evidence to prove guilt. Any other assumption would make public discussion of these and similar serious matters impossible. We therefore see no reason to assume that most members of the . . . community would be unable to draw the necessary distinction and to respond appropriately to any revelation . . . "

59. At para [60] he refused to accept that most members of the section of the public under consideration in that case would be unable to respond appropriately to the disclosure of the name of the applicant for anonymity in that case. The possibility that the media might publish articles critical of the applicant cannot normally be a reason why the identity of the applicant should not be disclosed.

60. There are exceptional cases where the court can be satisfied that the media reporting will be so critical as to amount to an interference with the applicant's Convention rights. The rights that may be interfered with may be under Arts 2 and 3, where reporting would be likely to lead to violence against the applicant. Such cases have occurred and were considered by the Supreme Court in *Guardian* para [27]. But there is no suggestion of anything so extreme in the present case.

61. In cases of alleged **blackmail**, where the defendant does not claim or assert a right to make the threatened publication, anonymity can be given to the claimant on the basis that that is necessary and proportionate for the prevention of crime. This is in accordance with Art 10(2): see eg *AMM v HXW* [2010] EWHC 2457 (QB) paras [24]–[28], [38]–[39]. But as already noted, there is no suggestion of **blackmail** in the present case.

62. Alternatively, the rights that may be interfered with may be the right of access to the court. A threatened publication may be a **contempt** of court, or an interference with the course of justice. This may occur where the threatened media reporting will discourage the claimant or a witness from giving evidence. Interference with the administration of justice is a crime. So a measure to prevent that can be necessary, in accordance with Art 10(2). But the threshold is a high one (as appears from para 7 above). There is no sufficient evidence of that in the present case.

63. I conclude that in the present case it is not necessary for there to be a departure from the principle of open justice, or any interference with the public's

rights under Art 10, such as would justify me in making an order prohibiting disclosure of the identity of the Claimant.

THE ERRORS THAT HAVE OCCURRED

64. In court Miss Addy took full responsibility for the failure of the Claimant to comply with his undertaking to issue a Claim Form. The failure was remedied immediately after the hearing. She and Miss Harris have both sent written letters of apology and explanation. I accept that **they acted in good faith.** The failure was contributed to by the fact that solicitors are in Manchester whereas Miss Addy was in London. **Applications such as these do impose great professional pressure on the legal representatives, since they require urgent action, and arise when the representatives may already have other urgent commitments. That is mitigation, not a justification for a failure.**

65. **Those advising clients on the making of applications for injunctions have a responsibility to read the Practice Direction 25A and to comply with it.** That Practice Direction is in plain English and is available on the **internet**. It requires no specialist expertise to follow it. It was inevitable that an undertaking would have to be given to the court to issue a claim form immediately, and preparations should have been made to do that. See para 25 above. Drafting a claim form is not a complicated task. The claim form as issued reads:

> "The Claimant's claim is for an injunction restraining the Defendant from misusing private information relating to the claimant".

66. **Where there has been a breach of an undertaking to the court, or a breach of the legal representatives' duties to see that correct legal procedures and forms are used, there must be an investigation by the court. An explanation must be provided. If the explanation is inadequate, then sanctions must follow. The sanctions open to the Court may be limited, in that the sanction must not itself be a disproportionate interference with the rights of a claimant, in particular the right of access to the Court under Art 6, and the rights under Art 8. In the present case I do not have to consider that matter further.**

CONCLUSION

67. It is for the reasons set out above that I made the order on 15 October 2010.

JIH v News Group Newspapers Ltd [2010] EWHC 2818 (QB) per Tugendhat J

Mr Justice Tugendhat:

1. In an action to restrain misuse of private information, in what circumstances should the court order that the claimant must not be named (an "anonymity order")? In what circumstances should the Court order **that even the nature of the information which is protected by an injunction must not be identified?**

2. This judgment requires consideration of these questions. I expressed views on them in the judgment I handed down on 21 October 2010 in **Gray v UVW** [2010] EWHC 2367 (QB) ("*Gray*") in the light of *In* **re Guardian News and Media Ltd** [2010] 2 WLR 325; [2010] UKSC 1 ("*Guardian*"). In *Gray* I had the benefit of argument from experienced counsel for the Claimant. But the Defendant was an individual who appeared in person. Nor did I receive representations in any form from any third party (although I was informed that newspaper publishers had been served). In this case both parties are represented by experienced counsel and the Defendant ("NGN") is a publisher of a national newspaper. In addition, as set out below, I have also had the benefit of submissions from Associated Newspapers Ltd, Express Newspapers Ltd, Guardian News and Media Ltd, MGN Ltd, Independent Print Ltd and Telegraph Group Ltd ("the Media Organsiations"). The views I express in this judgment therefore carry more weight.

3. It was also on 21 October 2010 that the parties in this action delivered to the Court a form of consent order, signed by both of them, which they asked the Court to make: see para 26 below. No other documents accompanied that form. It was clear (as has since been confirmed) that they expected the Court to make the order without consideration of any other documents. But the form of order contained derogations from the principle of open justice. The parties now accept that, **as I stated in Gray, an order for anonymity and reporting restrictions cannot be made simply because the parties consent: parties cannot waive the rights of the public (Gray para [34]).**

4. It may not always be necessary for there to be an oral hearing before the Court makes an order to which both parties have given their written consent, when that order includes provisions derogating from open justice. **But the court must always be provided with sufficient material upon which to decide the questions which it is required to decide. In a case where the derogation is said to be necessary to protect a Convention right there are two questions: (1) is any, and if so which, Convention right of any party is engaged? and (2), if it is, then is there sufficient general, public interest**

in publishing a report of proceedings which identifies that party to justify any resulting curtailment of the rights of that party and his/her family to respect for their private and family life? (Gray para [4] citing Guardian para [52]).

5. **Having read Gray the Claimant's solicitor Mr Shear made a witness statement,** and Mr Tomlinson provided a **Skeleton Argument**.

6. It is important to record that the arguments of the parties before me were not adversarial. The parties have reached an agreement, and neither of them has resiled from it. Both parties were asking me to make the order in the form they had consented to. However, both counsel were able to give their assistance to the court, and they did so from the perspective of a claimant and a defendant respectively.

7. The feature of the form of order in this case on which I asked for particular assistance was that it contained two provisions, either of which, by itself, might not have caused me concern, but which, when appearing together, call for an explanation. The first of these two provisions was that the Claimant be not named. The second of these two provisions was the substantive part of the order: it contained no information as to the subject matter of the action. The essential part reads (subject to exceptions):

   " . . . the Respondent must not publish . . . (a) all or any part of the information . . . described in the **Confidential Schedule** . . . , or (b) anything which might identify the . . . claimant as the person who has obtained the order . . . "

8. However, as Mr Tomlinson, expressed it in his skeleton argument:

   " . . . [where] the court has . . . accepted that the publication of private information should be restrained, . . . if the court is to avoid disclosing the information in question it must proceed in one of two *alternative* ways: (1) If its public judgment or order directly or indirectly discloses the nature of the information in question then it should be anonymised; (2) If the claimant is named in the public judgment or order then the information should not be directly or indirectly identified" (emphasis added).

9. If it is right, as in my judgment it is, that *anonymisation* **and** *withholding of information* about the subject matter of the action are **alternative** forms of protection for a claimant, then in the present case the agreement reached between the parties contains a derogation from open justice which requires particularly close scrutiny. The fact that the claimant has agreed to this form of order is not surprising. It is more surprising that NGN should have agreed to it.

10. In response to questions from the bench, Mr Tomlinson submitted that the

terms of this public judgment could cure any defect in the order. So it could. But the parties contemplated that this order would be made by consent, and without a public judgment. And the formulation in Mr Tomlinson's skeleton argument refers to both public judgment and order, and rightly so, in my view. **Pursuant to CPR r.5.4C(1)(b) it is also the general rule that a person who is not a party to proceedings may obtain from the court records a copy of a judgment or order given or made in public (whether made at a hearing or without a hearing).** That will apply to the order that I make in this case.

CHRONOLOGY OF PROCEEDINGS

11. NGN publishes a number of titles, including the News of the World and the Sun. Earlier this year NGN published articles in its newspapers concerning the Claimant. The first publication was without notice to the Claimant. Subsequently journalists approached the Claimant about other possible publications they might make concerning him.

12. On 13 August 2010 the Claimant applied to Nicol J sitting in the interim applications court, **for an interim Order before issuing proceedings.** The application was **supported by a witness statement from the Claimant**. In it he set out the facts, and gave reasons for his fear that, **unless an injunction was granted, he and other individuals would suffer distress and humiliation, and he explained the serious effect upon him and them that he feared might result.**

13. **Notice was given to NGN (and to no other media organisation) pursuant to HRA s 12 (2).** A hearing took place in the interim applications court. Counsel appeared for the Claimant and for NGN. They were counsel other than Mr Tomlinson and Mr Spearman who appeared at the hearing before me. Nicol J gave a judgment, a note of which is in the papers before me. The chronology of events is derived from that note, from the evidence before Nicol J, and from the recent witness statement of Mr Shear.

14. The hearing on 13 August lasted 2 hours and 20 minutes, finishing at 9.18pm. The judgment is not public. **It could not be public in the form in which Nicol J gave it, without defeating the purpose of the order that he made.**

15. **Nicol J asked himself the question that he was required to ask under HRA s 12(3): is the court satisfied that the applicant is likely to establish that publication should not be allowed?**

16. Nicol J said **"I have no doubt that the private life considerations of Art 8 are engaged here".** He then carried out the balancing exercise pursuant to the guidance in *Re S (A child)* [2004] UKHL 47; [2005] 1 AC 593 ("*re S*"), focussing on the comparative importance of the rights engaged, in this case the rights under Art 8 and Art 10 of the Convention. He concluded that he ought to grant the order sought. He then turned to the terms of the order. **He**

accepted submissions for NGN that the order sought was wider than was necessary, and granted it in the more limited terms which he considered were necessary. He made the substantive order, the essential terms of which are set out above in para 7.

17. Nicol J then turned to consider the **anonymity** order. He granted it saying:

> "if this was not included in the order it would undermine the **purpose** of the order itself. I note that it is common for such an order to be made, at least when the order is made to prohibit publication".

18. The Order of 13 August recites that Nicol J granted anonymity to the Claimant pursuant to CPR 39.2(4) and the inherent jurisdiction of the court because it appeared to him that:

> "(1) these proceedings were likely to attract publicity
>
> (2) that publicity revealing the identity of the Applicant is likely unfairly to damage the interests of the Applicant and/or frustrate the administration of justice in these intended proceedings".

19. Nicol J also accepted undertakings as required by CPR PD25A, and, as ancillary matters:

    i) heard the application in private pursuant to CPR r 39.2(3)(a), (c) and (g)

    ii) made an order under CPR r5.4C limiting the information that was to be available to the public from the court file

    iii) made the right (under CPR PD 25A para 9.2) of third parties affected by the order to obtain the order and the supporting evidence subject to an undertaking to be given to the Court by such third party.

20. On 13 August the **Order was served on the six Media Organisations.** Associated Newspapers Ltd sought a copy of the hearing papers and **provided the undertaking required by the Order.** The papers were served on them later that day. MGN Ltd asked to be informed as to the return date and whether they could be present at the hearing. This was agreed on behalf of the Claimant.

21. On 16 August 2010 the Claimant gave Notice of an application for an Order continuing the Order of 13 August. On the same day he issued a claim form. The relief claimed was

> "an injunction restraining the publication or disclosure of private information concerning the Claimant identified in the **Confidential Schedule** to the Order of Mr Justice Nicol dated 13 August 2010".

22. On 20 August 2010, by agreement between the parties, Nicol J continued his Order of 13 August, subject to the correction of one omission, until a return date specified as 20 September, or so soon after as the Court could

accommodate the parties. He gave directions for the service of evidence and skeleton arguments. The estimated time for the hearing was one day.

23. The Order of 20 August was served on the Media Organisations. **The Guardian News and Media Ltd sought a copy of the hearing papers and offered the required undertaking.** Papers were delivered on 25 August. MGN Ltd asked to be notified of the return date, which the Claimant agreed to do. None of the Media Organisations gave notice of any intention to apply for variation or discharge of the Orders of 13 or 20 August. Until I circulated the draft of this judgment (as described below) none of the Media Organisations, nor any third party, had made any representation to the Court, whether informally by letter (as is sometimes helpfully done) or by formal intervention. The point as to the scope of the Order on which I have sought the assistance of the parties was a point raised by the Court of its own motion. On receiving this judgment in draft MGN Ltd reminded the Court of *re S* para 35:

   "... **it is true that newspapers can always contest an application for an injunction. Even for national newspapers that is, however, a costly matter which may involve proceedings at different judicial levels. Moreover, time constraints of an impending trial may not always permit such proceedings. Often it will be too late and the injunction will have had its negative effect on contemporary reporting."**

24. In the event no further evidence was served pursuant to the Order for directions. The hearing before me was the return date. **By that time the parties had reached an agreement**. Parties to such a dispute are entitled to settle it by agreement, and thereby to give up such rights as they may claim to have, whether under Art 8 or Art 10. In this case it is NGN which has compromised its rights under Art 10. There is no reason for the Court to go behind that agreement, in so far as the parties have compromised their own rights. The Court is concerned only with the terms of the agreed form of order in so far as those terms affect the duties of the court and the rights of third parties.

25. There then followed the events described in para 3 above.

26. The form of consent order provides:

   " ... BY CONSENT THAT the interim Order of Mr Justice Nicol dated 13 August 2010 (as varied by paragraph 1 of the Order of Mr Justice Nicol dated 20 August 2010) be continued until final judgment or further Order in the meantime"

27. I am informed that the Claimant has agreed that he will not enter judgment in default of defence without giving 21 days notice. I have not been told what further steps, if any, are expected to be taken in the proceedings. I make no comment upon that aspect of the matter in this judgment. But this may well be the last time this matter comes before the court. What I am being asked

to make is not a Final Order in the technical sense of that term. But it may well be the last order the court makes in the action. As two of the Media Organisations have reminded the court in their submissions on receipt of this draft, in such circumstances Art 6 may apply: *Micallef v Malta* 17056/06 para 85. **This order may be more effective to protect the Claimant's rights than a true Final Order would be. As Eady J said in X & Y v Persons Unknown** [2006] EWHC 2783 (QB)**,** [2007] EMLR 290 **at para 72:**

> ". . . the *Spycatcher* doctrine [*Attorney-General v Newspaper Publishing Plc* [1988] Ch 333 at 375, 380] would go on inhibiting third parties from publishing the relevant information notionally pending a trial which would never actually take place. The *Spycatcher* doctrine, as a matter of logic, has no application to a permanent injunction since, obviously, there is no longer any need to preserve the status quo pending a trial. This doctrine is directed at preventing a third party from frustrating the court's **purpose** of holding the ring: see eg the discussion in *Att.-Gen. v Punch Ltd* [2003] 1 AC 1046 at [87]–[88] in the Court of Appeal and at [95] in the House of Lords; and *Jockey Club v Buffham* [2003] QB 462 (Gray J)."

28. The witness statement of the Claimant made on 13 August was directed primarily to the substantive relief claimed in the proceedings. It dealt only indirectly with the ancillary provisions of the order, such as the application for anonymity and other derogations from the principle of open justice.

29. Accordingly, in his statement of 22 October Mr Shear **addressed specifically the derogations from open justice**.

30. The evidence of Mr Shear brings the court up to date with the information which is in the **public domain**. It is not suggested that there has been any breach of the Orders of Nicol J. **The point made is that what is in the public domain is evidence of what is likely to occur if the anonymity and other derogations from open justice are not continued.** Much of the publicity about this case has been in the form of guesses, or invitations to the public to guess, the identity of the Claimant. There have also been similar publications and speculations on the **internet**. Such publications and speculations are not uncommon after the court grants an injunction on the application of an unnamed claimant.

31. Mr Shear's evidence is relevant to my conclusion as to the amount of information that could be given in this judgment, or my order, relating to the subject matter of the action. But I cannot set out what that evidence is without incurring the risk of identifying the Claimant.

THE LAW ON OPEN JUSTICE

32. I repeat what I wrote in my judgment on *Gray*. The principle of open justice

in English law long preceded the ECHR and the HRA. For recent cases on its importance see *R v Legal Aid Board ex p Kaim Todner* [1999] 1 Q.B. 966 per Lord Woolf MR at 977 and *R (Binyam Mohamed) v Secretary of State for Foreign and Commonwealth Affairs* [2010] EWCA Civ 65 at [38]–[42]. So far as material to this case the relevant parts of Art 6 are:

> " . . . Judgment shall be pronounced publicly but the press and public may be excluded from all or part of the trial . . . where the protection of the private life of the parties so require[s], or to the extent strictly necessary in the opinion of the court in special circumstances where publicity would prejudice the interests of justice".

33. In so far as Art 6 contains the words "to the extent strictly necessary in the opinion of the court in special circumstances where publicity would prejudice the interests of justice", it is similar in substance to the common law as summarised in *Guardian.* In *Scott v Scott* [1913] A.C. 417 at 438, 463 and 477 Lords Haldane, Atkinson and Shaw said:

> "(438) . . . unless it be strictly necessary for the attainment of justice, there can be no power in the Court to hear in camera either a matrimonial cause or any other where there is a contest between the parties. He who maintains that by no other means than by such a hearing can justice be done may apply for an unusual procedure. But he must make out his case strictly, and bring it up to the standard which the underlying principle requires. He may be able to show that the evidence can be effectively brought before the Court in no other fashion. He may even be able to establish that subsequent publication must be prohibited for a time or altogether. But this further conclusion he will find more difficult in a matrimonial case than in the case of the secret process, where the objection to publication is not confined to the mere difficulty of giving testimony in open Court. In either case he must satisfy the Court that by nothing short of the exclusion of the public can justice be done. The mere consideration that the evidence is of an unsavoury character is not enough, any more than it would be in a criminal Court, and still less is it enough that the parties agree in being reluctant to have their case tried with open doors . . . If the evidence to be given is of such a character that it would be impracticable to force an unwilling witness to give it in public, the case may come within the exception to the principle that in these proceedings, . . . a public hearing must be insisted on in accordance with the rules which govern the general procedure in English Courts of justice. A mere desire to consider feelings of delicacy or to exclude from publicity details which it would be desirable not to publish is not, I repeat, enough as the law now stands. I think that to justify an order for hearing in camera it must be shown that the paramount object

of securing that justice is done would really be rendered doubtful of attainment if the order were not made.

(463) . . . in public trial is to found, on the whole, the best security for the pure, impartial, and efficient administration of justice, the best means for winning for it public confidence and respect.

(477) . . . Only in proportion as publicity has place can any of the checks applicable to judicial injustice operate. Where there is no publicity there is no justice.' 'Publicity is the very soul of justice. It is keenest spur to exertion and the surest of all guards against improbity. It keeps the judge himself while trying under trial.' 'The security of securities is publicity.' But amongst historians the grave and enlightened verdict of Hallam, in which he ranks the publicity of judicial proceedings even higher than the rights of Parliament as a guarantee of public security, is not likely to be forgotten: 'Civil liberty in this kingdom has two direct guarantees; the open administration of justice according to known laws truly interpreted, and fair construction of evidence; and the right of Parliament, without let or interruption, to enquire into, and obtain redress of, public grievances. Of these, the first is by far the most indispensable; nor can the subjects of any state be reckoned to enjoy a real freedom, where this condition is not found both in its judicial institutions and in their constant exercise ".

34. The last clause of Art 6 also qualifies the word "necessary" with the word "strictly". It requires that an order be "strictly necessary" where the reason for making the order is that "publicity would prejudice the interests of justice". Lord Rodger did not mention Art 6 in *Guardian* and for the purposes of the present case it appears to add nothing to the principle of open justice as prescribed by *Scott v Scott.*

35. The relevant parts of Arts 8 and 10 are:

"Article 8 Right to respect for private and family life

1 Everyone has the right to respect for his private and family life, his home and his correspondence.

2 There shall be no interference by a public authority with the exercise of this right except such as is in accordance with the law and is necessary in a democratic society . . . for the prevention of disorder or crime, for the protection of health or morals, or for the protection of the rights and freedoms of others.

Article 10 Freedom of Expression

1 Everyone has the right to freedom of expression. This right shall include freedom to hold opinions and to receive and impart information and ideas without interference by public authority . . .

2 The exercise of these freedoms, since it carries with it duties and responsibilities, may be subject to such formalities, conditions, restrictions or penalties as are prescribed by law and are necessary in a democratic society, . . . for the prevention of disorder or crime, for the protection of health or morals, for the protection of the **reputation** or rights of others, for preventing the disclosure of information received in confidence, or for maintaining the authority and impartiality of the judiciary."

COMMON GROUND BETWEEN THE SUBMISSIONS

36. The parties accept that, as most recently stated in *Gray*, the following principles apply when the issue of anonymity is being considered (this being the formulation in Mr Tomlinson's skeleton argument):

(1) As a general rule, the names of the parties to an action should be included in orders and judgments of the court *(ibid,* para 1).

(2) There is no general exception for cases where private matters are in issue *(loc. cit.).*

(3) An order for anonymity is a derogation from the principle of open justice and an interference with the Article 10 rights of the **public at large**.

(4) Where the court is asked to restrain the publication of the names of the parties and the subject matter of the claim [on the ground that restraint is necessary under Art 8] the question is whether the there is sufficient general, public interest in publishing a report of the proceedings which identifies a party to justify any resulting curtailment of his right and his family's right to respect for their private and family life *(ibid,* para 4).

(5) An order for anonymity and reporting restrictions should not be made simply because the parties consent: parties cannot waive the rights of the public *(ibid,* para 33)

(6) An anonymity order made by a Judge, on the first hearing of an injunction application does not last for the duration of the proceedings but must be reviewed at the return date *(ibid,* para 34)

37. For the purposes of proposition (4) the Court must first find that Art 8 is engaged before proceeding to the question of public interest, as Nicol J did. Nicol J asked the question (in para 15 above) in the form approved by the Court of Appeal for without notice applications in ***ASG v GSA*** [2009] EWCA Civ 1574 para [5] (see also *Micallef v Malta* 17056/06 para 86). That is a different basis from that which applies at the return date. Waller LJ said in that case that the test is:

"Is there a sufficient degree of likelihood that the claimant will win

at trial to justify an ex parte injunction for *a short period* before a full inter partes hearing?" (emphasis added)

It follows from this (point (6)) that the ancillary provisions of the Orders of 13 and 20 August were, like the substantive provisions, to last only until the return date. **The Judge hearing the case at the return date must come to his own view as to the necessity for such derogations in the light of the facts as they are known to him at that time. An anonymity order made on a without notice application such as the one on 13 August is not to be understood as applying indefinitely.** The parties before me both accepted that was so.

38. In *Gray* at para [1] I cited *Lord Browne of Madingley v Associated Newspapers Ltd* [2008] 1 QB 103, [2007] EWCA Civ 295, [2007] EMLR 538 ("*Browne*") as authority for the proposition that claims for injunctions to restrain publication of private information enjoy no general exception from the principles of open justice. It is authority for that proposition, but, as Mr Tomlinson rightly submitted, it is not a clear example of that principle being applied. There is a distinction between cases where the applicant for such an injunction is successful, and cases where he is not. In *Browne* the proceedings were **initially anonymised and heard in private, both at first instance and on appeal.** The claimant was asking for an injunction in relation to five categories of information (*Browne* para [12]). He was successful in relation to two categories, but was unsuccessful in relation to three (paras [46] and [62]).

39. The Court of Appeal did not directly address the basis on which it made its decision to name the claimant. It said at para [3]:

> "granted that the judgment relates to some matters concerning the parties, there is no good reason why they should continue to be referred to anonymously".

THE LEVELS OF INFORMATION AN ORDER MAY SPECIFY

40. So far as the identity of a party is concerned, there is only one level of disclosure: the party will be named or not named. Further, as submitted on behalf of Guardian News and Media Ltd, and supported by Mr Spearman, if it is to be necessary to protect it pursuant to Arts 8 and 10(2), private information has to cross "**a certain level of seriousness**": *R (Wood) v Commissioner of Police of the Metropolis* [2009] EWCA Civ 414; [2010] 1 WLR 123 paras [22]–[23]. **This principle applies both to the identity of the Claimant, and to any information about the subject matter of the action.** To publish that a person has obtained an injunction restraining the publication of private information will not normally, of itself, cross that threshold, but will depend on all the circumstances. Whether the information is sufficiently serious may depend

upon the identity of a claimant. Resolution No 1165 (1998) of the Parliamentary Assembly of the Council of Europe on the right to privacy includes:

> **"6 . . . public figures must recognise that the special position they occupy in society—in many cases by choice—automatically entails increased pressure on their privacy.**
>
> **7. Public figures are persons holding public office and/or using public resources and, more broadly speaking, all those who play a role in public life, whether in politics, the economy, the arts, the social sphere, sport or in any other domain."**

41. So far as the subject matter of the action is concerned the position is more complicated. In *Browne* the Court differentiated between information at various levels of generality. At para [5] the Court distinguished between "referring in broad terms to the kind of information" and "detail". Amongst the categories of information for which the claimant was seeking an injunction were "the details of the **relationship** between himself and JC" (para [7]) and "the bare fact" of that **relationship** (para [12] category (c)).

42. The claimant succeeded in obtaining an injunction restraining publication of the details. He failed in respect of the bare fact of the **relationship**. But his failure on that category was only on account of the other categories of information (referred to as (b) and (d)) on which the claimant was unsuccessful. See para [61]. Categories (b) and (d) on which the claimant was unsuccessful related to information about misuse of the resources and **confidential information** of BP plc, of which the claimant was at that time the group chief executive. The Court accepted that category (c), the fact of the **relationship**, concerned the claimant's private life (para [60]) in that case.

43. Of course, in other cases, the fact of a **relationship** may not be private at all. A personal **relationship** between two individuals will be a matter of public record if there is a marriage or civil partnership. And there are many less formal personal **relationships** or partnerships which the parties are proud to publicise to all the world. So, too, business or official **relationships** may be either private or public, depending upon the circumstances of the case.

44. In *Browne* there were three levels of information concerning the **relationship** between the claimant and the individual referred to as JC. The Court was considering whether or not to enjoin (or permit to be disclosed) in its order information as follows:

    i) no information about the subject matter of the action

    ii) "the kind of information" the subject matter of the action

    iii) "the bare fact of the **relationship**"

    iv) "details of the **relationship**".

45. If the court is not minded to enjoin disclosure of details of the **relationship**, then it will obviously not enjoin disclosure of the other alternatives. But if it is minded to enjoin disclosure of the details of the **relationship**, then it will have to decide whether in its judgment or order it discloses:

i) no information at all about the subject matter of the action, or

ii) the kind of information to which the action relates, and,

iii) in some cases, the fact of any **relationship** to which the action relates.

46. Another example is *McKennitt v Ash* [2006] EWCA Civ 1714; [2008] 1 QB 73. It does not appear that the claimant in that case ever asked for anonymity. What she did ask for were orders to prevent disclosure of the information which was the subject matter of the action. Eady J made such an order, as did the Court of Appeal. The Order of the Court of Appeal is to be found at [2008] 1 QB at p77. The Court of Appeal strongly endorsed the way that Eady J had dealt with the matter, and gave its own brief reasons for the Order it made at paras [1]–[2] and [81] of the judgment of Buxton LJ. Eady J and the Court of Appeal described the information which was the subject matter of the action at paras [19]–[25]: some items are not explained at all (eg para [19] and [25]), others are generically described (eg para [23] "the state of the first claimant's health"). In the present case the interim order of Nicol J, and the form of consent order, disclose no information at all about the subject matter of the action. All that information is in the **Confidential Schedule**. I must consider whether in my Order and in this judgment I can disclose more information about the subject matter of the action, and thereby make a less serious derogation from open justice.

SUBMISSIONS OF MR TOMLINSON

47. Mr Tomlinson submits that in most cases it is the first of the two alternatives he mentioned in paragraph 8 above will be the appropriate one, **namely that the court should disclose *the kind or nature of the information* in question in the action, without naming the claimant.** But in some cases even that is not possible: the information about a claimant which is in the **public domain**, whether before or after an interim injunction is granted, may be such that the publication of any information at all about the subject matter of the action will in practice reveal to the public the facts of any **relationship** in question. In those cases the court should, as in the draft consent order, disclose no information at all about the subject matter of the action.

48. Mr Tomlinson submits that where the court is considering whether to disclose the name of the claimant **or, in the alternative**, some information about the subject matter of the action, **there are reasons why the court should in general prefer to disclose the subject matter rather than the name are.** Those reasons are as follows:

(1) In general, the public interest in open justice will be best served by knowing the subject matter of the proceedings rather than the "bare identity" of the claimant.

(2) It will often be the case that **public domain** information concerning the claimant will mean that the nature of the information in issue is obvious so that if the proceedings are not anonymised it will be clear that the identified claimant is seeking to prevent disclosure of information of a particular kind.

(3) If a claimant is named there will, almost inevitably, be speculation and rumour about the likely nature of the information covered by the injunction. Of course, unless the nature of the information is obvious, much of this speculation and rumour will be false and unfounded. Nevertheless it is established in Standard Verlags GmbH v Austria (No 2) Judgment of 4 June 2009, ECtHR, para 53 that

> "even **public figure**s may legitimately expect to be protected against the propagation of unfounded rumours relating to **intimate** aspects of their private life".

49. Mr Tomlinson relies on the following further points:

(a) The general public interest served by identifying this Claimant as a person who has obtained a privacy injunction is very limited. He contrasts the obvious public interest in identifying the individuals in the *Guardian News and Media* case. They had entered into public debates about matters of high public interest arising out of the proceedings, namely the appropriateness of Government counter-terrorism measures. The Claimant has not entered into any such debate.

(b) It is likely that the publication of the Claimant's name would lead to the public becoming aware of the nature of the information covered by the injunction in the particular circumstances of this case. This is not just a matter of "general speculation" as to the nature of the kind of information likely to be covered by an injunction of this type (as discussed in *Gray* [55]) but focussed and accurate inference in the light of the circumstances. In any event, "speculation" can itself be **intrusive**' (see *Standard Verlags GmbH* v *Austria (No2)*). This is not a matter of the press "abusing their freedom to report" but of interference with the Claimant's Art 8 rights as a direct result of the publication of his name.

(c) In any event, the publication of the Claimant's name would lead to large scale media **intrusion.** He would be photographed and questioned, and other people would be subject to unwanted media attention. This coverage and attention would, in itself, constitute a very substantial **intrusion** into the private and family life of himself and of any other individual concerned, and would be very distressing for all of them. Of course, such attention may be a necessary incident of a person invoking the Court's process, but it is a matter which the Court can properly take into account when balancing the relevant interests and performing its duty to ensure that the protections given to the Claimant's Art 8 rights are "practical and effective". There is a public interest in ensuring that individuals are not deterred from seeking legal redress through the courts by the consequences of court orders being made public.

(e) The defendant in this case is NGN, a major media organisation, and it has accepted that anonymity is appropriate.

SUBMISSIONS OF MR SPEARMAN

50. Mr Spearman submits that Mr Tomlinson overstates the importance of the public knowing the subject matter of the action, and understates the public interest in disclosure of a name. This is not a case where the claimant could say he would be deterred from coming to court. As illustrated by cases cited in *Guardian* and *Gray*, there are many types of litigation where individuals are not deterred from coming to court by the fact that even **intimate** details of their health and other private matters will be aired in public.

51. Mr Spearman refers to para [62] of *Guardian* where Lord Rodger explained the importance of identifying parties to litigation in the light of other recent decisions of the House of Lords, including *re S* para 34 and in *In re British Broadcasting Corpn* [2009] 3 WLR 142, 152, para 25. He said:

> **"What's in a name? 'A lot' the press would answer . . . "**

52. Mr Spearman submits that it is always important for the public to know who has obtained an injunction from the court. There are examples from the past of rich and powerful individuals who have repeatedly applied for orders from the court, and who, with hindsight, are now known to have been doing so abusively. The naming of claimants may also be important, not because their identity is important, but because if they are named it can be seen that others are not the subject of suspicion as being the persons about whom rumours or true information is circulating. The number of individuals whom the public might suspect of being the claimant is in many cases quite small, and it is unfair on those who are not the claimant (and their families) for there to be speculation that they might be the claimant.

53. Further he submits that if the claimant is not identified, there will in any event be speculation and rumours about the identity of the claimant. An anonymity order will not stop speculation and rumours. Even if the court can give some information about the subject matter of the action, the amount of information the court can give will be limited, because the more detail the court gives in its order or judgment the greater the likelihood of so called

jigsaw identification. So in truth it is impossible to give to the public at the same time both no information about the identity of the claimant and full information about the subject matter of the action. If the claimant is not named, the amount of information that can be given about the subject matter of the action will inevitably be small. So if the public is given the name of the claimant, there will be little lost in terms of information that will be given about the subject matter of the action. Whereas if the claimant is not named, the public will get very little information at all, whether as to the claimant's identity or as to the subject matter of the action.

54. On the facts of this case, and of many such cases, a claimant could not say that the prospect of being named will deter him from coming to court. In those cases where there is before the application is made for an interim injunction already substantial information in the **public domain** about the claimant (or a threat to put substantial material in the **public domain**), the choices open to a prospective claimant are likely to be limited. The choices are likely to be between submitting to continuing **intrusive** publicity without a court injunction, or obtaining an injunction which at least limits the scope of such publicity. In most cases an application for an injunction in which the claimant is named is unlikely to make the publicity worse from the claimant's point of view than it would be if he obtained an injunction anonymously.

55. If a claimant is named in circumstances where there is already information about him in the **public domain**, it does not follow that the subject matter of the injunction must be the information which has most recently been put in the **public domain**. Reasonable members of the public can be expected to understand that no such inference can be drawn. So the fact that a named person has obtained an injunction restraining misuse of private information will not of itself lead a reasonable person to conclude that the subject matter of the injunction is the information most recently put into the **public domain**. On the other hand, disclosure of some information about the subject matter increases the likelihood of the public correctly inferring the identity of the claimant. So an order that is to be effective in protecting the identity of the claimant will have to tell the public little or nothing. Such is the form of consent order in this case.

DISCUSSION

56. The evidence of the Claimant and Mr Shear does **not** include a statement that the Claimant **would have been deterred** from commencing this action if he had expected that his name would be identified in the court documents. It is difficult to see how a person in the Claimant's position could credibly make such a statement.

57. I accept Mr Spearman's submission that, in those cases where there is, or

there is a threat to put, substantial information in the **public domain** about the claimant before the application is made for an interim injunction, the choices open to a person considering whether or not to make a claim are limited. **The present case is not one where naming the claimant would put him in a worse position than he would have been if he had not applied for an injunction**. If he had expected to be named, that would have been unlikely to deter him from applying for the injunction on 13 August.

58. It is important to bear in mind what privacy injunctions are intended to achieve. **In some privacy cases the information sought to be protected will be truly secret. One example may be the paternity of a child where the mother has successfully withheld that information** (as happened in the case of a French Minister of Justice: "Minister's Mystery Baby" *The Observer*, Sunday 4 January 2009). Another example may be that the applicant is suffering from a particular condition or disease (eg the case of the late President Mitterand *Plon (Societe) v France* 58148/00 [2004] ECHR 200; 42 EHRR 36). Such cases bear some comparison to cases about trade or official secrets: if the secret is revealed there is nothing the court can do to undo **what has been done. In cases of trade or official secrets an injunction may thereafter be futile.**

59. But in many privacy cases the information sought to be protected is not secret in that sense, or, **even if it is, once the secret is revealed, there is still something to be achieved by an injunction**. Art 8 is about interference with a persons' private and family life. There may be **such interference by the repetition in the press of information even when that information is not secret or unknown**. As *Plon v France* (paras [14], [34] and [47]) illustrates, this is be because the **repetition of known facts** about an individual may amount to unjustified interference with the private lives not only of that person and but also of those who are involved with him (in that case his widow and children) in the matters which are the subject of the action. It may also lead to **harassment**: *von Hannover v Germany* (59320/00); (2005) 40 EHRR 1 para [68]. The widow and children were parties in the *Plon* case in the national courts. But the obligation of the Court under s 6 of the HRA (not to act incompatibly with Convention rights) obliges the Court to have regard to the Art 8 rights of persons **who are not parties to the action, as well as to the rights of the claimant.**

60. It is to be noted that in the *Standard Verlags* case in the first instance proceedings in Austria, as in *McKennitt,* there is no suggestion that the names of the individuals concerned were anonymised. The two men concerned were Mr Klestil, the Federal President of Austria and Mr Scheibner, the head of a parliamentary group. Mrs Klestil-Loefler was a **public figure** in her own right, as well as being first lady. The complainants to whom Standard Verlags Gmbh had been ordered to pay compensation were Mr Scheibner and

Mrs Klestil-Loefler. The names of all three are given in the judgment of the ECHR. **As a matter of practice, the ECHR does give anonymity to those whose private lives are said to be the subject of unnecessary or disproportionate interference, and could have done so in that case if it had thought it necessary to do so.** See *A v United Kingdom* 35373/97 (2003) 36 EHRR 51 paras [13] and [17], where the applicant and her family had been named in Parliament as "neighbours from hell", as a result of which she was harassed and had to move home.

61. The agreement by NGN to anonymity is relied on by Mr Tomlinson. **I attach little weight to it**. The court has not been given (and would not expect to be given) any information as to any agreement or arrangement that may have been made between NGN and the Claimant. It is open to the parties to settle litigation such this in consideration of an agreement for the publication of other information, or of other matters entirely unrelated to the subject matter of the action. **There may be an incentive upon a news publisher to agree that a claimant should enjoy anonymity in consideration of some other benefit the claimant may be able to give to the news publisher**. It is not to be assumed that news publishers are always concerned to protect the Art 10 rights of the public and their competitors. I do not suggest that in this case there has been such a bargain at the expense of the public. **I simply decline to attach weight to NGN's agreement to the form of consent order, in circumstances where there is no evidence as to why it has been agreed in that form.**

62. Having considered the evidence, I too have no doubt that the private life considerations of Art 8 are engaged here, both as to the subject matter of the action, and, to a much lesser extent, as to the identification of the Claimant. **The proceedings are likely to attract publicity, and if the Claimant is identified that will result in some interference with the private life of himself and his family**. There is no suggestion of any public interest or other possible justification in disclosure of the information which is the subject matter of the action.

63. **It is implicit in the form of the consent order, and I accept, that in the present case it would not be possible to make an order or give a judgment which disclosed any information about the subject matter of the action which did not thereby make it likely that the Claimant would be identified. To identify both the subject matter and the Claimant would defeat the purpose of the proceedings. Accordingly, the only practical question open to the Court is whether to withhold the identity of the Claimant, in addition to withholding all information about the subject matter of the action. In this case the alternatives canvassed by Mr Tomlinson (para 8 above) are**

theoretical not real. The only real choice is to allow the public to know the Claimant's identity or to allow them to know nothing at all about the action.

64. I remind myself that where the proposed justification for anonymity is that identification would prevent the attainment of justice, the test that the Claimant has to satisfy is that of strict necessity (paras 33 and 34 above). The Claimant has not shown to that high standard that the object of achieving justice in this case would be rendered doubtful if the anonymity order were not made. It is not possible to do perfect justice to all parties and to the public at the same time. In my judgment the proposed order will be effective to achieve justice, and will give all necessary protection the private lives of the Claimant and any others concerned**, if it identifies the Claimant, but gives information about the subject matter only in the Confidential Schedule.** It will be served on newspaper publishers (as the earlier Orders have been). They will know what they can publish in the future and what they cannot publish. Nothing will stop people from speculating in private. And the court cannot stop much of the speculation that takes place on the **internet**. **But an Order will limit the extent to which the private lives of the Claimant and others are interfered with notwithstanding that it identifies the Claimant.** So the general principle of open justice provides, in this case, sufficient general, public interest in publishing a report of proceedings which identifies the Claimant to justify any resulting curtailment of the rights of the Claimant and his family to respect for their private and family life

CONCLUSION ON ANONYMITY

65. Accordingly, I will not make an Order requiring that the identity of the Claimant be not disclosed. His identity will therefore be disclosed in any order I make. However, this must be subject to what is to happen during the period pending any appeal. Otherwise, by naming the Claimant, I would render the right of appeal nugatory.

OTHER PROVISIONS OF THE ORDER

66. Since I made clear that I would deliver an open judgment, the parties asked that I should add a new provision to the Order. It is that the **Defendant must not disclose (or cause anyone else to disclose) any information which identifies, or any information which is liable to lead to the identification of, the subject matter of this action (that is the information which is in the Confidential Schedule), save for that contained in any public judgment and Order of the court.**

67. **This is a form of order adapted from that made by Sharp J, and explained by her in her judgment in DFT v TFD** [2010] EWHC 2335 (QB)**, in particular in para [29]. Subject to the further matters mentioned below, I would be willing to include that provision in the order I make.**

68. Mr Spearman made submissions about other provisions of this Order. However, in the light of the conclusion that I had reached on anonymity when I circulated this judgment in draft, I invited the parties to submit to me a revised form of order. As I requested, the draft is a freestanding order which does not require the reader to read any earlier order. I consider that below.

69. The parties, and the other publishers to whom this judgment was circulated in draft, welcomed the giving of an open judgment in this case and cases like it. The giving of such judgment is clearly desirable in principle. **That is the primary means by which judges satisfy the public that they have given consideration to the matters they are required to consider before they make orders affecting the rights of the public**. But the holding of oral hearings and giving of detailed reasoned judgments require time and other resources. **Before such a judgment can be handed down, it must be circulated not only for the usual editorial corrections. The parties must have the right to make submissions as to matters which should be included and excluded**. That too is an exercise that can be costly in time and other resources. That may not always be necessary or proportionate: in some cases the reasons for giving anonymity will be obvious. In *Guardian* at para 2 Lord Rodger said:

> "the present appeals show that an order ("anonymity order") may be made, often by consent of both parties, without the court considering in any detail what is the basis or justification for it".

Those words, and the detailed consideration the Supreme Court gave to the anonymity orders both in that case and the case of *Secretary of State for the Home Department v AP (No 2)* [2010] UKSC 26, [2010] 1 WLR 1652, may be taken as guidance that judges should give detailed reasons for making anonymity orders. There are further models in the detailed judgments on anonymity given by the judges in Northern Ireland in *A (A minor) & Others v A health & Social Services Trust* [2010] NIQB 108 and *R A, Re Judicial Review* [2010] NIQB 27. On the other hand, the ECHR did not explain in its judgment in *A v United Kingdom* why it did not identify the applicant in its judgment dismissing her application. It may be inferred that the reason was obvious: in order not to give an occasion for further **harassment** of her.

70. As stated in para 4 above, where the Court is required to decide whether to grant (or continue) derogations from open justice, the information necessary for the Court to carry out its obligations under HRA s 6 **must be provided to the Court by the party asking for the order.** In most cases the information the Court requires should be **in the form of a witness statement from the party concerned and in a section of the statement clearly addressing the derogations that are asked for**. There should also be **a short skeleton argument directing the judge's attention to the applicable law**, to the **relevant parts** of the evidence and the **grounds of the application.** It cannot

be assumed that all judges will have at the forefront of their minds the applicable law, as Nicol J did in this case, particularly when asked to make such orders in urgent applications made out of hours. Advocates must have in mind their obligations to the court to see that **correct legal procedures and forms are used** (*Memory Corpn v Sidhu (No 2)* [2000] 1 WLR 1442, 1460). I make clear that I cast no blame on the parties in this case, or their legal representatives, given that the first judgment stating that anonymity orders could not be given by consent in privacy injunctions was *Gray*.

SUBMISSIONS FROM OTHER PUBLISHERS

71. **When I circulated this judgment in draft I asked the Claimant's solicitors to give me the names of those publishers who they had served with the orders of Nicol J**. They were the Media Organisations. All these publishers publish a number of different titles and web sites. **I circulated the draft of the judgment to each of these**. In doing so I invited them to make representations (if so advised) as to any matter which should, or should not, be included in the judgment, in addition to editorial corrections.

72. I received written responses, and have taken some of the representations into account in revising the preceding part of this judgment. Mr Tomlinson and Mr Spearman have made further submissions in writing in response. **Other complaints, representations and submissions from third parties included the following:**

    i) That they had not been given, but should have been given, **notice** of the application to Nicol J: Associated Newspapers Ltd, Express Newspapers Ltd, MGN Ltd, Guardian News and Media Ltd

    ii) Complaints that they had not been given **copies of the witness statement of Mr Shear and the skeleton argument** of Mr Tomlinson submitted to me on 22 October, and other documents: MGN Ltd

    iii) Complaints that the provisions of **CPR PD 25A para 9.2** (persons served with the order to be provided on request with materials read by the judge and a note of the hearing) had not been complied with: MGN Ltd

    iv) Complaints that the Claimant had not notified them of the **return date**: MGN Ltd (the Claimant has apologised to MGN Ltd for this omission), Guardian News and Media Ltd

    v) That applicants should be required to undertake to the Court to keep third parties who have been served with an order, and who are bound by it under the *Spycatcher* principle, **informed as to what is going to happen** in the action, including prior notice of any hearings: MGN Ltd, Guardian News and Media Ltd

    vi) That the **information relied** on in support of any application for a

derogation from open justice (see para 70 above) should be served on third parties: MGN Ltd

vii) The provisions of **CPR PD 25A para 9.2 should not be dispensed with,** or made subject to any condition (such as are in paras 5 and 6 of the draft Order set out below), alternatively any condition other than an undertaking to protect private information: all six Media Organisations.

73. **There has been no application by any third party to vary or discharge the Orders of Nicol J. These points are raised as matters of general principle.** They were not canvassed at the hearing on 22 October, and the parties have not responded to them for that reason. They are points that merit consideration, but not in this already long judgment. Some of these points are already the subject of other judgments (eg *TUV v Persons Unknown* [2010] EWHC 853 (QB) paras [10-[16]).

THE REVISED FORM OF ORDER

74. The revised form of draft order submitted by the parties includes the following as its substantive provisions, to run until the trial of this action or further order in the meantime:

"**The prohibited acts**

1. The Defendant must not publish, republish, syndicate, use, communicate or disclose to any person:

(a) Any information concerning the subject matter of these proceedings save for that contained in the public judgment of the Court handed down on 5 November 2010 and/or

(b) Any of the information set out in the **Confidential Schedule** to this Order (together "the Information").

PROVIDED THAT nothing in this Order shall prevent the publication, disclosure or communication of any of the Information:

(i) by the Defendant (1) to legal advisers instructed in relation to these proceedings for the **purpose** of obtaining legal advice in relation to these proceedings or (2) for the purposes of carrying this Order into effect or (3) for the **purpose** of these proceedings (including for the **purpose** of gathering evidence in relation to these proceedings) provided that any person to whom such information is disclosed must first be either given a copy of this Order or notified of its substance and effect;

(ii) by the Defendant of any part of the Information that is in the **public domain** as the result of national media publication (otherwise than as a result of breach of this Order).

[(iii) by or to any person named in the **Confidential Schedule** *for purely*

private and personal purposes and in confidence, (that is, on the express understanding that there will be no further disclosure of the Information), with their closest friends, their immediate family and professional advisers.]

Confidential information in Statements of Case

2. Anything which may reveal any information or purported information described in the **Confidential Schedule** to this Order shall be excluded from the statements of case served in this action, and included in a separate schedule served with the statement of case.

3. Pursuant to CPR 5.4C(4) any person who is not a party to this action may not obtain from the court records any copy of any confidential schedule served with any statement of case. Any non party seeking access to or copies of any confidential schedule from the court file must make an application to the Court, having previously given at least 3 days' notice of the application to the solicitors for the parties.

4. If any non-party at any time makes an application to the Court under CPR 5.4C(2) for permission to obtain from the Court records a copy of any other document, other than a statement of case, or of any communication, such non-party must give at least 3 days' notice of the application to the solicitors for all parties.

Provision of Documents and Information to Third Parties

5. The Claimant shall not be required pursuant to CPR 25 PD 9.2 or otherwise to provide any third party served with a copy of this order with:

(a) a copy of any materials read to or by the Judge, including material prepared after the hearing at the direction of the Judge or in compliance with the order; and/or

(b) a note of the hearing

save where the third party (1) specifically requests the same and (2) provides written undertakings to the court (i) that these documents will not be copied or reproduced except for the purposes of any application to vary or discharge this Order (ii) that they will be kept securely and (iii) that these documents and the information contained therein shall only be used (save to the extent that such information is already in the **public domain**) for the said purposes.

6. Any person who has made any such request may apply to the Court to vary these provisions or for directions.

Hearing in Private

7. Pursuant to CPR 39.2(3)(a)(c) and (g), the hearing of the application to which this order relates be heard in private and pursuant to section 6 of

the Human Rights Act 1998, there be no reporting of the same. For the avoidance of doubt, nothing in this provision shall prevent the reporting of the Court's public judgment dated 5 November 2010.

Variation or Discharge of this Order

8. The Defendant or anyone served with or notified of this Order may apply to the Court to vary or discharge this Order (or so much of it as affects that person), but they must first give not less than 48 hours written notice to the Claimant's solicitors. If any evidence is to be relied upon in support of the application, the substance of it must be communicated in writing to the Claimant's solicitors at the time of giving notice or as soon as possible thereafter".

75. In addition, the undertakings given to the Court by the Claimant are:

"Schedule 1

Undertakings given to the Court by the Claimant:

(1) If the Court later finds that this Order has caused loss to the Defendant and decides that the Defendant should be compensated for that loss, the Claimant will comply with any Order the Court may make.

(2) If the Court later finds that this Order has caused loss to any person or company (other than the Defendant) to whom the Claimant has given notice of this Order, and decides that such person should be compensated for that loss, the Claimant will comply with any Order the Court may make.

(3) If for any reason this Order ceases to have effect the Claimant will forthwith take all reasonable steps to inform, in writing, any person or company to whom he has given notice of this Order, or who he has reasonable grounds for supposing may act upon this Order, that this Order has ceased to be of effect.

(4) The Claimant will as soon as reasonably practicable give notice of this Order to the Defendant and will take all practicable steps to serve the Defendant with this Order and all supporting documents.

Schedule 2

Undertaking given to the Court by the Claimant's solicitors:

The Claimant's solicitors will prepare and retain until the conclusion of this intended action a full note of the hearing at which this Order was made."

76. The only provision not agreed between the parties is para 2(iii), which appears above underlined. This is referred to as a "friends and family clause".

77. Mr Spearman accepts that "NGN" is not entitled to seek the addition of this proviso in the light of the agreement between the parties.

78. Mr Tomlinson accepts that in principle such a clause may be appropriate in cases where the defendant is an individual, or where the claimant proposes to serve the order on a third party who is an individual, at least where the information the subject matter of the action is of a personal nature that such an individual may reasonably expect to discuss with friends and family. But he says that in this case there is no intention of serving the order on any third party who is an individual.

79. In the absence of full argument, I prefer to say nothing on this point, and to omit the proviso from my order.

CONCLUSION

80. This judgment is a public judgment. My conclusion is that the Claimant should not be granted anonymity. I will make the Order in the revised form agreed between the parties. But pending any order that may be made on any application for permission to appeal, the Claimant's name must remain anonymised.

Ntuli v Donald [2010] EWCA Civ 1276

Lord Justice Maurice Kay:

1. On 26 April 2010 Eady J granted an anonymised claimant an injunction restraining an anonymised defendant from doing specified but unpublishable things and further restraining the defendant and others from publishing the fact that the injunction had been sought and obtained. **This type of relief has become known as a superinjunction.** On this appeal the appellant/defendant seeks the discharge of the injunction in its entirety or, in the alternative, complains about its substantive terms. She also contends that the orders for anonymity and the non-disclosure of the application for and existence of the injunction were inappropriate. There is a cross-appeal whereby the respondent/claimant contends that the substantive injunction did not go far enough.

2. It will facilitate the writing and, indeed, reading of this judgment if I set out the result of the appeal and of the cross-appeal at the outset. **It is that the substantive injunction will remain but the order for anonymisation of the parties and the non-disclosure of the application for and the existence of the injunction will be discharged.** The judgment will be a public judgment. For this reason, some of it will be expressed in muted or anodyne terms.

3. The respondent/claimant is Howard Donald, one of the hugely successful "boy band" Take That. He has never married but he has had a number of **relationships** and he is the father of two children. The appellant/defendant is Adakini Ntuli. She is also a musician but is now a full-time single parent of two children. Mr Donald is not their father. During some of the time since 2000, Mr Donald and Ms Ntuli had a **relationship**. Its duration and intensity are matters of dispute. They did not cohabit. Mr Donald was also in other **relationships** during the same period. By the end of 2009 at the latest, the **relationship** between Mr Donald and Ms Ntuli seems to have come to an end. On 17 March 2010 she sent him a text message which included these words:

> "Why shud I continue 2 suffer financially 4 the sake of loyalty when selling my story will sort my life out?"

4. This led to communication between the parties and eventually between solicitors. Before the solicitors became involved, Ms Ntuli secured the services of **Max Clifford**, the well-known publicist, and she entered into negotiations with the **News of the World.**

5. On 25 March, Mr Donald made an *ex parte* application (on notice) to Eady J and obtained an interim injunction. **In addition to restraining the publication, use or disclosure of scheduled categories of confidential information** or **the existence of the proceedings, it provided for anonymisation of the parties**. It provided for a **return date** and the **privacy of the hearings,** together with the **sort of directions which are commonly used** in order to underwrite the security of such injunctions.

6. Following a two day hearing on the return date (30 March), Eady J reserved judgment until 26 April when judgment was handed down and, following submissions by counsel, the order which is the subject of the present appeal was made. It continued the anonymisation and the non-disclosure of the existence of the proceedings. In some respects it modified the terms of the substantive injunction. It will be sufficient for present purposes if I set out the selected parts of the order.

7. The principal substantive restraint in the original order restraining the publication of **confidential information** contains a proviso which was modified so as to read:

> **"PROVIDED THAT nothing in this paragraph of this Order shall prevent the Defendant from publishing, communicating or disclosing the following**
>
> **(a) any material that before service of this Order was already in, or that thereafter comes into, the public domain . . . ; or**
>
> **(b) the fact that the Claimant had a relationship with the Defendant;**

AND PROVIDED FURTHER THAT nothing in this paragraph of this Order shall prevent the Defendant from discussing any of the material which she has already discussed or wishes to discuss with any family member or close friend, nor from disclosing to any such family member or close friend the existence of these proceedings or the Claimant's interest in them."

8. **The Schedule of confidential information subject to the restraint upon publication, communication use or disclosure included this provision:**

   "Any **intimate**, personal or sexually explicit details about the **relationship** . . . including any facts of a sexual nature."

   Another category referred to "**intimate** or sexual activity". The order also contained undertakings by Ms Ntuli.

9. On this appeal, the respective stances of the parties are that Mr Donald maintains that the injunction ought to extend to a restriction upon publication, communication or disclosure of the mere fact of the fact of the **relationship** (subject to the family and close friend proviso), whereas Ms Ntuli maintains that, in the light of further undertakings which she offered to Eady J, there ought not to have been an injunction at all. **Alternatively, she contends that the injunction is too vague, particularly in relation to the use of the word "intimate".** In any event, her case is that the orders for anonymisation and non-disclosure of the existence of the proceedings are inappropriate. In this clash of human rights, Mr Donald seeks to uphold his privacy rights by reference to Article 8 of the ECHR and Ms Ntuli relies on her right to freedom of expression under Article 10. More mundanely, there is also an issue as to the order for costs made by Eady J. He ordered Ms Ntuli to pay two thirds of Mr Donald's costs of the application.

1. Should Eady J have granted an injunction?

10. Prior to the coming into force of the Human Rights Act 1998, the approach to cases such as this lacked coherence in domestic law. However, the basic principles of substantive law are now well-settled. In *Re: S (a child)(Identification: Restrictions on Publication)* [2005] 1 AC 593, at paragraph 17, Lord Steyn extracted four propositions from *Campbell v MGN Ltd* [2004] 2 AC 457:

    "First, neither Article [8 or 10] has *as such* precedence over the other. Secondly, where the values under the two Articles are in conflict, an intense focus on the comparative importance of the specific rights being claimed in the individual case is necessary. Thirdly, the justifications for interfering with or restricting each right must be taken into account. Finally, the proportionality test must be applied to each. For convenience, I will call this the ultimate balancing test."

11. So far as Article 8 is concerned, the ambit of private life was explained by Lord Nicholls in *Campbell* (at paragraph 21):

> **"Essentially, the touchstone of private life is whether in respect of the disclosed facts the person in question had a reasonable expectation of privacy."**

12. The authorities were rigorously reviewed by Buxton LJ in *McKennitt v Ash* [2008] QB 73, [2006] EWCA Civ 1714, where he said (at paragraph 11):

> ". . . in a case such as the present, where the complaint is of the wrongful publication of private information, the court has to decide two things. First, is the information private in the sense that it is in principle protected by Article 8? If 'no', that is the end of the case. *If 'yes', the second question arises:* in all the circumstances, must the interest of the owner of the private information yield to the right of freedom of expression conferred on the publisher by Article 10? The latter inquiry is commonly referred to as the balancing exercise."

13. He had previously (at paragraph 8) described that case as "what might be called old-fashioned breach of confidence by way of conduct inconsistent with a pre-existing **relationship**, rather than simply the **purloining** of private information". The present case can be so categorised.

14. In his judgment, Eady J adopted a distinction drawn by Lord Hoffmann (dissenting) in *Campbell* (at paragraph 60) where he said:

> **"The relatively anodyne nature of the additional details is in my opinion important and distinguishes this case from cases in which (for example) there is a public interest in the disclosure of a sexual relationship (say, between a politician and someone whom she has appointed to public office) but the addition of salacious details or intimate photographs is disproportionate and unacceptable. The latter, even if accompanying a legitimate disclosure of the sexual relationship, would be too obtrusive and demeaning."**

15. So far as "**salacious** details" are concerned, Eady J considered that **the court "should make every attempt to recognise" Lord Hoffmann's distinction** and grant relief accordingly in relation to facts of a sexual nature or other **intimate** personal details about a past **relationship**. He added that

> "**. . . these would be matters in respect of which the Applicant would have a reasonable expectation of privacy, unless it could be shown that there was a countervailing public interest or that such matters were already genuinely in the public domain.**"

16. He found no such countervailing public interest or **public domain** obstacle and, accordingly, he granted the injunction restraining publication of, amongst

other things, **"any intimate, personal or sexually explicit details about the relationship . . . including any facts of a sexual nature".**

17. Although this went further than the undertakings then offered on behalf of Ms Ntuli, she maintained and was willing to undertake before Eady J that she does not intend to publish any descriptions of sexual activity with Mr Donald. That remains her position. **Mr Hugh Tomlinson QC does not really dispute that the judge was right to ensure protection against publication of sexually explicit details,** although it is suggested that justice might be achieved by more expansive undertakings than were offered to Eady J. In that regard, as the scope of protection remains an issue, I do not think that the judge can be criticised for resorting to a prohibitory order. **The real complaint is that the judge was wrong to extend the injunction to cover "other information"** and that, in any event, the wording of the injunction lacks clarity. I shall consider these matters separately.

(1) "Other information"

18. **This ground of appeal focuses on what I may describe as "non-sexual information".** Accepting that some form of restraint is appropriate in relation to **sexually explicit** details, **Ms Ntuli's case is that the judge was wrong to extend the injunction to cover such information as conversations between the parties concerning the nature of their relationship, its future development and their non-sexual feelings.** Eady J expressed his conclusion in this way (at paragraphs 40 and 41):

> "I would certainly grant an injunction in respect of '**salacious** details' (to adopt Lord Hoffmann's phrase**), but I would go further and restrict the communication, with a view to publication to the media, of information as to intimate conversations or activities.** Wording of that kind would not prevent references to appearances or activities in public or social circumstances. **A similar distinction was recognized in Lord Browne of Madingley.** It has been acknowledged in that case and, for example, **in McKennitt v Ash that private communications between intimates** will generally give rise to a reasonable expectation of privacy under Article 8 . . . .
>
> "The mischief towards which the injunction is directed is that of revealing *publicly*, for **no good reason**, **intimate** details relating to a personal **relationship** in which each party has a reasonable expectation of privacy."

As I have related, the injunction does not extend to discussions with close friends and family.

19. The appeal on this issue is put on the basis that, although the judge correctly summarised the approach to be taken in accordance with "the new

methodology", he erred in his application of it in that he failed to carry out an analysis as to whether or not there was a reasonable expectation of privacy in relation to "the other information" but rather assumed that there was before carrying out "the ultimate balancing exercise". He then further erred by proceeding on the basis that Ms Ntuli had to establish a "substantial argument" for publication based on the public interest. At paragraph 34, the judge said:

> "I am not persuaded that there is any substantial argument for publication based on public interest. Applying the strict modern criteria to be found in the Strasbourg cases . . . ., **it seems to me that there is no reason to suppose that the revelation of the relationship would in any way contribute to a debate of general interest**. Nor would it serve to prevent the public being misled or lead to the exposure of hypocrisy."

20. The Strasbourg cases referred to include *Von Hannover v Germany* (2005) 40 EHRR 1, where the Court said (at paragraph 76):

> " . . . .the decisive factor in balancing the protection of private life against freedom of expression **should lie in the contribution that the published photos and articles make to a debate of general interest.** It is clear in the instant case that they made no such contribution since the applicant exercises no official function and the photos and articles related exclusively to details of her private life."

21. This reflects recent domestic jurisprudence, for example the speech of Baroness Hale in *Campbell*, where she said (at paragraph 149):

> **"The political and social life of the community, and the intellectual, artistic or personal development of individuals, are not obviously assisted by pouring over the intimate details of a fashion model's private life."**

22. Having criticised the judge for analytical shortcomings, Mr Tomlinson emphasises the following points. As to a reasonable expectation of privacy, he refers to (a) the fact that Mr Donald is a **public figure**, some of whose other **relationships** have received media coverage; (b) his own openness about some immature sexual activity about 20 years ago; (c) the fact that, unlike the claimant in *McKennitt*, he had never sought to extract a promise of non-disclosure from Ms Ntuli during the course of the **relationship**; (d) the unlikelihood of any significant damage to Mr Donald's career or family life in the event of disclosure; and (e) the nature and **purpose** of Ms Ntuli's desired publication, identified as the exercise of *her* Article 8 rights of self-development and autonomy and her Article 10 rights of freedom of expression. Turning to the balancing exercise as between the respective Convention rights of the parties, he submits that the "other information" is

not "core private information" but simply the story of a failed **relationship** which should be given a very low privacy value. He refers again to Mr Donald's past openness about **relationships** and the unlikelihood of significant damage resulting from publication. He places particular emphasis at this stage on Ms Ntuli's "need" to tell the story of a **relationship** that went wrong and the reasons for its failure as she sees them by reference to her rights to personal autonomy and self-development. In so doing, he seeks to resist the characterisation of her story as "vapid **tittle tattle**".

23. **I simply do not accept that the judge, who is steeped in litigation of this kind, failed to have regard to any of these matters**. It seems to me that they are all addressed, expressly or by implication in his judgment. At that stage, Ms Ntuli was represented by different Leading Counsel and it is plain from the skeleton argument before Eady J and the judge's references to the oral submissions that Mr Tomlinson's predecessor put the case a little differently. For example**, it needed Mr Tomlinson to put Ms Ntuli's desire to tell her story in the context of her right to personal autonomy and self-development.** However, I regard that, in the present case, as an **ex post facto dignification** which does not live easily with the evidence to which I referred, in truncated form, in paragraphs 3 and 4, above.

24. The judge clearly had regard to **Ms Ntuli's stated motives for wanting to sell her story** (see, for example, paragraph 32 of his judgment). He referred to Mr Donald's "admissions as to his past behaviour", adding that it "can be taken into account, and assessed in the general application of the 'intense focus' to the facts of the case but it cannot be a determinative factor or anything like it" (paragraph 30). He evaluated the information and, in my judgment, was right **to place a relatively low value on it** in the light of the authorities to which I have referred. He also had proper regard to the possible impact of publicity on **the parties' respective children (Mr Donald's being somewhat younger).**

25. I am satisfied that there was no analytical deficiency in the judgment and that Eady J came to the correct conclusion about the "other information".

(2) The terms of the injunction

26. It is axiomatic that any injunction

> **"should be to the highest degree clear and precise so that no publisher would be in any doubt whether he was infringing it or not." (Times Newspapers Ltd v MGN Ltd [1993] EMLR 443 at page 447, per Sir Thomas Bingham MR).**

27. Mr Tomlinson submits that the terms of the order in this case do not satisfy that requirement. His complaint is with the formulation

> "any **intimate**, personal or sexually explicit details about the **relationship**."

28. In particular, he criticises the use of the word "**intimate**" in this context. **He maintains that its meaning is unclear** so that Ms Ntuli cannot locate the boundary between what is lawful and what is not. It is suggested that exchanges between counsel and Eady J illustrate the problem.

29. **I accept that there is a degree of overlap between "intimate", "personal" and "sexually explicit". They are not mutually exclusive epithets. However, that does not necessarily establish ambiguity or a lack of clarity. Words of restraint often overlap, as for example "publishing, communicating or disclosing".** As developed before us, **the issue seems to be whether "intimate" has an essentially sexual connotation**. **I am convinced that it does not.** The same word was used in the order in *McKennitt v Ash*, where the **relationship** between the parties was not sexual. **What the judge had in mind in the present case is apparent from paragraph 17 of his judgment:**

> **". . . the court's protection should be extended to any facts communicated by the Defendant of a sexual nature** ***or other*** **intimate** ***personal details about their past*** **relationship."**

30. **Mr Sherborne submits that the attempt on behalf of Ms Ntuli to free herself from restraint in relation to "intimate" details is manifestly self-serving.** Her position is that it is not "sexually explicit" details that she wishes to publish but non-sexual details of (to use Mr Tomlinson's phrase) "a **relationship** that went wrong" for which she holds Mr Donald responsible. **I consider that there is force in Mr Sherborne's submission.**

31. The order expressly permits publication, communication or disclosure of "the fact that the Claimant had a **relationship** with the Defendant". **It would not breach the order to describe it as a sexual relationship.** No one would infer that an unadorned reference to "a **relationship**" in this context was anything other than a **sexual relationship**. **Within that relationship, however, the judge rightly decided that there were non-sexual but intimate and/or personal details in respect of which Mr Donald was likely to establish at trial that he has a reasonable expectation of privacy**. I do not consider that the terms of the order lack clarity.

2. The cross-appeal

32. By his cross-appeal, Mr Donald complains that the injunction granted by Eady J did not go far enough and that it should have restrained publication and disclosure of the very existence of the **relationship** pending trial. The refusal of the judge to go that far was founded on his application of section 12 of the Human Rights Act. The relevant provisions are as follows:

> "(1) This section applies if a court is considering whether to grant any relief which, if granted, might affect the exercise of the Convention right to freedom of expression.
>
> . . .
>
> (3) No such relief is to be granted so as to restrain publication before trial unless the court is satisfied that the applicant is likely to establish that publication should not be allowed."

33. Thus, the general principles relating to interim injunctions are modified because of the importance of freedom of expression.

34. Authoritative guidance on the approach to section 12(3) was provided by Lord Nicholls in *Cream Holdings Ltd v Banerjee* [2005] 1AC 253, [2004] UKHL 44, where he said (at paragraph 22):

> "Section 12(3) makes the likelihood of success at trial an essential element in the court's consideration of whether to make an interim order. But in order to achieve the necessary flexibility the degree of likelihood of success at the trial needed to satisfy section 12(3) must depend on the circumstances. There can be no single, rigid standard governing all applications for interim restraint orders. Rather, on its paper construction the effect of section 12(3) is that the court is not to make an interim restraint order unless satisfied that the applicant's prospects of success at trial are sufficiently favourable to justify such an order being made in the particular circumstances of the case. As to what degree of likelihood makes the prospect of success 'sufficiently favourable', the general approach should be that courts will be exceedingly slow to make interim restraint orders where the applicant has not satisfied the court that he will probably ('more likely than not') succeed at trial. In general, that should be the threshold an applicant must cross before the court embarks on exercising its discretion, duly taking into account the relevant jurisprudence on Article 10 and any countervailing Convention rights. But these will be cases where it is necessary for a court to depart from this general approach and a lesser degree of likelihood will suffice as a prerequisite. Circumstances where this may be so include . . . where the potential adverse consequences of disclosure are particularly grave, or where a short-lived injunction is needed to enable the court to hear and give proper consideration to an application for interim relief pending the trial or any relevant appeal."

With this in mind, I turn to the particular circumstances of the present case.

35. The witness statements filed by and on behalf of Mr Donald and Ms Ntuli provide different accounts of the duration and intensity of their **relationship**. They also differ as to the extent to which it was conducted in public, although

it seems to be common ground that it was not wholly secret and nor did Mr Donald ever seek to impose a condition of secrecy. It is unnecessary for me to rehearse the detail.

36. The judge assessed the matter in this way (at paragraph 37):

> "There seems to be something of a conflict, or at least a difference of interpretation, on how private the **relationship** actually was. I cannot resolve such a conflict on an application of this kind. **It seems to me right, therefore, to conclude that in this respect the Applicant has failed to persuade me that he is 'likely' to establish at trial that the relationship between them had been kept so private that he retained a reasonable expectation of privacy in respect of the mere fact that it existed.** To put it another way, it has not been demonstrated that it is necessary and proportionate to extend the injunction so far as to restrict the Defendant's freedom of expression in this respect."

37. The essential submission on behalf of Mr Donald is that, applying Lord Nicholls' approach, the judge ought to have put this case into Lord Nicholls' exceptional, "lesser degree of likelihood" category. Mr Sherborne emphasises the fact that at no time during the **relationship** or since it ended has there been any reference to it in the media**. He submits that this is a paradigm case for providing temporary relief pending trial (or, perhaps, a further inter partes hearing) at which the conflict of evidence would be resolved.** He seeks to derive support from *ASG v GSA* [2009] EWCA Civ 1574, in which this Court granted interim relief following a refusal of it at first instance.

38. **In my judgment, this case bears no resemblance to the cases that Lord Nicholls had in mind as exceptional**. *Disclosure of the mere fact of this past* **relationship** *which, on any view, was not entirely secret, does not carry with it particularly grave adverse consequences.* In view of the limited nature of the permitted disclosure and the other matters properly considered by the judge, it cannot be said that, in relation to this issue, he "erred in principle or reached a conclusion which was plainly wrong", that being the test to be applied on appeal: *Lord Browne of Madingly v Associated Newspapers Ltd* [2008] QB 103, [2007] EWCA Civ 295, at paragraph 45 (per Sir Anthony Clarke MR). Whilst it is true that there is no urgency in respect of this disclosure, nor is there a compelling reason to restrain it. Moreover, *ASG* does not assist Mr Donald because, not only was it fact-sensitive, more importantly it was concerned with the prior, *ex parte* stage.

39. For these reasons, I would dismiss the cross-appeal.

3. Costs

40. Ms Ntuli seeks to overturn the costs order made by Eady J. It was in these terms:

> **"The Defendant shall pay two-thirds of the Claimant's costs of and occasioned by this application (including, for the avoidance of doubt, the hearings on 30 and 31 March 2010 and on 26 April 2010), such costs to be assessed if not agreed."**

41. Mr Tomlinson acknowledges the wide discretion entrusted to the trial judge. However, he refers to *Desquenne et Giral UK Ltd v Richardson* [2001] FSR 1 CA as authority for the proposition that where an interim injunction is granted the court will normally reserve the costs of the application until the determination of the substantive issue. He, of course, concedes that this is not a hard and fast rule.

42. The judge explained his order in a brief judgment following the hand down of the main judgment. He was critical of Ms Ntuli because, on her own case, she had infringed Mr Donald's privacy in her dealings with the News of the World . . . "the plainest possible infringement". He concluded that, in the circumstances of this case, costs should follow the event, subject to a one-third reduction to reflect the extent to which Ms Ntuli had succeeded in narrowing the injunction. It is now submitted on her behalf that, in reaching that conclusion, the judge wrongly assumed things in Mr Donald's favour that will be in issue at trial. I do not consider that submission to be justified. **For my part, I would not interfere with the order.**

4. Superinjunction and anonymity

43. If the injunction is to remain, the next question is whether it should retain its superinjunction and anonymity elements. The original order of 25 March 2010 included provisions under the headings "Anonymity of the Parties" (paragraph 3) and "Injunction and Related Relief" (paragraph 5). Paragraph 5 stated:

> "Upon it appearing to the Judge (1) that these proceedings are likely to attract publicity, (2) that publicity revealing the identity of the Claimant or the Defendant [is] likely unfairly to damage the interests of the Claimant and (3) that accordingly publication of details revealing the Claimant's or Defendant's identity ought to be prohibited."

44. Paragraph 5 restrained Ms Ntuli from publishing, disclosing etc

> **". . . the existence of these proceedings or the Claimant's interest in these** proceedings."

45. These provisions continue in the order of 26 April. This followed some rather desultory written and oral submissions and may have been conditioned by the fact that the judge assumed that this appeal would be heard and determined by July at the latest. Because of these protections, the private judgment did not need to be and was not expressed in inhibited terms. On this appeal, Ms

Ntuli seeks to take issue with both the superinjunction and anonymity elements. She is supported by Ms Heather Rogers QC who has been permitted to make written and brief oral submissions on behalf of Guardian News and Media Ltd.

(1) The superinjunction element

46. It seems that the only argument advanced on behalf of Mr Donald at the *ex parte* stage was that a superinjunction provision was necessary because, without one, the media might publicise the fact that "a well-known popular musician" had obtained an injunction which prohibited the publication of (to put it neutrally) **salacious** details. **This is unpersuasive because protection against personal identification could have been achieved by a simple anonymity order.** Alternatively, the order could limit publicity to the fact that Mr Donald had obtained an injunction restraining Ms Ntuli from disclosing details of the **relationship** which existed between them.

47. Superinjunctions attract understandable controversy. **Sometimes it is the product of more heat than light.** Although the concept carries the nomenclature of novelty, there is much that is simply a reflection of general principles. The starting point is the principle of open justice, most notably expounded in *Scott v Scott* [1913] AC 417, where Lord Haldane LC said (at page 438):

> **"[The point] is one of principle . . . turning not on convenience but on necessity."**

Lord Atkinson added:

> **". . . in public trial is to [be] found, on the whole, the best security for the pure, impartial and efficient administration of justice, the best means for winning for it public confidence and respect."**

See also Lord Shaw of Dunfermline (at pages 476–478).

48. Needless to say, it is not an absolute rule. As Lord Diplock said in *A-G v Leveller Magazine Ltd* [1979] AC 440 (at page 450):

> ". . . since the **purpose** of the general rule is to serve the ends of justice it may be necessary to depart from it where the nature or circumstances of the particular proceeding are such that the application of the general rule in its entirety would frustrate or render impracticable the administration of justice . . ."

49. More recently, in *ex parte Kaim Todner* [1999] QB 966 Lord Woolf MR explained the principle in a contemporary context and added (at page 977):

> "Any interference with the public nature of court proceedings is therefore to be avoided unless justice requires it."

50. This line of authority (which includes numerous other examples) requires

open justice to apply because it furthers the interests of justice unless a countervailing consideration overrides it in the interests of justice. There are well-known circumstances in which to insist upon open justice would itself create a greater injustice.

51. It is submitted on behalf of Mr Donald that this is such a case. Mr Sherborne seeks to fortify that submission **by inviting us to dilute the test of necessity referred to in the earlier authorities on the basis that they preceded the Human Rights Act which,** in providing for competing qualified rights (private life and freedom of expression), requires a more nuanced approach. In this regard, he refers to the control order case of *Home Secretary v AP(No2)* [2010] 1 WLR 1652, [2010] UKSC 26, in which the anonymity of a successful appellant against a control order was continued.

52. **In my judgment, there is no need for a new approach.** Indeed, it is significant that Article 6 of the ECHR itself prescribes a test of strict necessity in the context of publicity being permitted to be restricted in the interests of justice. However, as part of its consideration of all the circumstances of a case, a court will have regard to the respective and sometimes competing Convention rights of the parties. In *AP(No2)*, this led Lord Rodger to formulate the question in these terms (at paragraph 7):

> " . . . whether there is sufficient general, public interest in publishing a report of the proceedings which identifies [AP] to justify any resulting curtailment of his right and his family's right to respect for their private and family life."

53. There, anonymity was continued because the public interest in publication "**has to give way to the need to protect AP from the risk of violence"** and the same public interest "would not justify curtailing *AP*'s right to respect for his private and family life" (paragraph 18). Whilst this is not the language of "necessity", it is not significantly different. Indeed, "has to give way" is qualitatively similar to a necessity test. Necessity remains the test for the residual power to order a private hearing under the Civil Procedure Rules (CPR 39.2(3)(g)).

54. **This is an essentially case-sensitive subject**. Plainly Mr Donald is entitled to expect that the court will adopt procedures which ensure that any ultimate vindication of his Article 8 case is not undermined by the way in which the court has processed the interim applications and the trial itself. **On the other hand, the principle of open justice requires that any restrictions are the least that can be imposed consistent with the protection to which Mr Donald is entitled.** In my judgement, **in view of the terms of the substantive injunction and the circumstances of this case, the appropriate restriction on publicity is one that limits reporting and publicity to what is contained in**

this judgment, together with any ancillary orders necessary to fortify such an order. I am simply unpersuaded that greater restriction is necessary at this stage. There is nothing in this judgment that is significantly invasive of Mr Donald's private or family life.

(2) Anonymity

55. It seems to me that what I have said in relation to the superinjunction element applies also to the question of anonymity. *Provided that publicity is limited to what is contained in this judgment, there is no justification for continued anonymity.* I have in mind the judgment of Lord Rodger in *Guardian News and Media Ltd* [2010] 2 WLR 325, [2010] UKSC 1, at paragraphs 63–64. **The material in respect of which Mr Donald has been found to have a reasonable expectation of privacy is not detailed in the judgment.** The material in the judgment does not attract a reasonable expectation of privacy. I note that an order restricting publicity to the contents of a judgment, in relation to which one party was anonymised but the other was not, was recently made by Tugendhat J in *Gray v UVW* [2010] EWHC 2367 (QB): see in particular paragraphs 44–63. There the continued anonymity of the defendant was justified by a significant risk that lifting his or her anonymity might have serious consequences for his or her private life which consequences might not be remediable. I do not consider that the same can be said of Mr Donald in the present case. In my view, it would have been possible and appropriate for Eady J to have written his judgment in a publishable form. **Moreover, to have done so would have avoided the risk that anonymisation can give rise to, namely that of "jigsaw" identification, whereby anonymisation may be undermined by correctly identifying someone as a result of relating separate snippets of information or, equally unfortunately, it may lead to the wrong person being identified by the media misaligning the snippets. We were shown one recent example of this.**

56. **I emphasise that my conclusion on the superinjunction and anonymity issues are confined to this appeal.** If the case goes to trial, matters such as the privacy of the hearing or parts of it will have to be revisited, as will the publicity or otherwise of the judgment. Much will depend on the issues as they are then identified.

Conclusion

57. It follows from what I have said that I would dismiss the appeal and the cross-appeal in relation to the substantive injunction but I would allow Ms Ntuli's appeal in relation to the superinjunction and anonymity issues. In the course of her submissions, Ms Rogers made a number of interesting procedural points of concern to Guardian News and Media Ltd (and, I suspect, to the media generally). They do not arise for decision on this appeal. It is

better that they be considered elsewhere, in particular by the committee set up by the Master of the Rolls, to consider such issues.

Lord Justice Sedley:

58. I agree.

The Master of the Rolls:

59. I also agree.

JIH v News Group Newspapers Ltd
[2010] EWHC 2979 (QB)

Mr Justice Tugendhat:

1. A week ago, on 5 November, I handed down my judgment in this matter: [2010] EWHC 2818 (QB) ("my judgment"). The Order I made that day ("my Order") included the following:

   "1 The Defendant must not publish, republish, syndicate, use, communicate or disclose to any person:

   (a) Any information concerning the subject matter of these proceedings save for that contained in the public judgment of the Court handed down on 5 November 2010 and/or

   (b) Any of the information set out in the Confidential Schedule to this Order

   (together "the Information") . . .

   10 The Claimant's application for an Order requiring that his identity be not disclosed be refused . . .

   12 It is ordered that the identity of the Claimant shall not be disclosed pending the renewal of his application for permission to appeal to the Court of Appeal . . ."

THE APPLICATION

2. On 10 November the Claimant gave notice of an application to vary para 10 of my Order so as to provide that the Claimant's identity be not disclosed. The reasons are set out in the second witness statement of Mr Shear also dated 10 November.

3. This was not an attempt to re-argue matters I had determined on 5 November. **The application is based on events that occurred subsequently, namely two publications in the press relating to my judgment and order.** No relief was

sought on this occasion against any person, other than the variation of the anonymity provided for in para 10 of my Order.

EVENTS SINCE MY ORDER

4. The first event was a publication in **the online edition** (and only the online edition) of the Daily Telegraph published at 7.00 am on 6 November. **The article reported my judgment**.

5. The second event was a publication in **both the online and the print editions of another newspaper** ("the other newspaper"). The article reported my judgment. It included a quotation which the Claimant submits breaches the terms of my Order.

6. On 5 November solicitors for the Claimant ("the solicitors") had prepared, and sent to the editor and the legal department of the publishers of the Daily Telegraph, Telegraph Media Group Ltd ("the Telegraph") and of the other newspaper (amongst others), **a letter which set out the effect of my Order.** On Monday 8 November they wrote to the Editor and Legal Department of the Telegraph, referring to my Order and to their previous letter, and complaining that the Telegraph was in breach of para 1(a) of my Order. No complaint is made of a breach of para 1(b).

7. The title to the **article contained words which the Claimant submits are a breach of the terms of my Order.** There is also a complaint of a breach of para 12 of my Order, by publication of information about the Claimant (although not his identity). The solicitors asked for the article to be removed. It was removed from the website that day.

8. Mr Anthony Hudson appeared before me **and apologised** on behalf of the Telegraph. **He explained how the publication had occurred, and the steps that had been taken to ensure that it would not occur again.**

9. The solicitors wrote a letter in similar terms to the other newspaper. There was a reply the same day stating:

   "The article was . . . taken down from the website immediately upon receipt of your e-mail. A warning has been circulated to all journalists not to repeat the matter referred to. A similar warning has been place on the electronic library cutting".

SUBMISSIONS

10. Mr Shear states that it is deeply troubling and distressing for the Claimant that these events have occurred, the more so because the Claimant had feared that they would occur. He referred to his previous witness statement which included passages about publications concerning the Claimant in the past.

11. Mr Sherborne submits that the effect of these two publications is that, **if and when the anonymity provision in my Order expires**, then the publication of the identity of the Claimant, taken together with these two publications that have already occurred, **will lead to the public knowing information about the subject matter of the action**. This will frustrate or undermine the **purpose** of para 1(a) of my Order. Therefore, in order to preserve the effect of my Order, the only possible step to take is to impose a new anonymity order.

12. Mr Sherborne submitted that this step is necessary to protect the Art 8 rights of the Claimant. He reminds me of para 62 of my judgment in which I said:

> "Having considered the evidence, I too have no doubt that the private life considerations of **Art 8 are engaged** here**, both** as to the **subject matter of the action**, and, to a much lesser extent, as to **the identification of the Claiman**t. The proceedings are likely to attract publicity, and if the Claimant is identified that will result in some interference with the private life of himself and his family. **There is no suggestion of any public interest or other possible justification in disclosure of the information which is the subject matter of the action."**

13. I accept that there is a prima facie case that the two publications complained of do disclose information about the subject matter of the action.

14. I make no determination as to whether either or both of these are a breach of my Order. If that issue arises in the future, then it will be necessary to give to the two publishers concerned an opportunity to make representations as to whether that is so or not. Mr Hudson's apology on behalf of the Telegraph was not an admission of **contempt** of court.

15. Mr Sherborne also submitted that:

> "At the time of lifting the anonymity order the Court regarded itself as being faced with two alternatives, namely to allow publication of the Claimant's identity or to allow publication of the nature of the material which was being injuncted and that since it would not be possible to do the latter (although that was not the submission of Counsel for the Claimant), it ruled that anonymity should be lifted".

16. **This submission is mistaken**. As my judgment makes clear, the Court **was never faced with a choice between the two alternatives referred to in para 8 of my judgment**. In the present case, on 22 October and now, the parties have been at one in presenting the court with only both alternatives together. The two together are to be found in the form of the consent order proposed on 22 October (para 7 of my judgment) and again in the form of consent order proposed following the circulation of my judgment in draft (para 74 of my judgment and para 1 of my Order). At no time, then or today,

has counsel for the Claimant submitted that I should allow publication of the subject matter of the action. On 22 October counsel (not Mr Sherborne) was precluded from doing so by the agreement that the parties had reached between themselves.

17. The position today is the same. I asked Mr Sherborne whether he was seeking an order in terms different from the draft consent order. He made clear he was not. So **the only choice** the court is offered today is the choice that it was offered on 22 October, and set out in para 7 of my judgment: to order **that there be no publication of the subject matter of the action together with anonymity, or to order that there be no publication of the subject matter of the action but without anonymity.**

18. Para 63 of my judgment reads:

> "It is implicit in the form of the consent order, and I accept, that in the present case it would not be possible to make an order or give a judgment which disclosed any information about the subject matter of the action which did not thereby make it likely that the Claimant would be identified. **To identify both the subject matter and the Claimant would defeat the purpose of the proceedings.** Accordingly, the only practical question open to the Court is **whether to withhold the identity of the Claimant, in addition to withholding all information about the subject matter of the action**. In this case the alternatives canvassed by Mr Tomlinson (para 8 above) are theoretical not real. **The only real choice is to allow the public to know the Claimant's identity or to allow them to know nothing at all about the action".**

19. That remains the position today. In saying what I said in that paragraph, I accepted what was implicit in the form of the consent order, and the submissions of both counsel that I should make the consent order as consented to by them**. I was not deciding any issue. There was no issue between the parties for me to decide**. I was simply endorsing a decision already made by the parties in the agreement by which they settled the action. As I said in para 6 of my judgment:

> "It is important to record that the arguments of the parties before me were **not adversarial**. The parties have reached an agreement, and neither of them has resiled from it. Both parties were asking me to make the order in the form they had consented to. However, both counsel were able to give their assistance to the court, and they did so from the perspective of a claimant and a defendant respectively."

20. I turn now to consider the Claimant's submissions as to the order that is necessary in the circumstances as they are today. **For this purpose I assume in favour of the Claimant that the two publications complained do in fact**

disclose information about the subject matter of the action (although not the information in the Confidential Schedule).

21. Mr Sherborne submitted that the information disclosed in the two publications complained of is **now in the public domain.** It follows that there **is a further risk of disclosure by other newspaper publishers.** It is not alleged that the Telegraph or the other newspaper are threatening to repeat what they have done.

22. Mr Spearman again made clear that the Defendant is bound by the settlement agreement and does not seek to resile from it. His submissions were, again, not adversarial, but with a view to assisting the court. He referred to **the public domain proviso** in para 1 of my Order. That reads:

 > **"PROVIDED THAT nothing in this Order shall prevent the publication, disclosure or communication of any of the Information:**
 >
 > **(i) . . .**
 >
 > **(ii) by the Defendant of any part of the Information that is in the public domain as the result of national media publication (otherwise than as a result of breach of this Order)".**

23. While **I have not determined today that there has been a breach my Order,** Mr Spearman submits that any editor considering whether or not to republish the information already published on 6 November would have to bear in mind the risk of an application to commit for **contempt** if he did that. The court considering the matter at that stage might have to determine whether there had been a breach of my Order by the Telegraph or the other newspaper. And if the court did have to decide that issue, **it might well decide that there had been a breach of my Order by one or other or both of the Telegraph and the other newspaper.** If so, the proviso would not assist the respondent to the motion to commit for **contempt**.

24. There is force in that submission. I need say no more than that. The effect of that consideration is, in my judgment, that the risk of any newspaper republishing what was published by the Telegraph and the other newspaper is not as great as Mr Sherborne would submit. The quick response of these two newspapers in removing the publications complained of on 8 November, immediately upon receipt of the solicitors' letters, also suggests to me that the risk of republication is not as great as Mr Sherborne submits it is.

25. Next I turn to consider the extent of the interference in the Claimant's private life that will occur if the Claimant's identity is disclosed in accordance with my Order. For this **purpose** I must assume either that there is no appeal, or that the appeal fails. If the appeal succeeds, the anonymity order will remain in place as the Court of Appeal may direct, and the publications complained

of today will not have interfered with the Claimant's private life (because he has not been identified).

26. Mr Hudson stated that according to the information at present available to the Telegraph there were about 12,000 hits on the article in question on the two days it was available to be viewed. There are no figures before me as to the circulation of the Daily Star, or the hits on its website. But I assume that there were many thousands of people who read the publication between 6 and 8 November.

27. Mr Sherborne submits that each of the readers of those publications will, when they know the identity of the Claimant, come to know the subject matter of the action, and that will constitute an interference with his private life.

28. I accept that submission. And I repeat that nobody (not the Defendant nor any of the Media Organisations) has ever suggested to the court that there is any public interest in the disclosure of the subject matter of the action.

29. On the other hand, the extent of the information disclosed by the Telegraph and the other newspaper is very limited. It does not include the information in the **Confidential Schedule**. Para 1(a) of my Order is similar to the order of Sharp J in her judgment in *DFT v TFD* [2010] EWHC 2335 (QB) (which I referred to in para 67 of my judgment). As she explained in paras [35] to [39], the **purpose** of that provision in that case was to reduce the risk of jigsaw identification of the claimant. The orders of Nicol J did not include the words that were inserted in Para 1(a) of my Order: they were added following submission on 22 October, with the support of counsel for both parties. In the present case, if and when the claimant is identified, that provision will have the effect of limiting the risk of jigsaw disclosure of the information in the **Confidential Schedule**.

30. A threatened interference with the Art 8 rights of a claimant is not, by itself, always sufficiently serious to necessitate the imposition of an injunction or anonymity order. Assuming, as I do, that there would an interference with the private life of the Claimant and others if and when his identity is disclosed, by reason of the publications on 6 November, I must consider what further order, if any, is necessary and proportionate to prevent that.

31. While I assume that what has been disclosed by the two publications complained of before me would in each case amount to an interference with the private life of the Claimant and others, on the scale of possible interferences, the disclosure does not rank high. What was published was at a high level of generality, lacking all detail. Further, in reaching this conclusion I have in mind the evidence of Mr Shear in his first witness statement. I referred to it

in paras 30 and 31 of my judgment. I cannot explain the relevance in more detail without undermining the **purpose** of my Order.

CONCLUSION

32. I conclude that having regard, as I must, to the need to protect the Art 8 rights of the Claimant and others concerned, it is not necessary to vary my Order. I will not order that the identity of the Claimant be not disclosed. In my judgment, notwithstanding the events that have occurred since 5 November, it remains the position that the general principle of open justice provides, in this case, sufficient general, public interest in publishing a report of proceedings which identifies the Claimant to justify any resulting curtailment of the rights of the Claimant and his family to respect for their private and family life

FURTHER OBSERVATIONS

33. What has occurred is a matter for great concern. Editors and others will take note of the submission of Mr Spearman set out in para 23 above. If the court is to give effect to Art 10 to the fullest extent, it is essential that editors and publishers have regard to the "duties and responsibilities" referred to in Art 10(2) itself. These duties and responsibilities include a requirement that they comply with orders of the court, and that they take all necessary steps to ensure that journalists understand this necessity.

KJH v HGF [2010] EWHC 3064 (QB)

Mrs Justice Sharp:

It is ordered that publication of any information as to the subject matter of these proceedings or the identity of the parties to these proceedings, is limited to that contained in this judgment

1. This judgment concerns an application heard in private at a with notice hearing, for the continuation until trial or further order of an interim injunction, in privacy and confidence. The order was first granted by Eady J and has been continued twice since then, by myself and then Eady J.
2. I heard submissions on behalf of KJH from Hugh Tomlinson QC and evidence has been put before me in witness statements from two solicitors from Harbottle & Lewis and in a confidential witness statement from KJH and in exhibits to those witness statements. The Respondent to the application, HGF was given notice of this hearing but was not present or represented.
3. In considering whether KJH is entitled to the relief asked for I have applied

the principles of law referred to in paragraphs 13 to 19 of my judgment in *DFT* v *TFD* [2010] EWHC 2335 (QB). I am also required to consider section 12(4) of the Human Rights Act 1998 (HRA) and whether the threshold test for interim relief affecting the convention right to freedom of expression in section 12(3) of the HRA is satisfied in accordance with the approach of the House of Lords in *Cream Holdings v Banerjee* [2005] 1AC 253.

4. The evidence establishes to a high degree of probability that KJH was the victim of **blackmail** involving the threat of the revelation of stolen private and **confidential information**. In those circumstances, I am satisfied that KJH is likely to establish at trial that publication of the information in question should not be allowed. I am similarly satisfied that there has been no waiver of KJH's privacy rights, and that there is no public interest justification for the publication of the information.

5. In my judgment the privacy interests engaged are strong, as is the claim in breach of confidence, but for the avoidance of doubt the information does not reveal (by way of example) that KJH was conducting an extra marital affair, or any other affair, nor does it reveal wrongdoing of any description (whether sexual or otherwise) by KJH or any other person. I am also satisfied that there is a continuing risk that the private and **confidential information** stolen from KJH will be made public, and that an interim injunction is therefore necessary.

6. I have considered whether it is possible to give more details as to the underlying narrative of the case. However, in the particular circumstances of this case it is not possible in my view, to give more details than the extremely limited ones I have referred to already without there being a significant risk that notwithstanding the other orders which I have made, which are referred to in paragraph 12 below, KJH's identity will become public, as will the private and **confidential information** which this action is brought to protect.

7. The circumstances in which it is necessary to derogate from the principle of open justice, in particular by holding hearings in private, ordering the anonymisation of the parties, ordering that there should be no report of the existence of the proceedings themselves or by restricting the information in public judgments have been considered in a number of recent cases including *Terry (previously LNS) v Persons Unknown* [2010] EWHC 119 (QB); *DFT* v *TFD* [2010] EWHC 2335 (QB); *AMM v HXW* [2010] EWHC 2457 (QB); *Bernard Gray v UVW* [2010] EWHC 2367 (QB); *JIH v News Group Newspapers* [2010] EWCA 2818; *JIH v News Group Newspapers Ltd* [2010] EWHC 2979 (QB) and *Ntuli v Donald* [2010] EWCA Civ 1276.

8. As Maurice Kay LJ said in *Ntuli* at [54]:

> "This is an essentially case-sensitive subject. Plainly Mr Donald is

> entitled to expect that the court will adopt procedures which ensure that any ultimate vindication of his Article 8 case is not undermined by the way in which the court has processed the interim applications and the trial itself. On the other hand, the principle of open justice requires that any restrictions are the least that can be imposed consistent with the protection to which Mr Donald is entitled."

9. In *AMM*, Tugendhat J considered those principles in the context of a **black-mail** case, and said this at [21]:

> " . . . where a claimant alleges he is being **blackmail**ed, the court may be faced with limited choices. One choice is to refuse an anonymity order. But in that case, if the **blackmail**er's threat is to be thwarted, the court will restrict publication of the information which is the subject matter of the action. The alternative is for the court to grant the anonymity order. The court can then permit publication of some of the facts about the action, including the allegation of **blackmail**. If the court adopts that course, then the anonymity order should suffice to prevent publication of the fact that it is the applicant who has been **blackmail**ed."

10. He went on to say this at [38] to [39]:

> "The fact that a person is making unwarranted demands with threats to disclose information does not of itself mean that that person has no right to freedom of expression. As Lord Atkin pointed out in *Thorne*, the **blackmail**er may even be under a duty to disclose the information. But if a person is making unwarranted demands with threats to publish, that is a factor in deciding whether that person has any Art 10 rights, and, if so, then the weight to be accorded to them in balancing them with the applicant's Art 8 rights.
>
> In my judgment, the need to have regard to the Art 8 rights of the Claimant, and to promote the public Interest in preventing and punishing **blackmail** are both factors which weigh strongly in favour of the grant of an anonymity order. There is a strong case that Defendant has no right to publish the information which she seeks to publish . . . On this view her Art 10 rights are not strong. And as an alleged **blackmail**er, her Art 10 rights are much weaker. If the Claimant fails at trial to establish any part of his case, then position of the Defendant and her rights will fall to be considered afresh."

11. The strong public policy considerations to which Tugendhat J referred, and which justify the protection of the identity of victims of **blackmail** arise in both criminal and civil proceedings: such persons should not be deterred from seeking the protection of the courts for fear that the information which the **blackmail**er has threatened to reveal will be exposed or their identity as

the victim of **blackmail** will be made known. Although as Tugendhat J said, a final determination of the matter must await trial, granting anonymity at the interim stage serves not only the interest of the applicant in protecting his or her Article 8 rights but the public interest as Tugendhat J also said, in promoting the prevention and punishment of **blackmail**.

12. Having regard to those matters, and in all the circumstances I am satisfied it has been necessary to derogate from the principle of open justice by holding the hearing in private in accordance with CPR 39.2(3)(a)(c) and (e). I am also satisfied that it is necessary that both parties to the application should be referred to by their initials rather than by their names. I have for the same reasons continued the order already made restricting access to documents on the court file, so that none of the witness statements or annexures to the witness statements or the names of the parties would be provided to non parties without further order of the court.

13. I have ordered that KJH is not required to provide the material provided to the court, or a note of the hearing to those third parties served with the order unless they specifically ask for that material and give undertakings to protect the use of that material and the information it contains. It should be noted however that I have been told that KJH does not intend to serve copies of the order on any media organisation at present, and intends to serve the order on a third party only if there is a threat of publication by that third party.

    I have also ordered that publication of any information as to the subject matter of these proceedings or the identity of the parties to these proceedings is limited to that contained in this judgment. I made an order to the same effect in *DFT*, as the Court of Appeal did in *Ntuli* and as Tugendhat did in *JIH (No 1)*. I have drawn attention to that part of my order at the beginning of this judgment.

JXF (A Child Suing by His Mother and Litigation Friend KMF) v York Hospitals NHS Foundation Trust [2010] EWHC 2800 (QB) per Tugendhat J

Mr Justice Tugendhat:

1. Should the Court make an **anonymity order** in respect of the Claimant when **approving a compromise** by or behalf of a **protected** party?

2. I did make such an order in this case, and stated that I would give my rea-

sons later. These are they. **The application was made in relation to a hearing under CPR 21.10 for approval of a settlement.**

3. In this case the Claimant asked for an order that contained various provisions to ensure that his identity be not disclosed. These included that he be referred to **only** by the letters **JFX** in the documents filed with the Court, and that documents already filed **be disclosed to third parties** under CPR r5.4 only **subject to appropriate adjustments**. The Claimant had in his Application Notice also asked for the hearing to be in private, but Mr Maskrey **did not pursue that,** and it was held in public. **The application is not opposed by the Defendant.**

4. CPR 21.10 provides :

   "(1) Where a claim is made—

   by or on behalf of a child or protected party;

   . . .

   no settlement, compromise or payment (including any voluntary interim payment) and no acceptance of money paid into court shall be valid, so far as it relates to the claim by, on behalf of or against the child or protected party, without the approval of the court".

5. The reasons for this provision are explained in the notes to the White Book (2010) 20.10.1 as follows:

   "Rules 21.10.1 and 21.11 and the Practice Direction provide a comprehensive code the objects of which are:

   (a) To protect the interests of children and protected parties. This may involve protecting the child from any lack of skill or experience of their legal advisers which might lead to a settlement of a money claim for far less than it is worth; see *Black v Yates* [1992] Q.B. 526 ; 4 All E.R. 722 . (claim by child dependants for compensation greater than amount awarded by a foreign court).

   (b) To provide means by which a defendant may obtain a valid discharge from a child or protected party's claim. At common law a contract of compromise out of court does not bind such a claimant unless it can be proved to have been for their benefit. No prudent defendant would wish to take a risk on this point. A judgment in proceedings or an order approving a settlement of proceedings under r.10 does bind the claimant child or protected party and gives the defendant a discharge.

   (c) To make sure that money recovered by or on behalf of a child or protected party is properly looked after and wisely applied. Rule 21.11 provides for the control of money recovered.

(d) To ensure that the interests of all dependants entitled to a possible share in the settlement are properly defined and protected; see para7 of the Practice Direction . . . ."

6. **The Order for anonymity was sought under CPR 39.2 which, so far as material, provides:**

"(1) The general rule is that a hearing is to be in public. . . .

(4) The court may order that the identity of any party or witness must not be disclosed if it considers non-disclosure necessary in order to protect the interests of that party or witness".

7. Applications under CPR 20.10 are **normally** held in **public**. But counsel inform me that **there has been an increase in the number of applications for anonymity.** In *In re Guardian News and Media Ltd* [2010] 2 WLR 325; [2010] UKSC 1 ("Guardian") para 22 Lord Rodger stated the general rule, which applies to personal injury cases as to other cases:

"In the United Kingdom, until the recent efflorescence of anonymity orders, the general rule both in theory and in practice was that judicial proceedings were held in public and the parties were named in judgments. Their names would also be given in newspaper reports and in the law reports. That is still usually the position—as can be seen from the frequent press reports of, say, employment tribunal hearings and decisions where details of personal and **sexual relationships** among the warring parties are a common feature".

8. In para 2 he said:

"the practice of referring to parties by initials has increased at all levels in recent years. Even assuming that the use of initials was justified in many cases, the present appeals show that an order ("anonymity order") may be made, often by consent of both parties, without the court considering in any detail what is the basis or justification for it. This happens despite Sir Christopher Staughton's warning, in *R v Westminster City Council, Ex p P,* (1998) 31 HLR 154, 163, that "when both sides agreed that information should be kept from the public, that was when the court had to be most vigilant." Lord Woolf MR quoted the warning with approval in *R v Legal Aid Board, Ex p Kaim Todner* [1999] QB 966, 977D-E."

THE FACTS

9. The facts of the present case can be stated only in general terms. To do otherwise would defeat the **purpose** of the anonymity order that I have made. The Claimant is **still a child**. His claim was for **negligence** relating to **treatment** provided at the hospital managed by the Defendant**. His dis-**

abilities are fortunately much less than in other cases which have come before the courts, and that is in part the reason why anonymity is sought. It is expected that he will need , but it is also expected **that he will be of full capacity when reaches the age of 18.** It follows that he has an **awareness** of his condition that makes him **more sensitive** to it than some other claimants would be. It also follows that even if his money is in a trust for him, it will be a bare trust, so that he will, if he wishes, be able to require the money to be paid to him. **He will also be able to participate in normal social life to a greater extent than some other claimants**. For these reasons he will be **more vulnerable** than other claimants. There are means by which the financial interests of claimants under a disability may be protected for the whole of their lives, if they lack capacity. These are set out in CPR 20.11. But a claimant who has capacity, or will have it at the age of 18, **will not be protected in this way**. He may became a **target** for those who would wish to **profit** from his money or **deprive** him of it.

10. The sum of money which is the subject of this settlement is substantial. It is information that the Claimant is to receive **so large a sum** of money that is sought to be **protected** by the **anonymity** order. In the present case the application has not been based on the sensitivity of any medical or other private information.

11. One of the purposes of these proceedings for approval is as stated in sub-para (c) of para 5 above: to ensure the money paid to the claimant **is looked after and wisely applied.** If the naming of a claimant will make him vulnerable to losing the money to **fortune hunters or thieves**, then it follows that the **purpose** of the approval hearing will be defeated.

THE PRINCIPLE OF OPEN JUSTICE

12. The requirement that there be **open justice** now rests on **two bases**. The oldest basis is that of the **common law**, as set out in cases such as **Scott v Scott** [1913] AC 417, as noted in *Guardian* para 23. **Another basis is the ECHR**. In *Scott v Scott* the justification contemplated for any derogation was not the right to private life of any of the parties. The derogation in question there was a hearing in private, but the same principles apply to anonymity. As Lord Haldane put it, in the passage starting at p438:

> "I think that to justify an order for hearing in camera it must be shown that the paramount object of securing that justice is done would really be rendered doubtful of attainment if the order were not made."

13. Art 6 may add nothing. No mention of Art 6 was made in *Guardian*. **It may be that Art 6 would not apply to applications under CPR 21.10.** That would be so if such applications do not involve **"the determination of [a party's] civil**

rights and obligations": *Y v HM Attorney General* [2003] EWHC 1462 (Ch). I have heard **no argument** on this, and **say no more** about it.

14. In *Guardian* the justifications contemplated for any derogation from the principle of open justice include **respect for private life**. The reason, and the basis, for the court's jurisdiction to make anonymity orders was explained as follows:

> "29. In fact, however, in these cases the courts have gone further: they have not only used initials in their judgments but have made anonymity orders addressed to other people–in effect, to the press. Having the power to make orders of this kind available is one of the ways that the United Kingdom fulfils its positive obligation under article 8 of the Convention to secure that other individuals respect an individual's private and family life . . .
>
> 30 To comply with article 8, United Kingdom law must have a remedy of this kind available for use in appropriate cases . . . In *In re S (A Child) (Identification: Restrictions on Publication)* [2005] 1 AC 593, . . . speaking for all members of the appellate committee, Lord Steyn affirmed, at p 605, para 23, that the court did have jurisdiction to make an order of this kind and that "the foundation of the jurisdiction to restrain publicity in a case such as the present is now derived from Convention rights under the ECHR." More recently, in *In re British Broacasting Corpn* [2009] UKHL 34; [2009] 3 WLR 142, 161, para 57, Lord Brown of Eaton-under-Heywood indicated that the powers of the High Court to make such an order "arise under section 6 of the [Human Rights Act 1998] read in conjunction with section 37 of the [Senior Courts Act 1981].""

15. In para 34 Lord Rodger stated that by making **anonymity** orders

> "the courts have interfered with the article 10 Convention rights of the press to impart information which either is, or normally would be, available to them".

16. The relevant parts of Arts 8 and 10 are:

> "Article 8 Right to respect for private and family life
>
> 1 Everyone has the right to respect for his private and family life, his home and his correspondence.
>
> 2 There shall be no interference by a public authority with the exercise of this right except such as is in accordance with the law and is necessary in a democratic society . . . for the prevention of disorder or crime, for the protection of health or morals, or for the protection of the rights and freedoms of others.
>
> Article 10 Freedom of Expression

> 1 Everyone has the right to freedom of expression. This right shall include freedom to hold opinions and to receive and impart information and ideas without interference by public authority . . .
>
> 2 The exercise of these freedoms, since it carries with it duties and responsibilities, may be subject to such formalities, conditions, restrictions or penalties as are prescribed by law and are necessary in a democratic society, . . . for the prevention of disorder or crime, for the protection of health or morals, for the protection of the **reputation** or rights of others, for preventing the disclosure of information received in confidence, or for maintaining the authority and impartiality of the judiciary."

17. Having considered how the court should balance the rights under the two articles, Lord Rodger concluded:

> "In the present case M's private and family life are interests which must be respected. On the other side, publication of a report of the proceedings, including a report identifying M, is a matter of general, public interest. Applying Lord Hoffmann's formulation, the question for the court accordingly is whether there is sufficient general, public interest in publishing a report of the proceedings which identifies M to justify any resulting curtailment of his right and his family's right to respect for their private and family life."

18. There are therefore **two questions** for the court to consider **before making an anonymity order** based on the need to protect Convention rights. **The first question is**: are the Art 8 rights (or any other Convention rights) of the applicant engaged at all? In the case of a claimant in a personal injury action, his or her Art 8 rights will **often be engaged**, to a greater or lesser extent, because of the **sensitivity of the medical and financial information** under discussion. In the case of a defendant, that is much less likely to be the case. Defendants which are public authorities **do not, in any event, normally have Art 8 rights**, and are most unlikely to have them in respect of such claims.

19. If the Claimant's Art 8 rights are engaged, then the **second question** for the court is: is there sufficient general, public interest in publishing a report of the proceedings which identifies the **Claimant to justify any resulting curtailment of his right and his family's right to respect for their private and family life?**

20. One argument commonly advanced for claimants, which is also advanced in this case, is the **fear of intrusive media reporting.** In the present case there is **no specific evidence** as to why that should be a real concern. I do not doubt that there is likely to be press reporting, as both counsel submitted.

But there is **no history of unduly intrusive reporting** in this case, or any similar case to which I have been referred.

21. In *Guardian* at paras [62] and [72] Lord Rodger put that argument in its proper context. **At para [62] he explained the importance of a name for reports of proceedings.** And at para [72] he dealt with **possible abuse** as follows:

    "72 . . . the possibility of some sectors of the press abusing their freedom to report cannot, of itself, be a sufficient reason for curtailing that freedom for all members of the press. James Madison long ago pointed out that "Some degree of abuse is inseparable from the proper use of everything, and in no instance is this more true than in that of the press": "Report on the Virginia Resolutions" (1800), in *Letters and Other Writings of James Madison* (1865) Vol 4, p 544. The possibility of abuse is therefore simply one factor to be taken into account when considering whether an anonymity order is a proportionate restriction on press freedom in this situation."

22. There is only one case decided since *Guardian*, to which I have been referred, and in which the court has considered **anonymity** in relation to a **claim involving medical matters**. That case did **not** concern **an approval** hearing. It is *A (A minor) & Others v A health & Social Services Trust* [2010] NIQB 108. It was a highly unusual claim for an alleged breach of duty in relation to **IVF treatment** by two children who were born **with a skin colour different from that of their parents**. The claim was dismissed on the merits. In that case Gillen J gave careful consideration to the application for anonymity in paras [39]–[44]. He excised from the judgment details of the case, and **granted anonymity to protect the Art 8 rights** of the claimants and their family (para [49], [51]).

23. Another case since *Guardian* in which anonymity orders have been considered is also from Northern Ireland. It is *R A, Re Judicial Review* [2010] NIQB 27, in which the court was asked to quash a decision of a District Judge who had refused to extend a reporting restriction in relation to the publication of the applicant's name. The Court refused to quash the order (although that does not appear from the name of the case). **Again the court gave detailed consideration to the question in a manner which is rarely found in cases where anonymity was granted before Guardian.** The **ground** for refusing anonymity was that the applicant's name had been **disclosed earlier** in the proceedings, so that the risk of harm to him would not be averted by an anonymity order: paras [6], [13] and [29]. If judges give judgments like these, Lord Rodger will **not have occasion** to say in the future that anonymity orders are being made **"without the court considering in any detail what is the basis or justification for it"** (see para 8 above).

24. The reasons given in *Kaim Todner* for adhering to the general rule of naming the parties to litigation apply to personal injury claims. They are set out at p977 as follows:

> " . . . it is so important not to forget why proceedings are required to be subjected to the full glare of a public hearing. It is necessary because the public nature of proceedings deters inappropriate behaviour on the part of the court. It also maintains the public's confidence in the administration of justice. It enables the public to know that justice is being administered impartially. It can result in evidence becoming available which would not become available if the proceedings were conducted behind closed doors or with one or more of the parties' or witnesses' identity concealed. It makes uninformed and inaccurate comment about the proceedings less likely."

25. The need for **public confidence** to be maintained applies as much to the exercise of the court's jurisdiction **to protect the interests of children** and other protected parties as any to other proceedings before the court. And in personal injury cases publicity is an important means by which **exaggerated claims can be detected and deterred.** Exaggerated personal injury claims are **not infrequent**. If there is **publicity**, then neighbours and relations of a claimant whose claim has been exaggerated may know that fact, **and will be able to report it to the defendant**, usually a hospital authority or insurance company. The risk of exaggerated claims may be smaller where the claims are made by children. And there is no suggestion of that at all in this case. **But if anonymity became routine, then the risk would increase**. And as was also said in *Kaim Todner* immediately before the passage cited above:

> **"The need to be vigilant arises from the natural tendency for the general principle to be eroded and for exceptions to grow by accretion as the exceptions are applied by analogy to existing cases".**

26. In carrying out the balancing act required between Arts 8 and 10 (as explained in *In Re S*) the court **must focus on the particular facts of each case.**

DISCUSSION

27. In the present case I accept that there are **factors which expose the claimant to a risk of interference with his private life**. But I regard these factors as weak in this case. The size of awards of compensation is private information, but it is information of a kind that is very commonly reported, and the reports serve a **useful function in keeping the public informed.** The family's concern about media **intrusion** is genuine, but there is **nothing wrong with responsible reporting.** There is no evidence in this case to give rise to a reasonable fear that there would be any other kind of reporting. **A stronger point may be that the claimant has an awareness of his condition that makes him more**

sensitive to publicity than some other claimants would. But there is **little explanation** in the evidence of **how significant** that sensitivity may be.

28. I also accept that there is the risk that the **purpose** of the approval hearing will be **defeated** if the claimant is named, as explained in paras 9 and 11 above. **This is a strong argument in the present case.**

29. On the other hand, there is the general interest in publishing a report of these proceedings, including the name of the Claimant. That is the general interest that prevailed in *Kaim Todner,* and the general interest in naming claimants which is referred to in *Guardian* at para 62. **There is no general public interest in naming the claimant in these proceedings which is based on any fact specific to this case.**

CONCLUSION

30. **I concluded that in the present case naming the claimant would create the risk that the purpose of the approval hearing would be defeated, for the reason given in para 11 above.**

CDE and FGH v MGN Ltd and LMN [2010] EWHC 3308 (QB) per Eady J:

Publication of any report as to the subject matter of these proceedings or the identity of the Claimants is limited to what is contained in this judgment

Mr Justice Eady:

1. On 28 and 29 July 2010 I heard an application on the Claimants' behalf to continue an interim injunction originally granted on 16 July. Further submissions in writing were received in August, September and October from both sides. Then in November there was yet further evidence submitted and even a request for another oral hearing. Eventually, by the first week in December the parties decided that this was unnecessary but that I should receive more written submissions (on the maintenance of anonymity). The last were received on 13 December. This accounts for the considerable delay in delivering the judgment. **It has led to regrettable additional anxiety and stress for those immediately concerned.**

2. **The claim is based upon apprehended infringements of rights of confidence and/or privacy under Article 8 of the European Convention on Human Rights and Fundamental Freedoms**. This is a jurisdiction in which the decisions to be made are rarely straightforward. **By contrast** with the suggestion made by Lord Woolf CJ in the Court of Appeal in *A v B Plc* [2003] QB 195, it has proved, following the House of Lords' decisions in *Campbell v MGN Ltd* [2004]

2 AC 457 and in *Re S (A Child)* [2005] 1 AC 593, **that the answer in most cases is far from obvious**. Nevertheless, Parliament has clearly imposed upon judges, through s 12(3) of the Human Rights Act 1998, the burden of determining at this preliminary stage, **almost always on incomplete or partial evidence,** whether an injunction is likely to be granted at trial. **Guidance has been given by the House of Lords in Cream Holdings Ltd** *v Banerjee* [2005] 1 AC 253, but that does not make it any easier. There are **no hard and fast rules**. It is a question of weighing up competing Convention rights and forming a judgment on the **unique facts of each case.**

3. As is so often required in these cases, I shall need to tread a careful path, so as to make my reasons **comprehensible to any interested reader** while, at the same time, trying not to include material that would be **unnecessarily intrusive or embarrassing to the parties.**

4. The First Claimant often **appears on television** and is married to the Second Claimant. **They have always guarded their private lives closely and have never sought publicity.** They have **teenage children** whose interests they are also concerned to safeguard. The application is **intended to protect** them all, so far as possible, against the inevitable **intrusion** a newspaper publication would make into their private and family lives.

5. The Second Defendant is a **single mother in receipt of disability benefit**. It seems from the evidence that she had suffered from time to time with **mental health problems.** She has only ever met the First Claimant face to face on two occasions, in April 2009, when he made brief visits to her home. She nevertheless conducted a kind of **quasi-relationship with him "on and off"** between about March 2009 and February 2010 by means of telephone, texts, emails and tweets**. Intimate and personal thoughts were exchanged and there was also a good deal of flirtation and sexual innuendo.** She now wishes to sell her story to the *Sunday Mirror*, although it is said that she is not motivated by money. **A "confidential agreement" has already been entered into with the paper.** The **publisher of the newspaper has been joined** to these proceedings as the First Defendant.

6. Any such publication is likely to prove **distressing to the Claimants**, and **almost certainly to their children** also, and the proceedings are brought in an attempt to avoid that. Although there can be little doubt that the coverage contemplated would be **intrusive** upon the Claimants' family life and bring bewilderment and distress to their children, it is correspondingly true also of the Second Defendant's family. **She too has a young daughter (and another who is now an adult). I have no doubt that these are all persons whose Article 8 rights are currently engaged**: see now *Donald v Ntuli* [2010] EWCA Civ 1276 at [24]. It is also the case that the Defendants' Article 10 rights are in issue and have to be weighed alongside.

7. There **is evidence before** me as to the **likely impact** upon the Second Claimant's **health** and as to parental concerns about the **impact upon the children** in the school environment. As I understand the attitude of the newspaper, it is simply that a married man cannot be accorded greater rights or consideration by the court than a single man and, in so far as there may be any impact on his family, that is too bad. Yet it is now well established that the first question a court has to address on applications of this kind is whether Article 8 rights are engaged. As to that, **the threatened publication would undoubtedly engage the Article 8 rights of all the persons I have identified**. The fact that the First Claimant has a wife and children simply means that there **are more persons whose rights have to be taken into account**. They cannot simply be ignored on the basis of traditional arguments along the lines of who has a cause of action and who does not. Since they would at least potentially be affected by the exercise of the Defendants' Article 10 rights, **their Article 8 rights have to be weighed in the balance.**

8. There can be little doubt of the likely impact of publication on the First Claimant's life. It was articulated by the Second Defendant herself who told a *Sunday Mirror* journalist, in their initial conversation on 6 July, **"I just don't want it to wreck his life, because he doesn't deserve it . . . we all make mistakes, don't we, and I don't think we should crucify him for it".** It was hardly an exaggeration on her part to suggest that the lives of the Claimants and their family would be "wrecked"—at least for a significant time. Their counsel, Mr Desmond Browne QC, has laid emphasis on the protection afforded by Article 8, specifically, to family life and on the plea contained in the Second Claimant's evidence to be given the opportunity **to rebuild their marriage in private**. She herself has apparently lost a stone in weight.

9. The attitude of the Second Defendant was fairly consistent for several days at the beginning of July, in that she too regarded all this material as private and she herself then had no wish to see it exposed in the media. She first had an inkling of press interest when she was apparently **door-stepped** at the end of June by a female journalist representing the **News of the World.** She spoke of a "tip" that the Second Defendant and the First Claimant had had an affair and that he had left his wife. This was clearly inaccurate in that **no "affair" in the conventional sense of that term had taken place**. In so far as there was any such **relationship**, it could only be characterised as "virtual". Moreover, the First Claimant had only "left" the Second Claimant, for a few days in April 2009, in what has been described (by the Second Defendant) as a marital "blip". **It was so fleeting a separation that their children were not even aware of it.**

10. The *News of the World* journalist had gone on to use what Mr Browne called "the standard journalistic ploy" to secure co-operation from an unwilling

source. In the Second Defendant's words She was naturally anxious about it and spoke to the First Claimant. He was also concerned and feared that "his life was going to collapse". That conversation took place on the morning of 30 June, after he rang in response to a text message from her of the night before.

11. It seems, however, from the evidence of the Second Defendant's [**public relations adviser,** Mr X], that she had already seen him by this time. He claims that they first met on 29 June and there is no reason to doubt it. She says that she made contact with him on the recommendation and introduction of a Facebook "friend" (a journalist who wishes to remain anonymous). **She told Mr X at the first meeting that she wanted the story stopped if possible.** That seems to have been her **purpose** in consulting him. He gave some degree of encouragement to her on 2 July, stating that he thought that it would not get out. Unfortunately, rumours had already begun to appear on various websites. **How this story leaked out is not known, but there is clearly a limited range of possible sources.12. The Second Defendant texted the First Claimant that evening: "Bloody papers. My worst nightmare". She was still concerned about the story appearing in the media because of the impact on herself and her family; in particular, because she did not want to be portrayed as a person who had supposedly had an affair.**

13. The next day, 2 July, as she informed the First Claimant, she felt that she was "being pushed from all angles by everyone". She feared that she would be made to look like a "marriage wrecker". She again used the phrase "worst nightmare". Sadly, when she had been in a clinic in 2003 receiving treatment for mental health problems, she had been assaulted and abused by a male nurse—who has subsequently been convicted of a criminal offence. She received a large sum by way of compensation. He took advantage of her, it seems, while she was under the influence of prescribed drugs which he administered to her. She had then been suffering from anorexia and she was concerned that a photograph of her taken at that time, which showed her in an emaciated condition, might be resurrected and published in a newspaper. She had even been told by the *News of the World* journalist that *she* had such a **photograph** in her possession. **She was especially afraid about media coverage because her assailant might read all about it and recognise her.** The evidence suggests that the Second Defendant is, at least in some respects, **still a fragile and vulnerable person and that she has found this experience extremely distressing.**

14. During the afternoon of 2 July, she spoke to Mr David Price, the solicitor advocate who was giving advice to the First Claimant at that time. She told him that she had been to Mr X to try to stop the story coming out. She said that she just wanted to be left alone by everybody and not to be mentioned

in the press. She reassured Mr Price about her own intentions, when she said that she that she would not "do" a story and added: **"It goes against my morals. The only time I would ever talk about anything is if I was ripped to pieces and slagged off".** She also told him that she had been "friends" with the First Claimant and that she was "furthest from the kiss and tell type". It thus seemed to Mr Price at that time, not unreasonably, that there was a community of interest between her and his client. They both wished to avoid exposure in the press.

15. Her attitude at that time appeared to be that the whole **relationship** had been private. In her words, "**It's all private**. Me knowing [the First Claimant] is private. What happened between us is private. It's all private, but so is my illness". She told Mr Price, "I just want to be left alone as much as he does". She had no criticism to make of the First Claimant, saying that "[he] hasn't done anything really: neither of us have".

. . .

40. Although I was told in court by Mr James Price that the Second Defendant wished to publish her story by that stage, it is obvious from these exchanges that this was not always so. Indeed, even up to the time when she first consulted the solicitors introduced to her by Mr X, and who were also acting for the *Mirror*, **her wish (unlike that of the newspaper) was to avoid publication.** Moreover, **the pressure being exerted on her by Ms K (exemplified through her misrepresentations about David Price) is something to be borne in mind** when the court comes to carry out the balancing exercise as between Article 8 rights (including those of the Second Defendant) and the Article 10 rights of the two Defendants. It is clear, for example, from the Court of Appeal decision in *Murray v Express Newspapers Plc* [2009] Ch 481, at [36], that a judge needs to take into account *inter alia* " . . . **the circumstances in which and the purposes for which the information came into the hands of the publisher**". These are relevant considerations when it comes **to attributing a value** to the proposed *exercise of the Defendants' Article 10 rights as compared to the* **intrusive** *effect it would have upon the Article 8 rights of the Claimants.* **It is part of making an assessment of proportionality.**

41. Ms K's persistence seems eventually to have prevailed by the morning of 9 July, after she had given the Second Defendant the chance to "sleep on it". At 13.10 that afternoon, she texted David Price (still without in any way complaining about his behaviour):

> "Sorry, David. I'm being convinced this will very likely get out. If [the First Claimant] or I gag ourselves [i.e. by giving cross-undertakings], we'll have no defence opportunity."

42. It is worth noting that this reason for changing her mind, as being given at

that stage, has nothing to do with receiving "independent legal advice", as was later suggested in the course of submissions. It seems to have been brought about through her being persuaded (by Ms K and/or Mr X and/or by the solicitors he introduced) that the story would get out in the **public domain**—even if she withheld her co-operation. Yet no one ever offered her any rational explanation as to why that should be so. Nor was the prediction borne out by events.

43. **I must now come to the balancing exercise, as between the various competing Convention rights, and particularly having regard to the several public interest arguments presented on behalf of the Defendants.** This requires me to come to a conclusion as to the "likely" outcome at trial: see Lord Nicholls' speech in **Cream Holdings,** cited above. It is one of those cases in which there are conflicts of evidence, and of interpretation, such that the court has to labour at a disadvantage: **there has been no cross-examination to test the various accounts**. No application was made **for oral evidence** to be given and it would be a most **unusual step** to take in an application of this kind. One has, therefore, to decide what is **"likely"** to happen at trial **on the basis merely of what is so far available.**

44. **As to the Defendants' BBC argument,** there is a conflict between the Second Defendant and the production manager. She is said by the Second Defendant to have offered her protection on behalf of the BBC. This seems to me to be highly unlikely. . . .

45. **A second "public interest" point** was that there was a breach of s 127 of the Communications Act 2003, in that the First Claimant and the Second Defendant sent **intimate** images of themselves to one another by email. This is common ground. There is no need for me to go into detail. Whether this gives rise to a matter of public interest is rather doubtful. The point of whether such communications would give rise to criminal liability under the statute was expressly left open in relation to the telephone system in *DPP v Collins* [2006] 1 WLR 2223, where the legislative **purpose** of the provisions was analysed in the quite different context of racial abuse. As to telephone chat-lines, the position was referred to in passing at the end of Lord Brown's speech, he being the only member of the panel to address the question (*obiter*):

> "(Quite where that leaves telephone chat-lines, the very essence of which might be thought to involve the sending of indecent or obscene messages such as are also proscribed by section 127(1)(a) was not explored before your Lordships and can be left for another day)."

46. In any event, even supposing that their activities did technically amount to a breach of those statutory provisions**, it would not follow that the public**

interest in exposing this would be such as to justify the infringement of their privacy involved in newspaper exposure. There is nothing in either domestic or Strasbourg jurisprudence cited by Mr James Price that would support that proposition. It always remains a matter of balancing competing rights while paying due regard to proportionality: see e.g. the discussion in *Mosley v News Group Newspapers Ltd* [2008] EMLR 20 at [113]–[119].

47. Again, therefore, **I would conclude on the evidence at this stage that it is unlikely that, at trial, the exchange of intimate images would be held to be such as to justify the publication of allegations that would otherwise give rise to infringements of Article 8.** It is, incidentally, unclear as to how the revelation would be in the interest of the Second Defendant since, **if there was any significant wrongdoing, she would appear to be just as implicated herself.**

48. **A third public interest argument** presented on the Defendants' behalf was that the First Claimant had been exploiting a **vulnerable woman** for his own "gratification" and that this deserves, in the opinion of the relevant journalists, public exposure and condemnation. **There was no whisper of this from the Second Defendant herself until after she came into contact with the newspaper and its lawyers.** The evidence of the communications between them would appear to show quite clearly that **her participation** in the **explicit exchanges** was not only willing but **enthusiastic**. It is said that until she had the advantage of being advised independently, by the lawyers introduced by Mr X, she was not in a position to appreciate that she had been exploited. It was only the *Mirror* journalists who were perceptive enough to see this and, through the same lawyers, were able to make her realise that she had been a victim of the First Claimant (rather than a willing participant). **A number of points need to be made about this argument.**

49. **First**, it involves the assumption that the Second Defendant was vulnerable and not always capable of recognising when she was being exploited. The argument is two-edged, in the sense that if I make that assumption it would behove the court to take that vulnerability into account in assessing *any* act of exploitation. That is to say, I should be equally wary, when addressing the balance between her Article 8 rights and those under Article 10, as to her sudden change of heart about "going public". **If her apparently willing participation in the electronic and telephone exchanges is now not to be taken at face value, because of her vulnerability, why should the same caution not be applied to her recent volte face in deciding to allow her private life to be exposed in the tabloid newspaper?**

50 **Secondly**, the suggestion of **exploitation** *needs also to be assessed against the background of the* **Second Defendant's communications with other men** on Twitter. Once again, I shall not identify them or what passed between them,

but it is clear from paragraphs 35–37 of the First Claimant's second witness statement that she enjoyed sexually explicit and provocative exchanges not only with him **but with others** on the **Internet** generally what Mr James Price called "telephone sex". Indeed, on 29 January 2009 she herself described her Twitter account as "looking like a celeb stalkers function room". **This does not appear to be consistent with "victim" status.**

51. **Thirdly**, whether she was **exploited** by the First Claimant is an **issue of fact**, to be determined according to the available evidence (at this stage, of course, incomplete). It is not a matter of "independent legal advice". There is no evidence that points clearly to exploitation in the copious transcripts before me. It is an *interpretation* which the First Defendant and its lawyers now seek to put upon what happened. They invite the court to do the same but, in any event, argue that it is their interpretation which matters for present purposes and that it should prevail—whether the court is inclined to agree with it or not. But it seems to be clear, as a matter of legal principle, that it is for the court to decide whether the facts give rise to a **public interest in overriding relevant Article 8 rights (or are likely to do so at trial). It cannot be a trump card that one or more of the Defendants have been able to think up an interpretation of the facts, in hindsight, which happens to provide the makings of a public interest argument**. The court has to come to its own conclusion on the matter. Unlike the situation in *Mosley v News Group Newspapers Ltd* [2008] EMLR 20, which concerned the outcome of a trial, the court in the present case has to form a view about whether a public interest argument is **likely** ultimately to succeed. Nonetheless, it is still for the court to come to its own conclusion on that.

52. If it *were* relevant to address the issue of "**independent legal advice**", it would be necessary to have in mind the newspaper's interest in publishing a story about the private affairs of the Second Defendant and her clearly expressed wish, until she met the lawyers, to keep those matters private. That could be said to give rise to at least a potential **conflict of interest** which would, in itself, tend to undermine any argument based upon "independent legal advice".

. . .

73. More central to the decision I have to make is the issue of whether the proposed revelations, **intrusive** as they plainly would be, are **"likely"** at trial to be classified merely as **embarrassing tittle tattle or rather as serving some more valuable function**. Is it likely to be held that it would be in the public interest as contemplated, for example, in the Press Complaints Commission Code? Or would it contribute, in the words of the Court in Strasbourg, in *Von Hannover v Germany* (2005) 40 EHRR 1, to a "debate of general interest

to society"? **On the evidence before me, it seems clear that the answers would be in the negative**. Accordingly, I will continue the injunction, as in my judgment the Claimants are likely to succeed in obtaining a permanent injunction against **intrusions** of the kind contemplated by the Defendants.

74. I had in mind that this **anonymised** judgment should be publicly available and that to reduce the risks of "**jigsaw identification**", which are well known generally and evident in this case**, it would be appropriate to make an order of the kind proposed by Sharp J in DFT v TFD** [2010] EWHC 2335 (QB) **and by the Court of Appeal in Donald v Ntuli**, cited above. The need for such an order is rather confirmed by recent evidence which, Mr Browne suggests, indicates that the Second Defendant herself has regrettably been seeking ways in which to circumvent the existing order of the court. I took into account submissions on the form of order that was appropriate in the light of my rulings.

75. As I indicated at the outset of the judgment, the Defendants sought to argue, very late in the day, that the judgment should, after all, not be anonymised. This has been responsible for the further delay since it was first raised on 27 October.

76. There is no point in any longer anonymising the First Defendant, since I have identified MGN Ltd in paragraph [5] above and throughout the judgment. As to the individual parties, however, it seems to me self-evident that **to identify either of them would entirely defeat the court's purpose in granting the injunction.** That which it is intended should be kept private, until the trial, would to all intents and purposes become public: there would be no point in having a trial.

77. As has recently been re-emphasised by the Court of Appeal in *Donald v Ntuli*, at [54], and by the Supreme Court in *Secretary of State for the Home Department v AP (No 2)* [2010] 1 WLR 1652 at [7], the **question of anonymity is "an essentially case-sensitive subject".**

78. The desirability of open justice has long been acknowledged and was explained, for example, a century ago in *Scott v Scott* [1913] AC 417. Lord Diplock referred to that earlier decision in *Att-Gen v Leveller Magazine Ltd* [1979] AC 440, 449–50 and summarised the position succinctly:

> "If the way that courts behave cannot be hidden from the public ear and eye this provides a safeguard against judicial arbitrariness or idiosyncrasy and maintains the public confidence in the administration of justice."

79. To similar effect were the words of Woodhouse P in the New Zealand Court of Appeal in *Broadcasting Corp of New Zealand v Att-Gen* [1982] 1 NZLR 120, 122–3, where he referred to the importance of public access to justice and

the need for judges to carry out their responsibilities under **the eyes of their fellow citizens**. The **purpose** is to provide daily and public assurance, *inter alia*, that justice is being administered by a fair and balanced application of the law to facts as they really appear to be. He continued:

> **"It is a matter as well of maintaining a system of justice which requires that the judiciary will be seen day by day attempting to grapple in the same even fashion with the whole generality of cases."**

80. It is to be noted that in both these passages what is given emphasis, for obvious reasons, is **the need for the public to understand the court's reasoning processes** and how the law has been applied in different factual situations.

81. Nonetheless, it has always been recognised that in certain circumstances it may become necessary to impose restrictions on the principle of open justice for various reasons. Even so, where such circumstances arise, those restrictions need to be kept to the minimum necessary to achieve the particular **purpose**. As Lord Diplock observed in the *Leveller* case:

> ". . . since the **purpose** of the general rule is to serve the ends of justice it may be necessary to depart from it where the nature or circumstances of the particular proceeding are such that the application of the general rule in its entirety would frustrate or render impracticable the administration of justice or would damage some other public interest for whose protection Parliament has made some statutory derogation from the rule."

82. So too, Lord Loreburn noted in *Scott v Scott*, at 446:

> "In all cases where the public has been excluded with admitted propriety the underlying principle, as it seems to me, is that the administration of justice would be rendered impracticable by their presence, whether because the case could not be effectively tried, or the parties entitled to justice would be reasonably deterred from seeking it at the hands of the court."

His Lordship also commented that it may occasionally be necessary to exclude the public if **"justice will be frustrated or declined if the court is made a place of moral torture".** Of course, if those whose rights are threatened are "reasonably deterred from seeking [justice] at the hands of the court", then to that extent access to justice is denied and Article 6 rights are correspondingly undermined.

83. **It is obvious why anonymity is so regularly applied in breach of confidence and privacy cases. If the parties were identified, it would often mean that the confidentiality was lost.** As Sir John Donaldson MR put it in *Att.-Gen. v Newspaper Publishing Plc* [1988] Ch 333, **the ice cube would have melted**.

The court and litigants alike would be frustrated in giving effect to important rights that need to be recognised and implemented by reason now of the European Convention. Usually, there will be competing rights under Article 8, Article 6 and Article 10 that have to be reconciled. In some well known cases, Article 2 has also been engaged, but that is of no relevance here. In this case, it is a question of balancing the rights of the Claimants (and/or their family) under Article 8 and Article 6, on the one side, with those of the Defendants under Article 10. Additionally, however, there is the interest of the general public in open justice (another aspect of Article 6).

84. **The most important element of open justice in this case, as with many other privacy and confidence cases, is that interested observers and legal practitioners should be able to monitor the court's processes and form a view as to whether judges are applying a consistent, fair and balanced approach in the application of this recently developed jurisdiction to the facts of individual cases.**

85. As Maurice Kay LJ pointed out in *Donald v Ntuli*, however, any litigant in such a case is entitled to expect that the court will adopt procedures which ensure that any ultimate vindication of his Article 8 case should not be undermined by the way in which the court has processed any interim application. Thus it may be helpful to set about the balancing exercise, as between privacy rights and the public's interest in open justice, by posing the question in the form adopted by Lord Rodger in the *AP (No 2)* case. **Is there a sufficient general, public interest in publishing a report of the proceedings which identifies the person concerned to justify any resulting curtailment of his right and his family's right to respect for their private and family life (my emphasis)?** In this particular case, the rights of the parties' families are of considerable importance.

86. The central public consideration in this case is that **the reasoning of the court should be transparent.** Compared to that, **the social utility or value to be attached to identification, as such, is relatively low:** cf *XJA v News Group Newspapers Ltd* [2010] EWHC 3174 (QB) at [15]. **There may be cases in which it is possible to reveal the identity of one or more of the litigants involved and yet not defeat the purpose of the court's protection. If so, well and good**. It is plainly desirable that everything should be made public unless there is a sound reason to withhold any information—including the parties' identities. But I am satisfied that this is not such a case. It is necessary and proportionate to withhold their identities to ensure, so far as possible, that the information to which rights of privacy are said to attach should not be revealed pending trial. Otherwise a trial would serve no **purpose**.

87. After the draft judgment was circulated, a further hearing took place in private to enable me to hear the parties' submissions on the **consequential**

orders that would reflect my rulings. At that stage, Mr James Price invited me to consider **anonymising in the public judgment, apart from the parties, (a) the Sunday Mirror journalist, (b) his instructing solicitor, (c) the Second Defendant's public relations adviser and (d) his assistant. This was a very unusual request, but it will already have been noted that, not without hesitation, I agreed to comply with it.**

88. The reason for taking such an unusual course really springs from the nature of the exercise a judge is required to carry out under s 12(3) of the Human Rights Act. Although it might be thought that my conclusions do not reflect very well on those people**, I have been at some pains to emphasise that I am not making findings about them at this stage.** These hearings have not been part of a trial. All I am required to do is to try to decide on incomplete (and untested) evidence what is "likely" to be the outcome at trial.

89. Meanwhile, says Mr James Price, it might give rise to unfairness if casual observers interpret my observations as though they *were* the ultimate findings. It is true that much of what I have said is based on recordings and facts which are incontrovertible but, even so, upon closer examination facts sometimes emerge in a different light. That is why I was prepared to go along with counsel's suggestion for the time being. I was reminded of the decision in *R v Legal Aid Board, ex parte Kaim Todner* [1999] QB 966 and I bear in mind the important policy considerations addressed in that case but, for the reasons canvassed by Mr James Price, I will grant the anonymity to the non-parties on a temporary basis.

XJA v News Group Newspapers Ltd
[2010] EWHC 3174 (QB) per Sharp J

Mrs Justice Sharp:

Publication of any report as to the subject matter of these proceedings or the identity of the Claimants is limited to what is contained in this judgment

1. I am asked to approve a **consent order agreed** between the parties. It contains provisions (in particular relating to **anonymity**) which require the approval of the court since they derogate from the principle of open justice.
2. I have heard oral submissions from James Price QC on behalf of the Claimant, and written submissions from Richard Spearman QC on behalf of the Defendant.
3. All of the hearings to which this judgment refers, were **held in private**. I was satisfied it was necessary for the hearings which were held before me, to be

held in private pursuant to **CPR 39.2(3)(a)(c) and (e)** because otherwise the applications would be self-defeating.

4. The Claimant, XJA made an application **on short notice** to the Defendant for an interim injunction, restraining the publication of certain information, which the Defendant had informed XJA earlier that day, it intended to publish. It was said that publication would be a misuse of private information. The application was heard by Calvert-Smith J, and was opposed. The judge granted the relief asked for (including that the Claimant be **anonymised)** and provided for a very short return day for a full hearing between the parties, 2 days later. The matter then came before me, on an application for the continuation of the injunction, which was opposed. After Mr Price had made submissions on behalf of the Claimant however (including, to the effect that the central information with which the action was concerned was false) Mr Spearman, on behalf of the Defendant asked the court to adjourn the matter part-heard, for 7 days to enable further investigations to be carried out. This application was not opposed, and I granted it. The investigations were on-going, and on the day before the adjourned hearing was due to take place, the Defendant asked again, for a further 7 day adjournment. This was not opposed, and again, I granted the application.

5. By the time of the next adjourned hearing date, the parties had agreed a consent order, subject to the court's approval in relation to the provisions concerning open justice, which provided, amongst other matters, for the continuation of the interim relief granted by Calvert-Smith J until trial or further order.

6. On behalf of the Claimant, Mr Price submits that following the decision of the Court of Appeal in *Ntuli v Donald* [2010] EWCA Civ 1276, the relevant question on anonymity which has to be answered is that posed in the judgment of Lord Roger in *Home Secretary v AP (No 2)* [2010] 1 WLR 1652 at [7]:

   > " . . . the court must ask itself 'whether there is a sufficient general public interest in publishing a report of the proceedings which identifies [AP] to justify any resulting curtailment of his right and his family's right to respect for their private and family life.' The court [in *Re Guardian News & Media*] emphasised that the answer will depend on the facts of the particular case."

7. Mr Price emphasises that the Court of Appeal reiterated in *Ntuli* at [54] that **"this is an essentially case-sensitive subject".** It follows therefore that reference to earlier or other cases is unlikely to be of significant assistance in answering the relevant question.

8. On the facts of this case, he submits it is clear that the Claimant has a reasonable expectation of privacy in relation to the information that he is the

person who brought these proceedings and obtained an injunction to protect his privacy. The Claimant is a well-known pe rson**. If the Claimant's identity became public it would lead to intrusive questions and speculation which would be extremely distressing for him and his family**. The Claimant would be placed in a particularly invidious position because the central information with which this action is concerned is (on the Claimant's case) fictional. The Claimant would either have to remain silent when faced with questions and speculation, including questions from family and friends, which would lead to people supposing the information in issue was true, and very likely of an embarrassing or humiliating nature (in short, that he had acted appallingly and was trying to cover it up). Or he would have to explain, by saying the information is false which would to that extent, defeat the **purpose** of the injunction. **Either way, publication of the information would seriously affect the harmony of his family.**

9. **Mr Price also submits that the *bare fact* that a named claimant has obtained a privacy injunction covering unspecified private information serves no public purpose: it contributes nothing to the useful stock of public knowledge or to a debate of public interest.** On the contrary, it would simply feed useless and potentially damaging speculation. It is not a case of a report being **disembodied** (as in *Re Guardian News & Media* [2010] 2 WLR 325, see in particular paragraphs **[63]** and **[64]**): there is nothing to report about the case since the injunction is being continued by consent.

10. In *JIH v News Group Newspapers Ltd* [2010] EWHC 2818, *(JIH (No 1))*, Tugendhat J **refused anonymity** to a claimant, though the parties had consented to an order being made to that effect. Mr Spearman in his written submissions says that *JIH (No 1)* is currently listed before the Court of Appeal for permission to appeal, with the appeal to follow if permission is granted. There is also a direction that the application for permission is to be heard as soon as possible. In those circumstances, it does not seem sensible from the Defendant's perspective, to embark upon an argument on anonymity without the guidance that the Court of Appeal may give in that case; and the Defendant considers its position is fully protected by the terms of the consent order which provides for liberty to apply, which is unqualified.

Discussion

11. In *Ntuli*, Maurice Kay LJ said at [52] that "as part of its consideration of all the circumstances of a case, a court will have regard to the respective and sometimes competing Convention rights of the parties." He went on to say this at [54]:

> "This is an essentially case-sensitive subject. Plainly Mr Donald is entitled to expect that the court will adopt procedures which ensure

that any ultimate vindication of his Article 8 case is not undermined by the way in which the court has processed the interim applications and the trial itself. On the other hand, the principle of open justice requires that any restrictions are the least that can be imposed consistent with the protection to which Mr Donald is entitled."

12. **Nothing in the judgment should be taken as a comment on the merits of this case either way**. As Tugendhat J said in *JIH (No 1)* at [24], it is open to the parties to compromise their rights; the only concern therefore is whether those terms affect the duties of the court and the rights of third parties. In *JIH (No 1)* it appears that while the consent order provided that the interim order should be continued until final judgment or further order in the meantime, in light of other provisions agreed between the parties, that order might well be the last order the court is asked to make in that action (see paragraphs [26] to [27] of the judgment). In this case however, the parties have agreed to the continuation of the order made by Calvert-Smith J, **until trial or further order**; and there **is nothing to suggest that this case will not, in fact progress to a trial.**

13. Although it is **rare for cases such as these to go to trial,** in my view, at the interim stage, and in particular before there has been a full return day hearing, both as part of its consideration of the overall circumstances which apply in the particular case, and of the general public interest in open justice, the court may need to consider what might happen in the future. **Naming a claimant may well have an impact on what if anything can be said in a later public judgment,** including after a trial. There may be cases (*McKennitt v Ash* [2005] EWHC 3003 (QB); affd, [2008] QB 73, is one such example) where even if the claimant is named in an action in which he is ultimately successful, the nature of the information or the subject matter of the information could be revealed in a public judgment after a trial in general terms, without revealing the private information the action is brought to protect.

14. If however the case is one in which it would not be possible as a matter of reality, for the court to indicate the nature of the information without revealing it (and in my view, this is such a case) **naming a claimant at the interim stage may produce an undesirable restriction on what could be said in a subsequent judgment,** including a fully reasoned public judgment after a trial.

15. In this case, I have concluded on the facts, and having regard to the considerations to which I have referred above that there is no sufficient general public interest in identifying the Claimant at this stage of the proceedings, to justify any resulting curtailment of his right and his family's right to respect for their private and family life. The article 8 rights of the Claimant are engaged in my view, both as to the subject matter of the action and as to

the information that the Claimant is the person who brought these proceedings and obtained an injunction to protect his privacy. Identification of the Claimant could on the evidence before me, seriously affect his family life. It is material in my view, that the central information with which this action is concerned is said to be false, for the reasons Mr Price gives. The issue of truth or falsity is yet to be determined. But it seems to me it is a factor in this case which is relevant to the seriousness of the interference with the article 8 rights of the Claimant, and to the need for an anonymity order. As against that, there is nothing to report about this case, apart from **the bare fact** that an identified claimant has obtained a privacy injunction, and the court's consideration on the issue of anonymity, which cannot feed on itself to create a justification for identifying the Claimant.

16. I find therefore in all the circumstances, **that disclosure of the Claimant's identity would be an unjustifiable interference with his private and family life, which outweighs the rights of the public under article 10 and the need for open justice;** and that it is **necessary** therefore to continue the order that the Claimant shall not be identified. I make the order which the parties have put before me and agreed, which includes an order that there be **no report of these proceedings or the subject matter of these proceedings which is not included in this judgment.**

JIH v News Group Newspapers Ltd [2011] EWCA Civ 42

The Master of the Rolls:

Introductory

1. The courts are not infrequently asked to make orders preventing the publication of private information, concerning, for instance, the details of a person's **finances, health, sexual activities**, or **family life**. In such cases, the claimant is **normally** (but by no means always) a **public figure**, and at least one of the defendants is normally (but by no means always) a member of the national **media.**

2. When considering what order to make on such applications, it is normally necessary to balance two competing legal rights, each of which constitutes a **fundamental** feature of a **civilised** modern democratic society. Those competing rights are an individual's right to "respect for his private and family life", as stipulated in **Article 8** of the European Human Rights Convention and relied on by the claimant, and the more general right to "freedom of expression", relied on by the defendant and laid down by **Article 10** of the

Convention, which also refers to the "right . . . to receive and impart information and ideas".

3. In many cases, this **balancing** exercise is **difficult**. This is partly because the two rights are rather **different** in their **constituent factors**, partly because there are often powerful arguments pointing in **opposite** directions, partly because each case depends very much on **its own particular facts**, and partly because the exercise can involve a significant degree of **subjectivity.**

4. When the balance comes down in favour of preventing publication, a further **problem** sometimes **arises**, namely the **extent** to which, and **the way** in which, the parties' **evidence** and **arguments**, and the court's **reasoning** and **order**, in the particular case **can be reported.** It would be wrong to permit unrestrained reporting in the normal way, as that would involve publishing the name of the claimant and the details of the information whose publication he seeks to prevent, thereby rendering the court's order pointless. On the other hand, **public coverage** of court proceedings is a **fundamental aspect** of **freedom of expression**, with particular importance**: the ability of the press freely to observe and report on proceedings in the courts is an essential ingredient of the rule of law**. Indeed the right to a "fair and public hearing" and the obligation to pronounce judgment in public, save where it conflicts with "the protection of the private lives of the parties" or "would prejudice the interests of justice", are set out in Article 6 of the Convention.

5. The appeal in this case is concerned with this issue of reporting restrictions, and, as both Mr Hugh Tomlinson QC (who appears for the claimant with Mr David Sherborne) and Mr Richard Spearman QC (who appears for the defendant) contend, it therefore raises **a point of general concern** and of some importance. However, **the determination of the precise extent of what can be reported about the proceedings themselves** is every bit as fact-sensitive as the anterior exercise of deciding whether to make an order restraining publication of the private information in the first place.

6. As Maurice Kay LJ said in a recent case raising a somewhat similar issue, *Ntuli v Donald* [2010] EWCA Civ 1276, para 52, when deciding whether, and if so to what extent, to impose reporting restrictions in relation to legal proceedings, "as part of its consideration of all the circumstances of a case, a court will have regard to the respective and sometimes competing Convention rights of the parties." He went on to say this, two paragraphs later:

> "This is an essentially case-sensitive subject. Plainly [the claimant] is entitled to expect that the court will adopt procedures which ensure that any ultimate vindication of his Article 8 case is not undermined by the way in which the court has processed the interim applications and the trial itself. On the other hand, the principle of open justice requires that

any restrictions are the least that can be imposed consistent with the protection to which [the claimant] is entitled."

An outline of the facts

7. The facts of this case (in so far as they can fairly be set out in a publicly available judgment concerning information about the claimant's private life, which it is accepted should not be published, at least for the moment, and as they were described by Mr Tomlinson in open court) are as follows. The claimant, known for present purposes as JIH, is **a well known sportsman**, who has, for some time, been in an apparently **long-term** and **conventional relationship** with another person, to whom I shall refer as "XX". Since his **relationship** with XX had started, but before August 2010, a story had been published, **without JIH having received any prior notice**, suggesting that he had had a sexual liaison with another person, whom I shall call "YY".

8. The story whose publication JIH is seeking to prevent concerns an alleged **sexual encounter** he had with a **different person**, to whom I shall refer as "ZZ", last year. In August 2010, JIH discovered that the defendant, News Group Newspapers Ltd ("NGN"), had been told of this **alleged encounter by ZZ.**

9. On learning that NGN intended to publish a story in *The Sun*, based on the information provided by ZZ, JIH began the present proceedings in August 2010 without revealing his identity in the publicly available court papers. He immediately made an application seeking an order, on an interlocutory basis (i.e. **until the trial of his action**), preventing the publication of information contained in a "**Confidential Schedule".** That Schedule referred to **"[i]nformation concerning a sexual relationship or alleged sexual relationship between [JIH] and [ZZ] during the period of his relationship with [XX] . . . ., including the fact or any details of such relationship"** (and I think it is clear that "such **relationship**" is that with ZZ).

10. JIH's proceedings were served on seven other media companies, and the application was granted in the form of a short term injunction by Nicol J on 13 August 2010, **while NGN and the other media companies had the opportunity to consider their respective positions.**

11. Thereafter, having considered JIH's claim and, no doubt, having taken legal advice, NGN entered into **negotiations** with JIH, with a view to agreeing terms pending the trial of his claim. These negotiations **resulted in an agreed form of order** in which, to summarise the essence of the agreement for present purposes, until the trial of these proceedings (or further order in the meantime), (a) NGN would submit to an injunction preventing it from publishing "all or any part of the information contained in the **Confidential Schedule",** save to the extent that any such information **was in an open judgment of the**

court, and, crucially for present purposes, (b) the **identity** of JIH would not be disclosed, and (c) the hearing of the application be in **private**, and **not be reported**. The basis of the order was that NGN accepted that, at least until trial, publication of the information in the schedule would arguably infringe JIH's Article 8 rights, which would outweigh the Article 10 rights relied on by NGN.

12. When the draft agreed order ("the draft order") was presented for approval to **Tugendhat J**, he decided that he was **not prepared** to make the order, at least without having heard argument which persuaded him that it was appropriate to do so. In taking that course, he was following the approach which he had adopted in *Gray v UVW* [2010] EWHC 2367 (QB), where he had held that "**an order for anonymity and reporting restrictions cannot be made simply because the parties consent: parties cannot waive the rights of the public"** (quoting from the judgment below in this case, [2010] EWHC 2818 (QB), para 3). **I agree both with the principle there identified, and with the consequent right, indeed obligation, of a Judge to take the course which Tugendhat J took in this case on being presented with the draft order**, namely to call for argument to persuade him to approve any part of an order which restricts or prevents publication of any aspect of the proceedings, and about which he has any doubts or worries.

13. The reason that the Judge called for argument as to the terms of the draft order was not concerned with the principle of whether an interlocutory injunction restraining publication of the information in question should be made: **the Judge plainly thought that such an injunction was justified**. What **worried** the Judge was the **breadth of the draft order** so far as the **reporting restrictions** it contained: he thought that they went too far.

14. Having heard argument on the terms of the draft order concerning restraints on publication, Tugendhat J gave judgment on 5 November 2010. In that judgment, he concluded that the draft order should be approved, subject to the important exception that he should **refuse** JIH's application to continue Nicol J's order granting him **anonymity**—[2010] EWHC 2818 (QB). Although Tugendhat J **refused permission to appeal**, he sensibly **stayed** the implementation of the order so as to give JIH the opportunity to appeal to this court.

15. Thereafter, there was some media reporting of the case, which revealed more than was permitted by Tugendhat J's order of 5 November. As a result, JIH brought the matter back before the Judge, asking him to reconsider his refusal to accord JIH anonymity. That application was refused in a judgment given on 18 November—[2010] EWHC 2979 (QB). **The Judge refused JIH permission to appeal against that order also.**

The present application

16. JIH then applied**, initially in writing in the normal way**, for permission to appeal against both decisions to this court. I ordered that JIH's applications for permission to appeal against the two judgments should be heard by three members of the Court of Appeal**, with any appeal to follow immediately if either application succeeded**. This is not normally a procedure I favour, but, on this occasion, where there were **two potential appeals**, where any refusal of permission would have **resulted in a renewed application** which would have involved a hearing, where the matter was **urgent** for the parties, and where the issues raised might well be of **wider significance**, it seemed right to make such an order.

17. The hearing of the applications was **held in open court**. It was obviously right, as a matter of principle, to have the hearing in public if it was possible to do so. As both counsel very sensibly accepted, this was indeed possible**, on the basis that, at the hearing, the identity of JIH was not revealed,** and some of **the facts**, and some of the **contents of the documents** were referred to in rather coded or **referential terms.**

18. Mr Tomlinson argued that JIH should have been accorded anonymity, either on the basis of the position as it was as at the first hearing before Tugendhat J, or in view of the publicity which occurred thereafter. **Mr Spearman** presented the case for NGN to the contrary with **commendable restraint**, bearing in mind, on the one hand, that his client had agreed the order for anonymity, and, on the other hand, that he wished to give the court all the assistance that he could. **The case against anonymity was supported by written submissions from Ms Gillian Phillips, Director of Legal Services of Guardian News & Media, and from Mr Marcus Partington on behalf of The Media Lawyers Association.**

Open justice and the need for restraint

19. The cardinal importance of open justice is demonstrated by what is stated in Article 6 of the Convention. But it has long been a feature of the common law. It was famously articulated in the speeches in *Scott v Scott* [1913] AC 417—see particularly at [1913] AC 417, 438, 463 and 477, per Lord Haldane LC, Lord Atkinson, and Lord Shaw of Dunfermline respectively. The point was perhaps most pithily made by Lord Atkinson when he said "in public trial is to be found, on the whole, **the best security for the pure, impartial, and efficient administration of justice, the best means for winning for it public confidence and respect."** For a more recent affirmation of the principle, see *R(Binyam Mohamed) v Secretary of State for Foreign and Commonwealth Affairs* [2010] EWCA Civ 65, paras 38–42, per Lord Judge CJ.

20. However, as with almost all fundamental principles, the open justice rule is

not absolute: as is clear from Article 6, there will be individual cases, even types of cases, where it has to be qualified. In a case involving the grant of an injunction to restrain the publication of allegedly private information, it is, as I have indicated, rightly common ground that, where the court concludes that it is right to grant an injunction (whether on an interim or final basis) restraining the publication of private information, the court may then have to consider how far it is necessary to impose restrictions on the reporting of the proceedings in order not to deprive the injunction of its effect.

21. In a case such as this, where the protection sought by the claimant is an anonymity order or other restraint on publication of details of a case which are normally in the **public domain**, certain principles were identified by the Judge, and which, together **with principles contained in valuable written observations** to which I have referred, I would summarise as follows:

(1) The **general rule** is that the names of the parties to an action are included in orders and judgments of the court.

(2) There is no general exception for cases where private matters are in issue.

(3) An order for anonymity or any other order restraining the publication of the normally reportable details of a case **is a derogation** from the principle of open justice and **an interference with the Article 10 rights** of the **public at large**.

(4) Accordingly, where the court is asked to make any such order, it should only do so after **closely scrutinising** the application, and considering whether a degree of restraint on publication is **necessary**, and, if it is, **whether there is any less restrictive or more acceptable alternative than that which is sought.**

(5) Where the court is asked to restrain the publication of the names of the parties and/or the subject matter of the claim, on the ground that such restraint is necessary under Article 8, the question is whether there is **sufficient general, public interest in publishing a report of the proceedings** which identifies a party and/or the normally reportable details to **justify any resulting curtailment of his right and his family's right to respect for their private and family life.**

(6) On any such application, **no special treatment should be accorded to public figures or celebrities:** in principle, they are entitled to the **same protection as others**, no more and no less.

(7) An order for anonymity or for reporting restrictions should **not** be made **simply because the parties consent**: parties cannot waive the rights of the public.

(8) An anonymity order or any other order restraining publication made by a Judge at an interlocutory stage of an injunction application **does not last for the duration** of the proceedings **but must be reviewed at the return date.**

(9) Whether or not an **anonymity order** or an order restraining publication of normally reportable details is made, then, at least where a judgment is or would normally be given, **a publicly available judgment should normally be given,** and a copy of the **consequential court order should also be publicly available**, although some editing of the judgment or order may be necessary.

(10) **Notice of any hearing should be given to the defendant unless there is a good reason not to do so**, in which case the court should **be told of the absence of notice and the reason for it,** and should be satisfied that the reason is a good one.

22. Where, as here, the basis for any claimed restriction on publication ultimately rests on a judicial assessment, it is therefore essential that **(a)** the judge is first satisfied that the facts and circumstances of the case are sufficiently strong to justify encroaching on the open justice rule by restricting the extent to which the proceedings can be reported, and **(b)** if so, the judge ensures that the restrictions on publication are fashioned so as **to satisfy** the need for the encroachment in a way which **minimises the extent of any restrictions.**

23. In the present case, as in many cases where the court grants an injunction restraining publication of information, the claimant's case as to why there is a need for restraints on publication of aspects of the proceedings themselves which can normally be published is **simple and cogent**. If the media could publish the name of the claimant and the substance of the information which he is seeking to exclude from the **public domain** (i.e. what would normally be information of absolutely central significance in any story about the case—who is seeking what), **then the whole purpose of the injunction would be undermined,** and the claimant's private life may be **unlawfully exposed.**

24. In the course of his judgment, at [2010] EWHC 2818 (QB), paras 8 and 9, Tugendhat J accepted the proposition advanced before him by Mr Tomlinson for JIH that:

> "Where the court has accepted that the publication of private information should be restrained, if the court is to avoid disclosing the information in question **it must proceed in one of two alternative ways:**
>
> **(1) If its public judgment or order directly or indirectly discloses the nature of the information in question then it should be anonymised;**

(2) If the claimant is named in the public judgment or order then the information should not be directly or indirectly identified."

25. While that is not an unfair assessment in the present case, in other cases the position will sometimes be a little less stark. **However, in any case, it is plainly correct that, where the court permits the identity of the claimant to be revealed, it is hard to envisage circumstances where that would not mean that significantly less other information about the proceedings could be published than if the proceedings were anonymised**. Thus, if the identity of JIH could be published in the context of the present proceedings, it would not be appropriate to permit the publication of even the relatively exiguous information contained in paras 7–9 above. As the Judge went on to say, the obvious corollary is that, **if the claimant is accorded anonymisation, it will almost always be appropriate to permit more details of the proceedings to be published than if the claimant is identified.**

The reasoning of Tugendhat J in this case

26. The Judge gave a full and careful judgment on 5 November 2010, in which he concluded that **anonymity** should **no**t be accorded to JIH. While that decision did not involve the exercise of a discretion, it involved a balancing exercise, with which, at least as a matter of general principle, an appellate court **should be slow to interfere**. When considering an appeal against such a decision, an appellate court is normally exercising a **reviewing function**, and should not allow the appeal unless satisfied that the judge was wrong. As I said in *Flood v Times Newspapers Ltd* [2010] EWCA Civ 804, para 49, **"[w]here the determination is a matter of balance and proportionality, it is, generally speaking, difficult for an appellant to establish that the judge has gone wrong".** All the more so, where, as here, the Judge is **very respected** and **highly experienced** in the particular area of practice, and has given the issue very careful consideration.

27. However, in this particular case, I am satisfied that, owing to a **misunderstanding or an oversight**, the Judge's decision cannot stand. As he pointed out, the draft order was too restrictive in the extent to which it prevented the reporting of these proceedings. And, it should be added, it was only because of Tugendhat J's **vigilance** that this point was identified: had he not read and considered the draft order when it was sent to him for approval, and had he simply approved it, this point would have gone by default.

28. As the Judge held, the draft order was **too restrictive in that it both gave JIH anonymity and prevented the reporting of any aspect of the evidence.** As explained above, it is clear that, if anonymity was refused, so that JIH was identified in the media, the information contained in paras 7–9 above could not also be published. However, **if anonymity was granted, it seems equally**

clear that that information could be published, without undermining the purpose of the injunction. So the Judge was right in concluding that the **choice** to be made **was between revealing the identity of JIH or revealing the general nature of the information which he was seeking to keep private.**

29. The Judge's **decision to opt for revealing** JIH's **identity**, rather than revealing the **general nature of the information** sought to be protected, was based on the propositions that **(a)** it was **common ground** between the parties, as demonstrated by the draft order, that the general nature of the information should **not be revealed**, and (b) it had **not** been submitted on behalf of JIH that this should be reconsidered. Accordingly**, as even the general nature of the information was not to be published,** it followed that JIH's identity should **not be withheld** from the public, **given that restrictions on reporting should always be kept to a minimu**m. That this was the reasoning of the Judge is clear from what he said at [2010] EWHC 2818 (QB), para 63, and [2010] EWHC 2979 (QB), para 16.

30. In my view, this approach was, on analysis, erroneous, although I understand how the error arose. Once the Judge had, rightly, called for argument as to the terms of the draft order so far as reporting restrictions were concerned, **all aspects of the draft order in that connection were up for consideration.** Furthermore, although Mr Spearman's analysis of JIH's skeleton argument below has established how it might have been understood otherwise, and the point appears to have been made only relatively briefly in oral submission, I am satisfied that Mr Tomlinson did argue below that**, if the restrictions in the draft order on reporting this case were to be reduced,** it was the general details of the story which should be reportable in the media, and JIH's **anonymity** should be retained.

31. Accordingly, the Judge reached his conclusion in his judgment on a mistaken basis. In my view, we should therefore give JIH permission to appeal, and, as indicated when the application was listed for hearing, we should go ahead and decide the appeal. Furthermore, I consider that, rather than sending the case back, which would incur further delay and cost, we should decide the issue ourselves; indeed, the parties did not suggest otherwise.

Discussion

32. **As I have explained, the *choice* we face is either permitting JIH to be identified or permitting all the information contained in this judgment, and in particular in paras 7–9 above, to be published**. I have reached the conclusion that, on the facts of this case, it would be right to accede to JIH's claim **for anonymisation**, and that, as a result, the information contained in this judgment (but no other information about the facts about or giving rise to the case, at least if they could assist in JIH being identified) can be published.

33. If the identity of JIH is revealed, then the only details of the case which it would be realistically possible to permit to be **published, would be the fact that he is seeking a permanent injunction, and has obtained an interlocutory injunction, to restrain The Sun from publishing information about him which he contends is of a private nature**. At least on the face of it, there is **obvious force in the contention** that the **public interest** would be better served by publication of the fact that the court has granted an injunction to an **anonymous well known sportsman**, in the circumstances described in paras 7–9 above, than by being told that it has granted an injunction to an identified person to restrain publication of **unspecified information** of an allegedly private nature.

34. In *Re Guardian News and Media Ltd* [2010] UKSC 1, [2010] 2 WLR 325, para 22, Lord Rodger referred to the **"recent efflorescence of anonymity orders"**, although it is right to emphasise that this was in a rather different context from the present type of case. There is a belief in some quarters that there may be no way of assessing the extent to which, and the circumstances in which, the courts are granting orders preventing the publication of allegedly private or otherwise **confidential information**, because of the inclusion of reporting restrictions in such orders. There may be nothing in that belief, but in recent years there has been an increase in the number of such orders, which itself gives rise to concern, as does the fact that the belief is understandable.

35. The concern would, I think, be substantially **met if courts comply with the principle that judgments and orders are made available as mentioned in para 21(9) above, and those judgments and orders disclose as much as possible about the case**. More particularly, there is much in the point that the media will be generally better able to discover, and report on, what the courts are doing if they can publish **(a)** details of the **type of case** (for instance, as in this case, a sexual liaison between an unidentified well known sportsman, in an apparently monogamous **relationship**, and a third party) rather than **(b)** the name of the individual who is seeking to protect an unspecified aspect of his or her alleged private life by means of an injunction. **As Mr Tomlinson puts it, the former information would normally enable the public to have a much better idea of why the court acted as it did than the latter information.**

36. Having said that, I acknowledge the importance of being able to name JIH as the claimant. As Lord Rodger famously said, in the *Guardian case* [2010] 2 WLR 325, para 63, "**What's in a name? 'A lot' the press would answer**". Two paragraphs on, he explained that "**if newspapers can identify the people concerned, they may be able to give a more vivid and compelling account which will stimulate discussion**". And he went on to say that

"[c]oncealing . . . identities simply casts a shadow over entire communities." However, as Mr Tomlinson says, that was said in a context where there was no question but that the nature of the allegations and contents of the court order could be freely published. Unlike the present case, Lord Rodger was not concerned with a trade-off between revealing the identity of a party and publishing the substance of the allegations and order. Nonetheless, the judgment vividly illustrates the importance of being able to identify, and put a name to, parties to litigation which is potentially of **interest to the public**.

37. It is not, of course, for the media to dictate to the courts whether an anonymity order, or some other sort of order, is appropriate. However, as Mr Spearman points out, if a story is of less interest to the media and the public, it is less likely to be reported or read, and media reporting "**contributes to a debate of general interest"**—per the European Court of Human Rights in *Von Hannover v Germany* [2005] EHRR 1, para 63.

38. There are other arguments. **An anonymity order runs the risk of unintentionally encouraging suspicion and gossip in relation to innocent third parties.** In the present case, as even a casual inspection of blog and twitter sites would reveal, vouchsafing the fact that the injunction was granted at the request of a well known sportsman may well lead to suspicions or allegations against well known people other than JIH. On the other hand, it is true that, at least in many cases, identification of the claimant will be more likely to result in public speculation, or even deduction by journalists or members of the public, as to the nature of the information which he is trying to keep out of the **public domain**. Indeed, **there is something in the point that such speculation could be even more damaging to JIH than if no injunction had been granted at all.**

39. As I have already emphasised, when deciding on questions of this sort, each case will turn on its own facts. Accordingly, **it is not appropriate to suggest that there is some sort of general rule that anonymisation is more**, or indeed less, likely to result in greater interference with free speech and maintaining public scrutiny of the courts than precluding the publication of more extensive information about the proceedings.

40. In this case, I consider that the **crucial factor** is the previous story about JIH's alleged liaison with YY, **which had already been published, without JIH's prior knowledge or permission.** That earlier story involved a very similar allegation about JIH to that which NGN was proposing to publish as a result of ZZ's allegations. **If we permitted JIH's identity to be revealed without permitting the nature of the information of which he is seeking to restrain to be published, then it would nonetheless be relatively easy for the media and members of the public to deduce the nature of that information: it**

would be a classic, if not very difficult, jigsaw exercise. It is true that the very fact that this decision means that we are revealing that JIH is a person about whose alleged sexual activity a previous story has been published, and that this will immediately **narrow** the field for those seeking to identify him, but, in my view, **that point is of limited force:** there have been quite a few stories of this nature relating to different well known people published in the printed and electronic media in the past two or three years.

41. Given that I consider that, in the absence of the point just discussed, the argument would, from the point of view of NGN, be at best **very finely balanced,** it follows that I conclude that JIH is entitled to retain anonymity in connection with these proceedings—until trial or further order in the meantime.

Conclusion

42. For these reasons, I would allow JIH's appeal against the order of 5 November 2010 to the extent that I would direct **that he is to be granted anonymity in connection with these proceedings until trial or further order**. I would also direct that the extent to which the facts of, and individuals involved in, this case can be **reported is limited to the facts and matters in this judgment and the two judgments of Tugendhat J**. It is therefore unnecessary to consider JIH's appeal against the judgment of 18 November 2010, but it is right to record that, had I decided to uphold the decision of 5 November, I would have upheld the decision of 18 November. If the Judge had been right to conclude on 5 November that anonymity should be refused, he was well within the margin of discretion available to him to decide that the events subsequent to that date did n ot justify going back on that conclusion.

Lord Justice Maurice Kay:

43. I agree.

Lady Justice Smith:

44. I also agree.

In Private POI v The Persons Known as "Lina" [2011] EWHC 234 (QB) per Supperstone J

Mr Justice Supperstone:

By order dated 26 January 2011 publication of any information as to the subject matter of these proceedings or the identity of the Applicant, shall be limited to that contained in this judgment.

1. On 26 January 2011 I continued the injunction granted by Mr Justice Tugendhat on 12 January 2011 to restrain publication of **private information**, and other related orders until trial or further order.

2. The information the subject of the order was identified in the order as follows:

   "(a) Any information concerning the subject matter of these proceedings or any information identifying or tending to identify the Applicant save for that contained in this Order and in any public judgment of the court given in this action.

   (b) All or any of the private photographs ('the Photographs') or video ('the Video') of the Applicant or any information as to their contents or circumstances in which they were taken, as more particularly described in Confidential Schedule A at the end of this Order ('the Confidential information'); and

   . . . PROVIDED THAT nothing in this paragraph of this Order shall prevent the Respondent from publishing, communicating or disclosing any material that before service of this Order was already in, or that thereafter comes into, the public domain as the result of national media publication (other than as a result of breach of this Order or a breach of confidence or privacy)."

3. The Respondent was not present or represented at the hearing before me. However the injunction granted by Mr Justice Tugendhat was served on the Respondent by e-mail at 19.10 on 12 January 2011. The Respondent was informed that an application may be made to the court to vary or discharge the Order. The Respondent was also informed that the Order provided for a Return Date on 26 January 2011 when the Claimant would be returning to court to seek the continuation of the Order. The Respondent was told that the Respondent was free to attend this hearing and make representations should the Respondent so wish. The Claim Form was subsequently served on the Respondent on 13 January 2011. No response has been received from the Respondent.

4. On 25 January 2011 the Applicant's solicitors e-mailed the Respondent informing the Respondent that they would be serving a copy of the application to continue the injunction that afternoon. Immediately afterwards, the Claimant's solicitors received a failure notice informing them that the message had not been delivered to the address to which it was sent. **It would appear therefore that the e-mail account for the address to which the injunction and related documents and the Claim Form was served may have been closed down by the Respondent at some point following service of the Injunction and Claim Form on 12 and 13 January 2011 respectively.**

5. In *JIH v News Group Newspapers Ltd* [2010] EWHC 2818 (QB) Tugendhat J set out at **para 36** the principles that apply when the issue of **anonymity** is being considered. In the present case the material principles are as follows:

> "(1) As a general rule, the names of the parties to an action should be included in orders and judgments of the court . . .
>
> (2) There is **no general exception** for cases **where private matters** are in issue
>
> . . .
>
> (3) An order for **anonymity** is a **derogation** from the principle of open justice and an **interference with the Article 10** rights of the **public at large**.
>
> (4) Where the court is asked to restrain the publication of the **names** of the parties and the **subject matter** of the claim [on the ground that restraint is necessary under Art.8] the question is whether there is **sufficient general, public interest in publishing a report of the proceedings which identifies a party to justify any resulting curtailment of his right and his family's right to respect for their private and family life.**
>
> (5) An order for anonymity and reporting restrictions should **not** be **made** simply because the parties **consent:** parties cannot waive the rights of the public (*ibid*, para 33) . . .
>
> (6) An anonymity order made by a Judge, on the first hearing of an injunction **application does not last for the duration of the proceedings but must be reviewed at the return date . . .** "

6. I have applied those principles and reviewed the anonymity order made by Tugendhat J on 12 January 2011.

7. In my judgment the **Photographs** and/or the Video were taken in **circumstances** where the Applicant **has a strong basis for submitting that he has a reasonable expectation of privacy.** The evidence of the Applicant is that **no permission** was sought or given either for the taking of the images or the publication of them. In my view the Applicant also has a strong basis for submitting that the Respondent is attempting **to blackmail him**. I am satisfied in accordance with the Human Rights Act 1998 s 12(3) that the Applicant is **likely to establish** that publication should not be allowed. I have had regard to the matters set out in s 12(4). On the evidence before me there is **no real likelihood** of the Respondent being able to succeed in, or even to advance, an argument that it is or would **be in the public interest** for the material to be published.

8. In my view the position with regard to the Art.8 rights of the Applicant and

any rights of the Respondent under Art.10 has not changed since the hearing before Tugendhat J.

9. I bear in mind the observations of Tugendhat J in *AMM v HXW* [2010] EWHC 2457 (QB) which are relevant on the facts to the present case. As the judge said:

> "38. The fact that a person is making unwarranted demands with threats to disclose information does not of itself mean that that person has no right to freedom of expression. . . . But if a person is making unwarranted demands with threats to publish, that is a factor in deciding whether that person has any Art.10 rights, and, if so, then the weight to be accorded to them in balancing them with the applicant's Art.8 rights.
>
> 39. In my judgment, the need to have regard to the Art.8 rights of the Claimant, and to promote the public interest in preventing and punishing **blackmail** are both factors which weigh strongly in favour of the grant of an anonymity order. There is a strong case that [the] Defendant has no right to publish the information which she seeks to publish about a **relationship** with her former husband. On this view her Art.10 rights are not strong. And as an alleged **blackmail**er, her Art.10 rights are much weaker. . . . "

10. There is plainly a strong argument that the Art.8 rights of the Applicant are engaged; on the other hand the argument in support of any rights of the Respondent under Art.10 is weak. The balance, in my view, falls, as before, to be struck in favour of the protection of the Art.8 rights of the Applicant. **It is strongly arguable that the interference with the Claimant's right to respect for privacy and family life under Art.8(1) cannot be justified under Art.8(2).**

11. In the circumstances of this case an order for **anonymity** is, in my judgment, necessary in the interests of justice. As Tugendhat J said at para 8 when giving his reasons for granting an injunction on 12 January 2011,

> "The evidence of attempted **blackmail** includes evidence that there is some information about the case that has been put in the **public domain**. If the name of the Applicant were to be identified, then it is likely that persons who knew, or learned, both that the Applicant had issued these proceedings and what is already in the **public domain** would be able to deduce information about the contents of the images, or the circumstances in which they were taken, which is private information, and which the Applicant is likely to establish should not be published. It is likely that the policy of the law to protect those alleging they are victims of a **blackmailer** would be defeated."

12. I was satisfied that the hearing of the application before me should take

place **in private pursuant to CPR39.2(3)(a) and (c)** and for the reasons set out in this judgment that the order of Tugendhat J should continue until trial or further order.

ZAM v CFW & TFW [2011] EWHC 476 (QB) per Tugendhat J

Mr Justice Tugendhat:

1. **The Claimant is a married man. His wife is one of a number of beneficiaries of some substantial family trusts ("the trusts"). The First Defendant is one of her sisters, and another beneficiary of the trusts. The Second Defendant is the First Defendant's husband.**
2. On 25 February 2011 the Claimant applied urgently, without notice to the Defendants, for an interim injunction to restrain the further publication of words which had been published on four occasions identified in a letter before action from the Claimant's solicitors ("Farrers") to the Defendants dated 18 February 2011. Those occasions were (1) **two telephone calls to the public relations advisers of the Claimant's employers in late January and early February 2011, (2) a telephone call to the Claimant's employers about a week later, and (3) a letter to one of the brothers of the Claimant's wife and of the First Defendant also about a week later. The letter asked for a number of undertakings to be given by 25 February 2011.**
3. Each of those communications was made, or purported to be made, not by the Defendants themselves but instead by an individual who I will refer to as "X". The Claimant's evidence is that he has never met X, and that he does not know whether X is a real person. The Claimant also relied on communications from another person, who I will refer to as "Y". **The Claimant's evidence makes it appear likely that, whether X is a real person or a pseudonym for Y or for one or other or both of the Defendants, all the communications emanating from X and Y upon which the Claimant relies have been sent or made for and on behalf of the Defendants.**
4. The Claimant contended that there were compelling reasons why the Defendants should not be notified of the application on 25 February 2011 (see s12(2) of the Human Rights Act 1998), namely that, if notified, the Defendants would be likely to do the very thing which the Claimant was seeking to prevent, before the Claimant could gain access to the Court and obtain an injunction. He also contended that the present case was one of **blackmail.**
5. In support of those contentions, the Claimant relied, in particular, on various documents.

. . .

12. **The Claimant claimed that the words published are very seriously defamatory of him, and that there is no basis for any of the allegations in question. Among other things, he claimed that he is able to demonstrate by the evidence of independent persons and by documents that one of the allegations, relating to financial impropriety, is without foundation.**

13. **The Claimant also submitted that this is a clear case of harassment under the Protection from Harassment Act 1997 ("the 1997 Act").** He argued that (1) there is, and without an injunction there will continue to be, a course of conduct which amounts to **harassment** of the Claimant (see the reference in s7(2) of the 1997 Act to "alarming the person or causing the person distress" and the provision in s 7(3) that a "course of conduct" must involve conduct on at least two occasions), (2) the victim can apply for an injunction under ss1 (1A) and 3A of the 1997 Act, and (3) the Defendants could not show any of the grounds set out in s1(3) of the 1997 Act, in particular because their conduct is the reverse of reasonable.

. . .

17. **The words complained of consist of allegations of the most grave and serious kind, which, if true, would involve various forms of criminality.** Mr Spearman submitted that, as is virtually self-evident, publication of the material in question would cause **alarm and distress to the Claimant**. He also submitted that it is apparent, from the words of X himself, that, through his agency, the Defendants have both **understood and intended throughout that publication would cause alarm and distress to the Claimant. I accept those submissions.**

18. The Defendants personally **have not sought to justify or otherwise defend** the publication of those words (or the actions about which the Claimant complains) in any way.

19. However, on 2 March 2011 the Court received a fax which takes the form of a statement signed by X. That fax raises a number of issues. Perhaps most importantly, it asserts that the Claimant is the **"the subject of a variety of legal activities" in a foreign country in respect of an alleged incident of serious misconduct in that country**. However, no details are given of when or where that incident took place, as to the identity of any other person allegedly involved in it, or as to the alleged "legal activities". The fax also alleges that much of the Claimant's evidence may have been manufactured by his "family and relatives . . . who have been desperately trying to stifle growing criticism" of his financial dealings with assets of the trusts. Other points made in the fax include that the present proceedings are a waste of

the Court's time and an unwarranted and excessive stifling of the basic and civil human rights of other people; that this country is not the proper venue for these proceedings; that the email addresses used for the Defendants are not their true email addresses; that the address at which service has been effected on the Defendants is not their residence; and that there has been no personal service on the Defendants because they are abroad. At least one basis upon which this statement is sought to be put before the Court appears to be that my Order of 25 February 2011 has been served on the writer, and that the writer is accordingly entitled to apply to vary or discharge it at least so far as it affects the writer.

20. The Claimant states that the words complained of are completely untrue. In support of his contention that the words complained of are entirely false, he has not only filed and served a detailed witness statement with Confidential Exhibit which he himself has made but he has also filed and served detailed witness statements with Confidential Exhibits from (a) one of the other beneficiaries of the trusts, who (among other things) has had substantial involvement with representing the interests of the beneficiaries to the trustees, (b) the senior partner of the offshore law firm referred to above, who has been a trustee for the last 10 years of the relevant family trusts, and who considers the Claimant to be "a man of absolute integrity", (c) an investment adviser to the trusts, who details, by reference to supporting documents, what has become of the material investments, and (d) an officer of the corporate trustee of the relevant trusts, who states (among other things) that it is "inconceivable" that the trusts have been "raped" or that there has been any "on-going criminal enterprise" or "back-door dealings" as has been alleged by X.

21. As I have said, a letter of claim was sent on behalf of the Claimant on 18 February 2011. It is to be noted that the responses—none of them from the Defendants—do not give any indication that they are relying on any defence whether of justification or at all.

22. The fax of 2 March 2011 which was sent to the Court is devoid of the sort of detail which would be required before the Court could treat it as giving rise to a sufficient basis upon which a defence could credibly be advanced to the highly defamatory publications complained of, whether on the basis of justification or on any other basis. In any event, the bare assertions made in that fax have to be considered in context. This includes the fact that the fax contains assertions about the efficacy of service on, and notification to, the Defendants of these proceedings which there are strong grounds for believing to be self-serving and untrue.

23. It is well known that it is rare for the court to grant injunctions on interim

applications in defamation actions. However, the court has jurisdiction to do so and will do so in an appropriate case.

24. **On the information before me I am satisfied that there is a prima facie case of libel**, that there **remains a threat by the Defendants to publish** or further publish the words complained of, and that if publication or further publication occurs the Claimant **will suffer injury which cannot fully be compensated in damages**. I am in no doubt that the words complained of are **defamatory.** Nothing has been stated by the Defendants personally to the effect that they have a defence **of justification or any other defence.** Nor am I able to regard the fax of 2 March 2011 as providing any or any sufficient basis for saying that there may be a defence that will succeed at trial (see ***Bonnard v Perryman*** [1891] 2 Ch 269 and *Greene v Associated Newspapers Ltd* [2005] QB 972 per Brooke LJ at [57]).

25. **In any event, I consider that the Claimant has a clear basis for relief in reliance on the provisions of the 1997 Act**. It is apparent from *Thomas v News Group Newspaper Ltd* [2002] EMLR 78 that, in principle**, publications are capable of constituting harassment.** In *Howlett v Holding* [2006] EWHC 41, Eady J said at [5] "in some circumstances, the exercise of one's right of free speech can fall within the concept of **harassment**, provided the other necessary ingredients are present**. For example, it would have to be classified as unreasonable and oppressive conduct".** In my judgment, there are strong grounds for saying that this is such a case.

26. The Claimant **is likely** to establish that the publication complained of should not be allowed.

27. Turning to derogations from open justice, **it would frustrate the purpose of the injunctions sought if the Claimant's applications had the effect of making public the very allegations in respect of which he is seeking relief by way of injunction.** The Court has jurisdiction to make an Order for anonymity in accordance with s6 of the Human Rights Act 1998 and CPR 39.2(4). In a case like the present, where there is **a strong case** for believing there to be **an attempt at blackmail**, such Orders are frequently made in respect of both parties. There are strong policy reasons to discourage such conduct, which would be undermined if anonymity was refused. See *DFT v TFD* [2010] EWHC 2335 (QB); *AMM v HXW* [2010] EWHC 2457 (QB); *KJH v HGF* [2010] EWHC 3064 (QB).

28. It was also submitted by Mr Spearman that if anonymity were not to be ordered, the fact that the Claimant has had to seek relief would be capable of being made a story in its own right, and would be likely to lead to widespread speculation as to what story he has been concerned to prevent the Defendants from telling**. It would be unfair to him (and his family) that, as**

the price of preventing the publication of allegations that (ex hypothesi) he is entitled to prevent, he (and his family) should be exposed to invasive speculation of this sort. In this particular case, the public interest in open justice is better served by granting anonymity to the Claimant **and revealing such detail about the subject matter of the action as is contained in this public judgment**. See *JIH v News Group Newspapers Ltd* [2011] EWCA Civ 42.

29. The Defendants had an opportunity to appear and make representations to the court today. They did not do so. Nevertheless nothing in this judgment is to be taken as a finding of fact against them. I have made an order prohibiting publication or further publication of words complained of, or any other similar words defamatory of the Claimant. This judgment is to be read subject to any findings of fact that may be made at any trial. It is further subject to a provision I have made granting permission to the Defendants to apply to vary or discharge this order. I also made an order that the Defendants should pay the Claimant his costs of and occasioned by these applications, which, in light of the circumstances set out above, I assessed summarily in the full amount of the schedule of costs submitted by Farrers.

MNB v NGN Ltd [2011] EWHC 528 (QB) per Sharp J

Mrs Justice Sharp:

1. On 1 March 2011 Henriques J granted a **temporary injunction** with a **short return date** to prevent the disclosure of private information ("the information") about the Claimant. The hearing was on **short notice** to the Defendant. It was conducted **over the telephone**. It was also held in **private,** and the application that it should be was not opposed. The application for an injunction was however contested. The parties were represented by the same counsel who have appeared before me, that is, Hugh Tomlinson QC for the Claimant, and Richard Spearman QC for the Defendant. **The Claimant had been informed earlier that day of the Defendant's intention to publish a story in the Sun newspaper which concerned his sexual relationship with another person**; and two public interest justifications for its publication were advanced by the Defendant. **By the time of the telephone hearing, the principal public interest justification had been abandoned.**

2. A **full note of the hearing has been produced by the Claimant's solicitors**. The judge's attention was drawn to the relevant considerations of law including those relating to article 8 and article 10 of the ECHR and the provisions of section 12(3) of the Human Rights Act 1998. He concluded the Claimant was

likely to succeed in establishing at trial that publication of the information should not be allowed.

3. The judge ordered that the Claimant could be **anonymised**. Paragraph 1 of the order made prohibited the publication until the return date (4 March 2011) of:

> **"(a) Any information concerning the subject matter of these proceedings or any information identifying or tending to identify the applicant save for that contained in this Order and in any public judgment of the court given in this action.**
>
> **(b) Any information concerning the fact or details of any sexual relationship between the Applicant and the person named in the Confidential Schedule to the Order . . ."**

4. Paragraph 1 went on to provide that:

> **"nothing in paragraph 1 of this Order shall prevent the Respondent from publishing, communicating or disclosing any material that before the service of this Order was already in, or that thereafter comes into, the public domain as the result of national media publication (other than as a result of this Order or a breach of confidence or privacy)".**

5. At the start of the return date hearing before me, I was told the application for an interim injunction **was no longer opposed.** Subject to its right to apply to apply to discharge or vary the Order, the Defendant has agreed therefore that the order made by Henriques J should continue until trial or further order (including therefore a paragraph in the same terms as that set out in paragraphs 3 and 4 above). I indicated to the parties at the hearing, I approved those terms and therefore the interim order is now in place.

6. There is no doubt in my view that the Claimant's **article 8 rights** are engaged, both in relation to the **subject matter** of the action, and **the identification** of him as the Claimant. There is no doubt either that publication of the information as to the fact or details of the **affair will result in some interference with the Claimant's private life**. It is not currently suggested by the Defendant that there is a public interest in the publication of the information or that there is any other reason for it to be disclosed. It is not suggested for example that the information was in the **public domain**. I am satisfied in accordance with section 12(3) of the Human Rights Act 1998 that the Claimant is likely to establish at trial that publication of the information should not be allowed.

7. Because provisions in the order agreed between the parties derogate from the principle of open justice, they are **subject to the approval of the court.** In this case, I am satisfied that the particular provisions in it which derogate from that principle are **necessary.**

8. The issue now between the parties concerns an article published by the Defendant **after the hearing** before Henriques J ("the article"). The article was published in the Sun newspaper on 3 March 2011 and **remains available online**. It referred to the fact that an individual with a particular occupation had "gagged" the "Sun". The Claimant says its publication has led to the publication of articles in other newspapers and which continue to be available on the **internet** in substantially similar form to the article. **It is said the article's contents breach the order made by Henriques J.**

9. Mr Tomlinson submitted a written skeleton argument for the purposes of this hearing which dealt with whether the temporary injunction granted by Henriques J should be continued until trial or further order; Mr Spearman did not. **I was not provided with a written argument by either side on any of the matters which are now in dispute.** The Claimant's complaint about the article was raised the evening before the hearing, and to that extent, my adjudication on it, is not made as part of the return date hearing ordered by Henriques J.

Hearing in private

10. A further issue has been raised by the Defendant, albeit very briefly, as the hearing began concerning the hearing of this application in private. At the outset of the hearing, **Mr Tomlinson invited me to hear the matter in private pursuant to CPR 39.2(3)(a)(c) and (g). Mr Spearman invited me to consider making an order which permitted the public to remain, and to impose reporting restrictions in the event that anything was said which impinged on the Claimant's article 8 rights.** He said that it was possible for example to conduct appeals before the Court of Appeal in such cases in this way; and there shouldn't be one rule of thumb for hearings before the Court of Appeal and a different one at first instance.

11. At the outset of the hearing, before it was ordered to be in private, members of the public were present in court as were representatives of the press. **Mr Spearman did not address the consequences for the privacy interests of a claimant which may result from the inadvertent revelation to third parties of information the application is designed to protect, during the course of a hearing.** Mr Spearman did not suggest either a form of order the court might make, still less a mechanism to overcome the considerable practical difficulties which in my judgment would arise in preventing the dissemination of the information in the event of inadvertent disclosure; nor did he address the problems which might arise in the event that an inadvertent disclosure resulted in a subsequent "leak."

12. A hearing at first instance usually ranges widely over the facts and matters in issue; and this is what occurred in this case. **It would have been**

impossible in my view for the issues which arose to be properly explored without referring in some detail to the information concerned; and without revealing the identity of the Claimant, or matters which would be likely to lead to his identification. This problem was compounded by the absence of written arguments on the matters in issue and by the need to refer in some detail to the article. I considered it to be necessary therefore on the facts of this case for the hearing before me to be in private, though of course the matter has to be kept under review, including during the course of the hearing itself.

13. When a matter comes before the Court of Appeal, the position may well be different to the one faced by the court at first instance: in particular it is very likely that the matters in issue will have been narrowed and reduced to writing, and the parties and the Court are also much more likely to know what the factual "parameters" of the case are.

14. After the hearing, the Defendant's solicitors provided me with a copy of the decision of the President, Sir Mark Potter, in *Re Child X* [2009] EWHC 1728 (Fam). It was said it would be relevant to my consideration whether hearings like the present one are capable of being conducted in the presence of accredited media representatives without violating the article 8 rights of the claimants, a position which prevails in the Family Division. I do not think the positions are analogous. **The jurisdictional basis for the attendance of accredited media representatives at hearings which are private and which are not open to the general public in the family courts is statutory: the relevant FPR (10.28) was inserted into the FPR by statutory instrument. There is no jurisdictional basis so far as I am aware (and certainly none was suggested) which would permit this court to distinguish between the media and members of the public for this purpose.**

The article

. . .

25. Mr Spearman submits moreover that it is not appropriate to restrain publication because the details are already **in the public domain** and to that extent, an injunction would now serve no useful **purpose**. In this context, he refers me to publications in other newspapers which continue to be available online; and to *Vestergaard Fransden A/S v Bestnet Europe Ltd* [2009] EWHC 1456 (Ch), [2010] FSR 29 and **British Broadcasting Corporation v HarperCollins Publishers Ltd and others [2010] EWHC 2424 (Ch)**. The cases support, he submits, the proposition that if information is **no longer confidential** then no injunction should be granted to protect it, even as against a person who was under an **equitable duty** not to disclose it. Further he submits that if any of the details are likely to be put into a public judgment, in which the

Claimant is **anonymised**, it would be futile to make an order requiring what the Defendant has published to be taken down.

26. As to Mr Tomlinson's alternative argument, he submits, shortly, that the details cannot sensibly be called or categorised as private information of the nature the court should restrain, and the article doesn't raise the Claimant's article 8 rights at all in particular because it doesn't identify him. If it does, then the free speech, article 10 rights of the Defendant should prevail. The comments the Defendant is entitled to make about the grant of the injunction cannot be made without identifying the Claimant as having a particular occupation, and the inclusion of that fact is a vital part of the story.

Discussion

27. In *Ntuli v Donald* [2010] EWCA Civ 1276, the Court of Appeal had to consider the orders it was appropriate to make in cases involving allegedly private information. Maurice Kay LJ said this **[53]** and **[54]**:

> "This is an essentially case-sensitive subject. Plainly Mr Donald is entitled to expect that the court will adopt procedures which ensure that any ultimate vindication of his Article 8 case is not undermined by the way in which the court has processed the interim applications and the trial itself. On the other hand, the principle of open justice requires that any restrictions are the least that can be imposed consistent with the protection to which Mr Donald is entitled. In my judgement, in view of the terms of the substantive injunction and the circumstances of this case, the appropriate restriction on publicity is one that limits reporting and publicity to what is contained in this judgment, together with any ancillary orders necessary to fortify such an order. I am simply unpersuaded that greater restriction is necessary at this stage. There is nothing in this judgment that is significantly invasive of Mr Donald's private or family life. "
>
> "(2) Anonymity
>
> It seems to me that what I have said in relation to the superinjunction element applies also to the question of **anonymity. Provided that publicity is limited to what is contained in this judgment, there is no justification for continued anonymity.** I have in mind the judgment of Lord Rodger in *Guardian News and Media Ltd* [2010] 2 WLR 325, [2010] UKSC 1, at paragraphs 63–64**. The material in respect of which Mr Donald has been found to have a reasonable expectation of privacy is not detailed in the judgment**. The material in the judgment does not attract a reasonable expectation of privacy**. I note that an order restricting publicity to the contents of a judgment, in relation to which one party was anonymised but the other was not, was recently made**

by Tugendhat J in Gray v UVW [2010] EWHC 2367 (QB): see in particular paragraphs 44–63. There the continued anonymity of the defendant was justified by a significant risk that lifting his or her anonymity might have serious consequences for his or her private life which consequences **might not be remediable**. I do not consider that the same can be said of Mr Donald in the present case. In my view, it would have been possible and appropriate for Eady J to have written his judgment in a publishable form. **Moreover, to have done so would have avoided the risk that anonymisation can give rise to, namely that of "jigsaw" identification,** whereby anonymisation may be undermined by correctly identifying someone as a result of relating separate snippets of information or, equally unfortunately**, it may lead to the wrong person being identified by the media misaligning the snippets**. We were shown one recent example of this."

28. In *JIH v News Group Newspapers Ltd* [2011] EWCA Civ 42, the Court of Appeal considered the issue of **reporting restrictions** following the making of orders to prevent the publication of private information. The parties had agreed to an order in substantially similar terms to that made by Henriques J. (The claimant in that case was represented by Mr Tomlinson, and the Defendant, by Mr Spearman). The judge below had approved that part of the order which prohibited the publication of *"any information concerning the subject matter of these proceedings save* **for that contained in the public judgment of the court"** but refused to make an order that the identity of the Claimant should not be disclosed (though he imposed a temporary restriction on the Claimant's identification pending an appeal): see *JIH v News Group Newspapers Ltd No1* [2010] EWHC 2818; and *JIH v News Group Newspapers Ltd No2* [2010] EWHC 2979. **The Court of Appeal allowed the claimant's appeal, and directed that he be granted anonymity in connection with proceedings until trial or further order.**

29. At [21] the Master of the Rolls said this:

"In a case such as this, where the protection sought by the claimant is an anonymity order or other restraint on publication of details of a case which are normally in the **public domain**, certain principles were identified by the Judge, and which, together with principles contained in valuable written observations to which I have referred, I would summarise as follows:

(1) The general rule is that **the names of the parties to an action are included in orders and judgments of the court.**

(2) There is **no general exception for cases where private matters are in issue.**

(3) An order for anonymity or any other order restraining the publication of the normally reportable details of a case is a **derogation** from the principle of open justice and an **interference with the Article 10 rights** of the **public at large**.

(4) Accordingly, where the court is asked to make any such order, it should only do so after **closely scrutinising** the application, and considering whether a **degree** of restraint on publication is **necessary**, and, if it is, whether there **is any less restrictive or more acceptable alternative** than that which is sought.

(5) Where the court is asked to restrain the publication of the **names of the parties** and/or the **subject matter** of the claim, on the ground that such restraint is necessary under Article 8, the **question is whether there is sufficient general, public interest in publishing a report of the proceedings which identifies a party and/or the normally reportable details to justify any resulting curtailment of his right and his family's right to respect for their private and family life.**

(6) On any such application, **no special treatment should be accorded to public figures or celebrities**: in principle, they are entitled to the **same protection as others,** no more and no less.

(7) An order for anonymity or for reporting **restrictions should not be made simply because the parties consent: parties cannot waive the rights of the public.**

(8) An anonymity order or any other order restraining publication made by a Judge at an interlocutory stage of an injunction application **does not last for the duration of the proceedings but must be reviewed at the return date.**

(9) Whether or not an anonymity order or an order restraining publication of normally reportable details is made, then, at least **where a judgment is or would normally be given, a publicly available judgment should normally be given, and a copy of the consequential court order should also be publicly available, although some editing of the judgment or order may be necessary.**

(10) **Notice of any hearing should be given to the defendant unless there is a good reason not to do so**, in which case the court should be told of the absence of notice and the reason for it, and should be satisfied that the reason is a good one.

Where, as here, the basis for any claimed restriction on publication ultimately rests on a judicial assessment, it is therefore essential that (a) the judge is first satisfied that the facts and circumstances of the case are sufficiently strong to justify encroaching on the open justice rule by restricting the extent to which the proceedings can be reported, and (b) if so, the judge ensures that the restrictions on publication are fashioned so as to satisfy the need for the encroachment in a **way which minimises the extent of any restrictions."**

30. The Master of the Rolls also made at direction at [42] that:

> "the extent to which the facts of, and individuals involved in the case can be reported is limited to the facts and matters in this judgment and the two judgments of Tugendhat J."

31. The order made following the hearing in the Court of Appeal was in these terms:

> "Until trial or further Order in the meantime, the Respondent must not publish . . . any information
>
> (a) concerning the **sexual relationship** between the Appellant and the individual named in the **Confidential Schedule** or
>
> (b) concerning the identity of the Appellant as the claimant in these proceedings or as the person who has obtained this order, or
>
> (c) concerning the identity of the individual named in the **Confidential Schedule** as an individual with whom the Appellant had a **sexual relationship**."

32. An order such as the one made by paragraph 1 in this case, may be made when the court determines the claimant is entitled to an interim injunction in a case concerning private information, as the observations made in the cases cited above and the order made by the Court of Appeal in *JIH*, make clear. Such orders are made to give effective protection to the article 8 rights of a claimant, at least on an interim basis. The **precise ambit** of such orders needs to be decided on a case by case basis. It is not however suggested by the Defendant that such orders are wrong in principle. **Their obvious purpose is the protection on the one hand of the ability of the press to report the proceedings, and on the other, of the article 8 rights of the claimant against the risk in particular of "jigsaw identification" if he or she is anonymised**. This could defeat the **purpose** of an interim injunction, and indeed potentially, the **purpose** of the action itself.

33. **By its nature, jigsaw identification involves the separate publication by different entities of different items of information which do not identify the claimant when looked at separately, but do so or risk doing so, when they are put together. Such information therefore does not have to actually identify a claimant. Nor need it be private. The conjunction of publicly**

available information with the report of proceedings may well lead to "two and two" being put together.

34. It is to be noted that it does not appear that the Defendant addressed any specific argument to Henriques J on the material part of paragraph 1 of the Order. Indeed in the context of his argument on whether the Claimant should be anonymised (which the Defendant did object to) Mr Spearman appears from the solicitors' note of the hearing, to have accepted that the form of the order asked for, and ultimately granted by the judge, restricted what could be reported to the fact that an unnamed person got an injunction relating to a **sexual relationship** with another unnamed person.

35. I accept, as Mr Spearman submits, that the court should be wary of making findings of fact on matters which may be material in the event committal proceedings are taken. I make no finding of **contempt**; such issues must be dealt in due course, in the event they may later arise. I am also not exercising the court's jurisdiction to restrain an anticipated **contempt**, or in **contempt** proceedings, **(where the standard of proof may be a criminal, rather than a civil one: see for example, *Coe v Central Television plc* [1994] EMLR 433, at 441).**

36. However, in my view, the considerations to which Mr Spearman refers should not prevent the Claimant from seeking to protect his article 8 rights on an interim basis **(by preventing the publication of details which may lead to his identification);** nor should they inhibit the court from granting such an order in an appropriate case to ensure the orders that the court makes are not undermined and/or their underlying **purpose** is complied with.

37. I have not addressed all the arguments advanced by both sides, some of which might merit further evidence or argument, because it is sufficient for the purposes of this application for me to state the following. **First**, in my judgment the **purpose** of the order made by Henriques J was to prevent the publication of items of information which actually identified the Claimant or which tended to identify him (t**hat is, they might, in conjunction with other information as explained above**). **Second**, publication of the details to which particular objection is taken fall within the category of information which tends to lead to his identification**. Third**, the subject matter of the action is the **affair**; comment by relatives or others which reveal information about the affair (for example, its length, when it occurred, the parties' reaction to what has occurred, or their current status) **is therefore information concerning the subject matter of these proceedings.**

38. **Fourth,** the Claimant is **likely** to establish at trial that he is entitled to an order in the form or substantially in the form made by Henriques J in paragraph 1 of the Order. He is **likely** to do so on the ground that such an order

is **necessary** (i) to prevent the risk of jigsaw identification thus frustrating the **purpose** of the court's order prohibiting the publication of the information (whether on an interim or final basis); and therefore (ii) to protect his article 8 rights in the private information this action is brought to protect and in his **identification** as the person concerned–bearing in mind the principles set out in *JIH* to which I have referred above, and in accordance with the proper approach to such applications where the article 8 rights of the claimant and the article 10 rights of the defendant are engaged, as in my judgment they are here.

39. I bear in mind that **there is no public interest justification currently advanced for the publication of the central story itself**; I also bear in mind the concession made by the Claimant as to the details which are not objected to. I have concluded on the facts**, there is no sufficient general public interest in publishing the details to which I have referred to justify the seriousness of the interference with the article 8 rights of the Claimant, which would occur if he was identified and if the order made by Henriques J, and now continued by consent and with my approval, is thus undermined.**

40. **The need for such an order has been reinforced** by the publications which have taken place since the order made by Henriques J. Though Mr Spearman has said the Defendant's agreement to the terms of the Order I have already made (see paragraph 5 above) was without prejudice to its argument about the ambit of paragraph 1, **the publication of the article in my view, has reinforced the need for an order which protects the Claimant against the continuing risk of "jigsaw" identification.** In addition, what has occurred inevitably affects what may be said in any public judgment, and the nature of the orders it is now necessary to make which derogate from the principal of open justice.

41. The threshold of likelihood to which I have referred must be achieved because the grant of the relief which is asked for brings into play section 12 (3) of the Human Rights Act 1998. I have also considered section 12 (4) and specifically, section 12 (4) (a) (ii)—that is the extent to which the material has become available to the public. So far as the latter point is concerned, I do not think the point has been reached where an order made by the court will achieve no **purpose**. The continued dissemination of the details by the Defendant itself continues and is likely to increase the risk that the Claimant will be identified. The court is not (to adopt Mr Tomlinson's metaphor) holding back the tide, though this matter may need to be revisited in due course.

42. In consequence, the Claimant is entitled to an order which ensures his rights are protected to the extent necessary to prevent his identification, and in the manner intended by Henriques J. The Defendant will not therefore be entitled to continue to publish the article in its current form. It will be necessary

for me to hear the parties as to the precise terms of the order which should follow from the decision I have reached as recorded in this judgment.

Goldsmith and Sheherazade v BCD [2011] EWHC 674 (QB)

Mr Justice Tugendhat:

An outline of events

1. In December 2008 Zac and Sheherazade Goldsmith and Jemima Khan were the victims of a **crime**. An unidentified person **hacked into the e-mail** accounts of Mrs Goldsmith and Mrs Khan and **sent e-mails to a journalist** at a national newspaper, purportedly from Mrs Goldsmith herself, containing **personal information** about Mrs Goldsmith and her family. The journalist's suspicions were aroused and she alerted the Goldsmiths. This crime was also a flagrant breach of the civil law of **breach of confidence**. Since the nineteenth century this court has restrained such breaches of confidence by injunctions (eg *Argyll v Argyll* [1967] Ch 302). So the Claimants **made an urgent application to this court before even issuing the claim forms**, as the Civil Procedure Rules permit them to do.
2. Mrs Jemima Khan is Mr Goldsmith's sister. Each Claimant is, of course, well known to the public. They were all greatly distressed by what had occurred.
3. On 15 and 18 December 2008 I granted the interim injunctions the Claimants applied for ("the 2008 Orders"). At that time the Claimants were **anonymised** and there were three defendants, identified only by description, because the **true identity of the defendants was unknown.** On 23 December 2008 the Claimants obtained from the courts in **Northern Ireland** and in the **Republic of Ireland** orders in terms similar to the ones I had granted.
4. **In January the Claimant also obtained a third party disclosure order against Microsoft, the operator of their Hotmail accounts.** Microsoft was, of course, entirely innocent, but needed **the protection of a court order** before it could disclose the data from which the identity of the hacker might be discovered. The Claimants instructed an expert, a Mr Hall, to investigate. By the end of January there were grounds to suspect that the hacker was the person now identified as BCD. The Claimants reported the matter to the police, who arrested BCD in May 2009. **In August 2009 the police decided not to prosecute. BCD expressed remorse and accepted a caution.**
5. After reporting the matter to the police the Claimants **did nothing further to progress their claims in these actions.** The decisions of the police not

to prosecute, or the Claimants not to progress their claims, may well have been motivated by considerations of mercy. **But the Claimants overlooked that they had given undertakings to the court to serve the claim forms, which they did not do**. So they were in breach of undertakings to the court. That is a very serious matter. It could easily have been avoided by effecting service, or, alternatively, by an application to the court to vary the terms of the undertakings. But that was not done.

6. Meanwhile, the Claimants' solicitors had **notified a number of national newspapers of the 2008 Orders**. At least two national newspapers knew what this action was about, because a second journalist had also contacted Mrs Goldsmith. But no newspaper raised any objection to the terms of the orders I had made.

7. However, after hearing nothing further for two years, Farrer & Co for News Group Newspapers Ltd ("NGN") wrote to the Claimants' solicitors in December 2010. **They made the very strong point that by this time the anonymity provisions in the 2008 Orders were no longer necessary, and that the Claimants should agree to a variation of those orders accordingly.** The Claimants did not dispute that. But the letter from Farrer & Co prompted the re-opening of the file, which **led to the discovery that the Claimants were in breach of their undertakings** given to the court in December 2008, namely to serve the claim forms.

8. But for the breaches of the undertakings, the request by NGN would have been resolved by agreement, and it may well not have been necessary to have held an oral hearing in court. The orders could probably have been varied on paper. The reason why there had to be a hearing in this case was **because a breach of an undertaking is very serious,** and must be fully explained to the court, and the court must consider what to do in response to it.

9. The re-opening of the file also led to discussions between the Claimants' solicitors and BCD. **BCD had no defence to the Claimants' claims and wished to submit to judgment by consent** with as little trouble and cost as possible. That was agreed by her and by the Claimants. That would not have required a further oral hearing in court. That too could have been dealt with on paper, but for the breaches of the undertakings.

10. On 17 March 2011 I discharged the 2008 Orders and made new orders. I stated that I would give my reasons later in an open judgment, which I now do.

11. The substantive provisions of each of the two 2008 Orders and each of the two orders I made on 17 March 2011 were prohibitions on the disclosure of:

> **"any personal private information contained in or derived from personal and private e-mails received at or sent from [the Claimants']**

personal email addresses set out in the Confidential Schedule 3" [to each of the orders].

12. On 7 February 2011 the Claimants in each action had given notice of applications to vary the orders made in 2008 and for other relief. The orders made after the hearing on 17 March were finalised late on that day, **and the draft of this judgment was circulated the following morning. Some delay is necessary in the preparation of this public judgment. The reason is that, in cases such as this, it is necessary, in order to protect the interests of all parties, to circulate the judgment in draft so as to ensure that nothing confidential is inadvertently included in the public judgment which should not be included**, and equally that nothing is omitted which should be included.

13. In the claim forms and the 2008 Orders **three Defendants are listed as "persons unknown" followed by words of description**. Although the hacker has now been identified, it is necessary in the interests of justice that the identity of that person not be disclosed. The reasons for this are explained below. The other two descriptions of unknown defendants included in the claim forms and the 2008 Orders are now otiose.

The applications in December 2008

14. The evidence in support of the applications made to me in 2008 was **so strong** that I was easily satisfied (in accordance with the Human Rights Act 1998 s 12(3)) that the Claimants were **likely to establish** that publication of the contents of their e-mails should not be allowed.

15. But the **form of the 2008 Orders did include a departure from CPR Part 25 PD para 5.1**, in that they **did not include a return date**, that is a date at which the injunction would cease to apply, unless it was renewed or extended. The reasons for this are explained below. **A return date would be included in any interim order that were made today.**

16. The 2008 Orders did include a number of standard undertakings given to the court by the Claimants in each action, in particular:

    "4. as soon as practicable the Claimant will issue and serve a claim form claiming the appropriate relief".

Breaches of the undertakings of the court and of the rules

17. Each of the Claimants did issue a claim form in accordance with that undertaking**, but each omitted to serve the claim forms as soon as practicable once the identity of the Defendant became known**. As stated above, this was a serious breach, even if committed with good intentions. **Each of the Claimants has apologised to the court.** One of the matters which I address in this judgment is what I should do about these breaches.

18. Not only was there a breach of that undertaking by each of the Claimants,

but the four month time limit for service of claim forms prescribed by CPR Part 7.5(1) expired on 15 and 18 April 2009 respectively. **The Claimants made no application to extend the period, as they might have done, in accordance with CPR 7.6(1). It is now too late for them to do so.**

19. The Claimants therefore each asked the court for an order under CPR Part 6.16(1) dispensing with service of the claim form. That rule provides that the court may make such an order **"in exceptional circumstances"** and that such an order may be made at any time.

Service on the newspapers

20. As soon as the 2008 Orders had been made they were served on NGN, the publishers of The Sun, on MGN Ltd, the publishers of the Mirror and Sunday Mirror, and on Associated Newspapers Limited, the publishers of the Daily and Sunday Mail.

21. In the letter of December 2010 referred to above, Farrer and Co referred to a number of recent authorities including my judgments in *Gray v UVW* [2010] EWHC 2367 which had been handed down on 21 October 2010, *JIH v NGN* [2010] EWHC 3174 (QB), and the judgment of the Court of Appeal handed down on 16 November 2010 in *Donald v Ntuli* [2010] EWCA Civ 1276 [2011] 3 WLR 294**. These judgments all gave effect to the principles to be applied by the court when making anonymity orders** as explained by the Supreme Court on 27 January 2010 in *In re Guardian News Media Ltd* [2010] UKSC 1 [2010] 2 AC 697. NGN invited the Claimants to consent to the removal of the anonymity orders which I had made.

22. When the solicitors for the Claimants came to realise that their clients were in breach of the undertaking to serve the claim forms, the Claimants sought to remedy this situation. They issued the application notices of 11 February and they purported to serve BCD, albeit it long out of time. Her identity had been known to them no later than August 2009. The result was the agreement between the Claimants and BCD recounted above.

The hearing on 17 March

23. Accordingly, the order I made on 17 March **included a final judgment by consent against BCD.** BCD did not appear on 17 March, but submitted letters, including letters from medical advisors in support of her application for an order that her identity not be revealed.

24. Although the substantive hearing on 17 March was in private, **I sat in open court at the beginning of the hearing and again at the end of the hearing**. I did so in each case to hear submissions from Ms Marzec on behalf of Associated Newspapers Limited, and, at the end, to explain in open court that I would make a new injunction and later deliver this public judgment.

By that time Ms Marzec had had time to consider the draft of the orders that Mr Caldecott was asking me to make, and her submissions were confined to the form of those orders. She made no objection to the substance of the orders. Her submissions as to their form were of assistance to the court.

25. In addition I had the benefit of the written arguments on behalf of NGN in the correspondence addressed to the Claimants by Farrer & Co and on behalf of MGN Limited in their correspondence with the Claimants' solicitors. I also had the benefit of written submissions in a letter from Mr Marcus Partington of MGN Ltd addressed to me for the purposes of the hearing.

Derogations from open justice in the 2008 Orders

26. The evidence in support of the application for the substantive relief also justified the hearing of the application in December 2008 without notice, in accordance with Human Rights Act Section 12(2)(a). **There were at that time no practicable steps that the Claimants could have taken to notify the respondents whose identity they knew nothing about.**

27. This evidence also justified two further provisions derogating from open justice that I made in December 2008. The first of these was the order that **"the publication of all of the information relating to these proceedings or information describing them is expressly prohibited"** (this is a provision added to an ordinary form of injunction which is sometimes referred to as a "**super injunction**").

28. The second such provision of the order was that the proceedings be **anonymised** so that the Claimants each be referred to only by letters of the alphabet in all court documents and notices.

29. The reasons for including these two provisions are the following**. If the unknown Defendants (whoever they might be) came to know that the Claimants had commenced these proceedings and had obtained an order of the court before the Claimants could effect service of the claim forms on them, there appeared to me to be a real danger that the Defendants might either defeat the purpose of the proceedings by publishing the contents of the confidential e-mails, for example on the internet, or that they might destroy evidence which might lead to the identification of the Defendants**. See *Terry v Persons Unknown* [2010] EWCH 119 (QB), [2010] EMLR 16 at page 400 at para 138.

30. However, as already noted, if a similar application were to be made today**, the orders would include a return date which limited the time during which these two provisions of the order should ru**n. I shall explain below why there was not a return date.

The evidence

31. In so far as not already set out above, the evidence included the following. Mrs Goldsmith and Mrs Khan each gave evidence that they had encountered difficulties in logging onto their e-mail accounts..

. . .

What to do about the breach of the undertakings to the court

37. The facts of the ongoing police investigation and of the knowledge of BCD's ill-health together provide some explanation for the failure of the Claimants to fulfil their undertaking to serve the Claim Forms as soon as practicable. **But these facts do not amount to an excuse for that failure.** The Claim Forms could, and probably should, have been served in late January 2009. **If they were not served at that time, then they should, without doubt, have been served no later than about 12th August 2009 (subject to the Claimants having applied for the necessary extension of time).**

38. **In any event the court ought to have been kept informed of the non-compliance with the undertaking and any reason for that.** However, it was not until after receipt of letters from the newspapers who had been served with the order, that is the letters of December 2010, that the Claimants and their advisors properly addressed this matter.

39. The first question therefore is: what should the Court do faced with this breach of the undertaking for which there is no good excuse? **I accepted the apologies of the Claimants. While the breaches of the undertakings are culpable, they were not intended to achieve an improper purpose.**

40. Such is not always the case with failure by a claimant to fulfil such undertakings. **The Court must be vigilant to ensure that where such failures occur, they are dealt with in a way that is, so far as possible, consistent with justice and with the need to mark the seriousness of such breaches of an undertaking.**

41. One possible course for the Court to take would have been to discharge the 2008 Orders and strike out the actions. I gave consideration as to whether or not I should do that. I was persuaded by MrCaldecott that I should not do that. **Rather, I should grant the application for an order dispensing with service of the Claim Forms. The exceptional circumstances that make that course possible are as follows.**

42. The medical evidence made available to the Court by BCD, together with her own letter, **make clear that BCD's mental health remains fragile.** And BCD wishes to put this matter behind her.

43. If I were to discharge the 2008 Orders without making a fresh order, there would be nothing to stop the Claimants issuing new claim forms and

applying for fresh injunctions on the same day. While BCD has consented to judgment, and claims to have no intention of publishing e-mails or the contents of emails in the future, the evidence as to the past behaviour of BCD is such that I find that **there remains a risk to the Claimants from BCD from which the Claimants are entitled to be protected by an injunction restraining publication of the confidential material in question**. The **failure of BCD to refrain from the conduct which has led to these proceedings,** notwithstanding the police warning on the earlier occasion, provides sufficient material upon which to found a need for a fresh injunction.

44. It follows that to discharge the 2008 Orders without replacing them would be inconsistent with the overriding objective. The overriding objective is to deal with cases justly (CPR Pt 1.1). **Where it is possible for the Court to impose some penalty for breach of an undertaking to the Court which is consistent with dealing with the case justly, that is what the Court will do. In the present case such an option is not available. In practice, however, the Claimants have suffered for their failures. They have had to incur the not insubstantial costs of the oral hearing on 17 March (which would probably not otherwise have been necessary), and they have quite properly not asked for any order for costs in their favour against BCD.**

45. The fact that BCD wishes to consent to judgment to put this matter behind her, and not to undergo further legal procedures detrimental to her mental health, are, in my judgment, exceptional circumstances within the meaning CPR Part 6.16(1) which justify my dispensing with service of the Claim Forms in the present case, notwithstanding that the time for service of them has so long expired.

Why there was no return date in the 2008 Orders

46. The costs of access to justice in England and Wales are one of the biggest problems in the administration of justice today. Newspapers have much cause to complain about this, and have successfully invoked the European Convention on Human Rights to address the problem. As recently as January 2011 MGN Ltd won their case in Strasbourg, *MGN v UK* Application No 39401/01, on the costs involved in another breach of confidence case *Campbell v MGN Ltd* [2004] UKHL 22.

47. The reason why in this case (and in other cases heard in and about 2008) the court did not include a return date was in an attempt to keep down the costs of access to justice. The saving of expense is a part of the overriding objective set out in CPR Part 1.2(b). A return date puts claimants to the burden of incurring costs in coming back to the Court for a hearing which may be no more than a formality. In cases where, as here, there is evidence of a serious breach of confidence by an unknown person, it is not uncommon for claim-

ants to need a considerable time to identify and serve the defendant, if they ever succeed in doing so at all. And when such defendants are identified, it is not uncommon, as happened in this case, for the matter to be resolved by consent. So a return date can give rise to costs which are unnecessary.

48. In 2008 it was thought that the absence of a return date would be unlikely to cause any prejudice to newspapers served with the order. The 2008 Orders included, as such orders invariably do, a provision that:

> "Anyone notified of this order may apply to the Court at any time to vary or discharge this order (or so much of it as affects that person), but anyone wishing to do so must first inform the claimant's solicitors in writing".

49. It follows that any of the newspaper publishers served with the order in December 2008 could have applied to the Court then and there to vary or discharge the orders.

50. However, it is the experience of the court that newspapers and other third parties rarely avail themselves of the right to apply to discharge or vary an injunction. The reasons for this may be various. One reason may be that the journalists know from their own sources (as in this case) what the action is about. They may have no wish to publish anything about it. Another reason may be the risk of incurring costs if the third party makes an application to the court.

51. Regrettably, the well intentioned attempt by the court to save costs has given rise to serious unintended consequences. One problem is that the absence of a return date gives rise to a risk that claimants will fail (inadvertently or deliberately) to fulfil their undertakings to the court. If there had been a return date in the 2008 Orders, I think it unlikely that the Claimants would have allowed the time for service of the claim forms to expire without returning to the Court to seek any necessary extension of time.

52. Another problem is that in this case the derogations from open justice which were fully justified when ordered in December 2008 have lasted longer than was necessary. There is also concern that this may have happened in other cases, and Mr Caldecott informed me that newspaper publishers have written to claimants in other cases in terms similar to those of Farrer & Co's letter of December 2010. The perception that this is a problem in other cases has given rise to public concerns which led to the setting up of a committee chaired by the Master of Rolls.

53. By late 2009 it was apparent that the attempt to save costs by not including a return date in interim orders in cases of breach of confidence and privacy was giving rise to these problems. Therefore, on 2 December 2009, when I handed down a judgment in *G and G v Wikimedia Foundation Inc* [2009] EWHC

3148 (QB), at paras 21 to 25 I stated that there should be a return date in accordance with Part 25 Practice Direction para 5.2, and that orders should be drafted so as to have effect for no longer than is necessary and proportionate.

54. Under English law civil proceedings are adversarial, and the court expects parties to an action, or non-parties affected by an action, to apply to the court if they claim that their rights have been unjustifiably interfered with. The court endeavours to frame its orders so as to respect the rights of non-parties, but where it does not succeed, there should be no lasting damage if the non-parties make known their concerns by applying to the court. They may do this as soon as they are served with the order, or, if thought fit, at a later time. In order to assist media third parties in this regard, and for the benefit of those members of the public who are concerned about anonymised injunctions, there have been changes in practice. During the last year judges have generally adopted the practice of recording their reasons for granting an injunction that might affect the media in the form of written reserved judgments (like this one) which are made available on the **internet** at websites including www.bailii.org. In the past that information was not always provided to third parties unless they requested it.

55. NGN, Associated Newspapers Ltd and MGN have made such an application in this case. In raising the matter when they did in December 2010, NGN has caused there to be revealed an important breach of an undertaking of the court.

56. In some cases newspaper publishers served with such an order may be put in a difficult position, because they may not know what the subject matter of the action is. In the present actions that is not so, at least in the case of some newspaper publishers. It was in fact, as stated above, a journalist who brought to the attention of the Claimants the serious breach of confidence of which Mr and Mrs. Goldsmith were the victims. Mrs Goldsmith also gave evidence of an approach from a journalist on the other newspaper.

57. Responsible journalists would have had no difficulty in recognising that disclosure of the contents of personal e-mails exchanged between members of a family would be a breach of confidence. If any newspaper had thought that this material could lawfully be published, and was newsworthy, there was an opportunity to do so before the applications were made to the Court. The fact that they did not do so demonstrates that journalists and newspapers did act responsibly in relation to this case.

58. In reality the substantive injunction prohibiting publication of the contents of the e-mails involved no interference with the freedom of expression of anyone. Even in December 2010, what the newspaper publishers sought was

the removal of the anonymity and restriction on reporting the fact of the injunction. No-one has suggested that the personal emails exchanged within a family which are disclosed by a hacker should not be the subject of an injunction to restrain a breach of confidence in ordinary form.

59. However the order for anonymity and the order restraining "the publication of all of the information relating to these proceedings or information describing them" were interferences with freedom of expression and derogations from open justice. They were justified at the time they were made, for the reasons given above, but they should not have lasted longer than the period of time necessary to effect service of the Claim Forms.

An alternative way to avoid unnecessary costs

60. **The inclusion of a return date in such orders need not always involve claimants in substantial unnecessary legal costs. Of course, in the normal way a return date is an oral hearing attended by Counsel, which is a costly matter. But where at the return date the only relief that the claimant seeks is agreed with all parties concerned, or where it is an extension of time for service of the claim form, or an extension of an anonymity order, or some other ancillary provision, this can generally be done on paper.**

61. Solicitors acting for claimants can write to the Court setting out what has happened since the grant of the original injunction and why it is that an extension of the injunction to a new return date is required. If the explanation is, for example, that it has not yet been possible to serve the defendant, or that the defendant who has been served requires further time to consider the matter, or that the matter is subject to a police investigation during which it might be inappropriate for the Court to make a different order, then having seen the explanation, the Court can communicate with the claimant's solicitors to the effect that no oral hearing is required and the matter can be dealt with on paper, or, if such be the case, that an oral hearing is required.

62. When I refer to a case being dealt with on paper, I refer to provisions of the CPR including the following:

i) Part 1.4 (2):

"Active case management includes . . . (j) dealing with the case without the parties needing to attend Court."

ii) Part 3.1(2):

"Except where these Rules provide otherwise, the Court may . . . (d) hold a hearing and receive evidence by telephone or by using any other method of direct oral communication".

63. It is pursuant to CPR Part 1.4(2)(j) that in this case I have taken into consideration the written representations of BCD and of Mr Partington for MGN

Ltd. Where a third party considers that an order may have been made in terms which are inconsistent with the CPR, including its Practice Directions, or with the principles laid down in *In re Guardian News and Media Ltd* or any other applicable case law, then the third party should raise that with the claimant, as NGN did in this case. If there is then an agreed variation, and in some cases even where the matter cannot be resolved by agreement, then CPR Part 1.4(2)(j) may provide an inexpensive way for the matter to be put before the court.

Anonymity for the defendant

64. BCD has by letter asked for anonymity, and the Claimants support that application. It is, as already indicated, also supported by medical evidence. Notwithstanding the agreement between the parties, it is for the court to decide whether such a derogation from open justice is necessary.

65. The proper approach to applications for anonymity in cases involving confidentiality has recently been set out by the Court of Appeal in *JIH v News Group Newspapers Ltd.* [2011] EWCA Civ 42 at para 21. As stated at subparagraph (5):

> "Where the Court is asked to restrain the publication of the names of the parties and/or the subject matter of the claim on the ground that such restraint is necessary under Article 8, the question is whether there is sufficient general, public interest in publishing a report of the proceedings which identifies a party and/or the normally reportable details to justify any resulting curtailment of his right and his family's right to respect for their private and family life."

66. In the present case, so far as the anonymity of BCD is concerned, the Article 8 rights in question are not those of the Claimants**. It is the Art 8 rights of BCD with which I am concerned on this point**. Because of the fame of the Claimants there is a real fear that, if the identity of BCD is disclosed, BCD will be the subject of **intrusive** attention from journalists and others who are not as responsible as those who decided not to publish the **confidential information** in December 2008, even before an injunction was granted. There are real fears for the effect on BCD's health and well being.

67. The necessity of protecting the confidentiality of BCD's medical condition was one of the reasons why the hearing on 17 March had to be in private.

68. As I have already indicated, there is in the present case no interference with the freedom of expression of anyone arising from the substantive provisions restraining disclosure of **confidential information**. No responsible journalist would expect to publish the **confidential information**. Certainly none of the newspapers who have made representations to the Claimants or the Court in this case have indicated any wish to publish the confidential material in

question. **The only interference with freedom of expression, and the only derogation from open justice, in the orders I made on 17 March were those necessary to preserve the confidentiality of the information question and the anonymity of BCD.**

69. Having regard to the medical evidence, I have no hesitation in concluding that there is no sufficient general public interest in publishing a report of these proceedings which identifies BCD to justify the resulting curtailment of her right to respect for private life, which includes her health and well being.

70. It is for these reasons that I discharged the orders that I had made in December 2008, and made the new orders that I made on 17 March 2011.

OPQ v BJM [2011] EWHC 1059 (QB)

Mr Justice Eady:

1. On 29 January 2011 Cox J granted an injunction to the Claimant which I extended on 2 February (the return date), when its terms were also slightly varied: see [2011] EWHC 160 (QB). Its **purpose** was to restrain the First Defendant and her partner from publishing confidential material about the Claimant's private life. On that occasion, I described it as "**a straightforward and blatant blackmail case**".

2. The evidence at that stage showed that the First Defendant, probably through her partner, had been negotiating with a newspaper group **to sell intimate photographs and other information obtained in circumstances that were clearly private and in respect of which she owed the Claimant a duty of confidence.** There was also evidence as to the likely adverse impact of publicity **on the health and wellbeing of various members of the Claimant's family.**

3. It appeared on the material before me that a large sum of money was being discussed with Associated Newspapers Ltd but, at that point, someone acting on the First Defendant's behalf contacted the Claimant's solicitor on the evening of 29 January and told him that she would rather do "a deal" with him. **It was said that she thought that the Claimant might prefer to pay some money to make the problem go away for good.**

4. It was **obviously a case for the parties to be anonymised** with a view to protecting the Claimant's rights and **to reduce the risk of jigsaw identification:** see e.g. *JIH v News Group Newspapers Ltd* [2011] EWCA Civ 42 at [40].

5. Having decided that the rights of the Claimant and his family under Article 8 of the European Convention on Human Rights and Fundamental Freedoms were **engaged, as they so plainly were**, the court had to carry out a **balancing**

exercise in the light of an "**intense focus**" upon the particular facts of the case: see e.g. *Campbell v MGN Ltd* [2004] 2 AC 457 and *Re S (A Child)* [2005] 2 AC 593. Paying due regard to the Article 10 rights of the two Defendants, and those of Associated Newspapers, my conclusion was that there was no reason why they should prevail over the Article 8 rights of the persons concerned. There was, for example, **no public interest in the confidential information**; nor would it contribute to "**a debate of general interes**t", in the sense contemplated by the European Court of Human Rights in Strasbourg in **Von Hannover v Germany** (2004) 40 EHRR 1.

6. Since I was satisfied that the Claimant would be "**likely**" to obtain a permanent injunction to protect his rights at trial, it was appropriate for me to continue the interim injunction: see s 12(3) of the Human Rights Act 1998 and *Cream Holdings v Banerjee* [2005] 1 AC 253.

7. Very shortly after I continued the injunction, **copies of it were served on various media interests by the Claimant's solicitors, so as to notify them of the prohibition and of the court's intention to maintain the status quo until trial or further order.** This was with a view **to taking advantage of the so-called Spycatcher doctrine:** see *Att-Gen v Newspaper Publishing Plc* [1988] Ch 333 and *Att-Gen v Times Newspapers Ltd* [1992] 1 AC 191. **Anyone who revealed the confidential information, having knowledge of the court's order, and thereby thwarting its purpose, would be liable to be punished for criminal contempt of court**. As Lloyd LJ explained in *Att-Gen v Newspaper Publishing* at p 380:

> "At common law, if the court makes an order regulating its own procedure and the **purpose** of the order is plainly to protect the administration of justice, then anyone who subverts that order will be guilty of **contempt**."

8. In due course, since there was no answer to the claim, agreement was reached between the parties. This included provision for an undertaking to be given to the court not to publish any of the **confidential information**. **Thus the Claimant's legitimate objectives were achieved and there would be no longer any need for the proceedings to be continued against the Defendants or for a trial to take place.**

9. **It is generally thought that once a permanent injunction has been obtained following a trial, or by consent, or an undertaking has been given to similar effect, the Spycatcher doctrine will no longer apply. That is because the court's purpose, in holding the ring until trial, has been overtaken by events—there will be no need for a trial**: see *Att-Gen v Punch Ltd* [2001] QB 1028 at [87]–[88]; *Jockey Club v Buffham* [2003] QB 462; and *X & Y v Persons Unknown* [2007] EMLR 290. I have recently so held in a case which is due shortly to be heard in the Court of Appeal. The law may be reconsidered

at that stage but, in the meantime, I shall proceed on my present understanding of the position.

10. There is an application before the court to put into effect the terms of the proposed settlement, but that is for the moment adjourned. Currently, the interim injunction granted on 2 February remains in force and the *Spycatcher* doctrine continues to apply. As and when it ceases to have effect, however, Mr James Price QC on behalf of the **Claimant asks that fresh steps should have been taken to protect him against third parties, since there is good reason to believe that the allegations may well be published in the media once it is thought that the Spycatcher restraints fall away.** To that end, he invites me to grant an injunction ***contra mundum*; that is to say, an order that is of general effect.**

11. This is a jurisdiction which was widened, at first rather tentatively, in the immediate aftermath of the Human Rights Act 1998: see the observations of Lord Phillips MR in the Court of Appeal in *Re S (A Child)* [2004] Fam 43 at [98]–[99], set out below at [16].

12. The notion of an injunction ***contra mundum*** appears to run counter to the principle enunciated over two centuries ago by Lord Eldon in *Iveson v Harris* (1802) 7 Ves Jun 251, 256–7:

> " . . . I have no conception that it is competent to this Court to hold a man bound by injunction, who is not a party in the cause for the **purpose** of the cause."

13. By the time of the *Spycatcher* litigation just over 20 years ago, although it remained a fundamental principle that the courts act *in personam* in accordance with Lord Eldon's dictum, it had been recognised, that there were " . . . certain fairly limited exceptions of which the best established is wardship": *Att.-Gen. v Newspaper Publishing* at 377G, *per* Lloyd LJ. Indeed, not so long before, in *X County Council v A* [1985] 1 All ER 53, 55h, Balcombe J (as he then was) expressed the view that the power to grant an injunction other than *in personam*, and which was expressed to extend ***contra mundum***, was confined to the wardship jurisdiction.

14. The courts had long before inherited the sovereign's role as *parens patriae*, the nature of which was described, again by Lord Eldon, in *Wellesley v Duke of Beaufort* (1827) 2 Russ 1 at 20:

> " . . . it belongs to the King, as *parens patriae*, having the care of those who are not able to take care of themselves, and is founded on the obvious necessity that the law should place somewhere the care of individuals who cannot take care of themselves, particularly in cases where it is clear that some care should be thrown around them."

Where the court was exercising this jurisdiction, it was not confined by the ordinary constraints of *inter partes* litigation: see e.g. *Scott v Scott* [1913] AC 417, 483, where it was characterised by Lord Shaw as being "*intra familiam*".

15. Within a short space of time, however, Balcombe LJ (as he had by then become) was acknowledging in *Att.-Gen. v Newspaper Publishing*, at pp 388–9, together with Sir John Donaldson MR, that the power to grant a ***contra mundum*** injunction was not necessarily restricted to the *parens patriae* jurisdiction.

16. **This traditional terminology, and the constraints that tended to accompany it, have now largely been superseded as a consequence of the Human Rights Act.** The courts have recognised that there is now a "new era": see *Venables and Thompson v News Group Newspapers Ltd* [2001] Fam 430 at [100], *per* Dame Elizabeth Butler-Sloss p It was accepted that remedies had to be fashioned to meet the needs of the particular case in the light of the European Convention. Hence the observations of Lord Phillips MR in *Re S (A Child)* to which I referred above, at [98]–[99]:

> "98. Dame Elizabeth Butler-Sloss P, sitting in the Family Division, has asserted a jurisdiction to issue an injunction against the world in support of a private law right to confidentiality which is without precedent. In *Venables v News Group Newspapers Ltd* [2001] Fam 430 an application for an injunction was made by the child murderers of James Bulger, who were about to be discharged from prison, having each reached the age of 18. They were to be given false identities and each sought an injunction against the whole world, to continue for his entire lifetime, restraining publication that might lead to the identification of their identities or whereabouts. Dame Elizabeth Butler-Sloss P granted the injunction. In so doing she was strongly influenced by the fact that the claimants' human rights under Articles 2 and 3 would be threatened if their identities were disclosed. This decision was novel in at least two respects: (1) Dame Elizabeth Butler-Sloss P recognised a private law right to confidentiality protecting the identities and whereabouts of the two claimants valid against the whole world; (2) the President held that she had jurisdiction to grant an injunction in protection of private law rights against all the world.
>
> 99. In *X (formerly Bell) v O'Brien* [2003] EWHC 1101 (QB), Dame Elizabeth Butler-Sloss P made similar orders protecting the identity and whereabouts of Mary Bell and her daughter. These two decisions are not directly relevant to the present case. They exemplify, however, the manner in which the courts have extended both the scope of **confidential information** and the use of the injunction to protect this, thereby giving effect to the right to respect for private life conferred by Article 8 of the Convention."

17. This approach was developed and further explained by the House of Lords in the same case. Correspondingly, the significance of historical distinctions has rather faded into the background. The view was unanimously expressed by their Lordships that the earlier case law about the inherent jurisdiction need no longer be routinely considered**, since the foundation of the jurisdiction to restrain publicity could be regarded, since the advent of the Human Rights Act, as deriving from the rights guaranteed under the Convention**. It thus becomes, on the facts of any given case, a matter of carrying out the ultimate balancing test: [2005] 2 AC 593 at [17] and [23]. The court always needs to have in mind the following considerations when applying this new methodology in relation to conflicting Convention rights:

   i) neither article has as such precedence over the other;

   ii) where conflict arises between values under Articles 8 and 10, an "intense focus" is necessary upon the comparative importance of the specific rights being claimed in the individual cases;

   iii) the court must take into account the justifications for interfering with or restricting each right;

   iv) so too, the proportionality test must be applied to each.

18. **It is now acknowledged, therefore, that the court's power to grant an injunction *contra mundum* is not confined to the wardship jurisdiction; nor to children; nor to "individuals who cannot take care of themselves". The remedy is available, wherever necessary and proportionate, for the protection of Convention rights whether of children or adults.**

19. It so happened that in the early case of *Venables and Thompson* the court was concerned to protect their rights under Articles 2 and 3. Dame Elizabeth Butler-Sloss at that stage expressed some doubt as to whether she could have made such an order for the **purpose** solely of vindicating rights under Article 8. Those doubts were resolved, however, not long afterwards in the *Mary Bell* case, where the evidence fell short of establishing a need to protect her rights under Article 2 or Article 3. Account was taken of Strasbourg jurisprudence and particularly *Bensaid v United Kingdom* (2001) 33 EHRR 10. Her Ladyship referred, at [22], to the importance attaching to the physical and psychological integrity of human beings and the relevance of Article 8 in that context. This had been explained in *Bensaid* at [46]–[47]:

   "46. Not every act or measure which adversely affects moral or physical integrity will interfere with the right to respect for private life guaranteed by Art.8. However, the Court's case-law does not exclude that treatment which does not reach the severity of Art.3 treatment may nonetheless breach Art.8 in its private life aspect where there are sufficiently adverse effects on physical and moral integrity.

> 47. **Private life is a broad term not susceptible to exhaustive definition.** The Court has already held that elements such as **gender identification, name and sexual orientation and sexual life are important elements of the personal sphere protected by Art 8**. Mental health must also be regarded as a crucial part of private life associated with the aspect of moral integrity. **Article 8 protects a right to identity and personal development,** and the right to establish and **develop relationships** with other human beings and the outside world. The preservation of **mental stability** is in that context an indispensable precondition to effective enjoyment of the right to respect for private life."

She was accordingly prepared to grant relief to Mary Bell in respect of her Article 8 rights in the light of medical evidence about her mental fragility.

20. Mr Price referred also to the similar case of *Carr v News Group Newspapers Ltd* [2005] EWHC 971 (QB). Evidence was before the court which gave reason to suppose that the claimant's physical wellbeing was at some risk, but there too reference was made to Article 8 and to the analysis in *Bensaid*:

> "Of course the applicant's rights under article 8 of the Convention are also engaged. Those relate to privacy, which is a concept wide enough to include a person's physical and psychological integrity. The preservation of mental stability is recognised as being a necessary precondition for the exercise of rights under Article 8."

Accordingly, the need to protect her mental health was one of the grounds for granting her a *contra mundum* injunction.

21. The matter had been put beyond doubt a few months earlier by the decision of the House of Lords in *Re S (A Child)* where the court's jurisdiction was held, at [23], to be "not in doubt" whenever it became necessary to protect Article 8 rights:

> **"The foundation of the jurisdiction to restrain publicity in a case such as the present is now derived from Convention rights under the ECHR. This is the simple and direct way to approach such cases."**

22. Despite these clear statements of principle, earlier doctrinal distinctions have resurfaced in argument from time to time; for example, in the recent case of *Spencer v Spencer* [2009] EMLR 25 where, at [26], Munby J (as he then was) had to re-emphasise the wide reach of the Convention: "Adults and children are equally entitled to the protection of the Convention". Where necessary, the court has the power to give effect to Article 8 rights by granting what he described as a "blanket order preventing any publication".

23. The House of Lords again had the opportunity in *Re BBC* [2010] 1 AC 145 to revisit and further explain the jurisdiction identified in *Re S (A Child)*. The House of Lords, as any other court, **was bound to act compatibly with**

Convention rights and may thus be called upon to strike the appropriate balance in case of conflict and, where necessary, to make a *contra mundum* order.

24. In the present case there is solid medical evidence as to the health, including the mental health, of the Claimant and various family members. Their rights plainly need to be taken into account: see eg *Donald v Ntuli* [2011] 1 WLR 294 at [24]. It is clear that **publicity relating to the subject-matter of the present dispute could have very serious consequences**. It may well be that this is one of the main reasons why opposition was withdrawn by various newspaper groups shortly before Mr Price made his application before me. The Claimant's advisers had been notified that leading counsel was to be instructed on their behalf to resist the order, **but once the evidence was disclosed to them the matter was not pursued.** I have no idea, therefore, what the grounds of opposition might have been. **The only representations I have are in the form of a letter from MGN Ltd querying the jurisdiction (a concern I have endeavoured to answer) and urging that the order should contain a public domain proviso**. In those circumstances, I have to carry out the balancing exercise as best I can on the information before me.

25. There is **no material** on which I could conclude that any of the **protected information** is in the **public domain**; nor that there would be a l**egitimate public interest in its disclosure**; nor that there would be **any question of exposing or detecting crime**; nor that the information would make any contribution to "**a debate of general interest**": see *Von Hannover v Germany*, cited above, at [60] and [76]. As was said in *Leempoel v Belgium* (64772/01) on 2 November 2006:

> "Whilst the right for the public to be informed, a fundamental right in a democratic society that under particular circumstances may even relate to aspects of the private life of public persons, particularly where political personalities are involved . . . publications whose sole aim is to satisfy the **curiosity** of a certain public as to the details of the private life of a person, whatever their fame, should not be regarded as contributing to any debate of general interest to society."

A fortiori here, where the Claimant is a private citizen.

26. I therefore come to the same conclusion as on 2 February, when the case first came before me. There is no doubt that the Claimant has a reasonable expectation of privacy in respect of the information in question, or that the Article 8 rights of other family members are engaged. There is no reason why the Article 10 rights of the Defendants or indeed of anyone else should prevail and, therefore, the "ultimate balancing" comes down firmly in favour of protecting the Claimant's rights. **Furthermore, in view of the clear risk**

of publication in the media, there is unfortunately no other means open to the court of fulfilling its obligation under the Human Rights Act to protect those rights than to grant a *contra mundum* injunction. Accordingly, it is necessary and proportionate to do so.

MJN v News Group Newspapers Ltd [2011] EWHC 1192 (QB) per Sharp J

Mrs Justice Sharp:

1. This is the return date hearing pursuant to the order of Beatson J of 5 May 2011 who granted an interim injunction to MJN, the Claimant, on short notice. The Claimant **asks for a continuation** of the Order made on that occasion until trial or further order. The Defendant and Respondent to the application is and was News Group Newspapers Limited (NGN). Mr Hugh Tomlinson QC appears for the Claimant. NGN does not attend, though Mr Richard Spearman QC has sent to the court written submissions on NGN's behalf. As I shall explain below, **neither the application before Beatson J, nor that before me today has been opposed.** As I indicated at the end of the hearing I have granted the application to continue the Order made with some variations which have been discussed and agreed between the parties. These are my reasons.
2. Shortly before the application on the 5 May, **NGN notified the Claimant of its intention to publish in the Sun newspaper an account by an 18 year old lingerie model, Kimberley West, of her 'relationship' with the Claimant, a married premier league footballer.** NGN then declined to give an undertaking not to publish, and were notified of the Claimant's intention to apply for an urgent interim injunction **on short notice** to prevent the disclosure of private information.
3. The terms of the Order which the Claimant then invited the court to make (and which it did make) had been the subject of discussion between Mr Tomlinson, and Mr Spearman in advance of the hearing. The Order, discussed and made, permitted the publication of the story of the '**relationship**' by Ms West **provided only** that (i) **nothing is published which identifies or tends to identify the Claimant as the other party to the relationship** or **as the person who has applied to the court for an injunction**; and (ii) **what is published excludes sexual, salacious and/or other specified details.** It is not conceded by the Claimant that there is any lawful justification for the publication of the story itself. But it was, and is accepted by Mr Tomlinson, that sofar as the issue of **prior restraint** is concerned, the balance between the Article 8 and

Article 10 rights engaged could be struck in the way allowed for by that part of the Order **permitting Ms West to sell her story to NGN, and for its publication**, but for it **not to be told in a way which identifies the Claimant or which gives sexual or salacious details.**

4. Ms West and NGN appear **to have taken full advantage of this**, so that a story has now been published about the '**relationship**', and a further one, complaining about the injunction as well. Thus, on 6 May 2011 the Sun published an article **headed "MARRIED PREM STAR * GAGS SUN ON AFFAIR",** with a sub-heading, "*(Yes, another one)" illustrated by a picture of Ms West; and on 7 May 2011 a further story was published in the Sun headlined "MY FLING WITH PREM STAR" with the caption **"The only version of this story that rat's lawyers will let us print."**

5. As I have said, NGN did not oppose **(although it did not consent to)** the Order being made on the terms discussed between leading counsel until an early return date (11 May 2011). NGN have adopted precisely the same position in respect of its continuance.

6. NGN's stance is explained by Mr Spearman as follows:

   > "So far as continuing relief is concerned, NGN's stance on this Return Date is the same as it was before Beatson J. If the Court is satisfied by MJN that this is a proper case for an injunction, then NGN does not resist (but does not consent to) the continuation until trial or further order in the meantime of an Order in the terms made by Beatson J. Those terms include an entitlement for NGN (like anyone served with or notified of the Order) to apply to vary or discharge the Order without needing to show any change of circumstances. In addition, there is one change which NGN would propose, namely that paragraph 1(c) should be amended to make clear that what is prohibited is not publication of any **photograph** or video film of the Claimant or his house but only publication of such images relating to or in the context of his **relationship** with Kimberley West.
   >
   > In those circumstances, in order to save costs NGN's present position is that it does not intend to appear or be represented at the Return Date."

7. The position before me therefore is that NGN does not oppose the application. It does not seek to argue that the Order should not be continued (subject to the variations which I shall turn to in a moment, and which are agreed), or for example, that the Claimant has made hypocritical statements about his **relationships**, or that it is in the public interest for the Claimant to be named. Indeed, **no public interest justification for the publication of the story has been advanced in argument by NGN or any other media organisation at any stage.**

8. It is still necessary for the court to be satisfied independently that the Order asked for should be granted on the terms the Claimant asks for and which NGN does not oppose; **but I consider Mr Tomlinson is correct in submitting the fact that the very experienced legal advisers for NGN have taken the position that it is not appropriate to resist the granting of such an order on an interim basis is a material factor to be considered.**

9. I summarised the law which applies to applications to restrain what is said to be private information by interim injunction pending the resolution of the matter at a trial (if there is one) in *DFT v TFD* [2010] EWHC 2335 (QB) as follows:

> "14. **Interim relief before trial.** Since this is an application which, if granted, might affect the exercise of the right to freedom of expression, section 12 of the Human Rights Act 1998 applies and no relief is to be granted so as to restrain publication before trial unless the court is satisfied that the applicant is likely to establish that publication should not be allowed.
>
> > "As to what degree of likelihood makes the prospects of success 'sufficiently favourable', the general approach should be that courts will be **exceedingly slow to make interim restraint orders** where the applicant has not satisfied the court he will probably (**'more likely than not'**) succeed at the trial." See *Cream Holdings Ltd v Banerjee* [2005] 1 AC 253, at [22] per Lord Nicholls.
>
> 15. **Private information.** When considering whether the publication of information which is said to be private should be permitted, the court must first decide whether the information in question is private, that is whether the claimant has a **reasonable expectation of privacy** in respect of that information such that the claimant's rights under Article 8 of the European Convention on Human Rights are engaged (stage 1). If yes, the Court must then **engage in a balancing exercise**, weighing the Article 8 rights of the claimant against the Article 10 rights of the defendant (stage 2). See eg *Murray v Express Newspapers Plc* [2009] Ch 481 at [24], [27], [35] and [40].
>
> 16. In *Murray* the Court of Appeal said at [35] that the question at stage 1 is "**a broad one**" which "takes account of all the circumstances of the case". The Court of Appeal also quoted with approval Lord Hope's formulation of the test in *Campbell v MGN* [2004] 2 AC 457, [99]:
>
> > **"The question is what a reasonable person of ordinary sensibilities would feel if she was placed in the same position as the Claimant and faced the same publicity"**
>
> 17. Relevant considerations include the **attributes** of the claimant, the

nature of the activity in which the claimant was engaged, the **place** at which it was happening, the **nature and purpose of the intrusion**, the **absence of consent**, whether it was known or could be inferred that consent was absent and the effect (of disclosure) on the claimant (see *Murray* at [36]).

18. The Court should approach the balancing exercise at stage 2 in this way:

> "**First,** neither article has as such precedence over the other. **Secondly**, where the values under the two articles are in conflict, an intense focus on the comparative importance of the specific rights being claimed in the individual case is necessary. **Thirdly**, the justifications for interfering with or restricting each right must be taken into account. **Finally,** the proportionality test must be applied to each" per Lord Steyn in *Re S (a child)* [2005] 1 AC 593 at [17].

19. **Public Interest.** It is not enough for information to be **interesting to the public**. Publication of the information must be in the public interest. The modern approach in any event is to consider public interest as an aspect of proportionality: see *HRH Prince of Wales v Associated Newspapers Ltd* [2008] Ch 57 at [68]."

10. As Mr Tomlinson submits, there are therefore essentially two questions for the court. **First**, would a reasonable person in all the circumstances regard each item of information as private. **Second**, if so, is there in any event, some proper justification for its publication.

11. Evidence has been put before the court in witness statements from the Claimant, and his solicitors, Mr Hobbs and Mr Oakley**, and in confidential schedules to those witness statements.** No evidence has been put before the court by NGN. In summary it is said that the Claimant, a married Premier league footballer as I have said, and Ms **West had a brief sexual relationship and that their relationship was not conducted in public**. To the best of the Claimant's knowledge, **only one person knew about it** (a friend of the Claimant's) apart obviously from the Claimant and Ms West. The Claimant **understood that Ms West viewed the matter as confidential** and did not speak to any one about it either. It is also said the Claimant **has never courted publicity in relation to any aspect of his private life.** He says that the information concerned here is private and sensitive, and its publication would cause him and his wife enormous distress and **embarrassment**.

12. As for the **first question**, in my judgment the Claimant is likely to establish at trial that he has a reasonable expectation of privacy in relation to the information which he wishes to restrain such that his privacy rights are engaged. As was said by Eady J in *Mosley v News Group* [2008] EWHC 1777 (QB) at [98]

"anyone indulging in sexual activity is entitled to a degree of privacy—especially if it is on private property and between consenting adults" and that "**people's sex lives are essentially their own business**" at [98].

13. As for the **second question**, I also consider it to be plain and obvious, as Mr Tomlinson submits that the Claimant is likely to establish at trial that publication of the information which the Claimant seeks to protect, either identifying him as a party to a '**relationship**' with Ms West, **and/or as to the sexual, or salacious details of the relationship**, would constitute an unjustifiable interference with the Claimant's personal and family life.

14. It is accepted by the Claimant that the Article 10 rights of Ms West and NGN are also engaged. In my judgment, **the Claimant is likely to establish that there is no basis or justification for publication of the information which the Claimant now seeks to protect**, in particular in circumstances where Ms West has already **been permitted to tell her story of her relationship with the Claimant, albeit without naming him**. No public interest justification has been advanced for its publication as I have said; but in any event I consider the Claimant is likely to establish there **is no public interest in the fact that the Claimant had a short-lived affair or in its sexual/salacious details and that publication of the relevant information would not make any contribution to any debate of public interest:** see most recently, in this context, *ETK v News Group Newspapers* [2011] EWCA Civ 439. The relevant information here is **not in the public domain.**

15. I consider Mr Tomlinson is right therefore in submitting the balance in favour of the Claimant's Article 8 rights in the protection of private information about a **sexual relationship** is strong, when set against the Article 10 rights of NGN and Ms West, in the absence of any public interest justification, to add the identify of the Claimant and sexual and **salacious** details of the '**relationship**' to the story Ms West and NGN have already told; and thus that the balance between the parties' respective rights has been fairly struck at this stage.

16. I am therefore satisfied that the injunction granted by Beatson J, **the relevant terms of which are available in a public Order**, and which are summarised in paragraph 3 above, should continue until trial or further order, subject to one variation referred to by Mr Spearman in his written submissions and which Mr Tomlinson agrees should be made. **Paragraph 1 (c) of the Order shall be varied so there shall be no publication of any photograph or video film of the Claimant or the Claimant's house (but only if that photograph or video identifies or tends to identify the Claimant as being the person who applied for this Order).**

17. It is necessary further to consider the terms of the draft Order and any

derogation it makes from the principles of open justice. I am satisfied that it remains necessary for the Claimant to be anonymised for the reasons I have already given. **At the start of the hearing, Mr Tomlinson invited me to hear this matter in private.** In the event however, I was satisfied this was not necessary, provided an **order was made pursuant to CPR 31.22 that no use may be made by any person who is not a party to the action of any of the confidential schedules to the witness statements or the skeleton arguments read by the court and referred to in the course of the hearing; and that no person who is not a party to the action may obtain the documents from the court records.** Accordingly, the hearing was in public, and I made an order pursuant to CPR 31.22 in those terms.

18. Subject to that, I am further satisfied that the further provisions within the draft Order put before me which derogate from the principles of open justice **(and which, for example, permit information which may reveal the identity of the Claimant to be contained in confidential schedules to the witness statements and excluded from the statements of case)** are necessary to prevent disclosure of the information which is the subject matter of this application.

Mosley v The United Kingdom [2011] ECtHR 774

(Application no 48009/08)

JUDGMENT
STRASBOURG
10 May 2011

This judgment will become final in the circumstances set out in Article 44 § 2 of the Convention. It may be subject to editorial revision.

In the case of Mosley v the United Kingdom,

The European Court of Human Rights (Fourth Section), sitting as a Chamber composed of:

Lech Garlicki, *President,*
Nicolas Bratza,
Ljiljana Mijović,
David Thór Björgvinsson,
Päivi Hirvelä,
Ledi Bianku,
Nebojša Vučinić, *judges,*
and Lawrence Early, *Section Registrar,*

Having deliberated in private on 11 January 2011 and 12 April 2011, Delivers the following judgment, which was adopted on the latter date:

PROCEDURE

1. The case originated in an application (no 48009/08) against the United Kingdom of Great Britain and Northern Ireland lodged with the Court under Article 34 of the Convention for the Protection of Human Rights and Fundamental Freedoms ("the Convention") by a British national, Mr Max Rufus Mosley ("the applicant"), on 29 September 2008.
2. The applicant was represented by Collyer Bristow LLP, a firm of solicitors based in London. The United Kingdom Government ("the Government") were represented by their Agent, Mr D. Walton, Foreign and Commonwealth Office.
3. The applicant alleged that the United Kingdom had violated its positive obligations under Article 8 of the Convention, taken alone and taken together with Article 13, to ensure his right to respect for his private life.
4. On 20 October 2009 the Court decided to give notice of the application to the Government. It also decided to rule on the admissibility and merits of the application at the same time (Article 29 § 1).
5. The applicant and the Government each filed written observations (Rule 54 § 2 (b)). Third-party comments were also received from Guardian News & Media Ltd, The Media Lawyers' Association and Finers Stephens Innocent on behalf of The Media Legal Defence Initiative, Index on Censorship, The Media International Lawyers' Association, European Publishers' Council, The Mass Media Defence Centre, Romanian Helsinki Committee, The Bulgarian Access to Information Programme (AIP) Foundation, Global Witness and Media Law Resource Centre, which had been given leave by the President to intervene in the written procedure (Article 36 § 2 of the Convention and Rule 44 § 3 (a)).
6. A hearing in the case took place in public in the Human Rights Building, Strasbourg, on 11 January 2011 (Rule 59 § 3).

. . .

II. RELEVANT DOMESTIC LAW AND PRACTICE

A. The Press Complaints Commission

29. The Press Complaints Commission ("PCC") is an independent body set up to examine complaints about the editorial content of newspapers and magazines, and their websites, in the United Kingdom. If a complaint is upheld, a public ruling will be issued by the PCC and the newspaper or magazine concerned is obliged to publish the critical ruling in full and with due prominence.

30. On 18 November 2008 **the PCC upheld a complaint by Mr p Burrell that the News of the World had published an article about him which was inaccurate, in breach of clause 1 of the Editors' Code of Practice** (see further paragraph 31 below). **The newspaper had failed to approach him for comments prior to publication**. In its adjudication, the PCC noted:

"The [PCC] has previously said that failure to contact the subjects of articles before publication—while not obligatory—may constitute a lack of care under Clause 1 in some circumstances. It has never said that people have no right ever to comment on a story, or to be offered a right of reply, if they have misled people in another context.

The [PCC] was also aware of the newspaper's concerns about an undeserved injunction being granted. However, it did not consider that this meant that the requirements of the Code did not apply. Given the nature of the story, and how the newspaper wished to present it, the inclusion of the complainant's comments was necessary to avoid breaching the Code.

. . .

It has never been an absolute requirement for newspapers to contact those who are about to feature in articles. This would be impractical for a number of reasons: often there will be no dispute about the facts, or the information will be innocuous; the volume of people mentioned in straightforward stories would make it impossible; and legitimate investigations might on some occasions be compromised by such a rule. **However, in this case the newspaper made the wrong decision and the complaint was upheld."**

B. Codes of Practice

1. The Editors' Code of Practice

31. The PCC is responsible for ratifying and enforcing the Editors' Code of Practice ("the Editors' Code"). The Editors' Code is regularly reviewed and amended as required. Clause 1 of the Editors' Code provides, *inter alia*, that the press must take care not to publish inaccurate, misleading or distorted information, including pictures.

32. Clause 3 of the Editors' Code deals with privacy. At the relevant time, it provided as follows:

"3. *Privacy

i) Everyone is entitled to respect for his or her private and family life, home, health and correspondence, including digital communications. Editors will be expected to justify intrusions into any individual's private life without consent.

ii) It is unacceptable to photograph individuals in a private place without their consent.

Note—Private places are public or private property where there is a reasonable expectation of privacy."

33. Clause 10 of the Editors' Code sets out provisions on **clandestine** recordings:

"**10 *Clandestine devices and subterfuge**

i) The press must not seek to obtain or publish material acquired by using hidden cameras or **clandestine** listening devices; or by intercepting private or mobile telephone calls, messages or emails; or by the unauthorised removal of documents or **photographs**; or by accessing digitally-held private information without consent.

ii) Engaging in misrepresentation or subterfuge, including by agents or intermediaries, can generally be justified only in the public interest and then only when the material cannot be obtained by other means."

34. At the relevant time, the "**public interest**" was explained in the Editors' Code as follows:

"There may be exceptions to the clauses marked * where they can be demonstrated to be in the public interest.

1. The public interest includes, but is not confined to:

i) Detecting or exposing crime or serious impropriety.

ii) Protecting public health and safety.

iii) Preventing the public from being misled by an action or statement of an individual or organisation.

2. There is a public interest in freedom of expression itself.

3. Whenever the public interest is invoked, the PCC will require editors to demonstrate fully how the public interest was served.

4. The PCC will consider the extent to which material is already in the public domain, or will become so.

. . ."

35. **Paragraph 3** was **amended** in October 2009 to provide:

"Whenever the public interest is invoked, the PCC will require editors to demonstrate fully that they reasonably believed that publication, or journalistic activity undertaken with a view to publication, would be in the public interest."

36. The **Editors' Codebook** accompanies the **Editors' Code** and is intended to provide **guidance as to compliance with the Code's provisions**. It underwent

major revision in January 2011, providing updates on prior notification and "public interest". As **regards prior notification**, it now explains:

> "**There is wide agreement that prior notification of the subjects of stories ahead of publication, while often desirable, could not—and should not—be obligatory.** It would be impractical, often unnecessary, impossible to achieve, and could jeopardise legitimate investigations. Yet, at the same time, a failure to include relevant sides of the story can lead to inaccuracy and breach the Code. The PCC has set out guidance on how to square this circle:
>
> **1. If there is no doubt about the story's truth, it is unlikely that a failure to approach those involved for comment prior to publication will lead to a breach of Clause 1 of the Code [on accuracy];**
>
> **2. Where information has come from a source (especially an anonymous one), it may be prudent to seek the 'other side of the story' before the article appears;**
>
> . . ."

37. As to the "**public interest**" test, the Codebook notes:

> "In judging publications' claims that otherwise prohibited **information** or **methods** were justifiable in the public interest**, both the Code and the PCC set high thresholds**. The **burden is on the editor to demonstrate fully how the public interest was served.**"

38. It provides details of previous rulings of the PCC on the question of the "public interest" and identifies key questions as:

> **"Was it reasonable to believe that publication or journalistic activity would have served the public interest? The PCC would require a full explanation showing that the grounds were genuine and sound in the circumstances.**
>
> **If clandestine methods, subterfuge, harassment or payments to criminals or witnesses are involved, could the information have been obtained by other means?**
>
> **Is the information in the public domain, or likely to become so?**
>
> **If children are involved, is the public interest in publication exceptional?"**

2. The Ofcom Broadcasting Code

39. Broadcasters are subject to **the Ofcom Broadcasting Code** ("the Ofcom Code"). Section 7 of the Ofcom Code deals with fairness and provides, *inter alia*:

> "7.9 Before broadcasting a factual programme, including programmes

examining past events, broadcasters should take reasonable care to satisfy themselves that:

. . .

- **anyone whose omission could be unfair to an individual or organisation has been offered an opportunity to contribute."**

40. **Principle 8 of the Ofcom Code** addresses the need to avoid **any unwarranted infringement** of privacy in programmes and in connection with obtaining material included in programmes.

C. Remedies for publication of private information

41. Under English law, a number of remedies are available in cases of misuse of private information. An injunction can be sought to restrain publication of the private material. **Damages** are also available to compensate for the injury caused by any **intrusive** publication, including **aggravated damages** where additional features of the **intrusion** or the defendant's post-publication conduct makes the original injury worse. **An alternative to damages is an account of the profits made by the defendant.** The court can also order **delivery-up** of the offending material.

42. Further protection is offered by the **Data Protection Act 1998**, which makes provision for the regulation of the processing of information relating to individuals**, including the obtaining, holding, use or disclosure of such information.** It sets out in a schedule **eight data protection principles** which must be observed by data controllers in the United Kingdom. These principles include the principles that personal data shall be processed fairly and lawfully; that personal data shall be obtained only for one or more specified and lawful purposes; that personal data shall be adequate, relevant and not excessive in relation to the **purpose** for which they are processed; that personal data shall be accurate and up to date; and that personal data shall be processed in accordance with the rights of data subjects under the Act. Further requirements are stipulated in respect of "sensitive personal data", which includes information as to a person's sexual life.

43. However, section 32(1) of the Act provides a "**public interest**" exemption from the data protection principles where information is processed for journalism purposes:

> **"Personal data which are processed only for the special purposes are exempt from any provision to which this subsection relates if—**
>
> **(a) the processing is undertaken with a view to the publication by any person of any journalistic, literary or artistic material,**
>
> **(b) the data controller reasonably believes that, having regard in**

particular to the special importance of the public interest in freedom of expression, publication would be in the public interest, and

(c) the data controller reasonably believes that, in all the circumstances, compliance with that provision is incompatible with the special purposes."

44. Section 3 defines "**the special purposes**" as including the "**purposes of journalism**". Section 32(2) provides that the exemption relates to the data protection principles, except the seventh data protection principle which sets out the need for appropriate technical and organisational measures to be taken against unauthorised or unlawful processing of personal data and against accidental loss or destruction of, or damage to, personal data. Section 32(3) provides that compliance with any code of practice is relevant to the assessment of whether there was a reasonable belief that publication would be in the public interest.

45. Section 13 of the Act entitles a data subject to apply for compensation where there has been a contravention of the requirements of the Act and section 14 allows him to apply for rectification, erasure or destruction of personal data.

D. Interim injunctions

46. The position as regards interim injunctions under English law was set out in the case of **American Cyanamid Co v Ethicon Ltd** ([1975] AC 396). In particular, a claimant seeking an interim injunction was required to show that he had a "seriously arguable case" to be tried. Once this had been shown, it was for the courts to decide where the balance of convenience lay between the case for granting the injunction and that of leaving the applicant to his remedy of damages. If there were doubts as to the adequacy of a remedy in damages, the preservation of the *status quo* often prevailed, with the result that an interim injunction would be granted.

47. The position in cases engaging the right to freedom of expression was subsequently amended with the entry into force of the **Human Rights Act 1998. Section 12 of the Act provides:** . . .

48. The effect of the Human Rights Act, in particular section 12(3), was considered by the House of Lords in **Cream Holdings Limited and others v Banerjee and others** [2004] UKHL 44. Lord Nicholls of Birkenhead observed that:

"15. When the Human Rights Bill was under consideration by Parliament concern was expressed at the adverse impact the Bill might have on the freedom of the press. Article 8 of the European Convention, guaranteeing the right to respect for private life, was among the Convention rights to which the legislation would give effect. The concern was that, applying the conventional *American Cyanamid* approach, orders imposing **prior restraint** on newspapers might readily be granted by the courts to preserve the **status quo** until trial whenever applicants claimed that a threatened publication would infringe their rights under article 8. **Section 12(3) was enacted to allay these fears**. Its principal **purpose** was to **buttress the protection afforded to freedom of speech** at the interlocutory stage. It sought to do so by setting **a higher threshold** for the grant of interlocutory injunctions against the media than the *American Cyanamid* guideline of a 'serious question to be tried' or a 'real prospect' of success at the trial."

49. **He concluded that:**

> **"22. Section 12(3) makes the likelihood of success at the trial an essential element in the court's consideration of whether to make an interim order. But in order to achieve the necessary flexibility the degree of likelihood of success at the trial needed to satisfy section 12(3) must depend on the circumstances. There can be no single, rigid standard governing all applications for interim restraint orders. Rather, on its proper construction the effect of section 12(3) is that the court is not to make an interim restraint order unless satisfied the applicant's prospects of success at the trial are sufficiently favourable to justify such an order being made in the particular circumstances of the case**. As to what degree of likelihood makes the prospects of success 'sufficiently favourable', the general approach should be **that courts will be exceedingly slow to make interim restraint orders where the applicant has not satisfied the court he will probably ('more likely than not') succeed at the trial**. In general, that should be the threshold an applicant must cross before the court embarks on exercising its discretion, duly taking into account the relevant jurisprudence on article 10 and any countervailing Convention rights. **But there will be** cases where it is necessary for a court to depart from this general approach and a lesser degree of likelihood will suffice as a prerequisite. **Circumstances** where this may be so include those mentioned above: **where the potential adverse consequences of disclosure are particularly grave, or where a short-lived injunction is needed to enable the court to hear and give proper consideration to an application for interim relief pending the trial or any relevant appeal."**

50. Subsequently, in *Douglas & Ors v Hello! Ltd & Ors* ([2005] EWCA Civ 595), the Court of Appeal noted:

> **"258. Of course, as recently emphasised by the House of Lords in** *Cream Holdings Limited v Banerjee* [2004] 3 WLR 918, a claimant seeking an interlocutory injunction restraining publication has to satisfy a

particularly **high threshold test**, in light of section 12(3) of the Human Rights Act 1998."

E. The House of Commons Culture, Media and Sport Committee

51. On 9 February 2010 the House of Commons Culture, Media and Sport Committee ("the Select Committee") published a report on *Press standards, privacy and libel* (2nd Report of Session 2009–10, HC 362-I). The report was prepared following receipt of written submissions and the hearing of oral evidence from a number of stakeholders, including the applicant and the editor of the *News of the World*. A chapter of the report was dedicated to examining privacy and breach of confidence. **As regards the evidence received on the need for a rule of pre-notification, the report noted:**

> **"82. In his own case, Mr Mosley stated that he would certainly have sought an injunction if he had had advance notification of the** *News of the World*'s intention to publish. Mr Myler [the editor of the *News of the World*] told us that he and his colleagues at the newspaper were conscious of this: **'we knew that probably Mr Mosley would get an injunction, and I felt very strongly that this was a story that actually should not be stopped because of an injunction'."**

52. **According to the evidence received by the Select Committee, journalists contacted the subjects of their articles prior to publication in the great majority of cases.** However, there was some evidence before the Select Committee that editors sometimes **took a calculated risk** not to contact a subject because they knew or suspected that an injunction would be imposed in respect of an intended publication.The report noted:

> **"91. Clearly pre-notification, in the form of giving opportunity to comment, is the norm** across the industry. Nevertheless we were surprised to learn that the PCC does not provide any guidance on pre-notification. **Giving subjects of articles the opportunity to comment is often crucial to fair and balanced reporting**, and there needs to be explicit provision in the PCC Code itself."

53. **The Select Committee recommended** that the Editors' Code be amended to include a requirement that **journalists should normally notify the subject of their articles prior to publication**, subject to a **"public interest" exception,** and that guidance for journalists and editors on pre-notifying should be included in the **Editors' Codebook.**

54. As to the need for a legally binding pre-notification requirement, the Select Committee concluded that:

> **"93. . . . a legal or unconditional requirement to pre-notify would be ineffective, due to what we accept is the need for a 'public interest'**

exception. Instead we believe that it would be appropriate to encourage editors and journalists to notify in advance the subject of a critical story or report **by permitting courts to take account of any failure to notify when assessing damages in any subsequent proceedings for breach of Article 8**. We therefore recommend that the Ministry of Justice should amend the Civil Procedure Rules to make failure to pre-notify an aggravating factor in assessing damages in a breach of Article 8. We further suggest that amendment to the Rules should stipulate that no entitlement to aggravated damages arises in cases where there is a public interest in the release of that private information."

III. RELEVANT INTERNATIONAL MATERIALS

A. Relevant Council of Europe texts

1. The Parliamentary Assembly of the Council of Europe

55. On 23 January 1970, the Parliamentary Assembly of the Council of Europe adopted Resolution 428, containing a declaration on mass communication media and human rights. **As regards the duty of the press to act responsibly,** the declaration indicated that it would be desirable to put in place:

"(a) professional training for journalists under the responsibility of editors and journalists;

(b) a professional code of ethics for journalists ; this should cover inter alia such matters as accurate and well balanced reporting, rectification of inaccurate information, clear distinction between reported information and comments, avoidance of calumny, respect for privacy, respect for the right to a fair trial as guaranteed by Article 6 of the European Convention on Human Rights;

(c) press councils empowered to investigate and even to censure instances of unprofessional conduct with a view to the exercising of self-control by the press itself."

56. The declaration also noted that there was an area in which the exercise of the right of freedom of expression might conflict with the right to privacy protected by Article 8, and that the exercise of the former right should not be allowed to destroy the existence of the latter. **It observed that the right to privacy consisted essentially in the right to live one's own life with a minimum of interference and concerned private, family and home life, physical and moral integrity, honour and reputation, avoidance of being placed in a false light, non-revelation of irrelevant and embarrassing facts, unauthorised publication of private photographs, protection against misuse of private communications and protection from disclosure of information given or received by the individual confidentially**. The declaration

also stated that the right to privacy afforded by Article 8 should not only protect an individual against interference by public authorities, **but also against interference by private persons or institutions, including the mass media,** and that **national legislation should guarantee this protection**

57. On 26 June 1998 the Parliamentary Assembly adopted a further resolution, Resolution 1165, on the right to privacy, **focusing on public figures.** The Resolution noted that personal privacy was often invaded, even in countries with specific legislation to protect it, as people's **private lives** had become a **highly lucrative commodity** for certain sectors of the media. It continued:

> "8. It is often **in the name of** a one-sided interpretation of the right to freedom of expression, which is guaranteed in Article 10 of the European Convention on Human Rights**, that the media invade people's privacy,** claiming that their readers are entitled to know everything about **public figure**s.
>
> 9. Certain facts relating to the private lives of **public figure**s, particularly **politicians**, may indeed be of interest to citizens, and it may therefore be legitimate for readers, **who are also voters**, to be informed of those facts.
>
> 10. It is therefore necessary to find a way of balancing the exercise of two fundamental rights, both of which are guaranteed in the European Convention on Human Rights: the right to respect for one's private life and the right to freedom of expression."

58. The resolution reaffirmed the importance of every person's right to privacy and of the right to freedom of expression as fundamental to a democratic society. **It noted that these rights were neither absolute nor in any hierarchical order, since they were of equal value.** Further, the right to privacy afforded by Article 8 required protection against interference by private persons or institutions**, including the mass media**. The resolution also set out specific guidelines on the necessary content of national legislation:

> **"i. the possibility of taking an action under civil law** should be guaranteed, to enable a victim to claim possible damages for invasion of privacy;
>
> **ii. editors and journalists should be rendered liable for invasions of privacy by their publications**, as they are for libel;
>
> . . .
>
> iv. **economic penalties should be envisaged for publishing groups which systematically invade people's privacy;**
>
> . . .
>
> vii. provision should be made for anyone who knows that information or

images relating to his or her private life **are about to be disseminated** to **initiate emergency judicial proceedings**, such as **summary** applications for an **interim order** or an injunction postponing the dissemination of the information, subject to an **assessment by the court** as to the **merits** of the claim of an invasion of privacy;

viii. the media should be encouraged **to create their own guidelines for publication and to set up an institute** with which an individual can lodge complaints of invasion of privacy and demand that a rectification be published."

59. On 3 October 2008 Resolution 1636 (2008) on indicators for media in a democracy was adopted by the Parliamentary Assembly. It recalled the importance of freedom of expression of the press in a democracy and called on member States to assess their national media legislation bearing in mind the basic principle that there should be a system of media self-regulation including a right of reply and correction or voluntary apologies by journalists and that journalists should set up their own professional codes of conduct and that they should be applied.

2. The Committee of Ministers

60. At the Sixth European Ministerial Conference on Mass Media Policy in Cracow, 15–16 June 2000, the participating Ministers adopted a declaration on "A media policy for tomorrow". In the declaration, the representatives of the Contracting States agreed on a programme of action at pan-European level, to be implemented by the Steering Committee on Mass Media ("CDMM"). The programme of action included the following provisions:

"I. Activities relating to the balance between freedom of expression and information and other rights and legitimate interests

The CDMM should:

—step up its work on the balance between freedom of expression and information and the right to privacy;

—complete the work on the disclosure of information and the expression of opinions about political figures and public officials, the disclosure of information in the public interest, as well as media reporting on legal proceedings, so as to define common orientations for the whole of Europe as speedily as possible;

—examine the problems caused by the dissemination of material casting doubt on individuals' dignity and integrity, even in the traditional media;

—examine the implications of the on-line dissemination of information by individuals or other sources which may not be bound by professional journalistic ethics or codes of conduct."

61. Following the adoption of the programme of action, the CDMM established a Group of Specialists on freedom of expression and other fundamental rights ("MM-S-FR"). The MM-S-FR prepared a draft declaration of the Committee of Ministers on freedom of expression and the right to respect for private life which was reviewed by the CDMM at its meetings of 10 July 2003 and 21 January 2004. However, the CCDM did not invite the Committee of Ministers to adopt the declaration.

B. Law and practice in Council of Europe member States

62. According to the information provided by the parties or otherwise available to the Court, there is no pre-notification requirement as such in any of the legal systems of the Contracting Parties. However, some member States require the subject's consent to publication of material relating to private life, in many cases subject to some form of "public interest" exception. Thus the failure to obtain consent may have legal consequences in any subsequent civil proceedings commenced by the subject of the publication.

63. A number of member States have adopted codes of practice, generally not binding, which also contain some form of consent requirement.

C. Directive 95/46/EC of the European Parliament and of the Council of 24 October 1995 on the protection of individuals with regard to the processing of personal data and on the free movement of such data ("the EC Directive")

64. The EC Directive was adopted in order to ensure adequate protection for personal data. It applies to the 27 Member States of the European Union. It was transposed in the United Kingdom through the **Data Protection Act 1998** (see paragraphs 42–45 above). There is no reference in the EC Directive to the need to provide for a pre-notification requirement in privacy cases.

THE LAW

I. ALLEGED VIOLATION OF **ARTICLES 8 AND 13** OF THE CONVENTION

65. **The applicant complained that the United Kingdom had violated its positive obligations under Article 8 of the Convention, taken alone and taken together with Article 13, by failing to impose a legal duty on the News of the World to notify him in advance in order to allow him the opportunity to seek an interim injunction and thus prevent publication of material which violated his right to respect for his private life. The Government contested that argument**

66. In the Court's view, the complaint under Article 13 as to the absence of an effective domestic remedy is a reformulation of the applicant's complaint under Article 8 of the Convention that the respondent State did not ensure respect for the applicant's private life, and is subsidiary to it (see *Armonienė*

v Lithuania, no 36919/02, § 23, 25 November 2008, BAILII: [2008] ECHR 1526; and *Biriuk v Lithuania*, no 23373/03, § 23, 25 November 2008, BAILII: [2008] ECHR 1528). **The Court accordingly considers it appropriate to analyse the applicant's complaints solely under Article 8 of the Convention**, which reads in so far as relevant as follows:

> "1. Everyone has the right to respect for his private and family life . . .
>
> 2. There shall be no interference by a public authority with the exercise of this right except such as is in accordance with the law and is necessary in a democratic society in the interests of national security, public safety or the economic well-being of the country, for the prevention of disorder or crime, for the protection of health or morals, or for the protection of the rights and freedoms of others."

A. Admissibility

1. Victim status

a. The parties' submissions

67. The Government considered that the applicant was no longer a victim of any violation of the Convention. They noted that he had successfully pursued domestic proceedings and was awarded the sum of GBP 60,000 in damages and recovered GBP 420,000 in costs (see paragraph 28 above). They concluded that he had obtained a remedy before the domestic courts and considered that remedy to constitute adequate and proportionate reparation for the harm he had suffered. **They emphasised that the damages awarded in his case were the highest to date in the United Kingdom for an invasion of privacy**. The Government further noted that the applicant had **recovered damages in other jurisdictions** and that it seemed that he had **outstanding proceedings** in the United Kingdom and elsewhere in respect of the same or similar publications. **These included proceedings in Germany, which settled for EUR 250,000**, and civil and criminal proceedings in France and Italy regarding the publication which was the subject of the English proceedings.

68. The Government also emphasised that since commencing his legal action against the News of the World, the applicant had sought and obtained a **high profile** in the United Kingdom as a champion of privacy rights and, in that context, had submitted evidence to Parliament and had participated in a number of press and media interviews. **They questioned whether the effect of the publication was as detrimental to the applicant as he claimed.**

69. The applicant insisted that he remained a victim of a violation of the Convention notwithstanding the damages award in the domestic proceedings. **He argued that damages were not an adequate remedy where private and embarrassing personal facts and intimate photographs were deliberately**

exposed to the public in print and on the internet. This information could never be expunged from the minds of the millions of people who had read or seen the material and privacy could not be restored to him by an award of damages**. The only effective remedy in his case would have been an injunction, a remedy which he was denied by the failure of the newspaper to notify him in advance. Similarly, actions taken in other jurisdictions did not remove his victim status.** Such actions were aimed at requiring media and **internet** websites to remove explicit or highly personal information repeated or taken from the original publication by the *News of the World*. Indeed, his efforts in this regard **were evidence of how persistent and damaging the breach of his privacy had been.**

70. Finally, the applicant argued that any implication that he had not suffered from the breach of his privacy was both absurd and offensive. **He pointed to the intimate nature of the material disclosed and the humiliation occasioned by its public disclosure, as well as to the impact of the publication on his family.**

b. The Court's assessment

71. The Court accepts that the publication of the articles, **photographs** and video images of the applicant **participating in sexual acts** had a significant impact on the applicant's right to respect for his private life. The fact that, following the widespread dissemination of the material (see paragraph 11 above), the applicant has chosen to pursue what he perceives to be a necessary change in the law does not lessen the extent of any **humiliation or injury suffered by him as a result of the original exposure of the material**.

72. The Court notes the unusual nature of the applicant's complaint. Having won his case at domestic level and obtained damages, his argument before this Court is directed at the prevailing situation in the United Kingdom in which there is no legal requirement to pre-notify the subject of an article which discloses material related to his private life. Whether or not Article 8 requires, as the applicant has contended, the United Kingdom to put in place a legally binding pre-notification requirement is a matter to be considered in the context of the merits of the case. **However, it is clear that no sum of money awarded after disclosure of the impugned material could afford a remedy in respect of the specific complaint advanced by the applicant.**

73. In light of the above, the Court finds that the applicant can claim to be a victim in light of the specific nature of his complaint under Article 8 of the Convention.

2. Exhaustion of domestic remedies

a. The parties' submissions

74. The Government argued that in so far as the applicant sought to claim that the damages awarded in the domestic proceedings were not adequate, he had failed to exhaust domestic remedies as he did not appeal the judge's ruling on exemplary damages. **They further relied on the fact that the applicant had elected to pursue a remedy in damages, rather than an account of profits.** Finally, they noted that the applicant had **failed** to bring any proceedings under the **Data Protection Act 1998** (see paragraphs 42–45 above), **which would have allowed him to complain about the unauthorised processing of his personal information and to seek rectification or destruction of his personal data.**

75. The applicant reiterated that he was **not seeking further damages** from the newspaper but **was making a complaint about the absence of a law** which would have prevented publication of the article which violated his right to respect for private life. Accordingly, the additional remedies proposed by the Government were, in his submission, **irrelevant** to his complaint.

b. The Court's assessment

76. The Court reiterates the unusual nature of the applicant's complaint in the present case (see paragraph 72 above). **None of the remedies on which the Government rely could address his specific complaint regarding the absence of a law requiring pre-notification.** They are therefore not to be considered remedies which the applicant was required to exhaust before lodging his complaint with this Court.

77. The Government's objection is accordingly dismissed.

3. Conclusion

78. The Court has **dismissed** the Government's objections as to the applicant's victim status and exhaustion of domestic remedies. It notes that this complaint is **not manifestly ill-founded** within the meaning of Article 35 § 3 (a) of the Convention. Nor is it inadmissible on any other grounds. It must therefore be declared admissible.

B. Merits

1. The parties' submissions

a. The applicant

79. The applicant argued that a positive obligation could arise under Article 8 of the Convention even in the sphere of the relations of individuals between themselves. In the present case, he contended, the respondent State had an obligation to enable him to apply for an injunction by requiring that he be notified prior to publication of an article which interfered with his private life. The applicant emphasised that in his case details of the most **intimate**

parts of his private life were published on the front page, and in several inside pages, of a newspaper with **an estimated readership of approximately ten million people in the United Kingdo**m. **Highly intrusive** images made by means of **secret** recordings were also posted on the newspaper's website and inevitably reproduced **elsewhere on the internet**. The applicant considered that the judgment of Eady J made it clear that had he had an opportunity to apply for an injunction, an injunction would have been granted (see paragraphs 17–18 above).

80. In support of his argument that the law should provide for an opportunity to seek an injunction, the applicant emphasised, first, that where a conflict arose between competing interests under Article 8 and Article 10, **it was for the courts and not the newspapers to resolve it.** He highlighted the dangers of allowing journalists to be the sole judges as to where the balance between the right to freedom of expression and the right to respect for private life lay, as, he claimed, **the British press were largely hostile both to the need to protect private life and to the interpretation of that right by the judiciary**. Further, he considered that as the law currently stood, editors were encouraged not to notify subjects as, once an article had been published, **subjects often decided not to bring legal proceedings for fear of attracting further publicity** in respect of the invariably embarrassing or damaging details about their private lives. *Second*, the applicant argued that where the resolution of the conflict between Articles 8 and 10 occurred only after publication, there was insufficient protection for private life because, **once lost, privacy could not be regained**. Referring to the judgment of Eady J (see paragraph 27 above), the applicant noted that in defamation cases, it was a complete defence to prove the truth of the published material and that, as a result, damage done to **reputation** could be removed by proving that the allegations were false. **However, the same could not be said in relation to privacy, which was inherently perishable and therefore could not be restored to the victim of the interference**. Further, he was of the view that section 12 of the Human Rights Act 1998 provided significant protection for newspapers' right to freedom of expression **by setting a high threshold before an interim injunction would be granted (see paragraphs 47–50 above).** He emphasised that pursuant to the Court's jurisprudence on Article 10, there was a need for newspapers claiming protection to comply with the requirements of **responsible journalism**. In his view, these requirements included a pre-notification requirement.

81. The applicant accepted that the respondent State had a **margin of appreciation** but contended that it related solely to the scope or efficacy of any pre-notification requirement. **His complaint was not that he had received some warning but not enough; rather, he had received no warning at all.**

He considered that the absence of a uniform approach in other Contracting Parties requiring pre-notification was not decisive. He pointed to the fact that in a number of States, consent played an important role in the context of privacy law and contended that where consent was either required for disclosure or relevant to an assessment of whether the disclosure was lawful, there was no need for a separate pre-notification requirement. He further relied on what he called the **"unique nature of the tabloid press"** in the United Kingdom, highlighting the unlawful actions of some tabloid reporters and the criticisms made by the tabloid press of developing laws on privacy.

82. While the applicant agreed that the precise mechanics and scope of any system of pre-notification was a matter for the discretion of the respondent State, he considered the difficulties which the Government claimed would arise, for example, in formulating a pre-notification obligation, to be illusory or at the very least exaggerated, **given in particular that prior notification already occurred in the vast majority of cases (see paragraph 52 above)**. In his view, a pre-notification obligation in respect of an intended publication would arise, at the very least, where there were reasonable grounds to believe that the publication would infringe the right to respect for private life, having regard to all the circumstances of the case including any public interest defence. There was nothing unfamiliar about the legal concept of "reasonable belief". **He further pointed out that a form of pre-notification was already envisaged in the Ofcom Code, which imposed an obligation on broadcasters before broadcasting a factual programme to seek comments from anyone it would be unfair to exclude (see paragraph 39 above).**

83. The applicant accepted that any system would require exceptions in certain circumstances to allow for legitimate situations where it would **be either impractical or contrary to the public interest for the media to notify an individual in advance.** Thus where **all practicable steps** had been taken to notify or where there were **compelling reasons** not to notify, no sanction for a failure to notify would arise. He disputed that conceptual difficulties would arise in devising any public interest exception to the general requirement, pointing to the provision in the Human Rights Act 1998 **that a party seeking an injunction should notify the media in advance of the application and to the exception for "compelling reasons" to that general rule set out in the same Act (see paragraph 47 above).**

84. As to sanctions, the applicant considered that criminal or regulatory sanctions were required to enforce the pre-notification requirement (citing *KU v Finland*, no 2872/02, 2 December 2008). He pointed out that criminal proceedings against newspapers and editors for alleged **contempt** of court, obscenity or breaches of the Official Secrets Acts were possible.

b. The Government

85. While the Government accepted that Article 8 could give rise to positive obligations, they contended that a high threshold had to be crossed before Article 8 would be engaged in this way. They distinguished between three types of cases. **First**, where an applicant had suffered directly from State inaction, such as non-recognition of transsexuals, the case for a positive obligation was strong. **Second,** where positive action by the State was called for by an applicant to prevent interference by non-State bodies, such as in environmental and media cases, positive obligations were less readily invoked. **Third**, where an applicant alleged that positive action by individuals was called for, the extent of any positive obligation under Article 8 was at its weakest. The Government argued that relevant factors in determining the extent of the positive duty were the extent to which fundamental and essential aspects of private life were in issue; the prejudice suffered by the applicant; the breadth and clarity of the positive obligation sought to be imposed; and the extent of consensus among Council of Europe member States or internationally. With reference to these factors, they argued that they had no positive obligation to protect the applicant's privacy by providing for a legally binding pre-notification requirement.

86. If there was a positive obligation in the circumstances of the case, the Government contended that there was a significant **margin of appreciation** available to them in deciding where in domestic law to strike the balance between the requirements of Article 8 and Article 10 and that the current position fell within that range. **They argued that an inevitable consequence of a pre-notification requirement was that there would be an increase in the number of interim injunctions granted, which in themselves were a restriction on freedom of expression and for that reason should be approached with caution.**

87. The Government pointed out that there **was a consistent pattern among Council of Europe member States against a system of pre notification** and disputed in this regard that the tabloid press in the United Kingdom was unique in Europe. As to the role of consent in certain other States, the Government noted that it was not clear whether consent was a strict requirement in the cases mentioned by the applicant, nor was it clear whether there were exceptions. In any case, they considered it questionable whether this approach differed from the approach in the United Kingdom, where consent would be a complete defence to any action for invasion of privacy and failure to pre-notify would be taken into consideration in fixing any damages award. **Further, the Government emphasised that an insistence on compulsory pre-notification would be to depart from internationally accepted standards as established by the Council of Europe (see paragraphs 55–59**

above). In this regard, they noted in particular that the legal position in the United Kingdom complied with the guidelines set out in Resolution 1165 (see paragraph 58 above).

88. The Government also referred to the important role of the PCC and the Editors' Code in the system for protection of privacy rights in the United Kingdom. In particular**, they highlighted that the PCC had recently upheld a complaint where a newspaper had failed to seek the subject's comments prior to publication (see paragraph 30 above).** They also emphasised that the matter had recently been examined in the context of an inquiry by the **House of Commons Culture, Media and Sport Committee (see paragraphs 51–54 above**). After hearing evidence, the Select Committee had **decided against recommending a legal requirement of pre-notification (see paragraph 54 above).**

89. Finally, the Government considered that the fact that pre-notification was carried out as a matter of good practice in most cases did not mean that there were no insuperable difficulties in imposing a legal requirement to do so. In their view, the introduction of a pre-notification requirement would give rise to a number of practical and principled objections. Difficulties arose regarding the **formulation of the scope of any obligation**, including **the identification of the categories of press and media to which the obligation would apply** and the extent of the notification requirement and the circumstances in which it would be engaged, **as well as the operation of any "public interest" exception.** In this regard, they disputed the applicant's claim that the Ofcom Code provided an example of the kind of pre-notification duty called for, considering the obligation set out in Rule 7.9 of that code to be significantly different. **The question of sanctions for a failure to comply with a pre-notification requirement was also problematic**. The Government considered it clear that the applicant contemplated criminal sanctions and **expressed concern about how to define and enforce any criminal offence**. They also warned that an inadequately framed law could give rise to breaches of Article 10.

90. In conclusion, the Government invited the Court to find that the framework of legal regulation in place in the United Kingdom concerning publications which might contravene the right to respect for private life was sufficient to comply with any positive obligations which arose.

c. Third party submissions

i. Guardian News & Media Ltd

91. The Guardian News & Media Ltd ("the Guardian") argued that if the applicant's complaint were to be upheld by the Court, it would seriously and disproportionately fetter the right of the press to publish, and the public to

receive, information and opinions in the public interest. **A pre-notification requirement would thus have a serious and unjustified chilling effect upon the practical enjoyment of the right to freedom of expression**. It would, in their view, also be **inconsistent with the concept of responsible journalistic freedom** which the Court had consistently emphasised.

92. The Guardian stressed that while the applicant had formulated the pre-notification duty by reference to the facts of his case, its repercussions would be felt far more widely. **First**, they argued, an alleged breach could involve not only the media but also public authorities, non-governmental organisations or even private individuals. **Second,** logic dictated that pre notification would be required not only in privacy cases but in all cases requiring a balancing exercise pursuant to Article 10 § 2.

93. Referring to the wide **margin of appreciation** in this area, the Guardian considered that the appropriate balance had been struck in the United Kingdom. **They highlighted the absence of any European consensus that a pre-notification duty was required.** Further, although some countries required that consent be obtained before information regarding private life was disseminated, at least where the public interest was not implicated, a similar number of countries had no such provision. The Guardian also referred to the **Data Protection Act 1998 and its parent EC Directive, which did not provide for any pre-notification requirement** (see paragraphs 42–45 and 64 above). They further referred to the recent inquiry by a House of Commons Select Committee, which in its subsequent report rejected the argument that there was a need for a pre-notification requirement in the United Kingdom (see paragraphs 51–54 above).

94. Finally, the Guardian contended that any pre-notification requirement would be unworkable in practice. They considered that it would not always be obvious when the pre-notification rule would be triggered, nor was it clear how the need for a "public interest" exception could be catered for.

ii. The Media Lawyers' Association

95. The Media Lawyers' Association ("the MLA") contended that a pre-notification requirement was wrong in principle, would be unworkable in practice and would constitute a breach of Article 10 of the Convention.

96. The MLA emphasised the wide **margin of appreciation** in deciding what measures were required to satisfy any positive obligation in this field. They referred to the lack of any European consensus on the need for a pre-notification duty. They also pointed to the fact that a House of Commons Select Committee had recently rejected the suggestion that there should be a legal pre-notification requirement (see paragraph 54 above). The question whether there was a need to contact a subject prior to publication was, in their view,

a matter to be addressed in the **context of the ethics of journalism and the codes of practice governing the media.** These codes had evolved over time and demonstrated that the media were well aware of the duty to respect each individual's right to privacy. In particular, the MLA noted that the Editors' Code gave guidance as to what might be covered by "public interest" (see paragraphs 34–35 above).

97. The MLA contended that the duty for which the applicant argued was vague and uncertain in scope. They pointed out that a pre-publication duty would have wide ramifications, potentially applying not just to the media and journalists but to a far broader group. A number of practical questions arose, for example, as to who would have to be contacted by the media in respect of any intended publication, **whether the duty would arise in respect of photographs taken in the street of unknown persons, whether it would apply to images or text previously published and whether it would extend to notification of close family members of the subject, who might also be affected by the publication of the material.** The MLA further referred to the need for exceptions to any general duty, for example, where there was a good reason not to contact the subject or where there was a public interest in publication.

98. The MLA emphasised the importance of Article 10 and in particular the role of the press as "**public watchdog**". They considered that the availability and operation of interim injunctions continued to be a matter of concern in this area and contended that **prior restraint**s on publication constituted a serious interference with the right to freedom of expression. Accordingly, such restraints should only be granted where strictly necessary, and any order granted should be no wider than necessary. They emphasised that injunction proceedings in themselves inevitably led to delay and costs, even if no injunction was eventually granted, and any changes which would encourage the seeking of injunctions would therefore not be desirable. They argued that domestic law struck an appropriate balance between competing rights and interests.

iii. The Media Legal Defence Initiative, Index on Censorship, The Media International Lawyers' Association, European Publishers' Council, The Mass Media Defence Centre, Romanian Helsinki Committee, The Bulgarian Access to Information Programme (AIP) Foundation, Global Witness and Media Law Resource Centre

99. In their joint written submissions, the interveners referred to the importance of the right to freedom of expression. There would, in their view, be significant consequences were a pre-notification requirement to be introduced. It would delay publication of important news, **which was itself a perishable commodity,** in a wide range of public interest situations wherever the **public figure** could claim that his psychological integrity was at stake from publication of the truth. The interveners disputed that any balance was required

between rights arising under Articles 8 and 10, arguing that there was a presumption in favour of Article 10 and that **reputation** was a subsidiary right which had to be **narrowly** interpreted.

100. The interveners further argued that there was a wide **margin of appreciation** in this area. They emphasised the tradition in common law countries against **prior restraint**s on publication, arguing that a pre notification requirement would go against the long-standing approach in this area. Further, they pointed out, there was **no Europe-wide consensus as to a need for a pre-notification rule**. It was also noteworthy that questions of privacy protection had been regularly debated in the United Kingdom in recent years and had been the subject of various reports, including the recent Select Committee report (see paragraph 51–54 above). In that report, the applicant's case for a pre-notification requirement had been rejected.

101. The interveners also contended that privacy was inadequately defined to support a pre-notification requirement. **However, they accepted that there might be an argument for a notice requirement relating to medical records and photographs taken without consent in private places, for example, but only if reputation were no part of Article 8 and private information were properly defined.** In their view, as currently formulated, the requirement called for was so vague as to be unworkable.

102. The interveners considered that any general duty would have to be subject to exceptions, notably to an exception where there was a "public interest" in publication. This being the case, it was relevant that in the applicant's case, the editor of the *News of the World* would have published the story without notification even if there had been a legally binding pre notification requirement because he genuinely believed that there was a Nazi element to the activities which would have justified publication in the public interest (see paragraph 24 above).

103. **The interveners emphasised that even successfully defended injunction proceedings could cost a newspaper GBP 10,000; an unsuccessful newspaper could pay GBP 60,000.** It was simply not viable for the media to contest every case where compulsory notification would be followed by a request for an injunction. This was the chilling effect of a pre notification requirement.

2. The Court's assessment

104. The Court recalls that Eady J in the High Court upheld the applicant's complaint against the *News of the World* (see paragraph 25 above). He found that there was no Nazi element to the applicant's sexual activities. **He further criticised the journalist and the editor for the casual and cavalier manner in which they had arrived at the conclusion that there was a Nazi theme. In the absence of any Nazi connotations,** there was no public interest or justi-

fication in the publication of the articles or the images. Reflecting the grave nature of the violation of the applicant's privacy in this case, Eady J awarded GBP 60,000 in damages. **The newspaper did not appeal the judgment.** In light of these facts the Court observes that the present case resulted in a **flagrant** and unjustified invasion of the applicant's private life.

105. The Court further notes that as far as the balancing act in the circumstances of the applicant's particular case was concerned, the domestic court firmly found in favour of his right to respect for private life and ordered the payment to the applicant of substantial monetary compensation. The assessment which the Court must undertake in the present proceedings relates not to the specific facts of the applicant's case but to the general framework for balancing rights of privacy and freedom of expression in the domestic legal order. The Court must therefore have regard to the general principles governing the application of Article 8 and Article 10, before examining whether there has been a violation of Article 8 as a result of the absence of a legally binding pre-notification requirement in the United Kingdom.

a. General principles

i Article 8

106. It is clear that the words "the right to respect for . . . private . . . life" which appear in Article 8 require not only that the State refrain from interfering with private life but also entail certain **positive obligations** on the State to ensure effective enjoyment of this right by those within its jurisdiction (see *Marckx v Belgium*, 13 June 1979, § 31, Series A no 31). Such an obligation may require the adoption of positive measures designed to secure effective respect for private life even in the sphere of the relations of individuals between themselves (see *Von Hannover v Germany*, no 59320/00, § 57, ECHR 2004 VI, BAILII: [2005] ECHR 555; and *Stubbings and Others v the United Kingdom*, 22 October 1996, BAILII: [1996] ECHR 44, § 61–62, *Reports of Judgments and Decisions* 1996 IV).

107. The Court emphasises the importance of a prudent approach to the State's positive obligations to protect private life in general and of the need to recognise the diversity of possible methods to secure its respect (*Karakó v Hungary*, no 39311/05, § 19, 28 April 2009, BAILII: [2009] ECHR 712). The choice of measures designed to secure compliance with that obligation in the sphere of the relations of individuals between themselves in principle falls within the Contracting States' **margin of appreciation** (see, *inter alia*, *X and Y v the Netherlands*, 26 March 1985, BAILII: [1985] ECHR 4, § 24, Series A no 91; and *Odièvre v France* [GC], no 42326/98, § 46, ECHR 2003 III, BAILII: [2003] ECHR 86). However, this discretion goes hand in hand with European supervision (see, *mutatis mutandis*, Observer *and* Guardian *v the United*

Kingdom, 26 November 1991, BAILII: [1991] ECHR 49, § 59(c), Series A no 216; and *Lindon, Otchakovsky-Laurens and July v France* [GC], nos. 21279/02 and 36448/02, § 45, ECHR 2007 XI, BAILII: [2007] ECHR 836).

108. The Court recalls that a number of factors must be taken into account when determining the breadth of the **margin of appreciation** to be accorded to the State in a case in which Article 8 of the Convention is engaged. **First,** the Court reiterates **that the notion of "respect" in Article 8 is not clear-cut,** especially as far as the positive obligations inherent in that concept are concerned: bearing in mind the diversity of the practices followed and the situations obtaining in the Contracting States, the notion's requirements will vary considerably from case to case (see *Sheffield and Horsham v the United Kingdom*, 30 July 1998, BAILII: [1998] ECHR 69, § 52, *Reports* 1998 V). Thus Contracting Parties enjoy a wide **margin of appreciation** in determining the steps to be taken to ensure compliance with the Convention (see *Handyside v the United Kingdom*, judgment of 7 December 1976, BAILII: [1976] ECHR 5, Series A no 24, p 22, § 48; *Abdulaziz, Cabales and Balkandali v the United Kingdom*, 28 May 1985, BAILII: [1985] EHRR 471, § 67, Series A no 94; *Hatton and Others v the United Kingdom* [GC], no 36022/97, § 97, ECHR 2003 VIII, BAILII: [2003] ECHR 338; and *Armonienė*, cited above, § 38). In this regard, the Court recalls that by reason of their direct and continuous contact with the vital forces of their countries, the State authorities are, in principle, in a better position than the international judge to give an opinion on how best to secure the right to respect for private life within the domestic legal order (see, *mutatis mutandis*, *Handyside*, cited above, § 48; *A, B and C v Ireland* [GC], no 25579/05, § 232, 16 December 2010, BAILII: [2010] ECHR 2032; and *MGN Limited v the United Kingdom*, no 39401/04, § 142, 18 January 2011, BAILII: [2011] ECHR 66).

109. **Second**, the nature of the activities involved affects the scope of the **margin of appreciation**. The Court has previously noted that a serious interference with private life can arise where the state of domestic law conflicts with an important aspect of personal identity (see *Christine Goodwin v the United Kingdom* [GC], no 28957/95, § 77, ECHR 2002 VI, BAILII: [2002] ECHR 588). **Thus, in cases concerning Article 8, where a particularly important facet of an individual's existence or identity is at stake, the margin allowed to the State is correspondingly narrowed** (see *Evans v the United Kingdom* [GC], no 6339/05, BAILII: [2007] ECHR 264, § 77, ECHR 2007 IV; and *A, B and C v Ireland* [GC], cited above, § 232). The same is true where the activities at stake involve a most **intimate** aspect of private life (see, *mutatis mutandis*, *Dudgeon v the United Kingdom*, 22 October 1981, BAILII: [1981] ECHR 5, § 52, Series A no 45; and *ADT v the United Kingdom*, no 35765/97, BAILII: [2000] ECHR 402, § 37, ECHR 2000-IX).

110. **Third**, the existence or **absence of a consensus across the Member States** of the Council of Europe, either as to the relative importance of the interest at stake or as to the best means of protecting it, is also relevant to the extent of the **margin of appreciation**: where no consensus exists, the **margin of appreciation** afforded to States is generally a wide one (see *Evans*, cited above, § 77; *X, Y and Z v the United Kingdom*, 22 April 1997, BAILII: [1997] ECHR 20, § 44, *Reports* 1997 II; and *Dickson v the United Kingdom* [GC], no 44362/04, BAILII: [2007] ECHR 1050, § 78, ECHR 2007 XIII). Similarly, any standards set out in applicable international instruments and reports are relevant to the interpretation of the guarantees of the Convention and in particular to the identification of any common European standard in the field (see *Tănase v Moldova* [GC], no 7/08, § 176, ECHR 2010 . . .).

11. **Finally**, in cases where measures which an applicant claims are required pursuant to positive obligations under Article 8 would have an impact on freedom of expression, regard must be had to the fair balance that has to be struck between the competing rights and interests arising under Article 8 and Article 10 (see *MGN Limited*, cited above, § 142), rights which merit, in principle, equal respect (*Hachette Filipacchi Associés (ICI PARIS)* v *France*, no 12268/03, § 41, 23 July 2009, BAILII: [2009] ECHR 1425; compare and contrast Sunday Times *v the United Kingdom (no 1)*, 26 April 1979, BAILII: [1979] ECHR 1, § 65, Series A no 30).

ii. Article 10

112. **The Court emphasises the pre-eminent role of the press in informing the public and imparting information and ideas on matters of public interest in a State governed by the rule of law** (see *Financial Times Ltd and Others v the United Kingdom*, no 821/03, § 59, 15 December 2009, BAILII: [2009] ECHR 2065; *MGN Limited*, cited above, § 141; and *De Haes and Gijsels v Belgium*, 24 February 1997, BAILII: [1997] ECHR 7, § 37, *Reports* 1997-I). Not only does the press have the task of imparting such information and ideas but **the public also has a right to receive them**. Were it otherwise, the press would be unable to play its vital role of "**public watchdog**" (Observer *and* Guardian, cited above, § 59; Bladet Tromsø *and Stensaas v Norway* [GC], no 21980/93, BAILII: [1999] ECHR 29, § 62, ECHR 1999-III; *Gutiérrez Suárez v Spain*, no 16023/07, § 25, 1 June 2010, BAILII: [2010] ECHR 2225; and *MGN Limited*, cited above, § 141).

113. It is to be recalled that methods of objective and balanced reporting may vary considerably and that it is therefore not for this Court to substitute its own views for those of the press as to what technique of reporting should be adopted (see *Jersild v Denmark*, 23 September 1994, BAILII: [1994] ECHR 33, § 31, Series A no 298). However, editorial discretion is not unbounded. **The press must not overstep the bounds set for, among other things, "the**

protection of . . . the rights of others", including the requirements of acting in good faith and on an accurate factual basis and of providing "reliable and precise" information in accordance with the ethics of journalism (see *Pedersen and Baadsgaard v Denmark* [GC], no 49017/99, BAILII: [2004] ECHR 693, § 78, ECHR 2004-X; *Times Newspapers Ltd v United Kingdom (nos. 1 and 2)*, no 3002/03 and 23676/03, BAILII: [2009] ECHR 451, § 42, ECHR 2009 . . . ; and *MGN Limited*, cited above, § 141).

114. **The Court also reiterates that there is a distinction to be drawn between reporting facts—even if controversial—capable of contributing to a debate of general public interest in a democratic society, and making tawdry allegations about an individual's private life** (see *Armoniené*, cited above, § 39). In respect of the former, the pre-eminent role of the press in a democracy and its duty to act as a "**public watchdog**" are important considerations in favour of a **narrow** construction of any limitations on freedom of expression. However, different considerations apply to press reports concentrating on sensational and, at times, lurid news, intended to titillate and entertain, which are aimed at satisfying the **curiosity** of a particular readership regarding aspects of a person's strictly private life (*Von Hannover*, cited above, § 65; *Hachette Filipacchi Associés (ICI PARIS)*, cited above, § 40; and *MGN Limited*, cited above, § 143). Such reporting does not attract the robust protection of Article 10 afforded to the press. **As a consequence, in such cases, freedom of expression requires a more narrow interpretation** (see *Société Prisma Presse v France* (dec), nos. 66910/01 and 71612/01, 1 July 2003, BAILII: [2003] ECHR 715; *Von Hannover*, cited above, § 66; Leempoel *& SA ED Ciné Revue v Belgium*, no 64772/01, § 77, 9 November 2006, BAILII: [2006] ECHR 2002; *Hachette Filipacchi Associés (ICI PARIS)*, cited above, 40; and *MGN Limited*, cited above, § 143). While confirming the Article 10 right of members of the public to have access to a wide range of publications covering a variety of fields, the Court stresses that in assessing in the context of a particular publication whether there is a public interest which justifies an interference with the right to respect for private life, **the focus must be on whether the publication is in the interest of the public and not whether the public might be interested in reading it.**

115. **It is commonly acknowledged that the audiovisual media have often a much more immediate and powerful effect than the print media** (see *Jersild*, cited above, § 31; and *Peck v the United Kingdom*, no 44647/98, BAILII: [2003] ECHR 44, § 62, ECHR 2003 I). **Accordingly, although freedom of expression also extends to the publication of photographs, the Court recalls that this is an area in which the protection of the rights of others takes on particular importance, especially where the images contain very personal and intimate "information" about an individual or where they are taken on private**

premises and clandestinely through the use of secret recording devices (see *Von Hannover*, cited above, § 59; *Hachette Filipacchi Associés (ICI PARIS)*, cited above, § 47; and *MGN Limited*, cited above, § 143). Factors relevant to the assessment of where the balance between the competing interests **lies include the additional contribution made by the publication of the photos to a debate** of general interest as well as the content of the **photographs** (see *Krone Verlag GmbH & Co. KG v Austria*, no 34315/96, § 37, 26 February 2002, BAILII: [2002] ECHR 159).

116. The Court recalls that the nature and severity of any sanction imposed on the press in respect of a publication are **relevant to any assessment of the proportionality of an interference with the right to freedom of expression** (see, for example, *Ceylan v Turkey* [GC], no 23556/94, BAILII: [1999] ECHR 44, § 37, ECHR 1999-IV; *Lešník v Slovakia*, no 35640/97, BAILII: [2003] ECHR 124, § 63, ECHR 2003-IVl and *Karsai v Hungary*, no 5380/07, BAILII: [2009] ECHR 1974, § 36, 1 December 2009). **Thus the Court must exercise the utmost caution where measures taken or sanctions imposed by the national authorities are such as to dissuade the press from taking part in the discussion of matters of legitimate public concern** (see *Jersild*, cited above, § 35; and *Cumpănă and Mazăre v Romania* [GC], no 33348/96, BAILII: [2004] ECHR 692, § 111, ECHR 2004 XI).

117. **Finally, the Court has emphasised that while Article 10 does not prohibit the imposition of prior restraints on publication, the dangers inherent in prior restraints are such that they call for the most careful scrutiny on the part of the Court.** This is especially so as far as the press is concerned, for news is a perishable commodity and to delay its publication, even for a short period, may well deprive it of all its value and interest (see Observer *and* Guardian, cited above, § 60). The Court would, however, observe that **prior restraints** may be more readily justified in cases which demonstrate **no pressing need for immediate publication and in which there is no obvious contribution to a debate of general public interest.**

b. Application of the general principles to the facts of the case

118. As noted above (see paragraph 106), it is clear that a positive obligation arises under Article 8 in order to ensure the effective protection of the right to respect for private life. The question for consideration in the present case is whether the specific measure called for by the applicant, namely a legally binding pre-notification rule, is required in order to discharge that obligation.

119. The Court observes at the outset that this is not a case where there are no measures in place to ensure protection of Article 8 rights. **A system of self-regulation of the press has been established in the United Kingdom, with guidance provided in the Editors' Code and Codebook and oversight**

of journalists' and editors' conduct by the PCC (see paragraphs 29–38 above). This system reflects the 1970 declaration, the 1998 resolution and the 2008 resolution of the Parliamentary Assembly of the Council of Europe (see paragraphs 55 and 58–59 above). While the PCC itself has no power to award damages, an individual may commence civil proceedings in respect of any alleged violation of the right to respect for private life which, if successful, can lead to a damages award in his favour. In the applicant's case, for example, the newspaper was required to pay GBP 60,000 damages, approximately GBP 420,000 in respect of the applicant's costs and an unspecified sum in respect of its own legal costs in defending the claim. **The Court is of the view that such awards can reasonably be expected to have a salutary effect on journalistic practices**. Further, if an individual is aware of a pending publication relating to his private life, he is entitled to seek an interim injunction preventing publication of the material. Again, the Court notes that the availability of civil proceedings and interim injunctions is fully in line with the provisions of the Parliamentary Assembly's 1998 resolution (see paragraph 58 above). **Further protection for individuals is provided by the Data Protection Act 1998, which sets out the right to have unlawfully collected or inaccurate data destroyed or rectified (see paragraphs 42–45 above).**

120. The Court further observes that, in its examination to date of the measures in place at domestic level to protect Article 8 rights in the context of freedom of expression, **it has implicitly accepted that ex post facto damages provide an adequate remedy for violations of Article 8 rights arising from the publication by a newspaper of private information.** Thus in *Von Hannover*, cited above, the Court's analysis focused on whether the judgment of the domestic courts in civil proceedings brought following publication of private material struck a fair balance between the competing interests. In *Armonienė*, cited above, a complaint about the disclosure of the applicant's husband's HIV-positive status focused on the "derisory sum" of damages available in the subsequent civil proceedings for the serious violation of privacy. While the Court has on occasion required more than civil law damages in order to satisfy the positive obligation arising under Article 8, the nature of the Article 8 violation in the case was of particular importance. Thus in *X and Y v the Netherlands*, 26 March 1985, BAILII: [1985] ECHR 4, § 27, Series A no 91, the Court insisted on the need for criminal law provisions to achieve deterrence in a case which involved forced sexual intercourse with a sixteen year old mentally handicapped girl. In *KU v Finland*, no 2872/02, BAILII: [2008] ECHR 1563, §§ 46–47, 2 December 2008, the availability of civil law damages from an **Internet** service provider was inadequate where there was no possibility of identifying the person who had posted an advert in the name of the appli-

cant, at the time only twelve years old, on a dating website, thus putting him at risk of sexual abuse.

121. In the present case the Court must consider whether, notwithstanding its past approach in cases concerning violations of the right to respect for private life by the press, Article 8 requires a pre-notification rule in order to ensure effective protection of the right to respect for private life. In doing so, the Court will have regard, **first**, to the **margin of appreciation** available to the respondent State in this field (see paragraphs 108–110 above) and, **second**, to the clarity and potential effectiveness of the rule called for by the applicant. While the specific facts of the applicant's case provide a backdrop to the Court's consideration of this question, the implications of any pre-notification requirement are necessarily far wider. However meritorious the applicant's own case may be, the Court must bear in mind the general nature of the duty called for. **In particular, its implications for freedom of expression are not limited to the sensationalist reporting at issue in this case but extend to political reporting and serious investigative journalism. The Court recalls that the introduction of restrictions on the latter type of journalism requires careful scrutiny.**

*i. The **margin of appreciation***

122. The Court recalls, **first**, that the applicant's claim relates to the positive obligation under Article 8 and that the State in principle enjoys a wide **margin of appreciation** (see paragraph 108 above). It is therefore relevant that the respondent State has chosen to put in place a system for balancing the competing rights and interests which excludes a pre notification requirement. **It is also relevant that a parliamentary committee recently held an inquiry on privacy issues during which written and oral evidence was taken from a number of stakeholders, including the applicant and newspaper editors. In its subsequent report, the Select Committee rejected the argument that a pre-notification requirement was necessary in order to ensure effective protection of respect for private life (see paragraph 54 above).**

123. **Second**, the Court notes that the applicant's case concerned the publication of **intimate details of his sexual activities, which would normally result in a narrowing of the margin of appreciation** (see paragraph 109 above). However, the highly personal nature of the information disclosed in the applicant's case can have no significant bearing on the **margin of appreciation** afforded to the State in this area given that, as noted above (see paragraph 121 above), any pre-notification requirement would have an impact beyond the circumstances of the applicant's own case.

124. **Third**, the Court highlights the **diversity of practice** among member States as to how to balance the competing interests of respect for private life and

freedom of expression (see paragraphs 62–63 above). Indeed the applicant has **not cited a single jurisdiction in which a pre-notification requirement as such is imposed**. In so far as any common consensus can be identified, it therefore appears that such consensus is against a pre-notification requirement rather than in favour of it. The Court recognises that a number of member States require the consent of the subject before private material is disclosed. However, it is not persuaded that the need for consent in some States can be taken to constitute evidence of a European consensus as far as a pre-notification requirement is concerned. Nor has the applicant pointed to any international instruments which require States to put in place a pre-notification requirement. Indeed, as the Court has noted above (see paragraph 119), the current system in the United Kingdom fully reflects the resolutions of the Parliamentary Assembly of the Council of Europe (see paragraphs 56–59 above). The Court therefore concludes that the respondent State's **margin of appreciation** in the present case is a wide one.

ii. The clarity and effectiveness of a pre-notification requirement

125. The applicant considered that the duty should be triggered where any aspect of private life was engaged. It would therefore not be limited to the intended disclosure of **intimate** or sexual details of private life. As such, the duty would be a relatively broad one. Notwithstanding the concerns expressed by the Government and the interveners (see paragraphs 89, 94, 97 and 101 above) the Court considers that the concept of "private life" is sufficiently well understood for newspapers and reporters to be able to identify when a publication could infringe the right to respect for private life. Specific considerations would arise, for example in the context of **photographs** of crowds, but suitable provisions could be included in any law. The Court is further of the view that a satisfactory definition of those who would be subject to the requirement could be found. It would appear possible, for example, to provide for a duty which would apply to those within the purview of the Editors' Code.

126. However, the Court is persuaded that concerns regarding the effectiveness of a pre-notification duty in practice are not unjustified. **Two** considerations arise. **First**, it is generally accepted that any pre notification obligation would require **some form of "public interest" exception** (see paragraphs 83, 89, 94, 97 and 102 above). Thus a newspaper could opt not to notify a subject if it believed that it could subsequently defend its decision on the basis of the public interest. The Court considers that in order to prevent a serious chilling effect on freedom of expression, a reasonable belief that there was a "public interest" at stake would have to be sufficient to justify non-notification, even if it were subsequently held that no such "public interest" arose. The parties' submissions appeared to differ on whether "public interest" should be

limited to a specific public interest in not notifying (for example, where there was a risk of destruction of evidence) or extend to a more general public interest in publication of the material. The Court would observe that a **narrowly** defined public interest exception would increase the chilling effect of any pre-notification duty.

127. In the present case, the defendant newspaper relied on the belief of the reporter and the editor that the sexual activities in which the applicant participated had Nazi overtones. They accordingly argued that publication was justified in the public interest. **Although Eady J criticised the casual and cavalier manner** in which the *News of the World* had arrived at the conclusion that there was a Nazi element, he noted that there was significant scope for differing views on the assessment of the "public interest" and concluded that he was not in a position to accept that the journalist and editor concerned must have known at the time that no public interest defence could succeed (see paragraphs 23–24 above). Thus, in the applicant's own case, it is not unlikely that even had a legally binding pre-notification requirement been in place at the relevant time, the *News of the World* would have chosen not to notify in any event, relying at that time on a public interest exception to justify publication.

128. **Second**, and more importantly, any pre-notification requirement would only be as strong as the sanctions imposed for failing to observe it. **A regulatory or civil fine, unless set at a punitively high level, would be unlikely to deter newspapers from publishing private material without pre-notification.** In the applicant's case, there is no doubt that one of the main reasons, if not the only reason, for failing to seek his comments was to avoid the possibility of an injunction being sought and granted (see paragraphs 21 and 52 above). Thus the *News of the World* chose to run the risk that the applicant would commence civil proceedings after publication and that it might, as a result of those proceedings, be required to pay damages. **In any future case to which a pre-notification requirement applied, the newspaper in question could choose to run the same risk and decline to notify, preferring instead to incur an ex post facto fine.**

129. Although punitive fines or criminal sanctions could be effective in encouraging compliance with any pre-notification requirement, the Court considers that these would run the risk of being incompatible with the requirements of Article 10 of the Convention. It reiterates in this regard the need to take particular care when examining restraints which might operate as a form of censorship prior to publication. **It is satisfied that the threat of criminal sanctions or punitive fines would create a chilling effect which would be felt in the spheres of political reporting and investigative journalism, both of which attract a high level of protection under the Convention.**

iii. Conclusion

130. As noted above, **the conduct of the newspaper in the applicant's case is open to severe criticism**. Aside from publication of the articles detailing the applicant's sexual activities, **the News of the World published photographs and video footage, obtained through clandestine recording, which undoubtedly had a far greater impact than the articles themselves.** Despite the applicant's efforts in a number of jurisdictions, these images are still available on the **Internet**. The Court can see no possible additional contribution made by the audiovisual material (see paragraph 115 above), which appears to have been included in the *News of the World*'s coverage merely to titillate the public and increase the **embarrassment** of the applicant.

131. The Court, like the Parliamentary Assembly**, recognises that the private lives of those in the public eye have become a highly lucrative commodity** for certain sectors of the media (see paragraph 57 above). The publication of news about such persons **contributes to the variety of information available to the public and, although generally for the purposes of entertainment rather than education, undoubtedly benefits from the protection of Article 10.** However, as noted above, such protection may cede to the requirements of Article 8 **where the information at stake is of a private and intimate nature and there is no public interest in its dissemination**. In this regard the Court takes note of the recommendation of the Select Committee that the Editors' Code be amended to include a requirement that journalists should normally notify the subject of their articles prior to publication, subject to a "public interest" exception (see paragraph 53 above).

132. However, the Court has consistently emphasised the need to look beyond the facts of the present case and to consider the broader impact of a pre-notification requirement. The limited scope under Article 10 for restrictions on the freedom of the press to publish material which contributes to debate on matters of general public interest must be borne in mind. Thus, having regard to the chilling effect to which a pre-notification requirement risks giving rise, to the significant doubts as to the effectiveness of any pre-notification requirement and to the wide **margin of appreciation** in this area, the Court is of the view that Article 8 does not require a legally binding pre-notification requirement. Accordingly, the Court concludes that there has been no violation of Article 8 of the Convention by the absence of such a requirement in domestic law.

FOR THESE REASONS, THE COURT UNANIMOUSLY

1. *Declares* the application admissible;

2. *Holds* that there has been no violation of Article 8 of the Convention.

Done in English, and notified in writing on 10 May 2011, pursuant to Rule 77 §§ 2 and 3 of the Rules of Court.

Lawrence Early Registrar, Lech Garlicki President

ETK v News Group Newspapers Ltd [2011] EWCA Civ 439

Lord Justice Ward:

1. On Saturday 5th March 2011 the applicant made an application on short notice to Collins J. to restrain News Group Newspapers Ltd, the publishers of the News of the World, from publishing or communicating or disclosing to any other person:

   "(a) any information concerning the facts of this case and the individuals involved (including, in particular, any information identifying or in any way tending to identify the Applicant as being the person who has applied for this order), save for that contained in this order and in any public judgment of the court given in this action;

   (b) any information concerning the fact or details of the **sexual relationship** between the Applicant (who is a male working in the entertainment industry) and the person named in the **Confidential Schedule** (who is a female working in the entertainment industry)."

2. Having heard the matter in private, Collins J dismissed the application, refused permission to appeal but granted temporary relief in the terms set out above on the applicant's undertaking expeditiously to apply for permission to appeal. That was done, Sedley LJ adjourning the application to be heard by two Lord Justices on notice to the respondent. **Given the urgency, I directed that the full court should sit on Thursday 11th March to be able to hear the appeal if permission were granted and the parties were content for the appeal to follow.**

3. The case was listed to be heard in private. When it was called, Mr David Price QC intervened on behalf of that well known figure, Mr Benjamin Pell, who is regularly seen in the press benches of these courts reporting especially on matters in this field in which he has become quite an expert, to the extent even of his occasionally prompting learned counsel with references to relevant authority of which counsel was ignorant. Mr Price sought to persuade us to hear the matter in open court but we ruled that since the main argument would be fact-sensitive, it was necessary for the preservation of confidentiality to sit in private.

4. We granted permission to appeal, heard the appeal, and although we indicated the result, we formally adjourned in order to hand down this judgment in open court.

The background

5. **In about November 2009 the appellant, who is a married man, began a sexual relationship with another woman whom I shall simply call "X", who is herself married.** The source of the News of the World's information suggests that this **relationship became obvious to those with whom the appellant and X were working**. Towards the end of April 2010 the appellant's wife confronted him with her belief, formed either intuitively, or from information conveyed to her, that he was having an affair. **He admitted it.** This was deeply distressing for the wife but she and her husband determined, not least for the sake of their two teenage children**, to rebuild her trust and their marriage**. To that end the appellant accepted that he would **end his sexual relationship with** X and he so informed her.

6. **Continuing their working relationship was obviously awkward** and in discussion with his employers, the appellant told them that he would prefer in an ideal world not to have to see her at all and that one or other should leave but both accepted that their working commitments did not then make that possible. They agreed to conduct themselves with due decorum and to continue to perform their duties in a professional way as in fact they did.

7. In December 2010 their employers informed X that her services would **no longer be required,** explaining publicly that it was a convenient moment to make this change. **She was, understandably, upset and angry and may even have threatened to take proceedings against the employer**. The appellant only became aware of her departure whilst he was on holiday with his family over Christmas.

8. News of these events leaked to the News of the **World whose enquiries alerted the appellant to its wish to publish the fact of the affair** and that the affair was the real cause of X leaving her employment. He moved accordingly for this injunction**, supported not only by his wife, but also by X.**

The judgment under appeal

9. Collins J. gave a **short ex tempore** judgment. He found there was a **reasonable expectation of privacy**. He conducted a balancing exercise between the right of the newspaper to freedom of expression under Article 10 of the European Convention of Human Rights and the appellant's right to respect for his private and family life under Article 8 and he recognised that by virtue of section 12 of the Human Rights Act 1998 the appellant had to show that it was more likely than not that at trial the balance would come down in favour of Article 8. **He held that there was public interest in the effect of the adul-**

tery and so refused the injunction because the respondent intended to go no further than reporting the fact of the affair with the resultant dismissal of X . His "last concern" related to the children. As I shall show he held that the adverse effect on them could not tip the balance.

Discussion

10. The principles which govern an application like this for an interim injunction to restrain publicity of private information are by now well established.

(1) The first stage is to ascertain whether the applicant has a **reasonable expectation of privacy so as to engage Article 8;** if not, the claim fails.

(2) The question of whether or not there is a reasonable expectation of privacy in relation to the information:

> " . . . **is a broad one**, which takes account of **all the** circumstances of the case. They include **the attributes** of the claimant, the **nature of the activity** in which the claimant was engaged, **the place** at which it was happening, the **nature and purpose** of the **intrusion,** the **absence of consent** and whether **it was known or could be inferred,** the **effect** on the claimant and the **circumstances** in which and the **purposes** for which the information came into the hands of the publisher": see *Murray v Express Newspapers* [2009] Ch 481 at [36], cited in *TSE and ELP* [2011] EWHC 1308 at **para 18**.

The test established in *Campbell v MGN Ltd* [2004] UKHL 22, [2004] 2 AC 457 is to ask whether a reasonable person of ordinary sensibilities, if placed in the same situation as the subject of the disclosure, rather than the recipient, would find the disclosure offensive.

(3) The protection may be lost if the information is in th**e public domain.** In this regard there is, per *Browne v Associated Newspapers Ltd* [2008] QB 103 at [61],

> **" . . . potentially an important distinction between information which is made available to a person's circle of friends or work colleagues and information which is widely published in a newspaper."**

Whether **what may start** as information which is private has become information known to the **public at large** is a **matter of fact and degree** for determination in each case depending on its specific circumstances.

(4) If Article 8 is engaged then the second stage of the inquiry is to conduct "**the ultimate balancing test**" which has the **four features** identified by Lord Steyn in *In Re S (A Child) (Identification: Restrictions on Publication)* [2005] 1 A.C. 593 at [17]:

> "**First,** neither article [8 or 10] has *as such* precedence over the other.

> **Secondly,** where the values under the two articles are in conflict, an intense focus on the comparative importance of the specific rights being claimed in the individual case is necessary. **Thirdly**, the justifications for interfering with or restricting each right must be taken into account. **Finally**, the proportionality test must be applied to each." (It should be noted that the emphasis was added by Lord Steyn.)

(5) As *Von Hannover v Germany* (2004) 40 EHRR 1 makes clear at [76]:

> **"the decisive factor in balancing the protection of private life against freedom of expression should lie in the contribution that the published photos and articles make to a debate of general interest."**

(6) Pursuant to **section 12(3) of the Human Rights Act 1998 an interim injunction should not be granted unless a court is** satisfied that the applicant **is likely**—in the sense of more likely than not—to obtain an injunction following a trial.

A reasonable expectation of privacy?

11. Collins J. found in the appellant's favour. Mr Anthony Hudson, who appears for the respondent, undertakes to file a respondent's notice to challenge that finding. **He submits that the manner in which the appellant and X conducted their relationship was such that it became known to those with whom they worked with the result that knowledge spread in the work-place, reaching to the higher echelons of management.** Thus, he submits, the fact of the **relationship** was "**naturally accessible to outsiders**". He relies on observations of Eady J. in *X v Persons Unknown* [2007] E.M.L.R. 10 at [30] distinguishing between "**matters which are naturally accessible to outsiders and those which are known only to the protagonists**". That was a very different kind of case where the judge was drawing a distinction between a couple whose marriage was encountering difficulties (the "protagonists") and their acquaintances (the "outsiders") who knew of the marital tensions not from private revelation (which would be protected) but from some public manifestation of the discord e.g. an actual separation (which probably would not entitle the protagonists to a reasonable expectation of privacy). **Here the sexual relationship was essentially a private matter. One way or another it became known to work colleagues but their knowledge does not put the information into the public domain**—see *Browne v Associated Newspapers Ltd* cited at [10(3)] above. In my judgment the appellant was reasonably entitled to expect that **his colleagues would treat as confidential the information they had acquired whether from their own observation of the behaviour of the appellant and X or from tittle-tattle *and gossip* which larded the office**

conversation or from a confidential confession to a colleague. A reasonable person of ordinary sensibilities would certainly find the disclosure offensive.

12. In my judgment the judge was correct to hold that the appellant's Article 8 rights were engaged. I would therefore dismiss the respondent's cross-appeal.

The ultimate balance to be struck between Article 10 and Article 8

13. As for Article 10, everyone has the right to freedom of expression **but the ones with the greatest need for this constitutionally vital freedom are the organs of the media. In the interests of our democratic society we—and that includes the judges—must ensure that the press are freely able to enquire, investigate and report on matters of public interest. The press is the public watchdog. That freedom is, however, not unrestricted as Article 10(2) itself makes so** clear that it is worth repeating:

    "2. The exercise of these freedoms, since it carries with it **duties and responsibilities**, may be subject to **. . . restrictions** . . . as are **prescribed** by law and are **necessary** in a **democratic** society for the protection of the **reputation** or **rights** of others or for preventing the disclosure of information **received in confidence** "

    This restriction can only be justified if it is a **proportionate** and is **no more than is necessary** to promote the **legitimate object** of the **restriction**. To restrict **publication simply to save the blushes of the famous, fame invariably being ephemeral,** could have the **wholly undesirable chilling** effect on the necessary ability of publishers to sell their newspapers. **We have to enable sales if we want to keep our newspapers.** Unduly to fetter their freedom to report as editors judge to be responsible is **to undermine the pre-eminence of the deserved place of the press as a powerful pillar of democracy.** These considerations require the court **to tread warily** before granting this kind of injunction.

14. As for Article 8, weight must be given not only to the right to respect for the private and family life of the appellant himself, **but also to the rights of X and, in addition, the rights of the appellant's wife and his children**. It is not at all clear to what extent if at all, Collins J. had regard to the Article 8 rights of anyone bar the appellant. He did say of X:

    "8. The first question is whether there is a reasonable expectation of privacy. There was certainly a reasonable hope of privacy **shared** by the claimant and [X]. The fact that the **relationship** was adulterous does not mean that privacy was lost. Prima facie the **relationship** should be protected by Article 8. . . . "

    This suggests her rights were taken into account but other passages can be read as limiting his focus to the rights of the appellant alone for he said:

> "9. Thus, I have to consider the balancing exercise between the right of the newspaper under Article 10 and the right of the *individual* under Article 8. . . .
>
> 11. The News of the World argues that their rights outweigh those *of the Claimant*." [I have added the emphasis.]

15. As for the wife and children, the judge said this:

> "13. My last concern relates to the claimant's children. As Mr Tomlinson rightly points out, there is likely to be an adverse effect on them if the News of the World discloses the fact of the adultery. One recognises the concerns that this issue raises but unfortunately if one parent behaves in a way that attracts adverse publicity it will affect the children. This is not something which can tip the balance if there is otherwise no good reason to grant an injunction."

16. **Every allowance must be made for the fact that this was an ex tempore judgment delivered on a Saturday morning in an urgent application when no-one can expect verbal exactitude or detailed reasoning on every point of the argument. The exigencies of life as the out-of-hours applications' judge shackle perfection**. That said, I cannot but conclude that in this instance the **judge erred**. **First,** X's rights were at the very forefront of the story the News of the World wished to publish, namely that it was the fact of their adultery, not any lack of professional competence, that led to the termination of her services. She did not welcome the **intrusion** of the press, has made it plain to this Court that she has no intention of bringing proceedings either against her employer or the appellant who is associated with the employer and supports the application. **The evidence before the court is that X has made clear that she did not wish her privacy to be invaded at all.**

17. **The position of the appellant's wife is equally clear: she opposes publicity. Then there are the children**. The **purpose** of the injunction is both to **preserve the stability of the family while the appellant and his wife pursue a reconciliation and to save the children the ordeal of playground ridicule when that would inevitably follow publicity**. They are bound to be harmed by immediate publicity, both because it would **undermine the family as a whole** and because **the playground is a cruel place** where **the bullies** feed on personal discomfort and **embarrassment**. In another context, in *Beoku-Betts v Secretary of State for the Home Department* [2008] UKHL 39, [2009] AC 115, Lady Hale commented at [4] on the risk of:

> " . . . missing the central point about family life, which is that the whole is greater than the sum of its individual parts. The right to respect for

> family life of one necessarily encompasses the right to respect for the family life of others, normally a spouse or minor children, with whom that family life is enjoyed."

18. Collins J. may not have recognised the rights of the appellant's wife but he certainly did accept that the **adverse effect on the children** was relevant. Regrettably I cannot agree that the **harmful effect** on the children cannot tip the balance where the adverse publicity arises because of the way the children's father has behaved. The rights of children are not confined to their Article 8 rights. In *Neulinger v Switzerland* [2010] 28 EHRC 706 the Strasbourg court observed that:

    > "131. The Convention cannot be interpreted in a vacuum but must be interpreted in harmony with the general principles of international law. Account should be taken . . . 'of any relevant rules of international law applicable in the relations between the parties' and in particular the rules concerning the international protection of human rights. . . .
    >
    > 135. . . . there is currently a broad consensus—including in international law—in support of the idea that in all decisions concerning children, their best interests must be paramount."

    Support for that proposition can be gathered from several international human rights instruments, not least from the second principle of the United Nations Declaration of the Rights of the Child 1959, from article 3(1) of the Convention of the Rights of the Child 1989 (UNCRC) and from article 24 of the European Union's Charter of Fundamental Rights. For example, article 3(1) of the UNCRC provides:

    > "In all actions concerning children, whether undertaken by public or private social welfare institutions, courts of law, administrative authorities or legislative bodies, the best interests of the child shall be a primary consideration."

19. Thus it seems to me just as **"the court's earlier approach to immigration cases is tempered by a much clearer acknowledgement of the importance of the best interests of a child caught up in a dilemma which is of her parents' and not of her own making"** so too must the approach of the court to these injunctions have regard to the interests of children. The quotation is taken from paragraph 20 of the speech of the Baroness Hale of Richmond with whom Lord Brown and Lord Mance agreed in *ZH (Tanzania) v Secretary of State for the Home Department* [2011] UKSC4 which was a case concerned with the weight to be given to the best interests of children who are affected by the decision of the Home Secretary to remove or deport one or both of their parents from this country, more specifically with the question: in what circumstances is it permissible to remove or deport a non-citizen parent

(here the mother whose immigration history was described as "appalling") where the effect will be that a child who is a citizen of the United Kingdom will also have to leave? **I appreciate that the issue is far removed from that with which this Court is concerned but since the interests of the appellant's children are undoubtedly engaged, the universal principles cannot be ignored. The proper approach is, therefore, neatly summarised by Lord Kerr of Tonaghmore at paragraph 46 of that decision, namely:**

> "It is a universal theme of the various international and domestic instruments to which Lady Hale has referred that, in reaching decisions that will affect a child, a primacy of importance must be accorded to his or her best interests. This is not, it is agreed, a factor of limitless importance in the sense that it will prevail over all considerations. It is a factor, however, that must rank higher than any other. It is not merely one consideration that weighs in the balance alongside other competing factors. Where the best interests of the child clearly favour a certain course, that course should be followed, unless countervailing reasons of considerable force displace them. It is not necessary to express this in terms of a presumption but the primacy of this consideration needs to be made clear in emphatic terms. What is determined to be in a child's best interests should customarily dictate the outcome of cases such as the present, therefore, and it will require considerations of substantial moment to permit a different result."

However this learning must, with respect, be read and understood **in the context** in which it is sought to be applied**. It is clear that the interests of children do not automatically take precedence over the Convention rights of others.** It is clear also that, when in a case such as this the court is deciding where the balance lies between the article 10 rights of the media and the Article 8 rights of those whose privacy would be invaded by publication**, it should accord particular weight to the Article 8 rights of any children likely to be affected by the publication, if that would be likely to harm their interests.** Where a tangible and objective public interest tends to favour publication, the balance may be difficult to strike. The force of the public interest will be highly material, and **the interests of affected children cannot be treated as a trump card.**

20. How then does this approach square with the way Lord Steyn advised in *In Re S* that the ultimate balance should be struck, see [10(4)] above. He was confining himself to articles 8 and 10 and not ranging more widely to take note of the other Convention rights of children**. He expressed his opinion long before Neulinger called for a re-appraisal of the position**. In any event, the emphasis he added makes it clear that he was concerned strictly with the balance between article 10 and article 8 "*as such*", i.e. where the only

rights in balance were those conferred by articles 8 and 10. If, as he requires, an intense focus on the comparative importance of the specific rights being claimed in the individual case is necessary, then the additional rights of children are to be placed in the scale. The question then is whether the force of the article 10 considerations outweigh them given what I have said in paragraph 19.

21. Here there is no political edge to the publication. **The organisation of the economic, social and political life of the country, so crucial to democracy, is not enhanced by publication.** The intellectual, artistic or personal development of members of society is not stunted by ignorance of the sexual frolics of figures known to the public. As Lord Hope said of Miss Campbell (paragraph 120 of *Campbell v MGN Ltd*),

> " . . . it is not enough to deprive Miss Campbell of her right to privacy that she is a **celebrity** and that her private life is newsworthy."

22. In my judgment the benefits to be achieved by publication **in the interests of free speech are** wholly outweighed by the harm that would be done through the interference with the rights to privacy of all those affected, especially where the rights of the children are in play.

The decisive factor

23. The decisive factor is the contribution the published information will make to a debate of general interest. Is a debate about the reasons why X's employment terminated a matter of such public interest? Both the appellant and X will be known to a sector of the public though it is impossible to measure how large—or how small that sector is. Certainly some members of the public will have noticed the end of her employment: a proportion of them will even have speculated why she left. **But the reasons for her leaving give rise to no debate of general interest**. The reasons for her leaving may interest some members of the public but the matters are not of public interest. Publication **may satisfy public prurience** but that is not a sufficient justification for interfering with the private rights of those involved.

Conclusion

24. I have come to the firm conclusion that the **judge erred** and that this is a case where it is **more likely than not** that an injunction would be granted following a trial. In my judgment the appeal should be allowed and interlocutory injunctions granted in the terms sought.

Lord Justice Laws:

25. I agree.

Lord Justice Moore-Bick:

26. I also agree.

CTB v News Group Newspapers Ltd and Imogen Thomas [2011] EWHC 1232 (QB) per Eady J

1. During the afternoon of 14 April 2011 I granted a temporary injunction **until the return date on 20 April** against two defendants, who were News Group Newspapers Ltd and a woman called **Imogen Thomas**. It had emerged from a telephone conversation between her and one of the solicitors acting on the Claimant's behalf, shortly before the hearing, that **she had at some stage engaged the services of Mr Max Clifford as her publicist**. Earlier that day, there had appeared in *The Sun* newspaper an account, attributed to her **"pals"**, of a **sexual relationship she had with a footballer**. She was identified as the subject of the coverage, **probably with her consent**. The footballer in question was not, however, named. That was **because a Sun representative had given his solicitor an undertaking to that effect on the evening of 13 April (which was to expire at 4 p m. the following day).**

2. The initial application was made by Mr Hugh Tomlinson QC on behalf of the Claimant, who was referred to throughout as CTB. The **purpose** of the exercise was to restrain publication **not only of the identity of the Claimant but also of any further account, or purported account, of such a relationship**. According to his witness statement of 14 April, he had met Ms Thomas in September 2010 and on two further occasions, once in November and once in December. **There might thus appear to be a conflict between them as to the length and nature of the relationship**. According at least to **the published account** of Ms Thomas, it continued for about six months and would thus have involved **more frequent meetings** between them. So far, that account has not been set out in any witness statement. **To date, therefore, the Claimant's evidence on these matters remains uncontradicted.**

3. The Claimant is a **married man with a family.** It is well established, in such circumstances, that the court needs to take into account and have regard to **the interests of the claimant's family members**, and their rights under Article 8 of the European Convention on Human Rights and Fundamental Freedoms. This emerges clearly, for example, from a number of decisions in the Court of Appeal: see e.g. **Donald v Ntuli** [2011] 1 WLR 294, at [24], **Ambrosiadou v Coward** [2011] EWCA Civ 409 and, most recently, **ETK v News Group Newspapers Ltd** [2011] EWCA Civ 439.

4. On 14 April, News Group Newspapers Ltd was represented by leading counsel, Mr Richard Spearman QC, **who did not oppose the grant of an injunction over the short interval before the return date**. Ms Thomas was not represented, and **indeed had not been notified of the hearing**, since on the evidence **I was satisfied that there would otherwise have been a risk of**

further disclosure of private or confidential information prior to her being served with the order.

5. The Claimant's witness statement was to the effect that Ms Thomas had **made contact with him by various text messages** in March, which led him to conclude that she was at that stage **thinking of selling her story**, such as it was. She told him by this means that **she wanted, or "needed", a payment from him of £50,000**. It was against this background **that he agreed** (he says with some reluctance) **to meet her in a hotel** where he was staying in early April of this year in order to discuss **her demands**. Although he had no wish to meet, he eventually agreed **because he was concerned that she would go to the newspapers if he refused**. On that occasion, which was according to his evidence only the fourth time they had met, they were together for no more than 30 minutes. **She had asked him to provide her with a signed football shirt, which he did**, but he told her that he was not prepared to pay her the sum of £50,000.

6. The next development was that she asked to see him again, in a different hotel, a few days later (where he was also staying). He agreed with reluctance and on this occasion, as she had requested, provided her **with some football tickets.**

7. It now seems that the Claimant may well have been "set up" so that photographs could be taken of Ms Thomas going to one or other, or both, of the hotels. Although the position is not yet by any means clear, the **evidence before me on 14 April appeared to suggest that Ms Thomas had arranged the hotel rendezvous in collaboration with photographers and/or journalists**. He first began to "smell a rat" when she told him at the first April meeting, perhaps feigning innocence, that she had been followed and recognised when she visited the first hotel.

8. On 12 April, the Claimant sent Ms Thomas a message to say that he did not want any further contact with her. Then, in something of a quandary, he thought better of it and sent her a further message the following day. **This was to convey to her that he might be willing to pay her some money after all.** By this time, however, she made it clear that **she was looking for £100,000.** She later texted him to say that there was a **journalist outside her** house.

9. The evidence before the court **at that point**, therefore, appeared **strongly to suggest that the Claimant was being blackmailed** (although that is not how he put it himself). I hasten to add, as is obvious, that **I cannot come to any final conclusion about it at this stage.** I have to **make an assessment** of the situation **on the limited (and untested) evidence** as it now stands. (That is what is required **by s 12(3) of the Human Rights Act,** to which I shall return shortly.)

10. Ms Thomas made contact with the Claimant again on 13 April and asked him to call her. When he spoke to her, he formed the impression that she had someone with her—probably a journalist. At all events**, she told him that The Sun was thinking of publishing a story to the effect that they had had an affair for some six months and that this account would be supported by photographs of her at or near the hotels where the April visits had taken place.** She did not give any indication that she herself was in any way responsible for this. It is hardly likely that she would have done so, of course, if she was still hoping to extract money from the Claimant. It seems, nevertheless, that *The Sun* was ready to take advantage of these prearranged meetings in order to be able to put forward the claim that it was *The Sun* which had *found* him **"romping** with a busty Big Brother babe". **This was no doubt to give the impression, which Ms Thomas herself may have fostered, that a sexual liaison between them was still continuing at the time of the two hotel rendezvous in April.**

11. Shortly afterwards, still apparently seeking **to absolve herself** from any responsibility for the newspaper coverage, Ms Thomas sent a message to the Claimant to the effect that **one of his friends must have tipped off the newspaper.** According to his account, the Claimant knew this to be untrue, since he **had never** mentioned her to anyone.

12. The evidence before the court at that stage, therefore, appeared to indicate, **rightly or wrongly**, that Ms Thomas had arranged for **photographs** to be taken, having already agreed a payment or payments from the newspaper. Despite that, **she was still requesting £100,000 from the Claimant**. This was the background against which I had decided that there was ample reason not to trust Ms Thomas. It seemed reasonable, **in those circumstances, that the Claimant and his advisers should be excused the need to serve her in advance of the 14 April hearing.**

13. At all events, it seems probable that she had agreed at some point to contribute to the story in **The Sun that was published in its issue for 14 April** (i.e. prior to the hearing of the injunction application). **It is thus ironic that Ms Thomas has subsequently complained of the court's supposed unfairness in according anonymity to the Claimant but not to her.** She was already identified, **apparently of her own volition**, before any application was made to the court. **It seemed to me that the Claimant was fully entitled to the protection of anonymity at the time he came before the court on the first occasion—**not least for the reasons acknowledged and explained by the Court of Appeal in **JIH v News Group Newspapers Ltd** [2011] 2 All ER 324 **at [40].**

14. On the return date, being the last day of term, the application was renewed by Mr Tomlinson. Mr Spearman again appeared on behalf of News Group

Newspapers Ltd and, on this occasion, Ms Thomas was represented by Mr David Price QC, who had only recently been instructed on her behalf and took a largely "watching" role.

15. **It seems that Ms Thomas had instructed other solicitors for a short time,** with whom the Claimant's advisers had made contact on 15 April. On that date she had **signed a very brief witness statement accepting that she wished to publish her account of her relationship with the Claimant and that she was in discussion with the Mail on Sunday about that**. This was in support of a proposed application by Associated Newspapers Ltd to vary the terms of my order of 14 April because she had been advised that it "arguably" prevented her from doing so. In the event, that application did not materialise. Then there was a hiatus during which she had no legal representation before Mr Price was finally instructed. In the meantime, however, there were further publications over the weekend in other tabloids. **She appears to have collaborated at least in a Sunday Mirror article.**

16. On 20 April I was prepared to continue the injunction and, following detailed negotiations between counsel, I approved an agreed order on 21 April. I now set out more fully the reasons for granting the injunction on 14 April and for continuing it with effect from the return date.

17. I now wish to make it clear that, shortly before this judgment was handed down, **Mr Price stated on his client's behalf that she denies either causing the publication in The Sun on 14 April or asking the Claimant for money.**

18. The on applications of this kind is now so well established and so well known that there should be no need to explain it yet again.

19. **The courts are required to carry out a balancing exercise between competing Convention rights, as was always overtly acknowledged by the government prior to the enactment of the Human Rights Act 1998.** It was, for example, explained by the then Lord Chancellor, Lord Irvine, when the bill was before the House of Lords on 24 November 1997 (*Hansard*, HL Debates, Col.785). **He said that any privacy law developed by the judges following the enactment would be a better law because they would have to balance and have regard to both Article 8 and Article 10 (as indeed has been happening over the last decade). When the statute came into effect in October 2000, it explicitly required the courts to take into account Strasbourg jurisprudence when discharging those responsibilities.**

20. **Despite this long history**, it has for several years been repeatedly claimed in media reports that courts are **"introducing a law of privacy by the back door". Yet the principles have long been open to scrutiny**. They are readily apparent **from the terms of the Human Rights Act**, and indeed from the content of the **European Convention** itself. Furthermore, they were **clearly**

expounded seven years ago in two decisions of the House of Lords which was, of course, at that time the highest court in this jurisdiction: ***Campbell v MGN Ltd*** [2004] 2 AC 457 and ***Re S (A Child)*** [2005] 1 AC 593.

21. Since those decisions were promulgated in 2004, the law has been loyally applied by the courts in a wide variety of circumstances and **exhaustively explained in numerous appellate judgments.** In particular, there are a number of important decisions of the Court of Appeal in addition to those I have already mentioned: see **Douglas v Hello! Ltd (No 3)** [2006] QB 125; **McKennitt v Ash** [2008] QB 73; **HRH Prince of Wales v Associated Newspapers Ltd** [2008] Ch 57; **Lord Browne of Madingley v Associated Newspapers Ltd** [2008] QB 103; and **Murray v Express Newspapers** [2009] Ch. 481. This does not purport to be an exhaustive list, but it will suffice to establish beyond doubt the legal framework **within which the courts are required to operate on applications of this kind. It is widely known that the House of Lords refused permission to appeal with regard to each of the last four cases I have listed**. This can only, surely, have been on the basis that it was by that stage recognised that the principles were sufficiently clearly established.

22. The **majority of cases** over the last few years, in which the courts have had to apply those principles, would appear to be of the so called "**kiss and tell**" variety and they **not infrequently involve blackmailing threats**. **Blackmail** is, of course, **a crime** and in that context the courts have long afforded **anonymity** to those **targeted as a matter of public policy.** That has not hitherto been questioned. In the modern context, against the background of the Human Rights Act, it is equally clear that the courts have an obligation to afford remedies to such individuals**, to discourage blackmailers and to give some protection in respect of personal or private information where there is a threat of revelation.**

23. In circumstances of this kind, **there has to be a two stage process**. This accords with what has been described as **"the new methodology":** *Re S (A Child)*, cited above, at [23]. **First,** the court has to decide whether the subject matter of the threatened publication would be such as to give rise to a **"reasonable expectation of privacy**" on the part of the applicant. In this case, as in so many others, there can be no doubt on that score. It is concerned with conduct of an **intimate and sexual nature** and, what is more, there has been no suggestion in this case that the **relationship**, for so long as it lasted, was conducted publicly. **It is clear both from domestic and Strasbourg jurisprudence that such personal relationships are entitled to Article 8 protection:** see e.g. the discussion in *Mosley v News Group Newspapers Ltd* [2008] EMLR 20, and in particular at [100] and at [125]–[132] and, for yet another decision of the Court of Appeal, in this context, see also *ASG v GSA* [2009] EWCA Civ 1574.

24. Once that hurdle has been overcome, **the next stage is for the court to weigh against the claimant's Article 8 rights, and any duty owed to him under the traditional law of confidence, whether it would be appropriate for those rights to be overridden by any countervailing considerations**. In the present case, of course, it is necessary to weigh up the **Article 10 rights of Ms Thomas**, together with **those of any journalists** she has approached. Also, it is necessary to have **regard to the public interest and to the right of citizens generally to receive information.**

25. I have to consider whether there would be a **legitimate public interest** in the revelation of this particular information, **in so far as it is not already in the public domain**, and whether publication would **contribute to "a debate of general interest"**, in the sense conveyed by the European Court of Human Rights in such cases as *Von Hannover v Germany* (2005) 40 EHRR 1. **Would it help to achieve some legitimate social purpose, such as the prevention or detection of crime? Or again, echoing the terminology of the Press Complaints Commission Code, would publication in some way prevent the public from being seriously misled?**

26. As in so many **"kiss and tell"** cases, it seems to me that the answer, at stage two, is not far to seek. Indeed**, it was not even argued that publication would serve the public interest.**

27. Discussion **focused rather on the extent to which relevant material might already, at that time, be in the public domain**. In most of these cases, it will be appropriate, in accordance with established practice, to include within the terms of any court order what is called a "**public domain** proviso": see e.g. *Att.-Gen. v Times Newspapers Ltd* [2001] 1 WLR 885; *X and Y v Persons Unknown* [2007] 1 FLR 1567. **There may well be, in any given case, room for argument as to what truly is or is not in the public domain**; but **the principle is clear, namely that the court will not attempt to prevent publication or discussion of material that is genuinely in the public domain since, where that is so, there will no longer be any confidentiality or privacy to protect**. This is reflected in one of Lord Goff's "limiting principles", to be found in his speech in *Att.-Gen. v Guardian Newspapers (No 2)* [1990] 1 AC 109, 282B-F:

> "The first limiting principle (which is rather an expression of the scope of the duty) is highly relevant to this appeal. It is **that the principle of confidentiality only applies to information to the extent that it is confidential**. In particular, once it has entered what is usually called the **public domain** (which means no more than that the information in question is so generally accessible that, in all the circumstances, it cannot be regarded as confidential) then, as a general rule, the principle of confidentiality can have no application to it."

28. A **distinction was drawn, however, in Att.-Gen. v Guardian between government or state secrets and those relating to a person's private life**: see at p 260E-H (Lord Keith) and p 287C-D (Lord Goff). It is more difficult to establish that confidentiality or a reasonable expectation of privacy has gone for all purposes, in the context of personal information**, by reason of its having come to the attention of only certain categories of readers**: see also *R v Broadcasting Complaints Commission ex parte Granada TV* [1995] EMLR 16. It is not a black and white distinction between public and private in such circumstances, **but rather a matter of looking at the particular facts and deciding whether, notwithstanding some publication, there remains a reasonable expectation of some privacy.** It is regarded as **a question of degree**: a **distinction has sometimes been drawn, for example, in respect of private information between that which has been published in the national media and that which is only available on a more limited scale**: see e.g. *Venables v News Group Newspapers* [2001] Fam 430, 470–471 and the general discussion in *Carter-Ruck on Libel and Privacy* (6th edn) at 19.86 *et seq*. Each case has to be assessed on its own facts.

29. A **complicating factor** in the present case, **as the Claimant's advisers recognised**, was that the order had to be drafted in such a **way as to exclude from the general prohibition** not only information which could be categorised, broadly, as in the "**public domain"** but also, specifically, **that which had appeared in The Sun on the morning of 14 April**. This was simply a fact of life. Nothing could be done about it. The Claimant was not accepting either that the allegations in the newspaper would have been outside the scope of private or **confidential information**, prior to publication, or that they were true. **Nevertheless, in reality it was no longer possible to maintain an objection to publication**. That is why the order, and in particular the proviso, had to be drafted in specifically **tailored terms**, intended to reflect what had appeared in the newspaper that morning.

30. When the matter was before me, **I was not persuaded that there was by that time nothing left to protect in respect of which the Claimant still had a reasonable expectation of privacy.**

31. When applying the "**new methodology**" in this sort of case, it is necessary, where the court is required to carry out "**the ultimate balancing test**" between two or more competing Convention rights, to have regard to the following propositions identified in *Re S (A Child)* at [17]:

    i) **No** one Convention article has as such **precedence** over another.

    ii) Where conflict arises between rights under Article 8 and Article 10, an "**intense focus**" is required in the particular circumstances of the case upon the comparative importance of the specific rights being claimed.

iii) The court must take into account the **justification** put forward for interfering with or **restricting each right**.

iv) The **proportionality** test must be applied to each.

32. This approach, as adopted by their Lordships, was entirely consistent with that of the Council of Europe in Resolution 1165 of 1998:

> " . . . *the Assembly reaffirms the importance of every person's right to privacy, and of the right of freedom of expression, as fundamental to a democratic society. These rights are neither absolute nor in any hierarchical order, since they are of equal value.*"

33. It follows that **one can rarely arrive at the answer in any given case merely by reference to *generalities*.** It must all depend upon the particular facts of the case. It follows too that there can **be no automatic priority accorded to freedom of speech.** The relative importance of the competing values must be weighed by reference to the individual set of circumstances confronting the court. **Of course the court will pay particular regard to freedom of expression,** but that does not entail giving it automatic **priority**. All will depend on the value to be attached to the exercise or proposed exercise of that freedom **in the particular case**. **It will rarely be the case that the privacy rights of an individual or of his family will have to yield in priority to another's right to publish what has been described in the House of Lords as "tittle-tattle about the activities of footballers' wives and girlfriends**": see e.g. *Jameel v Wall Street Journal Europe SPRL* [2007] 1 AC 359 at [147]. It has recently been re-emphasised by the Court in Strasbourg that the reporting of "**tawdry allegations about an individual's private life**" does not attract the robust protection under Article 10 afforded to more serious journalism. In such cases, "freedom of expression requires a more **narrow** interpretation": *Mosley v UK* (App No 48009/08), 10 May 2011, BAILII: [2011] ECHR 774, at [114].

34. When an interim application is sought at this stage, with a view to maintaining the status quo until trial, the court has to proceed on the basis of evidence that may well be incomplete and has certainly not been tested in the witness box. But Parliament has imposed the obligation on judges in these circumstances to form a view, on such evidence as is available, as to whether the particular claimant is **"likely" to succeed**, at trial, in obtaining an injunction on a permanent basis to protect the information in question: see s 12(3) of the Human Rights Act. It has been established that "**likely**" in this context has generally to be equated to "**more likely than not**": *Cream Holdings Ltd v Banerjee* [2005] 1 AC 253 at [22].

35. It is obvious that by the time a case comes on for trial the totality of the material before the court may present a rather different picture. It is possible, for

example, that some of the evidence relied on at the early interlocutory stage will have been shown by then to be inaccurate or misleading. Nevertheless, the court is required to decide whether or not to grant an interim injunction on the evidence **as it stands at that time**.

36. The courts will have to apply this methodology unless and until Parliament decides to legislate to different effect.

37. On the evidence before me, **as at 14 and 20 April**, I formed the view that the Claimant would be **"likely"** to obtain a permanent injunction at trial, if the matter goes that far. As I have said, it remains uncontradicted. The information is such that he is still entitled to a "reasonable expectation of privacy" and **no countervailing argument has been advanced to suggest that the Article 10 rights of the Defendants, or indeed of anyone else, should prevail.** There is certainly **no suggestion of any legitimate public interest in publishing such material**.

38. Moreover, in so far as Ms Thomas wishes to exercise her Article 10 right by selling her life story, she is entitled to do so, but only subject to the qualification that **she is not thereby relieved of any obligation of confidence** she may owe, or free to intrude upon the privacy rights of others: **see e.g. McKennitt v Ash, cited above, at [28]-[32] and [50]-[51].** In so far as there are any conflicts of evidence or of recollection between her and the Claimant, it will be for the court to resolve them at the appropriate time. I will discuss with counsel whether it would be appropriate to order a speedy trial for that **purpose**.

CTB v News Group Newspapers Ltd and Imogen Thomas [2011] EWHC 1326 (QB) per Eady J

1. The background to the present applications is to be found in the circumstances which led to the earlier claim for an injunction against the Defendants restraining publication of material in respect of which the Claimant had a reasonable expectation of privacy and which might legitimately be regarded as confidential. The context is more fully set out in my judgment of 16 May at [2011] EWHC 1232 (QB). I now give my rulings following the subsequent arguments that took place on that date.

2. Mr Spearman QC for News Group Newspapers Ltd ("NGN") **seeks to vary** the terms of that injunction because, he submits, there has been **such widespread coverage** on the **Internet** since the order was first granted on 14 April 2011 that it would now be **pointless** for the court to maintain the Claimant's anonymity—**notwithstanding the absence of any legitimate public interest.**

He also argues, unusually, that in any event NGN should be allowed to pass on such information as it has, accurate or not, to the Claimant's wife. I shall need to return to that shortly in an attempt to explain the reasoning.

3. Although Ms Imogen Thomas was represented by Mr David Price QC, as she had also been on 20 April, **he took no part in the argument.** Her stance, once again, was that **she did not oppose the continuance of the injunction.**

4. Meanwhile, Mr Tomlinson QC for the Claimant applies **for an order under CPR 31.12 for specific disclosure of documents against NGN**. He recognises, of course, that disclosure applications are rarely made at such an early stage in proceedings. Nevertheless, he says that it is a course warranted by these particular circumstances. In particular, he argues **that it would be both necessary and proportionate to have disclosure of certain documents at this juncture because Mr Spearman seemed to be placing emphasis, in support of his application to vary the injunction, upon the "clean hands" of NGN and its employees**. He argues that there is no reason to blame NGN for the emergence of allegations or deductions on Twitter or elsewhere on the **Internet** and that, accordingly, it should not be placed at a disadvantage *vis-à-vis* its commercial rivals as to what it can publish. (That is not easy to follow, since NGN is in no worse position than any other media group served with the order.) **In effect, Mr Tomlinson submitted that I could not fairly decide the outcome of Mr Spearman's application to vary unless I had seen the extent of any email traffic passing between NGN staff and third parties on this subject-matter**. In other words, he invited the court to be sceptical and not accept Mr Spearman's "clean hands" case at face value.

5. I asked that Mr Spearman clarify to what extent he was actually relying on "clean hands", as opposed to merely observing that the Claimant's advisers had not produced any direct evidence of NGN collaboration with tweeters and bloggers. **He replied rather neutrally. I think the effect of what he said was that it would be rather time-consuming and burdensome for NGN to carry out the necessary research to enable them to advance a positive "clean hands" case.** All he was doing, therefore, was to point out that Mr Tomlinson could not directly attribute any responsibility, on the evidence as it stands at the moment, to NGN employees for the material appearing on the **Internet**. That is probably true, for the time being at least, but Mr Tomlinson was ready to draw realistic inferences and invited the court to do the same. **He suggests it is merely fanciful to suppose that no one at NGN has breached the confidence and/or sought to undermine the order.**

6. Nonetheless, for present purposes, there is a potentially important distinction between Mr Spearman's advancing a positive "clean hands" case, as he appeared to be doing at the outset, and his merely saying that the Claimant is unable to prove a direct link. **The potential significance is that the court**

does not have to make a finding on that point and, therefore, does not need disclosure to assist in its task.

7. **I am satisfied that Mr Spearman's application to vary the injunction can be resolved without a prolonged investigation of email traffic within NGN.** The outcome need not depend on the extent to which NGN employees have or have not leaked the Claimant's identity themselves. While I would not agree with Mr Spearman that the application is based on "flawed logic", **I do take the view that the disclosure sought is unnecessary and would be disproportionate to the present exercise.**

8. What Mr Tomlinson did rely on, however, were the terms of a broadcast by Mr Kelvin MacKenzie on BBC Radio on the morning of 30 April, when he claimed that he regularly passed on the identities of claimants who had been granted injunctions to anyone who asked him. He obviously does not approve of the current law of privacy and makes it his business to undermine court orders accordingly. He also likes to drop hints in his articles to give any interested readers a steer as to who might be covered by an order. Mr Tomlinson described this as "playing games". **It is necessary to remember in this context that Mr MacKenzie is no longer an employee of NGN. He seems to be, in legal terms, an independent contractor. His activities could not necessarily, therefore, be attributed to NGN.**

9. The order sought on the Claimant's behalf was that NGN should:

   a) conduct a search of its email system including any backup servers;

   b) disclose all emails located as a result of that search sent by Kelvin MacKenzie to any external email address during the period 14 April 2011 to 13 May 2011 which refer to the Claimant or tend in any way to identify the Claimant;

   c) disclose any other emails located as a result of that search sent by anyone employed by the First Defendant to any external email address during the period 14 April 2011 to 13 May 2011 which refer to the Claimant or tend in any way to identify the Claimant;

   d) disclose the recipient email address of any emails disclosed pursuant to (b) and (c) above;

   e) disclose any other documents including SMS text messages created by Kelvin MacKenzie between 14 April 2011 and 13 May 2011 which refer to the Claimant or tend in any way to identify the Claimant;

   f) disclose any other documents including SMS text messages created by anyone employed by the First Defendant between 14 April 2011 and 13 May 2011 which refer to the Claimant or tend in any way to identify the Claimant;

g) disclose each and every recipient of any document disclosed pursuant to (e) and (f) above.

10. What was suggested was that these requirements should be complied with by 20 May 2011, although Mr Spearman suggested that if it were to be carried out, the exercise would take far longer. I do not find that surprising. Mr Tomlinson accordingly confined his request at the hearing to a search for any documents evidencing traffic between NGN staff and Mr MacKenzie and also for any communications from Mr MacKenzie's *Sun* email address (as prominently displayed at the head of his weekly column) to third parties. **It still seems to me, however, to be unnecessary for the purpose in hand to spend precious time and money in enquiring into the detail of what Mr MacKenzie was up to. It would be something of a sledgehammer to crack a nut.**

11. There is another aspect to this application which causes me some concern. The proposed exercise, if carried out, might reveal attempts to undermine the orders of the court and thus suggest that one or more employees of NGN was committing **contempt** of court. **Although the law relating to self-incrimination in this context cannot be said to be crystal clear**, it would seem that the modern approach adopted by the courts is that such a risk cannot be regarded as an absolute bar when the court is invited, as a matter of discretion, to order disclosure, but it remains a factor to be taken carefully into account: see e.g. *Cobra Golf Inc v Rata* [1996] FSR 819, 830–832; *Dendron GmbH v University of California* [2005] 1 WLR 200; *C Plc v P (Att.-Gen. intervening)* [2008] Ch 1. **It would certainly need to be borne in mind if I were otherwise of the view that an order for disclosure should be made.**

12. **On the material before me, in any event, I would reject the Claimant's application for specific disclosure.**

13. Needless to say, if the Claimant's advisers have come to the conclusion that **contempts of court** have been committed, it is open to them to provide their evidence to the **Law Officers of the Crown**. It is they who have traditionally had the responsibility of representing the public interest in relation especially to allegations of criminal **contempt**: see e.g. *Gouriet v UPOW* [1978] AC 435, 483D–484B, 495E-F, 499G–500F and 518–519; *Att.-Gen. v Newspaper Publishing Plc* [1988] Ch 333, 362D, 367H–368A.

14. I turn next to Mr Spearman's **application to vary** the injunction and, in particular, so as **to remove the anonymity of the Claimant**. He says that many tens of thousands of people can, if they are sufficiently interested, find out who the Claimant is by making appropriate searches on the **Internet**, although it is fair to say that there **was speculation about a number of possible candidates**. Mr Spearman argues, as did Mr Kelvin MacKenzie in the

radio programme of which I was supplied with a transcript, that in effect privacy injunctions (and no doubt other forms of injunction also) have ceased to serve any useful **purpose** in the **age of the Internet**. Not only can information be put out on various networks from **within this jurisdiction**, but it can obviously be done also by anyone who wishes in **other jurisdictions**.

15. Parliament may at some stage wish to change the law and make specific provision in the light of these developments, but in the meantime the courts are obliged to apply the law as it currently stands. **The logical conclusion of Mr Spearman's argument is, perhaps, that the court should always refuse injunctive relief to applicants on the basis that, to a greater or lesser extent, the defendants or others may simply ignore its orders**. It would not be right, however, for courts to ignore their responsibilities and to refuse relief in circumstances where it is properly sought. My attention was drawn to a recent decision of King J in a case called **NEJ v News Group Newspapers Ltd, where a similar argument was apparently unsuccessfully advanced**. It is not clear to me, however, at the moment that the judgment has yet been made public. For this reason, I shall not make reference to its content, germane though it appears to be.

16. The principle, however, is **clear. One has only to pose the question for the answer to become obvious. Should the court buckle every time one of its orders meets widespread disobedience or defiance**? In a democratic society, if a law is deemed to be unenforceable or unpopular, it is for the legislature to make such changes as it decides are appropriate.

17. Meanwhile it is not right to say that the law of privacy is unclear or "confused". As I illustrated in the earlier judgment, there are a significant number of appellate authorities which have explained it in great detail. It is not easy to see, therefore, how any significant changes could be achieved other than by legislation.

18. Reference was made by Mr Spearman to the refusal of injunctive relief in yet another of his client's cases: *Mosley v News Group Newspapers Ltd* [2008] EWHC 687 (QB). It was there said:

> "The court should guard against slipping into playing the role of King Canute. Even though an order may be desirable for the protection of privacy, and may be made in accordance with the principles currently being applied by the courts, there may come a point where it would simply serve no useful **purpose** and would merely be characterised, in the traditional terminology, as a *brutum fulmen*. It is inappropriate for the court to make vain gestures."

The circumstances here are rather different. In Mosley, I took the view that there was no point in granting an injunction because, **even before the**

application was made, several hundred thousand people had seen the intimate video footage which NGN had put on line—conduct that was recently characterised by the European Court of Human Rights as a "flagrant and unjustified **intrusion**": *Mosley v UK* (App No 48009/08), 10 May 2011 at [104]. In a real sense, therefore, it could be said **that there was nothing left for the court to protect by an injunction.**

19. Here, the **Internet** allegations prayed in aid by Mr Spearman took place **after** the order was made. **Different policy considerations come into play when the court is invited to abandon the protection it has given a litigant on the basis of widespread attempts to render it ineffective**. Furthermore, unlike the *Mosley* case, **there is no doubt other information that Ms Thomas could yet publish, quite apart from this Claimant's identity, which is not yet in the public domain**. The injunction thus continues to serve a useful **purpose**, from the Claimant's point of view, for that reason alone, since she is amenable to the jurisdiction of the court. Otherwise, he would not seek to maintain it.

20. Mr Spearman's application is therefore quite **narrow**. He seeks only to vary the injunction so as to permit the Claimant to be identified. The basis of this argument appears to be closely related to one of the "**limiting principles**" explained by Lord Goff in *Att.-Gen. v Guardian Newspapers (No 2)* [1990] 1 AC 109, 282B-F, to the effect that the principle of confidentiality only applies to information to the extent that it is confidential:

> "In particular, once it has entered what is usually called the **public domain** (which means no more than that the information in question is so generally accessible that, in all the circumstances, it cannot be regarded as confidential) then, as a general rule, the principle of confidentiality can have no application to it."

The law thus recognises that a time may come, **at least in relation to state secrets or commercial confidentiality,** when the information in question has become so widely available that there is really nothing left for the law to protect. At an earlier stage in the same litigation, relating to *Spycatcher*, **Sir John Donaldson MR had famously likened confidential information to an ice cube**. Once it has melted, of course, it is simply too late to afford any effective remedy. That is Mr Spearman's argument in a nutshell.

21. Yet even at the time of the *Spycatcher* litigation in the House of Lords, over 20 years ago, **a distinction** was being already flagged up between **confidential information in the context of state or commercial secrets, on the one hand, and personal information on the other**: *ibid.* at 260E-H and 287C-D.

22. Whereas it may be possible to a draw **a bright line boundary as to commercial secrets between being public and private**, that is not so easy, **nor even**

generally appropriate, when it comes to publications infringing a person's rights under Article 8 of the European Convention on Human Rights and Fundamental Freedoms. As was explained in *Campbell v MGN Ltd* [2004] 2 AC 457, the law nowadays is required to protect information in respect of which there is a *reasonable* expectation of privacy and for so long as that position remains. **What is "reasonable" depends on the circumstances. It is a concept that is not susceptible in itself to bright line boundaries.**

23. It is important always to remember that the **modern law of privacy is not concerned solely with information or "secrets"**: it is also concerned importantly with **intrusion.** That is one reason why it can be important to distinguish between the way the law approaches **public domain arguments in relation to commercial or state secrets, for example, and that which is appropriate to personal information.** It also largely explains why it is the case that the truth or falsity of the allegations in question can often be irrelevant: see e.g. *McKennitt v Ash* [2008] QB 73 at [80] and [87].

24. It is fairly obvious that **wall-to-wall excoriation in national newspapers**, whether tabloid or "broadsheet", is likely to be significantly more **intrusive** and **distressing** for those **concerned than the availability of information on the Internet or in foreign journals to those, however many, who take the trouble to look it up.** Moreover, with each exposure of personal information or allegations, whether by way of **visual images** or verbally, there is a **new intrusion** and occasion for **distress or embarrassment**. Mr Tomlinson argues accordingly that **"the dam has not burst"**. For so long as the court is in a position to prevent **some of that intrusion and distress**, depending upon the individual circumstances, it may be appropriate to maintain that degree of protection. **The analogy with King Canute to some extent, therefore, breaks down.**

25. It may be thought that the wish of NGN to publish more about this "story", with a view to selling newspapers and perhaps achieving other commercial advantages, demonstrates that coverage **has not yet reached saturation point**. Had it done so, the story would no longer retain any interest. This factor tends, therefore, to confirm my impression that **the court's attempts to protect the Claimant and his family have not yet become wholly futile.**

26. In these circumstances, it seems to me that the right question for me to ask, in the light of *JIH v News Group Newspapers Ltd* [2011] 2 All ER 324 and *Re Guardian News and Media Ltd* [2010] UKSC 1, is whether there is a **solid reason** why the Claimant's identity should be generally revealed in the national media, such as to outweigh **the legitimate interests** of himself and his family in maintaining anonymity. The answer is as yet in the negative. **They would be engulfed in a cruel and destructive media frenzy.** Sadly, that may become unavoidable in the society in which we now live but, for the

moment, in so far as I am being asked to sanction it, I decline to do so. On the other side, as I recorded in my judgment on 16 May**, it has not been suggested that there is any legitimate public interest in publishing the story**

27. Mr Spearman raises the alternative argument, verging on the bathetic, that *The Sun* should at least be allowed to tell the Claimant's wife what it knows, or thinks it knows. This is a difficult one to follow. NGN is a media group legitimately interested in making profits from communicating to the world at large. It surely does not aspire to the role of social worker or "**relationship** counsellor". Its Article 10 rights are hardly engaged by this subsidiary argument at all. It was faintly suggested, therefore, that it should be allowed to pass on the story to the Claimant's wife in the furtherance or protection of *her* Article 8 right to family life. The Claimant regards this as so much humbug. The point of Article 8 is that it is not supposed to be any of NGN's business.
28. These are my reasons for rejecting the Defendant's application to vary the injunction.

CTB v News Group Newspapers Ltd and Imogen Thomas [2011] EWHC 1334 (QB) per Tugendhat J

Mr Justice Tugendhat:

1. At about 1430 this afternoon Eady refused NGN's application to remove the anonymity he had granted to the claimant on 20 April. He said at para 23 ([2011] EWHC 1326 (QB)) that "It is important always to remember that the modern law of privacy is not concerned solely with secrets: it is also concerned importantly with **intrusion**". **Intrusion** in this sense includes **harassment**.
2. Very shortly afterwards a name was mentioned by **Mr Hemming MP in the House of Commons** in the course of a question which **was interrupted** by the Speaker. On that basis NGN asked me to hear a further application shortly after 5pm **for the anonymity of the claimant to be removed**. As the public now know, anyone who wanted to find out the name of the claimant could have learnt it many days ago. The reason is that it is has been repeated thousands of times on the **internet**. NGN now want to join in.
3. It is obvious that if the **purpose** of this injunction were to preserve a secret, it would have failed in its **purpose**. **But in so far as its purpose is to prevent intrusion or harassment, it has not failed**. The fact that tens of thousands of people have named the claimant on the **internet** confirms that **the claimant and his family need protection from intrusion into their private and family**

life. The fact that a question has been asked in Parliament **seems to me to increase, and not to diminish the strength of his case that he and his family need that protection.** The order has not protected the claimant and his family from taunting on the **internet**. **It is still effective to protect them from taunting and other intrusion and harassment in the print media.**

TSE and ELP v News Group Newspapers Ltd [2011] EWHC 1308 (QB) per Tugendhat J

1. On 19 May 2011 I granted an injunction to prohibit the publication of **(a)** any information tending to identify the Claimants as having had a **sexual relationship** with one another; or tending to identify either of the Claimants as having had an affair, or **(b)** any other information identifying or in any way tending to identify the Claimants or either of them as being the persons who have applied for this order, save for that contained in the public part of the order I made on 19 May or in this public judgment.
2. **The hearing on 19 May was held in public. The order of 19 May is a public document. It is available to be inspected, except the Confidential Schedule.** The hearing on 13 May had been held in private. Sharp J did not deliver a public judgment in view of the imminence of the return date. This judgment includes all that needs to be said about the hearing on 13 May. A **detailed note** of that hearing was kept and has been provided to me. It was made by Laura Tyler of the Claimants' solicitors.
3. These are the circumstances in which I made the order and the reasons why I made it.
4. **The case concerns an adulterous relationship between the Claimants where both the man and the woman want to preserve their privacy. Neither of them is the source of NGN's information**. The male Claimant, referred to as TSE is a **married footballer.**
5. On 13 May Sharp J made an order substantially to the same effect. That order was stated to run until 19 May ("the return date"). On 16 May both the Claimants and the Defendant ("NGN") were represented by leading counsel. **NGN did not resist the injunction**, but it did not consent to it, **or offer undertakings to the court**. It adopted the same stance on 19 May. Mr Spearman submitted a written argument to the court stating that NGN did not resist the making of the order but did not consent to the making of it. He did make submissions on the form of the order, all of which Mr Caldecott accepted, with the result that when Mr Caldecott came to court he was able to produce

to me an order which was in terms which Mr Spearman had agreed were appropriate in the event that the court decided to make the order at all.

6. The form of the order I made, and the stance adopted by NGN are similar to another case in which Sharp J handed down a written judgment on 11 May: *MJN v News Group Newspapers Ltd* [2011] EWHC 1192 (QB).

NO CASE ADVANCED ON PUBLIC INTEREST

7. NGN did not advance any argument that publication ought not to be prohibited in the public interest. This point is considered further below.

THE BACKGROUND

8. On 12 May 2011 **a journalist** working for **The Sun** contacted a representative of the man's club to inform him that The Sun intended to run a story on 13 May alleging that the **man had conducted an adulterous relationship with the Claimant referred to as ELP.**

9. In a witness statement made by him the man states that the information in question has hitherto been private and explains the effect that he says that publication of this information would have if it were published**. It would have a devastating effect on his marriage, on his wife and particularly their children.** He states that it has become common for footballers whose private lives are exposed by the media to be **booed during games** and be the **subject of cruel chants.**

10. ELP states that a reporter from The Sun came to where she lived some months ago. She met him on the doorstep. **He referred to the relationship with the man and said that The Sun would be willing pay a lot of money for that story**. She said she would not talk and asked the reporter to leave. **She does not know the source of the story**. She did not, and **does not, want the story to be published**. She subsequently received messages from the reporter asking her to talk, but she did not reply. She received a call from Ms Tyler and instructed Schillings to act for her in these proceedings.

11. Ms Tyler made a witness statement dated 13 May. In it she recounts conversations between herself and Mr Walford of NGN. **In one conversation Mr Walford stated that NGN believed it was in the public interest to publish that the man was having an extra-marital affair because "we are exposing his hypocrisy**". That argument was **not advanced** to Sharp J and **has not been advanced before me**. No doubt NGN came to appreciate that, in the light of numerous judgments by different judges of the House of Lords, of the Court of Appeal, of this court and **of the European Court of Human Rights, it had no prospect of success**. Some of these cases are cited below.

THE HEARING BEFORE SHARP J

12. The Claimants asked for the hearing to be, and it was, held in private **because it was necessary to inform the court of the information in respect of which the Claimants were seeking an injunction**. A public hearing would have defeated the **purpose** of the application.

13. Ms Tyler asked for, and Sharp J granted**, anonymity** for the Claimants because they expected that if their names were given, that would lead to **serious intrusion** into the private lives of themselves and their families.

14. If an injunction to restrain the disclosure of private or **confidential information** is to be effective, the court must **either** grant **anonymity** to the claimants, **or refrain from giving any information in the order or any judgment about the nature of the information**. Naming the claimants in this case would in practice also disclose the nature of the information sought to be protected. So the Claimants asked not to be identified. Sharp J was satisfied that that was **necessary** if an effective order were to be made at all. I too am satisfied that that continues to be **necessary.**

15. On 18 May Ms Tyler made a second witness statement. In it she informed the court of the identities of the media organisations which had been **served with the order**: Associated Newspapers, Express Newspapers, Guardian Media Group, Independent News and Media, MGN, Telegraph Media and Times Newspapers.

THE LAW OF PRIVACY

16. The Court is bound by the Human Rights Act 1998 ("HRA"). According to that, the Claimant must first establish that his or her right to respect for private life under Art 8 **is engaged** (that is whether the information is in principle private), and second that relief is appropriate having regard to Art 10, the right to freedom of expression, and the matters set out in s 12(3).

    As to the first question, Mr Caldecott submits the following, which cannot be disputed. It is now clear the test is whether the Claimant had a reasonable expectation of privacy in relation to the information in question. **See McKennitt v Ash** [2008] QB 73 per Buxton LJ (with whom Latham and Longmore LJJ agreed, at **para 11**, further cited in Murray at **para 27**).

18. **The question is objective.** As Lord Hope put it in *Campbell v MGN Ltd* [2004] 2 AC 457: "*The question is what a* **reasonable person of ordinary sensibilities** *would feel if she was placed in the same position as the claimant.*" In *Murray v Express Newspapers Ltd* [2009] Ch 481 the Court of Appeal stated: "*The question of whether there is a reasonable expectation of privacy* **is a broad one**, *which takes account of* **all the circumstances** *of the case. They include the* **attributes** *of the claimant, the* **nature of the activity** *in which the claimant*

was engaged, **the place** *at which it was happening, the* **nature and purpose** *of the* **intrusion,** *the* **absence of consent** *and whether it was* **known or could be inferred**, *the* **effect on the claimant** *and the* **circumstances** *in which and the* **purposes** *for which the information came into the hands of the publisher."* **[para 36]**

19. **As to the second**, In *Re* S [2005] 1 AC 593 Lord Steyn identified four propositions as emerging from *Campbell v MGN Ltd* as *"the new methodology"* to be applied by the courts where both articles 8 and 10 are engaged:

    (i) Neither article has *as such* **precedence** over the other.

    (ii) Where the values under the two articles are in conflict, an **"intense focus"** on the comparative importance of the specific rights being claimed in the individual case is necessary.

    (iii) **The justifications for interfering** with or restricting each right must be taken into account,

    (iv) The **proportionalit**y test must be applied to each. For convenience Lord Steyn calls this **"the ultimate balancing test."**

20. **It is clear that the performance of Lord Steyn's** *'ultimate balancing test'* **requires an** *"intense focus on the comparative importance of the specific rights being claimed in the individual case"*; and that such applications *"fall to be decided* **not on the basis of rival** *generalities but by focussing on the* **specifics of the rights and interests** *to be balanced in the* **individual case**". See *In Re S (A Child) (Identification: Restrictions on Publication)* [2004] UKHL 47; [2005] 1 AC 593, at para 17 and *Clayton v Clayton* [2006] EWCA Civ 878; [2006] Fam 83 at para 64 (Sir Mark Potter P).

21. According to s 12(3) of the HRA, an injunction before trial is not granted unless the court is satisfied that the applicants are likely to establish that publication should not be allowed. And in coming to its finding on that the court is obliged to and does have regard to the matters set out in s 12(4), which reads:

    > "(4) The court must have particular regard to the importance of the Convention right to freedom of expression and, where the proceedings relate to material which the respondent claims, or which appears to the court, to be journalistic, literary or artistic material (or to conduct connected with such material), to—
    >
    > (a) the extent to which—
    >
    > (i) the material has, or is about to, become available to the public; or
    >
    > (ii) it is, or would be, in the public interest for the material to be published;

(b) any relevant privacy code."

22. The relevant privacy code in the case of NGN is that of the **Press Complaints Commission** which provides, so far as material:

 3.***Privacy**

 i) Everyone is entitled to respect for his or her private and family life, home, health and correspondence, including digital communications.

 ii) Editors will be expected **to justify intrusions into any individual's private life without consent**. Account will be taken of the complainant's own public disclosures of information.

 The public interest

 There may be exceptions to the clauses marked * where they can be demonstrated to be in the public interest.

 1. The public interest includes, but is not confined to:

  i) Detecting or exposing crime or serious impropriety.

  ii) Protecting public health and safety.

  iii) **Preventing the public from being misled by an action or statement of an individual or organisation.**

 2. There is a **public interest** in **freedom of expression** itself.

 3. Whenever the public interest is invoked**, the PCC will require editors to demonstrate fully that they reasonably believed that publication, or journalistic activity undertaken with a view to publication, would be in the public interest.**

 4. The PCC will consider the extent to which material is already in the **public domain,** or will become so.

 5. In cases involving children under 16, editors must demonstrate an **exceptional public interest** to over-ride the normally paramount interest of the child".

THE EVIDENCE IN RELATION TO PUBLIC INTEREST

23. No evidence has been produced by NGN that the Claimants have misled the public, nor has it argued or attempted to demonstrate that there is any basis of upon which the court should **"over-ride the normally paramount interest the child[ren]".** The editor of The Sun has not offered an explanation such as is referred to in para 3 of the paragraph headed Public Interest**. It is a requirement of the law as well as of the PCC Code that the Court should have regard to the impact of publication on the Claimants' children** (see, for example, **CDE & FGH v MGN Limited [2010] EWHC 3308 (QB) at [7]).**

24. For decades both the English Courts and the ECHR have recognised a reasonable expectation of privacy in relation to **sexual relationships; sexual conduct being "an essentially private manifestation of the human personality"** (*Dudgeon v UK* (1981) 4 EHRR 149 at [52] and [60]). **It is sometimes forgotten that ten years before the HRA *Stephens v Avery* [1988] Ch 449, afforded protection to information concerning an adulterous lesbian relationship.** At p455 Sir Nicolas Browne-Wilkinson, V.-C said "*To most people the details of their sexual lives are high on their list of those matters which they regard as confidential*". And this was consistently applied in what were then cases based on the law of confidentiality. In *Barrymore v News Group Newspapers Limited* [1997] FSR 600 Jacob J said: "*The fact is that when people kiss and later one of them tells, that second person is almost certainly breaking a confidential arrangement.*"

25. The present case is, as already stated, **not a case of kiss and tell**. It is one in which **both parties to the past relationship wish to keep it private.**

26. As recently as last week the ECHR restated the position in *Mosley v The United Kingdom*–48009/08 [2011] ECHR 774 (10 May 2011):

> "119 The Court observes at the outset that this is not a case where there are no measures in place to ensure protection of Article 8 rights. A system of self-regulation of the press has been established in the United Kingdom, with guidance provided in **the Editors' Code and Codebook** and oversight of journalists' and editors' conduct by the **PCC** (see paragraphs 29–38 above). This system reflects the 1970 declaration, the 1998 resolution and the 2008 resolution of the Parliamentary Assembly of the Council of Europe (see paragraphs 55 and 58–59 above). While the PCC itself has no power to award damages, an individual may commence civil proceedings in respect of any alleged violation of the right to respect for private life which, if successful, can lead to a damages award in his favour. In the applicant's case, for example, the newspaper was required to pay GBP 60,000 damages, approximately GBP 420,000 in respect of the applicant's costs and an unspecified sum in respect of its own legal costs in defending the claim. **The Court is of the view that such awards can reasonably be expected to have a salutary effect on journalistic practices.** Further, if an individual is aware of a pending publication relating to his private life, he is entitled to seek an interim injunction preventing publication of the material. **Again, the Court notes that the availability of civil proceedings and interim injunctions is fully in line with the provisions of the Parliamentary Assembly's 1998 resolution (see paragraph 58 above)**. Further protection for individuals is provided by the **Data Protection Act 1998,** which sets out the right to have unlawfully collected or inaccurate data destroyed or rectified (. . .).

> . . .
>
> 131. The Court, like the Parliamentary Assembly, recognises **that the private lives of those in the public eye have become a highly lucrative commodity for certain sectors of the media** . . . The publication of news about such persons contributes to the variety of information available to the public and**, although generally for the purposes of entertainment rather than education**, undoubtedly benefits from the protection of Article 10. However, as noted above, such protection may cede to the requirements of Article 8 where the information at stake is of a private and **intimate** nature and there is no public interest in its dissemination."

27. The HRA s 12 requires the court to have regard to the matters set out in sub-section (4) whether they are raised by a defendant or not. **So the fact that NGN has not argued before the court that it is in public interest for the material to be published, or that the material has, or is about to, become available to the public, does not relieve the court of the obligation to have particular regard to these matters.**

Public domain

28. For this reason Ms Tyler has put before the court **evidence of publication concerning these proceedings which have been made through various electronic media, including Twitter, in addition to the publications made on the print and online editions of The Sun and The Mail.**

29. The court does not grant injunctions which would be futile**. But the fact that these publications have occurred does not mean that the there should be no injunction in this case**. I explained the reasons in **JIH v News Group Newspapers Ltd** [2011] EMLR 9, [2010] EWHC 2818 (QB) (the subsequent judgment of the Court of Appeal did not affect this part of the judgment):

> **"58 It is important to bear in mind what privacy injunctions are intended to achieve. In some privacy cases the information sought to be protected will be truly secret**. One example may be **the paternity of a child** where the mother has successfully withheld that information (as happened in the case of a French Minister of Justice: "Minister's Mystery Baby" The Observer, Sunday 4 January 2009). Another example may be that **the applicant is suffering from a particular condition or disease** (eg the case of the late President Mitterrand *Plon (Societe) v France* 58148/00 [2004] ECHR 200; 42 EHRR 36). Such cases **bear some comparison to cases about trade or official secrets**: if the secret is revealed there is nothing the court can do to undo what has been done. **In cases of trade or official secrets an injunction may thereafter be futile.**

59. But in many privacy cases the information sought to be protected is **not**

secret in that sense, or, even if it is, once the secret is revealed, **there is still something to be achieved by an injunction**. Art 8 is about interference with a persons' private and family life. **There may be such interference by the repetition in the press of information even when that information is not secret or unknown.** As *Plon v France* (paras [14], [34] and [47]) illustrates, **this is be because the repetition of known facts about an individual may amount to unjustified interference with the private lives not only of that person and but also of those who are involved with him** (in that case his widow and children) in the matters which are the subject of the action. It may also lead to **harassment**: *von Hannover v Germany* (59320/00); (2005) 40 EHRR 1 para [68]. **The widow and children were parties in the *Plon* case in the national courts**. But the obligation of the Court under s 6 of the HRA (not to act incompatibly with Convention rights) obliges the Court to have regard to the Art 8 rights of persons **who are not parties to the action**, as well as to the rights of the claimant"30. In the present case the effect of the publications to which Ms Tyler referred me is that private information which was secret is **no longer secret**. **So to that extent one purpose of the injunction has been defeated.** But the **extent of the publications**, and **the tone of the publications** demonstrates that the evidence put before Sharp J was correct. **There is a pressing need for the injunction to prevent harassment and unjustified intrusion into the lives of the Claimants and the man's family.**

31. In the course of his submissions Mr Caldecott referred to **the difficulty that claimants may have in enforcing injunctions against those who publish private information on the internet**. The difficulties are well known. However, as the ECHR confirmed in the *Mosley* case, **whether or not an injunction is granted, claimants continue to have the right to claim damages, whether or not those who publish the information have had notice of any injunction.**

INFORMATION AND MISINFORMATION

32. **One of the purposes of handing down judgments such as this is to explain the law and to attempt to encourage informed reporting and to forestall misinformed reporting.**

33. At the hearing on 13 May NGN had told Sharp J that it would publish a report and that it would only refer to the man as a married premier league footballer. **However, on 14 May NGN published in The Sun an article headed "New ace gags Sun on romps revelation" and gave other information about him which limited the number of individuals who might be the claimant to very few.** Accordingly, Ms Tyler submitted that NGN has been in breach of the order. That is not an issue that I have to rule upon in this judgment.

34. But there is another effect of NGN giving the details it did give about the

Claimants. **It thereby put the other individuals who fitted the description it gave in the article under suspicion and exposed them to the risk of intrusion into their private lives and harassment. This is a consequence of the way The Sun chose to report the proceedings. It need not have been a consequence of the claimants' action in bringing the proceedings.**

35. The stance adopted by NGN in this case (neither resisting the injunction, nor consenting to it) had the consequence that The Sun's article about the case under the heading "New ace gags Sun . . . " was accurate, **whereas it would have been less easy to print such a headline if NGN had offered undertakings or otherwise avoided the need for the court to issue an injunction**. There are other types of cases in which Defendants neither resist an injunction nor consent to it. **An example are the cases where ISPs are ordered to provide to those wishing to make claims about interference with their privacy the information required to identify those who have made the publications complained of**: eg *G & G v Wikimedia Foundation Inc* [2009] EWHC 3148 (QB). In those cases the ISPs do that in order to have the protection of a court order as a defence if a complaint is made by the individual who has published the information on the **internet**. **There is no such reason why NGN should adopt this stance in this case, nor why NGN adopted it in the MJN case**. NGN does not explain why it adopts it. It is the court's experience that in the past NGN has submitted to injunctions which it could not defend, or settled cases, as it did in *JIH*. **If parties choose to exercise their right neither to oppose nor consent to injunctions, it has the further effect of taking up the time of the court that would be available to other litigants.**

36. Before leaving this case there is one further observation to be made. In this case the claimant is a footballer, and the injunctions granted in this court are **sometimes reported as being disproportionately of benefit to footballers and other sportsmen.** But as the other cases cited in this judgment show, there is **no stereotype which can be used to categorise claimants in privacy actions,** and **many of them are women, as is ELP**. The claimants in the following cases were **women and children**: *McKennitt, Campbell, Murray, S, FGH, Stephens, Plon* (the successful claimants were the widow and family of the late President Mitterrand), *von Hannover, Clayton.* **A number of the cases related to claimants who were gay or lesbian:** *Dudgeon*, *Stephens* and *Barrymore*. **This is not a case of a woman being silenced by an injunction:** ELP is an applicant for the injunction together with a man, **after she had resisted an offer of money to publish her story. FGH was also a woman**. Many of the cases are about information which is **not sexual**: *McKennit, Campbell, Murray, S, Plon, von Hannover, Clayton.*

37. The **variety of privacy claimants** was illustrated in the first edition of

Tugendhat & Christie on the Law of Privacy and the Media OUP, 2001) at p 218 (see p 548 of the 2nd edn, 2011), which included the following passage:

> "Since the *Douglas* case, the court has granted injunctions in confidence to **restrain the ex-girlfriend of a film actress's brother from disclosing to the press private family photographs of the actress** and her **young children** obtained during her **relationship** with the brother, **to stop the unauthorised publication of sexually explicit photographs of a pop singer**, to **prevent the publication of unauthorised photographs of a television actress walking around topless in a hotel garden**, and less **salaciousl**y, **to prevent further publication of an unauthorised photograph of Gracie Attard, the surviving, formerly conjoined twin".**

38. All of the claimants in that passage were **women or children, some rich, and some not rich**. The references in the footnotes are as follows: *W v W* (HC, 22 February 2001, Lloyd J); *A v B and C* (QBD, 2 March 2001, Mackay J); *Holden v Express Newspapers Ltd* (QBD, 7 June 2001, Eady J); *Re A* (Fam, 15/16 June 2001, Bennett J).

Sir Frederick Goodwin v News Group Newspapers Ltd and VBN [2011] EWHC 1437 (QB)

[This report is set out in full because: (a) it is a case of such high profile and public interest, (b) the court was at pains to give a thorough examination of the facts and the law, and the report is therefore a meticulous and definitive guide as to the approach to these cases.]

Mr Justice Tugendhat:

1. The Defendant ("NGN") publishes The Sun newspaper. It applies to vary an injunction dated 19 May. **That injunction prohibited the disclosure of information concerning a sexual relationship between Sir Fred Goodwin and a colleague of his at RBS.** The **relationship** continued while she was working for RBS and he was Chief Executive of that bank. The lady is referred to now as "**VBN**". The litigation has attracted very wide publicity. This is in part due to the **reputation** which Sir Fred Goodwin acquired as he led RBS, at first to a number of business successes, but in the end to the brink of collapse. NGN state that he did this by **cutting the number of employees** and through a series of acquisitions, the last of which was of ABN Amro**. RBS had to be rescued with vast sums of public money**. When Sir Fred Goodwin left the bank in November 2008 he was contractually entitled to severance terms which were in very large figures. **He has since attracted much adverse criticism in the media reflecting public resentment that he could receive such**

high rewards after presiding over the failure of one of the country's leading banks. A bank failure on this scale had not occurred in the United Kingdom since the nineteenth century. NGN state that Sir Fred Goodwin had at an earlier stage attracted much adverse criticism from those who disapproved of the policy he carried out at RBS **in cutting the number of employees.** It is common knowledge that Sir Fred Goodwin has figured very **prominently in the media** for a number of years, and that in recent years the coverage has been **increasingly hostile.**

2. These facts may well explain why NGN consider that articles about Sir Fred Goodwin will be of **interest to the public** to whom they wish to sell The Sun. But what is of **interest to the public** is not the same as what it is in the public interest to publish. **Newspaper editors have the final decision on what is of interest to the public: judges have the final decision what it is in the public interest to publish.**

3. The case raises important questions as to the circumstances in which the parties to a sexual relationship may or may not hold a reasonable expectation of privacy in respect of that relationship, and **when it may or may not be in the public interest for there to be disclosure in the media of the fact (but not the details) of a sexual relationship.**

4. VBN is not a claimant in the proceedings. She would be entitled to be a claimant if she wished, since her private life is as much engaged as that of Sir Fred Goodwin. But she does not have to be a party. **She is a party to this application for the reasons explained more fully below**. In brief, she is the person who will be the most affected if the variation to the injunction now sought by NGN is granted. Sir Fred Goodwin would not be directly affected by the proposed variation, **since the variation that permitted disclosure of his name was made at the hearing on 19 May**. VBN had been given no notice of that hearing and was not represented at it, so there had to be this further hearing.

THE HISTORY OF THIS LITIGATION

5. On the afternoon of 1 March 2011 a representative of The Sun contacted Sir Fred Goodwin regarding an allegation that he was having an affair with a lady who was an employee of the bank at a time. The journalist also gave the name of the lady and the department in which she worked. It was **suggested** to Sir Fred Goodwin that the public interest in publication of the story was the fact that **the lady was involved in determining his severance package when he left RBS**. I will refer to this as NGN's "first argument".

6. No evidence for this suggestion has ever been produced by NGN and there has been no explanation as to how it ever came to be advanced. **If true, it would have been a very serious matter. It would have involved a clear**

conflict between the lady's professional duties to RBS and her personal interest in assisting the man with whom she was in a relationship. Sir Fred Goodwin and the lady have **both denied that she had any involvement in determining his severance package and that denial is not challenged**. Since that initial conversation on 1 March no one on behalf of NGN has mentioned that suggestion again.

7. Later that same day Mr Tomlinson QC, on behalf of Sir Fred Goodwin, applied for an injunction against NGN to Henriques J. He was the Judge who was hearing out of hours applications at the time. **The application was made by a telephone in a conference call to which Mr Spearman QC was also a party, representing NGN. At that hearing no evidence or legal submissions had yet been put on paper**. That is a common situation in urgent applications. So each counsel told the Judge what he had been instructed his client would say about the facts, **and a detailed note was kept by the solicitors.** As the rules of court provide, an applicant for an injunction in those circumstances is required later to lodge a witness statement by him confirming the facts explained to the Judge on his behalf. **A defendant is not required to do that unless, at the next hearing to be held a few days later, the defendant opposes the continuation of the injunction.**

8. Mr Tomlinson asked for an injunction to prohibit the publication of any information concerning the subject matter of proceedings which Sir Fred Goodwin intended to commence**, or of any information tending to identify him (save for that contained in the court order and any Judgment), or of any information concerning the facts or details of any sexual relationship between Sir Fred Goodwin and the person named in the confidential schedule to the proposed order (now referred to as VBN**). At that time the proceedings were anonymised and Sir Fred Goodwin was referred to as MNB.

9. Mr Tomlinson submitted that Sir Fred Goodwin had a reasonable expectation of privacy in relation to information about his **relationship** with the lady because **the law generally recognises that sexual relationships are private unless the parties choose to make them public**. Further, he submitted, that there was **no public interest** in the disclosure of the fact that Sir Fred Goodwin and the lady had had this **relationship**.

10. For NGN Mr Spearman submitted that the affair was being conducted at the time of the disastrous acquisition by RBS of ABN Amro. That acquisition would have led to the collapse of RBS, but for the government **bail out** which was **made with public funds**. The argument for NGN was that Sir Fred Goodwin **might have been distracted by the affair in particular because of other circumstances of his private life (which he identified, but which cannot be set out in this judgment)**. Mr Spearman stated that it was not the intention of The Sun to say anything more than that Sir Fred Goodwin

was having an affair. **There would be nothing published about the details of the relationship.**

11. **It is important to note that Mr Spearman also said that the identity of the lady was not of significance for the story, nor was it significant that she was an employee of RBS, nor in what field of employment she worked**. Mr Spearman submitted that the only relevance of the fact that the lady also worked for RBS was that **that might have made the affair more distracting than it would have been with someone who Sir Fred Goodwin only came across at the weekend.** So for that reason the newspaper might wish to publish that she was a work colleague**. It will be seen that that argument was very different from the one advanced by NGN before me**. At that hearing NGN was expressly disavowing reliance on matters which it is putting at the forefront of its case before me.

12. **Thus the sole argument raised by NGN at that stage was that the relationship with VBN coincided with the disastrous business deal**. On that basis NGN submitted that it might have distracted Sir Fred Goodwin's attention from the business affairs of RBS **at the time which was critical to the disastrous takeover**. I will refer to this as NGN's "second argument".

13. Henriques J gave a short ex tempore judgment in private recording the submissions for NGN, and rejecting them. Applying the test in the HRA s12 (see below), he was satisfied on the information before him that Sir Fred Goodwin was likely to succeed at trial in establishing that publication of the information in question should not be allowed. He reached this conclusion after finding that Sir Fred Goodwin's rights under Article 8 were engaged, and that he had a reasonable expectation of privacy, whereas he found no countervailing public interest so as to make it necessary and proportionate to permit The Sun to interfere with that right in the exercise of its right of freedom of expression under Article 10. He held that it was necessary in the interests of justice that Sir Fred Goodwin's name should not be disclosed at that stage. He ordered that the matter come back before the court on 4 March.

14. **VBN was not present or represented at the hearing.** There was no requirement that she should be. **But judges are required to have regard to the effect that any order might have on third parties who are not before the court.** So Henriques J enquired as to the position of VBN, and, after making his decision, **required the parties to inform her of the order he had made.**

15. On 2 March 2011 a claim form was issued and Sir Fred Goodwin made a witness statement. In it he stated that the **relationship** between himself and the lady was an entirely private matter which neither of them had disclosed to the public, and which had not previously been discussed or mentioned in

the media. **He said that any suggestion that the lady was responsible for his severance packet was wholly untrue**, and that she had nothing whatsoever to do with it. He gave information as to her position in the company. **He denied that the affair could have had any impact on his judgment or distracted him from his work at the time of the take over of ABN Amro.** He set out facts about the takeover which were well known at the time and which he said demonstrated that his own role in the affair was that of one man amongst very many. There were two other banks involved in the take over (Fortis and Santander); **the proposal was approved overwhelmingly by the shareholders of all three banks**; there were **external advisors**; there was another British bank, Barclays, who had been pursuing a possible takeover in competition with RBS; **the deal had been approved by regulators in approximately fifty countries and by the FSA**; and **in December 2010 the FSA concluded that there had been no breakdown of corporate governance in relation to the takeover** and that there was no individual wrongdoing. He expressed fears as to the **intrusion** into his private life that would follow if there were publication of the information about the **relationship** in question.

16. On 4 March 2011 the matter came back before the court. Sharp J continued the injunction in substantially similar terms. At that hearing Sir Fred Goodwin was still referred to only by the letters MNB.

17. **NGN abandoned its second argument before the hearing on 4 March**. If NGN had wished to oppose the continuation of the injunction at the hearing on 4 March, it would have had to put evidence before the court as the basis of its legal submissions. **NGN put no evidence before the court.** The same applies to any other newspaper or person notified of the order. If any such third party had wished to oppose the continuation of the injunction on 4 March (or at any later date) it would have had to put evidence before the court, and make submissions. **No third party has done that**.

18. Sharp J gave a public judgment [2011] EWHC 528 (QB). This was a reserved judgment given on 9 March. In paragraph 1 of that judgment she recorded how the matter had come to be heard on 1 March 2011 by Henriques J. She stated that, of two public interest justifications for the proposed publication advanced initially for NGN, one had already been abandoned by the time of the hearing before Henriques J. In para 5 of her judgment she stated that, at the start of the hearing before herself, **she had been told that the application for an interim injunction was no longer opposed**. Subject to its right to apply to discharge or vary the order, NGN had agreed that the order should continue until trial or further order. **Thus the second public interest argument (that Sir Fred Goodwin might have been distracted by the affair) was also abandoned by then.**

19. Sharp J went on to state in para 6 of her judgment the following:

"There is no doubt in my view that the Claimant's article 8 rights are engaged, both in relation to the subject matter of the action, and the identification of him as the Claimant. There is no doubt either that publication of the information as to the fact or details of the affair will result in some interference with the Claimant's private life**. It is not currently suggested by the Defendant that there is a public interest in the publication of the information or that there is any other reason for it to be disclosed**. It is **not suggested for example that the information was in the public domain**. I am satisfied in accordance with section 12(3) of the Human Rights Act 1998 that the Claimant is **likely to establish at trial** that publication of the information should not be allowed."

20. The remainder of her judgment was devoted to explaining why the hearing was in **private**, why Sir Fred Goodwin was being granted **anonymity**, and **what could be published** about the case.

21. This part of **Sharp J's judgment has been substantially misreported**. It was reported that in Parliament Mr Hemming MP had said that she granted an injunction prohibiting calling Sir Fred Goodwin a banker. **She did not**. What she prohibited was reporting the proceedings in terms which identified Sir Fred Goodwin as the claimant. This prohibition included referring to the applicant for the injunction as a banker, because that would be information which might tend to identify Sir Fred Goodwin as being the applicant**. That would defeat the court's purpose in granting anonymity to him.** The reporting of the supposed injunction prohibiting the identification of Sir Fred Goodwin as a banker did not explicitly identify Sir Fred Goodwin as the claimant in this case, although some understood the publicity as giving a hint that it was him.

22. On 19 May 2011 in the morning there were numerous media reports that in the House of Lords Lord Stoneham, speaking on behalf of Lord Oakeshott, had identified Sir Fred Goodwin as the applicant for the injunction in question. **Lord Stoneham was frustrating the purpose of the court order and thus impeding the administration of justice**, but he was doing so under the protection of Parliamentary privilege. If he had identified Sir Fred Goodwin in words spoken outside Parliament he would have been interfering with the administration of justice, or committing a **contempt** of court, as it is called.

23. In the light of this development NGN gave notice to Sir Fred Goodwin that it would apply to vary the injunction so as to permit the name of Sir Fred Goodwin to be published in the newspapers as the person who had applied for the injunction. That afternoon there was a hearing before myself. Sir Fred Goodwin appeared as did NGN, MGN (the publisher of the Mirror and the Sunday Mirror) and Associated Newspapers Ltd ("ANL", the publisher of the Daily Mail and the Mail on Sunday). **At the start of that hearing Sir Fred**

Goodwin accepted that the injunction should be varied so as to permit the identification of himself as the claimant and applicant for the injunction.

24. At hearing **neither NGN nor the two third parties put any evidence before the court.**

25. NGN also sought a wider variation of the injunction, which I did not accept. The order continued in a form which **prohibited the publication of any information identifying, or tending to identify the person named in the confidential schedule, as being the person with who the claimant was alleged to have had a sexual relationship** (save for that contained in the order of the court and any public judgment of the court given in this action). The order **also prohibited publication of any information concerning the details of any alleged sexual relationship between the claimant and the person in question.**

26. But the order did permit NGN to apply to vary the order **on condition that if the variation it sought might affect the rights of the lady named in the confidential schedule or her family, she must be given three clear days' notice in writing of the application.** Notice was later given to the lady of the present application. It was not three clear days notice, but no point is taken on that.

27. On 23 May I handed down a public judgment [2011] EWHC 1309 (QB). In it I set out what had happened in the case, and my reasons for making the order that I made on 19 May. **These reasons included the fact that the lady had not been given any notice that the court was to be asked to withdraw the anonymity which the injunction of 4 March gave to her** (paras [24]–[26]). **I also corrected a number of inaccuracies that had been published about the case (paras [9]–[10]).**

28. ANL appeared at that hearing**, as any third party affected by an injunction is entitled to do.** ANL (then represented by Mr Caldecott QC) raised a new **(the third)** argument on public interest, **namely that if there was a relationship between Sir Fred Goodwin and a lady who was a work colleague**, then that by itself would be a serious failure of corporate governance and might be in breach of the RBS Group Code of Conduct on Integrity Matters (dated 2007) ("RBS Code"). I shall refer to this as the "**third argument".** However, as stated in paragraph [21] of the judgment, no notice of this new case had been given to Sir Fred Goodwin or to the lady, and there **was no evidence that it had been investigated by or on behalf of ANL or anyone else**.

29. **No one on behalf of NGN has ever asked VBN anything about this case.** On 1 March **NGN did not ask** for her comments on the suggestion that she had been involved in arrangements for Sir Fred Goodwin's severance package. **NGN has not adduced** any evidence as to the enquiries that it has made

with RBS (but see now para 149 below), or anyone else who might have been concerned in the ABN Amro takeover, **whether Sir Fred Goodwin was distracted, or as to any other aspect of the case**. But in the evidence for VBN adduced before me VBN states that it came to her knowledge that NGN had contacted RBS in February. **There is no other evidence about that contact.**

30. On 27 May the matter came back before the court for **the fourth time**. On this occasion **the applicant was VBN**, although she was not yet referred to in that way. Mr Tomlinson QC appeared for her. **He asked me to refer to the Attorney General a publication made in the issue of the Daily Mail dated 20 May 2011, which he submitted was in contempt of court**, in that it impeded the **purpose** the court had sought to achieve by making the previous orders in this case. **I declined to make the reference as requested, but I did set out a number of facts relating to the case which, if the Attorney General so chose, he would be able to consider.**

31. In the Daily Mail ANL had published certain pieces of information about VBN. She complained that some of the information was **accurate** and would **tend to identify her**. She also noted other information which had been printed which she said was **incorrect**. A piece of information she said was incorrect was that the Daily Mail said that she had been promoted while Sir Fred Goodwin was in charge of RBS. Counsel for ANL (Mr Caplan QC) did not disagree when Mr Tomlinson informed the court that **that information was false.**

32. **So up until this point, no evidence had been put before the court on behalf of NGN or any third party in opposition to the continuation of the injunction.**

THE PRESENT APPLICATION

33. On 26 May 2011 NGN gave notice of its intention to apply to vary the order I made on 19 **May so as to permit the identification of the lady named in the confidential schedule**. The form of draft order made clear that **there was no intention to seek a variation of the order which might permit publication of any sexual or salacious information, or any photographs of the lady or any members of her family.**

34. The application was supported by two witness statements, the first evidence to be put before the court by NGN in this case. **Mr Hawkes,** the business editor of The Sun, raised two matters in his witness statement. **First** he stated that **he believed that the lady had been promoted while Sir Fred Goodwin was Chief Executive of RBS. The grounds for his belief that he gave were in a document.**

35. Miss Proudler of Olswang was by now instructed to act as solicitor by VBN (in addition to her previous instructions to act for Sir Fred Goodwin). In her witness statement dated 31 May 2011, Ms Proudler explained that **Mr Hawkes**

had **misinterpreted the document he referred to**. Ms Proudler stated that VBN has not been promoted as Mr Hawkes believed. **NGN now accept that that is the true position**. The suggestion that the lady had been promoted while Sir Fred Goodwin was Chief Executive is **no longer pursued** by NGN. I shall refer to this as NGN's fourth argument. It is the third argument that has been abandoned.

36. The second point advanced by Mr Hawkes in his witness statement related to the position in RBS held by VBN, and to the fact, as he asserted it to be**, that there had been no disclosure to anyone else at RBS of the relationship between herself and Sir Fred Goodwin**. Mr Hawkes stated that the **relationship** between them **led to a serious conflict of interest** on the part of both of them. This is the third argument, the one initially raised on 19 May by ANL.

37. The **RBS Code includes the following provisions on page 11.**

> "*Conflicts of Interest*
>
> So that you can undertake your job properly, maintain your objectivity and impartiality and ensure that your judgment could not be compromised, you should not put yourself in a position where your personal interests could conflict with the interests of the Group. For these purposes the term "Interests of the Group" is taken in its widest sense.
>
> You have a responsibility to act in the interest of the Group and must not misuse your position or any information obtained in the course of your employment to further your private interests—or those of anyone you have a **relationship** with . . .
>
> *How will I know if I have a conflict of interest?*
>
> If, in the context of performing your duties, it could be suggested that you are acting in your own interests or those of another person with whom you have a **relationship**, rather than in the interests of the Group, you may have a conflict of interest.
>
> *Possible conflicts of interest* **relationships** *and associations.*
>
> For these purposes, the term "**relationship**" is taken in its widest sense—from playing football with a customer to sharing membership of the same private club or society with a supplier **to forming a close personal relationship with a colleague.**
>
> While the Group entirely respects the right of every one of us to form friendships and personal **relationships** at work, there will be occasions when it will be **appropriate to tell your ma**nager about a **relationship** that may impact on your work by creating a conflict of interest.
>
> Here are some examples of when it would be appropriate to notify your manager of a potential conflict of interest:

—You are working under a dual control procedure and **have a close personal relationship** with your dual control partner

—You are conducting an investigation or a hearing under the disciplinary procedure in which an employee with whom you have a **personal relationship** is implicated . . . "

38. At page 12 of the RBS Code it is stated that the onus is on the employee to identify when it is appropriate to inform a manager of any **relationship** or association that had potential to create a conflict of interest.

39. At page 29, in a part of a section of the RBS Code of Conduct related to Group Security, and under the heading "Making a Disclosure within the Group", there is guidance as to what amounts to an event which ought to be notified to more senior management. These events include matters which are commonly referred to as **whistle blowing**. The guidance is that such matters should first be raised with an employee's immediate line manager, and if this is felt to be inappropriate, then it should be raised with a more senior manager or other persons whose job description is given in the RBS Code.

40. Mr Hawkes also referred to a publication from the FSA encouraging whistle blowers to "first use whistle blowing procedures in the workplace".

41. Mr Hawkes went on to state that the position in RBS held by the lady is sufficiently senior that she might be a person to whom a whistle blower might turn to make a disclosure. The fact that she was in a **relationship** with Sir Fred Goodwin while he was Chief Executive created the obvious risk (he said) that **confidential information** disclosed to her might, perhaps inadvertently, be disclosed to him, or that she might feel herself to be in a position where her duty to RBS conflicted with her personal obligations to him in relation to the disclosure made to her. Mr Hawkes stated that any employee who might have wished to consider making a disclosure to the lady would be entitled to know of her **relationship** with the Chief Executive. That may be relevant to the employee's decision whether to address concerns, or give notification, to the lady or to some other senior manager.

42. Mr Hawkes stated that it is a matter of public interest that Sir Fred Goodwin and the lady permitted this state of affairs to continue whilst he was Chief Executive.

43. Mr Hawkes referred to press cuttings about three other cases where a **relationship** between the Chief Executives of a large corporation and an employee had given rise to conflicts of interest. In one case the cutting reported that the lady had left the company, in another it was the Chief Executive who was ousted and in a third the Chief Executive had resigned.

44. Mr Hawkes referred to the investigation which the FSA is currently making into the allegations about the **relationship** between Sir Fred Goodwin and

the lady. He stated that there should be full public discussion of these matters at this stage and that such discussion should not await the outcome of that investigation.

45. He further exhibited an article in the Financial Times dated 24 May 2011. He noted that, according to that article, **an internal enquiry by RBS has concluded that the lady "played no part in key strategic decisions at the bank" and "did not compromise the bank in any way".** But **he stated** that that misses the point that is important in the present application. **The public is still entitled to discuss these matters, and discussions are not concluded by that internal investigation.**

46. The article in the Financial Times also reports a source who is not identified as saying "We have only known about this for several weeks" and the writer adds:

> "It is **not believed** Sir Fred or the woman in question disclosed the alleged **relationship** to their superiors—**neither** Sir George Matthewson nor Sir Tom McKillop, who both held the role of chairman when Sir Fred ran the bank, were told. Similarly, the Financial Services Authority is **not thought** to have had prior knowledge of the alleged affair . . . "

47. The application is also supported by a witness statement from Mr Hancock, who is the Member of Parliament for West Suffolk. He worked as an economist at the Bank of England until 2005. He now sits on the Public Accounts and Standards Privilege Select Committees. **He stated that it is his belief that it is strongly in the public interest that there be published the information that the lady holds the senior position that she does with RBS, and that she did so during the time she was having an affair with Sir Fred Goodwin at the time when he was head of the bank and the affair was not disclosed.** He refers to the number of employees for whom the lady is likely to have had responsibility and **that that responsibility included possible whistle blowing disclosures**. He stated that the matter cries out for independent investigation and that public confidence in any investigation can only be maintained if the public are given the facts now.

48. Mr Hancock's evidence is not evidence of any fact in the case. It was adduced in support of an argument which NGN has advanced, but which, in the event, I have not had to consider. **The argument is that a reasonable belief on the part of an editor that a matter is of public interest is a factor that the court has to take into account in deciding whether it is in the public interest for something to the published.**

THE EVIDENCE FOR VBN

49. Ms Proudler stated that **VBN did not notify her relationship to her manager (and the person she reports to is identified) "because there was no rela-**

tionship that might impact on her work by creating a conflict of interest". RBS has known about the **relationship** since February 2011, when they were informed by a journalist from The Sun. **An internal investigation has been conducted by RBS. VBN has not been criticised or disciplined as a result and it has not been suggested to her by anyone at RBS that she was in a position of conflict or in breach of the RBS Code**. The parts of the Financial Times article referred to by Mr Hawkes are consistent with VBN's understanding of the position, namely that **RBS is satisfied that there was no necessity for her to disclose a personal relationship with the Chief Executive Officer.**

50. VBN remarked that NGN has provided no explanation of why any conflict of interest should arise out of a **relationship** between the Chief Executive Officer, who is responsible for strategic direction of a substantial business, and a person in her position, which she described.

51. VBN confirmed that no employee of RBS had ever made a whistle blowing disclosure to her, and she stated that it was not likely that any would do so. She described dedicated arrangements that RBS has put in place for whistleblowers.

52. Ms Proudler also gave a very brief account of the personal circumstances of VBN. **VBN stated that she is a private person, with a family, who has never spoken to the media about any private matters.** She first met Sir Fred Goodwin in the company of large numbers of other people in the course of her work, but when she met him "personally" it was "in a social context". She did not say anything about her own marital status. She mentioned "a number of family members and associates**", but refers specifically to only one member of her family**. She identified that person in order to explain her concerns about **the humiliation that person might suffer if her name were to be published by NGN**. She made clear that at some point **some people had come to know about her relationship with Sir Fred Goodwin**, but she did not make clear when or how they came to know about it. Nor did VBN state in terms whether she told anyone at work about it. All that she said is that "there has already been disclosure identifying details" about her in a national newspaper and that "this has led to her being identified by a number of people with whom she works and with whom she has business **relationships**". **I infer from this that she is saying that no one with whom she works knew about her relationship with Sir Fred Goodwin before the publication in the national newspaper,** and the publication was in relation to these proceedings, and so in 2011.

53. VBN stated that publication of her name by NGN would be a very serious **intrusion** into her private and family life. She referred to occasions when her identity has been published, **but states that in spite of that, it has not**

become generally known. She distinguishes such publications from publication in the press and broadcast media which would inevitably come to the attention of those she deals with on a daily basis, which she stated would be extremely **intrusive**. She referred to people known to her who have already been persistently approached by journalists, and she fears that such approaches would intensify if the injunction were varied to permit NGN and the press and broadcast media to identify her.

54. Ms Proudler stated that VBN asked her "not to go into details of these matters because she is concerned that material put before the court may find its way into the **public domain**".

55. The court has powers to prohibit the publication of information provided to the court, and all the orders made in this action have included provisions designed to achieve that. VBN is entitled to choose what evidence she puts before the court, whatever her reasons for that choice may be. **But if she does choose not to put evidence before the court, the court will be able to act only upon the evidence that is before the court.**

56. While there is more evidence than I can set out in this judgment, the upshot nevertheless is that **there is very little evidence indeed before the court about the personal circumstances of either Sir Fred Goodwin or VBN.**

57. Mr Spearman did not ask me to doubt, and there is no reason to doubt, the truth of what VBN stated about the facts of her business and family position and the approaches she and others have received.

THE EVIDENCE OF SIR FRED GOODWIN

58. **Sir Fred Goodwin did not adduce any evidence for the purpose of this application**. But his witness statement of 2 March is before the court. In it he too gives **very little detail** about his personal circumstances.

59. Sir Fred Goodwin stated that:

> "the nature of any **relationship** between me and [VBN] is an entirely private matter. In so far as it is necessary to do so, I am content for the Court to proceed on the basis that there was a **relationship** as stated by The Sun to my representative. I have not disclosed any such **relationship** to the public and it has not been discussed or mentioned in the media. **I am advised that, for the purposes of an application to restrain the misuse of private information, the truth or falsity of The Sun's claims is legally irrelevant and I will not say anything further about it . . .**
>
> **I am a private man. I have never discussed my personal life or relationships in public. . . .**
>
> I believe that publication of the **Confidential information** would also lead

to considerable **intrusive** and disturbing speculation as to my private life and **relationships**, including on the **Internet**. If the **Confidential information** were disclosed publicly, this would inevitably also reach friends, colleagues and other business contacts, not just in the United Kingdom but worldwide. This would have a very substantial impact on the way in which friends, colleagues and business contacts relate to me and therefore **a serious negative impact on my personal life and career".**

60. I infer from this that Sir Fred Goodwin is content that the court proceed on the basis that he did have a **relationship** with VBN, as alleged by The Sun, that he had not told any of his friends or colleagues at work about it, and that his friends and colleagues would view the **relationship with serious disapproval**, albeit for **reasons which are not there set out.**

THE APPLICABLE LAW

61. Mr Spearman for NGN and Mr Tomlinson for VBN each submit that the law requires the application of a two stage test. They cite the decisions of the Court of Appeal in *McKennitt v Ash* [2008] QB 73 at para [11], *Lord Browne of Madingley v Associated Newspapers Ltd* [2008] QB 103 at para [37] and *ETK v News Group Newspapers Ltd* [2011] EWCA Civ 439 at para [10].

62. **Mr Spearman set out the position in his skeleton argument, in terms which I adopt (with some alterations), as follows:**

a. The starting point is the Human Rights Act 1998. By s 6 the court (as a public authority) is required to act compatibly with Convention Rights. By s 1(1) the court is also required to take into account judgments of the European Court of Human Rights ("the Strasbourg court"). That is what Parliament, not the judges, has decided. The Convention rights in question in this case are the rights to freedom of expression of NGN and the right of the general public to receive information, which are protected by Article 10 and by the common law, and the right to respect for private life protected by Art 8. So far as material to the present case these provide:

Article 8

(1) Everyone has the right to respect for his private and family life, his home and his correspondence.

(2) There shall be no interference by a public authority with the exercise of this right except such as is in accordance with the law and is necessary in a democratic society . . . for the protection of the rights and freedoms of others.

Article 10

(1) Everyone has the right to freedom of expression. This right shall

include freedom to hold opinions and to receive and impart information and ideas without interference by public authority and regardless of frontiers.

(2) The exercise of these freedoms since it carries with it duties and responsibilities, may be subject to such formalities, conditions, restrictions or penalties as are prescribed by law and are necessary in a democratic society . . . for the protection of the **reputation** or rights of others, for preventing the disclosure of information received in confidence . . .

b. The exceptions in Article 10 relating to the protection of the **reputation** or rights of others and the disclosure of information received in confidence can apply only where three conditions are satisfied. The restrictions must (a) pursue a legitimate aim or aims, (b) be "prescribed by law" (i.e. be easily accessible and formulated with sufficient precision for the ordinary citizen to rely upon them to regulate his conduct) and (c) be necessary in a democratic society for the protection of the legitimate aim or aims: the protection of the **reputation** or rights of others, or for preventing the disclosure of information received in confidence. They must also be proportionate to the end pursued, securing what is necessary for the protection of these aims and no more.

c. In accordance with the guidance given by the House of Lords in *Re S* [2005] 1 AC 593, Lord Steyn at [17], the correct approach to the balancing exercise where both Article 8 and Article 10 rights are involved is that: (i) neither Article as such has precedence over the other (ii) where the values under the two Articles are in conflict, an intense focus on the comparative importance of the specific rights being claimed in the individual case is necessary (iii) the justifications for interfering with or restricting each right must be taken into account (iv) finally, the proportionality test—or "ultimate balancing test"–must be applied to each.

d. When deciding whether information is in principle protected by Article 8 and, if so, whether Article 8 must yield to some countervailing right or rights, the Court considers the matter in two stages:

(1) The first question is whether there is a reasonable expectation of privacy. This is the **threshold question**, and it is an **objective test**. See *Murray v Express Newspapers plc* [2009] Ch 481, where Sir Anthony Clarke MR said at [35]:

"In these circumstances, so far as the relevant principles to be derived from *Campbell v MGN Ltd* [2004] 2 AC 457 are concerned, they can we think be summarised in this way. The first question is whether there is a reasonable expectation of privacy. This is of course an objective question. The nature of the question was discussed in *Campbell v MGN Ltd*. Lord Hope emphasised that the reasonable expectation was that of the person who is affected by the publicity. He said at [99]: "The question is what a reasonable person of ordinary sensibilities would feel if she was placed in the same position as the claimant and faced with the same publicity." We do not detect any difference between Lord Hope's opinion in this regard and the opinions expressed by the other members of the appellate committee".

(2) If and only if that question is answered in the affirmative, the Court proceeds to the **second part of the two-stage** approach which is laid down by the authorities. See *Murray v Express Newspapers plc* [2009] Ch 481, where Sir Anthony Clarke MR said at [27]:

"[There are] two key questions which must be answered where the complaint is of the wrongful publication of private information. They are, first, whether the information is private in the sense that it is in principle protected by article 8 (ie such that article 8 is in principle engaged), and, secondly**, if so, whether in all the circumstances the interest of the owner of the information must yield to the right of freedom of expression conferred on the publisher by article 10?"**

e. It is also clear from the authorities that the correct application of this approach requires the Court **to give separate consideration to different items or classes of information.** See, for example, *Lord Browne of Madingley v Associated Newspapers Ltd* [2008] QB 103, Sir Anthony Clarke MR at [37]:

"If, in respect of particular information, there is a reasonable expectation of the privacy, article 8 is engaged. The question is then whether interference with those rights should be permitted under article 8.2. Where, as in the present case, the article 8 right is based on the protection of private information, the basis for that interference will usually, though not in every case, be found in the rights and freedoms created by article 10".

f. In addition, because the relief sought will affect the Convention right to freedom of expression of the Defendant(s) and of third parties who are served with the injunction, **s12 HRA applies**. This includes the following:

"12.–(1) This section applies if a court is considering whether to grant any relief which, if granted, might affect the exercise of the Convention right to freedom of expression . . .

(3) No such relief is to be granted so as to restrain publication before trial unless the court is satisfied that the applicant is likely to establish that publication should not be allowed.

(4) The court must have particular regard to the importance of the

Convention right to freedom of expression and, where the proceedings relate to material which the respondent claims, or which appears to the court, to be journalistic, literary or artistic material (or to conduct connected with such material), to-

(a) the extent to which-

(i) the material has, or is about to, become available to the public; or

(ii) it is, or would be, in the public interest for the material to be published;

(b) any relevant privacy code.

g. As to s12(3) HRA, the correct approach appears from decision of the House of Lords in **Cream Holdings Ltd v Banerjee** [2005] 1 AC 253, [22]–[23]. As at the time of a hearing such as the present hearing, the threshold requirement that the applicant for an injunction must satisfy is generally that it is **"more likely than not"** that s/he will be able to establish at trial that publication should not be allowed:

> "As to what degree of likelihood makes the prospects of success 'sufficiently favourable', the general approach should be that courts will be exceedingly slow to make interim restraint orders where the applicant has not satisfied the court he will probably ('more likely than not') succeed at the trial. In general, that should be the threshold an applicant must cross before the court embarks on exercising its discretion, duly taking into account the relevant jurisprudence on article 10 and any countervailing Convention rights."

h. Turning next to s12(4) HRA, so far as concerns journalistic material the Court is required to have regard to **the extent to which such material has or is about to become available to the public, the public interest in publication, and "any relevant privacy code".** The PCC Code of Practice is such a code, and relevant provisions of it include the following:

3.***Privacy**

i) Everyone is entitled to respect for his or her private and family life, home, health and correspondence, including digital communications.

ii) Editors will be **expected to justify intrusions** into any individual's private life without consent. Account will be taken of the complainant's own public disclosures of information.

The public interest

There may be exceptions to the clauses marked * where they can be demonstrated to be in the public interest.

1. The public interest includes, but is not confined to:

i) Detecting or exposing crime or serious impropriety.

ii) Protecting public health and safety.

iii) Preventing the public from being misled by an action or statement of an individual or organisation.

2. There is a public interest in freedom of expression itself.

3. Whenever the public interest is invoked, the PCC will require editors to demonstrate fully that they **reasonably believed that publication, or journalistic activity undertaken with a view to publication, would be in the public interest."**

63. On an application for an interim injunction the effect of s 12(3) is that it is for the applicant to satisfy the court that she is likely to succeed at trial. In the present case, the application is by NGN and it is for a variation of an injunction. But VBN is opposing the application by contending that the injunction granted on the application of Sir Fred Goodwin (and subsequently varied) should be maintained. **She is in the position of an applicant for an injunction. It follows that the burden is upon her to satisfy the court of the matters upon which it is required to be satisfied by HRA s 12.**

64. In the law of privacy there has been some recognition in the authorities of the concept of a **public figure**, defined as those who exercise public or official functions (as appears from the words I have italicised in the following citations).

65. In *Campbell v MGN Ltd* [2004] AC 457 Baroness Hale said at [158–159]:

"There are undoubtedly different types of speech, just as there are different types of private information, some of which are more deserving of protection in a democratic society than others. Top of the list is **political speech**. The free exchange of information and ideas on matters relevant to the organisation of the economic, social and political life of the country is crucial to any democracy. Without this, it can scarcely be called a democracy at all. *This includes revealing information about* **public figures**, *especially those in* **elective office,** *which would otherwise be private but is* **relevant to their participation in public life.** Intellectual and educational speech and expression are also important in a democracy, not least because they enable the development of **individuals' potential to play a full part in society and in our democratic life**. Artistic speech and expression is important for similar reasons, in fostering both individual originality and creativity and the free-thinking and dynamic society we so much value. No doubt there are other kinds of speech and expression for which similar claims can be made. But it is difficult to make such claims on behalf of the publication with which we are concerned here. The political and social life of the community, and the intellectual, artistic or personal development of individuals, **are not obviously assisted by pouring over the intimate details of a fashion model's private life."**

66. In the same case Lord Hoffmann said at [56] and [60]:

"Take the example I have just given of the ordinary citizen whose attendance at NA is publicised in his local newspaper. **The violation of the citizen's autonomy, dignity and self-esteem is plain and obvious**. Do the civil and political values which underlie press freedom make it necessary to deny the citizen the right to protect such personal information? Not at all. While there is no contrary public interest recognised and protected by the law, the press is free to publish anything it likes. Subject to the law of defamation, it does not matter how trivial, spiteful or offensive the publication may be. **But when press freedom comes into conflict with another interest protected by the law, the question is whether there is a sufficient public interest in that particular publication to justify curtailment of the conflicting right**. In the example I have given, **there is no public interest whatever in publishing to the world the fact that the citizen has a drug dependency.** The freedom to make such a statement **weighs little in the balance against the privacy of personal information** . . . The relatively anodyne nature of the additional details is in my opinion important and **distinguishes this case from cases in which (for example) there is a public interest in the disclosure of the existence of a sexual relationship (say, between a politician and someone whom she has appointed to public office)** but the addition of **salacious details or intimate photographs is disproportionate and unacceptable. The latter, even if accompanying a legitimate disclosure of the sexual relationship, would be too intrusive and demeaning."**

67. The majority opinion in *Von Hannover v Germany* (2004) 16 BHRC 545; (2004) EMLR 21 stated (among other things) the following:

"(1) a fundamental distinction needs to be made between reporting facts—even controversial ones—capable of contributing to a debate in a democratic society relating to ***politicians*** *in the exercise of their functions*, for example, **and reporting details of the private life of an individual who, moreover, as in this case, does not exercise official functions.** While in the former case the press exercises its vital role of '**watchdog**' in a democracy by contributing to 'imparting information and ideas on matters of public interest' it does not do so in the latter case" [63];

> (2) . . . the decisive factor in balancing the protection of private life against freedom of expression **should lie in the contribution that the published photos and articles make to a debate of general interest"** [76]".

68. **This test of contribution to a debate of general interest was adopted by the Court of Appeal in *Ntuli v Donald* [2011] 1 WLR 294 at para [20].**

THE SUBMISSIONS OF THE PARTIES

69. There is no dispute that the fact that parties are in a **sexual relationship** may, in principle, be a fact in respect of which they have a reasonable expectation of privacy. What I set out next was not in dispute between the parties, except where indicated.

70. Mr Spearman accepts that where there might otherwise be such an expectation, **it will not necessarily be defeated by the fact that the two parties to the relationship work for the same employer.**

71. In the case of RBS, the RBS Code expressly recognises that RBS **"entirely respects the right of every one of us to form friendships and personal relationships at work".** What the Code requires is that on occasions "it will be appropriate to tell your manager about a **relationship** that may impact on your work by creating a conflict of interest". **As Mr Tomlinson points out, the RBS Code does not require that anyone else be told, and in particular it does not require that the newspapers be told.**

72. In **ETK** at para [11] Ward LJ held that the parties to **the sexual relationship between two people who were working together had a reasonable expectation that their work colleagues who knew about the relationship would keep that information confidential**. But in that **case there was no argument to the effect that the parties to that relationship did not have such a reasonable expectation**, save on the basis that the fact that it was **known to some other** people might itself defeat that expectation (in effect, that it might have been in the **public domain**). **It does not appear to have been a case where one party was a very senior executive and the other an executive of some less senior rank.**

73. There are various categories of information which may be the subject of a reasonable expectation of privacy, and some of these were considered by the courts in *Browne*. Two that are material to the present case were "**(b)** the **alleged misuse** of BP's resources and manpower to support and assist JC" and "**(c)** the **bare fact** of the past **relationship** between JC and Lord Browne". At that time Lord Browne was the group chief executive of BP.

74. At para [53] the Court of Appeal held that **"it was open to the judge to hold that the claimant had no reasonable expectation of privacy with regard to**

the use of BP equipment and resources". The court was approving the reasoning of Eady J at para [50] of his judgment. He had held that the claimant had failed at the first stage of the enquiry. He had asked himself at para [43]:

> "43 . . . One may ask whether there can be a reasonable expectation that the law will protect the privacy of a senior executive, in relation to the use of corporate information and resources, when the effect would be to keep such allegations from those who might ordinarily be expected to make the relevant judgments, or exercise supervision; that is to say, shareholders and colleagues on the board of directors. For example, they might wish to know that a company was set up (to enable JC to deal in ring-tones for mobile phones) with the assistance of [BP] personnel. It is at least accepted by the claimant that his personal assistant helped with "secretarial tasks". The company no longer trades.
>
> 44. Mr Spearman [who then appeared for Lord Browne] has argued that these matters, if they are to be criticised at all, should be regarded as relatively trivial. There is, for example, a dispute as to the *extent* to which [BP] personnel were involved in the project. He may well be right, but it seems to me that it is not desirable for the court to make a value judgment on such behaviour in a corporate context: more specifically, **if the circumstances call for a judgment to be made on relative gravity, it is not for a judge to help him keep the information from those whose right and responsibility it is to make it."**

75. Having upheld the judge's decision on that point, the Court of Appeal went on to consider whether publication of **the bare fact** of the **relationship** between the claimant and JC should be permitted. At para [59] the Court held that there was

> **"a sufficient reason to permit publication of *the bare fact* of the relationship. Publication of the information in categories b) and d) would make no sense without publication of the nature of the relationship between the claimant and JC" (the information in category (d) was an alleged breach of a duty of confidence owed by the claimant to BP in discussing BP's affairs with JC)**.

76. In the present case Mr Spearman did not clearly distinguish in his submissions between the first and the second stages of the court's approach as laid down in cases such as *McKennitt*. As he summarised his written submissions:

> "Any confidentiality or reasonable expectation of privacy that the lady (and [Sir Fred Goodwin]) may succeed in establishing at trial with regard to the revelation of the identity of the lady (or at least the role she had at RBS) would be outweighed by the Article 10 rights of the freedom

of expression of NGN to impart and of the general public to receive information and ideas".

77. Mr Tomlinson submits that the real and only question in the present case is the one that arises at the second stage, and that Mr Spearman had effectively conceded the first stage, namely that Sir Fred Goodwin and VBN did have a reasonable expectation of privacy.

78. It is true that the main weight of Mr Spearman's submissions did appear to be directed mainly to the second stage, but I did not understand him to concede that the first stage was satisfied in this case. **It seems to me that Mr Spearman's submissions are better considered at the first stage of the enquiry. That is how the Court of Appeal approached a similar issue in Browne as I note in para 74 above.**

79. I have sympathy with Mr Tomlinson in that the case for NGN has changed at each hearing of these proceedings (as described above), **and the case advanced before me on this application is a case that could have been, but was not, advanced at an earlier hearing.**

80. Moreover, although the case now advanced on public interest is one that is open to NGN on the basis of the evidence adduced before me, it is remarkable that that is all the evidence that NGN has chosen to advance. As Mr Tomlinson points out, **NGN has not given evidence as the investigation it has made into this matter, it has not asked any questions of VBN, and the only evidence of investigation is the approach to RBS referred to by VBN herself, and the initial and very limited approach to Sir Fred Goodwin on 1 March which caused him to set these proceedings in motion**. Thus it has had to rely on the article in the Financial Times as the only source of information that it has disclosed. There must, of course, also have been a report by a source to NGN about the **relationship, but journalists do not normally disclose their sources**, and it is not surprising that NGN gives no evidence about that.

81. **NGN submits that in this case** there was no reasonable expectation of privacy in respect of this particular **relationship** between Sir Fred Goodwin and VBN, **because he was Chief Executive of RBS at the time and she was an employee holding a senior position**. In the alternative, Mr Spearman submits that, if the second stage is reached**, it is in the public interest that the fact of the relationship be disclosed**. He stresses that all that is in question is the fact of the **relationship**, **not any intimate or salacious details, or even photographs.**

82. Mr Tomlinson submits that a reasonable expectation of privacy is a concept which must be applied with some flexibility in the light of the circumstances of the case. There may be a reasonable expectation of privacy confined to a

very small class of other persons, or one that extends to a larger class, or no such expectation at all.

83. As I understand the submission, it can be illustrated by the examples given in the RBS Code. **So, if two employees of RBS working under a dual control procedure have a close personal relationship with one another, they cannot have a reasonable expectation that their relationship will be kept so private that no one else working for RBS may know about it.** If such a couple were to attempt to keep the fact of their **relationship** unknown to anyone at RBS, then a third employee of RBS who came to know about it would be entitled, and may be bound, to notify a manager at an appropriate level of seniority—**in other words to blow the whistle.**

84. Mr Tomlinson refers to the distinction drawn by the Court in *Browne* at **para 61:**

> **"It appears to us that there is potentially an important distinction between information which is made *available to a person's circle* of friends or work colleagues and *information which is widely published in a newspaper*".**

DISCUSSION

Reasonable expectation of privacy

85. The right to respect for private life embraces more than one concept. Dr Moreham summarises what she calls the two core components of the rights to privacy: **"unwanted access to private information and unwanted access to [or intrusion into] one's . . . personal space"** (see Law of Privacy and the Media (2nd edn, 2011, Warby, Moreham and Christie eds) paras 2.07, 2.08, 2.16 and 12.71). I shall refer to the two components of the right as **"confidentiality"** and **"intrusion".** In 1988 Lord Goff spelt out the distinction between **private facts and official secrets**, and **between the publication of a private fact and the harm that might be caused by a later repetition of the same fact to a different readership**: *Att.-Gen. v Guardian Newspapers (No 2)* [1990] 1 AC 109 at p260E-H. The distinction is **well known to media lawyers**, as illustrated by the following cases. In *Blair v Associated Newspapers Ltd* (QBD, 10 March 2000) Morland J issued an injunction to stop further publication of The Mail on Sunday, **despite widespread publication** of the first edition and the fact that the story had been picked up by other Sunday papers. See also *West v BBC* (QBD, 10 June 2002, Ouseley J), *McMennitt v Ash* [2005] EWHC 3003 (QB), [2006] EMLR 10 para [81]; *X & Y v Persons Unknown* [2006] EWHC 2783 (QB), [2007] EMLR 290 para [64]; *JIH v News Group Newspapers Ltd* [2010] EWHC 2818 (QB); [2011] EMLR 9 paras [58]–[59], *TSE v News Group Newspapers Ltd* [2011] EWHC 1308 paras [29]–[30] and *CTB v News Group Newspapers Ltd* [2011] EWHC 1326 (QB) para [23].

86. The scope of the rights referred to in Art 8 and Art 10(2) is one important respect in which the law of privacy differs from the earlier English law of confidentiality, under which matters such as these came before the courts before about 2000. **The first significant change** in English law came in 1997 when the **Protection from Harassment Act** gave a right to protection from **intrusion.** It was soon recognised that this applied to newspapers: *Thomas v News Group Newspapers Ltd* [2001] EWCA Civ 1233; [2002] EMLR 4 (Law of Privacy and the Media para 10.59). Parliament developed English law further to give protection against **intrusion** by enacting the Human Rights Act 1998. **These developments made legally enforceable the principles already accepted voluntarily by the press in the PCC Code.**

87. The court does not address questions of privacy in terms of generalities. According to the authorities set out above, the question must be whether this particular person (usually a claimant, but here also VBN) has a reasonable expectation of privacy **in respect of the particular information** at issue. **So anyone commenting upon this case without reference to the specific evidence before the court will be approaching the issues in a way in which Parliament has not permitted judges to approach them.**

Confidentiality

88. The particular information at issue in the present **case is *the bare fact* of the relationship between the two individuals concerned**, or, if she is not named, then **the bare fact** of the **relationship** between Sir Fred Goodwin and the lady anonymised as VBN, **together with a description of her position at work with RBS.**

89. In this case the parties both accept that **the *details* of a sexual relationship** is information of a kind which will very commonly give rise to a reasonable expectation of privacy on the part of the individuals concerned, **but details are not what this case is about.**

90. However, **the fact that *details* of a sexual relationship are confidential or private does not necessarily mean that *the bare fact* of a sexual relationship is private** (Law of Privacy and the Media para 5.42). **Ntuli is a clear example of this.** In *Ntuli* the judge at first instance had granted an anonymised claimant an injunction restraining an anonymised defendant from publishing, amongst other information "the fact that the Claimant had a **relationship** with the Defendant" (paras [1] and [7] of the judgment of Maurice Kay LJ). The Court of Appeal varied the injunction, and named the parties. Maurice Kay LJ said at para [55] "**The material in respect of which Mr Donald has been found to have a reasonable expectation of privacy is not detailed in the judgment. The material in the judgment does not attract a reasonable expectation of privacy.**" The material in the judgment which

did **not** attract a reasonable expectation of privacy included the following at para [3]:

> **"The respondent/claimant is Howard Donald, one of the hugely successful "boy band" Take That. He has never married but he has had a number of relationships and he is the father of two children. The appellant/defendant is Adakini Ntuli. She is also a musician but is now a full-time single parent of two children. Mr Donald is not their father. During some of the time since 2000, Mr Donald and Ms Ntuli had a relationship. Its duration and intensity are matters of dispute. They did not cohabit."**

91. **The legal test requires consideration of all the circumstances:** *Murray* para [27]. One difficulty with privacy cases is that the court is often unable to set out all the relevant circumstances in the judgment. **The information not detailed in the judgment in Ntuli may have cast light on why the information that was detailed was held not to attract a reasonable expectation of privacy** and why other information was held to attract that. **Ntuli is not authority for the proposition that the bare fact of a relationship never attracts a reasonable expectation of privacy.**

92. As I have noted above, both Sir Fred Goodwin and VBN have been **reticent as to the circumstances** of this case: paras 54 and 58 above. It is correct (as noted by Sir Fred Goodwin) that **information need not be true in order for it to attract a reasonable expectation of privacy.** But that **does not mean that the circumstances of the parties are irrelevant**. As I have already remarked, **if the parties choose not to give to the court details of the circumstances of their case, the court cannot take them into account.**

93. There are **a number of reasons why the bare fact of a relationship may, or may not, attract a reasonable expectation of privacy.** The question depends on the particular circumstances of each case.

94. One reason why, in particular cases, the parties to a **relationship** will have a reasonable expectation that they can keep the bare fact of it confidential was mentioned in argument. **It is when an abusive family will not allow the couple to be together.** This is a situation well known in the Family Division and the criminal courts, but not yet, to my knowledge, in the context of a privacy injunction. There are literary examples to be found in *Romeo and Juliet*, and the gangster society portrayed in *West Side Story*. **Juliet needed to keep confidential the bare fact of her relationship with Romeo in order to avoid being forced into marriage with a man imposed upon her by her father.** Shakespeare invites the audience to sympathise with Juliet. **The audience will consider that she had a reasonable expectation of privacy, at least for the period until she had exchanged her marriage vows with Romeo and**

they were out of danger from revenge attacks from their violent friends and families.

95. But there is a more mundane reason why the courts **commonly prohibit the disclosure of the bare fact of a relationship**. It is explained by the court of Appeal in *JIH v News Group Newspapers Ltd* [2011] 2 All ER 324, [2011] EMLR 15, [2011] EWCA Civ 42 at **para [35]** as follows:

> "there is much in the point that the media will be generally better able to discover, and report on, what the courts are doing if they can publish (a) details of the type of case (for instance, as in this case, a sexual liaison between an unidentified well known sportsman, in an apparently monogamous **relationship**, and a third party) rather than (b) the name of the individual who is seeking to protect an unspecified aspect of his or her alleged private life by means of an injunction. **As Mr Tomlinson puts it, the former information would normally enable the public to have a much better idea of why the court acted as it did than the latter information."**

96. In other cases the details of the **relationship** have been disclosed in the media in an anonymised form before an injunction is sought, **with the result that if a name is published** it will be linked in readers' minds to the details already known. **So if the court is to give the applicant any protection in such a case, the only means of doing it is to prohibit the publication of the bare fact of a relationship.**

97. **Reasons why the bare fact of a relationship may not attract a reasonable expectation of privacy include the following. In general, parties to a relationship are proud, or at least content, to disclose the relationship. Not all relationships are sexual: relationships** include other family **relationships**, as well as membership of communities of many different kinds, business **relationships** and the like (as recognised in the RBS Code). **The first thing that people generally want to know about one another is the relationships of each other with one another and with other people**. Each person wants to know whether there is any common **relationship**, or any **relationship** which might preclude, or limit, the development or continuation of the **relationship** between the two of them. **The most important information about an acquaintance or colleague is: are they friend or foe, trustworthy or untrustworthy, and what relationship each can form or develop with the other (in the broadest sense of those terms).**

98. **In the case of sexual relationships, this is one reason why in the tradition of England women have generally worn engagement and wedding rings, and married men increasingly wear rings too. It is one reason why marriages and civil partnerships are public institutions. It is one reason why**

spouses and partners often like to take each other with them when they go to meet their friends.

99. **If a person does not wish to disclose an existing relationship, for whatever reason, there is a real risk that that will lead to misunderstanding or deception**. Recent examples in public life abound. In the parliamentary expenses scandal a prominent MP made a claim for accommodation expenses which he should not have made. The claim would have been a proper one, if the person to whom he claimed the money was payable had not been in a **sexual relationship** with the MP**. But it was not proper, because there was a sexual relationship. The problem was not the relationship, but the deception perpetrated in an attempt to keep it confidential.**

100. Returning to the facts of the present case, **the evidence about the relationship of the parties and their personal circumstances which they have put before the court is so *sparse* that I cannot be satisfied that Sir Fred Goodwin and VBN are likely to establish that they have a reasonable expectation of privacy in respect of the *bare fact* of their relationship.**

101. But I do find **that there is one fact in the case which in any event presents an obstacle to them establishing that they have such an expectation**. That fact is that Sir Fred Goodwin was the Chief Executive of RBS, the company for which VBN worked. As Mr Spearman submitted**: "The role of both parties, but perhaps more particularly that of the Claimant, is a matter of legitimate public interest and concern, and (it may be) censure, and these issues can only be ventilated if the lady (or at least her role) can be identified".**

102. **First**, it is obvious that if an employee has a **sexual relationship** with a more senior person in the company **there are any number of possible misunderstandings and grievances** (whether well found or unfounded) that can arise if the fact of the **relationship** is not known, at least to the work colleagues of the more junior of the two partners to the **relationship**. **Colleagues of the junior partner who speak candidly in her presence (whether as whistle blowers or not) about the senior partner without knowing of the relationship could reasonably feel that they had been trapped or misled, if and when the relationship comes to light.** And sooner or later the **relationship** is likely to come to light, as has the **relationship** in the present case. **There are few things that people are more sensitive to than signs that two other people are in a relationship. It is rarely realistic for partners in a relationship to expect that the *bare fact* of their relationship will remain confidential between the two of them for a long or indefinite period.**

103. **Second**, the extent to which men in positions of **power benefit from that power in forming relationships with sexual partners** who **are less senior**

within the same organisation is also a matter which is **of concern to an audience much wider than the work colleagues** of either partner in the **relationship**. In the present case Sir Fred Goodwin had a **reputation** as an exceptionally forceful businessman. And he was Chief Executive of one the largest publicly quoted companies in the United Kingdom, doing business on a global scale. **Whatever limits there may be to the legal concept of a public figure, or of a person carrying out official functions, in my judgment Sir Fred Goodwin came within the definition**. This **distinguishes him from sportsmen and celebrities in the world of entertainment, who do not come within that definition**. But even in the case of sportsmen**, there may be a public interest if the sexual relationship gives rise to conflicts with professional interest or duties, for example to his team.**

104. **For these reasons I am *not* satisfied that VBN will establish that she ever had a reasonable expectation of privacy in respect of the *bare fact* of her relationship with Sir Fred Goodwin.**

105. One circumstance which has not influenced me in reaching this decision is the fact that, after Sir Fred Goodwin had ceased to be Chief Executive Officer, RBS came to be under **the effective control of the state. That does not seem to me to affect this point materially**. But if it does, then it can only strengthen the point.

106. But that is not the end of the matter. **I accept the submission of Mr Tomlinson that there are *degrees of privacy*.** What matters in this application is whether, notwithstanding the conclusion I have reached so far, **nevertheless there remained a reasonable expectation of privacy held by Sir Fred Goodwin and VBN in the circumstances of this case such that the court should prohibit the disclosure in the press of the name or the *work position* of VBN.**

107. In the case of Sir Fred Goodwin the question of whether he should be named no longer arises. **On 19 May he accepted that he should be named**. It will be clear from what I have said above that, on the evidence before the court, **I take the view that he was well advised to accept this (albeit that the reasons I have given are in addition to the reasons why he made the concession he did make on 19 May: his reasons related to the publicity that had already occurred that day).**

108. But the fact that his identity as the claimant has now been published in the media **has enabled Mr Tomlinson to submit that the name of Sir Fred Goodwin and the fact that VBN is a work colleague is the only information that should be published**, and that no further variation of the injunction should be made.

109. I repeat that in this part of my judgment **I am considering privacy in the**

sense of *confidentiality*, and will consider intrusion or harassment separately. Given the position in public life that Sir Fred Goodwin held at the time when the **relationship** was formed, **I take the same view in the present case as Maurice Kay LJ** expressed in *Ntuli* at para [55] as follows:

> **"Provided that publicity is limited to what is contained in this judgment, there is no justification for continued anonymity.** I have in mind the judgment of Lord Rodger in *Guardian News and Media Ltd* [2010] 2 WLR 325, [2010] UKSC 1, at paragraphs 63–64."

110. And since this case has attracted so much publicity, readers of this judgment should be able know what Lord Rodger said without having to follow that link. Lord Rodgers was talking about freezing orders in the context of anti-terrorism legislation. He said:

> "63**. What's in a name? "A lot", the press would answer.** This is because stories about particular individuals are simply much more attractive to readers than stories about unidentified people. It is just human nature. And this is why, of course, even when reporting major disasters, journalists usually look for a story about how particular individuals are affected. Writing stories which capture the attention of readers is a matter of reporting technique, and the European Court holds that article 10 protects not only the substance of ideas and information **but also the form in which they are conveyed**: *News Verlags GmbH & Co KG v Austria* (2001) 31 EHRR 8, para 39, quoted at para 35 above. More succinctly, Lord Hoffmann observed in *Campbell v MGN Ltd* [2004] 2 AC 457, 474, para 59, "**judges are not newspaper editors."** See also Lord Hope of Craighead in *In re British Broadcasting Corpn* [2009] 3 WLR 142, 152, para 25. This is not just a matter of deference to editorial independence. **The judges are recognising that editors know best how to present material in a way that will interest the readers of their particular publication and so help them to absorb the information.** A requirement to report it in some austere, abstract form, devoid of much of its human interest, could well mean that the report would not be read and the information would not be passed on. **Ultimately, such an approach could threaten the viability of newspapers and magazines, which can only inform the public if they attract enough readers and make enough money to survive.**
>
> 64. Lord Steyn put the point succinctly in *In re S* [2005] 1 AC 593, 608, para 34, when he stressed the importance of bearing in mind that
>
>> "from a newspaper's point of view a report of a sensational trial without revealing the identity of the defendant would be a very much **disembodied** trial. If the newspapers choose not to contest such an

injunction, they are less likely to give prominence to reports of the trial. Certainly, **readers will be less interested and editors will act accordingly. Informed debate about criminal justice will suffer."**

Mutatis mutandis, the same applies in the present cases. A report of the proceedings challenging the freezing orders which did not reveal the identities of the appellants would be **disembodied**. **Certainly, readers would be less interested and, realising that, editors would tend to give the report a lower priority. In that way informed debate about freezing orders would suffer."**

111. The reasons that VBN has given in her brief evidence in support of maintaining the injunction all relate to **intrusion**. I shall consider them under that heading. So far as **confidentiality** is concerned, in my judgment **VBN does not have a right to keep the fact of the relationship confidential**, or, to the extent that she does, then it **would not be necessary or proportionate to restrict NGN's freedom of expression to prevent disclosure of that information. Her position at work, and to a lesser extent her name, are each important parts of the story, for the reasons given by Lord Rodger.**

112. If VBN's position in RBS were at a level at which there are many other women, it might be possible to identify her position in the company without identifying herself. But in the present case that is not likely to be possible. **Her position is sufficiently senior that identification of her status or the department in which she works is likely to identify her name**. It was on this basis that **VBN asked me to refer to the Attorney-General the information published in the Daily Mail.**

Intrusion

113. NGN has been criticised in the courts for **intrusion** and **harassment** on more than one occasion in relation to The Sun. But other readers of this judgment may be less familiar than NGN with the distinction in privacy law between **confidentiality** and **intrusion**.

114. In **Thomas** The Sun had published a number of articles referring to the claimant. In two of these she was described as a 'black clerk', and the paper criticised her involvement in a dispute over a racist comment made by police officers at her place of work (paras [5] and [9]). **The Sun disclosed her name and work address.** The court recognised that there are many actions that foreseeably alarm or cause a person distress that could not possibly be described as **harassment** (para [29]). The court stated that "**In general, press criticism, even if robust, does not constitute unreasonable conduct and does not fall within the natural meaning of harassment**" (para [34]). The court held that it was at least arguable that it was foreseeable that the publication of the articles complained of by Ms Thomas would lead

Sun readers to address hostile letters to her, causing her additional distress (para [46]). **The court stated that the test for whether the articles amount to harassment**

> "requires the publisher to consider whether a proposed series of articles, **which is likely to cause distress to an individual**, will constitute an abuse of the freedom of press **which the pressing social needs of a democratic society** require should be curbed".

115. The fact that Ms **Thomas** was black was obviously not something which was claimed to be confidential. Nor did she claim that her name or place of work were confidential. **What she complained of was harassment**. She complained that the cause of her **distress** and **fear** was the **repetition** in the articles of these personal facts concerning her. Of course that judgment was on an application to strike out the claim, and so in refusing to strike out the claim **the Court was not reaching any conclusion other than that the case was arguable.**

116. In that case Ms Thomas's claim was under the 1997 Act, and under that Act the definition o**f harassment** ***includes a requirement that there be a course of conduct which is unreasonable.*** **Intrusion which the court could prohibit under the Human Rights Act does not necessarily have to amount to harassment within the meaning of the 1997 Act. But the test will otherwise be substantially the same.**

117. More recent occasions on which NGN has been criticised for **Intrusion** are *Mosley v News Group Newspapers Ltd* [2008] EWHC 1777 (Eady J at first instance) and *Mosley v The United Kingdom*-48009/08 [2011] ECHR 774 (10 May 2011, by the Strasbourg court). The Court endorsed the criticisms made by Eady J of NGN, saying that case:

> "the newspaper was required to pay GBP 60,000 damages, approximately GBP 420,000 in respect of the applicant's costs and an unspecified sum in respect of its own legal costs in defending the claim. The Court is of the view that such awards can reasonably be expected to have a salutary effect on journalistic practices."

118. I accept that on the facts of the present case the fears of **intrusion** expressed by VBN are **well founded** to the extent relevant in this application. Thus I am satisfied that **she would be likely** to establish that publication by NGN of any information ***in addition*** **to her name and job description** (and the information contained in this judgment) **would be likely to cause distress to her which would constitute an abuse of the freedom of press which the pressing social needs of a democratic society require should be curbed**. So in my view NGN is well advised in not seeking a variation of the injunction which would permit it to publish more information than that.

119. **The issue between the parties is limited to VBN's name and job description: see para 33 above**. But even that issue is a **narrow** one. Mr Spearman expressly submitted that VBN's name was not significant. **He said it was her role that was significant, but that as soon as her role is published it will tend to identify her name.**

120. I consider first whether **VBN's name** should be published. In my judgment **publication in The Sun (or any other print or broadcast medium) of VBN's name would be a *significant* intrusion into her private and family life from which she is entitled to be protected** (as she is **likely** to establish at trial). And I am satisfied that **she is likely to establish that the interference with NGN's Art 10 right which would be involved in prohibiting publication of her name is *necessary* and *proportionate* for the protection of that right of hers.**

121. I consider next whether **the *role* or *job description*** of VBN should be published. **While publication of her job description would lead many people to identify her, and would also be an intrusion into her private and family life, in my judgment the information about her job description is an *important feature* of the story**. I am **not satisfied that she is likely to establish that the interference with NGN's Art 10 right, which would be involved in prohibiting publication of her job description, is necessary and proportionate for the protection of her rights.**

122. There is a further reason**. As VBN's evidence makes clear, her name has already become known to some of her acquaintances, in some cases by reason of publications outside the press and broadcast media. The additional publication of her name that is likely to follow from publication of her role in the press and broadcast media is not, in my judgment, likely to be so great a *further* intrusion into her private life as to make it necessary and proportionate to interfere with the Art 10 rights of NGN.**

123. **Accordingly, I shall vary the injunction to remove the prohibition upon publication of VBN's *job description*, while leaving in place the prohibition upon publication of her *name*.**

124. In reaching this decision I am aware that many individuals with access to blogs and other **internet** means of communication may publish the name of VBN. **If my purpose was to keep her name confidential, that would render the injunction futile, and I would not adopt the course I have decided upon**. Courts do not grant injunctions that would be futile.

125. But the degree of intrusion into a person's private life which is caused by internet publications is different from the degree of intrusion caused by print and broadcast media. Important though this story is, there are very many people who will not take the trouble to find out from VBN's job description what her name is. And there are many people who would not be sufficiently interested in the story to learn VBN's name unless it were exposed in The Sun. They include people who would not normally read a story about Sir Fred Goodwin or RBS, but would read a story about VBN, because they already know VBN. **As everybody knows, there is a big difference between making a criticism without naming names and making a criticism of named individuals.** This is so even if, in the former case, most readers or listeners in fact known the names of the individuals at whom the criticism is addressed. **Once a person's name appears on a newspaper or other media archive, it may well remain there indefinitely. Names mentioned on *social networking* sites are *less likely* to be permanent.**

126. Some people who have commented on this litigation have made comparisons between English law and the law of the USA. They should know that of the three examples produced by NGN of other cases of chief executives in **sexual relations** with work colleagues (para 43 above), two are reported in English newspapers and one in an American newspaper. **The name of the lady concerned is given in each of the English newspapers. In the American newspaper, The New York Times, neither her name nor her role is given.** She is referred to there as "a female Boeing executive".

127. **There is another case which also illustrates why it can be appropriate for the court to anonymise a party whose name can be readily discovered by a reader of a judgment**, if that reader is sufficiently motivated to follow up the references. It is *A v United Kingdom* 35373/97 [2002] ECHR 811; (2003) 36 EHRR 51. In that case the applicant had been named by an MP in Parliament as the "neighbour from hell" about whom the MP's constituents were complaining. As a result she was named in the newspapers. Before the Strasbourg court the applicant sought to challenge the doctrine of Parliamentary privilege in so far as it provides an absolute defence to a claim for defamation. She failed.

128. But the Strasbourg Court recorded that there is no means by which a person may obtain redress for any injustice or harm a person may suffer by reason of being named in Parliament, and in the consequential press reports of the Parliamentary debate. Before the Strasbourg court the applicant denied the truth of the majority of the allegations. **The MP never tried to communicate with her regarding the complaints made about her by her neighbours, and never attempted to verify the accuracy of his comments made in his speech either before or after the debate.**

129. The result of her being named in Parliament in this way was catastrophic for her and her family. The court described the consequences as follows:

> "15. The applicant was approached by journalists and television reporters asking for her response to the MP's allegations and her comments were

summarised in each newspaper the same day, although they were not given as much prominence.

16. The applicant subsequently received hate mail addressed to her at 50 Concorde Drive. One letter stated that she should "be in houses with your own kind, not in amongst decent owners". Another letter [contained a tirade of abuse]

17. The applicant was also stopped in the street, spat at and abused by strangers as "the neighbour from hell".

18. On 7 August 1996 a report was prepared for the SHA by a group which monitors racial **harassment** and attacks. The report found that "it has now come to the point where [the applicant] has been put in considerable danger as a result of her name being released to the public". The report recommended that the applicant be re-housed as a matter of urgency. She was re-housed in October 1996 and her children were obliged to change schools."

130. **Notwithstanding the extensive publicity given to her name in Parliament and in the consequential press reports, the Strasbourg court anonymised the title of the judgment and did not repeat the applicant's name.** No doubt the court was concerned not to precipitate further **intrusion** and **harassment.** That is my concern in this case, albeit that I would not expect that the **intrusion** into the life of VBN and her family to be as grossly offensive as the **intrusion** that happened in that case.

Public interest

131. In the light of the conclusion that I have reached on reasonable expectation of privacy, **the question of public interest at the second stage of the enquiry does not arise**. However, I shall state may findings on the arguments in case I am held to be wrong on the conclusions that I have reached.

132. If I had held that in respect of the **relationship** between Sir Fred Goodwin and VBN either of them was likely to establish that they had a reasonable expectation of keeping the matter private (in the sense of confidential), I would have held that they were not likely to establish that publication of the job description of VBN should be prohibited. In my judgment the position of Sir Fred Goodwin as Chief Executive of RBS is a matter which NGN would be likely to establish in light of the position that it is in the public interest for it to publish.

133. I do not reach this conclusion on the ground that NGN would thereby expose serious impropriety, still less crime**. I reach it because in my judgment it is in the public interest that there should be public discussion of the circumstances in which it is proper for a chief executive (or other person holding public office or exercising official functions) should be able to carry on a**

sexual relationship with an employee in the same organisation. It **is in the public interest that newspapers should be able to report upon cases which raise a question as to what should or should not be a standard in public life**. The law, and standards in public life, must develop to meet changing needs. **The public interest cannot be confined to exposing matters which are improper only by existing standards and laws, and not by standards as they ought to be, or which people can reasonably contend that they ought to be.**

134. On the evidence before me I am satisfied that Sir Fred Goodwin or VBN would be likely to establish that the trial judge should make no finding of any breach of the RBS Code. There is no evidence in this court of such a breach, (assuming, in any event, that the question whether there is a breach or not is a matter for this court to decide).

135. **On the evidence before me I am also satisfied that Sir Fred Goodwin or VBN would be likely to defeat any case NGN might make to the effect that the relationship between them had an impact on the financial difficulties of RBS**. I regard the suggestion as most implausible, and there is no evidence before me to support it.

136. But there is a further reason. **Everyone has difficulties in life which might distract them from doing whatever job they hold.** A senior executive will commonly have a family. Families give rise to any number of serious concerns that can be distracting. Family members suffer illness and bereavement. Children encounter difficulties at school or university, and difficulties with their friends. These can be very worrying for parents. As a matter of principle, the right to respect for private life of persons holding responsible positions cannot be overridden in the interests of freedom of expression simply because a newspaper alleges that they might have a worry that might distract them from doing their jobs. If there really is distraction, and the newspaper can put the evidence for it before the court, then it may be that the fact of the distraction can be reported. Such evidence might that the person falls asleep at meetings, or misses them altogether It may be possible to report that without interfering with the person's private life.

137. **It cannot be right that the press should be free to interfere with a person's private and family life by exposing confidential information, and then seek to justify that by speculating that the information might have distracted him from doing his job**. In the present case there **is no evidence that Sir Fred Goodwin was distracted from doing his job by his relationship with VBN. It is speculation by NGN.**

138. As Mr Spearman submitted the law is as follows:

"In order to establish a public interest defence at trial the defendant does not necessarily have to establish that the allegation which it proposes to make (or may already have made) by way of use of the (ex hypothesi) private or **confidential information** is true. See Lord Goff in *A-G v Guardian Newspapers Ltd (No 2) [Spycatcher]* [1990] 1 AC 109, 283:

'In any event, a mere allegation of iniquity is not of itself sufficient to justify disclosure in the public interest. Such an allegation will only do so if, following such investigations as are reasonably open to the recipient, and having regard to all the circumstances of the case, the allegation in question can reasonably be regarded as being a credible allegation from an apparently reliable source. (emphasis added by Mr Spearman)'"

139. **On the evidence before me, NGN has failed to show that it has conducted such investigations as are reasonably open to it to support the allegations it makes that there has been any breach of the RBS Code, or that Sir Fred Goodwin was distracted from his job as Chief Executive by the relationship with VBN.**

THE JUDGMENTS OF HENRIQUES AND SHARP JJ

140. Nothing in this judgment should be taken as expressing or implying any disagreement on my part with anything said or done by Henriques J or Sharp J.

141. On the contrary, I can say with confidence that if I had been the judge at the hearings on 1 and 4 March, and if the same submissions had been made to me as NGN made to those judges, I would not have said or done anything different. I repeat that neither NGN nor any third party had put any evidence before either of those two judges. The case advanced to me by NGN on this application is a case which NGN expressly disavowed at the hearing on 1 March, and on 4 March NGN did not oppose the grant of an injunction.

142. **The case advanced on this application is an entirely new case.** The hearing before me is the fourth occasion the case has come before a judge, but is the first occasion on which the court has had from NGN's side the benefit of evidence in the form of written witness statements and written submissions from counsel. There was no time for those to be prepared before the hearing on 1 March. And on 1 March Mr Spearman had to respond to the application made by Sir Fred Goodwin with virtually no time to reflect on the submissions that could best be made for NGN. It is no criticism of him that he did not advance on 1 March the arguments that he advanced before me.

143. It might have been expected that on 4 March there would have been the full argument that was advanced before me. But that did not happen. The continuation of the injunction was not opposed. That was a decision by NGN made for reasons which have not been explained in evidence.

144. On many occasions since 1 March people have commented publicly on the case, criticising the injunction in the pages of newspapers and elsewhere. **Much of this reporting contained many factual errors about the case, as I have noted above**. Judges read newspapers, but judges cannot vary court orders on the basis of what the public are told by the media**. If persons affected by a court order want it to be varied, they must make an application to the court**. As appears from the events of 19 May, they can do this quickly and informally, if it is urgent.145. English law develops in two ways. **First,** it is made by Parliament. The **Prevention from Harassment Act 1997** and the Human Rights Act 1997 are two privacy statutes referred to in this judgment. **Second** it is developed by case law, as judges apply the statute to particular cases. At the second stage it is essential that the parties to litigation put their evidence and submissions before the court. It is by weighing up arguments and counter arguments that judges are best able to interpret the law. The circumstances of injunctions applied for out of hours on the telephone are not favourable to a considered development of the law. That is one reason why judges order cases to come back before the court for full consideration on the evidence. That happened on 4 March. **But there was no argument then because NGN chose not to argue its case. And other media organisation notified of the injunction chose not to argue the case in court.** To the extent that media defendants choose not to submit evidence and **argument to the courts, judges will find it difficult to develop the law of privacy to meet the needs of society**.

CONCLUSION

146. For the reasons given above, this application succeeds in part and fails in part. The injunction will be varied to permit disclosure by NGN of the job description of VBN, but not disclosure of her name.

147. This judgment in draft to enable the parties to correct errors and omissions. The suggestions of the parties have been incorporated into the final version. At the same time I invited the parties to submit a form of order to be agreed if possible, or settled at the time the judgment is handed down.

148. Notwithstanding the decision I have reached**, I have not identified in this judgment the job description of VBN. The reason is that my decision may be the subject of an appeal**. By drafting it in the form I have, my intention is that it can be published and reported in full immediately, whether or not there is an appeal. **Nor have I given details of all the evidence submitted to the court. That is not possible, since it would disclose private information.** As with many **judgments in privacy cases, the fact that some of the evidence cannot be revealed, and the complicated provisions of the law, each requires the judge to write the judgment in ways that make it difficult to read.**

149. On 8 June solicitors to NGN sent to me copies of an exchange of letters between themselves and RBS dated 2, 7 and 8 June. On 2 June the solicitors had asked RBS to provide information about the internal enquiry regarding this matter. On 7 June RBS declined to do so. It stated that it could confirm that RBS had been contacted by the FSA in connection with this matter and is co-operating fully. On 8 June the solicitors wrote to RBS objecting it taking this stance. I have added this paragraph to the judgment in the light of para 29, which is in the form of the draft that was circulated.

NEJ v Helen Wood and Persons Unknown [2011] EWHC 1972 (QB)

MR JUSTICE KING:

1. This is the return date of the order made by Mr Justice Blake on 9th April 2011 preventing disclosure of private information relating to the applicant. In the form as ordered by Mr Justice Blake, **it prevents publication by reference to the confidential schedule, of sexual relationships between the claimant applicant and any woman in Dublin, Ireland in December 2009 and of information of photographs or film taken in Dublin at the time of sexual relationships referred to above.**
2. In the form granted, it has provision preventing any publication of any information concerning the facts of the case and individuals involved, **save for that containing the order and that in any public judgment given in the action.** There is provision for **anonymity,** and **for confidential information** in the statements of case, and also for **the hearing to be in private** and for the restriction on the provision of documents and information to third parties. I do not for present purposes go into the fine detail of the orders made in this respect.
3. **The basic facts underlying this application are that the applicant is an actor, well-known to the public. He accepts on the material I have seen that he has had sexual encounters with a prostitute. He is a married man, and he is a father.**
4. The named first respondent **Miss Helen Wood, who was originally granted anonymity by Mr Justice Blake, is the prostitute concerned.** In the order of Mr Justice Blake, there was a second respondent, namely the person unknown who has offered information about the applicant to the publishers of The Sun newspaper. Before me today, Mr Tomlinson QC appears for the applicant and Mr Spearman QC appears for News Group Newspapers Limited, the publishers of The Sun. **It is clear that the prostitute concerned is the person who has offered information about the applicant to the pub-**

lishers of The Sun newspaper. There is no issue on the material before me that she seeks through The Sun newspaper to publish her account, as it is put, of the shared sexual experience with the applicant. She herself does not seek anonymity.

5. Before identifying the crucial issue which arises before me as between Mr Tomlinson and Mr Spearman and minded that I am that **the first respondent herself is not before me,** I rehearse the basic principles applicable to the grant of this type of order, set out in Section 12 of the Human Rights Act 1998. I start with section 12(1), which provides:

   "This section applies if the court is considering whether to grant any relief which if granted might affect the exercise of the convention right to freedom of expression."

   Sub-section 3 provides:

   "No such relief is to be granted so as to restrain publication before trial unless the court is satisfied the applicant is likely to establish that publication should not be allowed."

   I interpose that it is well-established through the House of Lords decision in *Cream Holdings v Banerjee* [2005] 1 AC 253 that to construe "likely" in the sub-section as meaning " more likely than not in all situations" would be to set the test too high. The effect of the sub-section is that the court should not make an interim restraint order unless satisfied that the applicant's prospects of success are sufficiently favourable to justify the order being made in the light of all the circumstances in the case. In general, the threshold the applicant has to cross before the court embarks on exercising its discretion is to satisfy the court he would probably succeed at a trial.

   Sub-section (4) provides:

   "The court must have particular regard to the importance of the Convention right to freedom of expression, and, where the proceedings relate to material which the respondent claims, or which appears to the court to be journalistic, literary, or artistic material (or to conduct connected with such material) to- (a) the extent to which (I) the material has or is about to become available to the public; or (ii) is or would be, in the public interest for the material to be published; (b) any relevant privacy code."

6. I turn first to consider whether I am satisfied that the applicant is **likely** to establish that publication should not be allowed at trial. In my judgment, that threshold is crossed insofar as the proposed publication would identify the applicant and would go into the detail of his sexual encounters with the respondent.

My reasoning I can put shortly. I have first to be satisfied that the applicant is likely to establish at trial that the information concerned is private in the sense that it is in principle protected by Article 8 of the European Convention on Human Rights Convention. **Put another way, I have to be satisfied that the applicant is likely to establish at trial that the information concerned has the necessary quality of confidence about it, in that by its very nature the applicant has a reasonable expectation that it should be kept private**. I am satisfied that the applicant is likely to establish that he has a reasonable expectation that that which he does in his private life by way of sexual encounters **albeit with a prostitute, should be kept private.**

7. But then of course before I can say that he is likely to establish the publication would not be allowed at trial, I have to consider whether there is any countervailing public interest, likely to be found by the court at trial as being in favour of publication, and likely to outweigh that claim to privacy. It is at this stage that the court has to have in mind the competing rights of the applicant under Article 8, and those, both of the respondent herself and the media, in particular in this context The Sun newspaper, under Article 10 of the European Convention.

8. It is always worth rehearsing what Article 10 says:

> "Everyone has the right to freedom of expression. This right should include freedom to hold opinions and receive and import information, ideas, without interference by public authority and regardless of frontiers."

But of course paragraph 2 of Article 10 has the qualification:

> "The exercise of these freedoms since it carries with it duties and responsibilities may be subject to such formalities, conditions, restrictions or penalties prescribed by law and are necessary in a democratic society . . . for the protection of the . . . rights of others, for preventing the disclosure of information received in confidence . . ."

9. In fact, **no one has submitted before me** that there is any countervailing public interest, even taking on board the full impact of Article 10, in the full publication of the applicant's identity and the full publication of all the details of the sexual encounter concerned. **This is not a case in which it has been submitted that because of any public stance taken by the applicant with regard to his marital status or with regard to issues of morality, that he should be exposed in the public interest as, for example, a hypocrite**. I am satisfied on the material before me that there would be no justification for a finding that there was a public interest in such full publication on this or any other basis. **This is why I am satisfied that the applicant is likely to establish that the publication should not be allowed,** and subject to what

I am now going to consider, I am satisfied that in principle the applicant is entitled to an interim injunction designed to prevent his identification and his identification as someone who has been involved in such sexual encounters in private with a prostitute.

10. **Mr Tomlinson himself accepts that the respondent herself has an Article 10 right to share with the public her experiences so long as that which is published does not in any way identify the applicant**. He accepts that in the interests of the respondent herself in Article 10 terms and indeed of the public generally in Article 10 terms**, that there should be some publication of some information concerning her sexual encounters with a person of the applicant's status.**

11. **The point being emphasised by Mr Tomlinson is rather that the court should be slow to permit any publication which would tend to identify the applicant,** and in particular the court should be slow to permit a process of jigsaw **identification** so that little by little the applicant's identity can be revealed. **On the other hand, Mr Spearman has put a strong argument before me that there is a public interest that the media should be enabled to debate in public the general issue of the grant by the courts of this type of injunction the effect of which is to protect the private life of those who have public persona.**

12. I accept that which Mr Spearman says to me, namely that there is a live public debate about the justification for the grant of these injunctions which can have the effect of suppressing from public scrutiny the private conduct of public persons, **which some might think offend notions of social morality according to one's view of social morality.** This is a different point from that which is not being pursued before me in this particular case, namely that there is a public interest in the publication of the applicant's identity in respect of his private conduct, on the basis that it shows him up as a hypocrite in his public presentation.

13. Put shortly, the applicant through Mr Tomlinson accepts that there should be a qualification to the order granted by Mr Justice Blake in paragraph 1 of the injunction so that the proviso would now read:

> **"Provided that nothing in this paragraph of this order shall prevent the publication, communication or disclosure of the fact that the respondent had a sexual relationship with a prominent person who works in the entertainment industry and the respondent's account of that relationship."**

In the order granted by Mr Justice Blake, that proviso did not appear, the only material proviso being that nothing should prevent in effect publication of any material which before service of the order was already in or that which thereafter comes in to the **public domain** as the result of national media publication (other than as a result of breach of the order or a breach of confidence or privacy).

14. Mr Spearman seeks an order which would be more particular in the description of the class of person to which the applicant belongs. **By way of counter concession, Mr Tomlinson would accept Mr Spearman's proposed use of the phrase 'a world famous celebrity' and would accept 'a leading actor' as a description.** Mr Tomlinson's point however is that to put further detail into the description and **to include the fact of the applicant being married and being a father, would go too far and would raise too high a risk of his being identified.**

15. As always in a case of this sort, the court is having to balance competing rights and interests. I have already indicated that I am satisfied that the applicant is likely to establish at trial the right to keep private his identity and to keep private the fact of his personal sexual encounters conducted in private. It is perhaps stating the obvious that not only is he likely to establish, as I have found, the reasonable expectation that these matters should be kept private, **but the impact of any publication of these matters upon him and his family, who themselves have Article 8 rights, would be significant.**

16. Mr Tomlinson fairly emphasises to me that I have to have regard to the way in which such publication even in the form which it is accepted should be published, will be **intrusive** upon him personally and those who know already that it refers to him. On the other hand, I accept the principle that limitations on the freedom of expression should only be those which are necessary in order to protect the competing rights in this instance of the applicant, and that "necessity" should be the touchstone in a democratic society. **I also accept that there is a public interest in a public debate concerning whether injunctions of this sort should be granted.**

17. Ultimately, the decision I come to is one of discretion.

18. Mr Spearman did put before me as a freestanding ground for permitting publication, that that which he seeks to be allowed to publish **is in fact already in the public domain. He has drawn to my attention articles published today by the Daily Telegraph, but in particular by the Daily Mail newspaper. The Mail article is headed prominently, "Actor wins injunction over private life claims".**

19. Mr Spearman prays in aid the general *"Spy Catcher"* principle concerning that which is in the **public domain**, namely that the court should not seek to achieve the impossible and prevent further publication of that which is already public.

20. This, of course, is to express the principle too broadly. **The Daily Mail have**

not appeared in front of me, but my provisional view is that that which has been published in the Daily Mail is a breach of the order of Mr Justice Blake in the terms it was granted. Paragraph 1(a) of that injunction, subject for present purposes to immaterial provisos, **prevented publication of any information concerning the facts of this case and the individuals involved**, including in particular any information identifying in any way or intended to identify the applicant as being the person applying for this order, save for that contained in this order and in any public judgment the court has given in this action. This article on its face would appear to amount to publication of information concerning the facts of this case going beyond the publication allowed for in that Order

21. This provisional view leads me, despite the strong submissions of Mr Spearman, not to put any significant weight in coming to the decision I have, on the fact of this publication by the Daily Mail. **If it were the case that a publication in breach or apparent breach of an existing court order would of necessity compel a court on the return date of the order, to the conclusion that because the dam has been breached there is nothing the court can do to repair the breach, this would be a sad day for the rule of law**. The court should not readily condone such breaches of court orders, if ultimately of course it be established there have been such breaches. I stress of course that my view on the question of breach is only a provisional one.

22. **In my judgment, there has not been such widespread publication of that which appears in the Daily Mail today as to lead to the inevitable conclusion that there is no justification either in law or in terms of practicality in continuing the order of Mr Justice Blake.** I much prefer to approach this case on the basis I have, which is to assess and weigh against each other the competing rights of the applicant to privacy (and indeed those of his family), and those of the respondent and the media in freedom of expression.

23. Ultimately what I have concluded is that the respondent and the media should be allowed **to publish the fact that the respondent has had a sexual relationship with a leading actor, and indeed, if they so wish, to include the expression of his being a world famous celebrity**. I will also allow publication of the fact that the actor is married and a father. It seems to me that this is material to the public debate about the class of person who is seeking these injunctions and the status they are seeking to protect when preventing the publication of private sexual encounters. In many ways, the debate before me has been about the extent of the particularity which is justified, in the description which is to be published of the class of person from whom the applicant comes.

24. **I do not consider that the risk of the applicant being identified by publication of the fact that he is a leading actor, married, and a father is such that**

this should lead me to conclude that it is necessary in Convention terms for the Press to be prevented from publishing to the extent I have indicated.

25. This deals with the main issue between Mr Tomlinson and Mr Spearman, but I should record that I am satisfied that there is justification for the continuation of the other aspects of restrictions on open justice contained within the order of Mr Justice Blake and then the draft order before me.

26. I repeat that those restrictions do not now include restriction on the publication of the identity of the respondent. There is however justification for anonymity of the applicant since without such an anonymity order the **purpose** of the order I now grant will be wholly frustrated unless of course this court chooses not to give any sort of judgment publicly accessible. **As has been said with authority in the Court of Appeal, the better preference must be for an anonymity order coupled with a public transcript which allows the public to understand why an order has been made, and indeed to identify the class of person to whom the applicant does not belong, for example a politician or other holder of public office, and to enable the public to understand what is not being restricted, for example publication of wrongdoing in public office.**

27. **I am also satisfied that there is justification for the restrictions on access to the court file and for orders restricting the provision of documents and information to third parties and general restrictions on the preservation of the hearing papers.** I have already in this hearing ruled that this hearing itself should be heard in private and that there should be no reporting of the same, save for the reporting of any public judgment of the court, and the order itself. I have had regard in this context to the provisions of CPR Part 39.2 sub-paragraphs 3(a), (c) and (g). In the round, these restrictions are justifiable in order to prevent the **purpose** of this order being frustrated.

28. For all these reasons, I will continue the injunction in principle, but subject to the provisos I have indicated and subject to any other submissions being made to me.

Christopher Hutcheson (Formerly known as "KGM") v News Group Newspapers Ltd and Ors [2011] EWCA Civ 808

Lord Justice Gross

INTRODUCTION

1. This has been the appeal of the Appellant, "KGM" as he was originally styled,

from the Judgment of Eady J, dated 1st December, 2010 ("the judgment"), refusing him a "privacy" injunction against the First Respondent ("NGN"). The judgment also dealt with an issue which arose between KGM and the Second and Third Respondents ("MGN" and "ANL" respectively).

2. **At the conclusion of the hearing, we indicated that KGM's appeal in respect of NGN would be dismissed, with our reasons to follow. These are my reasons.**

3. Various consequences followed from giving our decision at once. **First,** it necessarily followed that KGM can now be referred to by his name—Mr Christopher Hutcheson ("Mr Hutcheson")–a course I propose to follow in this judgment. **Secondly**, this judgment can be and is a public judgment. **Thirdly**, there was no longer any need for the judgment of Eady J to remain a Judgment in Private, albeit that some very few redactions remain in place, for extraneous reasons which need not take up time here. **Fourthly**, the issue between Mr Hutcheson and MGN and ANL became academic, so that no more need be said of it.

4. In essence these proceedings concerned Mr Hutcheson's application to restrain NGN from publishing information in the **following categories**:

   i) As to the fact of his **relationship** with Frances Styles;

   ii) As to the fact that he is the father of Christopher and Victoria (of whom more below);

   iii) As to Frances and their children (i.e., Christopher and Victoria) being Mr Hutcheson's "second family".

5. I gratefully adopt, from the judgment, Eady J's concise summary of the factual background:

   "10. The information in respect of which the Claimant seeks to maintain confidentiality falls within a very **narrow** compass. In 1968 he married a lady with whom he had four children, who are now grown up. The marriage still subsists. In the meantime, from about 1976 he developed a **relationship** with another woman with whom, in 1979 and 1981 respectively, he had two children. Obviously, they too are now adults. For many years, however, the Claimant managed to keep the information about his 'second' family secret, to a greater or lesser extent. How far he succeeded in this intention has been a matter of debate in the light of the limited evidence available. The position now is that, finally, all members of the Claimant's 'first' family are aware of the situation, although I am told that one of his daughters was only informed two or three weeks ago. She was told by her husband, who himself had known of the 'second' family only since the beginning of last year.

11. The Claimant's case is that the information is no more widely known than among his two families and that it is **not 'public knowledge'.** He says that he still has a reasonable expectation of keeping his 'second' family secret, in the sense that he should not be identified as being the father of the two children in question or as having had a **relationship** with their mother.

12. I need to explain how it is that the information has become of interest at this point and why *The Sun* newspaper wishes to make it public by way of an 'exclusive' story.

13. **It so happens that the daughter who only found out recently about her father's 'second' family is married to the chef and businessman Gordon Ramsay**. The Claimant was until recently associated with Gordon Ramsay in business. **He was the chief executive of Gordon Ramsay Holdings Ltd** and Gordon Ramsay Holdings International Ltd which, together with various subsidiaries, constitute the Gordon Ramsay Group. In October of this year [ie 2010], however, **the Claimant was dismissed.**

14. Since that time, there has **been a very public slanging match between Gordon Ramsay and the Claimant in the columns of various newspapers.** Each of them has been making unappetising allegations about the other. This has not been confined to business matters. I was shown, for example, an 'open letter' from Gordon Ramsay to the Claimant's wife in which he refers to her estrangement from her daughter (Mrs Ramsay) and her grandchildren and calls for a degree of reconciliation. On the other hand, the Claimant for his part puts the blame for the estrangement on Gordon Ramsay. "

6. As recorded by Eady J (judgment, at [15]—[16]), *The Sun* (part of NGN) wished to pursue an allegation**, based on an unidentified "source",** that Mr Hutcheson was dismissed from Gordon Ramsay Holdings **because he had been using company monies to fund his second family.**

7. In the event, Eady J refused to grant the relief sought by Mr Hutcheson. The learned Judge based himself on the well-established test, with which neither party could nor did take exception:

"5. . . . it is clear that an applicant who seeks to restrain publication of personal information will need to approach the matter in **two stages. First**, it is necessary to demonstrate that he has a reasonable expectation of privacy in respect of the subject-matter in question, having regard to Article 8 of the European Convention on Human Rights and Fundamental Freedoms. If that hurdle is overcome, it next has to be shown that there is no countervailing public interest sufficient to outweigh his right to protect that information. **At the second stage**, the court will apply what has been termed **'an intense focus'** to the **particular circumstances** of the case, in order to arrive at a determination of where the balance lies between the competing rights concerned . . . . . . "

8. As to the first issue, namely whether Mr Hutcheson could persuade the Court that he had a "reasonable expectation of privacy" in respect of the information about his second family, the Judge's conclusion was as follows (at [36]):

   "36. I would accept that article 8 is certainly engaged so far as concerns the Claimant and the members of both his families. Yet there is **no question** of intruding, by any proposed publication, **into intimate matters internal to the 'second family' or to the Claimant's extra-marital relationship**. It is **a 'bare fact' case**; that is to say, the court is concerned only with **the bare fact** of the familiar **relationship** . . . . . . Factual information of that kind may sometimes involve **a relatively low degree of intrusion**. It may be reasonable to treat it discreetly, but that is not the same as enforcing a right to keep it secret *vis-à-vis* the right of another to exercise freedom of speech by referring to it. In the circumstances of this particular case, I would hold that there is, at this stage, **no reasonable expectation of privacy as to the fact of the 'second family'. "**

9. Strictly speaking, as Mr Hutcheson had failed at the first hurdle, Eady J's conclusion—that there was no reasonable expectation of privacy as to the fact of the second family—was sufficient to decide the application adversely to him. Nonetheless, Eady J went on to consider the "ultimate balancing exercise" required at the second stage. Here, the Judge's conclusion, again adverse to Mr Hutcheson, appears from the following paragraphs of the judgment:

   "40. In the present case, . . . [NGN] . . . wish to have the opportunity, in reliance upon **their well placed source**, to publish allegations relating to the supposedly true reason for the Claimant's dismissal from the Gordon Ramsay Group, which was said to involve his having misapplied corporate resources in some way connected with his 'second family'. **That the newspaper is entitled to do subject, of course, as always, to the constraints of the law of libel. The Claimant cannot rely on the law of privacy to prevent that . . .**

   41. Furthermore, I referred earlier to the Claimant's highly publicised attacks on Gordon Ramsay, both in relation to the way he runs his business and as to this supposed responsibility for the breakdown of relations between his wife and her parents. **It seems that there may be another side to this, and that the estrangement may not be wholly**

unconnected with the Claimant's double life and Mrs Ramsay's recent discovery of the true position. The Claimant can hardly expect to have it all his own way and to use the court's processes to cover up the true position **or to prevent Gordon Ramsay from responding to his allegations by using the full facts at his disposal.** It can thus be readily understood, in this particular case, that it would be very difficult to draw hard and fast boundaries between '**zones**'—whether business or familial in nature. According at least to this newspaper's source, the two seem to be intertwined."

10. Ultimately (at [42] of the judgment), the Judge observed that there was much in dispute and that it was impossible for the Court to come to a "definitive conclusion" as to where the truth lay regarding **"these very public quarrels—relating, as they do, to both business and family matters".** In the circumstances, Eady J posed the question, as required by s 12(3) of the Human Rights Act 1998 ("the HRA"), whether Mr Hutcheson was "likely" to succeed at trial in establishing his entitlement to a permanent injunction; the Judge concluded that he was not so persuaded and therefore declined to grant the interim relief sought. Eady J said this (ibid):

   "I cannot say that it would be **necessary or proportionate,** either in the interests of the administration of justice or for the protection of the Claimant's legitimate expectations in respect of Article 8, to restrict the freedom of expression of any of these Respondents."

11. Relatively little needs to be added by way of factual outline. Nothing more need be said as to Mr Hutcheson's "first family", save that, as is clear from the judgment, **both his wife and the children of that family all already knew—**by the time of the hearing before Eady J–of the information Mr Hutcheson was seeking to restrain NGN from publishing.

12. So far as concerned Mr Hutcheson's second family, a number of matters of relevance are in evidence and are conveniently mentioned here:

   i) Frances Styles **at some time called herself "Mrs Hutcheson" and changed her name, by deed poll, to "Frances Hutcheson".**

   ii) Although Mr Hutcheson's name was not on the birth certificates of Christopher and Victoria, **the children took his name.** Subsequently, when Victoria married in the USA in 2007**, her marriage certificate recorded Mr Hutcheson as her "father/parent"**. Both the birth certificates and the marriage certificate are in **the public domain.**

   iii) Mr Hutcheson provided financially for the "second family". In his evidence, he has said that he loved all his children immensely and was very proud of them. As to Christopher and Victoria, he had **"played a full role in their upbringing".** Subsequently, however, Mr Hutcheson added that his **relationship** with Frances had been conducted "**surreptitious**ly"; given his business commitments and the requirements of his first family, the amount of time he could spend with his second family was "greatly restricted". It followed that he had played a "much fuller role" in the upbringing of the children of his first family. **He had, however, attended meetings at Christopher's and Victoria's schools, such as parents' evenings**; those at the school knew him as Mr Hutcheson but, he said, did not know that he had another family. When Christopher and Victoria had reached an appropriate age (about 10 to 12), it had been explained to them that he did not live with them because he had another family with whom he lived; thereafter, they had understood the need for "discretion". In short, having regard to living arrangements, social functions and holidays, he had " . . . **publicly played the role of father to Christopher and Victoria on a very limited number and type of occasions** . . . ". No one who knew him in connection with the second family (other than the second family itself) knew of his first family—an essential matter if he was to keep knowledge of the second family from his wife and children of the first family. Likewise, apart from professional advisors and one other person, **no one outside of the second family knew of its existence—until he began informing his first family of the second family's existence.**

13. As to the impact of publication of the information, Mr Hutcheson forthrightly made it plain that he **was not concerned with the effect it would have on his own reputation.** There would be some who would criticise his actions and think less of him; that, however, was of no concern to him. **His concern lay elsewhere, with the distressing intrusion into the lives of his wife, Frances and the children**. In that regard, however, all the evidence as to the impact of publication on members of his first and second families came from Mr Hutcheson. **There was no evidence from Mr Hutcheson's wife, from Frances, or from any of his children.**

14. Eady J referred in the judgment to the termination of Mr Hutcheson's employment with the Gordon Ramsay Group. The letter of dismissal, addressed to Mr Hutcheson and signed by Mr Ramsay, was dated the 16th October, 2010 ("the letter of dismissal"). It spoke of a preliminary investigation into the Group which had revealed:

> " . . . .a number of serious instances of misconduct, including: misrepresentation, making false representations on insurance policies, accounting errors, misuse of the directors' loan account, personal use of company credit cards, failure to invoice for work done, mis-management of Group income and breaches of internal accounting procedures. The investigation has revealed serious breaches of the Group's internal

> policies and procedures, as well as contractual, fiduciary and statutory breaches. "

It further said that the misrepresentations made on the Group's insurance policies alone constituted gross misconduct and left Mr Ramsay with "no option but to summarily dismiss" Mr Hutcheson. **In fairness to Mr Hutcheson, it may be noted that there is no reference in the letter of dismissal to him using company monies to fund his second family.**

15. **The public "spat"** which has followed the termination of Mr Hutcheson's employment, played out by Mr Ramsay and Mr Hutcheson in the newspapers and as described by Eady J in the judgment, **does not appear**, at least on the evidence to which we have been taken**, to reflect well on anyone concerned.** Statements attributed to Mr Ramsay contain what may be veiled references to Mr Hutcheson's second family. More importantly for present purposes, are remarks made by Mr Hutcheson himself (as reported in *The Mail on Sunday*, 31st October, 2010). Mr Hutcheson said that he did not know why Mr Ramsay had turned on him; he:

> " . . . robustly denies any financial impropriety, admitting to using a company credit card and taking out loans but insisting everything was paid back. "

Mr Hutcheson added that he had taken money out of the company—just as Mr Ramsay would have done—but he had not used it "unethically, without anyone knowing, without accountants knowing or Gordon knowing". Mr Hutcheson placed the blame for the rift on Mr Ramsay—in the process of doing so, making a variety of personal criticisms of him-and spoke of the "impressive empire" they had built together. **He also made reference to the support he had given Mr Ramsay in keeping his marriage together when he (Mr Ramsay) had been accused of "cheating" his wife (Mr Hutcheson's daughter).** Overall, Mr Hutcheson claimed that he had been made a scapegoat for the Group's difficulties.

16. *The Sun's* position appears from a witness statement of a **Mr Pharo, its Head of News,** dated 16th November, 2010. Mr Pharo said this:

> "10. On Wednesday 10 November 2010 one of the reporters in my team told me that he had spoken to one of his sources about the Claimant and the reasons for his dismissal from Gordon Ramsay Holdings. **I cannot reveal the identity of the source because the information they had provided to the reporter was given on a confidential and/ or 'off the record' . . . .basis**. However, I am aware of the identity of the source and can confirm that **the source is a reliable and regular source**, having provided us with information previously which has been **accurate, reliable and resulted in published stories**.

> 11. The reporter went on to tell me that during his conversation with the source, **the source confirmed** . . . .that the reason the Claimant was sacked from Gordon Ramsay Holdings was because it had been alleged that the Claimant had **been using company monies to fund his 'second family' . . . ..**"

Mr Pharo explained (at para 3) that he was making the witness statement rather than the reporter concerned, because **he believed that if the reporter was identified it would reveal the identity of "the confidential source".** Mr Pharo spoke (at para 13) of the public interest in the story being published quickly. **He also—and frankly—emphasised the commercial interest of NGN in being free to publish the story, having spent time and money researching it and while it remained "a current matter of public debate".** If not free to do so, he was concerned that the news value of the story would "perish" or that the information might be published elsewhere (perhaps outside the jurisdiction), thereby losing for NGN the exclusivity of the story.

THE LEGAL FRAMEWORK

. . .

[Articles 8, 10 and 12 recited]

21. *(2) General statements:* So far as general statements are concerned, they serve to illuminate, first, the nature of the rights under consideration here; secondly, the inter-**relationship** between them; and, thirdly, the issue/s for decision.

22. I turn first to the judgment of Sir Anthony Clarke MR (as he then was) in *Murray v Express Newspapers plc* [2008] EWCA Civ 446; [2009] Ch 481, at [24], helpfully summarising the principles stated by Lord Nicholls in his speech in *Campbell v MGN Ltd* [2004] UKHL 22; [2004] 2 AC 457, esp. at [12]—[22], as follows:

> ". . . **(i)** The right to freedom of expression enshrined in article 10 of the Convention and the right to respect for a person's privacy enshrined in article 8 are vitally important rights. **Both lie at the heart of liberty in a modern state and neither has precedence over the other** . . . **(ii)** Although the origin of the cause of action relied upon is breach of confidence, since information about an individual's private life would not, in ordinary usage, be called 'confidential', the more natural description of the position today is that such information is private and the essence of the tort is better **encapsulated now as misuse of private information . . .** (iii) The values enshrined in articles 8 and 10 are now part of the cause of action and should be treated as of general application and as **being as much applicable to disputes between individuals as to**

> **disputes between individuals and a public authority . . . (iv)** Essentially **the touchstone** of private life is whether in respect of the disclosed facts the person in question had a reasonable expectation of privacy **. . . (v)** In deciding whether there is in principle an invasion of privacy, it is important to distinguish between that question, which seems to us to be the question which is often described as whether article 8 is **engaged**, and the subsequent question whether, if it is, the individual's rights are nevertheless not infringed because of the combined effect of article 8(2) and article 10 . . ."

23. Another most helpful summary, encapsulating the learning from a number of authorities, is that found in the judgment of Maurice Kay LJ, in *Donald v Ntuli* [2010] EWCA Civ 1276; [2011] 1 WLR 294:

> "10. Prior to the coming into force of the Human Rights Act 1998 the approach to cases such as this lacked coherence in domestic law. However, the basic principles of substantive law are now well settled. In *In re S (A Child) (Identification: Restrictions on Publication)* [2005] 1 AC 593, para 17, Lord Steyn extracted four propositions from *Campbell v MGN* . . . .:
>
> '**First,** neither article [8 or 10] has *as such* precedence over the other. **Secondly**, where the values under the two articles are in conflict, an **intense focus on the comparative importance of the specific rights** being claimed in the individual case is necessary. **Thirdly**, the justifications for interfering with or restricting each right must be taken into account. **Finally**, the **proportionality test** must be applied to each. For convenience I will call this the ultimate balancing test.'
>
> .
>
> 12. The authorities were rigorously reviewed by Buxton LJ in *McKennitt v Ash* [2008] QB 73 where he said, at para 11:
>
> 'in a case such as the present, where the complaint is of the wrongful publication of private information, the court has to decide two things. **First,** is the information private in the sense that it is in principle protected by article 8? If 'no', that is the end of the case**. If 'yes',** the second question arises: in all the circumstances, must the interest of the owner of the private information **yield to the right of freedom of expression** conferred on the publisher by article 10? The latter inquiry is commonly referred to as the balancing exercise . . . . . .' "

24. *(3) Art. 8:* In addressing the question of whether Mr Hutcheson is entitled to assert a claim to privacy in respect of the second family, it is next helpful to highlight **various features of Art. 8,** beginning with the identification in the authorities of "**private information as something worth protecting as**

an aspect of human autonomy and dignity": *Campbell v MGN Ltd (supra)*, at [50]. The cause of action focuses upon (*ibid*, at [52]):

> **". . . the protection of human autonomy and dignity—the right to control the dissemination of information about one's private life and the right to the esteem and respect of other people."**

Picking up on the same theme in the context of a free society, Laws LJ said this in *R (Wood) v Comr of Police of Metropolis* [2009] EWCA Civ 414; [2010] 1 WLR 123:

> "21. The notion of the **personal autonomy** of every individual marches with **the presumption of liberty enjoyed in a free polity**: a presumption which consists in the principle that every interference with the freedom of the individual stands in need of objective justification . . . . . . .an individual's personal autonomy makes him—should make him—**master of all those facts about his own identity, such as his name, health, sexuality, ethnicity, his own image** . . . ..He is the presumed owner of these aspects of his own self; **his control of them can only be loosened, abrogated, if the state shows an objective justification for doing so.**
>
> 22. This **cluster of values**, summarised as **the personal autonomy of every individual** and taking **concrete form** as a presumption against interference with the individual's liberty, is a defining characteristic of a **free** society. We therefore need to preserve it **even in little cases**. At the same time it is important that this core right protected by article 8, **however protean**, should **not be read so widely that its claims become unreal and unreasonable**. For this **purpose** I think there are three safeguards, or qualifications. **First**, the alleged threat or assault to the individual's personal autonomy must (if article 8 is to be engaged) attain 'a **certain level of seriousness**'. **Secondly,** the touchstone for article 8(1)'s engagement is whether the claimant enjoys on the facts a 'reasonable expectation of privacy' . . . . . . .Absent such an expectation, there is no relevant interference with personal autonomy. **Thirdly**, the breadth of article 8(1) may in many instances be greatly curtailed by the scope of the justifications available to the state pursuant to article 8(2) . . . . . . "

That, in the event, this judgment of Laws LJ was a dissenting judgment, is neither here nor there on the questions of principle canvassed in the passage cited.

25. It should further be noted that the mere fact that otherwise private information is known—and thus "public"—**but within a limited circle of people**, does **not,** without more, preclude a claim to prevent publication to the world at large.

26. As will be apparent, **a complaint of misuse of private information is necessarily fact sensitive.** That Art. 8 may be, in principle, applicable (or "engaged") does not by itself mean that there has been a breach of its provisions: *Harrow LBC v Qazi* [2003] UKHL 43; [2004] 1 AC 983, at [47], *per* Lord Hope. Further, the nature of the information requires careful consideration. There may, for instance, **be a difference (both at this stage and when conducting the balancing exercise) between information as to the bare fact of a relationship and information as to the contents or detail of that relationship**: see, *Browne v Associated Newspapers Ltd* [2007] EWCA Civ 295; [2008] QB 103, at [57] *et seq*. Further still, evidence is required as to the Art. 8 rights of the individuals said to be affected; as Tugendhat J expressed it, in *Terry and Persons Unknown* [2010] EWHC 119; [2010] EMLR 16, at [65]:

> **"Respect for the dignity and autonomy of the individuals concerned requires that, if practicable, they should speak for themselves."**

27. There **is no question of Art. 8 furnishing an absolute right to privacy**. Art. 8.2 qualifies, in terms, the right conferred by Art. 8.1. The claims of privacy must of course also be read with the right to freedom of expression provided by **Art. 10** (in this jurisdiction, **to be read together with s 12 of the HRA**). Moreover and, in my view, with respect, wisely, Laws LJ emphasised in *Wood (supra)*, at [22], that the **purpose** of the "safeguards" or "qualifications" to which he referred was to ensure that **the " . . . core right protected by article 8 . . . should not be read so widely that its claims become unreal and unreasonable"**.

28. *(4) Art. 10 and the balancing exercise:* Art. 10 enshrines another **vitally important right in a free society,** that of freedom of expression. It is unsurprising that the balancing exercise between the competing values of Arts. 8 and 10 may be difficult and necessarily requires an "intense" focus on the facts of the individual case. As US Appellate Judge and jurist, Richard A. Posner observed (in *How Judges Think*, 2008, at p 246):

> **". . . when cases are difficult to decide it is usually because the decision must strike a balance between two legitimate interests, one of which must give way."**

29. **In the area of sexual conduct,** the decision in *Terry (supra)* raises a question which (while it does not have to be resolved in this case) highlights the conflict or tension between these two competing fundamental rights. Against the background of Eady J having upheld, at trial, a claim to privacy in respect of sadomasochistic conduct in *Mosley v News Group Newspapers Ltd* [2008] EWHC 1777; [2008] EMLR 20, counsel in *Terry* (seeking an interim injunction in respect of information about an alleged adulterous **relationship**) appears to have submitted that the conduct of one person in private

must be unlawful before another person should be permitted to criticise it in public. In a powerful passage, Tugendhat J disagreed, emphasising (at [99] *et seq*) the importance of public discussion and the freedom to criticise. Tugendhat J observed (at [101] and [104]):

> "**It is not for the judge to express personal views on such matters, still less to impose whatever personal views he might have.** That is not the issue. The issue is what the judge should prohibit one person from saying publicly about another . . .
>
> . . .
>
> . . . There is no suggestion that the conduct in question in the present case ought to be unlawful, or that any editor would ever suggest that it ought to be. But in a plural society there will be some who would suggest that it ought to be discouraged . . . **Freedom to live as one chooses is one of the most valuable freedoms. But so is the freedom to criticise (within the limits of the law) the conduct of other members of society as being harmful or wrong . . . .It is as a result of public discussion and debate that public opinion develops . . ."**

See too, the thoughtful discussion in *Tugendhat and Christie, The Law of Privacy and the Media* (2nd ed.), at paras 12.208–12.216, under the heading "plurality of opinion".

30. *(5)* **Prior restraints on publication:** In striking the correct balance, **prior restraints on publication give rise to particular concerns**. In this jurisdiction, elaboration is unnecessary; such concerns are **given statutory force** by the clear wording of s 12 of the HRA (set out above).

31. *(6)* **Burden of proof:** So far as the burden of proof is concerned, it is, in my judgment, unnecessary to take time over a somewhat theoretical discussion as to legal, evidentiary and shifting burdens. Suffice to say that it is for the applicant for interim relief to make out the case of an infringement of his Art. 8 rights and for the respondent to raise a case of freedom of expression under Art. 10. But, ultimately, in a matter such as this, it is plain that the burden rests on the applicant to satisfy the requirements of s 12(3), HRA, or fail.

32. *(7)* **Appeals:** Throughout this case, I have been very mindful that we have not been hearing it *de novo* but on appeal, for that matter, from the decision of a vastly experienced Judge in this field. As it seems to me, this Court should be slow to interfere with the Judge's assessment in a case such as this and should not do so unless persuaded that the Judge has gone wrong. Insofar as this approach has been articulated in somewhat varying terms (cf. *Browne, supra*, at [45] on the one hand and *Flood v Times Newspapers Ltd* [2010] EWCA Civ 804 at [49], together with *JIH v News Group Newspapers Ltd*

[2011] EWCA Civ 42; [2011] EMLR 15, at [26] on the other], these formulations, with respect, appear more to reflect theoretical distinctions than to give rise to practical differences.

33. *(8)* **Pulling the threads together:** The foundation for the application for an interim injunction in cases of this kind is the (alleged) infringement of *privacy*. **By contrast with the law of defamation** (perhaps more familiar, at least to common lawyers), **the fact that the information is true is, of itself, no bar to the obtaining of an injunction**; instead and often, if not invariably, the fact that the information is true is **the reason why injunctive relief is sought.**

34. To some, applicants in privacy claims may seem unattractive. However, to others, **intrusive** media coverage of matters of sexual conduct, **particularly if it includes salacious detail**, may be equally unattractive. That said, for sections of the media, developments in privacy law impinging on their ability to publish such matters, may not only give rise to issues of principle as to freedom of expression in the individual case **but also to real commercial concerns–which, at least to the extent of the general public interest in having a thriving and vigorous newspaper industry, representing all legitimate opinions, may also be argued to give rise to a relevant factor for the court to take into account.**

35. To grapple with such issues, the Court can only have recourse to the legal framework discussed above. The starting point must therefore be the right to privacy, keeping well in mind that it is **not for the Judge to impose whatever personal views he or she might have**: *Terry, supra,* at [101]. That right must not, however, be read so widely that its claims become unreal and unreasonable: *Wood, supra,* at [22]. The Judge must in any event balance the claim to privacy (if the Art 8 right is *prima facie* infringed) with **the equally fundamental Art. 10 right** to freedom of expression, in the public interest and including the freedom to criticise: *Terry, supra,* at [104]. When considering interim injunctions (and, so, **prior restraint** on publication), s 12 of the HRA provides what might be termed **a statutory steer, which it is incumbent on the Court to follow**. How the Court strikes the balance in any particular case will, necessarily, be fact specific. Thus guided, I turn to the central issues in dispute on this appeal, under the convenient headings of: (1) Art. 8; and (2) the balancing exercise.

ART 8

36. *(1) The rival cases:* For Mr Hutcheson, Mr Tomlinson QC submitted that the Judge had fallen into error at [36] of the judgment. The Judge's finding that Art. 8 was "engaged" determined that there was a reasonable expectation of privacy—and thus that Art. 8 would be infringed by publication. All that remained was the balancing exercise (Art. 10) and the question of pre-trial

relief (s.12). A **sexual relationship** was "close to the core of private information"; keeping it private was a choice Mr Hutcheson was entitled to make and the fact that it was necessarily known to a small circle of people did not mean that he could not seek to prevent tabloid publicity. That Mr Hutcheson's conduct might be regarded as "morally blameworthy" was neither here nor there.

37. For NGN, Ms Page QC submitted that there had been no error on the part of the Judge**. He had been entitled to treat the engagement of Art. 8 and the question of a reasonable expectation of privacy as two distinct questions**. In any event, the criticism of the Judge in this regard was semantic only and lacking in merit. As Ms Page put it in her skeleton argument:

> **"Thus in this case Article 8 is clearly 'engaged' in the sense that Article 8 is applicable; the fact of the second family is a fact relating to the Appellant's family life. But that provides only limited assistance on the question whether Article 8 is 'engaged' in the sense that the Appellant has a reasonable expectation of privacy in relation to that fact, such that publication of it in a newspaper requires special justification."**

As to whether there was a reasonable expectation of privacy, the Judge had been right; this was a case. There were a **variety of public incidents attaching to that relationship,** going to the birth and marriage certificates already mentioned, together with Mr Hutcheson's own evidence as to active parenthood. In any event, the essential reason for privacy had gone: his wife and the children of his first family now knew of the second family. **There was an important distinction between not wanting publicity and having a reasonable expectation of privacy, such as to justify intervention on the part of the Court.**

38. *(2) Discussion:* For my part, I do not think that the criticism based on Eady J's approach is well-founded; in any event, it is, at most, semantic. **Art. 8 may be "engaged" in the sense that information relates to family life without it necessarily following that there is a reasonable expectation of privacy in the information in question: see, *Harrow LBC v Qazi* (supra).** While it may often be as or more convenient to treat the question of the "engagement" of Art. 8 as encompassing the question of its infringement as well**, the Judge cannot be faulted for approaching the issue in stages.** To such extent at least, I am unable to accept Mr Tomlinson's submissions.

39. The critical question under this heading, however, is whether Mr Hutcheson had a reasonable expectation of privacy in respect of the information he has sought to restrain NGN from publishing. As will be recollected, at [36] of his judgment, Eady J held that there was no such expectation, underlining that this was a "bare fact" case.

40. There is, it may be said, force in Mr Tomlinson's submission, arising both from the sexual and family nature of the **relationship**, together with the fact that for decades the existence of the second family has remained "secret". That a limited number of people knew of it does not, as already underlined, equate to *carte blanche* for the tabloids, or for any other section of the media. That said, the Art. 8 issue in the present case is not straightforward. **First**, this is a **"bare fact"** or **"fact of the relationship case". Secondly**, there is the unavoidably public nature of certain aspects of the life of the second family. **Thirdly,** the knowledge the first family now has of the second family has **removed at least much of the rationale for a claim to privacy.**

41. In the circumstances and given the view which I take on the balancing exercise (see below), it is, in the event, unnecessary to reach a conclusion as to whether Mr Hutcheson has made good the first limb of his case—namely, that the information is, in principle, protected by Art. 8. I am content instead to proceed by *assuming,* without deciding, that the information is so protected. I add only this; had I reached the conclusion that the information was protected by Art. 8, given the countervailing arguments already flagged, this conclusion would at most have been of a borderline nature. I turn to the balancing exercise.

THE BALANCING EXERCISE

42. *(1) The rival cases:* Mr Tomlinson focused on the Judge's key conclusions, at [40]—[41] of the judgment (set out above). The first, at [40], related to the allegation of misconduct; namely, Mr Hutcheson's alleged use of company monies to fund his second family. That allegation depended on hearsay material from an anonymous source. This was an insufficient foundation for a serious allegation and lacked plausibility, especially when contrasted with the letter of dismissal (set out above)—where no such allegation was advanced, despite a good many others being averred. So far as concerns the Judge's reasoning at [41] of the judgment, it was all too speculative; moreover, Mr Ramsay could not (as Mr Tomlinson put it) be described as "backward in coming forward". It followed, Mr Tomlinson submitted, that the balancing exercise involved a manifestly private **relationship** on the one hand with a very speculative claim to publication in the public interest on the other. On this footing there could be only one possible outcome at trial and Mr Hutcheson's application for interim relief satisfied the requirements of s 12.

43. The foundation of Ms Page's submissions was **the public interest** in the **exposure of wrongdoing**. NGN could not be restrained from publishing an allegation that Mr Hutcheson had been dismissed from the Gordon Ramsay Group for diverting funds to private purposes; **but that would be an allegation shorn of content. NGN** needed to publish **the fact of the second family**

to authenticate the allegation made to it by the confidential source. That allegation sufficed, on its own, to justify publication and prevent Mr Hutcheson satisfying the requirements of s 12. The letter of dismissal did not suggest otherwise; it reflected a preliminary investigation only and identified general headings of misconduct without underlying particulars. In any event, the allegation made by the source did not stand on its own. Publication was justified in the public interest, as Eady J held at [41] of the judgment**, to ensure that the public was not misled**. The publicity generated by Mr Hutcheson (and Mr Ramsay) in pursuing their dispute was such as **to make it wrong and artificial to prohibit publication of the fact of the second family; an injunction would risk the presentation of a distorted picture to the public.**

44. *(2) Discussion:* As already recounted, after conducting the balancing exercise, Eady J concluded that it was neither necessary nor proportionate to restrict NGN's freedom of expression. The Judge was not persuaded that Mr Hutcheson was likely to succeed at trial in establishing his entitlement to a permanent injunction, so that he failed to satisfy the test furnished by s 12(3) of the HRA. In my judgment, Eady J was right; at all events, these were conclusions to which Eady J was amply entitled to come. Accordingly, I am of the clear view that, even assuming the information to be protected in principle by Art. 8, this is not a case in which this Court should interfere with the decision reached by the Judge. My reasons follow.

45. First, I begin with a focus on the public interest in publication of the fact of Mr Hutcheson's second family. I have already referred to the very public dispute between Mr Ramsay and Mr Hutcheson, much ventilated in the media. To my mind, those who choose to conduct their quarrels in such a fashion take the risk that they may not be able to insist thereafter on clear boundary lines between what is public and what is private—regardless of whether they were, hitherto, only public personalities in a very limited sense. In the present case, as it seems to me, there is a very real risk of a distorted and partial picture being presented to the public of this dispute, were an injunction to be granted as sought by Mr Hutcheson. With respect to Mr Tomlinson's submissions, there is nothing speculative about this conclusion; the tenor of Mr Hutcheson's press interview of the 31st October, 2010 speaks for itself. The Judge's conclusion at [41] of the judgment, **that business and family matters had become intertwined, cannot be faulted;** on any view**,** that was a conclusion the Judge was entitled to reach and it suffices to demonstrate a powerful interest in publication.

Ferdinand v MGN Ltd [2011] EWHC 2454 (QB)

Mr Justice Nicol:

1. On 25th April 2010 the *Sunday Mirror* published an article under the headline "My Affair with England Captain Rio". In very similar terms the article also appeared on the website www.mirror.co.uk between 25th and 30th April 2010. The Defendant is the publisher of the newspaper and website. **The Claimant is the well known footballer, Rio Ferdinand**. He claims that the article in both formats was **an unjustified infringement of his right to privacy, a misuse of his private information and a breach of confidence**. The Defendant defends its publications as **a legitimate exercise of its right of freedom of expression**.
2. The article gave an account of the Claimant's **relationship** with **Ms Carly Storey**. They had met in 1996 or 1997 when he was a teenager and she was 17. They drifted apart from 2000, when the Claimant moved to Leeds United, until 2002. In 2002 they resumed contact via phone and text messages and also met up. The last time they met was in May 2005. They were not then in contact for nearly 2 years. They resumed contact in October 2007 and continued to have frequent text message exchanges until some time in 2009. After a gap of several months the Claimant and Ms Storey exchanged text messages in December 2009 and January 2010. They did not meet again. **On 5th February 2010 the Claimant was appointed captain of the England football team in replacement for John Terry**. On 6th February Ms Storey sent him a text concerning this appointment. The Claimant sent her a short response the same day. There was no further contact between them.
3. **The article said more about the relationship between the two of them. I shall need to come back to this.**
4. **The Defendant did not contact the Claimant about its proposed article in advance of publication**. He did not have the opportunity**, which he said he would otherwise have taken**, to apply for an injunction to prevent its publication. **It is admitted that the newspaper has a circulation of about 1.4 million and a readership of about 4 million.** The readership of the **website was agreed to have been substantial** until the Defendant voluntarily (and without admitting any obligation to do so) took it down.
5. On 28th June 2011 (and so the week before the trial began) Eady J. **made orders temporarily restricting public access to specified parts of the Statements of Case, an unredacted version of the article, a confidential schedule to the Claimant's witness statement, the text messages which had passed between the Claimant and Ms Storey and which had been disclosed in the action, the skeleton arguments and Ms Storey's witness statement until**

the trial. With minor changes I continued those orders until judgment. Having heard full argument, **Eady J. also considered that in principle the trial should be divided into a public and private parts**. He rejected the Defendant's argument that the widespread dissemination of the newspaper and online article rendered further restriction unnecessary. **He left open for further argument at trial where precisely the line should be drawn between the public and private parts.**

6. I was not willing to re-open the argument of principle, but I heard further submissions as to how the division should be made. **I made clear that my decision that restricting public access to part of the trial was a temporary measure and would not necessarily be reflected in my judgment.**

7. The Claimant gave evidence and was cross examined in both public and private sessions. **There were two other witnesses. Justin Rigby, the Claimant's public relations agent, gave evidence on his behalf. Nicholas Owens, a senior reporter at the Sunday Mirror, gave evidence for the Defendant**. Their evidence was exclusively given in the **public part of the proceedings**.

8. **Carly Storey had provided a witness statement** and, I was told, she had been expected to give evidence for the Defendant. However, shortly before the trial she went abroad and was unavailable. Her witness statement was admitted as **hearsay evidence**. Of course the weight that I could give to it had to reflect the fact that its contents had not been subject to cross examination.

9. On 19th July 2011 the Court of Appeal gave judgment **in Christopher Hutcheson (formerly known as 'KGM') v News Group Newspapers Ltd** [2011] EWCA Civ 808. I invited the parties to make submissions in writing as to its impact on the present case. The Claimant and the Defendant did so on 28th July (in the Defendant's case supplementing a letter dated 22nd July) and the Defendant replied to the Claimant's submissions on 4th August 2011. I have taken all of these into account.

Further detail about the Defendant's article

10. In order to make my decision comprehensible it is necessary to say more about the article which the Defendant published. On the front page of the *Sunday Mirror* there was a trail **[redacted]** and **photographs** of the heads of the Claimant and Ms Storey. Readers were directed to the story which appeared over two of the inside pages. There the story was published under the headline "**My affair with England captain Rio**" and in large type a quotation from Ms Storey, **[redacted]**

11. The article itself, which was written by Gary Anderson, began by quoting what the England manger, Fabio Capello, had said when appointing the Claimant as captain in place of John Terry, "**I ask always that the captain**

is an example to the young, for the children, for the fans...a role model outside the game—in life as well." It described how the Claimant and Ms Storey had met when they were teenagers and continued on and off for 13 years until, it was alleged, the Claimant had ceased contact with her on becoming the England captain in February 2010.

12. **In the article Ms Storey said that the relationship became a sexual one within a few weeks, but said they drifted apart in 2000 when the Claimant met Rebecca Ellison. He and Ms Ellison began to live together in Yorkshire** when he moved from West Ham United to Leeds United. In 2002 the Claimant played for England in the World Cup competition. He moved to Manchester United.

13. The article went on to describe how Ms Storey and the Claimant got back in touch in 2002**. Again the relationship was a sexual one, with at least 10 meetings, usually in London hotels. The last occasion was in May 2005**. In the article **Ms Storey alleged that the Claimant had misled her about his relationship with Ms Ellison.** Ms Storey said she was **very upset when she learned through the press that Ms Ellison was pregnant with the Claimant's first son and Ms Storey said she avoided him for 18 months.** The Claimant became **engaged to Ms Ellison in July 2007.**

14. In October 2007, according to the article, the Claimant contacted Ms Storey again and suggested that they meet up again. **[redacted]** at the Grove Hotel, Herts... At the time the England squad were holed up there ahead of a vital Euro 2008 qualifier against Estonia on the 13th."

15. In the article Ms Storey said that she did not show up because she had been going through bad depression and did not feel good about herself and didn't want the Claimant to see her in that state. **[redacted]** She said that the Claimant tried to arrange another meeting just before an important league match [redacted] but then cancelled because of the security arrangements in place at the hotel. Details were given of other attempted meetings **[redacted].**

16. The Claimant married Ms Ellison in June 2009, **[redacted]**

17. **Following his appointment as England captain, Ms Storey said the Claimant sent one brief text but after that the phone went dead and she had no further contact with him.**

18. In a separate box, there was an additional piece under the heading, "Rio Reformed". It said,

> "Rio Ferdinand earned a **reputation** in his early career as a football bad boy with **driving convictions, sex scandals and a missed drugs test ban.**
>
> But when he was about to become a father in 2006, he vowed to change

his ways, saying, 'I've strayed in the past but I'm going to be a family man now. My **priority** now is Rebecca, the baby and having a stable family life.'

Rio also recognised that failing to consign his wild man ways to the past could harm his career playing for Man United under Sir Alex Ferguson, **'You have to take charge of your conduct and the way you live outside football or you'll be out of the door,'** he said.

Rio set about transforming his image. He signed up as the **Prince's Trust** patron and in 2008 announced plans for his own **charity,** The Rio Ferdinand Live the Dream Foundation to help disadvantaged youngsters. **[redacted]** He also invested in a record label and became the face of his own **celebrity** life style magazine #5. **Recently he was described as a 'role model' in press releases for Dead Man Running**—a film starring rapper 50 cent which he helped finance.

[redacted.]"

19. Among the illustrations for the article were 5 screen shots of some of the texts and a **photograph** of Ms Storey and the Claimant together in 1997.

20. **The online version of the article was in virtually the same terms except that it did not include the photograph of the Claimant and Ms Storey or screen shots of any of the text messages.**

Further evidence in relation to the article

21. The Claimant disputed whether he and Ms Storey had met as many as 10 times in the period 2002-2005, he said he thought it was only a couple of times. **The exact number does not matter. In his opening note, Mr Tomlinson said that for present purposes the court could accept that it was not just one casual encounter.**

22. **[redacted].**

23. The article had said that the Claimant sent texts to Ms Storey in October 2009. That is not borne out by the phone records. However, **further text messages were exchanged in January 2010**. **[redacted]**

24. The Claimant noted that the text from Ms Storey on 6th February 2010 had said, "Oh my you taking over jt what a joke, maybe its time I cashed in seen as you want 2 blank me." The Claimant's response had been to text, "Wot chattin about". A week later Ms Storey had replied "Sorry I sent you that text the other day it was supposed 2 be a joke, I can see that it might of upset you and I didn't mean 4 that, I hope al is good anyway. Remember always friends." **Ms Storey says that she contacted the well known publicity agent, Max Clifford in late February 2010. She was in due course paid £16,000 by the Defendant for the information which appeared in the article.**

25. The Claimant said, without challenge, that he would change his mobile phone from time to time and it is agreed that he did so around the end of February 2010. The Claimant said that this was nothing to do with cutting off contact with Ms Storey. There had previously been gaps in their phone or text contacts. Thus, there had been no exchanges for several months at the end of 2009. The interval between their texts at the beginning of February and the appearance of the article at the end of April was considerably shorter. I agree with the Claimant in this regard. **That interval is too short to draw an inference that the Claimant had terminated contact with Ms Storey out of concern for the impact which the relationship might have on his professional career.**

26. The Claimant accepts that there is no legal obligation for a person to notify someone in advance of publishing private information—see **Mosley v UK** App. No. 48009/08, judgment of 20th May 2011, **but it was striking that the Defendant had not done so in this case although that would be common practice in the media industry.** The witness statement of Mr Rigby, the **Claimant's publicity agent** went further. He said that he had been **tipped off** about a possible story, but when he spoke to the journalist in question, Nick Owens, on 24th April 2010 (i.e. the day before the story was published) **he denied that the newspaper had a story on the Claimant.** Mr Rigby was referring to Nicholas Owens. I gave leave to the Defendant to adduce evidence from him in reply. Mr Owens' witness statement said that he could not recall this conversation with Mr Rigby. If asked, he would have said that *he* was not working on a story on the Claimant, **but he would definitely not have said that the newspaper did not have a story on him.** Journalists often worked on their own stories of which Mr Owens was unaware. In cross examination Mr Rigby candidly accepted that he could not be certain about the conversation and whether Mr Owens had been referring only to what he personally was working on or whether he was speaking more generally about the paper as a whole. **In these circumstances, Mr Tomlinson QC, on behalf of the Claimant, properly did not press the argument that the Defendant had positively misled Mr Rigby.**

27. **Mr Tomlinson did observe that there was a complete dearth of evidence as to how the story had come to be published, what had been the editorial considerations behind it or why the Claimant had not been asked to comment before publication.** Mr Millar responded that the questions of whether there was public interest in the article and whether the Defendant's freedom of expression should prevail over any claim that the Claimant might have to preserve his privacy were matters to be decided objectively. **He submitted that the views of the journalist and editors were not relevant to these issues—see Mosley v News Group Newspapers Ltd** [2008] EMLR 20 **at [135]–[137].**

Press publicity concerning the Claimant's private life before publication of the Defendant's article

28. **At least before 2006 the Claimant seems to have had something of a wild reputation**. In 2000, he and some friends went for a holiday to Ayia Napa in Cyprus. They met up with some women and the Claimant allowed himself to be filmed having sex with one of them. The incident received widespread publicity and the film itself (which the Claimant says was stolen) was also, without his consent, made widely available. The Claimant was also, apparently, disqualified from driving for being over the prescribed alcohol limit. In 2003 he missed a drugs test and was banned from playing football for his teams for several months in consequence.

29. Between 2002 and 2006 numerous articles were published (some by the Defendant, some by other newspapers) alleging that the Claimant had had affairs with other women and had been "cheating" on his long term partner, Ms Ellison. **The Claimant makes the point that none of these had been published with his consent or co-operation. There was no evidence that he had.** But they were part of the **reputation** which he had gained by the time Ms Ellison was pregnant with their first child.

30. On 29th January 2006 the **News of the World published a lengthy interview** with the Claimant. In his evidence, the Claimant explained that the interview had been set up by his commercial agent who dealt with endorsements and the media**. He accepted that the quotes in the article came from him**. In that article, the Claimant said, "**I've strayed in the past—but I'm going to be a family man now**." He admitted "succumbing" to other women during his five year **relationship** with Rebecca Ellison and saying, "**I'm not proud of it ... You do get girls coming on to you and sometimes I admit that I have succumbed. You are a young guy and there are temptations. Yeah, I've made mistakes—show me someone who hasn't**". The article continued, "**But the Man United defender—who has been linked to a string of other beauties including model Holly Maguire—reckons he's tackled his infidelity and is ready to grow up and take on the responsibility of fatherhood. 'I think everyone has seen over the last few years how I have matured. ... The key when you make mistakes is to learn from them. My priority now is Rebecca, the baby and having a stable family life.'**" The headline to the article (for which, of course, the Claimant was not responsible) said **"I've been a cheat before ... but I'll be a great dad."** On his behalf, Mr Tomlinson realistically accepted that the Claimant had been speaking of having affairs in the past and his intention to mend his ways in the future including in relation to his past infidelities towards Ms Ellison**. In his cross examination the Claimant accepted that the references to a stable family life and fatherhood, did not conjure up the image of someone having extra-marital affairs, quite the opposite.**

31. The Claimant published his autobiography, *Rio My Story* in September or October 2006. The dust jacket said,

> "You can't ignore him. Every football fan has an opinion on Rio Ferdinand. He is one of the most gifted footballers these shores have ever produced. Twice breaking the British transfer record and hugely admired, but he courts controversy in equal measure...He has been embroiled in sensational tabloid headlines involving women and partying."

> In the course of a section on the Ayia Napa incident, the Claimant wrote

> "The truth is some women will do anything to crack on with footballers and, let's be fair, which young players would pass up the opportunity to take them up on some of their offers? Some birds will buy you drinks all night, strip for you, get shagged with other people in the room and do all sorts of tricks. Some of the stories you hear... I admit I got carried away with it at times but you get older, more responsible and leave that sort of thing behind. You see it for what it's worth—that they aren't interested in you, just the notoriety and fame of being with a footballer, or anyone famous for that matter."

Describing how he and Ms Ellison set up home together when they moved to Yorkshire he said,

> "I was no longer the single lad, another thing which helped curb my lifestyle!"

In his cross examination the Claimant said that by "lifestyle" he meant clubbing and things that were detrimental to football. He denied that this was meant as a reference to his previous involvement with other women. Whether that was what he intended or not, **I consider that this statement would be taken by at least some readers as embracing that aspect of his previous life style and the passage would be understood as meaning that this aspect was also something which the Claimant had abandoned.**

In his autobiography the Claimant also commented,

> **"I have realised that we do have a responsibility off the field because children look up to us and want to be like us. It took me a long time to understand that."**

32. An interview with the Daily Telegraph published on 25th November 2006, said of him,

> "Ferdinand reads all the headlines (besides Beckham and Rooney, he is probably the country's most talked-about player) and he knows his own **reputation**: loud, arrogant, flashy, with an eye for the ladies and an inability to say no to any kind of party."

He is quoted as saying,

> **"'This year is the first year I didn't go on a proper lads' holiday and just get steaming every night for seven days. Rebecca was heavily pregnant so I went away for a weekend—I drank a fair bit, nothing like as much as I would have done before. It's good man. It's almost like having reins on you'. He thinks again. 'But then it's not like reins because you want to go home and see your baby, be a family.'"**

In cross examination the Claimant accepted that he was **saying that his priority was his family. There was more in his life than football and the family, but certainly no relations with other women.**

33. On 25th March 2008 the Claimant was appointed captain of the England football team by Fabio Capello. This was part of Mr Capello's strategy of trying out different players as captain. The following day the *Mail Online* published a story. It quoted Mr Capello saying the team captain would be a

> **"symbol on and off the pitch . . . I have to know the man, not only the player . . . He's a symbol of the England team . . . he has to be a big player but a symbol . . . A symbol is a good player, a good man and he has to represent the England team in every situation."**

The article was published under the headline "Good role model? Rio Ferdinand named England captain despite drug testing and roasting rows." The reference to "roasting", as the second paragraph made clear, was to the incident in Ayia Napa. *Mail Online* commented that "Ferdinand's talent on the pitch has made him the most expensive British player of all time, but his off the field antics have often made the headlines." The Claimant was quote**"If you can't be forgiven for failings when you were young then that is not a good thing. If you learn from those mistakes then you've every right to aim as high as you want. Since then, I have applied myself to a different level on the pitch, the training field and in my private life as well."**

34. In an interview with *The Times* on 20th May 2008 the Claimant was quoted as saying, in the same article as saying,

> "Getting the captaincy at United and with England against France has had a big impact on what people think about me. **I think people now believe my managers would not give me this job if they didn't trust me or didn't think I was responsible, so that makes people believe I am a reformed character.**
>
> You mature coming to a club like Manchester United, too, because if you don't grow up here, you won't do it anywhere. The workload of playing so many games means you cannot afford to go out because if you do, you won't be ready on Tuesday or Wednesday. When I left London for

> Leeds United it was a conscious decision because I was enjoying the finer things rather than football, but I have never done that since joining Manchester United [in 2002]. I've been a good professional in terms of picking the right times to go out. **The manager would come down on you if you were misbehaving outside the football club, but there has never been that need with me because I am not out partying or getting drunk."**

35. In an interview in *The Observer* for 1st June 2008 in the context of (among other matters, the Ayia Napa incident) the Claimant spoke of moving to Leeds United,

> "I left London, which was probably the biggest turning point in my career . . . I had time to reflect and think, 'If I don't knuckle down now, when will I achieve?' **And I got a girlfriend . . . and now I've got a family, and you mature.'"**

36. *Mail Online* published an article on 6th February 2010 under the head line "Boozer, love cheat and drug-test dodger. Meet the NEW England captain Rio Ferdinand." The story began,

> "England's new football captain Rio Ferdinand hardly represents a return to the Corinthian ideals; an eight month ban for missing a drugs test in 2003 will forever blight his record. **Perhaps the most persuasive argument to the Manchester United defender's promotion is that he has belatedly matured, to become the least worst of potential Terry replacements."**

The article concluded

> **"His home life is settled, it seems. Last year he married his long-time girlfriend and mother of his two children, Rebecca Ellison, in a ceremony which was not sold to a celebrity magazine. Miss Ellison had shown considerable forbearance in previous years as the footballer was linked with a number of models, including the then ubiquitous Abi Titmuss. Now aged 31 and articulate in interview, Ferdinand seems to have put his wilder days behind him. Time will tell."**

37. In an article in *The Times* for 6th February 2010, it was said:

> "The missed drugs test was the nadir but there were other indiscretions, too, among them four driving disqualifications and that infamous Ayia Napa sex tape in 2000. **At some point, though, the penny dropped, coinciding—it seemed—with the birth of the first of his two young boys, Lorenz, almost 3 ½ years ago. 'I think I have changed in many ways in the last few years', Ferdinand said in an interview with The Times last year. 'Having kids, you realise your responsibilities. I think you get to a point in your life when you know yourself.'"**

The Framework in which this claim has to be decided

38. Like in other privacy claims brought against the media, the Court has to grapple with the tension between two different rights set out in the European Convention on Human Rights—that in Article 8 to respect for private life and that in Article 10 to freedom of expression.

Article 8 of the ECHR provides:

> "(1) Everyone has the right to respect for his private and family life, his home and his correspondence.
>
> (2) There shall be no interference by a public authority with the exercise of this right except such as is in accordance with the law and necessary in a democratic society or the economic well-being of the country. For the prevention of disorder and crime, for the protection of health or morals, or for the protection of the rights and freedoms of others."

Article 10 of the ECHR says,

> "(1) Everyone has the right to freedom of expression. This right shall include the freedom to hold opinions and to receive and impart information and ideas without interference by a public authority and regardless of frontiers. This article shall not prevent States from requiring the licensing of broadcasting, television or cinema enterprises.
>
> (2) The exercise of these freedoms, since it carries with it duties and responsibilities, may be subject to such formalities, conditions, restrictions or penalties as are prescribed by law, and are necessary in a democratic society, in the interests of national security, territorial integrity or public safety, for the protection of health or morals, for the protection of the **reputation** or rights of others, for preventing the disclosure of information received in confidence, or for maintaining the impartiality of the judiciary."

39. Although at first sight, Article 8 appears to be directed at interferences by the State in a person's private life, **it is now beyond argument that it also encompasses a positive obligation to put in place a system to protect an individual's private life from interference by non-state entities such as the media:** see **Von Hannover v Germany** (2005) 40 EHRR 1 and **Campbell v MGN Ltd** [2004] 2 AC 457.

40. Article 8 accords protection (at least on a qualified basis) to "private life", "home" and "correspondence". Of these, "private life" is perhaps the most nebulous. According to the House of Lords in *Campbell* the question whether a Claimant's private life is in issue is to be decided by asking whether the person concerned had a "**reasonable expectation of privacy**" in that matter.

41. Article 8(2) and Article 10(2) make clear that the respective rights in Article

8(1) and 10(1) are not absolute. Neither is broken if the interference is prescribed by law, for a **legitimate aim** and is **necessary** in a democratic society. Where both rights are in play, the Court has to conduct a balancing exercise to decide which should prevail. As Lord Steyn said in *Re S (A Child)* [2005] 1 AC 593 at [17],

> "**First**, neither article has as such precedence over the other. **Secondly**, where the values under the two articles are in conflict, an intense focus on the comparative importance of the specific rights being claimed in the individual case is necessary. **Thirdly**, the justification for interfering with or restricting each right must be taken into account. **Finally**, the proportionality test must be applied to each."

42. Thus the parties in this case were agreed that the Court's approach should be that expressed by Buxton LJ in **McKennitt v Ash** [2008] QB 73 CA at [11] namely,

> "where the complaint is the wrongful publication of private information, the court has to decide two things. **First**, is the information private in the sense that it is in principle protected by article 8? If 'no' that is the end of the case. **If 'yes'**, the second question arises: in all the circumstances, must the interest of the owner of the private information yield to the right of freedom of expression conferred on the publisher by article 10? **The latter inquiry is commonly referred to as the balancing exercise . . .**"

Was the information in the article in principle protected by Article 8?

43. I am here addressing the first of Buxton LJ's questions in *McKennitt*. Sometimes, that is expressed alternatively as whether Article 8 is "**engaged**", but there is a danger in becoming distracted by terminology.

44. The Claimant submits that the information plainly was in principle protected by Article 8. The text messages from the Claimant were a form of "correspondence" which is expressly covered by Article 8(1). Furthermore, private **relationships**, especially those said to involve sexual affairs, are quintessential examples of matters in which individuals have a reasonable expectation of privacy—see for instance *Mosley v News Group Newspapers* [2008] EMLR 20 at [98]—[104]. This would cover the Claimant's entire **relationship** with Ms Storey. **In addition, the article was illustrated by a private photograph of the Claimant and Ms Storey which was taken in a hotel room in 1997**. The Claimant had a reasonable expectation that that, too, would remain private. In addition the publication of the article impinged on the private lives of **Ms Ellison and his family.** That has a direct effect, **since the Court is obliged to protect their Convention rights**. It also has an indirect effect because the

Claimant was distressed as a result of the impact which the article had on them.

45. The Defendant submits that the position is not so straightforward. There was **nothing in the Claimant's evidence to suggest that his relationship with Ms Storey in the period 1996—2000 was a secret.** Ms Storey's evidence was that she and the Claimant would **go out in public all the time** and their **relationship** was **completely open**. In cross examination, the Claimant had agreed that he and Ms Storey went out, though not, he said, as a couple. Between 2002 and 2005 the Claimant and Ms Storey **met in hotels**. The Claimant did not try to keep this a secret. On the other hand, **he did not tell her that their relationship had to be hidden.** He said in re-examination that **he expected her to keep the communications confidential**. The text messages (so far as they had been retained) were available in their entirety at the trial, but what the Claimant has to show is that what was published contravened his reasonable expectation of privacy. **Quotations from the texts in the articles were extremely limited. The 1997 photograph was openly taken by one of the other two people present in the room. The Claimant and Ms Storey are fully clothed. He is talking on a mobile phone. He is paying no attention to her. It is unexceptionable and conveys no private information beyond that which was said in the article, namely that they were at this stage friends.**

46. The Defendant also observes that in *Murray v Express Newspapers Ltd* [2009] Ch 481 at [36] the Court of Appeal commented,

> "As we see it, the question whether there is a reasonable expectation of privacy is **a broad one**, which takes account of **all the circumstances** of the case. They include the **attributes** of the claimant, **the nature** of the activity in which the claimant was engaged, **the place** at which it was happening, the **nature and purpose of the intrusion**, the **absence of consent** and whether it was known or could be inferred, **the effect on the claimant** and the **circumstances** in which and the **purposes** for which the information came in**to the hands of the publisher**."

47. The Defendant submits that it is relevant in this context that **the Claimant is a public figure in a broad sense** and, as such, he must accept and expect that his actions **will be more closely scrutinised by the media**—see **A v B plc (Flitcroft v MGN Ltd)** [2003] QB 195 at [11 (xii)]. **Further, the Defendant argued, the Claimant was saying that he was entitled to protect the privacy of an adulterous affair.** The Defendant did not ask the Court to make a moral judgment but submitted that what was at stake was significantly less important than in *Campbell* (**recovery treatment for a drug addict**) or *Re S (a child)* (**the impact on a young child of court reporting of her mother's trial for murder**). Additionally, the Claimant had published information about the Ayia Napa incident **in his biography.** In the January 2006 interview with the

News of the World he had **admitted to "cheating"** with other women while he was in a **relationship** with Ms Ellison. There had been the other articles to which I referred about those **affairs**. The Claimant had not denied them, nor had he taken any action in relation to them. **As a result, explicit details of the Claimant's sex life were already in the public domain and the Claimant could no longer have a reasonable expectation of privacy in this type of information.**

48. In addition, the Claimant had **behaved recklessly in his text messages** to Ms Storey **[redacted].**

49. I was invited to be sceptical of the distress which this article had caused the Claimant, given that he had taken no action over other disclosures. In **KGM v News Group Newspapers** *Ltd* [2010] EWHC 3145 (QB) Eady J. said that **it was often important to make an assessment of the Claimant's own attitude towards the maintaining of privacy**. The judge considered that the Claimant in that case was a robust character and that was a factor to be taken into account. **His judgment was upheld by the Court of Appeal under the name Hutcheson v News Group Newspapers Ltd (see above).**

50. As for the impact on the Claimant's family, Mr Millar observed that there had been **no witness statement or other evidence from Ms Ellison**. As Tugendhat J. said in *Terry (previously 'LNS') v Persons Unknown* [2010] EMLR 16 at [66],

> "The court is being asked by LNS to have regard to the Article 8 rights of the other person and the interested persons**. Respect for the dignity and autonomy of the individuals concerned requires that, if practicable, they should speak for themselves**. . . . If it is not practicable or just that the other person or anyone else should not give evidence personally, the court should know why."

This passage was approved by the Court of Appeal in *Hutcheson* (above) at [26]. **The Claimant's witness statement said that his children were too young to fully understand the article.**

Conclusions on whether the information was in principle protected by Article 8

51. **In my judgment the information in the article was in principle protected by Article 8. I emphasise that I am here addressing only the first of Buxton LJ's questions.** It is but an intermediate step on the way to deciding whether or not publication of the information did constitute a wrong.

52. The Claimant agreed that he and Ms Storey went out prior to 2000 and may have been seen in clubs at the same time. **However, they were not seen as a couple.** This differs from Ms Storey's witness statement that the two of them were completely open, but here I give more weight to the Claim-

ant's evidence which was tested in cross examination whereas Ms Storey's was not. The Claimant was also entitled to rely on Ms Storey's own words as they appeared on the cover of the newspaper and in large type with the story itself, **[redacted].** The article was also billed as an "**exclusive**". Neither description suggests that this was information which had previously been widely disseminated.

53. In any case, **even on Ms Storey's evidence, knowledge of their relationship was confined to their circle of family and friends** and that is not conclusive of the issue of whether the information is still in principle protected from publication in the mass media—see, for instance, **Lord Browne of Madingley v Associated Newspapers Ltd** [2008] QB 103 at [61]. **Furthermore, this was not an example of publication of the bare fact of a relationship between the claimant and another and in this respect the position is to be contrasted with Hutcheson.**

54. **The 1997 photograph is closer to the borderline**. It was taken openly on Ms Storey's account and the Claimant (who could not remember the occasion) was unable to contradict her. It shows nothing remarkable, **but it does show the two of them together in a hotel bedroom**. I am prepared to accept that this, too, was information which in principle was capable of protection and whose publication would, subject to the balancing test, infringe the Claimant's rights under Article 8. **Wood v Commissioner of Police for the Metropolis** [201] 1 WLR 123 confirms that an **intrusion** must **reach a certain level of seriousness** before it is even in principle capable of being protected by Article 8. **The Court of Appeal concluded that the mere taking of photographs of demonstrators in the street did not reach that level of seriousness, but it was different when it came to the retention of the photographs**. Laws LJ (with whom, on this issue, the other members of the Court agreed) made clear at [31] that he was not considering the *publication* of **photographs**. In my judgment neither the facts nor the principle of *Wood* assists Mr Millar.

55. I accept as well that the **texts are examples of "correspondence"** and so, again, in principle, subject to protection.

56. Sexual behaviour in private is part of the core aspects of individual autonomy which Article 8 is intended to protect. That does not mean that information about an individual's sexual activities will invariably be in principle protected, **but I was not persuaded by Mr Millar's arguments that the Claimant was unable to satisfy Buxton LJ's first question in this case.** His public position as a footballer and (at the time) captain of the England football team will need to be considered more closely in the context of the balancing exercise (Buxton LJ's second question), but it has no effect on the first question as to whether in principle the information which was published about him was

entitled to protection. Nor do I think that the earlier publicity which he had attracted affects this first question. He said in evidence that he had considered very carefully how much of his private life he wanted to discuss in the media. **There is no basis for arguing that, by his own public statements on his private life he had forsaken a reasonable expectation of privacy in connection with his relationship with Ms Storey**. In **KGM v News Group Newspapers Ltd** at [38] Eady J. said that **"The so-called 'zonal' argument has become discredited since at least the decision of the Court of Appeal four years ago in McKennitt v Ash."**

57. Mr Millar argued that there has been a material change since *McKennitt.* Section 12(4) of the Human Rights Act requires the Court to have regard to the terms of "any relevant privacy code" when considering whether to grant relief which may affect a person's right to freedom of expression. One of those Codes is The Press Complaints Commission's Editors' Code. Although the Code has been in existence for some time, the section on privacy was amended in October 2009 by adding the words which I have italicised in the quotation below.

> " 3. *Privacy
>
> (i) Everyone is entitled to respect for his or her private and family life, home, health and correspondence, including digital communications.
>
> (ii) Editors will be expected to justify **intrusion**s into any individual's private life without consent. **Account will be taken of the complainant's own public disclosures of information.**
>
> (iii) **It is unacceptable to photograph individuals in private places without their consent."**

58. I am not persuaded that this change makes any difference in the present context. **As I have already said, the Claimant had not, before the article, disclosed anything about his relationship with Ms Storey**. It is not necessary to consider whether in an extreme case there would be some merit in the argument that widespread and extensive discussion by a person of similar aspects of their private life would disentitle them to have a reasonable expectation of privacy. The present case is nowhere near that extreme. **In this context, the Claimant was also entitled to say that the articles alleging affairs with other women were not published with his consent and the fact that he had not litigated them could not be taken as his tacit acceptance of another article, let alone another article about a different woman.**

59. In my judgment the Claimant's **recklessness in his behaviour was not such** as to mean that he had no reasonable expectation of privacy. In **Mosley v News Group Newspapers Ltd** [2008] EMLR 20 at [226] Eady J. considered this question, but in the context of an assessment of damages. He said in

terms that such **recklessness did not excuse the intrusion into the Claimant's privacy.** The issue of damages, of course, is only relevant once liability is established and the question I am presently considering is relevant to the existence of liability. **Similarly, the level of distress which the Claimant himself suffered would be material as and when damages need to be assessed.** In the nature of things**, the subject matter of the article is private information which is likely to have caused even a phlegmatic character some embarrassment and, as such, this supports the existence of a reasonable expectation of privacy.**

60. This is sufficient for me to find in the Claimant's favour on this first question. I should add, though, that I thought the Defendant was on stronger ground in saying that I could place little weight on the impact of the article on Ms Ellison's private life or expectation of privacy. There is no witness statement from her and that is material. The Claimant himself accepted that his children were too young to fully understand. They were aged three and one at the time of publication.

The Balancing Exercise

The legal principles

61. I have already referred to the speech of Lord Steyn in Re S (a child) who said that the balancing competing rights between Article 8 and Article 10 called for an intense focus on the comparative importance of the two rights in the specific context of the particular case. Section 12(4) of the Human Rights Act 1998 says that the court must have particular regard to the importance of the Convention right of freedom of expression, but case law (including *Re S (A Child)* has made clear that **neither Article has automatic precedence over the other.**

62. Freedom of expression applies to banal and trivial expression as well as matters of public interest, but where that right has to be balanced against the rights of others to protect their privacy, the extent to which the content is of public interest or contributes to **a debate of general interest** assumes a much greater importance. Indeed, the contribution which the publication makes to **a debate of general interest** is the decisive factor in deciding where the balance falls between Article 8 and Article 10—see *Von Hannover* at [76]. In this context it has frequently been said that there is a difference between what is in the public interest and what is of **interest to the public**. As the European Court of Human Rights has said in **Mosley v UK** App No. 48009/08 Judgment 10th May 2011, BAILII: [2011] ECHR 774 at [114],

> **"The Court also reiterates that there is a distinction to be drawn between reporting facts—even if controversial—capable of contributing to a debate of general public interest in a democratic**

> **society**, and making tawdry allegations about an individual's private life...In respect of the former, the pre-eminent role of the press in a democracy and its duty to act as a **'public watchdog'** are important considerations in favour of a **narrow** construction of any limitations on freedom of expression. However, different considerations apply to press reports concentrating on sensational and, at times, lurid news, intended to titillate and entertain, **which are aimed at satisfying the curiosity of a particular readership regarding aspects of a person's strictly private life . . . Such reporting does not attract the robust protection of Article 10 afforded to the press.** As a consequence, in such cases, freedom of expression requires a more **narrow** interpretation....While confirming the Article 10 right of members of the public to have access to a wide range of publications covering a variety of fields, the Court stresses that in assessing in the context of a particular publication **whether there is a public interest which justifies an interference with the right to respect for private life, the focus must be on whether the publication is in the interest of the public and not whether the public might be** interested in reading it."

63. **It is not the case that the public interest is confined to the exposure of conduct which is illegal. Tugendhat J. rejected that proposition in Terry** at [100]. He added,

> **"[101] It is not for the judge to express personal views on such matters, still less to impose whatever personal views he might have. That is not the issue. The issue is what the judge should prohibit one person from saying publicly about another. . . .**
>
> **[104] There is much public debate as to what conduct is or is not socially harmful. Not all conduct that Is socially harmful is unlawful . . . The fact that conduct is private and lawful is not, of itself, conclusive of the question whether or not it is in the public interest that it be discouraged.** There is no suggestion that the conduct in the present case ought to be unlawful or that any editor would ever suggest that it should be. But in a plural society there will be some who would suggest that it ought to be discouraged. **That is why sponsors may be sensitive to the public image of those sportspersons whom they pay to promote their products.** Freedom to live as one chooses is one of the most valuable freedoms. **But so is the freedom to criticise (within the limits of the law) the conduct of other members of society as being socially harmful, or wrong.** Both the law, and what are, and are not, acceptable standards of behaviour have changed very considerably over the years, particularly in the last half century or so. During that time these changes (or, as many people would say, this progress) has been achieved as a result of

public discussion and criticism of those engaged in what were, at the time, lawful activities. The modern concept of public opinion emerged with the production of relatively cheap newspapers in the seventeenth century. Before that there was no medium through which public debate could be conducted. **It is as a result of public discussion and debate that public opinion develops."**

64. In *Hutcheson* (above) at [29] the Court of Appeal said that it was not necessary to resolve the issue in the context of that case, but it described the views of Tugendhat J. as "powerful". I respectfully agree. Freedom of expression, after all, is one of the human rights guaranteed in the Convention because it is an integral part of the foundation of a democratic state and **pluralism has long been recognised by the Strasbourg Court as one of the essential ingredients of a democracy** (see for example *Handyside v UK* (1979-80) 1 EHRR 737 at [49]). While I accept that the subjective perception of a journalist cannot convert an issue into one of public interest if it is not (see paragraph [27] above), **the Court's objective assessment of whether there is a public interest** in the publication must acknowledge that in a plural society there will be a range of views as to what matters or is of significance in particular in terms of a person's suitability for a high profile position.

65. *One facet of the public interest can be correcting a false image.* The PCC Code (to which, as I have said, the Court is obliged to have regard by s.12(4) of the Human Rights Act 1998) marks with a star certain of its provisions. These are ones which are subject to a public interest qualification. Clause 3 on privacy is one of those provisions. The Code then goes on to comment on the public interest. It says that this includes, but is not limited to,

> **"(i) detecting or exposing crime or serious impropriety; (ii) protecting public health and safety; (iii) preventing the public from being misled by an action or statement of an individual or organisation."**

66. One example of correcting a false image was *Campbell v MGN Ltd* [2004] 2 AC 457 where the model Naomi Campbell **had publicly denied taking illegal drugs or being an** addict. In her subsequent claim for infringement of her privacy she accepted that these statements had been untrue. She accepted that the newspaper had the right to correct the false image which she had projected.

67. Generally in a claim for publication of private information **the Court is not concerned with whether the information is true or false.** A Claimant is **not, for instance, expected to admit the truth of what has been published as the price of obtaining redress**. As Longmore LJ said in *McKennitt v Ash* (above) at [85],

> **"The question in a case of misuse of private information is whether**

the information is private not whether it is true or false. The truth or falsity of the information is an irrelevant inquiry in deciding whether the information is entitled to be protected and **judges should be chary of becoming sidetracked into that irrelevant inquiry."**

68. However, in the context of a defence of public interest based on correcting a false image, truth is important, as the Court of Appeal went on to acknowledge in *McKennitt*. **This defence can only begin to succeed if the Claimant's image is indeed false and if there is therefore something to be corrected.**

69. Naomi Campbell's action nonetheless succeeded because the House of Lords considered that the article **unnecessarily included a photograph and details of her attendance at Narcotics Anonymous.** This was an added and important **intrusion** into her private life which went beyond what was justified for the **purpose** of correcting her misleading image.

70. In *Re S (A child)* Lord Steyn said that the balancing act required an intense focus on the relative importance of both rights. Thus even if a Claimant succeeds in passing Buxton LJ's first test (that in principle the information is protectable), it may be necessary to revisit the Article 8 side of the balance to see quite how important the information is.

71. In this case the Defendant invokes **its own Article 10 right** to freedom of expression, **but it relies as well on the rights of Ms Storey.** Plainly she had a right of expression under Article 10 (subject, of course, to the balancing exercise). Mr Millar argued that she had a right under Article 8. He relied on what Munby J. said in **Re Angela Roddy (A Minor)** [2004] EMLR 127 **that the right to personal autonomy which Article 8 guarantees includes a right to impart information about one's private life rather than to keep it secret**. In the context of a case such as the present, however, such a right is likely to march in step with the Article 10 right. Both are qualified rights. Both have to be balanced against the competing Article 8 right of the Claimant.

The parties' contentions as to the balancing exercise

72. The Defendant contended that the Claimant had projected an image of himself as a reformed character. In the *News of the World* interview and on many subsequent occasions he had given the impression that he had put aside his past wild ways. He had matured. He had settled down with Ms Ellison and his children and he was committed to his family. **However, Ms Storey's account showed that this was not so**. **[redacted].**

73. Furthermore, these attempted meetings with Ms Storey impinged on his professional life. They had in the past taken place in hotels where the Claimant was staying with his football team. At least some of the meetings planned **[redacted]** were intended to do likewise. **The Claimant acknowledged that this was in breach of his obligations as a team member.**

74. The Defendant argued that the Claimant had embarked on a wider campaign since 2006 to project a more responsible and positive image than the **reputation** which he had had in the past. **His charitable and business activities were part of this**. Here, too, the Defendant argued, there was a public interest in demonstrating that this was misleading because **his relationship with Ms Storey had continued long after the time when he was supposed to have changed.**

75. In addition, the Defendant argued, **there was a public debate as to whether the Claimant was a suitable person to be appointed as England captain following the dismissal of John Terry.** Terry had been dismissed **because of his extra-marital affair**. Mr Capello and many commentators had observed that the England captain was expected **to be a role model for young fans and a high standard was therefore** demanded of the person who filled that role—both on and off the pitch.

76. In its defence, the Defendant argued additionally **[redacted]** the Communications Act 2003, but Mr Millar did not pursue this aspect at trial and I need say no more about it.

77. The Claimant responded that Ms Storey's account did not show that the Claimant had lied when he gave his interview to the *News of the World* in January 2006. He was not then promising to the world to remain in a monogamous **relationship** with Ms Ellison ever after. The past mistakes which he was intending to put behind him were those which had previously marred his professional career. Pre-eminently this was a reference to missing his drugs test which had led to him being banned from playing football for several months. It also included clubbing and partying which might also affect his play. He and Ms Storey never had met after 2005. **Since his marriage to Ms Ellison in 2009 they had not even made any arrangements to meet.**

78. Mr Tomlinson submitted that the Claimant's business activities had nothing whatever to do with the case. Nor did his charitable activities. **The Claimant was keen to encourage young boys to take part in sport and to discourage them from being involved with guns, knives, drugs or criminality. Nothing in the article had anything to do with that at all.**

79. Even taking into account all his public activities, the Claimant was simply not in the same category as politicians who might have to accept a greater public debate about their private lives.

80. The Claimant also submitted that his appointment as England captain provided no legitimate excuse for the publication of this private information. **John Terry had been dismissed, not simply because he had had an extra-marital affair but because the affair had been with the girl-friend of a team mate.** It was that aspect of the matter which had **undermined the trust and**

authority which was essential for a captain. In addition, the appointment of the Claimant had taken place at the beginning of February 2010. Ms Storey had approached her public relations agent at the end of February. **The article had not appeared until the end of April. This delay was incompatible with the article genuinely being a contribution to the debate about the England captaincy.** Furthermore, there had been **no evidence of any reaction at all to the publication of the article**. That showed it **did not impact at all on the public's view of the suitability of the Claimant to hold the post of captain.**

81. The Claimant submitted that Ms Storey's rights, whether under Article 10 or Article 8 were entitled to very little weight. While the article had given her account of the **relationship** with the Claimant, it had been published and would be read because of what it said about the Claimant. **It was his story rather than hers.** There was a parallel in this respect with *McKennitt v Ash* (above) where the findings of Eady J. at first instance were echoed by Buxton LJ in the Court of Appeal who said at [31] of Ms Ash, "**She gives vent to many complaints about the first claimant; but the interest of those is that they are complaints about the first claimant, and not at all that the complaints are made by the first defendant**." And he added at [51] "**As a result the first defendant had no story to tell that was her own as opposed to the first claimant's**." Furthermore, as Ms Storey had said in her text of 6th February, now was the time for her to cash in. She had done so, being paid £16,000 for her information by the Defendant.

82. In any case, the Claimant argued, the article intruded on the Claimant's private life further than could possibly be justified. Whatever the merit of the defence in relation to the texts that passed between the Claimant and Ms Storey in 2007-2010, they provided no justification for the disclosures and their **relationship** between 1996 and 2005. **The article went well beyond publication of the bare fact of the relationship during that period. It included, for instance, allegations about the number of times the two of them had had sex.** The **photograph** of the Claimant and Ms Storey from 1997 made no contribution to the public interest **and Von Hannover and Campbell v MGN showed that there was a particular sensitivity over the publication of photographs**. This was **not** a case where a publication had been produced under **great time pressure** and, where, as a result the Court might be tempted to allow additional **latitude** to a journalist. This article appeared months after the Claimant's appointment, weeks after Ms Storey had approached Max Clifford and with no explanation for what had happened in the interval.

83. Had the Defendant been confident about the claimed public interest in the article, it would have contacted the Claimant in advance of publication. The House of Commons Culture Media and Sport Select Committee reported that this was normal practice in the newspaper industry (see the quotation from the Committee's report of 9th February 2010 in *Mosley v UK* at [52]). **There was no evidence from the Defendant to explain this departure from the norm,** but the court could infer that the Defendant knew that if it did give the Claimant notice, it recognised that he would have applied for, and been granted, an injunction to prevent publication.

Balancing exercise: discussion

84. In my judgment there was a public interest in this article. At one level it was a "kiss and tell" story. Even less attractively, it was a "kiss and paid for telling" story, but stories may be in the public interest even if the reasons behind the informant providing the information are less than noble. The interview with the *News of the World* was significant. This was not a casual encounter with a reporter who elicited an off the cuff remark. **As the Claimant explained, the interview was set up by his publicity agent.** He did quite clearly wish **to portray himself as a reformed character**. He confessed past mistakes. They included his missed drugs test which had directly impacted on his career. But they were not restricted to matters so closely related to the football pitch. Even though he had played no part in the articles about women with whom he had allegedly had affairs while living with Ms Ellison, those stories had contributed to his wild image and it was that image to which he confessed in the article and said he was now putting behind him. He contrasted his past behaviour with where he was in the present—older, more mature, and, critically, in a stable family **relationship** with Ms Ellison. The article was accompanied by a picture of the two of them together. She was heavily pregnant and he was cradling her 'bump'. The picture reinforced the message of the article: Rio Ferdinand is now a family man and has given up the ways of his past including 'cheating' on Ms Ellison.

85. Mr Tomlinson is right to say that the article could not be construed as a promise through to an indefinite time in the future that the Claimant would remain faithful to Ms Ellison. But nor would it be right to approach the article in the way that a contract lawyer would analyse a pre-contract representation. **Through that article he projected an image of himself and, while that image persisted, there was a public interest in demonstrating (if it were to be the case) that the image was false.**

86. The *News of the World* article was followed by the Claimant's autobiography and numerous other articles **in which the same theme echoed**: Rio was **now reformed**. Some of these articles were published after he had resumed contact with Ms Storey. **I do not find it significant that he only married Ms Ellison in 2009. For many people infidelity with a long term partner is little, if any, different from adultery. It was 'cheating' on Ms Ellison to which the Claimant confessed in his News of the World interview in 2006 at a**

time when they not even engaged, but had, by then been living together for some 6 years. That was part of the behaviour that he said in that interview he had put behind him. Nor do I regard it as of any great weight that he and Ms Storey did not actually meet in the period 2007-2010. **[redacted]**

87. I also agree that a further factor in the public interest case is the Claimant's appointment as captain of England, first, on a temporary basis, in March 2008 and then in replacement of John Terry in February 2010. Mr Tomlinson may be right that what interests some managers, players and fans is only a captain's performance on the pitch**. John Terry's affair certainly had the extra dimension that it had involved the girl friend of a fellow team member and so was likely to make dressing room relations tense to say the least.** But on the evidence presented in this case, it is by no means a universal view that the captain's role is confined to what happens on the pitch or what affects the players' performance. The phrase "role model" is somewhat ubiquitous. In *A v B plc* [2003] QB 195 Lord Woolf CJ spoke at [11(xii)] **of a public figure who**

> "may hold a position where higher standards can be rightly expected by the public. The **public figure** may be a role model whose conduct could well be emulated by others. He may set the fashion. The higher the profile of the individual concerned the more likely will that be the position. **Whether you have courted publicity or not, you may be a legitimate subject of public attention**. If you have courted public attention then you have less ground to object to the **intrusion** which follows. In many of these situations it would be overstating the position to say that there is a public interest in the information being published. It would be more accurate to say that the public have an understandable and so a legitimate interest in being told the information."

Lord Woolf went on at [43 (vi)] to say specifically **that footballers were role models and undesirable behaviour on their part can set an unfortunate example.**

88. In *McKennitt v Ash* (above) Buxton LJ said at [62] that the width of the rights given to the media by *A v B plc* could not be reconciled with *Von Hannover*. He went on to add (at [65]) that Lorenna McKennitt, the Canadian folk singer who was the Claimant in the case before him, did not hold a position where higher standards of conduct could be rightly expected by the public. That, Buxton LJ said, "**is no doubt the preserve of headmasters and clergyman, who according to taste may be joined by politicians, senior civil servants, surgeons and journalists**." Ms McKennitt had, at most, been an involuntary role model and it was clear that Lord Woolf thought that role models anyway

were only at risk of disclosure of disreputable conduct which had not been the position in her case.

89. To return to the present case. The Claimant voluntarily assumed the role of England captain. **It was a job that carried with it an expectation of high standards**. In the views of many the captain was expected to maintain those standards off, as well as on, the pitch. By way of example, in 2008, Brian Barwick, the Chief Executive of the Football Association said,

> "one of the most important early decisions [Fabio Capello] will have to take will be to decide who is going to be his captain. . . . There isn't the degree of importance laid at the door of captains of other countries, but Fabio is aware of the importance of this decision . . . the captaincy, currently held by John Terry, **is a very significant part of the English sporting and social fabric** . . . **England players are special players. And that carries with it an extra weight of expectancy and responsibility** . . . **If you are an England player you are living out the dreams of thousands and thousands of kids and millions of people.** And while you don't want that weight of moral expectation weighing too heavily on anybody's shoulders, it is part of your responsibility. They have to accept that off the field they are role models."

At a press briefing on 26th February 2010 Fabio Capello said why he had taken the captaincy away from John Terry,

> "It was not good because I always asked **that the Captain is an example for the young, the children**, for the fans. It was not good. This is the reason and I told him this . . . The England shirt is very important and for me this will be one of the most important points we speak about . . . part of that is to talk about how important it is to behave well when you are representing England."

Mr Tomlinson emphasised that Mr Capello had added that it was only the problem with Wayne Bridge (the team mate with whose girl friend John Terry was said to have had an affair) which caused him to dismiss Terry. But for some commentators at least (e.g. *Mail Online* 28th February 2010), **this qualification was to distinguish the affair from other, quite separate, alleged misdemeanours of Terry.**

In any event, Mr Capello's remarks about the captain needing to set an example for young fans were in line with his remarks in March 2008 (see above) when the Claimant was temporarily made captain, that the captain was expected to be a symbol on and off the pitch.

Similarly, in February 2010 the Sports Minister, Gerry Sutcliffe was quoted as saying,

> "On the field John Terry is a fantastic player and a good England captain,

but to be captain of England you have got to have wider responsibilities for the country, and clearly if these allegations are proven—and at the moment they are only allegations—then it does call into question his role as England captain."

90. **Buxton LJ's list of those from whom higher standards were expected certainly was not meant to be closed.** The captain of England's football team, for a substantial body of the public, would come comfortably within it. In *Sir* **Frederick Goodwin v NGN** *Ltd* [2011] EWHC 1437 (QB) Tugendhat J. said at [103] that the Claimant, an exceptionally forceful business man, **came within the concept of a public figure** and that distinguished him from sportsmen and celebrities in the world of entertainment. However, as can be seen from the remarks that I have quoted there are many who would indeed see the captain, at least, of the England football team as a role model.

91. Of course, as Buxton LJ mentioned, the Strasbourg jurisprudence has developed since *A v B plc*. Princess Caroline of Monaco established that her rights under Article 8 had been violated in *Von Hannover* because German courts had not given her a remedy for the publication of **photographs** of her **going about ordinary activities.** But **there was nothing in the private information which had been published in that case which called into question her fitness to perform the ceremonial duties which her status required.** The Defendant's argument here is that Ms Storey's account did call into question the Claimant's fitness to be the role model which was expected of an England captain.

92. During the course of the hearing I asked the parties whether it was incumbent on me to decide whether the Claimant *was* fit to be England captain. Thankfully they agreed that it was not. **The issue is rather whether the Defendant's article reasonably contributed to the debate as to his suitability for that role.**

93. In paragraph [36] above I quoted the *Mail Online* article from 6th February 2010 which had the headline "Boozer, love cheat and drug-test dodger. Meet the NEW England captain Rio Ferdinand." The journalist who wrote that article would expect his (or her) readers at least to regard being a "love cheat" as not a good qualification for being England captain. The article went to say that the most persuasive argument in the Claimant's favour was that he had "belatedly matured" and **that, of course, was precisely the image which the Claimant had sought to project from the News of the World article onwards**. But the Defendant's article showed that, at least as far as women were concerned, **the image of change was a false one.**

94. **I was not convinced that the gap of almost three months between the Claimant's appointment as captain and the publication of the article took**

the matter much further. Ms Storey had said that she contacted Max Clifford towards the end of February. I could only speculate as to why there was then a further two months before the article appeared. **But in any case, the qualifications needed to be England captain seems to have perennial interest and the suitability of the captain of the moment is debated not just at the time of his appointment.** One example in evidence in this case was the article from *Mail Online* for 24th March 2011 where seven former England captains discussed their views of the role.

95. Nor did the absence of media comment in the wake of the Defendant's publication have much bearing. **Liability needs to be determined as of the date of publication and therefore in advance of any reaction.** If there was a subsequent response that might be evidence that the publication did contribute to a public debate, **but the absence of any such response is, at best, only weak evidence of the reverse proposition.**

96. There is a further aspect of Ms Storey's account where the correction of a false image and the suitability of the Claimant to be England captain overlap, namely the Claimant's admission that on occasions he either did, or tried to, sneak Ms Storey into a hotel where he and the other members of his team were staying. **He acknowledged** that this was against the rules set by the team's management. **[redacted].**

97. **Mr Tomlinson observed that this was not said to have happened (and indeed the Claimant had not tried to meet Ms Storey) since he had been made England captain.**

98. **I did not find this answer persuasive**. In his evidence the Claimant said that Mr Capello had told him to be professional, not only on the pitch but "**around the hotel**". **In the past the Claimant had not behaved in a professional manner around the hotels into which he had tried to sneak Ms Storey**. Whether or not he had done that in the few weeks since he had been made the permanent captain of England, **his relatively recent past failings could legitimately be used to call into question his suitability for the role.**

99. Nor was I persuaded that the Defendant's article excessively intruded into the Claimant's private life. *Campbell v MGN* was an example of a case where this was so. The essential story—that Ms Campbell had lied when she said she was not a drug addict—**was in the public interest**, but the newspaper went beyond what was reasonable by **publishing additional details of her treatment at Narcotics Anonymous and the covertly taken photograph of her leaving one of the NA meetings**. In this case, Mr Tomlinson argued that there was no justification for publication of the details of the **relationship** between the Claimant and Ms Storey prior to 2005, nor for the **photograph** of the two of them in a hotel room in 1997.

100. In my judgment, though, the Defendant was entitled to place the **relationship** between the Claimant and Ms Storey in context. **[redacted]** They had known each other for many years. Mr Tomlinson makes the point that they did not actually meet in the period from 2007. Yet it would be unreal to disguise the fact not only that they had known each other long before, **[redacted].**

101. **Publication of photographs can constitute an unacceptable intrusion into privacy even if a verbal report of the same occasion would not. Von Hannover, Campbell, and Murray are all examples**. But even if the occasion is private (as this one was) the "intense focus" of which Lord Steyn spoke in *Re S (A Child)* has still to be brought to bear. The Claimant could not remember the occasion when the picture was taken. Ms Storey says that this and other **photographs** were taken openly by one of the other people in the room. Given the size of a typical hotel room, that would seem likely. **This was not, therefore, covert photography as had been the case in Von Hannover and Campbell.** When Mirror Group Newspapers complained to Strasbourg that the House of Lords' judgment (both in substance and in relation to the order that it pay Ms Campbell's costs) had violated their right to freedom of expression, the Court dismissed the claim. It observed that,

> **"Photographs appearing in the tabloid press are often taken in a climate of continual harassment which induces in the person concerned a very strong sense of intrusion into their private life or even of persecution."**—*MGN Ltd v UK* Application No 39401/04 Judgment 18th January 2011, BAILII: [2011] ECHR 66 [143].

102. The House of Lords in *Campbell* placed great emphasis on the added degree of **intrusion** from the publication of the **photograph. It was part of the additional details to do with Narcotics Anonymous which was both superfluous to the exposure of Ms Campbell's dishonesty about drugs and potentially harmful to her recovery**. Furthermore, the **photograph** added nothing to the credibility of the story because the reader depended on the newspaper to explain what the picture showed (see Lord Hope at [123]). **Here, the picture showed the Claimant and Ms Storey clothed.** They are **not even engaging with each other.** The Claimant is speaking on a mobile phone. It is an unexceptionable picture. It was taken in a private room**, but its publication could have caused nothing comparable to the additional harm** that was referred to in *Campbell* and none of the **embarrassment** that pictures of sexual activity may cause (see for instance *Theakston v MGN Ltd* [2002] EMLR 22). In this case, the picture did provide an element of support to the story because it showed the Claimant and Ms Storey together. It was of limited value because of the age of the **photograph** but to that limited extent it did do more than the picture in *Campbell.* The Claimant said he was surprised and angry at the publication of the **photograph** as it was clearly a very old **photograph** and

yet the article was making out that the **relationship** was much more recent. I do not agree that the article misrepresented the position. It stated the date of the **photograph**. The **relationship** between the Claimant and Ms Storey had continued until January 2010. **Unlike in Campbell, I find that publication of the picture did not cause the Claimant justifiable additional distress**. Mr Millar argued that the Court should be slow to take on the role of editor and, at a micro-level, judge what was or was not acceptable for inclusion in the story. He is, of course, right that judges are ill equipped to be editors but Mr Tomlinson was equally entitled to respond that editorial discretion did not give *carte blanche* to intrude on privacy and the House of Lords in *Campbell* had indeed found in the Claimant's favour because the additional details (including the **photographs**) had been part of the publication. The resolution of this issue lies, in my judgment, in Lord Steyn's intense focus on the competing rights. Here, although the Claimant did have a reasonable expectation that such a **photograph** would remain private (and so, as I have held, he succeeded on Buxton LJ's first question), **its unexceptionable character meant that the right was of relatively low importance.** Publication of the **photograph** did provide some corroboration for the story (although, as I have accepted, of a relatively modest kind). **It supported the case that Ms Storey and the Claimant had known each other since 1997** and that, too, was a legitimate ingredient of the Defendant's argument as to why the Claimant had not, in fact reformed. I conclude that publication of this picture does not tip the balance in the Claimant's favour.

103. **Mr Tomlinson's emphasis on the absence of prior notice to the Claimant was in my view, with respect, a red herring**. He suggested that this was only explicable on the basis that the Defendant feared being subject to an interim injunction if notice had been given and this fear betrayed a lack of confidence in the reliance that they now placed on freedom of expression. **I do not find this line of argument helpful. Partly, that is because it is entirely speculative as to why no notice was given to the Claimant. More importantly, I have to decide where the balance lies between these competing rights as an objective matter.** The arguments which the Defendant now advances will either succeed or fail. The Defendant's internal assessment of their merits at some earlier stage is neither here nor there.

104. I did agree with Mr Tomlinson that, for the reasons he gave, Ms Storey's rights under Articles 8 and 10 did not assist the Defendant.

105. Overall, in my judgment, the balancing exercise favours the Defendant's right of freedom of expression over the Claimant's right of privacy.

The claim in breach of confidence

106. The action for misuse of private information has grown out of the older

equitable claim for breach of confidence. Breach of confidence in its original form does still have a life of its own and may be relevant, for instance, where the Claimant is not in a position to invoke Article 8. However, I did not understand Mr Tomlinson to argue that the Claimant had grounds for succeeding in breach of confidence even if he failed in relation to the newer, human rights based, cause of action. It is not necessary, therefore, for me to say any more about it.

Conclusion

107. For all of these reasons, this action is dismissed.

Case Digest Keywords Concordance

Introductory Note

This Keywords Concordance is provided in place of a conventional index for the Case Digest. Page references are exclusively to the Case Digest. Note that the Table of Cases and the Table of Legislation both cover the entirety of the work.

Index

Introductory Note

Note that this Index does not cover the Case Digest, for which a separate Keywords Concordance is provided. As exhaustive tables of cases and legislation are also provided, references to cases and legislation are, with very limited exceptions, omitted from this Index. References such as '178–9' indicate (not necessarily continuous) discussion of a topic across a range of pages. Wherever possible in the case of topics with many references, these have either been divided into sub-topics or only the most significant discussions of the topic are listed. Because the entire work is about 'privacy' the use of this term (and certain others which occur constantly throughout the book) as an entry point has been restricted. Information will be found under the corresponding detailed topics.